TAMA DAY

The SAGE Handbook *of*
Action Research

The SAGE Handbook *of*

Action Research

Participative Inquiry and Practice

Second Edition

Edited by
Peter Reason
Hilary Bradbury

SAGE Publications
Los Angeles ▪ London ▪ New Delhi ▪ Singapore

First published 2008

SAGE Publications Ltd
1 Oliver's Yard
55 City Road
London EC1Y 1SP

SAGE Publications Inc.
2455 Teller Road
Thousand Oaks, California 91320

SAGE Publications India Pvt Ltd
B 1/I 1 Mohan Cooperative Industrial Area
Mathura Road
New Delhi 110 044

SAGE Publications Asia-Pacific Pte Ltd
33 Pekin Street #02-01
Far East Square
Singapore 048763

Library of Congress Control Number: 2006938718

British Library Cataloguing in Publication data

A catalogue record for this book is available from
the British Library

ISBN 978-1-4129-2029-2

Typeset by C&M Digitals (P) Ltd, Chennai, India
Printed in Great Britain by The Cromwell Press Ltd, Trowbridge, Wiltshire
Printed on paper from sustainable resources

Contents

Editorial Board

Preface

Welcome to the second edition of the *Handbook of Action Research: Participative Inquiry and Practice*!

This volume, published five years after the original Handbook, builds on the original work and extends it. Because most of the material in the first edition will continue to be available in the 'concise paperback edition' (Reason and Bradbury, 2006), we have put together a collection of all new material. Some chapters are revisions and developments of key chapters in the first edition (Gaventa and Cornwall, Chapter 11; Schein, Chapter 18) or completely new articulations (Kemmis, Chapter 8). In other chapters we address similar themes and issues to the first edition, but have invited different authors to address them in order to provide a different perspective (e.g. Swantz, Chapter 2; Rahman, Chapter 3; Ison, Chapter 9; Gergen and Gergen, Chapter 10). We have added some important practices that were omitted from the first edition (e.g. Chambers on Participatory Rural Appraisal and related approaches, Chapter 20; Pedler and Burgoyne on Action Learning, Chapter 21; Wakeford et al. on Citizen's Jury, Chapter 22). Finally, we have chosen both a completely new set of exemplars which demonstrate significant developments in quality since the first edition and extended the section of skills.

In editing we have actively tried to develop four important themes which we thought underdeveloped in the first edition. First, we have attempted to show more fully the interrelationship of a wide range of ideas and practices in which action research is grounded. Chapter 1, organized primarily by Patricia Gayá Wicks, introduces what we think is a strong Groundings section by drawing on accounts provided by the Handbook Editorial Board of the range of theoretical and practical influences on their practice.

Second, we have attempted to contribute to the active debate about the scope and scale of action research, which we began in the first edition (particularly with the chapters by Gustavsen and Martin) and which has been carried forward in particular in the pages of the journal *Concepts and Transformations* (now the *International Journal of Action Research*; see Volume 8(1) and 8(3)). In this volume Swantz, Rahman, Gustavsen, Brown and Tandon, Martin, Wakeford, Stringer, and Mead in their different ways address issues that arise when action research is taken beyond the face-to-face group in an attempt to have an impact at a regional, national or international level. While in important contrast, Heron and Lahood, Mullett, Chowns, Chiu, Johns, McArdle and others demonstrate that if we wish to do work of significance and to influence changes in society toward justice and democracy, we not only need to build large-scale networks of inquiry but also to engage in transformations of consciousness and behaviour at personal and interpersonal levels. While it is true that we cannot make large-scale change on the basis of small cases, neither can we build truly effective and liberating political networks of inquiry without developing significant capacities for critical inquiry in the individuals and small communities that constitute them.

Third, we have recognized the importance of non-propositional, presentational forms of knowing in action research. The theme of voice and audience is foregrounded by Fine and Torre (Chapter 27), with particular emphasis on how we may speak out from a participative inquiry process to a wider audience and influence a range of stakeholders; the nature of presentational knowing in an extended epistemology is explored by Heron and Reason (Chapter 24); Chambers points to how visual and tangible ways of expressing knowing can be empowering (Chapter 20); the use of presentational forms is exemplified by Mullett (Chapter 30), Guhathakurta (Chapter 35), Kowlaski (Chapter 34); and the need to find appropriate form in writing explored by Marshall (Chapter 48).

Fourth and finally we have addressed the question of skills and education of action researchers. As Morten Levin argues in this volume, 'No other role in social science demands a broader spectrum of capacities bridging practical problem solving, reflective, and analytical thinking than that of an action researcher'. The final section of this volume addresses some of the personal, interpersonal, and political abilities that are demanded of an action researcher.

ACKNOWLEDGEMENTS

Our thanks must go to all those who have contributed to putting this volume together: To the Editorial Board for helping us think through what was needed for this revised volume and supporting our editorial work. To the contributors for their willingness to work closely with us through the process of draft and re-draft, for reviewing each others' chapters thoroughly and creatively, for taking the comments and criticisms of their own writing seriously and responding thoughtfully. To the participants and co-researchers in action research endeavours around the planet who have been part of the learning reflected here; a few of them are recognized in this volume as co-authors, but of course many remain unnamed. We are grateful for the help we have received from Kiren Shoman, Anne Summers, Katherine Haw and the editorial and production teams at Sage London, who have been responsive and efficient at all times. And we wish to appreciate each other and our efficient, supportive and where necessary challenging trans-Atlantic and pretty much 'virtual' relationship.

As with the first edition, we hope that the production of this work has been congruent with the action research philosophies and practices we espouse.

Peter writes:
I am enormously grateful for my friends, colleagues and students (and these roles are often indistinguishable!) who are associated with the Centre for Action Research in Professional Practice at the University of Bath. We do seem to have developed a genuine community of learning and practice which has some quite extensive influences both in the theory of action research and its practice and of which I am extremely proud. I am also grateful to the collaborative relationships with action researchers and others all round the world with whom I feel close through the curious phenomenon of the internet, and with whom I feel close connections as we develop this work of action research together.

Thank you to my extended family, who continue to bring with their love and nurture a quality of intellectual and emotional conversation. In particular I greet my grandchildren with delight, gratitude and enormous love: Otto, Liberty, Nathaniel and Aiden. Thank you also to my network of friendships, some new, some forged over 60 years.

My primary concern these days is for the state of the ecology of Planet Earth and for the challenges to her integrity coming from anthropogenic climate change, species extinction, and degradation of eco-systems everywhere. I am shocked by the speed with which these issues of sustainability have grown in significance over recent years and even months, as more evidence from the scientific communities becomes available and as the human community continues to evidence its inability to respond. Ten years ago I was concerned; now I am seriously alarmed.

There are many practical things we can do to lessen our impact on ecosystems, but I do not believe we will be able to move into a sound relationship with planetary ecosystems until we recognize that we humans are participants in the life of the planet, members of the community of beings. I hope that the participatory ethos expressed throughout this volume plays some part in influencing this essential shift in worldview.

Hilary writes:

Though written last, a preface is read first. It's therefore an ideal punctuation point at which to marvel over the Handbook and express the gratitude that arises.

My gratitude goes first to Peter. It astounds me how much we accomplish, how easily and with how much grace and humor. When we first started out as collaborators, on the first *Handbook of Action Research*, I did not understand just how unusual productive partnership actually is. And in all these years of working with such a maestro I have also learned, in the way one just does when learning in a context of practice, how to be a better partner and hopefully a better editor and a better action researcher. We have learned to create space for each other's contributions while also aiding each other in articulating what was sometimes inchoate. Our commitment and conscientiousness has led to real insight and better practice for me. I hope we still have some more innovations left to complete as a duo. Thank you Peter for being a gifted teacher, colleague and Bodhisattva.

Thank you to George Roth, Phil Mirvis, Bill Pasmore and Eric Neilsen who were my buddies in chapter writing. In holding you all as knowing so much more than I, I could ask questions I have been noodling for years. In writing I therefore could share some of the things I have also learned with and from you. I hope our readers will find it as useful for their own practice and understanding.

Through the editorial work for the Handbooks and the Journal, the community of action research has become a real community for me. I am simply stating a happy fact when I say that all my friends are action researchers! Happily many of those I have met through the virtual work of editing have also become real people for me. I especially love it when visitors from distant communities of action research – say from Australia – arrive in Los Angeles and we get to have lunch and discuss upcoming chapters and papers! I have truly appreciated the alacrity of all writers in the 'exemplars' chapters to which I devoted most of my energies. I thank you all for being flexible and responsive. To my task as editor, I brought my genuine interest in learning from you. I hope I communicated that in asking those questions of your work that I needed to have answered for my own practice, all readers would also, hopefully, benefit. I look forward to testing that assumption in the next few years with the graduate students to whom I assign the book in class (and who happily never seem that reluctant to share their opinions!).

Editing means getting to read what I might not otherwise have read. My own practice is that much richer as a result. I bring improvements to my work at the University of Southern California where we seek to engage business leaders in creating innovations in the world of sustainable development so that their own companies and society can benefit. I understand that each of us in this book is a pebble creating a ripple effect. Call me prescient, but I feel that in a decade, hopefully less, the ripple effect will appear far beyond our community. Action research will be more fully appreciated as an *essential* contribution on our way to co-creating a sustainable world. I therefore dedicate this work and all benefit that arises to our children (especially my Riane and Peter's grandchildren – all of whom have appeared since the last volume), their children and all the children of all the species for all time.

Peter Reason, Centre for Action Research in Professional Practice
University of Bath, England
Hilary Bradbury, Center for Sustainable Cities,
University of Southern California, Los Angeles, USA
2007

REFERENCES

Reason, P. (2004) 'Action research and the single case: a response to Bjørn Gustavsen', *Concepts and Transformations*, 8 (3): 281–94.

Reason, P. and Bradbury, H. (eds) (2006) *Handbook of Action Research: Concise Paperback Edition*. London: Sage.

Contributors

Arnold Aprill, a theater artist who has worked in Chicago's public schools for 25 years, has a lengthy background in the arts. He founded and directed the City Lit Theater Company, an interracial company that adapted literary works for the stage, and has taught arts education courses at the graduate level at the School of the Art Institute of Chicago. He is the founder of the Chicago Arts Partnership in Education (CAPE), and was a Leadership for a Changing World award recipient sponsored by the Ford Foundation and the Advocacy Institute in 2003. He is collaborating with the University of Chicago and the University of Illinois at Chicago to add college students to the CAPE approach. Arnie is motivated by two powerful imperatives: the urgent need to address the shameful inequities in urban public education in America and the need to reclaim the arts as a potent force for activating participative democracy.

Jørgen Bloch-Poulsen is an external lecturer at the Masters of Conflict Resolution Programme at Copenhagen University, Denmark, and associated with Partner in Dialog, a consultancy firm (www.dialog-mj.dk). He is a former Associate Professor in Philosophy of Science at Roskilde University in the history of ideas. Trained as a psychoanalyst, he teaches philosophy of science and interpersonal organizational communication at the Master of Conflict Resolution Programme. He works as a consultant with organizational development through dialogue with, for example, Bang & Olufsen, CSC, Danfoss, Lego, Novo, and Vestas. The action research project deals with involvement as a dilemma in team-based organizations shared in this volume and Associate Research Professor.

Hilary Bradbury When not editing work related to action research, Hilary Bradbury is Director of Sustainable Business Research at the USC Center for Sustainable Cities. Her expertise is in organizational change and transformation. Her PhD is from the Carroll School of Management at Boston College where she focused on a learning approach to sustainability. She brings over a dozen years' experience in the field of sustainable enterprises as an executive educator and action researcher. Previously she served as Associate Professor of Organizational Development at Case Western Reserve University. She has published widely in management journals, and conducted practice-based research funded by the National Science Foundation focused on multi-national corporations and their pursuit of sustainable development. Having grown up in Ireland, she now enjoys the sunshine living with her family in Los Angeles, California. Hilary is politically active in the sustainability movement and has been elected to serve on the regional school board.

L. David Brown is Associate Director for International Programs at the Hauser Center for Nonprofit Organizations and Lecturer in Public Policy at the Kennedy School of Government. Prior to coming to Harvard he was President of the Institute for Development Research, a non-profit center for development research and consultation, and Professor of Organizational Behavior at Boston University. His research and consulting has focused on institutional development, particularly for civil society organizations and networks, that foster sustainable development and social transformation. He has written or edited *Transnational Civil Society: An Introduction* (with Srilatha Batliwala), *Practice-Research Engagement for Civil Society in a Globalizing World*, *The Struggle for Accountability: NGOs, Social Movements and the World Bank* (with Jonathan Fox), and *Managing Conflict at Organizational Interfaces*. He has been a Fulbright Lecturer in India and a Peace Corps community organizer in Ethiopia.

Peter Bryant Having worked on participatory development processes in South Africa for the UK's Department for International Development, and throughout the UK, Peter now runs the Community Involvement Group, which specializes in participatory and deliberative processes such as citizens' juries and participation learning and action. He is also Vice-Chair of the World Development Movement and was a founding member of Right 2 B Heard.

Mary Brydon-Miller is an Associate Professor of Urban Educational Leadership and Educational Studies at the University of Cincinnati. She is a participatory action researcher who engages in both community-based and educational action research. She co-edited the volumes *Traveling Companions: Feminism, Teaching, and Action Research* (with Patricia Maguire and Alice McIntyre), *From Subjects to Subjectivities: A Handbook of Interpretive and Participatory Methods* (with Deborah Tolman), and *Voices of Change: Participatory Research in the United States and Canada* (with Peter Park, Budd Hall and Ted Jackson). She serves as director of the new interdisciplinary Action Research Center housed in the College of Education, Criminal Justice, and Human Services at the University of Cincinnati, which also sponsored the 2006 North American Action Research Summit. She teaches courses in action research, the theoretical foundations of urban educational leadership, and research ethics.

John Burgoyne is Professor of Management Learning in the Department of Management Learning and Leadership at Lancaster University, and also at Henley Management College. He is interested in individual and organizational learning, and the design, implementation and evaluation of management, leadership and organizational development.

María Teresa Castillo-Burguete was born in Chiapas, Mexico, and joined the Department of Human Ecology of Cinvestav, Mexico, in 1991. She obtained her PhD in Social Anthropology at the Universidad Iberoamericana of Mexico City in 2002. She is currently Senior Researcher at the Department of Human Ecology, where she teaches qualitative methods. Over the last ten years, she has studied gender relations in community participation in Yucatan and developed participatory research. She is co-author of a chapter in the first edition of the *Handbook of Action Research*.

Robert Chambers is a Research Associate in the Participation, Power and Social Change Team at the Institute of Development Studies. His main operational and research experience has been in East Africa and South Asia. His work has included aspects of rural development, public administration training, seasonality, irrigation system management, agricultural research and extension, perceptions of poverty, professionalism and participation. His books include *Rural Development: Putting the Last First* (1983), *Challenging the Professions* (1993), *Whose Reality Counts?* (1997), *Participatory Workshops* (2002) and *Ideas for Development* (2005). He is currently working mainly on participatory methodologies, how we know, do not know, and get it wrong in development, community-led total sanitation, and personal and institutional learning and change.

Lai Fong Chiu is a Senior Research Fellow of the University of Leeds. She previously held senior positions in the areas of public health and health promotion and health management in the United Kingdom National Health Service. She is committed to working to improve access to health services among minority ethnic and low-income communities. She has recently extended her work to migrant groups in continental Europe as an advisory member to the Task Force of the Migrant-Friendly and Culturally Competent Healthcare Organizations of the World Health Organization. She is also the coordinator of the Patients and Community Empowerment Working Group of the Task Force. While tasked with producing a set of standards and guidance on patients and community empowerment for healthcare organizations internationally, she continues to work locally with communities and health professionals in various projects to bring about change.

Gillian Chowns has spent most of her working life in one or other of the UK's major statutory agencies – Social Services, Education and the NHS. A local authority social worker for many years, specializing in children and families, she also taught in primary, secondary, sixth form and further education settings, both in England and Africa. In 1997 she moved into the palliative care field, establishing an innovative social work post within the East Berks Macmillan Palliative Care Team, specifically to support children whose parents were facing a life-threatening illness. From 1999 she combined this with a post as Senior Lecturer at Oxford Brookes University, in the School of Health and Social Care, where she teaches on the Palliative Care degree course. More recently she completed a PhD at the University of Southampton, researching through collaborative inquiry the pre-bereavement needs of children. One outcome of this research has been the video 'No – You *Don't* Know How We Feel!' Her other research interest is in international palliative care education.

David Coghlan is a faculty member of the School of Business, Trinity College Dublin, Ireland and is a Fellow of the College. He specializes in organization development and action research and is active in both communities internationally. He is currently on the editorial review boards of *Action Research, Journal of Applied Behavioral Science, Systemic Practice and Action Research, Irish Journal of Management* and the *OD Practitioner*. His recent co-authored books include: *Changing Healthcare Organizations* (Blackhall, 2003), *Managers Learning in Action* (Routledge, 2004), *Doing Action Research in Your Own Organization, 2nd edn* (Sage, 2005) and *Organizational Change and Strategy* (Routledge, 2006).

David Cooperrider is a professor of organizational behavior at the Weatherhead School of Management at Case Western Reserve University, and Faculty Director at the Center for Business as an Agent of World Benefit at Case. In Organizational Development (OD), David Cooperrider developed the methodology for organizational renewal known as Appreciative Inquiry. In the field of Corporate Social Responsibility and Sustainability, David leads the movement towards a more sustainable future, as mainfested in many international forums and gatherings, such as the Global Forum 'Business as an Agent of World Benefit: Management Knowledge Leading Positive Change'.

Andrea Cornwall is a fellow of the Institute of Development Studies at the University of Sussex, and member of the IDS Participation, Power and Social Change team. She has written widely on participation and participatory research and is author of *Beneficiary, Consumer, Citizen: Perspectives on Participation for Poverty Reduction* (Sida Studies, 2000), and co-editor of *Realizing Rights: Transforming Approaches to Sexual and Reproductive Wellbeing* (with Alice Welbourn, Zed Books, 2002), *Pathways to Participation* (with Garett Pratt, IT Publications, 2003) and *Spaces for Change? The Politics of Citizen Participation in New Democratic Arenas* (with Vera Schattan Coelho, Zed Books, 2006).

Federico Dickinson is a physical anthropologist with a PhD in human ecology, and he is a founder of the Department of Human Ecology of the Merida campus of Cinvestav, in Yucatan, Mexico. Since 1992 he has been researching the changes in the social fabric of rural communities when participatory research (PR) is applied, the social and cultural characteristics of those members of the community who take part in PR, and what happens, in cultural and societal terms, to the PR agents – both the facilitators, who belong to the community, and the acompañantes, who do not belong to the community – as the PR process develops through time.

Jennifer Dodge is a Research Associate at the Research Center for Leadership in Action at the Robert F. Wagner Graduate School of Public Service, New York University, and a doctoral candidate at the Wagner School. She is an active participant in the NYC Research and Organizing Initiative, a collaboration of organizing, research and policy groups committed to strengthening research for social change. Her interests include the policy role of nonprofit organizations, nonprofit management, social change leadership, and anti-poverty and environmental policy. Previously, she worked at MDRC, a policy research nonprofit, on a national employment and community development initiative. She has published articles in journals and edited volumes including *Action Research*, *Public Administration Review*, and *Advances in Appreciative Inquiry: Constructive Discourse and Human Organization* (ed. David Cooperrider and Michel Avital).

Chris Dymek is a scholar/practitioner who recently earned a doctorate in organization change from Pepperdine University. She also holds an MA in Philosophy from Wayne State University, a BA in Philosophy from the University of Michigan and a second BA in Computer Science from Wayne State University. Chris has held managerial positions in various industries, and is now helping to manage a major change initiative in a healthcare setting. Her industry and scholarly work focus on IT-related change.

Michelle Fine is Distinguished Professor of Social Psychology, Women's Studies and Urban Education at the Graduate Center, CUNY, and has taught at CUNY since 1990. She is a member of the Participatory Action Research (PAR) Collective at the Graduate Center and dreams wildly about critical inquiry, social theory and the politics of social justice for youth. With the craft of PAR, our projects seek to reveal theoretically and empirically the contours of injustice and resistance while we challenge the very bases upon which traditional conceptions of 'expert knowledge' sit. Recent publications include: *Sexuality Education and Desire: Still Missing After All These Years* (with S. McClelland); *Working Method: Social Research and Social Injustice* (with L. Weis); *Off White: Essays on Race, Privilege and Contestation* (with L. Weis, L. Powell Pruitt and A. Burns); and the multiple authored *Echoes of Brown: Youth Documenting and Performing the Legacy of Brown v. Board of Education* and *Changing Minds: The Impact of College in a Maximum Security Prison* (www.changingminds.ws).

Erica Gabrielle Foldy is an Assistant Professor of Public and Nonprofit Management at the Wagner Graduate School of Public Service at New York University. She is affiliated faculty with the Research Center for Leadership in Action, based at Wagner. She is also affiliated as a researcher with the Center for Gender in Organizations at the Simmons School of Management in Boston. Her research interests include identity and diversity in organizations, organizational learning and reflective practice, and the role of leadership in individual, organizational and social change. Prof. Foldy has published articles in a variety of journals and edited volumes, including *Public Administration Review* and *Journal of Applied Behavioral Science*. She also co-edited, with Robin Ely and Maureen Scully, the *Reader in Gender, Work and Organization*, published by Blackwell. She holds a BA from Harvard College and a PhD from Boston College. She was a Post Doctoral Fellow at Harvard Business School in 2002–3.

Victor J. Friedman, EdD, is Associate Professor of Organizational Behavior with a joint appointment in the Behavioral Sciences and Sociology-Anthropology at the Max Stern Academic College of Emek Yezreel. His life's work has been to help individuals, groups, organizations, and communities learn through 'action science' – ongoing experimentation and critical reflection in everyday life – and he has recently co-authored a book, *Demystifying Organizational Learning*. He has worked with educational, social service, and business organizations to promote organizational learning, social entrepreneurship, and social inclusion. He is a founder and co-chairperson of the Action Research Center, which promotes 'learning partnerships' between the College and local community activists for the purpose of mutual development and promoting social change. He is a senior associate of the Action Evaluation Research Institute and a member of the editorial board of *Action Research*.

Wendy Frisby is a Professor in the School of Human Kinetics in the Faculty of Education and Chair of Women's and Gender Studies in the Faculty of Arts at the University of British Columbia. She conducts feminist participatory action research (FPAR) with citizens and practitioners in the field to analyze how the social and living conditions experienced by those living in poverty, which are often exacerbated by existing policies, programs, and structures in community sport and recreation, create barriers to participation. She recently received Social Sciences and Humanities Research Council (SSHRC) funding (2006–9) to examine participatory policy development with Chinese immigrant women and sport/recreation policy-makers at the local, provincial, and federal government levels. The community-based organization WOAW (Women Organizing Activities for Women) that formed in conjunction with the research grant has received provincial and civic awards for its work to promote accessibility to sport and recreation for low-income populations.

Ronald E. Fry is Associate Professor of Organizational Behavior at Case Western Reserve University where he directs the Weatherhead School of Management's new Masters Program in Positive Organizational Development and Change. Ron was part of the group that originated the Appreciative Inquiry approach and continues to both apply and study the applications of AI in the field. His most recent book is *Appreciative Inquiry: A Positive Approach to Building Cooperative Capacity*, with Frank Barrett. He also recently co-edited *Appreciative Inquiry and Organizational Transformation: Reports from the Field* (Quorum, 2001). With Professor David Cooperrider, he co-directs the CASE Weatherhead International Certificate Program in Appreciative Inquiry for the Betterment of Business and Society. He is Editor and Chief of the CASE Center for Business as Agent of Work Benefit's global inquiry and directs the Center's Institute for Advances in Appreciative Inquiry. He currently oversees AI applications in a variety of systems including World Vision, Lubrizol, Roadway Express, and the US Navy.

John Gaventa is a fellow and member of the Participation, Power and Social Change team at the Institute of Development Studies, University of Sussex, and the director of the Development Research Centre on Citizenship, Participation and Accountability, based at IDS. He formerly was staff member and director of the Highlander Center in Tennessee. He has written widely on issues of participatory research, power and participation, including his books *Power and Powerlessness* (1980), *We Make the Road by Walking: Conversations on Education and Social Change with Myles Horton and Paulo Freire* (1990, co-edited with Brenda Bell and John Peters) and *Global Citizen Action* (2001, co-edited with Michael Edwards.)

Patricia Gayá Wicks is a Lecturer in Leadership Studies at the University of Exeter. Her research draws primarily on action research practices and on participatory worldviews to explore how individuals and communities can take effective action in the face of overwhelming circumstances, most particularly as in the case of our current ecological crisis. Her recently completed doctoral work develops Spinoza's notion of 'repose' as a way of engaging with complex, difficult issues in a manner which continues to foster joy and energy in meeting the challenges of these situations. Patricia completed her PhD at the Center for Action Research and Professional Practice at the University of Bath. As a member of faculty at the Centre for Leadership Studies, Patricia teaches on the undergraduate Management with Leadership programme, the MA/MRes in Leadership Studies programmes, and on Continuing Professional Development courses.

Kenneth J. Gergen is a Senior Research Professor at Swarthmore College, and the President of the Board of the Taos Institute, a non-profit organization dedicated to the promulgation of social constructionism in practice. Gergen has been a long-standing critic of traditional empiricist methods of research, and an ardent interlocutor in the development of alternative conceptions and practices of inquiry. His major writings include *Toward Transformation in Social Knowledge*, *Realities and Relationships*, *The Saturated Self*, and *An Invitation to Social Construction*.

Mary Gergen, Professor Emerita, Psychology & Women's Studies, Penn State University, Delaware County, is a scholar at the intersection of feminist theory and social constructionism. Her most recent book is *Feminist Reconstructions in Psychology: Narrative, Gender and Performance*. With Kenneth Gergen, she has edited *Social Construction, A Reader,* and written a primer, *Social Constructionism, Entering the Dialogue*. She is also a founder and Board member of the Taos Institute, a non-profit educational organization. She has been active in promoting alternative methodologies and presentational forms for many years.

Jill Grant is Assistant Professor in Social Work and Community Health at the University of Northern British Columbia. She has a PhD in Social Work from Wilfrid Laurier University. Her social work practice background is in community mental health practice, sexual and physical violence, and restorative justice. She conducts community-based participatory action research with mental health consumer/survivors, with a focus on the participation in mental health services of those who have used services and mental health housing.

Davydd J. Greenwood is the Goldwin Smith Professor of Anthropology and Director of the Institute for European Studies at Cornell University where he has served as a faculty member since 1970. He has been elected a Corresponding Member of the Spanish Royal Academy of Moral and Political Sciences. He served as the John S. Knight Professor and Director of the Mario Einaudi Center for 10 years and was President of the Association of International Education Administrators. He also has served as a program evaluator for many universities and for the National Foreign Language Center. His work centers on action research, political economy, ethnic conflict, community and regional development in Spain and the USA. His current work focuses on the impact of corporatization on higher education with a particular emphasis on the social sciences.

Meghna Guhathakurta is currently Executive Director of Research Initiatives, Bangladesh (RIB), an organization giving research support for poverty alleviation. RIB specializes in community-based action research and focuses on those marginalized groups who have been neglected by mainstream developmental actors. She was Professor of International Relations at the University of Dhaka until very recently. Dr Guhathakurta has written extensively on gender, development, South Asian politics and migration and is currently working on a study on access to justice for indigenous people. Her first book was the *The Politics of British Aid* Policy *Formation: the Case of British Aid to Bangladesh, 1972–1986* (Centre for Social Studies, Dhaka, 1990).

Bjørn Gustavsen is senior researcher at the Work Research Institute in Oslo, research director of the 'Value Creation 2010' programme, and visiting professor at the Vestfold University. He has helped create workplace development programmes in several countries and has written extensively on the relationship between theory and practice, workplace democracy and the use of programmes to create development – and innovation effects.

Agneta Hansson is lecturer at the Halmstad University, School of Social and Health Sciences. She was one of the Founders of the Centre for Working Life Research and Development and was also, in a period, its director. Her research interests focus on action research and on practical strategies for creating equal conditions for women and men in economic life.

John Heron is currently a co-director at the South Pacific Centre for Human Inquiry in New Zealand. He was Founder and Director of the Human Potential Research Project, University of Surrey, UK; Assistant Director, British Postgraduate Medical Federation, University of London; Director, International Centre for Co-operative-Inquiry, Tuscany, Italy. He is a researcher, author, facilitator and trainer in peer self-help psychotherapy, co-operative-inquiry, educational development, group facilitation, management development, personal and transpersonal development, professional development in the helping professions. His books include *Feeling and Personhood* (1992), *Co-operative-Inquiry* (1996), *Sacred Science* (1998), *The Complete Facilitator's Handbook* (1999), *Helping the Client* (2001) and *Participatory Spirituality* (2006).

Amparo Hofmann-Pinilla is an Associate Director for the Research Center for Leadership in Action at the Robert F. Wagner Graduate School of Public Service at New York University, where she oversees the Research and Documentation component of Leadership for a Changing World. Amparo's research interests include identity and social movements, especially among immigrants, and social change leadership. Amparo has collaborated in a series of studies on Leadership and new Latino communities, sponsored by the Wagner School. She also served as a program director in community-based HIV service agencies, and directed a peer and social service study/intervention to help persons living with HIV/AIDS adhere to their medications at Harlem Hospital/Columbia University. Amparo has taught as an adjunct lecturer in the Sociology Department at New York University (CUNY), Hostos Community College Social Studies Division and the Columbia University Spanish and Portuguese Department. She received an LLB at the Universidad Externado de Columbia in Bogota, Columbia, and an MA Phil in Sociology at New York University.

Ian Hughes Building on professional community development experience with Indigenous Australian communities, Ian Hughes is a Senior Lecturer in Community Health in the Faculty of Health Sciences at the University of Sydney, where he teaches in the gerontology programme. He has an established international reputation in action research, has taught action research in Australia, Singapore and Cameroon and coordinates the Action and Research Open Web (www.fhs.usyd.edu.au/arow). His current research integrates complex adaptive systems theory with action research in community health and organizational settings, including international graduate education, doctoral research supervision, community leadership and communication, healthcare decision-making, and medication safety with older people. Dr Hughes is a member of the editorial board of several international journals.

Ray Ison has been Professor of Systems at the UK Open University since January 1994 where he was foundation Director of the Postgraduate Programme in Environmental Decision Making and facilitated the launch of an MSc in Information Systems. He has been actively involved in the production of new Systems Practice courses and is foundation Director of the Open Systems Research Group with research foci on Systems Thinking and Practice, Information Systems and Sustainable Development. His own research has involved developing and evaluating systemic, participatory and process-based environmental decision-making, natural resource management, organizational change and R&D methodologies. He has pioneered and developed systemic approaches including second order R&D; systemic inquiry; soft systems methodology; systemic action research; managing for emergence; managing complexity; information systems; conceptual modelling; communities of practice and participatory institutional appraisal.

LaDon James is a field organizer for the Center for Community Change in Washington, DC. The Center provides policy and organizing expertise on a range of issue areas and works to establish and develop community organizations across the United States to bring attention to major national issues related to poverty and to help insure that government programs are responsive to community needs. LaDon also serves on the Advisory Board of Make the Road by Walking. She has been Co-chair of the Board of Directors of Community Voices Heard in New York City. In that role she participated as a 2001 award recipient in the Leaders for a Changing World program of the Ford Foundation and the Advocacy Institute.

Mariann Jelinek is Richard C. Kraemer Chair of Business Strategy at the Mason School of Business at the College of William and Mary in Williamsburg, Virginia. From June 1999 until August of 2001, she served as Director, Innovation and Organizational Change Program at the National Science Foundation, where she directed solicitation, assessment and awards for research projects on topics of organizational innovation. Her own research interests have centered on innovation, technology and organizations, in high technology firms and mature industries. She also investigates cognitive and organizational factors affecting innovation in a variety of industry settings. Her most recent project centered on industry–university relations around intellectual property. She holds a PhD from the University of California at Berkeley and a DBA from Harvard University's Graduate School of Business.

Taj Johns is adjunct faculty at St Mary's College in Orinda, California. Teaching in the Art of Leadership Masters Program, her specialty in building cross-cultural capacity and cultural competency has been developed by providing diversity trainings, working in city government organizing communities of diverse populations and facilitating SASHA workshops. Taj has a strong interest in understanding the effects of internalized oppression on human development and consequently co-founded SASHA, an acronym for Self Affirming Soul Healing Africans. SASHA is both a group and model which helps people explore and understand the impact of oppression in their lives. Her doctoral research is on the usefulness of the SASHA model towards reducing the personal effects of internalized oppression.

Stephen Kemmis is Professor of Education, School of Education, Charles Sturt University, NSW 2678, Australia. He is co-author with Wilfred Carr of *Becoming Critical: Education, Knowledge and Action Research* (Falmer, 1986), and co-author (with Robin McTaggart) of the chapter 'Participatory Action Research: Communicative Action and the Public Sphere' in Norman Denzin and Yvonna Lincoln (eds) *The Sage Handbook of Qualitative Research, 3rd edn* (Sage, 2005).

Rita Kowalski, a recent graduate of the MS in Positive Organizational Development and Change (MPOD) from Case Western University's Weatherhead School of Management, Rita is an OD Practitioner in The Veteran Health Administration's National Center for Organization Development (NCOD). She was an original member of the Project Team for the Stress and Aggression Project in the Department of Veterans Affairs and is continuing her work in action research on a variety projects. She is also a consultant member of the Society for Organizational Learning (SoL). Her interests are collaborative action inquiry, learning, knowledge transfer and poetry.

Marianne Kristiansen is Associate Professor and Founder of the Centre of Interpersonal Organizational Communication at the Department of Communication, Aalborg University, Denmark (www.vaeksthuset.hum.aau.dk) and is associated with Partner in Dialog, a consulting firm (www.dialog-mj.dk). Trained as a psychoanalyst and body therapist, she has done action research with high school students on 'quiet girls' and social interaction, with adult teachers on professional presence, with social workers on empowering social practice, with managers and employees in private organizations on mentoring, dialogue, and power. At present, she works with employees and managers on traditional and modern dilemmas in team based organizations. She teaches and counsels Masters and PhD students in interpersonal organizational communication at Aalborg University and Copenhagen University.

Gregg Lahood is a social anthropologist and antenatal educator with research interests in the transpersonal dimensions of birth-giving for both women and men. He has facilitated group inquiries in collaborative ritual-making and the transpersonal dimensions of consciousness for 20 years in New Zealand, Australia and England.

Morten Levin is a Professor at the Department of Industrial Economics and Technology Management in the Faculty of Social Sciences and Technology Management at the Norwegian University of Science and Technology in Trondheim, Norway. He holds graduate degrees in engineering and in sociology. Throughout his professional life, he has worked as an action researcher with a particular focus on processes and structures of social change in the relationships between technology and organization. His action research has taken place in industrial contexts, in local communities, and in university teaching where he has developed and been in charge of a three successive PhD programs in action research.

James D. Ludema has a PhD in Organizational Behavior, from Case Western Reserve University and is Professor in the PhD program in Organization Development at Benedictine University. His research focuses on appreciative inquiry, organization change, positive organizational scholarship, business as an agent of world benefit, and whole system methodologies for strategic change. His most recent book is *The Appreciative Inquiry Summit: A Practitioner's Guide for Leading Large Group Change*. He is an internationally recognized consultant and pioneer in the use of appreciative inquiry for large-scale corporate change initiatives.

M. Brinton Lykes, PhD, is Professor of Community Cultural Psychology and Associate Director of the Center for Human Rights and International Justice at Boston College. She has extensive experience in community-based participatory action research at the interface of

Euro-American and traditional native cultures with a particular focus on responding to and understanding the effects of structural violence including war, poverty and gender oppression. She continues her research with rural Maya women in Guatemala and collaborates in interdisciplinary and inter-professional PAR with immigrant communities and post-deportee families in Boston, and in a new initiative in post-Katrina New Orleans. Brinton's feminist activism includes work with local and international feminist and human rights NGOs.

Jenny Mackewn is an organizational consultant, trainer, psychotherapist and author. In the business context, Jenny's work focuses on the process of people management, organizational change, organizational culture and sustainable development. She specializes in executive mentoring and strategic development for leadership teams. She is particularly inspired and informed by the perspectives of complex adaptive systems, collaborative action research and creative approaches. She has developed a training programme of facilitation as and for action research which she offers at the University of Bath.

Amelia Mallona, PhD, has worked as an assistant professor at the School of Human Services, Springfield College, Manchester, NH, for the past eight years. She received her doctorate in Developmental and Educational Psychology from Boston College in 1998. Prior to her academic career, Amelia worked for over 10 years on economic and organizing projects in low-income communities in Nicaragua. She continues to be active in her Boston, MA, community, volunteering with City Life/Vida Urbana, a grassroots organizing agency.

Judi Marshall is a professor of Organizational Behaviour in the School of Management, University of Bath, UK. Judi's main research interests have been: managerial job stress; women in management (publications include *Women Managers: Travellers in a Male World*, 1984; *Women Managers Moving On: Exploring Career and Life Choices*, 1995; and analyses of careers, communications and job stress); change; and self-reflective, action-oriented forms of inquiry. Issues of representation and form in writing are long-term areas of exploration. In 1997, Judi and colleagues launched the MSc in Responsibility and Business Practice, designed to address issues of environmental and social justice within business education. Its educational approach is founded in principles and practices of action research. In 2005, Judi received a European Faculty Pioneer Award from the Aspen Institute, World Resources Institute and EABIS for championing attention to sustainability issues in business education.

Ann W. Martin is an Associate with Praxis Consulting Group and a part-time faculty member at The Norwegian University of Science and Technology where she teaches writing and methodology in EDWOR, an action research doctoral programme. She has taught and facilitated dialogue, conflict resolution, and organizational development, often engaging where there is a need for change in a large system or a complex of systems. In 20 years as an adult educator at Cornell University's School of Industrial and Labor Relations, Ann learned the value of including diverse perspectives in action for change. Ann holds an EdD in Adult Education from Columbia University and Masters degrees from the School of Industrial and Labor Relations at Cornell and the Harvard Graduate School of Education.

Kate Louise McArdle is a lecturer in organizational behaviour at the University of Bath, working on undergraduate management programmes and the postgraduate programme at the Centre for Action Research in Professional Practice. Kate's PhD work at CARPP focused on second-person inquiry processes with young women managers in a multi-national organization. Ensuing interests in the variety of issues involved in the development of inquiry practice (particularly around issues of quality, scale, facilitation practice and skill building for change) are explored through a broad spectrum of academic and consulting work. Kate also runs, swims, rides horses and loves being outdoors.

Geoff Mead had a 30-year career in the UK police service, holding a variety of senior management and leadership roles, and is now an independent organizational consultant working mainly in the area of leadership development in public services. He is the founding director of Hermes Consulting and a Visiting Research Fellow at the Centre for Action Research in Professional Practice at the University of Bath where, in 2002, he received a PhD in Action Research for his work on Living Inquiry. His work is increasingly focused on the role of story and narrative in leadership and organizational development. He is also a performer, teaching and telling traditional wonder tales to aspiring storytellers and international audiences.

Philip Mirvis is an organizational psychologist whose research and private practice concerns large-scale organizational change and the character of the workforce and workplace. A consultant to businesses in the USA, Europe, and Asia, he has authored eight books on his studies including *The Cynical Americans* (social trends), *Building the Competitive Workforce* (human resource investments), and *Joining Forces* (the human side of mergers). His most recent is a business transformation story, *To the Desert and Back*. Mirvis is a fellow of the Work/Family Roundtable and Corporate Branding Initiative, and a board member of the Foundation for Community Encouragement. Mirvis has a BA from Yale University and a PhD in Organizational Psychology from the University of Michigan. He has taught at Boston University, Jiao Tong University, Shanghai, China, and the London Business School. He is currently a senior research fellow, Boston College School of Management, Center for Corporate Citizenship.

Terry L. Mitchell has a PhD in Community Psychology from the University of Toronto. She is a registered psychologist with a background in counseling and community practice. Her research focus is community-based participatory action research on health equity and cancer survivorship with women and medically underserved populations, in particular Aboriginal peoples. Dr Mitchell is an assistant professor in the Department of Psychology at Wilfrid Laurier University where she teaches community psychology and trains graduate students in qualitative and participatory methods.

Jennifer Mullett is a Community Psychologist in private practice (Action Research Consulting). Her former positions include Research Scholar in Community Based Research supported by the Michael Smith Foundation for Health Research and Director of Research and Evaluation for the Ministry of Health in British Columbia. Involved in several community projects, her main expertise is mentoring community workers in methods appropriate for action research directed towards creating healthy communities for the development of families, children and youth. She is also an Adjunct Professor in the faculty of Human and Social Development, University of Victoria, Canada.

Bano Murtuja A Senior Associate and the Director of Vis-à-Vis Research Consultancy, Bano's recent work has included research relating to the mental health needs and understandings of South Asians at a local level, BME confidence in the criminal justice system in the UK and capacity building needs of faith-based communities. She was responsible for drawing up the reports on ministerial meetings, 'Tackling Extremism Together'. Bano is a Visiting Research Associate at Newcastle University. A founding member of Right 2 B Heard, she was one of ten commissioners on the UK's recent power inquiry, sits on a number of advisory panels for a diverse range of research programmes, and facilitates a Café Scientifique programme in Blackburn.

Eric Neilsen is Professor of Organizational Behavior at the Weatherhead School of Management, Case Western Reserve University. He received his BA degree from Princeton University (1965) and his MA and PhD degrees from Harvard University (1970) in sociology, and was an Assistant Professor of Organizational Behavior at the Harvard Business School. He founded and was the first director of the masters in Organization Development and Analysis program at Case in 1975. He is the author of *Becoming an OD Practitioner* and has published articles in many books and journals, including *Academy of Management Review*, *Administrative Science Quarterly*, *Harvard Business Review*, *Human Relations*, and the *Journal of Management Education*. Professor Neilsen's research interests are in the application of attachment theory to organizational change and development.

Geoffrey Nelson is Professor of Psychology and member of the graduate program in Community Psychology at Wilfrid Laurier University. Geoff served as the Senior Editor of the *Canadian Journal of Community Mental Health*, and together with the Canadian Mental Health Association/Waterloo Region Branch, he received the Harry V. McNeill Award for Innovation in Community Mental Health from the American Psychological Foundation. He is the author of five books and over 100 journal articles and book chapters. His research has focused on issues related to psychiatric consumer/survivors (housing, self-help/mutual aid) and primary prevention programs for children.

Sonia Ospina is a Professor of Public Management and Policy, and Co-Director of the Center for Leadership Development, Dialogue and Inquiry at the Robert F. Wagner Graduate School of Public Service at New York University, where she also serves as the Research Director of the Research and Documentation of Leadership for a Changing World.

William Pasmore is a Partner at Mercer Delta and also serves as the global practice leader for the organizational research group. Before joining Mercer Delta in 1997, Bill was a tenured full professor in the Weatherhead School of Management at Case Western Reserve University, where he taught courses in the school's MBA, Executive MBA, PhD and Executive PhD programs. He was a visiting professor at INSEAD and Stanford and a faculty member in the executive education programs there. As a thought leader in the field of organization development, he has published 19 books and numerous articles, including *Designing Effective Organizations* (1988), *Creating Strategic Change* (1994), *Research in Organization Change and Development* (2005), and *Relationships that Enable Enterprise Change* (2002). He is a frequent keynote speaker and his work is recognized internationally. He has been a leading consultant to executives in North America and abroad for over 30 years. He holds a BS in Aeronautical Engineering/Industrial Management and a PhD in Administrative Sciences, both from Purdue University.

Mike Pedler is an academic and consultant on management and leadership development. He is Professor of Action Learning at Henley Management College and holds visiting professorships at the universities of York and Lincoln. He is an Honorary Senior Research Fellow in the Department of Management Learning at Lancaster University and a partner in the consultancy practice Whole Systems Development.

Michel Pimbert is currently Director of the Sustainable Agriculture, Biodiversity and Livelihoods Program at the UK-based International Institute for Environment and Development (IIED). Michel is an agricultural ecologist by training. He previously worked at the International Crops Research Institute for the Semi Arid Tropics (ICRISAT) in India, the Université François Rabelais de Tours in France, and the World Wide Fund for Nature in Switzerland. His work centres on the political ecology of natural resource and biodiversity management, sustainable agriculture, food sovereignty and citizenship as well as participatory action research and deliberative democratic processes. Over the last 20 years he has published extensively in these areas, linking theory with practice. His latest co-edited books include *Social Change and Conservation*, *The Life Industry: Biodiversity, People and Profits* and *Sharing Power: Learning by Doing in the Co-management of Natural Resources throughout the World.*

Thoralf U. Qvale is senior researcher at the Work Research Institute in Oslo and visiting professor at the University for Technology and the Natural Sciences in Trondheim. He has extensive experience as initiator and manager of workplace development projects and has written broadly on action research, socio-technical perspectives, learning and regional development.

Md. Anisur Rahman taught economics at Dhaka and Islamabad University and coordinated the Programme on Participation and Organization of the Rural Poor of the International Labour Office from 1977 until 1990. He is currently associated with the Research Initiatives, Bangladesh (RIB) in Dhaka.

Peter Reason is Professor of Action Research/Practice and Director of the Centre for Action Research in Professional Practice in the School of Management at the University of Bath, which has pioneered graduate education based on collaborative, experiential and action oriented forms of inquiry through the Postgraduate Programme in Action Research and the MSc in Responsibility and Business Practice. His major academic work has been to contribute to the development of a participatory worldview and associated approaches to inquiry, and in particular to the theory and practice of co-operative inquiry. He is currently leading a large-scale action research project exploring the introduction of potentially low carbon technology in industry. Peter's major concern is with the devastating and unsustainable impact of human activities on the biosphere which, he believes, is grounded in our failure to recognize the participatory nature of our relationship with the planet and the cosmos. This is an area in which action research can make a major contribution.

Colleen Reid is a postdoctoral fellow with Simon Fraser University's Faculty of Health Sciences and the British Columbia Centre of Excellence for Women's Health. She earned an Interdisciplinary PhD from the University of British Columbia in 2002. Dr Reid's postdoctoral work is focused on better understanding and measuring the social determinants of women's health. She is conducting feminist participatory action research to examine the relationship between women's employability and health. The project is currently underway in four communities in British Columbia and is intended to actively involve community groups and their constituents and to generate useable findings for improving policy and practice. Over the last 10 years she has collaborated with groups including the Vancouver Women's Health Collective, AIDS Vancouver, the Positive Women's Network, REAL Power Youth Society, Promotion Plus, and Literacy BC.

Anita M. Rees is the Associate Director of LIFETIME: Low-Income Families' Empowerment through Education, and a single mother of a teenage son, Alex. While on welfare, Anita graduated from the University of California, Berkeley with a Sociology degree in 1997. Having experienced the challenges of juggling family, school, and work responsibilities while on welfare, Anita is committed to LIFETIME's goal of helping low-income parents enroll in, continue, and successfully complete higher education and training programs. Anita received the Ford Foundation and Advocacy Institute's 2003 Leadership for a Changing world Award, and serves on the board of directors for East Bay Area Local Development Corporation (EBALDC), the California Family Resource Association (CFRA), and the Transportation and Land Use Coalition (TALC).

Tim Rogers lectures in communication and management courses in the School of Management at the University of South Australia. He holds degrees in both Drama and Psychology. His recently completed PhD examined the difficulties of working in the interprofessional healthcare context and the potential contribution of action science to this field. His academic interests also include the philosophy of the social psychological sciences in general and critical realism in particular.

George Roth is currently leading the Enterprise Change Research Program, a part of MIT's Lean Aerospace Initiative (LAI) program, a joint management–engineering effort transforming aerospace companies and government. His efforts examine and develop initiatives that promote learning and improvement initiatives across multiple organizations by prioritizing improvements in products and services within their value streams. This focus builds upon his ongoing research in organizational culture, leadership, learning, and change. George has a PhD in Organizational Studies, an MBA in Marketing and Finance, and a BS in Mechanical Engineering. His hobbies include sailing, running, bicycling and skiing. He, his wife, and two teenage daughters live in southern Maine.

Jenny W. Rudolph's research probes the cognitive and emotional bases of Murphy's Law in high-stakes situations. Many of the things that can go wrong do go wrong in organizations when people feel the social or physical stakes are high. Her current work explores diagnostic problem-solving under time pressure, the impact of workload pressure on accidents and errors, and the role of reflective practice and root cause analysis in organizational learning. As a teacher, Jenny attempts to create experiential learning environments where students can observe, analyze, and experiment with changing their habitual cognitive routines and ways of interacting. Jenny is an Assistant Professor of Health Policy and Management at Boston University School of Public Health. She is also on the faculty of the Center for Medical Simulation in Cambridge, MA, where she and her colleagues have pioneered the use of reflective practice in debriefing high-fidelity medical simulations. Jenny is a graduate of Harvard College, was a visiting scholar in system dynamics at the MIT Sloan School of Management, and received her PhD in Management from Boston College.

Edgar H. Schein is the Sloan Fellows Professor of Management Emeritus at the MIT Sloan School of Management, where he taught from 1956 to 2004. He has done research on career development, process consultation and organizational culture. His work on clinical research and organizational therapy is the primary basis for much of his writing. His recent books are *Process Consultation Revisited* (Prentice-Hall, 1999), *The Corporate Culture Survival Guide* (Jossey-Bass, 1999), *DEC is Dead: Long Live DEC* (Berrett-Kohler, 2003), *Organizational Culture and Leadership, 3rd edn* (Jossey-Bass, 2004) and *Career Anchors, 3rd edn* (Jossey-Bass/Pfeiffer, 2006).

A.B. (Rami) Shani is Professor and Chair of the Management Area at the Orfalea College of Business. He received his PhD in Organizational Behavior from Case Western Reserve University in 1981 and has held visiting professorship appointments at Stockholm School of Economics, Politecnico di Milano and Recanati Graduate School of Business Administration, Tel Aviv University. His main research interest concerns work and organization design, organizational change and development, collaborative research methodologies, and learning in and by organizations. His most recent co-authored books include *Behavior in Organizations, 8th edn* (McGraw-Hill/Irwin, 2005), *Creating Sustainable Work Systems* (Routledge, 2002), *Learning by Design: Building Sustainable Organizations* (Blackwell, 2003), and *Collaborative Research in Organizations: Foundations for Learning, Change, and Theoretical Development* (Sage, 2004).

Jasber Singh Deputy Director of Co-Inquiry at the PEALS Research Centre, Newcastle University, Jasber has been involved in a range of UK-based participatory work such as the Nanojury and Community X-change. Both projects used participatory techniques to allow community perspectives to be articulated in relation to science-related issues, such as nanotechnology and climate change. A founding member of Right 2 B Heard, he has also managed regional participatory action research at St Martins College, Lancaster, on investigating the barriers to employment faced by ethnic minorities in Lancashire, England. At the local level, Jasber carries out youth and community development work on several levels: as a street youth worker in deprived housing estates, with Asian Muslim youths, and with a multi-ethnic youth group, which has just completed a participatory video on the lives of young men in Lancaster. Currently, Jasber is carrying out action research on the barriers faced by ethnic minorities in accessing places of environmental beauty as part of his work on environmental justice.

Ernie Stringer After an early career as primary teacher and school principal, Ernie spent many years as lecturer in teacher education at Curtin University of Technology in Western Australia. From the 1980s he worked at Curtin's Centre for Aboriginal Studies where he worked collaboratively with Aboriginal staff and community people to develop a wide variety of innovative and highly successful education and community development programmes and consultative services. Their activities with government departments, community-based agencies, business corporations and local governments assisted those organizations to work more effectively with Aboriginal people. In recent years, as visiting professor at universities in New Mexico and Texas, he has taught action research to graduate students and engaged in projects with African American, Hispanic and other community and neighborhood groups. He is author of the texts *Action Research* (Sage, 1999), *Action Research in Education* (Pearson, 2004), *Action Research in Health* (with Bill Genat, Pearson, 2004) and *Action Research in Human Services* (with Rosalie Dwyer, Pearson, 2005).

Marja Liisa Swantz is the former Director of the Institute and Director of Research in Development Studies, University of Helsinki. She has been a Lecturer in Science of Religion and has acted as professor in Social and Cultural Anthropology and a visiting professor in the World Institute of Development Economics Research, in Helsinki. She is a graduate of the University of Helsinki and Turku, Finland and received her PhD from the University of Uppsala, Sweden. Marja Liisa has pioneered Participatory Action Research in Tanzania and has made use of it in large research programmes in the field of Anthropology and Development Studies.

Rajesh Tandon is an internationally acclaimed leader and practitioner of participatory research and development. He founded the Society for Participatory Research in Asia (PRIA)

23 years ago, a voluntary organization providing support to grassroots initiatives in South Asia, and has continued to be its chief functionary since 1982. With a PhD from Case Western Reserve University, a degree in electronic engineering IIT (Kanpur) and in management (IIM Calcutta), Dr Tandon has specialized in social and organizational change. His contributions to the enhancement of perspectives and capacities of many voluntary activists and organizations revolve around issues of participatory research, advocating for people-centred development, policy reform and networking in India, South Asia and beyond. He has advocated for a self-reliant, autonomous and competent voluntary sector in India and abroad. He is currently promoting local government bodies (panchayats and municipalities) as institutions of local self-governance in South Asia with a special focus on women and marginalized sections. Building alliances and partnerships among diverse sectors in societal development is another current area of his work. Under his leadership, PRIA has innovated numerous methodologies of participatory learning and training, participatory bottom-up micro-planning, and participatory monitoring and evaluation.

Steven S. Taylor is an assistant professor of management at the Worcester Polytechnic Institute in Worcester, Massachusetts, USA. His research focuses on organizational aesthetics and reflective practice. The organizational aesthetics work is focused on theorizing how arts-based modalities such as storytelling and theatrical performance within organizations function; writing plays about organizations; and inquiring into the aesthetics of everyday organizational actions, such as beautiful interventions into small group dynamics. His work in reflective practice is based in the action science/action inquiry traditions and is focused on extending these traditions with tools for reflection and arts-based practices. Steve's work has been published in journals including *Action Research, Human Relations, Organization Studies, Journal of Management Inquiry, Journal of Organizational Change Management*, and *Management Communications Quarterly.*

William Torbert, now Professor of Management at the Carroll School of Management at Boston College and a founding member of its Leadership for Change executive program, has consulted widely and served on the boards of organizations such as Harvard Pilgrim Health Care and Trillium Asset Management (the first and largest independent social investing advisor). With regard to scholarship, the 2004 Berrett-Koehler book, *Action Inquiry: The Secret of Timely and Transforming Leadership,* presents his theories, cases, surveys, and lab and field experiments in regard to developmental transformation at both the personal and organizational levels, as well as within science itself. His numerous other books and articles include the national Alpha Sigma Nu award-winning *Managing the Corporate Dream* (Dow Jones-Irwin, 1987), the Terry Award Finalist book *The Power of Balance: Transforming Self, Society, and Scientific Inquiry* (Sage, 1991), and the April 2005 HBR article 'Seven Transformations of Leadership', which won the worldwide Association of Executive Search Consultants Award for Best Published Research on Leadership and Corporate Governance.

María Elena Torre is chair of Education Studies at Eugene Lang College of The New School. Her research focuses on youth activism, urban education, and youth and community engagement in participatory action research for social justice. She is a co-author of *Echoes of Brown: Youth Documenting and Performing the Legacy of Brown v. Board of Education* and *Changing Minds: The Impact of College in a Maximum Security Prison*, and has been published in *Urban Girls, Revisited* (NYU Press, 2007), *Beyond Resistance: Youth Activism and Community Change* (Routledge, 2006), *Letters to the Next President: What We Can Do About the Real Crisis in Public Education* (Teachers College Press, 2004), *Qualitative Research in*

Psychology: Expanding Perspectives in Methodology and Design (American Psychological Association, 2003), and in journals such as *Action Research, Teachers College Record*, the *Journal of Social Issues, Feminism and Psychology*, and the *International Journal of Critical Psychology*. She has served as a consultant for New York City and state governments, and community groups and colleges interested in establishing college-in-prison programs in facilities such as San Quentin and Sing-Sing.

María Dolores Viga de Alva is from Tabasco, currently living in Yucatan, Mexico. She works at the Human Ecology Department of the Center for Research and Advanced Studies at the IPN, Mérida Unit. She has a PhD in Management Sciences from the National Polytechnic Institute, with a research topic focused on the design of an environmental model for a biosphere reserve in Yucatan. She was honored for her research and now this model has been applied to other communities on the Yucatecan coast. She has a particular interest in research on Natural resources, human well-being and environmental culture, including participatory research as a main methodology to promote responsible environmental behavior.

Tom Wakeford, having spent time as an ecologist, geneticist and science writer, succumbed to participatory action research while teaching at the University of East London in the mid-1990s. He has since been involved in a diverse range of initiatives on four continents, particularly focusing on areas of controversial knowledge and contested expertise. Currently Director of Co-Inquiry at the PEALS Research Centre, Newcastle University, and a Visiting Fellow at the International Institute for Environment and Development (IIED), his books include *Liaisons of Life, Democratising Technology* and *Teach Yourself Citizens' Juries*. He is on the editorial board of Participatory Learning and Action and is a founding member of Right 2 B Heard.

Lyle Yorks is an Associate Professor in the Department of Organization and Leadership at Teachers College, Columbia University, where he is director of the AEGIS doctoral program in adult education. Articles authored and co-authored by Lyle have appeared in the *Academy of Management Review, California Management Review, Adult Education Quarterly, Teachers College Record*, and other scholarly journals. Among his recent publications is a chapter on action research methods in *Research Methods in Organizations* (R. Swanson and E. Holton, III (eds), Berrett-Koehler) and *Collaborative Inquiry in Practice: Action, Reflection, and Meaning Making*, co-authored with J. Bray, J. Lee, and L. Smith (Sage). His current research interests center on action learning, collaborative inquiry, and organizational learning. He is currently Associate Editor of *Human Resource Development Review*.

Danielle P. Zandee teaches in the Masters in Positive OD and Change Program (MPOD) and other programs at Case Western Reserve University where previously she received her PhD in Organizational Behavior. Originally from the Netherlands, she obtained ample experience in human resources, corporate training & OD, and management development in the Royal Dutch Shell Group and at Nyenrode University before making the shift to an academic life. Guided by her perception that our global society is in dire need of bold social and organizational innovations, she wants to make scholarly contributions with practical transformative impact.

Introduction

Peter Reason and Hilary Bradbury

Action research is a family of practices of living inquiry that aims, in a great variety of ways, to link practice and ideas in the service of human flourishing. It is not so much a *methodology* as an *orientation to inquiry* that seeks to create participative communities of inquiry in which qualities of engagement, curiosity and question posing are brought to bear on significant practical issues. Action research challenges much received wisdom in both academia and among social change and development practitioners, not least because it is a practice of participation, engaging those who might otherwise be subjects of research or recipients of interventions to a greater or less extent as inquiring co-researchers. Action research does not start from a desire of changing others 'out there', although it may eventually have that result, rather it starts from an orientation of change *with* others.

Within an action research project, communities of inquiry and action evolve and address questions and issues that are significant for those who participate as co-researchers. Typically such communities engage in more or less systematic cycles of action and reflection: in action phases co-researchers test practices and gather evidence; in reflection stages they make sense together and plan further actions. And since these cycles of action and reflection integrate knowing and acting, action research does not have to address the 'gap' between knowing and doing that befuddles so many change efforts and 'applied' research.

Action research can be described conceptually – and you will find such descriptions in the volume. Action research primarily arises, however, as people try to work together to address key problems in their communities or organizations – some of which involve creating positive change on a small scale and others of which affect the lives of literally millions of people. The scope and impact of action research is perhaps best grasped through illustration from exemplars in this book.

Meghna Guhathakurta (Chapter 35) describes how 'theatre of the oppressed' is adapted in a Bangladeshi marginalized 'sweeper' community in a way that helps the people themselves understand and reflect on issues and problems they experience – both their low status in the wider community and tensions within the community – and thereby to develop a consciousness with the potentiality to transform. The variety of activities based in theatre holds up a mirror to the people, so their experiences can be discussed more openly.

Gillian Chowns (Chapter 39) set up a co-operative inquiry group with children who have a parent dying of cancer, which both directly helped the children understand and manage the stresses they experienced and also brought their voices, usually ignored, to the wider community of palliative care practitioners.

These are examples of engagement with a small community or group. They are important because through such micro-practices people increase their ability to make sense of their world and act effectively. Of course, from such face-to-face work people also develop the ability to influence a wider context. But in recent years, practitioners have been developing ways of using action research on a much larger scale.

Bjørn Gustavsen and his colleagues (Chapter 4) describe the development of action research in helping develop the quality of working life in Scandinavia over the past 40 years, work that is rooted in national agreements among industry, unions, and government. He shows how practice has developed from individual 'field experiments' working intensively at one site; through establishing development coalitions of several organizations engaged in shared learning; to a current practice of continuous widening of the circle of participating actors to build networks of inquiry and development across whole regions.

Ernie Stringer (Chapter 38) was invited by the government of newly liberated East Timor to use participative action research as a means of both formulating and implementing national education policy. With a new emerging government, very little funding and many schools destroyed in the liberation struggle, this project helped develop effective parent–teacher associations devoted to improving local education, and also worked with a wider group of stakeholders, including the Ministry of Education, to develop national policy and to develop democratic capacities.

On an even wider scale, action research projects and programmes such as these can also be seen as part of social and political movements for liberation and development working on a national and international scale. As we finalize our drafts for publication, we celebrate the award of the Nobel Peace Prize to Mohammed Yunus and the Grameen Bank in Bangladesh. While we have yet to more fully understand Yunus' work from the perspective of action research, we quote from the work of our colleague at Harvard's Hauser Center, itself an action research think tank, who describes Grameen as an action research process: 'Yunus tested the

hypothesis that accountability to peers might replace collateral as an incentive for poor borrowers to repay small loans, and helped create the practice innovations for a micro-credit movement that now serves millions of borrowers around the world' (Brown, 2002: 32). Certainly Yunus' work has changed our theory of why loans are repaid and has profoundly influenced the lending practices of global bodies such as The World Bank, as much as he changed the lives of those heretofore left out of the economy altogether, especially women. The Nobel committee's recognition of the work of someone actively engaged with complex and difficult issues is heartening. We see this as an indication of how action researchers may play a part in constructive large scale change. The degree to which participation and partnership ethic was practised – or could be more so in the future – is an important one for the whole micro-credit 'industry' to grapple with as it evolves. From an action research perspective, the challenge to all working with large scale change efforts will be in the extent to which we are able to respond to the challenge of participation – which gets harder, not easier as more people become involved. We must all sit with the question of how to engage stakeholders in a continuing process of participative inquiry and practical experimentation which keep our original visions and partnership ethics manifest.

Action research has influenced and been influenced by civil rights and anti-racism movements, feminisms, community development and so on, and can be seen as reciprocally contributing to the development of such social movements (Gustavsen, 2003a). One means of doing this is to link grassroots activity with the formal structures of international aid and development:

Dave Brown and Rajesh Tandon (Chapter 15) describe how practical efforts at consciousness raising and empowerment of the marginalized people around the world has attracted the attention of policy-makers in international institutions. They point to the importance of coalitions of institutions which span the 'North–South divide', which are both grounded in local issues and can have access to policy-makers.

The origins of action research are broad: they lie in the work of Lewin and other social science researchers around at the end of the Second World War; in the liberationist perspective that can be exemplified in Paulo Freire (1970); philosophically in liberal humanism, pragmatism, phenomenology, critical theory, systemic thinking and social construction; and practically in the work of scholar-practitioners in many professions, notably in organization development, teaching, health promotion and nursing, and community development both in Western countries and in the majority world. None of these origins is well linked to the mainstream of academic research with its conventional if unsupportable notions of objectivity in either North America or Europe: objectivist, hypothetico-deductive research retains a dominance, and although this has been strongly challenged by qualitative and interpretive approaches to research, the emphasis of the latter has been on *representation* of the world rather than *action* within it (Greenwood and Levin, 2001). Nor has action research always sat easily with Marxist thinking and socialist politics, as Marja Liisa Swantz's account shows (Chapter 2). As a result, the family of practices called action research has inhabited the margins of academia for many years. As Argyris (2003) points out, the pursuit of knowledge in the service of justice and effectiveness has often been held in disrepute. Moreover, Levin and Greenwood point out, the structure and ethos of universities often work against the processes of action research. So those who champion action research often need to build institutions to nurture and support themselves and the practice – coalitions of the kind Brown and Tandon describe; independent institutions such as PRIA (Participatory Research in Asia, New Delhi), RIB (Research Initiatives Bangladesh, Dhaka); government supported institutions like the Work Research Institute in Oslo; community and professional networks such as the Action Research Issues Association that has supported community and university-based action research in Victoria, Australia over 20 years, and ALARPM (Action Research, Action Learning and Process Management) also based in Australia which has been so successful in sponsoring the series of World Congresses of Action Research; and research centres and informal networks within universities such as those that can be found at Aalborg, Bath, Boston College, Case Western Reserve, Cornell, College of Emek Yezreel, Southern Cross, Pepperdine Trondheim, Southern California and others. Formal and informal institutions such as these are key in giving support to individual reflective practice in a context of supportive collegial relations.

Through examples such as those mentioned above, action research – which may be quite intimate or may seek influence on a large scale – demonstrates an inquiry-in-action that positively shapes the lives of literally hundreds of thousands of people everyday around the world. Indeed we might respond to the disdainful attitude of mainstream social scientists to our work that action research practices have changed the world in far more positive ways than has conventional social science. Indeed it is more useful to compare action research to the clinical practice of physicians (and Edgar Schein uses that term for his work, see Chapter 18) than to the work of conventional social scientists. We are intrigued that in the USA the National Institute of Health now regularly calls for 'participative action research' when soliciting grant proposals, and that the World Bank publishes a Participation Sourcebook (see http://www.worldbank.org/wbi/sourcebook/sbhome.htm). And we also note the concerns expressed by Gaventa and Cornwall in Chapter 11 concerning the dangers of the co-option of participation by global institutions.

So a first description of action research is that it:

- is a set of practices that responds to people's desire to act creatively in the face of practical and often pressing issues in their lives in organizations and communities;
- calls for engagement *with* people in collaborative relationships, opening new 'communicative spaces' in which dialogue and development can flourish;

- draws on many ways of knowing, both in the evidence that is generated in inquiry and its expression in diverse forms of presentation as we share learning with wider audiences;
- is values oriented, seeking to address issues of significance concerning the flourishing of human persons, their communities, and the wider ecology in which we participate;
- is a living, emergent process that cannot be predetermined but changes and develops as those engaged deepen their understanding of the issues to be addressed and develop their capacity as co-inquirers both individually and collectively.

Definitions of action research often emphasize an empirical and logical problem-solving process involving cycles of action and reflection, sometimes going back to Lewin's definition: 'It proceeds in a spiral of steps, each of which is composed of a circle of planning, action and fact finding about the results of the action' (1946/1948: 206). Lewin's account of action research was of course much wider than this, emphasizing the importance of practical democracy and education in the practice of inquiry (for a recent review of Lewin's contribution see Bargal, 2006). Our own working definition of action research, adapted slightly from the one we set out in the first edition of this Handbook, remains appropriate:

> action research is a participatory process concerned with developing practical knowing in the pursuit of worthwhile human purposes. It seeks to bring together action and reflection, theory and practice, in participation with others, in the pursuit of practical solutions to issues of pressing concern to people, and more generally the flourishing of individual persons and their communities.

What we want to say to all our readers is that we see action research as a practice for the systematic development of knowing and knowledge, but based in a rather different paradigm from conventional academic research – because it has different purposes, is based in different relationships, has different ways of conceiving knowledge and its relation to practice. These are fundamental differences in our understanding of the nature of inquiry, not simply methodological

niceties. We have found that the five dimensions of action research, which we introduced in the first edition of this Handbook and which are shown in Figure 1, remain a useful way of considering features of practice that are broadly shared, while at the same time accepting that practice is hugely varied.

A primary purpose of action research is to produce practical knowledge that is useful to people in the everyday conduct of their lives. A wider purpose of action research is to contribute through this practical knowledge to the increased well-being – economic, political, psychological, spiritual – of human persons and communities, and to a more equitable and sustainable relationship with the wider ecology of the planet of which we are an intrinsic part.

So action research is about working toward practical outcomes, and also about creating new forms of understanding, since action without reflection and understanding is blind, just as theory without action is meaningless. And more broadly, theories which contribute to human emancipation, to the flourishing of community, which help us reflect on our place within the ecology of the planet and contemplate our spiritual purposes, can lead us to different ways of being together, as well as providing important guidance and inspiration for practice (for a feminist perspective would invite us to consider whether an emphasis on action without a balancing consideration of ways of being is rather too heroic).

As we search for practical knowledge and liberating ways of knowing, working with people in their everyday lives, we can also see that action research is participative research, and all participative research must be action research. Human persons are agents who act in the world on the basis of their own sensemaking; human community involves mutual sensemaking and collective action. Action research is only possible with, for and by persons and communities, ideally involving all stakeholders both in the questioning and sensemaking that informs the

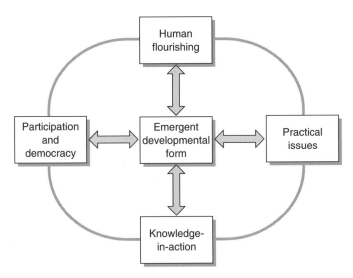

Figure 1 *Characteristics of action research*

research, and in the action which is its focus. And action research without its liberating and emancipatory dimension is a shadow of its full possibility and will be in danger of being co-opted by the status quo.

Since action research starts with everyday experience and is concerned with the development of living knowledge, the process of inquiry can be as important as specific outcomes. Good action research emerges over time in an evolutionary and developmental process, as individuals develop skills of inquiry and as communities of inquiry develop within communities of practice. Action research is emancipatory, it leads not just to new practical knowledge, but to new abilities to create knowledge. In action research knowledge is a living, evolving process of coming to know rooted in everyday experience; it is a verb rather than a noun. This means action research program is less defined in terms of hard and fast methods, but is, in Lyotard's (1979) sense, a work of art emerging in the doing of it.

These five interdependent characteristics of action research emerge from our reflections on practice in this developing field. Together they imply a 'participative turn' and an 'action turn'

in research practice which both builds on and takes us beyond the 'language turn' of recent years: the language turn drew our attention to the way knowledge is a social construction; the action turn accepts this, and asks us to consider how we can act in intelligent and informed ways in a socially constructed world (for a fuller exploration of these five dimensions see Reason and Bradbury, 2001/2006).

We start from these assertions – which may seem contentious to some of the academic community, while at the same time obvious to those of a more activist orientation – because the purpose of knowledge-making is so rarely debated. The institutions of normal science and academia, which have created such a monopoly on the knowledge-making process, place a primary value on pure research, the creation of knowledge unencumbered by practical questions. In contrast, the primary purpose of action research is not to produce academic theories based on action; nor is it to produce theories about action; nor is it to produce theoretical or empirical knowledge that can be applied in action; it is to liberate the human body, mind and spirit in the search for a better, freer world. We therefore suggest that in action research knowledge may be defined as what we've learned working in a context of action and that is the result of the transformation of our experience in conversation with both self and others that allows us consistently to create useful actions that leave us and our co-inquirers stronger.

FIRST-, SECOND-, THIRD-PERSON RESEARCH/PRACTICE

We have found that the terms first-, second-, and third-person research/practice have been quickly adopted by many action researchers. We used the terms in the first edition of the Handbook (following Torbert's original 1998 formulation) as an organizing framework. We continue to develop our thinking about them and see them as a helpful way of describing the diversity of action research practices (see also Reason and Torbert, 2001; Torbert and Taylor, Chapter 16).

- First-person action research/practice skills and methods address the ability of the researcher to foster an inquiring approach to his or her own life, to act choicefully and with awareness, and to assess effects in the outside world while acting. First-person research practice brings inquiry into more and more of our moments of action – not as outside researchers but in the whole range of everyday activities. In our action research practice, first-person inquiry provides a foundational practice and disciplines through which we can monitor the impact of our behaviour (Marshall and Mead, 2005; this issue is exemplified, for example, in Chapters 3 and 16).
- Second-person action research/practice addresses our ability to inquire face-to-face with others into issues of mutual concern – for example in the service of improving our personal and professional practice both individually and separately. Second-person inquiry starts with interpersonal dialogue and includes the development of communities of inquiry and learning organizations.
- Third-person research/practice aims to extend these relatively small scale projects to create a wider impact. As Gustavsen points out, action research will be of limited influence if we think only in terms of single cases, and that we need to

think of creating a series of events interconnected in a broader stream – which we can see as social movements or social capital (Gustavsen, 2003a, 2003b). So third-person strategies aim to create a wider community of inquiry involving persons who, because they cannot be known to each other face-to-face (say, in a large, geographically dispersed corporation), have an impersonal quality. Writing and other reporting of the process and outcomes of inquiries can also be an important form of third-person inquiry.

Chandler and Torbert (2003) have developed the idea of first-, second-, and third-person inquiry, offering a conceptual step forward by pointing to the temporal dimension – inquiry can be concerned with past, present, and future – unlike conventional research which is entirely limited to what happened in the past. They also usefully distinguish between first/second/third person *practice* and first/second/third person *voice*. They therefore describe:

1. the subjective, first-person voice;
2. any given particular set of intersubjective, second-person voices; and
3. the objectivity-seeking third-person voice. (Chandler and Torbert, 2003: 140; this framework is extended in Chapter 16).

We suggest that the most compelling and enduring kind of action research will engage all three strategies: first-person research practice is best conducted in the company of friends and colleagues who can provide support and challenge; such a company may indeed evolve into a second-person collaborative inquiry process. On the other hand, attempts at third-person research which are not based in rigorous first-person inquiry into one's purposes and practices is open to distortion through unregulated bias. Thus, to take just one example, Anisur Rahman (Chapter 3), in discussing the sensitization of 'animators' to stimulate and facilitate the process of participative action research, argues that they themselves must go through a process of (first person) self-inquiry in order to fully understand how to facilitate self-inquiry and self-initiatives in others. They may benefit by joining with others in (second person) collective inquiry for support and challenge in developing their experiences and skills. All this in the service of the wider (third person) purpose of human development and for 'downtrodden people to create their own history [and] their own science'.

A FAMILY OF APPROACHES

We have described action research as a 'family of approaches', a family which sometimes argues and falls out, whose members may at times ignore or wish to dominate others, yet a family which sees itself as different from other researchers, and is certainly willing to pull together in the face of criticism or hostility from supposedly 'objective' ways of doing research. We have come to appreciate the richness and diversity of this family, and our motivation as editors to create communicative spaces where the different members can come together in conversation has increased. We thoroughly agree with Robert Chambers' call in Chapter 20 for an 'eclectic pluralism [which] means that branding, labels, ownership and ego give way to sharing, borrowing, improvisation and creativity, all these complemented by mutual and critical reflective learning and personal responsibility for good practice' (p. 312). For some, action research is primarily an individual affair through which professionals can address questions of the kind 'How can I improve my practice?' For others, action research is strongly rooted in practices of organization development and improvement of business and public sector organizations. For many in the majority world, action research is primarily a liberationist practice aiming at redressing imbalances of power and restoring to ordinary people the capacities of self-reliance and ability to manage their own lives – to 'sharpen their minds' as villagers in Bangladesh describe it. For some the key questions are about how to initiate and develop face-to-face inquiry groups, while for others the primary issues are about using action

research to create change on a large scale and influence policy decisions. And for some action research is primarily a form of practice in the world, while for others it belongs in the scholarly traditions of knowledge generation hankering back to Socrates.

Our aim as editors is to honour and value all these different orientations. We want to insist that good action researchers will appreciate and draw on the range of perspectives and approaches that are available to them. It upsets us when we see action research as narrowly drawn; when, for example, we review an article that only sees action research as short-sighted consulting, seems to argue that one approach is the true form of action research, or traces action research back through just one discipline stream to one set of founding (usually masculine) authorities. We want you to delight in and celebrate the sheer exuberance and diversity that is available to you and be creative in how you use and develop it.

This of course also means there can never be one 'right way' of doing action research. We have addressed this question in the first edition of this Handbook and elsewhere (Bradbury, in press; Bradbury and Reason, 2003; Reason, 2006), arguing that this diversity of action research opens up a wide range of choices for the conduct of inquiry. We argue that a key dimension of quality is to be aware of one's choices, and to make those choices clear, transparent, articulate, to yourselves, to your inquiry partners, and, when you start writing and presenting, to the wider world. This is akin to the 'crafting' of research that Kvale (1995) advocates or, following Lather (2001), away from 'validity as policing toward 'incitement to dialogue'.

Those who involve themselves in the action research this book represents are aligned around three important purposes. The first purpose is to bring an action dimension back to the overly quietist tradition of knowledge generation which has developed in the modern era. The second is to expand the hold over knowledge held traditionally by universities and other institutes of 'higher learning'. The examples of action research in this book show how this can be done. At the same time our purpose is to contribute to the ongoing revisioning of the Western mindset – to add impetus to the movement away from a modernist worldview based on a positivist philosophy and a value system dominated by crude notions of economic progress, toward emerging perspectives which share a 'post-modern' sentiment (in the widest sense of that term). This Handbook offers many grounding perspectives which contribute to this, including our own understanding of an emergent participatory worldview which we articulate in the Introduction.

We address ourselves to an audience of scholar-practitioners whether inside, on the margins of, or outside academia. We clearly want to influence academic practice. Over the past 25 years, post-positivist research has received a great deal of attention in graduate and professional education, as evidenced by the attention to postmodernism and by developments in qualitative research (Denzin and Lincoln, 2005). Indeed the so-called 'campus paradigm wars' in the USA may be understood as a debate about how social science ought to be practised by inquiring into the role of the intellectual in a postmodern world. We wish to add to this debate by bringing to the foreground the many innovations in action approaches to social science, to delineate the possibilities for a 'turn to reflexive action' (Reason and Torbert, 2001) which offers new understandings of the relationship between ideas and practice. We also want to contribute to the development of new thinking about validity and quality in research, to show that good knowing rests on collaborative relationships, on a wide variety of ways of knowing, and an understanding of value and purpose, as well as more traditional forms or intellectual and empirical rigour.

Bringing scholarship and praxis back together, thereby drawing on long cultural traditions, our immodest aim is to change the relationship between knowledge and practice, to provide a model of social science for the 21st century as the Academy seeks additions and alternatives to its heretofore 'ivory tower' positivist model of science, research and practice.

CENTRAL INSIGHT OF PARTICIPATION: LIVING AS PART OF THE WHOLE

Action research is rooted in participation, which in turn supports key values of purpose and practice in action research efforts. As Kemmis puts it, the participative orientation is about 'opening communicative spaces' (Kemmis, 2001/2006), or as Heron has it, it is a situation in which all those involved can contribute both to the thinking that informs the inquiry and to the action which is its subject (Heron, 1996). This is especially clearly articulated in participatory action research (Fals Borda, 2001/2006) which concerns 'self-investigation by under-privileged people [which] naturally generates action by them' in a 'truly 'subject–subject' relation with the outside researchers' (Rahman, Chapter 3).

Most of us educated within the Western paradigm have inherited a broadly 'Cartesian' worldview which channels our thinking in significant ways. It tells us the world is made of separate things. These objects of nature are composed of inert matter, operating according to causal laws. They have no subjectivity or intelligence, no intrinsic purpose or meaning. And it tells us that mind and physical reality are separate. Humans alone have the capacity for rational thought and action and for understanding and giving meaning to the world. This split between humanity and nature, and the abrogation of all mind to humans, is what Weber meant by the disenchantment of the world. As Fals Borda has put it, participation is one way through which we may 're-enchant our plural world'.

Of course, participation is more than a technique. But it is also more that an epistemological principle or a key tenet of political practice. An attitude of inquiry includes developing an understanding that we are embodied beings part of a social and ecological order, and radically interconnected with all other beings. We are not bounded individuals experiencing the world in isolation. We are already participants, part-of rather than apart-from. Writers such as Jorge Ferrer

(2002) and Richard Tarnas (2006) have pointed to this deeper quality of human participation in a creative and intelligent cosmos. We would follow Thomas Berry in arguing that we will not be able to address the ecological devastations wrought by humans until we fully experience the universe and Earth as a community of subjects rather than as a collection of objects. To fully grasp the nature of participation calls for a profound shift, as Senge and his colleagues point out:

> When we eventually grasp the wholeness of nature, it can be shocking. In nature, as Bortoft puts it, 'The part is a place for the presencing of the whole'. This is the awareness that is stolen from us when we accept the machine worldview of whole assembled from replaceable parts. (Senge et al., 2005: 7)

In a more immediately human sense, the critical, systemic, and social constructionist perspectives emphasize a shift from the individual to relationships in which we all participate (Kemmis, Chapter 8; Ison, Chapter 9; Gergen and Gergen, Chapter 10). Thus an attitude of inquiry seeks to recognize the profundity of this active and increasing participation with the human and more than human world.

At a more immediate and practical level, participation in inquiry means that we stop working with people as 'subjects' (which, in actuality means to hold them as objects of our gaze) (following a linguistic twist better illustrated in Orwell's prescient novel *1984*). Instead we build relationship as co-researchers. Researching with people means that they are engaged as full persons, and the exploration is based directly on their understanding of their own actions and experience, rather than filtered through an outsider's perspective. Participation is also political, asserting people's right and ability to have a say in decisions which affect them and claim to generate knowledge about them. And, in addition to producing knowledge and action directly useful to a group of people, it can also empower them at a second and deeper level to see that they are capable of constructing and using their own knowledge (Freire, 1970; Reason, 2005).

REFERENCES

Argyris, C. (2003) 'A life full of learning', *Organization Studies,* 24 (7): 1178–92.

Bargal, D. (2006) 'Personal and intellectual influences leading to Lewin's paradigm of action research: towards the 60th anniversary of Lewin's *Action Research and Minority Problems* (1946)', *Action Research,* 4 (4).

Bradbury, H. (2007) 'Quality, consequence and "action-ability": what action researchers offer from the tradition of pragmatism', in R. Shanis et al. (eds), *Handbook of Collaborative Research.* Thousand Oaks, CA: Sage.

Bradbury, H. and Reason, P. (2003) 'Action research: an opportunity for revitalizing research purpose and practices', *Qualitative Social Work,* 2 (2): 173–83.

Brown, L.D. (ed.) (2002) *Practice-Research Engagement and Civil Society in a Globalizing Society.* Cambridge, MA: Harvard University/The Hauser Center.

Chandler, D. and Torbert, W.R. (2003). 'Transforming inquiry and action by interweaving 27 flavors of action research', *Action Research,* 1 (2): 133–52.

Denzin, N.K. and Lincoln, Y.S. (eds) (2005) *The Sage Handbook of Qualitative Research, 3rd edn.* Thousand Oaks, CA: Sage.

Fals Borda, O. (2001/2006) 'Participatory (action) research in social theory: origins and challenges', in P. Reason and H. Bradbury (eds), *Handbook of Action Research: Participative Inquiry and Practice.* London: Sage. pp. 27–37. Also published in P. Reason and H. Bradbury (eds) (2006), *Handbook of Action Research: Concise Paperback Edition.* London: Sage. pp. 27–37.

Ferrer, J.N. (2002) *Revisioning Transpersonal Theory: a Participatory Vision of Human Spirituality.* Albany, NY: SUNY Press.

Freire, P. (1970) *Pedagogy of the Oppressed.* New York: Herder and Herder.

Greenwood, D.J. and Levin, M. (2001) 'Pragmatic action research and the struggle to transform universities into learning communities', in P. Reason and H. Bradbury (eds), *Handbook of Action Research.* London: Sage. pp. 103–13.

Gustavsen, B. (2003a) 'Action research and the problem of the single case', *Concepts and Transformation,* 8 (1): 93–9.

Gustavsen, B. (2003b) 'New forms of knowledge production and the role of action research', *Action Research,* 1 (2): 153–64.

Heron, J. (1996) *Co-operative Inquiry: Research into the Human Condition.* London: Sage.

Kemmis, S. (2001/2006) 'Exploring the relevance of critical theory for action research: emancipatory action research in the footsteps of Jürgen Habermas', in P. Reason and H. Bradbury (eds), *Handbook of Action Research: Participative Inquiry and Practice.* London: Sage. pp. 91–102. Also published in P. Reason and H. Bradbury (eds) (2006), *Handbook of Action Research: Concise Paperback Edition.* London: Sage. pp. 94–105.

Kvale, S. (1995) 'The Social construction of validity'. *Qualitative Inquiry,* 1 (1): 19–40.

Lather, P. (2001) 'Validity as an incitement to discourse: qualitative research and the crisis of legitimation', in V. Richardson (ed.), *Handbook of Research on Teaching, 4th edn.* Washington, DC: American Education Research Association. pp. 241–50.

Lewin, K. (1946/1948) 'Action research and minority problems', in G.W. Lewin (ed.), *Resolving Social Conflicts.* New York. Harper and Row. pp. 201–16.

Lyotard, J.F. (1979) *The Postmodern Condition: A Report on Knowledge* (G. Bennington and B. Massumi trans.). Manchester: Manchester University Press.

Marshall, J. and Mead, G. (2005) Special Issue: Self-reflective practice and first-person action research. *Action Research,* 3 (4): 233–332.

Reason, P. (2004) 'Action research and the single case: a response to Bjørn Gustavsen', *Concepts and Transformations,* 8 (3): 281–94.

Reason, P. (2005) 'Living as Part of the Whole', *Journal of Curriculum and Pedagogy,* 2 (2): 35–41.

Reason, P. (2006) 'Choice and quality in action research practice', *Journal of Management Inquiry,* 15 (2): 187–203.

Reason, P. and Bradbury, H. (2001/2006) 'Inquiry and participation in search of a world worthy of human aspiration', in P. Reason and H. Bradbury (eds), *Handbook of Action Research:* London: Sage. pp. 1–14. Also published in P. Reason and H. Bradbury (eds) (2006), *Handbook of Action Research: Concise Paperback Edition.* London: Sage. pp. 1–14.

Reason, P. and Torbert, W.R. (2001) 'The action turn: toward a transformational social science', *Concepts and Transformations,* 6 (1): 1–37.

Senge, P.M., Scharmer, C.O., Jaworski, J. and Flowers, B.S. (2005) *Presence: Exploring Profound Change in People, Organizations and Society.* London: Nicholas Brealey.

Tarnas, R. (2006) *Cosmos and Psyche.* New York: Viking.

Torbert, W.R. (1998) 'Developing wisdom and courage in organizing and sciencing', in S. Srivastva and D. Cooperrider (eds), *Organizational Wisdom and Executive Courage.* San Francisco, CA: New Lexington Press. pp. 222–53.

PART ONE

Groundings

INTRODUCTION TO GROUNDINGS

In this section of the Handbook we highlight some of the diverse personal, political, and theoretical perspectives that have influenced action research. Of course these influences are touched on again and again throughout the volume as contributors discuss their practices, describe projects they have been engaged in, and explore the skills required for action research.

Action research nearly always starts with a question of the kind, 'how can we improve this situation?'. Action research activities are usually driven by personal commitments to contribute to human flourishing, and these commitments are informed by an intellectual orientation that is systemic or aware of interdependencies, emancipatory, critical and participatory. There is a wholeness about action research practice so that knowledge is always gained in and through action. As Marja Liisa Swantz expressed it to us. 'I do not separate my scientific inquiry from my life'.

This interaction of understanding and practice is emphasized in Chapter 1. We wanted to include as wide a range of grounding perspectives as possible, so we asked the members of the Editorial Board to send us a brief outline of the most significant grounding philosophies, ideas and/or political perspectives that have informed their work. And while to be sure their responses told us a lot about their intellectual perspectives, it was important to realize how deeply these perspectives were integrated with their lives, their relationships, and the personal and political engagements to which they were committed.

We also realize that some of the most significant action research has taken place over a long timespan: it is not so much a project or a programme but a social movement which has developed sometimes over decades. So the next four chapters place different action research traditions in an historical context: In Chapter 2 Marja Liisa Swantz gives her account of the development of participatory action research (PAR) through the perspective of her work in Africa and in Chapter 3 Anisur Rahman gives a parallel account from his perspective in the International Labour Organization and in South Asia. These chapters are companion pieces to Orlando Fals Borda's account of PAR in the first edition of this Handbook (Fals Borda, 2001/2006). In Chapter 4 Bjørn Gustavsen and his colleagues sketch out the history of action research in the workplace in Scandinavia since the 1950s and show from this what they have learned about developing the scale and scope of action research to a regional and national level. And in Chapter 5 Hilary Bradbury and her colleagues offer an account of the relationship between action research and organization development. These accounts show the extent of the influence of action research endeavours, touching the lives of so very many people worldwide.

The next two chapters show how action research can be seen as located within social movements: Brinton Lykes and Amelia Mallona link participatory and action research with the broad movement for liberation/emancipation of oppressed peoples worldwide, showing how action research is linked to and informed by perspectives such as liberation theology. Colleen Reid and Wendy Frisby write from the perspective of the feminist movement(s) and show how these lead to the possibility of a specifically feminist participatory action research. These chapters are companion pieces to Ella Bell's chapter on race and action research and Patricia Maguire's on Feminisms and action research in the first edition of the Handbook (Bell, 2001/2006).

Having shown the importance of finding one's grounding in practice and values, we next turn to theory with four chapters that link action research to important intellectual trends of our time: Ray Ison writes about systemic thinking; Stephen Kemmis develops a powerful definition of participatory action research grounded in critical theory and the writings of Habermas; Ken and Mary Gergen show the close affinity of action research to the linguistic turn and the constructionist perspective; and John Gaventa and Andrea Cornwall build on their earlier writing on power and knowledge, providing also an important critique of power in participatory research.

There are of course other intellectual perspectives that have informed action research, some of which are touched on in Chapter 1. Among the most important are humanism (Rowan, 2001/2006) and the philosophy of pragmatism, which is discussed by Mike Pedler and John Burgoyne in the context of

Action Learning (Chapter 21) and again in George Roth and Hilary Bradbury's Chapter 23, in which their thoughts on how quality in action research is developed is also grounded in pragmatist thinking (see also Reason, 2003). Further explorations of the epistemological foundations of action research can be found in John Heron and Peter Reason's exploration of the extended epistemology that underlies co-operative inquiry (Chapter 24) and Peter Park's chapter in the Handbook's first edition (Park, 2001/2006).

The final three chapters explore contextual issues in action research practice. Mary Brydon-Miller provides readers with an introduction to research ethics within an action research context, including a critical analysis of power and privilege. Dave Brown and Rajesh Tandon demonstrate the importance of alliances that cross the South–North divide and link grassroots practice to the wider institutional field. Morten Levin and Davydd Greenwood provide a powerful critique of the Western university system and call for a major reorganization to structuring teaching and research through action research strategies.

What we hope, from the selection of groundings, is that potential action researchers will realize that they are not making a discrete 'contribution to the field of knowledge' when they undertake a piece of action research but are contributing to a stream of action and inquiry which aims to enhance the flourishing of human persons, their societies, communities and organizations and the wider ecology of which we are all a part. This stream of activity is full of lively debate about choices of life and political commitments, different intellectual perspectives and, as we shall see in later sections, practical approaches to action research. There is no one clear view, so each one of us, individually and with co-researchers, is challenged continually to make choices, to critically examine those choices, and to make them clear to others with whom we work.

REFERENCES

Bell, E.E. (2001/2006) 'Infusing race into the discourse of action research', in P. Reason and H. Bradbury (eds), *Handbook of Action Research: Participative Inquiry and Practice.* London: Sage. pp. 48–58. Also published in P. Reason and H. Bradbury (eds) (2006), *Handbook of Action Research: Concise Student Edition.* London: Sage. pp. 49–59.

Fals Borda, O. (2001/2006) 'Participatory (action) research in social theory: origins and challenges', in P. Reason and H. Bradbury (eds), *Handbook of Action Research: Participative Inquiry and Practice.* London: Sage. pp. 27–37. Also published in P. Reason and H. Bradbury (eds) (2006), *Handbook of Action Research: Concise Student Edition.* London: Sage. pp. 27–37.

Maguire, P. (2001/2006) 'Uneven ground: feminisms and action research', in P. Reason and H. Bradbury (eds), *Handbook of Action Research: Participative Inquiry and Practice.* London: Sage. pp. 59–69. Also published in P. Reason and H. Bradbury (eds) (2006), *Handbook of Action Research: Concise Student Edition.* London: Sage. pp. 60–70.

Park, P. (2001/2006) 'Knowledge and participatory research', in P. Reason and H. Bradbury (eds), *Handbook of Action Research: Participative Inquiry and Practice.* London: Sage pp. 81–90. Also published in P. Reason and H. Bradbury (eds) (2006), *Handbook of Action Research: Concise Student Edition.* London: Sage. pp. 83–93.

Reason, P. (2003) 'Pragmatist philosophy and action research: readings and conversation with Richard Rorty', *Action Research,* 1 (1): 103–23.

Rowan, J. (2001/2006) 'The humanistic approach to action research', in P. Reason and H. Bradbury (eds), *Handbook of Action Research: Participative Inquiry and Practice.* London: Sage. pp. 114–23. Also published in P. Reason and H. Bradbury (eds) (2006), *Handbook of Action Research: Concise Student Edition.* London: Sage. pp.106–16.

1

Living Inquiry: Personal, Political and Philosophical Groundings for Action Research Practice

Patricia Gayá Wicks, Peter Reason
and Hilary Bradbury

This chapter seeks to detail the scholarly and intellectual threads identified by members of the action research community, and to point to further reading for those interested in pursuing these. It shows some of the ways in which the thoughtful integration of various theoretical perspectives and life experiences gives rise to well-developed personal paradigms which both shape and explain action researchers' being and acting in the world.

A key objective for the second edition of this Handbook was to reflect the variety of ways in which action research is grounded in our lived experience and ideas. In keeping with the participative ethos of action research, and inspired by the success of the first paper of the inaugural issue of the journal *Action Research*, called simply 'Why Action Research?' (Brydon-Miller et al., 2003), we contacted members of the Handbook's Editorial Board and asked them to send us a brief outline sharing the most significant perspectives that ground their action research practice. We received many thoughtful and engaged responses to our request.

What struck us as particularly significant was the degree to which our colleagues underscored:

- the importance of *practice* and *life experiences* and these as integrated with – and often preceding – philosophical, political, and intellectual underpinnings;
- the *web* of relationships, events, influences, role models, and experiences which underpins action researchers' practice (and which has done so over time).

The contribution this chapter seeks to make is to detail the scholarly and intellectual threads identified by our colleagues and friends in the action research community, and to point to further reading for those interested in pursuing these. Additionally, we hope to offer evidence of some of the ways in which the thoughtful integration of various theoretical perspectives and life experiences give rise to well-developed personal paradigms which both shape and explain action researchers' being and acting in the world.

LIVING LIFE MATTERS

The majority of respondents place life experiences among the primary influences that underpin their action research. These experiences often sit alongside, or even give rise to, interest in particular philosophical and intellectual perspectives, so that both theory and practice are seen as providing grounding. For example our colleagues shared that,

> ... practice was my real learning ground ... (Yoland Wadsworth)
> ... My philosophical self is kept in motion by my pragmatic and practical self, and here my education has come from the community activists I've worked with over many years. (Mary Brydon-Miller)
> Conscientization and the cyclical action-reflection-action as articulated by Paolo Freire gave grounding to the notion that knowing can be rooted in critical reflection of one's actions; Myles Horton's practice at Highlander Center with literacy and voter registration in Appalachia and struggles against racial discrimination during civil rights movements provided practical validity to the notions of 'making the road while walking'. (Rajesh Tandon)
> The most significant philosophical and political influences continue to be the living theories of practitioner-researchers. (Jack Whitehead)
> My research, action and participation journey has been influenced more by field and life experiences and the excitement and fun of epistemological puzzles than by philosophical or political perspectives. (Robert Chambers)

Furthermore, a number of Editorial Board members responded to our request with detailed accounts representing their life journeys and describing the *web of influence* that has sustained and contributed to their work over time. These webs encompass a wide range of influences, including personal and collegial relationships; encounters with role models; political and other significant events; spiritual disciplines; literature (fiction and non-fiction); activism and engagement with practitioners. For example:

> My deepest understanding of the relevance of participatory forms of inquiry for action comes from my research experiences with practitioners and activists, first in Colombia and then in the US. I have shared with them the dream of a different world and their wisdom has contributed to transforming me as much as it has helped transform their practice and sharpen their skills to change the world. (Sonia Ospina)
> Thinking over the influences I draw on in my daily work, it seems to me that people and experiences have on balance been more important than ideas and theory, although the latter have been important too. (Bob Dick)
> It is difficult for me to clearly distinguish 'philosophical and political' influences from general intellectual and spiritual influences as well as from the experiences, practices, and relationships in which many of those influences are embedded. (Victor Friedman)

Some respondents describe a gradual and ongoing process of developing understanding, while others talk about 'Aha!' moments through which significant meaning emerges. Orlando Fals Borda was one of the last to respond to our request, and so was able to reflect on other responses in his own reply:

> I tend to identify such collective examination as a praxiological experiment. Theory and practice, thinking-persons and life-experiences (*vivencias*), how they interact, fuse, and react in the search for explanations to understand realities and promote social progress appear to have been a driving force for respondents. (Orlando Fals Borda)

Fals Borda's description of different influences interacting and fusing with one another in the search for explanations seems particularly apt. There is conscious and meaningful *integration* in people's stories: integration of theory and practice; of scholarship and activism; and more generally, integration of numerous perspectives and life experiences into meaningful accounts, each of which seems to be intimately tied to the particular context, place, time, and life history of each person. It is evident that each person's understanding and practice of action research does not stand in isolation from other aspects of their being-in-the world; instead, action research both emerges from and contributes to a complex and panoramic view of the world in which one lives and one's own particular place within it. Judi Marshall has described this elsewhere as 'living life as inquiry' (1999).

GROUNDING OURSELVES IN THE PARTICIPATIVE, INTERDEPENDENT ECOLOGY OF LIFE

A number of the contributors to this chapter refer – in different ways and with varying degrees of explicitness – to a participatory worldview underlying their work. For example, Werner Fricke refers to 'participation as a central dimension in human life as well as in nature and between humans and non humans' and in so doing points to the work of Peter Reason (1994) and of French philosopher and anthropologist Bruno Latour (1993), and specifically his 'parliament of things'. Furthermore, Fricke acknowledges the influence of the 'philosophy of process' formulated by German Marxist philosopher Ernst Bloch (1995), and puts forward the following perspective:

> Any situation, any context, any institution or structure we find ourselves in is just a historical moment within a process of permanent change. This means we are coming out of the past going into the future. Everything is changing and may be changed. Humans and society are open to the future. (Werner Fricke)

In his response, Orlando Fals Borda speaks of the 'moral urge [which] undergirds (participatory) action research', referring to a participatory epistemology which he locates in the work of Gregory Bateson (1972, 1979), Fritjof Capra (1982, 1996), Paul Feyerabend (1975), and more broadly,

systemic analysts and some quantum physicists. Certainly, Bateson's argument that the conscious, purposive human mind which sees itself as separate from the ecological whole leads to 'pathologies of epistemology' and parallels the concerns expressed by many within the action research community (see Reason, in press).

The participative nature of life was approached from a variety of perspectives: Yoland Wadsworth, for example, refers to the interconnectedness of life with a bow to the biological and ecological sciences:

> … Perhaps the earliest truly transformative influence of all was *The Web of Life* – a then-new Australian biology textbook in 1967 for upper secondary students – that opened my eyes at the age of 15 to an ecological perspective. When I edited the school magazine the following year I re-named it *Cell* and wrote a 'systems piece' as an Editorial on the varying meanings of 'cell' from biology to a monk's! And two years later in August 1970 in a sociology lecture I suddenly realized with a blinding flash EVERYTHING was connected – from humans to duckponds to women's magazines to mining companies. (Yoland Wadsworth)

Reference was also made to a range of religious and spiritual influences underpinned by participatory understandings. Mary Brydon-Miller refers to the Quaker notion that 'there is that of God in each of us, and in all of creation', pointing out that this is a philosophy that Quakers share with many other world religions. This perspective, although framed in religious terms, is in line with the epistemological challenge to subject–object and matter–consciousness dualisms articulated in other chapters of this Grounding section. Victor Friedman, drawing from the Hebrew Bible and a wide variety of Jewish thinkers, identifies a central influence in the view that 'people are partners with God, and each other, in an ongoing process of creation'. Along similar lines, Peter Reason identifies the 'Buddha's teaching that attachment to a sense of separate self is the cause of suffering' as an essential perspective influencing his work. Bill Torbert refers to the interplay of consciousness, knowledge, practice, and consequences to which he was first introduced by the work of Russian writer and mystic George Ivanovitch Gurdjieff (1963) and Russian mathematician, philosopher and journalist Peter D. Ouspensky (1931). He explains that 'these [authors] spoke of a secret and lost knowledge that linked the spiritual and material worlds through a work of continual self-observation that the aspirant must conduct within him or herself, with the help of others'. The resurgence of Buddhist practice in the West also plays with the same sense of locating the self in experience of the world, very far from discovering through intellectual effort alone.

The spiritual perspectives outlined by respondents lay emphasis on the conviction that life is not a spectator sport but that participation is *fundamental* to the nature of our being, or an *ontological given*, a view articulated both by action researchers (Heron, 1996; Heron and Reason, 1997; Reason and Bradbury, 2001) and other contemporary writers (Berry, 1999; Ferrer, 2002; Tarnas, 1991, 2006). These perspectives have clear implications for practice and for how our colleagues mentioned above choose to live and act in the world.

CONFRONTING THE QUESTION OF HOW WE KNOW IN A POST OBJECTIVIST WORLD

In addressing the epistemological questions of *how we know what we know* and *what it is that we value as knowledge*, many contributors referred to the theory of scientific revolutions and paradigm shifts articulated by Thomas Kuhn (1962). Similar mention was made of theories as changing social constructs as expounded by Karl Popper (1959), Paul Feyerabend (1975) and Stephen Toulmin (1990), amongst others. Peter Reason, for example, explains that he was particularly influenced by 'the historical argument of Stephen Toulmin which places Cartesian thought as in part a response to the

political needs of the times'. Meanwhile, Jack Whitehead explains that his advocacy of 'living epistemological standards of judgment' is strongly influenced by Feyerabend, 'when he wrote about the meaning of freedom being understood in the course of its emergence through practice'. Whitehead points to Habermas (1975), Foucault (2000), Bernstein (1983) and Winter (1989) as focusing his attention on the importance of transforming the epistemological standards of judgement in the Academy: 'I continue to use [Habermas'] four criteria of social validity in reaching understanding'.

For many, epistemological debates are closely linked with the social construction of reality perspectives articulated by Peter Berger and Thomas Luckmann (1966), John Searle (1995) and the 'linguistic turn' heralded by Ludwig Wittgenstein (1953) and Richard Rorty (1970). Kenneth Gergen commends this stream of work for 'demonstrating the ways in which assumptions about the real, the rational and the good issue from relationships'. 'Thus, we may use research not simply to reflect the past, but to create new futures'. Gergen also identifies perspectives on the pragmatics of language as a key influence: 'shifting from a picture theory of language to a use-based (or game) understanding of language raises questions about the aims of social science to develop general theory, and invites a more pragmatic and dialogically based orientation to research'.

Along similar lines, Victor Friedman is explicit about the influence of American mathematical social scientist Herbert Simon's (1969) argument that social life is a 'design' process. In line with Simon's interest 'not with how things are but with how they might be' (1969: xx), Friedman points also to the elements of choice and agency in processes of social construction. He identifies as a key influence the belief that 'there is a link between individual theories of action, collective theories of action, and the realities we create. Most important, we have choices about these realities'. In doing so, Friedman points to John Dewey's (1982) pragmatism and 'theory of inquiry'. The pragmatist position suggests that knowledge is acquired through responding to a real need in life, something also identified as a key influence by Morten Levin and Hilary Bradbury. Hilary also specifically highlights how, for her, pragmatism rescues our appreciation of learning from academic understanding and instead allows us to also emphasize active experimentation. Hence what GE managers may call 'quality improvement' – and indeed what Deming, the father of the quality movement in the USA, called 'quality' – is but one iteration of the action research cycle of reflection on action.

Stephen Kemmis's account suggests that, like many of the action researchers who responded to our request, he has played an active role in weaving together the different threads of influence with which he was presented over time, resulting in a well-grounded conviction that alternative epistemological standards were required:

> As a young researcher in educational psychology at the University of Sydney and then as a doctoral student at the University of Illinois at Urbana-Champaign, the 1970s debates in history and philosophy of science (Thomas Kuhn, Karl Popper, Imre Lakatos [1986], Paul Feyerabend, Stephen Toulmin, Donald Campbell [1974]), especially evolutionary epistemology, overthrew my 'inherited' empiricist and positivistic understanding of science, alerted me to the 'linguistic turn' (Wittgenstein) and pushed me towards interpretivism and historical understanding ... and what later became known as qualitative research. ... I began to explore dialectics through Hilary Putnam [1975] and the Marxist tradition, including a fine account of dialectics offered by the now-disgraced Mao Tse-Tung [1972]. I became convinced that a science was needed that properly acknowledged each person's capacity to develop knowledge – their own and others. (Stephen Kemmis)

CRITICAL PERSPECTIVES ON THE POLITICS OF KNOWLEDGE GENERATION

Many of the contributors reported being influenced by the tradition of critical social science. Kenneth Gergen, for example, notes the importance of wide-ranging theoretical domains which break the fact/value binary and demonstrate that all knowledge claims are political in their implications. As a result many responses were embedded within critiques of domination and marginalization, and referred to frameworks and traditions that advocate critical examination of issues of power, identity and agency. These include civil rights and feminist movements; liberationist adult and trade union education; postcolonial and critical race theory; and anti-war and ecological protests as well as the student democracy movement. L. David Brown, for instance, suggests that he was 'more influenced in the long term by the more macro perspectives than the social psychological tradition that [he] was steeped in as a graduate student', and refers to the perspectives on oppression and liberation voiced by Paulo Freire (1972), Frantz Fanon (2004), Karl Marx (1970), William Gamson (1992) and participatory researchers in Southern contexts. He mentions also the perspectives on power, conflict and collaboration given expression by such commentators as Stephen Lukes (1974), Lewis Coser (1998) and Ralf Dharendorf (1959). Along similar lines, Stephen Kemmis credits Pierre Bourdieu (2004) and Michel Foucault (2000) as key influences: 'In different ways, [they] enabled me to understand that structures of oppression could be described as well as "unmasked".' He continues:

> Anthony Giddens [1984] helped me understand the nature and role of agency in dialectical relationship with social structure – and the resistant and transformative possibilities of agency. Alain Touraine [1983] made this even clearer in his analysis of social movements (as disturbing and challenging settled social orders). (Stephen Kemmis)

That epistemological pathologies – including the notions of an objective, value-free, expert science – were responsible for perpetuating and reinforcing social injustices and inequalities is a perspective also held by Yoland Wadsworth. She gives due credit to those influences which, during the 1980s, provided 'a new epistemological paradigm of engagement [which went] beyond the narrow exclusivity of replicative and objectivist science'. This was made possible, she suggests, by sociologists like Howard Becker (1997) and Alvin Gouldner (1976) and feminists like Mary O'Brien (1981). Robin McTaggart also acknowledges the influence of critical social scientists such as David Held (1989), Walter Feinberg (1975) and Henry Giroux (1983) 'for showing us that thinking interpretively alone was defeatist and failed to inform transformative practices'.

The emancipatory power of critical perspectives on social science is emphasized in Patricia Maguire's account of the key influences which were significant to her. She explains that it was while simultaneously engaging in feminist community activism and studying feminist scholarship (including Shulamit Reinharz,1992, Renate Duelli Klein, 1985, Sandra Harding, 1987, Marjorie DeVault, 1991, Liz Stanley, 1992 and Ann Oakley, 1984) that she was able to 'see' the androcentrism or male-centredness of much early PAR work, and the conspicuous lack of attention to issues of gender dynamics, gender inequities and feminist scholarship. The 'Aha!' moment described by Maguire below appears to resonate with the experience of a number of respondents, for whom integration of a variety of perspectives and experiences in a specific time and place brought forth step changes in clarity and understanding:

> The early critiques (1980s) of the entire development paradigm and enterprise by feminists in the 'south' (e.g. DAWN with Peggy Antrobus [2004] and Patricia Ellis [2003], and the ISIS network) created a grand 'Aha!' for me. There ARE other ways to 'see' and make sense of the world, so make room for them at the table of meaning making. (Patricia Maguire)

Maguire explains that she is also influenced by the work of feminist action researchers such as Marjorie Mbilinyi (2003), Patti Lather (1991, 2007), Gunilla Härnsten (2001), Brinton Lykes (1996), Alice McIntyre (2000), Yoland Wadsworth (1997), Nimat Hafez Barazangi (2004) and Colleen Reid (2004), amongst others.

Like so many action researchers, women and men, for whom feminism offered a new lens through which a transformative vision of the world could come to consciousness, Hilary also mentioned the work of 'constructive feminists' (in contrast with critical theory feminists). These include ecofeminists (e.g Susan Griffin) and cultural theory feminists such as Riane Eisler. Eisler offers a vision of culture anchored no longer in the dominator hierarchies of a Barbarian past but rather in the partnership principles from the still deeper past of Minoan (Crete's) civilization. Hilary writes that 'while the historicity may still be contested, the language and vision of partnership has been so constructive in my thinking about action research'. Moreover, given her particular commitment to convening decision-makers from the business world to work collaboratively in action research mode in developing joint innovations that contribute to a more sustainable society – or at the very least, actions that create significant pollution reduction – the idea that we hold our ecological interdependence in our DNA is very empowering.

HOW DO WE TEACH GIVEN ALL WE KNOW?

Unsurprisingly, many respondents identified critical perspectives on pedagogy as a key influence. Frequent reference was made to Paulo Freire's (1972) work on the pedagogy of the oppressed, conscientization and liberationist adult education and to the work of Budd Hall (1978) and Mohan Singh Mehta (1974). Along similar lines, perspectives which problematized the institutionalization of education and called for 'de-schooling' and non-formal democratic education were singled out (including the work of Herbert Kohl, 1984, Neil Postman and Carl Weingartner, 1969). Robin McTaggart, for instance, explains that his interest in participatory action research originated from a profound sense of dissatisfaction with the 'educational research' tradition to which he was introduced as an undergraduate and postgraduate student training to be a high school science teacher:

> 'Educational research' was then really a form of applied psychological research and suffered the failings of psychology as a research field at that time, [the] preoccupation with emulating the natural sciences in social inquiry. I found the generalizations sponsored by educational psychology to have little applicability in the early days of my high school science teaching career. My problems were immediate, pedagogical and reflexive. I required the perspective of an educator, not a psychologist, or sociologist, or philosopher, or scientist, or teacher, or political economist, but all of them. (Robin McTaggart)

McTaggart and Kemmis both acknowledge the influence of the neo-Aristotelian perspectives put forward by the likes of Joseph Schwab (1969), which leads us to 'see natural science as a process of inquiry rather than the recitation of a "rhetoric of conclusions"' (McTaggart) and which emphasizes the distinction between *practical reasoning* from *technical thinking*. For a recent thorough exploration of the relevance of Aristotlean thought – and especially the concept of *phrónesis* – to action research, see Eikeland (2006).

McTaggart states that his interest in action research was particularly stimulated by its transformative potential, and by the attention given to the question: *How might we change things at the same time as studying them?* He explains that while the sociological studies of Samuel Bowles and Herbert Gintis (1976), for example, affirmed his view that educational institutions reproduced disadvantage, these approaches to research did little to suggest how things might change, despite the daily efforts and successes of teachers and school leaders. In stark contrast, Paulo Freire and the participatory research movement 'provided fine and often courageous examples of transformative research and educational practices and theories'.

In a similar vein, Patricia Maguire explains that alongside the feminist 'ah-ha' moments described earlier, she was also significantly affected by 'people and place': specifically, her relationships with people at and through the Center for International Education (University of Massachusetts, Amherst) in the early 1980s, where she 'came to understand the connections among empowering education, participatory processes, and knowledge creation in service to meaningful social change'. The following extract from Maguire's account highlights the important role played by personal meetings, interactions and collegial relationships in the development of one's own action research practice:

> CIE was well known for promoting Freirian, empowering, non-formal education in development projects. Many of us there grappled with how to make our research more congruent with the transformational possibilities of participatory non-formal education. A steady stream of visitors such as Paulo Freire, Myles Horton (Horton et al., 1990), and Ira Shor (1992), and faculty members David Kinsey (1978) and Peter Park (1993), introduced us to PAR. There I met Mary Brydon-Miller and continue to be influenced by her work on ethics in AR (see Brydon-Miller et al., in press) and linking participatory research and psychology. My AR work continues to be nourished by my collegial relationship with Mary. Through CIE I was introduced to the work of Peter Reason, Budd Hall and Rajesh Tandon (1983), and later Davyyd Greenwood (2002) – particularly Davyyd's work to link AR and democratic processes. I'm inspired by Davyyd's commitment to teach AR democratically. (Patricia Maguire)

Likewise, Anisur Rahman clearly articulates the ways in which pedagogical concerns were brought into relief through his engagement with marginalized community groups, realizations which were affirmed and reinforced through a reading of Freire:

> My interaction in 1976–77 with the Bhoomi Sena movement in the state of Maharastra (India) by way of participatory study of the movement with three other South Asian scholars (De Silva et al., 1979) made me deeply aware of the need for work to promote intellectual self-capacity and self-assertion of the underprivileged people to guide their self-development. Through this interaction I zeroed

in on two realizations: (1) self-reliant development was not possible with someone else's thinking; and (2) the formidable status of formal knowledge with its associated power had created a sense of intellectual inferiority among the ordinary people, making them surrender to or look up to the formally educated for guidance to promote their lives, and they needed help and stimulation from friendly and deeply sensitive quarters in the formally educated stream to recover their self-confidence in their own intellectual abilities. Reading Paulo Freire consolidated this new awareness in me. (Anisur Rahman)

KNOWING IN THE SERVICE OF PRACTICE

Practical know-how, a 'popular science of and for the people', is identified as a key influence by many of our colleagues. This is understood as the diverse and effective forms of knowledge generation long-practised by ordinary people, unencumbered by the intervention or so-called expertise of scientists and elites. This is closely related to the idea of an 'extended' epistemology which encompasses experiential and practical knowing. Significant credit for this perspective is given to Freire, and alongside him to Orlando Fals Borda (1988), Anisur Rahman (1993; see also Fals Borda and Rahman, 1991), Rajesh Tandon (1983), John Gaventa (1991) and Budd Hall (1978). Tandon identifies the knowledge of ordinary people as a key influence in his work, one that he continues to lean on and build from:

Indigenous knowledge based on life and living, linked to solving daily problems of survival, transmitted through various folk forms of music, theatre, dance, poetry, drama – oral and aesthetic traditions of knowledge production, documentation and communication; popular knowledge and wisdom, as revealed in ecological and healing traditions and sciences, now popularized by modern markets. (Rajesh Tandon)

Meanwhile, Sonia Ospina explains that sociological theories giving primacy to social interaction, meaning-making, language, culture, everyday life and local knowledge served to clarify and refine her own commitment to linking inquiry to participation and action. In this context, she refers to the work of Max Weber (1958), George Herbert Mead (1934), Herbert Blumer (1998) and Peter Berger (1963), and speaks of these as tempered by recent post-modernist influences and, even more recently, by '*feministas de la diferencia*' like Maria Milagros Rivera Garretas (1997).

The phenomenological and hermeneutical traditions propagated by Edmund Husserl (1989), Hans-Georg Gadamer (2000), Jürgen Habermas (1981), Paul Ricoeur (1981) and Maurice Merleau-Ponty (1962, 2004) are also often referred to by the contributors to this chapter. Marja Liisa Swantz, for example, describes how an orientation towards phenomenology and hermeneutics helped her to develop a practical appreciation of the forms of knowing expressed in symbol and ritual amongst people:

Paul Ricœur's (1981) idea that symbol precedes language and rational thought and Susanne Langer's (1979) human need for symbolization and differentiating discursive from presentational symbolism led me to the analysis of the symbols and rituals of the people I lived and worked with and whose way of life I struggled to understand. Anthropologists Victor Turner (1986) and Mary Douglas (2003) developed my ideas of symbolism further. This emphasis on presentational rather than rational symbolism was at the base of my belief that people who communicated with symbols had knowledge and understanding of life which could broaden the concept of development dominating people's lives. I found support from writers such as Robert Ulin's (2001) *Understanding Cultures*, Ernst Fischer's (1969) *Art Against Ideology*, Thomas Fawcett's (1971) *The Symbolic Language of Religion*, Don Ihde's (1986) *Consequences of Phenomenology* and William Barrett's (1990) *Irrational Man*, amongst others: … In spite of the emphasis on presentational symbolism I understood that it had to lead also to rational understanding of one's situation and that the way to it was through mutual communication (Swantz, 1970). (Marja Liisa Swantz)

The tradition of the human potential movement and the place of individual consciousness in influencing change in wider systems are identified as critical influences by

Hilary Bradbury and Yoland Wadsworth. Key insights are gleaned here from C. Wright Mills's (1963) relationship between 'private troubles and public issues'; Charles Hampden-Turner's (1981) work, identified by Wadsworth as 'a psychology of being – but also a methodology for becoming'; and Abraham Maslow (1968) and other humanistic or 'third force' psychologists. The humanistic perspective which advocates that persons have the capacity to direct their own lives in ways which are life-affirming and constructive for themselves and others in their social contexts is one which resonates with action researchers. Indeed, identifying and strengthening such potential could be seen as a key objective of action research practice, as suggested by Werner Fricke:

> The human desire and capacity for participation and self-determination is often suppressed (e.g. by life-long work under poor, monotonous, unqualified working conditions), but cannot be destroyed. We called the employees' participative capacity 'innovative qualifications' (Fricke, 1983). (Werner Fricke)

Friedman makes a related point when he refers to the subconscious as a storehouse of unutilized knowledge and a potent source of healing and learning, as described, for example, by psychiatrist and hypnotherapist Milton Erickson (1985). Friedman also makes particular reference to the work of Sigmund Freud (1961), Melanie Klein (1992), Kurt Lewin's (1958) ideas of 'psychological-social space', and Wilfred Bion's (1961) and Larry Hirschhorn's (1988) perspectives on 'social defences'. The psychoanalytic tradition is also identified as a key influence by Yoland Wadsworth. She refers specifically to Isobel Myers and Katherine Briggs' (1987) application of Jungian psychology to self and human understanding and to Isabel Menzies Lyth's (1988) work on social systems as a defence against anxiety. The influences delineated above speak of action researchers' commitment to the development of self-awareness, moment-to-moment reflexivity, and to the ongoing examination of patterns of thought, behaviour and relating.

CREATING THE FUTURE: WHY OUR WORK IS SIGNIFICANT

It will perhaps come as no surprise to readers of this volume that a desire to contribute towards 'a better future' is evident in many of the accounts offered to us. Anisur Rahman, for instance, is clear about the motivation and vision underlying his interest and move into action research. For him, the worth of P(A)R is in its potential to contribute to people's *self-development* and *self-reliance*:

> My departure from traditional research and development thinking was spurred by the War of Liberation of Bangladesh of 1971, when I was a Harvard-trained economist of 38. The independence of Bangladesh with its officially declared socialist ideology inspired me and many others to think that the country could and would march forward with whatever resources it had, relying principally on the energy and creativity of its vast population, however resource-poor the country was, without depending on external charity and submitting its autonomy to foreign powers seeking to impose on other countries an ideology of pursuit of private greed and dividing the nation's people into an elite and non-elite class. ... I [became] convinced that initiatives for *people's self-reliant development* was the way for the nation to march forward with its head high ... With this awareness I joined the ongoing intellectual movement to experiment with Participatory (Action) Research and to deepen its conceptual contours, as a movement to promote 'people's self-development', seeing P(A)R not as a research *method* but as an organic component of people's self-development. (Anisur Rahman)

Davyyd Greenwood explains that it was through his involvement in an action research project that he began to more critically engage with the political and axiological dimensions of knowledge generation:

> I was ushered into action research by William Foote Whyte (1991), who took advantage of my long-time anthropological research in the Basque Country to involve me in a project on the industrial cooperatives of Mondragón. In the context of that

collaboration … I gained a renewed sense of the potential value of the social sciences to create liberating social arrangements, the power and value of democracy (even under difficult conditions), and the degree to which real social problems exceed the pathetically narrow confines that the academic social sciences with their Fordist models of organization want to impose on them. (Davydd Greenwood)

Kurt Neilsen also emphasizes the transformative, value-driven potential of action research practice. From Robert Jungk (1954) and Ernst Bloch (1995) he takes the perspective that social imagination, dreams and utopian ideals are living parts of culture, and that integrating social imagination with practical change 'keeps alive hope' for the possibility of radical change. He quotes Robert Jungk's conviction that 'many futures are possible'. He refers also to the lessons learned from critical theory and psychoanalysis, including the suggestion that 'we all need an open and uninstrumental arena to reach awareness and to increase social imagination'. It is in this context that Neilsen identifies the real worth and contribution of action research: 'In action research we organize such arenas as social movement/ social learning.'

The question of how best to organize appropriate and significant arenas for social learning is one that is close to Bjørn Gustavsen's heart. Gustavsen's work focuses on a key challenge facing the action research tradition, that relating to the question of scale. His account emphasizes the evolutionary nature of action research practice, where experimentation and reflection on action give rise to new challenges and considerations about quality and effectiveness, and about how we might best position and organize ourselves so as to create better futures:

The problem was not action research or not, but how to improve on the specific action research tradition in which I found myself. Being strongly involved in efforts to create more democratic forms of work organization, we faced, in my view, two major issues: One was to democratize our own efforts to encompass many workplaces rather than a few experimental sites, the other was to further develop the notion of democracy to give

more specific guidelines in a project where scale emerged as the important issue.

Against this background I found critical theory, as it stood after 'the democratic turn' – represented in particular by Jürgen Habermas (1981) – to be a promising point of departure. The orientation towards society, rather than 'you and I' or the small group, was consistent with a need to reach scale and the emphasis on communication was consistent with the core tool of action research. Its weakness was too much of a one-way traffic from theory to practice to fit the more open and explorative use of action characterizing contemporary action research. This gave rise to a new challenge: how to change the relationship between theory and practice to provide more scope for action and experience in the development of a critical function in democratic society. To work out answers to this question has implied to embark on a process of action research and 'social constructivism' that has, by now, been going on for more than two decades. (Bjørn Gustavsen)

ON 'MAKING THE ROAD WHILE WALKING'

We conclude this chapter by drawing on those accounts which, in their own ways, consider how the integration of our life experiences and grounding perspectives help us action researchers to respond to the question of *how we should live our lives*. In other words, given the broad philosophical orientations described above, *what would effective practice look like?* Many of the accounts offered to us demonstrate that the translation of philosophical, theoretical and political perspectives into practical knowing and/or active engagement is considered of utmost importance.

A significant number of our colleagues explain that they were particularly drawn to role models or teachers who evidenced integration of theory and practice in their own lives. In talking about the various figures that were influential to him, Bill Torbert identifies effectiveness, integrity and the search for wisdom as key qualities. These are arguably the kinds of qualities which become evident through one's processes and acts of living in the world, and indeed, the influential figures he names are well-known for their activeness and for the practical contributions of their life's work:

> Thinking about it now, I realize that the first figure to have a major influence on me – Bill Coffin (1999), the Yale minister whom I first heard preach once a year at Andover and then allied myself with closely at Yale – was characteristic of the sort of elder from whom I sought guidance over the next 15 years. An early Peace Corps training camp director, a central figure in Civil Rights and anti-Vietnam political organizing, Coffin was at once an intellectual, a political actor, and a spiritual leader. ... Through Coffin, I met Paul Tillich (1952/1980), Al Lowenstein (1962), and Martin Luther King (1967). ... Without ever having verbalized this until now, I sought guidance from the sort of elder whom I imagined as visionary, charismatic, effective, committed to integrity, and a seeker of wisdom (not just knowledge). (Bill Torbert)

Torbert continues to explain that he was drawn to his long-time mentor, Chris Argyris, for similar reasons:

> I first met Chris Argyris during my sophomore year at Yale (1963), reading most of his books and interviewing him (as I did Coffin) ... on the relation between faculty members' scholarship and their day-to-day life values. ... Like Coffin, Argyris charismatically integrated theory and practice – in this case through his research, teaching, and consulting with major institutions such as IBM and the State Department. (Bill Torbert)

Torbert expresses admiration not only for the application of theory in practice (through the embodiment of Platonic and Socratic inquiry, for example), he also shows appreciation for political action and activeness and for learning from peers in interaction with one another.

Bob Dick also identifies the successful integration of theory and practice, and also of various other dimensions, as a key quality of Chris Argyris's – and also Don Schön's – work:

> I like the way they integrate the intrapersonal, the interpersonal and the systemic – theory and practice, diagnosis and intervention, and including a research methodology. (Bob Dick)

Along similar lines, Mary Brydon-Miller claims to have been deeply influenced by the careful manner in which role models Paulo Freire and Myles Horton appeared to embody their espoused ideals and beliefs in their everyday practice and being-in-the-world:

> Thanks to Peter Park, I had the opportunity while in graduate school to get to know both Freire and Horton, and I can remember being struck by how genuine both men were in their interactions with others, embodying in every moment the kind of respect and concern for others that was the central message of their written work. (Mary Brydon-Miller)

The ability to learn from and in collaboration with peers and colleagues, as well as from teachers and role models, is evidenced in many of the accounts offered to us.

For instance, the 'people and experiences' identified as especially important by Bob Dick include powerful role models from across his life-time, the earliest of which was his fifth and sixth grade teacher, Murray Hines, who 'ran involving and democratic classes which were very different to those I had previously been used to'. He also gives due credit to Rhoda Felgate, the director of the amateur theatre where he was active for a time in his late 20s, and whom he suggests 'had a greater influence than I think she realized'. In particular, she is one of the many persons whom Bob Dick identifies as having made space for him to learn on his own terms and through practical engagement and experimentation:

> She encouraged me to move beyond what I thought were my limits. ... When I did exceed my abilities and experienced failure she was there to help me pick myself up and learn from what happened. (Bob Dick)

In addition to learning from teachers, Dick emphasizes learning from his collaborations with skilled colleagues, clients, and students. He refers in particular to the university classes which he was responsible for teaching and which, for the most part, he chose to run in experiential and democratic ways.

I learned as much from the class members as they learned from me. The tutors with whom I co-facilitated those classes were for the most part skilled practitioners and were also a source of learning. (Bob Dick)

It is significant that Dick, like a number of the other respondents to our request, draws explicit attention to moments of deep learning and transformation:

Also important are the moments of desperation when my repertoire is inadequate and I have to create something on the spur of the moment. Many of the processes I now use were originally devised when I felt blocked. (Bob Dick)

Indeed, appreciation of 'Aha!' moments, or key moments in which people come to a meaningful and creative integration of understandings, is a key theme throughout the accounts. Robert Chambers, for instance, draws attention to the ways in which the puzzles and challenges which gripped him were grounded in, and became apparent through, life and field experiences. His response emphasizes the possibilities for ongoing learning and transformation which emerge through engagement with others in field experiences:

In this journey, 'aha!' moments have been significant: in South India, realizing how selective perceptions can be mutually reinforcing in a research team; in Ethiopia, learning that farmers could understand a histogram when they said 'You have drawn what we said'; in India, discovering that local people could make brilliant maps, representing their realities and far more detailed than 'ours'; being asked, when seeking to 'hand over the stick' to networks in the South, 'who are you to say that you have a stick to hand over?' (Robert Chambers)

Indeed, a theme running through many of the responses is that it is through ongoing critically-engaged conversations with one another and with other scholars and practitioners that we can better understand both how we are moulded by, and how we also contribute to shaping, the field. The most meaningful relationships with mentors, colleagues, students, and co-researchers are never straightforward: we learn both from the challenge of 'friends willing to act as enemies' (Torbert, 1976: 169), those who know us well enough to keep interrupting degenerate patterns; and of 'friends willing to act as friends' (Marshall and Reason, 1993: 122) who will continue to love us through all the crises living life as inquiry will throw at us.

CONCLUSIONS

In this chapter, we have sought to balance acknowledgement and appreciation of various intellectual traditions and philosophical perspectives with an understanding that each action researcher is involved in developing his/her own understanding and practice in ongoing ways and in particular socio-historical contexts. What we have found in putting together this 'bricolage' of perspectives is that action researchers themselves could be understood to have been acting as 'bricoleurs' over time, and in a very real sense, 'making the road while walking'. Indeed, the active process of integrating and making sense of various influences and perspectives and of developing one's own understanding seems to be central to many action researchers' accounts. Most notably, responses to our request demonstrated both vigour and rigour: these qualities are apparent in the robust and well-developed sense of critical engagement with a range of philosophical and theoretical perspectives, and also in the conscious development of praxis through ongoing and active integration of life experiences, grounding perspectives and complex webs of influence. Individually and in community, we have critically engaged with a range of perspectives; have followed our interests, instincts and questions; have sought to make meaning from these; and have developed comprehensive understandings capable of informing our practice.

ACKNOWLEDGEMENT

We would like to thank the following Editorial Board members for taking the time to respond so fully and energetically to our request: L. David Brown, Mary Brydon-Miller, Robert Chambers, Orlando Fals Borda, Bob Dick, Werner Fricke, Victor Friedman, Kenneth Gergen, Davydd Greenwood, Bjorn Gustavsen, Stephen Kemmis, Morten Levin, Patricia Maguire, Robin McTaggart, Kurt Nielsen, Sonia Ospina, Md. Anisur Rahman, Marja Liisa Swantz, Rajesh Tandon, William Torbert, Yoland Wadsworth and Jack Whitehead.

REFERENCES

Antrobus, P. (2004) *The Global Women's Movement: Origins, Issues and Strategies*. London: Zed Books.

Argyris, C. (1985) *Action Science, Concepts, Methods, and Skills for Research and Intervention*. San Francisco, CA: Jossey-Bass.

Argyris, C. and Schön, D. (1974) *Theory in Practice: Increasing Professional Effectiveness*. San Francisco, CA: Jossey-Bass.

Barazangi, N.H. (2004) *Woman's Identity and the Quran: a New Reading*. Gainesville, FL: University Press of Florida.

Barrett, W. (1990) *Irrational Man: a Study in Existential Philosophy*. New York: Anchor Books/Doubleday.

Bateson, G. (1972) *Steps to an Ecology of Mind*. San Francisco, CA: Chandler.

Bateson, G. (1979) *Mind and Nature: A Necessary Unity*. New York: E.P. Dutton.

Becker, H. (1997) *Outsiders: Studies in the Sociology of Deviance*. London: Free Press.

Berger, P.L. (1963) *Invitation to Sociology: a Humanistic Perspective*. Garden City, NY: Doubleday.

Berger, P.L. and Luckmann, T. (1966) *The Social Construction of Reality: a Treatise in the Sociology of Knowledge*. Garden City, NY: Doubleday.

Bernstein, R.J. (1983) *Beyond Objectivism and Relativism: Science, Hermeneutics, and Praxis*. Philadelphia: University of Pennsylvania Press.

Berry, T. (1999) *The Great Work: Our Way into the Future*. New York: Bell Tower.

Bion, W.R. (1961) *Experiences in Groups, and Other Papers*. New York: Basic Books.

Bloch, E. (1995) *The Principle of Hope (reprint edn)*. Cambridge, MA: MIT Press.

Blumer, H. (1998) *Symbolic Interactionism: Perspective and Method*. Berkeley, CA: University of California Press.

Bourdieu, P. (2004) *Distinction: a Social Critique of the Judgment of Taste*. Cambridge, MA: Harvard University Press.

Bowles, S. and Gintis, H. (1976) *Schooling in Capitalist America: Educational Reform and the Contradictions of Economic Life*. New York: Basic Books.

Brydon-Miller, M., Greenwood, D. and Maguire, P. (2003) 'Why action research?', *Action Research*, 1 (1): 9–28.

Brydon-Miller, M., Greenwood, D. and Eikeland, O. (eds) (in press) 'Ethics and action research: Special issue', *Action Research*, 3 (1).

Buber, M. (2000) *I and Thou*. New York: Scribner Book Company.

Campbell, D.T. (1974) 'Evolutionary epistemology', in P.A. Schilpp (ed.), *The Philosophy of Karl R. Popper*, LaSalle, IL: Open Court. pp. 412–63.

Capra, F. (1982) *The Turning Point: Science, Society and the Rising Culture*. London: Wildwood House.

Capra, F. (1996) *The Web of Life: a New Synthesis of Mind and Matter*. London: HarperCollins.

Coffin, W.S. (1999) *The Heart Is a Little to the Left: Essays on Public Morality*. Hanover, NH: University Press of New England for Dartmouth College.

Coser, L. (1998) *The Functions of Social Conflict*. London: Routledge.

Dharendorf, R. (1959) *Class and Class Conflict in Industrial Society*. London: Routledge and Kegan Paul.

De Silva, G.V.S., Mehta, N., Wignaraja, P. and Rahmam, M.A (1979) 'Bhoomi Sena: a struggle of people's power'. *Development Dialogue*, 2: 3–70.

DeVault, M. (1991) *Feeding the Family: the Social Organization of Caring as Gendered Work*. Chicago: University of Chicago Press.

Dewey, J. (1982) *Logic: the Theory of Inquiry*. New York: Irvington.

Douglas, M. (2003) *Mary Douglas: Collected Works*. London: Routledge.

Eikeland, O. (2006) 'Phrónêsis, Aristotle, and action research', *International Journal of Action Research*, 2 (1): 5–53.

Ellis, P. (2003) *Women, Gender and Development in the Caribbean: Reflections and Projections*. New York: Zed Books.

Erickson, M.H. (1985) *The Wisdom of Milton H. Erickson* (ed. R.A. Havens). New York: Irvington Publishers.

Fals Borda, O. (1988) *Knowledge and People's Power: Lessons with Peasants in Nicaragua, Mexico and Colombia*. New York: New Horizons Press.

Fals Borda, O. and Rahman, M.A. (eds) (1991) *Action and Knowledge: Breaking the Monopoly with Participatory Action Research*. New York: Intermediate Technology Pubs/Apex Press.

Fanon, F. (2004) *The Wretched of the Earth* (trans. Richard Philcox). New York: Grove Press.

Fawcett, T. (1971) *The Symbolic Language of Religion*. Minneapolis, MN: Augsburg.

Feinberg, W. (1975) *Reason and Rhetoric: the Intellectual Foundations of 20th Century Liberal Educational Policy*. New York: Wiley.

Ferrer, J.N. (2002) *Revisioning Transpersonal Theory: a Participatory Vision of Human Spirituality*. Albany: State University of New York Press.

Feyerabend, P. (1975) *Against Method: Outline of an Anarchistic Theory of Knowledge*. London: Verso.

Fischer, E. (1969) *Art Against Ideology*. New York: G. Braziller.

Foucault, M. (2000) *Power: Essential Works of Foucault 1954–1984, Vol. 3*. New York: The New Press.

Freire, P. (1972) *Pedagogy of the Oppressed*. London: Penguin Books.

Freud, S. (1961) *Civilization and Its Discontents*. New York: W.W. Norton.

Fricke, W. (1983) 'Participatory research and the enhancement of workers' innovative qualifications', *Journal of Occupational Behavior*, 4: 73–87.

Gadamer, H.G. (2000) *Truth and Method*. New York: Continuum.

Gamson, W. (1992) *Talking Politics*. Cambridge: Cambridge University Press.

Gaventa, J. (1991) *Participatory Education and Grassroots Development: the Case of Rural Appalachia*. London: International Institute for Environment and Development, Sustainable Agriculture Programme.

Giddens, A. (1984) *The Constitution of Society: Outline of the Theory of Structuration*. Cambridge: Polity Press.

Giroux, H. (1983) 'Ideology and agency in the process of schooling', *Journal of Education*. 165 (1): 12–34.

Gouldner, A.W. (1976) *The Dialectic of Ideology and Technology: the Origins, Grammar, and Future of Ideology*. New York: Seabury Press.

Greenwood, D.J. (2002) 'Action research: unfulfilled promises and unmet challenges', *Concepts and Transformation*, 7 (7): 117–39.

Gurdjieff, I. (1963) *Meetings with Remarkable Men: All and Everything*, 2nd Series. London: Routledge.

Habermas, J. (1975) *Legitimation Crisis* (trans. T. McCarthy). Boston: Beacon Press.

Habermas, J. (1981) *The Theory of Communicative Action: Reason and the Realization of Society, Vol. 1*. Cambridge: Polity Press.

Hall, B. (1978) *Creating Knowledge: Breaking the Monopoly: Research Methods, Participation and Development*. Paris: UNESCO.

Hampden-Turner, C. (1981) *Maps of the Mind*. New York: Macmillan.

Harding, S. (1987) *Feminism and Methodology: Social Science Issues*. Bloomington, IN: Indiana University Press.

Härnsten, G. (2001) 'The relationship between agency and structure – some challenges for education and educational research', in L. Holmstrand, G. Härnsten and D. Beach (eds), *Deltagarorienterad forskning. Bidrag till NFPF:s symposium om deltagarorienterad forskning i Stockholm, March. Arbetsrapporter från pedagogiska institutionen, Uppsala universitet*, 224.

Held, D. (1989) *Political Theory and the Modern State: Essays on State, Power, and Democracy*. Stanford, CA: Stanford University Press.

Heron, J. (1996) *Co-operative Inquiry: Research into the Human Condition*. London: Sage.

Heron, J. and Reason, P. (1997) 'A participatory inquiry paradigm', *Qualitative Inquiry*, 3 (3): 274–94.

Hirschhorn, L. (1988) *The Workplace Within: Psychodynamics of Organizational Life*. Cambridge, MA: MIT Press.

Horton, M., Bell, B., Gaventa, J. and Peters, J.M. (1990) *We Make the Road by Walking: Conversations on Education and Social Change*. Philadelphia, PA: Temple University Press.

Husserl, E. (1989) *Studies in the Phenomenology of Constitution*. Boston: Kluwer Academic.

Ihde, D. (1986) *Consequences of Phenomenology*. Albany: State University of New York Press.

Jungk, R. (1954) *Tomorrow Is Already Here*. New York: Simon & Schuster.

King, M.L. (1967) *Where Do We Go from Here: Chaos or Community?* New York: Harper & Row.

Kinsey, D.C. (1978) *Evaluation in Nonformal Education: the Need for Practitioner Evaluation*. Amherst, MA: Center for International Education, University of Massachusetts.

Klein, M. (1992) *Love, Guilt and Reparation and Other Works, 1921–1945*. London: Karnac.

Klein, R.D. (1985) *Rethinking Sisterhood: Unity in Diversity*. Oxford: Pergammon Press.

Kohl, H. (1984) *Growing Minds: On Becoming a Teacher*. New York: Harper & Row.

Kuhn, T.S. (1962) *The Structure of Scientific Revolutions*. Chicago: University of Chicago Press.

Lakatos, I. (1986) *The Methodology of Scientific Research Programmes: Philosophical Papers, Vol. 1*. (ed. J. Worrall, and G. Currie). Cambridge: Cambridge University Press.

Langer, S.K.K. (1979) *Philosophy in a New Key: a Study in the Symbolism of Reason, Rite, and Art.* Cambridge, MA: Harvard University Press.

Lather, P. (1991) *Getting Smart: Feminist Research and Pedagogy with/in the Postmodern.* New York: Routledge.

Lather, P. (2007) *Getting Lost: Feminist Efforts toward a Double(d) Science.* Albany: State University of New York Press.

Latour, B. (1993) *We Have Never Been Modern.* Cambridge, MA: Harvard University Press.

Lewin, K. (1958) *Resolving Social Conflicts: Selected Papers on Group Dynamics (1935–1946).* New York: Harper.

Lowenstein, A.K. (1962) *Brutal Mandate: a Journey to South West Africa.* New York: Macmillan.

Lukes, S. (1974) *Power: a Radical View.* London: Macmillan.

Lykes, B. (1996) *Myths about the Powerless: Contesting Social Inequalities.* Philadelphia, PA: Temple University Press.

Marshall, J. (1999) 'Living life as inquiry', *Systematic Practice and Action Research,* 12 (2): 155–71.

Marshall, J. and Reason, P. (1993) 'Adult learning in collaborative action research', *Studies in Continuing Education*, 15 (2): 117–32.

Marx, K. (1970) *Capital: a Critique of Political Economy.* (ed. F. Engels, trans. S. Moore, and E. Aveling). London: Lawrence and Wishart.

Maslow, A. (1968) *Toward a Psychology of Being.* Princeton, NJ: Van Nostrand.

Mbilinyi, M. (2003) *Activist Voices: Feminist Struggles for an Alternative World.* Dar es Salaam: E & D Ltd.

McIntyre, A. (2000) *Inner-city Kids: Adolescents Confront Life and Violence in an Urban Community.* New York: New York University Press.

Mead, G.H. (1934) *Mind, Self and Society.* Chicago, IL: University of Chicago Press.

Mehta, M.S. (1974) *Progress and Development of Adult Education in India.* Bombay: Gandhi Shikshan Bhavan.

Menzies Lyth, I. (1988) *Containing Anxiety in Institutions.* London: Free Association Books.

Merleau-Ponty, M. (1962) *Phenomenology of Perception* (trans. C. Smith). London: Routledge & Kegan Paul.

Merleau-Ponty, M. (2004) *The World of Perception.* London: Routledge.

Myers, I. and Briggs, K. (1987) *Introduction to Type: a Description of the Theory and Applications of the Myers-Briggs Type Indicator.* Palto Alto, CA: Consulting Psychologists Press.

Oakley, A. (1984) *Taking It Like a Woman.* New York: Random House.

O'Brien, M. (1981) 'Feminist theory and dialectic logic', *Signs*, 7 (1): 144–57.

Ouspensky, P.D. (1931) *New Model of the Universe: Principles of the Psychological Method in Its Application to Problems of Science, Religion and Art.* (trans. R. R. Merton). London: Routledge.

Park, P. (1993) *Voices of Change: Participatory Research in the United States and Canada.* Westport, CT: Bergin & Garvey.

Popper, K. (1959) *The Logic of Scientific Discovery.* London: Hutchinson.

Postman, N. and Weingartner, C. (1969) *Teaching as a Subversive Activity.* New York: Delacorte Press.

Putnam, H. (1975) *Mind, Language, and Reality.* Cambridge: Cambridge University Press.

Rahman, A. (1993) *People's Self Development: Perspectives on Participatory Action Research: a Journey through Experience.* London: Zed Books.

Reason, P. (ed.) (1994) *Participation in Human Inquiry.* London: Sage.

Reason, P. (in press) 'Education for ecology: science, aesthetics, spirit and ceremony', *Management Learning.*

Reason, P. and Bradbury, H. (2001) 'Introduction: inquiry and participation in search of a world worthy of human aspiration', in H. Bradbury and P. Reason (eds), *Handbook of Action Research: Participative Inquiry and Practice*, London: Sage. pp. 1–14.

Reid, C. (2004) *The Wounds of Exclusion: Poverty, Women's Health, and Social Justice.* Edmonton: Qual Institute Press, International Institute for Qualitative Methodology.

Reinharz, S. (1992) *Feminist Methods in Social Research.* New York: Oxford University Press.

Ricoeur, P. (1981) *Hermeneutics and the Human Sciences: Essays on Language, Action, and Interpretation* (ed. and trans. J.B. Thompson). Cambridge: Cambridge University Press.

Rivera Garretas, M.M. (1997) *El fraude de la igualdad.* Barcelona: Planeta.

Rorty, R. (1970) *The Linguistic Turn: Recent Essays in Philosophical Method.* Chicago, IL: University of Chicago Press.

Schön, D.A. (1983) *The Reflective Practitioner. How Professionals Think in Action.* London: Temple Smith.

Schwab, J. (1969) *College Curriculum and Student Protest.* Chicago, IL: University of Chicago Press.

Searle, J. (1995) *The Construction of Social Reality.* New York: The Free Press.

Shor, I. (1992) *Empowering Education: Critical Teaching for Social Change.* Chicago, IL: University of Chicago Press.

Simon, H.A. (1969) *The Sciences of the Artificial*. Cambridge, MA: MIT Press.

Stanley, L. (1992) *The Auto/biographical I: the Theory and Practice of Feminist Auto/biography*. Manchester: Manchester University Press.

Swantz, M.L. (1970) *Ritual and Symbol in Transitional Zaramo Society with Special Reference to Women*. Lund: Gleerup.

Tandon, R. (1983) *Participatory Research in Asia*. Australia: Australian National University, Centre for Continuing Education.

Tarnas, R. (1991) *The Passion of the Western Mind*. New York: Ballantine.

Tarnas, R. (2006) *Cosmos and Psyche*. New York: Viking.

Tillich, P. (1952/1980) *The Courage to Be*. New Haven, CT: Yale University Press.

Torbert, W.R. (1976) *Creating a Community of Inquiry: Conflict, Collaboration, Transformation*. New York: Wiley.

Toulmin, S. (1990) *Cosmopolis: The Hidden Agenda of Modernity*. New York: Free Press.

Touraine, A. (1983) *Solidarity: the Analysis of a Social Movement: Poland, 1980–1981*. Cambridge: Cambridge University Press.

Tse-Tung, M. (1972) *Mao Tse-Tung: an Anthology of His Writings*. New York: New American Library.

Turner, V.W. (1986) *The Anthropology of Performance*. New York: PAJ Publications.

Ulin, R.C. (2001) *Understanding Cultures: Perspectives in Anthropology and Social Theory, 2nd edn*. Oxford: Blackwell Publishers.

Wadsworth, Y. (1997) *Do It Yourself Social Research, 2nd edn*. Sydney: Allen & Unwin.

Weber, M. (1958) *Essays in Sociology* (ed. C. Wright Mills and H.H. Gerth). New York: Oxford University Press.

Whyte, W.F. (ed.) (1991) *Participatory Action Research*. Newbury Park, CA: Sage.

Winter, R. (1989) *Learning from Experience: Principles and Practice in Action-Research*. London: Falmer Press.

Wittgenstein, L. (1953) *Philosophical Investigations*. Oxford: Blackwell.

Wright Mills, C. (1963) *Power, Politics, and People: the Collected Essays of C. Wright Mills*. New York: Oxford University Press.

2

Participatory Action Research as Practice

Marja Liisa Swantz

This chapter describes participatory action research practice in Africa, particularly Tanzania, drawing on the author's experience over several decades. It explores the relationship between participatory research and national politics, the place of theory, the role of the participant researcher, and the significance of symbols in social transformation, and it provides vignettes of the development of participatory practice in a development context.

Participatory Action Research – PAR or P(A)R – is multidisciplinary and multiform; no one perspective can claim authority or authenticity. PAR adherents agree that it breaks from the positivist and empiricist science. When Orlando Fals Borda reviewed the history of P(A)R at the World Congress on Participatory Convergence in Knowledge in Cartagena in 1997, he found at least 32 schools associated with the idea of participation in social, economic and political research. P(A)R had no one disciplinary or political orientation, but its beginnings were closely connected with critique of mainline social sciences and it frequently lined up with revolutionary movements (Fals Borda, 1998: xii).

Alfredo Molano in his opening speech at the same Congress referred to the multiple beginnings of PAR. In his words, 'As with all great things, it had no single inventor. Nobody discovered it, it was the result of an atmosphere rarefied by the clash between clear-cut scientific explanations and a rough reality.' Referring to the changes that had taken place, he pointed out that tempering of the radical orientation in the use of PAR and the need for critical interpretation had brought about an ethical dimension of science. The time of Marxism and its rigid application were over and the concern was for the reconstruction of the actual lives which ordinary people live. Two points had shifted the emphasis. After 20 years of action research, researchers were interested in walking shoulder to shoulder with ordinary people rather than one step ahead. Second, the researchers had stopped fighting against the state, instead, they were participating, in spite of the weaknesses of the state (Molano, 1998: 5).

These two points were guiding thoughts when PAR started in Tanzania in the mid-1960s and apply particularly to the initial steps of a participatory approach to research and researchers' participation in people's actual lives. These beginnings were different from the start of action research in Latin America. This chapter describes beginning stages of PAR in the African, mainly Tanzanian, context and thus complements other chapters on the development of PAR in Latin America, Asia, and India in this volume and in the first edition of this *Handbook* (Fals Borda, 2001/2006; Hall, 2001; Rahman, Chapter 3). Much of the beginnings refer to the work of the writer, and for this reason first-person language is used.

When describing the roots of their own work, pioneers of P(A)R like Fals Borda trace the epistemology and theoretical groundings and the theoretical paths they followed, rather than the political or practical context. Latin American scholars had their training in the universities of the USA and became aware of the political implications of the modernization theories and the myth of objective science. The dependency theories first developed in Latin America, which condemned the trickle-down and diffusion-of-innovation theories, spread quickly to centres of social science in other parts of the world in the 1970s. The social scientists in Tanzania gained inspiration from books by Andre Gunder Frank and Walter Rodney (1972) and the University of Dar es Salaam soon became the hot spot of radical political theory. However, in Tanzania PAR did not start from such a political theory or action as in Latin America. It started from the practical need to connect research to national development and to avoid separating the university from practical reality and the nation's stated political goals, which demanded mutual communication between researchers and people, in political jargon, 'peasants and workers'. Participant research in action was an outcome

of a sense that 'the license to practice the irrelevant has expired' (Nash, 1981: 236).

After the publication of Thomas Kühn's *Structure of Scientific Revolution* (1962), new possibilities for paradigmatic change emerged in the social sciences and PAR was an obvious way to break the false objectivism of positivist social science. Personally, I leaned on Gunnar Myrdal's (1970) critique of objectivism. I also discovered that John Galtung, professor for peace research from Oslo, had after his visit to Cuba come on an alternative model, which he called non-violent social science in which the general rule would be not to do research *on* people but *with* people (Galtung, 1975: 273–6). However, masculine concepts still prevailed also in new radical science, and there was a further need for a change of paradigm in women's studies. In the Tanzanian context these broke through to challenge the dominating social concepts and the 'scientific knowledge' that had suppressed people's knowledge in general and that of women in particular.

STARTING PAR IN TANZANIA

I learned participant research while immersed in village life some 50 km north of Dar es Salaam in 1965–70. I became part of a traditional community in which ritual and symbolic communication formed the base of social life and women were illiterate. A prominent medicine man adopted me as his daughter and thus integrated me into a family system with its responsibilities and privileges. My own family shared a Swahili house with a local family. In the words of a village woman to my daughter 20 years after:

> She did not come as a European. She came as one of us. She was Mswahilii.[1] Can you say that there is a difference between her and me because she is a European? No, there is no difference. We see her as one of us; exactly the same. (Tripp, 1991: 52)

Even if taken for what such statements are worth, they do indicate a basic condition for PAR. Participation means identification (Swantz, 1970, 1986b).

Participatory approach to research had its start with university students when I was locally employed as a Senior Research Fellow in the University of Dar es Salaam in 1972–5. The university supported students as research assistants during their long vacation. It enabled me to recruit students and give them training in the new approach. The departure point was educational. Tanzania needed academic people who were not divorced from their background and who would bring the wisdom and knowledge of the grassroots to the academy.

From the start PAR aimed at making research an agent of transformation in the rural community. It had to be of immediate interest to the people in the studied community, involving them in formulating the study problems and in finding solutions. In order to realize the educational and motivational potential of such a study it needed to be a common effort with villagers, elders, administrators, educators and researchers. It took some time to have such an unconventional approach approved by research authorities.

Research in action, later called PAR, was first developed with students over a three year period. The first group of 12 male students studied income-earning potentials of the school leavers in five coastal villages in 1973. Together with the youth they decided to start gardening, carpentry and fishing projects. Sharing work with the village youth was an instructive experience both for the students and the school leavers while they learned to plan and implement projects, consult village authorities, and make the projects viable. A Tanzanian colleague and I visited the students and analysed the situations with them. Funds became available from a trust fund for purchasing equipment. The students' attitudes towards the villagers changed radically, as they recorded in their reports. I quote from one:

Colleague, Ruth Besha and I have come to realise that this was a unique programme. While the traditional research methods take the people as objects of research, ours took them as actors, in fact as the stars of the whole process. This was a revolution in

itself. Despite the problems, the method whereby researchers stay and work together with the local people is the best one, as besides bringing youth of different educational levels together, it also gives the local people opportunities for learning from the researchers. ... At the same time we learned a lot from the local people. People talk freely with people with whom they are acquainted. (Swantz, 1976b: 119–26; 1982: 117–38)

In the following year women students were engaged in a participatory study with families having malnutrition problems. Each shared life with five families, in which the mother had been with a child for rehabilitation in a nutrition centre. The students made notes on daily life, keeping sets of questions in mind but forms out of sight. When mutual confidence was gained the problems could be discussed openly. Comparison with the living conditions of the healthy neighbours helped to focus on the economic and social differentials.

Other female students organized literacy classes for women cleaners of the university and the Ministry of Education in which they engaged women in lively talks and writing about their lives. The exercises encouraged the women to be active in advancing their social and educational level. One female student worked in a cashew nut factory, which employed over a thousand women workers. She experienced their work-related hazards of corrosive acid on bare hands and helped mobilize the women to take the poor working conditions to the workers union. Some women students gained deeper understanding in their home region of the reasons why women left their homes to become prostitutes in cities and on return established themselves as respectable farmers (Swantz, 1985c).

Participation and action made research contextual. The roles of the researchers and the researched interchanged in the course of communication through which there was a mutual development of knowledge and learning to understand people's problems. The students learned to question the role of the researcher and analyse how her/his presence influenced the research situation. PAR was in line with the political theory in which peasants and workers were to be the builders of the nation. The students' changed attitudes impressed the chief education officer of the university who recommended the approach for use in all the university departments when students were engaged as research assistants (Swantz, 1976a, 1976b).

With a Swedish colleague, Jan Rudengren, we developed a participatory approach in an ILO-supported pilot survey.[2] With some organizational assistance the villagers in 46 villages of Bagamoyo and two other districts assessed their educational level and the extent of utilization of skills and natural resources. The self-conducted survey raised active discussions in village meetings before and after the survey. The results made villagers aware of big gaps in skills and unused resources. In spite of statistical weaknesses in the survey, villagers' involvement in it and their self-assessment made them aware of their development potentials. The weakness was in the follow-up: the research settings seldom allowed the researchers' contact with local participants to continue. The written documents benefit the academy rather than the participants, who learn from the guided action, analysis and reflection, which is the educational component in participation (Swantz, 1979).

These first participatory projects prepared the way for four years of full participatory action research on development and culture built on the contacts gained in Bagamoyo District. The project was launched in 1975 in co-operation between Tanzanian and Finnish researchers under the Ministry of Culture and Youth and the Academy of Finland. Issues needing research and action arose in many areas: there were imminent problems resulting from the government intention of moving people to planned villages; government officers had problems getting Maasai boys to schools; cattle keepers were experiencing poor relations with the authorities. The start of PAR coincided with the government programme intended to foster self-reliant development. People soon nicknamed the project Jipemoyo, 'take heart', as Bagamoyo referred to the beating hearts of slaves who during the slave trade were brought to the coastal town, Bagamoyo, for sale (Swantz, 1981).

The aim of research was to gain a deeper view of people's own concepts of development, what assets their own cultural ways could contribute and what conflicts they caused. Seven Tanzanian and Finnish researchers of five disciplines along with some assistants became involved with intent to write doctoral theses after the four years of participatory research. Two worked with the Parakuyo Maasai, one with Kwere artisans, and an ethnomusicologist with his artist wife lived many years in Miono village with their three children, one born there, learning the Zigua music and dance. A geographer recorded people's moves to new villages, drawing maps for the ward office, and an ethnologist befriended women of Msoga. The project secretary engaged also in research on people's conceptions of ethnicity (Donner, 1977; Hurskainen, 1984; Jerman, 1997; Kiyenze, 1985; Mustafa et al., 1980; Sitari, 1983; Vuorela, 1987). The researchers lived with the people, renting village houses. Seminars were arranged to give a forum for village historians to relate past histories, people of same occupations discussed their work in groups, young people entertained in song and dance, and artists illustrated leaflets for distribution.

The government policy of concentrating population in bigger villages was aimed at improving people's access to health and educational services and at facilitating communal cultivation, but it also raised many difficulties. When people from scattered areas refused to move, force was often used. On the other hand, the intended aim of communal cultivation was never fully carried through; instead, people were told to join individually cultivated plots into unified fields for easy ploughing. People found ways to get around the orders instead of openly resisting. Today, 30 years later, the difficulties arising from mismanaged implementation of villagization belongs to the past: while some have returned to their home plots, the benefits from village dwelling can be seen in the village-based local government system. It has facilitated the application of PRA (i.e. Participatory Rural Appraisal) in village planning.

However, at that time the researchers could mediate between people and authorities. They learned people's reasoning and helped their voices be heard when local officers did not dare to bend the orders and the elected leaders would not risk their positions by expressing people's views. For example, Msoga village in Bagamoyo District was well situated along a river with good soil for vegetable gardens and a large maize field was ploughed with a hired tractor. The arbitrary plan made on an office drawing board had located the new village a few kilometres away along the main road. The school and dispensary had been moved there, but half of the people refused to move. Visiting the village we carried a tape-recorder, which the villagers at work on their gardens spotted. It prompted them to record their village story in songs and in a brief written history. They took for granted that we would take it to the president. The tape reached President Nyerere, with the result that they could stay in old Msoga and start a fresh.[3]

Also the Parakuyo Maasai of Bagamoyo District seized the opportunity through PAR to express their dissatisfaction at the dealings of the government, which in the early 1970s had taken their grazing and watering grounds along Ruvu river to start a state cattle farm run by the Chinese. The government had also failed to provide veterinary services, medicines and training. The Maasai had been ostracized from colonial times because of their different lifestyle and dress (or lack of it). They decided to organize a two-day seminar with the backing of the Jipemoyo researchers and were ready to butcher two cows to feed the participants. They wanted to speak to the regional veterinary officer residing in the capital and invited him to participate. When he didn't initially turn up, they delayed the start of the seminar until he finally arrived, after having been reminded by phone 15 km away.

The women researchers met with Maasai women separately since the Maasai men could not consume meat with women present, nor could they yet think of sending girls to school. PAR would play a role in bringing about changes too, these are described below.

One issue arose from the government assumption that the Maasai herds were growing in size and the consequent order to arrange annual sales. The Maasai initially resisted the proposed counting of the cattle, but after they analysed the situation with the researchers they co-operated in the count, which evidenced that the numbers were diminishing, not growing. The discovery put a halt to the forced marketing. Many individual herds were in fact too small for supporting a household. The researchers recorded the differentiation, which was taking place among the Maasai, dividing them into three income groups. Only the richest had enough cattle for reproducing themselves (Mustafa, 1989; Mustafa et al., 1980: vol 3, 64–87).

Through PAR the contacts with the veterinarians were encouraged and after Jipemoyo the regional veterinary officer organized a training seminar for the same group of Maasai. They could have also taught much to the officer about cattle, the locations of good grasses for grazing, and the best spots for digging wells or water pools. The contrast between the Latin names of cattle diseases that the veterinarian wrote on the blackboard and the experience of men sitting at desks became evident. The men, many illiterate, listened for a while but soon took the initiative to make the training officer listen to their questions, such as whether their practice of castration was harmful. The Maasai were quick to learn but their opportunities for an encounter with the livestock officers had been few – previously one visit to a government cattle farm had given them new ideas.

The conflict between the development policies and cultural traditions in relation to women placed the researchers in a sensitive situation. A woman elder approached me in a Maasai craal with the problem of clitoridectomy, which they practised but which she had doubts about. I pointed out its dangers and she shared our discussion with fellow women sitting in the moonlight. The change of harmful customs takes place gradually after some families break off the custom. In this, as in the schooling of girls, the Maasai who had become Christians saw first the need for change and others followed. Today many girls go to school and during my recent visit I ate meat with men.

Issues brought up in seminars and personal contacts during the four years of PAR (1975–9) began also to change discriminatory attitudes toward the Maasai. Shared research opened new perspectives and raised wide interest. When the Maasai Prime Minister learned of the progress made in settling the conflicts between the cattle herders and farmers, he initiated a seminar in Dar es Salaam between his local government officers and representatives of Lugoba Maasai and farmers. A Maasai woman in her blue apparel and red beads drew attention and the bureaucrats were impressed by the well-formulated arguments of the Maasai headman.

The leadership of the Academy of Finland followed closely the implementation of its first development research in Africa. The evaluation seminar in Helsinki drew participants from 14 different countries. The evaluator of the research methodology was a Swiss expert of PAR theory, Heinz Moser. In time five doctoral theses presented in universities of Dar es Salaam and Helsinki and some other degrees were the academic result of the Jipemoyo researchers who have become professors and development researchers. The immediate results of Jipemoyo were in the communication, analysis, action and reflection at the research scene. PAR also had political connotations. It made oppressed people visible and facilitated hearing them and solving their problems. It increased awareness and made power holders conscious of people's right to speak for their own defence.

Budd Hall edited an issue of the journal *Convergence on Participatory Research* in 1975 (Hall, 1975) in which he elaborated the basic principles of PAR, referring to my initial paper. He became the General Secretary of the International Council of Adult Education (ICAE) and was the main organizer of the First World Assembly of Adult Education in Dar es Salaam in 1976, during which some Latin American researchers visited a Jipemoyo research site. As the centre for PAR networks ICAE co-ordinated the Participatory Research Project (PRP) in Africa, Asia, Europe, Latin America and North America. Under its auspices regional and international conferences were held in which methodologies, theory and practice of PAR were debated. The Mzumbe conference in Tanzania gathered representatives from six African countries, in which educational and popular theatre projects had been started (Kassam, 1982).

POLITICAL GROUNDS FOR PARTICIPATORY ACTION RESEARCH

Critiques of the colonial scholarship, imperialistic history, and continuing neo-colonialist presence prepared the ground for new research approaches. Disinterested social science was declared false. Nationalistic spirit guided people being freed from colonial fetters. The experiences in the former colonial states converged when students met in universities and research-conferences. Social scientists were caught with the political inspiration of the new nations while they also were critical of the national politics. In Africa people supported parties and national governments which lined up against the colonial and neo-colonial forces, even if they differed in the degree to which they trusted their governments. The role of the state was different in Africa from that in Latin America. Building a nation was seen as building a strong state, which would take care of social needs and build a strong national economy.

In Latin America the struggle was against the North American economic and political power over their governments and bourgeoisie which lined up with these forces. Action research, later PAR, related to the struggle against the oppressive governmental force. The state became the enemy, with the exception of countries with socialist governments. Activists such as Mexican Gustavo Esteva resisted also the foreign developmental emphasis in people's struggle (Esteva, 1996). PAR was developed with and for the oppressed groups. Similarly in Asia PAR embraced a liberationist perspective (see Rahman, Chapter 3; Brown and Tandon, Chapter 15): people organized themselves to resist the power of landowners or moneylenders. In such situations the resistant groups embraced revolutionary ideology in differing ways.

In Tanzania, the relation of people to the state was different. Hardly any resistance groups emerged. People rallied around the President Julius Nyerere and his TANU party, Tanzania National Union.[4] In 1967 TANU had adopted the policy of *ujamaa*, communalism, formulated by the National Executive in Arusha and thus called the Arusha Declaration. The self-reliant socialist politics, which claimed traditional roots in *ujamaa*, assumed that people would cultivate communally and join in the fight against capitalism. People's political aspirations were to be given space within the one party state. The government structure provided fairly democratically elected village governments, committees and ten house cell groups, though the National Executive Committee could influence local choices of candidates. PAR accorded with President Nyerere's self-reliant development policies in which peasants and workers would be the main actors. The Marxist economic theory guided the fight against capitalism, but Nyerere declined to accept Marxism as the philosophy of life. As a Catholic, Marx could not overrule religion; further, while Nyerere built on tradition he disclaimed its oppression of women.

However, as with Latin America countries claiming to be socialist, so in Tanzania the ruling elite did not always live up to the stated policies. Bureaucracy and the self-interest of officials brought about a separation between the Party elite and the people which often led to oppressive treatment of ordinary people, especially in implementing villagization, where it met people's passive resistance. In contrast, PAR built on the people's interests.

FURTHER DEVELOPMENTS IN THE USE OF PAR

PAR researchers found themselves in similar situations to which the anthropological method of participant observation had earlier led researchers. The initial PAR projects had similarities with Action Anthropology, which Sol Tax initiated in 1948 with students doing research practice in the Meskwaki Indian settlement in Iowa, challenging the ideal of disinterested science: 'people are not rats and not to be treated like them. … Community research is thus justifiable only to the degree that the results are imminently useful to the community and easily outweigh the disturbance to it.' The early action anthropologists asked, 'Are the researchers in the position to know what is useful to the researched community? Can the doctoral theses as the academic outcome be considered commonly researched results?'(Mertens, 2004: 34–4). PAR researchers have had to deal with such problematics and place themselves as actors within the total research context. This means withdrawing from the action into periods of reading and reflection and placing oneself in the larger picture. The problems are widely dealt with in reflections on AR and PAR (Ragland, 2006).

In early 1960s when the university was established in Tanzania, foreign natural and social scientists went there with the background of disinterested science. This was inappropriate in situations in which the need for practical solutions was urgent. One of the initial solutions led to the application of the participant approach to research. In contrast with Sol Tax's work with the Meskwaki, the intention was not to assist people; rather, the 'informants' were to become co-researchers. The research problems were identified together and research was conducted with members of the community. The practice could be criticized, but the principles were clearly stated. It meant a common search for interpreting the situations, with the knowledge of researchers complementing the practical knowledge of the people. The researchers' formulation of the scientific problems was part of the evolving ideas and the attempts to analyse them.

Action researchers today might face the same criticism as Sol Tax for 'not producing a high-quality ethnographic portrait' (Mertens, 2004: 34–4). The rich literature of the social applicability of anthropology is relevant for further analysis of action research and its role in development. By and large, the anthropological methodology has not openly recognized research as a common endeavour for common goals with its informants in spite of the fact that anthropological research is a shared activity. The researcher only thanks the informants (Swantz, 1985b, 1986a).

In PAR the researcher needs to be open to learn from others and to adopt a genuine learner's attitude even in situations in which apparent ignorance tempts her to become a teacher. For example, the participatory malnutrition study was different from traditional nutrition studies, which analyse measured portions of food consumed by malnourished children basing the analysis on exacting knowledge of the nutritional values. The use of PAR drew the attention of nutritionists in Finland and Norway to the significance of human relations in research and it resulted later in further participatory nutritional studies and seminars (Swantz, 1985c: 96–121).

PAR rejects science as the dominating knowledge and bases the problems on everyday knowledge; the researcher and the researched share their knowledge as equals. The researcher genuinely recognizes that she does not know the life world, wisdom or meaning of central symbols of life of the co-researchers. The term 'informant', which anthropologists use of the local holders of knowledge, and also the term 'field study'

distance the scholar from the local partners and context. Reference to 'peasants' places a community into another class and emphasizes the difference, as does 'indigenous knowledge'. Such terms separate the academics into another category, class or nationality.

Harvard economist Stephen Marglin, in the book titled *Dominating Knowledge*, suggests the use of the concepts *episteme* and *techne* to differentiate knowledge systems of theoretical origin from technical or practical knowledge (Marglin, 1990). His and his wife's research team at UNU-WIDER,[5] in Helsinki, of which I was privileged to be part, struggled to give *techne* knowledge the credit it deserves. In another book with the telling title *Decolonizing Knowledge*, Aili Mari Tripp and I wrote an article based on PAR in fishing communities of Tanzania (Swantz and Tripp, 1996). Through PAR conducted prior to the evaluation of the foreign-sponsored training project we discovered that artisan fishermen's knowledge, an integral part of their daily work gained over many lifetimes, was ignored in fishing officers' technical training on the same shore. In the words of a graduating student of the Mbegani Fisheries Development Centre: 'We learn higher and higher knowledge, it has nothing to do with fishermen.' Yet 98 per cent of fish caught in the country were caught by artisan fishermen and women.[6]

Keeping the two categories of knowledge separate reduces the meaning of people's work. The cultural variables in the organization of work determine the satisfaction and the success of work, not only the type of knowledge applied in work performance. Knowledge, which is not integrated into the cultural context, is not holistic, not related to the community and its capabilities. (Marglin, 1990). The technical individualistic training models presage failure. The lack of contact with fishermen in training fishing officers discovered through PAR was emphasized in the evaluation of the training in its relation to the fisheries' sector. It uplifted the status of fishermen and also the fisherwomen, who had been identified only as buyers of the left-over fish (Swantz and Tripp, 1996).

PAR was developed into participatory evaluation in monitoring ongoing health work as an effort to integrate participation of the clients into evaluation. In Tanzania the total health sector had been evaluated in 1978–9 and a closer look at the grassroots was required. The Ministry of Health needed information about how the health services met women's needs. In place of one-time assessment, a proposal was accepted to work out continuous participatory monitoring and build it into the health workers' training system. Health workers during their training could learn to work with people, look at their future work from the viewpoint of the patients and assess the quality of the service given together with clients. The Tanzanian Ministry of Health and Finnida, the Finnish Development Co-operation, supported the plan and Finnish medical doctors through their NGO for Social Responsibility took part in it over a period of ten years. The project introduced participatory learning into the health workers' training in the medical training institutes and integrated participatory action into the periods of practical learning.

In one- or two-week training seminars all the levels of health workers were learning through participation a shared human approach to village health. Participants visited village homes, and some villagers were invited to the training venues. In group meetings participants analysed what they had experienced and how the health personnel could better meet people's real needs. All the 90 training institutes were involved and a participatory component was introduced into the syllabus for medical doctors' training. Materials for participatory learning and training were prepared and distributed by the Ministry of Health, so that the project influenced a large number of medical workers during the years. The researcher's role was to analyse the process (Swantz, 1992a, 1994). A follow-up was possible within participatory development in southern Tanzania. The chief medical officer had taken part in participatory training and he put it into practice. Materials available in the Ministry of Health

were upgraded and meetings were held between health workers and traditional healers. Participatory learning was an important tool when cholera hit the area and people had to deal with it. Research went side by side with participatory practice and was published in articles and chapters in books. However, the institutional continuity of participatory practice is difficult to maintain with the change of personnel.

Participatory evaluation, PE, was also done in 1982 when Finnida supported a group of six women to assess the effects of its projects on women in Tanzania, three studying the documents, three staying in project areas (Kivelä, 1985; Stude, 1985). PE assumes that the beneficiaries are the best judges of the effects of the projects, consequently they become part of the evaluation process. PE carried out alongside development projects makes development people-centred and reaches actual beneficiaries and, if applied, reduces the number of evaluation missions which consider people as 'targets' of development. Instead of people working from their own premises, external criteria formulated by the funding agents' interests are imposed on them (Swantz, 1985a, 1992b). Monitoring, in which the clients could participate, was attempted in Regional Integrated Project Support (RIPS) in southern Tanzania, to which a separate monitoring department was attached. Even then the people involved in the implementation did not always participate in the evaluation process.

For 12 years RIPS incorporated Participatory Rural Appraisal, PRA, and also research based on PAR into its programme. (Freling, 1998; Swantz in Seppälä, 1998: 157–94). Robert Chambers (see Chapter 20) participated in a training seminar and other PRA experts came from India, but the main work was carried out by Tanzanians, among them such experts in PRA as Mwajuma Masaiganah and M.G. Kajimbwa. Training in PRA methods was carried out in all 11 districts and village people learned to assess their resources and needs. As an important outcome the approach became part of national policy to be promoted throughout the country. Before the external support ended in 2005 it was declared to be a national model. Teams were to be trained in all the villages for assessing their potentials and for making village plans as the basic documents for rural development. To simplify the approach the Ministry for Local and Regional Government recommended later an approach in which opportunities and obstacles were analysed.

THE PLACE OF THEORY

In all of the PAR projects I have described the starting point was a practical situation. PAR was related to the development impetus of the country. The experiments of PRA became part of the theoretical debate in social sciences. Orlando Fals Borda was the initiator and President of the Research Committee on Innovative Processes in Social Change of the International Sociological Association, ISA. It had its beginning in a controversy within the research committee on Modernisation and Diffusion of Innovation in Varna in 1970. Fals Borda gathered an international conference in Cartagena in 1977, in which the innovative P(A)R scholars from five continents debated against the minority holding on to diffusion-of-innovation theories. The committee met again in the Tenth World Congress of Sociology in Mexico in 1982, in which Ulf Himmelstrand from Uppsala, then President of the ISA, also took part as a member. He had contributed a paper in Cartagena in 1977 of which Fals Borda remarked that he provided a bridge towards sceptical academicians. Their chapters in a book of the Committee spelled out the diametrically opposed perspectives (Himmelstrand, 1982).

Action Research in the context of urban social problems in the USA stimulated ideas for starting the experimental PAR in Tanzania, but those studies did not incorporate community members as active partners in the research. The poor reputation of instrumental science shadowed pragmatism,

but the trend was moving in that direction. The critique of John Dewey's pragmatism by Novack (1975) was in line with early PAR researchers when historical materialism ousted pragmatism.

Developments in social science eventually created space for the actor and everyday life. In Alain Touraine's *Le retour de l'acteur* (1984), the actor again had a role in the analysis, but Touraine had warned against the P(A)R proposed by Fals Borda in which the researcher becomes committed with the actors.[7] According to Anthony Giddens the majority of the newer or newly discovered schools of social science veered to the subjectivist side and research subjects were seen as beings capable of understanding the conditions of their actions, acting intentionally and having reasons for what they did. The 'sociological' direction of modern philosophy involved a recovery of the everyday (Giddens, 1987: 52–72).

The culture as a broad concept was an essential part of everyday life and people's identity in Africa. Symbolic conceptualization of life formed the basis for communally celebrated rituals and people's decisions were often based on visions and dreams. Some Jipemoyo PAR researchers and associates, in analysing the changing kin and age-grade-based societies, interpreted the cultural phenomena in line with the prevailing Marxist theories, according to which culture was the superstructure and cultural phenomena depended on the economy as the base. Anthropology was considered a colonial discipline and not a subject in the university. A South African anthropologist, Archie Mafeje, was a vocal critic. In his words, traditional African forms of society and religious practices were 'forms of oppression and mental enslavement, which should be judged as such for the benefit of the present day society' (Ranger, 1972).

Other Marxist anthropologists argued that kin relations were not determined by the economic infrastructure nor by relations of production (Godelier, 1973), so that it was possible to build development on interrelated concepts of culture and economy, using a broad concept of culture to comprise all human activity which did not reduce culture solely to dependence on economy. Material means were always mediated by meaning making – 'Rational production of gain is in one and the same motion the production of symbols' (Sahlins, 1976: 212, 215). For Paul Ricoeur (1967) symbols preceded all interpretation, and for Susan Langer (1951) the basic human need is symbolization preceding all action. Transformation of symbols indicated human capacity of symbolic conceptualization, which could evolve to self-shaped development (Swantz, 1986b: 378–82).

The political theory based on historical materialism eclipsed all other theoretical approaches in the University of Dar es Salaam in the 1970s. In the struggle to study development in relation to culture, phenomenology was criticized as being bourgeois, concentrating on appearances. In contrast the materialist phenomenology transformed appearances and thus was a way to transform the meanings of action, production and reproduction of symbolic universes from subjective to objective knowledge (Mustafa, 1977, 1989: 19–20; Rigby, 1977). This theorizing maintained to the end the distance between the researchers' rationalism and the life world of the research partners. This materialist perspective meant that no effort was made to fit aspects of this life world into any of the theoretical construction. Significant aspects of village culture – such as the witch-finding experts who controlled the minds of villagers; or the lame woman *mganga's* (healer's) claim that she was taken up to a tree by a wind to find solutions to a patient's problem – were simply ignored.

It was hard to accept 'class conditioned consciousness' as the motor of social development in societies in which 'classes' and 'proletariat' seemed misguided, inappropriate concepts. Even if one tuned in with the idea that the domination of social and economic forces could not be changed with gradual transformation of symbols, culture as

a larger concept had a role to play. Rejection of culture as a social force is a major deterrent still in the development of countries like Tanzania, although there are some signs that it is now gaining momentum. In formulating the *ujamaa* socialism, President Nyerere had seen the significance of culture as a trajectory of development. The scholars rejected Nyerere's socialism for its lack of theoretical grounding as they commonly reject efforts to learn directly from different conceptualizations of life. Perhaps here the way forward would be Peter Reason's contemplation on future participation finding Bateson's ability to 'peer over the edges of different frameworks' a way to reflect on and choose the premises of understanding and action (Reason, 1994: 37).

The women researchers in Jipemoyo analysed the women's role in peasant commodity production and the patriarchal relations of production. Whether in agricultural or pastoral societies, women were subjected to men's power; the structure of the kin-based societies made them dependent and the system worked against them. Their socially bound position, which they traditionally could utilize in favourable situations for their own benefit, deteriorated with the petty commodity and capitalist economies (Bryceson, 1980). The Marxist researchers saw the solution in a historical materialist framework, which to me erased women's rich ritual contribution with its symbolic values and potential for meaningful participation in knowledge creation. Participation was the best way to learn to understand women's views of their life situation, even if the researchers' final analysis of the factors affecting women differed from the women's own understanding.

The Jipemoyo scholars found support from Habermas, who in his *Theory and Practice* claimed to develop *the* theory of society. Historical materialism for him at that time (1971)[8] was 'an explanation of social evolution which is so comprehensive that it embraces the interrelationships of the theory's own origins and application' (Habermas,

1974: 1). In 1977 (English version, 1984) his *Theory of Communicative Action* opened up new ways of looking at social theory. The proletariat disappeared as the motor of revolutionary force and resistance broke into protest movements. Eventually Tanzania's weak economy eroded the adherence to state socialism, and after President Nyerere's resignation in 1985 the country adopted the multiparty system. Gradual opening to outside markets became a necessity but the structural adjustment policy forced by the World Bank on the developing countries brought new pressures on the economy.

Stephen Kemmis (2001/2006; also this volume), leaning on Habermas's theory of knowledge constitutive interests, divides AR into three groups: *empirical-analytic* (or positivist), *hermeneutic* (or interpretative) and *critical* approaches in research theory and practice. The context of the described cases of PAR does not fit solely into any one of these categories. Different approaches were combined with AR and PAR, and the political undercurrent and participatory reflection gave research critical overtones. I identify my own approach as being hermeneutic and phenomenological, critical of my person in relation to partners and seeing that I have a role in bringing into people's consciousness connecting factors for their own analysis.

THE ROLE OF THE PARTICIPANT RESEARCHER AND THE CRITERIA FOR VALIDITY

When I first introduced participatory research I rejected the conventional participant observation as alienating and formulated my own position as the researcher:

> Any scientific inquiry, which is made on the level of human encounter, involves the inquirer in an interpersonal exchange. The inquirer has to gain the confidence of the community with which she works. The centres of human existence can be reached only if there is common trust that the encounter takes

place for the benefit of people involved. This means that there is in last resort no mere observer position in such an encounter; there is common search for common good.... I feel justified in writing the result of my encounter with the Mwambao Zaramo only because of the knowledge that in it there was ... this mutual spirit of search for health as well as truth. (Swantz, 1970: 359–60)

Orlando Fals Borda called such an approach 'sympathetic participation'. In Latin America, changing the class *in* itself into class *for* itself was the principle of the researcher who saw the revolutionary challenge. The researcher could with social analysis raise people's consciousness to see their alienation in a corrupted society and to become conscious of their role in history.[9] For Fals Borda traditional 'sympathetic participation', in which the researcher puts him/herself in the place of the researched, was not enough. The researcher had to enter into the process which he/she studies as a full partner, getting an insider's view yet being aware that he/she represented a different class or social group. This made the researcher face the question of political involvement. In Moser's interpretation Fals Borda's action research bound science and action together, and thus in Latin America it meant that traditional ahistoric sociology changed from political equilibrium to a conflict and social crisis model. Fals Borda was developing a new kind of science but remained within social science (Moser, 1978: 176–9). The militant researchers would join the revolutionary movement and their theoretical frame would be a theory of revolution.

In clarifying the role of the researcher Heinz Moser wanted to give the researcher a definite role in PAR. In this he differed from those who represented more politically motivated participation – 'A researcher who acts like a superior practical worker is of no use to the people.' He has to trust people's expertise in their practical work. The researcher's role is to organize systematic reflection as a co-worker while identifying with the aims of a project. True knowledge could be validated through communication. In Moser's view the researcher should maintain his role and not become one of the researched group or community, otherwise he has no business being there as an outsider (Moser, 1978: 176–9).

The subjectivist approach was gaining ground when the positivist grip on social research was giving way. PAR broke off from the rule of keeping distance as a participant in a community, but it was neither desirable nor possible for foreign researchers to engage politically or become one with the community: identification did not mean 'going native', to use the anthropologists' critical term. In Jipemoyo the researchers identified with the interests of the local people, which gave people confidence in the researchers and they soon forgot that the project was supported by the government. Yet people comprised, not only one group with unified ideas. The researchers' contact with the Maasai caused some apprehension among other ethnic groups, as did also differing positions the women researchers took on women's issues, which were analysed in separate sessions with women. Researchers recognized that to treat 'the people' as one category was a gross simplification (see Gaventa and Cornwall, Chapter 11).

PAR could not be validated with the conventional scientific criteria. Practice verifies the success of action research and for the practitioner successful action suffices as criteria. The role of the researched community in proving the validity of results has not been considered sufficiently. For a scientist, practical success verifies the usefulness, but it does not fulfil the conventional scientific criteria. To serve as a proof the same research cannot be repeated as such. The researchers deal with such complicity of life that creating similar research situations hardly would serve as criteria.

Heinz Moser was invited in 1980 to give the main critique of the four years of the Jipemoyo research, theory and practice based on 800 pages of writing. Considering the traditional criteria of validity irrelevant to the new paradigm, he had earlier formulated theoretical foundations and criteria for validity of PAR. He had suggested three criteria (Moser, 1975: 122–4). The first one was transparency, which meant that all the participants were able to trace the whole process of the PAR, its functions, aims and methods. The second criteria was compatibility of the aims with the methods and means with which they are reached. The researcher who participates in research with the community cannot claim the traditional researcher's distance and thus have a view as an independent observer. Thirdly, the participant researcher should be able to claim that she knows the situation better than does any outside observer and that she has honestly set forth all the aspects she had become aware of.

ROLE OF SYMBOLS IN SOCIAL TRANSFORMATION AND PAR

The domination of a symbolic conceptualization of life was reflected in PAR cases in Tanzania. Ulla Vuorela, with researchers from the University of Dar es Salaam, was involved in a participatory theatre in Msoga village. She also found that storytelling was still a living tradition and recorded a hundred stories, relating them within their social context. Stories were open-ended, inviting the listeners to comment on them and debate about their meaning. Many stories, such as Monster as a Husband and Rebellious Girl, related to women and thus to the inner dynamics of the Kwere matrilineal culture, but a story could carry a multiplicity of meanings. Vuorela related the image of the Lost Woman to the importance of women in human reproduction; the concern of the community for continuity and the threat to it reflected the external elements in a story (Vuorela, 1991).

Before Msoga village was broken up I had been introduced to *changa cha mulungu*, literally translated 'a hut of god', used for a communal offering at the time of sowing and harvesting. Before harvesting the crop individually the home fires were extinguished and new fire fetched from the spirit hut where men and women together celebrated the offering of the first cobs of maize. The symbolic rite bound the community together. The villagers' eagerness to talk about their threatened culture was the initial incentive for participatory action research on culture and development starting from Msoga.

Jipemoyo researcher Bernhard Kiyenze discovered in his communication with the Kwere women potters the influence of bodily symbols on their occupation. Pregnant women or women with suckling babies were not allowed to dig clay nor take any part in pot-making lest the pots break and the child be harmed in contact with the high potency of the woman in her state of reproduction (Kiyenze, 1985: 50). Woman was closely related to nature and the pot was a central symbol of woman's womb. It was used in teaching the young girls about the bodily functions. The myths of the Zaramo, close relatives of the Kwere, credited the discovery of the domestic use of plants to the original woman who taught her husband the use of them. Woman's breast had mythical powers and she could exert final power over a disrespectful son by striking her breast (Swantz, 1986b: 148, 259).

I have interpreted the dominating symbolic conceptualization to have great potentiality for creative development, which if recognized would embolden people's initiative. Stage by stage evolving ritual planning could also serve as a model for development planning. Nothing is as well planned in Tanzania as feasts, since planning of them has a long tradition. Development planners should study the essentials of ritual planning.

The significance of cultural tradition was recognized by Terrence Ranger, Professor of History in the University of Dar es Salaam in the 1960s. He conducted research on the traditional religious movements as social movements of Africa, significant for moving African countries toward self-understanding.

He appreciated also my reconstruction of cultural transformation, which meant change from one symbolic system to another, instead of solely replacing people's capacity for self-reliant development with a materialist view of life. Ranger saw in it a counter argument to the view that African religious beliefs constitute a force opposing development, writing that 'there is a counter argument – namely that in the past change had been mediated through ritual and sanctioned by religious authority and that if we wish modernising change on a communal basis we need to understand these rhythms of innovation' (Ranger, 1972: 42; see also Swantz, 1986b: 359–68).

This can be verified by participation which is sympathetic to the symbolic view of life. The Bagamoyo Maasai have been turning to Christianity because of the vision their *laiboni*, ritual leader, has had. It has led to changes in lifestyle and acceptance of education for girls. The evidence is plentiful that symbols, dreams and visions are part of life in Africa, but the rational North ignores it and pretends it disappears if you do not pay attention to it (cf. Sundkler, 1960: 25–31).

For a Finnish researcher Finnish national development has served as an inspiration and as a historical precedent for the use of PAR. The revival of Finnish culture, including the collection of over a million verses of folk poetry and inspiration drawn from it for music, art and literature, laid the foundation for an independent Finland and Finnish as the official and academic language. It was crucial for the national self-understanding and economic development of the country since independence from Sweden and Russia was achieved.

In Tanzania the Ministry of Culture and Youth placed high hopes on Jipemoyo research. It was expected to identify a significant role for culture in national development, but the time was not ripe for it. The interest in culture is now revived when there is sufficient distance from the colonial past and the potential for new interpretations can be spelled out.

CONCLUSION

The introduction of PAR in relation to development has made possible its long time application in Tanzania. PRA (Participatory Action Research) shifted to PAR (participatory rural appraisal), which Anisur Rahman calls 'techniques' and Ponna Wignaraja a 'toolkit' (see also Chambers' discussion of PRA in Chapter 20). In the Tanzanian case it is important to note that the PRA in its different forms, including the Jipemoyo story, and most significantly PRA, have influenced the politics of the state in a major way. The capabilities of the villages to make their own plans and enabling the bureaucrats to work with the villagers are central aspects in the present local government reform.

We have witnessed the potential of the research approach based on participation and communication. Together with breaking the monopoly of privileged knowledge, also the monopoly of bureaucratic and technocratic power is broken. It is crucial that research is not separated from life. Knowledge gained through research needs to become part of people's lives. PAR cannot be only participatory practice, it has to be integrated into the way knowledge is created. PAR can become an accepted part of professional training, as it already is in parts of the world. The big question is how PAR-related training combined with academic research can break the domination of the bureaucratic and technocratic Western society, which keeps ordinary citizens at a distance.

I return to the speech of Alfredo Molano in Cartagena in 1997. When in the first participatory conference in Cartagena 20 years earlier many of the participants knew where they were going, in 1997 Molano claimed that by 'good fortune … we have no idea where are we going'. False certainty can lead researchers astray. Participatory action research can be used as a compass in realizing history, which has no presaged destination.

NOTES

1 A Swahili speaking person like her from the coastal region.
2 The project was run by the Ministry of Development Planning and had participation from ministries of Education, Agriculture and Labour, the Statistical Bureau and the Research Unit of the Institute of Adult Education (Swantz, 1979).
3 The newly elected President Jakaya Kikwete comes from Msoga. Ulla Vuorela, now professor in women's studies in Helsinki University, stayed there and later wrote her doctoral thesis on the women's question based on Msoga (Vuorela, 1987).
4 Tanzania became independent in 1961, and in 1964 it united with Zanzibar, forming the United Republic of Tanzania. In 1977 TANU and the Zanzibar Afro-Shirazi Party joined together and the name *Chama Cha Mapinduzi* (CCM, Revolutionary Party) was adopted.
5 United Nations University – World Institute of Development Economics Research, WIDER.
6 Mwajuma Masaiganah was employed by the Centre and started her PRA career in that research project.
7 Quote in Himmelstrand (1982) based on Touraine (1979) *La Voix et la Regard. Essai de sociologie.* Paris: Fayard.
8 *Theorie und Praxis* was published in German in 1971, in English in 1974.
9 This was part of the discussion first in the African workshop in Mzumbe and then in Cartagena in 1977, in which Fals Borda's earlier Columbia experience was criticized and he responded to it (Bryceson and Mustafa, 1982; Fals Borda, 1977).

REFERENCES

Bryceson, F.D.M.M. and Mbilinyi, M. (1980) 'The changing role of Tanzanian women in production', in A.O. Anacleti (ed.), *Jipemoyo, Development and Culture Research, Vol. 2.* Uppsala: The Scandinavian Institute of African Studies. pp. 85–116.

Bryceson, D. and K. Mustafa (1982) 'Participatory Research: Redefining the relationship between theory and practice' in Y.O. Kassam and K. Mustafa (eds) *An Emerging Alternative Methodology in Social Science Research.* New Delhi: Society for Participatory Research in Asia.

Donner, P. (1977) 'Integrating ethnomusicology with dialectics: first experiences from studying development of music in Tanzania', in A.O. Anacleti (ed.), *Jipemoyo: Development and Culture Research,*

Vol. 1. Uppsala: The Scandinavian Institute of African Studies. pp. 22–32.

Esteva, G. (1996) 'Hosting the otherness of the other: the case of the green revolution', in F. Apffel-Marglin and S. A. Marglin (eds), *Decolonizing Knowledge.* Oxford: Clarendon Press. pp. 249–78.

Fals Borda, O. (1977) 'For Praxis: The Problem of How to Investigate Reality in order to Transform it.' A paper at the Cartagena Symposium on Action Research and Scientific Analysis, Colombia. pp. 78–112.

Fals Borda, O. (1998) *People's Participation: Challenges Ahead.* Bogota: FAIEP.

Fals Borda, O. (2001/2006) 'Participatory (action) research in social theory: origins and challenges', in P. Reason and H. Bradbury, *The Handbook of Action Research: Participative Inquiry and Practice,* London: Sage. pp. 27–37. Also published in P. Reason and H. Bradbury (eds), *The Handbook of Action Research: Concise Paperback Edition.* London: Sage. pp. 27–37.

Frank, A.G. (1977) 'Sociology of development and underdevelopment of sociology', *Monthly Review Press.* p. 108.

Freling, D. (ed.) (1998) *Paths for Change: Experiences in Participation and Democratisation in Lindi and Mtwara Regions, Tanzania. Rural Integrated Project Support (RIPS) Programme Phase II.* Mtwara, Helsinki: Finnagro.

Galtung, J. (1975) *Peace: Research, Education, Action. Essays in Peace Research Vol. 1.* Copenhagen: Christian Ejlers. pp. 273–76.

Giddens, A. (1987) *Social Theory and Modern Sociology.* Cambridge: Polity Press.

Godelier, M. (1973) 'Structure and contradiction in capital', in R. Blackburen (ed.), *Ideology in Social Science.* New York: Vintage Books. pp. 334–68.

Habermas, J. (1974) *Theory and Practice.* London: Heinemann.

Habermas, J. (1978) *Knowledge and Human Interests.* London: Heinemann.

Habermas, J. (1984) *The Theory of Communicative Action.* Boston: Beacon.

Hall, B. (ed.) (1975) *Special Issue: Convergence on Participatory Research, Vol 2.*

Hall, B. (2001) 'I wish this were a poem of practice of participatory research', in P.B. Reason and, H. Bradbury (eds), *Handbook of Action Research: Participative Inquiry and Practice.* London: Sage. pp. 171–8.

Himmelstrand, U. (1982) 'Innovative processes in social change', in T. Bottomore, S. Novak and M. Sokolowska (eds), *Sociology: The State of the Art.* Beverly Hills, CA: Sage. pp. 37–66.

Hurskainen, A. (1984) *Cattle and Culture the Structure of a Pastoral Parakuyo Society.* Helsinki: The Finnish Oriental Society.

Jerman, H. (1997) *Between Five Lines.* Helsinki and Uppsala: The Finnish Anthropological Society and Nordic Arica Institute Bryceson.

Kassam, Y.K.M. (1982) *Participatory Research: an Emerging Alternative Methodology in Social Science Research.* New Delhi: Society for Participatory Research in Asia.

Kemmis, S. (2001/2006) 'Exploring the relevance of critical theory for action research: emancipatory action research in the footsteps of Jürgen Habermas', in P. Reason and H. Bradbury (eds), *Handbook of Action Research: Participative Inquiry and Practice.* Thousand Oaks, CA: Sage. pp. 91–102. See also P. Reason and H. Bradbury (eds) (2006), *Handbook of Action Research: Concise Student Edition.* London: Sage. pp. 94–105.

Kivelä, M. (1985) *Effects of Finnish Development Cooperation on Tanzanian Women: Women and Water Technology.* Helsinki: Institute of Development Studies (IDS), University of Helsinki.

Kiyenze, B.K.S. (1985) *The Transformation of Tanzanian Handicrafts into Cooperatives and Rural Small-Scale Industrialization.* Helsinki: Finnish Anthropological Society.

Kühn, T. (1962) *Structure of Scientific Revolution.* Chicago: Chicago University Press.

Langer, S. (1951) *Philosophy in a New Key. A Study in the Symbolism of Reason, Rite and Art.* London: Oxford University Press.

Marglin, S. (1990) 'Losing touch: the cultural conditions of worker accommodation and resistance', in S. Marglin (ed.), *Dominating Knowledge: Development, Culture and Resistance.* Oxford: Clarendon Press. pp. 217–78.

Mertens, R. (2004) 'Where the action was', *University of Chicago Magazine,* [April], pp. 30–5.

Molano, A. (1998) 'Cartagena revisited twenty years on', in O. Fals Borda (ed.), *People's Participation: Challenges Ahead.* Bogota: Conciencias, IEPRI, TM Editores. pp. 3–10.

Moser, H.H. (1975) *Aktions forschung als kritische Theorie der Sozialwissenschaften.* Munich: Kös Verlag.

Moser, H.H. (1978) 'Einige Aspekte der Aktionsforschung im internationalen Vergleich', in H.H. Moser (ed.), *Internationale Aspekte der Aktionsforschung.* Munich: Kösler. pp. 173–89.

Mustafa, K. (1977) 'Notes towards the construction of a materialist phenomenology for socialist development reasearch on the Jipemoyo project', in M.-L.H.J. Swantz (ed.), *Jipemoyo: Development and Culture Research, Vol. 1.* Uppsala: Scandinavian Institute of African Studies (SIAS). pp. 33–51.

Mustafa, K. (1989) *Participatory Research and the 'Pastoralist Question' in Tanzania: A Critique of the Jipemoyo Experience in Bagamoyo District, Vol. 7.* Helsinki: Scandinavian Institute of African Studies (SIAS).

Mustafa, K., Matwi, M. and Ruben, J. (1980) 'A preliminary survey of pastoralist development in Mindu Tulieni Village', in A.O. Anacleti (ed.), *Jipemoyo Development and Culture Research, Vols 3 and 9.* Helsinki and Uppsala: IDS, SIAS and Finnish Anthropological Society. pp, 64–87.

Mustafa, D. and Mustafa, K. (1982) *Participatory Research: Redefining the Relationship Between Theory and Practice. Participatory Research. An Emerging Alternative Methogology in Social Science Research.* Society for Participatory Research in Asia, New Delhi.

Myrdal, G. (1970) *Objectivity in Social Research.* London: Gerald Duckworth & Co.

Nash, J. (1981) 'Ethnographic aspects of the world capitalist system', *Annual Review of Anthropology*, 10: 393–423.

Novack, G. (1975) *Pragmatism versus Marxism. An Appraisal of John Dewey's Philosophy.* New York: Pathfinder's Press.

Ragland, B.B. (2006) 'Positioning the practitioner-researcher: five ways of looking at practice', *Action Research*, 4 (2): 165–82.

Ranger, T. (1972) 'Development, tradition, and the histrorical study of African religion', *African Religious Research, 2* (1): 46–9.

Reason, P. (1994) 'Future Participation', in P. Reason (ed.), *Participation in Human Inquiry.* Thousand Oaks, CA: Sage. pp. 30–9.

Ricoeur, P. (1967) *The Symbolism of Evil* (trans. E. Buchanan). New York: Evanston, London: Harper & Row.

Rigby, P. (1977) 'Critical participation, mere observation, or alienation: notes on research among the Baraguyu Maasai', in M.-L.H.J. Swantz (ed.), *Development and Culture Research.* Uppsala: Scandinavian Institute of African Studies. pp. 52–79.

Roderick, R. (1986) *Habermas and the Foundations of Critical Theory.* New York: St. Martins.

Rodney, W. (1972) *How Europe Underdeveloped Africa* Dar es Salaam and London: Bogle-L'Ouverture Publications.

Sahlins, M. (1976) *Culture and Practical Reason.* Chicago: University of Chicago Press.

Seppälä, P.B.K. (ed.) (1998). *The Making of Periphery: Economic Development and Cultural Encounters in Southern Tanzania.* Uppsala: Nordic Africa Institute.

Sitari, T. (1983) *Settlement Changes in the Bagamoyo District of Tanzania as a Consequence of Villagization.* Helsinki and Uppsala: Scandinavian Institute of African Studies and IDS.

Stude, T. (1985) *Effects of Finnish Development Cooperation on Tanzanian Women: The Case of Uyole Agricultural Centre 1973–1982.* Helsinki: IDS and University of Helsinki.

Sundkler, B. (1960) *The Christian Ministry in Africa.* Uppsala: Swedish Institute of Missionary Research.

Swantz, M.-L. (1970) *Symbol and Ritual in Traditional Zaramo Society with Special Reference to Women.* Lund: Gleerup.

Swantz, M.-L. (1973) *Research in Action as a Programme for University Students.* Dar es Salaam: BRALUP, University of Dar es Salaam.

Swantz, M.-L. (1976a). 'Research in action in Dar es Salaam', *Overseas Universities,* 22: 19–22.

Swantz, M.-L. (1976b). The role of participant research in development', *Geografiska Annaler, 56 B 2*: 119–127.

Swantz, M.-L. (1977) 'Bagamoyo research project "Jipemoyo": introduction to its general aims and approach', in *Jipemoyo: Development and Culture Research, Vol. 1.* Helsinki, and Uppsala: IDS and SIAS. pp. 3–15.

Swantz, M.-L. (1978). 'Participatory research as a tool for training', *Les Carnets de l'Enfance/Assignment Children,* 41: 93–109.

Swantz, M.-L. (1979). 'Research as an educational tool for development', in H. V. H. H. Hinzen (ed.), *Education for Liberation and Development.* Hamburg: UNESCO Institute for Education. pp. 229–38.

Swantz, M.-L. (1981). 'Culture and development in Bagamoyo District of Tanzania', in P. R. Reason (ed.), *Human Inquiry: a Sourcebook of New Paradigm Research.* New York: John Wiley. pp. 283–92.

Swantz, M,-L. (1982) 'Participatory research as an instrument for training: The youth development project in the coast region of Tanzania', Y.O. Kassam and K. Mustafa (eds) *Participatory Research: An Emerging Alternative Methodology in Social Research.* Participatory Research Project, African Adult Education Association, Nairobi. Participation Research Network Series No. 2. Society for Participatory Research in Asia, New Delhi. pp. 117–138

Swantz, M.-L. (1985a). *Effects of Finnish Development Cooperation on Tanzanian Women: Concluding Report.* Helsinki: Institution of Development Studies.

Swantz, M.-L. (1985c). *Women in Development: a Creative Role Denied?* London/New York: C.Hurst/ St. Martin.

Swantz, M.-L. (1986a). 'Anthropology: applied and pure', *Suomen Antropologi (The Journal of Finnish Anthropological Society),* 1: 2–9.

Swantz, M.-L. (1986b/1970). 'The Contribution of anthropology to development work', in H. O. Skar (ed.), *Anthropological Contributions to Planned Change and Development*. Gothenburg: Acta Universitatis Gothoburgensis. pp. 118–32.

Swantz, M.-L. (1986c). *Symbol and Ritual in Traditional Zaramo Society with Special Reference to Women*, 2nd edn. Uppsala: Scandinavian Institute of African Studies.

Swantz, M. L. (1990). *The Medicine Man among the Zaramo of Dar es Salaam*. Uppsala and Dar es Salaam: Scandinavian Institute of African Studies and University Press, DSM.

Swantz, M.-L. (1992a). 'Evaluating health projects: how could it be done better?', *Journal of Social Medicine*, *29*: 277–85.

Swantz, M.-L. (1992b). 'Participation and the evaluation of the effects of aid for women', in L. O. S. Berlage (ed.), *Evaluating Development Assistance, Approaches and Methods*. London: Frank Cass. pp. 104–19.

Swantz, M.-L. (1994) 'Community participation in health care', in K.S. Lankinen, S. Bergstrom, P.H. Mäkelä and M. Peltomaa (eds), *Health and Disease in Developing Countries*. London: Macmillan pp. 433–41.

Swantz, M.-L. (1998) 'Notes on research on women and their strategies for sustained livelihood in southern Tanzania', in P.B.K. Seppala (ed.), *The Making of Periphery*. Uppsala: Nordic Africa Institute. pp. 157–94.

Swantz, M.-L. and Tripp, A.M. (1996) 'Development for "big fish" or for "small fish"? A study of contrasts in Tanzania's fishing sector', in F.S.A.M. Apffel-Marglin (ed.), *Decolonizing Knowledge: From Development to Dialogue*. Oxford: Clarendon Press. pp. 44–66.

Swantz, M.-L., Wild, Z. and Salome, M. (1995) *Blood, Milk, Death: the Regenerative Symbols of the Zaramo*. Westport, CT: Bergin & Garvey.

Swantz, M.-L. and Vainio-Mattila, A. (1988) 'Participatory inquiry as an instrument of grassroots development', in P. Reason (ed.), *Human Inquiry in Action*. Thousand Oaks, CA: Sage. pp. 127–43.

Touraine, A. (1979). *La Voix et la Regard*. Paris: Fayard.

Touraine, A. (1984). *Le Retour de l'Acteur. Essai de Sociologie*. Paris: Fayard.

Tripp, A.M. (1991) 'Close encounters, human dimensions of fieldwork in a Tanzanian setting', in G. Jeremy (ed.), *A Different Kind of Journey: Essays in Honor of Marja-Liisa Swantz*. Helsinki: Finnish Anthropological Society. pp. 45–64.

Vuorela, U. (1987) *The Women's Question and the Modes of Human Reproduction: An Analysis of a Tanzanian Village*. Helsinki: Finnish Anthropological Society.

Vuorela, U. (1991) 'From oral to written: themes of the lost woman in some Tanzanian narratives', in J. Gould (ed.), *A Different Kind of Journey*. Helsinki: Finnish Anthropological Society. pp. 65–91.

3

Some Trends in the Praxis of Participatory Action Research

Md. Anisur Rahman

This chapter traces some trends in the praxis of PAR starting with work in Germany and Moser's theoretical reflection on the validity of such research. It refers to Fals Borda's emphasis on developing an endogenous 'science of the proletariat' and development of the Participatory Research Network of the International Council for Adult Education. Thereafter it traces the development of a South Asian trend in PAR evolving into a global programme under the International Labour Organization, in which concepts/questions like people's liberation and people power, the 'animator' in PAR and the validity of PAR as research have been visited. Recent PAR work in Bangladesh is touched upon at the end.

Participatory (Action) Research – PR/PAR – has diverse perspectives. This chapter traces the praxis of PAR in the last century of trends with which the present author has been personally involved or by which he has been theoretically stimulated, concluding with recent PAR experiments in Bangladesh with which he is currently associated. The central thinking in this perspective is that ordinary, underprivileged people will collectively investigate their own reality, by themselves or in partnership with friendly outsiders, take action of their own to advance their lives, and reflect on their ongoing experience. In such PAR, self-investigation by underprivileged people naturally generates action by them (including inaction if they so choose) to advance their own lives, so that *action unites, organically, with research*. The 'action' content of the term PAR refers specifically to action by the people themselves, not excluding any action taken by outside partners in such research.

The philosophical root of PAR thinking is traceable to the philosophy of Marx and Engels calling the working class to create their own history, a vision they cannot logically realize without the 'means of mental production', and not only the 'means of material production', under their control.

Paradoxically, the formal left has shown little interest in promoting anything remotely akin to participatory research. In recent times the concept of *conscientization* of Paulo Freire, also with a radical vision of social change, has inspired micro-level grassroots work with oppressed groups in many parts of the world with the aim of advancing their collective self-reflected awareness and action, independently of the formal left. Other quarters have also been working, independently of allegiance to Marxism or Freirianism, to promote *conscientization* and self-development initiatives of oppressed groups guided by their own thinking, from a general social concern for promoting popular participation, grassroots self-reliance and broad-based development with a better balance in the distribution of social power and product.

'EMANCIPATORY RESEARCH' IN GERMANY

Perhaps the earliest reference to and theoretical reflection on PAR is found in the writings of Heinz Moser about a trend in Germany (Moser, 1980a,1980b). Moser refers to growth of 'emancipatory research' in Germany working for the interests of the people with the political change of 1969, in which 'participatory action research found a certain basis', constituting a 'certain kind of 'transition' of the new [political] philosophies into research strategies' (Moser, 1980a: 3). Referring to field PAR work in Germany in this period, Moser reflects in particular upon the question of the *validity of PAR as research*. He argues that PAR belongs to a different paradigm of social inquiry than positivist research, so that it is not answerable to the positivists' question of validity or objectivity of the findings; instead, PAR has its own criterion of validity which is a matter of 'dialogical argumentation', with the 'truth' being a matter of consensus rather than of verification by any externally determined standards (Moser,

1980a: 12; 1980b: 9). For more on Heinz Moser's thinking on validity of PAR as research, see Marja Swantz (Chapter 2 in this volume) wherein, interestingly, one also notices a parallel of the birth of 'emancipatory research' in Germany with that of participatory research in Tanzania, both emerging from an awareness, inspired by a new pro-people political climate, of connecting research with popular practice.

A LATIN AMERICAN TREND

A Latin American trend that started in the 1970s is associated with the name of Orlando Fals Borda, who gave conceptual as well as experimental leadership to PAR on that continent. One of Fals Borda's incisive earlier writings on this subject was his analysis of action research that was going on in Colombia in the 1970s (Fals Borda, 1979). This research was purportedly inspired by the philosophy of historical materialism of Marx and Engels, calling for work toward establishing a society led by the proletariat, and hence, as Fals Borda logically argued, to be dominated in its thinking by a 'science of the proletariat' or 'popular science' (1979: 48) as against a science of the bourgeoisie, with the proletariat able to impose upon society its own system of interpreting reality. Fals Borda observed that the Colombian search in its action research for a 'science of the proletariat' had remained inconclusive, with its action researchers in their 'characteristic impatience' imposing on the people 'certain general theses of historical materialism as developed in other contexts and social formations' (1979: 49) and not derived by the people from their actual conditions. Fals Borda called for such action research to give the people a true sense of *ownership* of the inquiries so as to autonomously develop their own independent analysis of the reality lived by them, in a truly '*subject-subject*' relation with the outside researchers (Fals–Borda, 1988: 88).

PR NETWORK OF THE INTERNATIONAL COUNCIL FOR ADULT EDUCATION

When working in Tanzania in 1970–4 for the International Council for Adult Education (ICAE) based in Toronto, Canada, Budd L. Hall was influenced profoundly by the participatory thoughts of Julius Nyrere and other pro-people Tanzanian leaders of the time, a visit by Paulo Freire to Tanzania in 1971, the 'participant research' work of Marja Swantz and her Tanzanian colleagues with women and others in the coastal region of Tanzania (reported by Swantz in Chapter 2 in this volume), and the First World Assembly of the ICAE that took place in Dar es Salaam in 1976 where ideas on more qualitative and ethnographic approaches to adult education were presented. Back in Toronto in 1976, Budd Hall with other colleagues started the 'Participatory Research Project' at the ICAE.

The Budd Hall group interacted with Fals Borda and radical intellectuals from many parts of the world who assembled to seek new directions for research at a major conference on action research at Cartagena in April 1977. Stimulated by this interaction, the Toronto PR group launched the International Network on Participatory Research in September 1977 with major autonomous and self-directing nodes in Toronto, New Delhi, Dar es Salaam, the Netherlands, and Venezuela.

This network presented the first definitional statement of participatory research, as reproduced by Budd Hall from a paper he had presented in 1997:

1. PR involves a whole range of powerless groups of people – the exploited, the poor, the oppressed, the marginal.
2. It involves the full and active participation of the community in the entire research process.
3. The subject of the research originates in the community itself and the problem is defined, analyzed and solved by the community.
4. The ultimate goal is the radical transformation of social reality and the improvement of the lives of the people themselves. The beneficiaries of the research are the members of the community.
5. The process of participatory research can create a greater awareness in the people of their own resources and mobilize them for self-reliant development.
6. It is a more scientific method or research in that the participation of the community in the research process facilitates a more accurate and authentic analysis of social reality.
7. The researcher is a committed participant and learner in the process of research, i.e. a militant rather than a detached observer. (Hall, 1997: 5)

The Participatory Research network expanded throughout the late 1970s and 1980s and has been responsible for giving visibility to the above concepts and to practices aimed at materializing these concepts in different parts of the world, stimulating social movements and social policy scholars and activists until today.

A SOUTH ASIAN TREND

About the same time a particular South Asian trend in PAR was growing independently. This trend started with the coming together of a team of South Asian social scientists, including the present writer, to jointly articulate the vision of an alternative paradigm of rural development with people's collective self-initiatives as the core of this thinking. After a preliminary articulation of their vision (Haque et al., 1977) the team visited the *Bhoomi Sena* ('Land Army'), a political movement for self-determination of a very oppressed tribal people in Palghar Taluk in Maharastra, India. This team undertook a study of the Bhoomi Sena movement in collaboration with the leaders and cadres of the movement and a number of external activists helping the movement with self-reliance-promoting pedagogy (de Silva et al., 1979; Rahman, 1981a). As the study recounted, the assertive leaders and cadres of Bhoomi Sena looked for guidance from friendly outsiders 'not for telling us what we should do' but to 'help us think about our problems on our own' (De Silva et al., 1979: 45). This defined in a classic way the task of friendly external intellectuals in promoting people's intellectual self-thinking and, for that matter, 'popular science' as Fals Borda had conceived it. Among the external activists working with Bhoomi Sena an educationist, Dutta Savle, helped the movement develop a method of *lok chetna jagoran* 'raising people's awareness', coinciding with Paulo Freire's notion of *conscientization*), through collective self-reflection and analysis. Over time, and with its passionate concern for popular self-determination, Bhoomi Sena developed a unique model of its own of decentralized decision-making, with the centre encouraging spontaneity of village-level organizations, itself facilitating and coordinating their activities including organizing systematic periodic collective reviews of the experiences of people's struggles at various levels, thus promoting people's praxis – action-reflection rhythm – and never dictating people's action. The centre, thus, consciously nourished the development of true people power with the capacity of turning even against the centre itself, thus constituting 'countervailing power' which people power in the ultimate analysis must constitute (for elaboration of this concept see Rahman, 1981b; 45–6, 2000: 115–17). The Bhoomi Sena movement was so firm in its own autonomy vis-à-vis any external forces that it rejected overtures of the Indian Communist Party to join it although it considered the Party an ally in the overall struggle of the country's oppressed against structural oppression. In thus asserting its autonomy vis-à-vis the Communist Party, Bhoomi Sena sharply illustrated the problematic of macro-structural change to promote people's (working class) power to which the formal left is committed, insofar as the formal left has been unable to address the task of truly releasing the energies of the people, which calls for release of people's *spontaneity* within the framework of 'centralism' to which the formal left is wedded.

The Concept and Sensitization of the 'Animator'

Having interacted with Bhoomi Sena, the above study team decided to explore whether people's autonomous initiatives could be unleashed by methods similar to Bhoomi Sena's in a different social context, as in villages in Sri Lanka from which two of the study team members came. For this, external 'animators', as the term was adopted, had to be recruited and 'sensitized', to work as 'keys' to unlock self-thinking and self-initiatives of the people. The conventional term 'training' of animators was used with reservation as it was perceived that none can be 'trained' to respond creatively to dynamic field situations as the task of the animators would be, and that one could only try give to the would-be animators the needed sensitivity to the challenge of their task so that they could be constantly their own judge while pursuing this challenge. 'Animation', in fact, does not and cannot follow any methodology but is an art in which one can, with practice and reflection, develop one's skill, given the necessary commitment, creativity and sensitivity to the specifics and dynamics of a given situation.

It was also conceptualized that the animators should themselves experience intellectual self-reliance so as to be motivated to pass this urge on to the people. Operationally, this meant that an animator also must not be *taught* ('trained') but must be taken through a process of self-inquiry to discover how one would pursue one's own charge of animation to unlock people's spirit of self-inquiry. Such an experience of self-inquiry ('first person inquiry' as discussed in Chandler and Torbert, 2003; Marshall, 2004; Wadsworth, 2001; see also Chapters 16 and 46) would also give the would-be animators a fulfilment which they might also want to pass on to the people, for those who are 'taught' rather than stimulated to search for themselves are in turn prone to 'teaching' others in their charge rather than to stimulate their self-inquiry. With this conceptualization, 'sensitization' of would-be animators was initiated as a process of their own collective self-inquiry on ways to face the challenge of their task, followed by field action to try out their understanding and thoughts and team-reviews of ongoing experiences – i.e. a process of the animators' own *praxis*.

The experiment with sensitizing animators in Sri Lanka had successes in promoting self-reliant participatory processes of oppressed villagers who found their own paths for getting out of dependent structures once, as they expressed themselves, the 'rust in our brains is … removed' (Tilakaratna, 1985: 8). This subsequently induced Susanta Tilakaratna to conceptualize the very term 'animator' as one who facilitates liberation of intellectual self-thinking of oppressed groups (Tilakaratna, 1987: 23) previously given to dependence on others' thinking. One can easily see the relevance of this concept of 'animator' to Fals Borda's notion of the working class building its own science, and for that matter of the implicit Marxian notion of the working class re-appropriating the 'means of mental production' to create their own history – for both of which the working class may need assistance from the conventional intellectual stream in a very special way, as Bhoomi Sena had also experienced and observed. This may be contrasted with the Leninist concept of 'revolutionary intellectuals' with presumed 'advanced consciousness' appropriating the task of intellectually leading the working class rather than helping them recover their own intellectual potentials, a concept that contains seeds of domination of the working class by such intellectuals (Rahman, 1993c).

The Sri Lankan experiment also conceptualized the need for progressive *withdrawal* of the external animators as a test of their success in liberating the collective intellectual potentials of the people. The experiment was remarkably successful in this regard in several places, with 'internal animators' from within the people taking over the task of animation of people's groups, the external animators progressively moving on to other locations to initiate similar animation work (Tilakaratna, 1985).

ILO'S 'PORP' PROGRAMME – ASIA

By then a global programme called Participatory Organizations of the Rural Poor (PORP) had been started in the International Labour Organization directed by the present writer, for whom participation in the study of Bhoomi Sena was a deeply transformative experience. In addition to collaborating with the Bhoomi Sena study and Sri Lankan experiment, the programme initially launched participatory research projects through national action researchers in South Asia and in the Philippines, which developed their own respective methodologies of research.

In India, a model of participatory research was developed by activists working with a tribal peasant movement in another part of Maharastra (Paranjape et al., 1984). The research theme was conceived as the tensions and contradictions in self-reliant development of the movement, to be explored not merely as research for its own sake but to promote resolution of these contradictions. The research methodology centred on organizing a series of people's workshops for which the participants were first invited to develop polar, alternative positions on a set of major issues in the question of self-reliance, e.g. individual vs. collective self-reliance, and participation in the wider labour movement in issue-based joint fronts vs. a more permanent affiliation to a larger federation. Presentation of these polar positions and debates made the people aware of the contradictions and alternatives in their struggle and also of the need for concrete choices among alternative positions. On some of the issues thus debated, concrete choices were made in the process of the research itself, and a heightened level of awareness gained in this exercise contributed to reaching a conscious or unconscious synthesis of other contradictions subsequently.

PAR was taken to another dimension in a project in India in which a number of forest-based people's movements and organizations got together for joint inquiry and articulation on the subject of 'forest, ecology and the oppressed'. Coordinated by The People's Institute for Development and Training based in New Delhi, representatives of these organizations first met in a ten-day workshop to identify issues for investigation and to design ways of recording people's perceptions. They then returned to their respective areas for detailed investigations. While doing this they were also visited by members from participating organizations from other areas. The data thus collected were passed on to a smaller research team composed of social activists in contact with these movements, who analysed the data and interviewed those who had visited the various movements. On the basis of these, the research team developed a set of case studies on the experiences of life and struggle of the people concerned, problem-wise analyses, and an analytical synthesis based on all these. These were presented in a second workshop attended by all groups who had participated in the first. The final report was prepared by the research team incorporating the deliberations of this workshop (Das Gupta, 1986).

In the Philippines, a PAR study (Women's Research Committee et al., 1984) of a women settlers' movement initiated the formation of a research coordination team, with two members taken from the leadership of a 14-member 'vanguard group' of the women settlers and two from an activists' organization helping the movement. Members of the vanguard group provided inputs into the research using minutes of weekly meetings of the women settlers, initiating group discussions with women on their life and struggle and preparing papers on various issues pertaining to the movement. These inputs were woven into two dramas which were staged by the women settlers. All women participants in the movement were invited to witness these dramas to validate the data collected and to synthesize their experiences.

The final study incorporated the feedback received from the audience and discussed the benefits from the research, saying that this provided an opportunity to the vanguard group for a first comprehensive review of their first two years of organizing effort, from which the strengths and weaknesses of their effort were identified; and that the process of research enabled the settlers, particularly the vanguard group, to develop their capacity to understand immediate micro issues in relation to broader macro issues.

Theoretical Reflections

Meanwhile, close collaboration between PORP and the Latin American trend had started after Fals Borda read the report on Bhoomi Sena and saw in this movement illustration of 'the basic principles of PR' (Fals Borda, 2001/2006: 27). At his invitation Rahman presented theoretical reflections on PR at the World Congress on Sociology in Mexico in 1982, wherein he presented the ideological standpoint of PAR, calling for 'rethinking the meaning of "liberation"':

> Liberation, surely, must be opposed to *all* forms of domination over the masses. The dominant view of social transformation has been preoccupied with the need for changing existing, oppressive structures of relations of *material* production. This is certainly a necessary task. But – and this is the distinctive viewpoint of PAR – domination of masses by elites is rooted not only in the polarization of control over the means of material production but also over the means of *knowledge* production including, as in the former case, the social power to determine what is valid or useful knowledge. Irrespective of which of these two polarizations sets off a process of domination, it can be argued that one reinforces the other in augmenting and perpetuating this process. By now, in most polarized societies, the gap between those who have social power over the process of knowledge generation – an important form of 'capital' inasmuch as knowledge is a form of social power – and those who have not, have reached dimensions no less formidable than the gap in access to means of physical production. History shows that a convergence of the latter gap in no way ensures convergence of the former; on the

contrary, existence of the latter has been seen to offset the advantages of revolutionary closures of the former and has set off processes of domination once again. (Rahman, 1985: 119)

In this presentation Rahman also dwelt on the question of 'objectivity' and 'validity' of PAR as research. Developing from Moser's position on this, Rahman argued that 'objectivity' in research is a question of moving from individual 'subjective' positions to collectively agreed positions, and standards of objectivity of research are set by individual research schools as collectively agreed positions within the given school. Thus 'objectivity' and 'truth' are not absolute questions but are questions of *consensus* within a particular school, and in this sense 'truth' is always *relative* and not *absolute*. Hence with systematic consensual procedures among the participants involved, PAR also can and does generate and validate 'objective truth' as against individual and hence 'subjective' truth un-validated by collective consensus (Rahman, 1985: 127–8).

PORP IN LATIN AMERICA

Soon thereafter Fals Borda initiated PORP participatory research exercises in Colombia, Nicaragua and Mexico. Of these three, the Nicaragua exercise stood out both in its breadth and depth, and also because this was the first ever known participatory research in a revolutionary 'socialist' country. As the coordinator of this participatory research, Malena de Montis had personally explained to the author the unusual fact of people's research being initiated in socialist Nicaragua as due to the Sandinistas not having been a party but a social movement, in which the people were often ahead of the intellectuals who gave theoretical articulation to the movement, and there were elements within the government (e.g. Paul Oquist, a foremost theoretician in action research) committed to action research. The exercise was undertaken in El Regadío in 1983 (de Montis, 1985; Rahman, 1993b) with a peasant community

which had become organized and had been playing its own role in the socialist reconstruction of the country. A research team was formed to undertake the initial task of investigation, composed and coordinated by de Montis, one educationist, some coordinators of the National Programme of Adult Education and representatives of mass organizations and cooperatives. The team drafted the design of an inquiry into the history of the community, and a survey on the current socio-economic characteristics of El Regadío, as well as on the ideological transformation of the community. The draft design was presented to a larger coordination committee constituted for the research, which discussed and modified it. Members of the larger committee were given training in survey work. While undertaking house-to-house surveys they explained the participatory character of the whole exercise to members of the households, with the promise to return to them the information obtained for their reflection and analysis.

After the survey the results were tabulated in workshops where other members of the community also participated. The whole community was invited thereafter to an assembly where the information obtained was presented on boards, and the participants deliberated on the data thus presented. Finally, delegates of state institutions and mass organizations at the municipality level were invited to a meeting with the community to coordinate their programmes in the light of the findings of the survey, and to jointly seek solutions to problems. The coordination committee also planned methods for disseminating the information and knowledge obtained through the survey, such as through a pamphlet and audio-visual documentation. For producing the pamphlet – *the people's own research report* – members of the committee learnt to use a wooden mimeographing machine and also diagrammatic and other techniques for presenting data, and improved their writing ability even though they cared only to communicate without necessarily writing full sentences.

Interestingly enough, one conclusion of this exercise privately communicated to the author by de Montis, was that this – i.e. participatory research – was considered by the people researchers of El Regadío as real literacy for the people, while the much-publicized adult education programme of revolutionary Nicaragua was criticized as a programme in which the people were being taught!

Useful Techniques to Promote People's Countervailing Power

In a report (Fals Borda, 1985) on the PAR exercises in the three Latin American countries taken together, Fals Borda, equating the notion of 'people power', as 'countervailing powers', as the Bhoomi Sena study had also conceptualized it, presented four techniques indicated by the three experiences as useful in the establishment of people's power:

1. *Collective research:* ... the use of information collected and systematized on a group basis, as a source of data and *objective* [*italics added*] knowledge of facts resulting from meetings, socio-dramas, public assemblies, committees, fact-finding trips, and so on. This collective and dialogical method not only produces data which may be immediately corrected or verified but also provides a social validation of objective knowledge which cannot be achieved through other individual methods based on surveys or fieldwork. ...
2. *Critical recovery of history:* ... an effort to discover selectively, through collective memory, those elements of the past which have proved useful in the defence of the interests of exploited classes and which may be applied to the present struggles to increase conscientisation. Use is thus made of oral tradition, in the form of interviews and witness accounts by older members of the community possessing good analytical memories; the search for concrete information on given periods of the past hidden in family coffers; data columns and popular stories; ideological projections, imputation, personification and other techniques designed to stimulate collective memory. ...
3. *Valuing and applying folk culture.* ...the recognition of essential core values among the people. ...This allows account to be taken of cultural and ethnic elements frequently ignored in regular political practice, such as art, music, drama, sports, beliefs, myths, story-telling and other expressions related to human sentiment, imagination and ludic or recreational tendencies.
4. *Production and diffusion of new knowledge:* ... an integral part of the research process because it is a central part of the feedback and evaluative objective of PAR. It recognizes a division of labour among and within base groups ... [incorporating] various styles and procedures for systematizing new data and knowledge according to the level of political conscience and ability for understanding written, oral or visual messages by the base groups and public in general. (Fals Borda, 1985: 94–7)

As Fals Borda wrote: 'This systematic devolution of knowledge complies with the objective set by Gramsci transforming "common" sense into "good" sense or critical knowledge' (Fals Borda, 1985: 96).

In a further reflection of the PR experiences in the above three countries, Fals Borda reaffirmed the need for development of people's endogenous science, reinforcing Rahman by arguing that

forms and relationships of knowledge production should have as much, or even more, value than forms and relationships of material production. ... The elimination of exploitative patterns at the material or infrastructural level of a society does not assure, by itself, that the general system of exploitation has been destroyed ... it becomes necessary to eliminate also the relationship governing the production of knowledge, production which tends to give ideological support to injustice, oppression and the destructive forces which characterize the modern world. (Fals Borda, 1987: 337)

PORP IN AFRICA

In working with PAR in Africa PORP collaborated with the Organization of Rural Associations for Progress (ORAP) in Matabeleland, Zimbabwe, an apex organization of village associations in more than 500 villages for promoting people's initiatives for their own development with the philosophical guidance of Sithembiso Nyoni and her close activist associates (Nyoni, 1991). ORAP, started in 1981 with participatory research in a number of villages, is an outstanding example of continuing participatory research by way of people's self-deliberations, action and reviews – i.e. people's praxis – at various levels from grassroots groups up to the apex organization. While they are being assisted in various technical matters by a team of outside experts, all the decision-making powers of ORAP – by way of planning and implementation of small-scale cooperative activities and bigger-scale development works and reviews of ongoing experiences – are in the hands of bodies of people, from family clusters to village groups to higher level people's organizations.

Participatory research was started in six villages in the zone of Bamba-Thialene in Senegal in 1975 and has since then spread to other areas of the country. The process started as a spontaneous inquiry initiated in the homes of friends on economic problems of the villagers, leading to the formation of a delegation to different parts of the zone to conduct censuses on human, agricultural and livestock resources of the zone and the needs of the population. An educated professional joined their search, and people of other villages also started joining the investigations leading to inter-village reflection sessions. Gradually village level sub-committees started forming in different villages, leading finally to the formation in 1977 of a Committee for Development Action in the Villages of the Zone of Bamba Thialene. The Committee initiated collective developmental actions in poultry, agriculture, animal husbandry etc., with collective reflection becoming a most important method both before launching any initiative and also for reviewing their experiences. With assistance from PORP a major people's self-review exercise of their activities was undertaken in 1987, leading to the crystallization of important lessons from their experience and consolidation of future tasks (Marius, 1987).

In Burkina Faso, the traditional 'Naam' groups started getting transformed into developmental organizations, sparked off in 1976 by a group of Naam leaders and their European friends. The groups sought to maximize the mobilization of their internal resources supplemented by outside grants and loans, channelling them into group income-generating activities, collective infrastructure-development activities and health and education activities. The local groups themselves define their programmes of activities by collective discussion and review their ongoing experiences (Egger, 1987; Swadogo and Ouedraogo, 1987).

PEOPLE'S SELF-REVIEW IN HUNGARY

The last participatory research project launched by PORP was for people's self-reviews in Hungary during 1989–90, inviting communities to get together and review their experience with 'socialism' and identify collective perspectives and tasks for the future (Biro and Szuhay, 1990).

The people's self-review exercise in the village of Tök in northern Pest was revealing of the coercive imposition of 'collectivism' on a peasant society which had created hierarchical structures in which the villagers had lost their previous culture of mutual sharing of problems and concerns that had given way to suspicion and fear. The animators had a hard task of getting the people to come together for collective inquiry and deliberation. When finally the villagers did get together, they reconstructed the history of the village, inviting recounting from elderly people, and underlined the gradual erosion of the autonomy and identity of the village and loss of decision-making power on matters pertaining to village life as the village had become merged with a neighbouring larger village to form one mega administrative unit. Reviewing this history, the villagers reached a consensus on the need to assert the autonomy and identity of Tök as an independent village, asserting their own historical traditions, customs, values and social aspirations. In conclusion, they decided to initiate a public campaign to achieve an independent administration of their own. Eventually this people's self-review work got integrated into the political process as a result of the animator-researchers directly entering the political arena where they promoted the ideas that emanated from the grassroots.

Another village, Dormand in Heaves county in northeast Hungary where the people's self-review was initiated, had consisted mostly of day labourers on big farms and in railway and excavation works. These labourers had clearly benefited from cooperativization of land in the village under communist rule. They viewed the changes after 1945 as very positive, with full employment and secure income. While being critical of the abuses of power that had crept into the cooperative over time and desirous of increasing their incomes further, their expectation was higher salaries or wages, and they did not respond to the animator's challenge to them to search for their own solutions to the question of improving their livelihood through enterprises of their own.

The people's self-review project in Hungary also worked with a gypsy community in a settlement in northeast Hungary, and this stimulated the community to mobilize themselves to campaign against social prejudices against them and for better housing facilities.

Significantly, PORP itself was discontinued in the ILO soon after the fall of the Berlin Wall, when the importance of keeping a 'progressive front' within the organization weakened. This exemplified part of the problem of finding space for supporting PAR through international establishments that depend on the global political climate.

'GONOGOBESHONA': PAR BANGLADESH VINTAGE

Following the country's liberation war in 1971 with an officially declared 'socialist' ideology, a number of NGOs created in Bangladesh after independence adopted Paulo Freire's pedagogy of 'conscientization' as an approach to adult education. By the end of 1975 reactionary forces had consolidated political power, and grassroots work by NGOs shifted toward a micro-credit operation, attracted in particular by the international acclaim of and support for the Grameen Bank with its de-emphasis on any kind of social awareness-raising work and all-out emphasis on credit as the panacea for alleviating mass poverty. The country continued to remain one of the poorest in the world, with the 'microcredit programmes [not having] been very successful in including the hard core poor, who constitute about half of the poor in Bangladesh' (Ahmed, 2004: 131).

Disillusionment with micro-credit as an answer to mass poverty is generating interest in the search for alternative ways of assisting the low-income groups in the country. Explicit PAR work started here in December 2002, assisted by a newly created poverty-research supporting agency – Research Initiatives, Bangladesh (RIB; see website www.rib-bangladesh.org). The first PAR exercise with RIB support was initiated in Belaichondi union in Dinajpur district with 228 members – more than half female – of economically very depressed families who were themselves invited to deliberate, in small groups and in inter-group sessions, on the causes of their poverty and to seek ways of economic advancement. Two principal animators were elected for this exercise through mutual ranking by 18 candidates for animators themselves after a five-day dialogical workshop. This six-month PAR exercise had an electrifying effect on the personality of the participants. Previously used to seeking sympathy and charity, they now transformed into positive personalities proud of their identities as 'gono-gobeshoks' (people-researchers) seeking self-understanding for themselves to advance their own lives. The exercise promoted solidarity among the participants listening to and offering solutions to each others' problems, forming solidarity groups to advance their joint livelihood by various means like collective savings and different types of economic action, minimizing wasteful practices like gambling, and reducing oppression of women (Azad, 2003).

The *Belaichondi* PAR exercise was followed by further animation work to promote *gonogobeshona* (people's research) in the district of Nilfamari in northern Bangladesh starting in November 2003, led in particular by a senior animator in the *Belaichondi* work. The work resulted in the formation within 10 months of 176 *gonogobeshona* groups of underprivileged villagers in 15 unions – 161 female groups with 4347 members and 15 male groups with 405 members – who met once or twice a week as a rule to discuss mutual problems. This has resulted in the participants initiating numerous individual or cooperative economic activities to improve their livelihoods. The female groups included four groups of young girls, most of them students, whose general performance in school has considerably improved, for some dramatically so, much to the surprise of their guardians and teachers.

The *gonogobeshona* culture in the area is spreading like a positive virus beyond the RIB-supported project, with village mothers spontaneously forming their own *gobeshona* groups to discuss better child-rearing practices; village youth forming groups to discuss among themselves as well as with their school/college teachers and parents how they can improve their scholastic performances, giving up anti-social activities and being more useful members of their families; and small children of 3 to 6 from underprivileged families forming their own *shishu* (child)-*gobeshona* groups for overall self-development in healthy, playful interaction with each other. This kind of spontaneous spread of the culture of *gonogobeshona* has not been seen or heard of before by the present writer, who personally visited a number of these groups and was astonished by the eager recounting to him of members of such various groups on how they have found a new meaning of life in the culture of *gonogobeshona:* this is giving them self-confidence and a sense of belonging to each other amidst their poverty and transforming their despondency into a sense of mission to face life together with their own individual and collective intellect without depending on outside patronage, wisdom and/or charity and with positive social values.

One of the profoundest stories heard by the present author in one of his visits to Nilfamari was of an elderly man who used to listen as a bystander to discussions of a female *gonogobeshona* group, and volunteered one day to share his own reflections. He said that he was stimulated by the *gonogobeshona* of the women to do some *gobeshona* by himself on why his daughter-in-law hated him so much. Ultimately he deduced the reason to be that he had completely destroyed his daughter-in-law's father by charging a large dowry on the occasion of his son's marriage. The realization, as well as the public admission of guilt, were of profound socio-psychological significance, suggesting that the culture of *gonogobeshona* is generating a kind of solidarity and sense of belonging to each other among its participants from which this senior man had felt isolated and to belong to which he had felt a deep longing that had induced him to recognize and admit in public his profound guilt at his greed.

RIB-assisted PAR in Bangladesh has also been conducted with members of the *dalits*, an 'untouchable' community in Shatkhira district in southwest Bangladesh working as tannery labour or cleaners of jungles and city wastes. Members of the *dalit* class have gotten together in groups to discuss their problem of social exclusion and associated poverty, have formed their own organization for promoting their rights and livelihood, have organized rallies and representations to state officials to assert their rights and to union chairmen for redress of oppressions upon them. From a historical tradition of accepting their fate without questioning, they are now asserting that the 'Creator' has not created humans as unequal and that 'untouchability' must give way to equality between all humans. Their struggle for human right remains a hard one, and only a small beginning has been made (Das et al., 2005).

Exciting PAR work with another 'untouchable' (sweeper) community in

Kushtia town in western Bangladesh, using drama for conscientization, is reported separately by Meghna Guhathakurta in this volume (see Chapter 35). Further PAR work with socially excluded communities has been launched with RIB support and is showing encouraging response from the concerned communities forming assertive solidarity groups and engaging in collective deliberations on their problems and collective actions and struggles to promote their livelihood and social status and to resist injustices and oppression.

CONCLUSION: CASE FOR MODESTY

The positive experiences of Bangladesh PAR work are balanced by some negatives as well as deep questions about their future, and a few reflections in this direction are presented by way of concluding this chapter. The effort of RIB to promote PAR in Bangladesh has had failures as well, due principally to its inability to always choose the right PAR researcher/animator(s). Some researchers have been attracted by RIB funds to present themselves as PAR-promoters without the necessary commitment or skill, and their work has produced anything but PAR. Effort at sensitization of animators through 'sensitization workshops' has 'sensitized' different animators to different degrees, with some working with 'vanguardist' tendencies and some dropping out. Encouragingly, in many areas 'internal animators' belonging organically to the concerned communities and spontaneously picking up animation work stimulated by the PAR process itself have emerged; but they have their limitation of time for animation work due to their need to do other work to make a living. The vibrancy of PAR processes is as a result declining in some places after stoppage of RIB-support for animation work, although internal motivation to continue the PAR praxis seems to remain strong, and inspiring voluntary animation work by internal animators is continuing in their spare time. The supply of appropriately sensitive animators able also to give time for animation work without continued RIB support seems to be a major constraint in the way of sustaining the full initial momentum of PAR works that are being initiated by RIB.

The question of 'scaling up' of PAR processes in the country – a question for PAR in any country that Gustavsen, Hansson and Qvale in Chapter 4 in this volume have called the 'diffusion or dissemination problem' – is also rather problematic. Apart from the question of continued funding of animation work, the task is up against the formidable batting of a host of NGOs doing 'development delivery' work with external resources and technical expertise that naturally attracts many in the poverty groups, limiting to that extent the space for PAR work with its non-delivery nature. Some NGOs have even started 'co-opting' PAR work with their big money, seeing its appeal as an alternative to micro-credit-type operations, and would-be PAR researchers attracted more by the funding than by the philosophy are not hard to find. PAR in the country is also facing strong competition from PRA – Participatory Rural Appraisal – another action research approach oriented to using participatory techniques in externally controlled research upon the poverty groups that is attracting donor funding on a rather significant scale. Adding to this the watchdog eyes of government agencies to ensure that grassroots development work does not take any 'uncomfortable turn' from the point of view of the powers that be, and with their power to cut off the supply line of foreign funding for such work on which RIB itself also depends, it will be prudent not to be too optimistic about the continued growth of quality PAR work in the country to anything like a significant enough scale.

In final conclusion, PAR is clearly a 'radical' philosophy, whether PAR researchers show allegiance to any radical 'ism' or not. As a 'macro ideology' it is wedded to the concept of a central administration that respects grassroots autonomy sufficient to preserve grassroots identity and creativity, as Bhoomi Sena of India and the villagers of Tök in Hungary have asserted, so that people can really 'create their own history'. However, like the 'dictatorship of the proletariat', no blueprint for such a centre exists, nor can it be articulated outside its endogenous process carrying its own dialectics with it, so that the ultimate macro-outcome of the process remains unsure, including the possibility of serious distortion/cooptation, as in the case of the 'dictatorship of the proletariat' or, for that matter, of conventional 'democracy' as well. With such imponderables, PAR at this stage remains no more than a search for life of the people involved, with the vision – whether of Marx or of particular PAR visionaries – for the downtrodden people to create their own history for which they need to build their own science, no more than an inspiration to practical PAR work that awaits macro-validation by history.

REFERENCES

Ahmed, Salehuddin (2004) 'Microcredit and poverty: new realities and new issues' *Economics and Altruism: Random Thoughts*. Dhaka: The University Press Limited. pp. 114–42.

Azad, Lenin (2003) *Hato daridryoder daridryo bimochoner shangram: onushilaner ak bikalpo dhara* (Struggle of the Ultra Poor for poverty alleviation: and alternative approach). Mimeographed Research report. Dhaka: Research Initiatives.

Biro, Andras, and Szuhay Peter, (1990) *People's Self Review: Three Case Studies from Hungary*. Rural employment Policy Research Programme Working Paper, World Employment Programme, Geneva: International Labour Office.

Chandler, Dawn and Torbert, Bill, (2003) 'Transforming inquiry and action: Interweaving 27 flavors of action research' *Action Research*, 1(2) October: 133–52.

Das, Milan, Das Ashim, and Hossain Faruq, (2005) *Dalit/Antyojder Arthik o Shamajik Protibandhokjotar Bisleshon ebong Protikarer upar Bishayak Prak Karmomukhi Gabeshona* (Analysis of and pre-action research on economic and social handicaps of Dalits/low caste communities). Mimeographed Research report. Dhaka: Research Initiatives, Bangladesh.

Das Gupta, Subhachari (1986) *Forest, Ecology and the Oppressed (A Study from the Viewpoint or the Forest Dwellers)*. New Delhi: People's Institute for Development and Training.

De Montis, Malena (1985) 'Potential for people's education in the social transformation of rural areas: The case of El Regadío (Nicaragua)' in Fals Borda (1985) pp. 106–109).

De Silva, G.V.S., Mehta Niranjan, Wignaraja Ponna, and Md. Rahman Anisur, (1979) 'Bhoomi Sena: a struggle for People's Power', *Development Dialogue*, 2: 3–70.

Egger, Philippe (1987) *L'Association Six 'S' – Se servir de la saison seché en Savane et au Sahel – et les groupement Naam: note sur quelques observations*. (mimeographed). Geneva: International Labour Office.

Fals Borda, Orlando (1979) 'Investigating reality in order to transform it: the Colombian experience', *Dialectical Anthropology*, 4: 33–55.

Fals Borda, Orlando (ed.) (1985) *The Challenge of Social Change*. London: Sage Publications.

Fals Borda, Orlando (1987) 'The application of participatory research in Latin America', *International Sociology*, 2(4): 329–47.

Fals Borda, Orlando (1988) *Knowledge and People's Power Lessons with Peasants in Nicaragua, Mexico and Colombia*. New Delhi: Indian Social Institute.

Fals Borda, Orlando (2001) 'Participatory (action) research in social theory: origins and challenges'. in Reason and Bradbury (2001/2006) *Handbook of Action Research Participative Inquiry and Practice* pp. 27–37. Also published in P. Reason and H. Bradbury (eds) (2006), *Handbook of Action Research: Concise Student Edition*. London: Sage. pp. 27–37.

Hall, Budd L. (1997) '*Looking Back, Looking Forward: Reflections on the Origins of the International Particpatory Research Network and the Participatory Research Group in Toronto, Canada*'. Paper presented at the Midwest Research to Practice Conference in Adult Continuing Education, Michigan State University, East Lansing, Michigan, 15–17 October.

Haque, Wahidul, Mehta Niranjan, Md. Anisur Rahman, and Wignaraja Ponna, (1977) 'Towards a theory of rural development', *Development Dialogue*, 2: 11–137.

Marius, Dia (1987) '*L'Experience en matière d'autodeveloppement du Comité d'Acton pour le Developpement des villages de la Zone Bamba-Thialéne. Report on People's Self-review*' (mimeographed). Research Report submitted to the International Labour Office, Geneva.

Marshall, Judi (2004) 'Living systemic thinking', *Action Research*, 2(3) September: 305–26.

Moser, Heinz (1980a) '*Participatory action research – the German case*'. Paper presented at the International Forum on Participatory Research, Ljubljana, Yugoslavia, April.

Moser, Heinz (1980b) '*Action research as a new research paradigm in the social sciences*'. Paper presented at the International Forum on Participatory Research, Ljubljana, Yugoslavia, April.

Nyoni, Sithembiso (1991) 'People's Power in Zimbabwe', in Orlando Fals Borda and Md. Anisur Rahman (eds), *Action and Knowledge, Breaking the Monopoly with Participatory Action Research.* London: Intermediate Technology Publications: 109–20.

Paranjape, P.V., Kanhare Vijay, Sathe Nirmala, Kulkarni Sudihindra, and Gothaskar Sujata (1984) 'Grass-roots self-reliance in Shramik Sanghatana, Dhulia District, India' in Rahman (1984). pp. 60–92.

Rahman, Md. Anisur (1981a) *Some Dimensions of People's Participation in the Bhoomi Sena Movement.* Participation Occasional Paper, United Nations Research Institute for Social Development (UNRISD) Participation Programme. Geneva. Republished in Rahman (1993a).

Rahman, Md. Anisur (1981b) (Guest editor) *Development, Seeds of Change, Village through Global Order.* Issue 1. Rome: Society for International Development. Republished in Rahman (2000).

Rahman, Md. Anisur (1984) *Grassroots Participation and Self-reliance: Experiences in South and Southeast Asia.* New Delhi, Oxford and IBH.

Rahman, Md. Anisur (1985) 'The theory and practice of participatory action research', in Orlando Fals Borda, (ed.) (1985), *The Challenge of Social Change.* London: Sage Publications. pp. 107–132. Also published in *IFDA dossier* (1982) 31:17–30 ; reprinted in Shadish and Reichart (eds) (1987); and in Rahman (1993a).

Rahman, Md. Anisur (1993a) *'People's Self-Development, Perspectives in Participatory Action Research, A Journey through Experience.* London: Zed Books, and Dhaka: University Press Limited.

Rahman, Md. Anisur (1993b) 'The praxis of PORP: A programme in participatory rural development', in Rahman (1993a).

Rahman, Md. Anisur (1993c) 'People's self-development', in Rahman (1993a) pp. 178–201.

Rahman, Md. Anisur (ed.) (2000) *Participation of the Rural Poor in Development.* Dhaka: Pathak Shamabesh. Reproduction of Rahman (1981b).

Reason, Peter and Bradbury Hilary, (eds) (2001/2006) *Handbook of Action Research: Participative Inquiry and Practice.* London: Sage Publications.

Shadish, Wiliam R. Jr. and Reichard, Charles S. (eds) (1987) *Evaluation Studies Review Annual,* Vol 12. London: Sage Publications. pp. 135–60.

Swadogo, A. R. and Ouedraogo, B. L. (1987*) Auto-evaluation de six groupements Naam dans la province du Yatenga* (mineographed). Draft report submitted to the International Labour Office, Geneva.

Tilakaratna, Susanta (1985) *The Animator in Participatory Rural Development: Some Experiences in Sri Lanka.* World Employment Programme Working Paper WEP 10/WP 37. Geneva: International Labour Office.

Tilakaratna, Susanta (1987) *The Animator in Participatory Rural Development (Concept and Practice).* Geneva: International Labour Office.

Wadsworth, Y. (2001) 'The Mirror, The Magnifying Glass, The Compass and the Map – Facilitating participatory action research', Chapter. 43 in *Handbook of Action Research* (eds), Peter Reason and Hilary Bradbury (2001/2006). pp. 420–32.

Women's Research Committee, Farmers' Assistance Board Inc. and Women's Health Movement, Philippines (1984) 'The Struggle Toward self-reliance of organized resettled Women in the Philippines', in Rahman (1984), pp. 93–120.

4

Action Research and the Challenge of Scope

Bjørn Gustavsen, Agneta Hansson and Thoralf U. Qvale

In aiming for generalities in research, the tradition is to study a case or a set of cases and draw conclusions with reference to all cases of a similar kind. While this kind of thinking has been strongly criticized even in descriptive-analytic research, it can be even more strongly criticized in action research. If action research is seen as social constructions made jointly between research and other actors, we cannot remove the active participation of research after 'the first case' and let theory speak alone. Instead, the need is for a process of social construction that can, in itself, encompass the challenge of reaching out in scope. This implies network building and similar efforts that can bring a broad range of actors to share ideas and practices. This chapter presents an example of a development of this kind, showing the successive widening of action research efforts from small workplaces to substantial regions, and the intermediate steps and challenges.

INTRODUCTION

The major advantage of action research compared to the production of 'words alone' is the creation of practices. While words often have a slippery relationship to reality, forms of practices *are* reality. Intentions, meanings, goals, values are expressed in patterns of organization, behaviour and action.

When helping to construct forms of practice, the problem is that action research is dependent upon working with specific people in specific contexts. Often, this means working with groups of relatively few people. The groups can claim to represent other people – they may, for instance, be the management of corporations or the leadership of NGOs – but it remains that the direct relationship to and, consequently, the element of direct influence from action research on human practices is constrained to the small group. Out of this there emerges a challenge: How can action research achieve scope, magnitude, or mass in its impact? The traditional answer is to create theory with a claim to validity beyond the case, or cases, out of which it emerges. The assumption is that others can learn from the theory and do likewise.

From our experience in the action research tradition in working life in Scandinavia, that by now spans a period of four decades and throws much light on the diffusion problem, a core learning is that there is no direct diffusion via general theory from one or a few cases to many cases. To reach out in society it is necessary to travel a far more complex road. Below, some of the main parts of this road will be presented and discussed.

THE POINT OF DEPARTURE

In the 1960s, Norway was the seat of a series of field experiments with new forms of work organization (Emery and Thorsrud, 1969, 1976). Developed jointly by the Work Research Institute in Norway and the Tavistock Institute in the UK, the main point was to break with highly specialized – Taylorist – forms of work organization to replace them with forms giving the workers more autonomy in terms of decision-making rights, possibilities for learning and for the development of social relationships in the workplace. Behind what Miller and Rose (2001) call 'The Tavistock Programme' was, however, not only the idea of introducing something new; the idea was, literally speaking, to introduce it on a world scale (Emery and Trist, 1973; van Ejnatten, 1993). From four field sites in Norway the process was supposed to spread to other workplaces in Norway and to the neighbouring countries and from this platform to conquer the world.

Where was the line from Norway to the world broken? The first point to be noted was that the process of diffusion within Norway was slow (Bolweg, 1976; Gustavsen and Hunnius, 1981; Herbst, 1974). Second, that the processes emerging in other countries seemed to differ in important respects from the one that had been launched in Norway. This was the case in particular in Sweden, which was seen as critical, since this was the only Scandinavian country that could, at the time, be expected to influence broader developments in the industrialized world. In a sense the development in Sweden took off more rapidly and dramatically than in Norway (Sandberg, 1982) but it was, from the beginning, distributed over several initiatives. While a series of field experiments along the same lines as in Norway were launched (Björk et al., 1972), there were also two other initiatives emerging. One was linked to the work of a number of public commissions that were set down to study and promote participative democracy in the sectors of working life under state ownership (Karlsson, 1969), another to the Swedish Employers Confederation where a special department was established to promote new forms of work organization (Agurên and Edgren, 1979). These three initiatives partly developed in different directions, partly entered into a relationship of competition. Extending the perspective to other countries – i.e. Denmark (Agersnap, 1973), Holland (Van Beinum and Vliest, 1979), Germany (Fricke, 1975), the UK (Hill, 1971) and the USA (Duckles et al., 1977) – it was seen that whatever emerged in terms of initiatives within the area represented still further differentiations compared to the original point of departure.

AN ALTERNATIVE APPROACH: LOCAL CONSTRUCTIVISM

Against the background of diffusion problems indicated above, the Norwegian research group found it necessary to reconsider how to achieve wider impact and scope. If the enterprises were reluctant to join a process of diffusion of specific forms of work organization, it was reasonable to ask what forms of work organization they would like to pursue.

Although the question was quite obvious, the issue of how to pose it was less so. One could imagine developing a questionnaire aiming at a sample of workplace actors. This was found unsatisfying, first and foremost because work organization is a question of *relationships:* something that exists *between* people. To elicit adequate answers it would be necessary to pose the question to workplace collectivities rather than to individuals. Could we, however, expect to get any meaningful answers at all? Experience indicated that ideas about work organization are inseparably linked to efforts to *do* something about work organization. It is only when embarking on a process of improvement that the issues involved become identifiable and the choices between different patterns realistically grounded.

The possibility of posing the question in an appropriate way emerged when the social partners, in 1982, made an agreement on workplace development (Gustavsen, 1985). The social partners did not, however, aim at promoting specific forms of organization; their purpose was to make their members become more conscious about the issue of work organization and more oriented towards developing their own initiatives. The core measure to be introduced was the notion of meetings, or conferences, where workers and managers in each enterprise could engage in discussions of their needs and options, without being under the pressure of having to accept or reject any specific form. This gave research the opening needed to participate in a broad discourse on work organization.

EARLY EXPERIENCE

Throughout the 1980s, altogether about 450 conferences were organized between labour and management, largely in individual enterprises, in a few cases in networks of enterprises. Research was asked to help develop an adequate conference model and came, in this way, to influence the design of these events.

Central in this context was the notion of democratic dialogue and its expression in a number of design criteria (Gustavsen, 1992, 1993, 2001, 2006; Gustavsen and Engelstad, 1986.)

Research could not participate directly in more than a limited number of these conferences. However, through participation in the board set up by the social partners to supervise the implementation of the agreement, it was possible to gain an overview of what came out of them (Gustavsen, 1993). First, there was no turn away from autonomous forms of work organization, but the importance of giving attention to the contexts of implementation was stressed, in particular to the myriad details that have to be confronted to make a specific form of organization work in a specific context. Second, in efforts to diffuse new forms of work organization there was a need to give more attention to issues of process. Third, there was a need to develop a new relationship between figure and ground. Whereas the diffusion process was built on using the pioneer cases as figures, and new sites of implementation as background, the conference participants generally wanted the reverse: each workplace and enterprise, and its problems and challenges, should be the main issue; examples of what others had done should recede more into the background and be taken forth only when they could help provide useful points in understanding or acting within the primary context (Engelstad and Ødegaard, 1979). This gave rise to a fourth point: each unit of development had to be understood as a unique combination of elements. Elden (1983) introduced the notion of 'local theory' in this context. Fifth, making the process emanate from local circumstances and actors implied that local resources could carry much more of the process than what was assumed in the experimental period.

These points provided a basis for the continued work but they also reinforced the challenge associated with scope, or 'critical mass' as it was generally called at the time. If scope could not be reached when there was a belief in the power of the good example in combination with general theory, how could we hope to advance towards scope under the kind of local constructivism implicit in the points above? This question formed the point of departure for a series of efforts, actions, considerations and reconsiderations that have by now been going on for more than two decades. Much of the efforts have been expressed in workplace development programmes organized jointly by research, the labour market parties and public institutions, for instance research and development councils. First out was the LOM (Leadership Co-ordination and Co-operation) programme in Sweden (1985–90) organized by the Work Environment Fund in co-operation with the labour market parties. Second, Enterprise Development 2000 (1994–2000) organized by the Research Council of Norway in co-operation with the labour market parties and Innovation Norway. Third, Value Creation 2010, a continuation of Enterprise Development 2000 with the same partners.

THE LOM PROGRAMME AND THE IDEA OF LOCAL GROWTH POINTS

While the co-operation with the labour market parties in Norway made it possible to develop the notion of dialogue and local co-operation, there was no programme to provide a broader funding for research. The first initiative to provide this was the LOM programme in Sweden (Gustavsen, 1992). The labour market parties had made an agreement on development parallel to the Norwegian one (Gustavsen, 1985), but in Sweden there also existed a Work Environment Fund with, among other things, the task of turning this agreement into reality (Oscarsson, 1997). This programme made it possible to focus more strongly on the problem of how to combine scope with locally constructed initiatives.

First, it was necessary to establish the local platforms: the process of organization had to begin with challenges and ideas as expressed by the enterprise level actors locally. As a complement to this, the idea of

local research support was introduced. Instead of letting the programme emanate from one research centre, it was decided to support a number of geographically distributed research groups so as to make the programme as sensitive to local-regional conditions as possible.

Whereas these two ideas can be said to work towards differentiation, in order to create local links the idea was introduced that the basic unit of development should be four organizations in co-operation not only with research but also with each other. The main point was that each participating organization should engage in development experiences together with other organizations from the beginning of the process. In addition, when such groups of four were established, they should function as 'recruitment nodes' to pull in further organisations, eventually ending up with broader networks (Engelstad, 1996). Through this approach, the issue of diffusion was defined as a process of growth emanating from a number of local nodes.

While the participating organizations had to carry their own costs, finance was made available to research conditional on each research group demonstrating that the agreement was in place with an adequate number of organizations for joint development work. The support offered by research to the participating organizations was mainly focused on process: on how to organize the development work so as to achieve participation from all concerned and adequate forms of interaction between them. Various organizational expressions of the notion of democratic dialogue – in conferences, workplace meetings, project groups and similar – constituted the main tools (Gustavsen, 1992; Naschold, 1993: esp. pp. 63–6).

With altogether 64 researchers participating to a greater or lesser extent, distributed among about 15 different institutions, the LOM programme was the most broadly framed action research programme to appear in Sweden. The programme was not only intended to generate specific results within its own time frame of five years but also – and even more importantly – to lay the ground for a long-term development of a number of action research groups in Swedish working life.

In an evaluation performed around the time of the termination of the programme, one main conclusion was that the programme had succeeded quite well in reaching out broadly in working life and in creating significant improvements in employee participation in more than 80 per cent of the cases where specific projects had actually emerged. However, such specific projects had occurred in only about half of all the 148 organizations that made an effort to relate to the programme (Naschold, 1993). The number of organizations that had used the improvements in participation to develop more radical innovations in organization and technology were about 10 per cent of those who had developed a project – a seemingly meagre figure. The evaluation commission saw the main reason for this in the relatively short running time of each project within the programme.

The overall purpose of building geographically distributed research-enterprise combinations that could form nodes or growth points in a strategy for diffusion was achieved in a number of cases. Most of the research-enterprise combinations that were created by the programme were, however, too fragile to survive the termination of the programme. The exceptions largely occurred in situations where the development towards the formation of networks had moved relatively far (Engelstad and Gustavsen, 1993). On the other hand, although advanced results were achieved in a few cases only, the programme demonstrated that such results *could* be reached through this kind of local-regional strategy with a far smaller research input per case than in field experiments.

THE ENTERPRISE DEVELOPMENT 2000/THE VALUE CREATION 2010 PROGRAMMES AND THE CHALLENGE OF THE LEARNING REGION

In 1990, it was decided to revise the agreement on workplace development between the social partners in Norway. The agreement had been a success in terms of number of users, but had led to more deep-going changes in only a modest number of organizations (Gustavsen, 1993). It was decided to strengthen the measures associated with the agreement using an action research approach and through this to develop regional growth points. It took several years to prepare the ground for a programme, but in 1994 Enterprise Development 2000 was launched, in co-operation among the social partners, the Research Council of Norway and Innovation Norway.

The Norwegian initiative built on experiences from the LOM programme, in particular the point that a five year programme cycle was too short to establish and consolidate a number of research-enterprise combinations with the potential for growth. From the beginning, a six-year cycle time instead of five was established with the promise from the social partners to back a prolongation if the first cycle was reasonably successful. The focus as the programme started was to ensure the establishment of the most viable groups of researchers and enterprises as was possible. Much work was put in by the programme secretariat on this point. Altogether seven research-enterprise combinations – called modules – were developed (Gustavsen et al., 2001, and Levin, 2002, contain broad presentations of the programme, its evaluation and results).

While each of the modules could show ups and downs in terms of participating enterprises and programme impact, the overall picture was one of a steady increase in number of participating enterprises. With background the labour market parties decided to initiate a new programme – Value Creation 2010 – with a 10 year running time. In addition to continuing the developments on enterprise and network levels, this programme came to place a stronger focus on the regional dimension and on some of those issues that are often referred to as governance. To illustrate not only the overall character of the developments initiated by the programme but, more specifically, the emergence of the last dimensions, we will turn to a sample case.

THE GRENLAND CASE

With seven large processing plants owned by different corporations, employing about 5000 people and with an annual turnover of about €2 billion, the Grenland area – located on the east coast of Southern Norway about 150 km south of Oslo, and with a population of 100,000 – constitutes the largest concentration of processing industry in Scandinavia.

In the 1960s and early 1970s it was the seat of some of the most highly profiled field experiments with new forms of work organization, first in a fertilizer plant (Emery and Thorsrud, 1976) and later in several other plants in the complex belonging to Norsk Hydro, the largest industrial group in Norway. These experiments pioneered patterns of work organization that have later become common in processing industry, such as integrated work groups with responsibility for the running of the plant as a whole instead of the previous pattern of specialized work roles and corresponding dividing lines between operators and foremen, process and maintenance, production and quality, control room and factory.

The processes to be triggered off in the host corporation were not unlike those that came to characterize the national scene: much interest and discussion but also the emergence of various factors that made a broad strategy for implementation of the ideas difficult. In a sense the ideas were kept pending, eventually to start gaining ground again with the later emergence of new productivity concepts.

More or less sporadic contacts were maintained between the Work Research Institute (WRI) and the Grenland industry, and in 1998 researchers at the WRI launched an initiative that came to encompass plants from this region, together with plants from other parts of the country. The initiative was called Forum for New Manufacturing Concepts in the Process Industry and was based on meetings every sixth month, site visits and informal contacts across enterprise boundaries (Qvale, 2000). This initiative must be seen against the background of the major pressure for change that emerged in the 1990s. Cost cutting through downsizing and outsourcing, in combination with ideas like lean production and on-line quality management, hit the processing industry with full force. Characteristic of the plants joining the Forum and, consequently, also of most of the Grenland plants, was a conscious effort to meet the new conditions without renouncing on worker participation and without laying off people against their will. The result was an increase in the efforts to create – or recreate – patterns of work organization based on worker autonomy, in combination with plans for personnel reductions that could be supported jointly by management and the local unions.

By 1999 it was recognized that plant level strategies were insufficient. Most of the plants, in spite of having state of the art technology, were losing money, suffering from a 10 year period of low rates of investments, a high rate of exchange for Norwegian currency, low prices on the world market and high Norwegian wages and duties, within a national regime that did not promote policies supportive of this kind of industry. All historical advantages, such as cheap energy, were gone and work organization – however advanced – could not alone compensate for this. Rather than continue to focus on internal processes within each plant, it was deemed necessary to start exploiting the possibilities inherent in co-operation *between* plants. This was the situation when the Grenland group of enterprises was invited to join the VC 2010 programme.

The programme imposed certain requirements on its users. The regional representatives of the labour market parties were to be involved in a steering or advisory position and the research aspect had to be strengthened. The social partners had for a decade worked closely together to use their joint political influence to help develop new regional policies for education, economic growth and public administration. They were, consequently, involved in a number of other aspects pertaining to regional development and could pull these into the co-operation.

With the new configuration of actors it was necessary to renew the co-operation platform. For this purpose a dialogue conference was organized in January 2002. In addition to bringing new actors into the process, the conference came to represent a breakthrough in terms of what kind of effort the processing plant actors were willing to explore together. Among the new efforts could be found joint maintenance teams, a joint facility for the handling of emergencies and associated training, a joint occupational health centre, joint specialized workshops in areas like machining, electrical engines and valves, and a project in regional logistics. For the employees and the unions to accept plant crossing initiatives like this, they needed a high degree of trust in the willingness of management to pursue goals associated with the long-term growth of the plants and not short-term rationalization effects.

The WRI has made continuous efforts to continue the process of expanding the scope of the conferences, in terms of participants as well as in terms of topics. Some of the new actors represent other industrial branches, such as a network of local engineering firms. Some represent new initiatives, like a biological laboratory, an initiative that to some extent has its roots in competence from the time when all the processing plants had their own laboratories.

While the continuous widening of the circle of participating actors makes it possible to pull in a continuously widening circle of issues and stepwise approach that can be called a regional innovation process, the relationships between the 'older' actors are also continuously changing. One experience is that issues that could create conflicts and lock-ins often disappear, or are cast within a new framework, when new actors enter the scene. In this way they are, if not always

solved, at least not allowed to block the process.

The Grenland area is of modest size from an international perspective, and to keep the regional process moving and growing there is a need to transcend the boundaries constituted by this area. How this is to be done is one of the main challenges. It is not a simple issue of, say, including the whole of the administrative region of which Grenland is a part. The rest of the region is largely based on agriculture and tourism and does not necessarily provide interesting partners for Grenland industry. In light of the increased pressure for fruitful regional frameworks the Norwegian government has (like many other European governments) initiated a process towards merging areas to form larger regions. This process is in its infancy and has so far given rise to limited concrete results.

The development sketched above can be linked to a set of concepts. Some of the concepts – like local understanding, dialogue and regional growth points – have roots in the 1980s while other concepts – such as those associated with regional organization of change – are of more recent origin. While the concepts can, from the position of today, be seen as pointing at different aspects of one and the same reality, the fact that they have appeared over time indicates their background in a moving discourse.

DIALOGUE

The core element in all activities is the notion of dialogue as the main constructive force. The reasons for placing dialogue in the centre have been spelled out in other contexts (for instance Gustavsen, 2001/2006) and will be mentioned only briefly.

The point of departure was practical experience. Even if the purpose is to conduct a field experiment it is hardly possible to avoid conducting conversations with those concerned. Since this is the case one may as well ask if all conversations are of equal value or if certain forms provide more fruitful outcomes in terms of ideas and agreements than others.

Second, workplace development in Norway plays itself out against the background of a specific social order where democracy is a core element. In all democratic constitutions free or open dialogue is a basic condition, expressed in principles like the freedom of speech, the right to form associations, the right to be heard before authorities who are making decisions pertaining to the individual, and similar. Principles of this kind are not automatically applicable in a workplace context; they form points of orientation rather than operational criteria. The point in this context is to ground the notion of dialogue in the order of society and not in existential or psychodynamic mechanisms. The ability to master dialogue is identical to the ability to enter into discourses of reason and fruitfulness with people one does not know. The reason lies in the procedure, not in personal knowledge.

While practical and institutional concerns have been the main ones, the kind of action research that forms the background for this contribution has not remained uninfluenced by the various 'turns' that have come to characterize much social research in general, such as the linguistic turn, the communicative turn, the pragmatic turn and the constructivist turn. None of these concepts are particularly precise, and they open up for large fields of discourse more than for the identification of specific positions. However, they all point at the independent weight carried by language in the formation of human understandings and actions and at the need to anchor joint action in a joint language. They also generally share the view that the linguistic tools available to a set of actors are strongly linked to the practical context in which they exist and have to find solutions to challenges. In this way these 'turns' do, in a sense, also turn theory in a practical direction and make, in this way, a contribution to the arguments for action research.

The first practical expression of the notion of democratic dialogue was the dialogue conference, originally introduced as a part of the agreement on workplace development among the labour market parties in Norway, later further developed within the LOM programme in Sweden. Essentially, these conferences were designed to place all participants on an equal footing while at the same time promoting the production of ideas and the ability to reach joint action platforms. A presentation of design criteria and modes of functioning can be found in the first edition of the Handbook (see Gustavsen, 2001/2006). Around the dialogue conferences a number of other measures are grouped. Efforts have been made to make other arenas adopt more or less of the same dialogue criteria, to make these arenas function in support of dialogue as well. In ED 2000 it was, for instance, seen that enterprise councils and health and safety committees could be oriented in this direction (Bakke, 2001), a development that can be seen in the Grenland case as well. Claussen (2003) describes the introduction of a new kind of shop floor encounter, developed to increase the dialogue arenas accessible to production workers, and a type of encounter based on locating SWOT analyses within the framework of dialogue conferences.

CHANGE AND HYBRIDS

One recognition to emerge out of the failure of field experiments to trigger off broader change in working life was the need for understanding each workplace, each organization, as a unique phenomenon (Elden, 1983). If we look at the processing plants that constitute the core of the Grenland development the need for plant specific understandings and solutions is verified. They still, however, work together. Why is that?

At this point the notion of hybrid, as developed by Latour (1998), can help explain the mechanism that comes into force when organizations are learning from each other. When an organization makes an improvement, or an innovation, it generally means to use known elements but to put them together in a new way. The trigger mechanism in this context is often what other organizations are doing. The impulses that come from other organizations join experiences and impulses from one's own organization, and out of this a new pattern emerges. The new pattern is, however, original in the sense that it is not a replication of the patterns exhibited by any other organization.

A dynamic network co-operation between enterprises is characterized by an exchange of hybrids. Drawing upon its own experiences as well as systematically utilizing impulses from other enterprises, each organization continuously restructures itself and, at the same time, sends new impulses to the other network members.

When change is mainly a sequence of hybrids, 'diffusion' cannot be a linear process. In fact, diffusion is not at all possible if diffusion is taken to mean that the same pattern is transferred from one organization to the next (Gustavsen, 2003). While the recognition that linear diffusion is not possible emerged quite early, and is perhaps the most basic recognition to emerge out of the period of field experiments, it took a long time to create an alternative framework for achieving scope in the development.

GROWTH AND RELATIONSHIPS

While dialogue conferences were initially organized for single organizations, they have, since the mid-1980s, also been extensively used for the purpose of creating relationships *between* and among organizations.

To make each participating organization open to co-operation with others, four organizations were introduced as the basic unit of development as early as from the beginning of the LOM programme. Four is not a magic figure and in later programmes this issue has been more open. The point is that each organization from the beginning of the process works with some other organizations, to create its experiences in interplay

with other organizations. Such smaller groups of organizations were intended to form the basis for the formation of networks with a larger number of members. The assumption was that by utilizing existing local-regional relationships the difficulties associated with reaching new organizations could be reduced. To a large extent this assumption has proven valid. On the other hand, as the Grenland case demonstrates, the passage from smaller groups of organizations to larger networks has been far from linear and has implied a number of new challenges.

In achieving scope, the emphasis is less on the single conference than on the relationships *between* conferences (Shotter and Gustavsen, 1999). The conferences need to form a pattern with the potential for reaching a continuously widening circle of actors without losing those that are already within the network. Many of the efforts of the ongoing Value Creation 2010 programme have been oriented towards this challenge. The programme has clearly been most successful in contexts of the Grenland type: regions made up of smaller communities where people know each other and where there exist social links and ties ('social capital'). However, when a network is emerging it is important that actors in other communities can join the process, since each community will often be too limited to house the sufficient mass of enterprises. We see, consequently, that in parts of the country where there are small communities of the relevant type, but long distances between them – such as in the northernmost parts – the network formation process is generally unable to reach sustainable mass. A parallel problem – but for the opposite reasons – can be found in the big cities, in particular Oslo. The city has about 60,000 enterprises and is, in this respect, rich in network potential. There are, however, few smaller local environments where social relationships can be founded and there have been major problems associated with anchoring the Value Creation 2010 efforts with specific actors.

DISTRIBUTIVE AND LOW-INTENSITY FORMS OF ACTION RESEARCH

Basing broad change on the use of encounters like dialogue conferences means that many of the actors involved are exposed to the impulses from research at intervals and relatively briefly each time. It is obvious that intensive contact with one single workplace over a period of time that can go on for years implies certain advantages. Research can deal with all problems – large and small – hands on, and it is possible to gather detailed data on everything that happens. No country has so far invested the resources necessary to combine high-intensity efforts with scope in number of workplaces involved. All change-generating actors are facing the challenge of how to reach out in scope with limited resources.

In principle, the answer has to be distributive and low-intensive approaches, as far as possible based on mobilizing the actors concerned to themselves sustain the process. When a strategy of this kind is launched it must, however, be kept up in a way that is consistent with its own characteristics. If, for instance, conflicts, blockages, or other problems appear, the core strategy must be to bring new partners into the discourse rather than attack the problems head-on (Pålshaugen, 2004). Conflict agendas can, in themselves, be seen as hybrids, and by bringing in new actors there will often be a change of agenda that makes the conflict disappear, or at least make the actors able to move on. In this way, conflicts are used to broaden the circle of actors in a way consistent with the basic characteristics of the strategy. To freeze and dig deeply into the conflict in the hope of solving it like a court of law is counterproductive.

Even if conflicts do not dominate the scene it is important not to freeze the participation. This point is demonstrated by the Grenland case where new actors are pulled in all the time, even though a group of processing plants constitute a permanent nucleus. The point is not only to use each new event to widen the circle but to make the participants as accustomed as possible to continuously working with new people and to draw advantages from this. It can be added, from the point of view of action research, that relationships with dynamic, problem-solving capacity do not emerge by themselves. There is, today, a vast literature on, for instance, networking in the context of discourses on clusters, innovation systems, regional development and even network society. Generally, this literature grossly underplays the constructive efforts associated with actually creating these networks, be it efforts that face action research or other actors.

DEVELOPMENT CONFIGURATIONS

The need to utilize existing social relationships indicates that action research cannot create social change on its own. Something has to be present in the context where change is to take place; this something is often referred to as trust. What quality of relationship and how much trust need to be present for successful development to emerge, are questions that often appear. Rather than make a large initial effort at mapping out the social capital existing in, say, a region, as an action research programme Value Creation 2010 is based on moving directly into action and seeing what happens. The process is, however, not blind. Various mechanisms, for instance contacts with the regional representatives of the social partners, are brought to bear on the challenge of finding a fruitful entry point. As events unfold, new impulses that help refine the course emerge, while successful joint action in itself promotes trust. In this way research-enterprise nodes have been developed in all major parts of the country, although they show, as indicated above, different degrees of ability to grow. Among the most sharply featured configurations that have emerged so far, Grenland is one. Another can be found in the Rogaland-Hordaland area where as many as 10 different enterprise networks have emerged in parallel (Claussen, 2003; Haga, in prep.). A further example is constituted by the Raufoss industrial district (Johnstad, in prep.) where an old munitions factory has been converted into about 30 new companies that have, in turn, triggered off about 40 new local suppliers. With about 50 owner organizations and a further 100 users, Nordvest Forum is a more loosely structured learning network where experiences from enterprise level projects are shared through direct contacts as well as through network events (Hanssen-Bauer, 2001). Some of the configurations have not attained contours of a sharpness comparable to these examples, and are still in a more emergent phase. Nor is it true that the strategy pursued by the VC 2010 programme will necessarily be successful in all parts of the country. So far the advances at each end of the urbanization scale – Northern Norway and Oslo – are modest and there is no guarantee that they will be more pronounced in the future.

KNOWLEDGE, DIFFUSION AND SOCIAL MOVEMENTS

When the issue of work organization first entered the scene as an issue of broad concern, the road to change was defined as the use of spearhead projects to create and sustain a general theory of participative organization as well as to provide telling examples of their advantages in terms of productivity and innovation. Neither general theory nor spearhead projects proved, however, to have much persuasive power. Instead, it became necessary to embark on a process of slow constructivism, beginning with local units where each unit was allowed to take its own problems and challenges as a point of departure, but where the local actors could, when they had launched their own process of development, be brought to consider external cases as sources of ideas. To recognize that the development of participation needs participative strategies was, however, not the core point; this discovery has been made many times, in action research and elsewhere. The

challenge is, this notwithstanding, to create a process that can reach out in scope. Participative democracy is not a kind of social order that can survive in small corners and lacunae in an otherwise hierarchically structured world. This has implied the stepwise development of networks and other linking structures to allow each point of change to relate to new actors and help the new actors orient themselves towards participation as a core issue. The generalizations possible from each separate site of experience reach no further than the social links that surround them.

The region thus far appears as the level of social organization where the closeness to the problems needed in order to deal with work organization can be combined with the need for adequate scope, or mass. This corresponds to a perspective emerging in studies of innovation where the current tendency is to identify the region as the most significant level of organization (Asheim, 1996; Cooke, in prep.). Even global actors – such as the pharmaceutical industry – today locate their innovation processes in specific regions generally characterized by a high density of actors with relevant knowledge and experience, rather than try to link actors across the globe in one and the same process.

This does not mean that impulses cannot travel across regional boundaries, but the interplay between regions follow the logics of mutual exchange of hybrids, not the logics of each region subordinating itself to the same general truth (Ennals and Gustavsen 1998). Insofar as patterns of action become synchronized across regional boundaries, the most appropriate characteristic of the pattern to emerge is *social movements* (Gustavsen, 2003), of which there are a number in play, often in several versions. Examples can be the women's movements, the movements for ecological consciousness and balance, the movements for peace, and even the one dealt with in this chapter: the movement for participative democracy. 'To be in the movement' means to share experience with others and work for a common goal, but not to become part of a system of uniform elements.

How well has the movement towards participative democracy as expressed in autonomous forms of work organization succeeded so far? This is a substantial topic of discussion in its own right. The optimism that could be seen in the 1970s and into the 1980s has been replaced by a more pessimistic outlook (Ennals, 2003). However the global situation may be assessed, the Scandinavian countries show a picture where autonomous forms of work organization are at least more widespread than what is generally the case in Europe (Gallie, 2003; Lorenz and Valeyre, 2005). It would be pretentious to argue that this is owing to the efforts of action research. In fact, in a social movement there is no single type of actor that can claim to be the cause of what other actors do. When 'Scandinavian exceptionalism' is explained in terms of historically given patterns of co-operation between such actors as the social partners, it is, however, overlooked that not even the social partners in Scandinavia co-operate beyond the point where co-operation creates results that both partners find fruitful. A general commitment to co-operation explains far less than the actual fruits of specific forms of co-operation and for any fruits to be picked at all there must be actors who take initiatives, organize events, link processes and perform other tasks needed for practical experience to be created. This is where action research finds its role.

REFERENCES

Agersnap, F. (1973) *Experiments with Labour-management Co-operation in the Iron- and Metals Industry* (*Samarbejdsforsøg i jernindustrien*). København: Foreningen af verkstedfunktionærer i Danmark/ Centralorganisationen af metalarbejdere i Danmark/ Sammensludningen af arbejdsgivere indenfor jern- og metalindustrien i Danmark.

Agurên, S. and Edgren, J. (1979) *New Factories*. Stockholm: The Swedish Employers' Confederation.

Asheim, B.T. (1996) 'Industrial districts as learning regions: A condition for prosperity?', *European Planning Studies*, 4: 379–400.

Bakke, N.A. (2001) 'Report to the benchmarking group', in B. Gustavsen, H. Finne and B. Oscarsson (eds), *Creating Connectedness: the Role of Social Research in Innovation Policy*. Amsterdam: John Benjamins. pp. 41–58.

Björk, L., Hansson, R. and Hellberg, P. (1972) *More Democracy in Work* (*Økat innflytande i jobbet*). Stockholm: Personaladministrativa Rådet/ Utvecklingsrådet för samarbetsfrågor.

Bolweg, J. (1976) *Job Design and Industrial Democracy*. Leiden: Nijhoff.

Claussen, T. (2003) 'Participation and enterprise networks within a regional context: examples from south-west Norway', in W. Fricke and P. Totterdill (eds), *Action Research in Workplace Innovation and Regional Development*. Amsterdam: John Benjamins. pp. 83–102.

Cooke, P. (in prep.) 'Learning regions: a critique and revaluation of regional innovation systems', in B. Gustavsen, R. Ennals and B. Nyhan (eds), *Learning for Local Innovation – Promotion of Learning Regions*. Thessaloniki: CEDEFOP. www.cewc.org/cedefop/upload.

Duckles, M.M., Duckles, R. and Maccoby, M. (1977) 'The process of change at Bolivar', *Journal of Applied Behavioural Science*, 13 (3): 387–99.

Elden, M. (1983) 'Democratization and participative research in developing local theory', *Journal of Occupational Behaviour*, 4 (1): 21–34.

Emery, F. E. and Thorsrud, E. (1969) *Form and Content in Industrial Democracy*. London: Tavistock Publications.

Emery, F.E. and Thorsrud, E. (1976) *Democracy at Work*. Leiden: Nijhoff.

Emery, F.E. and Trist, E. (1973) *Towards a Social Ecology. Contextual Appreciation of the Future in the Present*. London: Plenum Press.

Engelstad, P.H. (1996) 'The development organization as communicative instrumentation: experiences from the Karlstad progreamme', in S. Toulmin and B. Gustavsen (eds), *Beyond Theory: Changing Organizations through Participation*. Amsterdam: John Benjamins. pp. 89–118.

Engelstad, P. H. and Gustavsen, B. (1993) 'A Swedish network development for implementing a national work reform strategy', *Human Relations* 39 (2): 101–16.

Engelstad, P.H. and Ødegaard, L.A. (1979) 'Participative redesign projects in Norway: summarising the first five years of a strategy to democratise the design process in working life', in The Quality of Working Life Council (ed.), *Working with the Quality of Working Life.* Leiden: Nijhoff. pp. 327–38.

Ennals. R. (2003) 'Regional workplace forums and the modernisation of work', in W. Fricke and P. Totterdill (eds), *Action Research in Workplace Innovation and Regional Development.* Amsterdam: John Benjamins. pp. 289–312.

Ennals, R. and Gustavsen, B. (eds) (1998) *Work Organization and Europe as a Development Coalition.* Amsterdam: John Benjamins.

Fricke, W. (1975) *Work Organization and Competence (Arbeitsorganisation und Qualifikation).* Schriftenreihe des Forschungsinstitut der Friedrich Ebert Stiftung. Bonn: Neue Gesellschaft.

Gallie, D. (2003) 'The quality of working life: is Scandinavia different?', *European Sociological Review,* 19 (1): 61–79

Gustavsen, B. (1985) 'Technology and collective agreements: some recent Scandinavian developments', *Industrial Relations Journal,* 16 (3): 34–42.

Gustavsen, B. (1992) *Dialogue and Development.* Assen: van Gorcum.

Gustavsen, B. (1993) 'Creating productive structures: the role of research and development', in F. Naschold, R. Cole, B. Gustavsen and H. van Beinum, *Constructing the New Industrial Society.* Assen: van Gorcum. pp. 133–68.

Gustavsen, B. (2001/2006) 'Theory and practice: The mediating discourse', in P. Reason and H. Bradbury (eds), *Handbook of Action Research.* London: Sage. pp. 17–26. Also published in P. Reason and H. Bradbury (eds) (2006), *Handbook of Action Research: Concise Student Edition.* London: Sage. pp. 17–26.

Gustavsen, B. (2003) 'Action research and the problem of the single case', *Concepts and Transformation,* 8 (1): 87–93.

Gustavsen, B. and Engelstad, P.H. (1986) 'The design of conferences and the evolving role of democratic dialogue in changing working life', *Human Relations,* 39 (2): 101–16.

Gustavsen, B. and Hunnius, G. (1981) *New Patterns of Work Reform: the Case of Norway.* Oslo: Oslo University Press.

Gustavsen, B., Finne, H. and Oscarsson, B. (eds) (2001) *Creating Connectedness: the Role of Social Research in Innovation Policy.* Amsterdam: John Benjamins.

Haga, T. (in prep.) 'Training for innovation', in B. Gustavsen, R. Ennals and B. Nyhan (eds), *Learning for Local Innovation – Promotion of Learning Regions.* Thessaloniki: CEDEFOP.

Hanssen-Bauer, J. (2001) 'The Nordvest Forum Module', in B. Gustavsen, H. Finne and B. Oscarsson (eds), *Creating Connectedness: the Role of Social Research in Innovation Policy.* Amsterdam: John Benjamins. pp. 203–18.

Herbst, P.G. (1974) *Socio-technical design: Strategies in Multidisciplinary Research.* London: Tavistock Publications.

Hill, P. (1971) *Towards a New Philosophy of Management.* London: Grower Press.

Johnstad, T. (in prep.) 'Raufoss – from a learning company to a learning region', in B. Gustavsen, R. Ennals and B. Nyhan (eds), *Learning Together for Local Innovation – Promoting Learning Regions.* Thessaloniki: CEDEFOP.

Karlsson, L.E. (1969) *Democracy in the Workplace (Demokrati på arbetsplatsen).* Kalmar: Prisma.

Latour, B. (1998) 'From the world of science to the world of research', *Science,* 280: 208–9.

Levin, M. (ed.) (2002) *Researching Enterprise Development.* Amsterdam: John Benjamins.

Lorenz, E. and Valeyre, A. (2005) 'Organizational change in Europe: national models or the diffusion of "one best way"?'. Paper presented at CIRCLE Workshop, Lund, 14–15 September (www.circle.lu.se).

Miller, P. and Rose, N. (2001) 'The Tavistock programme: the government of subjectivity and social life', in M. Wetherell, S. Taylor and S.J. Yates (eds), *Discourse Theory and Practice.* London: Sage. pp. 364–79.

Naschold, F. (1993) 'Organization development: national programmes in the context of international competition', in F. Naschold, R. Cole, B. Gustavsen and H. van Beinum, *Constructing the New Industrial Society.* Assen: van Gorcum. pp. 3–120.

Oscarsson, B. (1997) '25 years for the renewal of working life' *(25 år för arbetslivets förnyelse).* Stockholm: Rådet för Arbetslivsforskning.

Pålshaugen, Ø. (2004) 'How to do things with words: Towards a linguistic turn in action research', *Concepts and Transformation,* 9 (2): 181–203.

Qvale, T.U. (2000) 'The development coalition as method for simultaneous development and diffusion of knowledge' (Utviklingskoalisjonen som metode for kunnskapsutvikling ogspredning i ett grep), in Ø. Pålshaugen and T.U. Qvale (eds), *Forskning for bedriftsutvikling* (Research and enterprise development). Oslo: Arbeidsforskningsinstituttet, Publikasjoner 9/2000: 149–94

Sandberg, T. (1982) *Work Organization and Autonomous Groups.* Lund: Liber.

Shotter, J. and Gustavsen, B. (1999) *The Role of Dialogue Conferences in the Development of Learning Regions: Doing from within Our Lives Together What We Cannot Do Apart.* Stockholm: Swedish Centre for Advanced Studies in Leadership, Stockholm School of Economics.

Van Beinum, H. and Van der Vliest, R. (1979) 'Q.W.L. developments in Holland: An overview', in The Quality of Working Life Council (eds) *Working for the Quality of Working Life.* Leiden: Nijhoff.

Van Ejnatten, F. (1993) *The Paradigm that Changed the Workplace.* Assen: Van Gorcum.

5

Action Research at Work: Creating the Future Following the Path from Lewin

Hilary Bradbury, Phil Mirvis, Eric Neilsen
and William Pasmore

What is the relationship between action research and organizational change and development? In this chapter we take four intersecting perspectives on this dynamic relationship, tracing the lineage from Kurt Lewin, whose contributions to action research and change in the workplace began shortly after the Second World War, through socio-technical work design, organization development programs, and appreciative inquiry, to its latest applications to sustainability and redefining the role of business in society.

Pasmore begins with a review of how Lewin's ideas informed the socio-technical school of work design. He shows how its methods emphasized the systemic study of the workplace, took account of the values, objectives, and powers of the parties involved, and stressed people's participation in defining their situations, in choosing new options, and evaluating the results – all central tenets of Lewin's formulation of action research (c.f. Bargal, 2006). Mirvis then takes up action research as applied to group dynamics and collective behavior that builds on frameworks developed originally in the study of T-Groups and in small group

change. This analysis shows how Lewinian distinctions between 'task' and 'process' activities of a group and his models of how social fields influence behavior take on new meaning when action research is extended in its scale ('getting the whole system in the room') and scope ('to effect system-wide change').

Lewin's concept of *Einstellung*, or the perceptual disposition people bring to a situation, stresses the importance of 'self-knowing' by people as they study themselves in action. This is a point of departure for Neilsen who delves into the emotional attachments of people at work and shows how new forms of intervention, chiefly appreciative inquiry, may help people to attain the sense of security and psychological safety needed to cope with massive changes launched in today's organizations.

Finally, today we experience challenges to the natural and human environment where work organizations and working people are both a partial source of and solution to what threatens the human condition. The chapter concludes with Bradbury's thoughts on the relevance of action research to issues of sustainability and global change. Here we see how, as in Lewin's time, researcher-activists are sharing knowledge and working together to face daunting societal challenges. And, as Lewin did before them, they are joining hands with leading-edge practitioners to apply scientifically-derived knowledge to practical problems and to promote a democratic, value-full, and egalitarian social order.

LEWIN'S INFLUENCE ON THE STUDY OF WORK

The story of Lewin's influence on work begins with Alex Bevalas, one of his students at the University of Iowa, who worked with Alfred Marrow's Harwood manufacturing company to conduct action research into ways to enhance job performance by having workers participate in experimental changes in work methods. The conditions they created resulted in what we would call a 'learning organization' today: workers were encouraged to experiment with different methods, to discuss them among themselves, and to choose the methods which they agreed were most effective. Groups of workers increased their own quotas after discovering and employing new methods and increased their job satisfaction as well (Marrow, 1969).

Coch and French (1948) continued experimentation at Harwood and showed how, more broadly, participation was a prime means to reduce resistance to change. They demonstrated that participative management methods, in which workers discussed changes with their supervisors, were more effective than traditional approaches to change, in which industrial engineers specified the new processes workers should use.

In his classic formulation of field theory, Lewin (1951) held that behavior is influenced by its environment, the context within which it occurs. His thinking was a challenge to Freudian psychology, the dominant paradigm at the time, which held that all behaviors could be explained by deep-seated aspects of the personality. Lewin's action research demonstrated clearly that behavior varied across time and under the influence of different environmental forces. This theory and related findings became a central tenet of what would be called the socio-technical school as well, as it allowed for the possibility that by changing aspects of the workplace, behavioral changes could be produced. It would not be necessary to change the personalities of workers in order to produce new behaviors; the potential for a wide range of behaviors, triggered by different environmental stimuli, already existed in the individual.

TAVISTOCK AND THE ORIGINS OF SOCIO-TECHNICAL SYSTEMS[1]

Eric Trist met Kurt Lewin in 1933 during Lewin's visit to Cambridge, where Trist was a student. Trist continued his studies in the United States and began his career as an applied psychologist, building on and extending Lewin's thinking with colleagues at the Tavistock Institute in London.

Following the Second World War, Lewin and Trist turned their attention to matters of national recovery. No longer supported by military funding, Trist's historical account of the early years of the Institute (Trist and Murray, 1990) makes it clear that their intellectual productivity was born of need. Trist could have joined a university faculty after the war but was perhaps influenced by Lewin in his desire to create an organization that would stand between academia and practice, acting as a bridge between the two rather than a captive of either. Tavistock would be dedicated to action research and, despite failures and miscalculations, persisted in advancing its thinking through practical experiments in organizations involving significant and pressing problems.

One early project was an observation of coal-mining practices (Trist and Bamforth, 1951). Coal was in short supply compared to national demand for its use in the post-war recovery of the industrial sector. New methods, based upon advances in above-ground industrial engineering (conveyor belts, Taylorism, job specialization), had been applied to the mines but had not yielded the results promised. Ken Bamforth, a fellow at the Institute, knew of mines that used the new technology in novel ways. Trist was interested in coal mining practices and, with the support of the British Coal Board, began detailed studies of the differences in work arrangements used in high production and low production mines. Using painstaking ethnographic methods, Trist began to formulate theories that would explain the differences in outputs he observed. Interviewing workers after hours in pubs and in their homes, he pieced together the tenets of what would later become socio-technical theory.

Briefly, the workers in the highly productive, innovative mines operated more as self-managing groups. Their leaders, when confronted with the need to employ new technology, turned to them for advice on how to implement new methods rather than following the technical advice of industrial engineers who, after all, had never worked underground and didn't know the myriad factors that made coal mining challenging and dangerous.

The miners informally devised systems that allowed them to be multi-skilled and self-directing, rather than highly specialized and dependent upon external leadership, as was the case in lower-productivity mines. The multi-skilled, self-directing arrangement made it easier for the group to adjust to circumstances as they evolved, rather than trying to apply a mechanical process to changing underground conditions. Drawing on systems thinking, Trist provided graphic evidence of how systems must possess requisite variety in order to adapt to changing external conditions (Ashby, 1960). He was also able to demonstrate that the social system and the technical system of an organization operated in an interdependent fashion.

Through his ethnographic methods, Trist deduced that the social systems in the more productive mines were more consistent with the self-image of the miners and protected them from the many dangers that accompany work underground. In contrast, in the low performance mines, workers felt alienated from their work, trapped in a system they could not influence, and constantly exposed to risks over which they had no control. The industrial engineers had failed to see that the work system itself made control impossible; that the complex technology and fragmentation of work roles had led to coordination needs that could not be met in the dark, noisy, dangerous, ever-changing underground environment. No matter how advanced the technology, it would fail in practice if not mated with a social system designed to operate the technology effectively. This principle, known as *joint optimization*, was to become the cornerstone of socio-technical systems theory:

> Inherent in the socio-technical approach is the notion that the attainment of optimum conditions in any one dimension does not necessarily result in a set of conditions optimum for the system as a whole … The optimization of the whole tends to require a less than optimum state for each separate dimension. (Trist et al., 1963)

This conclusion is classically Lewinian, in its 'emphasis on the total situation' as Bargal

(2006) notes whereby principles of behavior are 'always to be derived from the relation of the concrete individual to the concrete situation' (Lewin, 1935: 41).

SOCIO-TECHNICAL SYSTEMS THEORY

While Trist, A.K. Rice, and others were pioneering Tavistock's work in the field, Fred Emery, who joined Tavistock in 1951, was leading efforts to develop theory that could explain what the group was discovering. In 'Characteristic of Socio-Technical Systems', Emery (1959) conveyed important principles of socio-technical work design, hewn largely from the coal mining studies and weaving experiments in the group's formative years. Drawing on open systems theory, Emery explored the nature of technical systems, social systems, and the work relationship structures that bring the two systems together. Emery argued that because organizations employ whole persons, it is important to pay attention to human needs beyond those required for the routine performance of tasks dictated by the technology. His psychological requirements for individuals include: some control over the material and processes of the task; that the task itself be structured to induce forces on the individual toward aiding its completion; that the task have some variety and opportunity for learning; and that the task be interesting and meaningful.

Emery's paradigm was in violent conflict with the master/servant relationship that characterizes many workplaces. Some managers have mistaken this concern for the influence of workers in decision-making to be a veiled form of advocacy for communism. In fact, Emery was a staunch supporter of free market economies. His primary concern was with the effectiveness of work systems, not with who owned them. Emery also helped us to understand that the continued extreme fractionation of work, best represented by the assembly line, can and often does produce less than optimal results. Taking a systems perspective, Emery clarified that the fractionation of work creates an inability to control the system as a whole, rather than promoting greater control, as assumed by designers of the system. Because the system seldom operates perfectly, even small problems can create large systemic impacts. In highly fractionated work systems, the single worker is powerless to correct the situation. Each person is 'tied to the job' or machine, and cannot change the technical system to compensate for the disturbance. Instead Emery proposed that the basic unit for design of socio-technical systems must itself be a socio-technical unit and have the characteristics of an open system. By this, he meant a small (8–10 person) self-managing group of workers who, among the members of the group, possess the skills and authority to control the operation of their technology.

At a larger system level, the success of each group would depend on the linkages among the groups, and the logic of control (in this case, self-control) behind those linkages. Three principles of design emerged from this analysis (Pasmore, 1988): first, that the best design for a productive system is one in which each part of the system embodies the goals of the overall system; second, that the parts should be self-managing to the point that they can cope with problems by rearranging their own use of resources; and third, that members that make up the parts of the system are multi-skilled in ways that allow them to cope with anticipated needs to rearrange themselves around problems or opportunities that might arise.

Trist's original coal mining studies laid the foundation for socio-technical systems theory but were not true examples of action research, since Trist and his team were only observers of naturally occurring experiments rather than collaborators in their planning and evolution. The blending of action research and socio-technical systems thinking would take place in subsequent experiments in England, India, Australia, Norway, Sweden, the Netherlands, and the United

States, often under Trist's first-hand guidance or inspiration, and often undertaken by his students and followers. This, too, extends the Lewinian tradition whereby a community of researchers and practitioners develop a body of theory and shared sense of mission in the context of addressing, in this case, socio-technical problems.

LEWIN ON GROUP AND ORGANIZATION DEVELOPMENT

Kurt Lewin's formulation of action research had applications in the workplace well beyond its socio-technical design. Toward the end of his career, and particularly during his association with Douglas McGregor at MIT's Research Center for Group Dynamics, Lewin became more interested in the effects of groups on the behavior of individuals. Lewin and McGregor experimented with applications of action research to group dynamics in efforts to bring about changes in industry, educational institutions and society. One of these efforts, in connection with the Connecticut State Inter-Racial Commission, led to the founding of the NTL Institute, which continues to offer training in group dynamics following the methods of open and honest participative inquiry among members of groups developed by Lewin over 50 years ago.

The T-Group, a form of 'laboratory' education where individuals (typically 8–15) would join together in a leaderless group, proved an ideal medium for action research into the psychological processes of influence and change and, as the method developed, for self-study of these processes by participant-learners. Accordingly, he stressed the need for 'self-critical reconnaissance' on the part of people as they studied themselves in action. Later, as he observed participants struggling to understand the import of their own behavior in a training group, he said, 'One must be helped to re-examine many cherished assumptions about oneself and one's relations to others (Lewin, 1948)'.

The underlying notion was that self-study in T-groups helped to expand people's awareness of 'taken for granted assumptions' about individual and group behavior and thereby allowed them to make choices about their behavior. Indeed, some proponents likened labs to 'therapy for normals' (Weschler et al., 1962).

In the 1950s and 1960s, there were variations in labs within NTL, as well as more psycho-analytically oriented programs offered by the Tavistock Institute and a variety of encounter groups on the US west coast. There were also variations in the make-up of participants: stranger labs, family labs involving supervisors and subordinates in leaderless groups, plus laboratory education moved into organizations, including Union Carbide (Doug McGregor), Esso (Herb Shepherd), and the US State Department (Marrow, Argyris, and others).

Action research concerning group dynamics took a very practical turn in the decades that followed. Richard Beckhard (1969), as an example, developed a diagnostic model and protocol for team building and trainers began to promulgate frameworks, exercises, and instruments for human relations training in industry. Meanwhile, 'process issues' that might arise in a group were to be addressed with the aid of a facilitator or 'process consultant'. Mirvis (1988) makes the case that explorative aspects of action research ebbed during this period and it became primarily a 'technology' to improve work groups.

FROM TEAM TO COMMUNITY BUILDING

Interestingly, laboratory-type education has had a rebirth in recent years and draws on action research in new ways. M. Scott Peck (1987), as one example, developed a 'community building' process that has the same unstructured form as the T-group but involves larger numbers of people (upwards from 50 to 75) and draws from psycho-spiritual principles to frame and interpret group development.

William Isaacs (1999), in turn, drew on the work of David Bohm (1986, 1989) to propose a group conversation framework called 'dialogue' that has some similar characteristics but applies principles of quantum mechanics to group life. In these contexts, action research methods are used to deepen the capacity of individuals and the group-as-a-whole to understand itself.

Their application, however, emphasizes different behavior than in the T-Group days. For instance, drawing from the tenets of humanistic psychology in the 1950s and 1960s, many group trainers and team builders stressed the importance of dealing directly with 'here and now' behavior and regarded interpersonal feedback as integral to the 'helping' relationship. Indeed, to heighten self-awareness in training programs, people were encouraged to share their reactions to others' behavior and, in some circles, to offer interpretations. By contrast, participants in community building or dialogue groups are urged to self-reflect, and be aware of their filtering and judgments, in service of emptying oneself of what gets in the way of truly hearing another person. The idea is that by 'observing the observer' and 'listening to your listening', self-awareness of thoughts, feelings, and experiences, past and present, seep gently into consciousness.

In turn, the notion of offering Rogerian-type counseling in a group – to help people see themselves more clearly through questioning or clarifying – is discouraged in dialogue. Instead, the focus is on collective dynamics and interpretive comments, if offered at all, are aimed at the group-as-a-whole. Furthermore, the intent is not to 'work through' these dynamics by confronting them directly. Rather, the group serves as a 'container' – to hold differences and conflicts up for ongoing exploration. This keeps 'hot' conversation 'cooled' sufficiently so that people can see the 'whole' of the group mind. This facilitates development of group consciousness by counteracting tendencies toward 'splitting' in group dynamics whereby people identify with the 'good part' of their group and reject the 'bad part'.

Behind this view is a model of what some call the 'quantum universe'. From the study of particle physics, it is believed that observation of a particle influences the quantum field around it – meaning literally that observing affects the observed. David Bohm (1986, 1989), the physicist whose theories stimulated development of the dialogue process, generalized the point to human communication and gatherings. By simultaneously self-scanning and inquiring within a group, in his view, people create a connective field between observer and observed. By 'holding' this field, in turn, a group can 'contain' both energy and matter, and investigate more fully what it is producing. And in uncovering this 'tacit infrastructure' lies the possibility of creating new collective dynamics.

TRANSFORMING A COMPANY

These ideas have informed widespread experiments in developing community in the workplace (Mirvis, 1997). One of the most interesting applications concerns the Unilever's Food Business, first in Holland and later in Asia. The change program began in 1995 when Tex Gunning, then president of the business, took over the Dutch food company in financial trouble – aging plants, quality problems, eroding margins, close to being sold off. To effect a turnaround, Gunning assembled over 10,000 pallets of waste product, from various locales, into a massive warehouse. Buses arrived from three nearby factories. Managers and their cost accountants, quality experts and production workers, some 1600 employees in total, toured aisles of spoilt material, counted the massive loss of money, and contemplated the waste of their own time and talents. This evocative 'wake up' call was followed by outbursts and resentment, then analysis and confrontation, and later acknowledgment of 'what's what' and first steps toward a new way forward.

How to explain the dynamic? Ed Schein (1995), who was trained by Alex Bavelas, found Lewin's theorizing crucial in his study of attitude changes among prisoners of the chinese Communists during the Korean War:

> I found contemporary theories of attitude change to be trivial and superficial when applied to some of the profound changes that the prisoners had undergone, but I found Lewin's basic change model ... to be a theoretical foundation upon which change theory could be built solidly. The key was to see that human change ... was a profound psychological dynamic process that involved painful unlearning without loss of ego identity and difficult relearning as one cognitively attempted to restructure one's thoughts, perceptions, feelings, and attitudes

The warehouse began a painful unlearning experience for the Dutch workers. As one recalled:

> At the warehouse we were told what we were doing was not right. We got more information. We got to see the numbers. Quality problems. That was a shock for me because the people did their best and they were never told. This factory is our bread. If it goes bad with the factory, it goes bad with us.

The subsequent transformation of the company involved a unifying vision, captured in the slogan 'competing for our future'. It was implemented by a mix of 'hard' and 'soft' changes. The hard side of change involved restructuring, asset sales, and staff reductions, along with the formation of business units and the introduction of profit and loss accounting and responsibilities. On the soft side, Gunning created a community of over 120 leaders at every level of the company, and through a series of periodic gatherings – in the forests of the Ardennes, mountains of Scotland, and deserts of Jordan – led his team through multi-day dialogues for purposes of personal and organization development. An annual learning conference engaged the two thousand employees in community building as well. The results: double-digit growth and deep and lasting bonds formed within the company.

The change process was documented with an action research methodology called a 'learning history' (see Roth and Bradbury, Chapter 23 in this volume). A learning history is a means to develop and test 'action theories' about change processes in organizations. Every employee in the company, select managers in Unilever, and various suppliers and contractors contributed to the findings. It involves, in its essence, a spiraling process of data collection, feedback, and collective problem-solving, the essence of the Lewinian model of action research. The company here added the elements of a reflective retreat, in the form of a journey, and of storytelling, as a means of transforming information into action. A moving journey to Jordan that engaged leaders and employees in reflection and storytelling was an historic event in the company's timeline and carried the lessons forward with added emotional relevance (Mirvis et al., 2003).

THE SOMATIC DEVELOPMENT OF ACTION RESEARCH

Action research at the individual, group and organizational levels has been invigorated in recent years by more robust cognitive frameworks for understanding collective problem solving, by the development of routines for self-monitoring and self-reflection, by interventions that enable and encourage the integration of multiple stakeholder viewpoints, and by even further interventions of an organic nature that allow people to learn both from and through their bodies as they encounter novel settings and challenges. Yet another line of innovation can be found in recent developments in the neurophysiology of the brain, and in particular, in new insights into the role of emotions in decision-making and the importance of secure attachments both among individuals and between individuals and their organizations in promoting effective action research.

While psychologists had been studying the interplay between cognition and emotion since long before Lewin, recent developments in neurobiology have provided a more robust basis for articulating those dynamics. The neurobiologist Antonio Damasio, in his seminal work, *Descartes' Error* (1994) provided new evidence that emotions are integral to human decision-making. Patients in his studies who had suffered damage to the emotional centers of their brain were shown to be capable, for instance, of describing multiple routes from the doctor's office to their homes and of exploring the pros and cons of each, but were incapable of making a choice as to which route to take. Damasio theorized that human preferences are built up over time in part by the accumulation of somatic markers, that is, changes in body states (heart rate, muscle contractions, etc.) that accompany ongoing experience, the memories of which are also stored in the brain. As the individual encounters new events that evoke memories of old ones, the act of doing so re-engages not only the cognitive memory of them but also their associated somatic markers, and the brain reads the latter changes as feelings (Damasio, 2003). Somatic markers vary in the valence of the feelings they induce. Experiences with rewarding or adaptive outcomes generate somatic markers that produce positive feelings and encourage further engagement in similar scenarios. Those with negative outcomes generate somatic markers that produce negative feelings and encourage fight, flight or other defensive reactions to similar scenarios. Thus, new events in a person's ongoing experience constantly evoke somatic markers that remind the individual in the exquisite shorthand of feelings, and often subconsciousnessly and far more quickly than conscious reasoning, of the quality of his/her experience of similar events in the past. Those feelings in turn provide us with our preferences and priorities. To wit, 'Emotions steer the decision-making process based on the net valence of past experience' (Neilsen et al., 2005: 309).

Damasio found that not only new experience but also the very process of remembering past events or imagining new ones derived from them re-engages somatic markers. The same parts of the brain are activated regardless of the source. Moreover, he hypothesized that, for whatever reasons, when individuals experience an ongoing stream of positive somatic markers they move toward a general state of joy. Their bodily systems exhibit smooth equilibrium, flexibility, readiness for and openness to new experience and learning. By comparison, when an ongoing stream of negative somatic markers is experienced, the body reacts self-protectively, gets ready to fight or flee, is less flexible and less open to novel experience and learning. Finally, he noted that somatic markers do not control individual behavior directly. Our cognitive frameworks and reasoning skills can intervene, allowing us to put our urges and feelings in context, and in many cases to choose a more adaptive course of action than our emotions would invite.

Damasio's findings can also be combined with attachment theory (Bowlby, 1969, 1988) to generate important insights into human collaboration, because the generation of positive and negative somatic markers is integral to the formation of human relationships as well. Attachments to primary caregivers in childhood are so important from an evolutionarily adaptive viewpoint that even the temporary loss of attachment can generate powerful anxieties, i.e. negative somatic markers. Consequently, children learn to accommodate to their caregivers' styles in order to maintain their attachment to them. Caregivers who are both sensitive and instrumentally supportive equip their children with the capacity to be both sensitive and supportive to others. Those who are too wrapped up in their own emotional worlds to maintain consistent emotional sensitivity to their children induce the latter to become preoccupied with their caregivers' emotions and lose capacity to deal realistically with difficult situations on their own. Those who have survived their own upbringing by blocking their emotions induce their children to do so as well. And those who behave destructively and erratically raise children whose own capacity for attachment is driven by fear and disorganization.

While most healthy children grow up with at least some training in maintaining and enhancing secure relationships, they also are likely to have learned to use the other styles in dealing with less sensitive caregivers. Moreover, there is a growing body of research to suggest that people learn to use all four styles in their relationships with romantic partners (Bartholomew and Horowitz, 1991; West and Sheldon-Keller, 1994), other members of groups to which they belong (Eldad and Mikulincer, 2003; Mikulincer and Schaver, 2001), as well as with their organizations (Neilsen, 2005). Consistent with Lewin's premise that behavior is a product of both personality and environment, they may use different styles under different conditions at any of these system levels.

The implication for action research as an egalitarian, collective problem-solving activity rooted in interpersonally sensitive and mutually supportive dialogue is that things will go better when those involved experience secure relationships on as many levels as are relevant to the activity. Conversely, defects in the underlying quality of their relationships in the context of an action research activity can divert energy from collective thought and experimentation and turn it inward toward defensiveness and rigidity. While most students of action research have yet to integrate the implications of these ideas into their theorizing, the perspective they provide lends new insights into one of the field's more promising techniques, appreciative inquiry (Neilsen, 2005)

Appreciative inquiry (see also Cooperrider and Zandee's and Ludema and Fry's articles in this handbook for detail) was born as a reaction to the encroaching rationalization of OD technology in the 1970s and 1980s. Appreciative inquiry is touted as unleashing positive conversation and change, unseating existing reified patterns of discourse, creating space for new voices and discoveries, and expanding circles of dialogue to provide a community of support for innovative action. Traditional problem-solving approaches, by contrast, promote deficit based thinking that contains conversation, silences marginal voices, fragments relationships, erodes

community, and contributes to broad cultural and organizational enfeeblement. Quite aside from these arguments, here we want to point out the potency of the technique from a neurobiological perspective.

The multi-phase process starts with the selection of a positive topic, one that focuses on the best of what is in the organization and especially the best of what people have experienced with respect to the particular issues being addressed. The participants involved in the activity then interview each other in an appreciative manner, helping them relive the experience in the moment and articulate the conditions that allowed it to occur (Discovery). Subsequent phases involve the sharing of the interview data and the building of common visions for the future (Dream), its use as a basis of collaborative redesign (Design), and action planning to implement new organizational practices that will increase the incidence of positive experiences in the future (Destiny).

From a neurobiological standpoint, the potency of the technique comes from the likelihood that the appreciative interview process at the beginning of the intervention cycle evokes robust streams of positive somatic markers in the minds of everyone involved (Neilsen et al., 2005). That, in turn, elicits the experience of secure attachments among participants, thereby freeing their energy for mutual learning and exploration. Perhaps most important, it also increases tolerance for the discomfort that normally accompanies any redesign effort. As noted earlier in this chapter, new designs and their juxtaposition against current realities create almost inevitable tensions, often calling for actions that shift resources and reconfigure individual advantages and opportunities. Just as children in secure relationships with their caregivers are capable of sustaining momentary separations and of returning to exploratory play once their caregivers have returned (Ainsworth and Bell, 1970), organizational colleagues who have secure relationships with each other are more capable than their less secure counterparts of holding the discomfort brought on by the need to re-examine old assumptions and experiment with new perspectives and behaviors, and of moving on more quickly to create new and more consistently satisfying organizations.

While not always acknowledged explicitly, one might argue that highly effective action research activities have always attended to the need to create a positive atmosphere and establish mutually sensitive and supportive relationships either as a prelude to or concomitantly with more intellectual activities. The more recent work reported here provides an incentive to revisit past interventions for further insights into how positive somatic markers and secure relationships can be produced.

WORKING FOR THE WHOLE: OD IN THE FUTURE

From its original focus on discrete teams inside one organization, we see action research applied to work moving outside the organization to embrace the larger world that organizations affect. Newer methods engage large numbers of people, involve gatherings of people from all parts of the world, and even send people on journeys to remote parts of the world, not to mention engaging them virtually through the web or teleconferencing. This is essential as organizations and their members are grappling with a broader, global, and much more complex set of challenges and needs than ever before.

While spread across regions and time zones, additional concern for broader stakeholder engagement and satisfaction is coming to be integrated with perennial concerns about profit. We see the trend toward this broader mandate, often referred to as a concern for sustainability, among diverse companies such as Dow Chemical, Honda, HP, GE, IKEA, Toyota, Unilever and Wal-Mart, to name but a few. Naturally, some firms are rightly criticized for seeking to avoid real change, by 'greenwashing' or buffering their business from external pressures with symbolic gestures. Yet

others are finding opportunities to create new institutional forms that reflect deeply held values while simultaneously serving their shareholders.

For those companies seeking to do the right thing, however, there are many obstacles. Even after getting technology right – say in the form of hybrid energy or sustainably harvested wood – there remains the even larger issue of the cultural change required inside the organization and reverberating through its salient stakeholders. Many companies concerned with sustainability have not created the conditions for a sustainable culture.

The insights of Lewin and the socio-tech school, and the processes that build on them, such as community building and appreciative inquiry, are as relevant today as in the past. In the arena of sustainability, the application of action research to change in organizations could come to be useful for the broader world. Even as technical insight about what is required to create sustainable enterprise in a sustainable society accumulates, there has been too little attention to human, behavioral factors that support sustainable change on the massive scale required to move us from the exploitive industrial era to the possibility of sustainability. Changing behavior is rarely easy. Lewin located change inside a force-field with positive and negative forces. Launching initiatives and maintaining momentum is a great challenge.

DEVELOPING A GLOBAL COMMUNITY AT WORK

The case of Unilever is one example of a company trying to effect the behavior change necessary to support sustainability. When Tex Gunning was transferred from Holland to Asia, community building in Unilever began to span the globe. Some 250 leaders from Asia began to join with westerners in annual learning journeys aimed at creating community in the company. These were tribal gatherings in that leaders typically woke at dawn, dressed in local garb, exercised or meditated together, hiked from place-to-place, ate communally, swapped stories by the campfire, and slept alongside one another in tents. In daily experiences they might meet monks or a martial arts master, talk with local children or village elders, or simply revel in the sounds and sights of nature. Considerable time along the way was spent in personal and collective reflections.

The Asian leaders tried to 'get into the skin' of others. Shared storytelling was part of this. 'In listening to other people's stories, you hear your own story,' remarked one leader. 'Other people's stories often clarify things in your own mind – what your past is and what drives you.' Sharing such stories established bonds of mutual understanding and empathy. The leaders were urged to self-reflect in group discussion, and be aware of their filtering and judgments, in service of emptying oneself of what gets in the way of truly hearing another person. On their journeys, the leaders sometimes spoke in smaller, 15-to-20 person groups, and sometimes as a full community of 200 plus, all sitting in a circle, with everyone given the opportunity to speak, irrespective of rank or tenure. The expectation was set to speak openly and frankly, and to deal with the 'difficult issues' that would otherwise be avoided or denied. There was also space for 'process comments' – observations about how the collective is operating – and periodic moments of silence so that leaders could reflect quietly on what's been said and what they next wanted to say.

The leadership community evolved to a stage where leaders could talk about sensitive subjects, like 'saving face', and confront the assumptions and cultural values behind each others' points of views. 'Whilst there are differences in our appearance, speech and food,' said an Indian manager, 'sharing inner most feelings and fears so openly has bonded us emotionally.'

On a collective scale, the Asian leaders' journeys were consciousness-raising experiences, aimed at stimulating inquiry into leaders' personal missions and the very purpose

of their company (Mirvis and Gunning, 2006). Knowledge of and exposure to human and environmental calamities can of itself be a 'wake-up call' and stimulus to fact-finding and action. But consciousness-raising requires some internalization of the problem-at-hand and the placing of one's self psychologically into the situation (Prochaska et al., 1994).

On the journey to Sarawak, for instance, the Asian leaders experienced, firsthand, the terrible costs incurred in the clear-cutting of tropical rainforests. They first learned about the state of the natural environment through a talk by a director of a global natural resources group. Then, to get closer to the scene and symbolically lend a hand, the execs cleaned a nearby beach of industrial flotsam and tourist trash. A trip upriver in hollowed-out wooden canoes took them to the village of the Penan. There they met villagers and hunters, in tribal dress and loincloths, talked through translators to the chief, medicine man, and tribesmen, and took a long walk with them through their clear-cut forests. The reflections of one leader exemplify the impact of this experience:

> The beauty of the nature and the majesty of the place helped deepen our insights about our roles as leaders and individuals on this earth. To be in the jungles of Borneo helped us feel and see the potential in this region, almost feel and touch the vision. We were able to move from discovering self to building a mental picture about the future with a clear direction of where you want to go and where you want to be.

This, in turn, led to calls to incorporate sustainability into regional strategic plans.

The next year these leaders traveled to rural China. Here they worked side by side with manual laborers as they swept streets, herded buffaloes, formed cement building blocks. They also led schoolchildren in play. Still others repaired bicycles, built roads, cooked noodles. The business leaders met villagers in rural China whose income was less than US $125 per annum. 'Seventy per cent of our 140 million is similar to the family of the man I met today,' said a Pakistani, 'while only 5 percent has a lifestyle similar to mine. I need to respect them and to value them for who they are and what they deliver to all of us.' An Indonesian added: 'I am Asian, 40 years old, living in a country that is 80 per cent rural, but I have never planted a tree nor talked to rural people who buy our products everyday. This is critical when we aim to improve their nutrition, their health, their happiness, life and future.'

The third year's meeting in India carried the consciousness-raising deeper and further. There the leaders were formed into 25 small groups to 'self-study' communities in India – including Mother Theresa's hospital, the Dalai Lama's monastery, a Sikh temple, cloth-spinning communes, ashrams and spiritual centers, and so forth. Through reflections on their experience and collective dialogue, the Unilever leaders came to a new vision of their business. Said one: 'The communities we visited reminded me of an 'itch' that has been bugging me for the longest time, that is, to give my time and effort to a cause which is beyond myself (and even beyond my family). I have been blessed so much in this life that the least I can do is to help my fellow men. I need to act now.' In turn, collective commitments were made to pursue a worthy mission that would emphasize the healthy, nourishing aspects of food (Ayas and Mirvis, 2004). This would mean dropping several current offerings in the market. And it would lead to the launch of a children's nutrition campaign to bring affordable foods to the 'bottom of the pyramid'.

In their most recent journey to Sri Lanka, where leaders went to offer service following the devastating tsunami, the sense of collective consciousness-raising was palpable. They spent several days cleaning up debris in schools and public buildings, helping local merchants to assess inventory and connect with suppliers, playing with children, and talking deeply with Sri Lankans, individually and in large gatherings. The report of a leader about his first encounter with a tsunami survivor illustrates the depth of the experience:

'This man who had lost two of his family members told me how God has been kind to him – his neighbor had lost all of his five family members. He made me realize that there is such goodness in simple lives – where I have never bothered to look.'

What did this soulful work teach the leaders? 'We listened to the fears and hopes of the mothers, fathers, and children left behind in this beautiful but devastated country. We shed tears of pain, hope, and love,' recalled one leader. 'We shed even more tears when we realized that by simply sharing our spirit with them we made an incredible difference not only to their lives but also to our own. It continues to surprise me how care and service for others helps me discover my own love.'

It is far too early to tell how new consciousness and business models will evolve at Unilever. What is apparent is that the Lewinian example of practical experimentation and continuous interaction between researchers and practitioners has informed Gunning's leadership model and sparked a change in the way these Unilever companies do business.

TRENDS IN OD FOR THE FUTURE

Three continuing trends in ODC scholarship allow for the possibility that OD scholarship can offer much to those concerned with issues of sustainability. In this way OD can meet the largest challenge of our generation by helping to design the next industrial revolution.

- Systems thinking – working with the whole system
- Relational know-how – engaging people collectively and fully.
- Generativity – defining ourselves through what we wish to create for the future.

Systems thinking – working with the whole system. Since the 1990s, more people from more organizations have been gathering inside and across organizations in networks, partnerships and joint ventures (Crossan and Guatto, 1996). Thinking of organizing through the lens of collaborative learning suggests a learning imperative that may allow us to remain adaptive and innovative in increasingly turbulent environments. As much as collaboration is demanded, the average organizational member does not learn to develop collaboration or partnership skills along the course of the traditional Western education. There is, rather, a chasm between learning to play nicely together in kindergarten and the requisite team development skills required of really understanding and working with the 'Other', etc. OD efforts are therefore often to remediate learning.

Developments in the field of ODC have been bringing attention to how we *grow* change rather than execute change in a more mechanistic way. For example, Weick has rendered useful Heidegger's idea of 'thrownness' for scholars of change (see Boland and Callopy, 2004). The concept helps remind us that we find ourselves always, already muddling around in human systems. We cannot so easily 'freeze and unfreeze' these constantly living systems quite as much or as easily as we might pretend. As such we might help change agents think of finding opportunities for change within what is *already happening* as we keep our eye on a goal of establishing collaborative agency.

Relational know-how – engaging people collectively and fully. The tools of large group change and community building have aimed at engaging at broadening and deepening people's engagement in the change process in organizations and society. The leaders on Unilever's journeys, for example, use personal journaling and dialogue to ask: 'How am I reacting to this situation? To this person? What do my reactions tell me about my own assumptions about life and people?' Schein (2003) calls this 'listening to ourselves'. At the same time, attention also turns to imagining: 'What has this person's life been like? Why do they see things the way they do?' This is a different sort of self-listening in which the self makes inferences

about what makes others tick and how they relate to their world.

Still, in the competitive business culture it is difficult to 'lower the guard', as one Unilever leader put it. 'The initial step of sharing personal information was difficult,' he recalled, 'But once you sense the value of truly connecting, building on it seemed relatively easy.' 'The important thing is to engage in the search and the inquiry into each other's cultures and mindsets, and into the relationship we have,' said another. 'To achieve this, one has to be open with oneself, understand one's own basic core values, and accept other people's differences "as is". This acceptance needs to be sincere and from the heart; without any prejudice, judgments and expectations.'

Empathizing is central to what Erich Fromm calls the 'art of loving' (1956). It too is integral to socialization and growth. Indeed, psychologists posit that just as seeing the world through another's perspective helps people to grow beyond egocentrism, so empathizing with another is the antidote to human selfishness. Kohn (1990), among others, suggests that empathy, more so than sympathy, is the basis for the 'helping relationship'. It is this kind of relational know-how that is essential to developing deep working and personal relationships across peoples from around the world.

Generating the future. Recent developments in positive psychology (Fredrickson, 2001; Snyder and Lopez, 2002), positive organizational scholarship (Cameron et al., 2003), and appreciative inquiry (Cooperrider, 1999, see also Chapter 12) assert that efforts to understand human interaction have been overly colored by 'deficit assumptions' about human nature. It would seem timely to help bring more focus to the positive emotional elements in people's engagement and build on people's desire to be a partner in something that has meaning.

Putting together the idea of bringing the whole system to learn together, developing deeper relationships among system members, and focusing generative images for the future, a group of scholars was convened to think together about how change occurs in complex human systems. In the following we notice that the principles distilled have much in common with Lewin's original formulations.

ACTIONALIZING KNOWLEDGE: SUPPORTING SYSTEMIC CHANGE

In December 2003, a group of social scientists were invited to gather for a couple of days at Case Western Reserve University. Co-convened by the Case/Weatherhead Institute for Sustainable Enterprise and The Natural Step, a global, sustainability NGO, the goal was to think together about how change happens in complex social systems.

The group consisted mostly of professors but included representation from the World Bank, the UN and other 'think tanks'. Our purpose was to think together and develop a consensus statement. The question considered was:

> How can we fundamentally change the ways in which we live and organize work together – with all living beings and systems – so that future generations not only survive but thrive?

Over time the conversation boiled down to a handful of ideas that together allow us to say: In effective social change we:

- **address immediate needs, linking them to larger, systemic issues**
  Successful change connects single-issue efforts with the web of political, cultural, economic and environmental factors.
- **raise awareness of how social systems support and resist change**
  Successful change engages people working at multiple levels – individual, organizational, national, international, etc. – in experiencing how the status quo is maintained.
- **involve diverse people in partnering for action**
  Successful change is fueled by a mix of 'unusual' suspects – from those at the periphery of power to those closer to the center – in co-producing alternative futures.
- **elevate expectations**
  Successful change celebrates many small victories, personal learning and further action, continually building momentum to evolve the system as a whole.

- **support positive innovations**
  Successful change disturbs the status quo, encourages the natural course of innovation and supports the evolution of the system as a whole.

CONCLUSION

It has been quipped that the tradition of AR/OD is a collection of 'footnotes to Lewin' (Bradbury, 2006). Our chapter illustrates that indeed OD efforts draw strongly – if not always explicitly – on Lewin's original ideas. Lewin had survived the Holocaust and worked with a commitment to offer a path away from the slaughter of those deemed 'other'. In a field in which the relationship between knowing and doing is particularly problematized, Lewin offered a path out of the post-Cartesian split that made doing a derivative of thinking. He reconceived knowing and doing in a cyclical relationship in which the quality of one was the quality of the other. Moreover, this was but one move in his generally more holistic approach to scholarly practice in support of participative change. From this worldview and the many practices it bred – from sociotechnical design to large-scale change efforts, to appreciative inquiry to culture change in support of sustainability, to name just those that are discussed in our chapter – we see that flourishing workplaces work with these core ideas: people are understood to reside within social fields in which the role of psychological as much as physical and physiological forces are at play. Our default social condition veers more easily toward autocracy than democracy. There are always both opposing and supportive forces that must be addressed for successful change. Productivity and success ensue when the individual can help shape the social environment. Effective action requires participation of actors beyond mere conceptualization of action. These ideas remain important as we create the organizations of the future. Today our challenges are even bigger than a human holocaust – between global climate change and continuing human warfare with even smarter bombs, all life on the planet is now threatened. OD practitioners can understand that our discrete efforts are also aligned around a large systemic purpose. That purpose is the recreation of organizations to give life to a truly postmodern era of collaboration and the possibility that life may indeed flourish on this planet for future generations yet unconsidered.

NOTE

1 Readers are also directed to William Pasmore's Chapter 3 in the first edition of the *Handbook of Action Research* that deals in more detail with the socio-technical tradition.

REFERENCES

Ainsworth, M.D.S. and Bell, S.M. (1970) 'Attachment, exploration and separation illustrated by the behavior of one-year-olds in a strange situation', *Child Development*, 41: 49–67.

Ashby, W. (1960) *Design for a Brain*. New York: Wiley & Sons.

Ayas, K. and Mirvis, P.H. (2004) 'Bringing "mission" to life: Corporate inspiration from Indian communities', *Reflections*, 5 (10): 1–12.

Bargal, D. (2006) 'Personal and Intellectual Influences Leading to Lewin's Paradigm of Action Research. Towards the 60th Anniversary of Lewin's Action Research and Minority Problems (1946)', *Action Research*, 4 (4): 367–88.

Bartholomew, K. and Horowitz, L.M. (1991) 'Attachment styles among young adults: a test of a four category model', *Journal of Personality and Social Psychology*, 61: 226–44.

Beckhard, R. (1969) *Organization Development: Strategies and Models*. Reading, MA: Addison-Wesley.

Bohm, D. (1986) *Wholeness and the Implicate Order*. London: Ark.

Bohm, D. (1989) 'On Dialogue', David Bohm Seminars, Ojai, CA.

Boland, R.J. and Collopy, F. (eds) (2004) *Managing as Designing*. Stanford, CA: Stanford University Press.

Bowlby, J. (1969) *Attachment*. London: Penguin.

Bowlby, J. (1988) *A Secure Base: Parent–Child Attachment and Healthy Human Development*. New York: Basic Books.

Bradbury, H. (2006) 'Editorial', *Action Research*, 4 (4): 363–5.

Cameron, K.S., Dutton, J.E. and Quinn, R.E. (eds) (2003) *Positive Organizational Scholarship: Foundations of a New Discipline*. San Francisco, CA: Berrett-Koehler.

Coch, L. and French, J. (1948) 'Overcoming resistance to change', *Human Relations*, 1: 512–32.

Cooperrider, D.L. (1999) 'Positive image, positive action: the affirming basis of organizing', in S. Srivastva and D.L. Cooperrider (eds), *Appreciative Management and Leadership*. Euclid, OH: Williams Custom Publishing. pp. 91–125.

Crossan, M.M, and Guatto, T. (1996) 'Organizational learning research profile', *Journal of Organizational Change Management*, 9 (1): 107–12.

Damasio, A. (1994) *Descartes' Error*. New York: Harcourt.

Damasio, A. (2003) *Looking for Spinoza*. New York: Harcourt.

Eldad, Rom and Mikulincer, Mario (2003) 'Attachment theory and group process: the association between attachment style and group-related representations, goals, memories and functions', *Journal of Personality and Social Psychology*, 84 (6): 1220–35.

Emery, F. (1959) *Characteristics of Socio-technical Systems (Doc. 527)*. London: Tavistock Institute.

Fredrickson, B.L. (2001) 'The role of positive emotions in positive psychology: the broaden-and-build theory of positive emotions', *American Psychologist*, 56 (3): 218–26.

Fromm, E. (1956) *The Art of Loving*. New York: Harper & Row.

Isaacs, W. (1999) *Dialogue and the Art of Thinking Together: A Pioneering Approach to Communicating in Business and Life*. New York: Doubleday.

Kohn, A. (1990) *The Brighter Side of Human Nature: Altruism and Empathy in Everyday Life*. New York: Basic Books.

Lewin, K. (1935) *A Dynamic Theory of Personality*. New York: McGraw-Hill.

Lewin, K. (1936) *Principles of Topological Psychology*. New York: McGraw-Hill.

Lewin, K. (1948) *Resolving Social Conflicts: Selected Papers on Group Dynamics*. New York: Harper & Row.

Lewin, K. (1951) *Field Theory in Social Science: Selected Theoretical Papers*. New York: Harper & Row

Marrow, A. (1969) *The Practical Theorist*. New York: Basic Books.

Mikulincer, Mario and Shaver, Phillip R. (2001) 'Attachment theory and intergroup bias: evidence that priming the secure base schema attenuates negative reactions to out-groups', *Journal of Personality and Social Psychology*, 81 (1): 97–115.

Mirvis, P.H. (1988) 'Organization development: Part I – An evolutionary perspective', in R.W. Woodman and

W.A. Pasmore (eds), *Research in Organizational Change and Development, Vol. 2.* Greenwich, CT: JAI Press. pp. 1–58.

Mirvis, P.H. (1997) '"Soul work" in organizations', *Organization Science,* 8 (2): 193–206.

Mirvis, P.H. and Gunning, W.L. (2006) 'Creating a community of leaders', *Organizational Dynamics,* 35 (1): 69–82.

Mirvis, P.H., Ayas, K. and Roth, G. (2003) *To the Desert and Back: The Story of One of the Most Dramatic Business Transformation on Record.* San Francisco, CA: Jossey-Bass.

Murray, H. (1990) *The Transformation of Selection Procedures: The War Office Selection Boards.* Philadelphia, PA: University of Pennsylvania Press.

Neilsen, Eric. H. (2005) 'Using attachment theory to compare traditional action research with appreciative inquiry', Proceedings of the 65th Annual Academy of Management Meeting, Academy of Management Best Conference Paper: ODC E1-6, Academy of Management.

Neilsen, Eric H., Winter, Mary and Saatcioglu, Argun (2005) 'Building a learning community by aligning cognition and affect within and across members', *Journal of Management Education,* 29 (2): 301–18.

Pasmore, W. (1988) *Designing Effective Organizations: The Sociotechnical Systems Perspective.* New York: Wiley & Sons.

Peck, M.S. (1987) *The Different Drum: Community Making and Peace.* New York: Simon & Schuster.

Prochaska, J.O., Norcross, J.C. and DiClemente, C.C. (1994) *Changing for Good.* New York: William Morrow.

Rice, A. (1958) *Productivity and Social Organization: The Ahmedabad Experiment.* London: Tavistock Publications.

Rom, E. and Mikulincer, M. (2003) 'Attachment theory and group processes: the association between attachment style and group-related representations, goals, memories, and functioning', *Journal of Personality and Social Psychology,* June 84 (6): 1220–35.

Schein, E.H. (1995) 'Kurt Lewin's change theory in the field and in the classroom: notes toward a model of managed learning.' www.solonline.edu.

Schein, E.H. (2003) 'On dialogue, culture, and organization learning', *Reflections,* 4 (4): 27–38.

Snyder, C.R. and Lopez, S.J. (2002) *Handbook of Positive Psychology.* New York: Oxford University Press.

Trist, E. and Bamforth, K. (1951) 'Some social and psychological consequences of the longwall method of coal-getting', *Human Relations,* 4: 3–38.

Trist, E. and Murray, H. (1990) *Historical Overview: The Foundation and Development of the Tavistock Institute.* Philadelphia, PA: University of Pennsylvania Press.

Trist, E., Higgin, G., Murray, H. and Pollock, A. (1963) *Organizational Choice: Capabilities of Groups at the Coal Face Under Changing Technologies: the Loss, Re-discovery & Transformation of a Work Tradition.* London: Tavistock Publications.

Weick, K. (2004) 'Designing for thrownness', in R.J. Boland and F. Callopy (eds), *Managing as Designing.* Standford, CA: Standford University Press.

Weschler, I., Massarik, R. and Tannenbaum, R. (1962) 'The self in process: a sensitivity training emphasis', in I. Weschler and E. Schein (eds), *Issues in Human Relations Training.* (Selected Readings, No. 5). Washington, DC: NTL. pp. 33–46.

West, M.L. and Sheldon-Keller, A.E. (1994) *Patterns of Relating: an Adult Attachment Perspective.* New York: Guilford Press.

6

Continuing the Journey: Articulating Dimensions of Feminist Participatory Action Research (FPAR)

Colleen Reid and Wendy Frisby

The primary aim of this chapter is to begin to articulate dimensions of feminist participatory action research (FPAR). In developing the dimensions, we considered the following questions: What are the advantages of integrating feminist research, participatory action research, and action research into a FPAR framework? What epistemological and methodological dimensions should be integrated into FPAR? What questions could those involved in FPAR ask themselves to continually refine and advance how they go about conducting this type of research? We begin the chapter by providing a brief overview of recent developments in feminist research. In some depth and with the aid of guiding questions, we then articulate the dimensions of FPAR that are, in part, based on our experiences. They include: (1) centering gender and women's experiences while challenging patriarchy; (2) accounting for intersectionality; (3) honoring voice and difference through participatory research processes; (4) exploring new forms of representation; (5) reflexivity; and (6) honoring many forms of action.

With the emergence of social movements such as the women's movement and the peace movement, new and different forms of activism have arisen (Ledwith and Asgill, 2000). The ideals of social critique, emancipation, and collective action that characterize these movements have also filtered into the academy and various approaches to research.

Feminist research (FR), participatory action research (PAR), and action research (AR) are critical approaches that focus on democratizing the research process, acknowledging lived experiences, and contributing to social justice agendas to counter prevailing ideologies and power relations that are deeply gendered, classed, and racialized. FR, PAR and

AR have been critical of the academy's control over knowledge generation practices and have struggled with straddling the community/academy divide (Chrisp, 2004; Lykes and Coquillon, 2006).

We argue that FR, PAR and AR are three research traditions that share some mutual goals and ongoing dialogue could create synergies between them, while addressing their respective oversights and limitations. Traditionally, PAR and AR researchers have seldom seen the need to focus on how gender shapes the construction of identities, behavior, and social relations, in part, because they believed women were included in generic terms like 'the community' or 'the oppressed' (Maguire, 1987). While PAR and AR are increasingly engaging marginalized women, rarely are feminist analyses or gender relations fully considered and women's activities are sometimes trivialized, ignored, misrepresented, or homogenized (Mohanty, 2003; Reinharz, 1992). FR, on the other hand, despite espousing action and social change agendas, has been slower in articulating specific strategies that can contribute to activist agendas (Naples, 2003). Since feminism and women's studies became instituted in the academy, the growth and development of highly theorized forms of feminism has, in some cases, distanced feminist goals of social change from marginalized groups who feminists initially set out to hear from and serve. As a result, 'many action-oriented feminist researchers have been frustrated by the lack of an articulated framework for translating feminist insights into concrete actions aimed at achieving social change' (Maguire et al., 2004: xii).

We believe that FR, PAR and AR researchers would be mutually well served if they became allies. As a result, we are calling for feminist participatory action research (FPAR) approaches that build on the strengths and overcome the limitations of these three research traditions. Not only are they more powerful as a larger and connected community, but epistemologically and methodologically they serve to buttress one another

(Maguire, 2001/2006; Brydon-Miller and Wadsworth, 2004; Greenwood, 2004; Lykes and Coquillon, 2006). Feminism's theoretical and epistemological debates, while honoring the agency and lived experience of women as it is historically and culturally situated, can serve to strengthen PAR and AR's ability to understand its communities and the implications of an action orientation (Reid et al., 2006). Likewise, participatory and action research, with its deliberate and long-standing tradition of advocating action towards social change, can help feminist researchers move out of the academic armchair by engaging in more transformative research that better serves women's diverse communities (Meyerson and Kolb, 2000).

The primary aim of this chapter is to begin to articulate dimensions of FPAR. In developing the dimensions, we considered the following three questions: What are the advantages of integrating FR, PAR and AR into a FPAR framework? What epistemological and methodological dimensions should be integrated into FPAR? What questions could those involved in FPAR ask themselves to continually refine and advance how they go about conducting this type of research? While we hope that this articulation becomes a conversation between diverse community members, practitioners, and researchers, we acknowledge that we write from within the academy and are linking FPAR's dimensions to theoretical and methodological debates that at times use complex and specialized language. Our aim in including 'guiding questions' is to make the framework more accessible and open to critique and revision given the unique aspects of different FPAR projects.

We identify ourselves as feminist participatory action researchers, located in the academy, who strive to conduct research towards social justice. We share many privileges as we are both white, heterosexual, married mothers from middle-class backgrounds who are well educated, able-bodied, and employed in Canada. At the same time, we have shared the challenges, difficulties, and rewards of engaging in FPAR projects for over seven years with diverse women on low income in political, academic, and community environments that are sometimes hostile towards this type of research. Before articulating the dimensions of FPAR that are, in part, based on our experiences, we provide a very brief overview of recent developments in FR to frame our discussion.

DEVELOPMENTS IN FEMINIST RESEARCH (FR)

While there has never been a fixed view on gender oppression, a unified vision of women's liberation, or a common approach to knowledge production, different approaches to FR share a concern for understanding the myriad of ways that gender impacts women's lives, conducting research that is politically and ethically accountable, and transforming unjust power relations. For Ramazanoglu and Holland (2002: 16), what makes the growing array of feminist methodologies distinctive 'is the extent to which they are shaped by feminist theories, politics, and ethics, while being grounded in diverse women's experiences'. The dramatic growth in feminist theoretical positions, methodological stances, and research strategies is viewed as 'a healthy sign of the vitality of feminist studies' (Fonow and Cook, 2005: 2213). Researchers are now working across epistemologies and methods to theorize how gender intersects with race, nation, sexuality, class, physical ability, and other markers of difference in more complex ways (McCall, 2005). Postcolonial theories, queer theories, and critical race theories represent just a few of the more recent theoretical developments that are raising new questions about how gender relations are constructed, sustained, and resisted (Harding and Norberg, 2005; Mohanty, 2003). Ramazanoglu and Holland (2002: 19) agree that FR is challenging conventional approaches to research, grappling with postmodern thought, and articulating

differences between women in largely productive ways, although many gaps and silences remain. The problem with feminist inspired PAR and AR is that theoretical stances are not often clearly identified, nor do such projects always set out to build or extend existing feminist theory.

A significant challenge for FR has been the development of methodologies for studying multiple forms of marginalization. Intersectional theory is based on the idea that 'different dimensions of social life cannot be separated into discrete or pure strands' (Brah and Phoenix, 2004: 76). It suggests that we need to move beyond seeing ourselves and others as single points in some specified set of dichotomies, male or female, white or black, straight or gay, scholar or activist, powerful or powerless (McCall, 2005). Rather, 'we need to imagine ourselves as existing at the intersection of multiple identities, all of which influence one another and together shape our continually changing experience and interactions' (Brydon-Miller, 2004: 9).

With increased calls for participatory research designs, more attention is being paid to the importance of insider-outsider roles and remaining reflexive about each other's social positioning, how this shifts over time and possibly confounds knowledge generation and plans for collective action (Lykes and Coquillon, 2006; Reid, 2004a; Reinharz, 1992). Some feminist researchers have explored the unique challenges and opportunities of conducting research with women in interpersonal and relational frameworks, with some arguing it is necessary to create close relations, while others warn of the risks of building trust, rapport, and disclosure with participants (Cotterill, 1992; Finch, 1993; Williams and Lykes, 2003). For example, Yoshihama and Carr (2002: 100) discussed the tensions around participation in FPAR for Hmong women in a male-dominated social order, as the women became vulnerable to criticism and rejection from their own families and neighbors because the topic of violence was not welcomed by the community. This illustrates why reflexivity and developing non-colonial research practices are so central (Tuhiwai Smith, 2005). What remains unclear is the extent to which FR researchers are aware of the growing number of FPAR studies that are drawing and building upon the participatory and action tenets of PAR and AR.

Nonetheless, FR continues to grapple with who is privileged epistemologically and how this affects the representation of voices and the interpretations of findings. Questions about how and who can speak for women of colour, lesbians, working-class women and postcolonials, for example, continue to be pivotal in helping feminists clarify the links between theory, method, and action (Fonow and Cook, 2005). Feminists agree that there is a need to develop a range of research methods that address diversity and divergence as well as commonalities in women's lives (Olesen, 2005), and experimentation with novel data collection techniques is important (Lykes in collaboration with the Association of Maya Ixil Women, 2001/ 2006). Exploring different methods of representation can help cut across difference to understand the contextualities of women's experiences of discrimination, prejudice, and disadvantage and how they are located in their particular social, economic, political, and cultural contexts (hooks, 1990; Mohanty, 2003; Reinharz, 1992; Wolf, 1996).

Despite a commitment to action-oriented research, FR have been slower to articulate specific strategies that can contribute to such agendas (Cancian, 1992; Naples, 2003). Possibly, those who are most marginalized have questioned the relevance and utility of the Western feminist movement and feminist theory and have identified with other social movements that are more directly action-oriented. Yet Harding and Norberg (2005: 2010) point out that social change has occurred due to 'politically engaged research on violence against women, on women's double day of work, and on the costs to men of maintaining norms of masculinity'. In these ways, feminist researchers can use their power to affect social policy, but FPAR argues that this can be enhanced through collective action with women who are the intended beneficiaries of action. For example, Wang, Burris and Ping (1996) used a photo novella methodology so rural Chinese women who could not read or write could inform policy makers about their lives and health needs. Three policy outcomes represented action arising from this study that challenged patriarchy through the provision of daycare, midwives, and education for girls.

By naming and mapping out initial dimensions of FPAR below, we hope to encourage stronger links between FR, PAR and AR because there is a recognition that 'existing systems of conducting and evaluating research must be reframed if our scholarship is to be consistent with the values we espouse' (Maguire et al., 2004: xvi).

TRAVELING NEW VISTAS: PROPOSING DIMENSIONS OF FPAR

From the outset we caution that we are not calling for an idealized set of FPAR dimensions that are impossible to achieve. We have seen researchers discount their work because it did not fully engage women in all phases of research, for example (Frisby et al., 2005). Rather, we hope to acknowledge different types and levels of FPAR. By presenting these highly interrelated dimensions, researchers may be able to reflect upon and evaluate FPAR projects as they are initiated, unfold, and are either sustained, disbanded, or partially completed. We do not present these dimensions definitively; rather, we invite others to critique, modify, connect, and extend them. We envision that each new attempt can open up new possibilities for engaging in more reflexive, collaborative, and transformative FPAR. The guiding questions are not meant to be asked only at the beginning of FPAR; they can be re-visited as projects unfold and are evaluated.

Centering Gender and Women's Diverse Experiences While Challenging Forms of Patriarchy

Gender and women's experiences are central to FPAR in several ways – in understanding how different forms of patriarchy create domination and resistance, in identifying key issues for research, and in giving explicit attention to how women and men, and those who do not identify with either of these binary gendered categories, benefit from action-oriented research (or not). Smith (1992, 1997) draws attention to how social relations are embedded and embodied in women's everyday activities, and how rendering them visible can become a starting point for political action. Our own research showed how some Canadian women living in poverty internalized oppression and sometimes saw themselves as being responsible for their own situations. When they engaged in dialogue with other women through a FPAR process, they more fully questioned how their everyday lives were tied to patterns of subordination within their families, workplaces, communities, and society at large, but their interpretations and plans for action differed depending on their age, family situations, ethnicity, and a number of other factors (Frisby et al., 2006; Reid, 2004a).

Such an analysis involves defying 'patriarchal truths' that women are naturally inferior to men and considering how women generally live in different material and social circumstances due to gendered power relations and globalization (Hartsock, 1983; Ramazanoglu and Holland, 2002). Mohanty (2003) argues that patriarchy and gender should not be treated as universal constructs and judged by Western standards, because such analyses often situate non-Western women as inferior powerless victims who lack agency to interpret, resist, and subvert the contexts shaping their lives in different ways. For example, Barazangi (2004) discusses how some academic feminists have dismissed Muslim women's views as 'religious' and considered the prevailing Muslim males' interpretations as representative of Islamic views on gender. Ignoring different constructions of patriarchy and gender as they are historically and culturally constituted will make it more difficult to develop strategic coalitions across difference (Ledwith and Asgill, 2000; Mohanty, 2003). Therefore, we argue that focusing on women's divergent daily experiences as embedded in larger relations of power should be a starting point in FPAR endeavors.

Guiding questions:

- What issues are of central concern to girls and women participating in FPAR projects and how are these issues tied to their everyday experiences?
- How are experiences tied to gendered, classed, and racialized power relations?
- What is the larger historical, cultural and political context that the study is situated within and what are the implications for the research?
- How will experiences with the issues identified be uncovered, interpreted, and collectively analyzed?
- How do experiences vary and what accounts for this?
- What forms of patriarchy exist and how do they shape/challenge researcher/participant worldviews?
- Could challenges to dominant patriarchal norms put participants and/or researchers or others at risk How will we know this, and what strategies will be used negotiate risk?

Accounting for Intersectionality

Feminists have argued that additive and interlocking conceptualizations of oppression have inadequately captured women's experiences and that intersectional analyses can be productively advanced by adopting a FPAR framework. A first step towards grappling with the sophisticated analyses of women's intersectionalities is to foster and support sustained, deliberate, and open dialogue with research participants and ourselves. While Ledwith and Asgill (2000) do not explicitly label their approach as FPAR, they do offer a model to help create alliances across difference based on respect for persons who are different, but whose interests in social justice are similar. Brydon-Miller, Maguire and McIntyre (2004) and Lykes and Coquillon (2006) provide examples of studies at the interstice of FPAR, FR, PAR, and AR that have problematized how power shapes and is shaped across these intersections and how crucial such analyses are for understanding the complexities of women's lives and conceptualizing meaningful possibilities for activism and social change.

Exploring these tensions 'can help reveal privilege, especially when we remember that the intersection is multidimensional and not fixed, including intersections of both subordination and privilege' (Wildman and Davis, 1996; cited in Brydon-Miller, 2004: 9). Affirming, attending to, and authorizing the voice of the oppressed is dependent on our ability to realize our own First-World researcher roles as oppressors (Brabeck, 2004). Through open dialogues with both our participants and ourselves, we can begin to understand the nature of oppression, domination, and exploitation as they intersect and interrelate with gender, race, class and other forms of advantage and disadvantage.

Guiding questions:

- How can intersectionality be considered and what complexities and tensions could this create?
- How does intersectionality shape identities, experiences, and relationships; and how does this shift over time?
- What non-colonial collaborative processes are in place to build relations and work across differences in gender, class, race, culture, sexuality, ablebodiedness and other markers of difference?
- How will intersectionality be taken into account when deciding on research questions, collecting and analyzing data, and deciding upon action plans?

Honoring Voice and Difference Through Participatory Research Processes

FPAR is an approach to producing knowledge through democratic interactive relationships that are committed to making diverse women's voices more audible by facilitating their empowerment through 'ordinary talk' (Maguire, 2001/2006). The aim is to connect the articulated and contextualized personal with the often hidden or invisible structural and social institutions that define and shape our lives. This can foster the development of strategies and programs based on real life experiences rather than theories or assumptions, providing an analysis of issues based on a description of how women actually hope to transcend problems encountered (Barnsley and Ellis, 1992).

However, in their poststructuralist critique, Cooke and Kothari (2001) argue that participatory approaches can impose rather than alleviate entrenched power relations, especially if communities are wrongly assumed to be homogeneous. They argue further that local knowledge has been romanticized through participatory approaches that leave broader exclusionary processes and institutions unchanged. Kesby (2005) counters that while participation is infused with power relations, it can be maneuvered to challenge more domineering and destructive forms of power.

> Power is not concentrated; nor is it a commodity to be held, seized, divided, or distributed by individuals. It is a much more decentered and ubiquitous force acting everywhere because it comes from everywhere. ... Neither is power inherently negative, limiting, or repressive; rather it is inherently productive of actions, effects, and subjects, even when most oppressive. (Kesby, 2005: 2040)

Like PAR, FPAR researchers argue for participatory strategies that involve participants in the design, implementation, and analysis of the research that can be deepened through collective dialogue, even though this can be fraught with conflict and challenges (Frisby et al., 2005; Naples, 2003). Collins (1990) suggests that wisdom is derived not necessarily from having lived through an Other's experiences, but from having engaged in an empathetic centerless dialogue with an Other in which the power dynamics are fluid. FPAR researchers hold a great responsibility in seeking the means through which the subaltern can find voice and can be empowered to represent her own interests (Brydon-Miller, 2004).

Participatory approaches include the co-generation of the research questions themselves, but these attempts often fall short of creating genuinely inclusive, safe, and unbiased spaces of relevance for people who live on the 'margins' of society. This helps to explain why FPAR is sometimes rejected by the very people whose lives it tries to explain (Barazangi, 2004; Reinharz, 1992). Yet, the feminist ideals of using participatory research techniques to give voice to people's experience and create change by focusing on action aimed at social transformation have not been fully realized. According to Maguire (1987: 35), how knowledge is created and who retains control over the knowledge generation and dissemination 'remains one of the weakest links in feminist research'.

Guiding questions:

- Who is and is not participating in FPAR projects, how are they participating, and what are the consequences?
- How will the voices and experiences of women in relation to broader structural conditions be heard?
- How will research questions be decided upon and who sees them as being relevant?
- What opportunities will women have to participate in all phases of research?
- Could participation put too much of a burden on some participants and how will we know and account for this?
- Is attention being given to barriers to participation (e.g. childcare, transportation, language, inscribed gender roles)?
- What sources of conflict, power imbalances, and silences are emerging and how will these be anticipated and dealt with?

Exploring New Forms of Representation

A related FPAR dimension is exploring new ways of representing data by testing the boundaries of prescribed ways of conducting research (Hertz, 1996). FPAR researchers have challenged, pushed, explored, and disrupted boundaries that have traditionally been set up by researchers and the researched (Edwards and Ribbens, 1998). They 'continue to seek authentic ways in which the subaltern may articulate her experience and speak on her own behalf in ways that can be heard and understood by members of the dominant culture' (Brydon-Miller, 2004: 12–13). Yet tensions are inherent in representing women's voices and experiences because questions are continually raised about 'who has the authority to represent women's voices and to what end', 'what forms of the representation will best capture the dynamics involved', 'who decides whether they are credible', and 'do representations reinscribe rather than transcend dominant power relations?'. As Lather indicates below, it is necessary to grapple with such tensions to continue to uncover counter-practices for less exploitative and more creative ways of collecting, interpreting, and communicating research findings.

> The necessary tension between the desire to know and the limits of representation lets us question the authority of the investigating subject without paralysis, transforming conditions of impossibility into possibility, where a failed account occasions new kinds of positionings. Such a move is about economies of responsibility within non-innocent space, a 'within/against' location. (Lather, 2001: 204)

Diaries and journals; dialogic and interactive interview formats; participatory workshops; poetry, photography, film and art; practices such as co-writing are just some examples of 'counter-practices' being explored in FPAR projects (Brabeck, 2004; Frisby et al., 2005; Lather, 2001; McIntyre and Lykes, 2004; Reid, 2004a; Wang et al., 1996; Williams and Lykes, 2003; also see Fine and Torre (Chapter 27), Chui (Chapter 34), and Chowns (Chapter 39) in this volume). Yet, 'we must trouble any claims to accurate representation to raise new possibilities for knowing and for what is knowable' (Fonow and Cook, 2005: 2222), and we cannot assume that women will want to collaborate and co-construct representations of their lives (Brueggemann, 1996: 19).

While such representations will always be shifting, partial, and contested, working with women to explore the advantages and risks of alternative ways of co-producing knowledge is a key consideration in any FPAR project.

Guiding questions:

- What forms of representation of subaltern and other voices are being explored?
- Who has authority over representation and how was this determined?
- How will data be collected, interpreted, analyzed, and communicated?
- What advantages and challenges are posed through this exploration?
- How might these new forms be received or resisted in the community, the policy arena, and in the academy?
- How are forms of representation connected to action plans?

Reflexivity

Considering the previous FPAR dimensions implicates the role of researchers whether they are from within the academy or not. It is widely agreed that reflexivity is a principle of good FR practice, but what it means and how it can be achieved is more difficult to pin down (Coleman and Rippin, 2000; Edwards and Ribbens, 1998; Fonow and Cook, 1991; Hertz, 1996; Lather, 1991; Reay, 1996; Rose, 2001). Generally, reflexivity means attempting to make explicit the power relations and the exercise of power in the research process. It involves critical reflection on a number of levels: the identification of power relationships and their effects in the research process; the ethical judgments that frame the research and mark the limits of shared values and political interests; and accountability for the knowledge that is produced (Ramazanoglu and Holland, 2002: 118–19). Feminist action researchers are expected to be transparent and attentive to the methodological, epistemological, and political influences, contradictions, and complexities in all stages of research (Ristock and Pennell, 1996). Reflexivity has also come to mean the

way researchers engage in self criticism and consciously write themselves into the text (Brabeck, 2004; Lykes and Coquillon, 2006). At its core, reflexivity is about reflecting on power, a researcher's power to perceive, interpret, and communicate about their research participants (Frisby, 2006; Frisby et al., 2005; Reid, 2004a, 2004b).

Feminist action researchers, with their explicit commitment to participatory research processes and meaningful engagement with research participants, question deeply their power and positions in the research process. Thus feminist action researchers are placed at the edges between public knowledge and private lived experiences. This 'liminal' position not only applies to the research process and product, but also concerns researchers personally in their own lived experiences (Reid, 2004a). Fine (1994) refers to the liminal position as the 'hyphen.' When we opt to engage in social struggles with those who have been exploited and subjugated we work the hyphen, revealing more about ourselves, and far more about oppression and discrimination. By working the hyphen, researchers probe how we are in relation to Others, understanding that we are all multiple in those relations.

Questioning 'chosen silences' as control mechanisms is central in FPAR (Chataway, 1997). Paradoxically, efforts at working reflexively may in fact perpetuate silences and thwart feminist efforts at the authentic representation of both ourselves and our research participants (Reid, 2004a). As women and men engaged in research for social change, it has been much harder to recognize the times that we have ourselves held power over others and possibly used our power in disempowering ways. As white middle-class and educated researchers, for instance, it is essential for us to engage in self-education about our own privilege and to co-create conditions for anti-racist work in order to be able to engage in more equitable dialogue with participants of colour.

FPAR researchers require a great deal of humility, patience, and reflexive dialogue between themselves and their participants so they can learn from their failures and partial successes (Williams and Lykes, 2003). By working through the struggles of developing relationships, FPAR researchers can learn the significance of tolerance, acceptance, and humility in the development of reciprocal relationships (McIntyre and Lykes, 2004). Maguire (2004) refers to this as 'shared vulnerability', a willingness to examine deeply held beliefs and to try new ways of thinking about gender, sexism, racism, heteronormativity, and oppression to explore new ways of being FPAR researchers. From this perspective, the beginning of the journey begins from within (Maguire, 2004). FPAR researchers are in a position to develop truly reflexive texts that leave both the author and the reader vulnerable, so they must think carefully about the intended and unintended consequences of their research (Reid, 2004a). Yet with the importance of being self-critical we cannot just 'write ourselves into the text'; we must also write ourselves into action and activism and use our self-reflections to generate actions of self-discovery within the research process (Reid et al., in press). This can become a resource to account for power imbalances while also facilitating and possibly transforming them.

Guiding questions:

- What are the intended and possible unintended consequences of the research?
- What are the power relations within and surrounding the project and what steps are being taken to level imbalances and mobilize power?
- What ethical issues are framing the research and its representation?
- Who owns the research, how will it be produced, communicated, and acted upon?
- How are the researchers accounting for their own social location and insider/outsider status?
- What emotions and struggles are being encountered in building relationships?

Honoring Many Forms of Action

FPAR projects need to seek clarity about the emancipatory goals for their research while articulating how they understand action, which is a dynamic process. What actions are desired is based on one's social, economic, and political situations and it can occur at both individual and collective levels (Reid et al., in press). People with problems figure out what to do by first finding out the causes and then acting on insight (Park, 2001/2006). Reinharz (1992) contends that the act of obtaining knowledge creates the potential for change, because the paucity of research about women accentuates and perpetuates their powerlessness, even though they have agency. It is through action that we learn how the world works, what we can do, and who we are – we learn with heart and mind – and this is how we can become aware and emancipated. Action is an integral part of reflexive knowledge, and can be conceptualized as speaking, or attempting to speak, to validate oneself and one's experiences and understandings in and of the world (Gordon, 2001/2006). However, in some FPAR studies it is not always clear what action was taken, by whom, what effect the action had, and how all of this was interpreted by different participants over time and space. Above all, we want to prevent situations where it is privileged researchers who benefit most by publishing the work.

Intersectional theory suggests that agency, or taking action, is complex and that women consent to, resist, and reshape social relations of power within a complex matrix of domination and subordination. Although FPAR no longer seeks single consciousness-raising events that will inspire all women to action, they increasingly recognize that examining and enacting action is a fruitful avenue for theory and praxis (Fonow and Cook, 2005). Fraser and Naples (2004) suggest that straddling the more conceptual feminist world with the action-oriented AR world, while being unified in similar visions and goals, can be simultaneously theoretical and engaged:

We all know of the theoretical work that, however brilliant, is so abstract and disengaged that it surrenders the capacity to illuminate political practice. But the reverse is equally problematic; when scholarship is too immediately political, too myopically focused on practical application, it loses the capacity to pose questions about the big picture. The trick, of course, is to keep both concerns simultaneously in view – but in such a way that avoids subordinating one to the other, and so preserves the integrity of each. (Fraser and Naples, 2004: 1106–7).

Another critical consideration is whether individual and local actions eventually link up to a larger social change agenda. What this should look like and what steps could be taken to accomplish this are seldom clear.

Guiding questions:

- What are the emancipatory goals associated with the project and how are these being decided upon?
- What forms of action/in-action were being taken before the project began?
- What different forms of action are (or could be) taken and by whom?
- What forms of action were unrealized but may be taken in the future?
- Who is benefiting (or not) from the actions being taken?
- Are the actions contradictory or being resisted or too risky/difficult to implement and what are the implications of this?
- Do the actions contribute to a larger social change agenda, and what steps could be taken to accomplish this, if desired?

CONCLUSION

As FPAR researchers we draw strength in continuing the journey towards linking FR, PAR and AR. These research traditions complement one another as approaches that are liberating, transformative, and that can, if we act with care and honesty, contribute to new ways of relating, new ways of constructing knowledge, new ways of confronting privilege, new criteria for what is valued in society, and new directions for implementing research processes that lead to social justice (McIntyre, 2000). Maguire (2004) contends that it remains impossible for PAR and AR to be transformative approaches to knowledge creation until more is learnt about feminism, with all its diversity. This involves critically examining their own multiple identities and

implications for their work, and incorporating feminist voices and visions (Maguire, 2004). Indeed, the most reasonable response to overcoming marginalization is to form alliances with others concerned with social change and democratization (Greenwood, 2004).

In this chapter we argued that there are numerous advantages of integrating FR, PAR, and AR into a FPAR framework. We proposed six initial dimensions with guiding questions, and invite further dialogue, critique, and refinement. While we remain passionate about FPAR and believe that it holds many promises, we also recognize that it is not a panacea as it is fraught with tensions, challenges, ambiguities, and contradictions. The greatest lesson we have learned in our own research and from reading about others is the importance of living in places of mutual growth and discomfort, taking action, and not becoming paralyzed while grappling with important questions (Brydon-Miller and Wadsworth, 2004). Inevitably, the researcher can never 'get it right' and we share Chrisp's challenge that:

> My hope is that maybe I will get it more right than the last time. … The tensions require constant deconstructing, complexities explored and acknowledged openly, and dilemmas made transparent. Along with the search for new or uniquely reworked knowledges, there is an urgent need for a courageous search for and utilization of new research processes. (Chrisp, 2004: 92).

It is impossible to rid ourselves of the legacy of discrimination that shapes every aspect of our culture, and we can never truly resolve the issues of power and privilege that continue to affect our interactions with others. However, we can hope to remain vigilant, humble, and open to instruction (Brydon-Miller, 2004). In this process, as FPAR researchers we can perhaps contribute to the long-term goal of social change – indeed, 'the long haul struggle to create a world in which the full range of human characteristics, resources, experiences, and dreams are available to all of our children' (Maguire, 2001/2006: 66).

REFERENCES

Barazangi, N.H. (2004) 'Understanding Muslim women's self-identity and resistance to feminism and participatory action research', in M. Brydon-Miller, P. Maguire and A. McIntyre (eds), *Traveling Companions: Feminism, Teaching, and Action Research*. Westport, CT: Praeger. pp. 21–39.

Barnsley, J. and Ellis, D. (1992) *Research For Change: Participatory Action Research for Community Groups*. Vancouver, BC: Women's Research Center.

Brabeck, K. (2004) 'Testimonio: bridging feminist and participatory action research principles to create new spaces of collectivity', in M. Brydon-Miller, A. McIntyre and P. Maguire (eds), *Traveling Companions: Feminism, Teaching, and Action Research*. Westport, CT: Praeger. pp. 41–54.

Brah, A. and Phoenix, A. (2004) 'Ain't I a woman? Revisiting intersectionality', *Journal of International Women's Studies*, 5 (3): 75–86.

Brueggemann, B.J. (1996) 'Still life: representations and silences in the participant-observer roles', in P. Mortensen and G.E. Kirsch (eds), *Ethics and Representations in Qualitative Studies of Literacy*. Urbana, IL: National Council of Teachers of English. pp. 17–39.

Brydon-Miller, M. (2004) 'The terrifying truth: interrogating systems of power and privilege and choosing to act', in M. Brydon-Miller, P. Maguire and A. McIntyre (eds), *Traveling Companions: Feminism, Teaching, and Action Research*. Westport CT: Praeger. pp. 3–19.

Brydon-Miller, M. and Wadsworth, Y. (2004) 'Conclusion', in M. Brydon-Miller, P. Maguire and A. McIntyre (eds), *Traveling Companions: Feminism, Teaching, and Action Research*. Westport, CT: Praeger. pp. 179–86.

Brydon-Miller, M., Maguire, P. and McIntyre, I. (eds) (2004) *Traveling Companions: Feminism, Teaching, and Action Research*. Westport, CT: Praeger.

Cancian, F.M. (1992) 'Feminist science: methodologies that challenge inequality', *Gender and Society*, 6 (4): 623–42.

Chataway, C.J. (1997) 'An examination of the constraints on mutual inquiry in a participatory action research project', *Journal of Social Issues*, 53 (4): 747–65.

Chrisp, J. (2004) 'The negotiation of divergent demands when community research is located in the academy: the mother-adolescent son project', in M. Brydon-Miller, P. Maguire and A. McIntyre (eds), *Traveling Companions: Feminism, Teaching, and Action Research*. Westport CT: Praeger. pp. 79–95.

Coleman, G. and Rippin, A. (2000) 'Putting feminist theory to work: collaboration as a means towards organizational change', *Organization Symposium*, 7 (4): 573–87.

Collins, P.H. (1990) *Black Feminist Thought: Knowledge, Consciousness, and the Politics of Empowerment*. New York: Harper Collins.

Cooke, B. and Kothari, U. (2001) 'The case for participation as tyranny', in B. Cooke and U. Kothari (eds), *Participation: The New Tyranny?* London: Zed. pp. 1–15.

Cotterill, P. (1992) 'Interviewing women: issues of friendship, vulnerability, and power', *Women's Studies International Forum*, 15 (5/6): 593–606.

Edwards, R. and Ribbens, J. (1998) 'Living on the edges: public knowledge, private lives, personal experience', *Feminist Dilemmas in Qualitative Research: Public Knowledge and Private Lives*. London: Sage. pp. 1–23.

Finch, J. (1993) 'It's great to have someone to talk to: ethics and politics of interviewing women', in M. Hammersley (ed.), *Social Research: Philosophy, Politics and Practice*. London: Sage. pp. 166–79.

Fine, M. (1994) 'Working the hyphens – reinventing self and other in qualitative research', in N.K. Denzin and Y.S. Lincoln (eds), *Handbook of Qualitative Research*. Thousand Oaks, CA: Sage. pp. 70–82.

Fonow, M.M. and Cook, J.A. (1991) 'Back to the future: a look at the second wave of feminist epistemology and methodology', in M.M. Fonow and J.A. Cook, *Beyond Methodology: Feminist Scholarship as Lived Research*. Bloomington: Indiana University Press. pp. 1–15.

Fonow, M.M. and Cook, J.A. (2005) 'Feminist methodology: new applications in the academy and public policy', *Signs: Journal of Women in Culture and Society*, 30 (41): 2211–30.

Fraser, N. and Naples, N. (2004) 'To interpret the world and to change it: an interview with Nancy Fraser', *Signs: Journal of Women in Culture and Society*, 29 (4): 1103–24.

Frisby, W. (2006) 'Rethinking researcher roles, responsibilities, and relationships in community development research', *Leisure/Loisir*, 30 (1): 437–45.

Frisby, W., Reid, C., Miller, S. and Hoeber, L. (2005) 'Putting "participatory" into participatory forms of action research', *Journal of Sport Management*, 19 (4): 367–86.

Frisby, W., Reid, C. and Ponic, P. (2006) 'Levelling the playing field: promoting the health of poor women through a community development approach to recreation', in P. White and K. Young (eds), *Sport and Gender in Canada*. Don Mills, ON: Oxford University Press. pp. 120–36.

Gordon, G.B. (2001/2006) 'Transforming lives: towards bicultural competence', in P. Reason and H. Bradbury (eds), *Handbook of Action Research: Participative Inquiry and Practice*. London: Sage. pp. 314–23. Also published in P. Reason and H. Bradbury (eds) (2006), *Handbook of Action Research: Concise Student Edition*. London: Sage. pp. 243–52.

Greenwood, D.J. (2004) 'Feminism and action research: Is "resistance" possible, and if so, why is it necessary?', in M. Brydon-Miller, P. Maguire and A. McIntyre (eds), *Traveling Companions: Feminism, Teaching, and Action Research*. Westport, CT: Praeger. pp. 157–68.

Harding, S. and Norberg, K. (2005) 'New feminist approaches to social science methodologies: an introduction', *Signs: Journal of Women in Culture and Society*, 30 (4): 2009–15.

Hartsock, N.C.M. (1983) 'The feminist standpoint: developing the ground for a specifically feminist historical materialism', in S. Harding and M.B. Hintikka (eds), *Discovering Reality: Feminist Perspectives on Epistemology, Metaphysics, Methodology and Philosophy of Science*. London: Reidel. pp. 283–310.

Hertz, R. (1996) 'Introduction: ethics, reflexivity and voice', *Qualitative Sociology*, 19 (1): 3–9.

hooks, b. (1990) 'Choosing the margin as a space of radical openness', in A. Garry and M. Pearsall (eds), *Women, Knowledge and Reality: Exploration in Feminist Philosophy*. New York. Routledge pp. 48–55.

Kesby, M. (2005) 'Retheorizing empowerment-through-participation as a performance in space: Beyond tyranny to transformation', *Signs: Journal of Women in Culture and Society*, 30 (4): 2037–65.

Lather, P. (1991) *Getting Smart: Feminist Research and Pedagogy Within the Postmodern*. New York: Routledge.

Lather, P. (2001) 'Postbook: working the ruins of feminist ethnography', *Signs: Journal of Women in Culture and Society*, 27 (1): 199–227.

Ledwith, M. and Asgill, P. (2000) 'Critical alliance: black and white women working together for social justice', *Community Development Journal*, 35 (3): 290–9.

Letherby, G. (2003) *Feminist Research in Theory and Practice*. Buckingham: Open University Press.

Lykes, M.B. and Coquillon, E. (2006) 'Participatory and action research and feminisms', in S. Hess-Biber (ed.), *Handbook of Feminist Research: Theory and Praxis*. Thousand Oaks, CA: Sage. pp. 297–326.

Lykes, M.B. in collaboration with the Association of Maya Ixil Women (2001/2006) 'Creative arts and photography in participatory action research in Guatemala', in P. Reason and H. Bradbury (eds), *Handbook of Action Research: Participative Inquiry and Practice*, London: Sage pp. 363–71. Also published in P. Reason and H. Bradbury (eds) (2006), *Handbook of Action Research: Concise Student Edition*. London: Sage. pp. 269–78.

McCall, L. (2005) 'The complexity of intersectionality', *Signs: Journal of Women in Culture and Society*, 30 (3): 1771–1800.

McIntyre, A. (2000) *Inner-city Kids: Adolescents Confront Life and Violence in an Urban Community*. New York: New York University Press.

McIntyre, A. and Lykes, M.B. (2004) 'Weaving words and pictures in/through feminist participatory action research', in M. Brydon-Miller, A. McIntyre and P. Maguire (eds), *Traveling Companions: Feminism, Teaching, and Action Research*, Westport, CT: Praeger. pp. 57–77.

Maguire, P. (1987) *Doing Participatory Research: a Feminist Approach*. Amherst, MA: The Center for International Education, University of Massachusetts.

Maguire, P. (2001/2006) 'Uneven ground: feminisms and action research', in P. Reason and H. Bradbury (eds), *Handbook of Action Research: Participative Inquiry and Practice*. London: Sage. pp. 59–69. Also published in P. Reason and H. Bradbury (eds) (2006), *Handbook of Action Research: Concise Student Edition*. London: Sage. pp. 60–70.

Maguire, P. (2004) 'Reclaiming the F-word: emerging lessons from teaching about feminist-informed action research', in M. Brydon-Miller, P. Maguire and A. McIntyre (eds), *Traveling Companions: Feminism, Teaching, and Action Research*. Westport, CT: Praeger. pp. 117–35.

Maguire, P., Brydon-Miller, M. and McIntyre, A. (2004) 'Introduction', in M. Brydon-Miller, A. McIntyre and P. Maguire (eds), *Traveling Companions: Feminism, Teaching, and Action Research*. Westport, CT: Praeger. pp. ix–xix.

Meyerson, D.E. and Kolb, D.M. (2000) 'Moving out of the "armchair": Developing a framework to bridge the gap between feminist theory and practice', *Organization*, 7 (4): 553–71.

Mohanty, C.T. (2003) *Feminism Without Borders: Decolonizing Theory, Practicing Solidarity*. Durham, NC: Duke University Press.

Naples, N.A. (2003) *Feminism and Method: Ethnography, Discourse Analysis, and Activist Research*. London: Routledge.

Olesen, V. (2005) 'Early millennial feminist qualitative research', in N.K. Denzin and Y.S. Lincoln (eds), *Handbook of Qualitative Research*. London: Sage. pp. 235–78.

Park, P. (2001/2006) 'Knowledge and participatory research', in P. Reason and H. Bradbury (eds), *Handbook of Action Research: Participative Inquiry and Practice*. London: Sage. pp. 81–90. Also published in P. Reason and H. Bradbury (eds) (2006), *Handbook of Action Research: Concise Student Edition*. London: Sage. pp. 83–93.

Ramazanoglu, C. and Holland, J. (2002) *Feminist Methodology: Challenges and Choices*. London: Sage.

Reay, D. (1996) 'Dealing with difficult differences: reflexivity and social class in feminist research', *Feminism and Psychology,* 6 (3): 443–56.

Reid, C. (2000) 'Seduction and enlightenment in feminist action research', *Resources for Feminist Research,* 28 (1/2): 169–88.

Reid, C. (2004a) *The Wounds of Exclusion: Poverty, Women's Health, and Social Justice*. Edmonton, AB: Qualitative Institute Press.

Reid, C. (2004b) 'Advancing women's social justice agendas: a feminist action research framework', *International Journal of Qualitative Method,* 3 (3) (online) http://www.ualberta.ca/~ijqm/english/engframeset.html.

Reid, C., Tom, A. and Frisby, W. (2006) 'Finding the "action" in feminist participatory action research', *Action Research,* 4(3): 315–32.

Reinharz, S. (1992) *Feminist Methods in Social Research*. New York: Oxford University Press.

Ristock, J.L. and Pennell, J. (1996) *Community Research as Empowerment: Feminist Links, Postmodern Interruptions*. Toronto, ON: Oxford University Press.

Rose, D. (2001) *Revisiting Feminist Research Methodologies: a Working Paper*. Ottawa, ON: Status of Women Canada.

Smith, D.E. (1992) 'Sociology from women's experience: A reaffirmation', *Sociological Theory,* 10 (1): 88–98.

Smith, D.E. (1997) 'Comment on Hekman's truth and method: Feminist standpoint theory revisited', *Signs: Journal of Women and Culture,* 22 (2): 392–8.

Tuhiwai Smith, L. (2005) *Decolonizing Methodologies: Research and Indigenous Peoples*. London: Zed Books.

Wang, C., Burris, M.A. and Ping, X.Y. (1996) 'Chinese village women as visual anthropologists: a participatory approach to reaching policymakers', *Social Science and Medicine,* 42 (10): 1391–1400.

Wildman, S.M. and Davis, A.D. (1996) 'Making systems of privilege visible', in S.M. Wildman (ed.), *Privilege Revealed: How Invisible Preference Undermines America*. New York: New York University Press.

Williams, J. and Lykes, M.B. (2003) 'Bridging theory and practice: using reflexive cycles in feminist participatory action research', *Feminism & Psychology,* 13 (3): 287–94.

Wolf, D.L. (1996) 'Situating feminist dilemmas in fieldwork', in D.L. Wolf (ed.), *Feminist Dilemmas in Fieldwork*. Boulder, CO: Westview Press, pp. 1–55.

Yoshihama, M. and Carr, E.S. (2002) 'Community participation reconsidered: Feminist participatory action research with Hmong women', *Journal of Community Practice*, 10 (4): 85–102.

7

Towards Transformational Liberation: Participatory and Action Research and Praxis

M. Brinton Lykes and Amelia Mallona[1]

This chapter discusses the liberatory and transformational potential of participatory and action research. We begin by situating participatory and action research within its historical roots in the majority world. We describe some of the contemporary social realities facing a growing number of people, particularly the ever-increasing poverty and violent conflicts that shape life for many in the global community. We argue that the transformational and liberatory goals of participatory and action research offer resources for engaging with communities in challenging these structural inequalities. Drawing upon the theoretical contributions of liberation theology, we suggest that a preferential option for the poor and a politically contextualized psychology are critical to renew participatory and action research to more fully realize the radical changes envisioned by its founders. We conclude with a discussion of the challenges, possibilities, and contradictions facing those seeking to engage in transformational liberatory research within a globalized world, particularly those of us working within or from the base of university systems of power and privilege.

During the past 30 years participatory action research, action research, and participatory research have developed from marginalized efforts on the part of community residents and activists, social scientists, development workers, educators, and social movement activists and analysts to 'legitimate' fields of inquiry and instruction in major research universities, development circles, non-profits, international organizations, public sector and grassroots organizations and local, regional, national, and international policy arenas (see Reason and Bradbury, 2001, among others, for a review of the depth and breadth of action research and its contemporary reach). Yet, despite these processes of institutionalization and growth, social inequalities and structural, that is, gendered, racialized, sexual, and economic oppressions and their intersectionalities,[2] which participatory and action researchers seek to challenge and transform, are evermore entrenched. This has not, of course, been a linear process of unchecked oppression and success of power-elites but rather a complex history of resistance – sometimes in the form of armed rebellion – and further repression as well as of technological shifts that have created global opportunities contributing to capital formations wherein multi- and trans-national corporate structures have annual profits that outstrip the GDP of many countries in the majority world.[3] It is within this latter context, that is, the majority world, that some of us, including the authors of this chapter, have embraced participatory action research as *vivencia*.

In this chapter we explore the liberatory and transformational potential of participatory and action research within the context of our life-work or *proyecto vital* [life project] as we strive to rearticulate our *preferential option for the poor* within global communities of the 21st century. Specifically, we suggest that a preferential option for the poor and a politically contextualized psychology are critical to developing participatory and action research that more fully realizes the radical changes envisioned by their founders. We begin by situating participatory and action research within its historical roots in the majority world and refer to select social and revolutionary movements (in Latin America and the United States) that deeply inform our understanding of oppression and liberation and situate the challenges facing us today. We draw on the theoretical contributions of liberation theology to situate the challenges facing contemporary participatory and action research. We turn to liberation psychology to explore the individual–collective dialectic of liberation and transformation. We conclude with a discussion of the challenges, possibilities, and contradictions facing those who seek to engage in transformational liberatory participatory and action research within a globalized world, particularly those of us working within university systems of power and privilege.

SOCIALLY SITUATING OURSELVES: PARTICIPATORY AND ACTION RESEARCH IN SOCIO-HISTORICAL CONTEXT

As Euro- and Latin American women of differing ages, social statuses, and economic backgrounds, we have engaged social change and participatory action research projects in a range of community-based and educational contexts. We have grown increasingly alarmed by social realities that define life in the 21st century for the majority of the world's population, including 'growing transnational inequalities' (Farmer, 2005: 18). Evidence of these inequalities are found in, among many others, alarming child death rates from malnutrition and lack of immunization (2 million each year according to UNICEF, 2005) as well as deaths from treatable diseases (e.g., tuberculosis, malaria and AIDS), these despite the availability of medical knowledge and technology (see, e.g., Farmer, 2005). Social indicators from the WHO, UNICEF, UNHCR, and other international bodies offer testimony to the effects of colonialism, patriarchy and global capitalist formations wherein the economic, social, political and cultural rights of a majority of the world's population are denied, excluding them from access to that which supports well-being (Prilleltensky and Nelson, 2002).

Contemporary global realities and the socio-historical context.

Processes of globalization are key contributors to some of these alarming social indices, and have a profound influence on how we understand the possibilities for transformational liberatory participatory and action research today. We understand globalization as a complex set of economic, social, and political processes related to increased economic trade and international financial independence; the proliferation of rapid communication technologies; the development of international judicial and political bodies; the increased movement of populations across borders; and increased cross-cultural influences, particularly that of industrialized Western nations on cultures throughout the world (see, e.g., Friedman, 2000; Kitching, 2001). Among the conflicting legacies and potentials globalization offers for transformational liberatory participatory and action research are, on the one hand, that shifting populations, power structures, and nation–citizen relationships create new spaces for advocacy, and rapid communications technologies can link organizers across the globe. On the other hand, the economic gap between rich and poor is growing, and increased global communication both deeply constrains and facilitates local processes.

The increasing interconnectedness of persons and spheres geographically removed from one another is an aspect of globalization that has influenced the way that people think about the relationship between the state and society, as the traditional nation-state now coexists with the concept of global civil society (Stahler-Sholk, 2001) and has created new transnational organizations and actors (Smith and Johnston, 2002). Political scientist Richard Stahler-Sholk (2001) observed that:

> the increasing concentrations of capital and new inequalities [on a global scale] tend to reinforce a transnational stratification of classes, changing the way power is contested, e.g. in Latin America. … As economic activity is integrated at a higher level on a global scale, the locale of decision-making power becomes further removed from the social subjects, creating something like the 'democracy deficit'. (p. 505)

Alternatively, social movement organizations are increasingly non-nation-based with membership drawn from 'dispersed geographical locations, encouraging the extensive use of new forms of communications technology which enable simultaneous action in diverse places' (Eschle, 2001: 68). Rapid modern communications technologies have contributed to international organizing and advocacy efforts as diverse as, for example, the Zapatistas in Mexico (Stahler-Sholk, 2001) and the United States-based International Campaign to Ban Landmines (1998–2005).

The Internet in particular offers the possibility of greater access to knowledge globally. This poses particular challenges for participatory and action researchers who have been committed to challenging hegemonic knowledge systems and recognizing multiple 'ways of knowing' (Belenky et al., 1986). Moreover, particular forms of contemporary knowledge may circulate more easily through cyberspace than the 'vernacular'; Stahler-Sholk (2001) criticizes the Internet's potential as a space in which to democratize knowledge, noting that it 'does not necessarily ensure democratic equality of access for all viewpoints' (p. 513).

In addition, the Internet and other forms of global communication disseminate a particular set of cultural symbols and practices, affecting individual identity and social subjectivity. Psychologist Jeffrey Jensen (2002) suggests that many people in the world today develop what he calls 'a *bicultural identity*', in which 'part of their identity is rooted in their local culture while another part stems from an awareness of their relation to the global culture' (p. 777, emphasis in original). Although not all peoples are equally influenced by globalization, due to differing access to technologies and different lifestyles, this 'global identity' is an additional force to be engaged in participatory processes of conscientization and transformative change.

Defining transformational liberation from within the socio-historical context

Movements for liberation and struggles for transformation have deeply informed participatory and action research throughout their history, which has, in turn, imbued discourses generated in a wide range of social and revolutionary movements with multiple meanings. In the academy, scholars have sought to distinguish liberation from transformation, defining each construct in terms of its user's ontological and epistemological framework (see, for example, Gottlieb and La Belle, 1990). Early practitioner-theorists of participatory and action research and critical pedagogy, including Paolo Freire (1970), Mohammed Anisur Rahman (1985/1983), and Orlando Fals Borda (1979; Fals Borda and Rahman, 1991), embraced both liberation and transformation, to emphasize the need for and commitment to radical change as a prerequisite for building more just societies.

In their analysis of Freire's discourse, Gottlieb and LaBelle (1990) suggest that Freire conceived of liberation as well as oppression as 'states of being'. Rahman (1991, see also this volume), however, makes reference to the social context when he talks about transformation. In explaining the lack of success of revolutionary movements he described the vanguard's failure to foster participatory egalitarian processes that valued the base's knowledge and praxis, and questioned whether sufficient weight was placed on social transformation in people's revolutionary struggles for liberation. He thus implied that liberation and transformation have different meanings, but that the processes and outcomes must be interdependent for radical change to be realized in the other and in the collectivity. Despite this focus on structural transformation as a precondition for freedom, Rahman (1990) remained convinced that the 'liberation of the mind is the primary task, both before and after structural change' (p. 313).

In the 1960s and 1970s in Latin America, liberation was associated with taking control over the state through armed struggles (Fals Borda, 2001/2006). Thus liberation and transformation, although understood as two separate realities, were interrelated and both were necessary preconditions for freedom from oppression and freedom towards a 'full humanity'. Gaventa and Cornwall (2001/2006), however, suggest that the meanings of liberation and transformation emergent in the early years of participatory and action research have changed in recent decades. Rather than armed struggle or contesting 'power over', contemporary participatory and action researchers draw on Foucauldian constructions of multiple discourses of power, referring to liberation as the creation of an alternative political, social and economic model which implies a redress

of poverty, oppression and violence, a 'meta-narrative pluralistic socialism' (Fals Borda, 2001/2006). Drawing upon this work, we distinguish liberation, transformation, and transformational liberation in the following manner. Liberation, as influenced by Freire's 'states of being', is understood as partial freedom from oppressive social, economic, and/or political conditions, whereas transformation is conceived of as a process of individual and/or collective change made through conscientization and praxis. Transformational liberation represents a process through which a shift in consciousness is attained through recognizing individual *and* collective potential and praxis. Specific oppressions are dismantled within a deeply contextualized historical moment and at least partial justice is attained, a process that is reflective of the ideal state of 'full humanity' described by Freire. In what follows we explore the potential of participatory and action research in the struggles for transformational liberation.

PARTICIPATORY AND ACTION RESEARCH: RADICAL HUMANISM AND STRUCTURAL TRANSFORMATION

Participatory and action research was conceived within the majority world in the 1970s and 1980s to systematize and amplify local knowledge, transforming it into social activist movements that contested the power of elites and struggled for greater socioeconomic justice, often through collaboration with external agents of change who were frequently based in universities. Participatory and action research and the broad-based social movements of the time were 'walking a long road together' and, in the best of circumstances, contributed to self- and social consciousness among social actors who constructed participatory and transformative grassroots movements towards social transformation. Participatory and action research were thus situated as a resource at the interface of radical humanism and structural transformation.

Critical consciousness as radical humanism

Writing about participatory and action research in the late 1960s and 1970s, Indian and Latin American educators and social change advocates acknowledged the centrality of Paolo Freire's praxis of critical consciousness, that is, *conscientização* [conscientization], for their work. Conscientization is 'a process of critical self-inquiry and self-learning and of thereby developing the confidence and capability to find answers to questions *on one's own*' (Rahman, 2004: 18, emphasis added).

Despite an early emphasis on the community's self-initiative, educators and community activists situated themselves as catalysts, generating participatory processes that tapped into and engaged local knowledge producers to facilitate their developing their own emancipatory practices. Rahman (1985/1983, see also this volume) argued that people need to develop 'their own endogenous process of consciousness raising and knowledge generation' and the 'social power to determine what is valid or useful knowledge' (p. 119). Through their own social processes people establish their own collectives and their own verification systems, thereby establishing themselves as 'fully scientific'. Rahman (1990) characterized the particular contribution of participatory and action research to transformational processes as the engagement of people in a process of 'creative development' (p. 313), thus aligning himself with Freire's emphasis on personal transformation or what we are describing here as radical humanism.

Radical structural change

Although participatory and action research emphasized micro-level, community-based change strategies, many early theorists argued, on the one hand, that micro-level change needed to be situated within an analysis of macro-level social inequalities, and further that participatory and action research were fundamentally concerned with transforming macro-level power relations towards greater socio-economic justice (Fals Borda, 1979). In many ways participatory and action research reflect one of multiple responses through which academic researchers sought to liberate their analytic and critical skills from a sterile search for 'knowledge for knowledge's sake' and engage with the majority populations in their struggles for radical social change. In the United States, the 1960s, 1970s, and 1980s were characterized by a wide range of civil rights protests and non-violent and sometimes violent actions with varying effects on dominant power systems. In Latin America during the same period massive protests were frequently met by repression and the installation of military dictatorships which sometimes gave rise to armed conflict. Mass-based urban and rural guerrilla movements such as the Nicaraguan Sandinista movement (FSLN), the Salvadoran Frente Farabundo Martí para la Liberación Nacional (FMLN), and the Union Revolucionario Nacional de Guatemala (URNG) among others challenged repressive state-sponsored violence in struggles for economic rights and a redistribution of power in countries throughout Central and South America.

These efforts were framed and re-framed within wider geo-political and ideological struggles and much has been written, by those within and outside of these struggles, of their relative successes and failures. Participatory and action research with survivors of these armed struggles have contributed to critical analyses of these movements. Despite their contributions many of these political organizations and armed guerrilla groups were led by a vanguard whose vertical structures of power failed to prepare the base for embracing its own power.[4] In contrast, movements for personal transformation, including, for example, second wave feminism in the United States (Rosen, 2000), often achieved goals of consciousness raising yet failed to interrogate material constraints and power structures, thus failing to guarantee basic human needs to wider communities of women in whose name these struggles were frequently waged. Irrespective of the specific outcomes of these admittedly widely differing struggles for change, contemporary transformative discourse and praxis wrestles with and is challenged by this legacy.

INDIVIDUAL CONSCIOUSNESS, STRUCTURAL OPPRESSION, AND COLLECTIVE CHANGE

Paolo Freire's pedagogy was a critical resource for facilitating local people's appropriation of their indigenous knowledge systems as they assumed their positions within struggles to transform their environments. His adult literacy programs were a critical step in majority world community-based organizing to move from a culture of silence, fatalism, and resignation to a deep questioning of old values and the creative development of new forms of social organization. A parallel ideological force that has informed many community-based struggles for transformation during the 1960s and 1970s and that continues to inform current discourses was liberation theology.

Liberation theology and praxis

According to Philip Berryman (1987), liberation theologians sought to interpret Christian faith 'through the poor's suffering, their struggle and hope'. Leonardo Boff and Clodovis Boff (1986) date the emergence of this theological discourse and praxis to early efforts of Latin American Catholic and Protestant clergy and laity to re-read Biblical texts through the lens of the majority population's experiences of marginalization and exclusion. Many of these religious workers lived and worked among the poor, many of whom had begun to organize against the scandalous effects of development. They were informed by critical sociology and Marxism which provided lenses through which to analyze traditional hierarchies of power and the rampant development of centers of economic power within the Northern hemisphere that increasingly marginalized those at the periphery in the early to mid-20th

century. These theologians urged middle-class and privileged Christians, their brothers and sisters, to make a 'preferential option for the poor', that is, to align themselves with the interests of those most marginalized from power (see, e.g., Boff and Boff, 1986; Gutiérrez, 1973/1988). This is not only an ideological commitment but rather, as amply discussed by Gutiérrez (1984/2003), a call to live among and enter into the life struggles and the spiritual knowledge constructed through journeying at the margins.

Dialectics of oppression and liberation

Latin America, Asia and Africa thus witnessed the development of small grassroots efforts for social change wherein outside catalysts, including religious workers, participatory and action researchers and development workers, accompanied local communities working to improve their quality of life. Mary Ann Hinsdale, Helen Lewis, and Maxine Waller's work with communities in Appalachia (1995) offers a concrete example of participatory research deeply informed by liberation theology and a gender analysis within the US context. Despite this example, often missing from these early efforts was a critical analysis of, on the one hand, the complex interface of colonialism, racism and gender oppression, and, on the other, an understanding of the ways in which the oppressed, often people of color, indigenous peoples, and women, had internalized the images of themselves held by the white male dominant culture (see, e.g. Cone, 1970; Fanon, 1967, 1968; Martín-Baró, 1994; Moane, 1999; Ruether, 1983, among others). As importantly, infusing these analyses into participatory and action research can correct for what Bell (2001) has described as the absence of race and what Maguire (2001/2006), Cornwall (1996, 2001, 2003), Crawley (1998) and Lykes and Coquillon (2006) have found to be a problematic positioning of gender. They have documented how '[f]or many involved in participatory research or action, gender is a footnote, rather than a place from which to begin the analysis' (Crawley, 1998: 25).

Liberating psychology for liberatory praxis

Liberation psychiatrists and psychologists clarify the complex dialectic of the intra- and interpersonal and structural processes that facilitate and constrain the potential for self and social transformation among majority populations. Basque-Salvadoran social psychologist Ignacio Martín-Baró (1994) posited that a psychology that could explain and contribute to transforming the marginalization and impoverishment of the majority population should include: (1) a focus on the liberation of the collectivity as well as personal liberation; (2) a new epistemology wherein the truth of the popular majority is not to be found, but created, that is, wherein truth is constructed 'from below'; and, (3) a new praxis, wherein we place ourselves within the research-action process alongside the dominated or oppressed. This articulation of a 'liberation psychology' rooted at least in part in Freire's pedagogy (1970) and in liberation theology (Gutiérrez, 1973/1988) shifted the focus of psychological research and practice from the isolated autonomous individual to a contextualized, historical agent-in-community. For example, in one of his many essays, Martín-Baró deploys the critical analytic tool of de-ideologization to deconstruct the fatalism of the Central American peasant. His analysis of the repressive labor practices of global capital contributes to a critical understanding of the peasant's practices of resistance, all too frequently obscured by situating him as primarily or exclusively 'oppressed' and by a psychologization of his 'personality traits' (Martín-Baró, 1994, see especially Chapter 12, pp. 198–220).

Psychiatrist Frantz Fanon (1967, 1968), living and working in his native Martinique, in France, and in Algiers, resituated human psychology within sociopolitical and historical forces, demonstrating that human neurosis was rooted in specific historical and political consequences of colonization, not in intrapsychic dynamics (Bulhan, 1985). He argued that derogatory images of blackness were constitutive of the social structures as well as the discourse of dominant white societies, and infiltrated the unconscious of blacks, intruding through dreams and expressing themselves in phobias, symptoms or neuroses. He demonstrated how one effect of the trauma caused by the institutionalized violence of colonialism was blacks' profound experiences of depersonalization in repressive colonial cultures. Fanon thus identified the processes that constrained blacks' capacity to grasp the mechanisms of oppression within themselves and in their surrounding realities, adding a critical dimension to Freire's theory of conscientization and education for transformation by facilitating our understanding of the ways in which a group could thwart its own potential for liberation.

Parallels can be seen between Fanon's and Martín-Baró's work and that of African American and black psychologists who also draw heavily on black liberation theology and on Africanist religious traditions (see, among others, Gordon, 1973; Ajani ya Azibo, 1994). A commonality among these is the shift of psychologists' attention to the systemic or structural dimensions of the identified problem or concern, rather than its more typical focal point, that is, the individual victim abstracted from a multi-layered social, historical and cultural context. They stress further the need to de-ideologize reality, that is, to peel off the layers of discourse that naturalize violence and structural poverty, reducing the oppressed to an object who possesses 'problems' (including neuroses and psychoses) and 'traits' (e.g., fatalistic), and negating the complex subjectivity and sociality of these historical agents.

DEVELOPMENT: LIBERATORY DISCOURSE AND THE POLITICS OF CHANGE

As argued above, the 1960s and 1970s were characterized by mass-, community-, and issue-based social movements and armed struggles for social change. These were most frequently met by repressive counterinsurgencies and the installation of dictatorships, frequently funded by the United States and Europe, often in the name of 'National Security' and/or as a defense against the spread of communism. The latter half of the 20th century saw selective shifts in strategy, characterized by, on the one hand, mass genocide and gross violations of human rights, and, on the other, an interest in using human rights discourse to protect civil and political rights within developing and established democracies. As the number of armed struggles and mass-based movements for social change receded and the neoliberal project took hold in the developing democracies, the majority population was met by a civilian army of international development workers. International funds were available to local communities, particularly in rural areas of Latin America, India, and Africa. The dramatic growth of non-governmental organizations in these areas in the latter half of the 20th century, among other indicators, suggests that the presence and influence of development programs shifted dramatically in this period.

Much participatory and action research within the context of local communities in the majority world has been carried out as part of community economic or participatory development processes. Participatory and action research strategies, such as participatory rural appraisal (PRA) and farmer participatory research (FPR), as well as people-centered development movements (see, e.g., Korten, 1990, cited in Roodt, 1996), have been importantly constitutive of community development efforts over many years (see Chambers, Chapter 20 in this volume). In Latin America the work has been and continues to be strongly influenced by Paulo Freire's critical pedagogy and his theories of conscientization and empowerment. Similar approaches that assume that knowledge generates power and that people's knowledge is central to social change emerged in Asia (Fals Borda and Rahman, 1991) and in Africa (see Hope and Timmel, 1984–2000). An example is Anne Hope and Sally Timmel's (1984–2000) 4-volume series of popular education resources, *Training for Transformation,* which focus on local communities' indigenous knowledge and rely heavily on Freire's pedagogical decoding practices.

Many economic development, humanitarian aid, and crisis intervention workers engage significant numbers of people in small local projects while the majority of the world's resources continue to be controlled by a handful of people (UNDP, 2006). A vast literature has emerged documenting and evaluating individual development projects and the ways in which they have or have not contributed to social change (see Institute for Development Studies (www.ids.ac.uk), among others). Despite local contributions there is little evidence that the cumulative effect has either redressed social inequalities or reduced structural violence. Critical analyses of these community-based efforts further interrogate an essentialized discourse of 'the poor' and 'women' (see below) as well as the universality of democratic participation (Cooke and Kothari, 2001), questioning the discursive practices of liberation and transformation within these applied settings. Minimally these critiques assert that the meanings of liberation and transformation in the late 20th and early 21st centuries are not those of the mid 20th century and challenge development workers to re-situate their work in radical praxis (Hickey and Mohan, 2005). In the following we explore the challenges facing those seeking to interrogate current praxis towards transformational liberatory participatory and action research.

THE MORE THINGS CHANGE, THE MORE THEY STAY THE SAME: WHITHER PARTICIPATORY AND ACTION RESEARCH?

As suggested above, critical pedagogy (Freire) and liberation theologies (Berryman, Boff, Gutiérrez, Ruether, Cone) and liberation psychologies (Martín-Baró, Watts and Serrano-García, Moane) emerged within relatively similar historical moments characterized by widespread social upheavals including armed struggle and broad-based non-violent social movements. Although differing not only in the professional lenses through which they analyzed their work among the marginalized and the social contexts in which they emerged, the initiatives sought to develop solidarity between the educated, professional elite and poor and marginalized populations of the majority world. In each context the challenge was to move beyond the professional responsibility to provide charity through a welfare system or state (in the Northern Hemisphere) or economic development (in the Southern Hemisphere), to a transformational praxis (see Hope and Timmel, 1984–2000, for further discussion). Through theory and praxis participatory and action researchers as well as liberation theologians and psychologists sought to demonstrate how the oppressed could be producers of knowledge and creators of a new reality.

Contemporary trends: Reflections on participatory and action research in the academy

Despite these roots in a discourse of liberation and transformation, participatory and action research, and even liberation psychology and theology, are increasingly taught and applied within institutional settings (e.g., schools, hospitals, industry, etc.) or within international and humanitarian aid contexts in the service of welfare and/or development. Moreover, as our own experiences teaching participatory and action research in the academy suggest, these shifts create new contradictions and challenges. Amelia lived and worked in Nicaragua prior to completing her PhD in the United States and entering a US-based university that serves primarily first generation college students of color. Brinton has divided her time over the past 30 years between community-based participatory action research in war zones of rural Guatemala, Northern Ireland, and urban South Africa or among peoples of color in urban Boston and teaching in a Boston-based elite private Catholic university. We describe briefly some of the contradictions experienced by those of us who seek to engage a liberatory and transformative praxis while benefiting from an academy that sustains oppression and social inequality.

Amelia

I have found teaching participatory action research and social change challenging, even among a constituency and within an institution that provides fertile terrain. In the School of Human Services at Springfield College, we require facilitation of a community project across three consecutive terms to provide students with practical experiences in addressing social issues. Although the course is directly designed to promote personal and collective transformation, I found, to my surprise that it is one of the most anxiety producing courses for students and more difficult to teach (see also Shirley, in Stackpool-Moore et al., 2006: 30). Each student's readiness to commit to a community process differs greatly. Moreover, students have a variety of experiences, knowledge and skills in guiding a participatory process. Also some students have a profound internalization of the 'banking' model of education, overvaluing a rational way of knowing and operating due to a sense of hopelessness around solving systemic social problems. In addition, traditional criteria for grading non-traditional courses present profound contradictions for me as an instructor and are a major source of anxiety for students. For example, how does one grade a 'failed' project in which a student's own process of transformation has been significant?

Upon reflection on these experiences, I recognized the importance of scaffolding the teaching-learning process (see Stackpool-Moore et al., 2006). I have added a preliminary step of asking students to reflect on issues that affect them personally and then to contextualize the issue within a broader perspective. I have found that it is easier to engage a student in action toward social change when it relates to an issue in which he or she is invested. One student, a mother who was concerned about her teenage children, successfully engaged in a project to prevent teenagers from entering gangs. For her, a very personal concern grew to a deeper understanding of the social and structural causes underlying that 'problem'. The challenge for all of us is then to go beyond small local projects to a systemic approach which recognizes the global context and connections.

Brinton

Participatory Action Research is an 'elective' in Boston College's Lynch School of Education, although it regularly attracts a diverse group of students within and beyond the school. Through an ongoing partnership with a Boston-based NGO, Cooperative Economics for Women, and my ongoing collaborations in Guatemala, seminar participants have opportunities for deep engagement in nationally or internationally-based local communities. In these contexts students are challenged to interrogate their power and privilege reflexively and to risk 'just enough trust' to develop relationships and facilitate participatory work in the borderlands between US-based university power and privilege and urban neighborhoods in the United States or rural communities in war-torn countries characterized by violence and economic uncertainty. Class and race-based tensions often emerge as the insider–outsider dichotomy is challenged by students from an upper middle class background seeking to work with 'the poor' and students of color seeking to work within their own identity-based communities and within and across social classes.

There is a growing diversity among those who enroll in this course including, for example, 'interested bystanders'. Moreover, graduate students today encounter multiple practical challenges including 'balancing family, work, and school', 'completing a dissertation', or 'building a resumé'. The creature comforts of middle class or upper middle class academic privilege often swamp initial enthusiasm for this work. Juggling the demands of a university system and the rhythms of rural Guatemala or urban Boston is also challenging for learners and teachers. I am constantly challenged to respect the multiple practical burdens and differing personal realities that confront students today and to creatively explore how participatory and action research as *vivencia* can contribute, at least in some partial way, to their critical self-understandings and to their potential future embrace of this praxis. We are challenged by these practical limitations as we seek to extend the praxis of liberation and transformation from the base of the university and we discuss below some of the structural contradictions that shape these concrete experiences.

The power of the professorate

In a 1985 article Anisur Rahman suggested that despite its successes at inverting the assumption that knowledge can only be produced within the academy, participatory and action research failed to invert a second set of assumptions fundamental to its praxis, leaving intellectuals in their positions as consumers of material production rather than followers of change generated by those most directly affected by it. Clarifying their relations to power and powerlessness elucidates some of the challenges faced by university professors who seek to accompany those marginalized from power whose interests differ significantly from their own.

Recent critical reflections on Freire's work suggest that his pedagogical praxis was directed primarily to a group of 'liberated pcdagogucs' who would carry out liberatory educational projects with the oppressed rather than to the oppressed themselves (Bowers and Apffel-Marglin, 2005). Esteva, Stuchul and Prakash (2005) argue, for example, that Freire's failure to critique education itself created another layer of ideological obfuscation of indigenous people's knowledge or, the 'vernacular'. His work thus negated the people's developing understanding that the initiative and the struggle for a transformational liberation must come 'from within themselves rather than from external agents of change' (Esteva et al., 2005; 24) and reaffirmed the importance of accessing educational credentials outside of the community in order to succeed. Both criticisms challenge the sources of liberation within Freire's work and importantly resituate and re-characterize transformational change.

Eduardo and Bonnie Duran's (1995) *Native American Postcolonial Psychology* echoes these considerations, recognizing the centrality of the soul and psyche, of myths and dreams for generating transformative praxis, thereby affirming worldviews that differ fundamentally from those of Euro-American societies. These critiques and affirmations dislocate the professional, that is, the catalyst, animator, or researcher, reaffirming the transformational possibilities of indigenous systems of knowledge and people's powers as knowledge constructors and protagonists of their own transformation. It challenges those of us within the academy that are committed to transformational liberation to interrogate not only our positionality in the collaborative participatory and action research processes in which we are engaging, but also the basic assumptions of our theory and practice.

DISCUSSION

We conclude with some cautious responses drawing heavily on our personal journeys within and among Central American, South African, Northern Irish, and urban United Statesian communities and recognizing challenges facing us in the 21st century.

Preferential option for the poor

As professionals, particularly those of us situated within university communities, we are challenged to interrogate our personal and professional constructions of reality and de-ideologize our disciplines (Martín-Baró, 1994). Rod Watts and Irma Serrano-García (2003) argued that: 'Any hope for the formation of alliances across the divide of oppression requires that the beneficiaries of privilege first critically analyze their status and attend to their own sociopolitical development' (p. 76). Ignacio Martín-Baró challenged Central American psychologists to

face 'the disjunction between an accommodation to a social system that has benefited us personally and a critical confrontation with that system' (1994: 46). For him this meant not that psychologists should abandon their profession but rather that they should put themselves and the profession at the service of the 'poor and oppressed majorities in their effort to emerge into history, in their struggle to constitute themselves as a new people in a new land' (p. 46). Burton and Kagan (2005) caution that liberatory discourse is all too frequently limited to critique and debate, and rarely takes the next step towards creative engagement in articulating transformed social systems and structures. Moreover, they caution that although it may serve to uncover abuse and exploitation, all too often the root causes of these social problems are unexamined and the problems return.

Recently, Rahman (2004) urged grassroots activists to 'dispense altogether with the term 'poor' and with talk of 'poverty alleviation'' (p. 18), arguing that efforts to solve the 'problem of poverty' create de facto relations of dependency within the current global relations of capital. In contrast he proposed seven principles that should guide grassroots activism, urging those who would develop solidarity to press for a 'pragmatic collectivism' wherein people 'retain the surplus that they produce themselves' and develop power over the market as laborers, consumers, and producers. He embraces the language of empowerment and democratic participation, through which the 'subaltern, underprivileged, oppressed' contribute to the 'articulation of an ideological vision of a more humane world' (p. 16). Through this he seeks adequate discourse and praxis towards transformative liberation for these difficult and challenging times.

Elina Vuola (2002) and Simone Lindorfer (2006) raise similar critiques about the tendency of liberation theology to 'essentialize' the poor and feminist theology to 'essentialize' women. Drawing on experiences in Latin America (Vuola) and Northern Uganda (Lindorfer), they urge a discussion of praxis among liberation psychologists and theologians, one that more adequately responds to the lived experiences of poor women and children. In order to realize the preferential option for the poor, women's particular vulnerabilities related to poverty, that is, specifically, reproductive health (for Vuola) and violence against women (for Lindorfer), must be recognized and addressed.

Liberation theology and psychology and participatory and action research envision the possibility of transformational liberation. Work at their interface allows us to imagine radical change in both our material relations of power and powerlessness as well as in our individual and collective consciousness of oppression and liberation. Participatory and action researchers committed to praxis that moves towards transformational liberation are, little by little, creating some cross-race and cross-class gendered social spaces wherein protagonists engage in critically analyzing the interlocking systems of oppression that constrain and facilitate our sociality (e.g., Fine, 2006; Fine et al., 2001 2004). Those of us with access to university privilege and power are forging some relationships of 'just enough trust' through which we continually strive to deepen our understanding of the root causes of social illnesses and collectively engage in problem-posing alongside communities historically marginalized from power and resources. Through creative collaborations some of us are engaging in dialogical encounters with ourselves and others from differing racial, cultural, sexual, and social class statuses towards developing solutions that we hope will transform material relations and enable us not only to enact but to sustain new ways of being and doing.

In order to contribute to redressing power imbalances in global communities of the 21st century we research activists are also seeking to participate in contemporary social movements. As importantly we support community-, immigrant- and labor-based centers, among others, that serve as forums to promote the creation of knowledge from below, knowledge that energizes social movements (see, among others, Hale, 2007). Many of us also continue to sustain ourselves through teaching and learning in mainstream institutions. Within those contexts we participate within the global community at numbers of levels. We utilize the 'global identity' described briefly above as a resource for creating a global sense of community, identifying common concerns and common issues, and articulating global actions that could lead to global solutions. Through a renewed commitment to the transformation of individual and collective consciousness we seek to creatively explore the meanings of a 'new humanity' for all. For example, as university professors we organize forums to dialogue about the specific ways in which participatory and action researchers can 'transgress' institutional political correctness, voicing the ethical and moral commitments that enable us to stand in opposition to structural poverty and violence. We create daily possibilities for influencing institutions that support the status quo (e.g., universities, hospitals, human services organizations) in ways that more fully reflect a radical commitment to transformational processes as equal partners with marginalized communities of the majority world.

Yet, we recognize the limits and partiality of each of these efforts and the deep structural inequalities and gross violations of human rights that daily challenge the global majority. We have argued that the preferential option for the poor and liberation psychology contribute importantly to participatory and action research towards a liberatory transformative praxis. Yet we are still 'making the road as we go', ever aware of the contradictions described above and that transformational liberation is a process to be engaged in, not an endpoint or outcome that we have achieved. Working within the privileged US-based university context positions and situates our praxis, facilitating yet constraining our preferential option for the poor and thus our engagement in grassroots activists' struggles for radical social change.

NOTES

1 The authors thank Erzulie Coquillon for her extensive contributions to this chapter and John Gaventa, Roderick Watts, and Simone Lindorfer for insightful and thorough reviews of an earlier draft of this chapter. Despite these important contributions, the authors are fully responsible for the final chapter.

2 'Intersectionalities' refers to recent writings by postcolonial theorists, particularly women, who write at the intersection of race, gender and class analysis and position themselves critically vis-à-vis these structures of oppression.

3 Rather than the terms Third World or developing world, we use the term majority world to refer to countries outside the US and European orbit and to peoples of color within that orbit. These countries and these groups encompass a majority of the world's population and occupy a majority of the earth's land surface or geographical space.

4 A well known exception reflected in participatory and action and community based research is the experience at El Rigadío in Nicaragua in 1983 (see Rahman, Chapter 3 in this volume). The project took place at a moment during the early years of the development of the FSLN (the Sandinistas) when it was still organizing as a movement.

REFERENCES

Ajani ya Azibo, D. (1994) 'The kindred fields of black liberation theology and liberation psychology: a critical essay on their conceptual base and destiny', *Journal of Black Psychology*, 20 (3): 334–56.

Belenky, M.F., Clinchy, B.M., Goldberger, N.R. and Tarule, J.M. (1986) *Women's Ways of Knowing*. New York: Basic Books.

Bell, E.E. (2001/2006) 'Infusing race into the US discourse on action research', in P. Reason and H. Bradbury (eds), *Handbook of Action Research: Participative Inquiry and Practice*. London: Sage. pp. 48–58. Also published in P. Reason and H. Bradbury (eds) (2006), *Handbook of Action Research: Concise Student Edition*. London: Sage. pp. 49–59.

Berryman, P. (1987) *Liberation Theology: Essential Facts about the Revolutionary Movement in Latin America – and Beyond*. Philadelphia PA: Temple University Press.

Boff, L. and Boff, C. (1986) *Introducing Liberation Theology* (trans. Paul Burns). Maryknoll, NY. Orbis Books.

Bowers, C.A. and Apffel-Marglin, F. (eds) (2005) *Rethinking Freire: Globalization and the Environmental Crisis*. Mahwah, NJ: Lawrence Erlbaum Associates.

Bulhan, H.A. (1985) *Frantz Fanon and the Psychology of Oppression*. New York and London: Plenum Press.

Burton, M. and Kagan, C. (2005) 'Liberation social psychology: learning from Latin America', *Journal of Community and Applied Social Psychology*, 15: 63–78.

Cooke, B. and Kothari, U. (eds) (2001) *Participation: the New Tyranny?* London and New York: Zed Books.

Cone, J.H. (1970) *A Black Theology of Liberation*. Philadelphia: Lippincott.

Cornwall, A. (1996) 'Towards participatory practice: participatory rural appraisal (PRA) and the participatory process', in K. de Koning and M. Martin (eds), *Participatory Research in Health: Issues and Experiences*. Johannesburg: Zed Books. pp. 95–107.

Cornwall, A. (2001) *Making a Difference? Gender and Participatory Development*. (IDS Discussion Paper 378). Institute For Development Studies Discussion Paper. Available at http://www.ids.ac.uk/ids/bookshop/dp/dp/dp378.pdf

Cornwall, A. (2003) 'Whose Voices? Whose Choices? Reflections on Gender and Participatory Development', *World Development*, 31 (8): 1325–42.

Crawley, H. (1998) 'Living up to the empowerment claim? The potential of PRA', in I. Guijt and M.K. Shah (eds), *The Myth of Community: Gender Issues in Participatory Development*. London: Intermediate Technology Publications. pp. 24–34.

Duran, E. and Duran, B. (1995) *Native American Postcolonial Psychology*. Albany, NY: State University of New York Press.

Eschle, C. (2001) 'Globalizing civil society? Social movements and the challenge of global politics from below', in P. Hamel, H. Lustiger-Thaler, J.N. Pieterse, and S. Roseneil (eds), *Globalization and Social Movements*. New York: Palgrave. pp. 61–85.

Esteva, G., Stuchul, D.L. and Prakash, M.S. (2005) 'From a pedagogy for liberation to liberation from pedagogy', in C.A. Bowers and F. Apffel-Marglin (eds) *Rethinking Freire: Globalization and the Environmental Crisis*. Mahwah, NJ: Lawrence Erlbaum Associates. pp. 13–30.

Fals Borda, O. (1979) 'Investigating reality in order to transform it: The Colombian Experience'. *Dialectical Anthropology*, 4: 33–55.

Fals Borda, O. (2001/2006) 'Participatory (action) research in social theory: origins and challenges', in P. Reason and H. Bradbury (eds), *Handbook of Action Research. Participative Inquiry and Practice*. London: Sage. pp. 27–37. Also published P. Reason and H. Bradbury (eds) (2006), *Handbook of Action Research: Concise Student Edition*. London: Sage. pp. 27–37.

Fals Borda, O. and Rahman, M. A. (eds) (1991) *Action and Knowledge: Breaking the Monopoly with Participatory Action Research.* New York: Apex Press.

Fanon, F. (1967) *Black Skin, White Masks.* New York: Grove Press.

Fanon, F. (1968) *The Wretched of the Earth.* (trans. Constance Farrington). New York: Grove Press.

Farmer, P. (2005) *Pathologies of Power: Health, Human Rights, and the New War on the Poor.* Berkeley, CA: University of California Press.

Fine, M., Torre, M.E., Boudin, K., Bowen, I., Clark, J., Hylton, D., et al. (2001) *Changing Minds: The Impact of College in a Maximum-Security Prison: Effects on Women in Prison, the Prison Environment, Reincarceration Rates and Post-Release Outcomes.* New York: Graduate Center of the City University of New York & Bedford Correctional Facility.

Fine, M., Roberts, R.A., Torre, M.E., Bloom, J., Burns, A., Chajet, L., et al. (2004) *Echoes of Brown: Youth Documenting and Performing the Legacy of Brown V. Board of Education.* New York: Teacher's College Press.

Fine, M. (2006) 'Bearing Witness: methods for researching oppression and resistance: a textbook for critical research. *Social Justice Research*, 19 (1): 1–26.

Freire, P. (1970). *Pedagogy of the Oppressed.* New York: Seabury Press.

Friedman, T. L. (2000) *The Lexus and the Olive Tree.* New York: Anchor Books.

Gaventa, J. and Cornwall, A. (2001/2006) 'Power and knowledge', in P. Reason and H. Bradbury (eds), *Handbook of Action Research: Participative Inquiry and Practice.* Thousand Oaks: Sage. pp. 70–80. Also published in P. Reason and H. Bradbury (eds) (2006), *Handbook of Action Research: Concise Student Edition.* London: Sage. pp. 71–82.

Gordon, T. (1973) 'Notes on white and black psychology', *Journal of Social Issues*, 29 (1): 87–95.

Gottlieb, E.E. and La Belle, T. (1990) 'Ethnographic contextualization of Freire's discourse: consciousness-raising, theory and practice', *Anthropology & Education Quarterly*, 21 (1): 3–18.

Gutiérrez, G. (1973/1988) *A Theology of Liberation.* New York: Orbis.

Gutiérrez, G. (1984/2003) *We Drink from Our Own Wells: The Spiritual Journey of a People* [*Beber en su propio pozo: En el itinerario spiritual de un pueblo*]. (trans. M.J. O'Connel). Maryknoll, NY: Orbis Books.

Hale, C. (ed) (2007) *Engaging Contradictions: Theory, Politics and Methods of Activist Scholarship.* Berkeley, CA: University of California Press.

Hall, B. (2001) 'I wish this were a poem of practices of participatory research', in P. Reason and H. Bradbury (eds), *Handbook of Action Research. Participative Inquiry and Practice*, London: Sage. pp. 171–8.

Hickey, S. and Mohan, G. (2005) 'Relocating participation within a radical politics of development'. *Development and Change*, 36 (2): 237–62.

Hinsdale, M., Lewis, H.M. and Waller, S. M. (1995) *It Comes from the People: Community Development and Local Theology.* Philadelphia, PA: Temple University Press.

Hope, A. and Timmel, S. (1984–2000) *Training for Transformation: a Handbook for Community Workers* (Vols 1–4). London: Intermediate Technology Publications.

International Campaign to Ban Landmines. (1998–2005) *Possible Lessons for Other Campaigns.* Retrieved 1 February 2006 from http://www.icbl.org/tools/faq/campaign/lessons

Jensen, J. (2002) 'The Psychology of globalization', *American Psychologist*, 57 (10): 774–83.

Kitching, G. (2001) *Seeking Social Justice through Globalization: Escaping a Nationalist Perspective.* University Park, PA: Pennsylvania University Press.

Lindorfer, S. (2006) '*Sharing the pain of the bitter hearts: liberation psychology and gender-related violence in Eastern Africa'.* Unpublished dissertation. Departments of Theology and Psychology, University of Tübingen, Germany.

Lykes, M. B. and Coquillon, E. (2006) 'Participatory and action research and feminisms: towards transformative praxis', in S. Hesse-Biber (ed.), *Handbook of Feminist Research.* San Francisco, CA: Jossey-Bass. pp. 297–326.

Maguire, P. (2001/2006) 'Uneven ground: feminism and action research', in P. Reason and H. Bradbury (eds), *Handbook of Action Research: Participative Inquiry and Practice.* Thousand Oaks: Sage. pp. 59–69. Also published in P. Reason and H. Bradbury (eds) (2006), *Handbook of Action Research: Concise Student Edition.* London: Sage. pp. 60–70.

Martín-Baró, I. (1994). *Writings for a Liberation Psychology: Ignacio Martín-Baró.* (eds and trans. A. Aron and S. Corne). Cambridge, MA: Harvard University Press.

Moane, C. (1999) *Gender and Colonialism: a Psychological Analysis of Oppression and Liberation.* New York: St. Martin's Press.

Prilleltensky, I. and Nelson, G. (2002) *Doing Psychology Critically: Making a Difference in Diverse Settings.* New York: Palgrave MacMillan.

Rahman, A. (2004) 'Globalization: the emerging ideology in the popular protests and grassroots action research', *Action Research*, 2 (1): 9–23.

Rahman, M.A. (1985) 'The theory and practice of participatory action research', in. O. Fals Borda (ed.), *The Challenge of Social Change.* London: Sage. pp. 107–32. (previously published in *The Theory and*

Practice of Participatory Research (WEP 10/WP. 29/1983). Geneva: International Labour Office)

Rahman, M. A. (1990) 'The case of the Third World: people's self-development', *Community Development Journal* 25 (4): 307–14.

Rahman, M. A. (1991) 'The theoretical standpoint of PAR', in O. Fals Borda and M.A. Rahman (eds), *Action and Knowledge: Breaking the Monopoly with Participatory Action Research*. New York: The Apex Press.

Reason, P. and Bradbury, H. (eds) (2001) *Handbook of Action Research: Participative Inquiry and Practice*. London: Sage.

Roodt, M.J. (1996) '"Participatory development": A jargon concept?', In J.K. Coetzee, and J. Graaff (eds) *Reconstruction, Development and People*. Halfway House, South Africa: International Thomson Publishing. pp. 312–23.

Rosen, R. (2000) *The World Split Open: How the Modern Women's Movement Changed America*. New York: Penguin Putnam.

Ruether, R. (1983) *Sexism and God-talk: Toward a Feminist Theology*. Boston: Beacon Press.

Smith, J. and Johnston, H. (2002) 'Globalization and resistance: an introduction', in J. Smith and H. Johnston (eds) *Globalization and Resistance:*

Transnational Dimensions of Social Movements. Oxford: Rowman and Littlefield. pp. 1–10.

Stackpool-Moore, L., Taylor, P., Pettit, J. and Millican, J. (eds) (2006) *Currents of Change: Exploring Relationships between Teaching, Learning and Development*. Brighton: Institute of Development Studies.

Stahler-Sholk, R. (2001) 'Globalization and social movement resistance: the Zapatista rebellion in Chiapas, Mexico', *New Political Science*, 23 (4): 493–516.

UNDP (United Nations Development Program) (2006) *Global Partnership for Development*. [Annual Report]. New York: United Nations. Retrieved 4 August, 2006 from http://www.undp.org/publications/annualreport2006/english-report.pdf

UNICEF (2005) *Facts on Children: Immunizations*. Retrieved 30 January 2006 from http://www.unicef.org/media/media_9479.html

Vuola, E. (2002) *Limits of Liberation: Feminist Theology and the Ethics of Poverty and Reproduction*. London and New York: Sheffield Academic Press.

Watts, R. J. and Serrano-García, I. (2003) 'The quest for a liberating community psychology: an overview', *American Journal of Community Psychology*, 31 (1/2): 73–78.

8

Critical Theory and Participatory Action Research

Stephen Kemmis[1]

This chapter presents a set of arguments about action research drawing connections to aspects of the view of critical theory associated with the Frankfurt School, particularly the work of Jürgen Habermas. It draws together a succession of ideas about action research and the study of practice that lead me to a new overall view of critical participatory action research, synthesizing them in a new definition of critical participatory action research – or perhaps as a new thesis about what it is.

In this chapter, I present a set of arguments about action research drawing connections to aspects of the view of critical theory associated with the Frankfurt School (Jay, 1973; Wiggershaus, 1994), particularly the work of Jürgen Habermas. In my chapter in the first edition of this *Handbook*, I described ways in which developments in Habermas's theorizing were refracted in my changing views of action research. In our chapter for the third edition of the *Sage Handbook of Qualitative Research* (Kemmis and McTaggart, 2005), Robin McTaggart and I reflected again on how our views of action research had been changed by our reading of Habermasian critical theory.

In what follows, I draw together a succession of ideas about action research and the study of practice that have led me to a new overall view of *critical participatory action research*, synthesizing them in a new definition of critical participatory action research – or perhaps as a new thesis about what it is. The discussion draws attention to specific problems and issues which I believe to be crucial in understanding the nature of action research.

PRELIMINARY CONSIDERATIONS

Kemmis and McTaggart (1988) defined action research as:

a form of collective self-reflective enquiry undertaken by participants in social situations in order to improve the rationality and justice of their own social or educational *practices*, as well as their *understanding* of these practices and the *situations* in which these practices are carried out. (p. 1; emphases added)

This definition emphasized that the research should be undertaken by *participants* in social practices following Kurt Lewin's (1952) views of action research as involving participants *collectively* in researching their own situations, stemming from his findings about the role of group decision in securing participant commitment to social change. It emphasized *self-reflection* in the light of Lawrence Stenhouse's (1975) notion of the teacher as researcher, Donald Schön's (1983, 1987, 1991) views of the reflective practitioner, and also Jürgen Habermas's (1972) views about the interests that shaped the generation of knowledge (knowledge-constitutive interests) through different kinds of natural and social sciences – technical, practical and emancipatory interests.

Recent thinking about action research gives increasing emphasis to the *social*. Some views of action research focus on practitioners as individuals and on a naïve opposition of the individual and the group (construed as an aggregate of individuals) within a general view which Habermas (1987b, 1992) characterized as 'the philosophy of the subject'. This is the view that truth is the kind of category that can be applied to propositions apprehended in consciousness by knowing subjects – a matter on which advocates of the opposing perspectives of positivism (and its philosophical successors) and interpretivism agree. Habermas (1984, 1987a, 1987b) showed how 'the philosophy of the subject' can no longer be sustained, and proposed instead a 'post-metaphysical' philosophy in which 'truth' becomes manifest only in attempts at 'truth-telling', that is, through exploration of the validity of propositions in communicative action in which participants aim at intersubjective agreement, mutual

understanding and unforced consensus about what to do.

Moreover, Habermas has made a strong case against 'praxis philosophy' – the philosophy that, since Hegel and Marx, has supposed that a state (or other social 'totality') as a self-regulating macro-subject, could, through its own self-reflection, achieve a grasp of reality that would allow it to steer itself differently or transform itself in a coherent way out of unsatisfactory conditions, irrationality or contradiction. In *Truth and Justification* (2003c), Habermas argues against 'praxis philosophy', and in favour of a pluralism that he believes has replaced the kind of 'collectivism' that propelled communism in the 20th century.

Habermas's (1984, 1987a) analysis of social life in late modernity shows that no social structures of government or civil society can any longer claim to be fully integrated as 'wholes' or 'whole systems'. Instead of these totalities, we have only organizations and institutions and groups interacting and contesting with one another. Although he is a constitutionalist who believes that democratic societies can operate *as if* they were social wholes through basic law and a constitution, he recognizes that, in practice, there is no single steering centre that in fact has decisive and unitary steering power in contemporary Western democracies. Against praxis philosophy, he thus proposes (especially 1987b, 1996) a discourse theory which recognizes the existence of various kinds of open 'public spheres' or 'communicative spaces' in which individuals and groups thematize and explore issues and crises, not from the perspective of whole systems (either people or states or other social totalities as 'systems') but in terms of public discussions aimed at greater understanding and transformations of social life at the moments and places where specific crises occur. In particular, he has been interested in the 'boundary crises' that arise at the points where social systems (organizations, institutions, states and their structures and functions) collide with the lifeworlds (the forms of interpersonal, social life of real people and groups) which give meaning, solidarity and identity to those who inhabit them.

These arguments pose challenges to action research. They deprive action research of a simple understanding of itself as (a) transforming individuals as self-regulating persons and (b) transforming institutions, organizations or states as self-regulating social 'macro-subjects'. To be regarded as a rational enterprise, then, action research must find a way to work not just on the self-realization of persons or the realization of more rational and coherent organizations, but in the interstices between people and organizations, and across the boundaries between lifeworlds and systems. It must work *in the conversations and communications* of participants about crises and difficulties confronted by social systems and the lifeworlds in which people find meaning, solidarity and significance. It must become a process of facilitating public discourse in public spheres. To do this it must be rather different from what it has been.

Critical participatory action research, as I conceptualize it here, is a particular form of action research that aims to respond to these challenges. In the sections that follow, I present a number of arguments that suggest the form that critical participatory action research must take. The final part of the chapter synthesizes discussions presented in each preceding section, culminating in a new definition of critical participatory action research.

1 PARTICIPATORY AND COLLECTIVE RESEARCH TO ACHIEVE EFFECTIVE-HISTORICAL CONSCIOUSNESS IN AND OF PRACTICE AS *PRAXIS*

Studying Practice/Praxis

The Kemmis and McTaggart definition of action research (cited earlier) emphasized three foci for observation and possible transformation through action research:

practices, *understandings* and *situations*. While the term 'practice' is ubiquitous, different theorists of practice understand practice in very different ways (Kemmis, 2005, forthcoming a). Kemmis and McTaggart (2000) showed how practice is variously understood from either an 'objective' (external, outsider, observer, other) perspective or from a 'subjective' (internal, insider, participant, self) perspective – or *dialectically* in terms of both. To understand practice 'subjectively' is to focus on the person/s involved, as *they* see things; to understand it 'objectively' is usually to focus on practice as *others* see it; to understand practice dialectically is to attempt to understand practice in terms of the mutual-constitution, tensions and connections between the outside/inside and observer/participant perspectives. Similarly, practice is variously understood from the perspective of the individual (often a psychological perspective) or the perspective of the social (usually a sociological or systems-theoretic perspective) – or, occasionally, a dialectical perspective connecting both. Critical participatory action research aims at gaining a dialectical perspective on practice in both dimensions together (from outside and inside perspectives on individual participants and the social construction of their practice).

According to Carr and Kemmis (1986):

'Practice' in its commonsense meaning, is usually understood to refer to habitual or customary action. But it also means 'the exercise of an act', referring back to its origins in the Greek notion of *praxis*, meaning 'informed, committed action'. The action researcher distinguishes between practice as habitual and customary, on the one hand, and the informed, committed action of *praxis*, on the other. One way to describe the general aim ... of educational action research would be to say that [it is] interested in a critical revival of practice which can transform it into *praxis*, bringing it under considered critical control, and enlivening it with a commitment to educational and social values. (p. 190)

A special issue of the journal *Pedagogy, Culture and Society* (vol. 13, 2005) was devoted to exploring neo-Aristotelian views of *praxis*, and its distinction from *techné* (or technical, instrumental, means–ends, 'making' action). Contributors argued that the technical understanding of practice has now become so widespread as to deprive practitioners of a full understanding of the moral basis of their work, and of the traditions that have informed what it means to 'do' a practice or to 'be' a practitioner, especially the practitioner of a profession. To highlight the tensions and connections between these different perspectives, I use the term 'practice/*praxis*' to remind the reader that we are almost always concerned with practices as they are seen from the external ('objective') perspective of the observer *as well as* the internal ('subjective') perspective of the practitioner engaging in *praxis*.

Research that is Participatory – Individual and Collective Participation

In action research and in the social and educational sciences generally, we are normally concerned not solely with practices as the behaviour or intentional action of individuals, but also with the ways those practices are socially-constructed and 'held in place' by cultural-discursive, social and material-economic fields that precede and shape the conduct of practice/*praxis*.

If, as Carr and Kemmis (1986: 191) suggest, 'action research ... cannot be other than research into one's own practice', it also follows that if practice/*praxis* is collectively constructed, then practices must be understood not solely from the perspectives of the individuals involved, but also in terms of the collective understandings and collective effects of those involved and affected by the practice. Thus, action research must take into account the perspectives of the range of people involved or affected, or, preferably, involve them collectively in the research process. Since its inception, action research has been understood as a process in which participants can *be* or *become* researchers (see, for example, Lewin, 1952).

Furthermore, since changing or transforming practice/*praxis* requires not only changes

by individuals but also by those with whom they interact, changing practice/*praxis* also requires *extra-individual* changes – that is, changes in cultural-discursive, social, and material-economic dimensions in which practice/*praxis* is constituted (Kemmis, 2005, forthcoming a). The transformation of practice/*praxis* is therefore necessarily a social process, and, since changes are likely to have different consequences in terms of the self-interests of the different individuals and groups involved, the transformation of practice/*praxis* is also, inevitably, a political process.

Understanding and Interpretation: Towards Effective-Historical Consciousness

Since the dawn of modern social science, researchers have confronted the problem of how to understand the Other – whether a person, an object of art or social life (Outhwaite, 1975). The case is even more difficult when a participant in practice/*praxis* aims to understand her- or himself as *both* a subject and an object. Such a person can 'understand' themselves and their situation only from within their own conceptual resources, their own language and discourses, their own familiar ways of seeing.

Moreover, participants' interpretive categories are not theirs alone. Their ideas are generally the products of long histories and traditions of usage, carrying meanings that existed long before they came to use the ideas to understand their particular practice/*praxis* situation. So, too, particular practice/*praxis* situations are always pre-formed in local and wider histories. Thus, the person wishing to understand their own practice/*praxis* clearly must also attempt to understand the prejudices or perspectives built into their own ways of understanding – a task which may seem impossible. At one time, positivist science hoped to break free of misunderstandings by developing a transcendent 'objective' perspective – a hope that proved unattainable. By contrast, the perspective of interpretive science and history has sought ways to loosen the bonds of misunderstanding through the hermeneutical approach (hermeneutics being, historically, the interpretation of religious texts, but now applied to the interpretation of works of art, cultures and people). The contemporary classic account of hermeneutics is Hans-Georg Gadamer's (1975) book *Truth and Method*.[2] Gadamer rejects the notion that interpretation can be understood as a 'method' by analogy with 'scientific method'. He explores the nature of interpretation in a variety of contexts, with particular reference to the problem of interpretation faced by the historian who aims to understand a tradition while also being a product of that tradition. In particular, Gadamer describes the historian's (self) consciousness of how history is effective in her or his own historicality, actively influencing her or his interpretations (via 'prejudices' or taken-for-granted assumptions) – a state of intense historical self-awareness that Gadamer calls 'effective-historical consciousness' (pp. 267–9).

Action research must similarly conceptualize 'understanding' in a sophisticated way, not assuming that 'understanding' is a simple, unmediated process of grasping something in consciousness. It means also that we must think of interpretation as a process of interpreting ourselves as well as the object we are trying to interpret. And perhaps, taking a lead from Habermas (1989a; Holub, 1991), we might also conclude that it is possible to explore the linkages between language, labour and domination to discover some ways in which our language and thought are bound by ideology, shaping our ways of seeing and 'not seeing'. We might thus hope for a view of action research that includes not only a Gadamerian hermeneutics (effective-historical consciousness) but something more – the possibility of interrogating the range and limits of our language and thought by observing not only how they have been shaped by history, in usage, but also in the service of particular kinds of interests that can be read in the structures and consequences of particular kinds of work and

political life. As we shall see, Habermas's (1984, 1987a) *Theory of Communicative Action* and other writings provide resources for this task.

2   RESEARCH FOR CRITICAL (SELF-) REFLECTION

Critical

Max Horkheimer (1972), one of the founders of the Frankfurt School of critical theory, described critical theory as a form of theorizing motivated by a deep concern to overcome social injustice and the establishment of more just social conditions for all people. He contrasted critical theory and 'traditional theory', by which he meant positivistic science which aims to build scientific knowledge progressively by accumulating empirical knowledge of the world, taking for granted a distinction between facts and values. Critical theory, he said, 'has no specific influence on its side, except concern for the abolition of social injustice. ... Its own nature ... turns it towards a changing of history and the establishment of justice' (pp. 242–3).

The notion of 'critique' in critical theory means exploring 'existing conditions' (Marx, 1967) to find how particular perspectives, social structures or practices may be irrational, unjust, alienating or inhumane. More than this, it means finding how perspectives, social structures and practices are interlinked in ways that cause them to produce such consequences. The classical case was Marx's (1867/1887) analysis of class relationships under capitalism.

In critical participatory action research, participants aim to be 'critical' in this way, trying to find how particular perspectives, social structures and practices 'conspire' to produce untoward effects, with the aim of finding ways to change things so these consequences can be avoided. Being critical in this sense means acting negatively *against* identified irrationality, injustice and suffering, rather than positively *for* some predetermined view of what is to count as rational or just or good for humankind.

The 'Self' and Extra-Individual Features of Practice/Praxis

Critical participatory action researchers understand the notion of the 'self' differently from conceptions of the self in some other views of action research, for example, the notion of 'self' that appears in Schön's (1983, 1987, 1991) notion of the 'self-reflective practitioner'. First, on the basis of the argument about the individual and the collective in action research, the 'self' may now be read not as a singular and isolated individual, but as implying a plurality, a sociality that has shaped it as a 'self'.

Second, critical participatory action research understands the self as *constructed* through developmental-historical, cultural-discursive, social and material-economic interactions between people. As Habermas (1992: 26) remarks, following George Herbert Mead: 'no individuation is possible without socialization, and no socialization is possible without individualization'. Processes of individuation and socialization do not end at some point when a person becomes adult, but continue to shape individuals and social relationships in all settings. Thus, critical participatory action research is as much interested in changing the ways participants in an educational or social setting *interact* as it is in the changes *within* each individual.

Third, critical participatory action researchers take seriously the claim that both practices and the understandings of practice that action research aims to develop are formed in cultural-discursive, social and material-economic fields that are *extra-individual* (Kemmis, forthcoming a) – fields that exist in social spaces beyond particular individuals, even though the action of individuals may be necessary to (re-) constitute practices. Bourdieu (1977, 1990, 1998; Bourdieu and Wacquant, 1992) speaks of the formation of social practices in terms of 'habitus' and

'fields'. On the side of the individual, *habitus* is the set of dispositions or capabilities for action of the individual actor, like the dispositions and capabilities necessary to play football well. On the side of the cultural, social and economic, *fields* are the cultural, social and economic arrangements that pre-construct and *prefigure* (Schatzki, 2002: 210ff.) fields of action for the actors who enter them. The notion of fields draws attention to arrangements that generally precede and prefigure any practice; for example, a school and its resources, curricula and pedagogical practices all precede and prefigure the day-to-day enactment of the practice of education in the school, having 'a life of their own', as it were. As Kemmis (2005, forthcoming a) argues, transforming practices therefore requires not only changing the knowledge (or habitus) of practitioners and others who participate in a practice, but also changing these fields (and other extra-individual features of practice). Changing extra-individual features of practice can be difficult because cultures and discourses, social connections and solidarities, and material-economic arrangements exist between and beyond the individuals whose particular actions enact, but do not by themselves constitute, practices.

In critical participatory action research, the 'self' must thus be understood as a situated and located self. Each self is formed through a particular and unique developmental history; it is constructed in a particular cultural-discursive history; it is located in a particular and unique set of social connections and solidarities; and it sits within a particular history of material and economic exchanges in the world. 'Subjectivity' and 'identity' likewise must thus be viewed as fluid and dynamic, and as continually reconstructed in cultural-discursive, social and material-economic dimensions of interaction. 'Subjectivity' and 'identity' are not to be understood as fixed attributes of persons.

Understanding the self as situated and located in this way gives greater force to Gadamer's notion of effective-historical understanding. It becomes clear that the situations, settings, conditions and circumstances of practices cannot be adequately understood without also appreciating how practitioners understand them – *and* how the practitioner's interpretive categories are located in history, culture, discourses, social networks, material and economic exchanges. This view also gives more force to Habermas's objection against Gadamer that understanding does not occur in some pure form of language that transcends individuals. Understandings and the languages and discourses in which they are expressed are themselves already galvanized by relations of work and power, and they are the vehicles of work and power relations (as also amply evidenced in the work of Foucault, e.g. 1970, 1972, 1977, 1979, 1990).

Habermas (1974: 29) warns of dangers of solitary self-reflection:

> The self-reflection of a lone subject ... requires a quite paradoxical achievement: one part of the self must be split off from the other part in such a manner that the subject can be in a position to render aid to itself. ... [Furthermore], in the act of self-reflection the subject can deceive itself.

He thus argues that the organization of enlightenment is best understood as a social process, drawing on the critical capacities of groups, not just as an individual process drawing out new understandings in individuals. Together, people offer one another collective critical capacity to arrive at insights into the nature and consequences of their practices, their understandings, and the situations, settings, circumstances and conditions of practice. As we shall see, critical participatory action research opens communicative spaces that permit and foster such collective reflection.

3 RESEARCH THAT OPENS COMMUNICATIVE SPACE

Communicative Action

Habermas (1984, 1987a, 1987b) describes communicative action as action oriented towards intersubjective agreement, mutual understanding and unforced consensus about what to do. It is the kind of communication that occurs when people turn aside from strategic action (getting something done) to ask 'what are we doing?' In these cases, they may explore the four validity claims suggested in Habermas's theory of communicative competence:

- is it comprehensible (do we understand one another)?
- is it true (in the sense of accurate)?
- is it truthfully (sincerely) stated?
- is it morally right and appropriate?

As they work together to explore their practices, understandings and situations, participants in a critical participatory action research 'project' are interlocutors who *open communicative space* in which they encounter one another in a slightly unusual and slightly formal way – that is, with a shared commitment to communicative action. It is only 'slightly' unusual because people and groups frequently do interrupt themselves to explore questions of meaning, truth, truthfulness and moral rightness together. And only 'slightly' formal because the participants are usually aware in such circumstances that their discussions are moving to a meta-level at which these formal features of their communication and understandings are the objects of their collective reflection.

Placing the notion of 'opening communicative space' at the heart of a view of critical participatory action research is to emphasize the inclusive, collective, transformative nature of its aims – aims which serve and transcend the self-interests of individual participants. It is also to suggest that critical participatory action researchers undertake research into their own practices not just to 'perfect' or improve themselves as individuals, but also in the interests of acting rightly in terms of the historical consequences of their action.

In *Truth and Justification*, Habermas (2003c) gives an updated account of his view of communicative action, including the kind of communicative action we find in everyday life and in wider public spheres of argument about contemporary issues, including new insights about the presuppositions of argumentation:

> ... the rational acceptability of validity claims is *ultimately* based only on reasons that stand up to objections under certain exacting conditions of communication. If the process of argumentation is to live up to its meaning, communication in the form of rational discourse must, if possible, allow all relevant information and explanations to be brought up and weighed so that the stance participants take can be intrinsically motivated solely by the revisionary power of free-floating reasons. However, if this is the intuitive meaning that we associate with argumentation in general, then we also know that a practice may not seriously count as argumentation unless it meets certain pragmatic presuppositions.
>
> The four most important presuppositions are (a) publicity and inclusiveness: no one who could make a relevant contribution with regard to a controversial validity claim must be excluded; (b) equal rights to engage in communication: everyone must have the same opportunity to speak to the matter at hand; (c) exclusion of deception and illusion: participants have to mean what they say; and (d) absence of coercion: communication must be free of restrictions that prevent the better argument from being raised or from determining the outcome of the discussion. Presuppositions (a), (b) and (d) subject one's behaviour in argumentation to the rules of an egalitarian universalism. *With regard to moral-practical issues*, it follows from these rules that the interests and value-orientations of every affected person are equally taken into consideration. And since the participants in practical discourses are simultaneously the ones who are affected, presupposition (c) – which in *theoretical-empirical disputes* requires only a sincere and unconstrained weighing of the arguments – takes on the further significance that one remain critically alert to self-deception as well as hermeneutically open and sensitive to how others understand themselves and the world. (pp. 106–7; emphases in original)

Habermas then outlines (pp. 108–9) the universalizing capacity of argument as it appeals to wider and wider frameworks of justification, basing the search for justification and truth on a 'decentred' perspective that each participant gains as she or he becomes more sensitive to the views and perspectives of others, and by appealing to a wider community of potential participants who could engage in the discussion.

This taking-into-account of the perspectives and interests of others – what Habermas describes as 'decentring' (p. 109) and implying 'egalitarian universalism' (p. 107) – is at the heart of moral discourses about what it is right to do in any particular situation. It also describes the kinds of discussions that occur in many critical participatory action research initiatives.

From Subjectivity to Intersubjectivity

The communicative space opened by communicative action, and by participatory action research undertaken as a kind of process of communicative action, is an *intersubjective* space that exists between and beyond individual participants. Habermas (2003a) describes the linguistic grounding of intersubjectivity:

> As historical and social beings we find ourselves always already in a linguistically structured life-world. In the forms of communication through which we reach an understanding with one another about something in the world and about ourselves, we encounter a transcending power. Language is not a kind of private property. No one possesses exclusive rights over the common medium of the communicative practices we must intersubjectively share. No single participant can control the structure, or even the course, of processes of reaching understanding and self-understanding. How speakers and hearers make use of their communicative freedom to take yes- or no-positions is not a matter of their subjective discretion. For they are free only in virtue of the binding force of the justifiable claims they raise towards one another. The *logos* of language embodies the power of the intersubjective, which precedes and grounds the subjectivity of speakers.
>
> The *logos* of language escapes our control, and yet we are the ones, the subjects capable of speech and action, who reach an understanding with one another in this medium. It remains 'our' language. The unconditionedness of truth and freedom is a necessary presupposition of our practices, but beyond the constituents of 'our' form of life they lack any ontological guarantee. (pp. 10–11)

The intersubjective is not somehow 'above' individual understandings or self-understandings. The intersubjective exists in the communicative space in which speakers and hearers encounter one another – in speech and writing. The agreements they reach do not negate their individual subjectivity.

In terms of *justification*, such 'truth' as we can ever find will be *in communication*, and we will find it only through communicative action – searching with one another for intersubjective agreement, mutual understanding and consensus about what to do. Our ordinary conversations are never universal in the sense that they are all-inclusive; they never entirely escape the time and space in which they occur; and they frequently run aground in misperceptions, misunderstandings, disagreements or conflict. When they do run aground, all we can do is to pause until we are able to re-engage with one another on the basis of civility and reciprocal recognition of one another as persons worthy of respect. Nor will our conversations be completely coherent, fully argued and complete. The topics, themes and circumstances of our communicative action will forever be changing, leaving all our agreements incomplete and partial – halting steps and limited achievements on a path towards an unattainable *complete* agreement, *complete* understanding, and *perfect* consensus about what to do. Frail and fallible though it may be, all we have, and all we will ever have, is the conversation (Kemmis, forthcoming b).

This, then, is to take a fallibilist view of truth – a view that recognizes that current and new understandings are always open to revision in the light of as-yet-undiscovered knowledge or understandings – and a view that truth must always be justified discursively – through argument. The quality of the argument, and the ways people participate in it, is what gives life to being 'critical'.

Lifeworld and System

In Habermas's theory of communicative action, the 'domain' of *intersubjectivity*

replaces the idea that *truth is something apprehended in the consciousness of an individual*. Breaking with this tradition, in Habermas's view, is the key to escaping some of the dead ends that both 'objectivist' and 'subjectivist' philosophy and science has been led into. He breaks with 'the philosophy of the subject' by arguing that it is *in the space of the intersubjective* – the *lifeworlds* we inhabit, and in which we encounter one another as persons – that the possibility of truth and moral rightness resides, not in the consciousness of individuals participating in the discussion – although each individually has the communicative power to take 'yes' or 'no' positions with regard to the substance of arguments as they unfold.

Each of us inhabits a variety of lifeworlds, and the social world contains an indeterminate variety of lifeworlds – very different ways of life in different places. In Habermas's social theory and philosophy, the lifeworld is not only to be understood as a 'real' social space inhabited by particular people; it is also to be understood as a *court of appeal* (my phrase, not Habermas's) in which validity claims can be tested through argument or conversation. This is a convivial and human view of truth and justification that does not depend on appeal to a transcendental perspective (such as an omniscient God) to *make* a statement true.

Table 8.1 outlines the key elements and universal structures of the lifeworld identified by Habermas. It should be noted that he indicates that *particular* lifeworlds are diverse, characterized by multiplicity and diffusion, and that different lifeworlds overlap and interweave. The universal structures, however, give a clear idea of what is meant by the concept of 'the lifeworld'.

In the *Theory of Communicative Action* (1984, 1987a), Habermas distinguishes communicative action from strategic action (action oriented towards successfully achieving known outcomes by relevant means). In highly differentiated, complex societies, strategic action is usually guided by functional reason. Functional reason is expressed

Table 8.1 *Components of lifeworlds*

Culture	*Society*	*Person*
Reproduced via *cultural reproduction* which connects newly arising situations to existing conditions in *the semantic dimension.*	Reproduced via *social integration* which connects newly arising situations to existing conditions in *the dimension of social space.*	Reproduced via *socialization* which connects newly arising situations to existing conditions in *the dimension of historical time.*
Cultural reproduction secures continuity of tradition and coherency of knowledge.	Social integration coordinates action via legitimately ordered social relationships and lends constancy to the identity of groups.	Socialization secures the acquisition of generalized capacities for action for future generations and takes care of harmonizing individual life histories and collective life forms.
Cultural reproduction renews interpretative schemata susceptible of consensus ('*valid knowledge*').	Social integration renews legitimately ordered social relationships ('*solidarities*').	Socialization renews capacities for interaction ('*personal identities*').

in a language of goals and means, and, in the context of administrative systems, often in a language of roles, organizational functions and rules. *The Theory of Communicative Action* provides a critique of functional reason, arguing that communicative action offers a way out of being trapped in functional reason characteristic of the administrative systems that govern so much of contemporary life. Under contemporary social conditions, many different kinds of *systems* have become 'relatively autonomous' – that is, driven by their own local demands, and freed from their anchors in valid knowledge (claims to truth), social solidarities (morality and claims to justice), and individual understandings and capacities (authenticity). This autonomy means that systems become *uncoupled* from the lifeworlds that initially grounded them. Once uncoupled, systems thinking and functionality can then *colonize* lifeworld relationships, creating *rationalized* models of right action that are inappropriate for relationships between people wherever these should properly be based on valid knowledge, solidarity and personal capacities – as, for example, in relationships among members of a community of practice (like a profession), or in social welfare settings where people should be treated with recognition and respect.

Habermas identifies a number of pathologies in contemporary Western societies that are a consequence of the uncoupling of system and lifeworld and the rationalization

of the lifeworld. In his view, concerns about social integration, and maintenance of social order have become more insistent, pervasive and dominant with increasing social complexity, especially the increasing complexity of social life from the perspective of social systems. Moreover, more and more of the work of coordinating systems has been 'handed over' to the *steering media* of *money* and *administrative power* as bases for exchange between social subsystems. While this helps reduce the complexity of practical questions (because they are increasingly handled as questions about monetary exchange and administrative regulation, dealt with by functional reason and rational-purposive action), this transfer also permits further increases in the complexity of system relationships and coordination, to a crisis point – the point where a variety of kinds of crises begin to manifest themselves in the lifeworlds of participants (Habermas, 1987a: 143). Under these conditions, the smooth reproduction of lifeworlds can no longer be guaranteed because participants experience their lifeworld connections with others as fragmented and overburdened. Under such conditions, the regulation of social systems is increasingly difficult to manage, since the lifeworld anchoring necessary for system operation is no longer secure.

Critical participatory action research, working across the boundaries of lifeworlds and systems, creates opportunities to explore these boundary-crises by opening communicative space among participants and others involved in and affected by their actions.

Public Discourse in Public Spheres

It is not easy to establish the social and discursive conditions under which people can equally, openly and fearlessly ask and answer questions, and conduct themselves civilly towards reaching intersubjective agreement, mutual understanding and consensus about what to do Kemmis (forthcoming b). In practice, argumentation is frequently subject to distortion, deadline pressures and practical constraints on 'really' understanding one another's points of view. These limits and interruptions are not fatal, however, they are just *aporias* or gaps to be explored in other discussions – the openings for new conversations. What holds a group together is members' tacit or explicit agreement to continue the conversation. Intersubjective agreement, mutual understanding and mutual consensus are always situated and provisional. Action research initiatives can be understood as fora designed to open communicative space so emerging agreements and disagreements, understandings and decisions can be problematized and explored openly (Habermas, 1987b, 1996; Kemmis and McTaggart, 2005).

In Chapter 8 of *Between Facts and Norms*, Habermas (1996; see also 1992, Lecture XI) explores this kind of communication in terms of *public discourse* in *public spheres* (see also Kemmis and McTaggart, 2005). The kind of public discourse he has in mind is communicative action, the kind of public spheres he has in mind are communicative spaces constituted by participants themselves for dialogue in which there is voluntary participation; in which speakers have or take communicative freedom; and in which participants aim to be inclusive (both socially and in the language they use in addressing each other). Such communicative spaces may be created within an organization, but only by temporarily suspending, literally 'for argument's sake', the hierarchical roles and the functional imperatives of the organization as a system directed towards attaining particular objectives. More generally, communicative spaces are to be found at the margins of institutions, blurring boundaries and connecting with other public spheres. Conversations within these communicative spaces presuppose *communicative freedom*. They frequently arise in response to *legitimation-deficits* – in response to circumstances, policies or decisions which lack legitimacy in the eyes of those involved. Legitimation-deficits are frequently the central themes which give rise to social movements, becoming the foci for sustained practical and critical discussions about the nature and consequences of possible courses of action by those involved. And the outcomes of these discussions may be to influence an organization not directly but indirectly, by 'laying siege to the formally-organized political system by encircling it with reasons without, however, attempting to overthrow or replace it' (Baynes, 1995: 217). Habermas (1996) observes that communicative action in such groups builds *solidarity* among participants, in turn giving them a sense of *communicative power* and lending *legitimacy* to their emerging agreements, understandings and decisions – as a counter to the legitimation crisis which may have provoked the formation of a particular public sphere.

Critical participatory action research initiatives open communicative space beyond the sphere of immediate participants in a project or group. Very likely, their discussions will connect to a wider public sphere to which participants must ultimately refer in justifying their views, foreshadowing a universal public sphere which no actual conversation really reaches.

4   RESEARCH TO TRANSFORM REALITY

If *praxis* is right conduct in response to a particular situation at a particular time, informed by the agent's knowledge and by recourse to relevant theory and traditions, then the fruits of *praxis* are to be evaluated in history, in terms of its consequences, in hindsight. Action researchers are not passive about action as it unfolds, intervening *only afterwards* to revise or reconstruct plans that have gone awry; on the contrary, they intervene deliberately and actively in individual and collective practice/*praxis* with the intention of acting in ways likely to make things better than before.

In this sense, action research investigates reality in order to transform it, as Orlando Fals Borda (1979) put it and, equally, as Kemmis and McTaggart (2000) put it, action research also transforms reality in order to investigate it. Critical participatory action research is a form of *exploratory action* that *takes communicative action into social practice*, using social practice as a source of new understandings (Kemmis and Brennan Kemmis, 2003). It aims to 'write the history of the future' by acting deliberately to interpret and learn from what happens. It aims to 'feed' future reflection by collecting evidence about action as it unfolds, and about its unfolding historical consequences.

Much of Habermas's writing since *The Theory of Communicative Action* has been devoted to exploring contemporary problems and crises to re-think the world as a basis for doing things differently – transforming things. In *Between Facts and Norms* (1996), for example, he investigates theories of law to clarify what basic law constitutions must contain to preserve human and civil rights. In *Religion and Rationality* (2002), he takes up themes about religion raised by his account of religious belief and communities in *The Theory of Communicative Action*. He discusses communities of faith – and whether or not the idea of God can be replaced by intersubjectivity in the form of the *logos* of language. In *The Future of Human Nature* (2003a), he explores the moral and ethical questions posed by genetic modification of embryos, with profound implications for the self-understanding of our species. And in

Truth and Justification (2003c), he returns to questions about the nature of truth he last addressed intensively in the 1970s, especially in *Knowledge and Human Interests* (1972). He revises some of those old arguments, building on developments in analytic philosophy and developments in pragmatism, again through debates with key contemporary theorists in these fields.

Habermas has lived the role of the philosopher as public intellectual he describes in *Truth and Justification*. On the one hand, he has contributed to various kinds of philosophical debates with other leading thinkers of his times – for example,

- with Gadamer about interpretation (in *Theory and Practice*, 1974, and *Knowledge and Human Interests*, 1972),
- with the systems theorist Niklas Luhmann about the extent to which human society can be understood in terms of systems (in *Legitimation Crisis*, 1975, and in other works, including *The Theory of Communicative Action*, 1984, 1987a),
- with various poststructuralists and postmodernists (Derrida, Bataille, Foucault, Lyotard and others) about whether the thinking made possible in modernity is now obsolete and whether their criticisms of modernity and rationality are warranted (in *The Philosophical Discourse of Modernity*, 1987b),
- with the liberal theorist of justice John Rawls about the nature of justice and the constitutional state (in *Between Facts and Norms*, 1996, *The Inclusion of the Other*, 1998, and *The Postnational Constellation*, 2001), and
- with various interlocutors in the 'domestic disputes' within post-Marxist thought and critical theory (for example, in the Axel Honneth et al. edited volume *Interventions in the Unfinished Project of Modernity*, 1992).

On the other hand, through books and essays (often in the German press), he has continued to make interventions in the public political arena, commenting on such matters as German self-understandings of the National Socialist (Nazi) period (for example, in *The New Conservatism: Cultural Criticism and the Historian's Debate*, 1989b), on European and international legal and constitutional issues and structures (for example in *The Inclusion of the Other*, 1998), and in discussions of terrorism after 11 September 2001, in *Philosophy in a Time of Terror* (2003b, with Jacques Derrida, edited and introduced by Giovanna Borradori).

These interventions show that Habermas models the critical intention of critical theory – with an emancipatory and transformative intention both in relation to ideas and in relation to states of affairs in the world – whether modernity itself or more specific crises of national identity, international relations, or religious fundamentalism and terrorism. In terms of scale, these are grand interventions in contemporary issues.

Most critical participatory action research initiatives have a more modest scope. Interventions like those in Indigenous education of the Yolngu people of Australia's Northern Territory (Kemmis and McTaggart, 2000) had immediate goals of improving Aboriginal education in their communities, but also connected with much wider issues like issues of Indigenous rights and governance, post-colonial issues, and cross-cultural communication and education. The initiative addressed boundary-crises emerging at the point of collision between the lifeworlds of the Yolngu and systems that had colonized their country (government, administration, education, welfare, and of business). It also explored the collisions between the different lifeworlds of the Yolngu and the non-Indigenous teachers, administrators and others who had come to their country – involving different kinds of resources of culture, society and identity. Such initiatives aim to make the lived realities of people *less irrational* (in the dimension of culture, discourse and rationality), *less unjust* (in the dimension of society, justice, legitimacy and solidarity), and *less inhumane* (in the dimension of identity and personal capacity).

People already intervene through action research in many contemporary crises like those that occur at the boundaries between systems and lifeworlds, when identities, lifeworlds and forms of life are threatened by

- changing cultural and discursive conditions that threaten our understanding of ourselves, others and the world;
- changing social conditions that threaten solidarities and the legitimacy of established orders; or
- changing material-economic conditions that threaten the well-being and sustenance of people, families and larger social groups.

Careful, critical and continuously self-critical interventions like those of critical participatory action research create sites in which critical capacities are exercised and expressed. They can be launching-pads for wise and prudent social action on themes, problems and issues of contemporary concern. They offer ways of investigating existing conditions and exploring possible futures.

5 RESEARCH WITH A PRACTICAL AIM

Critical participatory action research occurs with the practical aim of *phronesis* – the commitment to acting wisely and prudently in the particular circumstances of a practical situation. It follows that participants in critical participatory action research deliberate differently about the situation in which they find themselves than they would if they regarded the situation as calling only for technical reasoning about the most efficacious, effective and efficient means to achieve known and accepted ends or goals.

Practical reason treats both ends and means as problematic. It is the form of reason employed whenever people have to act in a complex situation, in the knowledge that their action and its consequences will be judged in terms of complex and sometimes conflicting values. It is at its most evident in situations described as 'tragic' – where actors are forced to choose between conflicting sets of values (such as the classic moral dilemma of the parent forced by poverty to choose between respect for property and care for a family when deciding whether or not to steal food).

Research that aims to support and strengthen practical reason is necessarily addressed to actors as *agents* – people who must act, who must confront practical questions and make decisions about what to do. It addresses these actors as *persons* – knowing subjects – who might make wiser and more prudent decisions given a richer understanding of the situations in which they find themselves. Unlike a science aiming to support and inform technical reason, a 'practical science' aims not to achieve control of a situation but to educate actors or practitioners in ways that will help them to understand the nature and consequences of their actions more fully, and to assist them in weighing what should be done. Practical reason furnishes agents with better ways of *thinking about* action in the particular situations they confront, but its principal aim is to create better, more moral *actions*. *Praxis* is not *a way of thinking* about action, but *a particular kind of action* – morally-informed, wise, prudent, and oriented by reference to guiding traditions of thought and action, theory and practice.

Critical participatory action research is 'practical' in the sense that it aims at the production of the good for individual persons and for humankind by aiming for right conduct, the best one can do under the circumstances, knowing one will be judged by history. Action researchers document their actions because they expect to be judged by history and in terms of the historical consequences of their action.

6 RESEARCH WITH EMANCIPATORY AIMS

In *critical* reasoning about practice, researchers adopt a dialectical stance with respect to the 'objective' and 'subjective' and individual and social aspects of a setting. They treat others involved in the setting as co-participants who can work together collaboratively to *change* the ways in which they constitute it through their practice. While including elements of technical and practical reason, critical-emancipatory reasoning reaches beyond them. It manifests itself in attitudes of collaborative reflection, theorizing and social action directed towards emancipatory reconstruction of the setting (in terms of the personal and the political, the local and the global).

Critical participatory action researchers are committed to 'a communicative form of life'; they are committed to exploring and discussing issues relevant to the circumstances of their own lives. It is in their first-person roles as participants, together with others as equal subjects, that they must reach intersubjective agreements, mutual understandings and uncoerced consensus about what to do. They aspire 'to consider in each case all relevant points of view impartially and to take all interests equally into account' (Habermas, 2003c: 290).

It is here, to borrow the final words of *Truth and Justification*, that people in the end can and do find one another as persons, and thus as subjects who, like oneself, deserve respect:

> Given that different directions in life are existentially irreconcilable, it is always difficult for two parties whose identities have been shaped in different ways of life and traditions to reach agreement – be it at the international level between different cultures or between different subcultural collectivities within one and the same state. Here, it is all the more helpful to remember that an agreement on binding norms (ensuring reciprocal rights and duties) does not require the mutual appreciation for one another's cultural achievements and life styles, but instead depends solely on acknowledging that every person is of equal value precisely as a person. (p. 292)

The emancipatory impulse arises and finds expression in the light of this insight about the preciousness and indissoluble uniqueness of each human life. It arises in critical participatory action research when people seek to release themselves and others from constraints that narrow their lives and produce untoward consequences. It arises when people confront social structures and practices that are unjust in the sense that they cause or support domination (the constraint on self-determination) and oppression (the constraint on self-expression and self-development; Young, 1990). The emancipatory impulse springs from the eternal hope that things might be otherwise – more rational (in the sense of reasonable), more legitimate, more caring, and less apt to produce differential consequences of suffering and dissatisfaction.

This, in the end, is what makes critical participatory action research 'critical' in the terms in which Horkheimer (cited earlier) described critical theory. This is what motivates the commitment of critical participatory action researchers to cultural-discursive, social and material-economic transformation as well as the transformation of the lives and circumstances of individual people, and of oppressed groups.

Thus, critical participatory action research – and forms of 'engaged research' like it – often occurs in the context of social movements (Touraine, 1981; Habermas, 1987a: 391–6; 1992: 364–5; 1996: 373–84) in which there is a widening consciousness that current social structures or practices are producing untoward consequences; that they are illegitimate; that they exclude, dominate or oppress particular groups; or that they cause suffering or dissatisfaction. Under such circumstances, people do in fact undertake exploratory action to find *other* ways of thinking, relating to one another, and doing things that might have other, less unsatisfactory consequences. They often do so against seemingly overwhelming odds, often in small and cautious ways, taking heart from the understandings they reach with their fellows, the solidarity of working together, and the rewards of making a difference even if the achievements seem small and local. Out of such small steps, larger movements sometimes grow. These small steps make people feel 'alive' in a *universalistic* sense – making them feel connected to the circumstances of *all* people everywhere: alive *to* history, alive *in* history, and alive in *making* history – their own and others'. This is the emancipatory face of an 'effective-historical consciousness'

that aspires to a *better* history than the history we face if things go on as they are. It is the eternal other of human suffering – hope.

A NEW DEFINITION OF CRITICAL PARTICIPATORY ACTION RESEARCH

The arguments and perspectives presented in the preceding sections lead me to propose the following as a new (though long) definition of critical participatory action research – or a thesis about its nature. The numbers in this definition refer to the chapter's preceding sections.

Critical participatory action research

1. is research undertaken collectively by participants in a social practice to achieve historical self-consciousness (or 'effective-historical consciousness' aimed both at historical consciousness of an historical object and of the historicality of the person interpreting it) in and of their practice as *praxis* – that is, as morally-informed, committed action, oriented by tradition, that responds wisely to the needs, circumstances and particulars of a practical situation – not only by each as an individual but especially through collective deliberation aimed at collective self-understanding

2. as a process in which they reflect critically and self-critically on

   - their *praxis* as individual and collective participants in the practice (action that may perhaps turn out to be untoward in terms of its effects or longer-term consequences),
   - their historically-formed and intersubjectively-shared understandings of the practice (that may perhaps turn out to be ideologically or otherwise distorted), and
   - the historically-formed cultural-discursive, social and material-economic fields that constitute the conditions of their practice and the situations and settings in which their practice is conducted (conditions, situations and settings that may perhaps turn out to be destructive)

3. by opening communicative space – that is, space for collective reflection and self-reflection

through communicative action aimed at inter-subjective agreement, mutual understanding and unforced consensus about what to do – in which participants can strive together, subjectively and intersubjectively, to reach shared insights into and decisions about what to do in relation to the nature and historical formation of their practice in terms of

- how their practice has evolved over time in its intertwined (and sometimes contradictory or contested) cultural-discursive, social, material-economic and personal dimensions and
- themes and issues that arise as common concerns as a consequence of the tensions and interconnections within and between their shared *lifeworlds* (that provide content and resources constituted in the shared *logos* of language and shared background assumptions in the cultural dimension, solidarities in the social dimension, and competences and capacities in the personal dimension), on the one hand, and, on the other, the administrative and economic *systems* that structure and constrain possibilities for their action in the situation, and

4. by intervening in their unfolding collective history through exploratory action to investigate their shared reality in order to transform it and to transform their reality in order to investigate it, that is, by making changes in what they do and gathering evidence of the observable conduct and historical consequences of their actions for different people and groups involved and affected in terms of the cultural-discursive, social, material-economic and personal character, conduct and consequences of the practice,

5. with the practical aim of acting rightly (in terms of moral appropriateness) and with wisdom (based on critically-interpreted tradition and experience) and prudence in response to a current issue or concern that confronts them in their particular situation, and, in addition to this,

6. with the emancipatory aims of eliminating, as far as possible, character, conduct or consequences that are untoward, distorted, destructive or unsustainable because they are

- irrational (discursively unsustainable),
- unjust (causing or supporting domination or oppression), alienating or excluding (morally- and socially-unsustainable),

- unproductive (materially-economically unsustainable), or
- the unjustifiable causes of suffering or dissatisfaction for particular persons or groups
- and of enhancing participants' capacity for collective historical action, often in the context of social movements.

NOTES

1 I am grateful to Barbara Conlan and Roslin Brennan Kemmis for editorial work that significantly improved this chapter. The faults that remain are my responsibility.

2 Gadamer's argument against 'method' in the human and social sciences is elaborated in Joseph Dunne's (1993) *Back to the Rough Ground*, a masterful and scholarly exploration of *praxis* and its endangerment in contemporary times.

REFERENCES

Baynes, Kenneth (1995) 'Democracy and the *Rechsstaat: Habermas's Faktizität und Geltung'*, in S.K. White (ed.), *The Cambridge Companion to Habermas.* Cambridge: Cambridge University Press. pp. 201–32.

Bourdieu, Pierre (1977) *Outline of a Theory of Practice* (trans. R. Nice). Cambridge: Cambridge University Press.

Bourdieu, Pierre (1990) *The Logic of Practice* (trans. R. Nice). Cambridge: Polity Press.

Bourdieu, Pierre (1998) *Practical Reason: On the Theory of Action.* Cambridge: Polity Press.

Bourdieu, Pierre and Wacquant, Loïc (1992) *An Invitation to Reflexive Sociology.* Chicago: University of Chicago Press.

Carr, Wilfred and Kemmis, Stephen (1986) *Becoming Critical: Education, Knowledge and Action Research.* London: Falmer.

Dunne, Joseph (1993) *Back to the Rough Ground: 'Phronesis' and 'Techné' in Modern Philosophy and Aristotle.* Notre Dame, IN: University of Notre Dame Press.

Fals Borda, Orlando (1979) 'Investigating reality in order to transform it: The Colombian experience'. *Dialectical Anthropology*, 4: 33–55.

Foucault, Michel (1970) *The Order of Things: an Archaeology of the Human Sciences.* London: Tavistock.

Foucault, Michel (1972) *The Archaeology of Knowledge*, (trans. A.M. Sheridan Smith). London: Tavistock.

Foucault, Michel (1977) *Language, Counter-Memory, Practice* (ed. D.F. Bouchard, trans. D.F. Bouchard and Sherry Simon). Ithaca: Cornell University Press.

Foucault, Michel (1979) *Discipline and Punish: the Birth of the Prison* (trans. A. Sheridan). New York: Vintage.

Foucault, Michel (1990) *The History of Sexuality, Vol. 1: Introduction* (trans. R. Hurley). New York: Vintage.

Gadamer, Hans-Georg (1975) *Truth and Method*. London: Sheed and Ward.

Habermas, Jürgen (1972) *Knowledge and Human Interests*, (trans. Jeremy J. Shapiro). London: Heinemann.

Habermas, Jürgen (1974) *Theory and Practice* (trans. John Viertel). London: Heinemann.

Habermas, Jürgen (1975) *Legitimation Crisis* (trans. Thomas McCarthy). Boston: Beacon.

Habermas, Jürgen (1984) *Theory of Communicative Action, Vol. 1: Reason and the Rationalization of Society* (trans. Thomas McCarthy). Boston: Beacon.

Habermas, Jürgen (1987a) *The Theory of Communicative Action, Vol. 2: Lifeworld and System: a Critique of Functionalist Reason* (trans. Thomas McCarthy). Boston: Beacon.

Habermas, Jürgen (1987b) *The Philosophical Discourse of Modernity: Twelve Lectures* (trans. Frederick G. Lawrence). Cambridge, MA: MIT Press.

Habermas, Jürgen (1989a) *On the Logic of the Social Sciences* (trans. by Shierry Weber Nicholsen and Jerry A. Stark). Cambridge, MA: MIT Press.

Habermas, Jürgen (1989b) *The New Conservatism: Cultural Criticism and the Historians' Debate* (ed. and trans. Shierry Weber Nicholsen, with an intro. by Richard Wolin). Boston, MA: MIT Press.

Habermas, Jürgen (1992) *Postmetaphysical Thinking: Philosophical Essays* (trans. William Mark Hohengarten). Cambridge, MA: MIT Press.

Habermas, Jürgen (1996) *Between Facts and Norms: Contributions to a Discourse Theory of Law and Democracy* (trans. William Rehg). Cambridge, MA: MIT Press.

Habermas, Jürgen (1998) *The Inclusion of the Other: Studies in Political Theory* (ed. Ciaran Cronin and Pablo de Greiff). Cambridge, MA: MIT Press.

Habermas, Jürgen (2001) *The Postnational Constellation: Political Essays* (ed. and trans. Max Pensky). Cambridge: Polity Press.

Habermas, Jürgen (2002) *Religion and Rationality: Essays on Reason, God and Modernity* (ed. and with an intro. by Eduardo Mendieta). Cambridge, MA: MIT Press.

Habermas, Jürgen (2003a) *The Future of Human Nature* (trans. William Rehg, Max Pensky and Hella Beister). Cambridge: Polity.

Habermas, Jürgen (2003b) 'Fundamentalism and Terror' in Giovanna Borradori (ed.), *Philosophy in a Time of Terror: Dialogues with Jürgen Habermas and Jacques Derrida*. Chicago: University of Chicago Press. pp. 25–43.

Habermas, Jürgen (2003c) *Truth and Justification* (ed. and trans. Barbara Fultner). Cambridge, MA: MIT Press.

Holub, Robert (1991) *Jürgen Habermas: Critic in the Public Sphere*. London, New York: Routledge.

Honneth, Axel; McCarthy, Thomas; Offe, Claus and Wellmer, Albrecht (eds) (1992) *Interventions in the Unfinished Project of Modernity* (trans. William Rehg). MA: MIT Press.

Horkheimer, Max (1972) 'Traditional and Critical Theory', in Max Horkheimer, *Critical Theory*. New York: The Seabury Press. pp. 188–243.

Jay, Martin (1973) *The Dialectical Imagination: a History of the Frankfurt School and the Institute for Social Research, 1923–1950*. London: Heinemann.

Kemmis, Stephen (2005) 'Knowing practice: searching for saliences', *Pedagogy, Culture and Society*, 13 (3): 391–426.

Kemmis, Stephen (forthcoming a) 'What is professional practice?', in Clive Kanes (ed.), *Developing Professional Practice*. New York: Springer.

Kemmis, Stephen (forthcoming b) 'Participatory action research and the public sphere', in Petra Ponte and Ben Smit (eds), *Quality in Practitioner Research*. Amsterdam: Sense Publishers.

Kemmis, Stephen and Brennan Kemmis, Roslin (2003) 'Making and writing the history of the future together: exploratory action in participatory action research', in *Proceedings of the Congreso Internacional de Educación (Congreso V Nacional y III Internacional)* 9–11 October, 2003. Córdoba, Argentine Republic.

Kemmis, Stephen and McTaggart, Robin (1988) *The Action Research Planner*, 3rd edn. Geelong, Victoria: Deakin University Press.

Kemmis, Stephen and McTaggart, Robin (2000) 'Participatory Action Research', in N. Denzin and Y. Lincoln (eds), *Handbook of Qualitative Research*, 2nd edn. Thousand Oaks, CA: Sage. pp. 567–605.

Kemmis, Stephen and McTaggart, Robin (2005) 'Participatory action research: communicative action and the public sphere', in Norman Denzin and Yvonna Lincoln (eds), *The Sage Handbook of Qualitative Research*, 3rd, edn. Thousand Oaks, CA: Sage. pp. 559–603.

Lewin, Kurt (1952) 'Group decision and social change' in G.E. Swanson, T.M. Newcomb and F.E. Hartley (eds), *Readings in Social Psychology*. New York: Holt. pp. 459–573.

Marx, Karl (1867/1887) *Das Kapital/Capital*. Hamburg: Verlag von Otto Meissner (first published in English 1887, trans. Samuel Moore and Edward Aveling, ed. Frederick Engels; Moscow: Progress Press).

Marx, Karl (1967) *Writings of the Young Marx on Philosophy and Society* (ed. and trans. L.D. Easton and K.H. Guddat). New York: Anchor Books.

Outhwaite, William (1975) *Understanding Social Life: the Method Called Verstehen*. London: George Allen and Unwin.

Schatzki, Theodore (2002) *The Site of the Social: A Philosophical Account of the Constitution of Social Life and Change*. University Park, PA: University of Pennsylvania Press.

Schön, Donald A. (1983) *The Reflective Practitioner: How Professionals Think in Action*. New York: Basic Books.

Schön, Donald A. (1987) *Educating the Reflective Practitioner*. San Francisco, CA: Jossey-Bass.

Schön, Donald A. (ed.) (1991) *The Reflective Turn: Case Studies in and on Educational Practice*. New York: Teachers College Press.

Stenhouse, Lawrence (1975) *An Introduction to Curriculum Research and Development*. London: Heinemann Educational.

Touraine, Alain (1981) *The Voice and the Eye: an Analysis of Social Movements* (trans. Alan Duff). Cambridge: Cambridge University Press.

Wiggershaus, Rolf (1994) *The Frankfurt School: Its Histories, Theories, and Political Significance* (trans. Michael Robertson). Boston, MA: MIT Press.

Young, Iris Marion (1990) *Justice and the Politics of Difference*. Princeton, NJ: Princeton University Press.

9

Systems Thinking and Practice for Action Research

Ray Ison

This chapter offers some grounding in systems thinking and practice for doing action research. There are different traditions within systems thinking and practice which, if appreciated, can become part of the repertoire for practice by action researchers. After exploring some of these lineages the differences between systemic and systematic thinking and practice are elucidated – these are the two adjectives that come from the word 'system', but they describe quite different understandings and practices. These differences are associated with epistemological awareness and distinguishing systemic action research from action research. Finally, some advantages for action research practice from engaging with systems thinking and practice are discussed.

My primary purpose in this chapter is to introduce, albeit briefly, some of the different traditions within systems thinking and practice and to explore what action research (AR) practitioners may find useful by engaging with these traditions.

The history of systems thinking and practice can be explained in many different ways. Anyone can be a systems thinker and practitioner, but the narratives that are told are generally about those with recognized expertise. My perspective is that many well-known systems thinkers had particular experiences which led them to devote their lives to their particular forms of systems practice. So,

within systems thinking and practice, just as in other domains of practice, there are different traditions, which are perpetuated through lineages.

After exploring some of these lineages I elucidate how systemic and systematic thinking and practice are different – these are the two adjectives that come from the word 'system' but they describe quite different understandings and practices. These differences are associated with epistemological awareness, which is required, I claim, for moving effectively between systemic and systematic thinking and practice. I ground this claim in my own experience of doing AR which has led me to distinguish systemic action research from action research.

Finally, I suggest some advantages I, and others in the systems traditions, have found useful for AR from engaging with systems thinking and practice.

SYSTEMS TRADITIONS AND LINEAGES

Scene Setting

The word 'system' comes from the Greek verb *synhistanai*, meaning 'to stand together' (the word 'epistemology' has the same root). A system is a perceived whole whose elements are 'interconnected'. Someone who pays particular attention to interconnections is said to be systemic (e.g. a systemic family therapist is someone who considers the interconnections amongst the whole family; the emerging discipline of Earth Systems Science is concerned with the interconnections between the geological and biological features of the Earth). On the other hand, if I follow a recipe in a step-by step manner then I am being systematic. Medical students in courses on anatomy often take a systematic approach to their study of the human body – the hand, leg, internal organs etc. – but at the end of their study they may have very little understanding of the body as a whole because the whole is different to the sum of the parts, i.e. the whole has emergent properties (Table 9.1). Later I explain how starting off systemically to attempt to change or improve situations of complexity and uncertainty means being both systemic and systematic.

Many, but not all, people have some form of systemic awareness, even though they may be unaware of the intellectual history of systems thinking and practice as a field of practical and academic concern. Systemic awareness comes from understanding:

(i) 'cycles', such as the cycle between life and death, various nutrient cycles and the water cycle – the connections between rainfall, plant growth, evaporation, flooding, run-off, percolation etc. Through this sort of systemic logic water availability for plant growth can ultimately be linked to the milk production of grazing animals and such things as profit and other human motivations. Sometimes an awareness of connectivity is described in the language of chains, as in 'the food chain', and sometimes as networks, as in the 'web of life'. Other phrases include 'joined up', 'linked', 'holistic', 'whole systems', 'complex adaptive systems' etc;

(ii) counterintuitive effects, such as realizing that floods can represent times when you need to be even more careful about conserving water, as exemplified by the shortages of drinking water in the New Orleans floods that followed hurricane Katrina in 2005; and

(iii) unintended consequences. Unintended consequences are not always knowable in advance but thinking about things systemically can often minimize them. They may arise because feedback processes (i.e. positive and negative feedback) are not appreciated (Table 9.1). For example the designers of England's motorways did not plan for what is now experienced on a daily basis – congestion, traffic jams, emissions, etc. These unintended consequences are a result of the gaps in thinking that went into designing and building new motorways as part of a broader 'transport system'.

As I intimated earlier, many people either implicitly or explicitly refer to things that are interconnected (exhibit connectivity – Table 9.1) when they use the word 'system'. A common example is the use of 'transport system' or 'computer system' in everyday speech. As well as a set of interconnected 'things' (elements), a 'system' can also be seen as a way of thinking about the connections (relationships) between things – hence a process. A constraint to thinking about 'system' as an entity and a process is caused by the word 'system' being a noun – a noun implies something you can see, touch or discover, but in contemporary systems thinking more attention is paid to the process of 'formulating' a system as depicted in Figure 9.1. This figure shows someone who has formulated or distinguished a system of interest in a situation, i.e. a process. In the process a boundary judgement is made which distinguishes a system of interest from an

Table 9.1 Definitions of some generalized systems concepts likely to be experienced when encountering a system practitioner or for co-option into your own action research projects

Concept	Definition
Boundary	The borders of the system, determined by the observer(s), which define where control action can be taken: a particular area of responsibility to achieve system purposes
Communication	(i) First-order communication is based on simple feedback (as in a thermostat) but should not be confused with human communication, which has a biological basis
	(ii) Second-order communication is understood from a theory of cognition which encompasses language, emotion, perception and behaviour. Amongst human beings this gives rise to new properties in the communicating partners who each have different experiential histories
Connectivity	Logical dependence between components or elements (including sub-systems) within a system
Difficulty	A situation considered as a bounded and well defined problem where it is assumed that it is clear who is involved and what would constitute a solution within a given time frame
Emergent properties	Properties which are revealed at a particular level of organization and which are not possessed by constituent sub-systems. Thus these properties emerge from an assembly of sub-systems
Environment	That which is outside the system boundary and which affects and is affected by the behaviour of the system; alternatively the 'context' for a system of interest
Feedback	A form of interconnection, present in a wide range of systems. Feedback may be negative (compensatory or balancing) or positive (exaggerating or reinforcing)
Hierarchy	Layered structure; the location of a particular system within a continuum of levels of organization. This means that any system is at the same time a sub-system of some wider system and is itself a wider system to its sub-systems
Measure of performance	The criteria against which the system is judged to have achieved its purpose. Data collected according to measures of performance are used to modify the interactions within the system
Mess	A mess is a set of conditions that produces dissatisfaction. It can be conceptualized as a system of problems or opportunities; a problem or an opportunity is an ultimate element abstracted from a mess
Monitoring and control	Data collected and decisions taken in relation to measures of performance are monitored and controlled action is taken through some avenue of management
Networks	An elaboration of the concept of hierarchy which avoids the human projection of 'above' and 'below' and recognizes an assemblage of entities in relationship, e.g. organisms in an ecosystem
Perspective	A way of experiencing which is shaped by our unique personal and social histories, where experiencing is a cognitive act

(Continued)

Table 9.1 (Continued)

Concept	Definition
Purpose	What the system does or exists for; the raison d'être which in terms of a model developed by people is to achieve the particular transformation that has been defined
Resources	Elements which are available within the system boundary and which enable the transformation to occur
System	An integrated whole whose essential properties arise from the relationships between its parts; from the Greek *synhistanai*, meaning 'to place together'
System of interest	The product of distinguishing a system in a situation, in relation to an articulated purpose, in which an individual or a group has an interest (a stake); a constructed or formulated system, of interest to one or more people, used in a process of inquiry; a term suggested to avoid confusion with the everyday use of the word 'system'
Systemic thinking	The understanding of a phenomenon within the context of a larger whole; to understand things systemically literally means to put them into a context, to establish the nature of their relationships
Systematic thinking	Thinking which is connected with parts of a whole but in a linear, step-by-step manner
Tradition	Literally, a network of pre-understandings or prejudices from which we think and act; how we make sense of our world
Transformation	Changes, modelled as an interconnected set of activities which convert an input to an output which may leave the system (a 'product') or become an input to another transformation
Trap	A way of thinking which is inappropriate for the situation or issue being explored
Worldview	That view of the world which enables each observer to attribute meaning to what is observed (sometimes the German word Weltanschauung is used synonymously)

(*Source:* adapted from Wilson, 1984; Capra, 1996; and Pearson and Ison, 1997)

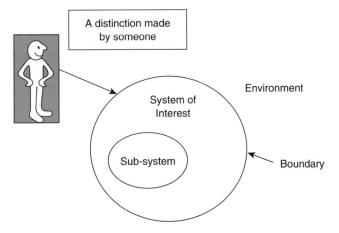

Key elements that result from systems thinking.

Figure 9.1   *Key elements of systems practice as a process which result from systems thinking within situations experienced as complex*

environment. It follows that because we each have different perspectives and interests (histories) then it is likely that we will make different boundary judgements in the same situation, i.e. my education system will be different to yours because we see different elements, connections and boundary. Contemporary systems practice is concerned with overcoming the limitations of the everyday use of the word 'system' as well as seeing the process of formulating systems of interest as a form of practice that facilitates changes in understanding, practice and situations.

Systems thinking embraces a wide range of concepts which most systems lineages have as a common grounding (Table 9.1). Thus, like *other* academic areas, 'systems' has its own language, as shown in Table 9.1. At this point it is worth noting that I have already used the word 'system' in a number of different ways: (i) the everyday sense when we refer to the 'problem with the system'; (ii) a 'system' of interest which is the product of a process of formulating or constructing by someone (Figure 9.1); (iii) the academic area of study called 'systems' and (iv) a systems approach – practice or thinking which encompasses both systemic and systematic thinking and action.

I now provide a brief overview of the history of systems thinking and practice which gives rise to the traditions of understanding out of which systemists think and act. This account is by no means comprehensive and reflects my own perspective on this history.

HISTORY AND OUR TRADITIONS OF UNDERSTANDING

Some historical accounts of systems lineages start with the concerns of organismic biologists who felt that the reductionist thinking and practice of other biologists was losing sight of phenomena associated with whole organisms (von Bertalanffy, 1968 [1940]). Organismic or systemic biologists were amongst those who contributed to the interdisciplinary project described as 'general systems theory' (GST; von Bertalanffy, 1968 [1940]). Interestingly, 'systemic biology' is currently enjoying a resurgence (O'Malley and Dupré, 2005). Other historical accounts start earlier – with Smuts' (1926) notion of practical holism – or even earlier with process thinkers such as Heraclitus who is reputed to have said: 'You cannot step into the same river twice, for fresh waters are ever flowing

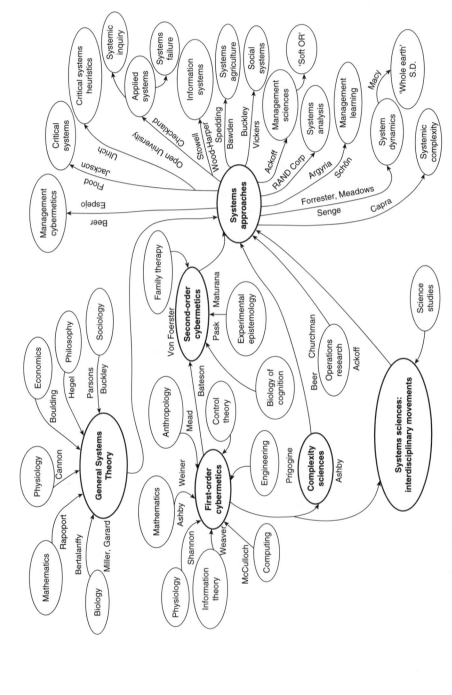

Figure 9.2 A model of different influences that have shaped contemporary systems approaches

in upon you.' Figure 9.2 gives an account of some of the influences that have given rise to contemporary systems approaches. Other historical accounts can be found in Checkland (1981), Flood (1999, 2001/2006), Francois (1997), Jackson (2000) or on Principia Cybernetica (2006).

In Figure 9.2 I identify five formative clusters that give rise to contemporary systems approaches. It is not possible to describe all these influences nor approaches in detail. Some of the motivation for the 'GST project' in interdisciplinary synthesis can be explained by the realization in many disciplines that they were grappling with similar phenomena. This project had its apotheosis in the interdisciplinary Macy conferences in the 1940s and 1950s which did much to trigger new insights of a systems and cybernetic nature and subsequently a wide range of theoretical and practical developments (see Heims, 1991). So, although GST, as an intellectual project, has not been sustained it has nonetheless left a rich legacy (Capra, 1996).

For example, Checkland (1981: 152) establishes a connection with Kurt Lewin's view of 'the limitations of studying complex real social events in a laboratory, the artificiality of splitting out single behavioural elements from an integrated system' (see also Foster, 1972). Checkland goes on to say: 'this outlook obviously denotes a systems thinker, though Lewin did not overtly identify himself as such' (p. 152). A central idea in Lewin's milieu was that psychological phenomena should be regarded as existing in a 'field': 'as part of a system of coexisting and mutually interdependent factors having certain properties as a system that are deducible from knowledge of isolated elements of the system' (Deutsch and Krauss, 1965, quoted in Sofer, 1972). Whilst Lewin may not have overtly described himself as a systems thinker, he was nonetheless a member of the Macy conferences 'core group'. He attended the first two conferences but died in 1947, shortly before the third conference, and his influence was lost to the group (especially his knowledge of Gestalt psychology).[1]

The next two clusters (Figure 9.2) are associated with cybernetics, from the Greek meaning 'helmsman' or 'steersman'. The term was coined to deal with concerns about feedback as exemplified by the person at the helm responding to wind and currents so as to stay on course. A key image of first-order cybernetics is that of the thermostat-controlled radiator – when temperatures deviate from the optimum, feedback processes adjust the heat to maintain the desired temperature. Major concerns of cyberneticians were that of communication and control (Table 9.1). As outlined by Fell and Russell (2000), the first-order cybernetic 'idea of communication as the transmission of unambiguous signals which are codes for information has been found wanting in many respects. Heinz von Foerster, reflecting on the reports he edited for the Macy Conferences that were so influential in developing communication theory in the 1950s, said it was an unfortunate linguistic error to use the word 'information' instead of 'signal' because the misleading 'idea of 'information transfer' has held up progress in this field (Capra, 1996). In the latest theories the biological basis of the language we use has become a central theme' (see first- and second-order communication in Table 9.1).

Fell and Russell (2000: 34) go on to describe the emergence of second-order cybernetics in the following terms: 'second-order cybernetics is a theory of the observer rather than what is being observed. Heinz von Foerster's phrase, "the cybernetics of cybernetics" was apparently first used by him in the early 1960s as the title of Margaret Mead's opening speech at the first meeting of the American Cybernetics Society when she had not provided written notes for the Proceedings (van der Vijver, 1997)'.

The move from first- to second-order cybernetics is a substantial philosophical and epistemological jump as it returns to the core cybernetic concept of 'circularity', or recursion, by recognizing that observers bring forth their worlds (Maturana and Poerkson, 2004; Von Foerster and Poerkson, 2004). Von

Foerster (1992), following Wittgenstein, put the differences in the following terms: 'Am I apart from the universe? That is, whenever I look am I looking through a peephole upon an unfolding universe [the first-order tradition]. Or: Am I part of the universe? That is, whenever I act, I am changing myself and the universe as well [the second-order tradition]' (p. 15). He goes on to say that 'Whenever I reflect upon these two alternatives, I am surprised again and again by the depth of the abyss that separates the two fundamentally different worlds that can be created by such a choice: Either to see myself as a citizen of an independent universe, whose regularities, rules and customs I may eventually discover, or to see myself as the participant in a conspiracy whose customs, rules and regulations we are now inventing' (p. 15). It is worth making the point that understandings from second-order cybernetics have been influential in fields as diverse as family therapy and environmental management. Some authors equate a second order cybernetic tradition with radical constructivism, although not all agree.

Operations research (OR) is another source of influence on contemporary systems thinking and practice. OR flourished after the Second World War based on the success of practitioners in studying and managing complex logistic problems. As a disciplinary field it has continued to evolve in ways that are mirrored in the systems community.

A recent set of influences have come from the so-called complexity sciences (Figure 9.2), which is a lively arena of competing and contested discourses. As has occurred between the different systems lineages, there are competing claims within the complexity field for institutional capital (e.g. many different academic societies have been formed with little relationship to each other), contested explanations and extensive epistemological confusion (Schlindwein and Ison, 2005). However, some are drawing on both traditions to forge exciting new forms of praxis (e.g. McKenzie, 2006).

Other recent developments draw on interdisciplinary movements in the sciences, especially in science studies. These include the rise of discourses and understandings about the 'risk' and 'networked' society (Beck, 1992; Castells, 2004), and associated globalization which has raised awareness of situations characterized by connectedness, complexity, uncertainty, conflict, multiple perspectives and multiple stakeholdings (SLIM, 2004a). It can be argued that this is the reformulation and transformation of an earlier discourse about the nature of situations that Ackoff (1974) described as 'messes' rather than 'difficulties' (Table 9.1), Shön (1995) as the 'real-life swamp' rather than the 'high-ground of technical rationality', and Rittel and Webber (1973) as 'wicked' and 'tame' problems. A tame problem is one where all the parties involved can agree what the problem is ahead of the analysis and which does not change during the analysis. In contrast, a wicked problem is ill-defined. Nobody agrees about what, exactly, the problem is. Schön, Ackoff and Rittel all had professional backgrounds in planning so it is not surprising that they encountered the same phenomena even if they chose to describe them differently.

An example of such a situation from my own work is that of water catchments; a 'catchment' (or watershed) has been historically regarded as a description of a biophysical entity, but today there are few catchments which do not have mixed forms of human activity (urban development, farming, extraction, mining etc.) interacting with biophysical or ecosystem functions. Catchments could thus be said to be socially constructed. On a global basis there is a shortage of water in relation to human-derived demands and often the quality of water available is no longer fit for purpose. In such situations more scientific knowledge can increase, rather than ameliorate, complexity and uncertainty, yet there is also a need to 'manage' catchments. This is the type of situation where systems thinking and practice and AR come together most fruitfully (SLIM, 2004a).

Table 9.2   The 'hard' and 'soft' traditions of systems thinking compared

The hard systems thinking tradition	The soft systems thinking tradition
oriented to goal seeking	oriented to learning
assumes the world contains systems that can be engineered	assumes the world is problematical but can be explored by using system models
assumes system models to be models of the world (ontologies)	assumes system models to be intellectual constructs (epistemologies)
talks the language of 'problem' and 'solutions'	talks the language of 'issues' and 'accommodations'
Advantages	**Advantages**
allows the use of powerful techniques	is available to all stakeholders including professional practitioners; keeps in touch with the human content of problem situations
Disadvantages	**Disadvantages**
may lose touch with aspects beyond the logic of the problem situation	does not produce the final answers; accepts that inquiry is never-ending

(Adapted from Checkland, 1985)

IMPLICATIONS FOR ACTION RESEARCHERS

Developments in systems thinking and practice have gone on in parallel – sometimes with mutual influences, sometimes in isolation – with other academic trends such as the emergence of discourse theory or post-structuralism or concerns with reflexivity, to name but a few. This should not pose problems for action researchers, rather it should offer more choices for practice. Awareness of the different systems traditions, the praxes that have evolved, their constituent concepts (e.g. Table 9.1) and the techniques, tools and methods that are used are all available for an action researcher to enhance their own repertoire.

One of the key concepts in systems is that of levels or layered structure (Table 9.1); this concept illuminates an important aspect of systems practice, the conscious movement between different levels of abstraction. In the next section I explore how it is possible, with awareness, to move between the systemic and systematic.

Not all the systems approaches depicted in Figure 9.2 have been influenced by the distinctions I have made; each has tended to focus on particular key systemic concerns, e.g. patterns of influence and the dynamics of stocks and flows in systems dynamics; critical theory and Habermasian understandings in critical systems approaches; phenomenology and interpretivism in applied 'soft systems', to name but a few. Those within each approach have generally evolved their own forms of praxis. Engagement with the different systems traditions also requires an ability to make epistemological distinctions – to be epistemologically aware. I explain why this is important in the next section.

SYSTEMIC AND SYSTEMATIC THINKING AND ACTION

Exploring the Systemic/Systematic Distinction

When Checkland and his co-workers, beginning in the late 1960s, reacted against the thinking then prevalent in systems engineering and operations research (two lineages depicted in Figure 9.2), and coined the terms 'hard' and 'soft' systems (Table 9.2), the case for epistemological awareness within systems began to be made apparent.

Systems practitioners, such as Checkland, found the thinking associated with goal-oriented behaviour to be unhelpful when dealing with messes and this resulted in a move away from goal-oriented thinking towards thinking in terms of learning, i.e. the purpose of formulating a system of interest as depicted in Figure 9.1 moves from naming, describing or discovering systems to orchestrating a process of learning which can lead to changes in understandings and practices. The epistemological shift was from seeing systems as 'real world entities' to models or devices employed in a process of action learning or research, i.e. the primary skill shifted to one of being able to build and use systemic models as epistemological devices to facilitate learning and change based on accommodations between different interests. 'Hard' systems approaches had typically been used within the lineage of 'systems engineering' which when it came to building bridges was fine, but when these people turned their attention to social issues it was not so easy to engineer new 'social systems' – in fact it proved dangerous to do so, with significant unintended consequences (a recent example is the attempt by the New Labour government in the UK to 'engineer' performance based on targets).

In our work at the Open University, driven by the need to develop effective pedagogy for educating the systems practitioner, we have rejected the hard/soft distinction because we experience it as perpetuating an unhelpful dualism – a self negating either/or. This is manifest, particularly among technology and engineering students, as 'hard approaches' (often quantitative) being perceived as more rigorous than 'soft'. Instead we employ the adjectives that arise from the word system: systemic thinking, thinking in terms of wholes and systematic thinking, linear, step-by-step thinking, as described earlier. Likewise, it is possible to recognize systemic practice and systematic practice. Together these comprise a duality – a whole rather than an unhelpful dualism (the Chinese symbol for yin and yang is a depiction of a duality – together they make a whole). Table 9.3 summarizes some of the characteristics that distinguish between systemic and systematic thinking and action.

The construction of Table 9.3 may suggest that the systemic and systematic are either/or choices. Historically, for many, they appear to have been. However, the capacity to practise both systemically and systematically gives rise to more choices if one is able to act with awareness. Awareness requires attempting to know the traditions of understanding out of which we think and act, including the extent of our epistemological awareness. I also refer to this as the 'as if' attitude, e.g. the choice can be made to act 'as if' it were possible to be 'objective' or to see 'systems' as real. Such awareness allows questions like: What will I learn about this situation if I regard it as a system to do X or Y? Or if you are a biologist, asking: How might I understand this organism if I choose to understand it as a system? Adopting an 'as if' approach means that one is always aware of the observer who gives rise to the distinctions that are made and the responsibility we each have in this regard. The systemic and systematic distinctions can be linked to the different traditions in systems – the systematic is akin to the first-order cybernetic tradition and the systemic builds on second-order traditions (Figure 9.2). Being able to work within both the systemic and systematic traditions is only possible with epistemological awareness.

My systemic and systematic distinctions extend the conclusions of Dent and Umpleby (1998) in their analysis of the underlying assumptions of systems and cybernetic traditions; they regard 'systems and cybernetics' as a collective worldview in which one strand is emerging with major assumptions about constructivism, mutual causation and holism and a traditional worldview comprising major assumptions of objectivism, linear causation and reductionism.

EPISTEMOLOGICAL AWARENESS

Epistemology is the study of how we come to know; within second-order cybernetics

Table 9.3 A summary of the characteristics that distinguish the epistemological basis of systemic thinking and action and systematic thinking and action

Systemic thinking	Systematic thinking	Some implications for AR
Properties of the whole differ and are said to emerge from their parts, e.g. the wetness of water cannot be understood in terms of hydrogen and oxygen.	The whole can be understood by considering just the parts through linear cause–effect mechanisms.	It is helpful to surface understandings about causality amongst participants in AR projects – using multiple cause diagramming is one way to do this; a choice can be made to see AR as a process of managing for emergence or to meet predetermined goals.
Boundaries of systems are determined by the perspectives of those who participate in formulating them. The result is a system of interest.	Systems exist as concrete entities; there is a correspondence between the description and the described phenomenon.	Awareness and choice are key concerns; awareness of the limitations of the everyday use of the word 'system' can help practice, especially surfacing boundary judgements.
Individuals hold partial perspectives of the whole; when combined, these provide multiple partial perspectives.	Perspective is not important.	Has implications for who participates in AR and how different perspectives are managed in the process of AR.
Systems are characterized by feedback – may be negative, i.e compensatory or balancing; or positive, i.e. exaggerating or reinforcing.	Analysis is linear.	Draws attention to the dynamics in a situation and how these may be understood differently by different participants. Need to avoid confusion between the (now) everyday notion of feedback and how it is understood cybernetically (Table 9.1)
Systems cannot be understood by analysis of the component parts. The properties of the parts are not intrinsic properties, but can be understood only within the context of the larger whole through studying the interconnections.	A situation can be understood by step-by-step analysis followed by evaluation and repetition of the original analysis.	For AR both have their place – it is useful to be aware of when and why it might be useful to begin, or act, systemically or systematically; starting off systemically will usually take you to a different place than starting off systematically.
Concentrates on basic principles of organization.	Concentrates on basic building blocks.	Involves shifting between process thinking and thinking in terms of objects or entities e.g. how do objects arise? What are relationships between entities?
Systems are nested within other systems – they are multi-layered and interconnect to form networks.	There is a foundation on which the parts can be understood.	Involve different ways of thinking about relationships.
Contextual.	Analytical.	Lead to different starting points and processes.
Concerned with process.	Concerned with entities and properties.	Both are relevant to AR.
The properties of the whole system are destroyed when the system is dissected, either physically or theoretically, into isolated elements.	The system can be reconstructed after studying the components.	May have implications for project managing in AR or how a study is set up.

(Continued)

Table 9.3 *(Continued)*

Systemic thinking	Some implications for AR	Some implications for AR
The espoused role and the action of the decision-maker is very much part of an interacting ecology of systems. How the researcher perceives the situation is critical to the system being studied.	The espoused role of the decision-maker is that of participant-observer. In practice, however, the decision-maker claims to be objective and thus remains 'outside' the system being studied.	In systemic action the AR role is that of participant-conceptualizer or co-conceptualizer; in systematic AR concern is primarily with understanding the action of others.
Ethics are perceived as being multi-levelled as are the levels, of systems themselves. What might be good at one level might be bad at another. Responsibility replaces objectivity in whole-systems ethics.	Ethics and values are not addressed as a central theme. They are not integrated into the change process; the researcher takes an objective stance.	It is not possible to reconcile 'objectivity' with ethicality and responsibility in the doing of AR – they belong to different traditions (not to be confused with doing some things systematically within a systemic framing).
It is the interaction of the practitioner and a system of interest with its context (its environment) that is the main focus of exploration and change.	The system being studied is seen as distinct from its environment. It may be spoken of in open-system terms but intervention is performed as though it were a closed system.	It is possible to think of all AR projects 'as if' they were systems to do ....; this would be a systemic approach whereas a systematic position might see an AR project 'as a' system.
Perception and action are based on experience of the world, especially on the experience of patterns that connect entities and the meaning generated by viewing events in their contexts.	Perception and action are based on a belief in a 'real world', a world of discrete entities that have meaning in and of themselves.	An awareness of epistemology is important to carry in AR practice.
There is an attempt to stand back and explore the traditions of understanding in which the practitioner is immersed.	Traditions of understanding may not be questioned although the method of analysis may be evaluated.	The AR practitioner is part of the situation and calls for a reflexive attitude

(Adapted from Ison and Russell, 2000)

knowledge is not something we have but arises in social relations such that all knowing is doing. From this perspective epistemology is something practical that is part of daily life. It is known (Perry, 1981; Salner, 1986) that personal change in epistemic assumptions is absolutely essential to any major breakthroughs in decision-making based on understanding and applying systems theories to practical problems. If, as Salner has found, many people are not able to fully grasp relatively simple systemic concepts (such as non-linear processes, or self-reflexive structures), they will not be able to rethink organizational dynamics in terms of 'managing' complexity without substantial alteration in the worldviews (their 'applied' epistemology).

Salner (1986), drawing on earlier work by Perry (1970, 1981) and Kitchener (1983), describes the prevailing theory on epistemic learning as involving the deliberate breaking down and restructuring of mental models that support worldviews. She acknowledges that this is not easy. Prigogine provides an additional lens on this theory in his discussion of 'dissipative structures' (Prigogine and Stengers, 1994). This theory provides a model of the dynamics of epistemic learning: each learner goes through a period of chaos, confusion and being overwhelmed by complexity before new conceptual information brings about a spontaneous restructuring of mental models at a higher level of complexity, thereby allowing a learner to understand concepts that were formally opaque. The shifts in understanding that concern these authors require circumstances in which there is genuine openness to the situation rather than a commitment to the conservation of a theory, explanation or epistemological position (e.g. objectivity) which is abstracted from the situation. Above all else it requires awareness that we each have an epistemology (or possibly multiple epistemologies).

Tensions and conflicts that arise in AR practice can often be attributed to differences in epistemology, although this cause may not be acknowledged or practitioners may not even

have the language to speak about it. A key component of AR projects is often some form of experiential learning – the Kolb (1983) learning cycle is often held up as an exemplar of an action research approach – but rarely is 'experience' understood in theoretical terms. Within the second-order tradition, experience arises in the act of making a distinction. Thus, another way of describing a tradition is as our experiential history. To do this requires language – if we did not 'live in' language we would simply exist in a continuous present, not 'having experiences'. Because of language we are able to reflect on what is happening, or in other words we create an object of what is happening and name it 'experience' (Helme, 2002; Maturana and Varela, 1987; Meynell, 2003, 2005; Von Foerster, 1984).

USING THE SYSTEMIC/SYSTEMATIC DISTINCTIONS IN ACTION RESEARCH

The example I use is a project working with stakeholders in the semi-arid pastoral zone of New South Wales, Australia (Ison and Russell, 2000). We used our understanding of systems thinking and systemic action research (AR based in the systemic understandings depicted in Table 9.3) to develop an approach to doing R&D (research and development) relevant to the context of the lives of pastoralists in semi-arid Australia. Our experience had been that many action researchers, whilst espousing a systemic epistemology, often in practice privileged a systematic epistemology without awareness that that was what they were doing, i.e. in practice they wished to conserve the notion of a fixed reality and the possibility of being objective (Table 9.3).

An outcome of our project was the design of a process to enable pastoralists to pursue their own R&D activities – as opposed to having someone else's R&D outcomes imposed on them. Our design was built around the notion that, given the right experiences, people's enthusiasms for action could be triggered in such a way that those with similar enthusiasms might work together. We understood enthusiasm as:

- a biological driving force (enthusiasm comes from the Greek meaning 'the god within'. Our use of 'god' in this context has no connection with organized religion – our position was to question the commonly held notion that 'information' comes from outside ourselves rather than from within in response to non-specific triggers from the environment);
- an emotion, which when present led to purposeful action;
- a theoretical notion;
- a methodology – a way to orchestrate purposeful action.

We spent a lot of time designing a process that we thought had a chance to trigger people's enthusiasms. Our process did in fact enable people's enthusiasms to be surfaced and led to several years of R&D activity on the part of some pastoralists, supported by ourselves but never determined by us (see Dignam and Major, 2000, for an account by the pastoralists of what they did). The process we designed did not lead to R&D actions (purposeful activity) in any cause and effect way, rather the purposeful activity taken was an emergent property of people's participation in the systemic, experiential learning process that we had designed. Our work has led to a four-stage model for doing systemic action research grounded in second-order cybernetic understandings (Figure 9.2). In summary these were:

(i) Stage 1: Bringing the system of interest into existence (i.e., naming the system of interest);
(ii) Stage 2: Evaluating the effectiveness of the system of interest as a vehicle to elicit useful understanding (and acceptance) of the social and cultural context;
(iii) Stage 3: Generation of a joint decision-making process (a 'problem-determined system of interest') involving all key stakeholders;
(iv) Stage 4: Evaluating the effectiveness of the decisions made (i.e., how has the action taken been judged by stakeholders?).

The way we went about designing the process (i.e of doing each stage) is described in detail in Russell and Ison (2000). The enactment of the four stages requires awareness of the systemic/systematic distinctions in action, i.e. as practice unfolds – they are not just abstracted descriptions of traditions. Our experience is that this is not easy as our early patterning predisposes us to take responsibility for someone else (tell them what to do), to resort to an assumption about a fixed reality and to forget that my world is always different from your world. We never have a common experience because even though we may have the same processes of perceiving and conceptualizing it is biologically impossible to have a shared experience – all we have in common is language (in its broadest sense) with which to communicate about our experience.

From my perspective systems thinking and practice are a means to orchestrate a particular type of conversation where conversation, from the Latin, *con versare*, means to 'turn together' as in a dance. To engage, or not, with systems thinking and practice is a choice we can make.

SOME ADVANTAGES FROM ENGAGING WITH SYSTEMS THINKING AND PRACTICE FOR AR

Many action researchers, including Kurt Lewin, have been influenced by systems thinking, but what is not always clear is the extent to which this is done purposefully – with awareness of the different theoretical and practical lineages depicted in Figure 9.2. I have already suggested that engaging with systems offers a set of conceptual tools which can be used to good effect in AR (e.g. Table 9.1). There are other potential advantages for AR practitioners. Firstly, systemic understandings enable reflections on the nature of research practice, including AR practice itself. This, I suggest, can be understood by exploring *purpose* (Table 9.1). Secondly, there is a rich literature of how different systems approaches or methodologies, including systems tools and techniques, have been employed within AR projects to bring about practical benefits for those involved (e.g.

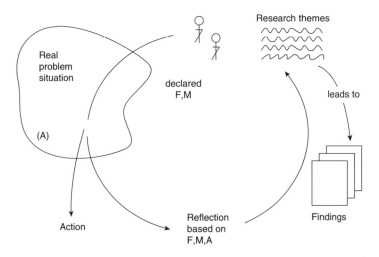

Figure 9.3 *The cycle of action research based on a declared framework of ideas (F) and methodology (M) and area of application (A) and articulated research themes* (*Source*: Holwell, 2004, following Checkland and Holwell 1998)

Checkland and Poulter, 2006). I explore some of these potential benefits in this final section.

Researching in Action Research

The distinctions between what constitutes research (within the phrase systemic action research or action research) and how it might be differentiated from 'inquiry' or 'managing' is, I suggest, contested.[2] AR has been a concern within the 'applied systems' lineage (Figure 9.2) for over 30 years (Checkland and Holwell, 1998a); within this lineage Holwell (2004) proposes three concepts that constitute action research as legitimate research: recoverability, iteration, and the purposeful articulation of research themes (Figure 9.3). She exemplifies her claims with a description of 'a program of action research with the prime research objective of understanding the … nature of the contracting relationship [within the UK National Health Service] with a view to defining how it could be improved' (p. 5). The project was 'complex in execution, including several projects overlapping in time' covering work from different bodies of knowledge, and was undertaken by a seven-member multidisciplinary team with different intellectual traditions. The issues explored crossed many organizational boundaries; the work was done over a four-year period and followed a three-part purposeful but emergent design (Checkland and Holwell, 1998b).

Within the Checkland and Holwell lineage they emphasize that the research process must:

(i) be recoverable by interested outsiders – 'the set of ideas and the process in which they are used methodologically must be stated, because these are the means by which researchers and others make sense of the research' (Holwell, 2004: 355);

(ii) involve the researcher's interests embodied in themes which are not necessarily derived from a specific context. 'Rather, they are the longer term, broader set of questions, puzzles, and topics that motivate the researcher [and] such research interests are rarely confined to one-off situations' (Holwell, 2004: 355) (I assume here they might also claim that themes can arise through a process of co-research or 'researching with' – see McClintock, Ison and Armson (2003) – and thus can be emergent as well);

(iii) involve iteration, which is a key feature of rigor, something more complex than repetitions of a cycle through stages 'if thought of in relation to a set of themes explored over time through several different organizational contexts' (Holwell, 2004: 356); and

(iv) involve the 'articulation of an epistemology in terms of which what will count as knowledge from the research will be expressed' (Checkland and Holwell, 1998b: 9). They further claim that the 'literature has so far shown an inadequate appreciation of the need for a declared epistemology and hence a recoverable research process' (p. 20). Likewise Russell (1986) claimed that what was lacking in almost all research calling itself action research was an adequate and thus useful epistemology.

What is at issue here are the differences between what I have called big 'R' (a particular form of purposeful human activity) and little 'r' research (something that is part of daily life, as is learning or adopting a 'researching or inquiring' attitude) although the boundaries are not always clear. Take recoverability. How in practice is this achieved? The most common form is to write an account of what has happened, ensuring that certain elements of practice and outcome, including evidence, are described (e.g. FMA in Figure 9.3). But writing is itself a form of purposeful practice, done well or not well as the case may be, which is always abstracted from the situation – it is always a reflection on action and is never the same as the actual doing. Of course recoverability could be achieved by other means – by participation (i.e. apprenticeship and the evolution of 'craft' knowledge) or through narrative, which may or may not be writing. It seems to me the key aspiration of recoverability is to create the circumstances where an explanation is accepted (by yourself or someone else) and as such to provide evidence of taking responsibility for the explanations we offer. It has a 'could I follow a similar path when I encounter a similar situation' quality about it. The alternative, as Von Foerster (1992) puts it, is to avoid responsibility and claim correspondence with some external or transcendental reality. For me the core concerns for AR practice are: (i) awareness; (ii) emotioning; and (iii) purposefulness.

In my own case I came to action research through my awareness that my traditional discipline-based research was not addressing what I perceived to be the 'real issues' – in terms elegantly described by Shön (1995), I had a crisis of relevance and rejected the high ground of technical rationality for the swamp of real-life issues. Warmington (1980) was a major initial

influence but my purpose was to do more relevant big 'R' research – for which I sought and successfully gained funding (Potts and Ison, 1987). It was during subsequent work on the CARR (Community Approaches to Rangelands Research) project, as reported in Ison and Russell (2000), that my own epistemological awareness shifted – something that I claim is necessary for the shift from action to systemic action research (Table 9.3). My experience is that such a shift has an emotional basis; thus the researcher can be seen as both chorographer (one versed in the systemic description of situations) and choreographer (one practised in the design of dance arrangements) of the emotions (Russell and Ison, 2005).

As acknowledged in the distinctions between participatory action research and action science (Agyris and Schön, 1991; Dash, 1997) and first, second and third person inquiry (Reason, 2001), there is a need to be clear as to who takes responsibility for bringing forth a researching system. Any account of big 'R' research needs to ask the question. who is the researcher at this moment in this context? Is it me, us or them? Answers to this question determine what is ethical practice, bounding, for example, what is mine from what is ours and what is yours (e.g. Bell, 1998; Helme, 2002; SLIM, 2004b).

Being Purposeful

Within systems traditions two forms of behaviour in relation to purpose are distinguished. One is *purposeful* behaviour, which Checkland (1981) describes as behaviour that is willed – there is thus some sense of voluntary action. The other is *purposive* behaviour – behaviour to which someone can attribute purpose. Following the logic of the purposeful and purposive distinctions, systems that can be seen to have an imposed purpose that they seek to achieve are called purposive systems and those that can be seen to articulate their own purpose(s) as well as seek them are purposeful systems. One of the key features attributed to purposeful systems is that the people in them can pursue the same purpose, sometimes called a *what*, in different environments by pursuing different behaviours, sometimes called a *how*. Note that I have deliberately not used the term goals, because of the current propensity to see goals as quite narrowly defined objectives. Certainly this was the way they were interpreted in the systems engineering tradition of the 1950s and 1960s and in the traditional OR paradigm (Figure 9.2; Table 9.2). My understanding of purposefulness is not a commitment to a deterministic form of rationalism because I recognize that in our daily living we do what we do and then, in reflection, make claims for what was done.[3] Being rational is a particular emotional predisposition; in doing big 'R' research it makes sense to me to act *as if* sustained rationality were possible. As I outlined earlier, an *as if* attitude signals epistemological awareness, a taking of responsibility, and is a means to avoid unhelpful dualisms.

So another feature of systemic action research is the extent to which there is some purposeful engagement with the history of systems thinking. If a system is conceptualized as a result of the purposeful behaviour of a group of interested observers, it can be said to emerge out of the conversations and actions of those involved. It is these conversations that produce the purpose and hence the conceptualization of the system. What it is and what its measures of performance are will be determined by the stakeholders involved. This process has many of the characteristics attributed to self-organizing systems; its enactment can, in reflection, usefully be considered as a 'learning system' (Blackmore, 2005).

Being aware of purpose and being able to ask about and articulate purposes can be a powerful process in AR.

Using Systems Tools, Techniques and Methods in AR

Within systems practice, a tool is usually something abstract, such as a diagram, used in carrying out a pursuit, effecting a purpose, or facilitating an activity. Technique is concerned with both the skill and ability of doing

or achieving something and the manner of its execution, such as drawing a diagram in a prescribed manner. An example of technique in this sense might be drawing a systems map to a specified set of conventions.

Several authors and practitioners have emphasized the significance of the term methodologies rather than methods in relation to systems. A *method* is used as a given, much like following a recipe in a recipe book, whereas a *methodology* can be adapted by a particular user in a participatory situation. There is a danger in treating methodologies as reified entities – things in the world – rather than as a practice that arises from what is done in a given situation. A methodology in these terms is both the result of and the process of inquiry where neither theory nor practice take precedence (Checkland, 1985). For me, a methodology involves the conscious braiding of theory and practice in a given context (Ison and Russell, 2000). A systems practitioner, aware of a range of systems distinctions (concepts) and having a toolbox of techniques at their disposal (e.g. drawing a systems map) as well as systems methods designed by others, is able to judge what is appropriate for a given context in terms of managing a process (Table 9.4). In Table 9.4 I list a range of diagramming tools which are introduced to systems students in OU courses as a means of engaging with complex situations. We have found these effective components of a systems practitioner's set of 'tools'; they can be used equally effective in AR.

Behind all systems methods there has generally been a champion, a promoter aided by countless co-workers, students, etc. To paraphrase the French sociologist of technology, Bruno Latour: we are never confronted with a systems method, but with a gamut of weaker and stronger associations; thus understanding what a method is, is the same task as understanding who the people are. This is the logic that underpins Figure 9.2.

A method, like any social technology, depends on many people working with it, developing and refining it, using it, taking it up, recommending it, and above all finding it useful. But not all technologies that succeed

Table 9.4   *Some forms of systems diagramming taught to Open University systems students for engaging with situations of complexity and the systems concepts associated with each (see Table 9.1)*

Diagram type	Purpose	Systems concepts employed or revealed
Systems map	To make a snapshot of elements in a situation at a given moment	• Boundary judgements • Levels – system, sub-system, supra-system • Environment • Elements and their relationships
Influence	To explore patterns of influence in a situation; precursor to dynamic modelling	• Connectivity via influence • System dynamics
Multiple cause	Explore understandings of causality in a situation	• Worldview about causality • Positive and negative feedback
Rich pictures	Unstructured picture of a situation	• Systemic complexity • Reveals mental models and metaphors • Can reveal emotional and political elements of situation
Control model	To explore how control may operate in a situation	• Feedback • Control action • Purpose • Measures of performance

are the best – it depends on who builds the better networks, particularly of practitioners. As you experience the use of a particular systems method and strive to make it a methodology, it is important to reflect on it critically – to judge it against criteria meaningful to you but above all to judge it in relation to your practice of it. It will be your experience of using an approach in a situation to which it fits that matters.

CONCLUSION

I have outlined some of the lineages which give rise to different forms of systems practice and what I consider to be involved in being systemic or systematic in relation to AR. For me, what we judge to be systems practice arises in social relations as part of daily life, but only when a connection has been made with the history of systems thinking as depicted in (but not restricted to) Figure 9.2. In practical terms systems practice can arise when we reflect on our own actions and make personal claims (purposeful behaviour) or when others observe actions that they would

explain in reference to the history of systems thinking (purposive behaviour). From this perspective what is accepted (or not accepted) as systems practice arises in social relations as part of the praxis of daily living. With this explanation someone who at first knew little of the history but had experiences of systems practice, appreciative inquiry, participatory action research, collaborative inquiry etc. as having many similarities could, through inquiry which linked with the histories, or lineages, begin to make finer distinctions of the sort that practitioners from each of these traditions had embodied. That is, I can recognize that in their doings different practitioners are bringing forth different traditions of understanding. In recognizing systems practice it would be usual that some engagement with, and use of, the concepts listed in Tables 9.1, 9.2 or 9.3 would be experienced.

NOTES

1 Magnus Ramage kindly drew my attention to a nice anecdote from a conversation between Margaret Mead and Gregory Bateson (both Macy

attendees), suggesting that Lewin's initial participation but early death was directly responsible for the introduction of 'feedback' into popular vocabulary in its rather loose sense – http://www.oikos.org/forgod.htm. Lewin is also sometimes described as a teacher of Chris Argyris (e.g. by Umpleby and Dent, 1999), but Lewin simply taught an undergraduate module that Argyris attended along with lots of others.

2   As evidence of this I cite the animated discussions within a forum run by Peter Reason and Fritjof Capra at the 2005 UK Systems Society Conference in Oxford.

3   For example, I would claim that intention arises in reflection and is not an a priori condition.

ACKNOWLEDGMENT

Figure 9.3 reprinted with permisson.

REFERENCES

Ackoff, R.L. (1974) *Redesigning the Future*. New York: Wiley.

Argyris, C. and Schön, D. (1991) 'Participatory action research and action science compared. A commentary', in William Foote Whyte (ed.), *Participatory Action Research*. Newbury Park, CA: Sage. pp. 85–96.

Beck, U. (1992) *Risk Society : Towards a New Modernity*. London: Sage.

Bell, S. (1998) 'Self-reflection and vulnerability in action research: bringing fourth new worlds in our learning', *Systemic Practice and Action Research*, 11: 179–91.

Blackmore, C. (2005) 'Learning to appreciate learning systems for environmental decision making – a "work-in-progress" perspective', *Systems Research and Behavioral Science*, 22: 329–41.

Capra, F. (1996) *The Web of Life: a New Synthesis of Mind and Matter*. London: HarperCollins.

Castells, M. (2004) 'Informationalism, networks, and the network society: a theoretical blueprint', in Manuel Castells (ed.), *The Network Society: a Cross-cultural Perspective*. Northampton, MA: Edward Elgar. pp. 3–48.

Checkland, P.B. (1981) *Systems Thinking, Systems Practice*. Chichester: John Wiley & Sons.

Checkland, P.B. (1985) 'From optimizing to learning: a development of systems thinking for the 1990s', *Journal of the Operational Research Society*, 36: 757–67.

Checkland, P.B. and Holwell, S. (1998a) 'Action research: its nature and validity', *Systemic Practice and Action Research*, 11 (1): 9–21.

Checkland, P.B. and Holwell, S. (1998b) *Information, Systems and Information Systems*. Chichester: Wiley.

Checkland, P.B. and Poulter, J. (2006) *Learning for Action : a Short Definitive Account of Soft Systems Methodology and Its Use for Practitioners, Teachers and Students*. Chichester: John Wiley & Sons.

Dash, D.P. (1997) 'Problems of action research – as I see it.' Working Paper No. 14, Lincoln School of Management, University of Lincolnshire and Humberside.

Dent, E.B. and Umpleby, S. (1998) 'Underlying assumptions of several traditions in systems theory and cybernetics', *Cybernetics and Systems*, 29: 513–18.

Dignam, D. and Major, P. (2000) 'The grazier's story', in R.L. Ison and D.B. Russell (eds), *Agricultural Extension and Rural Development: Breaking Out of Traditions*. Cambridge: Cambridge University Press.

Fell, L. and Russell, D.B. (2000) 'The human quest for understanding and agreement', in R.L. Ison and D.B. Russell (eds), *Agricultural Extension and Rural Development: Breaking out of Traditions*. Cambridge: Cambridge University Press. pp. 32–51.

Flood, R.L. (1999) *Rethinking 'The Fifth Discipline': Learning within the Unknowable*. London: Routledge.

Flood, R.L. (2001/2006) 'The relationship of systems thinking to action research', in Hilary Bradbury and Peter Reason (eds), *Handbook of Action Research: Partifipative Inquiry and Practice*. London: Sage. pp. 133–44. Also published in P. Reason and H. Bradbury (eds) (2006) *Handbook of Action Research: Concise Student Edition*. London: Sage. pp. 117–28.

Foster, M. (1972) 'An introduction to the theory and practice of action research in work organizations', *Human Relations*, 25 (6): 529–56.

Francois, C. (ed.) (1997) *International Encyclopaedia of Systems and Cybernetics*. Munich: K. Sauer.

Heims, S. (1991) *Constructing a Social Science for Postwar America: the Cybernetics Group 1946–1953*. Cambridge, MA: MIT Press.

Helme, M. (2002) 'Appreciating metaphor for participatory practice: constructivist inquiries in a children and young people's justice organisation.' PhD thesis, Systems Department, The Open University, Milton Keynes, UK.

Holwell, S.E. (2004) 'Themes, iteration and recoverability in action research', in B. Kaplan, D.P. Truex III, D. Wastell, A.J. Wood-Harper and J.I. Degross. *Information Systems Research: Relevant Theory and Informed Practice*. Boston, MA: Kluwer pp. 353–62.

Ison, R.L. and Russell, D.B. (eds) (2000) *Agricultural Extension and Rural Development: Breaking Out of Traditions*. Cambridge: Cambridge University Press.

Jackson, M. (2000) *Systems Approaches to Management*. New York: Kluwer.

Kitchener, K.S. (1983) 'Cognition, metacognition and epistemic cognition: a three level model of cognitive processing', *Human Development,* 26: 222–32.

Kolb, D. (1983) *Experiential Learning: Experience as the Source of Learning and Development.* Englewood Cliffs, NJ: Prentice Hall.

Maturana, H. and Poerkson, B. (2004) *From Being to Doing: the Origins of the Biology of Cognition.* Heidleberg: Carl-Auer.

Maturana, H. and Varela, F. (1987) *The Tree of Knowledge: the Biological Roots of Human Understanding.* Boston: Shambala Publications.

McClintock, D., Ison, R.L. and Armson, R. (2003) 'Metaphors of research and researching with people', *Journal of Environmental Planning and Management,* 46 (5): 715–31.

McKenzie, B. (2006) http://www.systemics.com.au/ (accessed June 2006).

Meynell, F. (2003) 'Awakening giants: an inquiry into the Natural Step UK's facilitation of sustainable development with sector leading companies.' PhD thesis, Systems Department, The Open University, Milton Keynes, UK.

Meynell, F. (2005) 'A second-order approach to evaluating and facilitating organizational change', *Action Research,* 3 (2): 211–31.

O'Malley, M.A. and Dupré, J. (2005). 'Fundamental issues in systems biology', *BioEssays,* 27: 1270–6.

Pearson, C.J. and Ison, R.L. (1997) *Agronomy of Grassland Systems, 2nd edn.* Cambridge: Cambridge University Press.

Perry, W.G. (1970) *Forms of Intellectual and Ethical Development in the College Years: a Scheme.* New York: Holt, Rinehart & Winson.

Perry, W.G. (1981) 'Cognitive and ethical growth: the making of meaning', in A. Chickering (ed.), *The Modern American College.* San Fransisco, CA: Jossey-Bass.

Potts, W.H.C. and Ison, R.L. (1987) *Australian Seed Industry Study* (Occasional Publication No. 1, Vols 1 & 2). Canberra: Grains Council of Australia.

Prigogine, I. and Stengers, I. (1984) *Order Out of Chaos: Man's New Dialogue with Nature.* London: Heinemann.

Principia Cybernetica (2006) http://pespmc1.vub.ac.be/ (accessed 8 January 2006).

Reason, P. (2001) 'Learning and change through action research', in J. Henry (ed.), *Creative Management.* London: Sage. pp. 182–94.

Rittel, H.W.J. and Webber, M.M. (1973) 'Dilemmas in a general theory of planning', *Policy Science,* 4: 155–69.

Russell, D.B. (1986) 'How we see the world determines what we do in the world: Preparing the ground for action research.' Mimeo, University of Western Sydney, Richmond, Australia.

Russell, D.B. and Ison, R.L. (2000) 'Designing R&D systems for mutual benefit', in R.L. Ison and D.B. Russell (eds), *Agricultural Extension and Rural Development: Breaking out of Traditions.* Cambridge: Cambridge University Press. pp. 208–18.

Russell, D.B. and Ison, R.L. (2005) 'The researcher of human systems is both choreographer and chorographer', *Systems Research and Behavioural Science,* 22: 131–8.

Salner, M. (1986) 'Adult cognitive and epistemological development in systems education', *Systems Research,* 3: 225–32.

Schlindwein, S.L. and Ison, R.L. (2005) 'Human knowing and perceived complexity: implications for systems practice', *Emergence: Complexity & Organization,* 6 (3): 19–24.

Shön, D.A. (1995) 'The new scholarship requires a new epistemology', *Change* (November/December): 27–34.

SLIM (2004a) 'SLIM framework: social learning as a policy approach for sustainable use of water' (see http://slim.open.ac.uk).

SLIM (2004b) 'The role of conducive policies in fostering social learning for integrated management of water', SLIM Policy Briefing No. 5. (see http://slim.open.ac.uk).

Smuts, J.C. (1926) *Holism and Evolution.* London: Macmillan.

Sofer, C. (1972) *Organizations in Theory and Practice.* London: Heinemann.

Umpleby, S. and Dent, E.B. (1999) 'The origins and purposes of several traditions in systems theory and cybernetics', *Cybernetics and Systems,* 30: 79–103.

van der Vijver, G. (1997) 'Who is galloping at a narrow path: conversation with Heinz von Foerster', *Cybernetics and Human Knowing,* 4: 3–15.

Von Bertalanffy, L.(1968 [1940]) 'The organism considered as a physical system', in L. von Bertalanffy, *General System Theory.* New York: Braziller.

Von Foerster, H. (1984) *Observing Systems.* Salinas, CA: Systems Publications.

Von Foerster, H. (1992) 'Ethics and second-order cybernetics', *Cybernetics and Human Knowing,* 1: 9–19.

Von Foerster, H. and Poerkson, B. (2004) *Understanding Systems. Conversations on Epistemology and Ethics* (IFSR International Series on Systems Science and Engineering, 17). New York: Kluwer Academic/ Heidelberg: Carl-Auer.

Warmington, A. (1980) 'Action research: its methods and its implications', *Journal of Applied Systems Analysis,* 7: 23–39.

Wilson, B. (1984) *Systems: Concepts, Methodologies and Applications.* Chichester: Wiley.

10

Social Construction and Research as Action

Kenneth J. Gergen and Mary M. Gergen

This chapter treats the significant relationship between the emergence of social construction-ist ideas in the social sciences and the concomitant flowering of action research. After out-lining major features of constructionist thought, attention is given to the dialogic relations between these ideas and action research developments. Strong convergences are found in the emphasis on research as political action, replacing methodological individualism with a collaborative epistemology, moving from a vision of research as mapping to one of world making, and the priority of pragmatics in evaluating research outcomes over vindicating theory. Additionally, the ways in which constructionist ideas can prove catalytic in the future development of action research is described. Special attention is given to advocacy as con-flict, collaboration across plural worlds, and the challenge of accumulating knowledge.

Long isolated and largely ignored within the behavioral sciences, action oriented research has become a major alternative to positivist conceptions and practices of research. Excitement now abounds as researchers from across numerous domains collect and com-municate about their practices and potentials in action research. Yet, how are we to account for this upward thrusting trajectory, the development of research forms, educa-tional programs, journals, conferences, and handbooks? What has shifted in the world of social science to bring about such an energetic

movement? In our view, one major answer lies in the broader intellectual currents sweeping the academy over recent decades. Broad and longstanding agreements on such issues as truth, objectivity, rationality, values, and progress have everywhere been thrust into question. Strands of such questioning are indexed in many ways: post-foundational, post-enlightenment, post-structural, and post-modern among them. For many scholars the significant strands have become intercon-nected under the rubric of *social construc-tion*. In effect, the growth of action oriented research is simultaneous with the emergence of a social constructionist view of knowledge. This is not to say that all action oriented researchers are steeped in constructionist theory, nor do all constructionist scholars engage in action research. However, there is a vital and significant kinship across these domains.

In the present chapter we wish to focus on this nexus between constructionist theory and action research, to explore and clarify the dimensions of this affinity. In doing so action researchers will find a rich body of thought adding both dimension and vitality to their endeavors. At the same time, there are certain lines of constructionist thought that may provoke reflection on current action practices. In illuminating these latter areas of tension we hope to facilitate the kinds of dialogue out of which new developments in both practice and theory can emerge. In effect, we wish both to celebrate the affinities and mine the tensions in the service of strengthening these related efforts. In order to achieve these ends it is first important to sketch the contours of constructionist thought.

SOCIAL CONSTRUCTION: DIALOGIC CONVERGENCES

The phrase, *social construction*, typically refers to a tradition of scholarship that traces the origin of knowledge, meaning, or understanding to human relationships. The term *constructivism* is sometimes used interchangeably, but most scholarship associated with constructivism views processes inherent in the individual mind, as opposed to human relationships, as the origin of people's constructions of the world. Although one may trace certain roots of social constructionism to Vico, Nietzsche, and Dewey, scholars often view Berger and Luckmann's, *The Social Construction of Reality* (1966) as the landmark volume. Yet, because of its alliance with phenomenology (mind as opposed to social discourse), and its lack of political critique, this

work has largely been eclipsed by more recent scholarly developments. One may locate the primary stimulants to the more recent development of social constructionist thought in at least three, quite independent movements. In effect, the convergence of these movements provides the basis for social constructionist inquiry today.

The first movement may be viewed as *critical*, and refers to the mounting ideological critique of all authoritative accounts of the world, including those of empirical science. Such critique can be traced at least to the Frankfurt School, but today is more fully embodied in the work of Foucault, and associated movements within feminist, black, gay and lesbian, and anti-psychiatry enclaves. The second significant movement, the *literary/rhetorical*, originates in the fields of literary theory and rhetorical study. In both cases, inquiry demonstrates the extent to which scientific theories, explanations and descriptions of the world are not so much dependent upon the world in itself as on discursive conventions. Traditions of language use construct what we take to be the world. The third context of ferment, the *social*, may be traced to the collective scholarship in the history of science, the sociology of knowledge, and social studies of science. Here the major focus is on the social processes giving rise to knowledge, both scientific and otherwise.

Our aim here is not to review the emergence of these three movements. There are numerous and detailed sources already available to the reader (see, for example, Gergen, 1994, 1999; Hacking, 1999). Rather, in what follows we shall briefly outline a number of the most widely shared agreements to emerge from these various histories. To be sure, there is active disagreement both within and between participants in these various traditions. However, there are at least four major lines of argument that tend to link these traditions and to furnish the major bonds among those who identity with social constructionism. This discussion will prepare the way for a treatment of contemporary issues and developments in action research.

The Social Origins of Knowledge

Perhaps the most generative idea emerging from the constructionist dialogues is that what we take to be knowledge of the world and self finds its origins in human relationships. What we take to be true as opposed to false, objective as opposed to subjective, scientific as opposed to mythological, rational as opposed to irrational, moral as opposed to immoral is brought into being through historically and culturally situated social processes. This view stands in dramatic contrast to two of the most important intellectual and cultural traditions of the West. First is the tradition of the individual knower, the rational, self-directing, morally centered and knowledgeable agent of action. Within the constructionist dialogues we find that it is not the individual mind in which knowledge, reason, emotion and morality reside, but in relationships.

The communal view of knowledge also represents a major challenge to the presumption of Truth, or the possibility that the accounts of scientists, or any other group, reveal or approach the objective truth about what is the case. In effect, propose the constructionists, no one arrangement of words is necessarily more objective or accurate in its depiction of the world than any other. To be sure, accuracy may be achieved within a given community or tradition – according to its rules and practices. Physics and chemistry generate useful truths from within their communal traditions, just as psychologists, sociologists, and priests do from within theirs. But from these often competing traditions there is no means by which one can locate a transcendent truth, a 'truly true'. Any attempt to establish the superior account would itself be the product of a given community of agreement.

These arguments have provoked antagonistic reactions among scientific communities. There remain substantial numbers in the scientific community, including the social sciences, that still cling to a vision of science as generating 'Truth beyond community'. In contrast, scientists who see themselves as generating pragmatic or instrumental truths find constructionist arguments quite congenial. Thus, for example, both would agree that while Western medical science does succeed in generating what might commonly be called 'cures' for that which is termed 'illness', these advances are dependent upon culturally and historically specific constructions of what constitutes an impairment, health and illness, life and death, the boundaries of the body, the nature of pain, and so on. When these assumptions are treated as universal – true for all cultures and times – alternative conceptions are undermined and destroyed. To understand death, for example, as merely the termination of biological functioning would be an enormous impoverishment of human existence. If a nourishing life is of value, there is much to be said of those who believe in reincarnation, the Christian dogma of 'a life hereafter', or the Japanese, Mexican, or African tribal views of living ancestor spirits. The constructionist does not abandon medical science but attempts to understand it as a cultural tradition – one among many.

The Centrality of Language

Central to the constructionist account of the social origins of knowledge is a concern with language. If accounts of the world are not demanded by what there is, then the traditional view of language as a mapping device ceases to compel. Rather, a Wittgensteinian view of language is invited, in which meaning is understood as a derivative of language use within relationships. And, given that games of language are essentially conducted in a rule-like fashion, accounts of the world are governed in significant degree by conventions of language use. Empirical research could not reveal, for example, that 'motives are oblong'. The utterance is grammatically correct, but there is no way one could empirically verify or falsify such a proposition. Rather, while it is perfectly satisfactory to speak of motives as varying in intensity or content, discursive conventions for constructing motivation in the 21st century do not happen to include the adjective 'oblong'. In this sense, all that may intelligibly be said about mental events is essentially derived from a linguist forestructure.

Social constructionists also tend to accept Wittgenstein's (1953) view of language games as embedded within broader 'forms of life'. Thus, for example, the language conventions for communicating about human motivation are linked to certain activities, objects and settings. For the empirical researcher there may be 'assessment devices' for motivation (e.g. questionnaires, thematic analysis of discourse, controlled observations of behavior), and statistical technologies to assess differences between groups. Given broad agreement within a field of study about 'the way the game is played', conclusions can be reached about the nature of human motivation. As constructionists also suggest, playing by the rules of a given community is enormously important to sustaining these relationships. Not only does conformity to the rules affirm the reality, rationality and values of the research community, but the very *raison d'etre* of the profession itself is sustained. To abandon the discourse would render the accompanying practices unintelligible. Without conventions of construction, action loses value.

The Politics of Knowledge

As indicated above, social constructionism is closely allied with a pragmatic conception of knowledge. That is, traditional issues of truth and objectivity are replaced by concerns with that which research brings forth. It is not whether an account is true from a god's eye view that matters, but rather the implications for cultural life that follow from taking any truth claim seriously. This concern with consequences essentially eradicates the longstanding distinction between *fact* and *value*, between is and ought. The forms of life within any knowledge-making community

represent and sustain the values of that community. In establishing 'what is the case', the research community also places value on their particular metatheory of knowledge, constructions of the world, and practices of research. When others embrace such knowledge they wittingly or unwittingly extend the reach of these values.

Thus, for example, the scientist may use the most rigorous methods of testing emotional intelligence, and amass tomes of data that indicate differences in such capacities. However, the presumptions that there is something called 'emotional intelligence', that a series of question and answer games reveal this capacity, and that some people are superior to others in this regard, are all specific to a given tradition or paradigm. Such concepts and measures are not required by 'the way the world is'. Most importantly, to accept the paradigm and extend its implications into organizational practices may be injurious to those people classified as inferior by its standards.

This line of reasoning has had enormous repercussions in the academic community and beyond. This is so especially for scholars and practitioners concerned with social injustice, oppression, and the marginalization of minority groups in society. Drawing sustenance in particular from Foucault's (1979, 1980) power/knowledge formulations, a strong critical movement has emerged across the social sciences, a movement that gives expression to the discontent and resistance shared within the broad spectrum of minorities. In what sense, it is often asked, do the taken for granted realities of the scientist sustain ideologies inimical to a particular group (e.g. women, people of color, gays and lesbians, the working class, environmentalists, communalists, the colonized) or to human well-being more generally? Traditional research methods have also fallen prey to such critique. For example, experimental research is taken to task not only for its manipulative character, but its obliteration of the concept of human agency.

From Self to Relationship

As discussed earlier, the constructionist dialogues shift attention from the individual actor to coordinated relationships. The drama here is substantial. On the broadest level, constructionism represents an unsettling of the longstanding Western investment in the individual actor. One of the major outcomes of Enlightenment thought was its privileging of the reasoning powers of the individual. It is the individual's capacities for reason and observation that should be valued, cultivated, and given power of expression in society. It is the individual who is responsible for his/her actions, and serves as the fundamental atom of society. Such presumptions continue into the present, as represented, for example, by concerns within both scholarly and professional circles with bringing about optimal states of cognition, emotion, motivation, self-esteem, and the like. Yet, as the constructionist proposes, all that we take to be rational and real emerge from a process of coordination. These are not possessions of the individual, but of people acting together. In the same way, neither the distinction between 'me' and 'you' nor the vocabulary of individual minds is required by 'the way things are'. It is not individuals who come together to create relationships, but relationships that are responsible for the very conception of the individual. The constructionist dialogues thus serve to undermine three hundred years of accumulated belief, along with the instantiation of these beliefs in the major institutions of society.

That the conception of individual selves is constructed is not in itself a criticism. Many would agree that precious traditions of democracy, public education, and protection under the law draw their rationale from the individualist tradition. However, to recognize the historical and cultural contingency of individualist beliefs does open the door to reflection. In particular, as many critics see it, there is a substantial dark side to constructing a world of individual agents. When a fundamental distinction between self and other is established, the social world is constituted by differences. The individual stands as an isolated entity, essentially alone and alienated. Further, there is a common prizing of autonomy – of becoming a 'self made man' who 'does it my way'. To be dependent is a sign of weakness and incapacity. To construct a world of separation in this way is also to court distrust; one can never be certain of the other's motives. And given distrust, it becomes reasonable to 'take care of number one'. Self gain becomes an unquestionable motive, both within the sciences (such as economics and social psychology) and the culture at large. In this context, loyalty, commitment, and community are all thrown into question, as all may potentially interfere with 'self-realization'. Such are the views that now circulate widely though the culture (see, for example, Bellah et al., 1985; Lasch, 1979). One may not wish to abandon the tradition of individual selves, but constructionism invites exploration into creative alternatives.

The most obvious alternative to the individualist account of human action is derived from constructionist metatheory itself. As the metatheory suggests, relationships may be viewed as the fundamental source of all intelligibility, including the intelligibility of all action in society. Thus, theorists from many different perspectives attempt to articulate a vision of a *relational self*. For example, as psychoanalytic theory has shifted toward 'object relations', therapists have become increasingly concerned with the complex relations between transference and countertransference (see, for example, Mitchell, 1995). No longer is it possible to view the therapist as providing 'evenly hovering attention', for the therapist's psychological functioning cannot be extricated from that of the client. From a separate quarter, many developmental theorists and educators are elaborating on the implications of Vygotsky's early view that everything within the mind is a reflection of the surrounding social sphere

(Wertsch, 1985). From this perspective there are no strictly independent thought processes, as all such processes are fashioned within particular cultural settings. Stimulated by these developments, cultural psychologists now explore forms of thought and emotion indigenous to particular peoples (Bruner, 1990; Cole, 1996). Discursively oriented psychologists add further dimension to relational theory by relocating so-called 'mental phenomena' within patterns of discursive exchange. For example, rather than viewing thought, memory, attitudes, or repression as processes 'in the head' of the single individual, they are reconstituted as relational phenomena. Theory and research have come to articulate reason as a form of rhetoric, memory as communal, attitudes as positions within an argument, and emotion as performance within relationship (see, for example, Billig, 1996; Middleton and Brown, 2005).

These four themes – centering on the social construction of the real and the good, the pivotal function of language in creating intelligible worlds, the political and pragmatic nature of discourse, and the significance of relational process as opposed to individual minds – have rippled across the academic disciplines and throughout many domains of human practice. To be sure, there has been substantial controversy, and the interested reader may wish to explore the various critiques and their rejoinders (see, for example, Nagel, 1997; Parker, 1998). However, such ideas also possess enormous potential. They have the capacity to reduce orders of oppression, broaden the dialogues of human interchange, sharpen sensitivity to the limits of our traditions, and to incite the collaborative creation of more viable futures. Such is the case in action research as it is in the global context.

CONSTRUCTION/ACTION CONJUNCTIONS

With this sketch of major contours of constructionist thought in place, we are now positioned to explore convergences and constructive tensions in relationship to action oriented research. Let us first consider the affinities uniting these endeavors. Here constructionist theory functions as a rich resource for sustaining and expanding action research endeavors. In turn, such endeavors represent illuminating instantiations of much that constructionist theory advocates. Let us consider, then, four significant convergences between social constructionist theory and practices of action research:

Research as Political Action

Action researchers have viewed themselves as politically engaged since the very inception of such endeavors. As Peter Reason and Hilary Bradbury (2001: 2) define it,

> A primary purpose of action research is to produce practical knowledge that is useful to people in the everyday conduct of their lives. A wider purpose of action research is to contribute through this practical knowledge to the increased well-being – economic, political, psychological, spiritual – of human persons and communities, and to a more equitable and sustainable relationship with the wider ecology of the planet of which we are an intrinsic part.

In part, it is just such engagement that initially served to marginalize action research from positivist social science. Positivists are traditionally committed to a view of scientific neutrality; facts are held to be separate from values, and the latter are a threat to valid and objective research outcomes. However, constructionist arguments demonstrate the fallacious character of this tradition. Regardless of the researcher's attempt to remain distanced from ideology and politics, all research is essentially a contribution to domains of meaning. And because domains of meaning are constitutive of forms of life, they will inevitably favor certain actions over others. Thus, in their selection of topics for study (e.g. aggression, attachment, attitude change), and the naming of subjects' actions (e.g. 'prejudice', 'biased judgment', 'conformity'), researchers enter for good or ill the public arena of meaning. Further, in the distance they maintain between themselves and their research subjects, the state of ignorance in which the subject is placed, and the use of experimental manipulation as a means toward knowledge, the positivist researcher serves as a cultural model for 'obtaining knowledge'.

In this context one may view with admiration the politically engaged posture of the action researcher. Here political, moral and ideological issues are not treated as irrelevant or suppressed. Rather, they often provide a vital source of motivation for the research. For example, the Highlander Research and Education Center in New Market, Tennessee (www.highlandercenter.org) is a resource center that has provided research assistance to citizens wanting to understand their environments and to influence public policy decisions. The center has provided skills to help in fighting against chemical companies that were creating toxic waste dumps on their land, and to educate the public on the effects of chemical wastes on public health.

In addition to active engagement in value relevant research, the action researcher also has the advantage of authenticity. First, for the sophisticated reader, traditional positivist research seems disingenuous. Researchers couch their findings in value neutral or realist terms, thus suggesting their purely objective status while suppressing the underlying value agenda. As Lewis (2001) has rightfully commented, 'deference to the experts allows science to be used to buttress political power and to disempower ordinary people' (p. 361). In contrast, action researchers are generally quite transparent regarding their valued forms of life. For example, Ella Edmonson Bell (2001/2006) openly proclaims that she is attempting to 'find better solutions for closing the gaps between humankind' (p. 56). One senses a significant degree of personal presence in the work of action researchers.

One may counter that this very willingness to reveal their value investments may repel many readers, especially those who do not wish to have others impose their values upon them. However, in our view such impositions of value are not characteristic of most action researchers. Rather, their research illustrates values in action, but they do not thereby prescribe or advocate universality based on their activities. In this sense, much action research reporting is more like storytelling than sermonizing. It says to the audience 'here is my story of the good', as opposed to 'I proclaim the universal good'.

Collaboration: Beyond Individualism

A second major way in which action practices have been cut away from traditional positive research is in their positioning of the researcher. Positivist methods of inquiry are wedded to an individualist vision of the world, in which each individual is essentially allotted 'a mind', and the activities of this inner region largely determine behavior. Thus the researcher, who embodies rigorous processes of reason and observation, sets out to study the less than rigorous mental processes of the research subject. The scientist emerges from the experimental process with 'knowledge', whereas the subjects of research remain in relative ignorance. Ultimately a hierarchy emerges in which a 'knowledge class' is granted authority over issues pertaining to human behavior. The claims of mental health professionals to superior knowledge of 'pathology', and the resulting classification system (DSM), rights to insurance payments, and support from the pharmaceutical industry are but one case in point.

In sharp contrast to this individualist orientation to research, action inquiry has from its very inception laid stress on processes of collaboration. Heron and Reason (2001/2006) specifically emphasize action research as a 'practice of co-operative inquiry', a domain of practice that researches '*with* people rather than *on* people'. As many believe, the emphasis on collaborating with one's 'subjects' has altered the fundamental understanding of the nature of social research (cf. Bopp and Bopp, 1998; Esteva and Prakash, 1998; Pyrch and Castillo, 2001).

This shift from an individualist to a collectivist orientation to research is in full harmony with the constructionist account of knowledge formation. As outlined earlier, constructionism recognizes the community as opposed to the individual as the fundamental source of intelligibility, and thus the origin of all that stands as rational or true. Action researchers extend the implications of this view in three ways. First, they do not work in separation from others, but with them. Their efforts are fundamentally collaborative. They recognize the essential condition of interdependence for the success of their work. Second, they do not sustain the traditional separation of communities between the professional community and those they study. Rather than creating barriers of incomprehension, they conjoin community and professional interests, intelligibility and outcomes. Finally, in their suturing these otherwise isolated communities, action researchers also undermine the incipient creation of knowledge hierarchies. Researchers and those with whom they work share whatever they can bring in the way of knowledge to the initiative at hand. Different forms of knowing may be useful in different ways, thus favoring a pluralist and instrumentalist view of knowledge.

This emphasis on collaboration brings forth a further synergy between constructionism and action endeavors: constructionist theory lends itself to an ontology in which relationship precedes the individual. To counter the problematic and pervasive ideology of individualism, constructionism invites the development of relational theory (see Gergen, 1999). At the current juncture, the development of relational theory is still in chrysalis form. However, it is at just this point that action research offers itself as a both an instantiation and stimulus to theory development. Many action research endeavors offer concrete illustrations of outcomes that cannot be separated from mutually constituting relationships. Typically, processes of interdependence take precedence over individual decision-making. At the same time, action research provides to the theorist a rich range of material for stimulating further theory development. For example, the practices of appreciative inquiry (Cooperrider et al., 2000, 2003 – see http://appreciativeinquiry.cwru.edu/intro/conference.cfm) and the work of the Public Conversations Project (www.publicconversations.org) have been enormously useful to us in developing a theory of transformative dialogue (Gergen et al., 2004).

From Mapping to World Making

In the traditional positivist program, the attempt by researchers is to move toward increasingly accurate accounts of the world. As many experimentalists see it, their challenge is to 'carve nature at the joint'. Yet, for the constructionist, this orientation is deeply problematic. First, the presumption that language can map the world of human behavior is conceptually fallacious. As we have seen, language is essentially an instrumental device enabling groups of people to engage in successful coordination. Within any particular group, language may be employed referentially (and thus as a map), but outside the network of shared understanding the language is empty. Second, the very concept of science as a mapping enterprise establishes an unfortunate relationship between scientists and their 'objects of study'. Essentially the scientific role is that of mastery of its objects. When the object is laid fully bare, and all its features are subject to control, knowledge is achieved. Not only is such an image degrading to those under study, but the results lend themselves to their exploitation by the powerful. Finally, in the case of the social sciences, the very forms of study and the articulation of outcomes enters into the cultural world as incitement to meaning. To carry out research in the positivist tradition alters the very territory – or forms of cultural life – that one attempts to map (Gergen, 1992). For experts to declare the existence of attention deficit disorder, for example, is to create a culture of the ill.

These constructionist critiques of traditional positivism provide impetus for a robust program of action research. At the outset, action researchers tend to eschew the metaphor of the map. Their purpose is not to test whether one set of words (hypotheses) is a more accurate map of the world than another. They also abandon the positivist assumption of the cultural world as a stable territory; rather, for action researchers the presumption of social change is foremost in focus. It is not the task of the action researcher to describe *the world as it is*, but to realize visions of *what the world can become*. In Tanzania, for example, action research was introduced over 30 years ago. Yet, until it was fully accepted by the social science departments of the universities, which were enmeshed in Western empirical practices, the results of communal change projects were 'disappointing'. Slowly participatory action research was accepted, and with the participation of the local population change projects began to flourish. Eventually the highest levels of governmental agencies were trained in action research methods; well understood was the need not to 'master an object of study' but to join with people in creating new futures (Swantz et al., 2001/2006).

From Theoretical to Practical Priority

In the positivist tradition, the ultimate goal of science is the development of general theory. Most hypothesis-testing research currently seeks to validate small-scale models of sweeping scope (e.g. models of decision-making, inter-group relations, mate selection, attitude change). Ultimately the attempt is to integrate disparate models into a singular or 'unified' theory of human behavior. These aspirations were most evident in the behaviorist era, sometimes viewed as 'the age of theory' (Koch, 1963). The 'cognitive movement' is typically viewed as the successor to behaviorism in terms of a general theory, with integrative attempts now seeking to incorporate both neurological and evolutionary theory. The major point, however, is that all research is placed in the service of

theory. In this sense, research results are not so very important in themselves, but rather as they may vindicate or challenge particular theoretical assumptions.

While constructionist critique of the mapping strategy undergirding this project has already been discussed, it is important at this juncture to underscore the general failure of such research to contribute significantly to society (Gustavsen, 1998). This is so in two major ways. First, because research findings are valued only as they speak to theory, such findings may be trivial in any other context. Experimental methods are typically remote from everyday life, stripped of cultural significance. Similarly, behavioral measures (e.g. pressing buttons, pushing levers, answering response restrained questionnaires, judging obscure stimuli) have little meaning outside the community of scientists. Second, the existence of abstract theory has no practical utility in itself. Abstract terms do not in themselves specify the particulars to which they apply. Thus, no application is possible until derivations are made, and there is no validity to the derivations outside a community of agreement.

In this context, action research provides a refreshing and highly productive alternative. Action research commences with problems or challenges in the world of everyday life. While there may be strong theoretical forestructures in place, the ultimate attempt is to generate change in existing conditions of life. Whether it be changing environmental policy, shifting practices in a local hospital, changing evaluation processes in a school, or discovering new community resources, the purpose of the research is very clearly to improve the lot of the people participating in the research and their surrounding community. Whether theoretical insights may be drawn from such work or not remains a question. We shall return to this issue shortly.

CONSTRUCTIONISM AS CATALYST

Overall, constructionist theory lends rich and extensive support to movements toward action research. In doing so it highlights significant strengths and potentials. At the same time, constructionist ideas are also significant in their catalytic value. They enable researchers to stand outside the realities created within the research endeavors themselves, and to consider ways in which they may be altered or enriched. It is in this context that we wish to reflect on certain practices of action research, with an eye toward generating productive dialogue and new futures. Three issues will be focal:

Advocacy as Conflict

Very often action research emerges in the context of oppression and injustice. Out of value convictions researchers offer themselves to groups whose cause they wish to champion. Governmental agencies oppress or ignore their citizenry; public utilities are not fairly distributed; corporate interests dominate over local health and welfare concerns; aid and other resources are diverted to intermediaries and never reach their rightful recipients – all of which are worthy issues to address. While such commitment provides a source of personal nourishment seldom available in the world of positivist research, there is important reason for reflection. There is a strong tendency in such research for the creation of a divide between the 'good' (supported by the researcher) and the 'evil' that is set against those the researcher supports. This is not to demean the values of the researcher or those whose interests are represented in the endeavor. However, it is first important to recognize that hierarchies of good and evil are divisive, and second that they are multi-hued. The construction of local realities is typically accompanied by a way of life suffused with a sense of the good. Thus, regardless of the obvious good of the causes we champion, those who are trampled by our success will suffer from the advance of evil. In effect, we might replace the nourishing but divisive myth of good vs. evil with a vision of conflicting goods.

In this context, it is useful to reflect on the potentials of various forms of action research. Rather than joining the cause that seems so obviously right, consideration might usefully be given to forms of inquiry that more fully recognize the existence of conflicting goods. For example, the Public Conversations Project in the Boston area has based much of its conversational work on the presence of participants with opposing viewpoints. In the paradigmatic case, opponents on the heated topic of abortion rights confronted each other. Efforts were made to generate a context of mutual trust, and to allow participants to speak both about what lay at the 'heart of the matter' to them, along with their ambivalence. The result was not a reduction of difference, but a substantial defusing of the animosity.

Collaboration in Plural Worlds

Closely related to this initial concern with the intertwining of advocacy and conflict is the issue of affirming and sustaining realities. When a researcher enters a group or organization, he or she is also entering a domain of the real. And, to participate in this world the researcher will almost necessarily be required to affirm this particular account of the real. A failure to do so would function as a token of bad faith. To embrace the local ontology maximizes the potential for coordinated action. At the same time, constructionist arguments warn against the constraining and blinding potentials of commitment to any given reality. The question arises, then, as to what extent an action researcher can function as a polyvocal agent. Under what conditions, and with what practices, can the researcher help alternative voices to be heard, enable movement across the borders of meaning, or introduce new worlds?

Effective examples of such work include the collaborative conferences designed by Bjørn Gustavsen and his colleagues (Gustavsen, 2001/2006) in Scandinavia. Here conferences are designed to improve the quality of life in large regions. The conferences include representatives from widely varied groups – business, government, voluntary, religious, and more. The major emphasis is on sharing in the diversity of views and concerns that each person brings to the event. By carefully listening to one another and sharing in some common experiences, they develop relationships that facilitate new activities into the future. In a similar manner, the practice of Appreciative Inquiry emphasizes the significance of sharing realities for organizational change. It is particularly useful, as well, when there is a high degree of conflict within the organization. Rather than focusing on failures, the appreciative process involves all the participants in a search for a commonly valued future (Watkins and Mohr, 2001).

The Question of Accumulating Knowledge

Let us finally consider a critique of action research often voiced within circles of positivist research. Even if one accepts the view of science as a social construction, it is said, it is possible within a positivist paradigm to make advances in knowledge. With continued hypothesis-testing research, one can make increasingly better predictions of certain restricted kinds of behavior (e.g. the effects of various drugs on performance). In contrast, it is said, action research is not cumulative. The field is composed of insular initiatives that seldom speak to each other. One doesn't contribute to an accumulation of knowledge through action research but, much like the domain of art, simply paints another in an expanding array of pictures.

On behalf of the action researcher, the constructionist first challenges the narrow conception of science presumed in such critique. As reasoned above, prediction and control are highly limited criteria of scientific utility. More interestingly, however, constructionist arguments challenge the action researcher to consider the potentials of such research for coherent advancement over time. For example, it is useful to view action research as a form of *practical art*. Employing this metaphor we can appreciate the way in which, like various arts and crafts, each practice makes a contribution to a range of future possibilities. Various schools of art contribute to ways of using perspective, color, collage, and so on to enrich the aesthetic experience. In a parallel manner, action research practices chart the many ways in which people can work together to create change (see also, Whyte, 1982).

However, we see additional possibilities for rendering such accumulation effective. It would be useful, for one, if researchers would acknowledge the ways in which they have drawn from preceding practices in order to bring forth change in any given circumstance. Virtually no research practice originates within itself; virtually all depend on a process of bricolage, that is, the piecing together of various, disparate modes of doing research. By acknowledging these sources, not only do we begin to see continuity, but we credit the process of collaboration that is so central to action research itself. There is also much to be gained by a scholarship of synthesis. We may usefully review various paradigms of action research to locate possibly transcendent communalities. It is in this vein that we have begun to assay various practices of *transformative dialogue*, with the purpose of establishing a vocabulary of practices (Gergen et al., 2004). By delineating such a vocabulary, the hope is to encourage practitioners to draw from it those resources most promising for the unique positions they confront.

Action researchers, themselves, have begun to appreciate the importance of sharing the narratives of various projects with one another. The published journals, *Action Research* and *Educational Action Research*, along with the on-line journals, *Action Research International* (www.scu.edu.au/schools/gcm/ar/ari/arihome.html), *The Ontario Action Researcher* (www.nipissingu.ca/oar), and

ARexpeditions (http://arexpeditions.mon-tana.edu/docs/about.html), are excellent examples of how research can be shared across international boundaries. The present handbook, and its predecessor (Reason and Bradbury, 2001), are also effective vehicles of sharing that allow practitioners of all varieties to gain wisdom from the stories handed from one practitioner to another.

REFERENCES

Bell, E.E. (2001/2006) 'Influsing race into the US discourse on action research', in P. Reason and H. Bradbury (eds), *Handbook of Action Research: Participative Inquiry and Practice*. London: Sage. pp. 48–58. Also published in P. Reason and H. Bradbury (eds) (2006), *Handbook of Action Research: Concise Student Edition*. London: Sage. pp. 49–59.

Bellah, R., Madsen, R., Sullivan, W.M. and Swidler, A. (1985) *Habits of the Heart*. Berkeley: University of California Press.

Berger, P. and Luckmann, T. (1966) *The Social Construction of Reality*. New York: Doubleday/Anchor Books.

Billig, M. (1996) *Arguing and Thinking, 2nd edn*. Cambridge: Cambridge University Press.

Bopp, J. and Bopp, M. (1998) *Recreating the World*. Calgary: Four Worlds Press.

Bruner, J. (1990) *Acts of Meaning*. Cambridge, MA: Harvard University Press.

Cole, M. (1996) *Cultural Psychology*. Cambridge, MA: Harvard University Press.

Cooperrider, D.L., Sorensen, P., Whitney, D. and Yaeger, T. (eds) (2000) *Appreciative Inquiry*. Champaign, IL: Stipes Publishing.

Cooperrider, D.L., Whitney, D. and Stavros, J. (2003) *The Appreciative Inquiry Handbook: For Leaders of Change*. Cleveland, OH: Lakeshore Publishers.

Esteva, G. and Prakash, M.S. (1998) *Grassroots Postmodernism*. London and New York: Zed Books.

Foucault, M. (1979) *Discipline & Punish*. New York: Vintage Books.

Foucault, M. (1980) *Power/Knowledge*. New York: Pantheon.

Gergen, K.J. (1992) *Toward Transformation in Social Knowledge, 2nd edn*. London: Sage.

Gergen, K.J. (1994) *Realities and Relationships: Soundings in Social Construction*. Cambridge, MA: Harvard University Press.

Gergen, K.J. (1999) *An Invitation to Social Construction*. London: Sage.

Gergen, M.M., Gergen, K.J. and Barrett, F. (2004) 'Appreciative inquiry as dialogue: generative and transformative', in D. Cooperrider and M. Avital (eds), *Advances in Appreciative Inquiry, Vol. 1*. Bristol: Elsevier Science Ltd. pp. 3–27.

Gustavsen, B. (1998) 'From experiments to network building: trends in the use of research for reconstructing working life', *Human Relations*, 51: 431–48.

Gustavsen, B. (2001/2006) 'Theory and practice: The mediating discourse', in P. Reason and H. Bradbury (eds), *Handbook of Action Research: Participative Inquiry and Practice*. London: Sage. pp. 17–26. Also published in P. Reason and H. Bradbury (eds) (2006), *Handbook of Action Research: Concise Student Edition*. London: Sage. pp. 17–26.

Hacking, I. (1999) *The Social Construction of What?* Cambridge, MA: Harvard University Press.

Heron, J. and Reason, P. (2001/2006) 'The practice of co-operative inquiry: research "with" rather than "on" people', in P. Reason and H. Bradbury (eds), *Handbook of Action Research: Participative Inquiry and Practice*. London: Sage. pp. 179–88. Also published in P. Reason and H. Bradbury (eds) (2006), *Handbook of Action Research: Concise Student Edition*. London: Sage. pp. 144–54.

Koch, S. (1963) 'Epilogue', in S. Koch (ed.), *Psychology: a Study of a Science, Vol. 3*. New York: McGraw Hill.

Lasch, C. (1979) *The Culture of Narcissism*. New York: Norton.

Lewis, H. (2001) 'Participatory research and education for social change: Highlander Research and Education Center', in P. Reason and H. Bradbury (eds), *Handbook of Action Research: Participative Inquiry and Practice*. London: Sage. pp. 356–62.

Middleton, D. and Brown, S.D. (2005) *The Social Psychology of Experience: Studies in Remembering and Forgetting*. London: Sage.

Mitchell, S. (1995) *Hope and Dread in Psychoanalysis*. New York: Basic Books.

Nagel, T. (1997) *The Last Word*. New York: Oxford University Press.

Parker, I. (ed.) (1998) *Social Constructionism, Discourse and Realism*. London: Sage.

Pyrch, T. and Castillo, M.T. (2001) 'The sights and sounds of indigenous knowledge', in P. Reason and H. Bradbury (eds), *Handbook of Action Research: Participative Inquiry and Practice* London: Sage. pp. 379–85.

Reason, P. and Bradbury, H. (eds) (2001) *Handbook of Action Research: Participative Inquiry and Practice*. London: Sage.

Swantz, M.-L., Ndedya, E. and Mwajuma S.M. (2001/2006) 'Participatory action research in southern Tanzania, with special reference to women', in

P. Reason and H. Bradbury (eds), *Handbook of Action Research: Participative Inquiry and Practice.* London: Sage. pp. 386–95. Also published in P. Reason and H. Bradbury (eds) (2006) *Handbook of Action Research: Concise Student Edition.* London: Sage. pp. 286–96.

Watkins, J. and Mohr, B. (2001) *Appreciative Inquiry: Change at the Speed of Imagination.* San Francisco, CA: Jossey-Bass Pfeiffer.

Wertsch, J.V. (1985) *Vygotsky and the Social Formation of Mind.* Cambridge, MA: Havard Univeristy Press.

Whyte, W.F. (1982) 'Social inventions for solving human problems', *American Sociological Review*, 47: 1–13.

Wittgenstein, L. (1953) *Philosophical Investigations.* New York: Macmillan.

11

Power and Knowledge

John Gaventa and Andrea Cornwall[1]

Participatory research has long held within it implicit notions of the relationships between power and knowledge. Advocates of participatory action research have focused their critique of conventional research strategies on structural relationships of power and the ways through which they are maintained by monopolies of knowledge, arguing that participatory knowledge strategies can challenge deep-rooted power inequities. Other action research traditions have focused more on issues of power and knowledge within organizations, while others still have highlighted the power relations between individuals, especially those involving professionals and those with whom they work. This chapter explores the relationship of power and knowledge. It begins by exploring some of the ways in which power is conceptualized, drawing upon the work of Lukes, Foucault and others. It then turns to considering the ways in which differing traditions of participatory research seek to transform power relations by challenging conventional processes of knowledge production. Finally, the chapter reflects on contemporary uses of participatory modes of knowledge generation and on lessons that are emerging from attempts to promote more inclusive participation in order to address embedded social and economic inequities.

Participatory research has long held within it implicit notions of the relationships between power and knowledge. Advocates of participatory action research have focused their critique of conventional research strategies on structural relationships of power and the ways through which they are maintained by monopolies of knowledge, arguing that participatory knowledge strategies can challenge deep-rooted power inequities. Other action research traditions have focused more on issues of power and knowledge within organizations, while others still have highlighted the power relations between individuals, especially those involving professionals and those with whom they work.

Power and knowledge are inextricably intertwined. A starting point for situating our analysis of power and knowledge in participatory research is to map out some of the different ways in which power is conceptualized and their implications for research. We then turn to considering the ways in which participatory research seeks to transform power relations by challenging conventional processes of knowledge production. We reflect on contemporary uses of participatory modes of knowledge generation and on lessons that are emerging from attempts to promote more inclusive participation in order to address embedded social and economic inequities.

CONCEPTUALIZING POWER

Earlier understandings of power in participatory research tended to dichotomize the notion: 'they' (structures, organizations, experts) had power; 'we' (the oppressed, grassroots, marginalized) did not. Participatory research was a means of closing the gap, of remedying the power inequities through processes of knowledge production, which strengthened voice, organization and action (see, for example, Fals Borda and Rahman, 1991; Gaventa, 1993; Hall, 1992a; Tandon, 1982/2005; Lykes and Mallona, Chapter 7 in this volume). Power, in these analyses, was often represented as if it were an attribute that some had and others lacked, something that could be won or lost. In recent years, as participatory research has come to be used by a diversity of actors and for an equally diverse variety of purposes, understandings of the relationship of knowledge and power in the participatory research process have had to become more sophisticated, taking into account the complexity and contingency of power relations.

Among the many theorists of power whose work has influenced the fields of social and political science, two stand out as the most influential: Lukes and Foucault. In what follows, we take as our starting point the three dimensions of power elaborated by Lukes (1974, 2005) and built upon by Gaventa (1980) in his analysis of quiescence and rebellion in rural Appalachia. We go on to explore the relational view of power emerging from the work of Foucault (1977, 1979) and his followers, and its implications for

understanding the dynamics of power in the participatory research process.

Lukes begins his argument by challenging the traditional view in which power is understood as a relationship of 'A over B': that is, power is the ability of A (the relatively powerful person or agency) to get B (the relatively powerless person or agency) to do what B might not otherwise do (Dahl, 1969). In this approach, power is understood as a product of conflicts between actors to determine who wins and who loses on key, clearly recognized issues, in a relatively open system in which there are established decision-making arenas. If certain voices are absent in the debate, their non-participation is interpreted as their own apathy or inefficacy, not as a process of exclusion from the political process.

Within this first dimension of power, knowledge or research may be conceived as resources to be mobilized to influence public debates. Practically, with this view, approaches to policy influence, knowledge and action relate largely to countering expertise with other expertise. The assumption is that 'better' (objective, rational, highly credible) knowledge will have greater influence. Expertise often takes the form of policy analysis or advocacy, both of which involve speaking 'for' others, based not on lived experience of a given problem, but on a study of it that claims to be 'objective'. Little attention is paid in this view to whose voices or whose knowledge are represented in the decision-making process, nor on how forms of power affect the ways in which certain problems come to be framed.

This pluralist vision of an open society, in which power is exercised through informed debate amongst competing interests, continues to affect many of our understandings of how power affects policy. However, this view has been widely challenged. Political scientists such as Bachrach and Baratz (1970) put forward a second understanding of power. They argued that the hidden face of power was not about who won and who lost on key issues, but was also about keeping issues and actors from getting to the table in the first place. Drawing upon the work of Schattschneider, they argued that political organizations 'develop a mobilization of bias ... in favor of the exploitation of certain kinds of conflict and the suppression of others. ... Some issues are organized into politics while others are organized out' (Schattschneider, 1960: 71). The study of politics, Bachrach and Baratz argued, must focus 'both on who gets what, when and how and who gets left out and how' (1970: 105).

In this view knowledge, and the processes of its production, contribute very strongly to the mobilization of bias. Scientific rules are used to declare the knowledge of some groups more valid than others, e.g. 'experts' over 'lay people', etc. Asymmetries and inequalities in research funding mean that certain issues and certain groups receive more attention than others; clearly established 'methods' or rules of the game can be used to allow some voices to enter the process and to discredit the legitimacy of others. Even where previously excluded actors do enter the policy process, they may be required to mimic the language and knowledge of the powerful, in order to begin to be heard.

From the second dimensional view, empowerment through knowledge means not only challenging expertise with expertise, but it means expanding who participates in the knowledge production process in the first place. It involves a concern with mobilization, or action, to overcome the prevailing mobilization of bias (see Gaventa, 1993, 1999). When the process is opened to include new voices, and new perspectives, the assumption is that policy deliberations will be more democratic, and less skewed by the resources and knowledge of the more powerful.

While the second dimension of power contributed to our understanding of the ways in which power operates to prevent grievances from entering the political arenas, it still maintained the idea that the exercise of power must involve conflict between the powerful and the powerless over clearly recognized grievances. This approach was then challenged by others such as Steven Lukes who suggested that perhaps 'the most effective and insidious use of power is to prevent such conflict from arising in the first place' (1974: 24). The powerful may do so not only by influencing who acts upon recognized grievances, but also through influencing consciousness and awareness of such grievances in the first place.

In this approach, the control of knowledge as a way of influencing consciousness is critical to the exercise of power. Knowledge mechanisms such as socialization, education, media, secrecy, information control, and the shaping of political beliefs and ideologies all become important to the understanding of power and how it operates. Power begins to resemble Gramscian notions of 'hegemony' (Entwistle, 1979) or Freirean ideas (1981) of the ways in which knowledge is internalized to develop a 'culture of silence' of the oppressed.

Countering power inequities involves using and producing knowledge in a way that affects popular awareness and consciousness of the issues and power relations which affect the lives of the powerless, a purpose that has often been put forward by advocates of participatory research. Here the discussion of research and knowledge involves strategies of awareness building, liberating education, promotion of a critical consciousness, overcoming internalized oppressions, and developing indigenous or popular knowledge. There are countless examples of how the transformation of consciousness has contributed to social mobilization, be they in the civil rights, women's, environmental or other movements. And, there are a number of intellectual traditions which may contribute to our understanding in this area. For instance, social movement theory recognizes the importance of consciousness by raising such issues as the development of collective identity, and of the constructions of meaning and of culture in galvanizing citizen action (Morris, 1984; Mueller, 1992). Feminist theory has long dealt with issues of the 'internalization of powerlessness', leading to a silencing of voices and an acceptance of the status quo, as well as how awareness building can be used as the basis for empowerment and social change (Kabeer, 1994; VeneKlasen and Miller, 2002). Building on the work of Paulo Freire, work in education explores the importance of 'learning for transformation', and puts forth various methods for doing so (Taylor and Fransman, 2004).

In each of these three approaches, there are implicit or more explicit conceptions of knowledge, and how it relates to power, as well as to strategies of empowerment. In the first view, knowledge is a resource, used and mobilized to inform decision-making on key public issues – issues of who produces knowledge, or its impact on the awareness and capacity of the powerless, are less important. In the second view, the powerful use control over the production of knowledge as a way of setting the public agenda, and for including or excluding certain voices and participants in action upon it. In response, mobilization of the relatively powerless to act upon their grievances and to participate in public affairs becomes the strategy – one in which action research is an important tool. In the third dimension, the emphasis is more upon the ways in which production of knowledge shapes consciousness of the agenda in the first place, and participation in knowledge production becomes a method for building greater awareness and more authentic self-consciousness of one's issues and capacities for action.

Beyond the Three Dimensional View

While over the years this three dimensional framework has provided a useful way of understanding power and knowledge in research, it has also been critiqued from a number of differing perspectives. For some, the approach is limited in its understanding of power as a 'power over' relationship – whereas for activism and organizing, the power to act and to act in concert with others ('power to' and 'power with') is fundamental to transformational social change. And, in some cases, power is seen as growing from within oneself, not something which is limited by others. This 'power within' is shaped by one's identity and self-conception of agency, as well as by 'the Other' (Kabeer, 1994; Nelson and Wright, 1995; Rowlands, 1995; VeneKlasen and Miller, 2002).

All three dimensions of power focus on the repressive side of power, and conceptualize power as a resource that individuals gain, hold and wield. Building on work by Foucault, others have argued that power is inherent in all social relations, and have explored its more productive and positive aspects. In this view, power becomes 'a multiplicity of force relations' (Foucault, 1979: 92) that constitute social relationships; it exists only through action and is immanent in all spheres, rather than being exerted by one individual or group over another. For Foucault, power works through discourses, institutions and practices that are productive of power effects, framing the boundaries of possibility that govern action. Knowledge is power: 'power and knowledge directly imply one another ... there is no power relation without the correlative constitution of a field of knowledge, nor any knowledge that does not presuppose and constitute at the same time power relations' (1977: 27).

Foucault's analysis of the micro-practices of power shows how the effects of power/ knowledge create particular kinds of subjects, who are subjugated through 'regimes of truth' that provide a means of policing the boundaries around the categories that knowledge defines. Foucault focuses on how power creates its subjects through the architecture of institutions, through the construction and reproduction of social mores and through the disciplining of the body itself. By placing the power effects of knowledge at the heart of his analysis, Foucault opens up a perspective on power that has often been misinterpreted as unduly negative. Rather, by showing how power/knowledge produces and sustains inequalities, Foucault affirms 'the right ... to rediscover what one is and all that one can be' (1979: 145).

Work by Hayward draws on Foucault to argue for 'de-facing power' by reconceptualizing it as 'a network of social boundaries that constrain and enable action for all actors' (1998: 2). She argues that freedom is the capacity to act on these boundaries 'to participate effectively in shaping the boundaries that define for them the field of what is possible' (1998: 12). This has a number of important implications for thinking about power and knowledge in participatory research. First, it shifts the analysis of power only from resources that 'A' holds or uses to include other broader ways in which spheres of action and possibility are delimited. If power is shaped by discourse, then questions of how discourses are formed, and how they shape the fields of action, become critical for changing and affecting power relations. From the perspective of participatory research, this is a crucial insight as the process of participatory research can in itself become a space in which dominant discourses are challenged and reframed, shifting the horizons of the possible.

Since this approach recognizes that power is part of all social relationships, in so far as power affects the field of what is possible, then power affects both the relatively powerful and the relatively powerless. From this perspective, power involves 'any relationship involving two or more actors positioned such that one can act within or upon power's mechanisms to shape the field of action of the other' (Hayward, 1998: 15). Power can exist in the micro-politics of the relationship of the researcher to the researched, as well as in broader social and political relationships; power affects actors at every level of organizational and institutional relationships, not just those who are excluded or at the bottom of such relationships.

Finally, this broader approach to power includes the more positive aspects through which power enables action, as well as how it delimits it. Power in this sense may not be a zero-sum relationship, in which for (B) to acquire power may mean the necessity of (A) giving up some of it. Rather, if power is the capacity to act upon boundaries that affect one's life, to broaden those boundaries does not always mean to de-limit those of others. In this sense power may have a synergistic element, such that action by some enables more action by others. Challenging the boundaries of the possible may in some cases mean that those with relatively less power working collaboratively with others have more, while in other cases it may direct conflict between the relatively powerful and the relatively powerless.

KNOWLEDGE AS POWER

If, in this expanded view, freedom 'is the capacity to participate effectively in shaping the social limits that define what is possible' (Hayward, 1998: 21), then we can also more clearly situate knowledge as one resource in the power field. Knowledge, as much as any resource, determines definitions of what is conceived as important, as possible, for and by whom. Through access to knowledge, and participation in its production, use and dissemination, actors can affect the boundaries and indeed the conceptualization of the possible. In some situations, the asymmetrical control of knowledge productions of 'others' can severely limit the possibilities which can be either imagined or acted upon; in other situations, agency in the process of knowledge production, or co–production with others, can extend these boundaries.

Throughout the literature on participatory action research, we find various theories and approaches which to some degree or another are premised upon the claim that democratic participation in knowledge production can enable otherwise marginalized people to exercise greater voice and agency, and work to transform social and power relations in the process (e.g. Hall, 1992a; Tandon, 1982/2005; Fals-Borda and Rahman, 1991; Rahman, Chapter 3 in this volume; Swantz, Chapter 2 in this volume). However, there are great variations within the 'schools' and traditions of participatory research as to how transformational social change occurs.

Below we illustrate and explore some commonalities and differences in these approaches, drawing especially (but not exclusively) from the approaches which have influenced our thinking the most. These are those associated with the Freirean tradition of 'participatory action research', and those associated with the work around PRA (participatory rural appraisal or participatory reflection and action) and PLA (participatory learning and action), an approach which has spread very quickly in the 1990s with an enormous impact on development thinking and practice.[2]

THE NATURE AND LOCATIONS OF POWER

For those early writers on participatory action research (PAR), power is understood as a relationship of domination in which the control of knowledge and its production was as important as material and other social relations. As Rahman put it many years ago:

> The dominant view of social transformation has been preoccupied with the need for changing the oppressive structures of relations in material production – certainly a necessary task. But, and this the distinctive viewpoint of PAR (Participatory Action-Research), domination of masses by elites is rooted not only in the polarization of control over means of material production, but also over the means of knowledge production, including control over the social power to determine what is useful knowledge. Irrespective of which of these two polarizations set off a process of domination, one reinforces the other in augmenting and perpetuating this process. (1991: 14)

The knowledge that affects people's lives is seen as being in the hands of a 'monopoly' of expert knowledge producers, who exercise *power over* others through their expertise (Hall, 1992a; Tandon, 1982/2005). The role of participatory action research is to enable people to empower themselves through the construction of their own knowledge, in a process of action and reflection, or 'conscientization', to use Freire's term. Such

action against 'power over' relations implies conflict in which the power of the dominant classes is challenged, as the relatively powerless begin to develop their new awareness of their reality, and to act for themselves (Selener, 1997: 23).

While in this earlier view of PAR power is located in broad social and political relations, later work by Chambers, more often associated with PRA, puts more emphasis on domination in personal and interpersonal terms. Starting with a focus on 'hierarchies of power and weakness, of dominance and subordination' (1997: 58), Chambers outlines two categories: 'uppers', who occupy positions of dominance, and 'lowers', who reside in positions of subordination or weakness. In his account of 'uppers' and 'lowers', power is less fixed in persons than in the positions they inhabit vis-à-vis others: people can occupy more than one position as 'upper', and may occupy both 'upper' and 'lower' positions depending on context. This relational portrayal of power relations mirrors Foucault's view of power as residing not in individuals but in the positions that they occupy and the ways in which discourses make these positions available to them.

Chambers describes the ways in which the taken for granted practices associated with the professions – what he calls 'normal professionalism' (Chambers, 1997) – create and reproduce power relations. By circumscribing the boundaries of what is knowable and treating other forms of knowledge as if they were mere ignorance, Chambers argues, professionals produce and reproduce hierarchies of knowledge and power that place them in the position of agents who know better, and to whom decisions over action, and action itself, should fall. His description of the ways in which professionals impose their 'realities' on 'lowers', with power effects that obliterate or devalue the knowledge and experience of 'lowers', resonates with Foucault's (1977) account of the ways in which 'regimes of truth' are sustained through discourses, institutions and practices.

Departing from a 'power over' perspective, PRA is characterized as a means through which a zero-sum conceptualization of power can be transcended: 'lowers' speak, analyze and act, in concert with each other and with newly sympathetic and enabling professionals who have become aware of the power effects of their positions as 'uppers'. Through analysis and action, 'lowers' are able to lay claim to their own distinctive versions and visions, acquiring the 'power to' and 'power within' that restores their agency as active subjects. By listening and learning, 'uppers' shed the mantle of dominance:

> From planning, issuing orders, transferring technology and supervising, they shift to convening, facilitating, searching for what people need and supporting. From being teachers they become facilitators of learning. They seek out the poorer and weaker, bring them together, and enable them to conduct their own appraisal and analysis, and take their own action. The dominant uppers 'hand over the stick', sit down, listen, and themselves learn. (Chambers, 1995: 34)

While offering an optimistic view of the possibilities of individual change, this view has also been critiqued for failing to analyse broader sources of oppression (e.g. Crawley, 1998) and also for being subject to misuse and abuse in a way that re-enforces the status quo (Cooke and Kothari, 2001). At the same time, those involved with PAR have also been critiqued for offering a broad analysis of social power relations, without clear starting points for change at the micro and personal level. (Many of those involved in organizational action research might also emphasize an intermediate level, which examines power in the organization and group, as a mediating level between individual power and broader social relationships.)

Part of the difference in views here is found in the level of analysis. Rather than thinking about these approaches as necessarily competing, it is perhaps more useful to think of them of as complementary, each with a differing starting point in addressing mutually re-enforcing levels of power. In his comparative work on PAR, 'co-operative-inquiry' and 'action inquiry', Reason also points to the necessary inter-linkages of each

of these levels and approaches. 'One might say that PAR serves the community, co-operative-inquiry the group, and action inquiry the individual practitioner. But this is clearly a gross oversimplification, because each of the triad is fully dependent on the others' (Reason, 1994: 336). If freedom, as defined earlier, is the capacity to address the boundaries of possibility which are drawn in multiple ways and relationships, then surely the multiple levels of change are each important.

POWER AND THE NATURE OF KNOWLEDGE

While differing approaches to action research may have differing understandings of the location of power, they all share an epistemological critique about the ways in which power is embedded and reinforced in the dominant (i.e. positivist) knowledge production system. The critique here is several-fold. First, there is the argument that the positivist method itself distorts reality, by distancing those who study reality (the expert) from those who experience it through their own lived subjectivity. Second is the argument that traditional methods of research – especially surveys and questionnaires – may reinforce passivity of powerless groups through making them the objects of another's inquiry, rather than subjects of their own. Moreover, empirical, quantitative forms of knowing may reduce the complexity of human experience in a way that denies its very meaning, or which reinforces the status quo by focusing on what is, rather than on historical processes of change. Third is the critique that in so far as 'legitimate' knowledge lies largely within the hands of privileged experts, dominant knowledge obscures or under-privileges other forms of knowing, and the voices of other knowers.

Against this epistemological critique, participatory action research attempts to put forth a different form of knowledge. On the one hand, such research argues that those who are directly affected by the research problem at hand must participate in the research process, thus democratizing or recovering the power of experts. Second, participatory action research recognizes that knowledge is socially constructed and embedded, and therefore research approaches 'which allow for social, group or collective analysis of life experiences of power and knowledge are most appropriate' (Hall, 1992b: 22).

Third, participatory action research recognizes differing ways of knowing, multiple potential sources and forms of knowledge. As can be seen in various essays in this volume (e.g. Heron and Reason (Chapter 24), Guhathakurta (Chapter 35), Fine and Torre (Chapter 27)), practitioners stress that feeling and action are as important as cognition and rationality in the knowledge creation process. While participatory research often starts with the importance of indigenous or popular knowledge (Selener, 1997: 25), such knowledge is deepened through a dialectical process of people acting, with others, upon reality in order both to change and understand it.

Resonating with the feminist critique of objectivity (see Harding, 1986; Reid and Frisby, Chapter 6 in this volume), writing on participatory research emphasizes the importance of listening to and for different versions and voices. 'Truths' become products of a process in which people come together to share experiences through a dynamic process of action, reflection and collective investigation. At the same time, they remain firmly rooted in participants' own conceptual worlds and in the interactions between them.

KNOWLEDGE, SOCIAL CHANGE AND EMPOWERMENT

While there is thus a certain amount of commonality in the various approaches in terms of their critique of positivist knowledge, and the liberating possibilities of a different approach to knowledge production, there are important differences across views as to what about participatory research actually contributes to the process of change. That is, what

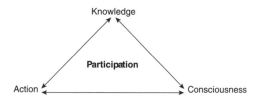

Figure 11.1 *Dimensions of participatory research*

is it in participatory research that is potentially transformatory of power relations?

In our earlier analysis of three approaches to power, we saw that each carried with it a distinctive approach to knowledge, and how it affects power relations. Participatory research makes claims to challenging power relations in each of its dimensions through addressing the need for:

- knowledge – as a resource which affects decisions;
- action – which looks at who is involved in the production of such knowledge; and
- consciousness – which looks at how the production of knowledge changes the awareness or worldview of those involved.

However, much of the literature, and indeed the practical politics of participatory research and struggles to reconfigure power relations and enhance agency, tend to emphasize one or the other of the above approaches. To do so, as we shall discuss below, is limiting, for it fails to understand how each dimension of change is in fact related to the other, as Figure 11.1 illustrates.

Participatory research as an alternative form of knowledge

Undeniably one of the most important contributions of participatory action research to empowerment and social change is in fact in the knowledge dimension. Through a more open and democratic process new categories of knowledge, based on local realities, are framed and given voice. As Nelson and Wright suggest, based on an analysis of PRA approaches, the change process here involves

> an ability to recognize the expertise of local farmers as against that of professional experts; to find more empowering ways of communicating with local experts; and to develop decision-making procedures which respond to ideas from below, rather than imposing policies and projects from above. (1995: 57)

Similarly, Chambers (1997) argues for the importance of participatory processes as a way of bringing into view poor people's realities as a basis for action and decision-making in development, rather than those of the 'uppers' or development experts. A number of case studies of participatory research have clearly demonstrated how involving new participants in the research process brings forth new insights, priorities and definitions of problems and issues to be addressed in the change process (see, for example, case studies in Park et. al., 1993, and others in this volume). Based on this view, for instance, the development field has seen a rapid expansion and acceptance of participatory methods to gather the 'voices of the poor' in the policy process, be it related to 'poverty', the environment or livelihoods (see, for example, Brock and McGee, 2002; Chambers, Chapter 20 in this volume).

The importance of using participatory methods to surface more democratic and inclusive forms of knowledge, as a basis of decision-making, cannot be denied. At the same time, by itself, this approach to using participatory research to reconfigure the boundaries of knowledge raises a number of challenges.

First, there is the danger that knowledge which is at first blush perceived to be more 'participatory', because it came from 'the community' or the 'people' rather than the professional researcher, may in fact serve to disguise or minimize other axes of difference (see critiques by Maguire 1987, 1996, on PAR; Guijt and Shah, 1998, on PRA; see also Brock and McGee, 2002; Cooke and Kothari, 2001; Cornwall, 2003; Cornwall

and Pratt, 2003). In the general focus on the 'community', an emphasis on consensus becomes pervasive. Yet consensus can all too easily masquerade as common vision and purpose, blotting out difference and with it the possibility of more pluralist and equitable solutions (Mouffe, 1992). By reifying local knowledge and treating it as singular (Cornwall et al., 1993), the possibility that what is expressed as 'their knowledge' may simply replicate dominant discourses, rather than challenge them, is rarely acknowledged. Little attention is generally given to the positionality of those who participate, and what this might mean in terms of the versions they present. Great care must be taken not to replace one set of dominant voices with another – all in the name of participation.

Moreover, even where differing people and groups are involved, there is the question of the extent to which the voices are authentic. As we know from the work by Freire (1970), Scott (1986, 1990) and others on consciousness, relatively powerless groups may simply speak in a way that 'echoes' the voices of the powerful, either as a conscious way of appearing to comply with the more powerful parties wishes, or as a result of the internalization of dominant views and values (hooks, 1994). In either case, participatory research implies the necessity for further investigation of reality, in order to change it, not simply to reflect the reality of the moment. Treating situated representations as if they were empirical facts maintains the dislocation of knowledge from the agents and contexts of its production in a way that is, in fact, still characteristic of positivism.

The dangers of using participatory processes in ways that gloss over differences amongst those who participate, or to mirror dominant knowledge in the name of challenging it, are not without consequence. To the extent that participatory processes can be seen to have taken place, and that the relatively powerless have had the opportunity to voice their grievances and priorities in what is portrayed as an otherwise open system, then the danger will be that existing power relations may simply be reinforced, without leading to substantive change in policies or structures which perpetuate the problems being addressed. In this sense, participation without a change in power relations may simply reinforce the status quo, adding to the mobilization of bias the claim to a more 'democratic' face. The illusion of inclusion means not only that what emerges is treated as if it represents what 'the people' really want, but also that it gains a moral authority that becomes hard to challenge or question.[3]

Participatory Research as Popular Action

For this reason, to fulfil its liberating potential, participatory research must also address the second aspect of power, through encouraging mobilization and action over time in a way that reinforces the alternative forms and categories of knowledge which might have been produced.

Though the action component of the participatory action research process is developed in all schools, it has particular prominence from the work of Lewin, and those organizational action researchers who have followed in his tradition. Action research focuses first on problem-solving, and more secondarily on the knowledge generated from the process. The emphasis of the process is not knowledge for knowledge's sake but knowledge which will lead to improvement, usually for the action researcher taken to mean in terms of organizational improvement, or for the solution for practical problems.

At the same time, while knowledge is not for its own sake, neither is action; rather the process is an iterative one. Through action, knowledge is created, and analyses of that knowledge may lead to new forms of action. By involving people in gathering of information, knowledge production itself may become a form of mobilization; new solutions or actions are identified, tested, and then tried again. Thus, in action research, knowledge must be embedded in cycles of

action-reflection-action over time (Rahman, 1991). It is through such a process that the nature of action can be deepened, moving from practical problem-solving to more fundamental social transformation (Hall, 1981: 12). The ultimate goal of research in this perspective is not simply to communicate new voices or categories, but

> the radical transformation of social reality and improvement in the lives of the people involved. … Solutions are viewed as processes through which subjects become social actors, participating, by means of grassroots mobilizations, in actions intended to transform society. (Selener, 1997: 19–21)

Participatory Research as Awareness Building

Just as expressing voice through consultation may risk the expression of voice-as-echo, so too action itself may represent blind action, rather than action which is informed by self-conscious awareness and analysis of one's own reality. For this reason, the third key element of participatory action research sees research as a process of reflection, learning and development of critical consciousness. Just as PRA has put a great deal of attention on the 'knowledge' bit of the equation, and action research on the action component, PAR, which grew from pedagogical work of Freire and other adult educators, placed perhaps the greatest emphasis on the value of the social learning that can occur by oppressed groups through the investigation process.

Here again, however, it is important to recognize that reflection itself is embedded in praxis, not separate from it. Through action upon reality, and analyses of that learning, awareness of the nature of problems, and the sources of oppression, may also change. For this reason, participatory research which becomes only 'consultation' with excluded groups at one point in time is limited, for it prevents the possibility that investigation and action over time may lead to a change in the knowledge of people themselves, and therefore a change in understanding of one's own interests and priorities. Not only must production of alternative knowledge be complemented by action upon it, but the participants in the knowledge process must equally find spaces for self-critical investigation and analysis of their own reality, in order to gain more authentic knowledge as a basis for action or representation to others. Such critical self-learning is important not only for the weak and powerless, but also for the more powerful actors who may themselves be trapped in received versions of their own situation. For this reason, we need to understand both the 'pedagogy of the oppressed' (Freire, 1970) and the 'pedagogy of the oppressor', and the relation between the two.

The important point is to recognize that the approaches are synergistic pieces of the same puzzle. From this perspective, what is empowering about participatory research is the extent to which it is able to link the three approaches, to create more democratic forms of knowledge, through action and mobilization of groups of people to act on their own affairs, in a way that also involves their own critical reflection and learning.

FROM MARGINS TO MAINSTREAM? POWER AND KNOWLEDGE IN 'NEW' POLICY SPACES

Much of the past literature on participatory research focused the use of these methodologies with or on behalf of relatively marginalized groups at the local level. Participatory action research was often associated with social movements, participatory rural appraisal with local planning and development projects, and action research with organizational change. As we have seen, the links between knowledge, power and empowerment are complex and difficult, even at these micro levels.

Over the last decade, practitioners of participatory research have faced new challenges as gradually participatory research moved from margins to mainstream, at least

in some quarters. In our chapter in the earlier edition of this Handbook, we wrote: 'rather than being used only at the micro level, it [participatory research] has been scaled up and incorporated in projects or programs working at regional, national or even global levels. Rather than being used by social movements of marginalized groups, its rhetoric and practice have been adopted by large and powerful institutions, including governments, development agencies, universities and multinationals.' In that earlier chapter we gave several examples of this, ranging from the World Banks's large scale 'Consultations with the Poor' exercise, which purported to use participatory research methods to gain views from poor people about their priorities and concerns (Nayaran et al., 2000), to national level participatory poverty exercises (Robb, 1999), to local level exercises in democratic consultation and participation. Towards the end of that essay we began to explore these challenges: What happens when participatory methods are employed by powerful institutions? Whose voices are raised and whose are heard? We suggested that there was a divergence of positions amongst proponents of participatory research – those who feared that the scaling up and incorporation of participatory approaches into policy processes would lead to serious misuse and abuse, and those who thought that they could contribute to new opportunities for change, especially for previously excluded groups. (See related discussion on the scope of participatory research by Martin (Chapter 26) and by Gustavsen et al., (Chapter 4) this volume.)

Some six years later, we close this essay by re-visiting these questions and exploring whether and how recent trends alter the relationships of power and knowledge as outlined in the earlier part of this chapter. From where we sit, especially as researchers working on issues of participation of relatively powerless and excluded groups in a development context, there have been some important shifts in the political terrain, which in turn shape how knowledge, action and awareness-building strategies associated with participatory research are taken up, and how they can be used to shape and expand 'the boundaries of the possible'.

First, around the world – including in our field – there has been an erosion of faith in 'expertise' to solve pressing problems and issues. Whether because of the failure of science adequately to predict or control risk (Beck, 1992), or because of a growing acceptance of differing ways of knowing, the 'monopoly' that positivist approaches to knowledge had on defining problems in the public arena – against which early participatory action research raised its critique – has to some extent been altered. As relates to the policy field, distinctions between expert and public knowledge to some extent have broken down (Fisher, 2000), and there is often increased recognition of the importance of different forms of knowledge – both professional and lay – as they inform the policy process. In the area of poverty, for instance, poverty policy is no longer only the province of economists, as there has been growing acceptance of the value of more participatory and qualitative ways in which poverty is understood (Brock and McGee, 2002). Similarly, in the area of the environment, there is growing acceptance of the importance of 'experiential expertise', and of methods like citizen juries, stakeholder consultations and the like in policy deliberations.

The broad trend towards pluralization of knowledge has been paralleled by another trend towards the opening up of new institutional spaces for democratic participation – and thus potentially the expansion of opportunities for people to contribute their knowledge to public debate. The stimuli for this expansion of the 'participatory sphere' (Cornwall and Schattan Coelho, 2006) are many and often contradictory. On the one hand, in many emerging democratic countries they are associated with a new wave of democratization and decentralization, sometimes driven by popular demands and struggle, other times from the neo-liberal agendas of international agencies, seeking to roll back and

weaken the state. On the other hand, in many 'mature democracies' concern over the emerging democratic deficits – declining rates of traditional forms of political participation, failing government performance and growing mistrust by ordinary citizens of political institutions – have contributed to a search for new approaches and 'spaces' for democratic engagement, in part perhaps to re-establish democratic legitimacy (Gaventa, 2006).

Whether resulting from the political project of creating more inclusive and participatory forms of democracy or from the project of simply making governments appear more responsive to shore up their own legitimacy, these new 'democratic spaces' have also opened up opportunities for a variety of participatory methods to be brought into the governance process. In places like the Philippines, Indonesia, and India, tools of participatory appraisal have been used in thousands of villages for participatory planning (Estrella and Iszatt, 2004; LogoLink, 2002) and for developing large scale approaches to service delivery such as in the areas of sanitation (Kar and Pasteur, 2005). In other countries, most notably Brazil, but now spread to many countries of North and South, participatory approaches are being used in budget processes, as well as in forms of citizen monitoring of government expenditure, with the effects in some cases of increasing levels of accountability and redirection of public services to lower-income communities (LogoLink, 2004).

Paralleling shifting understandings of science and knowledge and the opening of spaces for participation and consultation has also been the emergence of thinking about the role of 'deliberation' in policy processes, especially in the northern or Western democracies. The concept of 'deliberation' – in which, ideally, different stakeholders with different forms of knowledge deliberate to arrive at decisions which neither party would reach on their own – has added its own innovations to the field of participatory research, ranging from citizens' juries (see Wakeford et al., Chapter 22 in this volume), to ways of deliberative polling and forms of empowered stakeholder consultation or even 'empowered, participatory governance' (Fung and Wright, 2003). Deliberation places emphasis not only on the mobilization of differing actors and forms of knowledge into policy processes, but also on how their knowledge is shared, the micro-politics of speech and communication, and possibilities of creating new knowledge through consensus and debate.

The growing legitimacy of different forms of knowledge, the expansion of the 'participatory sphere' and the turn towards deliberation in some policy-making processes have all had a huge impact on the ways and opportunities through which knowledge links to policy-making. But we must also ask, how do these trends affect the relationship of knowledge and power? Have the growing legitimacy and scaling up of participation and participatory forms of research led to more equitable power relations, especially those affecting previously excluded groups?

We cannot make this assumption that the greater legitimacy of participatory research has produced the kinds of transformational change that is often claimed for it. Power, as we have argued earlier, is inherent in all social or political relations. If we use the various dimensions of power outlined earlier as our lens, than there is little in the new terrain that implies a diminishing of the relationship of power and knowledge in maintaining forms of exclusion, domination and inequality. On the other hand, the changing context may imply the need for new strategies through which the knowledge, action and awareness-building purposes of participatory research come to interact.

Simply creating new spaces for participation, or new arenas for diverse knowledges to be shared, does not by itself change social inequities and relations of power, but in some cases may simply make them more visible. As contributors to Cornwall and Schattan Coelho (2004, 2006) show, marginalized groups may enter these spaces but find themselves without voice within them, co-opted as tokens or manipulated by the powers that be. As this work makes clear, access to new spaces does not automatically imply greater presence or influence of new voices within them, as 'old' power also surrounds and fills such spaces. Despite new rhetoric of deliberation or inclusion, 'old ways' learnt in contexts like committees and public meetings tend to prevail. Public officials may be unused to having to explain bureaucratic procedures to citizens, or to conveying technical matters in plain language. Some may be unwilling to do so. Forms of argument and language which populate the spaces may serve to silence the voices or ways of speaking of some groups while enabling those of others. Those with greater experience of and access to the language of the state and its bureaucracies are more able to use these spaces to press their demands. For instance, retired teachers, community leaders, and NGO staff members may be able to take up invitations to participate and use them effectively, while more marginalized groups may enter the spaces for deliberation but still be silenced within them by how the meeting is conducted, or by their own internalized sense of powerlessness (as in the third dimension) which the new 'pluralism' in policy arenas has not changed.

On the other hand, in certain situations, such forms of 'invited participation' have created opportunities for people who may never otherwise have engaged in deliberation over public policy to get involved, learn and grow, e.g. to contribute to awareness building through the process of engagement. In Brazil, for instance, participatory budgeting has stimulated the creation of new social actors, as citizens come together with friends and neighbours to figure out their neighbourhoods' needs and register themselves as associations in order to participate. Over time, inequalities in mastery of technical language and voice between women and men have, Baocchi (2001) argues, diminished as these 'schools of democracy' teach all who enter them new skills and competencies. In some parts of the country, citizens from the poorest and most marginalized groups, often with minimal education, have come to take up positions as chairs of participatory policy councils and representatives of their neighbourhoods (Cornwall et al., 2006). In this sense, the awareness-building goals linked to participatory research emerge from engagement in new institutional arenas, not necessarily outside of them. Marginalized groups may need their own spaces in which they can develop arguments and confidence, and learn what it takes to participate effectively in these arenas (Agarwal, 1997; Kohn, 2000).

While institutionalized forms of participation may shift our focus to whose voices count *within* new policy spaces, we must remember that the second dimension of power – which affects whose voices and which issues enter such spaces at all – still has not gone away. In the development field, for instance, the discourses and policies of international donors affect what is legitimate for public debate in invited spaces for participation, and what is still to be dealt with behind closed doors. Perhaps no better example exists than the rapid growth of Poverty Reduction Strategy Papers for highly indebted countries, which mandated a process of consultation and participation with and by those living in poverty in developing national poverty alleviation plans. Initially met with enthusiasm by many civil society organizations as an opportunity around which to mobilize, increasingly the optimism has dampened as it became clear that certain significant causes of poverty were still off the public agenda, especially those involving macro-economic, trade and industrial policy (Rowden and Irama, 2004). In other cases the process has been more subtle, but still involved shaping certain understandings and voices of poverty into the policy process while excluding others. In such situations, some have argued, participation risks legitimating the status quo, re-enforcing structural inequities with a more 'participatory face' (Brock et al., 2004). Others have examined the cultural biases which concepts and practice of deliberation carry with them,

serving to create procedures and processes in which some groups feel more comfortable and adept to engage than do others (see, for example, the study of a national-level Canadian deliberative process that brought into sharp relief the contrast between styles of deliberation of 'Western' and aboriginal peoples; Kahane and Von Lieres, 2006).

The institutionalization of participation therefore does not negate the need for mobilization and action outside the 'new democratic spaces', both to continue to challenge the barriers that prevent certain issues for arising as well as to mobilize the knowledge and voices of those who are excluded from them. Yet, in practical terms, the nature of the mobilization often changes. On the one hand, citizens may mobilize around their 'experiential expertise' (Leach and Scoones, 2006, building on Collins and Evans, 2002, and Epstein, 1996), to challenge dominant understandings of science, such as in movements around occupational disease or against bioprospecting of plants. In other cases they may use forms of 'citizen science' to validate and call attention to their claims, a strategy long used in participatory research methods (see, for instance, Merrifield, 1993). On the other hand, the pluralization of knowledge and the greater contentiousness of science even amongst scientists themselves also means that popular movements can mobilize to enrol the support of accredited experts, and form alliances with them, as has been done very effectively by HIV/Aids activists in the USA (Epstein, 1996) or in South Africa (Robins, 2005). The need to be effective 'at the decision-making table' also means that citizen activists quickly learn the language and idiom of the experts themselves, sometimes at the expense of having their social and political energies drawn away from mobilization in their own spaces, through protests or building movements of their own constituencies (Mahmud, 2005). The net effect of these strategies is that 'boundaries between citizens and expert become more fluid and hybrids emerge', calling into question old dichotomies and strategies which simply pit popular and expert knowledge against one another (Leach and Scoones, 2006: 11).

The opening of new political spaces therefore brings to the fore questions of how to build alliances not only across forms of knowledge, but also between social movements working outside of the arenas of power, and experts and activists who are working on the inside. In turn, such alliance formation raises critical questions about who speaks for whom, with whose knowledge and with what accountability. Difficult enough at local level, such challenges of knowledge representation become all the more complex as we move from local to global arenas. In response, we see the emergence of new intermediary networks, associations, and international NGOs, increasingly referred to as global civil society, which attempt to bring citizen voices into global debates, such as negotiations on trade, environmental or agricultural standards. Yet who represents whom in such processes, and how the knowledge and voices of professional advocates in many global decision-making arenas are accountable to local actors, increasingly becomes an issue, as illustrated by the slogan of southern-based NGOs – 'not about us without us' – in challenging the right of their northern counterparts to speak on their behalf in the Make Poverty History Campaign. Effective engagement can be enhanced by participatory research and action at every level, but in an increasingly globalized world, new forms of vertical accountability that connect knowledge and actors across hierarchies are critical as well (Batliwala, 2002).

Ultimately, the trends towards pluralization of knowledge in policy processes, the growth of the participatory sphere and the reshaping of the local and the global do not alter our fundamental arguments in the earlier section about the relationships of knowledge and power. If anything they add to the importance of knowledge as a power resource both within and outside formal decision-making processes. In so doing, they bring to the fore more than ever the need to go beyond participatory research as a strategy for voice and participation but also as one for 'cognitive justice' which affirms 'the right of different systems of knowledge to exist as a part of dialogue' (Visvanathan, 2005). How such cognitive justice can be achieved, and what participatory research strategies are needed in the new context remain the enduring questions.

NOTES

1 Our thanks to Kate Hamilton and Mel Speight for research assistance for the original version of this article. Thanks also to Kate McArdle and Peter Reason for their comments on this version.

2 PRA evolved through innovation and application in the south in the late 1980s and early 1990s, influenced by Rapid Rural Appraisal (RRA), applied anthropology, participatory action research, feminist research and agro-ecosystems analysis (Chambers, 1992; Guijt and Shah, 1998). Core methodological principles include iterative, group-based learning and analysis, the use of visualization methods to broaden the inclusiveness of the process and enable people to represent their knowledge using their own categories and concepts, and an explicit concern with the quality of interaction, including a stress on personal values, attitudes and behaviour (see Chambers, Chapter 20 in this volume).

3 For examples of the dynamics of this in practice, see critiques by Brock and McGee (2002) and Brock, McGee and Gaventa (2004).

REFERENCES

Agarwal, B. (1997) 'Editorial: Re-Sounding the alert – gender resources and community action', *World Development*, 25 (9): 1373–80.

Bachrach, P. and Baratz, M.S. (1970) *Power and Poverty: Theory and Practice*. New York: Oxford University Press.

Baocchi, G. (2001) 'Participation, activism and politics: the Porto Alegre experiment and deliberative democracy theory', *Politics and Society*, 29: 43–72.

Batliwala, S. (2002) 'Grassroots movements as transnational actors: implications for global civil society', *Voluntas: International Journal of Voluntary and Nonprofit Organisations*, 13 (4): 393–409.

Beck, U. (1992) *Risk Society: Towards a New Modernity*. London: Sage.

Brock, K. and McGee, R. (2002) *Knowing Poverty: Critical Reflections on Participatory Research and Policy*. London: Earthscan.

Brock, K., McGee, R. and Gaventa, J. (2004) *Knowledge, Actors and Spaces in Poverty Reduction in Uganda and Nigeria*. Kampala: Fountain Press and Oxford: Africa Books Collective.

Chambers, R. (1992) 'Rural appraisal: rapid, relaxed and participatory', *IDS Discussion Paper, 311*. Brighton: Institute of Development Studies.

Chambers, R. (1995) 'Paradigm shifts and the practice of participatory research and development', in N. Nelson and S. Wright (eds), *Power and Participatory Development: Theory and Practice*. London: Intermediate Technology Publications. pp. 30–42.

Chambers, R. (1997) *Whose Reality Counts? Putting the First Last*. London: Intermediate Technology Publications.

Collins, H.M. and Evans, R. (2002) 'The third wave of science studies: studies of expertise and experience', *Social Studies of Science, 32* (2): 235–96.

Cooke, B. and Kothari, U. (eds) (2001) *Participation: the New Tyranny?* London: Zed Books.

Cornwall, A. (2003) 'Whose Voices? Whose Choices? Reflections on gender and participatory development', *World Development, 31* (8): 1325–42.

Cornwall, A. and Pratt, G. (eds) (2003) *Pathways to Participation: Reflections on PRA*. Brighton: Institute of Development Studies.

Cornwall, A. and Schattan Coelho, V. (eds) (2004) 'New democratic spaces?', *IDS Bulletin, 35*(2). Brighton: Institute of Development Studies.

Cornwall, A. and Schattan Coelho, V. (eds) (2006) *Spaces for Change? The Politics of Citizen Participation in New Democratic Arenas*. London: Zed Books.

Cornwall, A., Cordeiro, S. and Delgado, N. (2006) 'Rights to health and struggles for accountability in a Brazilian municipal health council', in P. Newell and J. Wheeler (eds), *Rights, Resources and the Politics of Accountability*. London: Zed Books.

Cornwall, A., Guijt, I. and Welbourn, A. (1993) 'Acknowledging process: challenges for agricultural research and methodology', *IDS Discussion Paper, 333*. Brighton: Institute of Development Studies.

Crawley, H. (1998) 'Living up to the empowerment claim? The potential of PRA', in I. Guijt and M.K. Shah (eds), *The Myth of Community: Gender Issues in Participatory Development*. London: Intermediate Technology Publications. pp. 24–34.

Dahl, R.A. (1969) 'The concept of power', in R. Bell, D.M. Edwards and R. Harrison Wagner (eds), *Political Power: A Reader in Theory and Research*. New York: Free Press, pp. 79–93. (reprinted from *Behavioral Science*, 2, (1957), 201–5).

Entwistle, H. (1979) *Antonio Gramsci*. London: Routledge and Kegan Paul.

Epstein, S. (1996) *Impure Science: Aids, Activism and the Politics of Knowledge*. Berkeley: University of California Press.

Estrella, M. and Iszatt, N. (2004) *Beyond Good Governance*. Quezon City, Philippines: Institute for Participatory Democracy.

Fals Borda, O. (1991) 'Remaking knowledge' in O. Fals Borda and M.A. Rahman (eds), *Action and Knowledge: Breaking the Monopoly with Participatory Action-Research*. New York: The Apex Press and London: Intermediate Technology Publications. pp. 146–66.

Fals Borda, O. and Rahman. M.A. (1991) *Action and Knowledge: Breaking the Monopoly with PAR*, New York: Apex Press and London: Intermediate Technology Publications.

Fisher, F. (2000) *Citizens, Experts and the Environment*, Durham and London: Duke University Press.

Foucault, M. (1977) *Discipline and Punishment*. London: Allen Lane.

Foucault, M. (1979) *The History of Sexuality, Part 1*. London: Allen Lane.

Freire, P. (1970) *Pedagogy of the Oppressed*. New York: Seabury Press.

Freire, P. (1981) *Education for Critical Consciousness*. New York: Continuum.

Fung, A. and Wright, E.O. (2003) *Deepening Democracy: Institutional Innovations in Empowered Participatory Governance*. London: Verso.

Gaventa, J. (1980) *Power and Powerlessness: Quiescence and Rebellion in an Appalachian Valley*. Urbana: University of Illinois Press and Oxford: Clarendon Press.

Gaventa, J. (1993) 'The powerful, the powerless, and the experts', in P. Park, M. Brydon-Miller, B. Hall and T. Jackson (eds), *Voices of Change: Participatory Research in the United States and Canada*. Westport, CT: Bergin and Garvey and Toronto: OISE Press. pp. 21–40.

Gaventa, J. (1999) 'Citizen knowledge, citizen competence, and democracy building', in S.L. Elkin and K.E. Soltan (eds), *Citizen Competence and Democratic Institutions*. University Park, PA: Pennsylvania State University Press. pp. 49–66.

Gaventa, J. (2006) 'Triumph, deficit or contestation? Deepening the deepening democracy debate', *IDS Working Paper*, 264. Brighton: Institute of Development Studies.

Guijt, I. and Shah, M.K. (1998) 'Waking up to power, process and conflict', in I. Guijt and M.K. Shah (eds), *The Myth of Community: Gender Issues in Participatory Development*, London: Intermediate Technology Publications. pp. 1–23.

Hall, B.L. (1981) 'Participatory research, popular knowledge and power: a personal reflection', *Convergence*, XIV (3): 6–17.

Hall, B.L. (1992a) 'Breaking the monopoly of action knowledge: research methods, participation and development', in R. Tandon (ed.), *Participatory Research: Revisiting the Roots*. New Delhi: Mosaic Books. pp. 9–21.

Hall, B.L. (1992b) 'From margins to center? The development and purpose of participatory research', *The American Sociologist*, 23(4): 15–28.

Harding, S. (1986) *Feminism and Methodology*, Bloomington: Indiana University Press.

Hayward, C.R. (1998) 'De-facing power', *Polity*. 31 (1), 1–22.

hooks, b. (1994) *Teaching to Transgress: Education as the Practice of Freedom*. New York: Routledge.

Kabeer, N. (1994) *Reversed Realities: Gender Hierarchies in Development Thought*. London and New York: Verso.

Kahane, D. and Von Lieres, B. (2006) 'Inclusion and representation in democratic deliberations: lessons from Canada's Romanow Commission', in A. Cornwall and V. Schatten Coelho (eds), *Spaces for Change? The Politics of Citizen Participation in New Democratic Arenas*. London: Zed Books. pp. 131–44.

Kar, K. and Pasteur, K. (2005) 'Subsidy or Self-respect? Community led sanitation. an update on recent developments', *IDS Working Paper, 257*. Brighton: Institute of Development Studies.

Kohn, M. (2000) 'Language, power and persuasion: toward a critique of deliberative democracy', *Constellations*, 7 (3): 408–29.

Leach, M. and Scoones, I. (2006) 'Mobilising citizens: social movements and the politics of knowledge', *IDS Working Paper*. Brighton: Institute of Development Studies.

LogoLink (2002) 'The International Workshop on Participatory Planning Approaches for Local Governance', Bandung, Indonesia; http://www.ids.ac.uk/logolink/initiatives/workshops/intlearnplan.htm (accessed 1 September 2006).

LogoLink (2004) 'International Workshop on Resources, Citizen Engagements and Democratic Local Governance', Porto Alegre, Brazil, http://www.ids.ac.uk/logolink/initiatives/workshops/ReCitEBrazil.htm (accessed 1 September 2006).

Lukes, S. (1974) *Power: a Radical View*. London: Macmillan.

Lukes, S. (2005) *Power: a Radical View, 2nd edn*. London: Macmillan.

Maguire, P. (1987) 'Towards a feminist participatory research framework: challenging the patriarchy', in

D. Murphy et al. (eds), *Doing Community–Based Research: A Reader*. Austin, TX: Loka Institute.

Maguire, P. (1996) 'Proposing a more feminist participatory research: knowing and being embraced openly' in K. de Koning and M. Martin (eds), *Participatory Research in Health: Issues and Experiences*. London: Zed Books. pp. 27–39.

Mahmud, K. (2005) *Coalition Politics in India: Dynamics of a Winning Combination*. New Delhi: Manohar.

Mahmud, S. (2006) 'Spaces for participation in health systems in rural Bangladesh: the experiences of stakeholder community groups', in A. Cornwall and V. Schattan Coelho (eds), *Spaces for Change? The Politics of Citizen Participation in New Democratic Arenas*. London: Zed Books. pp. 55–75.

Mahmud, S. and Kabeer, N. (2006) 'Compliance versus accountability: struggles for dignity and daily bread in the Bangladesh garment industry', in P. Newell and J. Wheeler (eds), *Rights, Resources and the Politics of Accountability*. London: Zed Book. pp. 223–44.

Merrifield, J. (1993) 'Putting scientists in their place: participatory research in environmental and occupational health', in P. Park, M. Brydon-Miller, B. Hall, and T. Jackson (eds), *Voices of Change: Participatory Research in the United States and Canada*, Westport, CT: Bergin and Garvey and Toronto: OISE Press. pp. 65–84.

Morris, A. (1984) *The Origins of the Civil Rights Movement*. New York: Free Press.

Mouffe, C. (1992) 'Feminism, citizenship and radical democratic politics', in J. Butler and J. Scott (eds), *Feminists Theorize the Political*. New York: Routledge. pp. 369–384.

Mueller, C.M. (ed.) (1992) *Frontiers in Social Movement Theory*. New Haven, CT: Yale University Press.

Narayan, D. Chambers, R. Shah, M. and Petesch, P. (2000) *Voices of the Poor: Crying Out For Change*, Washington, DC: World Bank.

Nelson, N. and Wright, S. (1995) 'Participation and power', in N. Nelson and S. Wright (eds), *Power and Participatory Development: Theory and Practice*, London: Intermediate Technology Publications. pp. 1–12.

Park, P., Brydon-Miller, M., Hall, B. and Jackson T. (eds) (1993) *Voices of Change: Participatory Research in the United States and Canada*. Westport, CT: Bergin and Garvey and Toronto: OISE Press.

Rahman, M.A. (1991) 'The theoretical standpoint of PAR', in O. Fals Borda and M.A. Rahman (eds), *Action and Knowledge: Breaking the Monopoly with Participatory Action-Research*. New York: The Apex Press and London: Intermediate Technology Publications. pp.13–23.

Reason, P. (1994) 'Three approaches to participatory inquiry', in K. Denzin and S. Lincoln (eds), *Handbook of Qualitative Research.* Thousand Oaks, CA: Sage. pp. 324–339.

Robb, C. (1999) *Can the Poor Influence Policy? Participatory Poverty Assessments in the Developing World.* Washington DC: The World Bank.

Robins, S. (2005) 'From "medical miracles" to normal (ised) medicine: Aids treatment, activism and citizenship in the UK and South Africa', *IDS Working Paper 252*, Brighton: Institute of Development Studies.

Rowden, R. and Irama, J.O. (2004) *Rethinking Participation: Questions for Civil Society about the Limits of Participation in PRSPs*, Washington, DC: ActionAid International USA and Kampala: ActionAid International Uganda.

Rowlands, J. (1995) 'Empowerment examined', *Development in Practice*, 5 (2): 101–7.

Schattschneider, E.E. (1960) *The Semi-sovereign People: a Realist's View of Democracy in America.* New York: Holt, Rinehart and Winston.

Scott, J.C. (1986) *Weapons of the Weak.* New Haven, CT: Yale University Press.

Scott, J.C. (1990) *Domination and the Arts of Resistance.* New Haven, CT: Yale University Press.

Selener, D. (1997) *Participatory Action Research and Social Change.* New York: The Cornell Participatory Action Research Network, Cornell University.

Tandon, R. (1982) 'A critique of monopolistic research', in R. Tandon (ed.), *Participatory Research: Revisiting the Roots* (2005). New Delhi: Mosaic Books. pp. 3–8.

Taylor, P. and Fransman, J. (2004) 'Learning and teaching participation: exploring the role of higher learning institutions as agents of development and social change', *IDS Working Paper, 219.* Brighton: Institute of Development Studies.

VeneKlasen, L. with Miller, V. (2002) *A New Weave of Power, People and Politics.* Oklahoma City, OK: World Neighbors.

Visvanathan, S. (2005) 'Knowledge, justice and democracy', in M. Leach, I. Scoones and B. Wynne (eds), *Science and Citizens: Globalisation and the Challenge of Engagement.* London: Zed Books. pp. 83–96.

12

Appreciable Worlds, Inspired Inquiry

Danielle P. Zandee and David L. Cooperrider

Twenty years after its introduction, appreciative inquiry is well-known as a strength-based collaborative approach for the study and change of organizational and societal realities. It is now commonly equated with a 'positive bias' in scholarship which is itself both welcomed and critiqued. This chapter's intent is to go beyond an understanding of appreciation as a focus on the positive with a return to the original call to appreciative inquiry as an invitation to re-awaken a 'spirit of inquiry' – a sense of wonder, curiosity, and surprise – in our pursuits of knowledge creation about the social world.

Appreciative inquiry celebrates the power of our imaginative mind. As a form of action research in pursuit of knowledge creation for social innovation, it invites us to be daring in our explorations and articulations of alternative possibilities for our shared and organized existence. At its best, appreciative inquiry becomes like art in enabling participants to see anew and to bring something fresh into the world – something that inspires thoughts and actions that truly help generate individual, organizational, communal, and global 'flourishing' (Reason and Bradbury, 2001: 1).

Two decades have passed since Cooperrider and Srivastva (1987) first conceptualized and presented appreciative inquiry as a generative approach to research into organizational life. This theoretical writing was a reflection on concrete organization development experience (Ludema and Fry, Chapter 19 in this volume) sparked by the question of how such inquiry can become a creative process of collaborative theorizing that leads to knowledge deemed relevant for the transformation of the practice in which it is grounded. The contours of appreciative inquiry as laid out in this ground-breaking piece have been successfully translated into a well known and globally utilized strength-based methodology for organizational and societal change and have informed the research perspective and agenda of many scholars (Cameron et al., 2003; Cooperrider and Avital, 2004). Indeed – especially in recent years with the rise of positive psychology (Linley et al., 2006; Seligman and Csikszentmihalyi, 2000) and positive organizational scholarship (Bernstein, 2003; Cameron and Caza, 2004) – a focus on what is now commonly known as the 'positive' side of organizing has gained tremendously in popularity and recognition.

This positive stance is presented as an effort to counterbalance the perceived predominance of a deficit discourse as manifested in a focus on problem-solving, human pathology, and negative organizational performance. This counterbalancing act, whilst providing a compelling antithesis, has evoked some noteworthy critiques. Fineman (2006), for instance, takes issue with how a privileging of 'positiveness' leads to a 'separation thesis' that artificially distinguishes between so-called positive and negative acts, experiences, and emotions. He states that 'in exclusively favoring positive narratives, appreciative inquiry fails to value the opportunities for positive change that are possible from negative experiences, such as embarrassing events, periods of anger, anxiety, fear, or shame' (2006: 275). His concerns are shared by Barge and Oliver (2003), who in addition caution not to equate the spirit of appreciation in conversation with technique through an excessive reliance on structuring devices such as the '4-D model' and the asking of 'unconditional positive questions' (pp. 127–8). A third important concern is that an overly positive bias may inadvertently obscure and maintain existing power differences by silencing or stigmatizing critical voices, and by providing elites with a new tool for manipulation and control (Barge and Oliver, 2003: 129; Fineman, 2006: 281).

These critical reflections call into question the meaning of appreciation in inquiry and the qualities that make inquiry a generative force that cherishes imaginative perceptions and co-constructions of novel organizational realities. The basic intention of appreciative

inquiry is to study that which gives life to a human system. As such it challenges us to find value and possibility in the full spectrum of human experiences and to overcome tendencies toward reductionist thinking in either/or (positive/negative) dichotomies. Like other action research approaches, appreciative inquiry invites the researcher to wholeheartedly engage with the complex, messy, and emergent nature of organizational and societal life. Such engagement asks for questions and methods that enable innovative research into the practice of a particular group in a specific time and place. It asks, in other words, for an intuitive approach to inquiry rather than a mechanical use of available techniques. An important premise of appreciative inquiry is that high quality inquiry depends on the presence of all participants in full voice. Such inquiry has the potential to challenge and transform, rather than maintain, the current state of affairs, including who has the right to speak and act. All of this, of course, is much easier said than done, and the current critique of appreciative inquiry makes that apparent.

Indeed, our understanding of *inquiry* in the appreciative/inquiry equation remains limited. As Cooperrider and Avital (2004: xii) note: 'While many are intrigued with the AI positive bias – toward the good, the better, the exceptional, and the possible – it is the power of inquiry we must learn more about and underscore.' In this chapter we explore the dynamics of inspired inquiry into appreciable worlds in order to enrich current notions of what such inquiry might entail. What does it mean to take an appreciative stance in inquiry? This first question leads us to revisit the original call to appreciative inquiry and especially its stated objective of being a form of inquiry with high 'generative capacity' (Cooperrider and Srivastva, 1987; Gergen, 1978). We then continue with a close look at five dimensions of appreciative inquiry in order to renew our comprehension of inquiry that is both inspired and generative. In our discussion of these dimensions we combine theoretical and practical perspectives by highlighting conceptual underpinnings as well as concrete examples of appreciative inquiry practice. We conclude this chapter with the proposition that 'mystical pragmatism' is perhaps the guiding value of appreciative inquiry, and an invitation to engage in this form of action research as spirited inquiry where together we discover and realize the noblest, most beautiful and meaningful possibilities for human existence on this planet.

TAKING AN APPRECIATIVE STANCE IN INQUIRY

The original call to appreciative inquiry asked researchers to become scholarly activists who set out to help create a better world through a process 'that affirms our symbolic capacities of imagination and mind as well as our social capacity for conscious choice and cultural evolution' (Cooperrider and Srivastva, 1987: 159). Appreciative inquiry itself was an imaginative conception of action research intended for 'discovering, understanding, and fostering innovations in social-organizational arrangements and processes' (p. 159). It was an answer to Gergen's daring invitation (1978, 1994a, 1994b, 1999) to heighten the 'generative capacity' of social science research, which can be summarized as the ability to challenge the status quo in organizational and social life, to create a sense of possibility, and to thereby open up new repertoires for thought and action. Gergen's notion of generative theorizing is radical in its focus on generating new reality – on being a catalyst for social transformation – by 'telling it as it might become' rather than 'telling it like it is' (Gergen and Thatchenkery, 1996: 370). As a process of generative theorizing, appreciative inquiry combines research and action, inquiry and intervention, by creating knowledge that enables the participants in this creation to engage in (almost) simultaneous practical experimentation and implementation of transformative ideas.

Appreciative inquiry is grounded in the belief that theory can be and should be of 'creative significance to society' (Cooperrider and Srivastva, 1987: 160). It is based on the premise that knowledge can enlighten and empower those who strive to change the environment in which they work and live. Thus it invites the researcher to develop and enable approaches to knowledge creation and usage that are liberating and 'promote egalitarian dialogue leading to social system effectiveness and integrity' (p. 159).

Appreciative inquiry is purposely not value free. As human inquiry with transformative and emancipatory intent, it 'invites, encourages, and requires that students of social life rigorously exercise their theoretical imagination in the service of their vision of the good' (Cooperrider and Srivastva, 1987: 140), and to join others in their visions of world betterment. Beyond a well-published bias towards the positive, appreciative inquiry is guided by a 'reverence for life' (Schweitzer, 1969). According to Cooperrider and Avital (2004: xiv) 'AI is perhaps best talked about as a way of living with, being with, and directly participating in the core of a human system in a way that compels each one of us to inquire into the deeper life-generating essentials and potentials of social existence.' In its most fundamental understanding, 'appreciation' means a valuing (in terms of discovery, description and explanation) of that – however small – which gives life to a human system (Cooperrider and Srivastva, 1987: 160). This central focus on what gives, promotes, and sustains life in human groups, organizations, and the larger world is directly related to Erikson's (1950, 1964) notion of generativity as 'the concern in establishing and guiding the next generation' (1950: 267). As guiding values, both appreciation and generativity inform inquiry as a nurturing of life into the future.

In their first articulation of appreciative inquiry, Cooperrider and Srivastva (1987: 159) made the assertion that the generative capacity of action research will advance when 'the discipline decides to expand its universe of exploration, seeks to discover new questions, and rekindles a fresh perception of the extra ordinary in everyday organizational life'.

One pathway toward such expansive explorations, creative questions, and fresh perspectives, is the employment of alternative metaphors (Gergen, 1994a). Where 'many commonly accepted explanations for human action are tied to prevailing metaphors within the culture' (1994a: 143), new metaphors may free neglected ways of seeing and thinking. Trying to escape the limits of problem-solving as a dominant mode of knowing, Cooperrider and Srivastva (1987) proposed to balance what they saw as the prevailing notion of 'organizing as a problem to be solved', with the root metaphor of 'organizing as a miracle, or mystery, to be embraced'. This metaphorical shift expands the terrain of inquiry from one defined by the issues at hand, to one that has no limits other than in our willingness to hold the marvel of life and our capacity to imagine desired futures. But how are we to engage in such inquiry? How do we overcome our habitual and sometimes pessimistic assumptions of reality in order to open ourselves to a more naïve learning stance implied by mystery?

The original call to appreciative inquiry was more than an invitation to embrace an activist agenda of social innovation through knowledge creation, life-centric guiding values, and an underlying metaphor of life as miracle. It was also a call to re-awaken a 'spirit of inquiry' that allows us to respond with a sense of 'awe, curiosity, veneration, surprise, delight, amazement, and wonder' (Cooperrider, 1996: 5) in our study of appreciable worlds. Such responses are important in propelling and sustaining generative processes of inspired and creative theorizing (Zandee, 2004). In the next section of this chapter, we discuss how a spirit of inquiry is nourished in a close-knit relationship between appreciation and inquiry.

GENERATIVE DIMENSIONS OF APPRECIATIVE INQUIRY

In the conclusion of their seminal paper, Cooperrider and Srivastva (1987: 165) made the assertion that we can train our 'appreciative eye' to 'see the ordinary magic, beauty and real possibility in organizational life'. Since that statement many have developed ways to heighten appreciation in inquiry and have encouraged others to engage in similar experimentation. We recognize five distinct dimensions of an appreciative stance in inquiry that together give the contours of what Grudin (1990) might call an 'ethos of inspiration', an interrelated practice of being, thinking, and acting that can elevate the generative capacity of our work. In what follows we give groundings to and concrete examples from appreciative inquiry and other action research practices for each of the dimensions. We also point to the practice elaborated in Ludema and Fry (see Chapter 19).

ILLUMINATING THE MIRACLE OF LIFE

The starting point of appreciative inquiry lies in its wish to hold and reveal the miracle of life. This first and fundamental dimension asks that we *appreciate life as mysterious*. In the academic and organizational context from which we write, this is a somewhat unusual request since modern society has worked hard to move into the opposite direction by transforming magic into science (Koestler, 1964: 261) in efforts to solve mystery and banish uncertainty. The wish for a re-enchantment of our world is expressed in the appreciative inquiry literature through discussions about wonder and childlike openness in inquiry (Cooperrider, 1990, 1996; Cooperrider and Barrett, 2002; Cooperrider and Srivastva, 1987). These discussions give illustrations of wondrous experiences of scientists and explore the metaphor of 'inquiry as art' to give compelling images of a more perceptive sensitivity to the mysterious realm.

Nissley (2004) notices these frequent references to the 'art of' appreciative inquiry, and moves beyond metaphor in his study of how 'practitioners *actually* engage organizations in the artful creation of positive anticipatory imagery' (p. 284). He makes connections with the emerging field of 'aesthetic discourse' (Strati, 1999) that is concerned with a more intuitive, sensuous – rather than a logico-rational – understanding of organizational life (p. 7). Indeed, our capacity to appreciate life as mysterious and to hold and express its delicate, ambiguous, and ineffable qualities may be heightened if we develop more artful approaches to inquiry. An example of 'appreciative inquiry as a process of creative inquiry that permits us to move beyond words alone' (Nissley, 2004: 286) is the use of artful creations such as drawings, poems, and songs during the so called 'dream phase' to express latent images of ideal futures. Such creations are forms of 'presentational knowledge' (Heron and Reason, 2001/2006; Reason, 1993) that act as a 'mediate for discovering and communicating shared meaning' (Nissley, 2004: 286).

QUESTIONING TAKEN FOR GRANTED REALITIES

The questioning and interruption of taken for granted realities is part and parcel of the notion of 'generative theorizing' (Gergen, 1978, 1994a, 1994b) that inspired the conception of appreciative inquiry. This scholarship of dislodgment and transformation challenges the status quo in order to invite people 'into new worlds of meaning and action' (Gergen, 1999: 116). It embraces a constructionist worldview that emphasizes that organizations and other social patterns and structures are products of human imagination and interaction 'rather than some anonymous expression of an underlying natural order' (Cooperrider et al., 1995). In this worldview nothing is fixed or given in how we perceive and create social reality and conceptions of truth will differ across time and space. The second dimension of appreciative inquiry asks us to take a questioning stance which is enabled when we can *appreciate truth as multi-faceted and impermanent.*

Ludema and Fry (Chapter 19) point out that appreciative inquiry practice commonly starts with the (re)framing of topics for inquiry. Deliberate shifts in topic definition liberate participants out of ingrained patterns of thinking and acting and spark their curiosity in a journey of discovery toward new, and otherwise possibly unconceivable, action strategies (Barrett and Cooperrider, 1990).

ENVISIONING NEW POSSIBILITIES

Appreciative inquiry takes guidance from the constructionist notion that 'words create worlds' in asserting that 'the artful creation of positive imagery on a collective basis may well be the most prolific activity that individuals and organizations can engage in if their aim is to help bring to fruition a positive and humanly significant future' (Cooperrider, 1990: 93). With this hopeful assertion, appreciative inquiry takes an 'affirmative postmodern' stance which 'includes more optimistic efforts to construct new construals of identity, knowledge, and community as alternatives to the modern worldview' (Sandage and Hill, 2001: 251). This third dimension reinforces the visionary potential of human inquiry, which is enabled when we *appreciate reality as limitless potential,* when we can imagine our social world as a playground of infinite possibility (Carse, 1986).

A key assumption of appreciative inquiry is that we awaken our imaginative capacity when we make deep connections with the core of what gives life to a human system. Such connections provide the inquiry participants with the ingredients and inspiration for the shared creation of evocative images of the future. Thoughtful, creative questions are used as the medium for the establishment of these vitalizing connections between existing strengths and future possibilities. Therefore, much time is dedicated to the crafting of such, so-called 'unconditional positive questions' (Ludema and Fry, Chapter 19 in this volume; Ludema et al., 2001/2006).

CREATING KNOWLEDGE IN RELATIONSHIP

Appreciative inquiry is based on the premise that high quality research occurs in moments of intimate human relationship. Its underlying constructionist worldview proposes the vision of a 'relational self' instead of individualistic accounts of human agency, and 'replaces the individual with the relationship as the locus of knowledge' (Cooperrider and Avital, 2004: xviii; Gergen and Gergen, Chapter 10 in this volume). This fourth dimension promotes knowledge creation as social endeavor. It asks us to *appreciate human existence as relational* and to truly see others as 'vital co-creators of our mind, our self, and our society' (Sampson, 1993: 109).

Grounded in the belief that we need to engage in dialogue if we want to change our organizations, communities and the larger world, appreciative inquiry practice facilitates large group 'whole system' conversations as 'narrative rich' environments in which participants share touching stories of accomplishment and aspiration (see Chapter 19). The experience is that such storytelling evokes the interpersonal connections and positive affect that allows participants to commit to a mutual process of inquiry.

Action research firmly embraces a 'relationality orientation' to inquiry (Bradbury and Lichtenstein, 2000). It clearly distinguishes itself from other research traditions in its emphasis on processes of collaboration (Gergen and Gergen, Chapter 10 in this volume) and many examples exist of successful participative inquiry approaches (Heron and Reason, 2001/2006; Ospina et al., Chapter 28 in this volume). However, much remains to be done if we fully want to make the shift from the so deeply ingrained individualistic worldview to a truly relational one. Action researchers are uniquely positioned to jointly promote this shift and to engage in shared inquiry to further develop the emerging contours of 'relational theory' (Gergen and Gergen, Chapter 10 in this volume).

ENABLING JUST AND SUSTAINABLE COEXISTENCE

The life-centric spirit of appreciative inquiry requires an expansion of our 'capacity of relatedness' (Cooperrider and Avital, 2004: xv) beyond specific organizations and communities and beyond the human group. Our constructions of localized social realities occur within a vast interrelated context and have the potential to impact global well being. For our inquiry to have truly life-giving capacity we need to remember our own embodied participation in a spirited, biological realm. This fifth dimension promotes inquiry as advocacy for worldwide justice and sustainability. Such global compassion is enabled when we can once again *appreciate our sensuous participation in a more-than-human world* (Abram, 1996).

Though appreciative inquiry relies heavily on a discursive way of knowing, it *does* hold an invitation to ground our linguistic practice in a bodily understanding of being. We can only fully nourish life through inquiry when we 'recall and re-establish the rootedness of human awareness in the larger ecology' (Abram, 1996: 261), and embrace our place in an interconnected 'web of life' (Capra, 1996). In its ideal form appreciative inquiry succeeds in awakening such global consciousness in participants by helping them to 'sense not just responsibility *for* but feel an intimacy *with* the whole' (Cooperrider and Avital, 2004: xxiii; Whitney, 2004).

Lately appreciative inquiry practice has aligned itself with efforts to promote a changing role of business in society. Through the Center for Business as an Agent of World Benefit (BAWB) it explores and facilitates the idea of sustainable and socially responsible enterprise (Bright et al., 2006). An important activity of the center is the so called 'world inquiry' through which exemplar stories of successful business innovations with positive societal impact are gathered, studied, and made available to the larger public. The center creates virtual meeting spaces through web-based conferences in its efforts to connect with the global community and to include as many voices as possible in the enabling of more just and sustainable forms of coexistence.

CONCLUDING THOUGHTS

Our discussion of the generative dimensions of appreciative inquiry shows the inseparable and dynamic relationship between the two words 'appreciative' and 'inquiry'. When we are able to take an appreciative stance we are free to choose and develop methods of inquiry that illuminate and create the fullest life-nourishing potential of human systems in the larger world. In similar fashion, our thoughtfully crafted approaches to inquiry may help others and ourselves to more sincerely embrace an appreciative perspective. Taken together, appreciation in inquiry invites open-ended, collaborative research that is sustained through responses like wonder, curiosity, imagination, heartfelt openness, and a sense of home in our explorations of appreciable worlds. Ideally we find ways to hold and heighten all five dimensions if we truly want to develop an 'ethos of appreciation' in our work.

Many of the methods that appreciative inquiry utilizes – sharing success stories, asking positive questions, creating artful future images, and organizing large group conversations – are appealing because they seem straightforward and easy to emulate. But the apparent simplicity of appreciative inquiry is in actuality rather 'profound' (Weick, 2004: 662). Indeed, inquiry methods that are not grounded in an appreciative stance can easily become mechanical, dull, and even manipulative techniques and a simplistic understanding of appreciation as 'being positive' will most likely not enable research approaches that can grasp and celebrate the living complexity of organizational and social life. Critical observations of appreciative inquiry practice (Barge and Oliver, 2003; Fineman, 2006) rightfully point to such pitfalls in the interpretation and utilization of appreciative methods in organization studies and development.

In the end, appreciative inquiry is perhaps best understood as a form of 'mystical pragmatism' which asks us to stand in the mysterious realm and from that position to help bring forth bold imaginations of possibility with practical beneficial significance for organized and social action. It invites us to explore how we might more openly relate to the miracle of life on this planet and thereby experience the power of appreciation more frequently and developmentally in each of our relations and initiatives as co-participants in a never ending quest to value and create. To take such a stance remains a choice, a leap of faith perhaps, that many of us involved in appreciative inquiry and other action research approaches are committed to make. Together we can further the theory and practice of inspired inquiry into appreciable worlds.

REFERENCES

Abram, D. (1996) *The Spell of the Sensuous: Perception and Language in a More-than-Human World.* New York: Random House.

Barge, K.J. and Oliver, C. (2003) 'Working with appreciation in managerial practice', *Academy of Management Review,* 28 (1): 124–42.

Barrett, F.J. and Cooperrider, D.L. (1990) 'Generative metaphor intervention: a new approach for working with systems divided by conflict and caught in defensive perception', *Journal of Applied Behavioral Science,* 26 (2): 219–39.

Bernstein, S.D. (2003) 'Positive organizational scholarship: meet the movement', *Journal of Management Inquiry,* 12 (3): 266–71.

Bradbury, H. and Lichtenstein, B.M. (2000) 'Relationality in organizational research: exploring the space between', *Organization Science,* 11 (5): 551–64.

Bright, D.S., Fry, R.E. and Cooperrider, D.L. (2006) 'Transformative innovations for the mutual benefit of business, society, and environment.' *BAWB Interactive Working Paper Series* 1 (1): 17–33. Retrieved 23 September 2006 from http://worldbenefit.case.edu/research/paperseries/?p=21

Cameron, K.S. and Caza, A. (2004) 'Introduction: contributions to the discipline of positive organizational scholarship', *American Behavioral Scientist,* 47 (6): 1–9.

Cameron, K.S., Dutton, J.E. and Quinn, R.E. (eds) (2003) *Positive Organizational Scholarship: Foundations of a New Discipline.* San Francisco, CA: Berrett-Koehler.

Capra, F. (1996) *The Web of Life: A New Scientific Understanding of Living Systems.* New York: Doubleday.

Carse, J.P. (1986) *Finite and Infinite Games: A Vision of Life as Play and Possibility.* New York: Ballantine Books.

Cooperrider, D.L. (1990) 'Positive image, positive action: the affirmative basis of organizing', in S. Srivastva and D.L. Cooperrider (eds), *Appreciative Management and Leadership.* San Francisco, CA: Jossey-Bass. pp. 91–125.

Cooperrider, D.L. (1996) 'The "child" as agent of inquiry', *OD Practitioner,* 28 (1): 5–11.

Cooperrider, D.L. and Avital, M. (eds) (2004) *Advances in Appreciative Inquiry: Vol. 1. Constructive Discourse and Human Organization.* Oxford: Elsevier Science.

Cooperrider, D.L. and Barrett, F.J. (2002) 'An exploration of the spiritual heart of human science inquiry', *Reflections: The SOL Journal,* 3 (3): 56–62.

Cooperrider, D.L., Barrett, F.J. and Srivastva, S. (1995) 'Social construction and appreciative inquiry: a journey in organizational theory', in D. Hosking, H.P. Dachler, and K. Gergen (eds), *Management and Organization: Relational Alternatives to Individualism.* Brookfield, VT: Ashgate Publishing. pp. 157–200.

Cooperrider, D.L. and Srivastva, S. (1987) 'Appreciative inquiry in organizational life', *Research in Organizational Change and Development,* 1: 129–69.

Erikson, E.H. (1950) *Childhood and Society* (35th anniversary edn). New York: W.W. Norton & Co.

Erikson, E.H. (1964) *Insight and Responsibility: Lectures on the Ethical Implications of Psychoanalytic Insight.* New York: W.W. Norton & Co.

Fineman, S. (2006) 'On being positive: Concerns and counterpoints', *Academy of Management Review,* 31 (2): 270–91.

Gergen, K.J. (1978) 'Toward generative theory', *Journal of Personality and Social Psychology,* 36 (11): 1344–60.

Gergen, K.J. (1994a) *Toward Transformation in Social Knowledge, 2nd edn.* London: Sage.

Gergen, K.J. (1994b) *Realities and Relationships: Soundings in Social Construction.* Cambridge, MA: Harvard University Press.

Gergen, K.J. (1999) *An Invitation to Social Construction.* London: Sage.

Gergen, K.J. and Thatchenkery, T.J. (1996) 'Organization science as social construction: postmodern potentials', *Journal of Applied Behavioral Science,* 32 (4): 356–77.

Grudin, R. (1990) *The Grace of Great Things: Creativity and Innovation.* New York: Ticknor & Fields.

Heron, J. and Reason, P. (2001/2006) 'The practice of co-operative-inquiry: research "with" rather than "on" people', in P. Reason and H. Bradbury (eds), *Handbook of Action Research: Participative Inquiry and Practice.* London: Sage. pp. 179–88. Also published in P. Reason and H. Bradbury (eds) (2006), *Handbook of Action Research: Concise Student Edition.* London: Sage. pp. 144–54.

Koestler, A. (1964) *The Act of Creation* (Arkana edn). London: Penguin Books.

Linley, P.A., Joseph, S., Harrington, S. and Wood, A.M. (2006) 'Positive psychology: past, present, and (possible) future', *The Journal of Positive Psychology,* 1 (1): 3–16.

Ludema, J.D., Cooperrider, D.L. and Barrett, F.J. (2001/2006) 'Appreciative inquiry: the power of the unconditional positive question', in P. Reason and H. Bradbury (eds), *Handbook of Action Research: Participative Inquiry and Practice.* London: Sage. pp.189–99. Also published in P. Reason and H. Bradbury (eds) (2006), *Handbook of Action Research: Concise Student Edition.* London: Sage. pp. 155–65.

Nissley, N. (2004) 'The "artful creation" of positive anticipatory imagery in appreciative inquiry: understanding the "art of" appreciative inquiry as aesthetic discourse', in D.L. Cooperrider and M. Avital (eds), *Advances in Appreciative Inquiry: Vol. 1. Constructive Discourse and Human Organization.* Oxford: Elsevier Science. pp. 283–307.

Reason, P. (1993) 'Reflections on sacred experience and sacred science', *Journal of Management Inquiry,* 2 (3): 273–83.

Reason, P. and Bradbury, H. (2001) *Handbook of Action Research: Participative Inquiry and Practice.* London: Sage.

Sampson, E.E. (1993) *Celebrating the Other: a Dialogic Account of Human Nature.* Boulder, CO: Westview Press.

Sandage, S.J. and Hill, P.C. (2001) 'The virtues of positive psychology: the rapprochement and challenges of an affirmative postmodern perspective', *Journal for the Theory of Social Behavior,* 31 (3): 241–60.

Schweitzer, A. (1969) *The Teaching of Reverence for Life.* New York: Holt, Rinehart & Winston.

Seligman, E.P. and Csikszentmihalyi, M. (2000) 'Positive psychology: an introduction', *American Psychologist,* 55: 5–14.

Strati, A. (1999) *Organization and Aesthetics.* London: Sage.

Weick, K.E. (2004) 'Mundane poetics: searching for wisdom in organization studies', *Organization Studies,* 25 (4): 653–68.

Whitney, D. (2004) 'Appreciative inquiry and the eleva-
tion of organizational consciousness', in D.L.
Cooperrider and M. Avital (eds), *Advances in
Appreciative Inquiry: Vol. 1. Constructive Discourse
and Human Organization.* Oxford: Elsevier Science.
pp. 125–46.

Zandee, D.P. (2004) 'A study in generative process: the
art of theorizing', unpublished doctoral dissertation,
Case Western Reserve University, Cleveland, USA.

13

Ethics and Action Research: Deepening our Commitment to Principles of Social Justice and Redefining Systems of Democratic Practice[1]

Mary Brydon-Miller

This chapter provides readers with an introduction to research ethics within an action research context. After a brief review of the fundamental principles upon which the guidelines for ethical research in general are grounded, the chapter discusses the relationship between the shared values of action research and these established codes of conduct, suggesting that the values articulated by action researchers not only reflect, but extend and more fully embody, these principles, providing a model for other forms of research. Following this a broad conceptual framework is outlined, grounded in these ethical principles and designed to represent the full range of contexts and processes we encounter in our practice as a means of broadening our discussion of the ethical challenges of action research. The importance of including a critical analysis of power and privilege is highlighted.

As action researchers we cross many boundaries. We come from a variety of disciplinary backgrounds, draw on distinct histories, develop diverse methodologies, and investigate a wide range of issues in communities across the globe. What does unite us to a large extent, however, are our aspirations. Read the definition of action research in the introduction to this volume, 'action research is a participatory, democratic process', or

Greenwood and Levin's 'we see AR as central to the enactment of a commitment to democratic social transformation through social research' (1998: 3), or Noffke's description of action research as 'a moral and ethical stance that recognizes the improvement of human life as a goal' (1995: 4), and you begin to understand that we are indeed engaged in 'a form of morally committed action' (McNiff et al., 1996: 3).

It is one thing to use this language of common values to define and inspire, and quite another to articulate what these terms mean in practice and to specify mechanisms through which we might determine the extent to which our efforts are successful in embodying these lofty goals. We cannot afford to be complacent. Asserting a belief in social justice does not insure that our actions will reflect this same high moral stance, for as Boser has noted, 'democratic intentions do not obviate the need for thoughtful examination of the ethical implications of the research' (2006: 14).

It is also critical that we understand that this need for ethical reflection extends beyond the confines of individual action and specific research endeavors to encompass the complex relationships within and among communities, academic institutions, governmental agencies, and funding sources. We must be sensitive to cultural differences and to the ways in which these inform our understandings of the ethical challenges we face in conducting research across cultural and national boundaries. And attention to the ethical implications of our work must persist across time as action researchers strive to bring about positive change in these systems and to engage in the ongoing cycles of action and reflection that define our practice.

Our common vision of research as a form of democratic action and a powerful force for social justice is currently threatened, due at least in part to the very success of action research. As our practice becomes more broadly accepted it is also at risk of being tamed, routinized, and redirected toward more mundane and less threatening objectives. Reclaiming our radical roots[2] depends in part on defining and communicating a clear understanding of the ethical foundations of action research. Having clarified this shared set of principles, our goal must then be to find ways of enacting these values in our practice as researchers, educators, community members, and social activists. As a community we must be united in demanding that work calling itself action research demonstrate a commitment to these principles.

I begin this exploration of the ethics of action research with a brief review of the fundamental principles upon which the guidelines for ethical research in general are grounded, with special attention to the ways in which they are represented in such documents as the Helsinki Declaration and the Belmont Report. I then discuss the relationship between the shared values of action research and these established codes of conduct, suggesting that the values articulated by action researchers not only reflect, but extend and more fully embody, these principles, providing a model for other forms of research. Following this discussion, I outline a broad conceptual framework grounded in these ethical principles and designed to represent the full range of contexts and processes we encounter in our practice as a means of broadening our discussion of the ethical challenges of action research. I then focus on the importance of including a critical analysis of power and privilege within any discussion of research ethics, concluding with an invitation to fellow action researchers to continue to engage these challenging questions of ethics openly and actively so that our highest aspirations might be realized within our shared practice.

A BRIEF HISTORICAL REVIEW OF RESEARCH ETHICS

Typically, considerations of research ethics are confined to an examination of the specific elements prescribed by human subjects review processes. Academic researchers complain mightily about the seemingly endless and intrusive demands of institutional review boards, but the truth is that to a large extent we brought it on ourselves. The legacy of unethical research includes notorious examples such as the biomedical research conducted by Nazi doctors and the Tuskegee Syphilis Study in the United States in which poor African American men were denied treatment for syphilis for years after effective treatments had been developed in order to observe the long-term effects of the disease (Jones, 1993; Thomas and Quinn, 1991).[3] These horrific practices along with other research such as Milgram's work on obedience (1963, 1983) or the Zimbardo prison experiment (Haney et al., 1973; Haney and Zimbardo, 1998) in which the harm, though admittedly not life-endangering and perhaps unintentional, was nonetheless serious and avoidable, have led to a general climate of skepticism and distrust regarding research and a conviction that any research involving human subjects requires a degree of governmental oversight in order to insure that it is carried out in a humane and ethical fashion.[4]

The Helsinki Declaration (Human and Fluss, 2001), originally adopted in 1964 and most recently amended in 2004, provides guiding principles for the ethical conduct of research, focusing on biomedical studies in particular. As Human and Fluss in their review of the history and impact of the Declaration note, countries from around the world including nations as diverse as Australia, China, Uganda, Israel, and India, all cite the Helsinki Declaration in their laws and policies regarding medical research.

In the United States the Belmont Report, which cites the Helsinki Declaration and was issued by the National Commission for the Protection of Human Subjects of Biomedical and Behavioral Research on 18 April 1979, was developed to address ethical concerns in research in both medical and social sciences disciplines. Its creators were charged with 'identifying the basic principles that should underlie the conduct of biomedical and behavioral research involving human subjects' (Department of Health, Education, and Welfare, 2000: 195). The three basic principles outlined in that report are:

- Respect for persons, i.e. 'that individuals should be treated as autonomous agents' and 'that persons with diminished autonomy are entitled to protection' (p. 198);
- Beneficence, i.e. 'do not harm' and 'maximize possible benefits and minimize possible harm' (p. 199); and
- Justice, i.e. 'research should not unduly involve persons from groups unlikely to be among the beneficiaries of subsequent applications' (p. 201).

These basic principles now form the foundation of the human subjects review processes at most governmental and academic institutions in the United States and many other countries and, along with additional considerations such as trust and scientific integrity, serve as the basis of most professional codes of ethics (Smith, 2000).

The Belmont Report goes on to define a number of specific applications incorporated into human subjects review processes and designed to put these principles into practice. These include:

- Informed consent – based largely on the first principle of autonomy, this includes the requirement that subjects are informed about the nature of the research, understand that information and, based on that understanding, choose to participate in the research without coercion or undue influence.
- Assessment of risks and benefits – reflecting the principle of beneficence, this requirement establishes that it is the responsibility of the reviewing body to determine whether the potential benefits of the research outweigh any possible risks, noting that 'the risks and benefits affecting the immediate research subject will normally carry special weight' (Department of Health, Education, and Welfare, 2000: 203).
- Selection of subjects – most closely tied to the principle of justice, this requirement includes stipulations that no individual or group be unfairly included or excluded from participation in research and provides special protections to individuals and groups whose capacity for informed consent might in some way be limited.

INTERSECTIONS BETWEEN ESTABLISHED ETHICAL PRINCIPLES AND THE SHARED VALUES OF ACTION RESEARCH

The shared set of values which underlie most forms of action research and which include participation in democratic processes, the improvement of human life, and engagement in morally committed action deepen, extend, and at times also complicate our understanding of the values outlined in such human subjects review processes.

Respect for persons, for example, under the guidelines of the Belmont Report and most sets of human subjects research guidelines, is limited to providing research subjects with the opportunity to decline to participate in a particular study and is assumed to be addressed through the informed consent process.

In action research, on the other hand, this principle extends to our conviction that all individuals have the capacity to contribute to the process of knowledge generation and the right to play an active role in shaping policies and processes that affect their own well-being and that of their families and communities. The very nature of action research itself is founded in this deep and abiding respect for persons as active agents of change.

At the same time action researchers might challenge the assumption that 'respect for persons' is actually best represented by the principle of autonomy as suggested by the Belmont Report, given that autonomy assumes a focus on individual good and self-governance versus collaborative decision-making and community benefit. Action researchers must remain mindful of the complex nature of balancing individual and collective action and the relationships of power and privilege which inevitably frame these processes of decision-making.

Action researchers might also question the perceived need for protection accorded those determined to have 'diminished autonomy', recognizing that such determinations often reflect deeply held prejudices toward individuals deemed less competent to participate in the public sphere and have also been used to disempower and control those whose actions challenge existing systems of power and privilege. We might also challenge the assumption that is often made by review boards that relationships between researchers and community participants necessarily imply coercion and constitute a breach of research ethics. This conflation of caring and coercion grows out of a model of research grounded in notions of objectivity and distance rejected in action research. This is not to say that coercion might not be an issue in action research, but understanding the nature of the problem within the context of the close, committed relationships that typify action research settings requires a more nuanced analysis than is commonly reflected in such review processes.

Similarly, the principle of beneficence, which in the Belmont Report and other similar documents while providing protection also tends to reflect the paternalistic nature of most medical and social research, might be recast by action researchers as a call to address social problems in a more collaborative and substantive manner. The notion of 'maximizing possible benefits' demands that research address significant social issues as these are defined by the members of communities themselves, rather than those deemed most important (read fundable) by researchers.

Action researchers might also challenge the assumption that the determination of what constitutes risks and benefits should be the purview of institutionally-based review bodies at all, suggesting instead that community review boards or other citizen-based processes of oversight would better reflect what members of the community consider an acceptable exposure to risk and desirable benefits, values espoused by documents such as the Belmont Report.

The notion of justice, too, which in the Belmont Report refers specifically to guaranteeing equal opportunities for participation in research (reflecting the insular worldview of many academic researchers), takes on a broader significance within action research, leading us to seek social justice more generally and demanding activism and political engagement. And here, too, action researchers would understand that a concern for justice must extend to participation in decisions regarding the funding of research, the application of research findings, and the generation, ownership, and dissemination of knowledge based on this research.

These now more broadly defined principles of respect for persons, beneficence, and justice apply across the board, not simply to our actions within the context of specific research projects, and so must inform all aspects of our practice as researchers, educators, administrators, and community members. The challenge, then, is to develop explicit strategies for remaining mindful of these principles within our individual practice, and attentive to how our collective responses to the practice of action research in general are addressing these concerns.

DEFINING THE BROADER INSTITUTIONAL, SOCIAL, AND CULTURAL CONTEXTS OF ACTION RESEARCH

Most considerations of research ethics focus solely on the details of a specific research project, and within this the majority of the attention is directed at a review of a written proposal for a research project specifying aspects of subject recruitment, data gathering, and analysis. Embedded within this review process is the assumption of the researcher or research team as a distinct entity operating independently of outside influence. The common vision of the practice of research, in its more positive incarnation, is of the heroic researcher alone in the laboratory late at night tirelessly engaged in collecting and analyzing data that lead after years of dedicated, selfless effort to a discovery that revolutionizes medical practice, or food production, or in some other way contributes to the good of humankind. In its more sinister version (fed no doubt by our collective viewing of films like *Frankenstein* and *The Fly*), the same lone researcher, though in this case with much more unruly hair, bends over the same laboratory table now strewn with random body parts fixated instead on destruction and domination – cue maniacal cackle. Determining research ethics in this instance is a straightforward case of individual good versus evil.

But the truth of all research, both for good and ill, is that it is a collective enterprise influenced by multiple forces within and beyond academic institutions, forces that intersect and influence one another's actions, efficacy, and ethics in complex, multilayered systems. This complex system influences all forms of research – it is simply more explicitly recognized in action research and open discussion of these competing forces more common. That said, it is also the case that action research – because it engages real issues and involves community partners – both addresses some of the ethical challenges inherent in more traditional approaches to research, but at the same time also generates a unique set of concerns. These ethical issues, and the often competing sets of values which underlie them, are present and compelling at each stage of the research process, and beyond the research process itself, in all aspects of our lives as action researchers and community activists.

Reader be warned: This is not a neat, tidy grid with clear indications of success and failure. Rather it is an attempt to capture elements of a complex, intersecting system in which multiple stakeholders operate with sometimes competing sets of interests and moral convictions that influence any attempt to bring about positive social change. But, acting under the assumption that 'most action researchers have disciplined themselves to believe that messes can be attractive and even exciting' (Brydon-Miller et al., 2003: 21), I offer the following framework representing the ethics of action research within broad institutional and social contexts followed by a consideration of strategies we might employ in more fully engaging these ethical principles in all levels of our practice.

Within the action research model, the individual researcher is but one of a collaborative group of investigators working together to define a research area, articulate a set of meaningful questions, and determine strategies for gathering and analyzing pertinent information. These researchers are collectively responsible for formulating and carrying out plans for action and determining the most effective means of disseminating the results of their work. Ideally, they represent a broad range of community and academic participants with a genuine respect for one another's contributions and long-term commitments to working together to address critical community concerns.

But researchers do not exist in isolation from other institutional and community influences. Academically-based researchers, for example, must address the concerns of institutional review boards, whose work in turn is a reflection of governmental regulations regarding human subjects research and is defined and constrained by these requirements (Brydon-Miller and Greenwood, 2006; Hemmings, 2006; Herr and Anderson, 2005). They must be ever cognizant of the demands of reappointment, promotion, and tenure committees in order to secure ongoing employment through presentations and publications considered legitimate within the academic sphere, and must address the demands for accountability as defined by both their own administration and those organizations or governmental offices funding the research if the work is to continue.

Community members participating in the research process likewise must deal with competing demands for their time and energy. If, for example, the research is being conducted with teachers in a school setting, the administration at the school and district levels have specific requirements defining when and how such work is to be conducted within the school. Here, too, funding agents determine many aspects of the research and reporting processes, and parents and other community members must be included in the process if the work is to truly reflect the values of participation central to action research (Zeni, 2001). These same complex and often competing forces operate in all settings in which action research takes place, whether that is health care (Minkler and Wallerstein, 2003), prisons (Weis and Fine, 2004), organizations and other workplaces (Hilsen, 2006), or community-based project sites (Lewis, 2006; Lykes, 2006).

At the same time, all of this exists within broader systems of political, social, and economic injustice that shape experiences of oppression on the basis of race, class, gender, sexual orientation, and other aspects of individual and community identity. Any consideration of research ethics must also take into account these multifaceted systems of power and influence (Brydon-Miller, 2004). And beyond the specific contexts within which the research itself takes place, our discussion must also acknowledge the ethical aspects of the processes of recruiting, training, credentialing, employing, promoting, publishing, reviewing, advocating, challenging, and creating change that are all part of our practice.

EMBODYING ETHICS WITHIN OUR PRACTICE AS ACTION RESEARCHERS

Clearly, given the vast range of activities noted above, it is impossible in this brief chapter to provide a detailed agenda for addressing the ethical challenges of action research at all levels and across contexts. Instead, drawing on specific action research based practices, I will outline a general process for examining the ethical implications of our practice within these broader systems starting at the level of individual reflection and moving toward the more collective and complex systems that define our shared practice and the contexts within which our work takes place.

Prior to entering a research setting of any kind, and ideally as a central component of any university-based action research course or other training program, we might begin with a critical examination of ourselves as individual researchers using a first-person action research approach (Chandler and Torbert, 2003). This process allows us to articulate our own value systems, our multiple identities and locations of power and privilege, and the ways in which these understandings influence our interactions with others and our research practices. In explaining this process to my own students, I often use the metaphor of dance training in which you are encouraged to find your center. Moving from the physical core of your body, you are balanced – able to move with grace and respond to the movements of other dancers around you with spontaneity and energy. Becoming aware of our own core values allows us respond to unexpected ethical challenges or issues with a similar sense of being morally grounded and confident in our actions. It also gives us the opportunity to re-examine these values and to confront contradictions in our ways of understanding the world. We can begin to achieve this sense of being centered through reflection, using specific strategies such as journaling, photovoice, or other practices (Meyer et al., 2004) that allow us the time and attention necessary to engage in open and honest processes of self-questioning and assessment. Again, like the dancer who constantly practices this skill, we cannot assume that we have somehow 'dealt with' the ethical challenges that face us all (Brydon-Miller, 2004). Rather we must remain mindful and open to the challenges that new relationships and experiences are bound to bring with them without allowing fear and self-defensiveness to prevent us from honestly examining our own feelings and actions.

This same process of self-reflection can enable us to engage in a critical examination of aspects of our individual and community identity and experience. Questioning how gender, race, class, educational attainment, sexual orientation, disability status, age and other aspects of our identity influence our own experience of and response to power and privilege is an important precursor to any engagement as action researchers, whether we intend to participate in such processes as insiders or outsiders in relation to the communities within which we propose to work.

At the next stage we enter into dialogue with potential research partners and begin to explore possible avenues for collaboration. At this point we need to be sure that the values and goals of all participants are clearly stated and that these sometimes differing points of view are received by all members of the group with respect and a commitment to honoring each individual's experience, concerns, and values. To extend our metaphor a bit further, we are joined at this point by other dancers, each with a unique repertoire of movements and gestures to contribute to the process. Our common task now focuses on developing a shared vision of the choreography we create as an ensemble. Open dialogue is key to this process, but a clear understanding of the hierarchies that exist everywhere within and outside our research settings can prevent us from naively assuming that simply bringing people together allows us to transcend preexisting relationships of power and privilege. Integrating on-going dialogue on the ethical implications of our research with all participants at each stage of the process offers opportunities for such discussion to reflect deepening understandings of the ethical challenges embedded in efforts to carry out such collaborative work and allows participants to develop greater confidence and conviction regarding their own ethical stance as well as a deeper appreciation of other points of view (Boser, 2006). Specific strategies such as the nominal group process (Delbecq et al., 1975) in which there are explicit mechanisms for guaranteeing that all participants have opportunities to contribute to the discussion can be helpful in this regard, but again, it is important to remain attentive to the dynamics of power in any group setting.

At the same time, the participants in collaborative research processes operate within broader institutional and community contexts which carry with them their own sets of values and systems of power. These might be likened to the orchestra, stage manager, composer, audience members and patrons, all of whom affect in direct and indirect ways both individual dancers and the nature of the performance as a whole. These systems can influence aspects of the research process in fundamental and quite explicit ways by controlling access to funding, time, and other resources and in more subtle ways by creating and sustaining expectations regarding social relationships and opportunities for achieving change. Honestly acknowledging the fact that there may be competing values systems between research partners and academic institutions, funding agencies, and the broader community is an important first step in addressing these issues effectively. It is also important to develop a clear understanding of the power dynamics that shape these relationships (Campbell, 2003).

Within academic settings negotiating this broader system might include, for example, working with members of university human subjects review committees to develop a greater shared understanding of the constraints within which they must operate and the shared mission of the review process and action research (Brydon-Miller and Greenwood, 2006; Hemmings, 2006). It can also entail using whatever power we have within academic institutions to create space for action research and other forms of community engagement within reappointment, promotion, and tenure review processes.

Our work with students, too, must reflect our recognition of the ethical demands of the teaching and mentoring relationships that form the basis of the educational experience. As individual members of faculty and within programs and departments we must monitor the nature of these relationships in order to model ethical behavior and to ensure that the best interests of the students, rather than our own personal interests, are our primary goals. At the same time we must provide specific learning experiences both through courses as well as in individual mentoring relationships to these students focused on a problem-oriented examination of challenges to ethical research and professional practice that make it clear that getting review board approval is just one step in the process.

Within the broader professional roles we fill, those serving as journal editors and reviewers might also work to insure that a discussion of research ethics with specific reference to appropriate forms of institutional ethical approval are included as expected components of all submissions (for an example see Löfman

et al., 2004). Creating highly visible venues for discussions of research ethics is also important, as in the designation of ethics as a focus for the 2006 World Congress of Action Research or the development of a special issue of the journal *Action Research* focused specifically on this subject (Brydon-Miller et al., 2006). Overall, in considering the ethical dimensions of our work within the academy, we 'must question the automatic belief in our own benevolence, the automatic equation between our own academic success and ethical behavior' (Newkirk, 1996: 14).

For those of us working in other organizational settings such as independent research centers, schools, and non-governmental agencies conducting action research projects, an attention to the ethical implications of our practice and of broader organizational policies and procedures is also critical (Hilsen, 2006; Holian, 1999). One perplexing question worth noting in this regard focuses on the notion of mandating action research and whether administrators and others responsible for leading change can ethically require participation in such processes or whether such demands fundamentally undermine the legitimacy of our practice (Judah and Richardson, 2006). Here again, an awareness of the complex set of relationships and of the differing levels of power within organizations can help to guide our decision-making.

At the broader community level, we must focus on developing strategies for acknowledging and dealing with areas of conflict while remaining grounded in our own personal and cultural values. Some of this involves developing skills in lobbying and community organizing that are often beyond the training or experience of academic action researchers. However, these are quite often areas in which our community research partners are extremely skilled, and as in any successful action research process, this ability to draw on the expertise of all participants is key. Learning to use the media effectively, to open dialogue with political figures, and to provide opportunities for community action can all be effective strategies in bringing these stakeholders into the process in constructive ways (Tandon et al., 2001).

ATTENDING TO ISSUES OF POWER AND BUILDING ON THE STRENGTHS OF COMMUNITIES

As noted throughout this chapter, power plays a critical role in framing the ways in which the basic principles of respect for persons, beneficience, and justice are understood and put into practice. Yet, too often the role of power is overlooked in contexts of action research and our broader professional practice. One strategy for developing a greater awareness of the dynamics of these relationships is to conduct analyses of the power relationships within our research settings. Beginning at the level of the individual researcher, we might ask what aspects of personal identity, experience, and professional position contribute to greater levels of power within the system and which undermine this authority. And at the broader, more systemic level, what are the sources of power held by specific institutions or stakeholders and how do they influence the action of other participants and the ways in which the research reflects basic ethical principles?

One model I have found especially useful in enabling research participants to visualize relationships of power and to better understand the implications of an ethic of respect for persons is Arnstein's Ladder of Citizen Participation (1969). Designed as a tool for analyzing power dynamics within systems, the point of Arnstein's model is not to suggest some sort of developmental stage theory of power in which groups must move from lower to higher levels, but rather to expose false promises of participation and encourage genuine citizen control. The lowest rung on Arnstein's ladder is that of manipulation, and it moves from there to therapy, considered a second level of non-participation, through levels of tokenism including informing, consultation, and placation, finally moving to three levels with increasing degrees of citizen power – partnership, delegated power, and finally, genuine citizen control.

Applying this analysis within our action research settings can assist us in challenging structures designed to give the pretense of participation to community partners and encouraging more authentic forms of involvement. Arnstein's ladder is especially useful in examining the ethical challenges involved in doing research in settings of highly unequal power, such as Chataway's (2001) project in the Kahnewake Mohawk community in Canada or Campbell's (2003) description of an HIV/AIDS prevention project in South Africa in which multiple stakeholder groups with very different levels of power and privilege were brought together to address the issue using an action research model. In both instances these white, nonnative researchers found themselves working within communities in which relationships of power influenced the control of resources and opportunities to take part in discussions about the research. Applying Arnstein's ladder in such situations can expose the ways in which power differentials within communities often influence who actually participates and controls community-based action research projects. For both Chataway and Campbell, these power dynamics influenced the direction of their action research projects in complex and, according to their own accounts, often confusing ways. Honestly acknowledging this confusion and the uncertainty they faced in trying to respond to these power differentials between the academic researchers and community participants, and among the community participants themselves, offers important insights into key ethical challenges facing these researchers and gives their accounts of their work a credibility and legitimacy that more sanitized accounts often lack.

Another approach to shifting our understanding of the role of power within the action research process and guiding us toward more ethical practice is to apply an asset-based analysis to our examination of our research settings. Based on the work of Kretzmann and McKnight (1997), this approach focuses on identifying the strengths of individual participants and groups of stakeholders within an action research project, reflecting the basic principles of justice and respect for persons. Again drawing on Campbell's work as an example, one facet of her analysis that most impressed me as a reader was her clear respect for the local women who carried out a sex worker peer-education program described in the volume, noting that they had 'succeeded in mobilizing strong and confident teams of sex worker peer educators in chaotic and disorganized community contexts with no pre-existing social organization of this nature' (2003: 101). Without in any way dismissing the economic and social oppression these women face or the culpability of the mine owners and governmental officials who profit from this oppression, Campbell at the same time refuses to depict the women themselves as simply 'victims' incapable of taking steps to address the issues facing their community. True action research is founded on this belief in the capacity of individuals and collectively within organizations and communities for critical reflection and action.

A final and critical reflection of power within action research settings demonstrating the broader definition of the principle of justice as reflected in greater levels of community engagement and control grows out of a reexamination of the processes of knowledge generation, dissemination, and ownership (Greenwood et al., 2006). To date the results of research have largely served to further the interests of researchers and their institutions, whether through mechanisms such as tenure and promotion, the overhead paid by granting agencies, or other forms of profit and prestige. But many action researchers have sought out innovative ways of making the results of their efforts both more accessible and more useful to their community partners. Whether this is through the development of materials useful in community development campaigns (Tandon et al., 2001) or strategies for engaging citizens in active public policy

debates (Wakeford, Chapter 22 in this volume), action research opens up the possibilities for a significant shift in who owns and controls the knowledge generated through research. At the same time, the continuing emergence of new venues for disseminating the results of research through the development of new technologies opens up the possibility for the democratization of knowledge.

Whether through new avenues for knowledge dissemination, the establishment of community-based review boards, or the development of innovative techniques for insuring broad community participation in action research efforts, shifts in power within the research setting away from the oversight and control of university-based experts and paternalistic oversight committees and toward ownership by members of communities themselves would better reflect the ethical principles of respect for persons, beneficience, and justice. This is a critical move if the full promise of these principles is to be realized in our practice as action researchers, but at the same time such redistributions of power and control carry unique challenges and genuine risks if we do not remain vigilant to the ethical implications of our practice. None of this should be viewed as a panacea for the current ethical challenges facing us as action researchers nor should the potential for positive outcomes blind us to the possibility of dire consequences should our attention to maintaining the highest possible ethical standards lapse. We strive to change the world – there is nothing more dangerous than that, and we must take responsibility for the possibility of risk inherent in this commitment to change.

CONCLUSION

'A respect for people and for the knowledge and experience they bring to the research process, a belief in the ability of democratic processes to achieve positive social change, and a commitment to action, these are the basic values which underlie our common practice as action researchers' (Brydon-Miller et al., 2003: 15). Living up to these values is the ethical challenge that must shape our action as scholars and change agents not only within the confines of our own research settings but beyond, extending across the academic institutions and organizations within which we work, into the broader contexts of our communities, to the issues facing us all on a global scale. Using the tools of action research, our common goal is to find ways to insure that the key ethical principles of respect for persons, beneficence, and justice, as embodied in the shared values of action research – participation in democratic processes, the improvement of human life, and engagement in morally committed action – remain at the core of our practice.

NOTES

1 I would like to thank Davydd Greenwood, Bjorn Gustavsen, Patricia Maguire, Peter Reason, and Bronwyn Williams for their thoughtful review and helpful suggestions on earlier drafts of this manuscript.

2 Patricia Maguire and I used this phrase as the title to a conference presentation and I think it captures my own hopes for the future of AR.

3 For a summary of recent research of attitudes toward medical research and factors influencing the willingness and ability of minorities to participate in health related research see the report from the National Institutes of Health published in the online journal *PloS Medicine* (6 December 2005) in which researchers discuss the barriers to participation and the multiple factors preventing such participation.

4 My dear friend and self-declared cynic, Davydd Greenwood, suggests that my analysis here overlooks the extent to which the increasing economic stakes of research for universities and the potential threat of litigation have driven the development of such review processes (personal communication). I think there is great merit in this observation but focus here on our own contributions to the problem. It's just too easy to always blame the lawyers.

REFERENCES

Arnstein, S. R. (1969) 'A ladder of citizen participation', *Journal of the American Planning Association*, 35 (4): 216–224.

Boser, S. (2006) 'Ethics and power in community-campus partnerships for research', *Action Research*, 4 (1): 9–21.

Brydon-Miller, M. (2004) 'The terrifying truth: interrogating systems of power and privilege and choosing to act', in M. Brydon-Miller, P. Maguire and A. McIntyre (eds), *Traveling Companions: Feminism, Teaching, and Action Research.* Westport, CT: Praeger. pp. 3–19.

Brydon-Miller, M. and Greenwood, D. (2006) 'A re-examination of the relationship between action research and human subjects review processes', *Action Research*, 4 (1): 117–28.

Brydon-Miller, M., Greenwood, D. and Eikeland, O. (eds) (2006) Ethics and Action Research [Special issue]. *Action Research*, 4 (1).

Brydon-Miller, M., Greenwood, D. and Maguire, P. (2003) 'Why action research?', *Action Research*, 1 (1): 9–28.

Campbell, C. (2003) *Letting Them Die: Why HIV/AIDS Prevention Programs Fail.* Bloomington, IN: Indiana University Press.

Chandler, D. and Torbert, B. (2003) 'Transforming inquiry and action: interweaving flavors of action research', *Action Research*, 1 (2): 133–52.

Chataway, C.J. (2001) 'Negotiating the observer-observed relationship: Participatory action research', in D. Tolman and M. Brydon-Miller (eds), *From Subjects to Subjectivities: a Handbook of Interpretive and Participatory Methods.* New York: New York University Press. pp. 239–55.

Delbecq, A.L., VandeVen, A.H. and Gustafson, D.H. (1975) *Group Techniques for Program Planners.* Glenview, IL: Scott Foresman & Co.

Department of Health, Education, and Welfare (2000) 'Belmont Report: ethical principles and guidelines for the protection of human subjects of research', in B.D. Sales and S. Folkman (eds), *Ethics in Research with Human Participants.* Washington, DC: American Psychological Association. pp. 195–205.

Greenwood, D.J. and Levin, M. (1998) *Introduction to Action Research: Social Research for Social Change.* Thousand Oaks, CA: Sage.

Greenwood, D., Brydon-Miller, M. and Shafer, C. (2006) 'Intellectual property and action research', *Action Research*, 4 (1): 81–95.

Haney, C. and Zimbardo, P. (1998) 'The past and future of U.S. prison policy: twenty-five years after the Stanford Prison Experiment', *American Psychologist*, 53 (7): 709–27.

Haney, C., Banks, W. and Zimbardo, P. (1973) 'Interpersonal dynamics in a simulated prison', *International Journal of Criminology and Penology*, 1: 69–97.

Hemmings, A. (2006) 'Great ethical divides: bridging the gap between institutional review boards and researchers', *Educational Researcher*, 35 (4): 12–18.

Herr, K. and Anderson, G.L. (2005) *The Action Research Dissertation: a Guide for Students and Faculty.* Thousand Oaks, CA: Sage.

Hilsen, A.I. (2006) 'And they shall be known by their deeds: ethics and politics in action research', *Action Research,* 4 (1): 23–36.

Holian, R. (1999) 'Doing action research in my own organisation: ethical dilemmas, hopes, and triumphs', *Action Research International*, Paper 3. Available online http://www.scu.edu.au/schools/gcm/ar/ari/p-rholian99.html (accessed 11 December 2005).

Human, D. and Fluss, S.S. (2001) *The World Medical Association's Declaration of Helsinki: Historical and Contemporary Perspectives, 5th draft.* World Medical Association, 24 July. Available: www.wma.net/ e/ethicsunit/helsinki.htm (accessed 11 December 2005).

Jones, J.H. (1993) *Bad blood: The Tuskegee Syphilis Experiment, rev. edn.* New York: Free Press.

Judah, M. and Richardson, G.H. (2006) 'Between a rock and a (very) hard place: the ambiguous promise of action research in the context of state mandated teacher professional development', *Action Research,* 4 (1): 65–80.

Kretzmann, J. and McKnight, J. (1997) *Building Communities from the Inside Out: a Path toward Finding and Mobilizing a Community's Assets.* Chicago: CTA Publications.

Lewis, H.M. (2006) 'Participatory research and education for social change: Highlander research and education center', in P. Reason and H. Bradbury (eds), *Handbook of Action Research: Concise Paperback Edition.* London: Sage. pp. 262–8.

Löfman, P., Pelkonen, M. and Pietilä, A. (2004) 'Ethical issues in participatory action research', *Scandinavian Journal of Caring Sciences*, 18: 333–40.

Lykes, M.B. (2006) 'Creative arts and photography in participatory action research in Guatemala', in P. Reason and H. Bradbury (eds), *Handbook of Action Research: Concise Paperback Edition.* London: Sage. pp. 269–78.

McNiff, J., Lomax, P. and Whitehead, J. (1996) *You and Your Action Research Project.* London: RoutledgeFalmer.

Meyer, H., Hamilton, B., Kroeger, S., Stewart, S. and Brydon-Miller, M. (2004) 'The unexpected journey: renewing our commitment to students through educational Action Research', *Educational Action Research*, 12 (4): 557–73.

Milgram, S. (1963) 'Behavioral study of obedience', *Journal of Abnormal and Social Psychology,* 67: 371–8.

Milgram, S. (1983) *Obedience to Authority: an Experimental View.* New York: Harper/Collins.

Minkler, M and Wallerstein, N. (eds) (2003) *Community-based Participatory Research for Health.* San Francisco, CA: Jossey-Bass.

Newkirk, T. (1996) 'Seduction and betrayal in qualitative research', in P. Mortensen and G.E. Kirsch (eds), *Ethics and Representation in Qualitative Studies of Literacy.* Urbana, IL: National Council of Teachers of English. pp. 3–16.

Noffke, S.E. (1995) 'Action research and democratic schooling: problematics and potentials', in S. Noffke and R.B. Stevenson (eds), *Educational Action Research: Becoming Practically Critical.* New York: Teachers College Press. pp. 1–10.

Smith, M. B. (2000) 'Moral foundations in research with human participants', in B.D. Sales and S. Folkman (eds), *Ethics in Research with Human Participants.* Washington, DC: American Psychological Association. pp. 3–10.

Tandon, S.D., Kelly, J.G. and Mock, L.O. (2001) 'Participatory action research as a resource for developing African American community leadership', in D.L. Tolman and M. Brydon-Miller (eds), *From Subjects to Subjectivities: a Handbook of Interpretive and Participatory Methods.* New York: New York University Press. pp. 200–17.

Thomas, S.B. and Quinn, S.C. (1991) 'The Tuskegee syphilis study, 1932–1972: implications for HIV education and AIDS risk programs in the black community', *American Journal of Public Health*, 81 (11): 1498–1505.

Weis, L. and Fine, M. (2004) *Working Method: Research and Social Justice.* New York: Routledge.

Zeni, J. (ed.) (2001) *Ethical Issues in Practitioner Research.* New York: Teachers College Press.

14

The Future of Universities: Action Research and the Transformation of Higher Education

Morten Levin and Davydd J. Greenwood

Higher education institutions worldwide are in the midst of a profound transition in which they are losing public credibility and support and are becoming increasingly subject to corporate forms of accountability and quality assurance. Though we support institutional accountability, we believe that this way of approaching the disconnection between higher education and the 'public good' is wrongheaded and ultimately destructive of the very idea of the university. Action research provides a way to promote knowledge generation that is intrinsically capable of producing public goods through concrete and practical problem-solving and of shaping deeper reflection processes through broad disciplinary and stakeholder participation in research-based discourses. We believe that universities should be reorganized to meet the challenges of redeveloping public support by structuring teaching and research through action research strategies. This means problem selection, analysis, action design, implementation, and evaluation by collaborative multi-disciplinary teams of academics and non-university stakeholders. It also means treating much teaching as apprenticeship to problem-oriented AR teams. Unless AR is used to break the Tayloristic and autopoetic structure of existing universities, the decline of public confidence and public support for higher education will continue.

INTRODUCTION: UNIVERSITIES IN TRANSITION

Higher education is in the midst of a great historical transition, parallel in scope to the creation of the medieval universities, the Neumanian English and American reforms in teaching and learning, the creation of the Humboldtian university that linked teaching and research inseparably, the rise of the great public universities, and the creation of the land-grant universities in the United States.[1] After each of these transitions, university life was fundamentally altered in ways that lasted for generations.

In Europe, the United States, Canada, and Australia, universities are no longer thought of unproblematically as 'public goods' and as unquestioned sources of value worthy of public support. After the long dominance of the Humboldtian and land grant legacies, teaching and research are being driven apart. Though the idea that university research is a some kind of 'public good' remains, entrepreneurial models of research generation, intellectual property control, and academic institutional management are being imposed throughout higher education systems. Governments and other regulatory bodies are imposing accountability regimes on all forms of higher education, converting the government into the regulators of higher education, the public into the customers of the university, and the faculty into service providers.

We believe AR can and should step forward to play a role in this transition for a number of reasons – some moral, some practical, and some professional. The moral and practical reasons are significant. AR's tenuous relationship to higher education is noticeable throughout this Handbook. Thus, it might seem that action researchers could afford to act as bystanders and let the managers and regulators commercialize and regulate universities, 'occasionalize' staffs, convert students and the private and public sector into 'customers', and be none the worse for it. We don't believe that standing on the sidelines and watching this spectacle is an option for action researchers because the neoliberal transformation of higher education is part of the commoditization and monopolization of knowledge and the imposition of ever greater inequality on communities, regions, and nation-states throughout the global system. Also, it is obvious that future action researchers are being trained at universities and so the kind of training they get partly determines the future of action research. If action researchers are to live up to our stated commitments to democratization, fairness, and respect for the diversity of knowledge systems, we must confront these forces everywhere, including in academic workplaces (see also this Handbook, Chapters 28, 46, and 47). Universities are important locations for this confrontation because they are one of the few remaining societal venues not already fully domesticated by market ideologies; they could be a launching ground for an effort to recreate a civil society that survives beyond the market's demands.

Many AR practitioners have shunned university life, viewing these institutions as bulwarks of the unfair political economy that they are attempting to overturn. Others have practiced AR on the margins of the university – in extension, outreach, and service learning settings – meeting important needs but readily accepting their marginality to the core of university life. Only rarely has AR become part of everyday university life. AR's democratizing agendas and necessary transdisicplinarity run right into the brick walls of academic professional silos and disciplinary control structures whose stated purpose is quality control but whose actual effect is to preserve professional disciplinary power and monopolies over positions and terms of employment and promotion in their disciplines (Silva and Slaughter, 1984; Slaughter and Leslie, 1997).

The professional reasons for AR's engagement in university reform center on skills action researchers could bring to the task. The current crisis in universities raises issues of organization and method that we believe AR is particularly capable of confronting effectively (see also Chapters 5, 9, 17, 24, 28, 45 and 47 in this Handbook).

For example, it is now a commonplace that universities are more firmly and tightly contextualized within local, regional, national, and global political economies than ever before. While this contextualization is not new, we now witness much more active interplay between universities and their contexts. In these emerging environments, universities that used to define themselves as superior to all outside of themselves no longer have the upper hand. Universities are required to justify themselves, to make visible, measurable contributions both to the welfare of the society generally and to economic development efforts in the areas surrounding them, and to do so visibly as a condition for their continued subsidization by the taxpayers and private sector organizations existence.

We believe the current transition in higher education creates a window of opportunity for AR. The outcome of the transition is not given a priori but will be the result of the involved stakeholders' capacities, interests, and actions. If AR is, to paraphrase Chris Argyris (et al., 1985), in the business of bringing about unlikely but liberating outcomes, then this is precisely the role that AR needs to play now with universities. Unlimited and unconditional support for academic knowledge generation in its conventional forms is gone and external oversight and quality control is here to stay, despite many professors' fantasies about an eventual return to the good old days. For universities to survive as more than either mass teaching institutions or as contract research shops for governments and the private sector, we must restructure the linkages between the way work is done within the university and the extra-university contexts of power, problem generation, and application (Greenwood and Levin, 2000). In other words, we must 're-contextualize' universities in concert with significant non-academic stakeholders, a kind of process that AR regularly engages in.

If we do not act, teaching and research will continue to separate; most of the academic workforce will end up on short-term, unprotected contracts; many faculty will have to raise their own salaries through grants and research revenues; students mainly will be taught by non-professorial staff; and rewards and research monies will be handed out according to scores on national and international accountability schemes and prestige rankings.

Without fundamental reforms dealing effectively with the interests of all the relevant internal university and extra-university stakeholders, public and private sector support for university research and teaching functions continue to diminish and the much more powerful external environment will impose itself willy-nilly on universities. If or when this happens, many of the research functions of universities will be taken over by non-university organizations. Even the training of elites, long a university monopoly, can easily become an in-house activity of central agencies and organizations with the corresponding hierarchization of the political and economic systems. The remnants of the 'public' character of university knowledge systems and practices and the remaining social and economic support for the special status of higher education institutions would then erode farther. If we were to deploy AR approaches to restructure university relationships, both within and in relationship to the surrounding context, some of the key positive elements of universities might be retained, some of their worst features might be moderated, and the public interest could be served more effectively than it currently is.

One could argue that the end of universities as we know them would be a good thing and we personally have had enough disappointing experiences in higher education to feel some sympathy for such a position. However, we believe that the rapid destruction of civil society and the privatization and marketization of practically everything under the sway of neo-liberal, globalizing ideologies exceeds even the ominous nightmares of Karl Polanyi in *The Great Transformation* (1944). We also believe the consequences are likely to be those that Polanyi predicted: the social impossibility of pure free market capitalism with its bloated 'haves' and miserable 'have-nots' will lead us back to profound social upheavals. Tensions do create windows of opportunities that, if intelligently handled by action researchers, might pave the way to significant improvements in both universities and the degree to which they support AR as an approach.

To make our views more concrete, we specify some of the major challenges universities face in the 21st century and show how these changes will impact both the general future of universities and the particular future of AR.

THE NEW 'PUBLIC MANAGEMENT' OF HIGHER EDUCATION

Though our portrait of the situation in contemporary universities can be understood as a 'gloom and doom' scenario, we think it is necessary to provide an empirical basis for our sense of urgency. The current situation in the British university system and the general direction of the 'Bologna Process' will serve as examples of the current crisis in higher education.

Only the most inattentive academics can ignore the rapid decline in public support for higher education. There are few exceptions to this trend. In many countries, this decline is already clear in the decreased national and state funding. It is also apparent in the increasing application of rhetorics and rules of neo-liberal public management and accountability that treat universities as institutions to be policed on behalf of the public, rather than as the 'public goods' and sources of national 'value' they once were.

This process is farthest advanced in the United Kingdom and Australia, visible across most of Europe, and now advancing quickly in the United States. Even in wealthy social democracies like Norway, where there is still reasonable public financial support for higher education and other major public sector institutions, there are strong demands for change that involve increased regulation and increased efficiency of universities. These processes are flying under the flags of quality assurance and efficiency improvement programs. Thus ideological changes, governmental policy directions, and new fiscal management instruments have fundamentally altered the educational and research context at universities.

England led the way in enacting these changes. The first Research Assessment Exercise in the UK took place in 1986 (there have been five RAE's so far) and, through them, UK policymakers reformed the higher education system from top to bottom, or so it appeared. In the 1980s, England had 38 universities and one in seven citizens got a university education. The Thatcher government decided to increase and broaden access to higher education and permitted the polytechnics that wanted to become universities to apply for university status. Simultaneously

the RAE was launched to assure that, with all these changes, the government was getting a proper return on its investment in research universities.

The RAE involves an evaluation of the supposed scientific merits of departments and institutions in which each academic department is graded on a quantitative scale derived from the aggregated scores of the individual faculty members. The RAE is the neo-liberal public manager's dream because it converts research efforts into numbers using publications and overall research productivity of each individual professor as the base. This is aggregated into scores for the unit to which the researcher belongs. Depending on these rankings, entire departments are closed or given more governmental research money.

It is no surprise that the RAE has completely unsettled British higher education with some famous departments (e.g. Cultural Studies at Birmingham) being summarily shut down. To survive in this environment, university faculty and administrators are forced to devote a great deal of effort to scoring highly on the RAE. Academic activity that is not measurable is irrelevant and is not privileged.

As this process was being repeated, it became clear that the RAE reinforces the hegemony of the prestigious older universities. It also further separates the disciplines and drives research and teaching apart, initially treating them as separate for evaluation, and then later as separable university functions. The Humboldt model of the combined teaching/research faculty thus is dead. The apparent move toward inclusiveness and fair competition that supposedly underlay the UK system has, by neo-liberal sleight-of-hand, reconsolidated elite power in higher education in the UK, occasionalized a large segment of the academic workforce, and generally diminished the quality of UK higher education for all but the elites. While the long-term effects of these changes on academic activities are hard to measure, the analyses conducted by David Rhind, Vice Chancellor of the City University of London and a close collaborator of the architects of the overall English policies found that the impact of this system on the social sciences has been devastating (Rhind, 2003).

Not surprisingly given the agenda, similar kinds of public management methods were applied to teaching through the creation of a unit of the Higher Education Funding Council for England (HEFCE) called the Quality Assurance Agency that has used similar schemes and metrics to score units on the quality of their teaching and learning systems.

From this beginning, this kind of academic management technology evolved into the Bologna Process and so the RAE story is not an isolated one. One might optimistically expect that the rest of Europe and the USA would view the RAE as a mistake to be avoided but, instead, most higher education systems are rushing headlong in this direction. The Bologna Process, begun in 1999 as a meeting of ministers of higher education from 29 countries who wanted to create a 'European area of higher education', is a broader application of these British strategies to most national systems. It now includes the educational systems of 40 European countries (and thus extends well beyond the European Union).

The apparently reasonable motive for this process was the need to enhance student and faculty mobility among European university systems by harmonizing degree and administrative structures. The ideal is that any student can take courses anywhere in Europe, have them fit their degree program, have them delivered by predictable means, and have the resulting degree understood and similarly valued in all countries. Any faculty member should have qualifications that can be understood in all European countries and should be able to move smoothly across the system, based solely on their competence.

There can hardly be a more transparent rendering of the neo-liberal 'free market' model than this. A look at any part of the Bologna Process websites will demonstrate the neo-liberal parentage of the approach (http://www.bologna-bergen2005.no/). The

emphasis everywhere is on metrics, quality assurance, homogenization (not harmonization) of systems, and responsiveness. Whatever the question is, homogenization of the institutions of higher education throughout Europe is the answer.

One immediate consequence has been a reduction in the diversity of educational programs and designs in exchange for a uniform structure that makes mobility easy and creates ample opportunities for academic management 'by the numbers'. The creative, critical, constructive and contextualized strengths of the diverse institutions in the current multi-faceted system are being cast aside or even treated as obstacles to the utopian free academic market forces that Karl Polanyi portrayed so eloquently over 60 years ago.

One need not be an action researcher to find it hard to believe that a large-scale, uniform and mono-dimensional system will serve the future of Europe best, even if it suits policymakers and authoritarian academic managers perfectly. It should also be clear that the diversity and uniqueness of many of the European national higher education systems that once created public goods of value, strengths, and possibilities for thinking 'outside of the box' are being destroyed. Now the move is to put all of higher education inside of one 'box'.

If, as often is claimed, the goal of the Bologna Process is to create a higher education system able to compete with the US system, then it is based on a radical misunderstanding of the US. The US 'system' contains community colleges, liberal arts colleges, denominational colleges, public state universities and colleges, private universities, land-grant universities, and a host of for-profit colleges and universities. Whatever the US system is, it is not homogeneous nor is it centrally managed.

What we really are seeing in the Bologna Process is an all out attempt to narrow the articulation between universities and their surrounding societies to a particular form of coercive accountability. This is a radical recontextualization of universities and higher education that is being transformed from a 'public good' into being 'managed' for a 'public' that has been politically reconstituted not as 'citizens' but as 'customers' (including governments, the private sector, and student 'clients') whose demands are to be satisfied and who must pay for what they learn. Education is increasingly treated as a means to enhance local, regional, national, and international economic performance, as providing needed support for solving problems that lie at the center of economic competitiveness, and as vocational training for roles in the global economy.

KNOWLEDGE GENERATION IN UNIVERSITIES

The broader functions of universities as sites for creative knowledge generation, for learning and critique, for the contrast and dispute of ideas and divergent interpretations, and engaging in constructive social redesign are now suppressed. Work that engages the non-university world now is mainly reduced to publicly-subsidized consulting (through tax exemptions, no overheads or direct grants). It is neither aimed at knowledge generation and sharing nor at improving society along dimensions other than competitiveness in profit taking for both the 'clients' and the university employees. This approach turns universities into industrial parks, venues for the development of the 'creative economy', and momentary stop-over locations for jet-setting academic entrepreneurs and highly paid academic 'managers'.

Whatever else this resolutely Tayloristic model of management does, it drives the disciplines ever farther apart by coercive review of the performance of the faculty in their disciplinary departments on a quantitative scale. Cooperation among disciplines and collaboration with non-university stakeholders (other than the private sector) is discouraged and quantitatively penalized. The utopian claim that this management technology will create a more accountable and useful university is false. These approaches rest firmly on the isolated disciplinary silos and use of autopoetic academic self-judgments, the very causes of university ineffectiveness to begin with.

'RAE world' clearly is not a scene in which AR can survive and prosper, not within higher education and nor within society in general. If AR stands for the value of the knowledge of all, for social processes that are collaborative and solidary, for mutual respect and duty rather than individual rights and exploitation, and for respecting the multi-disciplinary complexity of real world problems, then action researchers cannot stand by idly as these changes take place. But much more than the fate of AR is at stake as these processes challenge the essence of democracy.

Action researchers, in our view, have particular responsibilities in this scene because few other kinds of academics have the organizational process management skills and experiences of democratic knowledge development/practice needed to confront the neoliberal challenges. But using AR to address these challenges in higher education is not about saving universities as they are. There are far too many problematic features of university life as it currently exists to make any argument for preserving the past attractive.[2] It is about transforming universities into what they should be if they were to live up to their promise to be truly 'public goods'.

THE TRANSFORMATIONAL PROCESSES AND THE ROLE OF AR

We only describe this dire scene because we believe that better solutions are possible. Just as action researchers working in highly unjust and unhappy situations in communities and non-academic organizations are sustained by the knowledge and hope that significant positive transformations are possible, we know and believe that universities can be transformed into something better (see also Chapters 1, 13 and 47 in this Handbook). Rather than passively adjusting to the trends we have laid out, we think action researchers can use AR to improve the conditions and to help bring about a new and better era in higher education. This is obviously an enormous topic and we can only hope to outline an AR program of change in broad terms. To do this credibly, we will take up a few of the principal challenges that must be addressed to affect the transitions in contemporary higher education.

To imagine AR interventions, it is necessary to create a picture of the way the large-scale changes we have described affect everyday work in universities. It is at the level of organizational processes and behavior that AR can make the most significant difference because of AR's ability to promote alternative organizational processes and strategies based directly on the relevant stakeholders' experiences and hopes.

Many of the central knowledge production processes at universities are under scrutiny because the historically-created discipline-based knowledge systems of the Humboldtian and land grant systems are being challenged by intense societal demands for contextualized and transdisciplinary knowledge. This is, in some ways, precisely the demand that AR makes of universities.

But more is at stake. Also at risk are the concepts and practices of academic freedom and university autonomy. In confronting these neo-liberal pressures, it is vital to move from a radical individualist, free speech understanding of the concepts of academic freedom and institutional autonomy to understanding academic freedom and institutional autonomy as shared obligations to maintain open and democratic debates within the academic community and beyond. Such freedom and autonomy are also the basis of AR.

Thus, we believe that the conditions under which AR can prosper in universities are precisely those conditions necessary for the survival of universities as free spaces for teaching and learning, for knowledge development and critique. In what follows, we will take up a few of the most specific challenges to universities that we see and show how AR can address them:

- Societal changes in perception of the role of persons with a university degree (*from professionals to experts*)

- Changes in the expectations held for the professoriate (*from life in a tenured safe haven to entrepreneurial agility*)
- Changes in perception of what counts as knowledge (*from strong disciplinarity to contextualized transdisciplinarity*)
- Challenges to the integrity of knowledge generation in universities (*from individual academic freedom to academic freedom as a shared process*)

Before proceeding, we should be precise about what we see as the core traits of AR. Building on Greenwood and Levin (1998, 2006), we frame AR as a comprehensive strategy for research that is context bound (highly contextualized), as a process in which the users of the knowledge and the researchers participate together in the same knowledge generation process, as a process in which knowledge is built on the diversity of experiences of the involved actors, as a process where the research focus is on societal questions pertinent to the collaborators, and as a process in which the research creates actionable knowledge as an integrated part of the research process itself. The goal of AR is to bring about more liberated, solidary, healthful, fair, and sustainable social situations.

AR cannot and should not try to bring the dying models of the Humboldtian or land grant university back to life. The transitions that have taken place are not reversible and the old modes of operation are no longer adaptive. AR would support a way forward toward a new situation, toward a new university, one based on the democratic and solidary values of AR. The challenge for action researchers is to learn how the current transitions can be guided in these more desirable, more liberating directions and how we can learn to participate actively in the change process.

From professionals to experts

One key transformation, linked closely to the neo-liberalization of higher education, is the conversion of professionals into experts. This distinction is central to a major work by the sociologist Steven Brint (1994). Brint's work historically contextualizes current developments in the USA to show that there has been an overall change in the concept of the professions, a change that has radically affected higher education. He argues that the notion of professionals as a special group of educated persons whose combined knowledge and activity exerts a meaningful moral impact on society is evaporating. Rather, professionals now are splintered in many ways into different and much more instrumental, narrowly contextualized groups and functions. This change is accompanied by an increasing social conservatism and individualism among professionals. He sums up his argument by stating that professionals are being converted from 'social trustees' whose judgments were not only well informed but took into account the broader interests of society into 'experts' whose individual knowledge is easily marketed and valued in terms of the metrics of accountability and whose broader social concerns are reduced.

The contemporary professional, understood as someone with at least a master's degree from an institution of higher education, is now trained in so many different kinds of higher education institutions that she/he lacks shared educational experiences and a shared sense of social location and responsibility with many other academically-trained people. The ethical grounding of professional practice has been weakened by this de-socialization process. Consequently, there is no longer a unified public conceptualization of professionals and their social responsibilities.

These professional experts for hire can be found everywhere, marketing their services, all proclaiming to ground their practices in professional knowledge and practice. Facing these competing claims for their attention, the public has become both confused and quite suspicious of professionals because the public has no basis for making reasoned choices among the clamoring expert consultants (Berger and Luckmann, 1971; Heron, 1996).

The AR professional plays a very different role. The action researcher works directly with problem owners in collaborative problem identification and knowledge generation processes. By so doing, action researchers necessarily demonstrate, enact, and justify their values and professional skills in front of a collaborating group that includes a 'public' that is capable of judging them. One obvious outcome is that local participants learn in depth what kind of professional skills and standards an action researcher has and learn that such people are also flesh and blood human beings with their own strengths and weaknesses, skills and foibles. The public also learns that action researchers have substantive skills, the utility of which is not merely claimed but demonstrated in practice. They see that action researchers not only advocate values and strong standards of professional ethics but act them out in the context of the collaborative work and are willing to be judged by their collaborators. In short, the action researcher professional is fully present in the field situation, not hiding behind a purposely distanced 'expert' role.

Action researchers are, thus, engaged experts, striving to join with others in concrete problem-solving, and also are trained professionals whose training helps them set standards for the integrity of the collaborative research processes and for the examination of the quality and validity of the outcomes of these mutual learning processes. This is, it seems to us, very much the kind of professional 'expert' that the public can and should work with in a relationship built on trust. Action researchers work in the crossfire between different stakeholder groups and can only survive in this position though an engagement that is founded on personal integrity. But by playing this kind of role, action researchers regularly have the experience of gaining considerable respect from the stakeholders and renewing their enthusiasm for certain kinds of professional knowledge.

Action researchers, like everyone else, certainly are not neutral. We are committed to and advocate particular value positions based on our best judgment about rightness and fairness. However, these AR value positions are public because we practice collaboratively with the stakeholders in public and we neither can nor seek to hide their values, strengths, weaknesses, and uncertainties from the rest of the participants. In this regard, the AR professional is a model of the kind of 'transparent' professional that we think can both rebuild and deserve the public's confidence. Such professionals can do much to create faith in universities; indeed, this is the only path we can see for regaining public support for university-based knowledge generation.

FROM LIFE IN A TENURED SAFE HAVEN TO ENTREPRENEURIAL AGILITY

University professors in the United States seem remarkably unaware of the transitions we are discussing and the larger impacts these will have on their academic lives. The Europeans and Australians are much more alert to what is happening. Even though the rapid entrepreneuralization and individualization of academic professionals is obvious to many observers (e.g. Jennifer Washburn, 2005; David Kirp, 2003), many of our colleagues are proceeding with their lives as if business as usual were possible and as if the presence of management talk and corporate models at universities are just a temporary glitch that will correct itself. We, of course, believe this is quite wrong.

In *Ivy and Industry: Business and the Making of the American University, 1880–1980*, Christopher Newfield (2004) makes the case that the relationship between industry and higher education has always been an intimate one ever since the founding of US higher education institutions. He criticizes the mistaken notion that only now has the world of commerce influenced universities. The Tayloristic factory system that characterized industrial capitalism was mirrored remarkably well in the administrative structures of higher education with their intensely hierarchical arrangements with hermetic compartments (Greenwood and Levin, 2000).

Newfield argues that the liberal individualism that characterized the faculty's self-image was built on a clear 'deal' made between the faculty and administrators that put governance in the hands of administrators and academic pursuits in the hands of the professors. This division of labor is the same as that between bosses and workers in the Tayloristic factory system. According to Newfield, what has changed in recent years is not the invasion of the university by capitalism but shifts in the capitalist system to a global economy based on less hierarchical and bureaucratic business structures and on more agile and impermanent relationships.

In the academy, one sign of the arrival of this model is the emergence of the faculty member as national and international entrepreneur; another is alliances between faculty members and administrators to capture governmental and private sector resources through patentable research and research in which all parties have a shared financial interest. This process has drastically altered the US research universities in ways that, as yet, are barely visible in the state university systems of Europe. In the US research universities, the liberal individualist faculty member now either is an entrepreneur or is relegated to a secondary status and given lots of 'service' work to do (service now includes teaching, as if full-time research were the norm for university professors). In most institutions, those faculty members and units that do not contribute to the bottom line are made to understand their second-class status, and the internal university economy becomes much more like the 'winner-take-all' system that applies globally.

There are even starker examples of this entrepreneurialism in those cases where employees in higher education now only have a job as long as they bring in enough public and private sector research money to cover their own expenses. Another consequence of the move to entrepreneurialism is dismantling the academic tenure system and its substitution with a system of short-term employment contracts that allow universities to retool as the economic targets of opportunity shift. The tenured safe haven is already a relic of the past in many institutions and is on the way out at many more.

In Europe, this transition involves even more radical changes. Most US research universities, state or private, have budgets composed of tuition and fees, research grants and overheads, the income on alumni monetary and other gifts, and patent income. Emphasizing the entrepreneurial elements is a matter of focus in such systems, a way of enhancing some of the revenue streams that make up the budgets. However, in European state systems, based for generations on national funding allocations for teaching, the introduction of tuition, entrepreneurial research efforts, and capital campaigns to get funds from wealthy graduates are new, controversial, and rapidly spreading practices.

Given the above, we are amazed when the attempts to solve the funding and overcrowding problems in European universities are addressed by what some European higher education leaders call adoption of the 'American model'. They appear to mean something like a dynamic, entrepreneurial research university, a partial characteristic of perhaps 50 US universities that charge high tuition and fees. Actually, rather than the 'American model', what Europeans are mainly adopting is a set of neo-liberal policies that involve lowering public financial contribution to higher education, the de facto privatization of parts of the public system, and the purposeful conversion of many universities into second-class teaching institutions.[3]

AR does not oppose meaningful entrepreneurial behavior. Indeed action researchers often have an entrepreneurial/catalytical orientation and 'color outside the lines' by seeking direct engagement with problems in the world outside of university orbits and disciplinary trajectories. Funding for AR projects is rarely available in the current set-up of university life. To pursue AR interests,

faculty members have to be creative and innovative in obtaining funds for specific activities.

However, unlike conventional individualistic entrepreneurial researchers in universities, AR professionals do not limit themselves to seeking typical sources of funding. We are equally interested in seeking funding that can support research on pertinent problems for underprivileged groups. Public programs in Europe sometimes can be used to fund AR but gaining access to these monies demands entrepreneurial skills. But this type of entrepreneurial activity is quite different from that seen in the existing close relationships between industry and universities in which patents, intellectual property rights, and royalties are the currency of choice, the sort of entrepreneurial activity that the RAE and similar management models encourage.

FROM STRONG DISCIPLINARITY TO CONTEXTUALIZED TRANSDISIPLINARITY

The above analyses point to shifts in the understanding and contextualization of the role of academic professionals in both higher education and the larger environment. These views on professionals, however, do not address either the exact kinds of linkages existing between universities and society at large or the kinds of shifts taking place in the organization and character of knowledge production. This is what two widely discussed works, *The New Production of Knowledge: the Dynamics of Science and Research in Contemporary Societies* (Gibbons et al., 1994) and *Re-thinking Science: Knowledge and the Public in an Age of Uncertainty* (Nowotny et al., 2001), articulated successfully for European audiences. These works have given rise to a widely discussed framework that focuses explicitly on the organizational structure of the university/society linkage.

These works have generated a great deal of discussion about issues that should be central to the understanding of the future of higher education. These authors unfortunately are unaware of the ample tradition of systems analysis of organizations and organizational learning (Ackoff, 1999; Argyris and Schön, 1998; March and Simon, 1958) in which the distinction between closed system and open system dynamics is central. Still, their core arguments are based on a distinction between two modes of knowledge production: 'Mode 1', which is conventional knowledge production in academic settings in which knowledge is produced in the context of narrowly academic professional structures, and 'Mode 2', which is knowledge produced in the context of application much of which is external to the university itself.

They believe that knowledge production increasingly occurs in the context of application and not in the abstracted university environment. To respond to this, universities are forced to transgress their own internal and external boundaries in search of research opportunities in the *agora* and to garner financial support. In the process of capturing the needed resources, they are also captured by external forces.

This dynamic creates profound organizational and intellectual challenges. To transact successfully with forces interested in knowledge in the context of application, academics must move their work to the contexts of application. Further, knowledge in context is very rarely disciplinary knowledge but rather knowledge in a multi-disciplinary, multi-causal context. Under these conditions, the Tayloristic structures of higher education, rather than serving as a protection for academic inquiry, become a hindrance to it and must be transgressed by increasingly entrepreneurial faculty and administrators.

Were this not a sufficient challenge, the kind of knowledge that is valued is different. Within the context of Mode 1 knowledge production, the authors argue that the kind of knowledge that has long been privileged is what they call 'reliable knowledge'. This reliable knowledge is basically that knowledge deemed good by professional peers

using conventional modes of academic peer review and publication in the standard journals as legitimation. This is the much studied, defended and ridiculed set of practices that isolates academic knowledge production by discipline and also from public scrutiny.

Under Mode 2 conditions, this kind of knowledge is not valued very much. Rather what the authors call 'socially robust knowledge' is emphasized. This is knowledge that 'works' and is accepted as relevant in the context of application. That is, it is knowledge tested in action by actors who are in a position where the result of their work will determine if the knowledge is workable. The academics have no monopoly on determining if knowledge is socially robust; they must simply participate in the process as one more stakeholder.

This is not to say that Nowotny et al. have gotten it all right. Their arguments are extremely abstract. The structure of the knowledge construction arenas and co-generative learning processes happening in the context of application is nowhere clarified. More troubling, their discussion of socially-robust knowledge is uninformed by the extensive pragmatist and neo-pragmatist writings that define and operationalize very precisely the ways in which socially-robust knowledge is created (see for example Diggins, 1994, for an overview). That is, they are describing an arena in which the AR approach to co-generative learning and knowledge creation is essential. Unfortunately, they are not aware of generations of AR work on such processes.[4]

Action researchers have been practicing Mode 2 knowledge production since the first AR-based experiments took place in the 1940s and 1950s. The sociotechnical approach developed by the Tavistock Institute of Human Relations in London created the first viable transdisciplinary take on production system arguing for the close and interconnected relationship between technology and social systems. This framework argued that new solutions to organizational problems could not be achieved unless it was possible to change both the technology and work organization. That required an integrated activity.

No approach to creating Mode 2 situations is as promising as AR. By contrast, the 'new public management' in higher education creates just the opposite dynamic – splitting teaching from research, reifying disciplinary structures, supporting only research that seems 'profitable', and destroying the 'public goods' in higher education. This is not Mode 2 knowledge production; it is having consultants for hire with offices on university campuses. On this basis, we affirm that, to the extent that the fate of higher education depends on operating successfully in a Mode 2 world, then it turns on some version of pragmatic AR as its principal organizational mechanism for orchestrating those research processes.

FROM INDIVIDUAL ACADEMIC FREEDOM TO ACADEMIC FREEDOM AS A SHARED PROCESS

The depth and breadth of the challenge that Mode 2 knowledge production represents for academic business as usual is clear. While we welcome it as an opportunity to transform higher education, we are aware that many of our academic colleagues view the kinds of changes that Mode 2 knowledge production requires as infringements on their 'academic freedom'. The concept of academic freedom, despite the tendency of academics to use it at the drop of a hat, is actually poorly understood and little studied.

Conventional understandings of academic freedom make it synonymous with individual freedom of speech and action. This is especially the case in the USA. Two recently published books by Hollingsworth (2000) and Downs (2005) are typical in understanding academic freedom only as the freedom to express whatever the professors find it urgent to say. Academic freedom is understood as an individual right mainly exercised on university campuses.

We believe this view is wrong and anti-social. It is wrong to understand academic freedom as an individual possession or right. Academic freedom is a capacity achieved and guaranteed through daily, collaborative organizational activities, through the production of good, inclusive, and fair social processes of the sort AR seeks. Freedom is created through the social esteem that is gained from making constructive contributions to the resolution of important societal problems. Thus, academic freedom and institutional autonomy are the collaborative products of institutions committed to the constructive critique, thinking 'outside the box', and the consolidation and transmission of all kinds of knowledge.

The original formulation of concepts related to academic freedom is found in the Humboldt model. It was not then called academic freedom but it did center on the right of professors to teach what they considered important and the right of students to participate in only those classes they found valuable and interesting. Freedom of speech was part of this environment but the more important dimension was the collective, organizational environment that permitted voluntary encounters between the freedom to offer topics and the freedom to choose among them. Humboldtian academic freedom was constructed within the relationship between professors and students and involved mutual responsibility grounded in group life on campus.

The Humboldtian view shows that academic freedom was not some kind of special right given to the professoriate at institutions called universities but a constitutive principle of universities themselves. Menand (1996: 4) argues: 'Academic freedom is not simply a kind of bonus enjoyed by workers within the system. … It is the key legitimating concept of the [academic] enterprise.'

More than a few academics think that academic freedom has mainly been sustained, fought for and legitimated by academic professional associations (Haskell, 1996). They argue that the professional associations, in overseeing the quality and standards of practice of their practitioners, are best situated to determine what kinds of knowledge are professionally rigorous and to defend the rights of the members of the professions. We, of course, know the guardianship of professional associations of the academic freedom of the professions is a self-promotional idealization, a set of practices belied by known cases of political coercion, abuses, and blacklisting and the failure of professional associations to protect most of their members.

Yet, for a brief period what was said to be relevant and rigorous professional knowledge and standards of practice by the academic professions had ethical and even legal status in the public sphere. This status arose from the autonomous self-regulation of the professions that made them appear to be independent of particular political and economic considerations. Even though we do not see much evidence of the robust protection of academic freedom by these associations, it is worth noting that even this meaning of academic freedom implies that it is an organizational and collective product, rather than an individual right.

These very different examples show that academic freedom is fundamentally relational, that it is constructed and reconstructed in everyday relationships where authenticity in expression and effective and fair behavior is a central feature. Unless the prerogative of all parties to express authentic and un-coerced views is respected, there is no academic freedom.

For there to be academic freedom, universities must be organized in such a way that heterogeneity is encouraged and can prosper. For knowledge to be generated and used to contribute to constructive problem-solving with non-university stakeholders on problems of importance to society at large, there must be authentic communication and universities must support creativity, critique, and reflection for this kind of communication to be possible.

Universities that operate in this way are not just one more kind of business that aims to maximize the production of intellectual property from which income can be derived.

They are institutions that engage in understanding the conditions necessary for the successful creation of new ideas and new and better designs for living. As such, university inquiry, unlike proprietary research and vocational education, must be based on critical attitudes, multi-disciplinary coordination, and the collective academic freedom to think broadly and unconventionally that makes such inquiry possible.

Such a conception of academic freedom directly challenges the trend toward university attempts to protect and profit from intellectual property rights. A critical and constructive discourse on universities cannot take place if the knowledge generation processes are not freely accessible, open to critical inquiry, and controlled by the market rather than the results of democratic dialogue.

To summarize, academic freedom is not an individual right but a kind of freedom and openness of inquiry processes that is created in cogenerative, democratically-organized learning organizations and arenas. This kind of academic freedom is just as relevant to the context of application as it to a university campus because the freedom to think 'outside the box', to brainstorm without fear, and to subject one's own processes to reflective scrutiny is key to innovation and change in democratic societies. It is also the freedom to propose ideas and critiques of popular ideas and existing social and political arrangements without the immediate fear of punishment or dismissal.

These issues are vitally important to most university researchers and certainly to action researchers. After all, a major problem facing action researchers is the need to preserve personal and professional integrity in the face of social pressures. High involvement with external stakeholders is an essential ingredient in AR but maintaining this involvement without becoming the tool of the most powerful among the stakeholders is always a problem. To confront this, university-based action researchers must have the kind of job security that will support their ability to retain this integrity, the ability to 'speak the truth to power' as Freire put it (1970). Having a place to withdraw to – a platform on which to stand to resist pressures – is key. This is more fundamental in AR than in conventional social science research because democratic, pro-social values and commitments permeate AR's approach and inevitably create tensions when applied in authoritarian contexts both inside and outside universities. Nevertheless, it is vitally important for any kind of open, critical, and pragmatic inquiry at universities.

In the case of AR, projects with underprivileged groups depend on funding from third parties and this requires an explicit social contract about the *quid pro quos* for the funding. But, rather than allowing total control of projects by the funders, action researchers distribute control across the whole stakeholder group, including the funders (foundations, public agencies, or governments). Key in this are the specific terms of the funding and agreements on the collaborative evaluation of the projects and having a secure platform from which to negotiate these agreements.

Surprisingly, we have learned that many funders are willing to entertain these kinds of arrangements because they guarantee the relevance, quality, and social value of the work done, something that conventional academic expert professionals rarely do. Indeed, the discredit of the conventional academic professions has actually created opportunities for action researchers willing to demonstrate publicly the value of our work for all participants, including the funders, to see.

CONCLUSION

It seems for us obvious that the universities are at a crossroads created by both societal and internal institutional changes. Academics who believe they can keep their heads down and operate as in the past will lose all possibility of having an impact on the changes taking place and may find themselves eliminated by the change process itself. The professions, academic work, and the practices associated with academic integrity will take on new forms. Just what form they will take, however, is not set a priori. What emerges as the future university will depend on who engages in the current struggle, what interests they reflect, how they view academic work, and how they use their own power to support their interests and those of civil society. This is why we see AR as one of the most promising and viable options engaging in the reorganization of future academic life.

In this chapter we have argued that a major historical transition is under way toward the neo-liberalization of higher education. We believe that the current transitions raise issues of organization and method that we believe AR is capable of confronting effectively and that AR has the potential to make significant contributions to orchestrating positive change processes. We think that the deployment of AR to meet these needs seems a good way to resist the full-scale neo-liberalization of our societies because AR strengthens remaining pro-social and pro-democracy forces within higher education and links these to the wants and needs of a broad social spectrum of non-university stakeholders.

NOTES

1 Cardinal Newman's *Idea of the university* focused on universities as centers of training for ethical discernment and conduct based on broad education (Newman, 1907). The Humboldtian public university was the first to claim a systematic link between research and teaching as the basis for both scholarship and citizen education. The US land grant university was founded by the federal government to give each state in the union a university that engaged in combined teaching, research, and public service.

2 Much of academic life at research universities involves autopoetic processes for the direct benefit of the researchers, and often for the financial benefit of both the researchers and the university. The focus of a great deal of research is dictated by governmental grant priorities and private sector funding. It is all too often

the practice of universities to adjust to requirements framed by changing private and public funding, instead of developing and proposing viable alternatives based on the ethos of university-based knowledge generation. Of course, the private sector often determines governmental and foundation granting priorities anyway. This arena is highly competitive and heavily focused on the interests of the most powerful members of society (Kirp, 2003; Washburn, 2005).

3 This is not the place to develop the argument, but the notion that current academic management practices are applications of private sector management to higher education is quite wrong. Current private sector management and organizational development focuses on flattening hierarchies, multi-skilling, team-based production strategies, staying in constant touch with the 'customers', etc. Current higher education management is just the opposite. Hierarchy and administrative infrastructures are being increased, disciplinary boundaries are being reinforced, and faculty and staff are being managed in a way that produces competitive individualism. This is the old fashioned Taylorism of the early days of mass production industrial processes and is the approach to management that has broken the backs of companies like General Motors, U.S. Steel, etc. So the notion that contemporary management has taken over the university can only be believed by academics who know nothing about contemporary industrial systems.

4 For a more extended argument, see Levin and Greenwood (2001a, 2001b).

REFERENCES

Ackoff, Russell (1999) *Ackoff's Best: His Classic Writings on Management.* San Francisco, CA: Jossey-Bass.

Argyris, Chris and Schön, Donald A. (1998) *Organizational Learning II: Theory, Method and Practice.* Reading, MA: Addison-Wesley.

Argyris, C., Putnam, R., and McClain Smith, D. (1985) *Action Science: Concepts, Methods, and Skills for Research and Intervention.* San Francisco, CA: Jossey-Bass.

Berger, Peter and Luckmann, Thomas (1971) *The Social Construction of Reality.* London: Penguin Books.

Brint, S. (1994) *In an Age of Experts: the Changing Role of Professionals in Politics and Public Life.* Princeton, NJ: Princeton University Press.

Diggins, John (1994) *The Promise of Pragmatism: Modernism and the Crisis of Knowledge and Authority.* Chicago: University of Chicago Press.

Downs, Donald A. (2005) *Restoring Free Speech and Liberty on Campus.* Oakland, CA: The Independent Institute.

Freire, P. (1970) *The Pedagogy of the Oppressed.* New York: Herder & Herder.

Gibbons, Michael, Limoges, Camille, Nowotny, Helga, Schwartzman, Simon, Scott, Peter and Trow, Martin (1994) *The New Production of Knowledge: the Dynamics of Science and Research in Contemporary Societies.* London: Sage.

Greenwood, Davydd and Levin, Morten (1998) *Introduction to Action Research: Social Science for Social Change.* Thousand Oaks, CA: Sage.

Greenwood, Davydd and Levin, Morten (2000) 'Reconstructing the relationships between university and society through action research', in Norman Denzin and Yvonna Lincoln (eds), *Handbook of Qualitative Research, 2nd edn.* Thousand Oaks, CA: Sage. pp. 85–105.

Greenwood, Davydd and Levin, Morten (2006) *Introduction to Action Research: Social Science for Social Change, rev. edn.* Thousand Oaks, CA: Sage.

Haskell, Thomas (1996) 'Justifying the rights of academic freedom in the era of "power/knowledge"', in L. Menand (ed.), *The Future of Academic Freedom.* Chicago: University of Chicago Press. pp. 43–90.

Heron, John (1996) *Co-operative Inquiry: Research into the Human Condition.* London: Sage.

Hollingsworth, Peggie J. (2000) *Unfettered Expression: Freedom in American Intellectual Life.* Ann Arbor: University of Michigan Press.

Kirp, David (2003) *Shakespeare, Einstein, and the Bottom Line: the Marketing of Higher Education.* Cambridge, MA: Harvard University Press.

Levin, Morten and Greenwood, Davydd (2001a) 'Re-organizing universities and "knowing how": university restructuring and knowledge creation for the twenty-first century', *Organization,* 8 (2): 433–40.

Levin, Morten and Greenwood, Davydd (2001b) 'Pragmatic action research and the struggle to transform universities into learning communities', in P. Reason and H. Bradbury (eds), *Handbook of Action Reasearch: Participative Inquiry and Practice,* London: Sage. pp. 103–13.

March, James and Simon, Herbert (1958) *Organizations.* New York: John Wiley.

Menand, Louis (ed.) (1996) *The Future of Academic Freedom.* Chicago: University of Chicago Press.

Newman, John Henry Cardinal (1907) *The Idea of the University.* London: Longmans, Green & Co.

Newfield, Christopher (2004) *Ivy and Industry: Business and the Making of the American University, 1880–1980.* Durham, NC: Duke University Press.

Nowotny, Helga, Scott, Peter and Gibbons, Michael (2001) *Re-thinking Science: Knowledge and the Public in an Age of Uncertainty.* London: Polity Press.

Polanyi, Karl (1944) *The Great Transformation: the Political and Economic Origins of Our Time.* New York: Holt, Rinehart & Co.

Rhind, David (2003) *Great Expectations: the Social Sciences in Britain.* Commission on the Social Sciences, http://joni.soc.surrey.ac.uk/~scs1ng/C.Univ-Gt. Expectations.pdf.

Slaughter, Sheila and Leslie, Larry (1997) *Academic Capitalism: Politics, Policies and the Entrepreneurial University.* Baltimore: Johns Hopkins University Press.

Silva, Edward and Slaughter, Sheila (1984) *Serving Power: the Making of the Academic Social Science Expert.* Westport, CT: Greenwood Press.

Washburn, Jennifer (2005) *University, Inc.: the Corporate Corruption of Higher Education.* New York: Basic Books.

15

Action Research, Partnerships and Social Impacts: The Institutional Collaboration of PRIA and IDR

L. David Brown and Rajesh Tandon

This chapter explores the roles of participatory action research in shaping large-scale processes of development and social transformation through an institutional collaboration across the South–North divide. It describes the partnership between PRIA (The Society for Participatory Research in Asia) and IDR (The Institute for Development Research) in three programmes: (1) building civil-society capacity, (2) civil society and intersectoral influence, and (3) promoting participatory development by large donors. Each programme began as small initiatives that eventually grew to influence global concepts, debates, policies and practices. The chapter reflects on lessons that can be drawn from such collaboration in terms of increased resources and credibility, building programmes for long-term influence, working across local, national and transnational levels, and creating better integrated theories of social change.

The theory of action research grew out of the practice of problem-solving in groups and organizations. The theory of participatory research grew out of the practical efforts at conscientization and empowerment of the marginalized. These two streams of knowledge-action schools began to interact in the 1980s, and thereby emerged the stream of participatory action research.

The essential premise of such a knowledge-action stream has been the contribution of actionable knowledge to social transformation. Social development programmes in developing countries have, until recently, largely been based on distant and abstract concepts. Locally provided, actionable knowledge, from the perspectives of local protagonists, began to shape the design of such programmes only since the late 1980s/early 1990s. It is in this sense that action research has come to be recognized as an appropriate epistemology for the vision of a more just and equitable social transformation.

The potential of action research in 'uncovering' hidden realities and 'recovering' lost experiences at the grassroots level has begun to shape large-scale development actors nationally and globally. Action research methodology, with emphasis on participation of the excluded in knowledge construction itself, has come to influence the thinking of policy-makers and development professionals.

The growing complexities of social development problems, with partial solutions at local, national and global levels, imply the need for an understanding of causes and potentials from micro to macro levels. Such diversity of knowledge-action is not easy for a single institution to handle. It is in this sense that institutional collaboration across the South–North divide may create a system of knowledge-action, in the best traditions of Action Research, which has a wide scale impact on social policy and policy-makers.

This chapter explores this interrelated set of issues based on the experiences of institutional collaboration between IDR and PRIA. It attempts to describe the value of action research in producing actionable knowledge, from a variety of stakeholder perspectives, to shape policies and designs of social development. It also illustrates the unique value of long-term institutional collaboration in action research across the South–North divide to have large-scale social impacts. It thus highlights the potential of partnerships in the practice of action research and the long-term impacts such partnerships can generate.

Three programmes in particular illustrate the potential of long-term institutional collaboration across the chasms that separate the global South and North.[1]

- *Building civil society capacity.* In 1999 scores of organizations, including donor agencies (World Bank, USAID, EC, Ford Foundation, DIFD, etc.), Northern NGOs and Southern NGOs from many regions met for several days to discuss capacity-building for civil society. These discussions grew from a decade-long series of participatory action research initiatives spearheaded by PRIA and IDR with civil society support organizations in many regions. The network that emerged – the International Forum for Capacity Building (IFCB) – catalysed a series of discussions and agreements over the next several years to strengthen civil society in many countries. These discussions reshaped how scores of NGOs, donor agencies and governments engaged the challenges and potentials of civil society capacity-building.

- *Civil society and intersectoral influence.* In the mid-1980s civil society organizations in most developing countries regarded government and business as 'part of the problem' and saw little possibility of constructive engagement with either. By the turn of the century many aid agencies were hailing intersectoral partnerships as the best way to mobilize the resources required to solve intransigent development problems. Over more than a decade PRIA and IDR pioneered studies of civil society advocacy and collaboration across sector differences to create innovative development initiatives. The results of these studies have informed the strategies of countless civil society organizations as well as large donors (e.g. UNDP, USAID) and government officials.

- *Participatory development by large donors.* At the World Bank in 2000, a conference on the use of participatory development strategies in large development projects brought together dozens of Southern NGOs, Northern NGOs, and international development agencies to discuss the challenges and potentials of implementing participatory development strategies. The conference emerged from a decade-long campaign to foster more participatory strategies by the World Bank and the conference drew on studies of nominally participatory Bank projects carried out by a world-wide coalition of NGOs coordinated and trained by PRIA and IDR. The conference increased the pressure for participatory strategies by a wide range of large development actors.

The next section describes these initiatives in more detail, providing a window on the long-term institutional collaboration for PAR that transcends chasms between the South and North.

INSTITUTIONAL COLLABORATION IN PAR

PRIA (Society for Participatory Research in Asia) is a New Delhi-based organization whose mission is promoting the practice of participatory research as a contribution to knowledge building and social transformation. IDR (Institute for Development Research) was a Boston-based organization committed to action research and capacity-building for just, inclusive and sustainable development.[2] For almost two decades, PRIA and IDR worked closely together on a series of long-term participatory action research (PAR) programmes that had significant impacts on the roles of civil society organizations in development in many countries. A long-term action researcher on civil society and development characterized them as 'two beacons' that for many years led the field in identifying issues, generating knowledge, and informing policy and practice for civil society development.[3]

Three programmes in particular illustrate the potential of long-term institutional collaboration across the chasms that separate the global South and North. In these examples we briefly recount the streams of activity that produced large-scale long-term results and the patterns of collaboration associated with their outcomes.

1. Capacity-Building for Civil Society

In the mid-1980s PRIA began exploring with civil society leaders in India the capacities required to lead NGOs and social movements. It became clear that strategy and management problems were central to the effectiveness of many social transformation initiatives (Tandon, 1988). At the same time, IDR began action research with 'empowerment-oriented' international development NGOs and proposed revisions to existing organization development theory and practice required by such agencies (Brown and Covey, 1987). PRIA and IDR began to build knowledge about support organizations (SOs) from the field practices in India. They also began a long-term collaboration to train facilitators of support organizations for development NGOs. This initiative eventually trained scores of

facilitators and OD consultants in Asia and Africa.

Experience with organizational capacity-building also led to interest in the development of civil society as a sector of organizations. By 1990, PRIA and IDR, in cooperation with the Asian NGO Coalition (ANGOC), had launched a programme to strengthen civil society support organizations as a vehicle for sectoral capacity strengthening. This programme produced a series of consultations that focused on assessing and strengthening the roles of South Asian civil society support organizations (Almazan-Khan et al., 1995; Brown and Tandon, 1990; Tandon et al., 1997). During the early 1990s, PRIA built a network of regional support organizations (RSOs) for capacity-building to scale up its impact throughout India and supported the emergence of a similar network of South Asian support organizations. As a result, PRIA and IDR convened and coordinated an emerging international network of support organizations concerned with civil society capacity-building in Asia, Africa, Latin America and Eastern Europe.

The emerging knowledge from this network set the stage for wider attention to capacity issues. As civil society became a more important development actor and its need for capacity-building increased, PRIA, IDR and support organizations from Latin America and Africa persuaded the World Bank, the European Commission, USAID, UNDP and other major donors to support a series of research initiatives on issues of capacity-building for civil society in the developing world. These discussions led to the creation of the International Forum on Capacity Building (IFCB), which catalysed a series of regional and national discussions among NGOs, governments and donors that redefined capacity-building interventions from serving donor interests (e.g. accounting training to protect donors' funds) to responding more directly to the needs of southern civil societies (e.g. training in strategic thinking, coalition building and policy advocacy) in many countries (Tandon and Bandyopadhyay, 2003).

This 15 year collaboration began with research on organization capacity-building and evolved to influencing transnational discourses and policies on capacity-building. The ability of PRIA and IDR to influence the debate grew in part from their contributions to research and educational literatures (e.g. Brown and Kalegaonkar, 2002; Brown and Tandon, 1994). It also grew from their roles in mobilizing a worldwide network of civil society support organizations that could speak authoritatively about capacity needs in many different regions. In this initiative, debates that began at the local and national levels became transnational discourses about the roles of civil society, and PRIA and IDR were positioned to mobilize key stakeholders to join and support the IFCB – setting the stage for debating and redefining the nature and implementation of capacity-building for civil society.

2. Civil Society and Intersectoral Influence

For many years civil society activists rejected association with agencies from other sectors, such as government or business organizations. Their work with civil society sectors led PRIA and IDR to explore how civil society might engage those other sectors in development problem-solving. PRIA began exploring relations between civil society and government quite early (Tandon, 1989). Work with national NGO associations in the Philippines and India, for example, produced cases and frameworks to explain successful civil society *policy analysis and advocacy* on development projects (Gershman et al., 1997; Khan, 1997). These analyses were used to inform subsequent campaigns in those countries and in the region. PRIA worked closely with Indian national civil society associations and networks on a variety of advocacy campaigns; IDR convened international NGOs to share experience and

lessons from advocacy campaigns (IDR, 1997). Both organizations used their relationship to build knowledge grounded in diverse perspectives and then used their different linkages to disseminate results to interested Northern and Southern audiences.

A second strand of this work examined *cooperation* across sectors to solve development problems. In collaboration with the Synergos Institute and several regional networks, IDR and PRIA carried out research (based on 13 case studies) of cooperation between NGOs, grassroots groups and government agencies in 12 countries in Asia and Africa. This initiative brought representatives of the cases together with the coalition partners to build frameworks for understanding effective partnerships (Brown and Ashman, 1996, 1999; Brown and Tandon, 1993). In practical terms, the results of this initiative helped shape pro-partnership policies at UNDP and USAID (Brown and Tandon, 1993; Tandon, 1993; Waddell and Brown, 1997). PRIA and IDR later extended this exploration to assessing civil society development partnerships with business organizations based on research from India, South Africa and Brazil (Ashman, 2000). These studies again suggested that under some conditions such partnerships could serve development goals.

Today it is well established that civil society organizations can scale up their impacts through policy advocacy and intersectoral cooperation. Many actors and innovations have contributed to the shift from the isolated suspicion of two decades ago – and in this journey IDR and PRIA played critical roles in identifying possibilities and disseminating ideas about intersectoral relations. For over 10 years, the PRIA-IDR focus on intersectoral partnerships enabled civil society to gain confidence in engaging with governments and business; it also demonstrated the value of such partnerships in producing desirable development impacts from the vantage point of government and business.

3. Promoting Participatory Development Strategies

The value of participatory development strategies for catalysing sustainable transformations has long been recognized, but it has proved very difficult to mainstream participatory development strategies at some major international donors, such as the World Bank and USAID. In the early 1990s, IDR and PRIA were both elected to the NGO Working Group on the World Bank, a group of 26 NGOs from around the world that advised and advocated with the Bank. Over the next decade, they played central roles in a long-term campaign to mainstream participation in major international donors' projects and policies.

PRIA's experiences on issues of participation of the poor and the marginalized had generated knowledge about institutional constraints placed by government agencies and international donors (Tandon, 2002). Focusing on this issue, IDR and PRIA helped to design and organize a worldwide coalition to collect data on the Bank's efforts to promote participation in projects from every region in the world. IDR helped to develop the research approach and train case researchers, and PRIA led the analysis and interpretation of case results from Asia, Africa and Latin America. In collaboration with the Participation Group at IDS (UK), they convened a conference at the World Bank to share the knowledge with multilateral organizations (e.g. the World Bank, UNDP), bilateral aid agencies (e.g. USAID, DFID, and the Swedish International Development Agency) and NGOs in November 1998. This initiative produced a book-length analysis of major agency efforts to institutionalize participatory development strategies in their programmes (Long, 2001). It helped catalyse the formulation of standards for assessing Bank practices in fostering participation in the future and supported Bank staff who had been advocating for mainstreaming participatory approaches. The knowledge produced in the deliberations of the conference emphasized the need for internal institutional reforms to support participation. This was to become mainstreamed in the policy and project work of international donors. The internal changes at those agencies contributed to institutional reforms in recipient government organizations that were responsible for national project implementation.

INSTITUTIONAL COLLABORATION AND PARTICIPATORY ACTION RESEARCH

What does long-term South–North institutional collaboration have to offer for participatory action research for social transformation? We believe that at least four aspects of this collaboration contributed significantly to its impacts.

First, the combination of Southern and Northern bases enhances the intellectual capacities, perspective diversity and credibility of both partners. PRIA's perspective on development issues and its credibility with Southern activists added greatly to IDR's understanding and leverage with key stakeholders; IDR's access to research and its credibility with Northern NGOs and donors expanded PRIA's influence. IDR connected PRIA to the NGO Working Group on the World Bank and the coalition to explore intersectoral collaboration; PRIA linked IDR to a wide range of Southern support organizations and to the CIVICUS World Alliance for Citizen Participation. Together they could generate knowledge and influence a range of stakeholders beyond what either could accomplish working separately.

Second, the growth of a shared analysis of development problems, the recognition of shared values and the evolution of a relationship of mutual respect and trust meant that joint work was less dependent on particular projects and scarce funding. PRIA and IDR actively sought opportunities to pursue joint initiatives. They saw each other as long-term resources with common visions. The result was long-term collaboration, often supported by a patchwork of funding resources, that enabled cumulative results over long-term explorations, as in more than a decade of work with civil society support organizations. It also allowed expanding alliances, as in the growth of the support organization network from India to South Asia to a worldwide network.

Third, their long-term institutional cooperation enabled IDR and PRIA to evolve societal change theories across multiple levels – local, national, transnational – that are often required to catalyse sustainable social transformation. Although both organizations began their work with change theories grounded at the individual and organizational levels of analysis, their work together pressed for interorganizational, sectoral, intersectoral, national and transnational analysis that complemented their growing links to wider alliances and a more complex understanding of development problems. Their initial successes encouraged aspirations for wider impacts that depended on multi-leveled theories of change. Such an evolution was made possible through the multi-level partnership between PRIA and IDR that evolved over 20 years.

Finally, the conception of PAR that guided the work of IDR and PRIA evolved in interaction with their developing theories of social change. Early in their work together they recognized that 'participatory research' and 'action research' had much to learn from each other, and that future endeavors would have to grapple with research initiatives that were accountable to multiple stakeholders (Brown and Tandon, 1983). PRIA began with a conception of participatory research that emphasized solidarity with oppressed groups, and IDR was grounded in a theory of action research for organizational change. Together they evolved approaches to 'participatory action research' that engaged multiple stakeholders across organizational, sectoral, and national differences in shared inquiries on complex problems that eventually altered practices and

policies of many actors as well as produced new concepts and theories.

We live in a world where knowledge creation is increasingly important and knowledge grounded in practice and the insights of multiple disciplines as well as the demands of science is increasingly central (Gibbons et al., 1994; Nowotny et al., 2002). We believe that this increasingly interdependent world requires PAR that can integrate experiences and ideas from many levels and perspectives to produce new knowledge and innovations in policy and practice. Institutional collaboration across diverse worlds, such as the IDR-PRIA relationship, has much promise for bringing together the diverse resources and perspectives needed for transnational social learning and constructive social transformations. This is indeed the potential of participatory action research in generating more just social impacts in our different societies.

NOTES

1 The 'global South and North' refers not to geographic divisions but to concentrations of wealth and power (North) and concentrations of poverty and marginalization (South).

2 In 2001 IDR merged with World Education, another Boston-based development NGO.

3 Alan Fowler in the Symposium on Citizen Participation and Democratic Governance at the CIVICUS World Assembly, Glasgow, Scotland, 21 June 2006.

REFERENCES

Almazan-Khan, M.L., Tandon, R. and Brown, L.D. (1995) *Strengthening Civil Society: Contributions of Support Organizations in South Asia*. New Delhi: Society for Participatory Research in Asia.

Ashman, D. (2000) 'Promoting corporate citizenship in the global south: towards a model of empowered civil society collaboration with business.' Institute for Development Research, Boston, February.

Brown, L.D. and Ashman, D. (1996) 'Participation, social capital and intersectoral problem-solving: African and Asian cases', *World Development*, 24 (9): 1467–79.

Brown, L.D. and Ashman, D. (1999) 'Social capital, mutual influence, and social learning in intersectoral problem-solving', in D. Cooperrider and J. Dutton (eds), *Organizational Dimensions of Global Change.* Thousand Oaks, CA: Sage. pp. 139–67.

Brown, L.D. and Covey, J.G. (1987) 'Development organizations and organization development: toward an expanded paradigm for organization development', in R.W. Woodman and W.E. Pasmore (eds), *Research in Organizational Change and Development, Vol. 1.* Greenwich, CT: JAI Press. pp. 59–88.

Brown, L.D. and Kalegaonkar, A. (2002) 'Support organizations and the evolution of the NGO sector', *Nonprofit and Voluntary Sector Quarterly,* 31 (2): 231–58.

Brown, L.D. and Tandon, R. (1983) 'Ideology and political economy in inquiry: action research and participatory research', *Journal of Applied Behavioral Science,* 19 (2): 277–94.

Brown, L.D. and Tandon, R. (1990) *Strengthening the Grassroots: the Role and Nature of Support Organizations.* New Delhi: Society for Participatory Research in Asia Report.

Brown, L.D. and Tandon, R. (1993) *Multiparty Collaboration for Development in Asia.* New York: United Nations Development Programme Report.

Brown, L.D. and Tandon, R. (1994) 'Institutional development for strengthening civil society', *Journal of Institution Development,* 1 (1): 3–17.

Gershman, J., Boudreau, V., et al. (eds) (1997) *Policy Influence: NGO Experiences.* Manila: Ateneo Center for Social Policy and Public Affairs.

Gibbons, M., Limoges, C., et al. (1994) *New Production of Knowledge: the Dynamics of Science and Research in Contemporary Societies.* London: Sage.

IDR (1997) *Advocacy Sourcebook: Frameworks for Planning, Action and Reflection.* Boston: Institute for Development Research.

Khan, A.M. (1997) *Shaping Policy: Do NGOs Matter?* New Delhi: PRIA.

Long, C. (2001) *Participation of the Poor in Development Initiatives: Taking Their Rightful Place.* London: Earthscan.

Nowotny, H., Scott, P., et al. (2002) *Rethinking Science: Knowledge and the Public.* Cambridge: Polity Press.

Tandon, R. (1988) *Life Cycles in Voluntary Agencies.* New Delhi: Society for Participatory Research Report.

Tandon, R. (1989) *NGO-Government Relations: A Source of Life or a Kiss of Death?* New Delhi: Society for Participatory Research in Asia Report.

Tandon, R. (1993) *Holding Together.* New York: United Nations Development Programme Report.

Tandon, Rajesh (2002) *Participatory Research – Revisiting the Roots.* New Delhi: Mosaic Books.

Tandon, R. and Bandyopadhyay, K.K. (2003) *Capacity Building of Southern NGOs.* New Delhi: Society for Participatory Research in Asia Report.

Tandon, R., Singh, A., Cordeiro, A. and Nair, S.L. (1997) *Strengthening the Impact of Civil Society: Role of Support Organizations.* New Delhi: Society for Participatory Research in Asia Report.

Waddell, S. and Brown, L.D. (1997) 'Fostering strategic partnering', in Cathryn Thorup et al., *New Partnerships Initiative: Resource Guide.* Washington, DC: US Agency for International Development.

PART TWO

Practices

INTRODUCTION TO PRACTICES

In this section we offer descriptions of some of the key approaches to the doing of action research, which we have called 'practices'. We have chosen this rather than 'methods' or 'methodology' because we want to emphasize again that action research takes place in the doing of it rather than the abstract describing of it. The practices described in this section do indeed represent guides for 'how to do action research' but they are not formulaic: they require intelligent, choiceful application guided by the fundamental action research values and epistemologies which are explored elsewhere in this volume – notably a grounding in living issues, a participative/emancipatory ethos, and a spirit of inquiry.

Robert Chambers makes this very clear in Chapter 20 in writing that in PRA/PLA (Participatory Rural Appraisal/Participatory Learning and Action) practice comes before theory. There are some principles of practice which Chambers describes – methods; behaviour and attitudes; and sharing – which include some very visible and tangible 'tools', but these need to be crafted for the particular situation and tasks to hand. Victor

Friedman and Tim Rogers describe in Chapter 17 the approach of action science and again, while they outline initially five principles of this approach, they go on to demonstrate how these principles have been adapted by different people for application in different settings.

Action research is often described, following Lewin, as a 'spiral of steps, each of which is composed of a circle of planning, action, and fact-finding about the result of the action' (Lewin, 1946/1948: 206) or more simply as a cycle of plan–act–review. As Senge and his colleagues argue (Senge et al., 2005), this kind of formulation of learning through cycles of action and reflection, which they attribute originally to John Dewey, can so easily become superficial and unable to 'generate the depth of understanding and commitment that is required to generate change in truly demanding circumstances' (Senge et al., 2005: 87) when genuine invention in the face of novelty is required of us. We deepen our cycle of action and reflection through the kind of attention that Senge et al. refer to as 'presence' or Marshall and Reason (2006) have described as 'taking an attitude of inquiry'.

So we wish to emphasize again that action research is full of choices, and the key to quality is bringing these choices to awareness and understanding the consequences of those choices. It is straightforward to write, as do Heron and Reason, that in co-operative inquiry 'all participants work together in an inquiry group as co-researchers and as co-subjects', but how this fundamental idea is carried out is a matter of skilled practice which the description can barely hint at. So it is important to read these descriptions of practices alongside the descriptions of projects in the **Exemplars** section, and understand the kinds of skills needed to facilitate them in **Skills.**

What happens in many of the action research projects that we are familiar with is that we beg, borrow and steal from different approaches to create a form for that situation. In discussions of a major research project, someone might say, for example, 'if we started off with some kind of learning history approach, we would identify some of the key issues and build relationships with our partners. This could then lead to co-operative inquiries groups that would explore particular issues in more detail. And then maybe further along the road we could use some form of dialogue conference design to broaden the spread of the inquiry'.

But nevertheless, the individual practices must also be understood and appreciated in their own right as forms of practice that emphasize important principles of action research. One might decide, for example in the context of a PhD dissertation, to work primarily within the disciplines of action science or appreciative inquiry, or PRA, or co-operative inquiry, and demonstrate the depth of learning that can come from foregrounding one approach. Nevertheless, the way in which these practices unfold in practice will entail choices, which always have an emergent quality to them. My advice (Peter) to students describing their methodology for a PhD dissertation is to consider what they need to say at four levels: the overall personal/political/epistemological stance they are taking; the practices and approaches that have informed their approach; how they designed these into an approach which suited

their particular inquiry circumstances; what actually happened in practice. (Examples of action research theses conducted under this guidance can be found at www.bath.ac.uk/carpp/these.htm)

The first eight chapters in this section describe particular practices: Action Science, Action Inquiry, Clinical Inquiry, Appreciative Inquiry, PRA/PLA, Action Learning, Citizen's Jury, and Learning History. They are all written by originators or leading advocates of these approaches and thus demonstrate what action research may look like when seen through the eyes of this particular perspective. Heron and Reason then give a particular 'take' on the practice of co-operative inquiry by exploring in some detail the 'extended epistemology on which it is based' (this chapter complements their desciption of co-operative inquiry in Heron and Reason, 2001/2006); we should note in passing that several other chapters develop the idea of presentational knowing in practices (notably Chapters 20, 27, 30, 34, 35, 39, 43).

We then turn to some wider considerations of action research practice. Ian Hughes considers some of the ways in which action research has been applied in healthcare. Ann Martin picks up the theme of scale and develops her contribution in the first edition (Martin, 2001/2006) to explore the practices of action research on a large scale.

Michelle Fine and Maria Torre draw on their experience with participatory research to consider how to speak out. While Gustavsen and his colleagues argue that scale is approached through widening the network of inquiry, Fine and Torre ask what kind of voice may be needed to communicate to different audiences in order to make a political impact from participatory research. Sonia Ospina and her colleagues consider how it is possible to integrate action research practices with qualitative research working in the context of a major research grant and a prestigious US university where strong opinions are held about the legitimacy of action research. This chapter may be read in counterpoint to Levin and Greenwood's critique of the university as a home for action research (Chapter 14).

Finally, we should confess to the omissions. Robert Chambers in particular kept urging us not to exclude a whole range of approaches with which we were quite unfamiliar some of which he refers to in his chapter. We are aware that the tradition of teacher research is not included here although it has been well covered in other volumes (McNiff and Whitehead, 2002).

REFERENCES

Heron, J. and Reason, P. (2001/2006) 'The practice of co-operative-inquiry: research "with" rather than "on" people', in P. Reason and H. Bradbury (eds), *Handbook of Action Research: Participative Inquiry and Practice*. London: Sage. pp. 179–88. Also in P. Reason and H. Bradbury *Handbook of Action Research*: *Concise Paperback Edition*. London: Sage. pp. 131–43.

Lewin, K. (1946/1948) 'Action research and minority problems', in G.W. Lewin (ed.), *Resolving Social Conflicts*. New York: Harper & Row. pp. 201–16.

McNiff, J. and Whitehead, J. (2002) *Action Research: Principles and Practice, 2nd edn*. London: Routledge.

Marshall, J. and Reason, P. (2006) 'Keynote address: taking an attitude of inquiry.' Paper presented at the ALARPM 7th & PAR 11th World Congress, Groningen, The Netherlands, 22 August.

Martin, A.W. (2001/2006) 'Large-group processes as action research', in P. Reason and H. Bradbury (eds), *Handbook of Action Research: Participative Inquiry and Practice*. London: Sage. pp. 200–8. Also in P. Reason and H. Bradbury *Handbook of Action Research*: *Concise Paperback Edition*. London: Sage. pp. 166–75

Senge, P.M., Scharmer, C.O., Jaworski, J. and Flowers, B.S. (2005) *Presence: Exploring Profound Change in People, Organizations and Society*. London: Nicholas Brealey.

16

Action Inquiry: Interweaving Multiple Qualities of Attention for Timely Action

William R. Torbert and Steven S. Taylor

This chapter describes action inquiry, a kind of social science that can generate timely action. First, action inquiry studies not just the past, but also the present and future. Second, it is a form of research that is conducted simultaneously on oneself, the first-person action inquirer, on the second-person relationships in which one engages, and on the third-person institutions of which one is an observant participant. Third, it generates not just single-loop feedback that incrementally improves a stock of knowledge, but also double- and triple-loop transformations of structure, culture, and consciousness that influence ongoing interaction. The chapter describes how first-person action inquiry in the present explores four distinct but interweaving 'territories of experience,' which sometimes feel mutually aligned and sometimes dissonant. It further describes how second-person action inquiry on the emergent future crafts four distinct but interweaving 'parts of speech' to generate increasing shared vision and inquiring collaborative practice. It then offers and analyzes a few minutes of first- and second-person collaborative inquiry to illustrate these ideas. The chapter closes by introducing a third-person generalizable theory, and some of the quantitative empirical evidence supporting it, that describes how individuals, organizations, and science itself can transform to the point of practicing ongoing timely inquiry and action.

Developmental action inquiry (Fisher and Torbert, 1995; Torbert, 1976, 1987, 1991; Torbert et al., 2004) offers both a holistic approach and specific analytic tools to combine inquiry and action in the accomplishing of specific objectives, in the testing of one's data, interpretations, and assumptions, and in seeking to live one's life most fruitfully, valuably, and justly with others.

Developmental action inquiry is a process for searching, not just to distinguish between valid and illusory patterns in data from the past, but also for patterns and incongruities between strategy and performance in the present, as well as among possible visions, strategies, and specific goals for the future (Ogilvy, 2002; Senge et al., 2004; Torbert, 2000b, 2002). Also, developmental action inquiry studies not just things and practices outside the inquirer (third-person objects and practices), but also the inquirer's own changing practices, ways of thinking, and quality of attention (first-person research on 'my'-self), as well the interactions, norms, governance, and mission of the specific persons and groups with whom one is working or playing (second-person research on 'our' commun[ication]al process) (Chandler and Torbert, 2003).

Just as third-person quantitative and qualitative research seek validity through triangulating among different third-person methods, so does the developmental action inquiry approach offer the opportunity for triangulation among first-person subjective research methods (Ellis and Bochner, 2000; Foldy, 2005), second-person intersubjective research methods (Heron, 1996; Reason, 1994), and third-person objective research methods (McGuire et al., 2007). The goal is to inquire into and transform personal and social experiences *in a timely way* within three domains: the domain of objective, instrumental results; the domain of intersubjective ethical and political interactions; and the domain of subjective aesthetic and spiritual disciplines (Wilber, 1998). *The encompassing aims in action inquiry are to increase one's own and others' capacity to appreciate and cultivate transformation, integrity, mutuality, justice, and sustainability for ourselves, for our groups, and for our institutions.*

This type of experiential/empirical triangulation is accomplished, not primarily by adding to a third-person body of consensual knowledge through articles like this (although such work can play a part), but rather more by the growing capacity of the acting system (whether person, team, or nation) to experience and be in a productive and mutually emancipatory dialogue with difference, diversity, and incongruity in each event, *as is timely*. This occurs, in turn, through inquiry-based first- and second-person actions in the present and for the emerging future (as will be illustrated below) that treat ongoing experience at any given time as either harmoniously consonant, or as dissonant in one way or another, leading to adjustments. In the frequent case of experienced dissonance, there are four choices: 1) deny or externalize the dissonance (by far our most common minute-to-minute, day-to-day procedure as individuals, communities, and institutions); 2) to treat the dissonance as *single-loop feedback* (leading to a change in *practice* if the intended result is not being achieved); or 3) *double-loop feedback* (leading to a transformation of *strategy*); or 4) *triple-loop feedback* (leading to a change in quality of *attention*). (Complexity theory offers a different, but not incompatible, theoretical language for describing emergently complexifying (and de-complexifying) self-organizing *in medias res* by children; but the complexity theory approach offers little as yet in the way of first- and second-person tools for intentional adult action inquiry; Fischer and Bidell, 2006.)

In this chapter we describe and then illustrate the theory and practice of action inquiry. We start with first-person action inquiry in the moment and the associated analytic tool, the four 'territories of experience'. We then move onto second-person action inquiry and the associated analytic tool, the four 'parts of speech'. Next, we include an illustration of interweaving first- and second-person action inquiry. From there, we move to third-person action inquiry and two of the associated analytic tools, developmental theory and the Leadership Development Profile. Finally, we offer an example of a decade-long research project that interweaves first-, second-, and third-person in the service of organizational transformations, showing quantitatively how strong the association is between the intensity of the first- and second-person action inquiry processes in an organization and the likelihood that the organization in fact transforms as intended. Throughout, we must try to remember that these are but a very few illustrations of 81 possible kinds of research (3×3×3×3 [first-, second-, and/or third-person research voice, studying first-, second, or third-person practice, in the past, present, or future, with single-, double-, or triple-loop feedback/learning]).

FIRST-PERSON ACTION INQUIRY IN THE MOMENT

Let us now explore a closer view of first-person research by examining a generally quite unfamiliar form of research (even though it has existed as a form of spiritual practice in a great many cultural traditions): namely, practicing triple-loop meditation-in-action (Trungpa, 1970), or consciously acting in a way that simultaneously inquires into the current awareness-mind-body-situation interaction. This requires deliberate reflection and awareness expansion while engaged in outer action (Schön, 1983), a seemingly simple idea (but definitely a difficult practice) that warrants a brief digression. The dominant technical-rational mode of thought that characterizes the late 20th and early 21st century is based in a separation of mind and body that implies a separation of action and inquiry. We analyze and plan and then, based on that analysis, we act. We then analyze the results of the action and prepare to act again. This is the cycle at the heart both of most action research and most formal, academic inquiry (e.g. plan scientific experiment, collect data that tests hypotheses in single-loop fashion, etc.).

But action inquiry does not start from this separation of analysis and action, this separation of mind and body, this linear approach to inquiry. That is not to say that such off-line reflection is not useful, but simply that action inquiry is based in a holistic understanding that also tries to act and inquire *at the same time*. In this sense it is philosophically based in a craft, design, or artistic process tradition that generates productivity, transformation, and emancipation (Argyris et al., 1985; Flyvbjerg, 2001; Schön, 1983), rather than in a modern technical-rational tradition that generates mechanically or electrically caused enhancement of productivity. Like any craft or artistic process, action inquiry has tools and techniques. But just as painting is more than mastering the skills of composition, brush stroke techniques, and so on, action inquiry is fundamentally about the aesthetic whole of generating timely action, which is different from and not the sum of the techniques used to create that whole. Bearing this in mind, one tool or analytic technique for the practice of first-person research in the present moment is the effort to inquire into the four territories of first-person self-awareness as one acts.

Four territories of experience

The four 'territories of experience' described in Table 16.1 include: 1) *the outside world*, 2) *one's own sensed behavior and feeling*, 3) the realm of *thought*, and 4) the realm of *vision/attention/intention* (Torbert, 1972; Torbert et al., 2004). These four territories of experience are not mere analytic categories, but rather are all phenomenologically accessible territories of experience that exist simultaneously and continuously (see discussion of how each of us in our own first-person research can test this fundamental claim in Torbert, 1991: ch. 13), and that can potentially yield data and feelings of fit (*consonance*) or of incongruity (*dissonance*) as they become known to an acting system (through its *assonance*) in real time. Usually, in daily life, we take our attention and our categories of thought for granted, and apply them to judging what actions to take and what observations to make of the outside world. In action inquiry, we attempt to question all these taken-for-granted processes:

Table 16.1   *Four territories of experience of an individual person*

1) the outside world	objectified, discrete, *interval* units, of which 'I' am actively aware when 'I' notice the color and manyness of what 'I' see or the support the outside world is giving me through the soles of my feet (focused attention)
2) one's own sensed behavior and feeling	processual, *ordinal* rhythms in passing time, of which 'I' am actively aware when I feel what I am touching from the inside, or when I listen to the in-and-out of my breathing or the rhythms and tones of my own speaking (subsidiary, sensual awareness)
3) the realm of thought	eternal *nominal* distinctions and interrelations, of which I can be actively aware if my attention 'follows' my thought, if I am not just thinking, but 'mindful' that I am thinking (witnessing awareness)
4) vision/attention/intention	the kind of *noumenal* vision/attention/intention that can simultaneously interpenetrate the other three territories and experience incongruities or harmonies among them

Into which territories am I listening now? What am I hearing from the world beyond me? Am I acting from clear intent? Am I speaking in a language, tone, and rhythm that permits us to move toward shared intent and alignment? Am I discovering signs of our alignment or lack of alignment in your responses?

First efforts toward a triple-loop, first-person 'super-vision' that interpenetrates and embraces the other three territories of experience typically generate paralyzing self-consciousness of the teenage sort and are quickly forgotten. How to cultivate an ongoing, non-judgmental first-person awareness of how we are acting in the larger world is key to development, both personally and organizationally, and is itself a first-person inquiry practice for a lifetime. To listen to others as they speak, rather than just internally planning our own next comment, is hard (that is why we interrupt one another so often). To listen to 'myself' and the entire situation as 'I' speak is still harder. If we wish to become serious about such skills, we will seek the help of second-person communities and third-person traditions dedicated to such spiritual/aesthetic/educational research/practice methods. Examples of third-person traditions that through second-person tutelage introduce individuals to profound forms of first-person research range widely, from the Ignatian Spiritual Exercises of the Jesuits (Coghlan, 2005) to the Hindu Ramakrishna's disciples (Kripal, 1995), to the Buddhist lineage of Trungpa (1970), etc. Following the next section, a short 'case' will provide a more concrete sense of both the first- and second-person aspects of the four territories of experience.

SECOND-PERSON ACTION INQUIRY IN THE EMERGING-FUTURE

Now let us explore how second-person conversation during a team meeting or at a family dinner may be more or less action-inquiry-oriented depending on its degree of openness to inquiry into its own status as an ongoing activity. Speaking is the primary and most influential medium of action in the human universe – in business and politics, in school and in science, among parents and children, and between lovers. Does a given conversation go on without testing its own efficacy until it is interrupted by accident (e.g. the phone ringing), or by pre-arrangement (e.g. class time is over), or by someone's exit? Or is there regular inquiry about whether the participants understand one another's comments (typically generating single-loop changes in what one says to get the point across)? Is there also occasional double-loop inquiry about whether other conversational strategies may improve the creativity of the conversation? Is there ever triple-loop inquiry into the basic premises of the conversation and the possibility of reframing them?

Disciplined practice in recognizing and generating four parts of speech – framing, advocating, illustrating, and inquiring – roughly corresponding with the four territories of experience, has been found to transform practitioners' efficacy in some 30 years' experience of various communities of action inquirers (e.g. Argyris and Schön, 1974; Reason, 1994; Rudolph et al., 2001/2006; Torbert, 1976, 2000b). 'Inquiring' finds out about the outside world territory of experience. 'Illustrating' tells stories about actions. 'Advocating' mentally maps the world. And 'framing' suggests how the conversants may focus their attention overall amidst the current dilemma/opportunity/ activity. Table 16.2 offers fuller definitions and examples of the four parts of speech. In general, disciplined action inquirers find that they become increasingly effective in their speaking when they increasingly balance and integrate the four 'parts of speech' in seeking to assess and artistically give voice to the unique confluence of patterns in each current situation. You can test these claims in your own conversational experiments, especially if you can get a small group of two or three colleagues or friends to meet for an evening once a month just to practice ways of speaking in difficult conversations (McGuire et al., in press; Rudolph et al., 2001/2006).

Obviously, as we are treating them here, the four parts of speech are primarily kinds of moves or practices. But the 'framing' and 'reframing' part of speech alerts us to the possibility of changing 'the name of the game' – of redesigning norms, myths, and even the very mission of the conversation-relationship-project – of going beyond single-loop change to double- and triple-loop change.

AN EXAMPLE OF FIRST- AND SECOND-PERSON ACTION INQUIRY

The following illustration of attending to, and speaking from, the four territories of experience comes from a participant's journal during a week-long conference on 'Integral Epistemology' at the Esalen Institute in December 2005. It describes, from a first-person perspective, a few moments of first-person research during an intense conversation among some 20 senior academics and spiritual practitioners – the conversation itself an example of second-person research. The topic of that conversation was admittedly 'rarefied': whether a shared 'integral epistemology' about the nature-body-mind-attention continuum can be articulated. But the interest here is to trace, as one reads, the writer's attempt to evoke how his attention moves among the four territories of experience seeking to discover timely spoken action. Then, too, the four territories of experience can be thought of as just such an attempt to articulate the nature-body-mind-attention continuum. We suggest reading the following journal entry twice, the first time reading just the italicized journal, the second time pausing to review our parenthetical, analytic comments which are not italicized):

Richard Baker Roshi, co-founder in 1966 of the Tassajara Zen Mountain Center and founder in 1972 of the Green Gulch Zen Practice Community, continues in 2005 to presence as a powerfully-built, bushy-black-eyebrowed tower of silence and assertion, at least as I observed him during our four days together at the 'Integral Epistemology' workshop at the Esalen Institute.

Esalen, with its farm, its perfectly manicured organic gardens, its experimental elementary school, its daily sunset over the Pacific, its nude baths, its Tantric atmosphere of unreservedly friendly free choice, and its fine master classes in the various disciplines of the nature-body-feeling-mind continuum, strikes me as a contemporary Narnia – even in the way that it clings invisibly to Big Sur's plunging coastline, beneath the cement columns of one of Rt. 1's many graceful bridges on the winding stretch between St. Luis Obispo and Monterrey.

I began my acquaintance with Roshi Richard deeply suspicious of him because of his, as it seemed to me, unconcealed authoritative power mixed with his shadowy past, when he was accused, not without evidence, of messing with money and women in the community (Note author's haphazard <u>thoughts</u> on reports of the Roshi's <u>past actions in the outside world</u>, apparently clouded by pre-judgment and unclear <u>intention</u>). *As the conference proceeded, I could*

Table 16.2   *Four parts of speech (adapted from Tarbert et al., 2004)*

Framing   refers to explicitly stating what the purpose is for the present occasion, what the dilemma is that you are trying to resolve, what assumptions you think are shared or not shared (but need to be tested out loud to be sure). This is the element of speaking most often missing from conversations and meetings. The leader or initiator assumes the others know and share the overall objective. Explicit framing (or reframing, if the conversation appears off-track) is useful precisely because the assumption of a shared frame is frequently untrue. When people have to guess at the frame, they frequently guess wrong and they often impute negative, manipulative motives ('What's he getting at?').

For example, instead of starting out right away with the first item of the meeting, the leader can provide and test an explicit frame: 'We're about halfway through to our final deadline and we've gathered a lot of information and shared different approaches, but we haven't yet made a single decision. To me, the most important thing we can do today is agree on something … make at least one decision we can feel good about. I think XYZ is our best chance, so I want to start with that. Do you all agree with this assessment, or do you have other candidates for what it's most important to do today?'

Advocating   refers to explicitly asserting an option, perception, feeling, or strategy for action in relatively abstract terms (e.g., 'We've got to get shipments out faster'). Some people speak almost entirely in terms of advocacy; others rarely advocate at all. Either extreme – only advocating or never advocating – is likely to be relatively ineffective. For example, 'Do you have an extra pen?' is not an explicit advocacy, but an inquiry. The person you are asking may truthfully say, 'No' and turn away. On the other hand, if you say 'I need a pen (advocacy). Do you have an extra one (inquiry)?' the other is more likely to say something like, 'No, but there's a whole box in the secretary's office.'

The most difficult type of advocacy for most people to make effectively is an advocacy about how we feel – especially how we feel about what is occurring right now. This is difficult partly because we ourselves are often only partially aware of how we feel; also, we are reluctant to become vulnerable; furthermore, social norms against generating potential embarrassment can make current feelings seem undiscussable. For all these reasons, feelings usually enter conversations only if the relationship is close and risk is low, in which case there is little likelihood of receiving corrective feedback. The other time when feelings enter conversations is when they have become so strong that they burst in, and then they are likely to be offered in a way that harshly evaluates others ('Damn it, will you loudmouths shut up!'). This way of advocating feelings is usually very ineffective, however, because it invites defensiveness. By contrast, a vulnerable description is more likely to invite honest sharing by others ('I'm feeling frustrated and shut out by the machine-gun pace of this conversation and I don't see it getting us to agreement. Does anyone else feel this way?').

Illustrating   involves telling a bit of a concrete story that puts meat on the bones of the advocacy and thereby orients and motivates others more clearly. Example: 'We've got to get shipments out faster [advocacy]. Jake Tarn, our biggest client, has got a rush order of his own, and he needs our parts before the end of the week [illustration].' The illustration suggests an entirely different mission and strategy than might have been inferred from the advocacy alone.

You may be convinced that your advocacy contains one and only one implication for action, and that your subordinate or peer is at fault for misunderstanding. But in this case, it is your conviction that is a colossal metaphysical mistake. Implications are by their very nature inexhaustible. There is never one and only one implication or interpretation of an action. That is why it is so important to be explicit about each of the four parts of speech and to interweave them sequentially, if we wish to increase our reliability in achieving shared purposes.

Inquiring   obviously involves questioning others, in order to learn something from them. In principle, the simplest thing in the world; in practice, one of the most difficult things in the world to do effectively. Why? One reason is that we often inquire rhetorically, as we just did. We don't give the other the opportunity to respond; or we suggest by our tone that we don't really want a TRUE answer. 'How are you?' we say dozens of times each day, not really wanting to know. 'You agree, don't you?' we say, making it clear what answer we want. A second reason why it is difficult to inquire effectively is that an inquiry is much less likely to be effective if it is not preceded by framing, advocacy, and illustration. Naked inquiry often causes the other to wonder what frame, advocacy, and illustration are implied and to respond carefully and defensively.

If we are inquiring about an advocacy we are making, the trick is to encourage the other to *disconfirm* our assumptions if that is how he or she truly feels. In this way, if the other confirms us, we can be confident the confirmation means something, and if not, then we see that the task ahead is to reach an agreement.

---

see that, even when Richard disclosed personal stories in friendly openness, I interpreted them as self-aggrandizing (note a slight disentanglement of <u>thoughts</u> from outer <u>world behavior</u>, now recognized as two different territories of experience). *His style of rhetorical certainty certainly seemed to grate with the overt humility of my action inquiry style. (Of course, as I listened, I could* hear also how my own issues about marriage and money and the exercise of power heightened my sensitivities to Richard's past, not to mention my possible sense of competitiveness with a man of about the same age and length of awareness-practice [Further disentangling of thoughts from intentions, with inquiry into conflicting intentions]).

Our joint inquiry into the question, 'How do we know what we know about the nature-body-mind-attention/intention continuum?' had been convened by Esalen's Aslan, founder Michael Murphy, who looks a good 15 or 20 years younger than his actual age of about 75 and acts a good 30–40 years younger. Jay Ogilvy, one of the founding futurists of Global Business Network, and Jeff Kripal, Rice University's Chair of Religious Studies, facilitated a group of 20 who ranged from young art historian, Marcia Brennan (Modernism's Masculine Subjects 2001, Painting Gender, Constructing Theory 2004), to Sam Harris (author of the currently best-selling The End of Faith: Religion, Terror, and the Future of Reason 2005), and to Richard Shweder (a University of Chicago Distinguished Professor and cultural anthropologist).

For me, one critical, potentially-transformational moment in our joint inquiry came at mid-week. Roshi Richard had remarked on how the attention constitutes event-spaces as activities, such as the living room we 20 were then sitting in – with some of us attuned to the pink sunset glinting on the Pacific (the outer world territory), others attuned to the hills and valleys of our conversation (our own behaviors territory), and still others attuned to the framed photographs around the room, which showed it as a site for other very different activities at other times (body work, Japanese calligraphy, and so forth). He added that holding an intent in the present (attentional territory of experience) to constitute this or that kind of event-space can influence the emergent future.

This remark reminded me of an experience of a slightly different sort that I often have when planning a future event. I have learned that my earliest inclinations to plan the detailed agenda for an event are often driven by anxiety and produce only uncreative lists of issues to be addressed. Thus, I've learned to relax and not-take that first bait, but instead to let the question go until it returns again and again (entering own private territory of thought and remembering the double-loop experience of learning a new strategy for future planning). A time comes when the mind spontaneously produces a vision/fantasy of the deep-purpose-of-the-event-realizing-itself. Often, I have thereafter treated this image as the unifying creative thread with which to stitch the entire event-cloth, including the general rhythms of others' creative participation and influence. But in recent years, rather than grabbing such an event-pearl, I have sometimes continued with the presencing practice of

listening into the undifferentiated nature-body-mind-attention continuum, until a waterfall-like cascade of creative ideas and intuitions related to the event begins (Note another instance of first-person double-loop learning of a new future planning process which seems to introduce a first-person triple-loop learning process [the 'water-fall-like cascade']). From this cascade, I eventually choose various droplets to aid my listening, interpreting, and acting within the event-time itself.

NOW suddenly seems like a moment to speak, to help Richard disclose more of his approach, to encourage others to share any experiences they have of working with the emergent future, and to help me shape the next-day-forthcoming space/time-event when my work will become the focus of conversation. I share a taste of my experience (illustrating his idea) with Richard and the group, and I ask Richard, 'Do you have such experiences, or different ones, or how do you interpret mine?' (inquiring into others' thoughts). He shoots me a sideways glance, creates a brief pause by rearranging his legs (a non-verbal re-framing that draws the attention to him), and says, 'I try to pause til the last moment ... and then discover which way I move without pre-meditation (advocating his idea) – like the old saying, 'When you come to a fork in the road ... take it!' (illustrating his idea). The brevity and unfathomable surprise of this riposte draws a hearty round of laughter from the group.

I pause too, accepting the response silently, allowing the conversational rhythm of successive queries by others and responses by him to continue. Inside, however, I feel emotionally split between my continuing commitment to listening to the conversation and a sense of disappointment (dissonance within territory of own feelings/behavior). I feel he and I and we have missed an opportunity for further enlightenment (a sense of incongruity between the territory of feelings/behavior and the territory of intention): for I have been speaking of this progressive skill in empty-mind myself, intending to invite more than a well-rehearsed quip and a return to our prior speech-rhythms in response. Would it have made a difference if I had inquired of the rest of the group rather than Richard? Probably. (Single-loop feedback to self re: potentially more effective behavior.)

On the other hand, I discover over the next days that Baker Roshi's 'old saying' repeatedly reverberates within my present attention (triple-loop feedback) – such as the moment before 'my' session, when the scholar of Mircea Eliade, who is scheduled to comment on my article after me, suddenly proposes he go first: I pause imperceptibly at this fork, and then we reverse the planned structure on the spot, putting me more dramatically than before in the posture of first-person action inquiry in the present. Thank you, Baker Roshi, for transmitting, not so much an insight as a practice.

THIRD-PERSON INQUIRY AND DEVELOPMENTAL THEORY

Practicing first-person action inquiry in the moment and second-person inquiry for the emergent future may be complemented and sharpened by increasing familiarity with a broadly generalizable third-person developmental theory, applicable analogically to persons, to organizations, and to types of science, and testable through first-, second-, and third-person research methods (Torbert, 1991; Torbert et al., 2004). This developmental theory can both describe behavioral structures in the past and prescribe liberating structures-disciplines-designs for the future, whether we are engaged in the temporal structuring of a single meeting, a several-month project, a marriage of many years, one's entire career, or an inter-generational institution.

PERSONAL, INTERPERSONAL, AND ORGANIZATIONAL DEVELOPMENTAL ACTION-LOGICS

Table 16.3 offers a very brief overview of individual and organizational developmental action-logics, as these have been described in much greater detail elsewhere (Kegan, 1982, 1994; Torbert, 1976, 1987; Torbert et al., 2004; Wilber, 1999). An action-logic or theory-in-use is an internally coherent system of beliefs that we may not be fully aware of ourselves, but that directly shapes our actions and is difficult to transform (Argyris and Schön, 1974; Bachrach et al., 2000; Wilber, 1999). Each developmental action-logic can be reliably measured and has been found to be highly correlated with specific business actions and results (Merron et al., 1987; Rooke and Torbert, 1998, 2005). Here, we highlight only a few key points about the overall theory.

First, each later personal and organizational action-logic includes all the options and capacities of the earlier action-logics, plus new ones, gradually self-organizing to

the point of ongoing action and inquiry that spans the four territories of experience. In other words, the theory outlines the successive design-for-practice principles that any person or social system can potentially learn. As Table 16.3 suggests, a person gains some sense of control over the outside world to get what one wants in the very short-term at the Opportunist action-logic. Next, during the sometimes painful evolution to the Diplomat action-logic, one gains some sense of control over one's own behavior to meet one's routine weekly and monthly obligations, as well as to act within the norms of one's valued friendship circles. Then, if one makes the journey to the Expert action-logic, through engaging with craft disciplines, one gains some control over the world of thought and of the time horizons (3–18 months) necessary to complete projects. A great victory of the Achiever action-logic is that it coordinates the prior three action-logics and welcomes single-loop feedback, reliably permitting the person or team to plan, perform, test outcomes, and change performance to reach a goal. A further victory, won through transformation to the Individualist and Strategist action-logics, is an opening to double-loop feedback whereby the person's or organization's whole action-logic may transform, if the current strategic assumptions are not working (Merron et al., 1987; Fisher and Torbert, 1991). Transformation to the Alchemist action-logic (Torbert, 1996), wherein the system treats each moment as a new inquiry about how to distribute its attention through the other three territories of experience, permits one to test and recalibrate on a moment-to-moment basis, through triple-loop feedback, whether one's own and others' sense of lifetime mission, strategies, actions, and outcomes are aligned.

Second, transformation to later action-logics cannot be caused simply by external forces, but rather require an interaction between initiatives by the transforming system and challenging/supporting conditions in the environment. Consequently, people and organizations do not necessarily develop to later action-logics. In

Table 16.3 *Parallels between personal and organizational stages of development (adapted from Torbert et al., 2004)*

Personal development	Organizational development	
Impulsive Impulses rule behavior	**Conception** Dreams about creating a new organization	multiple, distinctive impulses gradually resolve into characteristic approach [e.g., many fantasies into a particular dream for a new organization]
Opportunist Needs rule impulses	**Investments** Spiritual, social network, and financial investments	dominant task: gain power [e.g. bike riding skill, capital] to have desired effects on outside world
Diplomat Norms rule needs	**Incorporation** Products or services actually rendered	looking-glass self: understanding others' culture/ expectations and molding own actions to succeed in their [e.g. a marketable product] terms
Expert Craft logic rules norms	**Experiments** Alternative strategies and structures tested	intellectual mastery of outside-self systems such that action = experiments that generate new ways of doing business
Achiever System effectiveness rules craft logic	**Systematic productivity** Single structure/strategy institutionalized	pragmatic triangulation among plan/theory, operation/ implementation, and outcome/evaluation – single-loop feedback acted upon unsystematically but regularly
Individualist Reflexive awareness rules effectiveness	**Social network** Portfolio of distinctive organizational structures	experimental awareness that diverse assumptions may complement one another both for inquiry and for productivity
Strategist Self-amending principle rules reflexive awareness	**Collaborative inquiry** Self-amending structure matches dream/mission	self-conscious mission/philosophy, sense of time/place, invites conversation among multiple voices and reframing of boundaries – double-loop feedback occasionally acted upon
Alchemist Mutual process (interplay of principle/action) rules principle	**Foundational community** of inquiry Structure fails, spirit sustains wider community	life/science = a mind/matter, love/death/transformation praxis among others, cultivating interplay, reattunement and continual triple-loop feedback among purpose, strategy, practice, and outcomes
Ironist Intergenerational development rules mutual process	**Liberating disiciplines** Structures encourage productivity and transformational learning through manageable conflict and vulnerable power	

samples of highly educated managerial and professional adults in different institutions, almost all between 25 and 55 years old, adding up to a total of 4310 as measured by the well-validated Leadership Development Profile, we find 5 percent scored as Opportunists, 12 percent as Diplomats, 38 percent as Experts, 30 percent as Achievers, 10 percent as Individualists, 4 percent as Strategists, and 1 percent as Alchemists (Rooke and Torbert, 2005). (It should be noted that many persons operating primarily at early action-logics experience occasional later action-logic moments or temporary states. Indeed, recognizing and cultivating such states through first- and second-person research can contribute to developmental transformation; Torbert and Fisher, 1992.)

Third, the personal action-logics alternate between those that are more agency-focused (Opportunist, Expert, Individualist) and those that are more relationally-focused (Diplomat, Achiever, Strategist). Likewise, the organizational action-logics alternate between those that tend toward centralization (Incorporation, Systematic Productivity, Collaborative Inquiry) and those that tend toward de-centralization (Investments, Experiments, Social Network). In the case of both individuals and organizations, the tension of these opposites declines at the later action-logics because those action-logics are increasingly win-win, both/and, paradox-welcoming, difference-friendly, transformational-not-static action-logics.

A fourth key quality of developmental theory is that the early action-logics up through the Achiever/Systematic Productivity action-logic do not recognize themselves as assumed and transformable frames around activity and thought, but rather treat their (unrecognized) assumptions as the very bedrock of reality (Torbert, 1991). Thus, these early action-logics assume everyone shares the same 'reality' and that significant deviations from one's own judgment represent lack of proper training, incompetence, or evil. Consequently, the early action-logics treat power as fundamentally a matter of unilateral enforcement in favor of the familiar and against the strange, with some peripheral inquiry whereby the strange may occasionally be transformed into the familiar. By contrast, the empirically rarer later action-logics treat power and inquiry as equally fundamental and recognize that only forms of mutual, transformational power generate double-loop and triple-loop learning; unilateral power is powerless to do so.

LEADER ACTION-LOGIC AND ORGANIZATIONAL TRANSFORMATION

According to these theoretical distinctions among developmental action-logics, we would expect that organizational leaders and consultants who measure at the later action-logics (e.g. Strategist, Alchemist), and who are themselves open to double-loop, transformational learning, will be more likely to succeed in supporting individual, team, and organizationally transformative learning than leaders and consultants at the earlier action-logics. Several third-person empirical studies statistically support this prediction (Bushe and Gibbs, 1990; Foster and Torbert, 2005; Rooke and Torbert, 1998). Likewise, we would expect that organizations exhibiting later action-logic qualities (e.g. Collaborative Inquiry, Liberating Disciplines) would be more likely to support individual transformation among their members than organizations at earlier action-logics. Once again, several statistical studies support this prediction (Manners et al., 2004; Torbert, 1991, 1994; Torbert and Fisher, 1992).

One study employing many interweaving first-, second-, and third-person action research methods shows that CEOs' and lead consultants' developmental action-logics account for an unusually large 59 percent of the variance (significant beyond the .01 level) in whether or not the 10 diverse organizations have positively transformed their action-logics (as measured by three trained scorers working independently and achieving .9 reliability) (Torbert et al., 2004: 112ff, 221ff). To be more specific, seven of the ten organizations successfully transformed, including all five of the organizations guided by CEOs measured as Strategists. By contrast, of the five organizations guided by CEOs measured at pre-Strategist action-logics, only two transformed. At the same time, three of the four lead consultants were measured as Strategists and the fourth as an Alchemist. The Alchemist consultant was the lead consultant in the only two cases where pre-Strategist CEOs were associated with successful organizational transformation. Thus, this consultant can be considered qualitatively more successful than the Strategist consultants.

We suggest that this result (accounting for 59 percent of the variance) is so much stronger than is usual for purely third-person science because the independent variable itself (the third-person Leadership Development Profile score of a person's action-logic) concerns the relative capacity of an individual to interweave first-, second-, and third-person action inquiry and to cultivate transformation in self or others through single-, double-, and triple-loop learning. Thus, it becomes conceivable that interweaving first-, second-, and third-person research, theory, and practice in the social sciences may dramatically improve their capacity to explain variance.

A later count of types of action inquiry initiatives tried by each of the ten organizations during the study confirms that the higher the combined CEO/Lead-Consultant action-logic score the more types of action inquiry the organization tried. For example, all ten CEOs took the Leadership Development Profile and received feedback about their performance (*third-person research on first-person practice in the past*). Also, all ten organizations engaged in senior management strategic planning with consultative support (*second-person research on third-person practice in the future*). Nine of the ten organizations participated in a senior management team self-restructuring (*second-person research on second-person practice in the future*) (the exception, in this case, was the one organization that regressed to earlier action-logics).

Only the seven organizations that successfully transformed created: 1) enhanced leadership roles for all senior team members (moving from a primary focus on departmental or divisional leadership to become a company-wide executive team) (enhancing each member's *first-person research on first- and second-person practice for the future*); 2) regular feedback on each senior team member's leadership effectiveness (*second-person research on first-person practice in the past*); and 3) distributed and rotated distinct leadership responsibilities within the team (e.g. agenda-planning, meeting management, inter-meeting follow-through, etc. – *second-person research on second-person practice*).

Also, the CEO/Lead-Consultant combinations associated with successful organizational transformation were: 1) most active in seeking out competitive information on industry practices (*first-person research on third-person practice in the past*); 2) most active in leading industry-wide associations in influencing public policy (*second-person research on third-person practice for the future*); 3) most active in offering frequent feedback to, and welcoming it from, senior team members (*first-person research on second-person practice and second-person research on first-person practice, in the present*); and 4) in offering developmental mentoring to senior management team members (*first-person research on second-person practice for the future*).

In these brief and distant mentions of different possible types of first-, second-, and third-person, the reader can begin to imagine how these different action inquiry disciplines may reinforce one another and increasingly create a climate for voluntary, mutual transformational practice within an organization. Of course, the sample size of the reported research is small. As more practitioners adopt such interweaving research disciplines and measures, the sample size can grow.

CONCLUSION

Action inquiry brings together action and inquiry by using multiple qualities of attention to embrace the complexity of our world. By consciously working with the ideas of first-, second-, and third-person research; first-, second-, and third-person practices; research on past, present and future; paying attention to the four territories of experience and to single-, double-, and triple-loop feedback among them, the four parts of speech, and the developmental action logics of self, projects, and organizations – well it's overwhelming to write (and we might guess read) about it, let alone try to do in practice. Worthy, perhaps, of a lifetime of inquiry? The illustrations of first- and second-person action inquiry during the Esalen conference and of the first-, second-, and third-person action inquiry over many years with the ten organizations offer some grounding and possibility for beginning practice.

We close simply by suggesting that action inquiry is a practice and as such is as much a voluntary, subjective, aesthetic choice and a mutual, inter-subjective, ethical commitment as it is an intergenerationally-sustainable, objective, epistemological science. However briefly, we have tried to analytically describe the mechanics of different brush strokes, the science of colors, and the theory of balance, knowing full well that painting isn't merely a matter of mechanics and theory. However, it is useful to know these things if one is going to paint. Action inquiry suggests a more explicit awareness of one's own practice than a traditional romantic image of a painter does – perhaps an Escher-like awareness, not of hands drawing themselves, but of us enacting our lives among others. An all-encompassing practice, perhaps, but a practice nonetheless, with all that suggests of discipline, study, and evolving voices within oneself and within one's evolving communities of inquiry.

REFERENCES

Argyris, C. and Schön, D. (1974) *Theory in Practice: Increasing Professional Effectiveness*. San Francisco, CA: Jossey-Bass.

Argyris, C., Putnam, R. and Smith, D. (1985) *Action Science: Concepts, Methods, and Skills for Research and Intervention*. San Francisco, CA: Jossey-Bass.

Bacharach, S., Bamberger, P. and McKinney, V. (2000) 'Boundary management tactics and logics of action: the case of peer-support providers', *Administrative Science Quarterly*, 45: 704–36.

Bushe, G. and Gibbs, B. (1990) 'Predicting organization development consulting competence from the Myers-Briggs Type Indicator and stage of ego development', *Journal of Applied Behavioral Science*, 26: 505–38.

Chandler, D. and Torbert, W. (2003) 'Transforming inquiry and action: interweaving 27 flavors of action research', *Journal of Action Research'*, 1 (2): 133–52.

Coghlan, D. (2005) 'Ignatian spirituality as transformational social science', *Action Research*, 3 (1): 89–107.

Ellis, C. and Bochner, A. (2000) 'Autoethnography, personal narrative, reflexivity', in N. Denzin and Y. Lincoln (eds), *The Handbook of Qualitative Research*. Thousand Oaks, CA: Sage. pp. 733–68.

Fischer, K. and Bidell, T. (2006) 'Dynamic development of action, thought, and emotion', in W. Damon and R. Lerner (eds), *Theoretical Models of Human Development. Handbook of Child Psychology*, 6th edn, Vol. 1. New York: John Wiley. pp. 313–99.

Fisher, D. and Torbert, W. (1991) 'Transforming managerial practice: beyond the achiever stage', in R.W. Woodman and W. A. Pasmore (eds), *Research in Organization Change and Development, Vol. 5*. Greenwich, CT: JAI Press. pp. 143–73.

Fisher, D. and Torbert, W. (1995) *Personal and Organizational Transformations: the True Challenge of Continual Quality Improvement*. New York: McGraw-Hill.

Flyvbjerg, B. (2001) *Making Social Science Matter*. Cambridge: Cambridge University Press.

Foldy, E. (2005) 'Claiming a voice on race (and responses)', *Journal of Action Research*, 3 (1): 33–54.

Foster, P. and Torbert, W. (2005) 'Leading through positive deviance: a developmental action learning perspective on institutional change', in R. Giacalone, C. Jurkiewicz and C. Dunn (eds), *Positive Psychology in Business Ethics and Corporate Responsibility*. Greenwich, CT: Information Age Publishing. pp. 123–42.

Heron, J. (1996) *Cooperative Inquiry*. London: Sage.

Kegan, R. (1982) *The Evolving Self*. Cambridge, MA: Harvard University Press.

Kegan, R. (1994) *In Over Our Heads*. Cambridge, MA: Harvard University Press.

Kripal, J. (1995) *Kahli's Child*. Chicago, IL: University of Chicago Press.

McGuire, J., Palus, C. and Torbert, W. (2007) 'Toward interdependent organizing and researching', in A. Shani et al. (eds), *Handbook of Collaborative Management Research*. Thousand Oaks, CA: Sage.

Manners, J., Durkin, K. and Nesdale, A. (2004) 'Promoting advanced ego development among adults', *Journal of Adult Development*, 11 (1): 19–27.

Merron, K., Fisher, D. and Torbert, W. (1987) 'Meaning making and management action', *Group and Organizational Studies*, 12 (3): 274–86.

Ogilvy, J. (2002) *Creating Better Futures: Scenario Planning as a Tool for a Better Tomorrow*. Oxford: Oxford University Press.

Reason, P. (1994) *Participation in Human Inquiry.* London: Sage.

Rooke, D. and Torbert, W. (1998) 'Organizational transformation as a function of CEOs' developmental stage', *Organization Development Journal*, 16 (1): 11–28.

Rooke, D. and Torbert, W. (2005) 'Seven transformations of leadership', *Harvard Business Review* (April): 66–77.

Rudolph, J., Foldy, E. and Taylor, S. (2001/2006) 'Collaborative off-line reflection: a way to develop skill in action science and action inquiry', in P. Reason and H. Bradbury (eds), *Handbook of Action Research: Participative Inquiry and Practice.* London: Sage. pp. 405–412. Also in P. Reason and H. Bradbury *Handbook of Action Research: Concise Paperback Edition.* London: Sage. pp. 307–14.

Schön, D.A. (1983) *The Reflective Practitioner: How Professionals Think in Action.* New York: Basic Books.

Senge, P., Scharmer, C., Jaworski, J. and Flowers, B. (2004) *Presence: Human Purpose and the Field of the Future.* Cambridge, MA: SoL (Society for Organizational Learning).

Torbert, B. and Associates (2004) *Action Inquiry: the Secret of Timely and Transforming Leadership.* San Francisco, CA: Berrett-Koehler.

Torbert, W. (1972) *Learning from Experience: Toward Consciousness.* New York: Columbia University Press.

Torbert, W. (1976) *Creating a Community of Inquiry: Conflict, Collaboration, Transformation.* London: Wiley Interscience.

Torbert, W. (1987) *Managing the Corporate Dream: Restructuring for Long-term Success.* Homewood, IL: Dow Jones-Irwin.

Torbert, W.R. (1991) *The Power of Balance: Transforming Self, Society, and Scientific Inquiry.* Newbury Park, CA: Sage.

Torbert, W. (1994) 'Cultivating post-formal adult development: higher stages and contrasting interventions', in M. Miller and S. Cook-Greuter (eds), *Transcendence and Mature Thought in Adulthood: the Further Reaches of Adult Development.* Lanham, MD: Rowman & Littlefield. pp. 181–203.

Torbert, W. (1996) 'The "chaotic" action awareness of transformational leaders', *International Journal of Public Administration*, 19 (6): 911–39.

Torbert, W. (2000a) 'The challenge of creating a community of inquiry among scholar-consultants critiquing one another's theories-in-practice', in F. Sherman and W. Torbert (eds), *Transforming Social Inquiry, Transforming Social Action.* Boston, MA: Kluwer Academic Publishers. pp. 161–88.

Torbert, W. (2000b) 'Transforming social science: integrating quantitative, qualitative, and action research', in F. Sherman and W. Torbert (eds), *Transforming Social Inquiry, Transforming Social Action.* Boston, MA: Kluwer Academic Publishers. pp. 67–91.

Torbert, W. (2002) 'Learning to exercise timely action now in leading, loving, inquiring, and retiring.' www.2.bc.edu/~torbert.

Torbert, W. and Fisher, D. (1992) 'Autobiography as a catalyst for managerial and organizational development', *Management Education and Development Journal*, 23: 184–98.

Trungpa, C. (1970) *Meditation in Action.* Boston: Shambhala.

Wilber, K. (1998) *The Marriage of Sense and Soul: Integrating Science and Religion.* New York: Random House.

Wilber, K. (1999) *Integral Psychology.* Boston: Shambhala.

17

Action Science: Linking Causal Theory and Meaning Making in Action Research

Victor J. Friedman and Tim Rogers

Action science refers to a broad approach to social practice that links human meaning making with the discovery and shaping of the causal theories that create our social world. This chapter focuses on the practice of action science inspired by the theory of action approach developed by Chris Argyris and Donald Schön. It describes five main features of this approach: communities of practice, theories of action, framing, testing, and change/design. The chapter then describes five applications of action science – Action Design, Debriefing with Good Judgment, Learning from Success, Action Evaluation/C3, and Organizational Learning in Action. These applications reflect a number of innovations or changes as well as the diversity of the field. The chapter concludes by arguing that action science is not a distinct method, but rather a set of value-based conceptual and practical tools that can be integrated into and enhance many forms of action research.

The term 'action science', originally coined by William Torbert (1976), was used by Chris Argyris (1980) and Donald Schön (1983) to describe research capable of explaining phenomena, informing practice, and adhering to the rational aims of science, while avoiding the 'inner contradictions' characteristic of 'normal' science techniques in the social realm. Argyris was inspired by Lewin's (1948, 1951) approach to action research, which retained the causal and theoretical imperatives of the natural sciences but rejected the positivist goal of the methodological unity of the natural and social sciences (Argyris, 1997; Robinson, 1993). Schön was inspired by Dewey's (1938) pragmatist epistemology that viewed experimentation in science as simply a special case of human beings testing their conceptions in action (Argyris et al., 1985: 6). Both projects were largely abandoned for many years as the social sciences became consumed with imitating positivist, natural science methodologies (Argyris et al., 1985). They were revived by Argyris et al. (1985), who set forth in great detail the idea of action science, its philosophical foundations and differences and similarities between action and normal science methodologies. [For further exploration of the action science and related action inquiry traditions see Chapters 16 and 46.]

Action science is closely related to, but distinct from, the 'theory of action' approach to professional effectiveness (Argyris and Schön, 1974) and organizational learning (Argyris and Schön, 1978, 1996). These two terms have often been used interchangeably, even by Argyris and Schön (e.g. 1991), but we believe that there are good grounds for retaining the distinction. Action science refers to a broad approach to social practice that links human meaning making with the discovery and shaping of the causal theories that create our social world. The theory of action approach is one manifestation of an action science with a very specific conceptual framework. Action science, on the other hand, may manifest itself in conceptual frameworks as diverse as field theory (Lewin, 1951), theory of inquiry (Dewey, 1938), theory of action (Argyris and Schön, 1974), and even the field theory of Pierre Bourdieu (1998).

This chapter will focus on the practice of action science inspired by the theory of action approach (Argyris, 1980; Argyris et al., 1985; Argyris and Schön, 1974, 1978; Schön, 1983, 1987). We begin by describing some of the main features of that approach. We then describe five applications of action science that represent advances in the field. Finally, we discuss the implications of these advances for the evolution of action science.

WHAT IS ACTION SCIENCE?

In the first edition of *Handbook of Action Research*, I (Friedman) defined action science as a form of social practice that integrates both the production and use of knowledge for the purpose of promoting learning with and among individuals and systems whose work is characterized by uniqueness, uncertainty, instability, and conflict. I also identified four key features of this approach: creating communities of inquiry within communities of practice, building individual and collective theories of action, combining interpretation with 'rigorous' testing of these theories, and creating alternatives to the status quo and informing change in light of values that are freely chosen by social actors (Friedman, 2001/2006). Today we would vary these features slightly and add a fifth one: the use of 'frames' to characterize the meanings inherent in theories of action.

Communities of inquiry. From an action science perspective, communities of inquiry integrate certain processes and norms of mainstream science, such as theory building and testing (see below), into everyday life. The norms necessary for this process include making behavior and the reasoning behind it transparent and open to the scrutiny of others, suspending judgment and persisting in inquiry until a common understanding is reached, actively seeking information that might disconfirm one's beliefs, and openly admitting error when confronted with evidence. In order to foster such norms, Argyris and Schön (1974, 1978) proposed that individuals and groups adopt a set of values they called 'Model II': valid information, free and informed choice, and internal commitment to choice and monitoring its implementation. Just as generating valid knowledge in a scientific community requires agreement among independent investigators, a community of inquiry regards uncertainty, difference, and conflict as opportunities for generating new knowledge through a process of experimentation and deliberation that leads to intersubjective agreement (Argyris et al., 1985: 13).

Theories of action. The basic conceptual tool of action science inquiry is mental 'theories of action' (Argyris and Schön, 1974, 1978; Argyris et al., 1985) that guide our behavior and enable us to make sense of the behavior of others. Theories of action are causal propositions consisting of three simple components: in situation X, do Y, in order to achieve goal Z. They may also include the assumptions underlying this causal connection and the values underlying goals. Theories of action are like mental programs that enable us to manage overwhelming amounts of information and respond almost automatically, and usually effectively, in most situations. The behavior of groups, organizations, and communities can also be seen as guided by collective theories of action that take shape through the interaction of individual theories (Argyris and Schön, 1978).

Argyris and Schön (1974) distinguished between the 'espoused theories' that express our intentions or how we think we act and the 'theories-in-use' implicit in our actual behavior. They found that people are generally unaware of their theories-in-use and the gaps between them and their espoused theories. Argyris and Schön (1974, 1978, 1996) also observed striking similarities in the action strategies people use in the face of uncertainty, conflict, and psychological threat. They posited the existence of a deeper, universal theory-in-use driven by values of unilateral control, protection of self and others, and rationality (Argyris and Schön, 1974, 1978, 1996). This theory-in-use, which they called 'Model I', accounts for much individual and organizational ineffectiveness and lack of learning. In order to facilitate learning, they proposed an alternative theory of action based on the 'Model II' values described above.

Theories of action provide a very simple, but powerful, tool for getting beneath the surface of individual, group, and organizational behavior. They enable us to systematically analyze and document behavioral patterns and the reasoning behind them, in order to identify the causal connections that explain effectiveness or ineffectiveness. They can also be used to produce 'actionable knowledge'; that is, new causal theories for generating desired outcomes (Argyris, 1993: 2–3).

Framing. 'Framing' refers to the logic or sense implicit in theories of action (Argyris

et al., 1985). This concept stems from the assumption that human beings do not have direct, unmediated access to objective reality. Rather we *construct* images of reality (Friedman and Lipshitz, 1992) or 'mental models' (Senge, 1990) from the raw materials of sense perception. Frames reflect the tacit choices we make in this construction process: what should be attended to, what should be ignored, and how to organize these data into meaningful patterns (Schön, 1983).

Frames are powerful sense-making mechanisms. They name the problem at hand, determine what solutions make sense, and shape the actions to be taken. They lend internal rationality to our theories of action and a sense of order and certainty to the world around us. Although we impose frames on our perceived reality, we usually act as if our perceptions were objective reality itself. For this reason, we may cling to our frames even if they lead to actions that are counterproductive. On the other hand, because we impose these frames, we have the ability to change, or reframe, them, opening the way for more effective actions (Friedman and Lipshitz, 1992).

Action science focuses inquiry on the way we frame the task, other people, and ourselves in problematic situations. Skilled reflection means knowing how to both impose a frame on a situation while at the same time being sensitive to where it does not fit, especially when we are at an impasse. 'Reframing' involves changing the internal logic of a frame by either bringing new information to bear or by reinterpreting the facts of a situation, giving them a different meaning. It enables people to discover opportunities for problem-solving and productive action that were previously missed.

Testing. From an action science perspective, our actions are not only attempts to achieve goals, but also a tacit form of experimentation in which we test our theories of action (Schön et al., 1984). Indeed, one of the implications of framing is that we should regard what we 'know' as hypotheses about reality rather than as facts – no matter how certain we may feel. Action science inquiry makes this experimentation process explicit and open to conscious reflection for the purpose of learning. Thus, when people disagree, the way forward is to jointly uncover and test their frames (Schön and Rein, 1994).

Action science attempts to do this by integrating the descriptive, contextual-rich power of interpretive, hermeneutic inquiry with the rigorous testing of validity demanded by the positivist mainstream (Argyris et al., 1985: 54). Thus, action science testing involves producing the 'core features of science' – 'hard data, explicit inferences connecting data and theory, empirically disconfirmable propositions subject to public testing, and theory that organizes such propositions' (Argyris et al., 1985: 12).

From an action science perspective, 'hard' behavioral data is as 'directly observable' as possible, such as audio and video recordings, against which we test our perceptions and interpretations. If, for example, we experience someone as having 'attacked' us, an analysis of their actual words might reveal that they were actually making reasonable, fair, and constructive criticisms. The use of such data is believed to make it more likely that inquiry will generate valid information and learning. For this reason, action science inquiry will almost always favor using directly observable data over verbal recollections or open discussion of a situation.

Action science utilizes 'personal cases' that people write about their experience in dealing with difficult situations. These cases include an illustrative sample of the actions that the person took, usually in the form of a discussion, using a 'two-column' format. On the right-hand column, case writers record the words they said as well as the responses of others. On the left-hand column, they record the thoughts and feelings they had as this discussion was going on. The left-hand column provides extremely rich data for inquiry into underlying frames, goals, values, and assumptions as well as for discovering gaps or contradictions within and between our reasoning and action. These two-column cases are considered to be directly observable

data about reasoning and behavior from which people can infer their own theories-in-use (Argyris, 1982: 41–2).

Action science addresses the problem of multiple interpretations by requiring that participants in a community of inquiry, including researchers, make their own frames explicit and open to public (intersubjective) testing. An action science tool for guiding this process is the 'ladder of inference' (Argyris et al., 1985: 57). The ladder is a metaphor for the reality-constructing process that enables people to trace the mental steps, or inferences, that lead from the bottom of the ladder (concrete, directly observable data such as the exact words spoken or actions taken) to increasing levels of interpretation (e.g. frames and theory building).

When we find ourselves in a disagreement, we can 'go down the ladder' until we discover the point where our interpretations diverged and then inquire into what led to the divergence. We can ask ourselves how our interpretations are connected to the directly observable data. In the process we may discover considerable gaps between the observable data and the inferences that were drawn from the data. We may also discover that some of our inferences were unreasonable or that other inferences make more sense. We may also reveal assumptions of which they were unaware and, if tested, could change the meaning of the phenomena. Finally, we may seek additional data that could disconfirm one, or both, of the interpretations. This process cannot guarantee that observers will agree or arrive at the 'right' interpretation but it can help people see that some interpretations are more reasonable than others (Weick, 1979).

Another well-known action science conceptual tool for testing is balancing 'advocacy' with 'inquiry'. Advocacy means putting forth our views directly and trying to convince others of their validity. Inquiry means exploring the views of others and questioning our own views in order to understand them better. Balancing advocacy means having strong opinions but holding onto them lightly. In other words, we state our views forthrightly *and* invite others to challenge them. We genuinely try to understand and see the sense in the other person's view while being open to questioning the sense in our own. Thus, deeply *valuing* valid information (Model II) is important because we need to be strongly motivated to avoid becoming defensive and to remain open to sometimes painful and embarrassing information (Argyris, 1993: 284).

Change/Design. Action science views people as 'designers' of their behavior and their 'behavioral worlds' (Argyris and Schön, 1974, 1978; Argyris et al., 1985). This design process occurs as we enact our mental theories of action through our behavior and our interactions with others. In doing so, we project our mental frames onto the external world, shaping relationships and the contexts in which we live. We are usually unaware of this design process and the outcomes are rarely what we intend, both because of our own limitations and the ways in which our theories interact with those of others. As a result, we often regard our behavioral world as an objective reality that is imposed upon us rather than as products of our design.

The objective of action science inquiry is to help us become more conscious designers so that we can shape our individual reasoning and behavior, as well as our behavioral worlds, and reconcile them with our intentions. It aims at making individual and collective theories-in-use explicit so that they can be critically examined and consciously changed. The theory of action concept provides a framework for systematic inquiry into the situation, goals, action strategies, assumptions, and values – and the links between them. It also provides a means for tracing the links between individual and collective theories-in-use, helping us discover our own causal responsibility for our behavioral worlds.

Action science takes a particular interest in the more intractable dilemmas and conflicts faced by organizations and society (Schön and Rein, 1994). It explicitly aims at helping people 'transform their world' by envisioning new possibilities and putting them into practice (Argyris et al., 1985: 71). One of the most widely cited, but often misunderstood, action science concepts is the distinction between 'single-loop' and 'double-loop' learning (Lipshitz, 2000). The difference between these two kinds of learning depends on which component of a theory of action is changed. 'Single-loop learning' occurs when action strategies are changed, but the rest of the theory-in-use remains constant. 'Double-loop' learning involves changes in goals, frames, assumptions, values, and/or standards for performance (Argyris and Schön, 1974; Friedman, 2001). Most of the action science literature has focused on double-loop learning, but productive single-loop learning is also very important and often requires considerable skill and effort (Lipshitz et al., 2006).

ADVANCES IN ACTION SCIENCE

In the following section we describe five applications of action science. They have been chosen because they all define themselves as having action science origins, constitute some innovation or change, and reflect the diversity of the field. Our objective is to illustrate rather than evaluate these advances, so we will not argue for their effectiveness. Because of the limitations of space, we will provide only brief sketches of each advance, but full descriptions of the concepts and methods can be found in the references.

Action Design. 'Action Design' refers to an extensive set of concepts and methods that have been developed to help people learn and apply action science methods, especially for the purpose of creating more effective relationships in work settings (McArthur et al., 2006; www.actiondesign.com). It was developed by Robert Putnam and Diana Smith, who were co-authors of *Action Science* (Argyris et al., 1985), and Phillip MacArthur. They have refined and reworked many of the original theory of action concepts and methods, creating clearer conceptual frameworks and employing language that is more 'user friendly'. For example, they have changed the concept of a person's 'theory-in-use' into a person's 'action model' that links 'framing', 'action', and 'results'.

A major contribution of Action Design has been the 'Learning Pathways' framework for inquiry. It is used to structure and guide inquiry into the underlying action models (theories-in-use) that produced ineffective behavior in situations such as those presented in two-column cases (see Rudolph et al., 2001/2006; Taylor et al., Chapter 46 in this volume). The Learning Pathways model begins by asking people to reflect on the results of their behavior and the extent to which these results were satisfactory or intended. It then works backwards, focusing on the specific actions, verbal or nonverbal, that account for these results. It then focuses on the underlying frames that contain the reasoning behind these actions. The model then looks outward to the features of the context that triggered this particular framing. Finally, it focuses on the person's action model – that is, the general patterns of reasoning and behavior that characterize this person and also produced particular framings in this kind of situation.

The Learning Pathways also guides strategies for change. If inquiry reveals that the actions were the source of ineffectiveness, then learning involves designing and putting into practice new action strategies (called 'reacting' in the model). However, if the frame was problematic, then learning needs to focus on reframing as a prerequisite to designing new action strategies. Finally, if the context and a person's action model significantly contributed to the framing, then learning requires 'redesign'. Redesign is the most complex and difficult learning pathway. On the one hand, it may mean changing aspects of the task system, organizational structure, or group norms. On the other hand, it also requires that learners acknowledge and alter tacit, but deeply embedded, beliefs and behavioral patterns.

Another Action Design innovation is the concept of 'relationship structures', which is drawn from the work of family therapist David Kantor (1999). Relationship structures show how one individual's frame shapes and is shaped by the frames of another. From an Action Design perspective, relationship structures constitute the building blocks of collective action and can be as powerful as formal organizational structures. They provide a basic unit of analysis for mapping and transforming key organizational conflicts and behavior patterns. As a consequence, organizational interventions based on productive conversation often focus on long-term coaching of pairs of managers.

Debriefing with good judgment. Action science has been applied to the process of 'debriefing' in medical education training programs that use simulations to help trainees learn from experience (Rudolph et al., forthcoming). Rudolph et al. (forthcoming) noted that instructors in such programs face a dilemma when providing negative feedback to trainees. If they take a 'judgmental' approach – simply telling trainees what they did wrong – they risk inhibiting learning by generating defensiveness and bad feelings. If they take a 'non-judgmental' approach – helping trainees reach their own conclusions – they risk inhibiting learning by withholding important information or by allowing trainees to learn the wrong thing.

Rudolph et al. (forthcoming) developed an alternative approach that they call 'debriefing with good judgment' through a rigorous reflection process (Rudolph et al., 2001/2006; Taylor et al., this volume). According to this approach, instructors help trainees become aware of and reflect on the frames underlying their action. In order to do so, instructors must exhibit real curiosity about trainee sense-making rather than simply asking leading questions aimed at proving a point. The key, however, is that instructors must also make the frames by which they evaluate trainee performance explicit and open to critical analysis. Frame differences are resolved by a process of public testing combining advocacy with inquiry, opening the possibility that instructors might be mistaken or change their view. By holding themselves to the same standards as they apply to the trainee, instructors not only create conditions for psychological safety and mutual respect, but they also open possibilities that they themselves might learn from the debriefing process. Debriefing with good judgment surfaces and helps resolve the clinical and behavioral dilemmas as well as other sources of confusion raised by the simulation experience.

Learning from Success. Learning from Success (LFS) is a systematic method for retrospective reflection developed by Jona Rosenfeld and Israel Sykes. LFS aims at generating actionable knowledge from successful individual, group, or organizational practice (Sykes et al., 2006). LFS began with Rosenfeld's (1981) observation that social workers and researchers who work with people in extreme poverty tend to focus on explaining their *failures*. Rosenfeld reframed the task as discovering the *successes* of the poor in order to learn from their strengths and the strategies that enable them to survive. The underlying assumption is that even people in the most dire straits have valuable knowledge to offer society.

Subsequently Rosenfeld was introduced to action science inquiry by Donald Schön. Together they facilitated a series of reflective seminars that researched examples of successful practice in areas where mainstream social services had consistently failed. These seminars brought together researchers, practitioners, clients, and policy-makers into a joint inquiry process in order to discover the underlying theories of action that account for success in these situations (Rosenfeld and Tardieu, 2000; Rosenfeld et al., 1996; Sykes and Goldman, 2000).

The experience of these seminars suggested that LFS could provide a means for transforming educational and social service systems that chronically fail to meet the needs of their client populations. Participants in the seminars were able to overcome bureaucratic and professional barriers and meet as equals in the context of the inquiry process. They also began to perceive each other in different and often more appreciative ways, overcoming alienation and

setting the stage for more productive relationships. Furthermore, the inquiry process had an energizing effect on the people involved, strengthening their motivation to continue with experimentation and reflection.

The obstacle to widely applying Learning from Success was the fact that it was closely associated with Rosenfeld's mastery and style. Therefore, it was necessary to turn this personal skill into a generalizable method that others could learn with a reasonable amount of effort. Sykes carried out a second-person action research with Rosenfeld about his practice and produced an explicit, ten-step format for facilitating the LFS inquiry process (Sykes et al., 2006):

1. Describing the context of the success.
2. Identifying a success that is worthy of study.
3. Concisely describing the success in terms of 'before' and 'after'.
4. Describing the positive outcomes, both objective and subjective, of the success.
5. Identifying negative 'side effects' and costs of success.
6. Examining whether the 'success' warrants further learning.
7. Identifying key 'turning points' between 'before' and 'after'.
8. Detailing the specific actions that led to success at these turning points.
9. Deriving the common elements that underlay the actions that led to success.
10. Identifying unresolved issues for further learning.

Each of the steps in the format generates data about the theories of action underlying a success. Step 1 produces a description of the situation or problem and of the conditions impinging on the success. Steps 3 to 5 lead to a description of outcomes (goals). Steps 7 and 8 specify the action strategies that produce these outcomes. Step 9 elicits the implicit framing. Step 6 represents rigorous testing of whether a particular experience can actually be interpreted as a success to be learned. The criteria for defining success are that an observable change has occurred (Step 3) and that the benefits of this change outweigh the costs (4 and 5). LFS inquiry format consciously avoids eliciting explanations of or the experience of success, but rather seeks concrete descriptions of *action* ('What did you *do*?') so as to produce actionable knowledge.

Because this format is extremely formulaic, it provides a very clear and structured method that can be used to produce actionable knowledge by novice facilitators with about a day of training and ongoing support. The format was first applied systemically in 45 Israeli high schools in a program entitled 'Learning from Success as Leverage for School-wide Learning' (Sykes et al., 2006). The primary goal of the program was to improve student achievement and performance by stimulating continuous renewal and organizational learning at the school and inter-school level. It involved creating 'learning workshops' within the schools that used the LFS inquiry format to generate actionable knowledge about their practice. The workshops brought together teachers, administrators, regional supervisors, and sometimes students and parents. They were facilitated by a member of the school staff who received training in the LFS inquiry format and ongoing support from an external consultant. The knowledge created by the workshop was documented in a specifically designed PowerPoint format so that it could be easily communicated and stored.

Each school applied the LFS inquiry format, but developed its own unique workshop and approach to learning. The learning workshops were supported by a network of teams at the school and regional level that included workshop facilitators, school principals, regional supervisors, outside consultants, and other key school staff. Knowledge dissemination and learning across schools was promoted through these teams as well as through meetings and conferences.

Action Evaluation/C3. Action Evaluation (AE)/C3 is a method for integrating systematic inquiry into the process of goal setting for social-educational programs and organizations (Friedman and Rothman, 2001; Rothman, 1997a). The name 'C3' is a play on words intended to emphasize that goals should express stakeholder identity at the individual, group, and inter-group levels. AE/C3 is somewhat unique as an action science method because it focuses on prospective reflection or 'invention' (Argryis et al., 1985) rather than on retrospective reflection.

Action Evaluation/C3 was developed by Jay Rothman, a researcher and mediator, who found that many good and hopeful conflict settlements fall apart in implementation. The problem, as he saw it, is the lack of effective methods for translating aspirations into well-structured programs of action. Defining goals for such programs is problematic because definitions of success in conflict resolution are varied, local, ambiguous, and contingent upon the nature of the conflict and the desires of multiple stakeholders with different agendas (Rothman and Ross, 2000). These conditions characterize many kinds of programs (not just conflict resolution) so that formal goals rarely reflect the aspirations of stakeholders and provide a poor basis for guiding, evaluation, and learning.

Rothman created Action Evaluation/C3 in order to engage these problems in goal-setting and program design, bringing together theory and practice from conflict resolution (Rothman, 1992, 1997a, 1997b), program evaluation (Chen, 1990; Fetterman, 1994), and action science (Argyris et al., 1985). He framed the problem of goal-setting involving multiple stakeholders as a process of constructing a shared identity that takes into account people's deepest needs, values, purposes, and definitions of self (Burton, 1990). Rothman argued that this process requires double-loop learning because stakeholders need to engage their differences up front by becoming aware of, questioning, and sometimes reframing, what they really want from a program. This kind of double-loop inquiry means getting 'underneath the members' initial commitments' and 'ask[ing] why they hold the positions they do and what the positions mean' (Argyris and Schön, 1996: 21).

In order to put these ideas into practice, Action Evaluation/C3 focuses on three questions: *What* are your definitions of success, or goals, for this program? *Why* are these goals important to you? *How* do you think the program should go about achieving these goals? In a typical AE/C3 process, these questions are asked of each individual stakeholder through a web-based questionnaire (www.ariac3.com). Individual responses are aggregated and analyzed at the stakeholder group level in order to yield a set of common, conflicting, and individual goals within each group. These goals become the starting point for a face-to-face process of forging consensus on common goals *within* each stakeholder group separately and then *among* the different groups.

The AE/C3 process places a great emphasis on the 'Why?' question as the springboard for goal inquiry. Before discussing the goals themselves, stakeholders are asked to jointly and openly reflect on why their goals are important to them and why they feel *passionately* about them. AE/C3 takes a normative position, based in the Model II values, that worthy program goals should be clear and understood (valid information), consensual (free and informed choice), and passionately held (internal commitment). Giving public expression to their deep motivations and the stories that explain them helps people understand and appreciate their own goals as well as those of others, paving the way for productively engaging differences in goal-setting (Friedman et al., 2006).

After the 'Why?' discussion, stakeholders engage in goal-setting based on analysis of the answers to the 'What?' question. When conflicts arise, the facilitator encourages balancing advocacy with inquiry in order to get at the underlying issues and to help participants work towards agreement. The goals of different stakeholder groups become the basis for a merge session in which the different groups attempt to reach consensus on common goals at the program level. The 'How?' data are then used to create an action plan that specifies what needs to be done to achieve the consensual goals. Finally, the results of the 'what', 'why' and 'how'

discussions are combined to create a causal 'program theory' of action (Chen, 1990; Friedman, 2001b).

Action Evaluations/C3 has been used in conflict resolution, social-education, and organization development programs ranging from two participants in a single stakeholder group to thousands of participants in many stakeholder groups. Most programs involve local facilitators who require only a few days of training and ongoing support. For example, the City of Cincinnati, Ohio, used AE/C3 to create a community–police relations improvement program after being confronted with a racial profiling lawsuit and tension between the African American community and the police that resulted in a three-day outbreak of civil unrest (Martin, Chapter 26 in this volume; Rothman and Land, 2004). With help from the news media, everyone who lived or worked in Cincinnati was invited to answer a questionnaire consisting of three questions: What are your goals for future police–community relations in Cincinnati? Why are those goals important to you? How do you think your goals can best be achieved?

More than 3500 people from eight stakeholder groups responded to this questionnaire (see Martin, Chapter 26 in this volume, p. 398). A total of 700 people attended small stakeholder group meetings to discuss their 'whys' and to agree upon their goals. Representatives of these groups then met and came up with a final set of five shared goals, which served as the platform for a formal settlement and program. Whereas previous investigative commissions and litigation produced no significant action, this program is now in its fifth year of implementation (The Cincinnati Collaborative Agreement, n.d.).

Organizational Learning in Action. In our own practice, we have applied action science along two main streams. The first stream has been developing methods for helping people learn and apply the theory of action approach to professional and interpersonal effectiveness (Friedman and Lipshitz, 1992). The second stream has been a series of formative evaluations aimed at helping experimental educational programs discover and improve the theories implicit in their practice (Friedman, 1997, 2001; Friedman et al., 2004; Lipshitz et al., 2006). These two streams have merged in a process that I call 'Organizational Learning in Action' (OLA).

The goal of OLA is to help organizational members discover and exercise conscious choice over the theories-in-use that shape their collective practice and behavioral world. Organizational theories of action are very difficult to grasp. Unlike individual theories-in-use, they cannot be thought of as existing in people's minds. Rather, they can only be constructed, like pieces of a puzzle, from what different organizational members do and say and from artifacts such as strategic plans, organizational charts, and reports. The OLA process attempts to put these pieces of the puzzle together so that organizational members can grasp the reality they have created and bring it into closer alignment with what they really want.

We begin OLA by defining substantive learning questions that focus on *task-related* uncertainties or problems. Focusing on *task* rather than on interpersonal relations at this stage reflects the assumption that most significant organizational conflicts are rooted in conflicting or inconsistent requirements for performance, even if they manifest themselves as interpersonal or inter-group conflicts (Argyris and Schön, 1978: Hirschhorn, 1990). We also create an 'organizational learning mechanism', such as a team, to inquire into these questions on behalf of the organization (Lipshitz et al., 2006).

Initial data about the learning questions are gathered through interviews and documentary evidence. These data are analyzed and the findings are 'mapped', preferably on a single page, so as to create a coherent and optimally comprehensive picture of the complex reality. Maps are usually constructed from components of theories of action (e.g. context, frames, action strategies, goals), but there is no fixed format because they need to reflect the unique contours of the specific organizational reality (for specific examples of maps see Argyris, 1993, Argyris et al., 1985, Argyris and Schön, 1978; Friedman, 2001, 2001/2006; Friedman and Lipshitz, 1994; Friedman et al., 2004; Lipshitz et al., 2006).

Maps provide organizational members with an opportunity to literally see and explore their shared reality. They give expression to different perspectives and highlight gaps, conflicts, and uncertainties in organizational theory-in-use. However, they also need to be tested for validity (Do they accurately reflect reality as you experience it?) and completeness (Is something important missing?) and revised accordingly. When organizational members question a feature of the map, we ask for disconfirming data and compare them with the data upon which we based our interpretations.

The maps provide a basis for reframing or more sharply focusing the initial learning questions. The next step is for learning team members to write two-column personal cases that illustrate those features of the map that have been chosen for deeper inquiry. The team then meets regularly to analyze and discuss these cases. Team members act as consultants to each other, but the facilitator plays an important role in using Model II skills to keep discussion productive. At this point, we introduce action science tools (e.g. ladder of inference, reframing, advocacy with inquiry) for helping a team to effectively manage differences and to enhance their learning.

These sessions are recorded and the transcripts analyzed in order to identify and conceptualize important patterns and themes. At the next session, these analyses are shared and tested for validity. In this way, the contours of the organizational theory-in-use emerge and are documented. If the emergent theories are consistent with what organizational members want, they can be used for dissemination and training. If they are inconsistent or problematic, inquiry then focuses on designing and implementing alternative theories of action. This iterative process of data collection, analysis, conceptualization and design may be repeated and expanded to involve new learning teams and new issues.

An example of OLA is a year-long intervention conduced with New Educational Environment (NEE), a program to help schools work more effectively with 'at risk' students (Friedman et al., 2004; Lipshitz et al., 2006). The OLA process was introduced after a period of rapid expansion which led program management to feel that it was losing control over program practice and inadequately harvesting knowledge gained in the field. At first the process was carried by a learning team consisting of the program management (the director and four regional managers) plus two veteran employees (consultants). Later it was expanded to include all 35 members of the program staff.

One of the important outcomes of this process was a significant reframing of the NEE intervention theory. The program faced a great deal of ambiguity over the definition of its target population (youth at risk? disadvantaged? underachievers?). Also it was not clear whether the 'real' target population was the school staff or the students or both. During OLA a new concept, 'social exclusion' (Rosenfeld and Tardieu, 2000), entered the discourse and struck the learning team members as remarkably descriptive of the experience of the students. Unlike terms such as 'at risk' or 'underachievers', which imply a deficit model, this new framing enabled the NEE staff to articulate what they knew – that the problem involved an ongoing dysfunctional relationship between these students and the school system. It also helped them see how teachers and administrators working with these students experienced exclusion as well. Finally, it led them to reframe their intervention as reversing the cycle of exclusion and fostering social inclusion. This reframing created the basis for developing a theory of inclusive educational practice that linked up with mainstream theory and research on social exclusion and inclusion (Razer et al., 2005). This growing body of practice theory was then used as the basis for developing an MA program in inclusive education at a college of education.

CONCLUSION

These examples illustrate that action science methods can be applied as first-, second-, and third-person action research across a wide range of professional fields, practices, and settings. None of these examples represents a distinct method called 'action science'. Rather each one uses the ideas of action science as conceptual and practical tools in the development of new methods for learning and change in a particular realm of practice. The action science roots of these methods may themselves be unseen by the participants in these processes or even by people who are trained as facilitators of these methods.

All these applications embody and reflect the features of action science described above: communities of inquiry, theories of action, frames, testing, and change/design. However, each one enacts these very differently, depending upon the unique interests, styles, and concerns of practitioners. Action Design and Debriefing with Good Judgment focus more on individual learning and increasing interpersonal effectiveness whereas Learning from Success, Action Evaluation/C3, and Organizational Learning in Action focus on collective learning and action. The latter three also have a more explicit research focus, providing formal means for conceptualizing and documenting the products of learning. Specific applications are often the result of integrating action science with existing theories and methods in fields such as family therapy (Kantor, 1999), conflict resolution (Rothman, 1997a; Stone et al., 1999), or program evaluation (Chen, 1990).

These applications have gone a long way to taking the 'mystery' out of the 'mastery' of the founders, Chris Argyris and Don Schön (Schön, 1987). They demonstrate that action science concepts and skills can be structured and systematized so that people can put them into practice at different levels of intensity. People can facilitate action science processes without necessarily becoming masters or undergoing extensive 'reeducation' (Argyris et al., 1985).

These examples of action science have developed in ways that are quite loosely coupled. To the best of our knowledge, there are no academic departments devoted to action science research and training, no institutes for the promotion of action science, no action science associations, and no action science journals. The lack of an institutional base and coordination limits knowledge sharing and cross-fertilization among people working in this field. It probably also limits action science's impact and action research in general and may threaten its continued development.

There are, however, advantages to this kind of evolution. First, it allows for diverse and creative applications; there appears to be no action science orthodoxy and few struggles over who has got it right. Although Model II values inspire and guide all of these applications, not one of them sets out to show people that they are Model I and that they need to learn Model II. In addition, Learning from Success and Action Evaluation/C3 represent significant departures from the early action science focus on retrospective learning from error, failure, and ineffectiveness (e.g. Argyris, 1982; Argryis and Schön, 1974, 1978).

These applications also shed light on the ambiguous role of 'rationality' in action science. On the one hand, 'be rational' was identified as a Model I value (Argyris and Schön, 1974). On the other hand, action science inquiry is heavily in favor of rationality – using reason, logic, and testing against empirical evidence to manage differences. Indeed, this preference is sometimes misinterpreted as an injunction against expressing feelings. However, as seen in Action Evaluation/C3, the expression of passion can be an important part of action science inquiry – and we believe this is implicit in the other approaches described here.

As we understand it, 'be rational', in the Model I sense, means suppressing subjective preferences and focusing on objective factors (Rogers, 2005). Diana Smith (1995: 11) suggested this interpretation in her analysis of boardroom power politics, where executives used strategies designed to prevent anyone from attributing their positions to self-interest. This suppression of self-interest forces subjective factors underground (deep into the 'left-hand column') where they wreak all sorts of havoc. Action science wants to legitimate the discussion of self-interest, moving more of this material to the 'right-hand column' where it can be made discussable and openly tested (Rogers, 2005).

Action science is more of a grounding of action research, like critical theory (Kemmis, 2001/2006), social constructivism (Lincoln, 2001), or participatory action research (Fals Borda, 2001/2006), than a discrete method or practice. It offers a number of very important contributions that can be integrated into many, if not most, action research practices. First, it offers a framework for bringing causal theories back into action research, not in the sense of demonstrating the relationship between discrete variables, but rather in the sense of knowledge that enables people to produce desired ends. This kind of causality is closely linked with how people make meaning as they seek to resolve problems or uncertainties. The second contribution is providing very specific and practical methods of testing that can help action researchers deal more effectively with questions of validity. Finally, the action science approach provides a means for tracing the recursive causal links between our own reasoning and behavior and the behavior of the social contexts in which we live. This knowledge is liberating because it enables us to shift from frames of helplessness to a proactive stance of discovering our causal responsibility and leverage. It enables us to transform obstacles into research questions and expand, if only in small steps, our ability to create the world we want.

ACKNOWLEDGMENT

We wish to thank Ariane Berthoin Antal, Orlando Fals Borda, James Ludema, Robert Putnam, Jay Rothman, and Israel Sykes for their helpful comments on earlier versions of this chapter.

REFERENCES

Argyris, C. (1980) *Inner Contradictions of Rigorous Research*. New York: Academic Press.

Argyris, C. (1982) *Reasoning, Learning and Action: Individual and Organizational*. San Francisco, CA: Jossey-Bass.

Argyris, C. (1993) *Knowledge for Action: a Guide to Overcoming Barriers to Change*. San Francisco, CA: Jossey-Bass.

Argyris, C. (1997) Kurt Lewin Award Lecture, 1997: Field theory as a basis for scholarly consulting. (Transforming psychology: interpretive and participatory research methods). *Journal of Social Issues,* 53 (4): 811–828.

Argyris, C., Putnam, R. and Smith, D.M. (1985) *Action Science: Concepts, Methods, and Skills for Research and Intervention*. San Francisco, CA: Jossey-Bass.

Argyris, C. and Schön, D. (1974) *Theory in Practice: Increasing Professional Effectiveness*. San Francisco, CA: Jossey-Bass.

Argyris, C. and Schön, D. (1978) *Organizational Learning: a Theory of Action Perspective*. Reading, MA: Addison-Wesley.

Argyris, C. and Schön, D. (1991) 'Participatory action research and action science compared', in W.F. Whyte (ed.), *Participatory Action Research*. Newbury Park, CA: Sage.

Argyris, C. and Schön, D. (1996) *Organizational Learning II: Theory, Method, and Practice*. Reading, MA: Addison-Wesley.

Bourdieu, P. (1998) *Practical Reason: On the Theory of Action*. Stanford, CA: Standord University Press.

Burton, J. (ed.) (1990) *Conflict: Human Needs Theory*. New York: St. Martin's Press.

Chen, H.T. (1990) *Theory-driven Evaluations*. Newbury Park, CA: Sage.

Dewey, J. (1938) *Logic: the Theory of Inquiry*. New York: Holt, Rinehart and Winston.

Fals Borda, O. (2001/2006) 'Participatory (action) research in social theory: origins and challenges', in P. Reason and H. Bradbury (eds), *Handbook of Action Research: Participative Inquiry and Practice*. London: Sage. pp. 27–37. Also published in P. Reason and H. Bradbury (eds) (2006), *Handbook of Action Research: Concise Paperback Edition*. London: Sage. pp. 27–37.

Fetterman, D. (1994) 'Empowerment evaluation', *Evaluation Practice*, 15 (1): 1–15.

Friedman, V. (1997) 'Making schools safe for uncertainty: teams, teaching, and school reform', *Teachers College Record*, 99 (2): 335–70.

Friedman, V. (2001/2006) 'Action science: creating communities of inquiry in communities of social practice', in P. Reason and H. Bradbury (eds), *Handbook of Action Research: Participative Inquiry and Practice*. London: Sage. pp. 159–70. Also published in P. Reason and H. Bradbury (eds) (2006), *Handbook of Action Research: Concise Paperback Edition*. London: Sage. pp. 131–43.

Friedman, V. (2001) 'Designed blindness: an action science approach to program theory evaluation', *American Journal of Evaluation,* 22 (2): 161–81.

Friedman, V. and Lipshitz, R. (1992) 'Shifting cognitive gears: overcoming obstacles on the road to Model 2', *Journal of Applied Behavioral Science*, 28 (1): 118–37.

Friedman, V. and Lipshitz, R. (1994) 'Human resources or politics: framing the problem of appointing managers in an organizational democracy', *Journal of Applied Behavioral Science*, 30 (4): 438–57.

Friedman, V., Razer, M. and Sykes, I. (2004) 'Towards a theory of inclusive practice: an action science approach', *Action Research*, 2 (2), 183–205.

Friedman, V., Rothman, J. and Withers, B. (2006) 'The power of why: engaging the goal paradox in program evaluation', *American Journal of Evaluation*, 27 (2).

Friedman, V. and Rothman, J. (2001) 'Action evaluation for knowledge production in social-educational programs', in S. Shankaran, B.Dick, R. Passfield and P. Swepson (eds), *Effective Change Management through Action Research and Action Learning: Frameworks, Processes and Applications*. Lismore, Australia: Southern Cross University. pp. 57–65.

Friedman, V., Razer, M. and Sykes, I. (2004) 'Towards a theory of inclusive practice: an action science approach', *Action Research,* 2 (2): 183–205.

Hirschhorn, L. (1990) *The Workplace Within: the Psychodynamics of Organizational Life*. Cambridge, MA: MIT Press.

Hollis, M. (1994) *The Philosophy of Social Science: an Introduction*. Cambridge: Cambridge University Press.

Kantor, D. (1999) *My Lover, Myself: Self Discovery through Relationship*. New York: Riverhead Books.

Kemmis, S. (2001/2006) 'Exploring the relevance of critical theory for action research: emancipatory action research in the footsteps of Jürgen Habermas', in P. Reason and H. Bradbury (eds), *The Handbook of Action Research: Participative Inquiry and Practice*. London: Sage. pp. 91–102. Also published in P. Reason and H. Bradbury (eds) (2006); *Handbook of Action Research: Concise Paperback Edition*. London: Sage. pp. 94–105.

Lewin, K. (1948) *Resolving Social Conflicts*. New York: Harper and Row.

Lewin, K. (1951) *Field Theory in Social Science*. New York: Harper and Row.

Lincoln, Y. (2001) 'Emerging sympathies: relationships between action research and social constructivism', in P. Reason and H. Bradbury (eds), *The Handbook of Action Research: Praticipative Inquiry and Practice*. London: Sage. pp. 124–32.

Lipshitz, R. (2000) 'Chic, mystique, and misconception: Argyris and Schön and the rhetoric of organizational learning', *Journal of Applied Behavioral Science*, 36: 456–73.

Lipshitz, R., Friedman, V. and Popper, M. (2006) *The Demystification of Organizational Learning*. Thousand Oaks, CA: Sage.

McArthur, P., Putnam, B. and Smith, D. (2006) *Productive Conversation: Manual of Tools and Concepts*. Newton, MA: Action Design.

Razer, M., Friedman, V. and Warshofsky, G. (2005) 'Social exclusion in education: Problem framing and intervention strategies.' Paper presented at the Social Policy Association Annual Conference – 'Well-being and Social Justice', University of Bath, UK.

Robinson, V.M.J. (1993) 'Current controversies in action research', *Public Administration Quarterly*, Fall: 263–90.

Rogers, T. (2005) *Creating Practical Knowledge for Managing Interprofessional Health Care Teams: the Promise of Critical Realism and the Theory of Action*. Adelaide: University of South Australia.

Rosenfeld, J.M. (1981) 'Learning from success: changing family patterns and the generation of social work practice', in *Family Life in the South African Indian Community*, Occasional Paper 20. University of Durban, Westville Institute for Social and Economic Research.

Rosenfeld, J.M. and Tardieu, B. (2000) *Artisans of Democracy: How Ordinary People, Families in Extreme Poverty, and Social Institutions become Allies to Overcome Social Exclusion*. Lanham, MD: University Press of America.

Rosenfeld, J., Schön, D. and Sykes, I. (1996) *Out from Under: Lessons from Projects for Inaptly Served Children and Families*. Jerusalem: Joint Distribution Committee-Brookdale Institute.

Rothman, J. (1992) *From Confrontation to Cooperation: Resolving Ethnic and Regional Conflict*. Newbury Park, CA: Sage.

Rothman, J. (1997a) 'Action evaluation and conflict resolution training: theory, method, and case study', *International Negotiation*, 2: 451–70.

Rothman, J. (1997b) *Resolving Identity-Based Conflict: in Nations, Organizations and Communities*. San Francisco, CA: Jossey-Bass.

Rothman, J. and Land, R. (2004) 'The Cincinnati Police–Community Relations Collaborative', *Criminal Justice*, 18 (4): 34–42.

Rothman, J. and Ross, M. (2000) *Theory and Practice in Ethnic Conflict Resolution: Conceptualizing Success and Failure*. London: Macmillan.

Rudolph, J., Foldy, E. and Taylor, S. (2001/2006) 'Collaborative off-line reflection: a way to develop skill in action science and action inquiry', in P. Reason and H. Bradbury (eds), *Handbook of Action Research: Participative Inquiry and Practice*. London: Sage. pp. 405–12. Also published in P. Reason and H. Bradbury (eds) (2006), *Handbook of Action Research: Concise Paperback Edition*. London: Sage. pp. 307–14.

Rudolph, J., Simon, R., Dufresne, R. and Raemer, R. (forthcoming). 'There's no such thing as "non-judgmental" debriefing: A theory and method for debriefing with good judgment', *Simulation in Healthcare*.

Schön, D.A. (1983) *The Reflective Practitioner*. New York: Basic Books.

Schön, D.A. (1987) *Educating the Reflective Practitioner*. San Francisco, CA: Jossey-Bass.

Schön, D. and Rein, M. (1994) *Frame Reflection: Toward the Resolution of Intractable Policy Controversies*. New York: Basic Books.

Schön, D.A., Drake, W.D. and Miller, R.I. (1984) 'Social experimentation as reflection-in-action', *Knowledge Creation, Diffusion, and Utilization*, 6 (1): 5–36.

Senge, P. (1990) *The Fifth Discipline: the Art and Practice of the Learning Organization*. New York: Doubleday Currency.

Smith, D.M. (1995) *Keeping a Strategic Dialogue Moving*. Retrieved 30 October 2002, from http://www.action-design.com/resources/theory/ksdm.htm.

Stone, D., Patton, B. and Heen, S. (1999) *Difficult Conversations: How to Discuss What Matters Most*. New York: Viking.

Sykes, I. and Goldman, M. (2000) *Learning from Success: Producing Actionable Knowledge by Reflecting on the Practice of a Successful Project ('Kesher')*. Jerusalem: Joint Distribution Committee-Brookdale Institute.

Sykes, I., Rosenfeld, J. and Weiss, T. (2006) *Learning from Success as Leverage for School-Wide Learning: a Pilot Program 2002–2005. The First Method, Learning from Past Success, the Retrospective Method*. Jerusalem: Myers-JDC Brookdate Institute.

The Cincinnati Collaborative Agreement (n.d.) http://www.acluohio.org/issues/police_practices/cinci_agreement.htm (accessed 30 July 2006).

Torbert, W. (1976) *Creating a Community of Inquiry*. London: John Wiley and Sons.

Weick, K. (1979) *The Social Psychology of Organizing, 2nd edn*. Reading, MA: Addison-Wesley.

18

Clinical Inquiry/Research

Edgar H. Schein

This chapter explains and illustrates the concept of clinical research by contrasting this form of empirical data gathering to the other major forms of research. The chapter tries to illustrate where each form of research is most appropriate and argues that clinical research, though driven by client needs, is not only a legitimate form of empirical research but actually has great advantages over the other forms of positivistic research when one is dealing with complex human systems.

The basic purpose of this chapter is to show that useful data can be gathered in situations that are *not* initiated by the researcher. Gathering data, building concepts and developing theory is the result of a research *attitude*, a desire to clarify what is going on and communicate that clarification to other researchers. It is my argument that some of the best opportunities for such inquiry actually arise in situations where the setting is created by someone who wants help, not by the researcher deciding what to study. Gathering useful data in settings that are defined by 'clients' who are seeking help is what I mean by clinical inquiry/research (Schein, 1987a, 1999a, 1999b, 2003, 2004).

The major implication of this way of thinking is that knowledge production is a byproduct of helping rather than a primary goal. The use of the word 'clinical' is therefore appropriate inasmuch as the inquiry always starts around some problem or issue that a client brings to a helper (therapist, consultant, coach, counselor). Even if the goal is couched in positive terms such as would be advocated by the proponents of appreciative inquiry (see Chapters 12 and 19), there is always under the surface some assumption of 'pathology', something that is wrong or could be better. Though clients prefer not to talk about pathology, from the point of view of the helper there is always pathology present and that needs to be understood. Indeed a better understanding of the pathology of a given situation is often the most profound research result of what I am calling clinical inquiry.

How is this idea connected to participatory action research (PAR)? By definition clients *participate* and are involved in the clinical process of working on their problems or issues, but they are not necessarily involved in 'research'. This is a crucial point in that the client may not have any interest in research at the beginning of the engagement and may, in fact, never get involved in the research component. Nevertheless, it is my argument that if the clinician helper has a research *attitude*, he or she may learn a tremendous amount during the helping process and such knowledge will often be more useful than what a formal researcher may find, *no matter what version of conventional or action research is used.*

Many would argue that 'action research' is precisely geared to this point. However, the original definition of action research was to take research subjects or targets of change programs and turn them into researchers by involving them in the research process. The research agenda is still defined by the researcher or change agent, and the 'subjects' or 'targets' become involved as a result of researcher initiatives. The researcher's skills in gathering and analyzing data are the primary bases for the quality of the outcome. Clinical inquiry research (CIR), by contrast, involves the gathering of data in clinical settings *that are created by people seeking help.* The researcher in these settings is called in because of his or her *helping* skills and the subject matter is defined by the client. If the helper takes an attitude of inquiry, this enhances not only the helping process but creates the opportunity for using the data that are produced to build concepts and theory that will be of use to others. The best examples come from medicine, particularly psychotherapy, where the publication of analyses of selected cases builds knowledge for fellow practitioners and interested researchers.

An additional argument for CIR is that once a helping relationship has been built with a client or client system (group or organization) the door is open for the researcher to seek additional data based in part on a greater willingness of the clients to provide data that they might otherwise wish to withhold or be unaware of (Schein, 1999a, 1999b). The clinician/helper can then migrate into other research roles and ask questions that subjects would ordinarily not answer because they might regard it as 'too private' or 'none of the researcher's business'. I suspect that ethnographers also have to become 'helpers' in some way or another before they begin to get more intimate data about the cultures they are studying.

To clarify what CIR means conceptually and operationally I need to locate it among various other forms of conventional research and action research. My goal is to show that in each of these types of research a somewhat different psychological contract develops between the researcher and the subject (client) which has consequences not only for the kinds of data that can be gathered and for issues of reliability and validity, but also for the welfare of the subjects.

Three basic dimensions differentiate various kinds of research with human systems, as shown in Figure 18.1; 1) whether the initiative for the inquiry is launched by the participant or the researcher; 2) the degree to which the researcher/inquirer becomes personally involved in the inquiry process; and 3) the degree to which the participant in the research becomes personally involved in the process.

These dimensions produce eight different kinds of inquiry models and psychological contracts. I will briefly describe each of these cells and give illustrations of the kinds of research or inquiry that characterize them. CIR will then stand out in sharp contrast to the other models of inquiry, and it is this contrast that most clearly defines the characteristics of CIR.

RESEARCHER INITIATED INQUIRY

The first four kinds of research that will be described below have in common that it is the *researcher* who makes the initial decision to get connected to some members of an organization, who advertises for 'research

		Researcher/consultant initiates the project	
		Subject/client involvement	
		Low	High
Researcher	Low	1. Demography	2. Experiments and surveys
involvement	High	3. Ethnography and participant observation	4. Action research

		Subject/client initiates the project	
		Subject/client involvement	
		Low	High
Researcher involvement tion and facilitation	Low	6. Internship	7. Educational interven-
	High	5. Contract research and expert consulting	8. Process consulting and clinical inquiry

Figure 18.1   *Types of researcher/consultant/subject/client relationships*

subjects' or who begins to make unobtrusive observations of some phenomenon he or she is interested in. If the research is to take place in an organizational context, the major up-front issues are: 1) how to get 'entry' into the organization and 2) how to elicit the co-operation of organization members so that they will become willing research subjects. How these issues are resolved depends on how involved the subjects become in the inquiry process and how involved the researcher becomes with the participants.

Cell 1: Low Researcher and Low Subject Involvement – e.g. Demography

In this form of inquiry a researcher decides on a topic and finds a way of gathering data that, at the extreme, may not involve the participants at all. At the same time the researcher attempts be objective and distances him or herself from the data. Examples would be to work with demographic variables or records. For example, when I was a consultant with Ciba-Geigy in the late 1970s my primary client was the head of management development. He was asked at one point to make some recommendations about the relative importance for executive development of cross-functional and

international assignments. He had records of the actual movement of all of the top executives for the past 20 years, so we jointly decided that the 'research' would be an analysis of these records to determine whether actual patterns of greater or lesser movement were related to career outcomes of various sorts. This required coding of the records and statistical analysis, which revealed clear patterns that later became the basis of recommendations for future executive career management.

The essence of this kind of research is that the participant may never be involved at all and the researcher takes a fairly uninvolved role. It is the research question, the data and the research methods that drive the process and that define the 'quality' of the research. Joseph Campbell's analyses of heroic myths and David McClelland's analyses of achievement motivation in different cultures based on analysis of their art and literature would be good examples.

Cell 2: Low Researcher but High Participant Involvement – Experiments and Surveys

This form of research also starts with the researcher formulating the question, issue, or problem but differs from Cell 1 in that the method chosen requires some direct involvement of the participants. The researcher develops a design that minimizes researcher bias such as a double-blind experiment, but the participant has to display some behavior, opinions, or feelings that become the primary data to be analyzed. In the organizational context experiments are rare, though Kurt Lewin was a genius in setting up experimental situations that enabled us to perceive what the dynamics were of different kinds of leadership and group climates (Lewin, 1952, 1999). Muzapher Sherif in his experiments with boys clubs showed us clearly what some of the dynamics of inter-group competition are (Sherif et al., 1961), and the Bavelas/Leavitt experiments on group communication patterns remain as classics showing the power of well designed experiments (Bavelas and Strauss, 1962; Leavitt, 1951).

Cell 3: High Researcher but Low Subject Involvement – Participant Observation and Ethnography

The classic form of this kind of research is participant observation or ethnography. In its pure form the assumption is made that the researchers become totally involved while, at the same time, trying to remain objective and to minimize their impact on the participants. It is important for ethnographers to be able to argue that their time spent in the culture did not influence the culture, hence their data could be trusted to be 'objective'.

In this kind of inquiry researchers have to work actively with the participants to gather the data even as they are concealing the purpose of the inquiry and the way in which the data will be analyzed (Van Maanen, 1979; Whyte, 1943). The evolution of projective tests can, in fact, be related to the need to have a measurement tool that the subject is unable to decipher, and may be used in either Cell 2 or Cell 3 as part of the inquiry process. However, I suspect that ethnographers cannot *not* influence the culture to some degree

and that becoming helpful in some way is, in fact, necessary for any valid data to be gathered. A seemingly trivial yet important example was Gideon Kunda's experience trying to gather data in an engineering group. They were quite aloof until one lunchtime Gideon helped to win a soccer game for the group. Suddenly he was one of the gang and his ability to get answers to questions increased dramatically (Kunda, pers. comm., 1992).

Cell 4: High Researcher and High Subject Involvement – Type 1 Action Research

Kurt Lewin's dictum that you cannot understand an organization until you try to change it is perhaps the clearest theoretical justification for the kind of research that occurs in this cell and that led to the label 'action research.' It is worth retelling the story of how a group of researchers at an early group dynamics workshop at Bethel, Maine, were sitting around one evening trying to analyze their group observations of that day. A number of participants drifted into the room and started to listen to what the researchers were talking about. At one point some of these participants heard analytical comments that did not fit what they remembered as having happened so they intervened and said that they wanted to tell their view of what had gone on. This led to a joint analysis of the data by both researchers and participants, which proved to be much richer than what the researchers had come up with themselves. Such joint analysis then came to be seen as a legitimate form of inquiry even though by Cell 1 standards it could be viewed as 'contaminating' the data.

In this kind of action research the researcher remains in control and defines the goals of the inquiry as in 'survey-feedback'. The design of the research process is geared to getting 'valid data' and the involvement of the participants is justified primarily by the assumption that the data will be that much better if they are involved. Where surveys are involved the researcher may train various managers to give feedback to the employees in order to initiate remedial action. Metaphors such as 'cascading the data down the organization' are used to highlight the action research elements and to show how the involvement of the participants in the data analysis will lead to improved organizational performance.

This form of action research differs from Cell 3 research in that the goal of the Cell 3 researcher is to gather data as a basis for action, whereas the Cell 4 researcher acknowledges that until the participants become involved in the gathering and analysis of the data we do not know enough to take the right kind of action and get the intended result. But this type of action research is also blind to the fact that the administration of the initial survey is itself already an intervention, whether or not the data are fed back to the participants. In summary, when the researchers choose the focus of the research, they have the problem of gaining entry into the research site and eliciting the cooperation of the research subjects. Even if subjects are only to be observed, they must agree to the researcher's presence and hopefully ignore the researcher sufficiently to allow the assumption that what is observed is not influenced in a major way by the researcher's presence. The researcher offers as his or her contribution to the psychological contract that the results will be fed back to the participants in some form or another, that the results may be helpful to the participants and, most importantly, that the participants will not be harmed. Hence confidentiality is promised and the researcher may offer to let the participants see what will be published about them. What remains unstated and often unexplored by either researcher or participants is the consequences of participation itself. Most researcher initiated research in all of the above cells assumes that the research process itself is more or less benign, that it 'precedes' intervention, and that the research process if anything will benefit the participants in that it gets them to inquire into their own processes.

Unfortunately most researchers operating in this mode have little or no training in how to assess the consequences of their research interventions for the participants. The assumption that research is benign allows researchers to proceed without worrying too much about the effects they may have on the participants.

CLIENT INITIATED INQUIRY

If an individual in a group or organization needs some kind of help or solicits some research to be done in the organization, the psychological contract is much more complex. We can no longer think of research 'subjects'; the participants now become 'clients' who will pay for the services rendered and will want to participate in various ways from the outset. Some level of entry into the organization is guaranteed, but the person invited in to help must have helping skills and must focus, at least initially, on the areas of concern defined by the client (Schein, 1999a). For many helpers, professional consultants or therapists, these considerations limit their self-concept to that of helper. They do not consider the possibility of gathering valid data in the helping context, and this self-perception is reinforced by the academic journal stance of not honoring case descriptions and other forms of qualitative research as legitimate 'science'. My argument is that not only should data gathering based on helping be considered legitimate research, but also such data are often deeper and more valid than any data gathered in the researcher initiated models (Cells 1–4).

What this means, in essence, is that client initiated inquiry is restricted in scope but is potentially much 'deeper'. It also means, however, that the research component must be governed by the *ethics of intervention*. If the helping process compromises the data and/or if certain kinds of data gathering would not be helpful they must be abandoned. The researcher must find ways of checking reliability and validity within the parameters of the intervention model and must build the research agenda around the possibilities that the client makes available.

As we will see, the boundaries between the four cells in this domain are not as clear-cut. Clinical research becomes possible to some degree in each cell. Nevertheless it is useful to distinguish some of the consequences of different degrees of involvement by the client and the researcher.

Cell 5: High Researcher, Low Client Involvement – Contract Research, Expert Consulting

One variant of this kind of inquiry results when the *client decides the research agenda and hires a researcher to implement it*. The client defines the problem, decides that some formal research is the way to solve it, decides who the researcher is to be and then empowers the researcher to proceed. Externally conducted employee or customer surveys, benchmarking studies of various kinds such as salary surveys and various other kinds of 'contract' research would fit this model. The most recent version is the desire by many organizations to do a 'cultural assessment'.

What the client wants in this model is data and information. The helper/consultant is hired to be an expert in providing it. If the data are primarily gathered outside the organization the model resembles traditional research. However, if the data are to be gathered inside the organization such as in an attitude survey, the issue of client involvement becomes complicated because the data gathering is itself an intervention of unknown consequences. One part of the client system launches an inquiry process that has possibly unknown and unintended consequences for other parts of the client system. Whereas an outside survey is justified to 'help some outside group gather information', if the outsider is doing the survey on behalf of some group inside the organization, the participant has to wonder what is going on inside the organization that has motivated this activity.

In terms of consulting models, this cell would include both what I have called 'purchase of expertise' where the consultant is hired to provide information and advice, and the 'doctor' model in which the consultant is hired to provide both diagnosis and a prescription (Schein, 1999a). The project is often defined as 'finished' when the consultant has delivered a recommendation and, in fact, some consulting models consider the delivery of a recommendation to be the very essence of consultation.

The ethical issue is especially sharp in this cell because the researcher has the license to gather data without having to worry about the consequences for the client because it is the client who has launched the inquiry. Contract researchers, if they are to be helpful, must understand the impacts of their data gathering methods and *must educate clients to those impacts before they undertake the data gathering*. Otherwise there is a risk that not only will parts of the client system be harmed by the research but that the data, may not be valid because of distortions introduced by employees who feel treated like 'guinea pigs'. They may be overly negative because 'finally someone is listening to us' or overly positive because 'even though they promised us confidentiality we better be careful what we say'. In either case management's decision to do the research signals their self-perception as having the right to gather such data, which in itself may be new information to the employees about their own culture. All too often employees have learned that this kind of inquiry is a prelude to some form of restructuring or reorganization which invariably involves layoffs. And, as much experience has shown, the expert or doctor often ends up delivering information and prescriptions that the client rejects because they do not fit the culture in some way or another, something the expert did not discover in the rush to do the contract research.

The recent trend to do culture surveys then provides a Catch 22 situation, in that the client system wants to find out what will work in its culture, but does not realize that the very act of assessing the culture is itself a cultural intervention of unknown consequence. For these reasons, Cell 5 'expert' inquiry should not be undertaken unless the client and clinician have established a relationship that allows full exploration of the consequences of the research before the research is undertaken (Schein, 1999a, 1999b).

Cell 6: Low Researcher, Low Client Involvement – Internship

This kind of inquiry is really a variant of the Cell 5 process but involves data gathering that is basically less involving to the helper/inquirer. Examples might be where the client asks for an analysis of demographic information or invites a graduate student to come in as an intern to 'learn' a bit about the organization or to do some 'exploratory research'. The client stays in control of what will be done and how, thereby limiting the involvement of the researcher. On the other hand, if the researcher is invited into the organization in an internship or participant role, all the positive possibilities of CIR are created.

Cell 7: Low Researcher, High Client Involvement – Educational Interventions, Facilitation

The potential for clinical research increases as the client's involvement in the total process of inquiry and getting help increases. If the client wants more than data and information, if he or she is willing to let the researcher enter the organization to a greater degree, even into settings where 'real work' is getting done, the helper can begin to observe 'real' organizational phenomena. The prototype of this level of inquiry is when the helper/consultant is brought in to facilitate a meeting or to make an educational intervention like running a workshop or giving a lecture to a group of executives. The helper is licensed to observe what is going on but not licensed to influence the situation beyond what the client has contracted for.

In my own experience, being the trainer in a T-group was the setting where I first encountered the power of this form of inquiry. I had extensive training in small group research yet discovered as I sat more or less silently in the group that most of what was really going on was not covered in the traditional research literature, yet seemed more real and relevant to group theory than what was in the literature. Even though the T-group was an artificial training environment, the group phenomena were very real and very vivid.

Years later at a management education conference the question came up of what material professors used in teaching about organizational phenomena. We discovered that each of us used illustrations from our consulting experience to a much greater extent than 'findings' from traditional research. The traditional research informed our thinking and provided models for what to observe, but the reality of what was going on usually went far beyond those models and forced us to develop new concepts and theories.

When we make educational interventions like running a seminar for managers we learn about them in part from their reaction to the material we provide. For many academic researchers such exposure to members of organizations serves as their primary database about what goes on in organizations. We enhance those data by putting participants through role-plays or simulations and thereby learn a lot about how the participants think, but unless we are dealing with teams from the same organization we cannot learn much about organizational dynamics per se.

The client implicitly or explicitly limits the domain by choosing the focus of the educational intervention, but also opens the door to the helper who may need to gather more information about the organization in order to design a better educational program. In that inquiry the helper can seek all kinds of information about the organization legitimately. In fact, the organization is often anxious to reveal itself so that the educational program will be relevant to that organization's issues.

Cell 8: High Researcher and High Client Involvement – Process Consultation and Clinical Inquiry

The clearest form of CIR occurs when the client and helper work together to decipher what is going on in the context of some problem that the client is trying to solve. On the surface this resembles the kind of action research that was described in Cell 4, but it differs greatly because it is driven by the *client's* agenda, not the researcher's.

The critical distinguishing features of this inquiry model are: 1) that the data come *voluntarily* from the members of the organization because they initiated the process and have something to gain by revealing themselves to the clinician/consultant/researcher, and 2) that the helper consultant actively involves the client in the inquiry process itself in order *to improve the quality of the helping process* (Schein, 1987b, 1988 [1969], 1999a). If the helping process is successful, the client is motivated to reveal more, hence the depths and validity of the data improve as the helping process improves. Valid data are the *result* of effective helping rather than the basis for choosing interventions.

Furthermore, as pointed out before, in the inquiry process the consultant/clinician is psychologically licensed by the client to ask relevant questions which can lead directly into joint analysis and, thereby, allow the development of a research focus that is now owned jointly by the helper and the client. Both the consultant and the client become fully involved in the problem-solving process and the search for relevant data becomes, therefore, a joint responsibility. The helper is committed to a joint inquiry and joint decisions on further interventions. In Cell 7 the helper can privately learn what he or she needs to know to produce a good educational intervention. In this cell the helper wants to build joint knowledge so that the client not only learns inquiry techniques but also becomes a co-researcher, which enables both the research and helping processes to go much deeper.

The consultant/clinician is not, of course, limited to the data that surface in specific diagnostic activities such as individual or group interviews. In most consulting situations there are extensive opportunities to hang around and observe what is going on, allowing the helper/researcher to combine some of the best elements of the clinical and the participant observer ethnographic models. The clinician can also gather demographic information and measure various things unobtrusively, but if the 'subjects' are to be involved at all, they must be treated as 'clients' and involved on their own terms around problems they have identified.

The clinical model reveals most clearly the power of Lewin's dictum that *one cannot really understand a system until one tries to change it.* Repeatedly I have found both in group training and in organizational consulting that most of the relevant data surfaced as a *consequence* of some specific intervention I made. In this model, intervention and diagnosis become two sides of the same coin. Everything the helper/clinician does is an intervention and, at the same time, every intervention reveals new data.

The power of this process is revealed as one uncovers causal phenomena that lie in deeper levels of group and organizational dynamics and that, when uncovered, lead to real 'insights' both on the part of the clinician and the client. And as the client becomes an active inquirer he or she sees new areas of relevant data to be collected that may never have occurred to the researcher.

The study of culture provides good examples of the complexity of these approaches (Schein, 1992, 1999b, 2004). In the 'expert model' the client has asked for a culture assessment and is prepared to pay for the research on a contract basis. If the researcher accepts the contract and initiates the study, ethnography, formal surveying, or individual interviewing with or without projective tests might seem like the methods of choice. The researcher would then take all the data and write a description of the culture, which might or might not be checked with participants, but the researcher would remain in control. The pitfalls of this approach were reviewed above.

In the process consultation CIR model I would first want to know what kind of help the client was looking for and what he or she meant by 'culture'. What issues, problems, or aspirations motivated the request for a cultural assessment in the first place? The reason for this initial step is that any cultural assessment that tries to be general and encompass the whole culture would require intensive observation and ethnographic interviews. A researcher who promises to do this with a questionnaire or survey would be limiting the project to the few questions that could be asked in a survey which would bias the cultural study toward the researcher's theories. I would point out to the client that the contract research model might reveal accurate but very limited data and those data might be quite irrelevant to the issues the client wanted to deal with. I would also point out that it would be much quicker and more efficient to work inside the client system as a helper around the questions that motivated the culture inquiry in the first place. If we involved the participants in deciphering their own culture this would help them to decide for themselves what kind of culture interventions might be appropriate. I would also argue that if they become co-inquirers we could go deeper into the culture and test the validity of what we find as we go along. Not only would it be more helpful to do the joint inquiry, but also the research data would be more valid and deeper.

ILLUSTRATION NO. 1: COLLABORATIVE INTERACTIVE ACTION RESEARCH

Lotte Bailyn and a team of researchers set out in the mid-1990s to study and intervene on work–family interactions in organizations under the auspices of a Ford Foundation grant (Bailyn et al, 2000). Initially the project appeared to fall in Cell 2 as being researcher initiated with low involvement of the researchers in the organizations studied but high involvement of the subjects who would have to reveal information about their work–family relationships. However, it was the intention of the researchers eventually to intervene in the client organizations to improve gender equity in work relations, placing the project into Cell 8 if they could get client involvement.

Several organizations were approached at high executive levels and permission was granted to *study* work–family relationships and gender equity in selected portions of these organizations. Permission and entry were secured through processes of involving the Human Resource Department contacts and the managers of the groups who were to become both the research subjects and clients. Bailyn and her team gained access to several engineering groups in a large corporation and launched their collaborative interactive action research in those groups.

In one group the research findings were that the engineers did not have enough time because of their demanding work schedule and the heavy overtime that they already put in just to get their regular work finished. When these data were fed back and worked on by both the clients and the researchers it was *discovered* that the engineers viewed 'work time as infinite' in the sense that the engineers worked until their work was done, even if that cut into family time. The relationship was not reciprocal, however, in that family time was bounded by the norm that you cannot skip work just because your 'family duties are not finished'.

The researchers, with the consent of the clients, then shifted the emphasis to the question of why the work schedule was so heavy in the first place? Working collaboratively with the researchers, who intervened primarily by being a mirror around the data collected, the engineers realized they had come to believe that high rates of interaction and teamwork were important, and that to facilitate such interaction they had to be available to each other *at all times*. This norm led to frequent meetings, people wandering in on each other all hours of the day, constant use of the telephone, and other interactive activities that prevented them from getting their individual work done until late in the day and on overtime.

With this insight there occurred a further shift in the role of the researchers toward becoming process consultants by beginning to work with the engineers on what might be done about the stressful situation they were experiencing. They jointly realized that the structure of the workday was negotiable, that the engineers did not have to be available to each other all day long. They decided on an experiment to declare certain hours during the 9–5 workday as 'private time' where no phone calls, meetings, or interruptions were allowed. To their own and the researchers' amazement they were able to get all of their work done in the normal workday which, parenthetically, solved the work–family conflict as well.

What is significant about this example is that there was not a step in the middle where results were published showing how work group norms of time management can become dysfunctional. The researchers moved seamlessly into a clinical role and, in that process, produced an intervention that changed the way the organization worked which, in turn, revealed the significant data that the actual workload was manageable within the normal workday. What this story also highlights is that the research and clinical agendas often overlap and that researchers have to be prepared to move into clinical roles just as much as clinician helpers have to be ready to gather data and put on researcher hats.

ILLUSTRATION NO. 2: DECIPHERING A FAILURE TO IMPLEMENT A NEW TECHNOLOGY

For several years I was a process consultant to a senior manager in a bank operations department, helping him with a variety of projects. One of his main goals was to introduce an effective new technology for handling various financial transactions. Several years had already been spent on developing the technology and contract research had been done to determine the feasibility of introducing the technology to the clerical workforce.

As the new technology was being installed, it became evident that many fewer clerks would be needed and it was then discovered that the bank had a powerful unbreakable norm that it would not lay anybody off. At the same time it was discovered that my client would not be able to relocate or retrain the many persons who would be displaced by the new technology. The existence of the 'no layoffs' norm was well known, but no one had any idea of how powerfully held it was until the technological change was attempted, and no one realized how overstaffed all the other departments of the bank were. The new technology was at this point abandoned as impractical.

In the traditional research model the existence of this norm would be a sufficient explanation of the observed phenomenon that a potentially useful technology failed to be adopted. But what I learned as a consultant to the head of this unit 'deepens' our understanding considerably. Once we discovered that the no layoffs norm was operating, I began inquiries about the source of the norm and learned that it was strongly associated with my client's boss for whom 'no layoffs' was a central management principle that he had made into a sacred cow. I had assumed from prior knowledge of social psychology that norms are upheld primarily by group members themselves. I found, instead, that in this situation it was the boss's fanaticism that was really the driving force, an insight that was confirmed three years later when he retired. Almost at once it became OK to lay people off but, surprisingly, the new technology was still not implemented. Our previous explanations would both have been *wrong*.

As a traditional researcher, I would not have been allowed to hang around for so long, so I would not even have discovered that the constraint on the new technology was something other than the no layoffs norm and the presence of its powerful originator. To explain further what was happening I had to draw on some other knowledge I had gained as a member of the design team for the initial change. I remembered that the group had had great difficulty in visualizing what the role of the new operator of such a computer program would be and what the role of that person's boss would be. The group could not visualize the career path of such an operator and could not imagine a kind of professional organization where such operators would be essentially on their own. I asked a number of people about the new technology and confirmed that people did not see how it could work, given the kinds of people who were hired into the bank and given the whole career and authority structure of the bank.

So what was really in the way of introducing the innovation was not only the norm of no layoffs, but some deeper conceptual problems with the entire socio-technical system, specifically an inability to visualize and implement a less hierarchical system in which bosses might play more of a consultant role to highly paid professional operators who, like airline pilots, might spend their whole career in some version of this new role. In fact, the no layoff norm might have been a convenient rationalization to avoid having to change deeper cultural assumptions about the nature of work and hierarchy in this bank.

What the clinical process revealed was that the phenomenon was 'over-determined', multiply caused, and deeply embedded in a set of cultural assumptions about work, authority, and career development.

THE ROLE OF TRAINING AND 'ON LINE' HYPOTHESIS TESTING

Hanging around organizations in a clinical consultant role reveals a lot, but is this valid knowledge? How do clinician researchers know when they know something? How do they avoid seeing what they want to see through their own cultural lenses? The first part of the answer to these questions is that perception is a *trained* skill. Just as artists have to learn to see before they can render something, so clinicians have to train in graduate programs to learn what to look for and how to avoid biases. Formal documentation, field notes, diaries, and dictations done immediately after an interview or site visit

are all essential tools to maintain objectivity. One should operate with self-insight and a healthy skepticism so that one does not misperceive what is out there to make it fit our preconceptions.

The second part of the answer is that we are constantly forming and testing hypotheses and expectations about what we will see and hear 'next', especially immediately after we have intervened by saying or doing something. Unexpected events are, in fact, one of the best sources of cultural data. Theory and concepts play a crucial role in training for this kind of work. We do not go into human groups and complex social situations without some knowledge of how individuals, groups, and organizations work. Formal knowledge gained in the other cells described above is necessary and useful, but usually not sufficient to reveal the detailed events of clinical situations so experiential learning is crucial, and the earlier we learn to observe real events the better.

If we are reasonably careful about our own hypothesis formulation and well trained in observing what is going on, we should be able to generate valid knowledge of organizational and cultural dynamics throughout any period of interaction with an organization.

But if such dynamic 'on line', 'here and now' confirmation or disconfirmation of our hypotheses and expectations is not enough validation, another criterion of validity is replicability, triangulation or crosschecking. If other observers see the same phenomenon that the clinician sees and if it occurs under conditions similar to the ones where the clinician first observed it, that adds confidence that the clinician is observing something real that is out there, not just in his or her head. In the cultural arena especially, evidence of shared tacit assumptions that is difficult to detect with questionnaires or interviews surfaces readily when one observes members of the culture in interaction. I have often checked with other outsiders at a meeting whether what I saw was also what they saw and found that the important cultural data are clearly visible to multiple outside observers.

LIMITATIONS OF CLINICAL RESEARCH

The major disadvantage of clinical data is that it is often not relevant to what the researcher might like to study. The psychological contract with the client entitles the helper to go deeper, but not really to change the subject and broaden it to some research concerns he or she might have. The client may not be part of the system that the consultant/researcher may want to study. On the other hand, seeing any organizational processes at work first hand seems more relevant than trying to infer them from more superficial data. Organizations and their cultures and sub-cultures are often like holograms in which seeing deeply into any part of the system reveals the whole to a considerable degree.

Some would argue that a further limitation is the requirement to remain as much an outsider as possible so as not to perturb and influence the system. In my own view that is a misconception based upon an outdated view of science. As I have argued all along, perturbing the system may be essential to obtaining data on how the system works, but such perturbation must be ethically circumscribed. Only when the client is seeking and getting help can the clinician validly make certain kinds of interventions. I would hypothesize, by the way, that good participant observers and ethnographers discover that the quality of their data improves as they become helpful to the organization in which they are working. It is inevitable that the insiders will not want someone to hang around who is not at least fun to talk to, to trade points of view with, and even to get advice from. In other words, good participant observation and ethnography inevitably become CIR though that aspect is often not written about or even admitted.

DOES CLINICAL EMPHASIS BIAS US TOWARD PATHOLOGY?

Many clients want help but don't want to admit that they have problems or poor health.

Calling what consultants do 'organizational therapy' is not popular even though accurate. However, this is mostly a linguistic semantic problem in that clients don't seek help unless they see something as 'wrong' or capable of improvement. By focusing on improvement one can sidestep confronting pathology, but at some point in the helping process the pathology has to be faced. Whether clients ask us to do contract research, support basic research, or hire us as consultants, are they not always trying to make things better, which clearly implies that they see something that is wrong or unsatisfying? It is almost the essence of life in organizations to overcome things that are not working as well as they could be, to achieve goals that are beyond what is possible in the present – in other words, to overcome the small and large pathologies of organizational life. By not using the word clinical or therapy we are not avoiding the existence of pathology or its effects; we are only denying our own ability to face pathology squarely, analyze it, and deal with it.

IMPLICATIONS FOR EDUCATION AND TRAINING

If we take this point of view seriously, what does it say about our graduate education and training? I would not wish to abandon the teaching of research as a logical process of thinking, nor do I want to abandon empiricism. In fact, in my view, clinical research, in that it deals with immediately observed organizational phenomena, is *more* empirical than much research that basically massages second and third order data. What is needed then is better training in how to be helpful and how to be a genuinely observant, inquiring person so that organizations will want our help and open themselves up to us more.

Some suggestions come to mind. Why don't we send all our graduate students off into organizations early in their graduate training with the mandate to find something where they can be helpful? Would it be that hard to locate organizations that would take interns for six months to a year, not to subject themselves to research but to have an intelligent, energetic extra hand to work on some immediate problems? The more immediate and practical the problems the better. Students would learn helping and inquiry skills fairly fast if they knew they would need them during their internship.

Why don't we teach our students basic interviewing and observational skills at the beginning of their graduate training? Instead of learning how to analyze tests or surveys, students might spend more time analyzing the everyday reality they encounter in a real organization. Particularly in the area of interviewing I have found most of my colleagues to be very naïve about the dynamics of this process, the degree to which researchers ask essentially rhetorical questions, and the degree to which they try to remain mysterious and distant from the subjects by excessive use of jargon.

Why don't we use more clinical materials in our graduate programs, books by Levinson (1972), Trist (Trist et al., 1963), Rice (1963), Kets de Vries (Kets de Vries and Miller, 1984, 1987), Miller (1990), Hirschhorn (1988) and others who try to lay out more systematically some of the dynamic processes they have observed? It is shocking that so little of the clinical tradition that was started in the Tavistock Institute studies in the 1940s has influenced US organizational research.

Finally, why don't we put much more emphasis on self-insight so that future clinician researchers can get in touch with their biases early in their career as a way of clarifying their vision?

CONCLUSION

The bottom line to all this, then, is that we need clinical skills for generating relevant data, for obtaining insights into what is really going on, and for helping managers to be more effective. We need more journals and outlets for clinical research, for case studies that are real cases, not demonstration cases to make a teaching point. We need to legitimate clinical research as a valid part of our field and start to train people in helping skills as well as in research skills. And we need more insight into our own cultural assumptions to determine how much they bias our perceptions and interpretations of what is going on.

REFERENCES

Bailyn, L., Rapoport, R. and Fletcher, J.K. (2000) 'Moving Corporations in the United States toward gender equity: a cautionary tale', in Linda Hass, Philip Hwang, and Graeme Russell (eds), *Organizational Change and Gender Equity*. London: Sage. pp. 167–79.

Bavelas, A. and Strauss, G. (1962) 'Group dynamics and intergroup relations', in K. Benne and R. Chin (eds), *The Planning of Change*. New York: Holt, Rinehart & Winston. pp. 587–91.

Hirschhorn, L. (1988) *The Workplace Within*. Cambridge, MA: MIT Press.

Kets de Vries, M.F.R. and Miller, D. (1984) *The Neurotic Organization*. San Francisco, CA: Jossey-Bass.

Kets de Vries, M.F.R. and Miller, D. (1987) *Unstable at the Top*. New York: New American Library.

Kunda, G. (1992) *Engineering Culture*. Philadelphia, PA: Temple University Press.

Leavitt, H.J. (1951) 'Some effects of certain communication patterns on group performance', *Journal of Abnormal and Social Psychology*, 46: 38–50.

Levinson, H. (1972) *Organizational Diagnosis*. Cambridge, MA: Harvard University Press.

Lewin, K. (1952 [1947]) 'Group decision and social change', in G.E. Swanson, T.N. Newcomb and E.L. Hartley (eds), *Readings in Social Psychology, rev. edn*. New York: Holt. pp. 459–73.

Lewin, K. (1999 [1939]) 'Experiments in social space', *Reflections: The Journal of the Society for Organizational Learning*, 1 (1): 7–13 (reprinted with the permission of the American Psychological Association, © 1997).

Ludema, J.D., Cooperrider, D.L. and Barrett, F.J. (2001/2006) 'Appreciative Inquiry: the power of the unconditional positive question', in P. Reason and H. Bradbury (eds), *Handbook of Action Research: Participative Inquiry and Practice*. London: Sage. pp. 189–99. Also published in P. Reason and H. Bradbury (eds) (2006), *Handbook of Action Research: Concise Paperback Edition*. London: Sage. pp. 156–65.

Miller, D. (1990) *The Icarus Paradox*. New York: Harper Business.

Rice, A.K. (1963) *The Enterprise and Its Environment.* London: Tavistock.

Schein, E.H. (1987a) *The Clinical Perspective in Field Work.* London: Sage.

Schein, E.H. (1987b) *Process Consultation: Lessons for Managers and Consultants.* Reading, MA: Addison-Wesley.

Schein, E.H. (1988 [1969]) *Process Consultation: Its Role in Organization Development, 2nd edn.* Reading, MA: Addison-Wesley.

Schein, E.H. (1992) *Organizational Culture and Leadership, 2nd edn.* San Francisco, CA: Jossey-Bass.

Schein, E.H. (1999a) *Process Consultation Revisited: Building the Helping Relationship.* Reading, MA: Addison-Wesley-Longman.

Schein, E.H. (1999b) *The Corporate Culture Survival Guide.* San Francisco, CA: Jossey-Bass.

Schein, E.H. (2003) *DEC is Dead, Long Live DEC.* San Francisco, CA: Berrett/Koehler.

Schein, E.H. (2004) *Organizational Culture and Leadership, 3rd edn.* San Francisco, CA: Jossey-Bass.

Schein, E.H. and Bennis, W. (1965) *Personal and Organizational Change through Group Methods: the Experiential Approach.* New York: Wiley.

Sherif, M., Harvey, O.J., White, B.J., Hood, W.R. and Sherif, C. (1961) *Intergroup Conflict and Cooperation: the Robber's Cave Experiment.* Norman, OK: University Book Exchange.

Trist, E.L. et al. (1963) *Organizational Choice.* London: Tavistock.

Van Maanen, J. (1979) 'The self, the situation, and the rules of interpersonal relations', in W. Bennis, J. Van Maanen, E.H. Schein and F. Steele (eds), *Essays in Interpersonal Dynamics.* Homewood, IL: Dorsey. pp. 43–101.

Whyte, W.F. (1943) *The Street Corner Society.* Chicago, IL: University of Chicago Press.

19

The Practice of Appreciative Inquiry

James D. Ludema and Ronald E. Fry

In this chapter, we discuss how to use appreciative inquiry (AI) as a generative form of action research. We define AI as a process of collective learning – a way to explore, discover, and appreciate everything that gives 'life' to organizations when they are most vibrant, effective, successful, and healthy in relation to their whole system of stakeholders. To illustrate these ideas, we walk step-by-step through an AI summit process with a large, North American transportation company, Roadway Express. We show how Roadway used AI to include marginal voices, strengthen relationships between labor and management, spark innovation, and produce significant short- and long-term business results. Based on the Roadway story, we offer five recommendations to enhance the effectiveness of AI as a catalyst for positive change. We conclude that although AI is primarily strength-based, it is much more than just a wish to be positive. It is a robust process of inquiry and anticipatory learning that enables participants in social systems to shape the world they most want by building new knowledge, spurring inventiveness, creating energy, and enhancing cooperative capacity.

In Chapter 12, David Cooperrider and Danielle Zandee provide an exploration of the conceptual underpinnings of appreciative inquiry. In this chapter, we discuss how to use appreciative inquiry as a form of action research. First, we introduce appreciative inquiry (AI) and its various forms of engagement. Second, we provide the example of an AI Summit (Ludema et al., 2003; Powley et al., 2004) with a large, North American transportation company as an illustration. Finally, we explore some of the factors that 'give life' to AI as a powerful catalyst for positive change.

A BRIEF INTRODUCTION TO APPRECIATIVE INQUIRY

Appreciative inquiry got its start in the early 1980s when David Cooperrider, then a doctoral student of organizational behavior at Case Western Reserve University, and his faculty mentor, Suresh Srivastva, were doing an organization change project with the Cleveland Clinic in Cleveland, Ohio. They found that when they used the traditional organization development (OD) approach of problem diagnosis and feedback, it sucked the energy for change right out of the system.

The more problems people discovered, the more discouraged they became; and the more discouraged they became, the more they began to blame one another for the problems. In fact, when Cooperrider and Srivastva noticed this same dynamic (discouragement and blame) occurring among themselves and their colleagues as they analyzed their interview data, they clearly saw the power of the questions they were using – on themselves! They and their colleagues saw first hand that the questions they asked were having an unexpected impact on the human system they were trying to understand and to help.

Second, they discovered that their work was more powerful when they let go of the very idea of intervening. Instead of *intervention* they framed their task as *inquiry* – simply to be students of organizational life, to learn, to discover, and to appreciate everything that gave 'life' to the system when it was most vibrant, effective, successful, and healthy in relation to its whole system of stakeholders. In their analysis of the data, Cooperrider and Srivastva engaged in a radical reversal of the traditional problem-solving approach. Influenced by the writings of Schweitzer (1969) on 'reverence for life', they focused on everything they could find that appeared to empower and energize the system, everything contributing to excellence and high performance at the clinic. Even though, in the early stages, they still asked some traditional diagnostic questions (such as 'Tell us about the biggest problem facing you as a chairman of your department'), they decided later, in preparing their feedback report, to emphasize all the generative themes: moments of success; experiences of high points; and stories of innovation, hope, courage, and positive change. Instead of doing a root-cause analysis of failure, they let go of every so-called deficiency and turned full attention to analysis of root causes of success.

The results were immediate and dramatic. Relationships improved, cooperation increased, and visible commitments by the physicians to change initiatives ensued. The Clinic Board was so enthused by the results that it asked to use the method with the entire organization of 8000 people. Cooperrider and Srivastva called the approach 'appreciative inquiry', and the term first appeared in a footnote in their feedback report to the Board. A few years later they published their classic article 'Appreciative Inquiry into Organizational Life' (Cooperrider and Srivastva, 1987), articulating the theory and vision of appreciative inquiry as a paradigm shift for the fields of action research and organizational change. It was a call, as they wrote, 'for a scholarship of the positive'.

Barrett and Fry (2005) describe AI as a strength-based approach to transforming human systems toward a shared image of their most positive potential (Cooperrider, 1990) by first discovering the very best in their shared experience. It is not about implementing a change to get somewhere; it is about chang*ing* … convening, conversing and relating with each another in order to tap into the natural capacity for cooperation (Bushe and Coetzer, 1995) and change that is in every system. At its core, AI is an invitation for members to leverage the generative capacity of dialogue (Gergen, et al., 2004; Ludema and DiVirgilio, 2006); to attend to the ways that our conversations, particularly our metaphors (Barrett and Cooperrider, 1990) and stories (Ludema, 2002), facilitate actions that support our highest values and potential. An appreciative inquiry effort seeks to create generative conversations that break the hammerlock of the status quo and open up new alternatives for organizing.

Toward a Positive Revolution in Change

Since the early 1980s, AI has grown extensively around the world. It has been used by thousands of people and hundreds of organizations in every sector of society to promote transformative change (see, e.g., Cooperrider et al., 2001; Watkins and Mohr, 2001; Fry et al., 2002; Ludema et al., 2003; Whitney and Trosten-Bloom, 2003; Cooperrider and Avital, 2004; Cooperrider et al., 2005; Stavros and Torres, 2005; Barrett and Fry,

2005; Cooperrider and Whitney, 2005; Thatchenkery and Metzker, 2006). Appreciative inquiry has also given birth to a variety of public-dialogue projects such as Imagine Chicago (www.imaginechicago.org), a citywide inquiry designed to promote civic discourse and innovation, Images and Voices of Hope (www.ivofhope.org), a worldwide inquiry to strengthen the role of media in building healthy societies, and Business as an Agent of World Benefit (BAWB; http://worldbenefit.case.edu), a world dialogue designed to engage executives, thought leaders, and change agents in reflecting on and convening around the subject of how the business sector might put its imagination, capacity, and resources to work on behalf of society and the planet.

Appreciative inquiry is also quickly developing a robust theoretical foundation. Yaeger, Sorensen, and Bengtsson (2005) estimate conservatively that since 1986 close to 400 publications and 80 dissertations have been written about AI, and many of these have received awards from the Academy of Management, the International Management Association, the Organization Development Network, the Organizational Development Institute, the American Society of Training and Development, and others. A variety of master's-level programs in management, organization development, education, and social change have incorporated AI into their coursework. At least two PhD programs in organization development/behavior, at Benedictine University (www.ben.edu/odhome) and Case Western Reserve University (http://weatherhead.cwru.edu/orbh), have made AI a cornerstone of their curricula. The emerging movements in positive psychology (www.positivepsychology.org) and positive organizational scholarship (Cameron et al., 2003; www.bus.umich.edu/positive) provide additional theoretical grounding to appreciative inquiry.

Finally, the community of AI practitioners around the world is growing dramatically, and an increasing number of resources are being made available. Appreciative Inquiry Consulting, (www.accon.suiting.org)

Benedictine University, Case Western Reserve University, Corporation for Positive Change (www.positivechange.org), NTL (www.ntl. org), the Positive Change Corps, (www.positivechangecorps.org), and the Taos Institute (www.taosinstitute.net) offer a variety of training programs for AI practitioners. The AI Listserv (lists.business.utah.edu/mailman/listinfo/ailist) allows anyone interested in AI to engage in online dialogue with others. The *AI Practitioner* (www.airpractitioner.com) is an up-to-the-minute quarterly journal that features new advances in the practice of AI from around the world. The AI Commons website (http://appreciativeinquiry.case.edu/) is a free, open-access resource bank at Case Western University that includes all things AI.

The Power of Appreciative Inquiry to Transform

At its core, appreciative inquiry is the study and exploration of what gives life to human systems when they function at their best (Cooperrider and Srivastva, 1987; Bushe, 1995). It is based on the assumption that every living system has a hidden and underutilized core of strengths – its positive core – which, when revealed and tapped, provides a sustainable source of positive energy for both personal and organizational transformation. Cooperrider and Sekerka (2003) relate this to the concept of *fusion energy* in the sciences. Fusion is the power source of the sun and the stars. It results when two positively charged elements combine into one. In organizations, when joy touches joy, strength touches strength, health touches health, and inspiration combines with inspiration, people are liberated and empowered to create ascending spirals of co-operative action.

The Appreciative Inquiry 4-D Cycle

As an approach to organization change, AI involves the co-operative search for the best in people, their organizations, and the world

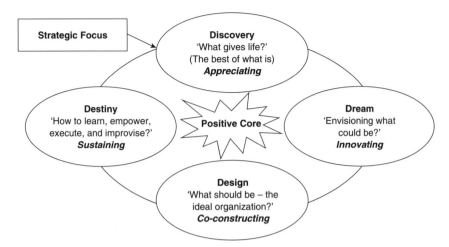

Figure 19.1   *Appreciative inquiry 4-D model*

around them. This is significantly different from conventional managerial problem-solving with its root cause analysis or gap analysis. The key task in problem-solving is to identify and remove deficits. The process typically involves: (1) identifying problems, (2) analyzing causes, (3) searching for solutions, and (4) developing an action plan.

In contrast, the key task in AI is to identify and leverage strengths. The steps include: (1) discovery of the best of what is, (2) dream to imagine what could be, (3) design what will be, and (4) destiny – to enact change learning to become what we most hope for (see Figure 19.1).

The purpose of the *discovery* phase is to search for, highlight, and illuminate those factors that give life to the organization, the 'best of what is' in any given situation. The list of positive topics for discovery is endless: high quality, integrity, empowerment, innovation, customer responsiveness, technological innovation, team spirit, and so on. In each case the task is to promote organizational learning by sharing stories about times when these qualities were at their best and analyzing the forces and factors that made them possible.

The second phase is to *dream* about what could be. When the best of what is has been identified, the mind naturally begins to

search beyond this; it begins to envision new possibilities. Because these dreams have been cued by asking positive questions, they paint a compelling picture of what the organization could and should become as it aligns with people's deepest hopes and highest aspirations.

The third phase is to *design* the future through dialogue. Once people's hopes and dreams have been articulated, the task is to design the organization's social architecture – norms, values, structures, strategies, systems, patterns of relationship, ways of doing things – that can bring the dreams to life. It is a process of building commitment to a common future by dialoguing and debating, crafting and creating until you get to the point where everyone can say, 'Yes this *is* the kind of organization or community that I want to invest my energies in. Let's make it happen.'

The final phase, *destiny*, is an invitation to construct the future through innovation and action. People find innovative ways to help move the organization closer to the ideal. Because the ideals are grounded in realities, the confidence is there to try to make things happen. This is important to underscore because it is precisely because of the visionary content, placed in juxtaposition to grounded examples of the

Table 19.1 *Forms of engagement of appreciative inquiry*

AI Summit: A large, multi-stakeholder group of people (30–thousands) participate simultaneously in a three- to five-day AI 4-D process.

Whole-System 4-D Dialogue: All members of the organization and some stakeholders participate in an AI 4-D process. It takes place at multiple locations over an extended period of time.

Mass Mobilized Inquiry: Large numbers of interviews (thousands to millions), on a socially responsible topic, are conducted throughout a city, a community, or the world.

Core Group Inquiry: A small group of people selects topics, craft questions, and conduct appreciative inquiry interviews.

Positive Change Network: Members of an organization are trained in AI and provided with resources to initiate projects and share materials, stories, and best practices.

Positive Change Consortium: Multiple organizations collaboratively engage in an AI 4-D process to explore and develop a common area of interest.

AI Learning Team: A small group of people with a specific project – an evaluation team, a process improvement team, a customer focus group, a benchmarking team, or a group of students – conduct an AI 4-D process.

Progressive AI Meetings: An organization, small group, or team goes through the AI 4-D process over the course of 10 to 12 meetings that are each two to four hours long.

extraordinary, that appreciative inquiry opens the status quo to transformations in collective action.

While this '4-D' cycle remains the most often used depiction of the AI process, it is important to remember that AI is a dynamic process and the 'D's' simply represent different, intentional sets of activities and conversations, all linked to an affirmative inquiry topic. The linearity of this diagram should not be mistaken for a 'forced march' agenda that one must follow. After Discovery, AI processes can take varied paths. Our colleague, Mac Odell, for instance, has modified his use of AI with thousands of Nepalese women to include seven D's: Discovery, Dream, Design, Destiny, Drumming, Dancing and Doing.

Forms of Engagement of Appreciative Inquiry

There are many different ways to use appreciative inquiry to promote positive change in organizations and in communities. Each AI process is designed to meet the unique needs and goals of the people, organization, or community involved. Table 19.1, adapted from Whitney and Trosten-Bloom (2003),

contains a brief description of the core forms of engagement of AI.

TRANSFORMING PERFORMANCE THROUGH PARTNERSHIP AT ROADWAY EXPRESS

Introduction

Roadway Express is one of the United States' larger unionized, 'less that truckload' freight carriers. Founded in 1930 and headquartered in Akron, Ohio, they are today a subsidiary of the Yellow Roadway Corporation. Revenues exceed $3.0 billion and they employ over 25,000 skilled and trained transportation professionals, the large majority of which are unionized teamsters. They have approximately 350 sites throughout the USA, Canada, Mexico and Puerto Rico ranging from neighborhood terminals with a handful of loading doors to their largest break-bulk hub with 460 doors in Chicago Heights, Illinois.

At a leadership development workshop with some 30 Roadway Express senior leaders who were being introduced to the concepts of AI, the then Chief Operating Officer made the following comment: 'I am beginning to see how this [AI] process might help me with some issues we face like diversity, involvement, or morale. But my main concern – the thing I lose sleep on – is margins. I have to find a way to increase our margins to stay competitive. Can AI help with that?' The result of the ensuing conversation was that a headquarters group would embrace the topic of optimal margins and sponsor three to four 'pilot' AI initiatives in the company to see if AI could really benefit their strategic objectives. They decided to begin by implementing an AI summit process with their two largest terminal sites.

The AI Summit (Ludema et al., 2003; Powley et al., 2004) is a method for accelerating change by involving a broad range of internal and external stakeholders in the change process in real time. It is typically a single event or series of events that bring people together to: (1) discover the organization's or community's core competencies and strengths; (2) envision opportunities for positive change; (3) design the desired changes into the organization's or community's systems, structures, strategies, and culture; and (4) implement and sustain the change and make it work. AI summits vary in size, anywhere between 30 and thousands of people. They typically consist of about two months of planning, three or four days of face-to-face, real-time summit activity, and several months of implementation and follow-up activities. What follows is a case description of the AI summit process at one of the Roadway sites and then a summary of other AI activities and results that occurred over the past four years, as Roadway continued to apply and adapt AI to help transform performance and organization culture.

Topic Choice

AI begins with (re)framing the situation or presenting issue in such a way as to attract interest and generate hope or positive anticipation. The effort here is intentionally to word the focus of the inquiry in such a way that it captures what people are really curious about and what they really want to see as a desired outcome of working together. This is often a re-framing exercise because of our tendency toward deficit discourse. We are trained to identify problems and often forget that chasing the solution may just create another problem for someone else, or not get us much further toward what we really wish for. Yes, we all want problems to go away, but why? What is the desired future on the other side of that problem? What is it we most wish for at the end of the day?

At Roadway's '211' Terminal, the initial problem or challenge was 'throughput'. Corporate headquarters had determined that 211 was lower than the overall company average in terms of the amount of time it took to transfer arriving freight onto another truck and get it out the gates to its next destination. They believed that if 211 could improve its performance in terms of the throughput metrics the company was using, it would have a direct effect on increasing margins, which was the overall company's focal topic: optimal margins. However, it was apparent from the start that if 'throughput' was to be the topic, few were going to be excited about working on it. As one 211 union steward put it, 'Throughput is just another management word for "speed up tactics", trying to get more out of us for nothing in return.'

At the 211 site, a design team was created consisting of the site manager, a district sales manager, a regional VP, several foremen, a clerk, an engineer, and three union stewards, consisting of a long and short-haul driver and a dock worker. The team was intentionally representative of the 'whole system' so that as many distinct perspectives (e.g., levels, functions, roles, affiliations) as possible would be included in planning and implementing the AI process. This group's first task was to convene for a day to reframe their topic. They did AI interviews with each other, probing into stories of when the 211 site had been at its best, when they had individually done something to speed the transfer of freight through the terminal, and their images of an ideal future when their site led the company in throughput measures. After finding common themes among their stories and preferred futures, they divided into three small sub-groups with a mix of job roles in each and proceeded to brainstorm possible topics that would be bold, exciting, a stretch for everyone, and affirmative – something all the stakeholders at 211 would want to strive for. The following affirmative topic was created by this group – *Winning with Employee-Driven Throughput: Crushing Non-Union Competition by Delivering Unsurpassed Speed and Leveraging Employee Pride and Involvement.*

One can see quickly how the 'management's voice' for speed got into the statement and how the union's voice for pride, involvement and crushing the non-union competitors also came to the forefront. The important thing is that everyone in the design team believed they could attract (vs. force or coerce) their constituencies to attend an AI meeting devoted to this topic, that their peers would really want to work to make this topic a reality.

The Summit: Engaging the 'Whole System'

The Design Team mapped all the stakeholder voices that needed to be involved in an inquiry into the affirmative topic (above). They then invited 128 stakeholders (of a total of approximately 1100) to convene in a local hotel ballroom for three days to engage in the AI summit process. The group again represented the whole system: drivers, foremen, management, union stewards, fork lift operators, dock workers, clerks, sales representatives, district executives, shop maintenance, and customers. This principle of wholeness is central to appreciative inquiry. When people engage each other and see interconnections among departments, processes, people, and ideas, they gain a deeper sense of empathy, a broader organizational mindset, and a better understanding of how to collaborate with others to get things done. If anyone is missing, there is much less potential for new discoveries, learning, cooperation, and innovative action (Ludema et al., 2003; Powley et al., 2004).

Discovery

After very brief welcomes, all participants were paired with people they did not know or work with to engage in appreciative interviews with each other. (The AI Commons website has a variety of appreciative interview guides, including those used at Roadway.) In any AI process, it is important to begin with these one-on-one interviews. They (1) give everyone equal voice; (2) establish a model of both sharing and listening in a deeply focused way; (3) offer every participant a chance to explore their own thinking in the relative safety of a one-on-one dialogue; (4) quickly generate a deep sense of connection among participants; and (5) draw out the appreciative foundations of the work to be done. Information, ideas, and stories that are generated during the interviews are referred to throughout the meeting.

In the case of Roadway, these interview conversations focused on stories of the best of the past at 211 in terms of things that related to the affirmative topic: unsurpassed speed, leveraging employee pride, involvement, and their ideal images of a 211 site that they most wished to work in. The pairs then combined into 'max-mix' groups of eight and began to theme the key success factors that were embedded in their stories. Max-mix groups are intentionally used in AI processes to allow people to learn and understand the organization from diverse perspectives. Each of these groups also noted key turning points and positive changes in the history of the 211 site on a timeline posted on one wall of the room. The result of this discovery process included a consensual validation of 211's history in terms of key industrial moments, company changes and local 211 changes that resulted in improvement or business growth, as well as a prioritized list of key factors at 211 that drive success in terms of margin growth and customer service.

As the latter were reported out from the various mixed stakeholder groups, they were posted on a large drawing of a truck on one of the meeting room walls. The truck cab was pulling two trailers. The first one was labeled 'Our Positive Core', and the most common strengths to preserve from the discovery interviews were summarized and posted on that trailer. Among the most mentioned common strengths to preserve were union pride, positive foreman–employee relationships, driver–customer interactions, low absenteeism, senior teamsters mentoring newer members, and cross-shift cooperation. Even at this early point in the process, several teamster participants were remarking that this was a different kind of meeting than what they expected; that people were listening to each other for a change.

An important part of the discovery phase was the involvement of the customer voice. Four customers were invited to sit on a panel during a working lunch. They were interviewed with similar questions to those that the pairs had used: tell a story of a highpoint experience with 211; tell a story of a time that 211 helped add value to your business; and share your ideal images of your company's future and how 211 can contribute to your future success. After responding to these questions in front of the whole group, an open question-and-answer session ensued. One of the important observations by the managers was how interested and curious the union members were in finding out more about how the customers saw things.

Dream

The dream phase of an AI summit is an invitation for the entire organization to engage in a spirited conversation about their organization's greatest potential. By doing this, the organization as a whole creates for itself positive guiding images of the future that expand the realm of the possible and spur innovation (Cooperrider, 1990). For many organizational members, this is often the first time they have been invited to engage in dialogue about the strategic future of their organization. Consistently, the process is both personally and organizationally inspiring.

At Roadway, with their strengths to preserve (positive core) in front of them, the multi-stakeholder groups began to share and analyze their greatest hopes and wishes for the future. They reviewed their images of the

ideal future 211 site from their interviews and pulled out the most common themes and ideas for change. Each group was then tasked to 'portray' some part of these images in the form of a skit, song, poem, newscast, etc. While one might expect a male-dominant, 'nuts and bolts' group like this to resist this kind of 'fun and games', the increased energy in the room was palpable. People could not wait to show their future images! The combination of humor, humility, and provocative implications in the various skits seemed to catalyze and unite the entire room. The key images conveyed through the presentations included drivers acting like sales agents with their local customers, the site interviewing customers to see if they qualified to be a preferred customer, dockworkers convening at the start of a shift without supervision to get organized for the day, an outgoing shift giving 'high fives' to the incoming shift at the main gate, and a union employee operating an electronic kiosk to access benefit information and to bid for work assignments.

The mixed groups were then asked to consider what they found most common and attractive in all the presentations, including their own, and to generate two or three actionable ideas that would accelerate 'Winning with Employee-Driven Thoughput'. These ideas were called out and posted on a large Opportunity Map on the wall (Ludema et al., 2003). Everyone then got to vote with sticky dots on the four ideas (out of approximately 65) that they felt were the most powerful and attractive to them to work on for the rest of the summit session. The voting produced seven clusters of ideas. Each of the seven were given a temporary label or title: Freight Ready Earlier; All Stakeholders Engaged – Communication; Educate and Leverage Employee Experience; Measurement, Technology and Equipment; Bridging the Gap – Attendance; Bridging the Gap – Positive Pride; Bridging the Gap – Bids.

Design

The entire group then reorganized around the seven opportunity areas. They 'voted with their feet' and walked to the specific opportunity area they most wanted to work on – at the summit *and* afterwards – to make it a reality. This idea of 'voting with your feet' (Owen, 1997) is essential to the design and destiny phases of appreciative inquiry. It allows people to follow their interests and passions rather than being forced or coerced to work on pre-determined priorities, and it invariably results in people gravitating toward activities where they have the highest level of expertise and can make the greatest contribution.

Design work began in each of the new teams with the creation of a 'provocative proposition' describing what success in this particular opportunity area should look like. Provocative propositions are statements of how organizational members plan to organize themselves in pursuit of their dreams. They are a set of principles and commitments about how people want to work together. They answer the question: 'What would our organization look like if it were designed perfectly to help us accomplish out dreams and produce the kind of performance (human, technical, financial, environmental) we want?' They provide positive anticipatory images for the groups to hold in front of them as they move toward specific action planning (Ludema et al., 2003). For example, the Freight Ready Earlier group crafted the following provocative proposition:

Freight Ready Earlier
Roadway Express is the #1 transportation provider in the world due to our unsurpassed throughput service. Team sell is contagious. Each employee is a stakeholder engaged in celebrating the success of the company. Customers are honored to have 211 employees handle their business. All customer contact work groups are key components in our success. They are recognized as the best trained, most highly motivated sales force in the universe.

Drafts of these propositions were shared with the entire stakeholder group and feedback was invited around two questions: 1) What do you like most or find most powerful in the statement – as it is now?; and 2) What would you add or edit to make it even more powerful and attractive? With this feedback, each team revised its proposition and proceeded to design specific targets and action plans. For the Freight Ready Earlier group, their action plans included the following:

Freight Ready Earlier

- One-Year Goals:
- 50% freight back by 15:30 hours
- 90% freight back by 17:00 hours
- City Wrap by 19:00 hours

Action Steps:

- If the customer has the freight ready, we need to be in position to pick it up. Credibility.
- Need to accept inefficiencies and fine tune as we go.
- Communicate to the Customer what we are trying to accomplish.
- Reduce number of spots and attempt to pickup live.
- Combine early peddles to improve productivity and get out timely.
- Focus on the most productive time for the city drivers. We can improve production for the bulk of our P&D business between 10:00-16:00.

In the other groups, action items included things like experimenting with shift start-up meetings with dockworkers taking the lead to organize the agenda and set plans for the day, short-haul (pick up and delivery) drivers becoming more active in generating new business from customers they knew best, a pilot mentoring program for senior teamsters to coach and educate newer members about the costs of absenteeism and its impact on their competitiveness and pension funds, reorganizing the docks and adding music to the area, and increasing the flow of information through electronic kiosks or message boards throughout the site

Destiny

Each opportunity group reported out their revised provocative propositions, short-term targets and key action steps to occur after the summit. After each report, a sensing of the whole group was obtained by asking every participant to hold up a green, yellow or red card to indicate their overall support of the action plan. While green cards dominated each presentation, those holding up yellow or red cards were tasked to give their feedback or questions and concerns directly to the team making the presentation during a break that came right after the reports.

To assist in follow-up after this summit, each of the seven teams was asked to find two volunteers to become part of a steering group that would convene regularly with the site manager to monitor progress and share best practices. It was also announced that there would be a one-day follow-up session in six months to share progress, celebrate victories, and involve more stakeholders who were unable to come to this event.

The summit ended with an 'open microphone' session where anyone could take a wireless microphone and say whatever they wished at that moment. Many of the comments were full of emotions. Some reported feeling like they could really speak their minds for the first time in decades of working for the company. Others remarked how much they enjoyed seeing everyone so positive about the company's future and willing to work together. Still others said how refreshing it was to engage without the bickering, complaining, or outright hostility that sometimes surrounded the workplace.

Immediate Results

The seven action teams met (approximately one hour per week) over the next several months. During this post-summit work, the teams experienced a mixed reaction from their peers; some were curious, interested, and eager to get involved, while others were skeptical and even resentful that the teams got permission to meet during work hours and they had to compensate for the absences. In addition, it was difficult in the rushed work atmosphere to convey a sense of the *experience* of the summit to those who had not been present. For this reason, the steering group felt it was important to involve new participants in the follow-up session.

Some changes occurred quickly (e.g. experimenting with union-led shift start-up meetings on the docks) while others took more time (e.g. re-organizing the dock layouts to make the movement of freight more efficient). One symbolic act was to permanently mount the Opportunity Map created at the summit (with the dot votes included) out in a central dock space. It remains there today, some 5 years later.

Six months following the summit, a one-day follow-up session was held. About 90 stakeholders were invited, including members from all the seven action teams and approximately 40 stakeholders who were not at the first summit. Each team presented progress and accomplishments-to-date, and then invited the new attendees to join in discussions about next steps. At the six-month follow-up meeting the following progress metrics, in terms of 'Winning with Employee-Driven Throughput' were reported:

- Average throughput improved 47% to 64%.
- Average transit speed reduced 2.3 days to 2.1 days.
- Average production efficiency increased 59% to 64%.
- Percent freight dispatched by 05:00 increased 16% to 27%.
- Reduced need for formal grievance mechanism (zero grievances for 105 days!).

Each of these results was considered positive and indicative of ultimate 'success' at Winning with Employee-Driven Throughput. Taken together they we deemed 'beyond expectation' by the terminal manager.

The Long-Term Generative Effect

After just two summits at Roadway terminals like the one described above, it became clear that common issues and opportunities were arising, regardless of the specific affirmative topic that each site had defined. Communication, mentoring, involving drivers in sales, dockworker involvement in designing their workspace, etc. were brought up across the system. Roadway thus began a program they titled Engagement through Education in the Fundamentals of Business to build a real partnership between the union and management.

They began to train and educate everyone with information to track their individual jobs to three key organizational metrics, including the union pension plan. These sessions were included as part of every AI summit, which they began to conduct on an annual basis. From 2001 through 2005, over 60 summits of two to three days in length were held, involving over 12,000 employees. Efficiency improvements from the change initiatives resulting from these AI interventions have been estimated at $10,234,603 in savings.

More telling is that in a totally separate, corporate-driven campaign in 2004 to cut costs from dock operations, the terminals where AI summits had occurred reported average savings of $95,584, compared to $14,135 coming from the non-AI sites. This suggests that the capacity of all stakeholders at a given terminal to work collaboratively and creatively to reduce costs was increased through the AI summit process, although the summit itself was not directly meant to address this. The discovery of real, shared strengths, common images of a more positive future, and high engagement in implementation of action initiatives resulted in *more willingness to engage in similar ways around new opportunities or challenges.*

At terminal 211, the amazing drop in filed grievances from over 300 in the months prior to the summit down to zero over 105 days (and thereafter averaging only 0–5 per month) signifies another example of a spread effect (Mantel and Ludema, 2000) coming out of the AI intervention. If only those employees who participated in the summit were somehow 'changed' to feel more engaged, committed, or willing to partner with management, then the other 85 percent of the system should be expected to behave as before. Something positive and generative was surfaced at the summit that began to influence the entire system – without any specific or formal mechanism, goal, plan, or process in place.

In sum, perhaps the deep, lasting transformation at Roadway from the application of AI practices is in what they term the 'qualitative' differences they are experiencing at the level of organization culture: employees becoming more educated as business people, more of an ownership mentality throughout the workforce, self-managed initiatives across the organization, the emergence of leaders at every level, and a new foundation of trust and partnership between union and management.

WHAT 'GIVES LIFE' TO EFFECTIVE AI PROCESSES?

As mentioned earlier, there are many different ways to do appreciative inquiry, and each AI process will be unique based on its purpose, the context in which it is done, the constellation of people involved, the skill and preferences of those leading or facilitating, the kinds of resources available, and perhaps most importantly, the surprises, innovations, and improvisations that occur along the way. At its best, AI is less a science than an art, less a prescriptive method than a dynamic commitment to engage with others in search and growth of that which gives, sustains, and enhances life in any given setting or situation (Cooperrider and Srivastva, 1987). That being said, when AI is used as a process for social and organizational change, there are a number of factors that influence its effectiveness. Below, we discuss five of these: agreeing on a clear, relevant, and compelling task; engaging the 'whole system'; emphasizing inquiry and learning; focusing unconditionally on strengths and pushing beyond discovery and dream to design and destiny. Certainly, there are many additional factors to be considered, but they remain beyond the scope of this chapter.

Agreeing on a Clear, Relevant, and Compelling Task

One of the basic assumptions of AI is that human systems move in the direction of what they study (Bushe, 2001). During an AI process, the task focus serves to organize inquiry and dialogue, and hence to establish direction for the organization's transformation. A clearly stated task, defined by a design team the represents the whole system, and a process carefully designed to keep the group on task are essential to success (Ludema et al., 2003). This is true for two reasons. First, the task determines what the group learns. For example, the topic for the Roadway 211 summit was 'Winning with Employee-Driven Throughput: Crushing Non-Union Competition by Delivering Unsurpassed Speed and Leveraging Employee Pride and Involvement'. It was selected by the project's design team, which was composed of people from multiple levels and functions to begin to represent the 'whole system'. They selected this topic because it was relevant to each of them at a *deep strategic and emotional* level. It would enable them to grow and to better accomplish their mission and goals as individuals and as an organization. This singular focus allowed everyone involved to learn more about throughput, speed, pride, and involvement than any of them imagined possible prior to the inquiry.

Second, a compelling task – or inquiry topic – attracts people to want to invest energy into it. Cooperrider (1990), Ford and Ford (1994), and Weick and Quinn (1999) make a compelling argument that, particularly within the context of continuous change, change occurs through a logic of attraction (Ford and Ford, 1994) rather than a logic of replacement (Ford and Backoff, 1988). People change to a new position because they are attracted to it, drawn to it, or inspired by it. There is a focus on moral power, the freedom of the change target, and the role of choice in the transformational process. In this model, to lead change is to 'pull' change by showing people what is possible (a logic of attraction) rather than 'pushing' change by telling people what to do (a logic of replacement).

At Roadway, a task that included both 'speed' and 'pride' was attractive to the whole organization. Everyone on the design team believed they could attract their constituencies to invest, at least for a period of time, in this task. As they got deeper into the inquiry, both at terminal 211 and at other terminals, they began to discover that there were other tasks that were equally, if not more, compelling for the organization. They began an inquiry into 'Engagement through Education in the Fundamentals of Business' to build deeper partnership between the union and management and to equip people to track their jobs on key organizational metrics. The attractiveness of these tasks has enabled Roadway to sustain energy, align their actions, and produce impressive results over more than a four-year period.

Engaging the Whole System

AI is grounded in social constructionist assumptions (Gergen, 1994, 1999; Cooperrider et al., 1995), including the idea that people invent and create their organizations and communities through conversation about who they are (identity) and what they want (ideals). From this perspective, organizations can be understood as networks of conversation (Ford, 1999) – multiple layers of conversations that are embedded in other conversations. This means that change agents work with, through, and on conversations to generate, sustain, and complete new conversations to bring about new patterns of action that result in the accomplishment of specific commitments (Ludema and DiVirgilio, 2006). This is the essence of AI; it changes conversations and relational space that characterize the status quo by infusing intentionally worded, affirmative inquiries and focusing on narratives of success to explore some affirmative topic and release pent up energy and ideas that people have not felt encouraged or able to express previously.

To do this well, it is essential to have as many relevant parties as possible engaged in the inquiry. When people inquire, converse, learn, and take action across previously polarizing boundaries, it has many benefits (Ludema, et al., 2003). First, it eliminates false assumptions and evokes trust. Second, it allows people to gain a sense of interdependence with others. Third, it lets people see, experience, and connect with a purpose greater than their own or that of their group or department. Fourth, it satisfies the fundamental human need to be part of a larger community. Fifth, it fosters a 'whole-organization' perspective, which creates new possibilities for action, possibilities that previously lay dormant or undiscovered. Finally, it establishes credibility in the outcomes. When everyone is part of the decision- and commitment-making process, it has a stronger chance of being put into practice. Public commitments engender personal responsibility.

It is particularly powerful when an AI process brings together 'improbable pairs', that is, people who may be on opposite extremes of a perceived dilemma. It is often precisely these people who need to come together to make significant new progress on a particular agenda. For example, in the case of Roadway, labor and management needed to come together to work on both speed and pride. Had the 'opposing' points of view not joined in dialogue, meaningful, lasting, sustainable progress would not have been made. They would have had to settle for 'business as usual'. In any AI process it is essential to include people who bring dramatically different points of view to the process. In this way all the voices get heard, new connections and relationships get made, and innovative solutions that were previously unimaginable get created.

Emphasizing Inquiry and Learning

Another basic assumption of AI is that 'human systems grow in the direction of what they most persistently, actively, and collectively ask questions about' (Ludema et al., 2001/2006). This reflects a fundamental commitment to *inquiry*; to learning as a way to change or develop (Barrett, 1995; Bushe and Khamisa, 2005). It comes not so much from a choice to share power but rather from a realization that managing a change from a typical command-and-control perspective is not achieving the intended results and that something else is being called for – and that we (leaders and members) need to discover (learn) what that is.

Quinn and Dutton (2005) offer one explanation for why this may be the case. They suggest that new patterns of conversation lead to new

forms of action by creating energy; energy, in the sense of being eager to act and being capable of action. Following Maslow, McGregor, Ryan and Deci (2000), and much of the job design literature, they argue that if a conversation supports *the experience* of autonomy, competence, and relatedness, it produces energy. According to Ryan and Deci (2000) autonomy suggests an inner endorsement of one's actions. The more autonomous the behavior, the more it is endorsed by the whole self and is experienced as action for which one is responsible. A context that supports autonomy encourages people to make their own choices and gives them freedom to express themselves, to create, and to lead. Competence is having the skills, abilities, and capacity to be successful. Contexts that contribute to feelings of competence during action can enhance intrinsic motivation for that action. Relatedness is the need people have to feel belongingness and connectedness with others. When people have a sense of relatedness, they feel like they are making a contribution to the greater whole and that the greater whole is making a contribution to them. AI enhances the experience of autonomy, competence and relatedness and generates energy for action by creating conversational contexts where people have equal voice, where collective strengths are validated, and where they can self-manage their destiny within strategic parameters.

In the case of Roadway, the design team developed a set of positive questions to guide the AI process. These questions were asked of everyone involved in the inquiry in order to bring forward best practices from across the organization. It unleashed system-wide learning and increased self-efficacy about effective models of organizing and the forces and factors that made them possible. This whole-organization learning, in turn, built energy for action by providing people with an increased sense of autonomy, competence, and relatedness and led to a flurry of innovation, such as shift start-up meetings led by dockworkers, short-haul drivers generating new business, a new mentoring program, reorganizing the docks, and increasing the flow of information through electronic kiosks and message boards. AI is based on the assumption that perhaps the most important thing a manager or change agent does is articulate questions. The questions we ask set the stage for what we 'find', and what we find becomes the knowledge out of which the future is constructed (Bushe, 2001).

Focusing Unconditionally on Strengths

When an organization decides to embark on an AI process, it is committing to an unconditionally positive approach to organization change. AI begins with a deep exploration of the organization's 'positive core' – its greatest strengths, assets, capacities, capabilities, values, traditions, practices, accomplishments, and so on. One of the reasons this is so important is that organizations find their point of highest vitality at the intersection of continuity, novelty, and transition (Srivastva et al., 1992). Vital organizations know how to innovate and create unexpected newness (novelty). They know how to launch and manage planned change (transition). But perhaps even more important, vibrant organizations are expert at connecting the threads of identity, purpose, values, wisdom, and tradition that support extraordinary performance (continuity).

Fredrickson's work (1998, 2003) suggests this is true, in part, because of the power of positive emotions. According to her 'broaden and build' model, negative emotions such as fear, hostility, anxiety, and apathy lead directly to 'fight or flight' behaviors, in essence narrowing a person's response options. Positive emotions, on the other hand, broaden a person's capacities. In the AI process of discovering strengths, sharing dreams, and designing and enacting the desired organization, positive emotions are activated such as interest, joy, hope, and pride in the association with others, the work, and the organization. These in turn lead to the enhanced thought–action repertoires associated with them. For example, interest leads to investigation, exploration, becoming involved, having new experiences, and incorporating

new information, all characteristics associated with learning. Joy leads to play, imagination, invention, and experimentation, all characteristics associated with innovation. Hope (Ludema et al., 1997) leads to seeing adversity as a challenge, transforming problems into opportunities, maintaining confidence, rebounding quickly after setbacks, putting in hours to refine skills, and persevering in finding solutions, all characteristics associated with achievement and goal accomplishment. Pride leads to supporting others, expressing gratitude and appreciation, connecting, and relating, all characteristics associated with cooperation, coordination, collaboration, and pro-social behavior. Thus, positive emotions generate energy by equipping people with the enhanced thought–action repertoires that enable them to feel 'eager to act and capable of action' (Quinn and Dutton, 2005). Over time, these emotional response patterns become enduring resources that buffer against depleting experiences and fuel high performance.

In the AI process, when a human group comes in contact with its positive core a sense of hope and pride is enhanced (Ludema, 2001). All stories about best past experiences (no matter the topic) will inevitably involve more than just the storyteller. Thus the capacity for cooperation is revealed in new ways during the discovery process of inquiring into stories of past success. This, in turn, fosters a desire to cooperate anew to utilize proven strengths or capabilities. 'I want's' are transformed into 'we can's'. As an example, in the Roadway 211 summit, many drivers came into the room with a pet peeve: why won't the company put air conditioning in the cabs as so many of our competitors have? After the discovery interviews in pairs, summarizing collective strengths from the individual stories at tables of mixed stakeholders, and sharing dreams of an ideal future, the expression of this concern became an action idea from one of tables: Let's do a study to determine the increase in margins or revenues that could allow for a capital expenditure to enhance all the cabs in the fleet. An unconditional focus on strengths allowed the group to take innovative action rather than get bogged down in disappointments. Over time, this strength-based approach became an enduring resource and created a spread effect throughout the terminal. This same effect proved true across Roadway; AI sites produced significantly better results in terms of innovation, cost reduction, and grievances than did comparison sites.

Pushing Beyond Discovery and Dream to Design and Destiny

Social architecture is also a key ingredient in the sustainability of large-scale change. Passionate action on an individual basis is essential to organization change, but organizational transformation is much more than the cumulative mass of personal transformations. It requires changes in the design of the organization. Time and again people in organizations who have used AI identify deep change in the social architecture of the organization as a primary factor in their sustained success. Thus, in any AI process meant to produce sustainable large-scale change, the design phase may well be the most important part (Mantel and Ludema, 2004). If overlooked or done poorly, it can breed cynicism when dreams and aspirations fail to be realized. If done well, it produces high levels of energy and performance by engaging a wide range of people in authoring the organization's future.

In the Roadway example, when asked to identify key organization design ideas for 'Winning with Employee-Driven Thoughput', the summit participants settled on seven opportunity areas. They then broke into small groups around these opportunity areas, discussed and wrote statements of how they wanted to organize in each area, got input (ideas, agreement, approvals, resource commitments, etc.) from others, and launched action initiatives to integrate their design ideas into the day-to-day operations of the organization. By the end of the summit, all of the small groups had the support of the whole system to take action on their new design ideas. This unleashed high levels of energy and cooperative action. Not only had the group discovered its positive core, strengthened relationships, and invented new possibilities for

the future, but it made those possibilities real and meaningful by designing them into the organization's social architecture.

The task of the destiny phase is to liberate and support action in service of the whole. It includes mobilizing key strategic action initiatives that will move the whole organization quickly and directly toward the commitments made in the design phase. It also includes supporting the dozens of improvisational initiatives (Barrett, 1998; Bushe and Khamisa, 2005) that inevitably are generated through the AI process. Support comes in many forms, such as time, people, funding, coaching, rewards and recognition, being an advocate for the work, integrating across teams, establishing a follow-up plan, or launching new waves of appreciative inquiry.

CONCLUSION

AI is first and foremost an approach to inquiry and anticipatory learning – not just a wish to be positive. It is based on the assumption that in any organization, knowledge and information are widely distributed and collaboratively created through conversation. By involving a broad spectrum of stakeholders and inviting them to inquire into the-best-of-what-is-and-can-be, AI enables organizational learning and spurs inventiveness throughout the system. It also builds cooperative capacity by allowing organizational members to understand one another's perspective and by providing them a direct and immediate connection to the 'logic of the whole'.

AI distinguishes itself as an exclusively strength-based approach. It privileges attention to strengths, life-giving forces, and success factors over root causes of problems, deficits, or breakdowns. This is based on the understanding that a deep connection with strengths provides organizational members with a sense of autonomy, competence, and relatedness, which in turn elicits positive emotions such as interest, joy, hope, and pride. Positive emotions enhance thought–action repertoires by broadening the scope of attention, cognition, and action and building physical, intellectual, and social resources, which lead to increased energy for action. AI creates energy for action by boosting positive emotions and increasing an organization's overall intelligence, creativity, resilience, and cooperative capacity.

AI has the exciting potential to bring 'every stakeholder into the center of strategic thinking, learning and planning' (Barrett et al., 2005), thereby tapping into a cooperative capacity that is still latent in most organizations – where every member honestly and enthusiastically considers the needs of the whole system with renewed confidence borne from seeing shared positive images of the future and proven abilities to cooperate and achieve shared aspirations.

REFERENCES

Barrett, F.J. (1995) 'Creating appreciative learning cultures', *Organizational Dynamics*, 24: 36–49.

Barrett, F.J. (1998) 'Creativity and improvisation in jazz and organizations: implications for organizational learning', *Organization Science*, 9: 605–23.

Barrett, F.J. and Cooperrider, D.L. (1990) 'Generative metaphor intervention: a new approach for working with systems divided by conflict and caught in defensive perception', *Journal of Applied Behavioral Science*, 26: 219–39.

Barrett, F.J. and Fry, R.E. (2005) *Appreciative Inquiry: a Positive Approach to Building Cooperative Capacity*. Chagrin Falls, OH: Taos Publications.

Barrett, F.J., Cooperrider, D.L. and Fry, R.E. (2005) 'Bringing every mind into the game to realize the positive revolution in strategy', in *Practicing Organizational Development*. San Francisco, CA: Pfeiffer. pp. 510–38.

Bushe, G.R. (1995) 'Advances in appreciative inquiry as an organization development intervention', *Organization Development Journal*, 13: 14–22.

Bushe, G.R. (2001) 'Five theories of change embedded in appreciative inquiry', in D. Cooperrider, P. Sorenson, D. Whitney and T. Yeager (eds), *Appreciative Inquiry: an Emerging Direction for Organization Development*. Champaign, IL: Stipes. pp. 99–110.

Bushe, G.R. and Coetzer, G. (1995) 'Appreciative inquiry as a team development intervention: a controlled experiment', *Journal of Applied Behavioral Science*, 31: 13–30.

Bushe, G.R. and Khamisa, A.F. (2005) 'When is appreciative inquiry transformational? A meta-case analysis', *Journal of Applied Behavioral Science*. 41 (2): 161–81.

Cameron, K.S., Dutton, J.E. and Quinn, R.E. (2003) *Positive Organizational Scholarship: Foundations of a New Discipline*. San Francisco, CA: Berrett-Koehler.

Cooperrider, D.L. (1990) 'Positive image, positive action: the affirmative basis of organizing', in S. Srivastva, D.L. Cooperrider et al., *Appreciative Management and Leadership*. San Francisco, CA: Jossey-Bass. pp. 91–125.

Cooperrider, D.L. and Avital, M. (eds) (2004) *Advances in Appreciative Inquiry: Constructive Discourse and Human Organization Vol. 1*. Amsterdam: Elsevier.

Cooperrider, D.L. and Sekerka, L.E. (2003) 'Inquiry into the appreciable world: toward a theory of positive organization change', in K.S. Cameron, J.E. Dutton, and R.E. Quinn (eds), *Positive Organization Scholarship*. San Francisco, CA: Berrett-Koehler. pp. 225–400.

Cooperrider, D.L. and Srivastva, S. (1987) 'Appreciative inquiry in organizational life', in W.A. Pasmore and W. Woodman (eds), *Research in Organizational Change and Development Vol. I*. Greenwich, CT: JAI Press. pp. 129–69.

Cooperrider, D.L. and Whitney, D. (2005) *Appreciative Inquiry: a Positive Revolution in Change*. San Francisco, CA: Berrett-Koehler.

Cooperrider, D.L., Barrett, F.J. and Srivastva, S. (1995) 'Social construction and appreciative inquiry: a journey in organizational theory', in *Management and Organization: Relational Alternatives to Individualism*. Aldershot: Ashgate. pp. 157–200.

Cooperrider, D.L., Sorensen, P.F., Yaeger, T.F. and Whitney, D. (eds) (2001) *Appreciative Inquiry: an Emerging Direction for Organization Development*. Champaign, IL: Stipes Publishing.

Cooperrider, D.L., Whitney, D. and Stavros, J.M. (2005) *The Appreciative Inquiry Handbook*. San Francisco, CA: Berrett-Koehler.

Ford, J.D. (1999) 'Conversations and the epidemiology of change', in R.W. Woodman and W.A. Pasmore (eds), *Research in Organizational Change and Development Vol. 12*. Stamford, CT: JAI Press. pp. 1–39.

Ford, J.D. and Backoff, R. (1988) 'Organizational change in and out of dualities and paradox', in R. Quinn and K. Cameron (eds), *Paradox and Transformation*, Cambridge, MA: Ballinger. pp. 81–121.

Ford, J.D. and Ford, L.W. (1994) 'Logics of identity, contradiction, and attraction in change', *Academy of Management Review*, 19: 756–85.

Fredrickson, B.L. (1998) 'What good are positive emotions?', *Review of General Psychology*, 2 (3): 300–19.

Fredrickson, B.L. (2003) 'Positive emotions and upward spirals in organizations', in K.S. Cameron, J.E. Dutton and R.E. Quinn (eds), *Positive Organizational Scholarship*. San Francisco, CA: Berrett-Koehler. pp. 163–93.

Fry, R.E., Barrett, F.J., Seiling, J. and Whitney, D. (2002) *Appreciative Inquiry and Organizational Transformation: Reports from the Field.* Westport, CT: Quorum Books.

Gergen, K.J. (1994) *Realities and Relationships: Soundings in Social Construction.* Cambridge, MA: Harvard University Press.

Gergen, K.J. (1999) *An Invitation to Social Construction.* Thousand Oaks, CA: Sage.

Gergen, M.M, Gergen, K.J, and Barrett, F.J. (2004) 'Appreciative inquiry as dialogue: generative and transformative', in D.L. Cooperrider and M. Avital (eds), *Advances in Appreciative Inquiry: Constructive Discourse and Human Organization, Vol. 1.* Amsterdam: Elsevier. pp. 3–28.

Ludema, J.D. (2001) 'From deficit discourse to vocabularies of hope: the power of appreciation', in D. Cooperrider et al. (eds), *Appreciative Inquiry: an Emerging Direction for Organization Development.* Champaign, IL: Stipes Publishing. pp. 265–87.

Ludema, J.D. (2002) 'Appreciative storytelling: A narrative approach to organization development and change', in R. Fry et al. (eds), *Appreciative Inquiry and Organizational Transformation: Reports from the Field.* Westport, CT: Quorum Books. pp. 239–62.

Ludema, J.D. and DiVirgilio, M.E. (2006) 'The role of energy-in-conversation in leading organizational change', *Research in Organizational Change and Development,* 16: 3–45.

Ludema, J.D., Cooperrider, D.L. and Barrett, F.J. (2001/2006) 'Appreciative inquiry: the power of the unconditional positive question', in P. Reason and H. Bradbury (eds), *Handbook of Action Research: Participative Inquiry and Practice.* London: Sage. pp. 189–99. Also published in P. Reason and H. Bradbury (eds) (2006), *Handbook of Action Research: Concise Paperback Edition.* London: Sage. pp. 155–65.

Ludema, J.D., Whitney, D., Mohr, B.J. and Griffin, T.J. (2003) *The Appreciative Inquiry Summit: a Practitioner's Guide for Leading Large Group Change.* San Francisco, CA: Berrett-Koehler.

Ludema, J.D., Wilmot, T.B. and Srivastva, S. (1997) 'Organizational hope: reaffirming the constructive task of social and organizational inquiry', *Human Relations,* 50 (8): 1015–52.

Mantel, M.J. and Ludema, J.D. (2000) 'From local conversations to global change: experiencing the worldwide ripple effect of appreciative inquiry', *Organization Development Journal,* 18 (2): 42–53.

Mantel, M.J. and Ludema, J.D. (2004) 'Sustaining positive change: inviting conversational convergence through appreciative leadership and organization design', in D.L. Cooperrider and M. Avital (eds), *Advances in Appreciative Inquiry: Constructive Discourse and Human Organization Vol. 1.* Amsterdam: Elsevier. pp. 309–36.

Owen, H. (1997) *Open Space Technology: a User's Guide, 2nd edn.* San Francisco: Berrett-Koehler.

Powley, E.H., Fry, R.E., Barrett, F.J. and Bright, D.S. (2004) 'Dialogic democracy meets command and control: transformation through the appreciative inquiry summit', *Academy of Management Executive,* 18 (3): 67–80.

Quinn, R.E. and Dutton, J.E. (2005) 'Coordination as energy-in-conversation', *Academy of Management Review,* 30 (1): 36–57.

Ryan, R.M. and Deci, E.L. (2000) 'Self-determination theory and the facilitation of intrinsic motivation, social development, and well-being', *American Psychologist,* 55 (1): 68–78.

Schweitzer, A. (1969) *The Teaching of Reverence for Life.* New York: Holt, Rinehart, and Winston.

Srivastva, S., Fry, R. et al., (1992) *Executive and Organizational Continuity: Managing the Paradoxes of Stability and Change.* San Francisco, CA: Jossey-Bass.

Stavros, J.M. and Torres, S. (2005) *Dynamic Relationships: Unleashing the Power of Appreciative Inquiry in Daily Living.* Chagrin Falls, OH: Toas Publications.

Thatchenkery, T.J. and Metzker, C. (2006) *Appreciative Intelligence: Seeing the Mighty Oak in the Acorn.* San Francisco, CA: Berrett-Kohler.

Watkins, J.M. and Mohr, B.J. (2001) *Appreciative Inquiry: Change at the Speed of Imagination.* San Francisco, CA: Jossey-Bass.

Weick, K.E. (1979) *The Social Psychology of Organizing.* Reading, MA: Addison-Wesley.

Weick, K.E. and Quinn, R.E. (1999) 'Organizational change and development', *Annual Review of Psychology,* 50: 361–86.

Whitney, D. and Trosten-Bloom, A. (2003) *The Power of Appreciative Inquiry: a Practical Guide to Positive Change.* San Francisco, CA: Berrett-Koehler.

Yaeger, T.F., Sorensen, P.F. and Bengtsson, U. (2005) 'Assessment of the state of appreciative inquiry: past, present, and future', *Research in Organizational Change and Development,* 15: 297–319.

PRA, PLA and Pluralism: Practice and Theory

Robert Chambers

PRA (participatory rural appraisal) and the more inclusive PLA (participatory learning and action) are families of participatory methodologies which have evolved as behaviours and attitudes, methods, and practices of sharing. During the 1990s and 2000s PRA/PLA has spread and been applied in most countries in the world. Among the multifarious domains of application, some of the more common have been natural resource management and agriculture, programmes for equity, empowerment, rights and security, and community-level planning and action. Related participatory methodologies which have co-evolved and spread widely as movements include farmer participatory research, integrated pest management, Reflect, Stepping Stones and Participatory Geographic Information Systems. Ideologically and epistemologically PRA/PLA seeks and embodies participatory ways to empower local and subordinate people, enabling them to express and enhance their knowledge and take action. It can be understood as having three main components: facilitators' behaviours, attitudes and mindsets linked with precepts for action; methods which combine visuals, tangibles and groups; and sharing without boundaries. Good practice has moved towards an eclectic pluralism in which branding, labels, ownership and ego give way to sharing, borrowing, improvisation, creativity and diversity, all these complemented by mutual and critical reflective learning and personal responsibility.

Since the mid-1970s there has been an accelerating evolution of participatory methodologies in development practice. One part of this has been a sequence known by its acronyms – rapid rural appraisal (RRA), participatory rural appraisal (PRA), and participatory learning and action (PLA). These are sets of approaches, methods, behaviours and relationships for finding out about local context and life. All three continue to be practised and are in various ways complementary. RRA began as a coalescence of methods devised

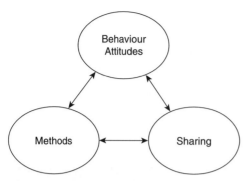

Figure 20.1 *Three principal components of PRA*
Source: Mascarenhas et al., 1991: 35A

and used to be faster and better for practical purposes than large questionnaire surveys or in-depth social anthropology. Its methods include semi-structured interviews, transect walks with observation, and mapping and diagramming, all these done by outside professionals.[1] In the late 1980s and early 1990s participatory rural appraisal (PRA) evolved out of RRA. In PRA outsiders convene and facilitate. Local people, especially those who are poorer and marginalized, are the main actors. It is they, typically in small groups, who map, diagram, observe, analyse and act. The term participatory learning and action (PLA) introduced in 1995 is sometimes used to describe PRA but is broader and includes other similar or related approaches and methods. Because of the continuities and overlaps, this methodological cluster or family is sometimes referred to as PRA/PLA or even RRA/PRA/PLA. Some, as in Pakistan, have sought to accommodate the shifts in practice by taking PRA to mean participatory reflection and action.[2] But increasingly practitioners in this tradition have moved beyond these labels and created new and specialized adaptations, some of these with other names. While continuing to use and evolve PRA methods and principles, many have become eclectic methodological pluralists.

In the early 1990s the main features of PRA emerged, with three principal components.

These were shown as three connected circles: methods; behaviour and attitudes; and sharing (Figure 20.1); Mascarenhas et al., 1991: 35A).

PRA methods, as they are often called, are visual and tangible and usually performed by small groups of people. These are the most visible and obviously distinctive feature of PRA. Maps and diagrams are made by local people, often on the ground using local materials but sometimes on paper. Many sorts of map are made – most commonly social or census maps showing people and their characteristics, resource maps showing land, trees, water and so on, and mobility maps showing where people travel for services. Using earth, sand, stones, seeds, twigs, chalk, charcoal, paper, pens and other materials, and objects as symbols, women, men and children make diagrams to represent many aspects of their communities, lives and environments. The methods include timelines, trend and change diagrams, wealth and wellbeing ranking, seasonal diagramming, Venn diagrams, causal linkage diagrams, and proportional piling. Matrix ranking and scoring are used for complex and detailed comparisons. And there are many variants and combinations of these and other methods or tools.[3]

Behaviour and attitudes, later construed as mindsets, behaviour and attitudes, were from early on regarded by many of the pioneers as more important than the methods. They were the focus of a South–South international workshop which led to the publication of *The ABC of PRA* (Kumar, 1996), where ABC stands for attitude and behaviour change. Some behaviours and attitudes were expressed as precepts (see Box 20.4) like 'Hand over the stick', 'Don't rush', 'Sit down, listen and learn' and 'Use your own best judgement at all times'.

Sharing initially referred to villagers sharing their knowledge, all sharing food, and the sharing of training, ideas, insights, methods and materials between organizations, mainly NGOs and government. By the mid-2000s the sharing circle has come to include relationships. The key phrase 'sharing without boundaries' (Absalom et al., 1995) came out of an international workshop of PRA practitioners and sought to make doubly clear the principle of openness and sharing between methodologies. It was also a pre-emptive strike against the claims of branding and exclusive ownership which go with some methodologies.

THE EVOLUTION OF PRA AND PLA

In the evolution of PRA there was much intermingling and innovation (Chambers, 1994, 1997). Among other sources were the approaches and methods of action science (Argyris et al., 1985; see also Chapter 17), reflection-in-action (Schön, 1983, 1987), popular education (Freire, 1970) and participatory research and participatory action research (BRAC, 1983; Rahman, 1984; Fals Borda and Rahman, 1991; see also Chapters 2 and 3). From farming systems research came recognition of local diversity and complexity (Norman, 1975), and from social anthropology the richness and detail of indigenous technical knowledge (e.g. Brokensha et al., 1980; Richards, 1985). The work of the Highlander Research and Education Centre in Rural Appalachia (Gaventa with Horton, 1981; Gaventa and Lewis, 1991; Gaventa, 1993) contributed the seminal insight that local people with little education were much more capable of doing their own appraisal and analysis than professionals believed.

In the origins of PRA, the largest stream, though, was the confluence of agro-ecosystem analysis (Gypmantasiri et al., 1980; Conway, 1985) with RRA (KKU, 1987). RRA had semi-structured interviewing at its core (Grandstaff and Grandstaff, 1987). Agro-ecosystem analysis crucially contributed sketch mapping, diagramming, transects and observation. The big breakthroughs were then the discoveries (or rediscoveries, for there are almost always antecedents) that with light and sensitive facilitation local people could themselves make the maps and diagrams, and that, especially when they worked in small groups, what they

presented demonstrated a complexity, diversity, accuracy and for many purposes relevance far superior to anything that could be elicited or expressed using earlier extractive or observational methodologies. This led to the practical principle that 'They can do it' applied to activity after activity, recognizing that local people had far greater abilities for analysis, action, experimentation, research and monitoring and evaluation than had been supposed by outside professionals or by themselves.

The stream flowed from RRA to PRA to PLA. PRA was most clearly identifiable in the first half of the 1990s. In 1995 the core publication for PRA experiences, still known as *RRA Notes*, was renamed *Participatory Learning and Action (PLA) Notes*.[4]

For both RRA and the PRA/PLA which grew out of it there was a multiplicity of parallel and simultaneous innovations which co-evolved, spread and inspired. The Sustainable Agriculture Programme at the International Institute for Environment and Development, in London, played a key part in the RRA-PRA-PLA evolutions, transitions and spread. In what was labelled PRA, several traditions developed. An early form in Kenya was evolved by Clark University and the National Environment Secretariat, adopted by Egerton University, and embodied in handbooks (e.g. PID and NES c.1989) which supported standardized training for a sequence of activities leading to community action plans. This approach was then applied in parts of East and West Africa, for example The Gambia (Holmes, 2001; Brown et al., 2002). In India, a few staff in two NGOs – the AKRSP (India) and MYRADA – were major contributors to an epicentre of PRA innovation which generated the more open-ended approaches which then spread much more widely in India and the world. These approaches in turn took different forms (Pratt, 2001): some stressed methods; others were more reflective and more concerned with quality of facilitation, attitudes and behaviours. In the early 1990s a proliferation of acronym labels marked an early stage of enthusiastic innovation and claims of ownership. Like the phyla of the Cambrian explosion or the steam engines of the early industrial revolution, many of these labels soon died out. What persisted were the practices and the acronyms PRA and PLA, the latter adopted, though sometimes used synonymously with PRA, in order to be more inclusive of other participatory methodologies in the spirit of sharing without boundaries.

In the 2000s PRA and PLA have diffused, borrowed and interpenetrated with other approaches. They have evolved and merged into a new creative pluralism (Cornwall and Guijt, 2004) in which earlier traditions survive but in which many methods have been evolved and adapted. Many of the early PRA practitioners have become more reflective and self-critical (Cornwall and Pratt, 2003). Others continue in earlier, sometimes routinized, traditions. In the mid-2000s it is not clear what the term PRA can or should now usefully describe. For many it remains associated with group-visual activities, and with behaviour, attitudes and relationships of facilitation which empower participants. In parallel with the persistence of traditional PRA, and of other established participatory methodologies, more and more practitioner/facilitators have become creative pluralists, borrowing, improvising and inventing for particular contexts, sectors and needs.

Reflecting critically on the evolution of PRA, theory has been implicit in and has co-evolved with practice. As with RRA earlier (Jamieson, 1987), theory has been induced from and fed back into practice. Practice itself was driven and drawn not by academic analysis, nor by a reflective analytical book like *Pedagogy of the Oppressed* (Freire, 1970), but by the excitement of innovation, discovery and informal networking. The main pioneers were not academic intellectuals but workers and staff in NGOs in the South, especially India, and a few from research institutes in the North, all of them learning through engagement in the field. And the detail of the methods came from the creativity and inventiveness of local people, once they had the idea of what they could do, as well as from the outside facilitators.

Spread and Applications

From 1990, the spread of PRA was rapid throughout much of the world (Singh, 2001; Holmes, 2002; Cornwall and Pratt, 2003). By 2000 practices described as PRA were probably to be found in well over 100 countries, of the North as well as of the South. They were being used by all or almost all prominent INGOs and many of their partners, by many donor and lender supported projects, and by a number of government departments, for example in India, Kenya and Vietnam.

With rapid spread, bad practice became rampant. The methods were so attractive, often photogenic, and so amenable to being taught in a normal didactic manner that they gained priority over behaviour, attitudes and relationships, especially in training institutes. Manuals proliferated and were mechanically taught and applied. Donors and lenders demanded PRA. Much training neglected or totally ignored behaviour and attitudes. PRA was routinized, people's time was taken and their expectations raised without any outcome, methods were used to extract information, not to empower, and consultants claimed to be trainers who had no experience. Communities were 'PRA'd'. Some in Malawi were said to have been 'carpet-bombed with PRA'. Just as academics began to wake up to what had been happening, there was much to criticize. The looseness of the one sentence principle – 'Use your own best judgement at all times' – could be liberating, giving freedom to improvise and invent; and it supported much brilliant performance and innovation. But equally, it could combine with an exclusive fixation on methods to allow sloppy and abusive practice.

Academic critics of PRA were not always able to draw on personal experience, or sometimes drew on their own defective practice. In consequence, some of the criticisms, for example in *Participation: The New Tyranny?* (Cooke and Kothari, 2001), were not well informed. Much was made of the well-known shortcomings of community public meetings, overlooking the value and widespread use of smaller groups. And criticisms that should have been made were overlooked, for example the common bias against women's participation inherent in PRA visual analysis since this tends to require undisturbed blocks of time usually harder for women to find than for men. Many practitioners, keenly aware of this problem, took determined steps to offset it. And from the mid-1990s, articulate practitioners were increasingly self-critical and reflective in a rich range of publications.[5]

In parallel, the applications of PRA approaches and methods, not alone but often combined and adapted with others, have been and continue to be astonishingly varied. They are constantly evolving and being invented. To at least some degree, all entail an element of participatory research. Most have never been recorded or published. An incomplete but illustrative list (see Box 20.1 and Box 20.2) can give a sense of the range.

Box 20.1   Natural Resource Management and Agriculture

- Participatory natural resource management (Probst and Hagmann et al., 2003; Borrini-Feyerabend et al., 2004; Pimbert, 2004) including agriculture, crops and animal husbandry (PRGA, c. 2002; *PLA Notes 45*, 2002
- Forestry, especially Joint Forest Management, and agroforestry (*Forests, Trees and People Newsletter*)
- Participatory irrigation management (Gosselink and Strosser, 1995)
- Participatory watershed management and soil and water conservation (Kolavalli and Kerr, 2002a, 2002b)
- Conservation and use of plant genetic resources (Friis-Hansen et al., 2000)
- Biodiversity, conservation, and protected area management (Pimbert and Pretty, 1997; Gujja et al., 1998; Roe et al., 2000)
- Integrated Pest Management (Dilts and Hate, 1996; Dilts, 2001; Fakih et al., 2003)

Box 20.2   Programmes for empowerment, equity, rights and security

- Participatory Poverty Assessments (Norton et al., 2001: Robb, 2002 [1999]) and understandings of poverty and wellbeing (White and Pettit, 2004)
- Consultations with the poor, in 23 countries (Narayan et al., 2000), as a preliminary for the *World Development Report* 2000/01 (World Bank, 2000) on poverty and development
- Women's empowerment and gender awareness (Guijt and Shah, 1998; Akerkar, 2001; Cornwall, 2003; Kanji, 2004)
- Applications with and by children (*PLA Notes 25*, 1996; Johnson et al., 1998; Cox and Robinson-Pant, 2003; Chawla and Johnson, 2004) including action research by primary schoolchildren on decision-making in their own classrooms (Cox et al., 2006)
- Work with those who are powerless and vulnerable, besides children including the homeless (AAA, 2002), the disabled, older people (Heslop, 2002), minorities, refugees, the mentally distressed, prisoners and others who are marginalized
- Identifying, selecting and deselecting people for poverty-oriented programmes
- Participatory analysis of livelihoods leading to livelihood action plans
- Emergency assessment and management, including participation by communities and their members in complex political emergencies
- Participatory human rights assessments and monitoring (Blackburn et al., 2004)
- Violence, abuses and physical insecurity (e.g. Moser and McIlwaine, 2004)
- Sexual and reproductive behaviour and rights (Cornwall and Welbourn, 2002; Gordon and Cornwall, 2004) and HIV/AIDS (International HIV/AIDS Alliance, 2006a, 2006b)

In addition, there have been innumerable applications in other rural and urban domains, not least in community and local planning (*PLA Notes 44*, 2002; *PLA Notes 49*, 2004; Swantz et al., 2001/2006), market analysis (*PLA Notes 33*, 1998), health (*RRA Notes 16*, 1992), food security assessment (e.g. Levy, 2003), water, sanitation (Kar, 2003, 2005), organizational analysis, personal experiential learning and change, and policy analysis. In multifarious domains there have been innumerable applications in participatory monitoring, evaluation and impact assessment (e.g. Guijt, 1998; Estrella et al., 2000; Mayoux and Chambers, 2005), with an increasing methodological pluralism and emphasis on learning and adaptation (Guijt, forthcoming).

Co-evolving Streams of Participatory Methodologies

Beyond this bald illustrative listing, more of a sense of what has happened can be given through eight examples of parallel and intermingling participatory research and action which have gone or are going to scale. Approaches, methods, ideas and experiences have over the past two decades flowed freely in all directions between these and RRA, PRA and PLA. The first five – farmer participatory research, integrated pest management, Reflect, Stepping Stones and Participatory GIS – are already widespread movements and are practised in many countries. The last three – the Internal Learning System, Participatory Action and Learning System, and Community-Led Total Sanitation – are promising approaches which are to varying degrees going to scale, and which illustrate the potentials of sensitive and inventive pluralism

1. Farmer Participatory Research

Farmer Participatory Research (Farrington and Martin, 1988; Okali et al., 1994) and Participatory Technology Development (Haverkort et al., 1991) have been a strong trend gaining increasing and now widespread acceptance. Important distinctions were made by Biggs (1988) indicating degrees of farmer

participation, from researcher design and control to farmer-design and control. From the late 1980s there has been a progressive shift towards the latter, as indicated by the many activities and publications of the system-wide Participatory Research and Gender Analysis programme of the Consultative Group for International Agricultural Research (see www.prgaprogram.org). As with streams of PRA and PLA, the capacities of local people, in this case farmers, were found to exceed by far what professionals had thought they were capable of. One example was the successive involvement of farmers in seed-breeding with scientists: in 1987 it had been radical to involve them in selection of later generations in the breeding process; but pioneering scientists (Witcombe et al., 1996) found that farmers' involvement in the whole process, including selection of the original crosses, substantially improved outcomes. Worldwide, farmers' research and participation in research have been spread through the international agricultural research centres, national agricultural research institutes, and INGOs such as World Neighbours.

2. Integrated Pest Management (IPM)

IPM has been a parallel movement, sharing characteristics with PRA and PLA. IPM in Indonesia started in the late 1980s, with the first training of trainers in 1989. Behaviour and attitudes of facilitators are considered critical (Pontius et al., 2002). IPM enables farmers to control pests in rice with sharply reduced applications of pesticide. By the early 2000s there were some one million farmer participants in Indonesia alone, and several millions worldwide. In IPM farmers are brought together in farmer field schools for *in situ* learning through their own action research. They observe, map, experiment and analyse, set up and study their own 'zoo' for insects and pests, and come to their own conclusions about how to manage and control them.

Even in a repressive and authoritarian social order, the farmer-centred approach of the farmer field schools provided 'a safe space for social learning and action' (Fakih et al., 2003: 95). In Indonesia, IPM groups came together and formed the IPM Farmers Association, in effect a national movement. The Association has engaged in advocacy to promote farmers' rights and discuss farmers' problems at local and district levels, and then nationally with a National Congress attended by the responsible minister (Fakih et al., 2003: 111).

3. Reflect

Reflect[6] is a participatory methodology which combines Paulo Freire's theoretical framework on the politics of literacy with PRA approaches and user-generated materials from PRA visualizations (*Education Action*, 1994–; *PLA Notes*, 1998; Archer and Newman, 2003; Archer and Goreth, 2004). Piloted through action research projects in El Salvador, Uganda and Bangladesh between 1993 and 1995, it has spread through the work of at least 350 organizations including NGOs, community-based organizations, governments and social movements, in more than 60 countries (Archer and Goreth, 2004). A standard manual was soon abandoned as too rigid (Phnuyal, 1999). Local differentiation and ownership are now marked. Reflect has taken many different forms with 'immense diversity' (Archer and Goreth, 2004: 40).

At the core of Reflect are facilitated groups known as Reflect circles. These meet regularly, usually for about two years, and sometimes continuing indefinitely. The balance between literacy and empowerment has varied. Analysis by circles, combined with networking, has confronted power and abuses and asserted human rights. Reflect's core principles include these: starting from existing experience; using participatory tools; power analysis; creating democratic spaces; reflection-action-reflection; self-organization; and recognition that Reflect is a political process for social change and greater social justice. These principles are manifest in *Communication and Power: Reflect Practical Resource Materials* (compilers David Archer and Kate Newman), the outcome of a widespread participatory process. First put together in 2003 in a loose-leaf form, its sections include written word, numbers, spoken word, images, and Reflect in action, with a strong emphasis on empowerment to enable people to do their own appraisal and analysis, leading to their own awareness and action.

4. Stepping Stones (SS)

Stepping Stones (Welbourn, 1995, 2002, in press) is an approach and methods to facilitate experiential learning concerned with social awareness, communication and relationships. It was evolved by Alice Welbourn and first tried in Uganda in 1994. Groups of people in communities meet for a sequence of interactions and reflections, especially on the inequalities that govern gender and other social relations in the context of HIV/AIDS. A review of evaluations by Tina Wallace (2006: 20) reported that SS had been adapted and used in over 100 countries. Most countries had no estimates of coverage but a World Bank estimate was that in Mozambique alone half a million people had been reached over four years.

Wallace's review found 'almost universal support for, and appreciation of, SS as a change process from those with first hand experience of using it or seeing it used' including 'better inter-generational communication, more openness about discussing sex, less stigma and more care for those with HIV and AIDS, and a willingness of PLWHA [People Living With HIV/AIDS] to be open' (Wallace, 2006: 10). Another evaluation summarized as follows:

> The response of communities across the globe has been overwhelmingly positive and the results extremely encouraging. Reductions in gender violence, increased self-esteem and confidence among women and girls, improved sex lives between married couples, radical reconfiguration of gender relations and the gender division of labour in the household, relinquishing harmful cultural practices, such as wife sharing and widow inheritance … are but a few examples of the reported impact. (Hadjipateras et al., 2006: 8)

5. Participatory Geographic Information Systems (PGIS)[7]

The new spatial information technologies, including Geographic Information Systems

(GIS), Global Positioning Systems (GPS), remote sensing software and open access to spatial data and imagery, empower those who command them. Differential access can lead to gains to powerful people and interests to the disadvantage of communities and local people, further marginalizing those already marginalized. PGIS is a generic term for approaches which seek to reverse this. By combining PRA/PLA and spatial information technologies, it has empowered minority groups and those traditionally excluded from spatial decision-making processes (Fox et al., 2006; Mbile, 2006; Rambaldi et al., 2006). Local people have been trained to use the technologies to construct their own maps and 3-D models (see Rambaldi and Callosa-Tarr, 2002, for modelling, and Corbett et al., 2006, and Rambaldi et al., 2006, for overviews) and use these for their own research. These maps and models differ from the ground and paper maps of PRA in their greater spatial accuracy, permanence, authority and credibility with officialdom, and have been used as 'interactive vehicles for spatial learning, information exchange, support in decision making, resource use planning and advocacy actions' (Rambaldi, 2005: 1).

Applications have been many. They have included (Rambaldi et al., 2006: 3): protecting ancestral lands and resource rights; management and resolution of conflicts over natural resources; collaborative resource use planning and management; intangible cultural heritage preservation and identity building among indigenous peoples and rural communities; equity promotion with reference to ethnicity, culture, gender, and environmental justice; hazard mitigation, for example through community safety audits (Mans, 2006); and peri-urban planning and research (Koti and Weiner, 2006). PGIS applications have been documented (Mbile, 2006; *PLA Notes*, 2006) for countries as diverse as Brazil (Amazon), Cameroon, Canada, Ethiopia, Fiji, Ghana, Indonesia, Kenya, Nepal, Namibia, Nicaragua, South Africa, Tanzania, and Uganda. In addition, there are 'hundreds of non-documented cases where technology-intermediaries (mainly NGOs) support Community-based

Organisations or Indigenous Peoples in using (Geographic Information Technology and Systems) to meet their spatial planning needs and/or achieve some leverage in their dealings with state bureaucracy' (Rambaldi et al., 2006: 4). An indicator of the power of mapping has been its restriction through the Malaysian 2001 Land Surveyors Law, passed after a community map in Sarawak had been instrumental in the legal victory of an Iban village against a tree plantation corporation (Fox et al., 2006: 103).

By the mid-2000s, PGIS had become a widespread form of 'counter mapping' (Rocheleau, 2005) enabling local people to make their own maps and models, and using these for their own research, analysis, assertion of rights and resolution of conflicts over land, and often reversing power relations with government organizations, politicians and corporations.

6. The Internal Learning System (ILS)

Pioneered in India by Helzi Noponen was conceived as a participatory impact assessment and planning system. The pictorial diaries and workbooks which are its most conspicuous feature were developed independently of PRA. Poor, often illiterate participants use them to keep their own records of changes over time. The intention is to reverse normal power relationships: poor participants 'are the first to learn about programme impact and performance, and alter plans as a result ... [they] are not only data gatherers, but they are also analysts, planners and advocates for change' (Noponen, in press). The ILS has evolved for different conditions including the work of the NESA (New Entity for Social Action) and its partners in South India for the empowerment of Dalit and Adivasi women and children (Nagasundari, in press); and of PRADAN (Professional Assistance for Development Action) and its partners in North India with self-help groups for the generation of sustainable livelihoods for poor rural people (Narendranath, in press). Among other outcomes have been action on social and gender issues previously too sensitive for discussion, and many micro-level manifestations of social change especially awareness and empowerment of women and others who are marginalized.

7. Participatory Action Learning System (PALS)

Pioneered by Linda Mayoux is 'an eclectic and constantly evolving methodology which enables people to collect and analyse the information they themselves need on an ongoing basis to improve their lives in ways they decide' (Mayoux, in press). Core features are the inventive use of diagram tools (Mayoux, 2003a), their integration with participatory principles and processes, linking individual and group learning, and the adoption and adaptation of approaches and methods from many traditions. Typically, diagram tools are designed and piloted, and incorporated in a manual for each context (e.g. Mayoux, 2003b). Applications and developments of PALS have included women's empowerment with ANANDI, an NGO in Gujarat (Mayoux and ANANDI, 2005), participatory monitoring and evaluation with KRC (Kabarole Research and Resource Centre) in Uganda, and impact assessment of micro-finance in several countries.

8. Community-led Total Sanitation (CLTS)

Pioneered by Kamal Kar in Bangladesh (Kar, 2003, 2005; Kar and Pasteur, 2005; Kar and Bongartz, 2006), CLTS is a remarkable initiative using PRA approaches and methods in which small communities are facilitated to conduct their own research and analysis into their practices of defecation and their consequences. This is done through mapping, transects, observation, calculations of quantities produced and ingested, and reflections on pathways from faeces to the mouth. This quite often leads to community decisions to dig holes and introduce total sanitation to become open defecation free. The approach has been introduced and is reported to have been adopted by thousands of communities spread over Bangladesh, Cambodia, India, Indonesia and other countries in South and Southeast Asia.

These eight examples are original and distinct methodologies which to varying degrees draw on and share PRA/PLA approaches, methods, behaviours and mindsets and which have creatively invented and evolved their own diverse and varied practices. Like Reflect, IPM and PGIS, all can be seen as forms of, or closely related to, participatory action research. All frame and facilitate sequences of activities which empower participants to undertake their own appraisal or research and analysis, and come to their own conclusions.

THEORY: UNDERSTANDINGS FROM PRACTICE[8]

Good theory and practice intertwine and co-evolve. Theory can exist as an intellectual abstraction without practice, but practice cannot exist without implicit theory. When theory and practice co-evolve, one or the other may exercise more influence. If theory and reflective practice have led relatively more in PAR, practice and experiential learning have led relatively more in the RRA-PRA-PLA sequence. At times, as in the 1989–91 explosion of PRA, not all the implicit theory was immediately made explicit. But critical reflection followed practice and principles were induced and articulated on the basis of experience. And this continues: among practitioners, researchers and activists engaged in the rapid spread of Participatory GIS, for example, there is a general consensus that PGIS practice is more advanced than the theory behind the applications (Rambaldi et al., 2006).

PRA/PLA practical theory appears robust.[9] It can be described at two levels. The first, as expressed by Jethro Pettit (pers. comm.), is more overarching: that most practitioners would share an epistemological or ideological perspective, articulated in the PRA literature, that expert and professional knowledge and ways of knowing need to be humble and to appreciate people's own knowledge and ways of knowing. Professionals, and people who are dominant in contexts and relationships ('uppers'), habitually underestimate the capabilities and the value of the knowledge of those who are subordinate in contexts and relationships ('lowers').[10] A role of the professional is to transform these relations by facilitating, enabling people to express and enhance their own contextual and specific knowledge. PRA behaviours, methods and orientations are a means towards this. The core is that uppers facilitate, support and protect processes through which lowers and local people empower themselves and power relations are transformed.

The second level supports the first. It is more detailed and can be induced from practice, from what has been found to work. Methods, approaches and methodologies have evolved through borrowing, inventing and experiential learning driven by the discipline, pressures and opportunities of engagement in the field. Innovation has taken place through improvisations forced by the challenge of immediate social situations. There will be, and should be, a range of views about this second level of theory. What is presented here is but one person's interpretation. Focusing on PRA experience and also drawing on the eight examples above, three clusters of principles can be distinguished. These are evolutions of the original three principal components of PRA (see Figure 20.1): behaviours, attitudes and mindsets: precepts for action; methods: visuals, tangibles and groups; and sharing: pluralism and diversity.

Behaviours, Attitudes and Mindsets: Precepts for Action

Empowering processes require changes of behaviours, attitudes and mindsets, and typically changes of role from teacher to facilitator and from controller to coach. To promote and sustain the spread of good PRA the practical theory has been expressed as short and simple precepts with the idea that these will embed and spread as expressions and behaviours; and that the experiences these bring will transform attitudes, predispositions and mindsets among uppers and transform relationships with lowers.

One basic reversal is through asking 'who?' and 'whose?' and answering with 'theirs', referring commonly to lowers, in practice often

local people and most of all to those who are poor, weak and marginalized. The overarching question 'Whose reality counts?' forces reflection on how powerful outsiders tend to impose their realities on local people, especially when they are bringing 'superior' knowledge or technology. The wide span of 'who?' and 'whose?' questions can be illustrated by the listing generated by a group of GIS practitioners (see Box 20.3). While some of these questions are specific to mapping, many apply more generally. All have implications for the behaviour and relationships of outsiders, facilitators and uppers, generally with insiders, local people and lowers. Some of the main behavioural precepts of PRA[11] which address these behaviours are shown in Box 20.4.

Methods: Visuals, Tangibles and Groups

Many PRA methods involve visual and tangible expression and analysis, for example mapping, modelling, diagramming, pile sorting, or scoring with seeds, stones or other counters. These are usually but not always small group activities. What is expressed can be seen, touched or moved and stays in place.[12] These visible, tangible, alterable and yet lasting aspects contrast with the invisible, unalterable and transient nature of verbal communication. Symbols, objects and diagrams can represent realities that are cumbersome or impossible to express verbally.

These visual and tangible approaches and methods reverse power relations and empower lowers in five ways. The first is group-visual synergy. As in Figure 20.2, group motivation, cross-checking, adding detail, discussing and cumulative representation generate a positive sum synergy through which all can contribute and learn. A facilitator can observe and assess the process for its rigour of trustworthiness and relevance.[14] The outcomes are then empowering through collective analysis and learning, and because they are at once credible and an output created and owned by the group.

The second is democracy on the ground (Chambers, 2002: 94–5, 186–7). Much PRA

Box 20.3   Whose reality counts?

Stage 1. Planning	**Stage 2. The Mapping Process**
Who participates? *Who decides on who should participate?* *Who participates in whose mapping?* *… and who is are left out?* ***Who identifies the problem*** *Whose problems?* *Whose questions?* *Whose perspective?* *… and whose problems, questions and perspectives are left out?*	*Whose voice counts? Who controls the process?* *Who decides on what is important?* *Who decides, and who should decide, on what to visualize and make public? Who has visual and tactile access?* *Who controls the use of information?* *And who is marginalized?* *Whose reality? And who understands?* *Whose reality is expressed?* *Whose knowledge, categories, perceptions?* *Whose truth and logic?* *Whose sense of space and boundary conception (if any)?* *Whose (visual) spatial language?* *Whose map legend?* *Who is informed what is on the map? (Transparency)* *Who understands the physical output? And who does not?* *And whose reality is left out?*

Stage 3. Resulting information control, disclosure and disposal

Who owns the output?
Who owns the map(s)?
Who owns the resulting data?
What is left with those who generated the information and shared their knowledge?
Who keeps the physical output and organizes its regular updating?
Whose analysis and use?
Who analyses the spatial information collated?
Who has access to the information and why?
Who will use it and for what?
And who cannot access and use it?
Ultimately …
What has changed? Who benefits from the changes? At whose costs?
Who gains and who loses?
Who is empowered and who is disempowered?

Ultimately …

What has changed? Who benefits from the changes? At whose costs?
Who gains and who loses?
Who is empowered and who is disempowered?

Source: Rambaldi et al., 2006: 108[13]

mapping and diagramming levels or reverses power relations by taking place on the ground. Those taking part have less eye contact, talk less, and can dominate less easily than in normal upright positions face-to-face. Hands are freer to move tangibles than mouths are to speak words. Those who are more powerful, sometimes older men, may not get down on the ground at all, whereas those who are younger and women may.

Box 20.4   Precepts of PRA

Precept ...	indicating
Introduce yourself ...	be honest, transparent, relate as a person
They can do it ...	have confidence in people's abilities
Unlearn ...	critically reflect on how you see things
Ask them ...	ask people their realities, priorities, advice
Don't rush ...	be patient, take time
Sit down, listen and learn ...	don't dominate
Facilitate ...	don't lecture, criticize or teach
Embrace error ...	learn from what goes wrong or does not work
Hand over the stick ...	or chalk or pen, anything that empowers
Use your own best	
judgement at all times ...	take responsibility for what you do
Shut up! ...	keep quiet. Welcome and tolerate silence

The third is the representation of complex realities and relationships. Visual and tangible approaches and methods enable local people and lowers generally to express and analyse complex patterns of categories, comparisons, estimates, valuations, relationships and causality across an astonishing range of topics, from social and census maps of communities to causal and linkage diagrams of causes and effects of poverty, from scored matrices for varieties of crops and domestic animals to different forms of violence, from characteristics of different sorts of sexual partners to seasonal analyses of work, income, debt, expenditures, sickness and other aspects of life, from on-farm nutrient flows to priorities for local development, and much, much else.

The fourth is using visuals as instruments of empowerment. Over the past decade rapid developments have generated a new repertoire for subordinate and marginalized people. The visual diaries of ILS in South India empower low-caste women, arming them with visual representations of their realities and experiences, enabling them to track and discuss changes in their lives over time, and to take action when patterns of marginalization (such as caste or gender discrimination) persist. The geo-referenced maps of forest and other peripheral people give them credible and potent aids for asserting and

securing their rights and boundaries. Making three-dimensional PGIS models has enabled local communities to express and display their knowledge and realities, and to plan, whether for land management, conservation, or cropping patterns. Large PGIS models can hardly fail to belong to communities and be retained by them. And they provide a natural and efficient locus for dialogue and decision-making (Rambaldi and Callosa-Tarr, 2000, 2002).

The fifth is participatory numbers. A diverse and versatile family of innovations has evolved to generate numbers and statistics from participatory appraisal and analysis (Barahona and Levy, 2003; Chambers, 2003; Levy, 2003; Chambers, forthcoming). Practical issues concerning standardization and commensurability, and ethical issues concerning ownership and use, have been recognized and tackled. To a striking degree, the numbers generated by lowers and local people through participatory methods and processes have been found to combine accuracy, authority and utility. In the Philippines, for example, when bottom-up statistics aggregated from village health workers replaced less accurate and less relevant top-down statistics, insights led to a policy change that reduced deaths (Nierras, 2002). In Malawi, when participatory methods were used to check the national census, the rural

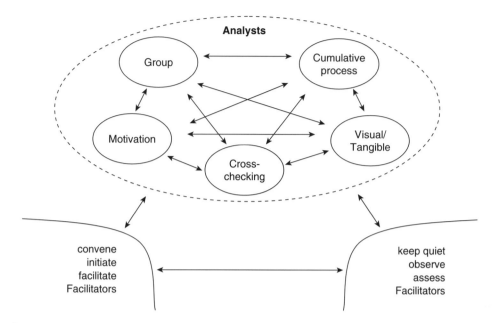

Figure 20.2 *Group-visual synergy*

population was revised upwards from 8.5 to 11.5 million (Barahona and Levy, 2003), with massive implications for the equity of national resource allocations.

These five ways in which visuals, tangibles and numbers empower often combine and reinforce each other. Their force is then more than their sum as parts. Together they have been found to be potent means for transforming power relations, strengthening the power of lowers and local people not just to understand their realities but to take action, and to negotiate with uppers and with outside powers-that-be.

Sharing, Pluralism and Diversity

Sharing without boundaries was a principle that emerged from a workshop of PRA practitioners in 1994 (Absalom et al., 1995). To be sure, there have been a few practitioners who might be described as PRA fundamentalists, who have sought or claimed some sort of exclusive expertise and ownership. But sharing was one of the three principle components of PRA enunciated in 1990, and a corollary of sharing and of 'use your own

best judgement at all times' is to endorse and celebrate pluralism.

It is striking how PRA, PLA, IPM, Reflect, PGIS and most of the other participatory methods have been open and porous, and how they have diversified creatively as they have spread. Methodological diversity is an enabling condition for creativity (Van der Mele and Braun, 2005). Those with standard manuals and detailed instructions have been less successful or have run into problems: Reflect's 'mother manual' was quickly abandoned when found to inhibit more than help. A key to good spread, and to becoming a movement, has often been holding firm to minimum principles, and then allowing and encouraging practices and behaviours which empower, through local creativity and ownership. An indicator of this is in the labels used: Reflect in Nepal, for example, is not known by its English name but has 16 different Nepalese names and identities (pers. comm., Bimal Phnuyal). Creativity, diversity and local ownership and responsibility have been at the core of the successful spread of these participatory methodologies.

This inclusiveness of sharing and borrowing raises questions about how the three components – of behaviours, attitudes and mindsets, of methods using visuals, tangible and groups, and of sharing, pluralism and diversity – can relate to other theories and theoretical frameworks. In PRA/PLA terms, an answer can be given by 'Use your own best judgement at all times'. For some who want a bounded and labelled methodology this will look and feel too loose, both personally and because it can appear to open the door for bad practice. For others it will turn responsibility back from an external authority or a predetermined process to personal reflective judgement, liberating through freedom to decide and choose what to learn from, borrow and adapt. It can then encourage eclectic opportunism and creativity to enhance local relevance and fit to contribute to the empowerment of others, especially lowers.

LOOKING FORWARD

Beyond PRA, brands and boundaries

The PRA label has been a problem, spreading often without PRA principles and practices. In the 1990s, by claiming some sort of ownership of PRA, a few consultants negated its spirit of sharing, but in the 2000s this has become less evident. Another problem has been how some have misunderstood PRA.[15] Sadly, too, some working in other traditions have regarded PRA as competitor rather than colleague. This may have contributed to some other action research practitioners' surprising lack of interest in the added value of PRA approaches and methods, and to their seeing PRA as extractive research conducted on local and poor people, not research conducted by and with them as in the movements, methodologies and applications described above. In these movements, as amply documented, practice and theory have been oriented towards empowering those who are marginalized and weak, using new approaches and methods to enable them to do their own appraisals and analysis, and to gain voice and take their own action.

Much of the discourse and practice has now moved beyond PRA. It is less clear than it was what PRA can usefully be said to be. The use of some PRA methods is quite stable and practical: wealth ranking (also known as wellbeing grouping), for example, is extensively used by INGOs and their partners as a means of enabling people in communities to identify those who are worse off according to their own criteria. At the same time, the best practice is often improvised and invented performance in ever changing conditions, leading to continuously evolving diversity.

The inclusive meaning of the term PLA has helped here, as for example by the International HIV/AIDS Alliance (2006b) for whom PLA is 'A growing family of approaches, tools, attitudes and behaviours to enable and empower people to present, share, analyse and enhance their knowledge of life and conditions, and to plan, act, monitor, evaluate, reflect and scale up community action' and 'a way to help people to participate together in learning, and then to act on that learning'.

When the objectives are to achieve both quality and scale, the agenda changes and moves beyond branding and boundaries. These can inhibit and limit more than help. It is no longer, if it ever was, the spread of PRA but inclusivity of participatory approaches, attitudes, behaviours, methods and mindsets that deserves priority; and that is something in which practitioners from all traditions can share.

Part of that is the capacity to adapt and innovate. There may always be trade-offs between standardization and scale on the one hand and creativity and quality on the other. But in moving from practice which is fixed, wooden and branded to practice which is more flexible, pliant and unlabelled, the frontier agenda shifts from reproducing methods to:

- modifying behaviour;
- enhancing repertoire – the range of things a person, a facilitator, knows to do; and
- fostering creativity to find new things to do and new ways to do them.

Paradigmatically, this is part of the shift from things to people, from top-down to bottom-up, from standard to diverse, from control to empowerment. Brands, boundaries, ego, exclusiveness and claims of ownership dissolve to be replaced by openness, generosity, inclusiveness and sharing.

Central to these transformations are personal reflexivity and institutional change. Critical self-awareness is part of learning and developing, and one key to facilitation. Change in institutions, especially in organizational norms, values, procedures, rewards and relationships, is an important complement to personal change. Congruence between the personal and the institutional is a predisposing condition for participatory processes in groups and communities, and for the continuous discovery together of ways of doing things which fit local contexts.

A New Eclectic Pluralism

In their review 'Shifting perceptions, changing practices in PRA: from infinite innovation to the quest for quality' Andrea Cornwall and Irene Guijt (2004), both early pioneers of PRA, review the excitement of the initial community of practice, the seeding of diversity, the poor practice that came with rapid spread in the latter 1990s, and how there came to be many PRAs and many pathways (see also Cornwall and Pratt, 2003). They highlight the quest for quality, and they also see a 'new pluralism'.

> Across a spectrum of areas of development work now are people who have engaged in some way with PRA. Participatory learning and action approaches have come to be used in a myriad of settings, in ways that are so diverse that they have given rise to entirely new areas of work – whether in policy research, learning, participatory governance or rights-based development work. (Cornwall and Guijt, 2004: 166)

The creative diversity of this new pluralism is brought to light by a review by Action Aid International of its participatory practices (AAI, 2006; Newman, in press). These are many and differ by country and within countries, and confront issues of participation, power and rights. While AAI may be exceptional among INGOs for encouraging

and reporting on such diversity, the NGO sector in general has in the past decade been a major seedbed for the creative proliferation of methodologies.

This new pluralism is eclectic. The approaches, attitudes, behaviours and mindsets variously identified and named as PRA and PLA are just one part of this. PRA group-visual methods remain powerful and useful, but many practitioners have moved on from relying on them as heavily as they did and now improvise more, borrowing and bringing to bear a wider range. So there are many springs as sources, and many mingling streams, confluences and branching flows. Besides those described above – PRA, farmer participatory research, Integrated Pest Management, Reflect, Stepping Stones, Participatory GIS, ILS, PALS, and Community-Led Total Sanitation – the many others include appreciative inquiry (see Chapter 19), theatre-based techniques (Abah, 2004; McCarthy with Galvao, 2004; Guhathakurta, Chapter 35), participatory video (Lunch and Lunch, 2006), Planning for Real (Gibson, 1996), Participatory Poverty Assessments (Norton et al., 2001; Robb, 2002 [1999]), participatory democracy (see Gaventa and Cornwall, Chapter 11), citizens' juries (Wakeford et al., Chapter 22), participatory budgeting, budget tracking, report cards, and social audits. And these and others can be adopted, adapted and improvised in a multitude of ways. The many manifestations of action research and participatory research contribute to this inclusive diversity. A new world of practice opens up. To suggest that participatory learning and action, as shown in the content and coverage of the journal of that title, might be an inclusive term for this borrowing, improvisation and creativity could be to fall into precisely the trap of naming and branding that is to be avoided. Paradigmatically, eclectic pluralism means that branding, labels, ownership and ego give way to sharing, borrowing, improvisation and creativity, all these complemented by mutual and critical reflective learning and personal responsibility for good practice.

As Heraclitus said, you cannot step into the same river twice. We move on. It is a question now of continuously opening spaces and encouraging the expression and experience of excitement, energy and creativity. It is a question of doing this in innumerable contexts, ever fresh and ever new, as part of a way of life. With a spirit of eclectic pluralism and sharing without boundaries, the potential for combinations and innovations is greater than it has ever been. From the PRA and PLA experiences, we learn that this is less a matter of methods and more of ways of living, being and relating. In participatory approaches and methods, there will always be a case for seeking common standards and principles. At the same time, by inventing and improvising each time anew for the uniqueness of each challenge and opportunity, the scope for adventure and discovery will never end.

ACKNOWLEDGEMENTS

I am grateful especially to Rosalind Eyben, John Gaventa, Emma Jones, Jethro Pettit, Peter Reason and Bill Torbert for many perceptive and constructive comments on drafts and to Jane Stevens for help with text and finding good sources for readers. As ever, responsibility for what is written is mine alone.

NOTES

1 The fullest introduction to RRA is the Proceedings of the International Conference held at Khon Kaen in Thailand in 1985 (KKU, 1987). For purposes of research by outsiders, well-conducted RRA is powerful and effective. It is unfortunate that it has been overshadowed by PRA. It deserves rediscovery and a renaissance.

2 Participatory reflection and action has the sequence of words wrong. It would be better putting action first, as participatory action and reflection, but the acronym PAR was already in use for Participatory action research. However, an advantage has been that more practitioners have abandoned their use of brand labels and become explicit about their pluralism (see e.g. Shah, 2003).

3 For what are known as PRA methods, typically including visuals and/or tangibles, see Jones (1996),

Chambers (1997), Shah et al. (1999), Mukherjee (2001), Kumar (2002), Jayakaran (2003), and International HIV/AIDS Alliance (2006b). See also www.ids.ac.uk/ids/particip for more.

4 *RRA Notes* Issues 1–21 (1988–94) was published by the International Institute for Environment and Development, whose Sustainable Agriculture Programme had much to do with the evolution and spread of PRA and which was documented in the Notes. Issue 22 in 1995 was renamed *PLA Notes* with the explanation: 'Participatory Learning and Action (PLA) has been adopted … as a collective term to describe the growing body of participatory approaches and methodologies.'

5 For a selection of critical reflections by practitioners of PRA/PLA see *PRA Notes* 24 (1995); the 32 individual contributions to *Pathways to Participation: Reflections on PRA* (Cornwall and Pratt, 2003); *Participation: From Tyranny to Transformation?* (Hickey and Mohan, 2003); and the 50th issue of *Participation Learning and Action* (2004), entitled *Critical Reflections, Future Directions.*

6 Reflect originally stood for Regenerated Freirian Literacy with Empowering Community Techniques, but this usage has been dropped and it is now referred to simply as Reflect.

7 For more on Participatory GIS visit www.iapad. org and www.ppgis.net. See also *Participatory Learning and Action* 54: *Mapping for Change: Practice, Technologies and Communication*, April 2006, and Peter Mbile (2006).

8 For an earlier and much fuller statement of PRA theory from practice see Chambers (1997: Chapter 7).

9 The word 'robust' is a response to reactions of colleagues to an earlier more modest draft of this chapter. They have argued against an apologetic stance which might imply that the RRA/PRA/PLA sequence was somehow a theoretical second-best because of the degree to which it was driven by experiential learning.

10 For elaboration and qualification of the concepts of upper and lower see Chambers (1997: 58–60, 207–10, 221–8).

11 Fuller listings of PRA-related precepts and behaviours can be found in *Participatory Workshops* (Chambers, 2002: 3 and 8).

12 Visuals and tangibles can, though, be vulnerable – on the ground to wind, rain and dust storms and trampling or eating by animals: hungry hens have been known to rapidly reduce matrix scores given by seeds. Paper is vulnerable to crumpling, smudging, fire, decay, and most of all retention or removal by NGO staff who take maps away from the communities who have made them.

13 This list of questions was built up progressively both at the Mapping for Change International Conference on Participatory Spatial Information Management and Communication held at the Kenya College of Communication of Technology, Nairobi, Kenya, 7–10 September 2005 and in subsequent

email exchanges between the authors of the paper (Rambaldi et al., 2006) and others.

14 The rigour of trustworthiness and relevance is expounded in more detail in Chambers (1997: 158–61).

15 PRA has, for example, been taken to stand for participatory research appraisal or participatory rapid appraisal. In *The Tyranny of Participation* (Cooke and Kothari, 2001: 88 and index) PLA is participatory learning analysis not participatory learning and action, despite the latter being the meaning of the periodical *PLA Notes* (now entitled *Participatory Learning and Action*).

REFERENCES

AAA (2002) *Basere ki Kahani (Story of Shelter): a Study of the Problems in the Night Shelters in Delhi Using Participatory Research*. Delhi: Aashray Adhikar Abhiyan.

AAI (2006) *From Services to Rights: a Review of ActionAid International's Participatory Practice*. [www.reflect-action.org] (available from ActionAid International, Private Bag X31, Saxonwold 2132, South Africa).

Abah, O.S. (2004) 'Voices aloud: making communication and change together', *Participatory Learning and Action,* 50 (October): 45–52.

Absalom, E. et al. (1995) 'Participatory methods and approaches: sharing our concerns and looking to the future', *PLA Notes,* 22: 5–10.

Akerkar, S. 2001 'Gender and participation: overview report', in BRIDGE (ed.), *Gender and Participation: Cutting Edge Pack*. Sussex: IDS [www.ids.ac.uk/ids/bridge].

Archer, D. and Goreth, N.M. (2004) 'Participation, literacy and empowerment: the continuing evolution of Reflect', *PLA Notes,* 50: 35–44.

Archer, D. and Newman, K. (compilers) (2003) *Communication and Power: Reflect Practical Resource Materials* [www.reflect-action.org] (available from ActionAid, London N19 5PG, UK).

Argyris, C., Putnam, R. and McLain Smith, D. (1985) *Action Science: Concepts, Methods and Skills for Research and Intervention*. San Francisco, CA: Jossey-Bass.

Barahona, C. and Levy, S. (2003) *How to Generate Statistics and Influence Policy Using Participatory Methods in Research: Reflections on Work in Malawi 1999–2002* (Working Paper). Sussex IDS.

Biggs, S. (1988) *Resource-Poor Farmer Participation in Research: a Synthesis of Experiences from Nine National Agricultural Research Systems*. The Hague: ISNAR (International Service for National Agricultural Research).

Blackburn, J., Brocklesby, M.A., Crawford, S. and Holland, J. (2004) 'Operationalising the rights agenda: participatory rights assessment in Peru and Malawi', *IDS Bulletin,* 36 (1): 91–9.

Borrini-Feyerland, G., Pimbert, M., Farvar, T., Kothari, A. and Renard, Y. (2004) *Sharing Power. Learning by Doing in Co-management of Natural Resources Throughout the World,* Cenesta, Tehran, IIED, London and IUCN (International Union for the Conservation of Nature)/CEESP/CMWG.

BRAC (1983) *The Net: Power Structure in Ten Villages*. Dhaka: Bangladesh Rural Advancement Committee.

Brock, K. and Pettit, J. (eds) (forthcoming) *Springs of Participation: Creating and Evolving Methodologies for Participatory Development*. London: ITDG Publications.

Brokensha, D., Warren, D. and Werner, O. (eds) (1980) *Indigenous Knowledge Systems and Development*. Lanham, MD: University Press of America.

Brown, D., Howes, M., Hussein, K., Longley, C. and Swindell, K. (2002) *Participation in Practice: Case Studies from The Gambia*. London: Overseas Development Institute.

Chambers, R. (1994) 'The origins and practice of participatory rural appraisal', *World Development,* 2 (7): 953–69.

Chambers, R. (1997) *Whose Reality Counts? Putting the First Last*. London: Intermediate Technology Publications.

Chambers, R. (2002) *Participatory Workshops: a Sourcebook of 21 Sets of Ideas and Activities*. London and Sterling, VA: Earthscan.

Chambers, R. (2003) 'Participation and Numbers', *PLA Notes,* 47: 6–12, August.

Chambers, R. (forthcoming) *Finding Out in Development: Endless Adventure,* London and Sterling, VA: Earthscan.

Chandler, D. and Torbert, W. (2003) 'Transforming inquiry and action: by interweaving 27 flavors of action research', *Journal of Action Inquiry,* 1 (2): 133–52.

Chawla, L. and Johnson, V. (2004) 'Not for children only: lessons learnt from young people's participation', *Participatory Learning and Action,* 50 (October): 63–72.

Conway, G. (1985) 'Agroecosystem Analysis', *Agricultural Administration,* 20: 31–55.

Cooke, B. and Kothari, U. (eds) (2001) *Participation: the New Tyranny?* London: Zed Books.

Corbett, J., Rambaldi, G., Kyem, P., Weiner, D., Olson, R., Muchemi, J., McCall, M. and Chambers, R. (2006) 'Overview: mapping for change – the emergence of a new practice', *Participatory Learning and Action,* 54: 13–19.

Cornwall, A. (2003) 'Whose voices? Whose choices? Reflections on gender and participatory development', *World Development,* 31 (8): 1325–42.

Cornwall, A. and Guijt, I. (2004) 'Shifting perceptions, changing practices in PRA: from infinite innovation to the quest for quality', *Participatory Learning and Action,* 50 (October): 160–7.

Cornwall, A. and Pratt, G. (eds) (2003) *Pathways to Participation: Reflections on PRA*. London: Intermediate Technology Publications.

Cornwall, A. and Welbourn, A. (eds) (2002) *Realizing Rights: Transforming Approaches to Sexual and Reproductive Well-being*. London: Zed Books.

Cox, S., Currie, D., Frederick, K., Jarvis, D., Lawes, S., Millner, E., Nudd, K., Robinson-Pant, A., Stubbs, I., Taylor, T. and White, D. (2006) *Children Decide: Power, Participation and Purpose in the Primary Classroom*. School of Education and Lifelong Learning, University of East Anglia, Norwich NR4 7TJ, UK [www.uea.ac.uk].

Cox, S. and Robinson-Pant, A. with Elliott, B., Jarvis, D., Lawes, S., Milner, E. and Taylor, T. (2003) *Empowering Children through Visual Communication*. School of Education and Professional Development, University of East Anglia, Norwich NR4 7TJ, UK.

Dilts, R. (2001) 'From farmers' field schools to community IPM', *LEISA*, 17 (3): 18–21.

Dilts, R. and Hate, S. (1996) *IPM Farmer Field Schools: Changing Paradigms and Scaling-up* (Agricultural Research and Extension Network Paper No. 596). London: ODI.

Education Action 1–20 (1994) ActionAid, London [www.reflect-action.org].

Edwards, M. and Gaventa, J. (eds) (2001) *Global Citizen Action*. Boulder, CO: Lynne Rienner.

Estrella, M. with Blauert, J., Campilan, D., Gaventa, J., Gonsalves, J., Guijt, I., Johnson, D. and Ricafort, R. (2000) *Learning from Change: Issues and Experiences in Participatory Monitoring and Evaluation*. London: Intermediate Technology Publications.

Fakih, M., Rahardjo, T. and Pimbert, M. with Sutoko, A., Wulandari, D. and Prasetyo, T. (2003) *Community Integrated Pest Management in Indonesia: Institutionalising Participation and People Centred Approaches* (Institutionalising Participation Series). London: IIED and Sussex: IDS.

Fals Borda, O. and Rahman, M.A. (eds) (1991) *Action and Knowledge: Breaking the Monopoly with Participatory Action-Research*. London: ITDG Publications.

Farrington, J. and Martin, A. (1988) *Farmer Participation in Agricultural Research: a Review of Concepts and Practices* (Agricultural Administration Unit Occasional Paper 9). London: Overseas Development Institute.

Forests, Trees and People Newsletter, International Rural Development Centre, Swedish University of Agricultural Sciences, Box 7005, 750 07 Uppsala, Sweden.

Fox, J., Suryanata, K. and Herschock, P. (eds) (2005) *Mapping Communities: Ethics, Values, Practice*. Honolulu: East-West Center.

Fox, J., Suryanata, K., Hershock, P. and Pramono, A.H. (2006) 'Mapping power: ironic effects of spatial information technology', *Participatory Learning and Action*, 54 (April): 98–105.

Freire, P. (1970) *Pedagogy of the Oppressed*. New York: The Seabury Press.

Friis-Hansen, E. and Shtapit, B. (eds) (2000) *Participatory Approaches to the Conservation and Use of Plant Genetic Resources*. Rome: International Plant Genetic Resources Institute.

Gaventa, J. (1993) 'The powerful, the powerless and the experts: knowledge struggles in a information age', in P. Park, B. Hall and T. Jackson (eds), *Participatory Research in North America*. Amherst, MA: Bergin and Hadley.

Gaventa, J. (1993) 'The powerful, the powerless and the experts: knowledge struggles in an information age', in P. Park, M. Brydon-Miller, B. Hall and T. Jackson, *Voices of Change: Participatory Research in the United States and Canada*, Ontario: OISE Press, pp. 21–40.

Gaventa, J. with Horton, B. (1981) 'A citizens' research project in Appalachia, USA', *Convergence*, 14 (3): 30–42.

Gaventa, J. and Lewis, H. (1991) *Participatory Education and Grassroots Development: the Case of Rural Appalachia* (Gatekeeper Series No. 25). London: IIED.

Gibson, T. (1996) *The Power in Our Hands: Neighbourhood Based – World Shaking* [available from Jon Carpenter, Charlbury, OX7 3PQ, UK].

Gonsalves, J. et al. (eds) (2005) *Participatory Research and Development for Sustainable Agriculture and Natural Resource Management: a Sourcebook. Vol. 1: Understanding Participatory Research and Development*. Laguna, Philippines: International Potato Center-Users' Perspectives With Agricultural Research and Development, and Ottawa: IDRC.

Gordon, G. and Cornwall, A. (2004) 'Participation in sexual and reproductive well-being and rights', *Participatory Learning and Action*, 50 (October): 73–80.

Gosselink, P. and Strosser P. (1995) *Participatory Rural Appraisal for Irrigation Management Research: Lessons from IIMI's Experience* (Working Paper No. 38). Colombo: International Irrigation Management Institute.

Grandstaff, T.B. and Grandstaff, S.W. (1987) 'Semi-structured interviewing by multi-disciplinary teams in RRA', KKU *Proceedings*, 129–43.

Guijt, I. (1998) *Participatory Monitoring and Impact Assessment of Sustainable Agriculture Initiatives: an Introduction to the Key Elements* (Sustainable Agriculture and Rural Livelihoods Programme Discussion Paper No. 1). London: IIED (available from IIED, 3 Endsleigh Street, London WC1H ODD, UK).

Guijt, I. (forthcoming) *Negotiated Learning: Collaborative Monitoring in Resource Management*, submitted to Resources for the Future.

Guijt, I. and Shah, M.K. (1998) *The Myth of Community: Gender Issues in Participatory Development*. London: Intermediate Technology Publications.

Guijt, I. and Van Veldhuizen, L. (1998) *What Tools? Which Steps? Comparing PRA and PTD* (Issue Paper No. 79). London: IIED.

Gujja, B., Pimbert, M. and Shah, M. (1998) 'Village voices challenging wetland management policies: PRA experiences from Pakistan and India', in J. Holland and J. Blackburn (eds), *Whose Voice?* London: ITDG Publishing. pp. 57–66.

Gypmantasiri et al. and Conway, G. (1980) *An Interdisciplinary Perspective of Cropping Systems in the Chiang Mai Valley: Key Questions for Research*. Chiang Mai University, Thailand: Multiple Cropping Project, Faculty of Agriculture, June.

Hadjipateras, A., Akuilu, H., Owero, J., Fatima Dendo, M. de and Nyenga, C. (2006) *Joining Hands: Integrating Gender and HIV/AIDS: Report of an ACORD Project Using Stepping Stones in Angola, Tanzania and Uganda*. Kampala, London and Nairobi: ACORD [hasap@acord.org.ug;info@acord.org.uk;info@acordnairobi.org].

Haverkort, B., Van der Kamp, J. and Waters-Bayer, A. (1991) *Joining Farmers' Experiments: Experiences in Participatory Technology Development*. London: Intermediate Technology Publications.

Heslop, M. (2002) *Participatory Research with Older People: a Sourcebook*. London: HelpAge Intl. [available from HelpAge Intl., PO Box 32832, London N1 9ZN, UK].

Hickey, S. and Mohan, G. (eds) (2004) *Participation: from Tyranny to Transformation? Exploring New Approaches to Participation in Development*. London and New York: Zed Books.

Holmes, T. (2001) *A Participatory Approach in Practice: Understanding Fieldworkers' Use of PRA in ActionAid The Gambia* (Working Paper No. 123). Sussex: IDS.

Holmes, T. (2002) 'Rapid spread through many pathways' in PG IDS *Pathways to Participation: Critical Reflections on PRA* : 4–5.

International HIV/AIDS Alliance (2006a) *All Together Now! Community Mobilisation for HIV/AIDS*. International HIV/AIDS Alliance, Brighton, UK [www.aidsalliance.org].

International HIV/AIDS Alliance (2006b) *Tools Together Now! 100 Participatory Tools to Mobilise Communities for HIV/AIDS*. International HIV/AIDS Alliance, Brighton, UK [www.aidsalliance.org].

Jamieson, N. (1987) 'The paradigmatic significance of rapid rural appraisal', in *KKU Proceedings*: 89–102.

Jayakaran, R. (2003) *Participatory Poverty Alleviation and Development: a Comprehensive Manual for Development Professionals*. China: World Vision.

Johnson, V., Ivan-Smith, E., Gordon, G., Pridmore, P. and Scott, P. (1998) *Stepping Forward: Children and Young People's Participation in the Development Process*. London: Intermediate Technology Publications.

Jones, C. (1996) *PRA Methods*, Topic Pack, Participation Group, IDS, Sussex.

Kanji, N. (2004) 'Reflection on gender and participatory development', *Participatory Learning and Action* 50 (October): 53–62.

Kar, K. (2003) *Subsidy or Self-respect? Participatory Total Community Sanitation in Bangladesh* (Working Paper No. 184). Sussex: IDS.

Kar, K. (2005) *Practical Guide to Triggering Community-Led Total Sanitation (CLTS)*. Sussex: IDS.

Kar, K. and Bongartz, P. (2006) *Update on Some Recent Developments in Community-Led Total Sanitation*, Sussex: IDS.

Kar, K. and Pasteur, K. (2005) *Subsidy or Self-Respect? Community Led Total Sanitation: an Update on Recent Developments* (Working Paper No. 257). Sussex: IDS.

KKU (1987) *Proceedings of the 1985 International Conference on Rapid Rural Appraisal*. Rural Systems Research and Farming Systems Research Projects, University of Khon Kaen, Thailand.

Kolavalli, S. and Kerr, J. (2002a) 'Mainstreaming participatory watershed development', *Economic and Political Weekly* (19 Jan.): 225–42.

Kolavalli, S. and Kerr J. (2002b) 'Scaling up participatory watershed development in India', *Development and Change*, 33 (2): 213–35.

Koti, F. and Weiner, D. (2006) '(Re) Defining peri-urban residential space using participatory GIS in Kenya', in P. Mbile (ed.), *Electronic Journal of Information Systems in Developing Countries: Special Issue on Participatory Geographical Information Systems and Participatory Mapping*, 25 (8): 1–12.

Kumar, S. (ed.) (1996) *The ABC of PRA: Attitude and Behaviour Change: A Report on a South-South Workshop on PRA: Attitudes and Behaviour in Bangalore and Madura*. New Delhi: Praxis [available from Praxis, 12 Patliputra Colony, Patna 800013, Bihar, India].

Kumar, S. (2002) *Methods for Community Participation: a Complete Guide for Practitioners*. New Delhi: Vistaar Publications.

Levy, S. (2003) 'Are we targeting the poor? Lessons from Malawi', *PLA Notes*, 47 (August): 19–24.

Lunch, N. and Lunch, C. (2006) *Insights into Participatory Video: a Handbook for the Field*. Oxford: Insight [www.insightshare.org].

McCarthy, J. with Galvoa, K. (2004) *Enacting Participatory Develpment: Theatre-based Techniques*. London and Sterling, VA: Earthscan.

Mans, G.G. (2006) 'Using PGIS to conduct community safety audits', in P. Mbile (ed.), *Electronic Journal of Information Systems in Development Countries: Special Issue on Participatory Geographical Information Systems and Participatory Mapping*, 25 (7): 1–13 [http://www.ejisdc.org].

Mascarenhas, J., Shah, P., Joseph, S. Jayakaran, R., Devavaram, J., Ramachandran, V., Fernandez, A., Chambers, R. and Pretty, J. (eds) (1991) *Proceedings of the February 1991 Bangalore PRA Workshop* (*RRA Notes* 13, August).

Mayoux, L. (2003a) *Thinking It Through: Using Diagrams in Impact Assessment* [www.enterprise-impact.org.uk].

Mayoux, L. (2003b) 'Participatory action learning system: an empowering approach to monitoring, evaluation and impact assessment, Manual.' Draft, June [www.enterprise-impact.org.uk].

Mayoux, L. (in press) 'Road to the foot of the mountain – but reaching for the sun: PALS adventures and challenges', in K. Brock and J. Pettit (eds), *Springs of Participation: Creating and Evolving Methodologies for Participatory Development*. London: ITDG Publications.

Mayoux, L. and ANANDI (2005) 'Participatory action learning in practice: experience of Anandi, India', *Journal of International Development*, March: 211–42.

Mayoux, L. and Chambers, R. (2005) 'Reversing the paradigm: quanitification, participatory methods and pro-poor impact assessment', *Journal of International Development*, 17: 271–98.

Mbile, P. (ed.) (2006) *Electronic Journal of Information Systems in Developing Countries: Special Issue on Participatory Geographical Information Systems and Participatory Mapping, Vol. 25* [http://www.ejisdc.org].

Moser, C. and McIlwaine C. (2004) *Encounters with Violence in Latin America: Urban Poor Perceptions from Colombia and Guatemala*. New York and London: Routledge.

Mukherjee, N. (2001) *Participatory Learning and Action, with 100 Field Methods*. New Delhi: Concept Publishing Co.

Nagasundari, S. (in press) 'Evolution of the internal learning system: a case study of the new entity for social action', in K. Brock and J. Pettit (eds), *Springs of Participation: Creating and Evolving Methodologies for Participatory Development*. London: ITDG Publications.

Narayan, D., Chambers, R., Shah, M. and Petesch, P. (2000) *Voices of the Poor: Crying out for Change*. Oxford: Oxford University Press.

Narendranath, D. (in press) 'Steering the Boat of Life with ILS: the Oar of Learning', in K. Brock and J. Pettit (eds), *Springs of Participation: Creating and Evolving Methodologies for Participatory Development*. London: ITDG Publications.

Newman, K. (in press) 'Can an international NGO practice what it preaches in participation? The case of ActionAid International', in K. Brock and J. Pettit (eds), *Springs of Participation: Creating and Evolving Methodologies for Participatory Development*. London: ITDG Publications.

Nierras, R.M. (2002) *Generating Numbers with Local Governments in the Philippines* (Working Draft). Sussex: IDS.

Noponen, H. (in press) 'It's not just about the pictures! It's also about principles, process and power: tensions in the development of the internal learning system' in K. Brock and J. Pettit (eds), *Springs of Participation: Creating and Evolving Methodologies for Participatory Development*. London: ITDG Publications.

Norman, D. (1975) 'Rationalising mixed cropping under indigenous conditions: the example of Northern Nigeria', *Samaru Research Bulletin 232*. Zaria, Nigeria: Institute for Agricultural Research, Samaru, Ahmadu Bello University (Also *Journal of Development Studies*, nd: 3–21).

Norton, A. with Bird, B., Brock, K., Kakande, M. and Turk, C. (2001) *A Rough Guide to PPAs: Participatory Poverty Assessment: an Introduction to Theory and Practice*. London: Overseas Development Institute.

Okali, C., Sumberg, J. and Farrington, J. (1994) *Farmer Participatory Research: Rhetoric and Reality*. London: Intermediate Technology Publications on behalf of the Overseas Development Institute.

Pathways to Participation (c. 2001) *Critical Reflections on PRA*. Sussex: IDS.

Phnuyal, B.K. (1999) 'Rejecting "the manual" for more critical and participatory analysis: REFLECT's experience in El Salvador', *PLA Notes*, 34 (February): 68–72.

PID and NES (1989) *An Introduction to Participatory Appraisal for Rural Resources Management*. Worcester, MA: Program for International Development, Clark University, and Nairobi: National Environment Secretariat, Ministry of Environment and Natural Resources.

Pimbert, M. (2004) 'Natural resources, people and participation', *Participatory Learning and Action*, 50 (October): 131–9.

Pimbert, M. and Pretty, J. (1997) 'Parks, people and professionals: putting "participation" into protected area management', in K.B. Ghimire and M.P. Pimbert (eds), *Social Change and Conservation: Environmental Politics and Impacts of National Parks and Protected Areas*. London: Earthscan. pp. 297–330.

PLA Notes 22–54 (1995–2006) Available from International Institute for Environment and Development, 3 Endsleigh Street, London WIH ODD, UK.

Pontius, J., Dilts, R. and Bartlett, A. (eds) (2002) *From Farmer Field School to Community IPM: Ten years of IPM Training in Asia*, Bangkok: FAO Regional Office for Asia and the Pacific. [available from Meetings and Publications Officer, FAO Regional Office, Phra Athit Road, Bangkok 10200, Thailand].

Pratt, G. (2001) *Practitioners' Critical Reflections on PRA and Participation in Nepal* (Working Paper 122, January). Sussex: IDS.

PRGA (c. 2002) *PRGA Program: Synthesis of Phase I (1997–2002),* Program on Participatory Research and Gender Analysis, CGIAR [www.prgaprogramme.org].

Probst, K, and Hagmann, J. with Fernandez, M. and Ashby, J.A. (2003) *Understanding Participatory Research in the Context of Natural Resource Management – Paradigms, Approaches and Typologies.* ODI Agricultural and Extension Network Paper 130, Overseas Development Institute, London.

Rahman, M.A. (1984) *Grassroots Participation and Self-reliance.* New Delhi: Oxford University Press and IBH.

Rambaldi, G. (2005) 'Barefoot mapmakers and participatory GIS', editorial, in *Participatory GIS, ICT Update* 27 (September). Wageningen: CTA Technical Centre for Agricultural and Rural Cooperation. [http://ictupdate.cta.int].

Rambaldi, G. and Callosa-Tarr, J. (2000) *Manual on Participatory 3-Dimensional Modelling for Natural Resource Management: Essentials of Protected Area Management in the Philippines, Vol. 7.* Los Banos, Philippines: NIPAP, PAWB-DENR.

Rambaldi, G. and Callosa-Tarr, J. (2002) *Participatory 3-Dimensional Modelling: Guiding Principles and Applications.* Los Banos, Philippines: ASEAN Regional Center for Biodiversity Conservation.

Rambaldi, G., Chambers, R. McCall, M. and Fox, J. (2006) 'Practical ethics for PGIS practitioners, facilitators, technology intermediaries and researchers', *Participatory Learning and Action*, 54 (April): 106–13.

Rambaldi, G., Kwaku Kiem, P.A., McCall, M. and Weiner, D. (2006) 'Participatory spatial information management and communication in developing countries', in P. Mbile (ed.), *Electronic Journal of Information Systems in Developing Countries: Special Issue on Participatory Geographical Information Systems and Participatory Mapping, Vol. 25* [http://www.ejisdc.org].

Richards, P. (1985) *Indigenous Agricultural Revolution.* London: Hutchinson and Boulder, CO: Westview.

Robb, C. (2002[1999]) *Can the Poor Influence Policy? Participatory Poverty Assessments in the Developing World, 2nd edn.* Washington, DC: World Bank.

Rocheleau, D.E. (2005) 'Maps as power-tools: locating "communities" in space or situating people and ecologies in place?', in J.P. Broisus Brosius, J. Peter, A. Lowenhaupt-Tsing and C. Zerner (eds), *Communities and Conservation: Histories and Politics of Community-Based Natural Resource Management.* Walnut Creek, CA: Altamira Press. Chapter 13.

Roe, D., Mayers, J., Grieg-Gran, M., Kothari, A. Fabricius, C. and Hughes, R. (2000) *Evaluating Eden: Exploring the Myths and Realities of Community-based Wildlife. Management, Series Overview.* London: IIED.

RRA Notes 1–21 (1988–1994) Available from International Institute for Environment and Development, 3 Endsleigh Street, London WIH ODD, UK.

Schön, D.A. (1983) *The Reflective Practitioner: How Professionals Think in Action.* New York: Basic Books.

Schön, D.A. (1987) *Educating the Reflective Practitioner.* San Francisco, CA: Jossey-Bass.

Shah, M.K. (2003) 'The road from Lathodara: some reflections on PRA', in A. Cornwall and G. Pratt (eds), *Pathways to Participation: Reflections on PRA.* London: Intermediate Technology Publications. pp. 189–95.

Shah, M.K., Degnan Kambou, S. and Monihan, B. (1999) *Embracing Participation in Development: Worldwide Experience from CARE's Reproductive Health Programs with a Step-by-Step Field Guide to Participatory Tools and Techniques.* Atlanta, GA: CARE.

Singh, K. (2001) 'Handing over the stick: the global spread of participatory approaches to development', in M. Edwards and J. Gaventa (eds), *Global Citizen Action.* Boulder, CO: Lynne Rienner. pp. 175–87.

Swantz, M.-L., Ndedya, E. and Masaiganah, M.S. (2001/2006) 'Participatory action research in Southern Tanzania, with special reference to women', in P. Reason and H. Bradbury (eds), *Handbook of Action Research: Participative Inquiry and Practice.* London: Sage. pp 386–95. Also published in P. Reason and H. Bradbury (eds) (2006) *Handbook of Action Research: Concise Paperback Edition.* London: Sage. pp. 286–96.

Van der Mele, P. and Braun A.R. (2005) 'Importance of methodological diversity in research and development innovation systems', in J. Gonsalves et al. (eds), *Participatory Research and Development for Sustainable Agriculture and Natural Resource Management: a Sourcebook. Vol. 1: Understanding Participatory Research and Development.* Laguna,

Philippines and Ottawa: International Potato Center-Users' Perspectives with Agricultural Research and Development and IDRC. pp. 151–6.

Wallace, T. (2006) *Evaluating Stepping Stones, a Review of Existing Evaluations and Ideas for Future M and E Work*. Johannesburg: Action Aid International [www.actionaid.org].

Welbourn, A. (1995) *Stepping Stones: a Training Package on Gender, HIV, Communication and Relationship Skills*, manual and video (Strategies for Hope). London: ActionAid.

Welbourn, A. (2002) 'Gender, sex and HIV: how to address issues that no one wants to hear about', in A. Cornwall and A. Welbourn (eds), *Realizing Rights: Transforming Approaches to Sexual and Reproductive Well-being*. London: Zed Books. pp. 99–112.

Welbourn, A. (in press) 'HIV and AIDS: the global tsunami – can participatory approaches stem the tide?', in K. Brock and J. Pettit (eds), *Springs of Participation: Creating and Evolving Methodologies for Participatory Development*. London: ITDG Publications.

White, S. and Pettit, J. (2004) 'Participatory methods and the measurement of well-being', *Participatory Learning and Action*, 50: 88–96.

Witcombe, J.R., Joshi, A. and Stharpit, B.R. (1996) 'Farmer Participatory crop improvement 1. Varietal selection and breeding methods and their impact on biodiversity', *Experimental Agriculture*, 32: 445–60.

World Bank (2000) *Attacking Poverty: World Development Report 2000/2001*, Oxford University Press for The World Bank.

21

Action Learning

Mike Pedler and John Burgoyne

As part of a wider family of action-based approaches to research and learning, action learning is distinguished by the primacy it accords to action and learning by the people actually facing the problems in question, and also for its scepticism on the views and advice of experts. Although best understood as a working philosophy and not a set of techniques or standard practices, a distinction can be made between action learning as specific method and action learning as 'ethos' or general way of thinking. Action learning is compared and contrasted with action research, and a 'praxaeology' or a general theory of human action based on pragmatism, critical realism and risk is outlined. The chapter concludes with an examination of the challenge to create a critical practice of action learning, offered in the spirit of peer inquiry and in the context of a mutual striving for useful action.

Action learning combines self-development with action for change. The motive to act and learn is both personal and political, based on a critique of how things are and a desire for something better; at the same time part of what is changed is the actor.

Action learning originates with Reginald Revans (1907–2003), who was variously an Olympic athlete, a student of nuclear physics, an educational administrator, and a professor of management. Like his contemporary, W. Edwards Deming, Revans was keenly interested in the improvement of human systems for the benefit of those who depend upon them. The philosophy of action learning is based on a fundamental pragmatism about what can and must be done, now;

and a deeply humanistic view of human potential:

> But, whatever our theoretical powers, the systems we need in order to understand the public services are not to be found in the libraries and computing rooms of universities. If they are to be found at all, it will be in such social laboratories as the back streets of Gateshead, and it is there that we shall need to learn how to work. Our problem at the moment is to get ourselves invited. (Revans, 1971: 492)

Revans owes a debt to Dewey, for his pragmatism and championing of experiential learning, and also to Mary Parker Follett, who, in the 1920s and 1930s, criticized hierarchical structures and positional authority, emphasizing the value of knowledge wherever it is to be found. She also advocated the contextual 'law of the situation and the importance of collaborative relationships' (Rosabeth Moss Kanter as reported by Graham, 1995).

Action learning is part of a wider family of action-based approaches to research and learning. It is distinguished by the primacy it accords to the people who actually face the problems or opportunities in question, and for its scepticism on the views and advice of experts. For problems beyond technical solution, it offers a way of learning a way through risky ground in the company of some trusted companions.

Action learning is perhaps best understood as a working philosophy rather than a set of techniques or standard practices. A distinction can be made between action learning as a specific method and its wider influence as an 'ethos' or general way of thinking.

In this chapter, we tackle the question of definition before surveying the development of action learning, particularly in management education. We then compare and contrast it with action research, and discuss action learning as a 'praxaeology' or general theory of human action. The chapter concludes with an examination of the current developmental challenge to create a more critical practice of action learning.

WHAT IS ACTION LEARNING?

A nurse: 'Professor Revans, I think that I have at last understood action learning!'

Revans: 'Very good, but now what are you going to do about it?'

Action learning starts and ends with purpose, the first question being always: 'What am I (or you) trying to do?' Revans was fond of quoting the Scottish philosopher John Macmurray – 'All meaningful knowledge is for the sake of action, and all meaningful action for the sake of friendship' (Revans, 1998: 2) – to emphasize that purpose is also the end point. In turn, purpose rests on values, the 'What am I trying to do?' tracking back to 'What do I stand for?'

Thus people facing paralysing dilemmas and difficult choices find that their way through lies via a consideration of purposes, ethics and values as much as through any technical and professional skills.

Some of the distinctiveness of action learning lies in its iconoclastic origins, less against positivism as against the dominance of the expert over the learner. Revans railed against the 'book culture' that he saw as dominant in British life: 'it is no longer by doing such things that one acquires prestige in Britain but by *writing and talking* about doing them' (1980: 189). This cultural bias encourages people to believe that talking about action is the same as doing it. Action learning is about helping people 'learn how to solve problems' (1980 [1966]: 5) and is expressly designed to correct this fault: 'there can be no learning without action; and no (sober and deliberate) action without learning' (in Pedler, 1996: 20).

He eschews any single definition of action learning, holding that it is rooted in ancient wisdom. This lack of precise definition may hinder transmission, but it also contributes to the generation of new practices and the renewal and re-vivification of the idea. Thus action learning itself changes in the light of, and the learning from, its practice. One definition is:

Action learning couples the development of people in work organizations with action on their difficult problems. ... [it] makes the task the vehicle for learning and has three main components – *people*, who accept the responsibility for action on a particular task or issue; *problems*, or the tasks which are acted on; and the *set* of six or so colleagues who meet regularly to support and challenge each other to take action and to learn. (Pedler, 1997: xxx)

And one can immediately quibble with this: action learning is not restricted to work organizations, a set can have any number of people in it; it is not just about problems but opportunities and so on. Despite the lack of an agreed definition, action learning seems to be well understood in terms of the key practice features. In a recent sample of

UK practitioners, more than 75 per cent agreed on the following features of action learning (Pedler et al., 2005: 56):

1. Sets of about six people
2. Action on real tasks or problems at work
3. Tasks/problems are individual rather than collective
4. Questioning as the main way to help participants proceed with their tasks/problems
5. Facilitators are used

And 65 per cent said that:

6. Tasks/problems are chosen independently by individuals

Beyond this, there are wide variations in practice and departures or developments of Revans' ideas. Among these are: its use for 'own-job' management development (action learning is intended as a means of tackling intractable organizational and social problems); the use of professional advisers or facilitators (where Revans warned against experts and favoured peer self-facilitation) and the embedding of action learning in otherwise taught programmes (Revans did not reject teaching (P or Programmed Knowledge) but subordinated it to Q (or Questioning Insight) via the questioning). One explanation for this is that action learning has spread as an 'ethos' or general way of thinking about learning and teaching, as well as a specific set of practices (Pedler et al., 2005: 64–5).

ACTION LEARNING IN MANAGEMENT EDUCATION AND ORGANIZATIONAL DEVELOPMENT

Management education is perhaps the most researched field where action learning has been applied, but it is certainly not to be confined here, being in principle applicable to all social situations where people are faced with messy problems unamenable to technical solution. Action learning is often found for example in public service, voluntary organizations and community settings and seems to appeal to people with professional as well as managerial identities, such as clinicians, teachers and researchers. Revans always sides with any people beset by problems, whoever they are, and not with any class or group. If action learning fits well with managers, it is because they are charged with sorting out the messy problems of organizations, and not because they are more deserving. In organizational life, action learning seems suited to leadership issues and the development of leadership ability, characterized (e.g. by Kotter, 1990) as preparing people for the creative resolution of problems and opportunities, rather than the more routine running of established management systems.

From the 1960s, action learning emerges as an alternative to traditional (i.e. US) business school practice. In 1965 Revans resigned his Chair at Manchester following negotiations over the new Manchester Business School, which he describes as a victory for the 'book' culture of Owens College over the 'tool' culture of the then Manchester College of Technology (later UMIST), which he favoured as being closer to the needs of industry and society (Revans, 1980: 197). He strongly objected to the importation of US business school practice, describing the MBA as 'Moral Bankruptcy Assured'.

Revans' criticisms anticipated or precipitated a continuing critique of the MBA, for example by Mintzberg (2004), who suggests that MBA might mean 'Maybe Best Avoided' and from Bennis and O'Toole (2004: 2) who suggest that US business schools are misled by 'physics envy': 'Too focused on "scientific" research, business schools are hiring professors with limited real-world experience and graduating students who are ill equipped to wrangle with complex, unquantifiable issues, in other words the stuff of management' (As a concluding footnote there is empirical research suggesting that firms implicated in corporate crime employ more MBAs (Williams et al., 2000)!)

Action learning has been recognized as an innovation in management education and development in the UK since the major initiative undertaken in the General Electric Company in 1975 (Casey and Pearce, 1977), but it has remained controversial. The use of action learning is now increasing as part of a wider expansion of management and leadership development activities and as part of a cluster of 'context specific' teaching/learning methods that have grown in relation to other educational and development approaches (Mabey and Thomson, 2000; Horne and Steadman Jones, 2001). According to this research, the significant growth of in-company development activities has apparently contributed to improved organizational performance. Other surveys also suggest that the use of action learning has grown substantially, alongside coaching and mentoring (Thomson et al., 1997; Institute of Management, 2001).

However, despite a wider awareness of newer learning theories such as situated learning and activity theory that provide a theoretical underpinning for action learning and other 'context sensitive' approaches, business school education remains dominated by traditional lecturing and case studies and action learning is not widely used here, nor are staff generally skilled in its use (Pedler et al., 2005). This indicates an 'espoused theory' of action learning in business schools rather than a 'theory in use' (Argyris and Schön, 1974: 7; see also Chapter 17) with the ability to translate theory into practice.

ACTION LEARNING AND ACTION RESEARCH: SIMILARITIES AND DIFFERENCES

Action learning is also part of a wider growth of interest in 'action approaches' to management and organization. Kurt Lewin is credited as the founder of 'action strategies' where 'knowledge is produced in service of, and in the midst of, action' in contrast to positivist approaches that separate theory from practice (Raelin, 1999: 117). Many varieties of practice are discussed in various surveys including multiple forms of action learning – self-managed, auto, on-line, business-driven & critical etc.; multiple forms of action

research – critical, educational, emancipatory, humanistic, participatory etc; together with many other forms of inquiry: action, appreciative, collaborative, co-operative, developmental action, etc. and including other cousins such as developmental evaluation and participatory rural appraisal (Elden and Chisholm, 1993; Brooks and Watkins, 1994; Greenwood and Levin, 1998; Marsick and O'Neill, 1999; Raelin, 1999; Pedler et al., 2005). Raelin proposes action research, participatory research, action science, developmental action inquiry, co-operative-inquiry and action learning as 'the burgeoning action strategies that are now being practiced by organization and management development practitioners around the globe' (1999: 115).

As part of a wider family of action-based approaches to research and learning, action learning and action research share many common values and positions on valid knowledge. For most practical purposes, it is their common heritage and not their different emphases that is important. Action learning and action research share common origins in a commitment to action and pragmatism, and a reaction against detached research generating abstract knowledge which is then disseminated through teaching from a position of assumed expertise. Both have their origins in a critique of the application of a positivist, natural sciences approach to social and human settings, and acknowledge the pragmatist philosophers in their emphasis on the importance of learning in a changing world. Both are characterized by cyclical processes that reflect the pragmatists' emphasis on the need for experiment, reflection and learning. Both are concerned with seeking pragmatic and meaningful solutions to social problems in organizations, communities and societies: what works best in helping people bring about the changes they seek? Both address the 'policy/implementation gap'; ideas are ten-a-penny, but what actually works? And how do we find out?

The differences between action learning and action research can best be seen in their starting points and development paths. One obvious difference that lends action learning an idiosyncratic iconoclasm is its continuing dependence upon the thought and practice of one man, Reginald Revans. Action research owes a great deal to Kurt Lewin, but this field also reflects the work of many other scholars and practitioners. Indeed, Revans has put himself in this tradition amongst others: for example, he variously describes the four-year Hospital Internal Communications (HIC) Project (1965–8) as action research, organizational development and operational research (1982[1966]). Wieland and Leigh (1971) described this project as an unusual approach to organization development, characterized by the bringing about of change through self-help teams. Clark endorses this, seeing Revans' work as 'non-directive' action research (1972: 119) and noting a distinctive characteristic of what would later be known as action learning:

> Though Revans defined a key problem area he deliberately did not propose a specific solution. Instead, he suggested that the problem of communication could be solved best by those working within the hospitals. (1972: 40)

Another apparently obvious difference is in the name: action *learning* versus action *research*. Action learning has become a radical alternative to teaching, whilst action research presents a striking juxtaposition to passive traditions of research, both positivist and interpretativist (participating ethnographically in events to render an authentic account of them).

Yet, despite continuing differences, traditions and cultural histories, distinguishing action learning from action research is made problematic by the many varieties of practice that exist in both. Finally, whilst practice boundaries are fuzzy and distinctions often hard to maintain, there is a convergence in both ethos and practice on seeing action as the basis for learning and for taking action on the basis of learning. Accepting this, some differences and differences in emphasis can be cautiously asserted:

Maturity

Action research is a more developed field, both in practice and especially theory and has

been developed and taken forward by a wider community of scholars than action learning.

Action or Knowledge?

McGill and Beaty suggest that action learning focuses on learning through action whilst action research is more research-oriented (2001: 20–2). In this argument, action research shares with all research the commitment to make a useful contribution to understanding and knowledge, and to show how this is arrived at methodologically, so that those to whom the new understanding is offered can see how it is arrived at, whether they agree with it and whether they want to 'replicate' the research in their own setting. The primary outcome is individual and collective understanding. Action learning seeks continuous improvement in systems and self-development through individual and collective action. Sensemaking is based on the actions taken, via reflection, honest observation and interpretation of the consequences of action. The purpose and outcomes are improved action and personal and collective learning.

This simple distinction between action/learning and research orientations may be a false dichotomy, because it can be argued that the purpose of the research in action research is primarily for the benefit of the people with the problem under study and not the university (Reason, 2006), but there does often seem to be a difference of emphasis in practice on the purpose of research.

Review or Research?

Alastair Mant provides a good illustration of the place and function of research in action learning:

> One of my consultancy assignments ... was to improve selection. The temptation was to spend a fortune on a very clever, very complicated testing procedure available from one of the glossier consultancy firms. The solution was to remember that all the rounds (principally for salesmen) were on file. A brief review ('research', if you insist) of the data there revealed that two of the line managers in the system had a genius for selection – not just for

choosing the right people but also for representing the organization accurately to them at interview. They were, in short, never wrong.

We could, I suppose, have studied these two men in fine detail, but it wasn't really necessary. All that was needed was to ensure their deployment at selection time and, where possible, to get other (and younger) managers to listen to them. (1983: 224)

The word 'review' signifies the primacy of action over codified knowledge; as soon as a way forward is spotted, the 'research' stops and the action begins. Beyond the requirements for action on real problems, action learning is generally less concerned with research as an activity. Whilst action research seems more naturally at home in the academy, action learning is more ambivalent and is happiest rooted in practice communities. The rejection of the scholastic tradition is much stronger in action learning than it is in action research.

Having said this, action learning is increasingly present in universities, both in research and qualification programmes. A growth of research both *by* and *into* action learning creates interesting problems for researchers. How does action learning research differ from other research practices? What can it contribute that is new?

The Book or the Tool?

Action learning's preference for the tool over the book makes for great adaptability, but also leads to a proliferation of practices, some of which, despite carrying the name, do not meet the basic requirements. Additionally, this flexibility carries the risk of action learning being co-opted as an implementation tool without any wider critique (McLaughlin and Thorpe, 1993; Vince and Martin, 1993; Wilmott, 1997). We return to the themes of a more critical perspective below.

Risk and Personal Development

Action learning is for people in circumstances of confusion, ambiguity and risk. In turn Revans stresses that the profound self-examination and self-development of the actor comes from

acting on problems carrying a significant possibility of failure (1998: 8–9). The relationship between the learner and the problem being tackled is personal as well as organizational: 'the problem is part of me and I am part of the problem' (Pedler, 1996: 20).

This emphasis on personal risk and self-development is highly distinctive to action learning, although some action researchers also argue for the importance of the personal as a key part of action research (see Gustavson et al., Chapter 4 in this volume).

The Set and other Distinctive Practices

Action learning has its own distinctive working practices, most particularly the set of peers working over time to provide support and challenge in helping each other achieve their goals. Action learning sets share various common practices including the primacy of questions and the provision of feedback. By focusing on action, pragmatic research, reflection and personal development, the set constitutes 'the cutting edge' of action learning (Revans, 1998: 10).

PRAXAEOLOGY: TOWARDS A GENERAL THEORY OF HUMAN ACTION

The power of action learning in adult, professional and managerial education stems from its philosophy of action. Whilst much attention has been given to theories of learning in various literatures, much less has been given to theories of action. Revans' attempt at a 'praxeology', or general theory of human action, rests on three assumptions or philosophical positions on 'how things are': critical realism, pragmatism and the risk imperative.

Critical Realism

Some interpretations of action learning take a simple realist perspective: 'To me ... Revans has a simple message: in action learning real managers share ideas and tackle real problems with their counterparts, which effects change in the real world' (Pedler, 1997: 65); others acknowledge the problematic nature of individual actions in complex systems and adopt a more constructionist approach, emphasizing aspects of collaborative inquiry and collective meaning making (Pedler, 1997: 69–73).

Critical realism may provide the most useful underlying orientation to action learning (Burgoyne, 2002). This starts with the ontological proposition that the world is neither the determinate machine of positivism or the 'anything goes' meaning-making of extreme social constructionism, but is an open system with emergent properties, containing some mechanisms or powers that can be relied on as stable. The notion that there are regular mechanisms in the world, that they are or are not activated, that they vary in their effects and outcomes as they interact with other mechanisms and contexts, fits the mix of interplay and interaction of predictability and emergence in Revans 'P' and 'Q' (1998: 4).

A critical realism stance on action learning is critical in two senses. First, it is critical of both strong positivism and extreme constructionism on pragmatic grounds: neither works. Secondly, following Mary Parker Follett (Follett, 1927; Graham, 1995), it is critical in its proposition that any action, taken on the basis of false assumptions about the situational reality, is bound to be destructive and dysfunctional.

Pragmatism

The philosophical position of pragmatism is commonly acknowledged as the basis for experiential learning (Dewey, 1929; Kolb, 1984) and in turn is commonly used to explain the process of action learning. Pragmatism holds that truth is not something absolute, but just that which is useful to choose and achieve worthwhile outcomes.

Action learning adopts a pragmatic stance: What are you trying to do? What is stopping you? Who could help you? (Revans, 1998). This stance is well expressed by the pragmatist philosopher William James, describing a furious debate with friends on a camping trip in the woods:

> The corpus of the dispute was a squirrel – a live squirrel supposed to be clinging to one side of a tree trunk; while over against the tree's opposite side a human being was imagined to stand. This human witness tries to get sight of the squirrel by moving rapidly round the tree, but no matter how fast he goes, the squirrel moves as fast in the opposite direction, and always keeps the tree between himself and the man, so that never a glimpse of him is caught. The resultant metaphysical problem now is this: Does the man go round the squirrel or not? He goes round the tree, sure enough, and the squirrel is on the tree, but does he go round the squirrel? In the unlimited leisure of the wilderness, discussion had been worn threadbare. (Thayer, 1982: 208)

James solves this problem by saying that it depends on what is 'practically meant' by 'going round'. For practical purposes, if it means that the man has circumnavigated the squirrel's position, then yes; if it means, did the man ever pass the squirrel, then no. What difference would it make if this rather than that were true? If no practical difference can be traced then the dispute is idle. Here truth is not a fixed, inherent quality but something that leads to a useful belief whose expectations are actually fulfilled: 'The truth of an idea is not a stagnant property inherent in it. Truth *happens* to an idea. It becomes true, is made true by events' (Thayer, 1982: 229).

James explains the pragmatic method as a way of dealing with otherwise irresolvable problems. Is the world one or many? Are we fated or free? Disputes about such issues tend to be circular and unending, and pragmatism interrupts this process to interpret each notion in terms of its possible outcomes and consequences. What difference would it make if this rather than that were true? What works best in helping people bring about the changes they seek? If no practical difference can be traced then, for pragmatists, the alternatives mean practically the same, and dispute is idle.

Action research has also been interpreted via contemporary representations of pragmatism such as those of Richard Rorty (Reason, 2003; see also Chapters 1 and 23). Philosophical pragmatism, action research and action learning hold much in common; the differences emerge in the respective emphases on thinking, researching, acting and learning.

The Risk Imperative

Revans' action learning is not a naive, risk-and-dilemma-free 'learning by doing' as sometimes depicted, but a practical and moral struggle for progress, cradled in risk and anxiety. Revans nominates 'managerial values' and the value system of the enterprise as the factor most likely to hinder effective action and learning: 'where those in charge do not know by what marks they are trying to navigate, they cannot delegate responsibility' (1971: 65).

Acting in challenging situations is characterized by conflicts of value and purpose, and also by the accompanying fear and risks – as much of inaction as of inappropriate action. Revans termed this *'the risk imperative'*:

> These attacks, whether upon problems or upon opportunities, must carry significant risk of penalty for failure. Those who are not obliged to assess the risk to themselves of pursuing, or of trying to pursue, such-and-such lines of action cannot, by their indifference to the outcome, explore their own value systems nor identify any trustworthy pattern of their own beliefs. Non-risk exercises, such as case discussions, often motivated by exhibitionism or a need for social approval, may draw from some participants declarations of belief that, while not misleading those who hear them, can help only to deceive those who express them. (1998: 8–9)

Systems Alpha, Beta and Gamma

Revans' most formal attempt to create a general theory of human action incorporates three interacting systems (1971: 33–67):

- Alpha – *the strategy system* based on the managerial value system, the external environment and the available internal resources;

- Beta – *the decision system or negotiation cycle* required to implement the decision or strategy – of survey, trial, action, audit and consolidation;
- Gamma – *the learning process* as experienced uniquely by each action learner, involving self-questioning and awareness of self and others.

System alpha summarizes what Revans had learned from his operational research experience where he applied his scientific training to studies of productivity in mines, factories, schools and hospitals: what opportunities exist in the external environment, and how may internal resources be deployed to exploit these (1971: 35–6)? In adding the managerial value system to this orthodoxy, as the basis for aims and decisions, he makes it clear that such choices are contested and moral in nature.

System beta is a direct application of scientific method to the project cycle of planning, action, reflection and learning. Revans points out that science, project methodology and learning all follow this same cycle.

System gamma is the vital learning theory component of Revans' model:

> System gamma was the essence ... it represents in its own way the structure of all intelligent behaviour, and offers, in conjunction with systems alpha and beta, one starting for a general theory of human action, for a science of praxeology. (1971: 58)

System gamma encapsulates the reflexive nature of action learning: when a person takes action on a situation, this affects the situation, but the effect of the change or action has a complementary effect upon the person (1971: 54–5). Additionally, Revans also sees system gamma as the means by which personal learning is linked to organizational learning in 'a cycle of institutional learning' illustrating 'the symbiotic nature of personal and institutional change' (1971: 129–30).

Although Cyert and March (1963) had already established the idea that organizations can be said to learn, Revans' particular contribution was to translate these ideas into the practice of action learning. This linking of individual action and development within the context of organizational change prefigures later preoccupations with organizational learning and the learning organization.

The Practice of Action Learning

Praxaeology denotes *praxis* – practice or doing – in the original Greek; but also as in Marx's usage, the inseparable unity of theory and practice, thinking and doing. Revans' adoption of this co-location is also reflected in other contemporary ideas such as reflective practice (Schön, 1983); action science (Argyris and Schön, 1978; Argyris et al., 1987); and also in more recent theories such as communities of practice theories (Lave and Wenger, 1991); activity theories (Engeström, 1987) and actor network theory (Law and Hassard, 1999). These more recent ideas locate knowledge and action in participative networks, in which individual 'actors' (including non-human ones) cannot easily be isolated. In the light of this, an adequate theory of action learning practice must now go beyond individuals to take account of the contextualized and situated nature of human actions and activities. Thus, action learning sets themselves may be viewed as activity systems and members of sets as 'actors-in-complex-contexts' (Ashton, 2006: 28).

Practice is a useful word for advancing Revans' theory of action, not only because it creates a unity from entities such as action and learning that might otherwise become polarized or mutually exclusive, but also because it can connect the individual actor with a wider, collective context of action. Revans re-capitulates action learning (and systems alpha, beta and gamma) in these terms, as change in three sets of relationships: with the external world (third-person), with oneself (first-person), with other practitioners (second-person) (1982: 724). Reason and Bradbury (2001/2006) make a parallel proposition for action research: experience, knowledge and research can be for the person, for the face-to-face inquiring group, and for the wider community.

TOWARDS A CRITICAL PRACTICE OF ACTION LEARNING

There are a number of unresolved and developmental issues for action learning, including the questions of definition, how best to link individual and organizational learning and the quest for a more critical action learning.

These three issues are related. Action learning 'means different things to different people' (Weinstein, 1995: 32) and Revans' 'classical principles' are often diluted, as in 'task forces' which report findings rather than take action (Dixon, 1997). In a survey of current practice, Pedler, Burgoyne and Brook (2005) suggest that action learning is usually seen as individual development in small groups with less evidence of sponsorship for tackling organizational issues as envisaged by Revans (1982: 280–6) or a key component in inter-organization or network learning (Coughlan and Coghlan, 2004). For organizational development to take place 'a connection must be secured between what has been learned by action learning participants and other members of the organization' (Donnenberg and De Loo, 2004: 167).

Given its protean nature, action learning is easily adapted to serve local circumstances and agendas. Wilmott's challenge – how can action learning avoid being 'selectively adopted to maintain the status quo'? (1994: 127) – promotes an aspiration for a more critical action learning which goes beyond the 'ordinary criticality' of reflective practice to a social and organizational critique. This is especially so in the context of management education, given the 'uncritical' nature of much current provision (McLaughlin and Thorpe, 1993; Burgoyne and Reynolds, 1997; Reynolds, 1999; Rigg and Trehan, 2004). As Reynolds and Vince (2004: 453) put it 'Do ideas brought into action-based discussions help to question existing practices, structures and associated power relations within the organization?' A critical action learning would distinguish between effective practice, reflective practice and critically reflective practice (Burgoyne and Reynolds, 1997: 1).

Questioning the Wisdom of Peers

This call for a more critical approach challenges one of action learning's basic tenets: its trust in the wisdom of peers:

> Action learning is to make useful progress on the treatment of problems/opportunities, where no solution can possibly exist already because different managers, all honest, experienced and wise, will advocate different courses of actions in accordance with their different value systems, their different past experiences and their different hopes for the future. (Revans, 1998: 28)

But from a critical perspective, set members are contained and encultured, unlikely to be able to mount an independent critique of their organizational and social world without some input of 'critical social theory' (Wilmott, 1997). However, action learning not only puts its trust in peers, but actively mistrusts experts (including those in critical social theory). This value preference gives it great power and distinctiveness, but does it also sometimes result in blindness to wider questions?

Action learning places great importance on 'insightful questions' (Revans, 1998: 6), and if critical theory can add value through the posing of good questions, then a critical practice of action learning might aim to combine this critique with the 'art of the possible' in terms of organizational change and personal practice. This can only happen, as both Revans and the critical theorists agree, via an understanding of, and a working with, the power relationships in any setting.

Critical Action Learning in Practice?

But what would this look like in practice? With honourable exceptions (e.g. Rigg and Trehan, 2004), the arguments so far have been mainly theoretical.

Because action learning is concerned with learning what 'works' as a basis for action, a critical practice must start from what works or does not work. The criticality is perhaps in a deeper examination of what counts as 'working', together with the moral, ethical and social justifications that are applied to the means as well as to the ends of any action.

Rigg and Trehan (2004) offer some rare examples of what critical action learning might look like in practice. Their action learners are working within an academic programme which provides critical theory inputs and which aims to encourage participants to become aware of their theories-in-use, to think critically and, through valuing their own experience and insights, to create their own theory from practice (2004: 152). Four illustrations are offered to support the authors' optimism that a critical action learning can contribute to a more critical management practice via a profound learning from experiences of emotions, power and diversity (2004: 162).

The illustrations are based on lengthy self-accounts that can only be glimpsed here. Here is part of Rav's story:

> Rav experienced 'intense rage of anger, and annoyance' and felt 'very lonely, isolated and devalued' in the early days of the programme. Rav was one of three Asian participants on the programme, and found himself in a set not only with the other two but also with an Asian facilitator. Experiencing deep emotions and conflicts, Rav took several actions including 'applying' to other sets for membership. Further strong feelings were provoked when he heard that they were 'considering my request (for entry)'. He continues:
> 'At this point I felt angry and humiliated, but to my surprise I decided to change my strategy. My other two group members were quick to point out that I had in fact experienced a covert act of rejection, which they had previously experienced in their own organizations. Suddenly, the bonding was back and we reaffirmed our commitment to complete the MSc and "show them how good we were". How dare they reject us, we were three experienced and talented Asian professionals who were capable and now willing to take on the world! ... To this end I didn't engage in any social interaction with the other groups, and our group very soon became detached and isolated from the "new organization". ... '.
> Reflecting later on his actions and feelings, he notes:
> 'Formulating this paper has forced me to conceptualise and analyse my actions and learning – Why did I behave in this manner? Do I have a

fear of white domination? Am I unable to accept rejection? Why did I feel the need to "overcompensate"? This experience does also force me to ask the question "How good am I at managing my emotion?"'

He specifically notes the value of critical theory in his learning:

'Habermas' work has certainly helped me to analyse and question my experiences and underlying beliefs and values, and thereby exposed my true development needs.' (Rigg and Trehan, 2004: 156–7)

Rigg and Trehan's analysis of their participants' experiences in general is that they demonstrate three interrelated themes: 'challenged perspectives on managing, transformed perspectives on self and adjustments to social relations' (2004: 155).

Can Action Learning Co-exist with Critical Theory?

We have suggested elsewhere that Lyotard's argument regarding three 'meta-narratives' or purposes of knowledge provides a framework for thinking about the positioning of action learning (Lyotard, 1984; Burgoyne, 1994; Pedler et al., 2005). These are: *speculative*: knowledge for its own sake, concerned with theoretical rigour; *emancipatory*: knowledge that helps us overcome oppression and attain the highest human potential; and *performative*: knowledge that helps action in the world, to resolve problems, to produce better goods and services (Figure 21.1).

Suppose that action learning now sits between the performative and emancipatory, and furthest from speculative. But, as in Revans' career it appears to have migrated to here from a position closer to that of operational research, it may be that the critical practice argument is now tugging action learning closer to a critical theory position between emancipation and speculation.

Whilst speculation is 'safe', the performative, whether driven by an emancipatory or other purpose, is inherently risky, with potential for either good or evil or both. The exercise of critical thinking and moral imagination require us to hold all possible interests in

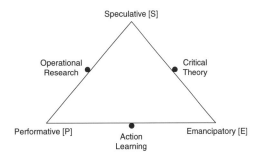

Figure 21.1 *Lyotard's triangle*

mind, whilst the action and risk imperatives of action learning demand that we take sides, choose, and commit. How can we continue to act, to good effect, whilst holding all these, and more, possibilities in mind? The tension in this position is reminiscent of Polanyi's scientist who wears commitment as 'a shirt of flame blazing with passion' whilst simultaneously holding the possibility that this firm belief might well be false (1962: 64).

Yet there remains some incompatibility and incommensurability of paradigms. The discomfort between action learning and the academy stems from the preference of academics for seeking to influence the world through ideas rather than activism. As academics, critical theorists can exercise moral imagination and accommodate multiple views without the need to subjugate them to a single commitment to action. When academics move into action they have the same problems as other people.

For example, the critical challenge of animal rights activists to the privileging of human over animal rights seems intellectually sound; but when it comes to action, its ends, means and justifiable limits, things become very problematic. The ethical dimensions emerge much more sharply in action than in when 'just' thought is involved. Revans understood this very well:

A man *may well learn to talk about taking action simply by talking about taking action* (as in classes at a business school) but to learn *to take action* (as something distinct from learning to talk about taking action) then he needs *to take action* (rather than to talk about taking action) and to see the effect, not of talking about taking action (at which he may appear competent) but *of taking the action itself* (at which he may fall somewhat short of competent). (1971: 54–5 original emphases)

And of course this insight is not new, as Revans noted in his frequent invocation of a passage attributed to the Buddha:

To do a little good is better than to write difficult books. The perfect man is nothing if he does not diffuse benefits on other creatures, if he does not console the lonely. The way of salvation is open to all, but know that a man deceives himself if he thinks he can escape his conscience by taking refuge in a monastery. The only remedy for evil is a healthy reality. (1980: 3)

A critical practice of action learning would mirror critical theory and, whilst refuting any claims to sovereignty by thinkers, conscious or unconscious, strive for a practical accomplishment which is no less demanding. Action learning can benefit from critical thinking, but only if this is offered in the spirit of peer inquiry and in the context of a mutual striving for useful action. It is the assumed superiority and hegemony of theory and theorists over practice and practitioners that is rejected, not the value of critical thinking.

REFERENCES

Argyris, C. and Schön, D. (1974) *Theory in Practice.* San Francisco, CA: Jossey-Bass.

Argyris, C. and Schön, D. (1978) *Organizational Learning: a Theory of Action Perspective.* Reading, MA: Addison Wesley.

Argyris, C., Putnam, R. and Smith, D. (1987) *Action Science.* San Francisco, CA: Jossey-Bass.

Ashton, S. (2006) 'Where's the action? The concept of action in action learning', *Action Learning: Research Practice*, 3 (1): 5–29.

Bennis, W.G. and O'Toole, J. (2004) 'How business schools lost their way', *Harvard Business Review*, May: 2.

Brooks, A. and Watkins, K. (1994) *The Emerging Power of Action Inquiry Techniques.* San Francisco, CA: Jossey-Bass.

Burgoyne, J.G. (2002) *The Nature of Action Learning: What Is Learned about in Action Learning?* Salford: University of Salford, The Revans Institute for Action Learning and Research.

Burgoyne, J. and Reynolds, M. (eds) (1997) *Management Learning: Integrating Perspectives in Theory & Practice.* London: Sage.

Casey, D. and Pearce, D. (eds) (1977) *More Than Management Development: Action Learning at GECl.* Aldershot: Gower Press.

Clark, P.A. (1972) *Action Research and Organisational Change.* London: Harper & Row.

Coughlan, P. and Coghlan, D. (2004) 'Action learning: towards a framework in inter-organisational settings', *Action Learning: Research & Practice*, 1 (1): 43–62.

Cyert, R. and March, J. (1963) *A Behavioural Theory of the Firm.* Englewood Cliffs, NJ: Prentice Hall.

Dewey, J. (1929) *Experience and Nature.* La Salle, IL: Open Court.

Dixon, N. (1997) 'More then just a task force', in M. Pedler (ed.), *Action Learning in Practice, 3rd edn.* Aldershot: Gower Press. pp. 329–38.

Donnenberg, O. and De Loo, I. (2004) 'Facilitating organizational development through action learning – some practical and theoretical considerations', *Action Learning: Research & Practice*, 1 (2): 167–84.

Elden, M. and Chisholm, R. (1993) 'Introduction to a Special Issue "Emergent Varieties of Action Research"', *Human Relations*, 46: 121–42.

Engeström, Y. (1987) *Learning by Expanding: an Activity-Theoretical Approach to Developmental Research.* Helsinki: Orienta-Konsultit.

Follett, M.P. (1927) 'Leaders and experts.' Paper presented at the Bureau of Personnel Administration, New York.

Graham, P. (1995) *Mary Parker Follett: Prophet of Management.* Boston: Harvard Business School Press.

Greenwood, D. and Levin, M. (1998) *Introduction to Action Research: Social Research for Social Change.* London: Sage.

Horne, M. and Steadman Jones, D. (2001) *Leadership: the Challenge for All?* London: Institute of Management & Demos.

Institute of Management (2001) *see* Mabey, C. and Thompson, M. (2001).

Jacobs, J. (1992) *Systems of Survival: a Dialogue on the Moral Foundations of Commerce and Politics.* London: Hodder & Stoughton.

Kolb, D. (1984) *Experiential Learning.* Englewood Cliffs, NJ: Prentice Hall.

Kotter, J.P. (1990) *A Force for Change: How Leadership Differs from Management.* New York: Free Press.

Lave, J. and Wenger, E. (1991) *Situated Learning: Legitimate, Peripheral Participation.* New York: Cambridge University Press.

Law, J. and Hassard, J. (1999) *Actor Network Theory and After.* Oxford: Blackwell.

Lyotard, J.-F. (1984) *The Postmodern Condition: a Report on Knowledge.* Manchester: Manchester University Press.

Mabey, C. and Thomson, A. (2000) 'The determinants of management development', *British Journal of Management,* 11 Special Issue: S3–S16.

McGill, I. and Beaty, L. (2001) *Action Learning: a Practitioner's Guide, 2nd rev. edn.* London: Kogan Page.

McLaughlin, H. and Thorpe, R. (1993) 'Action learning – a paradigm in emergence: the problem facing a challenge to traditional management education and development', *British Journal of Management,* 4: 19–27.

Mant, A. (1983) *Leaders We Deserve.* Oxford: Blackwell.

Marsick, V. and O'Neill, J. (1999) 'The many faces of action learning', *Management Learning,* 30 (2): 159–76.

Mintzberg, H. (2004) *Managers Not MBAs.* London: Financial Times, Prentice Hall.

Pedler, M. (1996) *Action Learning for Managers.* London: Lemos & Crane.

Pedler, M. (1997) 'What do we mean by action learning?', in *Action Learning in Practice.* Aldershot: Gower. pp. 61–75.

Pedler, M. (2002) 'Accessing local knowledge: action learning and organisational learning in Walsall', *Human Resource Development International,* 5 (4): 523–40.

Pedler, M., Burgoyne, J.G. and Brook, C. (2005) 'What has action learning learned to become?', *Action Learning: Research & Practice,* 2 (1): 49–68.

Polanyi, M. (1962) *Personal Knowledge: Towards a Post-critical Philosophy.* London: Routledge & Kegan Paul.

Raelin, J. (1999) 'Preface to a Special Issue "The Action Dimension in Management": Diverse approaches to research, teaching and development', *Management Learning,* 30 (2): 115–25.

Reason, P. (2003) 'Pragmatist philosophy and action research: readings and conversations with Richard Rorty', *Action Research,* 1 (1): 103–23.

Reason, P. (2006) 'Choice and quality in action research practice', *Journal of Management Inquiry,* 15 (2): 187–203.

Reason, P. and Bradbury, H. (eds) (2001/2006) *Handbook of Action Research: Participative Inquiry and Practice.* London: Sage.

Revans, R.W. (1971) *Developing Effective Managers.* New York: Praeger.

Revans, R.W. (1980) *Action Learning: New Techniques for Managers.* London: Blond & Briggs.

Revans, R. (1982) *The Origins and Growth of Action Learning.* Bromley: Chartwell-Bratt.

Revans, R.W. (1982 [1966]) 'Operational research and hospital administration', in *The Origins and Growth of Action Learning.* Bromley: Chartwell-Bratt. pp. 250–71.

Revans, R. (1998) *ABC of Action Learning.* London: Lemos & Crane.

Reynolds, M. (1999) 'Grasping the nettle: possibilities and pitfalls of a critical management pedagogy', *British Journal of Management,* 10 (2): 171–84.

Reynolds, M. and Vince, R. (2004) 'Critical management education and action-based learning: synergies and contradictions', *Academy of Management Learning and Education,* 3 (4): 442–56.

Rigg, C. and Trehan, K. (2004) 'Reflections on working with critical action learning', *Action Learning: Research & Practice,* 1 (2): 149–65.

Sayer, A. (1999) *Realism and Social Science.* London: Sage.

Schön, D. (1983) *The Reflective Practitioner.* New York: Basic Books.

Thayer, H.S. (ed.) (1982) *Pragmatism: the Classic Writings.* Indianapolis: Hackett.

Thomson, A., Storey, J., Mabey, C., Farmer, E. and Thomson, R. (1997) *A Portrait of Management Development.* London: Institute of Management.

Vince, R. and Martin, L. (1993) 'Inside action learning: an exploration of the psychology and politics of the action learning model', *Management Education and Development,* 24 (3): 205–15.

Weinstein, K. (1995) *Action Learning: a Journey in Discovery and Development.* London: HarperCollins.

Wieland, G.F. and Leigh, H. (eds) (1971) *Changing Hospitals: a Report on the Hospital Internal Communications Project.* London: Tavistock.

Williams, R.J., Barrett J.D. and Brabston, M. (2000) 'Managers' business school education and military service: possible links to corporate criminal activity', *Human Relations,* 53 (5): 691–712.

Willis, V. (2004) 'Inspecting cases: prevailing degrees of action learning using Revans' theory and rules of engagement as standard', *Action Learning: Research & Practice*, 1 (1): 11–27.

Wilmott, H. (1994) 'Management education: provocations to a debate', *Management Learning*, 25 (1): 105–36.

Wilmott, H. (1997) 'Making learning critical: identity, emotion and power in processes of management development', *Systems Practice*, 10 (6): 749–71.

22

The Jury is Out: How Far Can Participatory Projects Go Towards Reclaiming Democracy?

Tom Wakeford with Jasber Singh, Bano Murtuja, Peter Bryant and Michel Pimbert.

The citizens' jury has been wrongly viewed as a straightforward off-the-shelf method for public consultation. Instead, it has become a largely unregulated pseudo-trademark. It is attached to practices that can be placed along a continuum – from grassroots-based activism at one end, to attempts by policy-makers to re-engineer their systems of democratic account-ability, or at least to be seen to do so, at the other.

The use and abuse of the citizens' jury label by different practitioners, and other actors, illustrates the political interests that pervade attempts to create or validate knowledge. Citizens' jury style processes from four continents demonstrate how such initiatives can:

1. further marginalize groups already experiencing oppression if appropriate safeguards are not in place;
2. fail to link to social movements that are powerful enough to allow everyday people's voices to act as a counterweight to the ongoing transfer of power away from them;
3. suffer from a clash between the drive for short-term outputs and those who seek processes that could bring long-term improvements.

We conclude that brief and small-scale initiatives, such as juries, must become part of larger and long-lasting initiatives jointly owned by those who have been denied a voice in the past.

Over the last ten years the radical tradition of participatory action research (PAR) has been challenged in the UK and elsewhere. A new commercially driven and often politically biased consultation industry now threatens to undermine the work of previous decades. A particularly instructive case study is the recognition, modification and exploitation of the pioneering 'citizens' jury' (CJ) methodology, demonstrating how these forces (along with those identified by Chambers, Chapter 20 in this volume) threaten to undermine the potential of PAR to bring about social and environmental justice.[1]

Though diverse in their subject matter and style of delivery (see Box 22.2 and Table 22.1), CJs that embrace the broad principles of PAR include the following three elements.

1. The CJ is made up of 'jurors' – people who are usually selected 'at random' from a local or national population, with this selection process being open to outside scrutiny.
2. The jurors cross question expert 'witnesses' – specialists they have called to provide different perspectives on the topic – and collectively produce a summary of their conclusions, typically in a short report.
3. The whole process is supervised by an 'oversight' or advisory panel composed of a range of people with relevant knowledge and a possible interest in the outcome. They take no direct part in facilitating the CJ. Members of this group subsequently decide whether to respond to, or act on, elements of this report.

In the USA, where the term 'citizens' jury' was first used in the mid-1980s and where the Jefferson Institute subsequently trade-marked the term, the practice of CJs has been tightly regulated (Crosby et al., 1996). Outside the USA, however, CJs have been conducted in many different ways, and with many different objectives, and with varying success.

During the 1990s much of what had originally been presented as citizen participation became commercialized. In the UK at least, most CJs have become just one more item in a market researcher's portfolio, amidst a flurry of branding and re-branding of different consultation tools. This trend continues unchecked because of a lack of effective critical assessment of different participatory approaches. It is exemplified by the plethora of handbooks that claim to allow an informed 'choice' between the tools available whilst failing to explore the wider political and commercial context in which they are used (New

Economics Foundations, 1998; Involve, 2005; King Baudouin Foundation, 2005).

As with much PAR, there is a great deal of controversy over what constitutes good practice or professionalism in the area of public consultation (Pimbert and Wakeford, 2001; Irwin, 2006). Lacking the methodological self-regulation that exists in some areas of PAR, or the legal sanctions available to the owners of the CJ brand in the USA, consultation practitioners elsewhere are free to use almost whatever label they wish, without being limited to the approach taken by those who invented the particular tool. Conversely, many people have used all three elements above, yet called their processes by names other than a CJ, such as consensus conferences, citizens' councils, deliberative focus groups or, most commonly, citizens' panels (AEIDL, 2006; Satya Murty and Wakeford, 2001).

Our analysis here draws on our particular experiences, which are outlined in Box 22.1.

THE PARTICIPATION PARADOX

We estimate that research, community-based or commercial organizations have undertaken at least 500 CJ-type exercises in the UK between 1996 and 2006, with many more taking place in other countries. Perhaps the most striking aspect of the initial popularity, and subsequent scepticism, about CJs is how closely their history parallels that of another PAR technique called participatory rural appraisal (PRA), which had been introduced ten years previously.

PRA was named by Robert Chambers in the mid-1980s as a label for the introduction of participatory techniques to development work (Chambers, Chapter 20 in this volume; Richards, 1995; Pratt, 2001). PRA thus became part of a policy-shift towards consulting citizens. Backed by some of the world's major aid agencies, PRA techniques evolved and spread with such rapidity that by 1996 they were estimated as being used in at least a hundred countries and had been embraced by the World Bank (Narayan et al., 2000).

Box 22.1   Locating the authors

We are PAR practitioners who have been working together for several years. Along with others, we form part of a network called *Right to be Heard* – people from different backgrounds and locations who share a concern to see currently excluded voices influence policy via processes that are both participatory and inclusive. *Right to be Heard* includes facilitators, participants and funders of PAR initiatives. While benefiting from our interactions with many individuals over the years, this article is based on insights stemming from our role as facilitators.

Tom has been involved in promoting, planning and facilitating CJs in a range of contexts since the mid-1990s. He has been amongst those who have been critical of the model of CJs that employs them as a form of market research. He has attempted to develop co-production models that involve all participants both in CJ design and in the use of their outputs. All the authors worked together on CJs in East Lancashire, West Yorkshire (UK) or in India.

In the widely cited review that gives this estimate, Chambers and Blackburn (1996) suggest that PRA approach has 'much to offer the policy-making process'. 'It provides', they continue, 'a way to give poor people a voice, enabling them to express and analyse their problems and priorities'. 'Used well', the authors observe, 'it can generate important and often surprising insights which can contribute to policies which are better fitted to serving the needs of the poor' (p. 1). In the same breath, however, he acknowledges there is 'much debate about what constitutes "real" PRA'. '[T]he behaviour and attitudes' of those who bring it about are, he said, of greater significance than the methods used.

Though organizers of the first wave of CJs worked without reference to the PRA movement, the internationalization of the technique occurred in a post-Chambers political landscape in which decision-makers have increasingly commissioned their own politically ring-fenced consultation initiatives, using methods such as CJs. The declared aim is to facilitate a dialogue with fellow citizens. Yet, at the same time, many of the systems of accountability established during the last century have become weaker, while the proportion of populations that elect governments remain at an historic low (Electoral Commission, 2005; Norris, 1998; McDonald and Popkin, 2001).

In the UK and USA especially, attempts to deepen democracy have been against an intensified ideological background of competitive individualism and consumer capitalism. By contrast, structures that acknowledge humanity's mutual interdependence, or allow the development of collective action and solidarity, have struggled to survive. In richer nations this weakening of civil society has occurred even despite the widespread uptake of potentially empowering tools such as the internet, and a rise in single-issue campaigns such as those against animal experiments, mobile phone masts or wind turbines.

Many established democracies have, paradoxically, increased the number of government consultation initiatives, many of them CJs, accompanying a decline in the actual accountability and transparency of the decisions that are taken. An example of this paradox is new technology, which is the subject of some of the CJs described here. Many assume that technology is both capable of providing solutions to global problems and is open to democratic control. Yet, the last ten years has seen most of the same populations who have been consulted becoming ever more powerless to influence the pathway technology takes or its impact on our lives. A rare exception is the remarkable grassroots coalitions that have so far kept genetically modified foods out of farming systems in some of Europe and the world beyond.

Table 22.1   Summary and brief comparison of some citizens' juries (CJs) and similar processes that took place between 2000 and 2006

Name and date of the CJ or other initiative	Bringing co-inquirers together, including oversight	Ensuring, or not, equality between participants	Equality of exchanges (e.g. via specialist witnesses)	Impact on and/or response from policy-makers	Including and supporting marginalised groups	Role of organisers vs other co-inquirers writing the recommendations	Extent of replication or continuation of process	Co-ordination to communicate process outputs	Extent to which participants are helped to build an autonomous voice
Rad-Waste Consensus Conf. (2000)	Advert, overseen by MSP	Complaints by some cc-inquirers of bias.	Most witnesses had pro-nukes agenda.	Disputed.	None known.	Facilitators strongly guided the writing process.	Partially reconvened in 2002.	By funders and contractor.	None.
CJ on GM crops, Brazil (2001–2)	Via unions, no MSP.	Attempted by local facilitator against the odds.	Jurors got < 1 per cent of time to ask questions	Part of an ongoing NGO campaign.	Disputed	After deliberation, jurors answered an opinion poll.	Replicated, with modifications, in Brazil.	Wholly by ActionAid	None.
DIY CJs(2001–)	Electoral roll & local partners. MSP.	Comprehensive strategy	Witnesses dominant.	Initial hostility. Now ongoing dialogue.	Lack of support for under-21s & non-literate.	Jurors largely in control.	Ongoing in all locations. Replicated.	Newcastle University.	Yes, also R2BH.
Prajateerpu CJ, India (2001–3)	Via local university researchers. MSP	Women a majority. Local language.	Jurors dominant.	DFID changed policy. Ongoing.	Catered for non-literate status of most jurors.	Jurors largely in control.	Replicated, abroad, but not, as hoped, in India.	Local and UK NGOs together with jurors.	Ongoing through NGOs.
Citizens Council (2002–)	Advert. No MSP.	Some, of disputed impact.	Witnesses dominant.	No public response.	Included but sometimes suppressed.	Facilitators strongly guided the writing process.	Continued with revolving membership.	NICE	None
Deliberative Mapping (2002)	Commercial recruiters, with MSP.	Attention paid to gender difference.	Joint workshops, balance unknown.	None known.	Women given separate space.	Facilitators/academics largely in control.	None known.	By academic consortium to academic/policy-maker audience.	None known

(Continued)

Table 22.1 (Continued)

Name and date of the CJ or other initiative	Bringing co-inquirers together, including oversight	Ensuring, or not, equality between participants	Equality of exchanges (e.g. via specialist witnesses)	Impact on and/or response from policy-makers	Including and supporting marginalised groups	Role of organisers vs other co-inquirers writing the recommendations	Extent of replication or continuation of process	Co-ordination to communicate process outputs	Extent to which participants are helped to build an autonomous voice
CJ or GM food/crops. (2003)	Commercial recruiters. No MSP	Standard market research approach.	Witnesses dominant.	Funder accused of manipulation of the result.	None known.	Facilitators ensured jurors addressed funder's 'question'.	None.	Funder accused of distorting the recommendations.	None.
European Deliberation (2005–6)	Commercial recruiters, no MSP	Some scientific literacy assumed.	Literature and witnesses dominant	None known.	None.	Facilitators largely in control.	European Citizens Panel.	By consortium to media/policy-maker audience.	None known.
BBC CJ (2005–6)	Electoral roll & local partners. MSP	Possibly inhibited by BBC microphones.	Jurors dominant.	Meetings with senior politicians.	Young people disproportionately represented.	Jurors largely in control.	None at the time of writing.	Broadcast or web-cast via bbc.co.uk.	No, but R2BH.
Mali CJ on GM crops (2006–)	Use of PAR team. MSP.	Majority women and smallholder farmers.	Jurors dominant.	Strong political contacts ongoing.	Attention to literacy and deliberative confidence.	Jurors largely in control.	Ongoing.	Mali NGOs and IIED.	Yes, ongoing.

Key:
CJ–citizens' jury
MSP–oversight by a multi-stakeholder panel.
R2BH–Partcipants invited offered support to be involved in the Right to be Heard network

Box 22.2   Summary of the CJs compared in Table 22.1

Consensus Conference on Radioactive Waste Management (UK, 2000). Initiated by NIREX (UK government's radioactive waste disposal service). Followed a House of Lords sub-committee's recommendation that the government should 'seek to build public consensus before attempting to implement its chosen policy'. Early on in the process, one panel member resigned, complaining of bias in the process in favour of nuclear power. NGOs claim process was an officially sanctioned strategy to re-frame the debate. References: Kass, 2001; Wallace, 2001.

CJs on GM crops (Brazil, 2001–2). Initiated by ActionAid Brazil. Participants largely drawn from members of unions affiliated to the Landless Workers Movement (MST), the largest social movement in Latin America. A lawyer who was also a local member of parliament was pitted against local scientist as the main 'witnesses', with jurors getting 1 per cent of time to ask short questions. The CJ formed part of a wider and ongoing campaign by local and international NGOs. Reference: Toni and Von Braun, 2001.

DIY Juries (UK, 2001–). Initiated by Rowntree Trust/Newcastle University (UK). Replicated with modifications in Blackburn with Darwen, West Yorkshire, Reading and Norwich. Found that some potential participants found terms 'citizen' and 'jury' off-putting, to the extent that might reduce inclusivity of the process. Later initiatives used name 'community x-change'. Reference: PEALS, 2003b.

Prajateerpu (India, 2001–3). Initiated by Andhra Pradesh Coalition in Defence of Diversity (APCDD), International Institute of Environment and Development (IIED-UK). A local language PAR team identified marginalized farmers, especially women, across the state. CJ took place in the language used by poor people in the state (Telegu), rather than Hindi or English. State government and UK government's Department for International Development (DFID) were initially hostile. Later DFID changed its aid policy in the state. Most jurors were non-literate – reflecting status of majority of state's citizens – and female, reflecting their greater practical role, but lack of voice, in agriculture. Facilitators summarized and translated the final recommendations (made in Telegu) into English. Jurors played prominent role in local and international advocacy. Plans to replicate the process through the state prevented by a lack of state/NGO capacity. Informed similar processes in Zimbabwe, Mali (see below) and elsewhere. References: Pimbert and Wakeford, 2003; Wakeford and Pimbert, M. 2004.

Citizens Council (UK, 2002–). Initiated by National Institute of Clinical Excellence (UK). Facilitation unintentionally led to suppression of marginalized perspectives, such as racial minorities. Impact unclear at the time of writing. References: Davies et al., 2005; Barnett, 2006.

Deliberative Mapping (UK, 2002). Initiated by two universities (Sussex and UCL) and the Wellcome Trust. People's socio-economic background and gender listed in report, which was potentially disempowering. All analysis by academics and already powerful stakeholders, except final report, a draft of which was discussed by non-specialist participants. Reference: SPRU et al., 2003.

CJ on GM food/crops (UK, 2003). Initiated by the government's Food Standards Agency (FSA), delivered by Opinion Leader Research (OLR). Funder accused of manipulation of the result that made it suit its existing position (pro-GM food) when the result was broadly anti-GM crops. Major effort by FSA to 'spin' coverage to make jurors' result appear pro-GM. Condemned by some NGOs and PAR researchers for doing so. References: Genewatch, 2003a; PEALS, 2003a.

Meeting of Minds European Citizens' Deliberation (2005–6). Initiated by King Baudouin Foundation and European Commission. Potential participants were told the subject (brain science), leading to a bias in the sorts of people who volunteered. Process relied on written literacy and an interest in scientific research.

BBC CJ on the theme of 'respect' (2005–6). Initiated by BBC Radio 4 Today Programme and Newcastle University. BBC reporter and PAR team. Jurors took findings to leader of local council and UK government minister, reported by BBC. Low level of resourcing and short timescale adversely affected diversity and support to participants. Reference: BBC, 2005.

(Continued)

(Continued)

Citizens Space for democratic deliberation and the future of farming, Mali (2006–). Initiated by Regional Assembly of Sikasso, Mali and IIED, UK. Very similar methodology to Prajateerpu. Prompted a special meeting of the regional parliament. National and international publicity via written and broadcast media. Reference: IIED, 2006.

THE POLITICAL ECONOMY OF CJs

CJs were perhaps the inevitable product of two features of recent political systems, particularly in many Anglophone consumer-capitalist states: the thirst of politicians for political novelty, and their desire to be seen to be good rulers. Pierre Bourdieu's study of the French political elite concluded that 'no power can be satisfied with existing just as power, that is, as brute force, entirely devoid of justification' (Bourdieu, 1996: 265). This same logic can motivate other political elites as a justification to consult their citizens. In the UK, the intersection of these two increasingly pervasive trends provided a niche occupied by post-Thatcherite think-tanks, management consultants and sometimes action researchers.

The political marketing revolution of the 1990s transformed concepts of participation among policy-makers. Traditional opinion polling techniques were supplemented by qualitative research, particularly focus groups (Lees-Marshment, 2004). By the late 1990s, in the UK and USA at least, market research, rather than grassroots political debate, had become the primary mode by which politicians understood the potential behaviours of their electorate. The only exception was groups of voters who happen to make the difference between one national government being elected and another. In the UK these are the marginal parliamentary constituencies (Jon Cruddas in Joseph Rowntree Reform Trust, 2005), while in US presidential elections it is the swing states (Nusbaumer, 2004). These relatively small regions receive immense amounts of campaign funds for leafleting, door-to-door visits and media coverage, while sucking in resources that might have been used to engage residents of the rest of the country. The decline in direct contact between most voters and those in power has been accompanied by a shift of resources by both governments and competing political parties towards the skilful use of the mass media.

Focus groups have been used extensively by large corporations for market research from the 1950s onwards, allowing researchers to garner psychological and social insights to give an indication of the characteristics of the whole population. However, when transformed to the political arena, this approach fails citizens by denying them an opportunity to articulate their views to those representing them. Neither does it allow for dialogue or development of mutual understanding among citizens, or between citizens and their representatives.

The common feature of almost every one of the scores of consultation initiatives in a range of countries has been their failure to allow groups marginalized in society to influence the political process. Even those participating directly in such exercises are often left feeling their right to a voice has been violated (Skinner, 1997).

Presented as a significant response to what centre-left think-tanks saw as the growing divide between the Government and its electorate, CJs were embraced by many of those close to Tony Blair prior to Labour's election victory in 1997 (Crosby et al., 1996; Mattinson, 1998). Though rarely labelled as PAR, the UK has a rich history of community empowerment and citizen participation, remnants of which had even survived the 18 years of Thatcher government assault (Loney, 1983; Cockburn, 1977; Popay and Williams, 1994). However, while embracing and promoting the 'new' methods such as CJs, think-tanks such as the Institute for Public Policy Research (IPPR) failed to acknowledge either a past or future role for traditional grassroots-based processes of democratic participation (Coote and Lenaghan, 1997).

Within five years of having been first piloted, several hundred CJ-type exercises had been undertaken in the UK. These differed significantly in their aims and methodologies. Some are little more than adaptations of focus groups, while others are ambitious PAR initiatives aiming to build community capacity to directly influence policy. The small number of studies comparing these kind of initiatives (e.g. Kashefi and Mort, 2004; Smith and Wales, 2000; Wakeford, 2002) is symptomatic of the need for short-term impact, rather than a long-term view, that has underlain many of these initiatives.

INITIATORS OF CJs

The most common funders of citizens' juries in the UK and USA have been local and national government departments and agencies. Far behind them in frequency are academics studying the deliberative process or media organizations wishing to report on it. PAR activists, community organizations and other types of civil society organization make up a third group.

A safeguard against any citizens' jury process becoming biased by any single interest group or perspective is the control of key elements of a jury by a panel that contains representatives of 'a broad base of stakeholders' (Coote and Lenaghan, 1997). This involvement of organizations that can speak for a wide range of social interests via what is often called an oversight panel formed a key part of the original rationale of CJs in the USA and UK (Crosby, 1995).

The balance of different interests on an oversight panel can play a major role in vital

elements of the jury process such as the inclusivity of the jurors, witness choice and the use made of the jury's recommendations. As a result, whoever invites different organizations to join the oversight panel has the potential to shape the process.

Many of those initiating CJ in the UK after 1997 did not put the oversight of the processes in the hands of sufficiently diverse interest groups or make the contribution various organizations made to the jury process clear to jurors (Box 4 in PEALS, 2003a). Commissioning bodies have often preferred to restrict control over key aspects of the process – jury selection, choice of subject and witnesses – to a narrow spectrum of stakeholders, whose interests and perspectives coincide with those of the funding organization.

BRINGING TOGETHER CO-INQUIRERS

As in most processes of co-inquiry, there is a potentially immense diversity of groups who might have a role in a jury process. Figure 22.1 highlights three distinct groups of co-inquirers in a jury process – the funders, the facilitators and the jurors. Under the market research model of a jury, the relationships between these three groups is often merely contractual. Under this arrangement a funder pays a group of facilitators to conduct a jury process. One of these groups then invites the 'jurors', often with the offer of a payment for the time they will have given up to come along. At the other end of the spectrum, in a more PAR-based process – which we have called a DIY ('do-it-yourself') jury – funds or other resources come from community organizations which invite people from their own local area of work to be jurors.

CJs can involve people from a wide geographical area, such as the whole nation-state. However, the advantages of the symbolic national representativeness this provides must be weighted against the

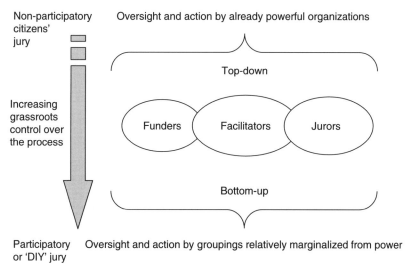

Figure 22.1 *Different co-inquirers involved in a jury process, showing the continuum between a non-participatory 'top-down' citizens' jury, and a more participatory 'do-it-yourself' jury that contains an element of grassroots control*

disadvantages. A nationwide spread is more expensive to run, and makes it much harder for jurors to continue their activities after the process has finished.

The inclusion of community-based organizations is also neglected in most CJs. If they are allowed to be co-producers of the process, these grassroots-based groups will find it easier to continue work with the jurors and other co-inquirers after the process has finished. Such alliances between citizens and community groups are at the core of DIY-jury approaches. They also make it more likely that policy recommendations that such juries generate will lead to policy change. Even on an issue that is national or international, local groups are far more likely to be able to achieve results that are measurable by people living locally.

The sorts of jurors who are drawn into a process will vary greatly depending on the strategy that is used to involve them. Attracting people via an advertisement in a local paper is unlikely to produce a process that is inclusive of the wide range of

backgrounds and perspectives that will be present in a local population. Such a mix requires a strategy of contacting and engaging groups that are normally excluded from consultation processes and are unlikely to push themselves forward. Facilitators attracted to this second, more challenging, approach are often those who are interested in using the exercise as a means of bringing about greater social justice.

Any organization that is funding a jury is likely to agree to help oversee its implementation. Other stakeholder organizations may, however, decide it is not efficient use of their resources, or perhaps not even in their interests, to associate themselves with the process. If such groups predict that the recommendations of a jury process are likely to be uncomfortable for them, they are faced with a dilemma: whether to become an 'insider' that is better able to make informed criticisms of the process, or an 'outsider' that is better able to either ignore the process or discredit it without being tainted by association (Wakeford and Pimbert, 2004).

FACILITATING WITNESSES AND DELIBERATIONS

There are many approaches to the facilitation of CJs. In processes set up to deliberate controversial issues, facilitation is particularly prone to challenge. The facilitator's key role in leading jurors through their interrogation of witnesses and the formulation of their final report can lead to suggestions that the process would have come to a different conclusion if the jurors had been left un-facilitated.

During the CJ meetings, facilitators should optimize the inclusivity and deliberative fairness of the process. Elements that are often key include: the time jurors have to deliberate, the equality of opportunity between different jurors in making their voice heard, and the attitudes to jurors shown by witnesses.

Time

Information provision in a CJ is usually by someone with specialist knowledge of the subject – a 'witness'. The balance between the time given to the witness for an initial presentation and the time jurors have to develop their questions and subsequently cross-question the witness is easily measurable. A public lecture may allow three-quarters of the time for the speaker, and one-tenth for questions for the audience. In a jury, reversing this balance and allowing three-quarters of the time for jurors to ask questions of witnesses, and discuss the answers they have had, ensures that jurors have a greater overall sense of ownership of the process and are more likely to find the information they receive useful.

Equality

One of the most comprehensive studies of a deliberative process ever conducted focused on a citizens' council, an adaptation of the classic CJ, which had been set up by the UK government via a market research company (Davies et al., 2005; Barnett, 2006; see also Table 22.1). The council met regularly over two years and was wholly controlled by a single stakeholder, the UK Department of Health.

The research included analysis of the time spent speaking by each different participants.

A process in which just one or two participants, among a dozen, get to speak is unlikely to be as inclusive of diverse perspectives than one in which everyone speaks. However, Davies and Barnett's research suggests that a simple measurement of time spent speaking could obscure more subtle processes of self-censorship in the presence of particularly vocal participants. Some members of the citizens' council made contributions that they presented as authoritative general statements, while others merely expressed monosyllabic assent or dissent on views articulated at more length by the more dominant members. This does not make their participation less valid. However, it raises the question of whether they would have enriched the deliberative process if they had fully articulated their thoughts, and whether facilitators allowed them sufficient opportunity to do so. The citizens council demonstrates the challenges of ensuring PAR processes are practically, and not merely rhetorically, inclusive (also see Lykes and Mallona, Chapter 7 in this volume).

Different styles of discussion will encourage jurors to articulate their views: not all will feel comfortable doing so in the full group, or in direct dialogue with particular witnesses. This is why we believe that facilitators in such processes should find ways to bring out as many different perspectives as possible from as many participants as would like to speak, including – but not restricted to – the questioning of witnesses and the formulation of the CJ's recommendations.

The inclusion of witnesses who speak from a variety of educational, professional and socio-economic backgrounds encourages jurors to engage with them. The greater the number of people that are present with the facilitation skills to allow potentially marginalized perspectives to have a space to be aired, the more likely it is to happen.

Witnesses

The choice of witnesses in a community-based jury process is key to ensuring a good process. Witnesses in a CJ have the dual role of information providers and interpreters of that information. Some use a style that is virtually unchanged from the professional context in which they normally communicate. In one CJ, a middle-aged safety expert gave evidence to a CJ using a projected series of computer slides as if he were at a meeting of fellow professionals. In another, a proud chemist passed a periodic table of elements that he kept in his wallet around the jurors.

Those jurors who are used to either receiving information in this form, or interacting with this type of person, will feel more confident in interacting with them. In contrast, a young woman witness with experientially-derived knowledge that she explains using personal stories might speak more directly to jurors with other backgrounds. We believe the socio-cultural profile of people who are invited to be witnesses is an important, yet often neglected, aspect of the analysis of jury processes. A CJ dominated by experiential evidence and providing no technical information relevant to policy-making might be criticized as being short on 'facts'. However, this is generally far less common than processes that become swamped by detailed statistical evidence to the exclusion of other forms of knowledge, in which there is a danger jurors will miss broader perspectives in forming their recommendations.

Balancing Deliberation and Capacity for Autonomy

We believe that CJs should not only be fair and competent deliberative forums, but also contribute towards the creation of an autonomous political space for those currently marginalized from power. Achieving this space requires careful thought about the necessary steps to allow a group of individuals, who are only connected by their joint attendance at jury meetings, to become a gathering of people who can attempt to built mutual respect and a common purpose.

Unfortunately, the scope of most CJs is limited by the perceived reality and institutional objectives of those funding the

process. Jurors are unable to organize their own autonomous political space, and as a result their opportunity to voice their views is circumscribed by funding constraints.

Facilitators have to work to a tight schedule. Time should be available for participants to discuss their values with each other and to acknowledge the value of hearing from different perspectives. Most important of all is to address the longer term challenge of bringing political change, towards which a CJ can be an important first step. However, this step is often neglected, even among CJs using the principles of PAR.

Minimizing Oppression and Facilitating Mutual Empowerment Within the Deliberations

Critics of styles of action research that use small groups of citizens have pointed to the danger of what they call 'groupthink' – the supposed tendency for people to passively accept the opinion of a particular member of a group (Cooke, 2001). This individual – perhaps a juror, or a facilitator – may be particularly charismatic, apparently better informed or just experienced at dominating discussion. Groupthink can be generated in a CJ if its funders and facilitators fail to design a process that allows all participants to feel their perspective is as valuable as everyone else's, and that they have an equal right to be heard.

Whether it is a group or an individual who perpetrates it, meetings can be sites of oppression, which may be based on opinions, ethnicity, gender, age, style of dress, disability or supposed lack of knowledge (Davies, et al., 2005; Kabeer, 2005). CJs cannot be opportunities to further the cause of social justice if the process they undertake does not promote a fundamental respect by every participant for each other.

Those who wish to stand outside a CJ process to study what happens, rather than adopting the PAR approach of co-producing every element of the process with participants, are in most danger of increasing the marginalization of certain groups via a CJ. While a purely academic approach may allow the facilitator to retain a greater distance and hence allow them to claim objectivity, in doing so they risk allowing a process to take place in which jurors are research subjects, rather than citizens with sufficient capacity to attain their right to have their voice heard in policy discussions.

Those undertaking CJs from a quantitative social research background are often keen that it is as statistically representative as possible of the population from which the jury is drawn. Most minority populations are already politically marginalized in society. Reproducing their numerical minority status on a CJ risks making it harder for them to have their perspective taken seriously by the majority of jurors who do not share this key element of their identity. For example, in an area of the UK where black and minority ethnic communities make up 7 per cent of the population, a jury of 24 people should, statistically, contain only two faces that are non-white – increasing the facilitation challenges of ensuring non-domination by particular groups.

The organizers of a CJ process in India made the decision to constitute a jury with a high proportion of members from Dalit and adivasi ethno-cultural heritage groups, and a majority of women, in the light of the substantial over-representation of high-caste and male perspectives in policy debates on the issues under debate (Pimbert and Wakeford, 2003). There is a trade-off between appearing balanced to the naïve observer and ensuring a space for those otherwise lacking a say in decisions. It is a choice between juries that are notionally representative of their populations – with greater legitimacy in the eyes of some decision-makers – and those CJs that allow oppressed or marginalized groups to have a greater influence on decision-making.

RECOMMENDATIONS

Only in very rare circumstances are CJ recommendations likely to fit neatly into a government decision-making process and timeframes. A potential exception could be the circumstances generated by the supposed 'yes or no' option of whether to grow GM crops in the UK in the spring of 2004. However, the extent to which the CJs that formed part of the public consultation influenced the subsequent decision is a matter of some controversy (Irwin, 2006). More commonly, the jurors will have to use their provisional conclusions as a first step in building political alliances and gathering more information, which will enable them to influence decisions. The more this is made explicit in the jury process, the more realistic participants can be about the process of achieving positive political change. Such an approach also ensures that jurors will not be disappointed that policy-makers do not instantly take radical action, or even respond coherently, to their recommendations.

Some of those facilitating CJs design a process in which jurors must reach a consensus on any recommendation being put forward. We, however, believe that this can lead to exactly the kind of marginalization of minority views described above. Establishing the level of support for various recommendations among the jury members can, if carried out sensitively, be an opportunity for informed deliberation, without certain perspectives becoming ridiculed.

We have observed that the prominence given to the inevitable short-list of recommendations that arises from a jury can direct those interested in the process from exploring the richness of the discussion within it. Stakeholders may comb the jury's 'verdict' for statements that support or potentially damage their interests, rather than engaging with the knowledge and insights the jurors have brought to the subject.

STANDARDIZATION AND COMMUNICATION

Participatory initiatives are most effective when they acknowledge that each situation will demand a unique design, using a new combination of tools as part of a continuous cycle of action and reflection. Because any participatory initiative contains a unique mix of people and institutions, each process will necessarily include elements from a range of approaches and methodologies. Misguided attempts to strictly standardize and replicate protocols, in line with conventional practice in laboratories and much positivistic social science, will undermine a CJ attempting to use PAR principles. Although we have produced a handbook for community groups interested in running a DIY jury, we tried to focus on principles and tools, rather than a prescriptive methodology (PEALS, 2003b).

In the politically controversial context in which CJs can sometimes be undertaken, facilitators may use additional means of demonstrating the fairness and competence of the process to complement the broad-based oversight panel described above. Audio and video recordings or transcripts which, with the jurors' consent, can be made available to members of the oversight panel and the public are another safeguard against criticisms of bias.

Having their voices recorded can affect the confidence of most people to be free with their opinions and insights. The CJ as a safe space in which to try out new ideas and express opinions that jurors may then want to retract is a vital element that may be compromised by the knowledge that their voices are being recorded (see Table 22.1). If they fear that they could be identified as holding a particular view, especially if it is unconventional, they may be less likely to express support for it. An extreme example of this was a jury process during which a national radio news programme, who had funded the initiative, expected to have access to the jury proceedings at all times, apart from a short period at the beginning of the first session when their presence was negotiated with the jurors (BBC, 2005).

One potential compromise between these two competing pressures is to create periods during the jury's deliberations where all recording equipment and outsiders – potentially even the facilitators – are excluded. However, the reasons for removing this safeguard on the transparency of the process must be made clear, especially to those outside the co-inquiry process.

The safe space provided by PAR-style CJ processes may become an opportunity for jurors to present evidence that contradicts information on the basis of which one or more powerful organizations have formulated their policies. If the contradictions between the two sets of evidence are publicized, for example by the media, the large organizations can choose either to open a dialogue with those involved with the jury, or try and discredit the process. If the CJ appears to expose significant flaws in an organization, participants may become viewed as whistleblowers, provoking a defensive reaction. Yet a more open approach to such challenges by organizations could ensure changes take place that satisfy both sides.

Although we know of many examples from around the UK and elsewhere, the best documented cases we have come across are in the case of CJ processes in Blackburn, UK (Wakeford et al., 2004) and Andhra Pradesh, India (Pimbert and Wakeford, 2003). Both cases showed the vulnerability of the CJ process to criticism from those in power, as with many non-traditional forms of social research. Our refusal as PAR practitioners to pretend that we are objective observers of a process, and instead to emphasise our active role in it, is double edged. On the other hand our more engaged approach makes it harder for juries' conclusions to be ignored.

CJS AND AUTHORITARIAN CREEP

Institutions

As we have seen, non-PAR CJs can all too easily end up as means by which powerful organizations can reduce citizens' influence on decision-makers, a tendency we call authoritarian creep. From our contact with a wide range of CJs over the last ten years, we suspect that by appearing to give grassroots communities influence, but actually re-legitimizing current power structures, non-PAR juries have tended to serve the interests of governments and corporate shareholders more than they have empowered those whose lives these institutions govern (Barns, 1995; Genewatch, 2003a, 2003b; Perdue, 1995; Wallace, 2001).

If well designed, CJs using the principles of PAR can help to forge new alliances that can help diverse groups of people build more participatory decision-making processes together. However, the timescales over which funders and facilitators of jury processes operate are usually much shorter than those required for genuine democratization. Funders often want to economize by providing short-term funding and to ensure media coverage to justify such an allocation of funds.

CJ facilitators are often freelance or short-term contract holders who are only able to raise funds for a process lasting a few months. Full-time staff who work on jury processes often do so in addition to their regular workload. CJs that attempt to use PAR principles will inevitably be seen as something unusual, likely to be tolerated rather than welcomed by colleagues who often have little knowledge of these approaches. Facilitators who have jobs within large organizations will generally experience pressure from their colleagues to return to their normal duties promptly, which is likely to adversely affect their maintenance of their ongoing involvement for a sufficient period necessary for the long-term impact of any PAR process.

The lack of institutional acceptance of PAR often fails both sides. Those commissioning the exercise are no nearer to overcoming the anti-participatory inertia in their organization. Jurors and their communities are not supported in their attempt to promote lasting change. Referring to his experience with one such organization, development analyst Nick Hildyard has suggested that:

perhaps the first thing that agencies serious about participation and pluralism might take is not to reach for the latest handbook on participatory techniques, but put their own house in order: to consider how their internal hierarchies, training techniques and office cultures discourage receptivity, flexibility, patience, open-mindedness,

non-defensiveness, humour, curiosity and respect for the opinions of others. (pp. 56–71)

Language and knowledge

Part of the popularity, and the controversy, that is associated with both community-led and more top-down CJs is their symbolism, which is drawn from the ancient tradition of legal trials by jury. Many organizations who are considering commissioning processes of public consultation are drawn to the CJ model, associated with decision-making that embodies fairness and justice. For potential jurors the appeal can include a sense that they are part of something important and that 'justice will be done'. However, critics have claimed that the appearance of fairness of a CJ can lead to participants and the wider population being deceived by seemingly pseudo-judicial processes that have few of the safeguards of their legal equivalents (Glasner, 2001).

Another dimension of the language used in a CJ is that it may reinforce the popular perception that people in power or with expert knowledge are in a separate category from the rest of us. The CJ is made up of people with generally less decision-making power or conventional expertise than those they are trying to influence. Some may not even have been accepted as 'citizens' of a nation-state, potentially leading them to feeling alienated, even from the CJ.

Jurors make their recommendations in relative isolation from the witnesses who have provided the information. Conventionally, these conclusions are then handed to those organizations who funded the process. Yet, any strategic long-term process of co-inquiry would involve mixed groups of people with all different sorts of relationships to power, and with different types of specialist and non-specialist knowledge of the subject under discussion.

Given PAR's aim of making the development of knowledge more of a co-inquiry among people from diverse backgrounds, it is perhaps ironic that CJs risk reinforcing a knowledge and power hierarchy. On something as technically complex as genetic modification (GM) or nanotechnology, jurors clearly need to be able to be equipped with the analytical tools to evaluate the information that is provided to them. However, there are three major dangers that arise from the brief interaction possible during a jury process. One is that they will not be allowed the time or deliberative tools to explore the technical information presented to them. Another is that they are not allowed the resources to analyse alternative ways of meeting the need addressed by witnesses, a particular failure of the juries on GM crops. Finally, like any of us, jurors will assess the evidence presented to them on the basis of the personal dynamics they develop with a witness, rather than on the information she has put across. As a result, CJs and similar processes can risk participants being so disempowered by the experience that they reject coinquiry approaches in favour of 'leaving it to the experts'.

Building Juries into Wider PAR Initiatives

Whether they be local councils, private corporations, national government departments or international agencies, large organizations exist as structures of power, with procedures that are generally unreceptive to the fundamental challenge to their way of making policy that PAR-orientated CJs represent, in common with many other PAR processes. However, as large organizations are increasingly experimenting with PAR (see Martin, Chapter 26 in this volume), we recommend two strategies be employed by facilitators working with marginalized communities to maximize their potential impact. Firstly, PAR practitioners should work to ensure that any process allows diverse members of marginalized communities to negotiate joint control of the participation process with those who fund them.

Initiatives should prioritize people, issues and perspectives typically excluded from conventional consultations, including, for example, people from minority ethno-heritage groups, disabled and young people, the over 50s, gay,

lesbian, transgender and bisexual people, the homeless and those with below-average incomes. Secondly, these marginalized groups should receive particular support to open discussions with decision-makers about more effective ways to involve them.

Two recent UK-based initiatives that are designed to work towards the objectives we have outlined here are Right to be Heard (www.right2bheard.org) and Involve (www. involving.org). Right to be Heard is a network of people from different backgrounds and locations who share a concern to see currently excluded voices influence policy via processes that are both participatory and inclusive of participants and facilitators. Some of its members are also associated with a network set up by Oxfam UK, Participatory Practitioners for Change. Involve is an organization of participation practitioners, particularly aimed at bringing together representative and participatory democracy. Both groups aim to improve the capacity of our elected representatives, policy-makers and the media to engage with participatory processes, particularly those that involve marginalized groups.

As realists we acknowledge that, for the foreseeable future, consultations will mostly be initiated by organizations with an interest in solving an immediate political problem of their own choosing, rather than one chosen by people who are marginalized from power. In the short term we can attempt to make these consultations a more two-way process where both top-down and bottom-up priorities can be addressed. However, in the long term, we believe that accessing alternative funding sources that can counter the power of large organizations is the only way that issues of importance to people who have been denied a voice for so long can become subject to truly emancipatory PAR processes.

Ten years ago the burst of enthusiasm in the UK for citizens' juries as a participatory magic-bullet was based on a mixture of the naiveté and ambition of some influential opinion-formers. We believe that juries can be a legitimate PAR tool. We would argue that the advantages of those CJs that are based on PAR principles, particularly as part of grassroots-led advocacy work, outweigh the disadvantages.

But, like other approaches to PAR, CJs very rarely become linked to social movements that are powerful enough to act as a counterweight to the perceived loss of control of our systems of global, national and local governance. Future generations may see CJs as having been little more than a gimmick – a historical footnote in the slide towards consumer-capitalist authoritarianism. However, we hope that CJs will eventually become legitimate tools of grassroots social transformation that can engage with powerful commercial and political forces, rather than be captured by them. As to whether such a transformation is possible, the jury is most definitely still out.

NOTE

1 This chapter is a shortened version of a report that is available for download via www.citizensjury.org

REFERENCES

AEIDL (2006) *Conclusions of the Conference to Launch the Initiative: European Citizens' Panel.* Brussels: AEIDL. [www.citizenspanel.eu]

Barnett, E. (ed.) (2006) *Citizens at the Centre: Deliberative Participation in Healthcare Decisions.* Bristol: Policy Press.

Barns, I. (1995) 'Manufacturing consensus: reflections on the UK National Consensus Conference on Plant Biotechnology', *Science as Culture,* 12: 199–216.

BBC (2005) *BBC Radio 4 Today Programme's Citizens' Jury on Respect.* Dedicated website and podcasts. [www.bbc.co.uk/radio4/today/reports/politics/citizenjury_reading_20050908.shtml]

Bourdieu, P. (1996) *The State Nobility.* London: Polity.

Chambers, R. and Blackburn, J. (1996) 'The power of participation: PRA and policy', *IDS Policy Briefing* 13. [www.ids.ac.uk/ids/bookshop/briefs/PB7.pdf]

Cockburn, C. (1997) *The Local State: Management of Cities and People.* London: Pluto Press.

Cooke, B. (2001) 'The Social psychological limits of participation', in B. Cooke and U. Kothari (eds), *Participation: the New Tyranny?* New York: Zed Books. pp. 102–21.

Coote, A. and Lenaghan, J. (1997) *Citizens' Juries: From Theory to Practice.* London: IPPR.

Crosby, N. (1995) 'Citizen juries: one solution for difficult environmental questions', in O. Renn, T. Webler and P. Wiedemann (eds), *Fairness and Competence in Citizen Participation.* Boston: Kluwer Academic. pp. 157–74.

Crosby, N., et al., (1996) *Citizens' Juries British Style: Features about Global Democracy.* Auburn University, USA. [http://fp.auburn.edu/tann/cp/ juries.htm]

Davies, C., et al., (2005) *Opening the Box: Evaluating the Citizens Council of NICE.* Open University, Milton Keynes, UK. [http://pcpoh.bham.ac.uk/publichealth/ nccrm/PDFs%20and%20documents/Publications/Cit izens%20council%20Mar05.pdf]

Electoral Commission (2005) *Election 2005: Engaging the Public in Great Britain.* Electoral Commission, UK. [www.electoralcommission.org.uk/templates/ search/document.cfm/14157]

Ewen, S. (1998) *PR!: a Social History of Spin.* New York: Basic Books.

Genewatch (2003a) 'Food Standards Agency hides unanimous findings of citizens' jury', *Press Release,* Genewatch, UK. [www.genewatch.org/Press%20 Releases/pr42.htm]

Genewatch (2003b) 'Written evidence', *Select Committee on Environment, Food and Rural Affairs, House of Commons,* September. [www.genewatch. org/Press%20Releases/pr42.htm] and [www.publi- cations.parliament.uk/pa/cm200203/cmselect/cmen vfru/1220/1220we04.htm]

Glasner, P. (2001) 'Rights or rituals? Why juries can do more harm than good', in M. Pimbert and T. Wakeford (eds), Special issue of *PLA Notes 40.* Co-published by The Commonwealth Foundation, ActionAid, DFID, Sida and IIED. [http://www.iied.org/NR/agbioliv/pla_ notes/pla_backissues/40.html]

IIED (2006) *Citizens' Space for Democratic Deliberation on GMOs and the Future of Farming in Mali.* London: IIED. [www.iied.org/NR/agbioliv/ag_liv_projects/ GMOCitizenJury.html]

Involve (2005) *People and Participation: How to Put Citizens at the Heart of Decision-making.* [www. involving.org/mt/ archives/ blog_13/ People%20and% 20Participation%20final.pdf]

Irwin, A. (2001) 'Constructing the scientific citizen: science and democracy in the biosciences', *Public Understanding of Science,* 10: 1–18.

Irwin, A. (2006) 'The Politics of talk: coming to terms with the new scientific governance', *Social Studies of Science,* 36: 299–320.

Joseph Rowntree Reform Trust (JRRT) (2005) *The Far Right in London: a Challenge for Local Democracy?* [www.jrrt.org.uk/Far_Right_REPORT.pdf]

Kabeer, N. (ed.) (2005) *Inclusive Citizenship: Meanings and Expressions.* London: Zed Books.

Kashefi, E. and Mort, M. (2004) 'Grounded citizens' juries: a tool for health activism?', *Health Expectations*, 7: 1–13.

Kass, G. (2001) *Open Channels: Public Dialogue in Science and Technology* (Report 153 of the Parliamentary Office of Science and Technology). (www.parliament.uk/post/pr153.pdf)

King Baudouin Foundation (2005) *Participatory Methods Toolkit. A Practitioner's Manual. (new edn).* Brussels: KBF. (www.kbsfrb.be/code/page.cfm?id_page = 153&ID = 361)

Lees-Marshment, J. (2004) *The Political Marketing Revolution: Is Marketing Transforming the Government of the UK?* Paper for the 2004 PSA Conference, University of Lincoln, April. (www.psa.ac.uk/cps/2004/Lees-Marshment.pdf)

Loney, M. (1983) *Community Against Government: the British Community Development Project 1968–78.* London: Heinemann Educational Books.

Mattinson, D. (1998) 'Market research meets democracy', *Pool* (March–April), Through the Loop Consulting Ltd, UK. (www.poolonline.com/archive/iss2fea3.html)

McDonald, M. and Popkin, S. (2001) 'The myth of the vanishing voter', *American Political Science Review*, 95: 963–74. (elections.gmu.edu/APSR%20McDonald%20and_Popkin_2001.pdf#search=%22%22The%20Myth%20of%20the%20Vanishing%20Voter%22%22)

Narayan, D., et al., (2000) *Crying Out for Change: Voices of the Poor.* Oxford: Oxford University Press.

New Economics Foundation (1998) *Participation Works: 21 Techniques of Community Participation for the 21st Century.* London: NEF. (www.neweconomics.org/gen/z_sys_PublicationDetail.aspx?PID=16)

Norris, P. (1998) *Elections and Voting Behaviour: New Challenges, New Perspectives.* Aldershot: Dartmouth.

Nusbaumer, S. (2004) 'Swing states: the battle for the few', *Intervention Magazine*, August. (Online). (http://www.interventionmag.com/cms/modules.php?op=modload&name=News&file=article&sid=825)

PEALS (2003a) *The People's Report on GM* (PEALS, UK) (www.gmjury.org/downloads/report.pdf)

PEALS (2003b) *Teach Yourself Citizens' Juries* (PEALS, UK). (www.citizensjury.org)

Perdue, D. (1995) 'Whose knowledge counts?', *Ecologist*, 25: 170–2.

Pimbert, M. and Wakeford, T. (eds) (2001) 'Deliberative democracy and citizen empowerment', Special issue of *PLA Notes 40.* Co-published by The Commonwealth Foundation, ActionAid, DFID, Sida and IIED (http:// www.iied.org/NR/agbioliv/pla_notes/pla_backissues/40.html)

Pimbert, M. and Wakeford, T. (2003) 'Prajateerpu, power and knowledge: the politics of participatory action research in development. Part I: Context, process and safeguards', *Action Research*, 1 (2): 184–207.

Popay, J. and Williams, G. (eds) (1994) *Researching the People's Health: Social Research and Health Care.* London: Routledge.

Pratt, G. (2001) *Practitioners' Critical Reflections on PRA and Participation in Nepal.* (Working Paper No. 122). Sussex: IDS. (www.ids.ac.uk/ids/bookshop/wp/wp122.pdf)

Richards, P. (1995) 'Participatory rural appraisal: a quick and dirty critique', *PLA Notes 24: Critical Reflections from Practice.* London: IIED. (www.iied.org/NR/agbioliv/pla_notes/pla_backissues/24.html)

Satya Murty, D. and Wakeford, T. (2001) 'Farmer foresight: an experiment in South India', in M. Pimbert and T. Wakeford (eds), Special issue of *PLA Notes 40.* Co-published by The Commonwealth Foundation, ActionAid, DFID, Sida and IIED. (http://www.iied.org/NR/agbioliv/pla_notes/pla_backissues/40.html)

Skinner, S. (1997) *Building Community Strengths: a Resource Book on Capacity Building.* London: Community Development Foundation.

Smith, G. and Wales, C. (2000) 'Citizen juries and deliberative democracy', *Political Studies,* 48: 51–65.

SPRU et al., (2003) *Deliberative Mapping Consultation on Options for Addressing the Kidney Gap.* SPRU, UK. (www.deliberative-mapping.org).

Toni, A. and von Braun, J. (2001) 'Poor citizens decide on the introduction of GMOs in Brazil', *Biotechnology and Development Monitor,* 47: 7–9. (www.biotech-monitor.nl/4703.htm).

Wakeford, T. (2002) 'Citizens' juries: a radical alternative for social research', *Social Research Update,* 37 (www.soc.surrey.ac.uk/sru/SRU37.html).

Wakeford, T. and Pimbert, M. (2004) 'Prajateerpu, power and knowledge: the politics of participatory action research in development. Part 2. Analysis, reflections and implications', *Action Research,* 2 (1): 25–46.

Wakeford, T., Murtuja, B. and Bryant, P. (2004) *Using Democratic Spaces To Promote Social Justice in Northern Towns.* University of Newcastle: IPP. (www.citizensjury.org)

Wallace, H. (2001) 'The issue of framing and consensus conferences', in M. Pimbert and T. Wakeford (eds), Special issue of *PLA Notes 40.* Co-published by The Commonwealth Foundation, ActionAid, DFID, Sida and IIED. (http://www.iied.org/NR/agbioliv/pla_notes/pla_backissues/40.html)

23

Learning History: An Action Research Practice in Support of Actionable Learning

George Roth and Hilary Bradbury

'Learning histories' are an action research practice developed to capture, assess and diffuse learning and change initiatives. The set of ideas that underpin them have developed into an integrated set of practices used by scholarly practitioners in evaluating organizational efforts. The chapter describes the rationale for the learning history, its background, and defining steps, and then we describe the processes by which we have conducted learning histories to illustrate the design. We conclude this chapter with our own reflections as to how quality is inscribed into the learning history process.

'Learning histories' are an action research practice developed to capture, assess and diffuse learning and change initiatives. The set of ideas that underpin them have developed into an integrated set of practices used by scholarly practitioners in evaluating organizational efforts.[1] The goal of a learning history is to capture what an innovating group learned and can transfer from their 'new knowledge' to other groups and organizations. The process involves convening salient stakeholders, or those participants with a stake, to reflect on their past and enable a future they desire, and in so doing, create materials that allow others to learn from their efforts. Collective reflection is the essence of the learning history process; a process that is facilitated by co-design and the use of 'shared narrative' from participant stakeholder interviews. In the process of creating a learning history, outside learning historians work with insiders in an organization, developing their inquiry skills and establishing processes that enable and support organizational reflection.

Four elements taken together form the design criteria for a learning history:

1. Multi-stakeholder co-design around notable accomplishments.
2. Insider/outsider teams leading reflective interviews.
3. Distillation and thematic writing.
4. Validation and diffusion with original participants and salient others.

In combining these elements, the learning history exemplifies the dimensions of quality that action researchers (Bradbury and Reason, 2001/2006; 2003) find important. The goal of a learning history is to create the kinds of conversations inside an organization that allow its members to enact the future they want. A learning history emerges from a concern for providing practical value to an organization, and through this orientation and a partnership between researchers and organizational members, it also generates conceptual insights. Value is also created by a judicious use of rigorous and relevant methods so that people are confident of the validity of the information that they are working with. Concern for disconfirmation and validation of data comes from explicit use of action science methods (Argyris et al., 1985; see also Chapter 17 in this volume) by the insider/outsider learning historian team when conducting interviews and facilitating discussions with organizational members. The validity concern is also present in the verification of the information within the document itself. Finally, the learning historian team aims to embed the process of the learning history so as to sustain the goals of the organization after the learning history is complete. We conclude this chapter with our own reflections as to how quality is inscribed in the learning history process. First, we describe the rationale for the learning history, its background, and defining steps, and then we describe the processes by which we have conducted learning histories to illustrate the application of its four aforementioned design criteria.

THE RATIONALE FOR THE LEARNING HISTORY

The content and process of a learning history stem from insights associated with different theoretical streams that also explain its name. The content design draws on theories of *learning*, which stress the importance of integrating reflection and action (Argyris and Schön, 1996; Freire, 1992; Kolb, 1984; Senge, 1990), and theories of social construction of reality, which emphasize the importance of *history* as an informant of organizational awareness, learning, and preferred action. The process design for the learning history is based on premises that conversation, and dialogue as a form of conversation (Bohm, 1987; Isaacs, 1998), allow for better thinking together. Conversation has been suggested as the most appropriate mode for integrating action and reflection (Baker et al., 1998; Ford, 1998; Roth, 2000) and inquiring into, and possibly transforming, the values from which one is operating (Nielsen, 1996; Schein, 1987; Torbert, 2001/2006). Written texts complement conversations by recording conceptual and pragmatic products of dialogue. Appropriately constructed texts offer a concrete platform for focused conversation from which praxis may evolve within communities of practice (Carlile, 2002; Nonaka and Takeuchi, 1995).

Noting that the work of organizational learning and change occurs through conversation (Ford and Ford, 1995) does not cover over the fact that not all people's words are equally heard or valued. Those with 'linguistic capital' (Bourdieu, 1991) speak with ease and authority and their words are accorded more value than those with less linguistic capital. The former have a capacity to direct or regulate the types of conversation considered important. They acquire linguistic capital and use it to create what accords with their interests, furthering a self-reinforcing dynamic. The learning history engenders a process that does not merely promote conversation, but allows an organization to enable its members to open up new conversations.

A learning history integrates perspectives of scholars and practitioners, making efforts to balance the distinctive interests of each group. It offers an opportunity for sets of people with their unique cultures and interests to create common ground in organizational life. This common ground enables practitioners to 'agree to disagree' about what requires action and simultaneously provides the basis for scholars to develop more theoretical work for academic colleagues.

Background

Developing the ideas, forms and contents of learning histories was itself a journey of learning and change for researchers and practitioners. A group of company representatives and 'researchers'[2] convened through the MIT Center for Organizational Learning (see Senge and Scharmer, Chapter 17 in Reason and Bradbury 2001/2006; Roth and Senge, 1996) developed these ideas starting in 1992, within a context of company-based organizational learning projects. The researchers, consultants, and company people undertaking the organizational learning projects were unanimous in their support and accolades for organizational learning. Yet, outside of those directly involved, there was little observable evidence of the learning taking place or its tangible impact beyond the project participants who often experienced dramatic improvements in their individual and group effectiveness. The personal nature of the learning therefore created a dilemma – while individuals were able to attest to the development of their own and others' capabilities, the link to uncontroversial results that could be reported to senior managers was unclear.

Initial attempts to document the learning projects were met with a range of resistance, especially when it was 'outsider' scholars doing the evaluation. Managers were making progress and did not need another person added to their team. One manager's key question helped galvanize efforts: 'if this documentation is a part of a learning initiative,' she said, 'why did the scholars' approach *not* support our learning?' This question raised a fundamental issue common in all action research pursuits. 'Objective' evaluation is impossible, so assessment should be located within the change that is underway. The learning history emerged in a context of responding to practical considerations concerning what action to take inside organizations, *along with* leading thinking from the application of social science disciplines.

What is a Learning History?

A learning history is both a product as well as a process. It is a process that assesses a change initiative through developing the capability of the people in the organization to evaluate their accomplishments in the service of creating materials with which to diffuse their learning to other interested parties. In combining these three elements, a learning history creates a cycle of organizational-level feedback. As documents, learning histories are typically 50 to 100 pages long, providing a retrospective account of significant events in an organization's recent past. Content comes from the stories, interviews, and other data collected from people who initiated, implemented, and participated in the original efforts, as well as non-participants affected by changes.

DESIGNING LEARNING HISTORY PROJECTS

The learning history involves reflecting, capturing, analyzing, distilling, writing, validating, and disseminating the collective learning. Others use the learning history to create their own experience as they read and talk about what is written in the document. In conversing with one another about learning and change, the readers work as a group to develop a shared understanding from the past to guide their future efforts. In the four sections that follow, we describe each of the design criteria for learning histories and illustrate them with examples from one learning history project, selected from many available.[3] This learning history is the 'Auto's Epsilon program learning history'.

1. Multi-Stakeholder Co-Design Around Accomplishments

Orienting Toward the Future by Making it Possible to Discuss Contradictions of the Past

The learning history project starts with a planning process that generates a list of what stakeholders consider to be the noteworthy outcomes of a project. A multi-stakeholder team is convened to establish these notable outcomes, as well as to define the conditions for conducting the learning history and using the document.

This initial phase takes considerable effort yet often seems to yield little progress. It is nonetheless crucially important for creating the conditions under which the project takes place and for how the learning history will be eventually used. Taking the time to develop notable outcomes starts the co-design of the process, guides the interviewing team and shapes the writing of the learning history document. The notable outcomes also become the basis for inquiry from participants in subsequent workshops.

Over the course of numerous projects, we have learned how important it is to involve people from different departments at the start of the learning history. For example, the use of a learning history in employee orientation, management training, or executive development programs is often discussed. Large corporations sponsor learning history projects to help them effectively engage many parts of their organization in the diffusion of learning around a new program. Specialists in training departments are often very detail oriented and have specifications

for their training materials. Making an early and overt effort to explain the learning history, its goals, content and format, engages these specialists. This early engagement develops an insider team with knowledge regarding the learning history and its process, establishing interest and confidence in the document as a training tool.

The Learning History at Auto's Epsilon Program

The learning project at AutoCo (pseudonym) had notable successes in reaching its goals and generated enthusiasm among team members. Other vehicle groups at AutoCo wanted to apply these learning concepts to this program, and requested training support. The AutoCo training and development department sponsored the learning history effort undertaken by the MIT Center for Organizational Learning and led by the first author. It provided $60,000 designated to the MIT research staff to support travel and salary expenses. Internal AutoCo staff from training and other corporate departments (with backgrounds in social science and organization development) worked as part of the insider/outsider learning history. The goal was to create a case study that AutoCo used in its training and that MIT might publish to wider management audiences (this learning history was published with commentaries in 1999 as *Car Launch: The Human Side of Managing Change*, Oxford University Press).

We have found with a few exceptions that the planning of a learning history project falls mostly to the outside learning historians who do the bulk of the work, while company insiders offer guidance. Although insiders commit to helping in coding, sorting and writing, we generally plan on outside learning historians still doing all this work. Most company people are event and activity driven, and can be interrupted with changing priorities when efforts are needed to accurately and adequately code, sort or write the learning history. Another aspect of planning and managing a learning history is to establish specific budgets for the stages of learning history work. As with any research or creative endeavor, it is possible to want more time. However, skilled researchers should be able to adjust their work pace to the time that is allotted, make trade-offs in the depth and sharpness of their analysis, and write to meet milestones.

2. Insider/Outsider Team Leading Reflective Interviews

Combining Practice and Scholarship Through the Synergy of Managers, Consultants, and Researchers Collaborating Beyond Pecuniary Relationships

A learning history, in seeking to engage participants in learning from experience, involves a process of capturing an organization's learning through the lens of provocateurs and participants. Learning historians interview these stakeholders about their experience in an open and inviting way. It is important that learning history team members together understand the importance of the breadth and depth of an organization's changes. A mixture of team member affiliations brings the perspective of the various audiences for the learning history. These audiences include managers and people in the company, in other companies, and academic audiences. Moreover, learning historians operate in a mode in which inquiry itself is a form of action. Interviews are not merely a means for extracting information but viewed as a powerful process that truly engages salient stakeholders. For example, by asking someone how he or she might have overcome an obstacle, one is also inviting him or her to consider how he or she might take action in the future. In this sense, inquiry is also a form of intervention.

A learning history team requires the involvement of corporate 'insiders'. The guide for good practice for insiders and outsiders on learning history teams comes from social science research. Spradley (1979) describes the development of 'key informants' as crucial to the ethnographic research. In developing this relationship, key informants become interested in the research; they become a sounding board for insights and help to navigate the complex cultural territory. Whyte's (1943) insights into Boston's street gangs were aided by the relationship he developed with his key informant, Doc. Not only did Doc introduce the Harvard student to people in the Italian slum, he later commented on Whyte's thinking about their social organization. Organizational insiders become key informants in learning histories. We pay particular attention to giving voice to their insights, choices, and abilities to generalize from details described in vignettes. Providing a way to note these insights contributed to the idea of writing learning histories in a two-column format, which we describe below. [For further exploration of organizational insiders in action research see Chapter 45.]

The reflective interviews are the primary method for data collection. In promoting reflection and inquiry, they draw upon techniques from ethnography (Sanday, 1979; Spradley, 1979; Van Maanen, 1988), oral history (see Yow, 1994), action science and organizational learning (Argyris, 1990; Argyris et al., 1985; Argyris and Schön, 1978; Senge et al., 1994) and process consultation (Schein, 1987). Ethnography provides the science for cultural investigation – an integrated approach of participant observation, interviewing, and archival research. The methods of oral historians provide a process honoring and capturing the story of the narrator. Action science, organizational learning and process consultation add inquiry skills and methods for developing people's capacities to reflect upon and assess the outcomes of their efforts. The transcripts of reflective interviews, and other textual material, create a rich database that learning historians later distill into a coherent written document.

The AutoCo Learning History Team and Interviewing Process

The learning history team for the AutoCo Epsilon was made up of five people: two MIT researchers, two people from the training department (both of whom were department veterans and one of whom was working on a PhD in organizational behavior at a local university), and an organizational development consultant from the corporate organizational effectiveness office. The OD consultant facilitated several of the team's learning events and was familiar with Epsilon's managers and engineers.

Learning history team composition is important. A paired team with an insider and an outsider generally conducts interviews. Pairing allows one person to lead the reflective interview while the other takes notes, develops possible follow-up questions, and tends to the tape recorder. At the start of the interview, these roles are explained, so that the respondent is informed of the process. Openness and transparency in the learning history team help to set those conditions for the reflective interview. Sharing notable results, a timeline of events and interventions, and asking questions for what influences produced results lets the respondent think about the whole of the changes, and describe the elements that he or she is familiar with.

In the AutoCo learning history we interviewed over 30 people, each time with a researcher paired with one of the AutoCo learning history team members. The people interviewed had been identified in the planning stage. They included vice-presidents responsible for multiple development programs, senior personnel managers, program and engineering leaders on the Epsilon project and from other programs, people from finance, purchasing and administrative functions, suppliers' engineers, and manufacturing engineers and managers from the assembly plant. The interviews also included several focus group sessions with engineering teams. The interviews took place over three months, with several visits made to the engineering and assembly facilities. It helped to conduct the interviews in rooms near actual work sites, so that it was easy to go and see what people wanted to show us.

3. Distillation and Thematic Writing

Combining Research, Pragmatic and Mythic Imperatives to Create an Interactive Text as a Part of Research and Practice

There comes a point in a learning history when all the interviews are done. The materials and perspectives start to feel familiar, and there is a sense that respondents have well described their learning. By this point, the learning team has amassed a formidable collection of notes, documents, and transcriptions. The analysis of these materials uses traditional qualitative data analysis processes (Corbin and Strauss, 1990; Miles and Huberman, 1994; Strauss, 1987). An emphasis of the analysis process is to develop grounded theory (Glaser and Strauss, 1967) based on what people said happened and how they dealt with the issues that faced them. These 'grounded theories' are the themes around which the learning history is organized and written. Because the goal of the learning history is to reflect the insight and learning of the organization, and not the testing of theory by researchers, we use the term 'distillation' to signify the efforts of this analytic process to maintain the essence and character of the participants' narrative.

Distillation is a process for making sense of the changes an organization has gone through, drawing upon the research and intuitive insights of the learning historians, and establishing an outline for the subsequent writing and editing process. It involves working with insiders to understand organizational phenomena while using the sensibilities of the outsiders to add greater meaning and present the insights in universal ways. Accomplishing these goals is not easy, as anyone who has written up qualitative research will know. The learning historian group, reflecting on its own experiences in writing multiple documents for sponsors, developed a way to address the challenges of maintaining integrity of the data, capturing the essence of the learning story, and providing appropriate feedback and critique to enable continued progress. It is difficult to focus on the minutiae of 'research', and make sure each branch of ethnographic description (the story) is triangulated by multiple sources and using multiple methods, at the same time that you are trying to distill a sense of the whole 'mythic' forest. And when people are told to take a 'pragmatic' stance – to produce a one-page memo that concisely communicates lessons learned – it's almost impossible to include the detailed 'research' data that would explain, using rigorous descriptions, why commonly known remedies are consistently overlooked.

We found that cycling between each of three orientations – research, mythic, and pragmatic, respectively – in an explicit fashion is necessary in addressing the requirement of each (Roth and Kleiner, 1998). As a team, we each had to acquire the dispassionate stance and in-depth knowledge of a 'research-oriented' behavioral scientist, immerse ourselves in storytelling, resonating with the 'mythic' archetypal struggles of the characters in epic tales, and take on the role of a master teacher, 'pragmatically' developing knowledge to face problems by putting yourself through various learning experiences. Depending upon our backgrounds, one role was more natural than another, but as a team, we could support and lead each other as we cycled through these orientations in distilling and writing the learning history. These three imperatives are not contradictory; they are complementary. The more you practice them together, the stronger you become in each.

Distilling the AutoCo Learning History Themes

We started by coding the textual materials from interview transcripts and other sources (see Corbin and Strauss, 1990). Meeting as a group, we presented the codes we created, writing them on 3M Post-its and sticking them on the wall of the conference room where we met (see Miles and Huberman, 1994). When all the codes were up, we started looking for patterns, sorting the Post-its by stacking similar concepts, and grouping them together when the concepts were associated with one another. From this organization, we started to get clusters – concepts and patterns that were adjacent and belonged together. The next step was to think about sentences that described these cultures, and provided a thematic orientation. There was a back and forth process to try to organize all the coded material into themes, and articulate themes in a compelling way. At this point, there is an impasse – trying to be true to and inclusive of all the data that underlies the codes, patterns and theme, while deriving a compelling statement that captures the essence of that theme. As this description illustrates, it is likely to be easier, particularly with researchers in the lead, to start with the research imperative and hold close to the data. However, this impasse is the mark of the time to cycle to the mythic imperative, and seek to express themes as archetypal stories.

In taking a mythic stance, the learning historian tries to help the organization through a catharsis. Most large organizations are 'mythically' deprived; official documents and presentations are bereft of stories. Managers talk in terms of highly rationalized, abstract explanations that do not typically tell how their numbers or policies really evolved. People in organizations get their myths the old-fashioned way – at the water cooler, in the washroom, over early morning coffee before everyone gets in, in late night 'watering holes', at remote meetings, or in the car-pool. Yet, these are the stories that have impact. To bring out the mythic force of the tale, learning historians may amplify key details and emotionally charged points. For example, many meetings go by without rancor, but the AutoCo learning history described only the 17th, where a breakdown occurred. A benevolent manager, challenged by his subordinates for micro-managing them, shouted at them: 'I don't trust you!' The meeting grew more volatile, but ended with an understanding of the dynamic of trust on that team.

Exhibit 23.1 The Six Themes of the AutoCo Learning History

1. **Hard results, soft concerns.** When managers pay attention to human issues like openness and fostering trust, would teams be able to produce better business results? In Epsilon, the focus on how managers think and interact started with nine months of working sessions in a cross-functional leadership team composed of most of the senior functional managers in the Epsilon program. These sessions aimed to foster shared vision and shared understanding of one another's mental models in the context of addressing the program's practical problems. Thus, the senior team management began the learning process long before the rest of the team, which enabled them to jointly design the evolution of the process.

2. **Setting an example of non-authoritarian leadership.** Many experts and consultants preach the need for a more non-authoritarian and participative approach to project leadership but can offer little help in how to develop and sustain such behavior. In Epsilon, this philosophy became reality as project leaders' behavior changed over time as a by-product of the tools and learning processes employed. For senior leaders, 'walking the talk' is not a trivial matter. It requires concerted effort and mutual partnership. And it can make a huge difference.

3. **Introductory learning labs: teaching techniques for thinking differently.** Eventually, a two-day 'learning lab', taught by program managers and MIT staff, was created to introduce many members of the Epsilon team to the learning tools and methods with which the leadership team had been working. 'Learning labs' may include a variety of techniques, but the key goal is inviting more in-depth conversation across functional boundaries, enabling people to focus on key business-related issues in a risk-free setting accessible to all.

4. **Combining engineering innovations with human relations:** the Harmony Buck. Combining new technical ideas with greater trust and new interpersonal skills (a 'human relations' approach) can enable people to apply the technical ideas more effectively. The 'Harmony Buck' speeded up prototyping by allowing people to come together and try out new engineering solutions. But it also built on the growing environment of involvement and openness and in turn contributed to that environment. The result was an increased flow of information among team members testing their ideas together.

5. **Partnerships.** Functionally-based people were drawn together in ways that bridged differences and focused on collaborative learning and action. An atmosphere which encourages experimentation across traditional boundaries leads to benefits that the senior leaders can't neccessarily predict or plan for.

6. **Process innovation in the context of a large organization.** Eventually, local process innovations are brought into larger management forums. The larger AutoCo organization responded to the Epsilon team in many ways, not always in ways Epsilon's members would have wished for. Innovative local line leaders often put their faith in proving that their innovations will lead to better business results, and that these results will bring credibility to their efforts. This assumption proved faulty for Epsilon's managers. Lacking senior management partners, they also lacked counsel on how to handle the larger system implications of their efforts.

Unpleasant 'truths' are not heard when they are too close to the mark or so harsh or pointed that they trigger emotional responses. 'Not being heard' is the danger we actively seek to avoid. We seek to find safe ways to bring forward the brutal truths, a way to consider them without blaming individuals or getting swept up in destructive battles. In utilizing this pragmatic imperative, we test the ability to hear the messages and take responsibility for what the receiver's reactions might be. We ask insiders on the learning history teams, because they know the organization's culture intimately, to take on the mantle of key managers they know or interviewed and project their reactions. They can draw attention to seemingly innocuous phrases or vignettes that will have devastating effects.

At AutoCo, we decided not to include an example where engineers overcame corporate bureaucracy. When AutoCo's corporate standards prevented it, the engineers used corporate credit cards to purchase several computers and software licenses to perform helpful design simulations. Later, when the corporate information technology group found out, they had corporate accounting take away all the team's credit cards. Using this story, which involved politics, would have infuriated corporate management. There were other examples of innovative approaches to constraining rules in the learning history, and by not including this example, it would improve the reception of corporate management to all of the Epsilon team's learning. We sacrificed including data to improve the organization's reception of the learning history.

4. Validation and Diffusion with Original Participants and Others

Seeking to Clarify What is Valuable and Useful to Make the Learning History 'Actionable'

Each element in a learning history process – planning, interviewing, observing, distilling (analyzing), writing, editing, validating quotes, circulating drafts, and conducting dissemination workshops – is intended to broaden and deepen learning throughout the organization by providing a forum for communicating, reflecting upon, learning from, and substantiating results. In that sense, consideration for making the work actionable is always a core facet of all parts of these efforts. The learning history process can be beneficial for not only the original participants, but also for those who advised them, and ultimately for anyone who is interested in the organization's change processes. The focus on broadening learning becomes a focus in validating the document by checking quotes and context, and in workshops oriented to use and diffuse the learning lessons.

A learning history is to be read and discussed and the ensuing conversations are understood to be the vehicle through which positive change can spread. It is important to understand how readers make sense of text when thinking about how people learn from a learning history. Reader-response theory is based on the understanding that the meaning of text resides neither in text alone nor in the author's intentions (Iser, 1989). Readers interpret and do not automatically accept 'authored' meanings. They bring their own background, experience and knowledge to what they read. While writers intend one meaning for their words, there are likely to be as many interpreted meanings of a text as there are readers. Meaning is created by the interaction of reader, text, and author's intentions (Yanow, 1994: 3).

Conversations that take place in skill building sessions are used to disseminate the information in learning histories. Providing a learning history to a group of people without giving them an opportunity to discuss its contents does not allow them to make collective sense. A facilitated workshop process, modeled on the concept of a 'managerial practice field' (Senge, 1990), has been used to create the settings where people develop their shared understandings of learning and change processes.[4]

The checking of individual quotes in isolation, then in context, and developing consensus for the material in the document as a whole before using a learning history in workshops helps an organization create safe and valid information for learning. The learning history team's attention to rigor and validity in creating a document that is accurate, engaging, and complete comes up against powerful preconceptions. People in organizations may be reluctant to accept a document as equally accurate about organizational matters as the information they get from a 'water cooler' conversation. Bringing these tendencies to light, and the desire to create and use valid information (Argyris and Schön, 1978) as the basis for learning, creates the context not only for using the learning history, but also for learning more broadly.

Diffusion and Change at AutoCo

In a workshop for sponsors of the MIT Center for Organizational Learning, a group of managers from AutoCo formed into one of over a dozen company teams. The workshop involved reading a section of the AutoCo learning history, drawing out lessons, and linking those insights to efforts in their own company. The specific section addressed the challenges in diffusing Epsilon's learning to the corporation. These AutoCo managers guessed that the disguised company was their own, and refused to participate. They claimed that they already knew what happened. They blamed the Epsilon program manager for shortcomings, stating that there was nothing that they could learn from a 'whitewashed and sanitized' account.

The AutoCo managers' orientation illustrates a challenge for all learners – 'leaping over the shadow of their own experience'. As individuals, it is difficult to see past our own perspectives and our sense of certainty about what we know. It was easier for these managers to blame a few individuals for the problems their organization faced than it was for them to examine conditions that they themselves were involved in creating. They illustrated the power of pre-existing biases, blaming, and stereotyping – all behaviors that have to be 'unlearned' in order for new learning to take place. In the learning history workshop, ironically, these AutoCo managers were producing the behaviors that they claimed to be a source of problems for Epsilon team.

AutoCo had a history of 'skunk works' projects. Unofficial projects took place under the radar of management scrutiny. Executives allowed efforts such as Epsilon's learning project to persist as long as they 'did not interfere with the focus on results'. When teams made changes, such as going around corporate computer systems standards or engineering change orders policies, their subversive actions were a part of behavior patterns that contributed to better results. AutoCo had no mechanisms for reflection that questioned and changed these policies for subsequent effort. Rather, the opposite happened. Executives sanctioned Epsilon's managers when they detected insurrections.

Results took time, and when they were recognized, the managers and team members were off on other endeavors.

The learning history and Epsilon team faced this challenge as the learning history document was completed. Individuals, in context, in sections and as a whole, with the original and another new team, had quote checked it. Both the original and new team agreed that it had important and useful lessons for AutoCo. The members of the Epsilon and learning history team, however, had moved on to other assignments. That situation left only one of the original proponents of the Epsilon learning project and one MIT researcher to address conditions for broader changes at AutoCo, as well as the review for release and external publication of the learning history. One option was to follow the skunk works approach – release the document, let teams use it, and executives react to its implications. Another option, the one that was chosen, was to make the effort to get on the President's calendar, and gain his support and approval. The learning project proponent worked with AutoCo's Human Resources Vice President to get his support, and a meeting with AutoCo's President. This President read the learning history, agreeing that the learning effort raised important issues that AutoCo needed to address. With his support, the Senior Vice President for Product Development wrote a forward to the document and sent the learning history to all engineering team leaders.

ENSURING QUALITY IN LEARNING HISTORIES

The goal of any learning history is to improve the quality and effectiveness of the conversations people have in their organization. The quality of the conversation that is achieved by people who read and discuss a learning history is an important indication of their abilities to manage learning and change in the future. Thus, what people do in using a learning history is a criterion for judging the document and process that created it. An essential requirement for a learning history is that the process for creating it improves the learning orientation. The learning history process is designed to create openness to inquiry and learning. Without cultivating this willingness to learn from experience, the learning history document will be ineffective and largely ignored. Just as an individual and a team need appropriate attitudes and skills to become more effective, organizations need collective processes and settings for reading, reflecting upon, and discussing learning histories.

Bradbury (cf. 2007) draws on the pragmatic tradition to propose core elements for assessing quality in action research. At the heart of pragmatic considerations is the consideration that the learning history must be actionable and moves stakeholders toward desired changes. Quality and actionability become synonymous, and thus can be considered by the ability of a learning history to: 1) add value, 2) engage and support participation and partnership, 3) utilize rigorous and culturally relevant inquiry, and 4) create infrastructure that leaves stakeholders stronger beyond the effort of the learning history itself. Each of these elements of learning history quality is discussed in the following sections.

LEARNING HISTORY QUALITY: ADDING VALUE

Practical value presumes that people prioritize their attention and efforts toward causes that they deem worthy. The primary questions raised by the consideration of practical value are 'what is needed' and 'by whom'. The initial planning and establishing the scope of a learning history project involves a collaborative process for articulating and organizing around these needs. In the world of organizational realities, processes must link research questions to organizational needs, to encourage ownership by salient stakeholders. It is critical to begin a learning

history project by creating an insider/outsider team that not only represents but includes these salient stakeholders. We find it helpful at the planning stage to develop a map of the system and then refine the focus of the learning history on areas that leverage change.

The learning history team brings the voices of participants that will speak to practical value into their daily activities. Connected to the delivery of practical value is the ability, from the start, to understand the salient stakeholders. While it is not possible or desirable to include all stakeholders directly, awareness of the organization's social and political groupings informs the selection of appropriate individuals for a robust insider/outsider team. For some stakeholders, recognition is sufficient to be a part of a change (especially if they have felt ignored); for others, active participation is needed for them to feel that they are a part of the effort.

LEARNING HISTORY QUALITY: WORKING AS PARTNERS

Participation, for action researchers, is the vehicle by which stakeholders become co-designers as well as implementers of desired changes. In their co-design responsibilities, stakeholders develop and test theory. Lewin's famous statement that 'nothing is more practical than a good theory' (Lewin, 1951) emerged in a context of regularly checking theory with practitioners. Participation starts with an initial crucial step of identifying salient stakeholders and continues with mobilizing those stakeholder who can best help make changes. 'Best help' may mean offering criticism. Stakeholders' involvement in change leads to continuously clarifying goals. Enjoining particular stakeholders to the action research project requires clarity about why some, and not others, are actively involved. That clarity comes from an understanding of project goals, and an involvement of stakeholders affected by the project.

LEARNING HISTORY QUALITY: UTILIZING RIGOROUS, VIGOROUS METHODS

Adequate methods are important for bringing in rich and valid information. Generally, participation will decrease if an overly rigid method is understood to offer merely 'scholarly' insight, or lack of rigor is implied by an overly pragmatic focus on 'best' practice. The consideration of adequate methods is one of generating robust data while simultaneously meeting the needs of those providing that data. The critical point is to consider how a method is used, rather than only discussing what method is used.

Learning historians draw on a range of methods. We draw especially on practices of qualitative researchers; however, we use these methods in ways to make them actionable and collective. The learning historians understand that inquiry itself is a form of action (see Chapter 12). For example, in interviewing stakeholders who need to be involved in a change, the questions asked can become vehicles for engagement and go beyond exchanges for merely gathering information. Validation meetings and subsequent follow-up processes, such as quote checking, can also be important steps toward developing skills and designing infrastructure to make sure action steps go beyond approving the use of quotes or the conversations in those meetings.

LEARNING HISTORY QUALITY: LEAVING STAKEHOLDERS STRONGER

How might the learning culture that has developed in the course of the learning history endure beyond the moment and continue into the future? One of the missing elements in a learning process in most large enterprises is an organizational infrastructure for reflection. Designing infrastructure for learning histories begins in its planning, when the stakeholders and purpose are determined. It is particularly important to enlist the decision-makers as early in the process as possible. Decision-makers might be prompted to ask: what do we need to institutionalize our learning? While the questions in establishing the context for a learning history include 'What information would change our minds about what we hold to be certain?', this does not address the pragmatic concerns of diffusing new insights broadly. At the final, discussion stage of the learning history, the conversation needs to turn to what will support people in moving from reflection and conversation to taking action based on their insights.

We have found it best to consider the development of infrastructure conceptually, rather than in the context of the implications for action from a particular question. When the focus is on particular questions there are political implications. Every action has consequences, and like any change, there are some that will gain and others that will lose from change. Asking the question about action conceptually avoids the limitations that come with reconciling the requirements of change with one's personal situation. For example, managers might need to use or change reward structures to reinforce new practices. Tracking impact – especially where qualitative and quantitative reports can be obtained – is particularly effective in providing people with a sense of progress which, in turn, creates the feedback that reinforces a virtuous learning cycle.

Learning Histories Advance the Whole Field of Organizational Learning

The planning of the learning history involves explicit discussions of the process by which new teams learn from the original team's experiences. Establishing conditions for reflecting, capturing, examining and transferring experience is an important aspect of the learning history planning. There have been numerous projects in which planning discussions surfaced preconditions for a learning history that did not exist. One example was a large telecom company in which stakeholders wanted to learn from its negotiations with the public utilities commission. The telecom company would then use the learning history to build upon its learning in the next round of negotiations, which would be several years away and involve a new team from the utility. The company was, however, unwilling to have their insights shared with the utilities commission or other companies, thus making it unsuitable for a learning history whose intent is to share and not sequester learning. Another example was a large manufacturing company in which different facilities had varying degrees of success with its corporate improvement programs. Some of its facilities had many units certified at the top levels, and other facilities had nearly all its units either not certified, or just achieving the very lowest level of certification. The sponsor for this potential study was more interested in knowing why certain facilities lagged behind others, so that he might gain, rather than in creating data to engage all facilities around what helped and what hindered performance improvement certification efforts. When the planning stage of the learning history process surfaced such unsuitable conditions, the researchers withdrew. Like other learning tools, learning histories are most effective for their intended purposes when they are broadly shared and discussed. It helps others learn from the original team's experience and helps the original team in that it makes that team's challenges universal – providing a sense that we are not alone or unique, but these are common challenges which others can learn from.

CONCLUSION

Most learning history efforts have been integrated with learning and change interventions, providing and creating opportunities for conversations as well as providing feedback to the progress of change. The learning is relevant not just to the specific organizational project, but intended to help develop knowledge across organizational projects. We have learned, through developing the methods and carrying out projects, teaching others, and working with practitioners, that learning histories can be rewarding for their practical value while they also contribute to scholarship. Learning history projects create a structure for action research, and thus can be assessed by the principles and choicepoints for quality in action research mentioned above (see also Reason and Bradbury 2001/2006).

Most organizations do not have ready places, uses, and processes for reflection. Many individuals reflect and learn, but often they do so in isolation or small groups, without public forums in which to develop and test their insights. Reflection is not a normal organizational process, but one that requires the development of processes and tools to enable it. The virtue of the learning history text is that is provides a common experience that can be discussed and assessed at different times and places. Using the learning history text provides opportunities for teaching and learning action science methods – surfacing and making visible individual and collective mental models that guide people's actions.

The goals for actionable processes that result from exemplary action research projects are interwoven into the design of learning histories. The process and skills for carrying out a learning history are something that an organization and its members learn by doing. The virtue of having insiders and outsiders on the team is that the skills associated with planning and carrying out the project are transferred to the organization. The people that support the learning history, in either its creation or use, learn and help model reflective practices. The abilities to reflect organizationally gradually become part of the organization's new repertoire.

An important question that we have raised in this chapter is the degree to which conventional research can be used in cultivating learning inside organizational life. We believe conventional research provides a solid foundation, and we draw extensively from qualitative research practices. It is not just a question of the methods, but *how* the methods are used. In the learning history there is a balance in the attention paid to adding value and the attention paid to getting the research 'very right'. Indeed this may be something that our conventional colleagues can learn from in terms of how to apportion their own efforts. While conventional research operates under the ethics and values of doing no harm, what we propose in learning histories is that there is a broader bandwidth for addressing issues of quality that are ultimately more actionable.

NOTES

1 Readers are also directed to Hilary Bradbury's Chapter 29 in the first edition of the *Handbook of Action Research*. There the focus was on the learning history as part of doctoral dissertation work.

2 Those who took part in the learning history projects include Linda Booth, Hilary Bradbury, Marty Castleberg, Brenda Cruz, Tony DiBella, Toni Gregory, Art Kleiner, Nina Kruschwitz, Virginia O'Brien, Ruthann Prange, George Roth, Ann Thomas, John Voyer, and JoAnne Wyer. We have also received help and suggestions from Ed Schein, John Van Maanen, John Carroll, Peter Senge, Ed Nevis, John Sterman, Chris Argyris, Don Schön, Bill Isaacs, Fred Kofman and Daniel Kim.

3 Numerous individuals and teams in dozens of settings have conducted learning histories. Some of these learning histories are used as company documents and available as working paper manuscripts (see www.sol-ne.org/res/wp/index.html), scholarly articles (Bradbury and Mainemelis, 2001), dissertations (e.g. Bradbury, 1998) and books (Roth and Kleiner, 2000; Kleiner and Roth, 2001; Mirvis et al., 2003).

4 Managerial practice fields are designed learning spaces where decision-makers can experiment, make mistakes, accelerate learning and test new behaviors. Practice fields, or 'learning laboratories', become an element of the infrastructure for learning that enables organizations to develop, capture, and disseminate new knowledge (Kim, 1993; Senge et al., 1994: 32–6).

REFERENCES

Argyris, C. (1990) *Overcoming Organizational Defenses, Facilitating Organizational Learning*. Boston: Allyn and Bacon.

Argyris, C. and Schön, D. (1978) *Organizational Learning: A Theory of Action Perspective*. Reading, MA: Addison-Wesley.

Argyris, C. and Schön, D. (1996) *Organizational Learning II: Theory, Method, and Practice*. Reading, MA: Addison-Wesley.

Argyris, C., Putnam, R. and Smith, D. (1985) *Action Science*. San Francisco, CA: Jossey-Bass.

Baker, A.C., Jensen, P.J., and Kolb, D.A. (1998) *Conversation as Experiential Learning* (Working Paper 98–4 [4a]). Cleveland, OH: Case Western Reserve University, Weatherhead School of Management, Department of Organizational Behavior.

Bohm, D. (1987) *On Dialogue*, David Bohm Seminars, PO Box 1452, Ojai, CA, 09023.

Bradbury, H. (1998) 'Learning with *The Natural Step*: cooperative ecological inquiry through cases, theory and practice for sustainable development.' Unpublished PhD dissertation, Boston College. Available though UMI: Ann Arbor.

Bradbury, H. (2001/2006) 'Sustaining sustainable development with action research', in P. Reason and H. Bradbury (eds), *Handbook of Action Research: Participative Inquiry and Practice*. London: Sage.

Bradbury, H. (2004) 'Varieties of action research'. Keynote address, Conference on Action Research. Aalborg University, Denmark, November.

Bradbury, H. (2007) 'Quality, consequence and actionability: what action researchers offer from the tradition of Pragmatism', in Shani et al. (eds), *The SAGE Handbook of Collaborative Research* (forthcoming). London: Sage.

Bradbury, H. and Mainemelis, C. (2001) 'Learning history and organizational praxis: non-traditional research', *Journal of Management Inquiry*, 10 (4): 340–57.

Bradbury, H. and Reason, P. (2001/2006) 'Conclusion: broadening the bandwidth of validity: issues and choice-points for improving the quality of action research', in P. Reason and H. Bradbury (eds), *Handbook of Action Research: Participative Inquiry and Practice*. London: Sage. pp. 447–55. Also published in P. Reason and H. Bradbury (eds) (2006), *Handbook of Action Research: Concise Paperback Edition*. London: Sage. pp. 343–51.

Bradbury, H. and Reason, P. (2003) 'Action research: an opportunity for revitalizing research purpose and practices', *Qualitative Social Work*, 2 (2): 173–83.

Bourdieu, P. (1991) *Language and Symbolic Power*. Cambridge, MA: Harvard University Press.

Carlile, P. (2002) 'A pragmatic view of knowledge and boundaries: boundary objects in new product development', *Organization Science*, 13 (4): 442–55.

Copleston, F. (1994 [1966]) *A History of Philosophy, Vol. 8: Modern Philosophy: Empiricism, Idealism and Pragmatism*. New York: Doubleday Press.

Corbin, J. and Strauss, A. (1990) *Basics of Qualitative Research*. Thousand Oaks, CA: Sage Publications.

Dewey, J. (ed.) (1938) *Experience and Education*. New York: Macmillan.

Dickstein, M. (1999) *The Revival of Pragmatism: New Essays on Social Thought, Law and Culture*. Durham, NC: Duke University Press.

Ford, J.D. (1998) 'Organizational change as shifting conversations', *Academy of Management Review*, August.

Ford, J. and Ford, L. (1995) 'The role of conversation in producing intentional change in organizations', *Academy of Management Review*, 20 (3): 541–70.

Freire, P. (1992) *Pedagogy of the Oppressed*. New York: Continuum.

Glaser, B. and Strauss, A. (1967) *The Discovery of Grounded Theory*. Chicago, IL: Aldine.

Habermas, J. (1971) *Knowledge and Human Interests* (trans. J. Shapiro). Boston: Beacon Press.

Isaacs, W. (1998) *Dialogue and the Art of Thinking Together*. New York: Doubleday Currency.

Iser, W. (1989) *Prospecting: From Reader Response to Literary Anthropology*. Baltimore: Johns Hopkins University Press.

James, W. (1978 [1908]) *Pragmatism and the Meaning of Truth*. Cambridge, MA: Harvard University Press.

Kemmis, S. (2001/2006) 'Exploring the relevance of critical theory for action research: emancipatory action research in the footsteps of Jürgen Habermas', in P. Reason and H. Bradbury (eds), *The Handbook of Action Research: Participative Inquiry and Practice*. London: Sage. pp. 91–102. Also published in P. Reason and H. Bradbury (eds) (2006), *Handbook of Action Research: Concise Paperback Edition*. London: Sage. pp. 94–105.

Kim, D.H. (1993) 'The link between individual and organizational learning', *Sloan Management Review*, Fall: 37–50.

Kleiner, A. and Roth, G. (2001) *Oil Change: Perspectives on Corporate Transformation*. New York: Oxford University Press.

Kolb, D. (1984) *Experiential Learning, Experience as the Source of Learning and Development*. Englewood Cliffs, NJ: Prentice Hall.

Lewin, K. (1951) *Field Theory in Social Science*. New York: Harper.

Miles, M.B. and Huberman, A.M. (1994) *Qualitative Data Analysis*. Newbury Park, CA: Sage Publications.

Mirvis, P., Ayas, K. and Roth, G. (2003) *To the Desert and Back: the Story of One of the Most Dramatic Business Transformations on Record*. San Francisco, CA: Jossey-Bass.

Nielsen, R.P. (1996) *The Politics of Ethics*. New York: Oxford University Press.

Nonaka, I. and Takeuchi, H. (1995) *The Knowledge-Creating Company: How Japanese Companies Create the Dynamics of Innovation*. New York: Oxford Universty Press.

Reason, P. and Bradbury, H. (eds) (2001/2006) *The Handbook of Action Research: Participative Inquiry and Practice*. London: Sage.

Rorty, R. (1996) 'Does academic freedom have philosophical presuppositions?', in L. Menand et al. (eds), *The Future of Academic Freedom*. Chicago, IL: University of Chicago Press.

Rorty, R. (1999) *Philosophy and Social Hope*. London: Penguin Books.

Roth, G. (2000) 'Constructing conversations: lessons from learning from experience', *Organizational Development Journal*, 18 (4): 69–78.

Roth, G. (2004) 'Lessons from the desert: integrating managerial expertise and learning for organizational transformation', *The Learning Organization Journal*, 11 (3): 194–208.

Roth, G. and Kleiner, A. (1998) 'Developing organizational memory through learning histories', *Organizational Dynamics*, Fall: 43–60.

Roth, G. and Kleiner, A. (2000) *Car Launch: The Human Side of Managing Change*. New York: Oxford University Press.

Roth, G. and Senge, P. (1996) 'From theory to practice: research territory, processes and structure at an organizational learning center', *Journal of Change Management*, 9 (1): 92–106.

Sanday, P. (1979), 'The ethnographic paradigm(s)', *Administrative Science Quarterly*, 24: pp. 482–93.

Schein, E. (1987) *The Clinical Perspective in Fieldwork*. Newbury, CA: Sage Publications.

Senge, P. (1990) *The Fifth Discipline: The Art and Practice of the Learning Organization*. New York: Doubleday.

Senge, P., Kleiner, A., Roberts, C., Ross, R. and Smyth, B. (1994) *The Fifth Discipline Fieldbook: Strategies and Tools for Building a Learning Organization*. New York: Doubleday Currency.

Spradley, J. (1979) *The Ethnographic Interview*, New York: Holt, Rinehart, and Winston.

Strauss, A. (1987) *Qualitative Analysis for Social Scientists*. New York: Cambridge University Press.

Torbert, W.R. (2001/2006) 'The practice of action inquiry', in P. Reason and H. Bradbury (eds), *The*

Handbook of Action Research: Participative Inquiry and Practice. London: Sage Publications. Also published in P. Reason and H. Bradbury (eds) (2006), *Handbook of Action Research: Concise Paperback Edition*. London: Sage. pp. 207–17.

Van Maanen, J. (1988) *Tales of the Field, On Writing Ethnography*. Chicago, IL The University of Chicago Press.

Whyte, W. (1943) *Street Corner Society*, Chicago, IL: The University of Chicago Press.

Yanow, D. (1994) 'Reader-response theory and organizational life: action as interpretation and text', paper presented at the Academy of Management Meeting, Dallas, TX.

Yow, V.R. (1994) *Recording Oral History, A Practical Guide for Social Scientists*. Thousand Oaks, CA: Sage Publications.

24

Extending Epistemology within a Co-operative Inquiry

John Heron and Peter Reason

Co-operative inquiry is a form of second-person action research in which all participants work together in an inquiry group as co-researchers and as co-subjects – not research on people or about people, but research with people. As co-researchers work together through cycles of action and reflection they engage in an 'extended epistemology' of experiential, presentational, propositional and practical ways of knowing. Our purpose in this chapter is to consider this extended epistemology in some depth. After an introductory overview, we consider each way of knowing in turn, first with some general remarks, then with a look at its role in the reflection phase, the action phase and the outcomes of a co-operative inquiry, including some examples from inquiry practice. We conclude with comments on issues of quality in the cyclic use of the four ways.

Co-operative inquiry is a form of second-person action research in which all participants work together in an inquiry group as co-researchers and as co-subjects. Everyone is engaged in the design and management of the inquiry; everyone gets into the experience and action that is being explored; everyone is involved in making sense and drawing conclusions; thus everyone involved can take initiative and exert influence on the process. This is not research on people or about people, but research with people

(Heron, 1971, 1996a; Heron and Reason, 2001/2006; Reason, 1988b, 1994, 1998, 1999, 2003; Reason and Torbert, 2001).

The inquiry group members work together through cycles of action and reflection, developing their understanding and practice by engaging in what we have called an 'extended epistemology' of experiential, presentational, propositional and practical ways of knowing. Our purpose in this chapter is to consider this extended epistemology in more depth than in previous conjoint writings.

After an introductory overview, we consider each way of knowing in turn, first with some general remarks, then with a look at its role in the reflection phase, the action phase and the outcomes of a co-operative inquiry, including some examples from inquiry practice. We conclude with comments on issues of quality in the cyclic use of the four ways.

A useful background to this chapter is our general introduction to co-operative inquiry (Heron and Reason, 2001). While the extended epistemology is foundational to co-operative inquiry, it is clearly not limited to it. It can be applied to everyday knowing and all forms of action research practice.

OVERVIEW OF THE FOUR WAYS OF KNOWING

The radical epistemology discussed here is a theory of how we know which is *extended* beyond the ways of knowing of positivist oriented academia. These we see as based primarily on abstract propositional knowledge and a narrow empiricism. However, we note the parallel developments in what Denzin and Lincoln (2005b) refer to as the later 'moments' in the development of qualitative research practices (Reason, 2006).

The four ways of knowing can be briefly defined as follows, both in terms of process and outcome. *Experiential knowing* is by being present with, by direct face-to-face encounter with, person, place or thing. It is knowing through the immediacy of perceiving, through empathy and resonance. Its product is the quality of the relationship in which it participates, including the quality of being of those in the relationship. *Presentational knowing* emerges from the encounters of experiential knowing, by intuiting significant form and process in that which is met. Its product reveals this significance through the expressive imagery of movement, dance, sound, music, drawing, painting, sculpture, poetry, story and drama. *Propositional knowing* 'about' something is intellectual knowing of ideas and theories. Its product is the informative spoken or written

statement. *Practical knowing* is knowing how-to-do something. Its product is a skill, knack or competence – interpersonal, manual, political, technical, transpersonal, and more – supported by a community of practice (Heron, 1981, 1992, 1996a).

Everyone naturally employs these four ways of knowing and tacitly interweaves them in all sorts of ways in everyday life. In co-operative inquiry they become intentional, and we say that knowing will be more valid if the four ways are congruent with each other: if our knowing is grounded in our experience, expressed through our images and stories, understood through theories which make sense to us, and expressed in worthwhile action in our lives. We also think of the intentional use of the ways in terms of a virtuous circle: skilled action leads into enriched encounter, thence into wider imaginal portrayal of the pattern of events, thence into more comprehensive conceptual models, thence into more developed practice, and so on.

EXPERIENTIAL KNOWING

We start from the position that all knowing is based in the *experiential presence* of persons in their world. Any form of inquiry that fails to honour experiential presence – through premature abstraction, conceptualization and measurement, or through a political bias which values the experience only of socially dominant or like-minded groups – ignores the fundamental grounding of all knowing.

Thus we can describe experiential knowing, at its simplest, as my direct acquaintance with that which I meet in my lifeworld: the experience of my presence in relation with the presence of other persons, living beings, places, or things. This kind of knowing is essentially tacit and pre-verbal. It is also profoundly 'real' – sound, solid and vibrant at the moment of experience – yet often elusive to express both to ourselves and to others. Geoff Mead describes the experiential grounding of his own inquiry:

As an integral part of my being in the world, my *living inquiry* is firmly anchored in the bedrock of my experience. ... I have actively sought new experiences and pushed my boundaries considerably in doing so, whether it be ritual menswork, separation and divorce, storytelling performances, or creating and delivering large-scale educational programmes for the police and other public services. ... Without such experiential grounding, I believe that action research remains as speculative and 'theoretical' as its reductionist cousins. (Mead, 2001: 66)

Our warrant for this assertion of the experiential as the ground of knowing is itself fundamentally experiential – although also rooted in a participatory worldview, as we explore below. Our work with co-operative inquiry, in mindfulness practices, ceremony and charismatic embodiment (Heron and Lahood, Chapter 29) and our attempts at aware everyday living all convince us that experiential encounter with the presence of others and of the world is the ground of being and knowing. This encounter is prior to language and art – although it can be symbolized in language and art. Our meeting with the elemental properties of the living world, the I–Thou encounter with a person (or other being), cannot be confused with our symbolic constructs: If you find yourself doubting this, try the simple exercise of opening yourself to the presence of another and compare that with thinking *about* her or him.

Experiential knowing is not a positivist grasping of other things in the world, for we say that the very process of perceiving is a meeting, a transaction, with what there is. When I hold your hand, my experience includes both subjectively shaping you and objectively meeting you. To encounter being or a being is both to image it in my way and to feel its presence, to know that it is there. To experience anything is to participate in it, and to participate is both to mould and to encounter, hence experiential reality is always subjective–objective, relative both to the knower and to what is known. Such encounter has greater immediacy and less mediation than our propositional knowing.

Experiential knowing is thus a ground for the symbolic frameworks of conceptual, propositional knowing, a necessary ground – but not an infallible one, because of the vulnerability of human sensibilities. The validity of the encounter can be described as 'declarative'. Worlds and persons are what we meet, and the reality of the relation of meeting, its qualitative impact, declares the tangible sense of the realness of the presence of each to each, and of each to herself or himself, and all of this in a shared field. Two people or a group in a meeting can open to and feel the quality of this shared field. We can only describe it metaphorically, but we can sense its qualitative shifts as the dynamic of the meeting unfolds. This quality of the field, whether harmonious or tense or joyful or blighted, is a living key to appropriate understanding and action in the situation, and a vital component of our experience of interpersonal reality.

Experiential Knowing and a Participatory Worldview

Experiential knowledge is close to what William James called 'knowledge of acquaintance', and he made the classic distinction between this and 'knowledge-about'. 'All the elementary natures of the world', he says, must be known by acquaintance or not known at all; and it is 'through feelings that we become acquainted with things' (James, 1890: 221).

For Whitehead, perceptual knowledge by acquaintance is rooted in 'prehension': a direct participative, emotional rapport with the environing field of events, rooted in the 'witness of the body' which is continuous with the rest of the natural world. Leslie Paul, following Whitehead, talks of the ineffable bed of sentience, a primary cosmic sensitivity, which gives an understanding of the interrelated web of being in which the organism is suspended (Paul, 1961).

The notion of basic, unitive engagement with the world is also important in the phenomenology of Merleau-Ponty. He argues that all language and discursive knowledge presupposes the pre-objective world of perception, consciousness-world union, which is anterior to every distinction including that of consciousness and nature. It is an unformulated consciousness of the totality which is body-and-world, the body being co-extensive with the entire field of possible perceptions, i.e. the world (Merleau-Ponty, 1962).

Our own view builds on this tradition. We hold that the very foundation of human perceptual sensibility is the capacity for feeling, which we define as a participatory relation with being and beings, integrating the distinctness of knower and known in a relational whole. Experiential knowing is feeling engaged with what there is, participating, through the perceptual process, in the shared presence of mutual encounter. We see this capacity for feeling as the quintessential nature of the life, the living energy, that is within us – the life that is the immanent pole of our embodied spirit (Heron, 1992, 1998).

Our notion of experiential knowing thus points toward a *participatory* view of the world. Our inherited 'Cartesian' worldview tells us the world is made of separate things: the objects of nature are composed of inert matter, operating according to causal laws. But as Thomas Berry puts it, the living world is not a collection of objects: it is a community of subjects of which the human community is part (Berry, 1999; Reason, 2001). Reality is both One and Many: the beings of the world are differentiated centres of consciousness within a unified cosmic presence (Heron, 1992, 1996a, 1998). Freya Matthews and other panpsychic philosophers hold that our primary relationship with our world is erotic: our knowing must be grounded in loving, not manipulation (Mathews, 2003; Skrbina, 2005). This places humans in the web of life as embodied participants, 'living as part of the whole' (Reason, 2005). Buddhist myth offers the image of Indra's net where all things both reflect and are reflected in all. Participation is our nature: we do not stand separate from the cosmos, we evolved with it, participate in it and are part of its creative force. (For further explorations of a participatory worldview see Abram, 1996; Eisler and Loye, 1990; Ferrer, 2002; Goodwin, 1999; Mathews, 2003; Skolimowski, 1994; Skrbina, 2005; Tarnas, 1991, 2000, 2006.)

Experiential Knowing in the Reflection Phases of Inquiry

One of the implications of this view for the practice of co-operative inquiry is that the co-inquirers are present, open to encounter with each other. In a successful inquiry group co-inquirers will develop a sense of pre-conceptual communion or resonance in their shared life-world, as a ground for subsequent reflection together. Of course, our participative worldview suggests that at some level this communion is going on tacitly and unintentionally as the very condition of being in a world. Co-inquirers don't have to generate it, they have only to open to it, honour it and enhance it intentionally and awarely. A variety of rituals and attunement practices can empower this natural process of mutual resonance (Heron, 1998, 1999; Heron and Lahood, Chapter 29).

Inquiry groups will also need to deal along the way quite explicitly with issues of inclusion, control and intimacy (Reason, 2003; Srivastva et al., 1977) for which appropriate facilitation may be needed. This process of interpersonal clearing can be enhanced by adopting further disciplines which provide a fertile ground for opening to communion, practices such as meeting in a circle, sharing time equally, listening attentively, and so on (see, for example, Baldwin, 1996; Randall and Southgate, 1980; McArdle, Chapter 42).

A group of graduate students and faculty at the University of Bath met for a workshop on Power and Participation. When we turned to discuss issues of power and participation within the group the feeling of tension greatly increased and strong feelings were expressed on both sides. We worked hard to understand, holding two disciplines: to listen to each person in turn fully without interruption; and to record their experience clearly in writing on the whiteboard. ... After a while several people commented on the shift in feeling in the group: we were quieter, more appreciative, more deeply understanding both our differences and the shared pattern of experience. In this sense we became more present with each other. (personal notes, Reason, 2005)

Experiential Knowing in the Action Phases of Inquiry

The action phases often involve co-inquirers being busy with their individual action inquiries in everyday life, apart from each other. Their inquiries will be enriched to the extent that they are able to deepen and extend their encounter with their world. We see this as happening in three ways. First, the very fact of being part of an inquiry will alert them to new dimensions of their world: once we join a group of people pursuing similar questions new aspects of our world are inevitably evoked. Indeed, it is often wise in the early stages of an inquiry for participants simply to notice how their new world looks to them. Thus, for example, the young women who accepted Kate McArdle's invitation to join an inquiry into young women in management simply through being part of that group noticed and felt more deeply the casual sexism that characterized their organization (McArdle, 2002, 2004).

Second and most important they can practise the bedrock skill of being present and open, of becoming intentional about, and make explicit in all its fullness, their participation in what is present. This includes open-hearted engagement with the relation of person-to-person meeting, being responsive to the changing qualities of its shared field as vital pointers toward relevant understanding and action in the situation. And third, they need to be alert to a tendency to become so engrossed in their everyday world, so engaged in the moment, that they forget they are part of an inquiry, and their experiential knowing reverts to becoming almost completely tacit. When this happens, interactions later on in reflection phases with other inquirers may enable the qualitative impact of their experiences to be rekindled and revisited.

Experiential Knowing as an Outcome of Inquiry

This kind of outcome is awkward for models of education and research which both presuppose and foster the value of dissociated intellectual excellence, but is fundamental for whole person education, learning and inquiry. Clearly, if the cultivation of radical presence in mutual resonance with other persons and in participative engagement with the world is a basic aspect of the inquiry process, then transformations of personal being, and of empathic relating both with the human world and the more-than-human world, are important outcomes.

These kinds of outcome are affirmed in the Heron and Lahood inquiry into the realm of the between (Chapter 29). Participants in an extended inquiry into transpersonal activities in everyday life agreed that transformations of personal being – e.g. 'a very important integration of deep face-to-face intimacy and the transpersonal' – were the most basic kind of outcome of the inquiry (Heron, 1998: 183). In a very different way, transformations of presence are evident as outcomes of the MSc in Responsibility and Business Practice at the University of Bath, which draws strongly on action research and experiential knowing in its educational principles (Coleman and Marshall, in preparation) and in the work of 'learning to love our black selves, described by Taj Johns in Chapter 32.

Such outcomes may be qualitatively specific to the focus of *any* kind of inquiry and, together with the practical life-skills that are co-involved with them, validate an inquiry in quite basic and long-lasting ways, through living repercussions and ripples, even if there are no written or presentational outcomes of any kind.

PRESENTATIONAL KNOWING

Presentational knowing is made manifest in images which articulate experiential knowing, shaping what is inchoate into a communicable form, and which are expressed nondiscursively through the visual arts, music, dance and movement, and discursively in poetry, drama and the continuously creative capacity of the human individual and social mind to tell stories. In all civilizations these products have been developed through imaginative discipline into a wide range of sophisticated cultural forms that independently symbolize our experience of the human condition. Presentational knowing is a fundamental part of the process of inquiry, and its expression is both a meaningful outcome in its own right, and a vital precursor to propositional outcomes.

However, the process of presentational knowing of our world, through intuiting significant patterns in our immediate experience, can have its great cognitive potential constrained by the conceptual power of language. The imaginal mind is continually creative in the transaction between the psyche and being, generating the visual, auditory and tactile images that participate in and disclose a world (Heron, 1992: 138–50). But this imaginal participation is entirely unconscious: I am only aware of the image, the outcome, and not of the imaging process. Moreover, I convert the image into an appearance of a world that seems to be quite independent of anything going on in me. This reification is massively reinforced by the use of language and the way in which its concepts and class names become embedded as an interpretative layer in our perceiving. This process of conceptualizing perception disrupts its transactional, participatory nature, breaking up the primordial synthesis of perceiver and perceived, and leading to a split between an alienated subject and an independent object (Heron, 1992: 25).

Once we enter the worlds of presentational knowing permeated by propositional knowing, the arguments of the language turn and the social construction of knowledge apply (see Chapter 10): knowledge mediated by language is a cultural construct formed from a certain perspective – in modern times a broadly Cartesian worldview, as mentioned

above – and for certain purposes (although, as we have argued, constructionist views tend to be deficient in any acknowledgement of experiential knowing; Heron and Reason, 1997).

The importance of presentational forms of knowing in their own right, and of releasing them from overcontrolling conceptual-rational dominance, has become increasingly apparent in the social sciences in recent years – notice for example Denzin and Lincoln's emphasis on the 'crisis of representation' (Denzin and Lincoln, 2005a: 18). Jerome Bruner makes the distinction between Mythos and Logos:

> There are two modes of cognitive functioning, two modes of thought, each providing distinctive ways of ordering experience, of constructing reality. The two (though complementary) are irreducible to one another. Efforts to reduce one mode to the other or to ignore one at the expense of the other inevitably fail to capture the rich diversity of thought. … Perhaps Richard Rorty is right in characterizing the mainstream of Anglo-American philosophy (which, on the whole, he rejects) as preoccupied with the epistemological question of how to know truth – which he contrasts with the broader question of how we come to endow experience with meaning, which is the question that preoccupies the poet and the storyteller. (Bruner, 1988: 99–100)

For Bruner stories are of the essence of Mythos, keeping the process of knowing open and creative. He argues that 'It is part of the magic of well-wrought stories that they keep these two landscapes intertwined, making the knower and the known inseparable' (2002: 27). And he makes the point that while we may 'come to conceive of the 'real world' in a manner that fits the stories we tell about it', it is nevertheless our good fortune that 'we are forever tempted to tell different stories' about the same events in the same world (2002: 103).

Presentational Knowing in the Reflection Phases of Inquiry

We argued above for the importance of co-inquirers developing a sense of pre-conceptual communion or resonance in their shared life-world, as a ground for subsequent reflection together. Presentational form can be of profound importance in shaping this communion: the possibility of mutually participative open encounter will be enhanced if co-inquirers meet in patterns which emphasize equality and mutuality. This may mean meeting in a circle of chairs or cushions without tables; with flowers or other centrepieces; with facilitation that is light and encouraging; with time shared reasonably equally between participants; and so on. For the patterns we manifest together in space and time – our postures, gestures and spatial relationships, our verbal distribution of time – symbolize fundamental qualities of our relating, and can be seen as a first, basic form of presentational knowing. Christina Baldwin and her colleagues exemplify this well in their process of 'calling the circle' (Baldwin, 1996; Baldwin and Linnea, 1999). Heron and Lahood in Chapter 29 recount how presentational forms of toning in mutual resonance, and of posture, gesture and motion in aware spatial interaction, can open up an empowering presence between those involved.

As the inquiry process develops, cycling between action and reflection, presentational knowing is the most basic way of making sense of our experience. Often this is in the form of stories which we bring back to our colleagues in the inquiry group. We will not rush quickly into propositions, but will hold open the presentational and imaginal space and allow it to do its sense-making magic, allowing our stories to resonate with those of other group members. We can play with the stories with a variety of storytelling practices (Mead, 2001; Reason and Hawkins, 1988). We can draw the stories, sculpt them in clay or psychodramatically with our bodies – thus countering our tendency to attribute one set of meanings to experience. In some forms of inquiry (see in particular Chapters 30, 34, 35) the use of presentational form such as theatre becomes a major vehicle for opening participants to new ways of seeing their experience.

Kate McArdle describes the importance of storytelling as a lead-in to the propositional for the members of a co-operative inquiry of young women in management (YoWiM).

> Taking time to 'tell our stories' mattered, and required much facilitative attention. … Through this process we were able to then create shared meaning and understanding around what we were talking about. This led us to move into the propositional – being able to name behaviours, processes and actions described in the stories and to feel that we were 'all on board' with what these names meant. (McArdle, in preparation)

Often the storytelling process is powerfully simple.

> The co-operative inquiry into holistic medicine sought among other things to understand the meaning of 'spirit' in general medical practice. Diana came to the group with a deeply moving account of a terminally ill woman who learned through a dream to let go of concerns for her family and die in peace surrounded by them. … The directness and simplicity of this story produced a prolonged silence in the group. It stimulated other doctors to remember and tell of similar quite simple times when 'spirit' had entered medical practice. It led the group to consider that 'spirit in general practice' was not esoteric, but could be seen as an everyday affair. (for full account of inquiry, see Heron and Reason, 1985)

Yorks and Kasl (2002) in their review of eight collaborative inquiries stress the role of presentational knowing in counterbalancing traditional academic overreliance on critical discourse and analytic forms of knowing. The diverse inquiries used video, film, a Brahms concerto for violin, reproductions of paintings, guided visualization, symbolic ritual movement, Black Angel cards, a game of tag, clay sculpture, watercolour design, birthing metaphors, stories about family, ancestors and progeny yet to be born. Such imaginal methods, Yorks and Kasl affirm, evoke experience, are a pathway for emotion, clarify and codify experience, and are pivotal in providing access to holistic knowing.

Presentational Knowing in the Action Phases of the Inquiry

Presentational knowing can help bring a quality of curiosity to the action phase of inquiry. If we are not going to find out what we already know, just as we must open ourselves to new encounters and new experiential knowing, we must also be open to new stories and metaphors, new patterns in space and time, with which to give form to that experience. In order to do this we may find it helpful to experiment with new presentational forms in our encounters with others

- Doctors in the holistic medicine inquiry experimented with dressing informally, re-arranging their offices, and with different non-medical ways of asking patients to tell of their ailments. (Heron and Reason, 1985; Reason, 1988a)
- The YoWiM group, seeking to engage other young women in the organization, changed the layout of the meeting room from its usual formality and decorated it with flowers and posters to create an atmosphere conducive to open conversation. (McArdle, 2004)
- In the Realm of the Between inquiry, presentational forms of toning, posture, gesture, movement and percussive rhythm themselves constitute the charismatic action phase of the inquiry. (Heron and Lahood, Chapter 29)
- Jennifer Mullett, in Chapter 30, describes how visual art, poetry and song were used by women in mid life as part of a women's health in mid-life project.

Action phases include keeping records of actions taken and of their significance – as reports to bring to subsequent reflection phases. There is great and highly relevant scope here for the use of presentational forms: dramatic accounts, poetic evocations, diagrams and line drawings, coloured graphics, choreographed mime, audiovisual recordings, and more. These are ways of keeping alive the comprehensive qualitative richness of actions and experiences more effectively than may be the case with the use of nothing but spare and bare verbal jottings in a diary.

Presentational Knowing as an Outcome of Inquiry

Traditionally, research findings are 'written up' in propositional form with evidential support from empirical data. If we take seriously

the interplay of Mythos and Logos, we can see that discoveries of a co-operative inquiry process may also be expressed in presentational form, either as stand-alone expressions or in conjunction with propositional text. A number of doctoral dissertations at CARPP include such presentational form. Geoff Mead (2001: 59–65) has worked this genre thoroughly, explicitly evoking the interplay of Mythos and Logos. This thesis includes, among other stories, *'Postcards from the Edge'* in which he seeks to 'deftly integrate' living and telling by offering a series of accounts of loving relationships over his life; *'The Men's Room'*, with narratives about men's retreats, men's support groups, friendship, and a co-operative inquiry into men's development in organizations (pp. 82–121). The Leadership for a Changing World programme (see Chapter 28) has posted on its website narrative accounts by members of co-operative inquiry groups. Gillian Chowns worked with children to produce a participatory video (Chapter 39), and Michelle Fine and Maria Torre theorize different forms of product in Chapter 27.

When co-operative inquiries are undertaken within postgraduate degrees, there is a noticeable tendency for discursive presentational outcomes, that is, stories and narratives (always together with propositonal outcomes), to be used rather than nondiscursive ones such as the graphic and plastic arts, dance and movement, and music. It indicates once again the dominating power of the written word prevailing in our academic institutions. The nondiscursive forms are more freely used in the ongoing reflection and action phases, where issues of readily assessing a final degree-bearing outcome are not at stake.

PROPOSITIONAL KNOWING

Propositional knowing is knowing 'about' something in intellectual terms of ideas and theories. It is expressed in propositions, statements which use language to assert facts about the world, laws that make generalizations about facts and theories that organize the laws. This is very familiar territory, as the propositional is the main kind of knowledge accepted in our society – not only in academic theories, but in the statements of politicians, propagandists, managers, marketeers and others who would define our world; and indeed in the more or less explicit theories each of us carry around which define who we are and the kind of world we tell ourselves we live in. In propositional form, 'knowing' easily becomes reified as 'knowledge'; and in this sense 'knowledge is power' and constitutes what Foucault (1980) described as 'regimes of truth' which create our reality.

The co-operative inquiry process can be very liberating in using different terms to 'redescribe' experience (to borrow a phrase from Rorty, 1989) in ways that are both more liberating and more fundamentally informative. Propositional knowledge is indeed essential for naming, in a well-rounded and grounded way, the basic features of our being-in-a-world in order to empower effective action in it.

However, propositional knowing needs handling with care, especially in the language-driven worlds of late-modernity. It has great conceptual power to divide the world into isolated mental subjects and independent non-mental objects. This split between humanity and nature, and the arrogation of all mind to humans, is what Weber meant by the disenchantment of the world and, we would argue, is one of the fundamental origins of the current ecological devastation. In contrast, writers since Gregory Bateson (1972) have argued that mind is immanent in ecological systems, and modern complexity theories demonstrate how the natural world is in a continual process of creative self-organization, a self-creative autopoesis (Maturana and Varela, 1987).

This process of objectification has been applied also to relations between persons. Traditional social science research is founded on the notion that the researcher alone does all the thinking associated with a research project, deciding what questions to explore, developing theory, asking questions, making sense of what is discovered.

The so-called 'subject' is the passive respondent to this attention and is seen as making no intelligent contribution to the research endeavour. Co-operative inquiry, along with all other forms of participative inquiry, aims to break this 'monopoly of knowledge' (Fals Borda and Rahman, 1991); and participative forms of social action, closely related to participative inquiry, aim in similar fashion to restore a sense of self-direction to those disempowered by this kind of political cognitive monopoly (e.g. New Economics Foundation, 1998).

In developing and using propositional knowing we must continually remind ourselves that 'the map is not the territory', as Korzybski pointed out to us a long time ago. But our tendency to confuse map and territory is usually closely linked up with social power (see Gaventa and Cornwall, Chapter 11 in this volume).

Propositional Knowing in the Reflection Phases of Inquiry

Co-operative-inquiry practice emphasizes the importance of research cycling so that propositions are continually tested in practice and thus rooted back in experiential knowing. This counters the tendency for ideas to fly off into a life of their own and to keep them grounded in experience and in participative relationship. Emphasis is placed on the epistemological heterogeneity which the whole of the extended epistemology articulates – the mutually enhancing effect between the four ways of knowing – rather than valuing propositional expression over and above the other forms.

On the other hand, propositional sense-making is important in giving the cyclic process focus and clarity, in transferring learning from a previous action cycle to fruitful planning of the next, and in producing carefully worded outcomes that can effectively influence social policy and social change. Charles and Glennie (2002) describe how the clarity of propositional knowing re-energized a tired inquiry group exploring the implementation of guidelines for child protection. Taking an active role as facilitators, they encouraged the group to identify four key inquiry questions and choose one to take forward. By doing this 'the group started to own the inquiry process and steer it, directing their energies into a sense making exercise' (Charles and Glennie, 2002: 216).

Propositional Knowing as an Outcome of Inquiry

While co-operative inquiry emphasizes the primacy of the practical (for which see below), nearly all inquiries have some kind of informative purpose: they aim to provide insight into social relations and to offer propositions and theories that will aid understanding. Such propositional outcomes are rarely simply descriptive but aim to be critical and emancipatory. They will resist the 'naturalization' of the social order which sees the 'socially/historically constructed order … as necessary, natural, rational and self-evident'; the domination of the interests of the powerful and the suppression of conflicting interests; the 'domination of instrumental reasoning'; and the 'orchestration of consent' whereby existing power relations and definitions of reality are taken for granted (Alvesson and Deetz, 2005: 74; see also Kemmis, Chapter 8).

We affirm that there are five main kinds of important propositional outcomes of a co-operative inquiry: those mentioned above that are informative about the domain or field of inquiry; those that report on the transformative practices undertaken, and on their effects; those that describe the inquiry process; those that evaluate the soundness of the inquiry process; and those that evaluate the soundness of its informative and transformative outcomes (Heron, 1996a: 109–10). However, it is also important to note that each of these kinds can be complemented by (as mentioned above under presentational outcomes), or even entirely replaced by, appropriate presentational outcomes.

PRACTICAL KNOWING

Practical knowing is knowing how-to-do, how to engage in, some class of action or practice. It is evident in the skills and competencies the inquirers develop, both in knowing how to do co-operative inquiry, and in knowing how to do those transformative actions in the world that the inquiry is engaged with.

As we have argued elsewhere, the argument for the primacy of the practical owes a lot to the philosophy of John Macmurray (1957), who holds that 'I do' instead of 'I think' is the starting point and centre of reference for grasping the form of the personal: the self is an agent and exists only as an agent. The self as thinking subject cannot exist as subject; it can be subject only because it is an agent. The self as knowing subject is in and for the self as agent. Knowing in its fullness is consummated in and through agency, and pure thought divorced from action leads to a lesser kind of knowing that is secondary, derivative, abstract, and negative.

We make a similar point that there is an 'up-hierarchy' of knowledge grounded in experiential knowing, which unfurls in presentational and then in propositional ways of knowing, and is consummated and fulfilled through practice. Practical knowledge, the realm of skills, is immediately supported by propositional knowing – i.e. by descriptive and prescriptive concepts and schema – but necessarily goes beyond these into the autonomous ineffability of knacks, of the very act of skillful doing. Such practical knowing is embodied in the individual; and in a shared 'culture of competence' in which particular practices are not only supported and valued but are embodied in the interactions of a whole community (Heron, 1992, 1996b).

Traditional academic thinking has difficulty with the notion of practical knowing, because, as Rorty (1999) argues, it is attached to the idea of theory as representing the world. If we give up the idea of knowledge as an attempt to represent reality and argue for the primacy of the practical, the relationship between truth claims and the rest of the world become causal rather than representational, and the issue becomes whether our propositional knowing provides reliable guides to the practical realization of our values.

Practical Knowing in the Reflective Phrases of Inquiry

The reflection phases of the inquiry, where co-researchers are meeting together, are important crucibles for the development of practical knowing. As we discussed in the section on experiential knowing, the quality of being together in fully mutual presence allows for the emergence of an attitude of inquiry, an open curiosity toward each other and to the experiences each brings to the group. Group members will develop and integrate skills of inquiry – both personal skills of aware openness, reflection and experimentation, and the skills associated with opening an inquiring space for others.

There is a specific way of practical knowing that is central to establishing full reciprocity among co-inquirers: knowing how to make decisions together. This skill involves a practical interplay, *within each co-inquirer, and between all,* of four basic political values: autonomy, active hierarchy, passive hierarchy, and co-operation (Heron, 2001: 122–3). Each person, in contributing to group decision-making, can move freely between four positions, and the first three positions are precursors to, and components of, the culminating fourth:

- Autonomy: I can identify my own idiosyncratic true needs and interests;
- Active hierarchy: I can identify options that promote the true needs and interests of all of us, individually and collectively;
- Passive hierarchy: I can identify an active-hierarchy proposal made by someone else as one that I can freely and authentically follow;
- Co-operation: I can co-operate with – that is, listen to, engage with, and negotiate agreed decisions with – my peers, celebrating diversity and difference as integral to genuine unity.

Active hierarchy here is the creative leadership which seeks to promote the values of autonomy and co-operation in a peer-to-peer inquiry. Such leadership is exercised in two ways. First, by the one or more people who take initiatives to set up the inquiry. And second, as spontaneously emerging and moving leadership among the peers, when anyone proposes initiatives that further enhance the autonomy and co-operation of all participating members.

The skill required for an individual person to manage these four positions, and to keep them in creative interplay while at the same time interacting with several other persons each of whom is busy with the same multiple interplay, is considerable. While there can be agreed procedural guidelines to support the process, the challenge to each person (and especially initiating leaders) to modify the demands of ego in the service of collaboration is formidable. Hence there can be occasions when confusion, chaos, individual frustration and interpersonal tension become acute – although these may also be fruitful opportunities for letting go of egoic compulsions, and for remarkable liberating zest when the breakthrough into creative and expanded social synchrony occurs.

This practical know-how has three areas of application in the reflection phase of an inquiry. The first is in decisions about managing the sequence of procedures for the whole phase; the second is in decisions about what sense co-inquirers have made of the previous action phase; and the third is in decisions to do with forward planning of the next action phase of the inquiry.

Practical Knowing in the Action Phases of Inquiry

What skills are needed in the action phase? In the informative strand of an inquiry, which asks whether, in the light of our experience, the world is the way we envisaged it, we need the skill of radical perception, being fully present and imaginally open to our experience, together with the ability to bracket off habitual conceptual frames and try out new frameworks, new ways of enacting the present situation. In the transformative strand, we need the skill of radical practice, the ability to maintain, while we act, an alert, intentional dynamic congruence among the motives of the action, its goals, the strategy or means it employs, its guiding norms (technical and moral), its ongoing effects, our beliefs about its context (Heron, 1996a). Torbert and Taylor (Chapter 16) describe this as congruence between the four territories of experience: the outside world, one's own sensed behaviour and feeling, the realm of thought, and attention/intention.

On the wider inquiry canvas, there are skills to exercise in our fundamental choices *about* action phases. How many action phases do we need for this particular inquiry and on what time scale? What is the appropriate balance between action and reflection? Do we use the action phases to converge on an increasingly focused question or to diverge over several main facets of the inquiry topic? Shall we take a more Apollonian or Dionysian approach to action? The Apollonian mode uses the reflection phase systematically to preplan, in the light of a review of the previous action phase, what is done in the next action phase; the Dionysian mode uses more presentational forms of knowing to review the previous action phase, and intentionally allows that learning to emerge in creative actions that arise spontaneously in response to future situations. Both have their place, and no inquiry is likely to follow a purely Dionysian or Apollonian approach (see Heron, 1996a; Heron and Reason, 2001/2006 for a fuller exploration of these issues).

Practical Knowing as an Outcome of Inquiry

The most basic, but not the only, outcome of co-operative inquiry is a transformative one, which crucially involves individual change of behaviour – the acquisition of new skills, new know-how – supported by peer inquirers. Thus

Geoff Mead (2001) relates how the inquiry context enabled a constraining and controlling manager to receive and elicit feedback that he could use to develop a more spacious and empowering style in his relations with staff.

Important issues then arise about the relation between changed individual practice and the occupational culture or sub-culture within which it is set. Traditionally there has been a fundamental asymmetry between an individual skill and such cultural development. Any radical agenda of transforming practice rested exclusively with the individual pioneer. Even where cultures of competence have promoted research and development, the breakthrough has come through the efforts of one or two individuals, sometimes vying with each other.

With the advent of co-operative inquiry and related forms of participative research, cultures of competence can become self-transforming *as collectives.* A co-operative inquiry group that is busy with transforming practice within a culture is involved with three interdependent kinds of skills outcomes, three kinds of transformation: new skills in transformative collaborative inquiry, new individual and co-operative working skills, new skills in regenerating the culture of competence within which those skills have their home. Thus a group of doctors who participated in the whole person medicine inquiry (Heron and Reason, 1985) went on to found the British Holistic Medical Association on participatory principles. Torbert has made a similar point in his emphasis on the development of communities of inquiry (Torbert, 2000, 2004); Gustavsen et al. (Chapter 4 in this volume) argue that action research must help develop the wider social movement within which separate inquiries are rooted.

INQUIRY CYCLING THROUGH THE EXTENDED EPISTEMOLOGY

We have articulated some of the key characteristics of four ways of knowing which together constitute cycles of action and reflection. Each of the ways of knowing makes its own contribution to the quality of the knowing that results from the inquiry cycle and is of value on its own account and in its contribution to the cycle as a whole.

Thus quality in *experiential knowing* is rooted in the openness through which we encounter the presence of the world. The threat to quality knowing here is that co-researchers create a defensive inquiry which guards against the discovery of the novel and different, and which reproduces in encounter the habitual social and personal taken-for-granted. Quality inquiry will courageously challenge habits, seek new encounters and deepen contact with experience.

Quality in *presentational knowing* arises through intuitive playfulness so that expressive forms articulate experiential knowing in creative ways, opening inquiry both back toward deeper experience and forward to new ideas and theories. The danger here is that co-researchers will stay with the same old stories and images and thus recreate existing realities and confirm existing beliefs. Quality inquiry will actively experiment with redescription and draw on a range of presentational forms to turn stories, accounts and images upside down and inside out in the pursuit of creative expression and imaginal range and depth.

Quality in *propositional knowing* articulates presentational form through conceptual schema. It depends on clarity of thinking and critical sense-making and carries with it a strong awareness of the links between propositional knowledge and social power. It will refuse to be held within a hegemonic paradigm and uncritical acceptance of taken-for-granted theories (and its identical opposite, the uncritical acceptance of the currently fashionable oppositional position!), but will engage accepted theory critically and forge new theoretical perspectives.

Quality in *practical knowing* is expressed in the ability of individuals, organizations and communities to accomplish worthwhile, desirable individual, social and ecological ends. It is rooted in the skills and knacks of individuals and more widely in cultural practices that support and co-ordinate such skills. The danger is always that individuals and groups will fool themselves about the efficacy of their actions and support practices for which there is no good evidence. The key quality question is whether, through cycles of action and reflection, sufficient good evidence is produced to support the practical claims that are made.

As we have argued, there is a strong case for seeing practical knowing as primary, the consummation of our inquiry as worthwhile action in the world, guided by propositional categories, inspired by presentational forms and rooted in and continually refreshed through experiential encounter. When co-inquirers are working together, there is a dynamic interplay between their actions and their state of being, mediated by intuitively grasping a significant pattern in their current behaviour and by conceptually naming the quality it reveals. Once this quality is identified and agreed, the inquirers can negotiate action to enhance or modify it. This alters their behaviour and the quality of the meeting. Co-sensitivity to the changing interactive qualities within a shared field, and co-acting to develop there an overall quality of human flourishing, are at the heart of excellence in a co-operative inquiry. In inquiry as in life, the basic call is to act intelligently, sympathetically, and creatively together to enhance the quality of our relationships with each other and our world.

REFERENCES

Abram, D. (1996) *The Spell of the Sensuous: Perception and Language in a More than Human World*. New York: Pantheon.

Alvesson, M. and Deetz, S. (2005) 'Critical theory and post-modernism: approaches to organizational studies', in C. Grey and H. Willmott (eds), *Critical Management Studies*. Oxford: Oxford University Press. pp. 60–106.

Baldwin, C. (1996) *Calling the Circle: the First and Future Culture*. Bath: Gateway Books.

Baldwin, C. and Linnea, A. (1999) *PeerSpirit Council Management in Business, Corporations and Organizations*. Langley, WA: PeerSpirit Inc.

Bateson, G. (1972) *Steps to an Ecology of Mind*. San Francisco, CA: Chandler.

Berry, T. (1999) *The Great Work: Our Way into the Future*. New York: Bell Tower.

Bruner, J. (1988) 'Two modes of thought', in N. Mercer (ed.), *Language and Literacy from an Educational Perspective, Vol. 1: Language Studies*. Milton Keynes: Open University Press. pp. 99–112.

Bruner, J. (2002) *Making Stories: Law, Literature, Life*. New York: Farrar, Straus Giroux.

Charles, M. and Glennie, S. (2002) 'Co-operative inquiry: changing interprofessional practice', *Systemic practice and Action Research*, 15 (3): 207–21.

Coleman, G. and Marshall, J. (in preparation) *Doing Management Education Differently: Course Participants' Experiences of a Management Degree Addressing Sustainability and Corporate Responsibility Issues*: Centre for Action Research in Professional Practice, University of Bath, UK.

Denzin, N.K. and Lincoln, Y.S. (2005a) 'Introduction: the discipline and practice of qualitative research', in N.K. Denzin and Y.S. Lincoln (eds), *The Sage Handbook of Qualitative Research, 3rd edn*. Thousand Oaks, CA: Sage. pp. 1–32.

Denzin, N.K. and Lincoln, Y.S. (eds) (2005b) *The Sage Handbook of Qualitative Research, 3rd edn*. Thousand Oaks, CA: Sage.

Eisler, R. and Loye, D. (1990) *The Partnership Way*. New York: Harper.

Fals Borda, O. and Rahman, M.A. (eds) (1991) *Action and Knowledge: Breaking the Monopoly with Participatory Action Research*. New York: Intermediate Technology Publications/Apex Press.

Ferrer, J.N. (2002) 'Toward a participatory vision of human spirituality', *ReVision*, 24 (2): 15–26.

Foucault, M. (1980) 'Truth and power', in C. Gordon (ed.), *Power/Knowledge: Selected Interviews and Other Writings, 1972–1977, by Michel Foucault*. New York: Pantheon. pp. 109–33.

Goodwin, B.C. (1999) 'From control to participation via a science of qualities', *Revision*, 21 (4): 26–35.

Heron, J. (1971) *Experience and Method: an Inquiry into the Concept of Experiential Research*: Human Potential Research Project, University of Surrey.

Heron, J. (1981) 'Philosophical basis for a new paradigm', in P. Reason and J. Rowan (eds), *Human Inquiry: a Sourcebook of New Paradigm Research*. Chichester: Wiley. pp. 19–36.

Heron, J. (1992) *Feeling and Personhood: Psychology in Another Key*. London: Sage.

Heron, J. (1996a) *Co-operative Inquiry: Research into the Human Condition*. London: Sage.

Heron, J. (1996b) 'Quality as primacy of the practical', *Qualitative Inquiry*, 2 (1): 41–56.

Heron, J. (1998) *Sacred Science: Person-Centred Inquiry into the Spiritual and the Subtle*. Ross-Wye: PCCS Books.

Heron, J. (1999) *The Complete Facilitator's Handbook*. London: Kogan Page.

Heron, J. (2001) *Helping the Client: A Creative Practical Guide*. London: Sage.

Heron, J. and Reason, P. (eds) (1985) *Whole Person Medicine: a Co-operative Inquiry*. British Postgraduate Medical Federation, University of London.

Heron, J. and Reason, P. (1997) 'A participatory inquiry paradigm', *Qualitative Inquiry*, 3 (3): 274–94.

Heron, J. and Reason, P. (2001/2006) 'The practice of co-operative inquiry: research "with" rather than "on" people', in P. Reason and H. Bradbury (eds), *Handbook of Action Research: Participative Inquiry and Practice*. London: Sage. pp. 179–88. Also published in P. Reason and H. Bradbury (eds), *Handbook of Action Research: The Concise Paperback Edition*. London: Sage. pp. 144–54.

James, W. (1890) *The Principles of Psychology, Vol. 1*. New York: Holt, Rinehart & Winston.

McArdle, K.L. (2002) 'Establishing a co-operative inquiry group: the perspective of a "first-time" inquirer', *Systemic Practice and Action Research*, 15 (3): 177–89.

McArdle, K.L. (2004) 'In-powering spaces: a co-operative inquiry with young women in management.' Unpublished PhD, University of Bath, UK.

McArdle, K.L. (in preparation) *Naming as Knowing: Participatory Methodology as In-powering Practice*.

Macmurray, J. (1957) *The Self as Agent*. London: Faber & Faber.

Mathews, F. (2003) *For Love of Matter: a Contemporary Panpsychism*. Albany, NY: SUNY Press.

Maturana, H.R. and Varela, F.J. (1987) *The Tree of Knowledge: the Biological Roots of Human Understanding*. Boston, MA: Shambhala.

Mead, G. (2001) 'Unlatching the gate: realising my scholarship of living inquiry.' Unpublished PhD, University of Bath, UK.

Merleau-Ponty, M. (1962) *Phenomenology of Perception* (trans.C. Smith). London: Routledge Kegan Paul.

New Economics Foundation (1998) *Participation Works: 21 Techniques of Community Participation for the 21st Century*. London: New Economics Foundation.

Paul, L. (1961) *Persons and Perception*. London: Faber.

Randall, R. and Southgate, J. (1980) *Co-operative and Community Group Dynamics ... Or Your Meetings Needn't Be So Appalling*. London: Barefoot Books.

Reason, P. (1988a) 'Whole person medical practice', in P. Reason (ed.), *Human Inquiry in Action*. London: Sage. pp. 102–26.

Reason, P. (ed.) (1988b) *Human Inquiry in Action: Developments in New Paradigm Research*. London: Sage.

Reason, P. (ed.) (1994) *Participation in Human Inquiry*. London: Sage.

Reason, P. (1998) 'Co-operative inquiry as a discipline of professional practice', *Journal of Interprofessional Care*, 12 (4): 419–36.

Reason, P. (1999) 'Integrating action and reflection through co-operative inquiry', *Management Learning Special Issue: The Action Dimension in Management: Diverse Approaches to Research, Teaching and Development*, 30 (2): 207–27.

Reason, P. (2001) 'Earth community: interview with Thomas Berry', *Resurgence*, 204: 10–14.

Reason, P. (2003) 'Doing co-operative inquiry', in J. Smith (ed.), *Qualitative Psychology: a Practical Guide to Methods*. London: Sage. pp. 205–31.

Reason, P. (2005) 'Living as part of the whole', *Journal of Curriculum and Pedagogy*, 2 (2): 35–41.

Reason, P. (2006) 'Choice and quality in action research practice', *Journal of Management Inquiry*, 15 (2): 187–203.

Reason, P., and Hawkins, P. (1988) 'Storytelling as inquiry', in P. Reason (ed.), *Human Inquiry in Action*. London: Sage. pp. 79–101.

Reason, P. and Torbert, W.R. (2001) 'The action turn: toward a transformational social science', *Concepts and Transformations*, 6 (1): 1–37.

Rorty, R. (1989) *Contingency, Irony, and Solidarity*. Cambridge: Cambridge University Press.

Rorty, R. (1999) *Philosophy and Social Hope*. London: Penguin Books.

Skolimowski, H. (1994) *The Participatory Mind*. London: Arkana.

Skrbina, D. (2005) *Panpsychism in the West*. Cambridge, MA: MIT Press.

Srivastva, S., Obert, S.L. and Neilson, E. (1977) 'Organizational analysis through group processes: a theoretical perspective', in C.L. Cooper (ed.), *Organizational Development in the UK and USA*. London: Macmillan. pp. 83–111.

Tarnas, R. (1991) *The Passion of the Western Mind*. New York: Ballantine.

Tarnas, R. (2000) 'A new synthesis', *Resurgence*, 199: 8–11.

Tarnas, R. (2006) *Cosmos and Psyche*. New York: Viking.

Torbert, W.R. (2000) 'The challenge of creating a community of inquiry among scholar-consultants critiquing one another's theories-in-practice', in F. Sherman and W.R. Torbert (eds), *Transforming Social Inquiry, Transforming Social Action: New Paradigms for Crossing the Theory/Practice Divide in Universities and Communities*. Norwood, MA: Kluwer Academic. pp. 161–89.

Torbert, W.R. (2004) *Action Inquiry: The Secret of Timely and Transforming Leadership*. San Francisco, CA: Berrett-Koehler.

Yorks, L. and Kasl, E. (eds) (2002) *Collaborative Inquiry as a Strategy for Adult Learning*. San Francisco, CA: Jossey Bass.

25

Action Research in Healthcare

Ian Hughes

This chapter provides specific recommendations for how to do good action research in the context of healthcare. It links to other appropriate AR practices as well as offering guidelines for intervention in diverse settings and questions for developing quality.

STATEMENT OF MAIN THEME

In this chapter I attempt to provide specific recommendations for how to do good action research in healthcare contexts, concrete guidelines for interventions, and explicit links to other AR practices. Action research has applications in healthcare as diverse as HIV/AIDs education in Tanzania (Mabala and Allen, 2002) and Ghana (Mill, 2001) and with prisoners in Malaysia (Townsend, 2001); improving care in nursing homes in Australia (Street, 1999) and the USA (Keatinge et al., 2000) and in British hospitals (Burrows, 1996; Crowley, 1996; Johns and Kingston, 1990); mosquito control in Malaysia (Crabtree et al., 2001); and supporting community-based health initiatives in all parts of the world.

The World Health Organization (1946) declares that 'health is a state of complete physical, mental and social well-being and not merely the absence of disease or infirmity'. Our health as individuals and communities depends on environmental factors; the qualities of relationships; our beliefs and attitudes; as well as bio-medical factors. To understand our health we must see ourselves as interdependent with human and non-human elements in the systems in which we participate. This holistic way of understanding health, looking at the whole person in context, is congruent with the participative paradigm informing this Handbook (see Introduction, Chapter 1; Reason and Bradbury, 2001/2006a). Health professionals, clients and communities are all part of a larger system (or system of systems), which we help to shape or influence through our actions, as it shapes and influences us. We cannot frame the health professional, the intervention and the client as independent

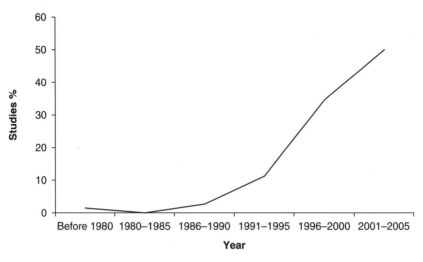

Figure 25.1 *Publication dates of community-based participatory research reports*
Source: based on Viswanathan et al., 2004a: 59, projected to 2005

and separate entities. They are mutually interdependent and participating actors in a larger system.

There is compelling evidence that factors including poverty, inadequate housing, air pollution, income inequality, racism, lack of employment opportunities, and powerlessness are associated with poor health outcomes and contribute to the growing health gap between rich and poor, white and nonwhite, urban and rural, North and South. Excluded communities have skills, strengths, and resources such as supportive relationships, community capacity, committed leaders, and community-based organizations to address problems and support health (Eng and Parker, 1994). Systematic reviews show increased use of participatory action research (PAR) in public and community health (Viswanathan et al., 2004a), health promotion (Green et al., 1995), hospitals (Waterman et al., 2001) and institutional settings to address these systemic health inequalities.

In healthcare, the participatory worldview which underlies action research (Reason and Bradbury, 2001/2006b) and the positivist paradigm underlying experimental research are in close relationship with each other. As I illustrate in Figure 25.2, there is not a wide gulf between positivist or bio-medical approaches and participative approaches to research, but participation, action and research can be combined, merged or separated in creative and flexible ways. Until maybe a decade ago action research and participatory approaches were a 'hidden curriculum' (Eikeland, 2001) in the health professions, with relatively few published reports. This is changing. A systematic review of community-based participatory health research in the USA shows half of all studies meeting their criteria have been published after 2000 (Figure 25.1).

CHOOSING ACTION RESEARCH

The contents pages of this volume show that action research is not one unified thing. The path of choices towards an action research project cannot be mapped in a simple decision tree, showing binary choices among alternative ways of doing research or engaging in action. Participation, action and research are combined in many ways in healthcare, and researchers may be confused about what counts as action research.

An Example

It is not possible to present a typical example of action research in healthcare, because the field is too varied, and not possible to select one outstanding example as criteria vary according to the purpose and situation of each project. Because there is not room for a full account here, I have chosen a project which is well reported (Maglajlic and RTK PAR UNICEF BiH Team, 2004; Maglajlic and Tiffany, 2006; Social Solutions, 2003a, 2003b; Zarchin, 2004) so that interested readers can follow up in greater detail.

In 2003 UNICEF initiated a participatory action research project to develop communication strategies for prevention of HIV/AIDS among adolescents in Bosnia Herzegovina. In each of three towns, the UNICEF Head Researcher worked with a non-government organization, which nominated a team of five young people as a research team. In the research teams, facilitator roles were split into different tasks, such as group process facilitator, record keeper and 'devil's advocate', and rotated among team members. Each team initiated a local research group of 20 young people. The average age of local research group members was 17, with a range from 13 to 19. (Maglajlic and RTK PAR UNICEF BiH Team, 2004).

A toolkit, including PAR guidelines and workshop activities, was developed as a resource for members of the local research groups (Social Solutions, 2003a). Each local research group, with the research team, decided what to research, how to research it, with whom and when. The three local research teams devised four questionnaires and surveyed adolescents (sample size ranging from 212 to 1611). One team also surveyed parents; another conducted face-to-face interviews; and the third team collected data through 'comment walls' during a basketball tournament. Statistical data were analysed through SPSS, and each local research group made sense of the data through content analysis, and worked with the research team to develop a proposal for a prevention strategy.

The major action outcome came in the implementation of the prevention strategies after the end of this action research project. There were two forms of action during the project. One local research group organized a two-day basketball tournament because they identified boredom and lack of activities as a reason for high levels of substance abuse. The second form of action lay in the action research process through which 15 research team members and 60 local research group participants received support, education and empowerment (Maglajlic and RTK PAR UNICEF BiH Team, 2004).

Why Researchers Choose Action Research in Health

Making a choice to use action research for a particular project or purpose may involve:

- Having some sense of what it might mean and its potential benefits over other approaches.
- Evidence from systematic reviews, research reports, textbooks and other literature.
- Information from within your organization, internet searches and non-peer reviewed sources.
- Opinions from peers or experts.
- Clinical data or other information gathered with clients, families, stakeholders, or co-researchers.
- Economic considerations including personnel, equipment and other resources.

Heather Waterman and her colleagues found five main reasons for choosing action research given in 48 British reports (Waterman et al., 2001: 21).

- The most common reasons for choosing action research are about encouraging stakeholders to participate in making decisions about all stages of research, or empowering and supporting participants.
- Frequent reasons include solving practical, concrete or material problems or evaluating change.
- Reasons associated with the research process included contributing to understanding, knowledge or theory; having a cyclical process including feedback, or embracing a variety of research methods.

- In 29 per cent of instances action research was chosen because it educates.
- And in a quarter, it was chosen because action research acknowledges complex contexts or can be used with complex problems in complex adaptive systems.

Ethical Choices, Aims and Purposes

Healthcare practice and research are ethical activities. Hippocrates' injunction that 'the physician must ... have two special objects in view ... namely, to do good or to do no harm (Hippocrates, 2004: 6) is cited as a fundamental ethical maxim for healthcare professionals. Action researchers in healthcare should help others, or at least do no harm. Collaboration and participation are valuable ethical safeguards.

One difficulty is that bio-medical research with obvious benefits that complies with funding or institutional ethics guidelines may also have effects that are harmful to some people. Foucault (1975) and others have shown how medical power and wealth are increased by building medical knowledge. Research funded by multinational drug companies supports an industry that distributes drugs unevenly round the globe. The research topics that receive funding often support an industry centred on professional interventions to cure diseases rather than action to build healthy and flourishing individual persons and communities (Reason and Bradbury, 2001/2006b). Those who make decisions about research funding in the illness industries have vested interests in existing knowledge and power structures. Participatory action research has a capacity to challenge these structures of knowledge and power. Participation of key stakeholders, especially those who are usually excluded from decision-making about research (such as clients, patients and community members), leads to projects that are more relevant to the lives of ordinary people, while good PAR is itself an empowering process.

In the 21st century, what happens in one part of the world can affect us all. As we develop global responses to HIV/AIDS and prepare for a bird flu pandemic it is truer than at any previous time in history that a complete state of health in one place depends upon other parts of the world. PAR can enable us to make sense of these interrelationships. Participatory understanding can lead us towards a sense of universal responsibility that is growing at this historical moment. As we all participate in webs of mutual interdependency, this universal responsibility is too important and too complex to delegate to professional or elected leaders. Each person has opportunities to participate in building healthy and whole communities, regardless of our occupation, formal education or health status. PAR is one way to do this. (For a more detailed discussion of ethics in action research see Chapter 13.)

Choices about Modes of Participation, Action and Research

This Handbook presents a rich diversity of approaches to action research. In addition, several authors have offered typologies of action research in healthcare. McCutcheon and Jung (1990: 145–7), Grundy (1988: 353), Holter and Schwartz-Barcott (1993: 301), McKernan (1996: 15–32; Waterman et al., 2001) and Masters (2000) each list three 'modes' of action research that arise from three underlying paradigms (Hart and Bond, 1995, identify four types). The three modes of action research can be labelled 'technical action research or action experiments'; 'action research in organizations or workplaces' (see Chapter 5), and 'emancipatory action research' or 'community-based participatory research' (see Chapters 2, 3, 8). These are not different research methods. The differences lie in the underlying assumptions and worldviews of the researchers and participants that lead to variations in the ways projects are designed, and who makes decisions (Grundy, 1982: 363). Technical action research is typically controlled by the

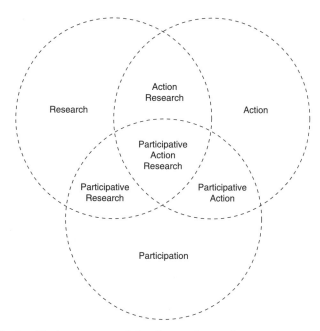

Figure 25.2 *Relationship between participation, action and research*

researcher, in the mode of Lewin's field experiments (Gustavsen, 2001/2006; Lewin, 1943). Action research in workplaces often involves collaboration or cooperation among a group of researchers or professionals, with the dual aims of increasing knowledge and contributing to improved practice. Participatory action research includes key stakeholders, including the disadvantaged, in making decisions through all phases of the research project.

A more pragmatic classification is illustrated in Figure 25.2. Following this diagram, an example of participative action is a community health programme designed and implemented by a coalition of professionals, community members and other stakeholders. Action research includes projects to improve professional practices through cycles of action and reflection, and can extend to clinical case studies without key stakeholders participating in decision-making. Participative research is conducted by a coalition of researchers, community members, patients,

health professionals or other stakeholders, and without a health intervention as an explicit part of the same project. Participative action research includes all three elements, systematic inquiry, professional practice intervention and participation in decision-making by key stakeholders. These categories are not discrete, but continuous, and the boundaries in the diagram are permeable or fuzzy. The proportions of participation, action and research are not usually decided in advance, but worked out as each project is designed and developed.

As a case in point, consider a report of action research to improve wound care in paediatric surgery (Brooker, 2000). Faced with increasing complexity in choosing the most effective of 400 different wound dressings, nurses collaborated with surgeons and other hospital staff to educate staff and monitor the use and effect of each dressing. Those who were most affected by the outcomes of the research (who were also the least powerful), the burned babies and

Table 25.1 *Hierarchy of levels of evidence in evidence based practice*

Level 1: Evidence obtained from systematic reviews of relevant and multiple randomized controlled
trials (RCTs) and meta analyses of RCTs
Level 2: Evidence obtained from at least one well designed RCT
Level 3: Evidence obtained from well designed non-randomized controlled trials or experimental studies
Level 4: Evidence obtained from well designed non-experimental research
Level 5: Respected authorities or opinion based on clinical experience, descriptive studies or reports of expert committees

children, and their parents, were not included in decision-making at any part of the project, and provided data passively (which was collected by nurses and medical staff monitoring progress). This project was seen as having some empowerment potential, for nurses in relation to senior medical staff, but it could not be described as empowering for the babies or their parents; nevertheless, this was a worthwhile project that produced useful practical knowledge.

Choices about participation, action and research are influenced by the available knowledge and information. Even with electronic access to literature, the information that we act on is heavily influenced by the educational and professional networks we belong to. A colleague who had been working on a project for two years told me she had just realized that what she has been doing is called action research, and there is a body of literature to inform it. She had been working in the next building, with access to an excellent academic library, without making the connection largely because the people in her network use a different approach to research.

Waterman and her colleagues (2001) found participation was the most commonly listed reason for choosing action research, but definitions of 'participation' vary. Some institutional ethics committees ask researchers to refer to people whose role is to provide data without making decisions about the conduct of research as 'participants', not 'research subjects'. Some researchers use the term 'participation' where others would describe working with health professionals or professional researchers as 'collaboration'. Waterman and her colleagues combined these.

Evidence-based choices

Since the 1990s healthcare knowledge systems known as 'evidence-based practice' have been developed to support health professionals in providing the best available care. Evidence-based medicine has been defined as 'the conscientious, explicit, judicious use of current best evidence in making decisions about the care of individual patients' (Sackett et al., 1996). From medicine, these principles were extended to other health professions and more recently, to include service development and management (Ottenbacher et al., 2002; Viswanathan et al., 2004a: 59). Evidence-based practice asserts that making clinical decisions based on best evidence, from the research literature and clinical expertise, improves the quality of care and the patient's quality of life.

Most texts on evidence-based practice present a hierarchy of evidence (see, for example, Holm, 2000; Madjar and Walton, 2001; Moore et al., 1995). Although wordings differ, the constructions are similar to Table 25.1.

Table 25.1 presents an absolute hierarchy of levels of evidence in which qualitative and action research approaches are ranked as inferior in the quality of knowledge they produce to the 'gold standard' randomized controlled trials. The argument is that the best evidence that a treatment or intervention is effective can only be obtained by controlling all influences on outcome other than the treatment, measuring the outcome and comparing that to the outcome without treatment, especially when this procedure is repeated at different places and times. Against this, others argue that we cannot evaluate a treatment properly unless we take the patient's perspectives into account and understand

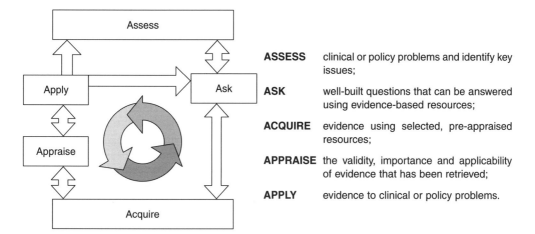

Figure 25.3 *Evidence-based information cycle*
Source: Hayward, 2005

their experiences in the context of their everyday lives. Statistical averages obscure important effects on some individuals in some contexts, and treatments must be adapted and tailored to each patient in his or her environment (Ovretveit, 1998: 36).

In clinical practice health professionals are advised to use evidence in ways that reinforce the hierarchy of evidence. In the evidence-based information cycle (see Figure 25.3), clinicians and policy-makers are invited to ask questions limited to 'questions that can be answered using evidence-based resources' and to acquire evidence only from 'pre-appraised resources' (Hayward, 2005). If healthcare practice is restricted only to information available from evidence-based data bases, fulfilling stringent criteria (that is, evidence from only one paradigm), this will limit the scope of approved practice strategies (Jones and Higgs, 2000). When clinical decisions go beyond patho-physiological concerns and when multi-professional teams work with complex problems, new situations or whole systems, evidence-based practice is too narrowly defined to support credible and effective practice.

If kinds of evidence are arranged as a continuum or a menu, rather than a hierarchy (Humphris, 2000; Whiteford, 2005: 39), then practice-based evidence and evidence generated through different research paradigms and approaches become equally available. Depending on the purpose, the nature of the problem and the situation, we can look for a 'best fit' between the question, type of evidence and research approach. What counts as good evidence, and the best ways to gather it, depends on the context and purpose of our inquiry. For example, in residential care of older people with dementia, the evidence of randomized controlled trials is relevant when recommending medication and dosage, but it is not helpful in considering policy or practice relating to sexual activity among older people with dementia.

Action researchers in health are responding to the challenge of evidence-based practice in a number of ways. Hampshire and her colleagues in the UK conducted a randomized control trial of action research in primary health care (Hampshire et al., 1999). Twenty-eight general practices were randomly allocated to two groups. Action research to improve pre-school child health services was facilitated in 14. The other 14 practices received written feedback alone (see Figure 25.4). Health professionals reported improvements in all 14 action research practices, and none of the others, but formal measures did not show any statistically significant changes. The authors

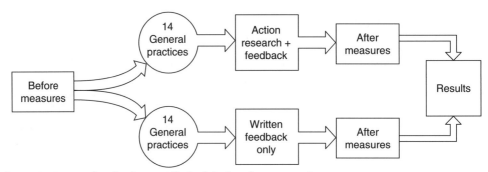

Figure 25.4   *Randomized controlled trial of action research*

conclude that action research is a successful method of promoting change in primary healthcare, but they found it difficult to measure the impact of action research.

The work of Hampshire and her colleagues demonstrates some difficulties in conducting randomized controlled trials of action research. There are recognized difficulties in making statistical measures of the effectiveness of interventions where there are many variables in complex situations. The RCT of action research did not use action research cycles in its own method (that would involve taking repeated measures of both the intervention and control group). They measured the change outcome and not the knowledge outcomes, that is, they evaluated action research as a change intervention, but not as a research approach. PAR would be difficult to study through RCT, as each local group is likely to devise a different project with different intended outcomes.

Choices About Quality and Rigour (Validity, Reliability, Relevance)

The claims that multiple randomized controlled trials are the 'gold standard' of evidence about the value of healthcare interventions are being challenged. Waterman et al. (2001) derive 20 questions to assess the quality of action research proposals and reports from their systematic review of 59 action research studies in UK healthcare settings including hospitals (56%), educational institutions (14%),

community health services (8%) and other health workplaces (see Table 25.2). Four questions (marked with an asterisk in Table 25.2) relate to defining characteristics of action research. The full report, including detailed subsidiary questions, is available online from http://www.hta.nhsweb.nhs.uk.

Guidelines for quality of participatory action research in health were prepared by the RTI Evidence-based Practice Center at University of North Carolina in a large systematic review of Community-Based Participatory Research (CBPR). They identified 1408 published articles and, after systematically applying exclusion criteria, reviewed 185 (Viswanathan et al., 2004a). Viswanathan and her colleagues systematically reviewed the quality of research method, the quality of community involvement, and whether projects achieved their intended outcomes.

The reviewers found few complete and fully evaluated CBPR reports, partly because length limitations in journals lead to incomplete documentation (Viswanathan et al., 2004a). Studies which they rated high for research quality did not achieve such high scores for participation, and from other data the reviewers found high-quality scores for participation associated with low-quality scores for research quality. Researchers applying for funds often failed to address conventional research quality criteria (Viswanathan et al., 2004a: 44). Despite this trend, the review uncovered several outstanding examples of high quality research combined with high-quality community

Table 25.2 *20 questions for assessing action research proposals and projects*

1. Is there a clear statement of the aims and objectives of each stage of the research?
2. Was the action research relevant to practitioners and/or users?
3. *Were the phases of the project clearly outlined?
4. *Were the participants and stakeholders clearly described and justified?
5. *Was consideration given to the local context while implementing change?
6. *Was the relationship between researchers and participants adequately considered?
7. Was the project managed appropriately?
8. Were ethical issues encountered and how were they dealt with?
9. Was the study adequately funded/supported?
10. Was the length and timetable of the project realistic?
11. Were data collected in a way that addressed the research issue?
12. Were steps taken to promote the rigour of the findings?
13. Were data analyses sufficiently rigorous?
14. Was the study design flexible and responsive?
15. Are there clear statements of the findings and outcomes of each phase of the study?
16. Do the researchers link the data that are presented to their own commentary and interpretations?
17. Is the connection with an existing body of knowledge made clear?
18. Is there discussion of the extent to which aims and objectives were achieved at each stage?
19. Are the findings of the study transferable?
20. Have the authors articulated the criteria upon which their own work is to be read/judged?

Source: Waterman et al., 2001: 48–50

participation throughout the research process (Webb et al., 2004). High quality research is expected in healthcare, and action researchers may be advised to pay more attention to ways in which high quality participation can enhance the quality of data collection and analysis to produce practical outcomes.

Overall, stronger or more consistent positive health outcomes were found with the better quality research designs. CBPR can also lead to unintended positive health outcomes, and to positive outcomes not directly related to the measured intervention. (For the guidelines that Viswanathan and her colleagues propose for the quality of CBPR please see Viswanathan, 2004a.) A more detailed checklist (though older and not based on wide systematic review) developed by Lawrence Green and associates (Green and Daniel, 1995) is available online from http://lgreen.net/guidelines.html. Action researchers need to provide evidence of high quality in participation and action and research. Assertions about the value of PAR will not convince seasoned reviewers of healthcare research.

Choices about Complexity and Action Research

Since the turn of the 21st century healthcare researchers have begun to apply complexity theory, including the theory of complex adaptive systems. Action research has special resilience and value in this emerging field of inquiry. A full explanation of complex adaptive systems is outside the scope of this chapter (but see, for example, Axelrod and Cohen, 1999; Fraser and Greenhalgh, 2001; Plsek and Greenhalgh, 2001; Plsek and Wilson, 2001; Wilson et al., 2001). In brief, complex adaptive systems include large number of autonomous agents (who adapt to change) and a larger number of relationships among the agents. Patterns emerge in the interaction of many autonomous agents. Inherent unpredictability and sensitive dependence on initial conditions result in patterns which repeat in time and space, but we cannot be sure whether, or for how long, they will continue, or whether the same patterns may occur at a different place or time. The underlying sources of these patterns are not available to observation, and observation of the system may itself disrupt the patterns.

Because the researcher is part of the complex adaptive system she or he studies, and because the sources of change are not all available for observation, it is impossible for one person to fully describe or understand a complex adaptive system. We need multiple perspectives, and because the situation may change in unpredicted ways, we need repeated observations and systematic feedback. Participatory action research meets these complex requirements. The collaboration and participation of co-researchers with different perspectives and ways of understanding, as well as iterative cycles of action and reflection, provide a robust model to increase our understanding of complex situations, while designing and monitoring interventions.

Because the action research cycles build feedback loops into ongoing research and action, they can be used for constant monitoring of complex adaptive systems, to try out interventions to see if they appear to have potential to lever disproportionate change, and provide feedback about interventions that are producing or not producing their intended effects. This leads to the development of local theories such as theories of change (ActKnowledge, 2003) or living theories (Whitehead, 2005).

Choices About Improving Healthcare Practice

Action research processes can be used to monitor and improve the quality of health services (Jackson, 2004). Action research cycles have much in common with the cycles of continuous quality improvement which inform healthcare quality management legislation in Australia, Canada, the UK, the USA and several other countries (ACCN, 1982; ACHS, 1985a, 1985b; ACSA, 2001; CARF, 1999).

Waterman et al. (2001) undertook a systematic review of 59 action research studies fitting their definition of action research as a period of inquiry that describes, interprets and explains social situations while executing a change intervention aimed at improvement and involvement. It is problem-focused, and founded on a partnership between action researchers and participants, is educative and empowering, with a cyclical process in which problem identification, planning, action and evaluation are interlinked.

This systematic review shows that action research can be useful for developing innovation, improving healthcare, developing knowledge and understanding in practitioners, and involvement of users and staff. Their findings indicate that action research is suited to developing innovative practices and services over a wide range of healthcare situations and demonstrates how the action research process can promote generation and development of creative ideas and implementation of changes in practice.

Organizational factors can facilitate or create barriers to action research. Meyer, Spilsbury and Prieto (1999) reviewed 75 reports of action research in health. Key facilitators and key barriers mentioned in 23 per cent or more of reports are summarized in Table 25.3. This review attended only to the action or change outcomes of action research and did not attempt to evaluate research rigour or the quality of participation.

CONCLUSION

Action research is increasingly used in various community and institutional healthcare settings. Action researchers in health work close to bio-medical researchers, and paradigm wars are giving way to sorting out the strengths and weaknesses of different research approaches for varied purposes and situations. Although the evidence-based practice movement has sparked new skirmishes between quantitative, qualitative and participative approaches in healthcare research, Waterman et al. (2001) point out how action research and evidence-based practice can work together.

We have seen that there is evidence that action research can combine research rigour, effective action and high-quality participation. Some well designed studies show high

Table 25.3　*Facilitators and barriers to action research*

Key facilitators	Key barriers
• Commitment • Talking/supportive culture • Management support	• Lack of time, energy, resources • Lack of multidisciplinary team work • Reluctance to change • Unstable workforce • Lack of talking/supportive culture

quality on all three dimensions. Many studies have been strong in one dimension, and weak in another, sometimes as part of an explicit research design (see Figure 25.2).

Waterman et al. (2001) recommend that health research funding will be appropriate for action research to:

- Innovate, for example to develop and evaluate new services;
- Improve healthcare, for example, monitor effectiveness of untested policies or interventions;
- Develop knowledge and understanding in practitioners and other service providers, for example, promoting informed decision-making such as evidence-based practice;
- Involving users and healthcare staff, for example, investigating and improving situations with poor uptake of preventive services; and
- Other purposes.

Action research 'seeks to bring together action and reflection, theory and practice, in participation with others, in the pursuit of practical solutions to issues of pressing concern to people, and more generally the flourishing of individual persons and their communities' (Reason and Bradbury, 2001: 1/2006a: 1). In the context of health and healthcare, this is about working towards complete physical, mental and social well-being. Experimental design and randomized controlled trials have an important place in healthcare research. These are most appropriate in well controlled situations such as drug trials. Well designed and implemented action research is the most appropriate approach for some other healthcare situations, where situations are truly complex or it is not possible to control many variables. We should recognize that statistical methods are often not the best way to measure complex

social change. Guidelines to inform choices about the quality and rigour of action research in health, based on sound evidence, have been published and need to be tested, and further refined. This may be an opportunity for a large-scale collaborative action research project. In the words of Laurence Green: 'If we want more evidence-based practice, we need more practice-based evidence' (Green, 2004/2006).

ACKNOWLEDGMENTS

Table 25.2 '20 questions for assessing action research proposals and projects', Waterman et al. (2001). Queen's Printer and Controller HMSE 2001. Reprinted with permission.

Figure 25.3 'Evidence-based information cycle', Hayward (2005). From http://www. cche.net/info.asp, The Centre for Health Evidence, University of Alberta, Edmonton, Alberta. Reprinted with permission.

REFERENCES

ACCN (1982) *A Guide to Quality Assurance: a Manual for Nurses Working in the Community.* Balwyn: Australian Council of Community Nursing, Nursing Advisory Committee.

ACHS (1985a) *Quality Assurance for Nursing Homes: Resource Kit.* Zetland: Australian Council on Hospital Standards.

ACHS (1985b) *Quality Assurance for Nursing Homes Information Kit.* Glebe, NSW: AMA/ACHS Peer Review Resource Centre.

ACSA (2001) *Continuous Improvement for Residential Aged Care.* Parramatta: Aged Care Standards and Accreditation Agency.

ActKnowledge (2003) *Theory of Change.* [http://www. theoryofchange.org/] (retrieved 23 November 2005)

Axelrod, R. and Cohen, M.D. (1999) *Harnessing Complexity: Organizational Implications of a Scientific Frontier.* New York: Free Press.

Brooker, R. (2000) 'Improving wound care in a paediatric surgical ward', *Action Research E-Reports,* 7 (available at: http://www.fhs.usyd.edu.au/arow/arer/007.htm.)

Burrows, D. (1996) 'An action research study on the nursing management of acute pain.' Unpublished manuscript, Buckinghamshire.

CARF (1999) *Commission on Accreditation of Rehabilitation Facilities.* [http://www.carf.org/default.aspx?site=ccac] (retrieved 13 July 2006)

Crabtree, A.S., Wong, C.M. and Mas'ud, F. (2001) 'Community participatory approaches to dengue prevention in Sarawak, Malaysia', *Human Organization,* 60 (3): 281–7.

Crowley, J. (1996) *A Clash of Cultures: Improving the Quaity of Care through an Action Research Process.* London: Royal College of Nursing.

Eikeland, O. (2001) 'Action research as the hidden curriculum of the Western tradition', in P. Reason and H. Bradbury (eds), *Handbook of Action Research: Concise Paperback Edition* London: Sage. pp. 145–55.

Eng, E. and Parker, E.A. (1994) 'Measuring community competence in the Mississippi Delta: the interface between program evaluation and empowerment', *Health Education Quarterly,* 21: 199–220.

Foucault, M. (1975) *The Birth of the Clinic: an Archaeology of Medical Perception.* New York: Vintage/Random House.

Fraser, S.W. and Greenhalgh, T. (2001) 'Complexity science: coping with complexity, educating for capability', *British Medical Journal,* 323: 799–803.

Green, L.W. (2004/2006) *If We Want More Evidence-based Practice, We Need More Practice-based Evidence.* [http://www.lgreen.net/] (retrieved 12 April 2006)

Green, L.W. and Daniel, M. (1995) *Guidelines and Categories for Classifying Participatory Research Projects in Health Promotion.* [http://lgreen.net/guidelines.html] (retrieved 9 September 2005)

Green, L.W., George, M.A., Daniel, M., Frankish, C.J., Herbert, C.P., Bowie, W.R. and O'Neill, M. (1995) *Study of Participatory Research in Health Promotion: Review and Recommedations for the Development of Participatory Research in Health Promotion.* Ottowa: Royal Society of Canada.

Grundy, S. (1982) 'Three modes of action research', *Curriculum Perspectives,* 2 (3): 23–34.

Grundy, S. (1988) 'Three modes of action research', in S. Kemmis and R. McTaggart (eds), *The Action Research Reader.* Geelong: Deakin University Press.

Gustavsen, B. (2001/2006) 'Theory and practice: the mediating discourse', in P. Reason and H. Bradbury (eds), *Handbook of Action Research: Concise Paperback Edition.* London: Sage. pp. 17–26.

Hampshire, A., Blair, M., Crown, N., Avery, A. and Williams, I. (1999) 'Action research: a useful method of promoting change in primary health care?', *Family Practice,* 16 (3): 305–11.

Hart, E. and Bond, M. (1995) *Action Research for Health and Social Care.* Buckingham: Open University Press.

Hayward, R. (2005) *Evidence-based Information Cycle* [http://www.cche.net/info.asp]

Hipprocrates (2004) *Of the Epidemics.* Whitefish: Kessinger.

Holm, M. B. (2000) 'Our mandate for the new millennium: evidence-based practice', *American Journal of Occupational Therapy,* 54 (6): 575–85.

Holter, I.M. and Schwartz-Barcott, D. (1993) 'Action research: what is it? How has it been used and how can it be used in nursing?', *Journal of Advanced Nursing,* 18 (2): 298–304.

Humphris, D. (2000) 'Types of evidence', in S. Hamer and G. Collinson (eds), *Achieving Evidence Based Practice: A Handbook for Practitioners.* Edinburgh: Bailliere Tindall. pp. 13–32.

Jackson, V. M. (2004) 'Medical quality management: the case for action learning as a quality initiative', *Leadership in Health Services,* 17 (2): i–viii.

Johns, C. and Kingston, S. (1990) 'Implementing a philosophy of care on a children's ward using action research', *Nursing Practice,* 4: 2–9.

Jones, M. and Higgs, J. (2000) 'Will evidence-based practice take the reasoning out of prctice?', in J. Higgs and M. Jones (eds), *Clinical Reasoning in the Health Professions, 2nd edn.* Oxford: Butterworth-Heinemann. pp. 307–15.

Keatinge, D., Scarfe, C., Bellchambers, H., McGee, J., Oakham, R., Probert, C., et al. (2000) 'The manifestation and nursing management of agitation in institutionalised residents with dementia', *International Journal of Nursing Practice,* 6 (1): 16–25.

Lewin, K. (1943) 'Forces behind food habits and methods of change', *Bulletin of the National Research Council,* 108: 35–65.

Mabala, R. and Allen, K.B. (2002) 'Participatory action research on HIV/AIDS through a popular theatre approach in Tanzania', *Evaluation and Program Planning,* 25: 333–9.

McCutcheon, G. and Jung, B. (1990) 'Alternative perspectives on action research', *Theory into Practice,* 24 (3): 144–51.

Madjar, I. and Walton, J. A. (2001) 'What is problematic about evidence?', in J.M. Morse, J.M. Swanson and A.J. Kuzel (eds), *The Nature of Qualitative Evidence.* Thousand Oaks: Sage. pp. 28–45.

Maglajlic, R.A. and RTK PAR UNICEF BiH Team (2004) 'Right to know, INICEF BiH: developing a communication strategy for the prevention of HIV/AIDS among young people through participatory action research', *Child Care in Practice*, 10 (2): 127–39.

Maglajlic, R.A. and Tiffany, J. (2006) 'Participatory action research with youth in Bosnia and Herzegovina', *Journal of Community Practice*, 14 (1–2): 163–81.

McKernan, J. (1996) *Action Research: A Handbook of Methods and Resources for the Reflective Practitioner, 2nd edn.* London: Kogan Page.

Masters, J. (2000) 'The history of action research', *Action Research E-Reports, 3*.

Meyer, J., Spilsbury, K. and Prieto, J. (1999) 'Comparison of findings from a single case in relation to those from a systematic review of action research', *Nurse Researcher*, 7 (2): 37–59.

Mill, J.E. (2001) 'I'm not a "Basabasa" woman: an explanatory model of HIV illness in Ghanaian women', *Clinical Nursing Research*, 10 (3): 254–74.

Moore, A., McQuay, H. and Gray, J.A.M. (1995) 'Evidence-based everything', *Bandolier*, 1 (12): 1.

Ottenbacher, K.J., Tickle-Degnen, L. and Hasselkus, B.R. (2002) 'Therapists awake: the challenge of evidence-based occupational therapy', *American Journal of Occupational Therapy*, 56 (3): 247–9.

Ovretveit, J. (1998) *Evaluating Health Interventions.* Buckingham: Open University Press.

Plsek, P.E. and Greenhalgh, T. (2001) 'Complexity science: the challenge of complexity in health care', *British Medical Journal*, 323: 625–8.

Plsek, P.E. and Wilson, T. (2001) 'Complexity science: complexity, leadership, and management in healthcare organizations', *British Medical Journal*, 323: 746–9.

Reason, P. and Bradbury, H. (2001/2006a) 'Introduction: inquiry and participatiion in search of a world worthy of human aspiration', in P. Reason and H. Bradbury (eds), *Handbook for Action Research: Concise Paperback Edition.* London: Sage. pp. 1–14.

Reason, P. and Bradbury, H. (eds) (2001/2006b). *Handbook of Action Research: Participative Inquiry and Practice.* London: Sage.

Sackett, D.L., Rosenberg, W., Gray, J., Haynes, R.B., and Richardson, W.S. (1996) 'Evidence based medicine: what it is and what it isn't', *British Medical Journal*, 312 (7023): 71–2.

Social Solutions (2003a) *RTK Bosnia & Herzegovina Toolkit Developed as a Resource Kit for Adolescents.* [http://www.actforyouth.net/documents/RTKtoolkitBiH.pdf] (retrieved 11 July 2006)

Social Solutions (2003b) *RTK Trip and Training Report for Bosnia and Herzegovina.* [http://www.actforyouth.net/documents/BiHRTKworkshopreport.pdf] (retrieved 11 July 2006)

Street, A. (1999) 'Bedtimes in nursing homes: an action-research approach', in R. Nay and S. Garratt (eds), *Nursing Older People: Issues And Innovations.* Sydney: MacLennan & Petty Pty Ltd. pp. 353–68.

Townsend, D. (2001) 'Prisoners with HIV/AIDS: a participatory learning and action initiative in Malaysia', *Tropical Doctor*, 31 (1): 8–10.

Viswanathan, M., Ammerman, A., Eng, E., Gartlehner, G., Lohr, K.N., Griffith, D., et al. (2004a) *Community-based Participatory Research: Assessing the Evidence. Evidence Report/Technology Assessment No. 99* (No. AHRQ Publication 04-E022-2). Rockville, MD: Agency for Healthcare Research and Quality.

Viswanathan, M., Ammerman, A., Eng, E., Gartlehner, G., Lohr, K.N., Griffith, D., et al. (2004b) *Exhibit 1: CBPR Reviewer and Applicant Guidelines* (July). [http://www.rti.org/] (retrieved 15 December 2005)

Waterman, H., Tillen, D., Dickson, R. and de Koning, K. (2001) 'Action research: a systematic review and guidance for assessment', *Health Technology Assessment*, 5 (23): 1–166.

Webb, L., Eng, E. and Viswanathan, M. (2004) *Community-Based Participatory Research: a Systematic Review of the Literature and its Implications.* Paper presented at the CCPH iLinc Web Conference, Washington, DC, December.

Whiteford, G. (2005) 'Knowledge, power, evidence: a critical analysis of key issues in evidence-based practice', in G. Whiteford and V. Wright St-Clair (eds), *Occupation & Practice in Context.* Sydney: Elsevier. pp. 34–50.

Whitehead, J. (2005) *What Is a Living Educational Theory Approach to Action Research?* [http://www.bath.ac.uk/~edsajw./] (retrieved 23 November 2005).

Wilson, T., Holt, T. and Greenhalgh, T. (2001) 'Complexity science: complexity and clinical care', *British Medical Journal*, 323: 685–8.

World Health Organization (1946) 'Preamble to the Constitution of the World Health Organization as adopted by the International Health Conference, New York, 19–22 June 1946', *Official Records of the World Health Organization*, 2: 100.

Zarchin, J. (2004) *Programme Experiences: RTK–Bosnia and Herzegovina Profile.* [http://www.comminit.com/experiences/pdsrtk/experiences-1840.html] (retrieved 11 July 2006)

26

Action Research on a Large Scale: Issues and Practices

Ann W. Martin

This chapter considers the challenges of doing action research in large scale change projects and what these challenges mean for practice in action research. Many of the demands of large scale projects may exist in smaller projects as well – issues of power and inclusion and implementation. But these issues become more complex when the numbers of participants and researchers increase and when the ground to be covered and understood is greater. Because the stakes are often high, politics and power are front and center. Engaging and utilizing a great diversity of perspectives is critical and more difficult to manage. Nonetheless, the possibilities for learning and the options for action increase exponentially as a large scale project develops. A central conclusion is that these challenges, possibilities and options place greater demands on the action research team themselves, to remain in continuous dialogue and reflection. The practice challenges are illustrated with experiences from two large scale projects in the USA.

In this chapter I consider the challenges of doing action research in large scale change projects and what these challenges mean for practice in action research. By large scale I mean projects where multiple systems – and large systems – are involved. These are most often community projects such as rebuilding a major harbor or reconstructing the twin towers in New York City might be, projects with a wide range of constituents and the potential for far reaching social and cultural consequences.[1] Many of the demands of such large scale action research projects may exist in smaller projects as well – issues of power and inclusion and implementation. But these issues become more complex when the numbers of participants and researchers increase and when the ground to be covered and understood is greater. With increased numbers of participants and constituent organizations comes increased diversity in perspectives and interests. This alone presents a challenge; it becomes much harder to get our hands around the project.

To begin, the matter of structuring a project to accommodate numerous participants and systems itself becomes difficult. Because the stakes are high, politics and power (and differing perceptions of power) are front and center.

As action researchers, we need to understand and appreciate these in order to engage all the relevant players. For example, in whose interest is it not to take action? What groups in the system are without voice? Since these differences will be central to co-generated learning, we need to take care as we construct – and reconstruct – the arenas for dialogue.

The possibilities for learning and the options for action increase exponentially as a large scale project develops. And so do the demands on the action research team members themselves to remain in continuous dialogue and reflection. Given the diversity and complexity of the systems, we must expect the unexpected and mine all action for the learning potential. When there are a great number of stakeholders, the conception of co-researchers is challenged; many of the potential participants may be far removed from decision-making forums. The knowledge held by those in the top and bottom levels of the system may be disparate because of the greater distance. However, we must include the broad range of views if we are to assure that the future is built on participant interests.

Finally, in large scale change where active participants may number 500 or more and where multiple systems may be impacted, we have to understand and live with, as well as try to manage, the iterative and developing nature of the learning project.

TO ILLUSTRATE LARGE SCALE CHANGE

I will use two projects to illustrate the scope of large scale change. Throughout the chapter I will refer to these and will occasionally make reference to another large scale project that is described in this Handbook (see Stringer, Chapter 35). The first case, a project for the School Boards Association of 29 school districts covering a population of nearly 300,000 and a school population of more than 40,000 students, was an action research project. The second, an attempt to heal relationships between the black community and the police of a large city, was never framed as an action research project, although it was built on principles of participation and inclusion that we think of as fundamental to action research.

The first project was situated in western New York State in the United States in a region that includes the City of Buffalo, population 215,000, the surrounding suburbs, and rural school districts all of which are included in Erie County. The Erie County Association of School Boards (governing boards for public schools) engaged my organization to research and recommend ways that the 29 school districts and two providers of special programs might collaborate to give every child in the region equal opportunity to meet state performance standards and reach his/her learning potential. Our recommendations were to address ways through collaboration and shared services to improve the efficiency, effectiveness, and equity of public education in Erie County.

The second project arose out of an historical community conflict in Cincinnati, Ohio. For years members of the African American community in Cincinnati had alleged unfair treatment at the hands of the city police. This history led to a proposed lawsuit against the police brought by the American Civil Liberties Union and the Cincinnati Black United Front. The judge assigned to the case sought a facilitated settlement of the charges, and in order to arrive at such a settlement invited a conflict resolution consulting firm, the ARIA Group, to guide a process that would inform such a settlement. This, then, was the project: to develop a set of guidelines for the settlement that would reflect the interests of parties in strong opposition to one another. Jay Rothman, president of ARIA, was asked by the Federal Judge to propose a process that the potential litigants would find acceptable as an alternative to litigation. ARIA launched a city-wide data gathering process that engaged eight stakeholder groups: youth, African American citizens, other minorities, business, educational leaders, foundations, white citizens, city officials and leaders, religious leaders, and social service agencies. With these groups, ARIA conducted what they called an 'action evaluation process' (rooted in principles of action research and more specifically action science, see Chapter 17) to assess the state of affairs and define the goals for a relationship between the African American community and the police.

SOME ASSUMPTIONS

The action research literature does not deal with the specifics of large scale change as a distinct approach, with the exception of what is written about dialogue in regional industrial change in Scandinavia (for example see Gustavsen et al., Chapter 4). While the guiding principles of action research as outlined by Elden and Levin (1991) and Greenwood and Levin (1998) may be conceptually consistent for both small and large scale projects, I hold that where large and multiple systems are involved, the link between inquiry, learning, and change should be made more explicit in the field than may be necessary in more bounded projects. Large scale change projects are political projects. The status quo before new action relies on existing power arrangements that will inevitably be challenged by change. A conscious inquiry (research) process as in action research establishes a context for learning among multiple stakeholders, a pre-requisite for sustainable change. Without this, as Dewey argues (1946), we risk domination of untested ideas that are held by one or another group in power. This risk is very great when the stakes are higher, as they are when large systems are in question. While we cannot always expect participants to see themselves as action researchers, we can make clear that we are engaging them in a mutual investigation and learning process. The framework of learning is the core concept that will enable participants to confront political realities, consider redirecting power, and recognize and value multiple interests. Learning as the central activity reduces the threat and

uncertainty experienced with imposed and undiscussable change.

MAKING SENSE AND DESIGNING FOR PARTICIPATION AND INQUIRY

In large scale action research, the first challenge is sensemaking in the use Karl Weick (1995) makes of the term: the development of possible explanations, not a body of knowledge. Who are the players? Where is the power? What will motivate the larger public to take an interest in any change? What are the relationships among the systems? As Weick suggests, these are only 'progressively clarified' (p. 11), not understood once, but subject to new insights. The second challenge is to design and implement processes that will engage multiple perspectives and support inquiry and learning within the political arena. I will undertake below first sensemaking and then design parameters.

1. Making Sense of the System and Who is in it

This is really making sense of the systems, figuring out just what systems will experience an impact from the change and, therefore, what systems it makes sense to include to understand the dimensions of the project. In the Erie County project, a project that included over 40,000 public school students, a city government and a county government as well as 31 separate school authorities, each governed by an elected board of at least seven members, and countless semi-public agencies from the State University to the Department of Social Services, we needed to be as inclusive as possible so that the ultimate recommendations would reflect what was actually do-able in such a broad community. But working within a very large system such as this raised a number of issues, which I will take up one by one:

a) Who should comprise the research team? And how to develop a co-generative research team with these actors?

b) What about the external research team?

c) Who would be the ultimate players?

d) Within multiple systems and a diversity of voices, whose knowledge is privileged?

e) Who makes the decisions about how to move forward with change? And what is consensus under these circumstances?

f) How can we bring the players to the discussion?

g) How do we treat the differences in values and perspectives, for example across class and racial divides in the inner city, the wealthy suburbs, and rural communities?

h) How do we, the external research team, manage the expectation that we are the experts and should 'take hold' and offer answers and solutions?

a) Who should comprise the research team? And how to develop a co-generative research team?

In Erie County, we collected nine outside researchers who would bring needed skills to the research team. We were data gatherers, data analysts, organizational change experts, and action researchers. Some had experience with large group processes; some had experience with interest-based problem solving.

Internally, the client for this project was already a team (the Collaboration Team) assembled three years prior to our entry by the County School Boards Association. Comprised of board of education members, school administrators, and county and university administrators, the team had already taken their collaboration cause to public forums and had framed a long list of information they wanted the 'hired' researchers to gather. They believed they had made sense of the landscape for their project and were initially taken aback when we wanted them to return to this sensemaking task with us.

In Cincinnati, ARIA assembled an advisory group of representatives of the key litigants, the Black United Front, the American Civil Liberties Union, and the Cincinnati police, to begin the project together. In Erie County, we had to teach action research from the very beginning, gentling, if you will, the

Collaboration Team into co-design and the practice of 'progressively clarifying' (Weick, 1995). In Cincinnati, the advisory group was assembled for the purpose of 'action evaluation', invited from the beginning to design a local stakeholder process based on a process ARIA had used elsewhere (see http://www. ariagroup.com/vision.html).

As is often the case in action research projects, the question of co-design is tricky. Insiders come to the external researcher group with the expectation that they will know how to design a change process. Of course, as action researchers, we do come with relevant knowledge and experience, but local knowledge is essential to achieving a process that will be meaningful locally. In large system change, it is unlikely that this local knowledge can be provided by a handful of local activists. Hence, in Cincinnati the advisory group used their knowledge of the local social map to guide the composition of stakeholder groups who would define a different future. In Erie County, we began our joint work with a daylong event to identify and map the stakeholders and their interests in school collaboration. In both cases, these initial activities laid an essential foundation for work in the highly politicized local environments.

But sensemaking required a further step – finding the means to access the broad spectrum of local opinions. In Erie County as soon as we had mapped the stakeholders we provided the team a seminar on communication in which we worked side-by-side to articulate just what it was we were trying to do in ways that we could be understood by the public. In Cincinnati, ARIA invited the media to the table, briefing them carefully on the process to occur and inviting them to cover all public meetings. In both cases, it was obvious that communication with a broader public was a strategic means to prime stakeholder interest and energize the dialogue to come. And in Erie County, this early work led to the first understanding by team members, both local and outside, of just how complex the system change we sought to effect was.

b) Some thoughts on external research teams

Working with a team of other researchers is always an adventure, great fun if the team is generous of spirit and open to learning, painful when differences are hard to resolve. The point in large system change is that the external research team must itself be large, and this inevitably 'ups the ante' and creates risks for collaborative learning. As director of our team in the Erie project, I began with enormous enthusiasm and little self-reflection. I failed to act on my own theory that differences should be surfaced and discussed and instead operated as if we were all in agreement. Not surprisingly, given that the team included conventional positivist researchers, we ended up with substantial differences over how to handle some of the data collection required by the project; we discovered through this experience (fairly late in the project) that we understood 'action research' quite differently. We could have used a good deal more mutual reflection and clarification as well as dialogue to surface differences and perceptions of power and authority in our own team before we began the project. Of course, with the large size of a team needed for large scale projects, such internal dialogues are complex and time consuming.

Although I have no data on the internal team in Cincinnati, I can report that Jay Rothman, the project leader, said in an interview that he felt alone and wished he had had a 'network' of other conflict resolvers and mediators (Portilla, 2003: 12). This speaks to the need for reflections with others when working in such complex systems. In practical terms, it not only shows the importance of a network of other researchers, but also of taking time to create an external reference group. To do this requires energy and attention, but it will strengthen the focus on research (inquiry and knowledge generation) that supports the active intervention in the project.

c) Who are the ultimate players in large system change?

This is the crux of the difference in large and small system action research. In large, multilayered systems, there are many, many players, often with political agendas that are tied to circumstances outside the scope of the action research. So, for example, in Erie County, some of the policy-level decision-makers – those who would control critical resources for change (superintendents of large public educational agencies, for example) – were beholden to a state Board of Regents for their jobs and their budgets. Others, the over 200 elected local Board of Education members, were subject to taxpayer revolts that could remove them from office at the next election. Social service agencies and non-profits that had an interest in collaborating with schools were subject to the decisions of their own boards and the contributions of their funders.

In Cincinnati, the ultimate players were police officials and policemen, city officials, a black community action organization, the American Civil Liberties Union, citizens, and a Federal Judge. For the officials and the Black United Front, there were high stakes in being perceived as strong. Their causes were being argued by lawyers, also with high stakes in visibility, who did not see themselves as stakeholders and had not participated in the vision and goal setting of over 3500 stakeholders. Once the several stakeholder groups had come up with goals, the attorneys for the parties were 'free' to play out their own agendas. However, Rothman makes the point that a number of times when the negotiators were ready to walk away and return to a litigation path, the mandate of the 3500 was a powerful disincentive to walk. Among other motives, no one wanted to be blamed for the failure given so much participation (and media) attention on getting that far (Rothman, pers. comm.).

An implication in both of these cases is that no matter how broadly stakeholders are involved in planning and considering alternatives in large scale change, the complexity of the system means the action research project may evolve in unpredictable ways. Another implication is that such complex processes warrant a very close look at this question of ultimate players, or final decision-makers. In Cincinnati, it might have been possible to forecast the lawyers' roles and, conceivably, had they been included in the reflection process all along, they might have been able to advocate for the collaborative agreement rather than reverting to adversarial positions (Rothman, forthcoming).

d) Within multiple systems and a diversity of voices, whose knowledge is privileged?

Political realities may mean that no matter what we do as action researchers to include all relevant stakeholder voices, someone(s) will call the shots simply by virtue of their position in the system. At the sensemaking stage, it becomes essential to figure out who those players are and how they may become open to alternative views. It is important to do an interest assessment to be sure that you understand their political and social needs so that they can be brought in to a mutual learning process without fear of losing.

The idealized assumption that all voices might be equal in a dialogue is not useful here (Gustavsen and Engelstad, 1986). As Rothman points out in his reflection on the Cincinnati project (forthcoming), where differences derive from individuals identities, conversations may need to confront the very issue of inequality. The political arena is such that all voices will not be experienced as equal. Our task is to figure out *where* they are not equal so we can create a design that legitimates alternative views.

In Erie County, our day of stakeholder mapping was partly aimed at this effort. We looked for what each group needed both from collaboration and from the larger public arena in order to feel successful. This early work guided our design, but in so complex a system political winds shifted continuously – elections were lost and won, budgets failed and 2000 municipal workers were laid off, hopes for school tax reform waxed and waned; the research process cannot not affect such contingencies, but in making sense of the system, they must be part of the understanding.

e) Who makes the decisions about how to move forward with change? And what is consensus under these circumstances?

In the attempt to make sense of decision-making in a large system I have been unable

to see that large groups of stakeholders can actually *decide* to move ahead with change. The decisions do rest in the hands of the few at the top, often politicians or others with referent power to make such decisions, though as the Cincinnati experience demonstrates, the few at the top may be significantly influenced by the attitudes and behaviors of those at the bottom. Formal consensus, an ideal in participatory decision-making, is not possible with so many actors. The best we can hope for is some groundswell of agreement on what is most important. In Cincinnati, stakeholder groups were able with ARIA's help to come up with five principles for the agreement between the Black United Front, the American Civil Liberties Union, and the Cincinnati police.

Implementation is another matter. The ultimate decision-maker on that agreement was a judge, but whether or not behaviors changed or will change depends on the will of hundreds if not thousands of people. The judge's decision was not and will not be the whole story.[2]

In Erie County, our external research team submitted final recommendations based on a 'sense' of what the local actors could support and develop. We built this 'sense' with the internal Collaboration Team, but we did not strive for formal consensus. The decisions about what to do belong with the 29 school boards, and implementation rests on their ability to influence other agencies. In effect, their consensus-building process is a long term project as they explore in groups of two or three or four boards how they might collaborate and share services based on the co-generated knowledge of the combined research team.

The complexity in projecting implementation in large scale change means action researchers need to take a long view. 'Results' are the learning and developed capacity for learning that we may hope to have supported through participation and inquiry.

f) How can we get the multiple players to the table?

The choices will be guided by what is manageable in terms of both size of group and maximizing the mix as well as who the stakeholders are. But strategies will also depend on understanding (making sense of) their interests. In Erie County our mapping exercise stopped short of what we needed. If we had taken the map as a guide to interview key players before we designed stakeholder meetings, we would have understood what the project could offer each group. As it was, we failed at bringing business interests into the discussions.

In Cincinnati, recognizing that it might be difficult to get youth to come together to develop goals, ARIA took a direct approach and hired 18 field workers to go out into the street to solicit interest and input from black youth. As a result, 750 youth shared their ideals and their input influenced very directly the final platform that shaped the negotiation agenda and final settlement agreement.

g) How do we treat the differences in values and perspectives, for example across the class and race issues of the inner city, the wealthy suburbs, and rural communities?

In Western society, and in particular in the USA, we find it hard to talk face to face about our identity-based differences. In local communities where there are divides along racial lines, people seldom acknowledge these or, if they do, choose not to explore them in depth. Whites are afraid of being seen as racists. Non-whites are afraid of being seen as troublemakers if they raise these issues (hooks, 1990). It is the same with divisions across class. Those who 'have' are afraid to be seen as politically incorrect if they mention poverty. The poor know they will risk being understood as lazy or 'begging' if they point out inequalities.

Yet to enter a large, multi-layered system as an action researcher one must make sense of the roles of class and race in the potential dialogue across constituencies. And so it becomes incumbent on us to raise the issues and generate the conversation so that these differences can inform action. Nonetheless, an outsider raising such issues risks being marginalized or kicked out of the project.

In Erie County, attitudes toward race and class were critical in planning for collaboration. One of the wealthiest suburban districts in

New York State and one of the poorest inner city districts in the same state were two of the 31 institutional stakeholders. Collaboration on any level – sharing of services, of staff, of curriculum, even an exchange of students – was fraught with inequalities or perceptions of inequality. For example, when we held a focus group interview with City of Buffalo teachers union leaders, they had little to say other than to ask sarcastically what the wealthier, whiter suburban districts could possibly want to share with them – certainly not resources such as computers in the classroom, certainly not students who would be afraid of the city environment.

As a research team we watched and waited for the stakeholders to take hold of the inequality issue. Finally, in a stakeholder meeting (c. 45 people from different occupations, status, and locations around the region), one school leader asked simply if the group meant 'all' when they said the goal of the project was to 'provide more effective, efficient, and equitable educational services for all children in Erie County'. This opened a discussion that we could not have opened successfully as outsiders. Sensemaking depended very much on co-generated learning and, we hope, on the safety we had created in ongoing dialogues. Once the question was asked, we could reflect the question back and support the stakeholders in their struggle to answer it honestly. In the end, the answer was clear: 'All means all', a politically risky conclusion, but a major milestone for the project. It enabled the Collaboration Team to advocate for 'all' in even the least diverse of their school communities.

h) How do we, the external research team, manage the expectation that we are the experts who should 'take hold' and simply offer answers and solutions?

Like many of the issues considered here, this arises in any action research project in which the participants are experienced in a hierarchical mode of learning. Also, like many of the issues considered here, the dilemma is exacerbated by the size of the project and the number of arenas engaged with it. Multiple institutions and associations touched by the project look at the time taken to connect with so many stakeholders and, counting time as money, wonder at the inefficiency. Why, they ask, should it stretch out for so long and involve so many people when the outside experts can just tell us what to do?

Our work then is to be persistent educators, teaching people through experience the value of involving many stakeholders. In practical terms, of course, the research team must be accessible and visible, willing to hear criticism and to listen carefully. In a public process, critics often protest that they know the answers even as they urge the experts to hurry up and give them the answers. In those ready answers may be the seeds of the developing solutions.

In *The Deliberative Practitioner* (2001), John Forester tells the story of a planner leading a multiparty process for design of the Oslo waterfront. In describing his work, Rolf Jensen, the planner, is quoted as saying, 'We tried to conceive from the first day that we are here to listen. We are here to try to understand. But we are also here to try to tell you a story – in other words why we are concerned about certain things' (p. 76). Forester labels this the (planner as 'negotiator'). The negotiator role is also what is required for the action researcher when making sense of and making sense in a large multi-system, multi-perspective project. We do bring expertise in the form of our questions and concerns, but we invite others to offer theirs as well and make clear that the different perspectives are all worthy of discussion.

2. What, then, can be the design parameters? What does it mean to take an action research approach to these issues in large scale projects?

a) Build the learning capacity of the research team

This should be a conscious, deliberate activity in the research process and cannot be taken for granted. With so many variables in large system change, so many agendas, so many players and so many levels on which to learn, the project can easily become daunting to both the external and internal participants on the research team. One way to manage this is to design for learning, making learning an explicit task of the combined team. In the hustle of activity – interviews, stakeholder meetings, large and small group planning sessions – schedule regular times to reflect together and review what has been learned. Ideally, agree that the team is itself a cooperative inquiry group, committing to and legitimizing the time and energy spent on mutual reflection. Frame the work explicitly within an action–reflection–learning spiral, and hold action up to that framework. In the swirl of activity and external events in a large system, we cannot take for granted that the learning will be captured and understood.

In Erie County we constructed joint learning activities very early in our work: the stakeholder mapping exercise, the communications workshop, and a workshop on change in which we, the external researchers, presented theory and challenged the internal team to see how the theory might apply to their context. We sought feedback on our developing ideas in public meetings. As a joint research team of 25 we met once a month to review progress and then I, as leader of the external team, provided a written reflection on each meeting. In Cincinnati, ARIA summarized regularly and fed data back to the larger stakeholder groups. This systematic approach to feedback feeds the cycle of action and learning..

b) Teach as you go about the co-generation of learning

In the United States and Canada and certainly in parts of Europe the public has come to expect that 'consultation' around big decisions or changes amounts to an information meeting – experts and/or leaders tell – with some question period. The questions are more likely to be understood as complaints rather than as recommendations for change. And so in a multi-system change process, such as the conflict resolution project in

Cincinnati or the recommendations for collaboration in Erie County schools, stakeholders need to be educated to learn in their role as contributors to a learning project. In Erie County, the representative group of stakeholders become an advisory group to the combined research team. We introduced early on the concept of *their* expertise and the importance of local context for the success of any recommendations that might come out of the project. In fact, our *mantra* was a quotation from the evaluation findings of a highly regarded national education reform initiative: 'Local context and design are crucial to a reform effort's success' (Annenberg Challenge, n.d.).

Modeling inquiry, ARIA sent back their consolidation of the 10,000 goals to the stakeholder groups for reaction and development. Rothman was explicit about their use of data to learn: 'We're action evaluators or interveners trying to use data to help them do the work they need to do to create the changes they want' (Portilla, 2003: 8).

c) Design opportunities for cross-cultural, multi-perspective dialogue; be determined and willing to take the time and expend the energy to learn from differences

The complexity of large system change is in the differences in position and perspective. The most critical role of the action researcher is to create a safe space for those differences to be acknowledged and recognized, though not necessarily reconciled. In *Justice and the Politics of Difference* (1990), Iris Marion Young argues against the ideal of community in favor of a vision of 'strangers in openness to group difference' (p. 256). Given the action goal of action research, the work should be grounded in the practical and temporal, and to assume that through the research a common ground can be found that erases difference is neither practical nor temporal. Rather the goal should be to learn enough from differences to be able to find practical means to move toward action. Where there is great diversity as there is in large systems, any agreement on action will have to meet divergent interests. This calls on action researchers in large system change to be

able to appreciate the productive potential in difference and work comfortably with conflict.

The scale of a large project means that researchers should work with not just one stakeholder group, but multiple stakeholder groups, enough to make sure that representatives from throughout the system(s) are heard and can hear. In Cincinnati, ARIA's eight stakeholder groups were designed to cover the territory of the dispute. Because the issue in Cincinnati was the differences in perspective of these groups, they met first as 'homogeneous' groups, police with police, African Americans with African Americans, and so on. Once these initial groups had established goals, the next step was for mixed groups with representatives from each homogeneous group to review the goals that had been generated and, with the help of an ARIA database, agree on a narrower list of goals. Ultimately, an even smaller mixed group, with one from each homogeneous group, arrived at the five goals that were included in the Collaborative Agreement. Jay Rothman, the leader of the Cincinnati project, brought with him years of experience working with groups in conflict, including Palestinians and Israelis.

In Erie County, we formed one large stakeholder group that met four times, sometimes for as long as a weekend. While the members did not clearly identify as one group or another, they did represent multiple perspectives and backgrounds. The group both brought in information and processed from their perspectives what information we gave back to them. In addition, we held several public meetings to which stakeholders were invited. We supplemented these with interest group meetings to feel reasonably certain that we had heard all perspectives. These groups ranged from an inner city church group to union leaders, to student groups, to social service agency leaders, to superintendents.

d) Take advantage of large group technologies

In a large scale change process, search conferences, dialogue conferences, and open space gatherings (Bunker and Alban, 2005) offer a means to bring multiple perspectives together and produce collective learning. But rather than hold one such conference, in a large scale project, we might hold several. Many large group processes combine small and large group work iteratively so that there is a gathering of local data from different perspectives and a building of collective knowledge that arises from reviewing in a large group the questions considered in small groups. Taking these principles, we could, as we did in Erie County, bring to a larger group the results of several smaller sessions of peer groups that had occurred at different times and in different places. The advantage of this more flexible approach was that we were able to reach many more people, and include more voices from each perspective than would have been manageable in even a large search conference.

It is worth noting that in the East Timor project described in this handbook, multiple community meetings were held all across the country in order to develop the model for parent participation in schools (Stringer, Chapter 38).

There is a risk in the practice of large group processes such as search and dialogue conferences that the client system experiences them as ends as much as means (Martin, 2000). The events themselves are demanding and often enlightening and inspiring. The results, a set of plans or agreements, feel to participants like an accomplishment. But from an action research perspective, the value of these processes is in what actions result. Oguz Baburoglu et al. (1996) have written about the need for a referent organization, preferably one that emerges from the conference itself, to carry out whatever plans are developed. Reason (pers. comm.) is working on a project that links specific issue inquiry groups in large scale events to create a network and movement for change. It seems imperative to position events such as these within the context of the larger research process. Whether or not you use one or several focused large group processes, the overall research design should include sessions and processes to follow up on whatever emerges. In other words, position such processes as moments in the ongoing learning process, not as ends in themselves.

e) Allow time and space for the system to learn

In participatory change, there must be a connection between top-down and bottom-up thinking and activity. Each informs and inspires the other. Creating that connection is not just a matter of creating arenas and events, but also of allowing enough time for enough of these to occur and reoccur so that the learning can progress. The structural means toward this end in the Value Creation 2010 (VC2010) project in Norway which prescribes regional networks of government, labor, local industry, and universities (Gustavsen et al., Chapter 4) is expected to be nationally funded for ten years. In the Erie project, albeit smaller than the national industrial development project of VC2010, we found one year entirely too little time to allow the layers of interest in the system to hear and learn from each other.

f) Accept, plan for, and respond to the non-linear progression of change in large systems

Essentially, you must design for the unknown, which means to design with flexibility in mind and be ready to change designs when the context calls for it. In Erie County, we were chosen as the action researchers for the project based on a design we submitted. The broad participation and co-generated learning we proposed were appealing to the Collaboration Team, but when, once we'd made some sense of the system and begun to extend to multiple stakeholders, we had to rethink our design, the team members were perplexed. We had planned three search conferences; we held none, deciding instead to extend focus group interviews and bring those results to the stakeholders. This redesign was as difficult for some of our own research team to accept as for the local team. Everyone who worried about such changes in design was worried that it 'looked like we didn't know what we were doing'. This is a problem, of course, because as researchers we are assumed to know what we are doing. What

I suggest here is that we be careful to define what it is we know we are doing, which is learning in action. It won't be useful to stick to a design if, once in the local context, we can see a more effective way to proceed. Once again, I argue for an explicit learning goal.

If we go to the pragmatic roots of action research in the work of John Dewey, we find his advice that our processes must be 'progressive and temporal' (as cited in McDermott, 1981: 23) as systems are living and not static. Expanding on the idea of research that is progressive and temporal, I pick up the biological framework of François Jacob (1982), cited by Greenwood and Levin (1998), which suggests that social outcomes, as biological ones, are the result of a dialogue between the actual and the possible (p. 97). This dialogue is ongoing. It is especially important in large scale projects to see that the process of learning and change is ongoing and is between the actual (right now) and the possible. There are too many factors, too many players, too many possibilities for change for the outcomes to be projected. Political vicissitudes, power players, seemingly unrelated local, national, and world events can all influence the development of change. What may seem impossible today may not be so tomorrow, and vice verse. The key, again, is that in action research these realities and the way they are perceived are all the subject of inquiry and learning.

g) Design for ongoing evaluation

Given that the context is so rich and diverse and located in real time, it may seem obvious that continuous evaluation is part of a large scale action research project. Certainly everything I've written here suggests continual reassessment. But here I argue for something more systematic that connects directly to the learning goals of action research. Introducing a participatory evaluation report, Michelle Fine says it so well: 'Participatory evaluation research leaves, within schools and other organizations, multiple constituencies for reform, a culture of inquiry, and a legacy of asking questions within a "safe context"' (Fine, 1996: 5).

As action researchers working on large system change, sometimes the best we can hope for is that we come away having fostered the energy for reform and the culture of inquiry. Ideally, once the project includes engagement of the local practitioners in inquiry about their goals and process as part of the work, there is less resistance in the form of 'taking too much time' or 'taking time away from the planning'. As action researchers, our mission should be to center evaluation so soundly in the core of the project that it becomes the avenue from one step in the project to the next.

It is significant that the ARIA project in Cincinnati was conceived of as participatory evaluation. The stated assignment for the stakeholder groups was to come up with goals for the relationship between the police and the African American community in the city. Their process was to inquire and listen and summarize, first in homogeneous stakeholder groups and then in groups that spanned experience, culture, and perspectives. In this case evaluation WAS the process.

What it Comes Down to: My Checklist

As I've written in this chapter, I've come to see challenges for my own practice as an action researcher. It is fine that I should strive to wax eloquent on inquiry and learning, but what does this mean I/we should actually do in the field? What is the practical value of this discussion? I find myself building an internal checklist, which is only fair to share. So, here it is:

1. Spend a lot of time with my own research team uncovering our values and differences, defining what we think the project calls for, what we each mean when we think of ourselves as 'action researchers'. And then, agree to check-in continually on what we see and how it fits with our espoused theories.
2. Learn how to 'sell' the significance of inquiry and group reflection so that these are experienced as productive by members of client systems. In an outcomes-based western society, hold out as Dewey did for the constructive value in learning.

3. Give much more time in the beginning of a project to individual and/or focus interviews to grasp different perspectives before we gather a great diversity of people together and expect them to talk across their differences.
4. Make participatory evaluation part of the project from its inception so that participants expect ongoing evaluation.
5. Let go. Understand that large scale change cannot be 'managed'.

Action research is based on a critical element of faith that when the opportunity is opened, there is great human capacity and will to learn and grow, and that, given a safe environment, people will engage in dialogue to learn from one another. This is certainly present in large scale action research where the project is undertaken in such a broad arena that it may impose on the initially unaware and/or uninterested participant. We proceed in the confidence that inquiry and dialogue will engage even skeptical participants. But this does not mean that action researchers, no matter how well able we are to understand systems or how skillful we are in design, can project or even speculate on the myriad potential connections and disconnections that can occur in interaction among players and systems. It is perhaps true in all action research, but certainly true in the context of large system change, that we have to be content with having fostered meaningful exchange of ideas and perspectives, an exchange that we hope, based on our faith, leads to some learning – a change or growth in perspective.

In his 1946 essay, Dewey described as '*the* problem of the public … the essential need for improvement of the methods and conditions of debate, discussion and persuasion' (p. 208). Dewey calls for a society were there is 'a more equable liberation of the powers of all individual members of all groupings' (p. 192). The greater the size of the systems in a change effort and the greater the diversity of participants, the greater is the need for inclusive and accessible arenas and methods. To be relevant and meaningful to the publics involved, the methods in large scale change must allow for

difference and create the space for learning from difference. As an action researcher, I am committed to Dewey's project to develop a more democratic society; just as important, I am committed to the values of inclusion and dialogue that we can hope will lead to the society where individuals can experience more power. What is most important as we contribute to large system change is that we foster learning so that, in face of their many differences, citizen participants can see their way to create positive change long after we are no longer involved.

ACKNOWLEDGMENT

I am particularly grateful to Jay Rothman, who graciously supported my use of his work in Cincinnati to illustrate my discussion.

NOTES

1 Of course, I could include in this list change within large corporations. The term 'far reaching social and cultural consequences' would still apply in such large systems, as would the issues considered in this chapter, including the political dimensions.

2 To learn more detail about ongoing challenges of implementing the Collaborative Agreement in Cincinnati, email friendscollab@gcul.org for access to the Collaborative Quarterly newsletter.

REFERENCES

Annenberg Challenge (n.d.) *Citizens Changing Their Schools: a Midterm Report of the Annenberg Challenge* [www.annenbergchallenge.org/pubs/citizens] (retrieved 13 April 2004).

Baburoglu, O., Topkaya, S. and Ates, O. (1996) 'Post search follow-up: assessing search conference based interventions in two different industries in Turkey', *Concepts and Transformations*, 1 (1): 31–50.

Bunker, B. and Alban, B. (2005) 'Special issue on large group interventions', *Journal of Applied Behavioral Sciences*, 41.

Dewey, J. (1946) *The Public and Its Problems.* Athens, OH: Swallow Press.

Elden, M. and Levin, M. (1991) 'Co-generative learning: bringing participation into action research', in

W.F. Whyte (ed.), *Participatory Action Research*. Newbury Park, CA: Sage. pp. 127–42.

Fine, M. (ed.) (1996) *Talking Across Boundaries: Participatory Evaluation Research in an Urban Middle School*. New York: City University of New York Graduate School and University Center.

Forester, J. (2001) *The Deliberative Practitioner: Encouraging Participatory Planning Processes*. Cambridge, MA: MIT Press.

Greenwood, D. and Levin, M. (1998) *Introduction to Action Research: Social Research for Social Change*. Thousand Oaks, CA: Sage.

Gustavsen, B. and Engelstad, P. (1986) 'The design of conferences and the evolving role of democratic dialogue in changing work life', *Human Relations*, 39 (2): 101–16.

hooks, b. (1990) *Yearning*. Toronto: Between the Lines.

McDermott, J.J. (ed.) (1981) *The Philosophy of John Dewey*. Chicago, IL: The University of Chicago Press.

Martin, A. (2000) 'Search conferences and the politics of difference.' Unpublished dissertation, Teachers College, Columbia University, USA.

Portilla, J. (2003) 'Jay Rothman, President of ARIA Group, Inc', in *Beyond Intractability.Org*. [www.beyondintractability.org/audio/rothman] (retrieved 9 July 2005)

Rothman, J. (forthcoming) 'Identity and conflict: collaboratively addressing police-community conflict in Cincinnati, Ohio', *Ohio State University Journal on Dispute Resolution*.

Weick, K. (1995) *Sensemaking in Organizations*. Thousand Oaks, CA: Sage.

Young, I.M. (1990) *Justice and the Politics of Difference*. Princeton, NJ: Princeton University Press.

27

Theorizing Audience, Products and Provocation

Michelle Fine and María Elena Torre

Drawing on two cases of participatory action research (PAR) – one conducted with women in a maximum security prison and the other with youth gathered together across a set of very diverse schools – this chapter is designed to raise questions about the politics and practice of PAR. In particular we focus on a theory of provocation, audience and products, asking readers to think with us about the kinds of 'actions' PAR seeks to undertake/provoke in politically very dark times. We end with a series of questions PAR collectives might engage with, as we seek to create PAR products as counter-hegemonic 'weapons of mass instruction'.

Readers of this volume are well equipped with the historic, theoretical and political framings of participatory action research (PAR). This 'practice' chapter draws readers' attention to an under-theorized aspect of PAR – questions of audience, product and provocation. Our participatory action research projects have been situated inside communities and institutions – prisons, schools – constituted through unjust distributions of resources, power and dignity.[1] Researching in collectives comprised of those on the 'inside' and not, we interrogate the very fabric of injustice in the (mal)distribution of resources, respect, opportunities, shame, failure and punishment and search for the tears where resistance survives. Our work strategically focuses on change – theoretical, structural and practice based. Our research

collectives deliberate together about the kinds of change we seek, whom we are trying to reach, and what products would most effectively provoke action. That is, we theorize audience, products and provocation, hoping that PAR will have 'legs' necessary to carry research into diverse domains – to reframe social issues theoretically, feed campaigns, nudge those with power and fill historic, documented memory with yet another instance of collective, informed resistance.

We have designed our participatory action research projects to inquire about a problem or struggle within the very institutions that substantial numbers of our researchers team are engaged in/working for/prisoners or students of. Thus provocation hovers as a goal and danger, teasingly co-dependent and spiking serious ethical considerations. That is, because our work is nested within institutions, and typically launched from the perspective of those with the least power, our research collectives must continually revisit questions of the research purpose – *for whom* is the work and *toward what ends*? In the 'ghostly haunts' (Gordon, 1997) of our work, we know that even with permissions, approvals and collaborations at the top, participatory action research is often quite inflammatory. And the ashes of vulnerability – no matter how hard we try to anticipate them – fall unevenly. Because of these delicacies, we must theorize audiences and change within, and beyond the local context. In these PAR projects, the global is intimately intertwined in the local.

We take you into two of these PAR projects – one launched in a women's prison and one grounded in a series of urban and suburban schools. In each case, we have had to pay close attention to questions of who cares, who needs to know, who is vulnerable, what products should be crafted, what impact/organizing needs to happen *within* the place and *outside of* or *across* places. The combination of these two cases allows to us think aloud about the choreography of insiders and outsiders, as well as deep work within an institution, across and way beyond.

PAR BEHIND BARBED WIRE

In 1995, President Bill Clinton signed the Violent Crime Control and Law Enforcement Act which discontinued prisoners' eligibility to apply for Pell Grants, noncompetitive, needs-based funds for low income college students in the United States. This effectively ended the few federal dollars that enabled women and men in prison to attend college. As a consequence, the vibrant, 15-year-old college program at Bedford Hills Correctional Facility, the maximum-security facility for women in New York State, closed, alongside more than 340 programs nationwide. Morale among the women in the prison plummeted, and even prison administrators and corrections officers

felt the effects. Fast forward: a task force of prisoners, prison officials, community leaders and local college presidents was launched to resurrect the college (for history of this amazing collaboration see www.changingminds.ws). Within a few months, the College Bound program, a consortium of colleges and universities donating faculty time, books, resources and mentors, was established. Since this unique rebirth, women in prison who pass the college entrance exam have been able to enroll in a BA in Sociology degree program. Those who do not pass can enroll in pre-college until they do. Pre-college serves as a crucial transition program for the 70 percent of women at Bedford who have neither a high school diploma nor a GED (high school equivalency diploma).

Today more than a third of the women in the prison are enrolled in college, while many of the remaining women are taking GED and pre-college courses. You can find study groups on Michel Foucault, qualitative research, and Alice Walker. One woman told us that on her cell block she has heard the staccato ticking of typewriter keys late into the night; another reported that 'young inmate[s] knock softly on [my] wall, at midnight, asking how to spell or punctuate.'

With the return of college, a number of the women prisoners decided that the program needed an evaluation; college in prison could no longer be taken for granted and its impact would have to be demonstrated, its value documented. After much deliberation with the prisoners and the administration, it was agreed that a participatory action research design, while difficult 'behind bars', would be essential. Two graduate students from The Graduate Center of the City University of New York co-taught a graduate seminar in the prison on research methods, reviewing the skills of critical research. Seven of the students in the course opted to join five Graduate Center women to form the College in Prison PAR collective.

The collective – Kathy Boudin, Iris Bowen, Judith Clark, Aisha Elliot, Michelle Fine, Donna Hylton, Migdalia Martinez, 'Missy', Melissa Rivera, Rosemarie A.

Roberts, Pam Smart, María Elena Torre and Debora Upegui – met every two to four weeks, over the course of four years. Hailing from New York, Jamaica, Maine, Puerto Rico and Colombia, some of us were immigrants and some US-born. Among us, we were lesbian, straight, bi and all of the above. Some of us were victims of violence, others accused of felony murder. All of us spoke English, and a number spoke Spanish too. We spent our 9–11 am sessions laughing, discussing, disagreeing, gossiping and writing; negotiating what was important to study, speak and hold quietly among ourselves.

We worked together for four years and elaborated a complex multi-method design that included archival research on years of college records and documents; nine focus groups with current students and drop outs; 20 interviews with former students now living on the outside; interviews with both sympathetic and hostile corrections officers; surveys by faculty and university administrators and a focus group with adolescent children of mothers in the college program. All of these methods were co-facilitated, to the extent possible, by Graduate Center and prisoner researchers. Simultaneously, we asked the New York State Department of Correctional Services (NYSDOCS) to undertake an extensive, quantitative longitudinal analysis of 36-month recidivism rates for thousands of women released from prison, stratified by those who participated in college and those who did not (see Fine, Torre, Boudin, Bowen, Clark, Hylton, Martinez, Missy, Rivera, Roberts, Smart and Upegui, 2001).[2] The NYSDOCS analysis revealed a dramatic disparity in recidivism rates: women without any college while in prison recidivated at 29.9 percent over three years, compared with 7.7 percent for women with some college.

The material gathered from qualitative and quantitative methods confirmed a substantial, positive impact of college in prison on women, their children, 'discipline' in the prison, post-release outcomes, the leadership

women provided in communities post-release and the tax benefits saved by society *not* having to subsidize those who are reincarcerated (at $30,000 per year). We refer you to the website for the full reporting of our methods and findings, www.changingminds.ws.

By the early part of year four, we had completed the research and we were trying to figure out *products*. We had very compelling data – charts, graphs, dollars, words of children, women's poetry, testimonials of wardens – documenting the profound benefits of college in prison. It was now time to wrestle with how we would write our report, who we would ask for endorsements, and where we would distribute it. Should our audience be primarily policy-makers? What about prisoners, college students and faculty? Prison activists? Should the text be written in a single authoritative voice? Or should we create a multi-voiced work filled with the questions and contradictions of participatory work? We debated between post-structural experimentation, feminist and critical race complexity and social science hypotheses. And what about authorship? Should we alphabetize? Separate prisoner researchers and Graduate Center researchers? Put Michelle's name first in the hope of gaining 'legitimacy'? Bury names of high profile prisoners' names to quiet concerns about perceptions? Or, should we place the most 'wanted' among us right up front to demonstrate the power of our collaboration? How do we anticipate resistance? And how do we not romanticize women who have been charged with violent crimes? That is, how do we re-present the women with a sense of humanity, re-present their crimes with complexity, and still contextualize the mass incarceration of men and women of poverty and color in a larger conversation about economic, racial and gendered (in)justice?

Our primary goal was to convince the New York State legislature to restore funds for college in prison programs. But we also wanted to produce *materials of use* for college campuses, other prisoners, prison advocacy groups, families of persons in prison, etc. So we decided to craft multiple products. Our primary document would be a single voiced, multi-method, rigorous and professionally designed report, widely available as a website. The prisoners wanted Michelle Fine to be the first name, and 'Missy' insisted on using only her nickname. The report was distributed to every governor in the USA and to every New York State Senator and Assembly Member. We sought to transform the public consciousness about prisons, re-present the face of women in prison, re-connect these women to the larger social communities from which they come, and influence social policy. To do so, we needed to engage and provoke those outside the prison – and not alienate those (administrators) within.

The women wanted a report that was polished and beautiful. We hired a graphic designer who brought in a draft cover for the report with bold black lettering on a stark white background: **CHANGING MINDS**. Those of us from the outside loved the drama of the image. The women inside were disappointed, and argued for a different cover, *'Give it life, color, excitement.' 'Make it sexy, give it lipstick!' 'They already think our life is so drab, make it vibrant.'* We all wanted the report to be irresistible, something people would want to touch, hold, place on their coffee tables. The text had to seduce, invite people to read and reacquaint themselves with women inside prison. Moreover, the report had to chip away at the stereotypic images of 'Monster Women'. The designer returned to the prison a few weeks later, with a brand new version of the report: the cover colorful and strong, the text inside layered with lowered reincarceration rates; cost benefit analyses; letters; photos; quotes from officers, prisoners and children – and even postcards. Capturing our desire for the data to jump off the page and move the reader to action, removable postcards were stitched into the report with varied messages, like: *'Dear Senator – Did you know that college in prison reduces recidivism rates from 30 per cent to 8 per cent? Get tough on crime – educate Prisoners'*. Underneath the postcards

were sequenced photographs of women's lives post-release, still photos of lives in motion. Pages surrounding them were draped in quotes from children: *'Now I tell people my mother is away at college!'* and corrections officers: *'I'm ambivalent about the college program, because I can't afford college for myself or my kids. But at least I know there will be less fighting at night, more reading ... and the women won't be coming back.'*

Mindful of the power of endorsements, we decided to gather well known and everyday people: prison reform advocates from the Left, prominent 'get tough on crime' voices from the Right, and families of murder victims interested in restorative justice. We invited, for instance, a mother whose daughter had been brutally murdered and has become well known for her anti-parole campaigns. Though we sat on explicitly different sides of the struggle against mass incarceration, she appreciated, with intelligence and generosity, the significance of educating those who would be released. The day her quote for the back of the report came across Michelle's email inbox, we (María and Michelle) both wept:

> Educating the incarcerated is not an exercise in futility, nor is it a gift to the undeserving. It is a practical and necessary safeguard to insure that those who have found themselves without the proper resources to succeed have these needs met before they are released. It is a gift to ourselves and to our children, a gift of both compassion and peace of mind. We are not turning the other cheek to those who have hurt us. We are taking their hands and filling them with learning so that they can't strike us again. (Janice Grieshaber, Executive Director, Jenna Foundation for Non-Violence)

Changing Minds was published on 10 September 2001. The report has been distributed across the USA at activist and scholarly meetings on prisons, schools, higher education and class/race/gender (in)justice in low-income communities. It has traveled to Australia, New Zealand, Wales, Alaska, Spain, Canada and Mexico. Members of the research team on the outside have presented on this work to traditional non-profit and faith-based organizations dedicated to sentencing and parole reform, education reform (both in and out of prison), humane treatment of prisoners, etc., as well as to meetings of governors, legislative assistants and correctional groups interested in 'what works'.

We have published scholarly chapters on critical epistemologies, design and methods (see for instance, Fine et al., 2003) in which our contradictions are interrogated, and more recently an article on the significance of higher education in prison as an extension of Affirmative Action policy (see Torre and Fine, 2005). For community organizing audiences, we produced 1000 organizing brochures in English and Spanish, carrying the results in a strong voice of advocacy, demanding justice and action.

In order to be globally accessible, over time, we created (and have sustained for five years) a website (www.changingminds.ws) where activists, organizers, students, faculty, criminal justice administrators, prisoners and their families can download free copies of the full report. To date, the website has received more than 5000 hits, with the California State Department of Corrections ordering 50 copies of the report and feminist and critical education faculty assigning the report in their classes. A father whose daughter committed suicide in prison decided to sponsor a college in prison project, and he too ordered copies for a number of prison administrators in his home state.

Lest this sound like a narrative of political victory and easy sailing, we offer a scene from another one of our 'products' – testimony at state legislative hearings. At one such hearing, the two of us (Michelle and María) presented the findings and concluded:

> College in prison is morally important to individuals, families and communities; financially wise for the state, and it builds civic engagement and leadership in urban communities. In fact, college in prison even saves tax payers money. A conservative Republican, as well as your more progressive colleagues, should support these programs … unless, of course, the point is simply to lock up Black and Brown bodies at the Canadian border.

To which one of the more progressive state legislators responded, '*Doctor, I'm afraid that is the point. You know that in New York, downstate's crime is upstate's industry.*'

Since then there has been some subtle movement toward rebuilding higher education programs in prisons in the USA, particularly in New York State and California. This reform has occurred, in part, because states saw their budgets depleted by the prison industrial complex. We find energy in these connective moments between social struggle and social policy, moments within which our projects can enter to transform and educate. When we enter these spaces we always speak with formerly incarcerated women, linking our research to larger issues of mass incarceration. With the report we show photos of our co-researchers, read their poetry, and say aloud the names of all the authors – even those who are 'otherwise detained'. We turn now to a PAR project launched across institutions – by educators and youth.

THE OPPORTUNITY GAP PROJECT AND *ECHOES OF BROWN*

In the Fall of 2001, a group of suburban school superintendents of desegregated districts gathered to discuss the disaggregated achievement gap data provided by the states of New Jersey and New York. As is true nationally, the test score gaps between Asian American, white American, African American and Latino students in these desegregated districts were disturbing. Eager to understand the roots and remedies for these gaps, a superintendent from one of the districts invited Michelle and colleagues from The Graduate Center to join the research team. We agreed, under the condition that we could collaborate with a broad range of students from suburban and urban schools to create a multi-year participatory action research project. Over the course of two years, more than 100 youth from urban and suburban high schools in New York and New Jersey joined researchers from The Graduate

Center to study youth perspectives on racial and class based (in)justice in schools and the nation. We worked in the schools to identify core groups of youth researchers drawn from all corners of the building – from special education, English language learner classes, gay/straight alliances, discipline rooms, student councils and AP classes. We designed a multi-generational, multi-district, urban-suburban database of youth and elder experiences, with the intent of tracing the history of struggle for desegregation from the US Supreme Court's 1954 decision that separate was *not* equal in *Brown v. the Board of Education, Topeka Kansas* to date, and analyzing social science evidence of contemporary educational opportunities and inequities by race, ethnicity and class (see Fine, Bloom, Burns, Chajet, Guishard, Payne, and Torre, 2005). Our work rested on a series of youth research camps that we created to develop our school/district-based research collectives, design our instruments, analyze data and theorize products.

At our first research camp, the 50 youth from six suburban high schools and three urban schools immediately challenged the frame of the research: *'When you call it an achievement gap, that means it's our fault. The real problem is an opportunity gap – let's place the responsibility where it belongs – in society and in the schools.'* And so we became the Opportunity Gap Project. Each research camp was held for two days at a time in a community and/or university setting. Immersed in methods training and social justice theory, we deconstructed what constitutes research, who can 'do' research, and who 'benefits'. The students learned how to conduct interviews, focus groups and participant observations, design surveys and organize archival analyses. Together, we designed a survey to assess high school students' views of race and class (in)justice in schools and the nation. The youth researchers were given a rough, 'wrong draft' of the survey and they dedicated a weekend to its revision, inserting cartoons, open-ended questions like, 'What's the most

powerful thing a teacher said to you?' and sensitive Likert scale items like 'Sometimes I think I'll never make it' or 'I would like to be in advanced classes, but I don't think I'm smart enough'. Over the next few months, we translated the survey into Spanish, Haitian Creole and Braille, and distributed it to 9th and 12th graders in 13 urban and suburban districts. At the second and third camps, other groups of youth researchers from the same schools (with some overlap) analyzed the qualitative and quantitative data from 9174 surveys, 24 focus groups and 32 individual interviews with youth. During the analysis phase, as we read what respondents had written in response to 'What are the causes of the achievement gap?', many of us were devastated. Racist slurs, genetic explanations and victim blaming characterized a number of the surveys. The youth researchers were visibly shaken as they realized that their own peers held these profoundly biased views – of them! From our PAR work in the prison we knew we had to address the depth of emotion that is embedded in social justice research (see Torre, Fine, Boudin, Bowen, Clark, Hylton, Martinez, Roberts, Rivera, Smart, and Upegui, 2001). One attempt to do so was the creation of a 'Graffiti Museum' in which youth researchers could document, on walls covered from floor to ceiling with paper, the most distressing, exhilarating and confusing comments they read. They scribbled poetry, sketched drawings and opened up streams of conversation with other youth researchers about the data. Eventually the Graffiti Museum became one of our most provocative products.

After the data were analyzed, teams of youth and adult researchers traveled from school to school presenting their findings to students, educators and community members. However, as we traveled, we witnessed the limits of talk. Some principals and superintendents welcomed the research. Others crossed their arms and tried to rationalize away the data. In one reporting session Kareem Sergent, an African American junior and youth researcher, presented a PowerPoint slide of the racialized patterns of school suspensions to his largely white teaching faculty:

> Now I'd like you to look at the suspension data, and notice that black males in high schools were twice as likely as white males to be suspended, and there are almost no differences between black males and black females. But for whites, males are three times more likely to be suspended than females: 22 per cent of black males, 19 per cent of black females, 11 per cent of white males and 4 per cent of white females.

The educators sat with crossed arms and challenged the data. Kareem continued, '*You know me, I spend a lot of time in the discipline room. It's really almost all black males.*' Hesitant nods were followed by immediate explanations from teachers about how in June '*it gets whiter*', and '*sometimes there are white kids, maybe when you're not there*'. Kareem persisted, turning to the charts projected on the screen: '*You don't have to believe me, but I speak for the hundreds of black males who filled out this survey. We have to do something about it.*'

While the session within the school was, perhaps predictably, filled with resistance, it revealed what we came to call the *power of the aggregate*. Youth researchers, like the rest of us, found comfort and power in the aggregate patterns that the survey and interview material provided. Frustrated with faculty unwillingness to listen to his analysis of the discipline data, Kareem tried to use his 'personal relationship' to the discipline room as a hook. When faculty resisted further, he took up the persona of the social scientist, simply reporting the evidence. He declared, calmly, that while they might choose to dismiss his particular case, they would nevertheless have to contend with hundreds of African American young men who completed the survey and told us the same. Kareem found confirmation and support in the aggregate data. But we worried about school-based presentations as our primary product and we grew concerned about the cognitive assumptions of social change embedded in these data-based presentations.

Though we saw most audiences nod in solidarity, we met far too many adults – like Kareem's faculty – who refused to listen to young people's complex renderings of *Brown's* victories and continuing struggles. We sat inside schools where it was clear that the 'achievement' gap – the latest face of segregation – was fundamentally built into the structures, ideologies and practices. We found ourselves trapped by obsessive audience questions pointing to poor youth and youth of color – *What's wrong with them? Even in the same school building, we have a gap? But if we stop tracking, how else can we teach students at their 'natural' levels?* And we became weary, even of sympathetic audiences, wondering, as we watched them tear up, if perhaps responsibility was being wiped away with their tissues.

Kareem's story is emblematic. A young person of color dares to raise a question about local injustice and the audience freezes in denial. Refusing responsibility, they treat the young person as though he has made it all up, is exaggerating or not taking responsibility. These dynamics are all too familiar. We know well from our work, and from the work of Jeanne Oakes (2005) and Julio Cammarota and colleagues (2006), that schools, public institutions, and boards of education typically deflect the critical commentary youth have to offer. As a result, we have come to understand that adult researchers have a responsibility to think through and, at times, find *audiences of worth* – those who deserve to hear, who will respect and engage the brilliance and passion of youth researchers. We speak here of audiences open to new and different knowledge that may destabilize what has become comfortable, audiences willing to cross institutional lines, audiences willing to be moved to action – full bodied, not just in the mind.

And so, in the Summer of 2003, with the milestone anniversary of *Brown* approaching, we decided to shift to *performance as public scholarship*. We extended our Social Justice and Social Research camps into a Social Justice and the Arts Institute. We recruited another radically diverse group of young people aged 13–21, who were interested in writing, performing, and social justice, and brought them together with community elders, social scientists, spoken word artists, dancers, choreographers and a video crew to collectively delve into the data from the Educational Opportunity Gap Project (Fine, Bloom, Burns, Chajet, Guishard, Payne and Torre, 2005); to learn about the legal, social and political history of segregation and integration of public schools; and to create *Echoes,* a performance of critical research, poetry and movement crafted to reflect on the 50th anniversary of *Brown* (Fine, Roberts, Torre, Bloom, Burns, Chajet, Guishard and Payne, 2004).

Together, we studied up on the history of *Brown,* Emmett Till, Ella Baker, and Bayard Rustin; finance inequity, tracking, battles over buses and bilingualism; the unprecedented academic success of the small schools movement; what it means to have separate schools for lesbian/gay/bisexual/transgender (l/g/b/t) students; as well as the joys, the dangers and 'not-yets' of integration. We sought to create a context in which young people could be exposed to history and contemporary research and then 'baste' their personal experiences in the seasoning of what has been, what is, and what could be. In this week-long Summer Institute, young people were educated alongside elders. The Institute was videotaped at the insistence of the young people, so that the process of youth PAR could be understood over time in all its complexity, and so that the work leading up to the performance would 'last more than one night'.

We struggled to help youth contextualize and historicize their 'personal experiences' as the project was not interested in simply producing a space for youth to 'give voice' to their 'individual' lives. Instead, we were committed, with the wisdom of historian Joan Scott (1990), to helping youth create products that would place their 'experience' critically in a sea of knowledge drawn from history, politics and research. The performances of two young people – Amir Bilal Billops and Kendra Urdang – illustrate how youth moved from 'personal experience' to critical research and performance.

In the midst of one morning's conversation about the expansion of the Harvey Milk school (New York City's school that focuses on l/g/b/t youth), a heated discussion ensued on the values and costs of 'integration'. Amir, an African American senior attending a desegregated high school, shared his deep disappointment with the unrealized promises of integration:

> When we were talking about the [black] dancer [Kathryn Dunham] and how she walked off the stage in the South during the 1940s because blacks were in the balcony, I realized that that happens today – with me and my friends. At my high school they put the special education kids in the balcony, away from the 'normal' kids. They [l/g/b/t students] may need a separate school just to be free of the prejudice. Putting people in the same building doesn't automatically take care of the problem.

That night he wrote 'Classification', a spoken-word piece he ultimately performed in *Echoes*:

> I was walking up the street with my boy Anthony and this other kid.
> Anthony was making jokes and the other kid turned around and asked, 'Are you in special ed?' My man said, 'Yes.'
> Soon after, being in my six person class, like yesterday I remember South Orange Maplewood School District classified me.
> It was 2000.
> She said I was 'eligible for special ed.'
> Possessing this label they gave me, I swallowed the stigma and felt the pain of being seen in a room with six people. Yeah, it fell upon me and the pain was like stones raining down on me. From the day where school assemblies seemed segregated and I had to watch my girl Krystal from balconies … Away from the 'normal' kids … to the days where I found myself fulfilling self-fulfilled prophecies.
> See I received the label of 'special education' and it sat on my back like a mountain being lifted by an ant – it just can't happen.
> It was my mind's master.
> It told me I was dumb, I didn't know how to act in a normal class. I needed two teachers to fully grasp the concepts touched upon in class, and my classification will never allow me to exceed track two.

So what is it that I do – so many occasions when the classification caused me to break into tears? It was my frustration.

My reaction to teachers speaking down to me saying I was classified and it was all my fault. Had me truly believing that inferiority was my classification.

Cause I still didn't know, and the pain WAS DEEP. The pain – OH GOD! THE PAIN!

The ridicule, the constant taunting, laughing when they passed me by.

Told me that community college should be my goal.

It wasn't until Ms. Cooper came and rescued me with her history class.

Showed me the importance of my history and told me the secrets my ancestors held.

She told me about the Malcolm Xs and the Huey Newtons.

She told me to speak out because this is the story of many and none of them are speaking.

And the silence is just as painful.

Amir's work provokes recognition of the sustained weight of oppression on those most adversely affected and the power of a single educator to interrupt and transform history.

In crafting a purposely diverse research team, we consciously invited young researchers/ performers from positions of substantial advantage to challenge the shiny armor of privilege they enjoyed in their schools. Kendra, a white, South African-Canadian-US student, created a spoken word piece about the racialized politics that constitute the tracking [leveling] in her desegregated high school. An excerpt of 'Go Blue!' reads:

and in the classrooms, the imbalance is subtle, undercurrents in hallways.
AP classes on the top floor, special ed. in the basement.
and although over half the faces in the yearbook are darker than mine,
on the third floor, everyone looks like me.
so it seems glass ceilings are often concrete.
....
so let's stay quiet, ride this pseudo-underground railroad,
this free ticket to funding from the board of ed.
racism is only our problem if it makes the front page.

although brown faces fill the hallways,
administrators don't know their names,
they are just the free ticket to funding,
and this is not their school.

When we travel with youth performers, or show clips from the video, we are always careful to represent the full range of collateral damage suffered by those students who have been unfairly marginalized and privileged, in order to reveal the perverse structural (de)formations in which youth are socialized and presumably educated.

Six months after the Summer Institute, on 17 May 2004, we performed *Echoes of Brown* for an audience of 800. It was a scholarly and aesthetic experiment that challenged the boundaries of time, geography, generation and discipline, and braided political history, personal experience, research and knowledge from a generation living in the long shadow of *Brown*. Guided by youth concerns about the fleeting nature of performance, we used the videotaped material from the Summer Institute to create a DVD and book, *Echoes: The Legacy of Brown v. Board of Education, Fifty Years Later* (Fine et al., 2004). The DVD holds $4\frac{1}{2}$ hours of video, interviews with youth, elders and educators about the persistent and growing (opportunity gap). The book contains photos; interviews with youth, elders and educators; youth spoken-word performances; statistical analyses of our research on the 'six degrees of segregation'; and a list of activist organizations committed to work on the opportunity gap. Paralleling the Graffiti Museum, that was recreated as a portable graffitti wall for the night of the performance, there is an internet-based chat room dedicated to ongoing conversation among educators and organizers who have used the video or clips from the DVD in their classrooms and in community settings. We have placed the book in mainstream bookstores, selected excerpts for use on websites (teacherscollegepress.com and whatkidscando.com), and published on the work with students and educators. As with the prison study, we have spent much time strategizing how to position texts, talks and performances into the hands and hearts of those most intimately and adversely affected by injustice … as well as those who naively believe they have been untouched by the severely inequitable distributions of educational resources, opportunities, hopes and dreams. With creative products and processes we seek to break open a small space in the fabric of global injustice, where young people can study, speak back, perform and provoke for justice.

CREATING WEAPONS OF MASS INSTRUCTION WITH PARTICIPATORY ACTION RESEARCH

Since our work in the prison and *Echoes*, we have been invited to collaborate with groups of youth nationally and internationally who are working on PAR projects through NGOs, on college campuses, suburban schools, community based organizations (CBOs), jail cells, urban schools and on the streets. Youth are crafting participatory research and organizing projects with activists, scholars, foundations, CBOs, and progressive educators, which critically investigate the social policies that construct and constrict their lives. Most exciting, they are taking this mix of activism and research and designing provocative products 'of use' (Cahill, 2004; Cammarota, Ginwright and Noguera, 2006; Torre and Fine, 2005). Through our research with the youth of the opportunity gap, *Echoes* and the women of Bedford Hills Correctional Facility, we have come to understand that these provocative products of PAR are essential in this most discouraging political moment. Products are significant to motivate a PAR collective toward a common end and products are crucial for establishing a material base that can be mobilized and expanded for future action.

Many have asked us to construct guidelines for PAR with youth. We typically decline. PAR is a deeply contextualized process for democratic and justice-based work that does not lend itself to a checklist of practices. Indeed, I (Michelle) recall having a conversation with Paolo Freire during one of his visits to New York when he confided that a great sense of sadness overcame him when he realized that his radical teachings were

being converted into lockstep curricula, checklists and structured principles. In the memory of Freire, I/we have long resisted creating such a list for PAR.

And yet, we have learned much and made mistakes about how to engage PAR projects with young people, and have come to think that there are a series of inquiries – conversations that action researchers and participatory action researchers should engage in as they move toward PAR with youth. We offer these questions in pencil, to help midwife thoughtful conversations about participation, products and provocation.

Audience

Participatory action research pivots toward change, but the question of who needs to be educated, mobilized, encouraged, convinced is rarely asked. We suggest that PAR collectives spend time thinking through audience by considering:

1. Whom do you want to reach, touch, mobilize, educate, provoke to action?
2. What are you asking readers/audiences to do? (For example, guilt is not a stance from which action is easily elicited; but collective responsibility may be.)
3. What resources have you provided to help shift a sense of collective responsibility into collective action?
4. What are the spatialities of change you envision? In other words, where do you want to incite change – in theoretical framing, in the next generation and elders, in community and institutions, in the local space of your work, across sites and/or beyond?

Products

Just as audience is a critical dimension of PAR, so too is the language and shape of your products. In what language will you produce your work? Will it be performed and/or presented as scholarly, policy study? Will it be narrated in a voice of outrage or distanced rationality? Who will be positioned as the speaker(s)? More specifically,

5. In what discourse do you choose to provoke – science, art, law, outrage, contentious politics?
6. In whose voice(s) do you write/perform/publish/reveal the depth of injustice?
7. Have you represented both the coherence of your collective and the rich differences among you?
8. How can you combine sharp social critique with an energizing sense of possibility?
9. How might your work be misused and how can you caution people against such misuse (For example, warning labels that read: this report should NOT be interpreted to suggest that ...)

Provocation

And then, finally, we encourage critical deliberation about the ethics of provocation and the uneven distribution of vulnerabilities. We recognize that all research is political. However, PAR is explicitly political. The task of provocation within PAR is always double – a goal and a danger. In this spirit we invite PAR collectives to consider:

10. Who is made vulnerable by the very products you have designed?
11. How does your project attach to other, ongoing struggles for social justice?
12. What happens to co-researchers and colleagues who are located squarely in the institution under scrutiny, the morning after? Are they connected to each other, to other social movements, to people in power who will protect them?

This is a most treacherous political moment for participatory research work. The relations of social research to social policy are badly misaligned – reflecting the severely strained relations between social policy and social justice (Fine and Barrerras, 2001). Locally and globally, the state has walked away from the needs of individuals, families and communities, particularly those who are poor, working class and of color. We face what French theorist Pierre Bourdieu has called 'a crisis of politics ... [in which we encounter] despair at the failure of the state as guardian of the public interest' (1998: 2). Bourdieu argues, further, that the neo-liberal

view of the state and the market have been represented as self-evident through a 'symbolic inculcation in which journalists and ordinary citizens participate passively and, above all, a certain number of intellectuals participate actively. ... This kind of symbolic drip feed to which the press and television news contribute very strongly ... produces very profound effects. And as a result neo-liberalism comes to be seen as an inevitability' (1998: 30).

Bourdieu insists, as do we, that social researchers have a public responsibility to disrupt the sense of inevitability – that bad people do bad things and deserve to end up in prison; some student will always fail, they just don't care about school – and to engage with communities around questions of justice and the inequitable distribution of freedom, goods and opportunities. Critically engaged, PAR has the potential to do just that. Whether launched in schools, communities, or prisons – around kitchen tables or in social movements – PAR provides a vital way of resuscitating and maintaining a questioning and participatory democratic practice, one with the potential to unleash a diaspora of radical struggle, hope and possibility across generations. Participatory action research is a strategic tool by which researchers' collectives can interrupt the drip feed, engage critical questions, produce new knowledge, provoke expanded audiences, and ask, in the language of the poet Marge Piercy (1973), how can we 'be of use?'

NOTES

1 Over the past decade, a loose and growing PAR collective has sprung up at the Graduate Center, CUNY. Each project has developed a unique set of situated, tailored products, designed to organize, shift public policy, provoke outrage and/or shift the epistemological grounds of social research. In addition to the two projects described in this chapter: Monique Guishard coordinated a project with mothers and youth in under-resourced communities of the Bronx organizing for educational justice, designing a compelling website on the history of educational

organizing in the South Bronx (Guishard et al., 2003; www.mothersthemove.com). Yasser Payne and the Street Life Collective researched men who lead a street life, producing a series of street conferences, and presentations in public schools (Payne, 2006). Caitlin Cahill, working with young women from the Lower East Side of New York, researched and contested the stereotypes of their being 'at risk' that litter their neighborhoods, and in response launched a massive sticker campaign in which the stereotypes were exposed and challenged (Cahill, 2004; www.feduphoneys.org). Roger Hart collaborated with youth in Nepal who participated in the design and construction of their boys' and girls' clubs (Hart, 2002). And María Elena Torre just completed a participatory project with students at an elite university, ostensibly working on 'diversity' issues and racism, where they sponsored a massive speak-out on students' experiences with racial, sexual, class and disability-based injustice (Torre, 2005b).

2. Following normal publication conventions this reference would be cited as (Fine et al., 2001). At the request of the authors we have intentionally broken with this convention to counter the privileging of the academic voice and to emphasize the fully participatory nature of this research. The first citation in each case lists all authors while subsequent references follow the normal publishing conventions – Eds.

REFERENCES

Bourdieu, P. (1998) *Acts of Resistance: Against the Tyranny of the Market.* New York: New Press.

Cahill, C. (2004) 'Defying gravity? Raising consciousness through collective research', *Children's Geographies*, 2 (2): 273–86.

Cahill, C., Arenas, E., Contreras, J., Jiang, N., Rios-Moore, I. and Threatts, T. (2004) *Makes Me Mad: Stereotypes of Young Urban Women of Color.* New York: Center for Human Environments at The Graduate School of the City University of New York. [www.fed-up-honeys.org]

Cammarota, J., Ginwright, S. and Noguera, P. (2006) *Youth, Democracy and Community Change: New Perspectives in Practice and Policy for America's Youth.* New York: Routledge Press.

Fine, M. and Barrerras, R. (2001) 'To be of use', *Analyses of Social Issues and Public Policy*, 1: 175–82.

Fine, M., Bloom, J., Burns, A., Chajet, L., Guishard, M., Payne, Y. and Torre, M.E. (2005) 'Dear Zora: a letter to Zora Neal Hurston fifty years after Brown', *Teachers College Record*, 107 (3): 496–529.

Fine, M., Roberts, R.A., Torre, M.E., and Bloom, J., Burns, A., Chajet, L., Guishard, M., and Payne, Y. (2004) *Echoes: Youth Documenting and Performing the Legacy of Brown v. Board of Education.* New York: Teachers College Press.

Fine, M., Torre, M.E., Boudin, K., Bowen, I., Clark, J., Hylton, D., Martinez, M., 'Missy', Rivera, M., Roberts, R.A., Smart, P. and Upegui, D. (2001) *Changing Minds: The Impact of College in a Maximum Security Prison.* New York: The Graduate School of the City University of New York.

Fine, M., Torre, M.E., Boudin, K., Bowen, I., Clark, J., Hylton, D., Martinez, M., 'Missy', Rivera, M., Roberts, R.A., Smart, P., and Upegui, D. (2003) 'Participatory action research: within and beyond bars', in P. Camic, J.E. Rhodes and L. Yardley (eds), *Qualitative Research in Psychology: Expanding Perspectives in Methodology and Design.* Washington, DC: American Psychological Association. pp. 173–98.

Gordon, A.F. (1997) *Ghostly Matters: Haunting and the Sociological Imagination.* Minneapolis, MN: University of Minnesota Press.

Guishard, M., Fine, M., Doyle, C., Jackson, J., Roberts, R., Staten, S., Singleton, S. and Webb, A. (2003) 'As long as I got breath, I'll fight': Participatory action research for educational justice', *The Family Involvement Network of Educators.* Harvard Family Research Project. [http://www.gse.harvard.edu/hfrp/projects/fine.html]

Hart, R. (2002) *Mirrors of Ourselves: Tools of Democratic Self Reflection for Groups of Children and Youth, Katmandu, Nepal.* New York: Children's Environments Research Group and the Save the Children Alliance.

Oakes, J. (2005) *Keeping Track: How Schools Structure Inequality.* New Haven, CT: Yale University Press.

Payne, Y.A. (2006) 'Participatory Action Research and Social Justice: Keys to Freedom for Street Life Oriented Black Men' in J. Battle, M. Bennett and A.J. Lemelle, Jr. (eds), *Free At Last? Black America in the Twenty First Century.* New York: Transaction Publisher. pp. 265–80.

Piercy, M. (1973) *To Be of Use.* New York: Doubleday.

Smith, L.T. (2001) 'Troubling spaces', *International Journal of Critical Psychology*, 4: 167–82.

Smith, L.T. (1999) *Decolonizing Methodologies: Research and Indigenous Peoples.* London: Zed Books.

Torre, M.E. (2005a) 'The alchemy of integrated spaces: youth participation in research collectives of difference', in L. Weis and M. Fine (eds), *Beyond Silenced Voices.* Albany, NY: State University of New York Press. pp. 251–66.

Torre, M.E. (2005b) *What's Your Issue? Questions of Diversity and Democracy on a College Campus.* New York: Eugene Lang College.

Torre, M. and Fine, M. (2005) 'Bar none: extending affirmative action to college in prison', *Journal of Social Issues,* 61 (3): 569–94.

Torre, M.E., Fine, M., Boudin, K., Bowen, I., Clark, J., Hylton, D., Martinez, M., Roberts, R.A., Rivera, M., Smart, P. and Upegui, D. (2001) 'A space for co-constructing counter stories under surveillance', *International Journal of Critical Psychology,* 4: 149–66.

28

Taking the Action Turn: Lessons from Bringing Participation to Qualitative Research

Sonia Ospina, Jennifer Dodge, Erica Gabrielle
Foldy and Amparo Hofmann-Pinilla

This chapter tells the story of our decision to introduce participation as a key feature of a qualitative research project about social change leadership. We analyze the context that influenced our choice to create a 'hybrid' design; discuss the subsequent choices we made about our 'positionality' vis-à-vis research participations and the kind of knowledge we produced; and reflect on the tensions these choices created with respect to control over the research process, its action orientation, and whose voice was represented. Embracing participation enriched the research but also provided hard-earned lessons about the trade-offs of taking the action turn.

This chapter tells the story of our explicit decision to introduce participation as a key feature of a large-scale, multi-year, US-based research project to study social change leadership. We invited those who would have been the 'subjects' of the research to co-inquire about their experience of leadership. Embracing participation opened up and enriched the research in many ways. It also generated tensions and challenges that would have been absent had we followed a more traditional qualitative research path. Given the action turn, more and more qualitative researchers are including elements of action

research in their work, yet this marriage is not straightforward. We provide hard-earned insights about the trade-offs of combining these approaches.

The research took place as part of a foundation-funded recognition program for social change leaders. Our decision to make the research participatory grew out of our position at the center of several competing interests: of participants, ourselves and our research community, and the funder. Choosing to honor each of these relationships led to a hybrid design that combined elements of action research and traditional interpretivist qualitative research. In this chapter we discuss the origins of the tensions we encountered, how they manifested themselves in the day-to-day life of the project, how we handled them, and their consequences.

This chapter begins by describing the institutional context of the research and the research design we created as a response to that context. We then discuss how that design resulted in choices we made related to 'positionality' (Herr and Anderson, 2005) and to the nature of knowledge that we wanted to produce. We then explore how these choices created tensions with respect to *control* over the research process, the *action* orientation of the research, and whose *voice* is represented – critical issues within the contested terrain of qualitative research paradigms (Guba and Lincoln, 2005), and within conversations around the nature and practice of action research (Gaventa and Cornwall, 2001/2006; Heron and Reason, 2001/2006; Park, 2001/2006).

SETTING THE STAGE: HOW HISTORY AND THE INSTITUTIONAL CONTEXT CREATED COMPETING DEMANDS

Our study grew out of the Research and Documentation component of a national, ongoing program called Leadership for a Changing World (LCW), funded by the Ford Foundation. The goal of the program is to 'recognize, strengthen and support leaders and to highlight the importance of community leadership in improving people's lives' (Leadership for a Changing World, 2006). It recognizes and provides a financial award to individuals and teams in social change organizations.

Program participants have included 165 individuals across 92 social change organizations, recognized in cohorts of 17 to 20 organizations from 2001 to 2005. These award recipients were selected because they demonstrated leadership that is strategic, is sustainable, bridges different groups of people, and gets results. They participate in the program for two years, and engage in various activities, including the research. Recipients represent community-based

organizations that effectively address critical social problems with a commitment to social change. Their work spans a broad range of policy domains, including community development, the arts, human rights, the environment, sexual and reproductive health, youth development, and education, among others. They also combine, in differing degrees, at least four types of activities: service delivery, organizing, advocacy and community building (Ospina and Foldy, 2005).

Competing Demands Emerging from Program Context. This context influenced our choices and contributed to three competing demands we faced as researchers. First, in addition to recognizing leadership for social change, the LCW program creators wanted to disseminate the notion that 'leadership comes in many forms and from many different communities' (Leadership for a Changing World, 2006). Therefore, our research was meant to change the way the broad public, as well as public officials and policy-makers, think about leadership. The research was part of an intervention for social change grounded on explicit value commitments (Toulmin, 1996) favoring the poor and disenfranchised, and supportive of social justice approaches. These requirements placed us closer to action research and other 'new paradigm' qualitative approaches that have taken the action turn, rather than to mainstream qualitative research, whether interpretivist or positivist, which assumes value neutrality as the starting point (Guba and Lincoln, 2005).

Second, because we came to this context located within an academic setting, schooled in the conventional demands of social science research, we wanted to influence the academic one as well. Both our school and the leadership field were clearly dominated by positivist orientations where objectivity, validity, and generalizability reign. Moreover, as interpretive qualitative researchers, we were attuned to the standards required by our own professional codes. For these reasons, we wanted to work with both conventional standards of qualitative research and at the same time meet the additional standards demanded by the action turn (Dodge et al., 2005).

Finally, the award recipients brought their own interests and demands. For most of them, engaging in research meant an opportunity to learn more about the issues they were passionate about: how to mitigate the effects of toxic sludge in their rivers, how best to design employee ownership programs, or the economic consequences of passing a living wage bill. While some also had questions about leadership practice and welcomed the opportunity for inquiry into this dimension of their practice, others were disappointed that research resources would not be directly and immediately applied to advance their own particular mission.

Placed at the center of these competing demands – from the funder, academic colleagues and program participants – we developed a hybrid design that, as much as possible, balanced these various interests. In the next section we describe the overall design and the specific choices arising from it.

CHOOSING A HYBRID RESEARCH DESIGN

Since research methods must be 'appropriate to the subject matter and interests at stake' (Toulmin, 1996: 204), our design considered the broader institutional context within which it existed. Our theoretical framework, research focus, methods and research stance reflect our attempt to create a hybrid approach that brought participation to the center of our practice. In turn, this choice had consequences for our positionality as researchers and for the nature of the knowledge we produced.

Theoretical Framework. Dominant, positivist theories hold up a 'heroic' version of leadership that is largely drawn from research in corporate and governmental organizations (Allen, 1990; Fletcher, 2004; Alimo-Metcalfe and Alban-Metcalfe, 2006). In contrast, our work focused on social change organizations and drew on a constructionist approach to leadership (Ospina and Sorenson, 2006), which views leadership

as the collective achievement of a group, rather than as the property of an individual (Pfeffer, 1977; Smircich and Morgan, 1982; Hunt, 1984; Tierney, 1987; Drath and Palus, 1994; Meindl, 1995; Pastor, 1998; Drath, 2001). Based on the notion that leadership emerges from the constructions and actions of people in organizations, our main research question was 'In what ways do communities trying to make social change engage in the work of leadership?'

Research Focus. This theoretical understanding had important implications for the focus of the research. If leadership is shared and relational, then research should focus on *the work* of leadership, as evidenced in collective action, rather than the behaviors or characteristics of individual leaders. For us, this meant collecting data from a wide variety of individuals involved in each organization, rather than just the award recipients themselves, and inquiring about how organizational members made sense of and carried out activities to exercise leadership in particular arenas.

Methods. We did this work by creating a multi-modal design with three parallel research methods: narrative inquiry, ethnography and cooperative inquiry. Offering participants an opportunity to choose their degree of involvement (given their limited time to engage in co-research while doing their regular work), we hoped that each participant (or a member of their organization) would agree to participate as co-researcher in at least one method.

The *narrative inquiry* involved site visits and extended interviews with participants and their colleagues focused on their work, in order to learn about aspects of leadership that the organization exemplified. These were summarized in a 'leadership story' for each group. In the *ethnographic inquiry*, ethnographers located near the organization's community worked with selected participants and their colleagues, for about three months, to paint a portrait of particular leadership issues or practices; *cooperative inquiry* groups, made up of six to eight participants, engaged in cycles of action and reflection to explore a burning question of their practice. We then integrated the fruits of all three streams, weaving together lessons from across methods and cohorts of participants, to develop a deeper understanding of practices involved in social change leadership.

In sum, this multi-modal design gave program participants, in theory, various ways of engaging in the research process. Each method afforded a unique angle from which co-researchers could reflect on their experience and offered opportunities for different degrees of participation. Incorporating a participatory perspective into our qualitative research had important implications for our research practice, in particular our 'positionality' as researchers vis-à-vis research participants.

Our position in relation to the research participants. Viewing action research as a broad concept covering many research practices, Herr and Anderson (2005) use the term 'researcher positionality' to describe the different stances researchers can take toward research participants. They propose a continuum of positions that range from (1) an insider studying her own practice to (6) an outsider working with insiders. Between these extremes, are other positions. From 'the inside' toward 'the outside', these include: (2) insiders in collaboration with other insiders; (3) insiders in collaboration with outsiders; (4) insider/outsider teams working in reciprocal collaboration; and (5) outsiders in collaboration with insiders.

While our understanding of our own positionality was implicit as we moved through the research process, we have used the concept to more fully understand our experience in the research. Our positionality was complicated by the competing demands we faced from the three major interests we wanted to honor. The conventional academic perspective suggested taking the sixth positionality, that of outsiders with a neutral stance controlling the research, but this was inconsistent with our interpretivist approach and with the demands of the program. Many LCW participants preferred the third positionality:

insiders in collaboration with outsiders, so they could use the research to investigate particular questions generated by their work. The foundation's original 'request for proposals' framed the invitation to do research about leadership as outsiders collaborating with insiders, or the fifth positionality. It encouraged outside researchers to draw extensively from participant practice to create new knowledge in the voice of the researcher.

Considering the context, we proposed the stance of co-research, inviting participants to study with us their experience of leadership. Doing so, we shifted the nature and goals of the research component from practice-oriented research (to learn *from* the practice of the LCW program participants) to a participatory research (to learn *with* LCW participants). The foundation welcomed this reframing. We thus aspired to take the fourth positionality Herr and Anderson (2005) describe: an 'insider/outsider reciprocal collaboration', which we felt provided the best response to the competing demands from participants, academics and the funder. However, despite valiant attempts at consistency, our footing has varied – ranging at different stages from 'insiders in collaboration with outsiders' to 'reciprocal collaboration' to 'outsiders in collaboration with insiders' and even 'outsiders working with insiders'. These shifts resulted from our responses to the interests of the various parties and the particular kind of knowledge most useful to each.

We found our positionality shifted most often in response to three specific tensions which we turn to now: *control* over the research process, the *action* orientation of the research, and the *voice* represented in the production of knowledge.

LIVING A HYBRID DESIGN: IMPLICATIONS FOR CONTROL, ACTION AND VOICE

Both action and qualitative researchers must address several difficult issues: who has power over the inquiry, how the research does or does not support action for change, and whose understandings are reflected in disseminated materials (Fals Borda, 2001/2006; Hall, 2001; Guba and Lincoln, 2005). Like Guba and Lincoln (2005), we acknowledge that these issues of control, action, and voice are interdependent, but we will look at them separately for analytical purposes. Below we provide a conceptual description of each issue, the choices we made to respond to each issue, the advantages and disadvantages of our choices including how they affected our positionality and, at the end of each section, an overall assessment of they way we approached the issue.

Control of the Inquiry

Control relates to the question 'how is knowledge created?' and to the interconnection between knowledge and power. Such issues as 'Who initiates [the research]? Who determines salient questions? ... [And] Who determines how data will be collected?' need to be addressed (Guba and Lincoln, 2005: 202). Engaging participants in research – sharing control with them – redefines the knowledge production process and outcomes in ways consistent with the quality standards of action research and its goals of 'participation and democracy' (Reason and Bradbury, 2001/2006).

Our research in practice: Tensions around control. In general, we aspired to generate what Herr and Anderson (2005) label the fourth positionality, 'reciprocal collaboration among members of an insider/outsider team' (p. 31), or what Chataway (1997) refers to as 'mutual inquiry', which implies sharing control equally. Herr and Anderson (2005) acknowledge that in an ideal world, this position represents the most democratic approach. Yet they also state that, because 'the notion of insider and outsider is often a matter of degree' (p. 38), in practice each position offers an equally respectable way of producing actionable knowledge, as long as the implications of one's choices are considered (see

also Reason, 2006; Reason and Bradbury, 2001/2006).

Indeed, in some instances, we have engaged in genuine reciprocal collaborations. However, given the complexity of our institutional context, we did not fully realize this aspiration. As expected, different individuals and leadership teams responded to the invitation to participate in different ways, from full participation and engagement in some cases, to willing collaboration in others, to partial and at times reluctant cooperation in yet others, to non-participation in a few. Given these choices, more often than not, we have been 'outsiders doing research in collaboration with insiders'. To respond to both the participants' interests in social change practice and the broader program's interest in generating new knowledge, we had to make choices about which research activities would prioritize practitioners' needs or academic needs. Importantly, these choices impacted positionality and who would control which streams of research.

For example, in cooperative inquiry, the projects were almost entirely driven by participants and required a significant time commitment from them. They reflected collectively on burning issues from their practice and worked with facilitators over five cycles of action and reflection to refine the question and answer it. The cooperative inquiry groups generated reports of their findings to contribute to knowledge production in the project, sometimes written by participants, sometimes by facilitators, and sometimes by both.

In contrast, participation in the narrative inquiry stream varied, from participants who shaped the inquiry from beginning to end, to those who only provided foci for the interview protocol, suggested interview participants, and gave us feedback on our analysis, then left it to the researchers to implement the rest. Even those quite involved in this stream did not participate in 'cross-site analysis', a piece of the research based in more traditional qualitative research practices that looks for common themes across organizations. The core research team managed and carried out this process: we identified key themes, carried out coding and analysis, and wrote academic articles, as well as developed a model of social change leadership (Ospina and Foldy, 2005).

Advantages. One of the key advantages of sharing control with participants is that the research process becomes more democratic, a worthwhile aspiration in itself. Given our theoretical, practical and philosophical motivations, we viewed program participants as owners of the experience of leadership rather than holders of attributes worth studying from afar. Therefore we saw the value of working with them to create knowledge, viewing them as insider 'agents' of the research project, rather than as 'objects' to be studied by outsiders.

A related advantage was that democracy also enhanced the quality of the knowledge generated. Given the scant availability of knowledge about leadership produced by applying a constructionist lens, we decided that it made sense to work *with* participants in the research, to share control over the research process so they would be involved with us in defining relevant research questions about leadership, choosing the best ways to carry out the research, and offering different ways to interpret findings. For example, in a summary report of all of the ethnographies we had done to date, we wrote about the power of this type of leadership for constructing social worth where others only saw problems. Because we created space for participants to identify topics of interest to them and propose ways to study them, we were able to learn about the important ways that they discovered and nurtured hidden assets to create positive social change in the most difficult circumstances.

Disadvantages. On the other hand, sharing control required us to spend additional energy doing tasks that, while present in more conventional qualitative research, are relatively bounded. Using participatory research meant ongoing negotiations over who would do what, who would take ownership over what,

and who would make decisions about which aspects of the research.

This challenge was intensified by the specific context of the broader program. New participants arrived every year, triggering anew the trust building process and requiring negotiations around control. Furthermore, the fact that the research was commissioned by a foundation influenced early decisions associated with control. For example, because the research was part of a broader funded intervention, we had to determine the general parameters of the research activities before participants arrived. The foundation's request for proposals required well-structured plans, and once we were recruited, they asked us for even further clarification of activities, schedules and products before the program started. Under these conditions, our original invitation for co-research was interpreted as imposing a rigid research design that was contrary to genuine collaboration and co-production. The first group of participants fought hard during the first program meeting to make it clear that they would not accept a position as unequal partners under a 'discourse' of co-research (Ospina et al., 2004). Given our position in relation to the various program stakeholders, we had to directly address suspicions that we were exploiting participants rather than engaging in a reciprocal relationship that would add value for everyone.

Assessment. We were most successful in sharing control with participants in cooperative inquiry and ethnography, where there was more room for negotiation over the insider/outsider collaboration, and where participants could create and use knowledge that would directly contribute to their work. As for narrative inquiry, while many participants appreciated it, in general they found the overall process and product more removed from the urgencies of their daily work and felt less interested in participating in all of its stages. We had most control over the cross-site narrative analysis, given our interest in producing public knowledge that met academic standards, and participants' lack of interest in engaging in this type of inquiry.

Though we strived to be egalitarian (Toulmin, 1996), we did not fully achieve it. Ultimately the initiative to do research did not come from participants nor was it organized to primarily help their work. Moreover, the basic structure and methods through which the inquiry was conducted were largely in place before the participants became involved. Also, as a result of the program's broader institutional context, the core team ultimately responsible for the research kept authority over resources designated for research.

Yet there were clear advantages to our hybrid approach. In sharing authority and control over the research agenda we engaged participants more fully, made the process more democratic and developed insights that we would not otherwise have done. Further, we created different kinds of knowledge, some of which has been directly useful to participants' work. In the next section, we explore how well these processes and products helped to create actionable knowledge.

INTEGRATING ACTION AND INQUIRY

Answers to the question of 'Knowledge for what?' bring to the forefront concerns about the extent to which inquiry and action are integrated or separated. In conventional social science research, action happens after the research is finished, by persons external to the inquiry (Ospina and Dodge, 2005). Applied researchers who advocate for 'pragmatic science' (Hodgkinson et al., 2001) may call for collaborating with those interested in future action, but even there, the expectation is that inquiry and action are distinct. In contrast, action is an integral part of the action research process; the *purpose* is to make positive change in the world, by developing local knowledge through participation (Toulmin, 1996; Reason and Bradbury, 2001/2006). This way, the process and products of action research are distinct, even from those

in applied and pragmatic research (Park, 2001/2006). Guba and Lincoln (2005) see a trend in qualitative research as it moves from 'interpretation and Verstehen, or understanding, toward social action' (p. 201). Their description of a 'mandate for social action, *especially action designed and created by and for research participants with the aid and cooperation of researchers*' (p. 202, emphasis added) illustrates how the action turn is bringing qualitative research and action research closer together.

Our Research Practice: Tensions around Action. The relevance research has for action is influenced largely by the kind of knowledge produced. This distinction between 'local' and 'public' knowledge is central here. Local knowledge is narrow and specific and is designed to support action at a particular place and time. Public knowledge consists of conclusions that are transferable to other contexts (Cochran-Smith and Lytle, 1993; Herr and Anderson, 2005).

Participants in our program were most interested in producing local knowledge that would enable them to advance the particular issues that drove their work – such as rights for day laborers or housing for people with HIV/AIDS. This would require a positionality of mutual collaboration. But the funder wanted public knowledge with broad appeal, even if it had no direct consequences for any given participant's work. Academics require a particular subset of public knowledge that is created according to particular rules of rigor, and that generalizes to either a population (positivist research) or a theory (interpretivist research) (Rubin and Rubin, 2005). Conventional researchers tend to choose the more traditional positionality of outsiders working with insiders for this work.

Our goal was to develop both local and public knowledge. We wanted to support the work of participants, find applications to other social change contexts and contribute to the theory of leadership. We believed we could do this by engaging in 'practice-grounded research', that is, research grounded in the perspectives of practitioners – independent of whether it is led by insiders or outsiders – but aimed at better understanding leadership practice in a way accessible to others outside the inquiry process. For the most part, our multimethod design allowed us to generate local knowledge for action while creating opportunities to build public knowledge, like other action research techniques do (see Roth and Bradbury, Chapter 23 in this volume).

Cooperative inquiries and collaborative ethnographies allowed participants to propose questions of relevance to their work, thus integrating research and action. One of the collaborative ethnographies grew from an agreement between two LCW organizations to document the factors that facilitated and hindered their efforts to engage in collaborative work given their differences – one worked with Latino immigrant workers to protect their rights; the other with a largely white, middle-class base that advanced the rights of gays and lesbians. The final narrative, however, provided insights about leadership and collaboration beyond the particular case.

Narrative inquiry, on the other hand, more directly addressed the need to produce knowledge for external practitioner and academic audiences. In our analysis of narrative transcripts, we searched for patterns across organizations using more conventional qualitative techniques. Our goal was to produce knowledge about leadership that contrasted with the heroic view that has guided previous research. We still sought to support action by producing public knowledge about a breadth of activities that contribute to leadership. For example, one of our papers explores how intensive dialogue with constituents experiencing a given problem leads to creative, grounded solutions (Dodge and Ospina, 2004). While still connecting inquiry to action, action was one level removed from participants' practice, and the researchers' positionality shifted from insider-outsider collaboration to outsider research in collaboration with insiders. The findings of this 'cross-site analysis' transcend the uniqueness of each context, and represent the perspective of outsiders, though they are still relevant for practitioners because they are based on participants' insider perspective.

Advantages. The most significant advantage of this approach was that we have successfully developed materials tailored to very different audiences: participants themselves, practitioners more broadly, and academics. One cooperative inquiry group explored how they, as community organizers, could effectively help others become more strategic, conceptual, and creative thinkers (Kovari et al., 2005). They remarked in their report on the importance of the inquiry for developing their own individual practice:

> We had originally asked how we could *teach* people to be more strategic, creative, and conceptual. What we began to understand during our inquiry was the importance of *engaging* others in the *experience* of strategic thinking. Our own actions and relationships with them would be part of the equation. To help people *learn* to be more strategic, creative, and conceptual, *we* would have to be *intentional* about being more strategic, creative, and conceptual *in relationship with them*. (p. 14)

The group finished the report by reflecting on how the 'cooperative inquiry process … had enabled these personal transformations' to take place (p. 15). While this inquiry was immediately useful to its participants, we have several testimonials from non-LCW practitioners indicating their interest in this and other materials. For example, a nearby consultant who was advising a different coalition in the region found a document we had written about fostering deep partnership in collaborative contexts, based on the narrative data, very useful for understanding how the collaboration operated (Dodge et al., 2004). This transfer of knowledge relates to Gustavsen's (2001/2006; see also Chapter 4 in this volume) notion of knowledge development in large-scale action research projects. He argues that knowledge is transferred when people begin to reference ideas that they learned from the work context of others. This is knowledge in action and represents a relational logic to knowledge development. Finally, we have contributed to academic conversations about leadership with multiple conference presentations and published manuscripts. This work is ongoing: we continue to develop materials for all three audiences. (For other examples, visit our website at www. wagner.nyu.edu/leadership).

Disadvantages. While our multi-modal design enabled us to flexibly respond to the different interests in the program, not all products were successful with participants. For example, we hoped that the 'leadership story' for each organization, produced during the first stage of the narrative inquiry, would be useful for marketing or fund raising. Indeed, some participants reported using them or simply enjoying seeing the portrayals of their work. However, based on participants' feedback, we decided that the stories' contribution did not warrant the labor involved.

A second disadvantage of our action orientation, given our position within an academic institution, is that many of our colleagues view the separation of action and inquiry as essential to rigorous scientific research. In taking the action turn, we risked facing challenges to the academic legitimacy of our research findings, and our standing as social science researchers within our own community of practice.

Assessment. Balancing needs for local and public knowledge risked the development of materials that satisfied neither academics nor practitioners. Keeping this in mind, we developed different materials to serve different audiences rather than cross-over materials that might potentially reach across audiences. While we were satisfied that we addressed the needs of the different stakeholders in the research, we were still disappointed that we were not able to produce products that could simultaneously serve different audiences.

As the research project moved from data collection to integration – of the insights learned across organizations, research methods and participant cohorts – we became increasingly aware of our overarching charge to change the public conversation about leadership. This meant becoming increasingly

removed from each local site as we strived to ensure that our findings would be transferable to other contexts and generalizable to the theory of leadership. Our positionality moved closer to traditional forms of qualitative research: outsiders working with insiders. However, we still wanted to honor the participatory spirit of the research by feeding this public knowledge back to the participants who made it possible. We are now beginning this process by translating some of our academic papers into practitioner-friendly formats. As we continue writing, we are faced with challenges of voice and representation, a task we take up next.

Voice and Representation

While issues of control, action and voice are deeply inter-related, perhaps the hardest distinction is between control and voice since whose voice is represented is generally decided by those who control the process. We distinguish them by relating control to the process and voice to the product of research. Voice and representation raise questions about 'knowledge from whose perspective?' As Guba and Lincoln (2000) indicate, 'Today voice can mean ... not only having a real researcher – and a researcher's voice – in the text, but also letting research participants speak for themselves' (p. 183). For action researchers, voice relates directly to power, with some equating action research with 'the right to speak' (Hall, 2001). Referring to representation, Gaventa and Cornwall (2001/2006) argue that in participatory research 'writing ... emphasizes the importance of listening to and for different versions and voices' (p. 74). While our discussion of control described decisions about *how* we created knowledge, in this section we describe *what* knowledge we created: the research products, the range of issues they explore, and the tensions over the material actually included in these documents. (The question of 'What knowledge is created' also invokes a discussion of validity requirements in conventional and new-paradigm qualitative research as well as in action research. For space reasons we will not engage this relevant discussion. For our approach to validity in this project, see Dodge et al., 2005.)

Our Research Practice: Tensions around Voice and Representation. With each document we created, we had to decide whose voice and whose representation of the world would dominate. While we designed a process to engage many voices at multiple points, each final product represents choices that inevitably excluded some representations. And here our positionality became particularly acute. Positionality represents power: who has the power to make those final choices? That question has arisen over and over in our work. Our choice to take the action turn influenced decisions that ranged from what topics to pursue to what findings to make public and how, and who, would author and write publications.

Because we wanted to learn from participants' direct experience, we designed the research to give participants great influence in the data collection process by naming the aspects of their work they felt deserved study. We wanted this diversity in topics because it would allow us to cast a wide net, and inductively identify issues relevant to the *work* of leadership rather then behaviors and characteristics of individual leaders. We also opened up the writing process in different degrees to ensure that the voices of participants were represented in final products. The diversity of topics reflects a diversity of perspectives; the process allowed new voices to represent their worlds in spaces previously closed to them.

Indeed, participants suggested and pursued a wide variety of issues that loosely fall under the larger umbrella of leadership. The focus of the leadership stories from *narrative inquiry* included topics as diverse as how participants developed and worked with unlikely allies (Walters et al., 2003a), the importance of cultural identity (Walters et al., 2003b) and the way day laborers are invited to use their voice at the policy table (Walters et al., 2003c). While mostly written

by our research team, these products were rich in quotations, and in some cases were written by participants.

Ethnographies included topics such as leadership development among community members (Weinberg et al., 2005) and the practice of shared leadership (Hufford et al., 2003). While these products were written by researchers, the process was directed by participants who exercised considerable control over their representations in final reports. *Cooperative inquiries* explored issues such as opening spaces for individuals to take up their leadership (Altvater et al., 2003) and using the arts to support social change work (Aprill et al., forthcoming). These products are mostly written collaboratively among participants, and although in some cases the group authorized the researchers to write final reports, they have done so in close collaboration. As a consequence, participants' voices have clearly been represented in research products.

In contrast, in the *cross-site analysis* used to develop academic papers, the research team identified the topics for further exploration, like the use of cognitive framing in social change leadership (Foldy et al., forthcoming), and the paradoxes of managing collaboration within coalitions (Ospina and Saz-Carranza, 2005), and took responsibility for writing these products. We also integrated the learning from across our data set in a tentative model of social change leadership (Ospina and Foldy, 2005). For the most part, as we moved toward cross-site analysis and writing, our positionality has been that of 'outsiders working with insiders' and our voice has been dominant. In a few cases, we have successfully woven together the voices of insiders and outsiders in academic work, by inviting participants to write their perspective into articles (Ospina et al., 2004; Yorks et al., Chapter 33 in this volume). We also continue to create opportunities for participants and other social change leaders to reflect on our interpretations, so that we can integrate their perspectives. For example, we have presented the social change leadership model at several practitioner forums which have included both LCW participants and other activists. Input from these sessions was folded into future analysis.

Advantages. This approach had advantages related to both the quality of the products as well as the research process. In relation to our products, we brought an often excluded voice, that of community-based leaders, into the public conversation about leadership. The diversity of voices allowed us to capture the complexity of the experience of leadership. Also, because of our commitment to include relatively unmediated representations of participants' voices, many of the products use a language, style and perspective that are more accessible to other members of the same communities. In other cases, we used photography and video to showcase participants more directly. Both these strategies increased the likelihood that the knowledge created would be of direct and immediate use to those involved. Finally, this approach enhanced validity, since those with the lived experience had an undeniable expertise. Regarding the research process, producing interpretations and conclusions that were sanctioned by participants reduced the likelihood of exploitative research that used people's experience and knowledge toward an end they did not support.

Disadvantages. One significant challenge of our hybrid design, given the goals of sharing ownership and honoring a broader range of voices as relevant for the research, was that we had less autonomy to interpret data and draw conclusions. Of course, as in more conventional qualitative inquiry, we were constrained by the rules of our research community to ensure that interpretations were the result of a systematic process. But traditional qualitative researchers, like their quantitative counterparts, have more degrees of freedom to pursue their own understandings of the data than action researchers do. By developing a hybrid approach, we were accountable not just to the data, and not just to standards of quality, but to participants who had a vested interest in research findings and the

knowledge that was ultimately drawn from the research.

This challenge manifested itself particularly in materials describing a single organization. We decided early on that materials of this type must be approved by the organization since they could potentially be damaging. Occasionally, this meant avoiding material that participants felt was inaccurate, misleading or potentially harmful to their work. For example, one ethnographer deleted a section of the report which included information that participants felt could harm a collaborative process that was underway. We also chose not to make public several leadership stories that participants ultimately decided did not accurately represent their work. We also ran into difficulties in one of our cooperative inquiries when participants of one group excised entire sections of the report that they felt represented the facilitator's point of view and not their own.

An additional constraint had to do with the fact that the design of our research favored positive assessments of the participants' work. Participants in LCW were chosen because they were exemplars of outstanding leadership. In our narrative research we used appreciative inquiry (see Chapter 19 of this volume) to surface what they were doing right, to better understand how effective leadership happens. The generative approach helped us connect to participants and overcome suspicions they had of us, as well as bringing depth and richness to the interviews. But it also determined the types of stories that we heard. Sometimes an appreciative approach was confused (by participants as well as by members of the research team) as an invitation to whitewash the messiness of real experience by downplaying its problematic dimensions. In addition, while we encouraged participants to invite stakeholders who might be critical of their work into the conversation, we ultimately spoke to the people that participants suggested, thus missing an opportunity to represent the work of leadership in contested contexts. We would have had difficulty establishing trust with the participants in any other way, but it does represent a limitation of our approach.

Moreover, the very diversity gained by making room for multiple voices and topics made generating clear and cogent learning a daunting task. *Integrating* the knowledge gained within each method, across the three different methods, and across the cohorts of LCW participants to generate transferable public knowledge has been very challenging. A more traditional design would have generated *comparable* local knowledge in order to produce a straightforward comparative analysis. Doing so would have made integration easier, but would have failed to capture the richness we gained. In other words, adopting a participatory approach – in terms of producing multi-vocal local knowledge – has added interpretive complexity to generate public knowledge.

Assessment. Action researchers have suggested that success of the research depends on the ability of practitioner-participants to bracket their insider perspective and take the position of an outsider, thus being able to view themselves in a different light (Heron and Reason, 2001/2006; Kemmis and McTaggart, 2005). But this can require support from skilled researchers, based on a sustained and intimate trusting relationship. In our case, while we were able to establish this type of relationship with some participants, the scale of the project precluded this across the board. For this reason, we have wondered about the advisability of 'doing action research with a large N' as one team member put it. The depth and quality of relationship that was necessary to maintain a critical stance while holding to the fourth positionality – 'reciprocal collaboration' – suggests working with a much smaller number of groups.

In sum, issues of voice arise in several arenas. Inviting multiple voices enhanced the diversity and richness of the data, but also posed challenges in creating a clear and consistent argument around the overall findings. Ultimately, those multiple voices represented multiple interests, each of which may have had a strong stake in what was concluded. Action research and qualitative research can diverge here, with each favoring a different stakeholder. While hybrids are certainly possible, they may fall short of the exacting standards of each type. Researchers entering this territory should take care to craft appropriate standards that draw from each approach (Dodge et al., 2005), and be satisfied that they will not be able to live up to the separate standards of each.

CONCLUSION

We have told our story, of qualitative researchers deciding to adopt participatory practices, in an effort to develop more insights about the very real challenges of combining action research with traditional qualitative designs (for a discussion of other challenges related to doing action research see Chataway, 1997; Kemmis and McTaggart, 2005). As we have documented, we began knowing that we had to satisfy three very different audiences with very different interests and preferences. We have had to meet the demands of the funder for public knowledge; we have had to establish trust with the participants, many of whom were suspicious of academia and craved immediately practical insight; and we had to answer to the research requirements of an academic community distrustful of participatory research. For the most part, we succeeded. While there are moment-to-moment decisions we would love to revisit, we do not believe that a significantly different design could have satisfied these divergent set of requirements. But we wanted to clearly illustrate the very real tensions that such a path brings with it. Calls for qualitative research to take the action turn may inadvertently suggest that such research involves a set of discreet, relatively straightforward decisions rather than an ongoing and intense grappling with competing demands that involves continual self-reflection, group discussion, and stakeholder negotiation. The issues of positionality and knowledge production point to the complex political landscape researchers enter by taking the action turn.

In addition to illustrating the trade-offs of moving towards more complex and responsive research, we also want to contribute to the development of more democratic research practices. Respect and appreciation for the diversity of paradigms to approach research problems was a pre-condition for crossing the boundaries to produce the hybrid research practice we believed would help us accomplish our research goals. In doing so, we embraced Toulmin's (1996) notion of 'methodological democracy' and, like him, rejected a fixed definition of social science as 'a single universal set of procedures, applicable in investigations of all kinds, regardless of the subject matter or interests involved' (p. 204). We agree that good social science comes in many forms that can be located within 'a spectrum of research fields, with varied goals, and different methods of investigation', all of them legitimate in their own way (p. 223). We hope that as many of us continue to experiment, the larger research community will develop tailored standards of quality that speak to multiple demands (Dodge et al., 2005). But as we open the door for hybrid practices, we ought to realize that legitimacy cannot be taken for granted. Instead, it must be earned step by step.

Reflections on our experience with hybridity offer important insights for those who may decide to pursue similar paths that mix paradigms and methodologies. The primary lesson we want to share is that bringing in a participatory perspective to more conventional qualitative research has produced important benefits, but it has also been extremely demanding. As qualitative researchers face Guba and Lincoln's call for action (2000, 2005) and Reason and Bradbury's (2001/2006) invitation to take the action turn, it is incumbent to keep in mind that the challenges of hybridity add yet another layer of uncertainty to the always thrilling and sometimes painful adventure of doing rigorous, useful and relevant research.

ACKNOWLEDGEMENT

Our experience in the Research and Documentation component of the Leadership for a Changing World (LCW) program informs the ideas we have developed in this article. We would like to acknowledge the many contributions of LCW co-researchers and our partners at the Advocacy Institute who, over the course of the years, have been active participants in shaping our learning. We would also like to thank the Ford Foundation for its generous support of the LCW research.

REFERENCES

Alimo-Metcalfe, B. and Alban-Metcalfe, J. (2006) 'More (good) leaders for the public sector', *International Journal of Public Sector Management,* 19 (4): 293–315.

Allen, K. (1990) *Diverse Voices of Leadership: Different Rhythms and Emerging.* Ann Arbor, MI: UMI.

Altvater, D., Godsoe, B., James, L., Miller, B., Ospina S., Samuels, T., Shaylor, C., Simon, L. and Valdez, M. (2003) *'Unpacking' Leadership Development: A Dance That Creates Equals* [http://www.wagner.nyu.edu/leadership/reports/files/ Unpacking.pdf].

Aprill, A., Holliday, A., Jeffers, F., Miyamoto, N., Scher, A., Spatz, D., Townsell, R., Yeh, L., Yorks, L. and Hayes, S. (forthcoming) *Can the Arts Change the World? The Transformative Power of the Arts in Fostering and Sustaining Social Change.*

Chataway, C. (1997) 'An examination of the constrains on mutual inquiry in a participatory action research project', *Journal of Social Issues,* 53 (4): 747–65.

Cochran-Smith, M. and Lytle, S. (1993) *Inside/Outside: Teacher Research and Knowledge.* New York: Teachers College Press.

Dodge, J. and Ospina, S. (2004) 'Dialogue and democracy: how social change non-profits use dialogue to respond to leadership challenges: findings from a narrative inquiry.' Paper presented at the Annual Conference of the Association for Research on Nonprofit Organizations and Voluntary Action (ARNOVA), Los Angeles, CA.

Dodge, J., Ospina, S. and Foldy, E.G. (2005) 'Integrating rigor and relevance in public administration scholarship: the contribution of narrative inquiry', *Public Administration Review,* 65 (3): 286–300.

Dodge, J., Ospina, S. and Sparrow, R. (2004) *Making Partnership a Habit: Margie McHugh and the New York Immigration Coalition*. [www.synergos.org]

Drath, W. (2001) *The Deep Blue Sea: Rethinking the Source of Leadership*. San Francisco, CA: Jossey-Bass.

Drath, W. and Palus, C. (1994) *Making Common Sense: Leadership as Meaning Making in a Community of Practice*. Greensboro, NC: Center for Creative Leadership.

Fals Borda, O. (2001/2006) 'Participatory (action) research in social theory: origins and challenges', in P. Reason and H. Bradbury (eds), *Handbook of Action Research: Participative Inquiry and Practice*. London: Sage. pp. 27–38. Also published in P. Reason and H. Bradbury (eds) (2006), *Handbook of Action Research: Concise Paperback Edition*. London: Sage. pp. 27–37.

Fletcher, J. (2004) 'The paradox of post heroic leadership: an essay on gender, power, and transformational change,' *Leadership Quarterly*, 15 (5): 647–61.

Foldy, E.G., Goldman, L. and Ospina, S. (forthcoming) 'Framing and the role of cognitive shifts in organizational leadership', *Leadership Review Quarterly*.

Gaventa, J. and Cornwall, A. (2001/2006) 'Power and knowledge', in P. Reason and H. Bradbury (eds), *Handbook of Action Research: Participative Inquiry and Practice*. London: Sage pp. 70–79. Also published in P. Reason and H. Bradbury (eds) (2006), *Handbook of Action Research: Concise Paperback Edition*. London: Sage. pp. 71–82.

Guba, E. and Lincoln, Y. (2000) 'Paradigmatic controversies, contradictions, and emerging confluences', in N. Denzin and Y. Lincoln (eds), *Handbook of Qualitative Research, 2nd edn*. Thousand Oaks, CA: Sage. pp. 163–88.

Guba, E. and Lincoln, Y. (2005) 'Pragmatic controversies, contradictions, and emerging confluences', in N. Denzin and Y. Lincoln (eds), *Handbook of Qualitative Research, 3rd edn*. Thousand Oaks, CA: Sage. pp. 191–216.

Gustavsen, B. (2001/2006) 'Theory and practice: the mediating discourse', in P. Reason and H. Bradbury (eds), *Handbook of Action Research: Participative Inquiry and Practice*. London: Sage pp. 17–27. Also published in P. Reason and H. Bradbury (eds) (2006), *Handbook of Action Research: Concise Paperback Edition*. London: Sage. pp. 17–26.

Hall, B. (1993) cited in Maguire, P. (2001) 'Uneven Ground: Feminisms and Action Research', in P. Reason and H. Bradbury (eds), *Handbook of Action Research: Participative Inquiry and Practice*. London: Sage Publications. pp. 59–70.

Hall, B. (2001) 'I wish this were a poem of practices of participatory research', in P. Reason and H. Bradbury

(eds), *Handbook of Action Research: Participative Inquiry and Practice*. London: Sage. pp. 171–9.

Herr, K. and Anderson, G. (2005) *The Action Research Dissertation: a Guide for Students and Faculty*. Thousand Oaks, CA: Sage.

Heron, J. and Reason, P. (2001/2006) 'The practice of co-operative inquiry: research "with" rather than "on" people', in P. Reason and H. Bradbury (eds), *Handbook of Action Research: Participative Inquiry and Practice*. London: Sage. pp. 179–89. Also published in P. Reason and H. Bradbury (eds) (2006), *Handbook of Action Research: Concise Paperback Edition*. London: Sage. pp. 144–54.

Hodgkinson, G.P., Herriot, P. and Anderson, N. (2001) 'Re-aligning the stakeholders in management research: lessons from industrial, work and organizational psychology', *British Journal of Management*, 12 (Special issue): S41–S48.

Hufford, M., McMackin, C., Bady, D. and Fout, J. (2003) *Waging Democracy in the Kingdom of Coal: OVEC and the Movement for Social and Environmental Justice in Central Appalachia*. [http://www.wagner.nyu.edu/leadership/reports/files/OVEC.pdf]

Hunt, S. (1984) 'The role of leadership in the construction of reality', in B. Kellerman (ed.), *Leadership: Multidisciplinary Perspectives*. Englewood Cliffs, NJ: Prentice-Hall. pp. 157–78.

Kemmis, S. and McTaggart, R. (2005) 'Participatory action research: communicative action and the public sphere', in N. Denzin and Y. Lincoln (eds), *Handbook of Qualitative Research, 3rd edn*. Thousand Oaks, CA: Sage. pp. 559–603.

Kovari, V., Hicks, R.T., Ferlazzo, L., McGarvey, G., Ochs, M., Alcántara, L. and Yorks, L. (2005) *Don't Just Do Something, Sit There: Helping Others Become More Strategic, Conceptual and Creative: a Cooperative Inquiry*. [http://www.nyu.edu/wagner/leadership/reports/files/ LeadersLearnersGuide.pdf]

Leadership for a Changing World (2006) *About the Program*. [http://leadershipforchange.org/program/]

Maguire, P. (2001/2006) 'Uneven ground: feminisms and action research', in P. Reason and H. Bradbury (eds), *Handbook of Action Research: Participative Inquiry and Practice*. London: Sage. pp. 59–70. Also published in P. Reason and H. Bradbury (eds) (2006), *Handbook of Action Research: Concise Paperback Edition*. London: Sage. pp. 60–70.

Meindl, J. (1995) 'The romance of leadership as a follower-centric theory: a social constructionist approach', *Leadership Quarterly*, 6 (3): 329–41.

Ospina, S. and Sorenson, G. (2006) 'A constructionist lens on leadership: charting new territory', in G. Goethals and G. Sorenson (eds), *The Quest for a General Theory of Leadership*. Cheltenham: Edward Elgar.

Ospina, S. and Dodge, J. (2005) 'Narrative inquiry and the search for connectedness: practitioners and academics developing public administration scholarship', *Public Administration Review,* 65 (4): 409–23.

Ospina, S. and Foldy, E.G. (2005) 'Toward a framework of social change leadership', Presented at the 2005 Annual Meeting of the Public Management Research Association, Los Angeles, CA.

Ospina, S. and Saz-Carranza, A. (2005) *Paradox and Collaboration in Coalition Work* [http://leadershipforchange.org/ insights/conversation/]

Ospina, S., Dodge, J., Godsoe, B., Mineri, J., Reza, S. and Schall, E. (2004) 'From consent to mutual inquiry: balancing democracy and authority in action research', *Journal of Action Research,* 2 (1): 47–69.

Park, P. (2001/2006) 'Knowledge and participatory research', in P. Reason and H. Bradbury (eds), *Handbook of Action Research: Participative Inquiry and Practice.* London: Sage. pp. 81–91. Also published in P. Reason and H. Bradbury (eds) (2006), *Handbook of Action Research: Concise Paperback Edition.* London: Sage. pp. 83–93.

Pastor, J.C. (1998) *The Social Construction of Leadership: a Semantic and Social Network Analysis of Social Representations of Leadership.* Ann Arbor, MI: UMI.

Pfeffer, J. (1977) 'The ambiguity of leadership', *Academy of Management Review,* 2 (1):104–12.

Reason, P. (2006) 'Choice and quality in action research practice,' *Journal of Management Inquiry,* 15 (2): 187–203.

Reason, P. and Bradbury, H. (2001/2006) 'Inquiry and participation in search of a world worthy of human aspiration', in P. Reason and H. Bradbury (eds), *Handbook of Action Research: Participative Inquiry and Practice.* London: Sage. pp. 1–15. Also published in P. Reason and H. Bradbury (eds) (2006), *Handbook of Action Research: Concise Paperback Edition.* London: Sage. pp. 1–14.

Rubin, H.J. and Rubin, I.S. (1995) *Qualitative Interviewing: the Art of Hearing Data.* Thousand Oaks, CA: Sage.

Smircich, L., and Morgan, G. (1982) 'Leadership: the management of meaning', *Journal of Applied Behavioral Science,* 18 (3): 257–73.

Tierney, W. (1987) 'The semiotic aspects of leadership: an ethnographic perspective', *American Journal of Semiotics,* 5 (2): 223–50.

Toulmin, S. (1996) 'Concluding methodological reflections: elitism and democracy among sciences', in S. Toulmin and B. Gustavsen (eds), *Beyond Theory: Changing Organizations through Participation.* Amsterdam: John Benjamins. pp. 203–26.

Walters, J., Reza, S., Ospina, S., Dodge, J. and Gomez, D. (2003a) *Sun of Justice Rising.* [http://www.nyu.edu/wagner/leadership/reports/ files/18.pdf]

Walters, J., Altvater, D. and Dodge, J. (2003b) *We Have to Reach Back.* [http://www.nyu.edu/wagner/leadership/reports/files/6.pdf]

Walters, J., Torres G. and Foldy E.G. (2003c) *From Services to Activism: How Latino Day Laborers and Domestic Workers are Advocating for Themselves.* [http://www.nyu.edu/wagner/leadership/reports/files/7.pdf]

Weinberg, L. (2005) *Leadership Development for Community Action: an Ethnographic Inquiry.* [http://www.wagner.nyu.edu/leadership/reports/files/NWFCO.pdf]

PART THREE

Exemplars

INTRODUCTION TO EXEMPLARS: VARIETIES OF ACTION RESEARCH

In this section we see how action researchers take a variety of practices that are oriented around grounding philosophies and use them to bring desired change to a particular system. In doing the work, action researchers engage the relevant stakeholders so that there is a seamlessness between planning and execution or reflection and action. The ordering of chapters suggests the varieties of scope, scale and intermingling of first-, second- and third-person practices that co-exist in the action research world. It also illustrates the variation in size of the research team, research impact and the degree to which the outcome brings relatively immediate results and/or brings about the deeper but slower change in belief structures and cultures.

THEMES FOR CONSIDERATION

We have looked across the varieties and wondered how to offer themes that allow us to see the individual chapters both for themselves and in relation to other chapters. We came up with the following set: context, leadership, first-, second-, third-person

modes of inquiry, level of impact and order of change. We hope they are useful for beginning to see how work that is marked by divergence can indeed sit under the umbrella term of 'action research'.

The context label refers to the different types of places and organizations in which action research takes place. By leadership we mean the core group of movers in the action research projects. We note throughout that first-, second-, third-person modes of inquiry often co-exist in one project. Nonetheless, for the sake of overview we find it helpful to note which predominates as the cause of the project's impact. The level of impact refers to the place in a system where impact is felt from individual, small group, organization, unit of community, to whole society. Finally, we suggest looking at the order of change. First-order change or single-loop change refers to the degree to which concrete results are experienced by project participants. Second-order or double-loop change refers to the change occurring at the level of operating theories and values from which results come.

In addition to the chapters in the Exemplar section that follow, the chapters in other parts of this Handbook contain both small and large examples of action research. Ludema and Fry in Chapter 19 offer an account of their practice within a business organization that not only brings about first-order improvements in practice, but changes the relationships and communication patterns among management, unions, employees and customers. Martin in Chapter 26 refers to two projects where quite large scale change is facilitated through action research. Gustavsen, Hansson and Qvale in Chapter 4 give an account of developments in Scandinavia over many years. And Brown and Tandon in Chapter 15 describe their practice of creating an inter-organizational structure that opens up larger scale or 'third-person' possibilities.

Context

The diversity of contexts in which action research is undertaken is really rather huge. Moreover, we see how truly international the community of action researchers is. We know that action research is happening in private spaces (see Heron and Lahood in Chapter 29 and Inj Drum), urban communities (see Yorks et al, Chapter 33.) and the ministerial offices of nation-states (see Stringer, Chapter 38). We know action research is happening in development contexts (see Guhathakurta, Chapter 35 and Castillo et al, Chapter 36.) and that it engages change in physical as well as cultural aspects of citizens' lives. We know it is happening in healthcare contexts (see Chowns, Chapter 39; Chui, Chapter 37; Kowalksi, Chapter 34) and that we can see it engaging different parts of the healthcare system, children of patients, patients and healthcare providers, respectively. Finally, we know it is happening in the business world (see Kristiansen and Bloch-Poulsen, Chapter 31 and Dymek, Chapter 40), both because of what outside consultants bring in and because managers inside can use it to develop desired results.

Leadership in Participation

In some cases those who led and generated the original design for the action research were those who also experienced it – as is the case

especially with the cooperative inquiry groups described by Heron and Lahood, Chapter 29; Taj Drum and Lyle Yorks et al., Chapter 33. However, in cases where larger groups were convened, a leadership group was separate from the original team of designers. This is especially evident where large groups of people were affected by the work, as in Ernie Stringer's project in East Timor (Chapter 38) and Meghna Guhathakurta's project (Chapter 35) that affected multiple Bangladeshi villages. We see that the most common mode for action researchers is to work either alone or in small teams at the start. For the novice this may seem like a contradiction to the principle of participation, but in fact it simply clarifies that as with most (research) projects, a core group of accountable people are leaders of the effort. These action researchers function both as designers and conveners of the work to which they then attract co-inquirers from the relevant set of stakeholders. The first-person challenge is then to provide leadership in a fashion that facilitates the emergence of participative inquiry.

Degree to Which Co-inquirers Co-design

Leadership in participation leads then to an important distinction concerning design. The work of John Heron and Taj Johns perhaps best exemplifies action research in which the co-participants are simultaneously co-designers of the process. Their meeting and desire to work together precedes a decision about how to work together. We also see that this is not that common. The other chapters exemplify how the action research core team designs with various degrees of participation from co-inquirers. Generally speaking, the larger the impact is in terms of scope, the smaller the proportion of co-inquirers are involved as co-designers. The core researchers must attend especially to questions of partnership and participation later on as is well exemplified by Castillo et al.'s work (Chapter 36) with residents of a town in

Mexico and Lai Fong Chui's work (Chapter 37) with healthcare consumers. As noted in the Introduction, action research projects are often emergent and so too design can emerge over time. Early design may be simply to open communicative space into which co-design can later develop.

Degree of Distance from Design

As a rule, one may say that to the degree the level of desired system impact is removed from the leadership team, then participative co-design is limited to those stakeholders who can carry the work into the larger system. Ernie Stringer's chapter perhaps best exemplifies this to the degree that the national level (school system in East Timor) was impacted by working with a small set of stakeholders that included ministers and other key decision-makers. In Stringer's example the carriers of the work are trained inside the original effort; the impact is thus made more directly by those who carry the message from the original research team onwards. In the original Handbook referred to this as 'creating infrastructure' for the future, in which the seeds of the later expansion of the work are designed in from the start. If there is no distance between core team and those impacted (as in Heron and Lahood's and Taj John's chapters), the issue of building infrastructure is moot, as the action research project itself is the place in which the stakeholders are left stronger and reach their desired goals.

Meghna Guhathakurta's chapter is particularly rich from the vantage point of leveraging small groups' efforts for a higher level impact. In it we see a small group of action researchers design the work of participative theatre and then carry it themselves, village to village, thereby making it an example of the migration from second- to third-person modalities. As a theatre piece it then attracts and engages many scores of people in participative inquiry on the treatment of minorities. There is little co-design inside the participatory theatre in the sense that the theatre stories are created at one point in time and then brought to the villages. Infrastructure building happens 'in situ' – that is, in the work of the theatre itself. A large number of people are directly impacted.

First-, Second-, Third-Person Inquiry Modes

We see that there is often a primary but rarely one exclusive mode of inquiry – be it as first or second person – in all the projects. More generally, we find that that it is unusual for a project to contain an equal focus on each mode. We are seeing an increase in attention to first-person inquiry as a foundation for other modes and it is safe to assume it is operating even where the focus of the report does not much mention it. In the concluding chapter we note an important trend of action research is to embrace first-person inquiry mode as the basis of the work, its seed of quality, so to speak. Much as great effort in the objectivist natural sciences is placed on the development of ever more refined measurements and instrumentation (e.g. microscopes), in action research the instrument of inquiry is understood to be ourselves, the action researchers. Taking time to reflect on self might be therefore seen as the equivalent to updating lab instrumentation in the natural sciences.

We see examples of first-person work that form the basis of their contribution in Kristiansen and Bloch-Poulsen's reflection on their work with managers, as well as in Mullett's work with women in mid life and Heron and Lahood's deeper exploration of everyday life. In each case the first-person inquiry anchors the action researchers' ability to bring significant change to the culture in which they find themselves. The other chapters place a great emphasis on second-person research practice.

First-, Second- and Third-Order Change

If first order change refers to change that operates at the level of changing the results that participants can experience as a benefit of action research, then we see that Chris Dymek's chapter illustrates how a successful IT system can be developed and that it offers good return on investment too. Similarly Ernie Stringer's chapter describes first-order change in the sense that the specific result of designing a new educational system was the goal of the action research – but see above that first-person changes lead inevitably to second-person shifts in relationship and framing.

Generally, though, we see that second-order change is most common in action research endeavors, where second-order change means that there is a questioning of the original conditions in which results were expected. In Taj John's chapter, there is a transformation of the experience of being black in America, from the objectification of racism to self-definition. Similarly in Jennifer Mullett's chapter we learn of women's work at the intersection of ageing and sexism as they transform their own image away from the objectification offered in popular media.

As a *general rule*, action research operates as a second-person practice, with increasing attention to first-person practice. Moreover, it operates as a mode in which second-order change is invited through reflection and dialogue. Thus there may be a time delay between reflection and action and therefore considerable difficulty in tracing cause and effect between action research and outcome. However, we are also seeing more attention to concern for first-order change, in which direct results of action research are evident. The premise is to leave the co-inquirers stronger after the action research. What we may take from this is to keep our eye on the elements we build into our work, all the time asking if we are best meeting the needs of the co-inquirers. For example, there is no reason why first-order change – because it is often more rapid – cannot be built into a second-order change project. Key elements to consider are the degree to which we are operating with regard to leadership and design, first-, second-, third-person mode and level of impact, and first- and or second-order results.

One might suggest that a better balance between first- and second-order outcomes would really help to commend the action research approach to practitioner participants. We need to be able to show evidence of results (or change practices) as well as provide opportunities for changes in the deeper currents of thought and culture.

We have noted before that the best way of understanding action research is to be immersed in a project. Perhaps the second best is therefore to read rich descriptions of exemplars. We commend the following to our readers as a way of deepening their own practice wherever they find themselves on the action research journey.

29

Charismatic Inquiry in Concert: Action Research in the Realm of 'the Between'

John Heron and Gregg Lahood

We report on long-term peer group action research in the realm between persons where a sacred presence may manifest. We characterize the core method as charismatic collaborative action inquiry and define what we mean by 'charismatic' and 'sacred'. We consider various forms of relation between spirituality and action research, and suggest that action research itself can be seen as a form of participatory and relational spirituality. We describe the general format of our charismatic inquiry meetings, outline the model of decision-making used, analyse the basic and supporting elements of the main inquiry process, and depict two forms of ancillary, structured co-operative inquiry which are used intermittently. We identify participants' perspectives on, and five primary kinds of outcomes of, these three interrelated kinds of inquiry, and then consider a wide range of issues about the quality and soundness of what we do. We end the chapter with an overview of related contemporary developments in the practice of embodied spirituality, and in transpersonal anthropology.

Denzin and Lincoln, in the closing chapter of their qualitative research handbook (1994: 583), assert that concerns of the spirit are returning to the human disciplines and that a sacred science is certain to emerge and make itself felt. In their introductory chapter to the first edition of this Handbook, Reason and Bradbury (2001/2006: 3–4) include spiritual practices and transpersonal sciences in their overview of various approaches to action research. Standing in these opening doorways, this chapter is about a form of action research which is a spiritual practice, one possible primitive prototype of a sacred science.

OVERVIEW

We report on long-term peer group action research in the realm between persons where a sacred presence may manifest. The group has been meeting regularly since 1995 (for 11 years at the time of writing) for two hours in the evening, currently every two weeks, with a five or six week break in the summer. Gregg, a transpersonal anthropologist (Lahood, forthcoming a, forthcoming b), joined the group in 1996. For a detailed history of its founding and early years see Heron (1998: 225–9).

The core method is collaborative action inquiry, an innovative variant of Torbert's action inquiry (2001/2006; Chapter 17 in this volume). It entails a spontaneity of toning, percussion, posture and movement that is interactively modulated by the participants, as in an improvisatory session of singers/musicians/dancers. The purpose of this is both to generate and be moved by, and thus inquire through this co-creative action into the nature of, a shared occasion of sacred presence in which we all participate and which is between us. We sometimes refer to such action as 'charismatic', by which we mean 'characterized by creative spontaneity and depth'. By 'sacred' we tentatively mean 'a combination of hallowed, holy, blessed, whole, generative, engaging, nourishing, nurturing, intimate, inclusive, numinous, awesome, mysterious'.

Our report covers the following: some background comments on spirituality and action research; a general account of the format of meetings; elements and properties of the main inquiry process; the three types of inquiry process; participants' perspectives and outcomes; issues of quality and soundness; related contemporary developments.

Our group has agreed a principle that any member can present a personal perspective on our inquiry, at the same time making clear the degree to which other members of the group have or have not collaborated. This chapter is the integration of John's and Gregg's perspectives, grounded on a comprehensive conceptual map of our inquiry process co-generated by the whole group.

SPIRITUALITY AND ACTION RESEARCH

In preparing this chapter it has been suggested to us that there may be many action researchers who draw on different spiritual traditions in their work, but usually conceal this because it is difficult to write about and people feel vulnerable. However, some practitioners, we have also been told, will talk openly: some meditate, some go to church, some pray, some talk about transpersonal experiences, and so on. An important distinction here is between bringing a spiritual practice *to* action research (Coghlan, 2005; Nolan, 2005), and action research itself, as such, being a spiritual practice, a sacred science (Reason, 1993).

One difficulty in construing action research itself as a spiritual practice is the subtle Cartesianism of recent transpersonal studies. This tacitly assumes that spirituality is a subjective experience, within a nonspatial individual consciousness, of transpersonal objects which transcend the everyday public space of social interactions (Ferrer, 2002). By contrast, we take a non-Cartesian view of spirituality as a shared transformative event, a shared occasion of enhanced human flourishing. It is generated by collaborative action for change taken together, the action itself in part shaping, and in part disclosing, inquiring into and being shaped by, the reality of the relational event. On this account spirituality is manifest in flourishing and liberating participatory events which persons-in-relation co-create with the reality of the presence between them in their situation (Heron, 1998; Ferrer, 2002).

The public event may be a shared transformation of behaviour into resonance with the presence of the between as such, as in our inquiry, or it may be a shared transformation of behaviour into greater organizational inclusiveness and empowerment as in other kinds of action research. In short, we do not believe there is necessarily any radical spiritual discontinuity between the unusual inquiry reported here and the inquiries reported elsewhere in this Handbook

(Chapters 30–44). From our perspective, all of them may be nascent and widely divergent approaches within a non-Cartesian spirituality of participatory events. In other words, all may be implicitly co-creative, in various liberating ways, with the reality of the presence between all the persons involved in the situation.

This approach to spirituality in terms of participatory, relational and transformative events has a resonance with Senge's account of 'presence' in terms of a group collectively and consciously participating in a larger field for change (Senge et al., 2005). Buber (1937) was a modern pioneer of relational spirituality, stressing the primacy of the I–Thou relation, the realm of the between, for attuning to the real. Authentic community, he held, is an event that arises out of the Centre between persons. This is echoed in the peer spirit circling of Christina Baldwin and Ann Linnea (2000). Also relevant is Hanh's (1995) notion of 'interbeing'; and an ancient precursor is the Shinto religious attitude and practice of intimacy (Kasulio, 1990). There is not space here to explore all these and other ramifications of relational spirituality, but we value the Gergens' account of the significance of relational processes (Chapter 9 in this volume).

THE GENERAL FORMAT OF MEETINGS

We describe here the process in our fortnightly two hour meeting in terms of Shekinah. Each person in the group has their own experientially-grounded belief system about what we do. There is no one correct account, but a family of related accounts with varying degrees of mutual overlap and resonance, and yet, we believe, with a central core in common. This is but one member of the family.

Shekinah in Hebrew means 'residence', 'dwelling'. In Jewish tradition it is the name for divine immanence, for the divine presence as it makes itself known in the material world, 'overshadowing', 'hovering', 'indwelling'. It is also associated with the feminine aspect of the divine, concerned with interpersonal relationships. In what follows Shekinah refers to the spiritual presence between humans, and between humans and presences in other realms. It is the spiritual heart of the relation of mutuality, in both these horizontal and the vertical dimensions, which the procedure we follow seems progressively to reveal.

As people arrive and gather we socialize with cups of various kinds of tea. All kinds of enlivened conversations occur, some spontaneously using language to seed the ground with transpersonal potentials, giving them room to grow; others are simply hilarious.

When we are well settled in, round a low table with candles and other items, someone proposes or starts a check-in round. This round accommodates a whole diversity of options: simple reportage of current life-events, routine, joyful, challenging or traumatic; an account of current spiritual, psi, psychological, interpersonal, energetic/sexual/somatic dynamics; a cathartic release of some current and/or archaic distress with self-generated insight; self-transfiguring spiritual assertions. Group members support and bear witness to the person checking-in, but rarely interact or comment, because the check-in is directed to what is between us. There may then be a period of silence, or this plus someone stroking the rim of a Tibetan bowl with a stick of wood to produce a tone.

At a certain point there is a distinct, spontaneous qualitative shift in the group energy field. One or two people are moved, and gradually and idiosyncratically each one is moved, to open their bodily, incarnate energy to the living presence within and between us, and between us and presences in other realms, by posture and gesture, by movement, by vocal toning, by rhythmic sounding of a diversity of rattles, drums, bells, tambourines, etc. This is both an opening of the heart and an exercise of alert discrimination. The posture, gesture, movement, toning and sounding are improvised in the moment out of a heart-communion with, and an aware inquiry into the nature and credentials of, this living presence – a marriage of appreciation and inquiry (Chapter 12).

This dynamic, charismatic, inquiring heart-opening goes on for a considerable period – on average about 45 minutes – with series of crescendos and diminuendos which are potently co-created with the rhythmic life of the between.

There is an unmistakable final diminuendo. We become entirely still. We draw together and hold hands, or sit silently apart, and for a long period feast on, and probe with the soul, the extraordinary depths and presence of Shekinah, also aptly named by one of our members as 'the band of golden silence'. This also has a clear ending. It may, or may not, be followed by a sharing, an affirmation, and a inquiring review, of what has been going on. Then we close the meeting and people depart for their homes.

What may be interwoven with the above are spontaneous episodes in which one or more members speak out of, and speak as, archetypal powers and presences interfused with the event.

If we are currently engaged in a co-operative inquiry (see below) into spiritual activities undertaken in everyday life between our fortnightly meetings, we will make space during the session for each person to report on and review the previous two weeks of activity, and in the light of that plan the next two weeks.

As well as the two-hour fortnightly meetings, we also meet for a three-day gathering at least once a year, for more intensive cycles of inquiry as described in a later section, and for attending more fully to personal and interpersonal dynamics that may be clouding the charismatic process.

As a professed peer-group, our model of decision-making seeks a creative balance between hierarchy, autonomy and co-operation. It is open to anyone to exercise a hierarchical or leadership initiative and propose some activity or direction for the group as a whole. Issues to do with the proposal are discussed, with time for each member to clarify their autonomous response; a vote is taken with arms more or less up, more or less down, or horizontal, to indicate degree of support, degree of rejection, or ambivalence. If there is

a minority of those who reject or are ambivalent, they speak to their position. This may cause some of the majority to change their position, in which case another arm vote is taken. Once unchanging positions are established, and the minority acknowledge they feel heard and understood and are open to accede to the majority, the majority vote holds. In our decisions, we are committed to celebrate diversity and variety in what individuals or subgroups may choose to do, as well as corporate and concerted actions.

ELEMENTS AND PROPERTIES OF THE INQUIRY PROCESS

This research is a mode of collaborative action inquiry in which our basic energies as embodied vital beings are opened up by spontaneous action to manifest, celebrate and inquire into the living spirit within and between us, and between us and the wider reaches of being. The basic elements are:

- Posture, gesture, facial expression, movement.
- Toning, with cycles of spontaneous crescendo and diminuendo.
- Musical rhythms with a variety of percussion instruments.
- Mutual resonance, with creative mimesis – building on what others do.
- Erotic energy as a component of mutual resonance.
- Relative position between us in the space of the room.
- Speaking out of altered states.
- Mutual trust.
- Exhilaration.
- Silent hand-holding after the charismatic expression, to bear witness to, be enfolded in, and inquire into the sacred presence between us.
- Charismatic disinhibition of these several modalities to open to the living spirit as it moves within and between and beyond, and this includes continuous internal adjustments of awareness – inquiring discrimination in keeping open to what there really is, locating and dissolving blocks, aligning energies, modulating idiosyncratic expression, attuning with others.

Supporting elements are:

- A check-in round early in a meeting.
- Freeform conversation, and structured dialogue.
- Feedback, conceptual review and authenticity checks.
- Peer decision-making, as described above.

Our practice has at least six basic properties. It is *relational*: it involves charismatic hybridization, that is, transformative mutual resonance with each other, and with what there is. It is *embodied*: it opens up the fundamental energies of being embodied – standing, posturing, gesturing, moving, breathing, sounding, perceiving, sensing – as gateways for the living spirit in which they are grounded. It is *autonomous*: it regards teacher, tradition and text as secondary to the primacy of the discriminating inquiring authority within each person. It is *peer*: it proposes that hierarchy rotates among peers to facilitate, sustain and enhance the flourishing of co-operation and creative autonomy as interdependent values. It celebrates *diversity in unity*: honouring idiosyncratic creativity and heterogeneous perspectives within an allowing and liberating whole. It is *political*: it is committed to make a difference in our daily engagement with social action in our lives.

THREE TYPES OF INQUIRY PROCESS

We engage in three types of inquiry. The first is our bedrock: the collaborative action inquiry which is the core of every fortnightly meeting. It is the active discrimination, exercised on-the-hoof – during our mutually resonant toning, percussion, posture and movement – with regard to what we are expressing, how we are doing so both individually and in concert, and in relation with whom or what, that is, with what presences or presence. This intuitive discrimination subsumes the continuous interplay of practical knowing (skilled action), presentational knowing (symbolic forms of sound, music, posture and movement) and experiential

knowing (encounter with each other and with that which is, Chapter 24; Heron, 1998: 228–9). It is conceptually elaborated in shorter and longer periods of reflective review, which occasionally involve a whole evening.

The second type of inquiry we use in our annual three-day meetings. This is a structured piece of co-operative inquiry (Heron, 1996; Heron and Reason, 2001/2006) built round our collaborative action inquiry (Reason, 1994). We co-decide an intentional project beforehand about how, and with what end, we do our charismatic expression, then do this, then share feedback on it and build this review into planning a second action-reflection cycle, and so on.

The third type embraces a series of structured co-operative inquiries, which bridge the gap between the fortnightly meetings and our engaged life in the world. Each of them runs for a specified period of time, involving several cycles of reflection and action, and they have occurred intermittently over the years. Part of a fortnightly meeting is used to plan individual or agreed spiritual practices to be taken as an action inquiry into daily life before the next meeting, when each of us report back on our action strand and develop a plan for the next two weeks of application. Shared topics, all focused on application in living, have been: transpersonal activities in everyday life, empowerment in everyday life, coming into being, gender issues, Shekinah in everyday life, presences and authentic intuition, authentic authority, terror, speaking from the heart. As well as the corporate topics – which individuals explore in their own way – there have also been a range of entirely idiosyncratic individual lines of action inquiry into transformations of daily living.

PARTICIPANTS' PERSPECTIVES AND OUTCOMES

When we review and make sense of what we experience during the procedures of our fortnightly meetings, there is a convergence of meaning in the various terms different members use to name the process: communion, attunement, resonance, alignment, and such like. There is a basic common ground about what this process engages with, particularly in the period immediately following the toning, percussion and movement. This was named by one of us 'the band of golden silence' – the sense of sacred presence indwelling the between, as we put it. Each person mediates their own nuanced account of this. There is also considerable divergence, involving both overlaps and varying connotations of the terms used, about other aspects of being we engage with. So we have: one's inner self; each other; powers and presences in complementary realities; the human race; nature/the biosphere/the earth; the solar system; galactic consciousness; extraterrestrials.

Many of us experience the procedure as a nonverbal, non-doctrinal version of worship, praise, high prayer, and dynamic meditation. One or two have expressed the theurgical view that our encounter with the divine changes the nature of the divine.

Here is an abridged account, from the notes taken by one of us, of impromptu declarations, made on 6 August 2004, of some individual perspectives on what we are doing. Each paragraph is a different speaker:

Ethereal alignment through sound.
    Invoking/inviting potent powers and presences.
    Culminating in co-dwelling in an in-between immediate sacred presence.
    Inquiring into how we can be together in many dimensions of living – from the practical to the transpersonal – and into how what we are doing here contributes to the wider society.
    A celebration of resting in my heart with others resting in their hearts; the ground of my human spirituality is between us as well as internal.
    A multidimensional attempt to create distress-free spirituality, to explore ritual life, how power is distributed, contested and re-contested, to feel the holding and support of others who are living a transpersonal life.
    Collectively touching into heartland, a shared intimacy generating a nectar-like quality, an alchemical exchange with a larger system of awareness, everyone distilling different metaphors and experiences.

Reclaiming my individual and collective spirit, tuning into the subtleties of how transpersonal spirit is brought forward, engaged with and expressed through sound, replenishing my essence in the process.

We identify five outcomes of this kind of relational inquiry, and believe them to be interdependent and mutually supporting (Heron, 1996). (1) Basic are the *transformations of being* which it brings about in the participants, and which they have variously named as attunement-alignment-harmonization-communion, bliss, softness, satisfaction, fulfilment, peace, nourishment, groundedness. These transformations, we believe, have a strong element of intersubjective hybridization, mutual cross-fertilization. (2) Intimately associated are the autonomous and co-operative *skills acquired* to effect such transformation, and (3) the idiosyncratic *insights into the nature of reality* which the aesthetic-expressive movement, toning and mutual resonance reveal. (4) An important applied outcome is *charismatic face-to-face transmission* and *transformation of practice* in relation to those we live, work, socialize and play with. This may be spontaneous or part of intentional practice within a type 3 inquiry as described earlier. These practical outcomes in everyday life are rich and complex and deserve a paper in their own right. One common thread is a sense of wholeness and groundedness which empowers whole relations with others. (5) Another important kind of public outcome are the *conceptual formulations* which we make in our review sessions to clarify what we do, how we do it, what we encounter, and with what soundness, which participants can share in the wider world, as in this chapter. Finally, we hypothesize, cautiously, about the possibility of *subtle activism*: the unknown (to us) possible effects at a subtle level on the immediate locality, and more widely on human affairs in this, that or the other respect (cf. Kelly, 2005). All these outcome claims are subject to issues of quality and soundness discussed in the next section.

ISSUES OF QUALITY AND SOUNDNESS

Reason and Bradbury (2001/2006: 450–4) propose five issues of quality: relational praxis, practical outcome, plurality of knowing, significant work, enduring consequence. To take these in turn, our group, as we see it: maximizes participation of the humans involved in its core process and engages the participation of wider reaches of being; has, as important practical outcomes, the liberation of participants from past spiritual colonization and the empowerment of their authentic spirituality in daily life; deepens and integrates multiple ways of knowing in appropriate methodology; affirms the significance of the sacred; and has sustained and developed its process for 11 years.

The devil's advocate will insist this is far too sanguine. 'Just how deluded and fanciful,' he or she will ask, 'is the co-creative enterprise of the fortnightly meetings? Is it simply a piece of improvisatory theatrical moving and toning without any ontological reference beyond what is evident to the sense-perception of anyone present in the room?' Here are a range of considerations that bear on these and other questions that relate to the five issues above and the soundness of what we are about.

Declarative validity Subtle realms, their resident powers and presences, sacred presence-as-such are what we meet in our state-specific enactments. They declare their ontological validity in and through these enactments. Crudely put: worlds, entities, presence-as-such are what we meet through our co-creations, and their reality is within the relation of meeting. Try it all and see.

Critical subjectivity and intersubjectivity The relation of meeting is itself constructed out of a dynamic discernment, an on-the-hoof expressively adjusting alignment, which involves both individual participative knowing and – by virtue of mutual resonance – co-operative participative knowing. Singly and together, in and through our moving and toning, we test for high quality ontological

soundness, for the most intimate and authentic embrace with the presence between.

Shared enthusiasm without psychic colonization The subtlety of listening and yielding to the experience of others, through mimetic linkage, while at the same time hybridizing it with one's own version, is at the heart of relational spirituality and its co-creative intersubjectivity. A declaration in any way nuanced with an authoritative voice, with tacit appeals to some authoritative spiritual tradition, blocks others from joining it and letting it blend with their imaginal worlds. By contrast, a 'clear' enthusiastic declaration, free from spiritual imperialism and the colonizing of consciousness, empowers others actively to yield: it invites a subtle mutual penetration and co-dwelling analogous to an erotic process (Lewis, 2003). Authentic co-creation flourishes when it steers clear of pontification and the colonization of consciousness on the one hand, and overly inhibited performances on the other.

Dionysian and Apollonian approaches Our inquiry is spanned between the poles of the Dionysian emergence of our process and the Apollonian preplanning of it (Heron, 1996). Over the years it has moved between the poles, always involving some degree of each. Of our three types of inquiry referred to above, type 1 inquiry is Dionysian, types 2 and 3 Apollonian. Too much Dionysian *enthusiasmos* and we are devoured by the divine, too much Apollonian preplanning and the spirit is unable to blow where it listeth. Learning to engage with the power of this polarity, in order to deepen the soundness of what we do, is a major dimension of our inquiry.

Group process and life process Another closely related basic polarity of our inquiry, which bears on soundness, is the group process within our meetings, and the life process in our daily existence between them. Over the years we have moved between combining our group process action inquiry with planning and reporting on our life process action inquiry, and just doing our group process without the life process planning and reporting – the assumption here is that the life process is then emergent. The soundness of the whole inquiry is critically to do with how the group process and the life process enhance each other,

Consensus collusion We occasionally use a devil's advocate procedure to raise questions about possible forms of unaware consensus collusion that may have us in their grip. One recent candidate was whether we were savouring Dionysian type 1 inquiry – our charismatic moving and toning – in part as a way of not engaging more fully with Apollonian type 3 inquiry – applications in everyday life – although, as already noted, these applications still go on in emergent, Dionysian mode. Another issue with which we confront ourselves is the degree to which we have interlocking structures of charismatic inhibition, that is, the extent to which we collude in the limits we set to our charismatic disinhibition.

Balance of hierarchy, co-operation and autonomy The model of peer decision-making we use seeks a balance of these three dimensions, as described in the section above on our procedure. John's role has shifted from taking strong hierarchical initiatives in setting up the series of inquiry workshops from which the group emerged, to a more ambiguous status as an intermittently influential peer, while hierarchical initiatives also move spontaneously among others in the group. Our model sometimes works superbly, sometimes relatively well and is sometimes – especially in the three-day gatherings – relatively chaotic with ego-burning confusion, tension and frustration. We have learnt to hang in with the chaotic phases. In burning up egoistic dross, these phases can presage both issues being disowned and denied, and also possibilities for the emergence of new and unexpected kinds of luminosity and order. There also times when the model is underused and habitual practice rules. We are still in the very early stages of developing peer decision-making as a fundamental kind of relational spiritual practice.

Personal and interpersonal tension A high percentage of the members participate in a local peer self-help counselling network and so have access to regular emotional housecleaning. Personal and interpersonal tensions triggered by our inquiry process, possibly distorting it in unacknowledged ways, pose a special challenge. It is an open question how far these tensions are resolved by the transmutative effect of our charismatic practices, and how far they both distort and are buried by the practices. Very little explicit healing is devoted to them in the two-hour fortnightly meetings. One purpose of the annual three-day gathering is to provide much more time for such work. And members do take material aroused in the group to sessions elsewhere. During the meetings we also use agreed nonverbal signs to give each other instant feedback about the felt quality – positive, ambiguous, negative – of our individual behaviours. In all these different ways, constant vigilance is required, continuously assessing our fluctuating levels of emotional and interpersonal competence.

Primacy of the practical and the correlative primacy of the between In our group process, the primacy of the practical – our moving and toning – is grounded in the correlative primacy of meeting – the experiential relation/the mutual resonance/the *presence*, between us, and others gathered with us. Practical and experiential knowing constitute primal poles of knowing, with imaginal knowing, as gestures in space and patterns of sound, mediating between them. In inquiry as in life, the basic dynamic is acting to enhance the quality of a shared life-field. Co-sensitivity to the changing state of the between-field and co-acting to enhance its overall flourishing, together entail cross-fertilization of co-inquirers' qualities and perspectives. This is at the heart of excellence in a collaborative action inquiry into embodied group process as a gateway to communion with what there is.

RELATED CONTEMPORARY DEVELOPMENTS

There is space briefly to mention some related approaches, alongside those in the opening section above. That the vital energies of the body can evoke the living spirit in which they are grounded, and whence they issue forth, is demonstrated in distinctive ways in each of the following: the holotropic breathwork of Stan Grof (1988) and the wide range of subtle and spiritual states it delivers; the paratheatrical research of Antero Alli (2003) with its comprehensive phenomenology of physical behaviours for cultivating 'resonance with vertical sources'; charismatic education and training (Heron, 1999) in the context of a dipolar account of spirit (Heron, 1998); aspects of the integral transformative practice of Leonard and Murphy (1995); the interactive somatic inquiries proposed by Marina Romero and Ramon Albareda (Ferrer, 2003) in their work on a fully embodied and vitalized spiritual life; the work of Michael Washburn (2003) asserting spiritual as well as instinctual energy in the Dynamic Ground of the human being, which can be awakened as an enlivening and guiding force within our bodies; Jorge Ferrer's (forthcoming) considered affirmation of embodied spirituality.

There are also relevant developments within anthropology. The once frowned upon going cognitively native has now become a major innovation, completely departing from early anthropology's monophasic bias – the gathering of data in the Eurocentric cognitive domain (Laughlin et al., 1993). There is a willingness to abandon early anthropology's spiritual or religious frigidity (Turner, 1993: 7), and to enter into states of consciousness, outlawed by scientific rationalism, as a demanding form of participant observation (Jules-Rosette, 1975; Peters, 1981; Laderman, 1991). Contemporary transpersonal anthropologists, interested in the field of waking dreams, make efforts to enter the alterity-scape of their host culture, seeing the experience as bearing essential forms of ethnographic data (Laughlin, 1994). They submit themselves to a profound process of cognitive re-structuring in a cultural milieu remote from secular materialism, and so embrace, in their direct knowing, a participatory epistemology.

This participatory turn in anthropology (Jackson, 1989; Tambiah, 1990) resonates with the participatory turn in transpersonal theory (Heron, 1992, 1998; Ferrer, 2002). Tambiah writes, 'participation is very much in place' in the world of qualitative science, and is pre-eminent 'as a mode of relating to and constructing reality'; this pre-eminence finds its zenith 'when describing aesthetic or religious orientations' because of its 'holistic and configurational grasping of totalities as integral to aesthetic enjoyment and mystic awareness'. The bridge to this mystical participation, he says, is to be found in the interconnectedness *between* persons and nature (1990: 106). This hybrid space of the between is an important research focus in both anthropology and co-operative inquiry.

The concept of hybridity draws from horticulture, meaning grafting or cross-pollination of two species to form a third, 'hybrid' species. Nineteenth century eugenics theory held that human cross-breeds and half-castes watered down an original pristine biological condition – the descent of white races from Adam and Eve. This dominant patriarchal idea of 'pure origins, pure lineages' in 'language, religion, nation, race, culture, status, class, gender … was preoccupied with divine or sacred origins' (Pieterse, 2004: 94).

With the development of Mendelian genetics in the 1870s, cross-breeding, cross-fertilization, polygenetic inheritance are seen as advantageous, invigorating and 'valued as enrichments to the gene-pool. Gradually this has been seeping through into wider circles; the work of the anthropologist Gregory Bateson (1972), as one of the few to connect the natural sciences and the social sciences, has been influential in this regard' (Pieterse, 2004: 71). The Creole, the half-caste, the cross-breed, the hybrid, find new status and have come to be valorized by many contemporary social theorists: Homi Bhabha has argued that all claims to the inherent purity and originality of cultures are in fact 'untenable', and that all cultural systems and articulations are constructed in what he names as the 'Third Space of Enunciation' (1994: 209).

It can be argued that this third space of the between, the space of hybridization, is where, largely unrecognized, the whole development of transpersonal theory and practice has been occurring. Within the micro-culture of our inquiry group, we seek to make it central in our co-creativity. This moment is akin, we believe, to what Bhabha, citing Salman Rushdie, calls 'the unstable element of linkage', the indeterminate temporality of the in-between, that has to be engaged in creating the conditions for 'newness to come into the world' (1994: 227).

CONCLUSION

The dynamic, charismatic format inaugurated when this inquiry was launched in 1995, and continuously refined through to the present day, is, as the authors see it, an intentional rebirthing of the spiritual potential within the basic energies of our embodiment. This rebirthing is relational – consequent upon the co-creative resonance among us all. And it empowers us to come into the presence between. In short: immanent spirit becomes manifest, through collaborative action, as relational and situational sacred presence. Participation in this presence engenders a liberating wholeness, a personal regeneration – which is given expression amidst the practicalities of everyday life and work, empowering whole relations with others.

REFERENCES

Alli, A. (2003) *Towards an Archeology of the Soul.* Berkeley, CA: Vertical Pool.

Bakhtin, M. (1981) *The Dialogical Imagination* (ed. M. Holquist, trans. C. Emerson and M. Holquist). Austin, TX.

Baldwin, C. and Linnea, A. (2000) *A Guide to PeerSpirit Circling.* Langley, WA: PeerSpirit Inc.

Bateson, G. (1972) *Steps to an Ecology of Mind.* San Francisco, CA: Chandler.

Bhabha, H. (1994) *The Location of Culture.* London and New York: Routledge.

Buber, M. (1937) *I and Thou.* Edinburgh: Clark.

Coghlan, D. (2005) 'Ignatian spirituality as transformational social science', *Action Research,* 3 (1): 89–107.

Denzin, N.K. and Lincoln, Y.S. (1994) 'The fifth moment', in N.K. Denzin and Y.S. Lincoln (eds), *Handbook of Qualitative Research.* Thousand Oaks, CA: Sage.

Ferrer, J.N. (2002) *Revisioning Transpersonal Theory: a Participatory Vision of Human Spirituality.* Albany, NY: SUNY Press.

Ferrer, J.N. (2003) 'Integral transformative practices: a participatory perspective', *Journal of Transpersonal Psychology,* 35 (1): 21–42.

Ferrer, J.N. (forthcoming) 'Embodied spirituality: now and then', *Tikkun: A Critique of Politics, Culture & Society* .

Grof, S. (1988) *The Adventure of Self-Discovery.* Albany, NY: SUNY Press.

Hanh, T.N. (1995) *The Heart of Understanding.* Berkeley, CA: Parallax Press.

Heron, J. (1992) *Feeling and Personhood: Psychology in Another Key.* London: Sage.

Heron, J. (1996) *Co-operative Inquiry: Research into the Human Condition.* London: Sage.

Heron, J. (1998) *Sacred Science: Person-centred Inquiry into the Spiritual and the Subtle.* Ross-on-Wye: PCCS Books.

Heron, J. (1999) *The Complete Facilitator's Handbook.* London: Kogan Page.

Heron, J. and Reason, P. (2001/2006) 'The practice of co-operative inquiry: research "with" rather than "on" people', in P. Reason and H. Bradbury (eds), *Handbook of Action Research: Participative Inquiry and Practice.* London: Sage. pp. 179–88. Also published in P. Reason and H. Bradbury (eds) (2006), *Handbook of Action Research: Concise Paperback Edition.* London: Sage. pp. 144–54.

Jackson, M. (1989) *Paths toward a Clearing: Radical Empiricism and Ethnographic Inquiry.* Bloomington: Indiana University Press.

Jules-Rosette, B. (1975) *African Apostles: Ritual and Conversion in the Church of John Maranke.* Ithaca and London: Cornell University Press.

Kasulio, T.P. (1990) 'Intimacy: a gerneral orientation in Japanese religious values', *Philosophy East and West,* 4 (4): 433–49.

Kelly, S.M. (2005) 'The Hidden Face of Wisdom: Towards an Awakened Activism.' [www.earthrainbownetwork.com/FocusArchives/HiddenFaceWisdom.htm]

Laderman, C. (1991) *Taming the Wind of Desire: Psychology, Medicine, and Aesthetics in Malay Shamanistic Performances.* Berkeley: University of California Press.

Lahood, G. (forthcoming a) 'Skulls at the banquet: near birth as nearing death', *Journal of Transpersonal Psychology.*

Lahood, G. (forthcoming b) 'Birth, death and alterity-scapes: comparing NDEs, shamanistic initiation and UFO encounters, with male reproductive crises', *Journal of Near Death Experience*.

Laughlin, C. (1994) 'Psychic energy and transpersonal experience: a biogenetic structural account of the Tibetan Dumo yoga practice', in D. Young and J. Goulet (eds), *Being Changed by Cross-Cultural Encounters: the Anthropology of Extraordinary Experience*. Peterborough, ONT: Broadview Press.

Laughlin, C., McManus, J. and Shearer, J. (1993) 'Transpersonal anthropology', in R. Walsh and F. Vaughan (eds.) *Paths Beyond Ego*. Los Angeles, CA: Tarcher. pp. 190–94.

Leonard, G. and Murphy, M. (1995) *The Life We Are Given*. New York: Tarcher/Putnam.

Lewis, I.M. (2003) 'Trance, possession, shamanism and sex', *Anthropology of Consciousness Journal,* 14 (1): 20–39.

Nolan, P. (2005) 'From first person inquiry to radical social action', *Action Research,* 3 (3): 297–312.

Peters, L. (1981) *Ecstasy and Healing in Nepal*. Malibu, CA: Undena

Pieterse, J. (2004) *Globalization and Culture: Global Mélange*. New York : Rowan & Littlefield.

Reason, P. (1993) 'Sacred experience and sacred science', *Journal of Management Inquiry,* 2: 10–27.

Reason, P. (1994) 'Three approaches to participative inquiry', in N.K. Denzin and Y.S. Lincoln (eds), *Handbook of Qualitative Research*. Thousand Oaks, CA: Sage. pp. 324–39.

Reason, P. and Bradbury, H. (eds) (2001/2006) *Handbook of Action Research: Participative Inquiry and Pratice,* London: Sage.

Senge, P., Scharmer, C.O., Jaworski, T. and Flowers, B.S. (2005) *Presence: an Exploration of Profound Change in People, Organizations and Society*. New York: Doubleday/Currency.

Tambiah, S. (1990) *Magic, Science, Religion, and the Scope of Rationality*. Cambridge: Cambridge University Press.

Torbert, W. R. (2001/2006) 'The practice of action inquiry', in P. Reason and H. Bradbury (eds), *Handbook of Action Research: Participative Inquiry and Practice*. London: Sage. pp. 207–18. Also published in P. Reason and H. Bradbury (eds) (2006), *Handbook of Action Research: Concise Paperback Edition*. London: Sage. pp. 207–17.

Turner, E. (1993) 'The reality of spirits: a tabooed or permitted field of study?', *Anthropology of Consciousness,* 3 (3): 9–12.

Washburn, M. (2003) *Embodied Spirituality in a Sacred World*. Albany, NY: SUNY Press.

30

Presentational Knowing: Bridging Experience and Expression with Art, Poetry and Song

Jennifer Mullett

This chapter describes the necessity for, and the effect of, presentational knowing. Participatory action research to educate women in mid-life about their choices for health evolved from straightforward community education into a deeper, more significant project. How and why creative forms of engagement such as art, song and poetry were crucial for subtle transformations in thinking in the action and outcome phases of the project are illustrated in this chapter.

Women between the ages of 45 and 65 lead very complex and sometimes very stressful lives. The women's health in mid-life project was designed to assist women to make informed choices in managing key mid-life health issues through health education and community action. The project followed the classic cycles of iterative action research progressing through the stages of: developing inter-sectoral partnerships, collecting information through various participatory methods, creating educational workshops and developing community supports in the action stages, and reflecting on the actions to plan for the future in repetitive cycles of reflection and action.

I will describe how the project morphed from an educational awareness and capacity building initiative into a deeper purpose, one that aimed to reconstruct for the women their vital place in their communities. I focus on key creative events that utilized presentational knowing in the action stages and then I describe how in the latter stages we struggled to convey the full realization of empowerment and capacity building, the outcomes, in the form of presentational knowledge to other audiences. Although this is a project concerned with women's mid-life health, the larger message is universal – it is about change, loss of self and transformation and the need to 'forge deep new purposes and bonds' in the developmental stage known as mid-life (Friedan, 1993: 499). In attempting to articulate the process of the transformation I rely on the theoretical principles of Vygotsky as they relate to the internalization of social dialogue.

PRESENTATIONAL KNOWING

In Chapter 24 Heron and Reason describe, as part of an extended epistemology, four kinds of knowing. This chapter is concerned with presentational knowing, the knowing that is the bridge between experience and the formal or discursive expression of our knowing. Woven throughout this chapter are descriptions of the evolving recognition of a developmental life stage. This understanding is expressed in the form of stories. In addition, and at the heart of this exemplar, are examples of how other forms of expression such as music and poetry were used to engage women and audiences in experiencing this understanding.

THE PROJECT

The women's health in mid-life project (nicknamed WHIM) began in a similar fashion to most other community health education/action projects. There are commonly three strategies. The first is providing information about health risks and how to avoid them with the hope that individuals, once informed, will change their attitudes or behaviour; a second approach recognizes the need to provide information and, in addition, to enhance personal motivation for change through self-empowerment; and, third, are community development approaches that seek to create contexts or supportive environments that facilitate change (Campbell, 2004). The community action initiatives to be described incorporated all three of these strategies. WHIM originated with the Ministry of Health in British Columbia,

Canada, tendering a 'call for proposals' for community agencies/groups to engage in a two-year women's health in mid-life project. Six community groups were subsequently funded based on successful competitive proposals. I was asked to conduct a collaborative action research evaluation across the six community projects in participation with the project coordinators from the communities (some projects already had participatory action research in their plans). Such an approach is described by Reason and Bradbury as: a participatory democratic process in which practical knowing is developed through the pursuit of practical solutions and the flourishing of individuals and communities (Reason and Bradbury, 2001/2006). I was responsible for a final report on the outcomes to the Ministry of Health.

OBJECTIVES OF THE PROJECT

The four objectives of WHIM were: raise awareness and empower women to take more responsibility for their own health; educate women about health issues related to menopause; raise awareness of the range of options available to women; increase women's confidence in discussing these issues with care professionals and build capacity in the community to enhance women's health. As the coordinators met with women in their communities to identify areas of focus they heard not only lists of physical and social health issues but, more importantly, they heard a profound sense of isolation, emptiness and worthlessness. From the very beginning it was clear that the purpose of the project needed to expand beyond the four objectives described.

THE CONTEXT AND THE COORDINATORS

The projects took place in small towns where the closest 'big' city is several hundred kilometres away. Average population of the towns is 10,000 with the largest having a population of 77,000. In rural settings, the founding 'industries' in the early 1800s were fur trading, gold mining, agriculture, ranching and forestry. Because they are stunningly beautiful locations, tourism and the resident colonies of artists now draw people to these areas as well. Some of the coordinators were already engaged in projects related to women's health and were very committed to women's issues. Two of them were nurses, while the others were experts in community development work.

GETTING STARTED

At the beginning stages of the project the six co-ordinators and I met on a monthly basis either in person or by telephone. The six small communities were located several hundred kilometres apart in the province. The project had a main co-ordinator, Lenore Riddell, at the BC Women's Health Centre in Vancouver. An electronic 'list serve' service was created to share ideas and resources as they were developed. At the first meeting I presented the purpose and process of action research methodology and ethics for data gathering. One of the projects was primarily concerned with identifying needs and will not be discussed here.

FIRST STAGE OF COMMUNITY ACTION WORK: INITIAL DATA GATHERING

There was a great variety in the methods of data gathering. Each community used a method that was appropriate to their purpose and population.

Williams Lake

In this small northern town and its surrounding small communities, gathering sessions

were advertised in a magazine developed for mid-life women and through the local media. Four gathering sessions were held with approximately 60 women attending each. Using the open space concept (Owen, 1997) women identified the main issues that concerned them: for example, communicating effectively with physicians; a more positive outlook in society towards mid-life; and a more positive image of mid-life women.

Nelson

In the interior of the province, 10 community meetings were held and advertised through the local media. As a result of these meetings 14 women volunteered to sit on a steering committee and various sub-committees to help organize events. Participants suggested the following main issues for which educational events or materials should be developed: alternatives to pharmaceutical therapies; prevention for mid-life health; wise women circles; stress, humour and life transitions and a question and answer column to be created in the local newspapers that included 'real women' in addition to professionals as the respondents.

Vernon

Community meetings and kitchen-table discussions (the coordinator went to women's homes) were held to establish a wise woman network. Participants at the gatherings were asked to suggest five names of women in the community whom they considered to be wise. Those women whose names recurred on the lists were invited to form a wise women network. This network constituted a focus group that provided advice for further development of the project.

Prince George

A diverse group of women were identified through existing networks and trained and supported to design and implement health education activities in their small communities surrounding Prince George. In preparation for these activities community meetings produced the following as issues of focus: 11 physical health issues followed by psychological and emotional issues such as 'body image, depression, grieving and major life changes, isolation and the invisibility of older women, mood swings, stress and guilt (the superwoman myth), self-esteem, and substance misuse'. Another group of issues characterized as 'social health' included acceptance, being a care giver, elder abuse, employability and responsibility in the 'sandwich' generation (looking after elderly parents while still caring for children and sometimes a spouse as well), self-esteem and youth worship (Anderson, 1999).

Sechelt

In the area known as 'the Sunshine Coast' the coordinator held small seminar and discussion sessions in Sechelt and on a smaller island. Through their already successful Sechelt Mature Women's Group, they were also able to consult with the women who met regularly to identify the issues of interest in their community. Finances and housing were two topics of primary concern to the mature women. An art therapist who had been working with some of the women asked them to rank topics of concern. The top four items were health, self-care, spirituality and creativity.

The Message Across the Communities

Across the five projects women said it was important to hear and learn from other women; take more control of their own health and make informed choices; and gain more understanding and validation of normal cycles and symptoms. The realization that they should take time for themselves was a significant outcome of the sessions. At the same time, the coordinators were distressed to hear how used up, isolated and disconnected from their communities the women felt. For example:

> We haven't had respect from the medical community and haven't felt empowered to take care of ourselves – everything was medicalized. We learned to do on a need to know basis. It is not just us and the way we think but the way we have been treated. With a forum of women there is trust for each other, everything can be talked about so learning is maximized.
>
> I am so tired of being 'invisible'.

The coordinators, all experienced community workers, knew that what they were hearing was more than women expressing their educational needs; they recognized that the planned venues would have to affirm and reconnect women in mid-life as vital, contributing members of their communities. The events would have to help women reconstruct a visible life for themselves.

PRESENTATIONAL KNOWING IN THE ACTION PHASES:

The first workshops developed in response to the data gathering sessions covered a broad range of topics. Some were presented in such a way as to evoke experiences that would, as Heron and Reason describe in Chapter 24, 'provide access to a greater understanding of themselves' for example, inspirational workshops designed to inspire authentic self-expression through creativity with writing, painting and dance. There are many details of the excellent community action initiatives created by the coordinators and their community partners that must be omitted due to space limitations.[1] Instead, two communities are highlighted here as examples: Prince George and Sechelt.

Prince George

A workshop specifically targeting body image included 'toe painting', a variation on finger painting for children. Different coloured paints were spread on the floor. The women created a painting by walking through the paint then standing on a piece of paper or paper pie plate. This encouraged new ways of moving one's body to create 'art' (and a lot of laughter). Another session was held with an artist and photographer to celebrate 'the wise woman within'. Women were asked to bring ads from magazines as well as their own photograph and talk about their favourite and their least favourite ads. They then created from their photo and art materials a representation of themselves in their 'own reality' for an art exhibit. This exhibit was displayed at the same time as the artist/photographer's work, a creative combination of artistic representations of body parts juxtaposed with mirrors that distort your shape.

Sechelt

A two-day retreat at a camp on the ocean brought women together to experience being creative and to try new forms of expression. There were mini workshops on drumming, singing, crafts, meditation and a massage therapy called 'Niha' that is done by oneself by lying on the floor with tennis balls. Everyone was rotated through each of these workshops after one hour. The women were hesitant at first in some of the workshops but were quickly involved by the facilitator. I attended the two-day retreat to observe and interview women who had agreed to tell their stories. I was struck by the effectiveness of the craft workshop in facilitating connectedness.

In this workshop women created a ribbon, two feet long by two inches wide to wear around their neck for the duration of the retreat. From bits and pieces of materials everyone had brought, we glued, sewed or pinned artefacts on to the ribbon to create a life 'line'. The artefacts represented important phases in our lives, for example where we were born, what type of work we did, children we had, traumatic or dramatic events in our lives and what we looked forward to for the future. At the end each woman told the story of her life line to others. Women wore their 'life' with pride throughout the two days and shared their stories with each other.

REFLECTION STAGE

At each of the above events, evaluations were conducted by written questionnaire or group discussion. In our monthly meetings the coordinators told stories of the women's experiences with the project and added their observations or interpretations. In this way we developed a collective knowledge of the issues but, more importantly, through the stories we came to a greater understanding of some women's suffering. We heard that some women associate the word menopause with 'old, dying, useless and no sex'. Also women appeared desperate for information. In almost every community the venues were overwhelmed by the number of women who wanted to attend them. For example, over 200 women attended a forum held in Williams Lake in a church basement while 80 more were turned away at the door. In one small remote town in the north, women drove 5 hours over icy roads to attend a symposium. In Vernon there was a 16 week waiting list for the educational materials at the library. It was clear that the women were learning a lot and, more importantly, were enjoying the opportunity to learn from and with each other.

FINAL PHASES OF ACTION

In the last stages of the project the coordinators planned the final events, some of which were large gatherings. I will describe one particularly successful activity from a large forum in Williams Lake: an unfashion show (Prince George also used this activity successfully). This event was videotaped, enabling us to view it later at our monthly meeting.

The Unfashion Show at Williams Lake

The 'unfashion show' was designed to celebrate women in mid-life. A local storyteller was hired to work with women in the community who volunteered to be 'performers'. She helped them to develop a short biography of their experience of mid-life, or to write or find a poem that represented them. The 'performers' chose from their own clothing something symbolic of themselves.

The storyteller began the show with an amusing story of how she became a 'crone'. She then introduced and narrated for the others. As each woman came down the runway, the storyteller read her biography or poem. The women strutted, walked or danced down a runway lit with lights to their favourite piece of music. Two women in particular 'brought down the house'. The first person to come down the runway was a woman dressed in jeans and her favourite t-shirt. She was heavily built, with a natural complexion devoid of make-up. She definitely was a contrast to a commercial image of a slim, young model. She danced down the runway to a popular rock song with such energy and joy that women howled with laughter while others cried with the impact of seeing such fun from a mid-life woman. Her short biography spoke of her love of life, her pride in having produced her wonderful children 'with the midriff to prove it' and the delight she has found in only looking after herself now that her children are grown.

The next 'model' was the local minister who came out of the wings wearing her white ministerial robes, holding her hands as if in prayer. At first, she danced slowly to the tune 'I believe in miracles', but when the lyrics reached the part: 'you sexy thing' she ripped open her gown, stripped it off to reveal her favourite sweater and jeans and threw the robe into the audience in mock imitation of a stripper. She danced in a fast tempo for the remainder of the song. The effect of seeing their minister let loose brought the women to their feet screaming and laughing. They embraced the 'life is good' spirit.

This hilarious and liberating beginning was followed by presentations from an expert panel on sexuality, bone health, and the pros and cons of both hormone replacement therapy and alternative approaches. Many questions from the audience of women focused on sexuality. The coordinator was convinced these questions would not have been asked if the women had not experienced the exhilaration of the unfashion show (based on her experience with the other events). In evaluation forms from the event and in later interviews, women said that in this conference 'learning with other women was a spiritual experience'. In all of the projects the educational materials were useful and helped women to make significant changes, but presented on their own they may not have been as effective.

PRESENTATIONAL KNOWING AT THE OUTCOME STAGE

Follow-up research to discern the effect of all this activity yielded 41 interviews, two focus groups and nine personal case stories as sources of data. In addition, evaluations had been collected throughout the project at all of the events. There were 388 of these evaluations. We focused on what the women had learned, how their thinking had changed and if they had made changes in their lifestyle. The coordinators and I discussed how these 'results' could be presented at an upcoming women's health conference in Victoria. We knew that it would be easy to lose the power of the projects to transform thinking if this information was presented in the usual conference presentation format. Also, collapsing the results of each community into an aggregate of achievements was likewise not appealing. Our first choice was to recreate an unfashion show for the audience. We knew that the music, poetry, humour and storytelling aspects of this medium would be entertaining, but we did not feel we could represent other women's biographies and it certainly would not make sense to do our own (only two of us were in mid-life). Also, when it came down to it some of us lacked the courage of the community women to dance down a runway in front of an audience! Conference sponsors generously included the travel costs of the coordinators but not women from the communities. Also, the unfashion show might have been amusing but would not have indicated the effects of the project. The coordinators were justifiably proud of what they had achieved, in particular the empowerment of the women in their communities. We convened another meeting to consider other ideas.

We were stuck on two points: We knew from the follow-up research that the women had experienced a profound transformation in their thinking about their health and themselves. We also knew from the follow-up interviews and our own reflection discussions that women said repeatedly that they found being with other women and learning together in a community of women a spiritual experience. How could we represent this so that the significance of it was recognized? What medium would do justice to the depth of the women's experience? How could we represent their discussions of such phenomena as love, grief, sickness, fear of loss of sexuality, self-esteem and dependence? These were the representational issues with which we struggled. We needed to be able to tell a story. Phenomenologist Van Manen (1990) described the importance of reading others' stories: 'we may be able to experience life situations, events and emotions that we would normally not have ... the opportunity of gaining insight into certain aspects of the human condition'. In describing the significance of poetry for understanding he captures the gist of what we were struggling with: 'A poet can sometimes give linguistic expression to some aspect of human experience that cannot be paraphrased without losing a sense of the vivid truthfulness that the lines of the poem are somehow able to communicate' (1990: 71). Each artistic medium has its own language of expression whether it is visual, tactile, auditory, etc. (Van Manen, 1990). We reflected on which 'language' would best convey the 'results' or our presentational knowledge.

COORDINATORS CONCEIVE A FORMAT FOR THE CONFERENCE

The coordinator from Vernon came up with a song to represent the transformation in her region. The others liked the idea and created a song for themselves. We decided on one song that combined the elements of the others. At the conference, to introduce the project each coordinator gave a short presentation on her community complete with photographs and a geography lesson and an overview of the activities. All of us then sang the song with the audience as follows. The audience was taught to sing a simple blues bar 'Ba BA ba bum'. As we sang the song the audience sang the blues bar as a chorus at the end of each line. The audience was hesitant at first but sang stronger with each repetition. Here is the song:

> Now ladies please listen
> We don't want to confuse
> Our message is simple
> And it's not in the news
> Gotta look for some wisdom
> Some stories and clues
> Now's the hour, find your power
> In these marvelous mid-life blues
>
> We're tired of the culture
> that says we're all through
> The ads and commercials
> The big companies too
> They see us as profit
> Just want us to buy
> We want respect, want to connect
> With a fabulous mid-life high

The audience was thus engaged in singing 'the results' of the project with us. They

Figure 30.1 *Singing the 'presentation'*

paid close attention to the words, the rhythm and the hand gestures of the coordinators. No longer in the passive state of 'audience', their senses were alert with anticipation, waiting for their cue, waiting to be part of the production. We were attempting to achieve what Heron and Reason have described in Chapter 24 as the purpose of presentational knowing: 'co-inquirers ... develop[ing] a sense of pre-conceptual communion or resonance in their shared life-world' (p. 369). In singing the song in unison with each other and on cue with us, the presenters, all of us transcended the duality of our roles.

In addition to our presentational knowledge format we were very fortunate that the Women's Conference had engaged a women's art cooperative to display their art throughout the conference centre. The art depicted women's bodies in a wide range of metaphorical representations. One life size figure of a plump woman was made of clay (mother earth) while another was a woman's torso decorated with flowers and gossamer wings (Figures 30.2 and 30.3). All of these

added to the sense of celebration of being a woman at a women's health conference.

GOING SOLO WITH THE RESULTS: PRESENTING NARRATIVES

The project ended, the final report was submitted and the coordinators and I went our separate ways. Yet I felt there was more for me to learn about presentational knowing and there was more in the women's stories to tell. I continued to investigate how to represent the results at other conferences. I read Riessman's (1993) monograph on narrative analysis. She describes the definition of a narrative as talk organized around consequential events. According to Riessman tellers take their listeners into a past world and in the telling of what happened to them make a point about their experience. Particularly pertinent to this chapter, Riessman suggests that respondents often narrativize their experience when 'there has been a breach between ideal and real, self and society' (1993: 3).

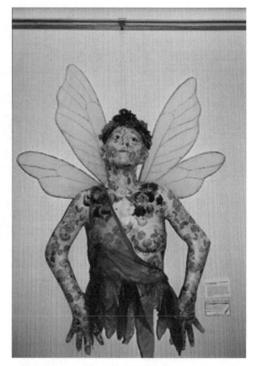

Figure 30.2 *Mother Earth greeter*
(Women's Art Cooperative)

Figure 30.3 *Fairy poised to soar*
(Women's Art Cooperative)

Nine personal narratives were told to me for the purpose of understanding how the women became involved in the project and what it had meant to them. I felt these stories were illustrative of transformational change. Riessman's rendering of a story into poetic structures seemed to be the language that might better convey the emotional impact of the women's story. As one who writes poetry myself I was intrigued. In fact, this project had inspired me to write a series of poems about mid-life that focused on disappearance and becoming invisible.

EXAMPLE OF A WOMAN'S STORY IN POETIC STRUCTURE

The following is an example of a short narrative told to me by a woman at the two-day retreat at Sechelt (some of the other coordinators attended this event as well). She had a great sense of humour, was obviously liked by others in the community and appeared to be laughing the entire weekend, but her story was quite different than her current happy state would suggest. It is her story that I felt would best be told in poetic structure. She began by saying: 'I was ignorant, sick and going crazy'. Applying Reissman's technique I created the following poetic structure. I intended to illustrate her transformation as she became connected to the women's health centre through the pot luck lunches for mature women.

I was going down
into a depression
and heading for Prozac
I was going through the change
– menopause – was irritable

My mother bounced off walls
threw things,
no one to turn to.
Afraid I was going there
Hard time of life

Diagnosis of osteoarthritis
and a lump in my breast

Just moved to the area,
Hard at this age
had to meet new people

I was in denial
Now, menopause is a pleasant thing
I am living healthier, walking more
I am going to be more creative

Audiences at conferences are quiet for the first few minutes after the reading of this poem. The first, standard part of my presentation explains the purpose of the community action and some of the detailed activities but this woman's poem allows the audience to feel her emotion and her fear of mental illness, particularly when read with dramatic inflection. On the first line: 'I was going down', the audience is immediately attentive. Through the reading some female audience members have been moved to tears while others, not so visibly moved, have confessed later to being affected. In the act of empathy, evoked by the artistic form, the audience experiences the life world of the woman. I was inspired to investigate how the interviews might be made more compelling.

THE INTERVIEWS IN POETIC STRUCTURE

Follow-up interviews with women asked them what issues they had become aware of with regard to mid-life health. I had amalgamated the responses into themes but the spiritual connection that they experienced was lost and the women's transformation trivialized in the coldness of academic discourse. They became soulless pieces of data. I experimented with different forms of poetic structures.

A haiku poem is composed of three lines which often do not rhyme. The first line has five syllables, the second line has seven and the last line has five. I removed the extraneous parts of the sentences and left the feelings, the actions and the thoughts in the form of the haiku poem in an attempt to reveal the transformative aspects. The following haiku is in response to the question: 'What issues have you become aware of with regard to your mid-life health through this project?'

I am too fragile,
develop emotional
And renewing self

And another:

Alone as a choice
A companion to oneself
Viable, valuable

In answer to 'Has this project changed the way you discuss things with your doctor?', a response in haiku form is this:

As I Doctor shop
More power, more personal
My health is my say

Through this form an audience can experience the essence of the project. In a recent class presentation a student (male) said that the rhythm of the poem draws you into the emotion. Van Manen (1990) suggests that in most research the results can be severed from the process of the research whereas in the presentation of phenomenological research 'you will listen in vain for the punch line, the latest information or the big news' (p. 13). He said that phenomenology like poetry tries an incantive, evocative speaking, a primal telling wherein we aim to involve the voice in an original singing of the world (Merleau Ponty, cited in Van Manen, 1990: 13). While this study was not a phenomenological study the coordinators and myself discovered experientially the meaning of Van Manen's and Heron and Reason's ideas as we struggled to represent what we were discovering about women's (human) consciousness.

CONCLUSIONS AND REFLECTIONS

The WHIM project attempted (and succeeded) to change the women's perception of mid-life and health by developing their self-esteem, their sense of empowerment, by increasing their knowledge and therefore choices and their connectedness to each other. The community coordinators, the main coordinator and I responded in particular to descriptions of the projects as 'a spiritual experience' and we wondered what it was about these events that was so powerful for women. Although we discovered that there was a lack of information on menopause and mid-life health, it is doubtful that the women on their own would have sought it or known what to do with it even where it was available. Learning with other women and from other women seemed to be more significant than the content of the educational sessions. Women needed first to find the joy in this life phase or, in Reason and Bradbury's words, how to 'flourish'. This appeared to motivate them to learn more in order to enjoy this developmental stage.

As a community psychologist I was particularly interested in what Sarason (1974) has called 'the psychological sense of community' that appeared to be missing for these women and their feelings of marginalization. Sarason suggested if we are to effect change we need to understand how the nature of our culture produced this reduced community feeling. One woman explained to me that as young women we make connections through our children or through our work but for older women there are no natural connections. Nelson and Prilleltensky (2005) describe this phenomenon in stronger terms. They refer to it as a social marginalization that can occur as individuals cycle through the life stages. They describe marginalization as being fundamentally related to the 'very meaning of what it means to be human' (p. 299). For those who are 'severely and involuntarily marginalized their selfhood, their humanity is threatened' (p. 300).

Reflecting on internalization of social dialogue

The Vygotskian perspective percolated for me as we tried to understand the nature of this social marginalization. As we reflected on the discussions with women we wondered how some had developed the idea that they were used up and finished, a perception that was distressing to witness. How is it that these older women came to feel so disenfranchised and disconnected from their community? Russian developmental psychologist Vygotsky is credited with explicating the process of internalization, the developmental relationship in which external processes are transformed to create internal processes. The Vygotskian formulation centres on two premises: internalization is primarily social and semiotic mechanisms (language) mediate the social and individual functioning (Wertsch and Stone, 1985). Interpsychological functioning becomes intrapyschological functioning as the external social dialogue becomes internal consciousness (Wertsch and Stone, 1985). In this project, the women felt stigmatized by negative views of mid-life and by a society that they perceived engaged in youth worship. The negative social (external) dialogue on ageing becomes internalized as a plane of consciousness so that the inner dialogue *with* oneself *about* oneself is negative. Vygotsky conceptualized internalization as a 'set of social relationships transposed inside'. This internalization is greater than simply a cognitive reflection of the environment but instead it is structurally dynamic with an emphasis on a person's 'interaction with the socially organized environment' (Valsiner, 1988: 142). We recognized that the women needed not only information for health but a way to find meaning in their lives at mid-life and to be engaged in a more positive social dialogue about mid-life.

Similarly, for Brazilian educator Paulo Freire, social dialogue is the mechanism by which human beings develop and progress (Gadotti, 1994). Freire developed educative strategies to bring the internalized thoughts to the surface of consciousness to be examined reflectively and critically. According to Freire, any educational strategy if it is to be liberating has to create authentic reflection on people and their relations with the world. Traditional didactic education is aimed at the submersion of consciousness while Freire's pedagogy of liberation strives for the emergence of consciousness (Freire, 1970). The key is to develop within people the 'power to perceive critically the way they exist in the world with which and in which they find themselves' (p. 64). Freire achieves this through the use of 'triggers': words, pictures, or any medium that begins the act of dialogue by bringing into consciousness that which has been internalized. He refers to this as 'conscientization', the process of learning to perceive social, political and economic conditions and to take action.

Reflecting on Community

In this project, the creative art forms, or Freirian 'triggers', used in the events facilitated this awakening to internalized attitudes and ways of being. The coordinators found ways to inspirit the women with a new life force. But there was another facilitator at work in this process: becoming part of a community through the process of engaging in the production of presentational knowing, or as Heron and Reason describe it in Chapter 24, 'develop[ing] a sense of pre-conceptual communion or resonance in their shared lifeworld' (p. 369).

A structural invisibility of the women at mid-life occurs as they lose their connections to societal institutions, for example their work and their children's school, etc. Through coming together for this project and the exploration of presentational knowing the women gained a connectedness in their community. Sarason (1974) articulates the characteristics of this psychological sense of community as the perception of similarity to others, an acknowledged interdependence with others. McKnight (1996) calls for a regeneration of community, a return to dependence on the collective efforts of citizens to provide support and comfort to each other instead of an individualistic reliance on professionals and institutions which in turn rely on consumers (clients) for their existence. This project facilitated the emergence of women out of their social marginalization and gave them the opportunity to develop new types of relationships and expectations for themselves. They were able to examine their old roles and develop new ones in the safety of a community of other women through art, poetry, music and laughter. This in turn inspired them to care for themselves and to become more fully a woman in mid-life.

ACKNOWLEDGEMENTS

This project had heart and soul because of the community coordinators. They are Linda Anderson, Heather Gordon, Barbara Levesque, Joan Meister, Patti Murphy, Carel Scott, and Celeste Wincapaw, and the main coordinator, Lenore Riddell. The two reviewers of this chapter, Hilary Bradbury and Rita Kowalski, gave excellent advice, detailed comments and enthusiastic reviews. Many thanks to all.

NOTE

1 Other sessions or classes included Celtic dance, Tai Chi, self-defense; drop-in 'pot luck' lunches and noon hour walks; healing circles, activities aimed at raising self-esteem. Practical issues such as financial planning and discussions of treatments for physical symptoms were discussed at other workshops in more traditional formats. Concurrently participants received specific information on depression, nutrition for health, exercises and ageing, menopause and hormone replacement therapy (facts and myths), bone health, sexuality, pros and cons of alternative therapies and some interactive media.

REFERENCES

Anderson, L. (1999) *Women's Health in Mid Life: a Report on Activities in the Northern Interior*. Northern Secretariat, Prince George, British Colombia: BC Centre for Excellence for Women's Health.

Campbell, C. (2004) 'Health psychology and community action', in M. Murray (ed.), *Critical Health Psychology*. New York: Palgrave Macmillan. pp. 203–22

Freire, P. (1970) *Pedagogy of the Oppressed*. New York: Continuum.

Friedan, B. (1993) *The Fountain of Age*. New York: Simon & Schuster.

Gadotti, M. (1994) *Reading Paolo Freire: His life and his Work*. Albany, NY: State University of New York Press.

McKnight, J. (1996) *The Careless Society: Community and Its Counterfeits*. New York: Basic Books.

Nelson, G. and Prilleltensky, I. (eds) (2005) *Community Psychology: In Pursuit of Liberation and Well-being*. New York: Palgrave Macmillan.

Owen, H. (1997) *Open Space Technology: a User's Guide*. San Francisco, CA: Berrett-Koehler.

Reason, P. and Bradbury, H. (eds) (2001/2006) 'Introduction: inquiry and participation in search of a world worthy of human aspiration', in P. Reason and H. Bradbury (eds), *Handbook of Action Research: Participative Inquiry and Practice*. London: Sage. pp. 1–14. Also published in P. Reason and H. Bradbury (eds) (2006), *Handbook of Action Research: Concise Paperback Edition*. London: Sage. pp. 1–14.

Riessman, C.K. (1993) *Narrative Analysis*. Newbury Park, CA: Sage.

Sarason, S.B. (1974) *The Psychological Sense of Community: Prospects for a Community Psychology*. San Francisco, CA: Jossey-Bass.

Valsiner, J. (1988) *Developmental Psychology in the Soviet Union*. Bloomington: Indiana University Press.

Van Manen, M. (1990) *Researching Lived Experience: Human Science for an Action Sensitive Pedagogy*. London, ONT: Western University Press.

Vygotsky, L.S. (1978) *Mind in Society*. Cambridge, MA: Harvard University Press.

Wertsch, J.V. and Stone, C.A. (1985). 'The concept of internalization', in J.V. Wertsch (ed.), *Culture, Communication and Cognition: Vygotskian Perspectives*. Cambridge: Cambridge University Press. pp. 162–179.

31

Working with 'Not Knowing' Amid Power Dynamics Among Managers: From Faultfinding and Exclusion Towards Co-learning and Inclusion

Marianne Kristiansen and Jørgen Bloch-Poulsen

The overall purpose of this chapter is to show how power manifested itself as an excluding and faultfinding discourse in a group of managers in a Danish company and how they and we changed this power mechanism towards co-learning and inclusion by means of dialogic inquiry. This cultural pattern emerged during the process when the managers were trained as mentors and had 'messy stuff' to deal with. Among other things, we learned to listen to our self-referential, emotional reactions when confronted with power mechanisms and to use them as points of departure for co-changing their culture.

This chapter is based on a videotaped, dialogic action research project that we carried out with a managerial group within the Research & Development Department of a major Danish company that produces televisions, loudspeakers, etc. The executive director, his two senior managers, their 22 managers, and some employees participated in the project. The main goal was to enhance employee involvement by training managers as mentors, i.e. to empower the employees by

empowering the managers as mentors (Kristiansen and Bloch-Poulsen, 2005).

The overall purpose of this chapter is to show how power manifested itself as a faultfinding discourse (Schiffrin, 1994) in the group of managers and how they and we dealt with and tried to change this disempowering mechanism.

First, we illustrate how this faultfinding pattern became apparent during the process. Managers and employees who, for example, admitted insufficiencies were excluded from being listened to or promoted. In line with Lewin's dictum (1948) that you get to know an organization when trying to change it, we happened to come across this pattern when we began training managers as mentors. We conceptualized this pattern as a power mechanism by means of which the managerial group maintained its own discourse of normality (Foucault, 1978, 2000), thereby creating a distinction between the included and the excluded.

Second, we show how the faultfinding pattern was not only co-created between managers and employees, but also between them and us (Kristiansen and Bloch-Poulsen, 2006). Our first-person inquiry (Torbert, 2001/2006; Torbert and Taylor, Chapter 16 in this volume) demonstrates how we did not understand this discourse at the beginning of the project, but adopted it due to our self-referentiality (Kristiansen and Bloch-Poulsen, 2004). Without knowing, we did not question our own a priori categories and ways of relating. Changing the pattern of faultfinding meant changing our self-referentiality, too.

Third, our second and third person inquiry demonstrates how we worked with the managerial group to collaboratively change the power mechanism from faultfinding and exclusion towards co-learning and inclusion. Later in the project this happened by changing the relations among them and between them and us into a dialogic inquiry where we all began problematizing the apparently natural, basic assumptions of their ways of living in organizational power mechanisms.

The authors' conceptual framework changed during the process, too. We originally understood power negatively as a juridical, positional concept, i.e. as an individual possession, for example located in the executive director, enabling him to constrain the scope of actions of his managers. Today, we also conceptualize power as a cultural pattern manifest in and co-produced by the discourse of all the managers in the department and by the interaction between them and us. It is a distributed network of social

alignments and relations, i.e. a strategic, relational and dynamic concept – or a specific regime of truth (Foucault, 1978, 2000; Gaventa and Cornwall, 2001/2006; Chapter 11 in this volume; Rouse, 1994). In our understanding, the consequences of power can vary to comprise excluding, constraining, empowering, and including.

In the following, we give a presentation that reflects the action research process itself. We do hope, though, that you will not lose the big picture, as we often did during the process! We believe action research can be developed through concrete descriptions, where we show changes in praxis, when things are messy and hurt; where we might experience happiness, co-create new concepts, models, and theories, when we ourselves are put at stake as persons, a place in which the distance between success and failure seems minimal.[1]

EMERGENT, MUTUAL INVOLVEMENT

The development process we worked on was convened to address the large personnel turnover in the software group of the R&D department particularly. By means of a Future Lab (Jungk and Müller, 1990) involving all employees and managers, it became clear that within this project organization the employees missed a managerial function dealing with their long-term personal and professional development. The Future Lab was organized because, alone, neither management nor we as action researchers could produce an adequate answer to the challenge of personnel turnover. It had to be the result of a joint effort involving the employees, too. Accordingly, the Future Lab decided that the managers were going to be trained as mentors. The concept of mentor was not co-produced until this moment. It described the wanted, but until now missing, management function.

During this project, we began conceptualizing our approach as emergent, mutual involvement (Kristiansen and Bloch-Poulsen, 2005). It is about being open to emerging, burning challenges dealing with job tasks and cooperation in ways that integrate organizational development as we tried to do with the Future Lab. The approach also implies co-developing concepts and models with the participants as illustrated by the concept of mentoring. Thus, we did not bring ready-made theories and models to be implemented in the programme.

It is our experience that no matter how well we prepare ourselves, we can never know what will emerge in the process. To us action research is about giving up the power of knowing in advance, albeit resting on many years of scholarship, inquiry and engagement with the questions of organization change, and instead being prepared to meet what is unexpected as, for example, the faultfinding pattern. Originally, we understood this as our naiveté, now we call it 'productive not-knowing'. We consider this to be a central part of emergent, mutual involvement more in line with a dialogic tendency within organizational development than with a strategic and instrumental one (Deetz, 2001).

DON'T ASK: 'WHAT IS A GOOD MANAGER?'

Already at our first training module with the 25 managers of the R&D department after the Future Lab, things were easier said than done. We met in the HR rooms of the company where we articulated our purpose and presented a preliminary outline of the mentor-training programme, which had been fine-tuned with the director and the two senior managers.

We experienced the atmosphere in the room as ranging between positive expectations and skepticism, e.g. when we began negotiating an idea of videotaping the whole process as a means to develop concepts and train the managers as mentors. We balanced expectations and continued asking: 'What is a good manager – especially a good mentor – according to your understanding?' We

intended to involve them, but the question created a subtle shift in the energy level in the room, as if the room stopped breathing for a moment. One of the two senior managers looked at the executive director in a way Jørgen interpreted as if something was wrong. Jørgen did not pay particular attention to this reaction because he was used to constantly being evaluated as a consultant. Marianne reacted by internalizing their reaction and began wondering if she could live up to their standards. Thus, we did not question our self-referentiality, but adapted to the situation, because deep down we were scared. Moreover, we did not have a plan for how to intervene when the going got tough. We were starting the process and were in doubt about the timing of our interventions. What did we dare to say without jeopardizing the whole project?

In retrospect, it has become clear to us that already at this time we met with an example of what all of us later termed a faultfinding pattern within the managerial group (see the section on 'The red pen' and onwards). We were being tested, although it was commonly known within the group that we had already done successful work with the organization which some of them had even participated in. We began realizing that the faultfinding pattern was not only out there between them, but also co-created in the relation between them and us. We might, for example, have intervened by questioning the subtle shift in energy and by asking whether we were up for a test because we experienced that we were being judged. By doing so, we could risk being excluded from their culture, but we might also have started a dialogue about it. We understand this as a dilemma of courage and timing of when to use the relations between them and us as a possible mirror of their culture. We chose to tiptoe on the tension.

At a later training session, one of the senior managers confirmed that at this moment they had been about to 'flunk' us, because they were tired of consultants merely asking questions. In the meantime, we had observed a meeting where all the managers discussed possible candidates for the next downsizing. Our feedback to them dealt with how managers asking open questions received no eye contact, were interrupted by judgemental statements, and not listened to, while those with unambiguous points of view accompanied by humour were mentioned in the minutes of the meeting. We experienced first hand that productive inquiry (Isaacs, 1999) worked as a way of being excluded from the managerial group, because practically all questions were ignored.

Without our knowing, mentor-training in dialogue and coaching could be experienced as a provocation to their culture. They were not used to asking for help and asking questions. In their daily work they acted mostly as advisers or experts. Would they respect help from a person (coach/dialogue partner) who did not know the right answer in advance? Would they respect us, if we practised dialogues and asked questions like 'What is a good manager?', or would we be excluded? We did not grasp, then, the possible impact of the disturbance created by the mentor-training project (Bateson, 1972).

In the next section, we unfold the fault-finding pattern between the managers and between them and us.

CAN A MANAGER LOSE FACE IN AN ORGANIZATION?

In the mentor-training, the managers dealt with their daily, burning issues and were simultaneously trained as coaches and dialogue partners based on concepts developed during the process. In the following clip from a coaching session, the coach, Asger, is also the day-to-day director of Børge, the problem holder or focus person. Their colleagues are gathered around them. They observe the conversation and give feedback to both parties afterwards. One of us is present, too. Børge's overall goal is employee involvement. He wants his employees, e.g. Karl, to become

'self-starters', i.e. to take more initiatives without depending on Børge. The purpose is to increase the efficiency of his project organized teams in the R&D Department:

Asger: And why [waves left hand] do you think Karl was unable to feel like a self-starter on this occasion? [quick smile]

Børge: [wry smile] I'm afraid that was perhaps because I piled on too much pressure, that I'm too ambitious ... that he perhaps says: 'OK, Børge has a grip on that, I can hear from Børge that he knows all about that, so I agree that something has to be done.'

Asger: [knits brows]

Børge: But he does nothing because he knows that I'll do it.

Asger: Does this mean that you take over and solve the task for him instead?

Børge: Yeah ... maybe [wry smile; nods], I do it, yes I do [looks up].

Asger: [leans over the table; smiles] Is that the mechanism?

Børge: Yes, I probably do that ... I probably do [smiles; looks up and then at Asger].

Asger: Have you been out and had a go at the machine?

Børge: Yes, I have [looks down].

Asger: [looks at Børge]

Børge: as recently as yesterday [laughs].

Asger: [laughs aloud; looks out into the training group – they/we laugh too] ... So it could be the mechanism [looks straight at Børge] which comes into force that means Karl doesn't take it?

Børge: [nods; looks straight ahead; moves body back and forwards] It could be ... it could be [5 secs.]. I don't know why [looks at Asger; with a wry smile].

Asger: [laughs; leans back]

Børge: I have to honestly admit.

There is a double asymmetry in this conversation. Asger is a coach and the executive director, too. The training group are observers, managerial colleagues and competitors, too. Besides, some of them refer to Asger as their day-to-day director. In this way, the training context is already integrated in the organizational context.

Asger keeps checking his notion that Børge solves a task for Karl ('Does this mean ... ?', 'Is that the mechanism ... ?', 'Have you been out ... ?', 'So it could be ... ?'). His repeated check is accompanied by loud laughter and eye contact with the training group laughing back. Børge answers by shifting between downgrading replies ('perhaps', 'maybe', 'probably') and admissions ('I do', 'Yes, I have', 'I have to honestly admit') at the same time smiling wryly and making a long pause before his final admission.

It is our interpretation that this conversation is turned into a disclosure of the insufficiencies of Børge in front of his colleagues and one of us, Jørgen. Four times, Asger asks the same Socratic question about Børge's possible shortcomings. A nonverbal alliance seems to be created in the training room between Asger, the training group, and Jørgen, by means of laughter and eye contact. By admitting a contradiction, Børge seems to be losing face within the managerial group (Goffman, 1967). In these ways, the conversation becomes an example of a faultfinding discourse. Asger and the training group can be interpreted as insiders and Børge as an outsider whose reality does not count (Chambers, 1995, 1997), but is met with laughter. Both the training group and Jørgen become co-witnesses to the disclosure of Børge. What was intended to be a helping or a generatively facilitated conversation in the training context became a disclosure in the organizational context.[2]

Even though the situation happened some years ago, Jørgen remembers it as if it were yesterday. At that time, he was puzzled. The same evening we watched a videotape of the conversation. It was not until Marianne exclaimed: 'What is this laughter about?' that Jørgen was able to express his discomfort and shame at having co-witnessed Børge's disclosure without intervening directly in the situation. As a consequence, the managerial culture seemed to be repeated in the training context. Was this due to Jørgen's unconscious identification with the faultfinding tendency of the executive director? By asking this question, we began problematizing our own a priori ways of relating, i.e. our self-referentiality. Today, we would probably have intervened by expressing our discomfort and checking what the special quality of this laughter was all about, using our emotional reactions as a vehicle for co-changing their culture.

In the following sections, we describe how we worked with the managerial group to collaboratively change the power mechanism from faultfinding and exclusion towards co-learning and inclusion.

THE RED PEN?

The faultfinding pattern is brought into the open in the following clip which presents a feedback conversation between Asger, the executive director, Leo, one of his experienced managers, and the two of us. We talk about their video-taped annual employee appraisal conversation. Along with Leo, we question Asger's 'red-line-behaviour':

JBP: The comments that we had written to you about that you – like me – sometimes appear to be evaluating, do you have any comment on them?

Asger: Yes, well, it is, of course, correct [all laugh]. I can't help evaluating and judging people.

Leo: We tease Asger a lot with a red pen.

Asger: I don't have a red pen, they're all blue [laughs]. It's nonsense.

Leo: It's again the phenomenon that no matter what we show you, you just can't help it ... it's again the bit about making it even better and developing it, eh? You add a line there and a dash there and then a bit over here [illustrates on a piece of paper]. And then you see what comes out of it. And we all know Asger's attitude is positive. But if you are a fusspot, then it isn't so easy. But if you have found out that he really does it because he genuinely means well, then it's great. But some people will think: 'that was pretty cruel, there isn't much left there.' But I think you know that yourself, you know, it isn't unknown for you?

Asger: No.

MK: But I was thinking that if you are not like Leo, but a bit more reticent ... then I think a person would have to push hard to make himself visible to you?

Asger: [nods]

MK: You get on best with strong employees?

Asger: Yes, I don't think the others have a chance. I don't notice their qualities ... That's probably right.

Earlier, we mentioned Jørgen's possible identification with the faultfinding tendency of the executive director, Asger. By using himself as an example, Jørgen shares his perspective with Asger and Leo and dares problematize Asger's faultfinding pattern ('The comments that we … on them?'). Asger and Leo confirm this pattern and Leo elaborates on it. Marianne changes perspective and questions whether some of Asger's more reserved managers experience his red marks as signs of exclusion or as invitations to learning. Asger confirms that he does not notice the reticent managers. Our inquiry is accompanied by laughter and we speak on an equal footing. Thus, we conceptualize this conversation as an example of a dialogue. We define dialogue as a collaborative inquiry characterized by sharing, daring and caring (Kristiansen and Bloch-Poulsen, 2005). In this dialogue, we share our points of views, we dare to problematize the red-pen tendency of the executive director, and we care to become wiser together. This dialogue could also be understood as an example of experiential knowing (Heron and Reason, Chapter 24 in this volume).

Leo understands Asger's red pen as a means of constantly developing projects and ideas in the R&D department (' … it's again the bit about making it even better and developing it, eh?'). In their daily work, faultfinding seems to be an important competence. We think Leo's remarks about the red pen illustrate a dilemma for this managerial group. On one hand, the red pen might function as faultfinding exclusion of the more reserved managers. On the other, Leo and people like him might experience it as knowledge sharing inclusion. In this way, Leo moves the perspective on power from Asger's individual psychology to the consequences of the red-pen tendency on managers.

We comprehend this red-pen dialogue as an initial, joint step of transforming their managerial faultfinding culture from an excluding towards a more empowering one.

HAS HE BEEN JUDGED FOREVER?

The following clips are from a group feedback conversation between seven managers, Ivar, the senior manager of some of them, and the two of us after a coaching session that we have all observed on the last training module. The executive director is not present. Bjarne, the focus person, is the day-to-day manager and mentor for a male employee who is very experienced, but 'on festive occasions he goes right at the women who happen to be present', as Bjarne mentions with a wry smile. The employee has applied for a job as a manager. Bjarne doubts whether is it in tune with his ethics to promote an employee with such behavior. The faultfinding pattern is here enlarged to embrace the culture in the whole department:

Bjarne: But this is problematic … What has happened right now is that the man has no real chance of becoming a manager here, ever, because we all share the same knowledge … Right now, I have a guilty conscience because I have in fact exposed the man. …

JBP: Let's just look at that. What do you mean by your guilty conscience?

Bjarne: Yes, it means there might never have been anybody who has pointed this out to him before. I've decided to go in and do that. But before he gets the chance to sort of do something about the situation, then he's, perhaps we've judged him in advance. And I'm the reason he's being judged. …

JBP: Who has judged him?

Bjarne: Well, I have a bit, haven't I, by involving you so he can be judged by you, too.

JBP: OK. We can check that. Has he been? [asks the group]

Ole: Well, he isn't the first employee to have made a right mess of things.

Bjarne: No, he sure isn't.

Ivar: And we don't necessarily judge them all.

Ole: We're all human beings, we can all mess up, etc.

Bjarne: Yes, OK. …

Ole: So I don't think so.

Bjarne: How many of you sitting here have really messed up?

Ivar: I could name a few of us.

Ole: But they have managed to move on.

JBP: I'll just check, is there anybody who judges him?

Leo: We could perhaps turn it around and say, why is it now Bjarne thinks the way he does? ... Once we have heard something, we can't avoid judging. And it's almost impossible not to.

Ole: We're bad at that, you're right.

MK: Does that mean that if you make a couple of mistakes, you're out?

Leo: No, one is enough actually, I'd say.

MK: One's enough?

Leo: Yes, if you can remember it then it's enough.

In this dialogue, Bjarne co-reflects with his colleagues and us on the consequences of sharing his knowledge about the employee in the training group. The conversation inquires into the same questions from different perspectives. Is the employee now excluded from becoming a manager ('I have in fact exposed the man')? Is it possible to share such knowledge within the managerial group?

The conversation starts out as an inquiry into Bjarne's 'guilty conscience'. Jørgen practises a dialogic competence that we call tracking. This is questioning a key expression, 'guilty conscience', that Bjarne has just used, followed by perspective reflection in a mutually affirming atmosphere. We co-developed the concept of tracking and other dialogic competencies during the project (Kristiansen and Bloch-Poulsen, 2005). Leo asks a perspective question: 'why is it now Bjarne thinks the way he does?' He understands Bjarne's way of thinking as an example of a judgmental tendency in the managerial group ('Once we have heard something, we can't avoid judging. And it's almost impossible not to'). Ole confirms this.

By changing from an individual to a managerial, group perspective, the group begins to inquire into the faultfinding discourse of their managerial culture and to question whether an employee is being excluded forever by them. Thus, the problem is no longer understood as only Bjarne's. It belongs to all of them. In the conversation above, we reached a new understanding of power, because Leo helped us again. Power changes from being conceptualized as an individual possession to also being understood as a discursive regime of truth with

different consequences for them and their employees. It is no longer only a question of whether Bjarne is going to use his power by, for example, rejecting the promotion of the employee. Thus, we began to conceptualize the faultfinding pattern as a shared culture in the department.

We intervene by checking: 'Who has judged him?' ... 'OK. We can check that. Has he been (judged)'? This is an example of a dialogic competence we came to call scanning, i.e. checking of ideas followed by perspective reflection in a mutually affirming atmosphere. We also intervene by asking: 'Does that mean that if you make a couple of mistakes, you're out?' This second loop question addresses a basic assumption about how many errors one is allowed to commit before being excluded and not promoted in this culture.

We remember a shift in energy or atmosphere when asking this question. Marianne felt all of a sudden alone in the group and began wondering if her question was wrong. We have had similar feelings in other groups when questioning basic assumptions about power mechanisms. We experience these second loop questions as trespassing an invisible border you did not know existed until you asked the question. We have learned it is important to be courageous, to keep sitting in the fire (Mindell, 1995), and continue the dialogue. As shown, this was not possible for us in the beginning of the project. At the described moment, we had co-operated for some time, developed mutual trust, and succeeded in co-establishing what we call a caring container (Kristiansen and Bloch-Poulsen, 2005), i.e. a dialogic space and rhythm where it becomes possible to meta-communicate about power mechanisms.

CATCH 22?

The group ends the conversation by concluding that Bjarne and they are caught in a Catch 22. No matter what Bjarne does, there will still be a problem:

JBP: The bit about your guilty conscience. Where is it now? Would you raise similar matters again?

Bjarne: Hmm ... yes, well, I think, it has been a good experience to bring it up, so as far as that is concerned, then I would probably ... But I would have to be very, very sure of my case, before I began to bring it up.

Ivar: Why is that, Bjarne?

Bjarne: Yes, well, because if I'm more unsure of my case, then there's a risk of the injustice being even greater, if we judge him, eh? ...

Aksel: But seen from the other side, if you, Bjarne, didn't tell anybody else about it, you were alone with it, and you decided to try it out on him, then you would also have a guilty conscience about that, I think.

Bjarne: Yes, because then I would not feel so clear in my head.

Aksel: So you would not know whether you really had any back up for doing something.

Ivar: So it's hardly surprising that it gives you a guilty conscience, no matter what you do.

Again, one of the managers, Aksel, changes the perspective of the conversation: 'But seen from the other side ...'. If Bjarne had not shared this knowledge, he would not have 'any back up for doing something'. We interpret Leo and Aksel's change of perspectives accompanied by confirming replies ('We are bad at that, you are right', 'Yes, because then I would not feel so clear in my head') and perspective reflections as examples of a dialogic use of the faultfinding pattern within the group. They question the limits of what they dare share in the training group without negative consequences for their employees. In this way, they problematize the boundaries of dialogues in organizations.

Apparently, we can change a cultural pattern by co-developing dialogues in the training context when we dare to share in a caring way, but this context is already integrated in the organizational context, so there seems to be a limit for dialogic action research, too.

CHANGING MANAGEMENT MEETINGS

Towards the end of the programme, the management group decided to address the faultfinding discourse of their management meetings. This decision was made at a plenary at a training module, where it turned out that it was not only us who experienced a judgemental atmosphere at their meetings. Some of the more reticent managers began talking about their stomach pains, their nervousness and physical discomfort when taking part in the meetings. These 'new voices' also said that colleagues in other departments felt as if they were being 'thrown to the lions' when they made a presentation in front of the group, as we felt in the beginning of the project.

Others remembered their feelings of being ashamed at not intervening directly, when Asger used 'the red pen' against one of their colleagues in a meeting. They felt the responsibility of co-witnessing, as they themselves were part of the managerial group.

Consequently, they decided to organize future management meetings by using a fishbowl model presented in the training. They would take turns as bystanders giving feedback regularly on communication patterns based on a more dialogic code of conduct written on a big poster in their meeting room. Collaboratively, we thus tried to organize their managerial meetings in new dialogic ways by moving their power mechanisms from an unspoken to a legitimate and open part of the agenda (Kristiansen and Bloch-Poulsen, 2000).

LEARNING THROUGH CHANGING

Changing the faultfinding pattern was not part of the mentor-training programme originally – it emerged during the process. The managers and we changed this all-embracing pattern by practising dialogues. This meant bringing the pattern into the open, questioning our self-referentiality, problematizing basic assumptions, and co-creating new ways of organizing their management meetings. The power mechanism was not suspended, but the faultfinding pattern was redirected from an excluding towards an including power mechanism.

Leo and Aksel helped us to look beyond an individual concept of power. Other managers also helped us to understand their culture – from 'the red pen' to being 'thrown to the lions'. In future projects, we will pay even more attention to the participants as our co-researchers and teachers.

Power is one of our teachers, too. In future projects, we expect to meet power mechanisms in organizational groups when questioning basic assumptions. We learned that it is important to listen to our (initial) self-referential, emotional reactions when confronted with power mechanisms and use them as points of departure for co-changing their culture. We learned, too, to pay more attention to energy shifts in the room. We try to remain congruent when we are uncomfortable and use our anxiety as a potentially knowledge-producing part of the process. Unless we are willing to run the risk of losing the project, questioning the given regime of truth, we will lose the process. Reviewing video clips turned out to be a helpful confrontation, changing our own blind and deaf spots into insight and new ways of acting.

We learned that action research is an ongoing process of transformative co-learning. As shown, this is sometimes a subtle, sometimes a rough and frightening change process balancing between courage, mutual trust, productive not-knowing, and timing. The more we gradually dared to share our reactions with them, even when this contributed to creating hot spots (Mindell, 1995), the more they dared to reflect and change their own culture and visa versa. The more managers began acting in dialogic ways towards each other, daring to ask difficult questions, addressing bodily and emotional reactions, considering faults not as reasons for exclusion but as points for learning (see Bradbury et al., Chapter 5 in this volume), the more they said they were able to help their employees as mentors (Kristiansen and Bloch-Poulsen, 2005: 273–4).

NOTES

1 In this chapter we have chosen not to enfold three major theoretical questions, which are present in embryo. They are about how to understand the relation between communication and organization, between the participants and us, and between dialogic change and organizational inertia.

2 As we did not ask the managers about their experiences, we cannot know if our interpretation is valid. However, when combined with the subsequent paragraphs where the managers validate the pattern, we think our interpretation offers the most comprehensive understanding (Kristiansen and Bloch-Poulsen, 1997).

REFERENCES

Bateson, G. (1972) *Steps to an Ecology of Mind*. New York: Ballantine Books.

Chambers, R. (1995) 'Paradigm shifts and the practice of participatory research and development', in N. Nelson and S. Wright (eds), *Power and Participatory Development: Theory and Practice*. London: Intermediate Technology Publications. pp. 30–42.

Chambers, R. (1997) *Whose Reality Counts? Putting the First Last*. London: Intermediate Technology Publications.

Deetz, S.A. (2001) 'Conceptual foundations', in F.M. Jablin and L.L. Putnam (eds), *The New Handbook of Organizational Communication*. Thousand Oaks, CA: Sage. pp. 3–46.

Foucault, M. (1978) *The History of Sexuality, Vol. I: an Introduction*. New York: Pantheon.

Foucault, M. (2000) *Power: Essential Works of Foucault, 1954–1984, Vol. 3*. New York: The New Press.

Gaventa, J. and Cornwall, A. (2001/2006) 'Power and knowledge', in P. Reason and H. Bradbury (eds), *Handbook of Action Research: Participative Inquiry and Practice*. London: Sage. pp. 70–80. Also published in P. Reason and H. Bradbury (eds) (2006), *Handbook of Action Research: Concise Paperback Edition*. London: Sage. pp. 71–82.

Goffman, E. (1967) *Interaction Ritual: Essays on Face-to-Face Behaviour*. London: Penguin Books.

Isaacs, W. (1999) *Dialogue and the Art of Thinking Together*. New York: Currency, Doubleday.

Jungk, R. and Müller, N.R. (1990) *Zukunftwerkstätten: mit Phantasie gegen Routine und Resignation*. Berlin: Verlag Volk und Welt.

Kristiansen, M. and Bloch-Poulsen, J. (1997) *I mødet er sandheden. En videnskabteoretisk debatbog om engageret objektivitet*. Aalborg: Aalborg Universitetsforlag.

Kristiansen, M. and Bloch-Poulsen, J. (2000) 'The challenge of the unspoken in organizations: caring container as a dialogic answer?', *Southern Communication Journal*, 65 (2/3): 176–90.

Kristiansen, M. and Bloch-Poulsen, J. (2004) 'Self-referentiality as a power mechanism: towards dialogic action research', *Action Research*, 2 (4): 371–88.

Kristiansen, M. and Bloch-Poulsen, J. (2005) *Midwifery and Dialogue in Organizations: Emergent, Mutual Involvement in Action Research.* Munich: Rainer Hampp Verlag.

Kristiansen, M. and Bloch-Poulsen, J. (2006) 'Involvement as a dilemma: between dialogue and discussion in team-based organizations', *International Journal of Action Research*, 2 (2): 163–97.

Lewin, K. (1948) *Resolving Social Conflicts: Selected Papers on Group Dynamics.* New York: Harper & Brothers.

Mindell, A. (1995) *Sitting in the Fire.* Portland, OR: Lao Tse Press.

Rouse, J. (1994) 'Power/Knowledge', in G. Gutting (ed.), *The Cambridge Companion to Foucault.* Cambridge: Cambridge University Press. pp. 92–114.

Schiffrin, D. (1994) *Approaches to Discourse.* Oxford: Blackwell.

Torbert, W.R. (2001/2006) 'The practice of action inquiry', in P. Reason and H. Bradbury (eds), *Handbook of Action Research: Participative Inquiry and Practice.* London: Sage. pp. 250–60. Also published in P. Reason and H. Bradbury (eds) (2006), *Handbook of Action Research: Concise Paperback Edition.* London: Sage. pp. 207–17.

32

Learning to Love Our Black Selves: Healing from Internalized Oppressions

Taj Johns

This inquiry did not begin as an action research project. Many years ago, I began to explore the effects of racism on my personal development. This exploration led me to seek out others who were struggling with how living in the United States as an African American affects personal growth and esteem. In this chapter I use the lens of action research to explain how my personal quest expanded to encompass both second- and third-person inquiries. My co-inquirers named our group SASHA, an acronym for Self Affirming Soul Healing Africans. The SASHA process that resulted from our inquiry is culturally specific to the needs of African Americans toward reducing the consequences of racism on their lives.

When I began my journey I was a victim of internalized racism. I had internalized the system's beliefs about me, judging myself from the dominant culture's standard. I did not feel worthy of love or respect. (Journal entry, 1989)

I begin by sharing a quotation from my personal journal, which describes the mindset that our work aims to address in the African American community. This chapter describes SASHA, an acronym for Self Affirming Soul Healing Africans that refers both to a group of people and to a healing process they created. By telling SASHA's story, I hope that others may learn from us and use our work in ways that help liberate other marginalized groups. This chapter is based on data I collected systematically from the SASHA archives, formal and informal interviews with SASHA participants, my own journals and finally my continued work on bridging cultural differences.

I frame our work in two related ways that extend and contribute to action research theory of practice. The evolution of SASHA was an organic interplay among the three levels of inquiry in action research which correspond to first-, second-, and third-person inquiry. Our SASHA experience provides a robust illustration of the extended epistemology described by Peter Reason and Hilary Bradbury in this Handbook's introduction. Our SASHA inquiry, which emerged from our experience and deep need to change our lives, engaged us in a wide variety of presentational ways of knowing. This inspired us to create a model that conceptualized how our SASHA process addressed the effects of internalized oppression on our community. The SASHA process changed all of us profoundly in the way we live our lives and carry out our work in the world.

The SASHA process is an experiential model. Participants are encouraged to engage in a series of exercises such as breathing, expressive movement, song, dance and giving voice to the stories that inform their worldviews. Sometimes participants just sit quietly in meditation, finding ways to integrate their new knowledge. These exercises are what distinguish the SASHA model from other cultural models that label stages of racial identity, but do not provide instruction for how to move through these stages.

A BRIEF HISTORY OF AFRICANS IN AMERICA

After 246 years of enslavement, many African Americans had internalized the negative images and ideas advanced by white preachers, writers and scientists. The sum total of their experience was the substitution of physical enslavement with a new system of mental enslavement. Embedded in the new system was the idea of white superiority and 'black' inferiority. (Molefi Kete Asante, 1995: 317)

A brief review of African Americans' history in the United States is essential for the reader to appreciate why healing models such as SASHA are necessary. This brief history shows how the components to oppress were established, eventually leading to internalization of that oppression.

During the development of America, human labor was needed for heavy work required on the farms that bolstered the Southern economy. A system of chattel slavery was established for this purpose and Africans were assigned to this system of servitude. As chattel, Africans were the property of European colonists who bought them. History reports many indignities associated with chattel servitude such as women being seen as a commodity to produce more slaves and children taken away from their families and sold to other colonists. African slaves in America were treated as savages, as less than human.

On 1 January 1863, as the nation approached the third year of civil war with the Southern states, President Lincoln signed the Emancipation Proclamation outlawing bondage. The proclamation only applied to the Southern states, which allowed slavery to continue in the north. By the time that the proclamation was ordered, the practice of racism was part of the American social structure. Africans in America were still faced with the attitudes of whites who continued to have the belief that we were less than human. Brutality against blacks is still documented today with the famous trial of the Los Angeles Police Department convicted of brutalizing Rodney King in 1992 and the brutal killing of James Byrd in Jasper, Texas, on 1998.

African American leaders during the emancipation and continuing to the present day worked to create structures that could promote racial equality. These structures involve establishing economic independence, social/political access, and educational opportunities. Movements to institute these strategies were formed based on the assumption that by providing access to educational, economic and social/political opportunities, African Americans would gain equal status with whites and share in the American dream. There are two reasons these strategies failed to produce the desired outcomes. First, the institution of racism did not offer the same opportunities and justice as provided for whites; secondly, the consequences of slavery had a profound effect on the psyche of the now free African.

In the modern era, these movements continue in parallel with other efforts. The 'Black is Beautiful' movement in the mid-1960s was an attempt to nurture the self-esteem of blacks (within a culture in which only white people's images were seen, where most dolls extolled European features). Affirmative action was an effort to offer preferential access to African Americans to educational and employment opportunities and one aspect of the civil rights movement focused on strengthening voters' rights and access to political institutions. This history suggests that the descendants of chattel slaves continue to suffer from the burdens of institutional racism, racism and internalized racism. Institutional racism refers to the systematic practices of institutions that create disadvantages for certain racial and ethnic groups. Racism is the belief that racial differences create a superior or inferior trait in a particular race. Internalized racism refers to the way people come to believe the derogatory messages about their racial group that are perpetrated by the dominant group. Once accepted as true, these messages lead to self-doubt and self-hatred. Ella Bell (2001/2006) suggests 'We must find new ways to dismantle both systemic and social dimensions of racial oppression' (p.56). I offer the SASHA process, as an action research method, to begin dismantling the lingering effects of historical oppression.

Desire to overcome the effects of racism both in my life and in the lives of 13 other African Americans was the reason SASHA was formed. We worked together for ten years. As we worked it became evident that our stories of marginalization and judging ourselves by taking on the perspective of our oppressor is a story common among African Americans who have internalized the oppression foisted on them by the larger society.

MY STORY

My feelings of unease with how racial stigma affects my personal progress in the world brought me into first-person action inquiry. I begin the SASHA story with my personal story to bring to life some of the history described above.

When I was 13 years of age, I was transferred to an all white school where I would spend the next three years of my life living in shame and embarrassment because of placement exams that assigned me to a slow track for my junior high school years. Although this was just three years of my life, it was an experience of shame that colored my life for the next 40 years. At my young age, I did not want to admit there was a difference created because of my skin color. Many years later a conversation with my therapist began to alter the way I look at the world and myself.

Me:	I remember feeling the embarrassment of being placed in the lower educational track throughout middle school. I was in classes with people who could not tell you the days of the week. These were people who could not read. I was in an all white school except for five other Black students and me. I think all but two of us were in the lower tracks in this school. I made 'A's' the whole time, all three years. I don't know why someone did not come and get me from these classes. When I went to high school, I made all A's and B's except in Civics.
Therapist:	It sounds like you were a victim of institutional racism.
Researcher:	I can't accept that. In order for me to accept that is to say that it was intentional. That people actually treated me this way because I'm black.
Therapist:	It is racist. (Journal entry, 1989)

My daily work was to find my way out of the maze of my secretive internal dialogue that said, 'You are not smart and have nothing worthwhile to contribute to society.' I struggled with proving to myself that I am worthy of my life. In an attempt to eliminate these feelings I have spent most of my adult years in school. I thought if I got enough education, I would be acceptable to myself and everyone else. Sitting quietly in a corner trying to understand some educational concept, I was constantly plagued with the feeling that I was not enough, I did not belong, and that I was stupid.

The reframing of my educational experience began my first-person inquiry. In order to understand my feelings of inadequacy, I began to attend workshops about self-improvement, on Adult Children of Alcoholics, and for self re-parenting. One process professed that this would be the last therapy you would ever need. After that workshop I attended another, which claimed to help me embrace my inner child. After that I tried meditation in order to eliminate my negative thoughts and construct a reality that was self-loving.

I continued to work hard – taking expressive writing classes, joining a Buddhist community, and learning Tai Chi. I was never able to eliminate the feeling of not deserving to be successful or belonging in this world. After years of trying, I was still left with the question, 'What can remove this feeling of being a mistake?'

What was not present in my first-person learning was an acceptance of my reality that race influenced the way I was treated in the educational system. I never understood that racial inequities impacted the way I perceived the world. Although I was on a journey that offered increasing access to self-reflection and new ways of thinking about the world I had not developed, in Peter Reason's term, 'critical subjectivity' but continued to suppress acknowledging the impact of institutional racism on my development.

FROM FIRST- TO SECOND-PERSON INQUIRY

After two years of struggling to understand how my life was shaped by race, I found three other women who were engaged in similar struggles. Even though we all had rewarding careers, we felt something restricted us from feeling complete or successful, so we wanted to understand the habits of mind that created our restrictive worldview.

In January 1991, when we convened the first meeting of our group, which would eventually evolve into SASHA, we knew nothing about action research. Four women, in our late 30s and early 40s, had come together to write a book about black women in recovery from racism.

Isis organized the first meeting with the intention of bringing the voice of African Americans into conversations of recovery. We used the term recovery, which is usually associated with addiction. We began to redefine this word to capture something different for ourselves. By recovery we meant recovery from feeling the emotional control of internalized racism. As Mariah would say 'We were recovering from white people.' We knew that racism moved us away from our goals. We all had a stake in the problem, which was feeling the limitation and effects that racial stigma, racism and stereotyping had placed on our lives.

We all lived in the San Francisco Bay area. Isis and I were in unstable relationships and were also single parents. Mariah and Fateema did not have children. Fateema was in a 15 year relationship with Harold. Later Harold would join our community and begin another group called the Black Men's Support Group. Three of us had family within 60 miles of where we lived; Fateema's family was from the Midwest where she was raised until she was in her mid-20s when she moved to the San Francisco Bay area.

Through our evolution we discovered that racism was the underlying facet of our recovery. We discovered that our ability to stay connected in body, spirit and mind was challenged each time we encountered a racial episode. We discovered through our work that when faced with racial issues (any type of traumatic situation) there are three possible reactions to the event. The mind can react by interrupting or denying the experience; the body may take a fight or flight stance; or the spirit may cause one to feel hopeless. These encounters offered temptations to numb or withdraw from the experience by using addictive patterned responses. We identified racism as the common variable that we needed to reframe. Identifying racism had become the impetus that would begin our recovery and reconstruction of feelings of self-worth.

As we continued to meet, the other women began to speak of concerns that revolved around being a strong black woman at the cost of our femininity, difficulties in learning to love our black men, understanding the impact of racism on our sexuality and a general sense of self-hatred. In one of Fateema's reflections (from the SASHA archives) she wrote about her lonely feelings that arose as she attempted to heal from internalized cultural hatred. She wrote:

> I was born and raised and continue to live in a country that hates me because of my African American heritage. All of my life I have been sensitive to this hatred. The color of my skin, the texture of my hair, the size of my lips all became badges of shame. I had internalized the dominant culture's negative beliefs about my Africanness. My journey of healing my self-hatred and learning to love myself as a black person has been a solitary one.

Although I had not seen my journey as one of recovery because I never saw racism as a phenomenon that required recovery, I soon discovered that I would spend the next years of my life 'recovering from white people' and the restraints of oppression. I realized during several reflection cycles that many of my years were spent evaluating myself from a white standard, a standard that influenced my relationships, my presentations in the world, and my love of self. In the following quote I expressed the pain of my high school years when I wanted to be accepted by whites and did not understand or appreciate the additional heritage I carried with my blackness.

> In high school I can now see I was an 'assimilated Negro'. (Assimilated Negro was a term used by some Black people in the 1960s and 1970s to describe blacks who choose to deny their culture, striving to live by the standards dictated by the dominant culture.) My internalized hatred of my blackness forced denial of my blackness. I felt, 'I am not like them, and cannot connect with them (black people).' I had been socialized for all intents

and purposes as a white girl in black skin. I had become frozen in my confusion, shame and pain of my blackness. (Journal entry, 7 January 1992)

After working together for five months, our group of four women became more systematic in trying to understand how racism affected our lives. I think of this as a time when my first-person inquiry shifted into our shared second-person inquiry. Our face-to-face encounters stimulated our empathy for each other through our stories that echoed each other's truth. Self-hatred, learning to love ourselves, our community, and a sense of a loss of our femininity and sexual expression were common themes. The most profound discovery that would guide us to our next learning was our shared history of attending workshops centered on recovery and race in what were essentially white arenas. From these endeavors, we all expressed feeling unsafe or, feeling we had to suppress our views. Isis recalls:

> Whenever you began to do your work, you had to defend what you felt around white people. They were quick to say, 'I am not responsible for what my great grandparents did to your ancestors,' or 'Why don't you all just let that go and live from today?' We did not have a space to explore our own experiences. (Archives, 1992)

It was apparent that we were trying to recover in a setting where participants did not know how racism had impacted and continued to impact our community. In addition, their desire to deny racism left a subtle imprint, suggesting that our experience was not important or valid, thus causing further confusion and injury. We realized we needed to create our own space if we were to heal. These interactions raised the question of why white people's resistance in accepting our perspective was important to us. As we continued the conversations with ourselves we began to see that our attitude regarding whites' resistance was yet another example of our need to recover from white people. We were still seeking acceptance and validation from outside ourselves. We had been meeting for five months when Fateema said:

We need to continue our healing before we can write a book about recovery. We have a big wound that we carry with us from racism. We will not be healed until we heal that racial wound. There is something about these racial issues we have internalized.

This epiphany redirected our learning and precipitated a new phase of second-person inquiry. This is how SASHA One was born.

BIRTH OF SASHA

Fateema and Isis had participated in a woman's healing circle that used Radiance Breathwork, a body-centered therapy created by Gay and Katherine Hendricks. Some of their technique derived from the work of Wilheim Reich. Radiance Breathwork is a process that encourages one to look at and release blocked energy through a series of breathing techniques. Fateema had made a connection with Amber and Leo, two white Breathwork facilitators, who agreed to work with us on our issues of oppression. For years each of us had worked individually with traditional therapists attempting to understand ourselves from a cognitive perspective. Breathwork seemed inviting because it offered insight about our body's memory, a memory most of us had not explored. The approach was holistic and could address our usual pattern of response which created the mind, body, spirit separation.

Amber and Leo had little knowledge of the Black American experience. We suggested several books that we felt help explain the African American's experience, such as *Black Rage* (Grier and Cobbs, 1969), *Ain't I a Woman?* (hooks, 1981), *The Color Complex* (Russell et al., 1993), and *There is a River* (Harding, 1983), just to name a few. These books would offer an appreciation for our struggle. In addition, Fateema and Isis engaged Amber and Leo in long conversations, educating them on how we wanted them to work with us around racism. We came to understand and appreciate that the expertise we needed really came out of our own experience. The approach

of using outside facilitators is similar to insider/outsider research teams. '[Insiders] interpret what the language, terms and even acronyms used in the [group] mean … they help to frame and provide an understanding of why certain results are important' (Roth and Bradbury, Chapter 23 in this volume). Isis and Fateema were our insiders, with knowledge of the work we wanted to embark upon while Amber and Geo were the outsiders. As outsiders, Amber and Leo were able to objectively observe our reactions to exercises, offer insight as to how we interacted with each other and maybe deepen our understanding of how our reactions to racism were stored in our body's memory. Isis recalls: 'Our training of them was very empowering because we were still in charge of how we wanted our healing to be and where the places were that needed to be explored. We were taking our healing seriously. We were very serious.'

Once we were satisfied that they understood our goal of uncovering and confronting the effects of racism, we hired them to begin teaching us how to use Breathwork. Ultimately, we wanted to develop this skill so we could begin to use breathing techniques in our community. This was a different approach for reframing the impacts of racism. From conversations with friends, families and acquaintances, we knew they also were longing for some alternative way to reduce the impact of racism on their lives.

We invited ten other African Americans who were friends or acquaintances willing to participate in the discourse and commit to the process of deconstructing old paradigms of self-hatred. As a group, these 14 African Americans would work together for the next year to support each other's, as well as their own, growth and racial healing. Our four person inquirer group had become a 14 person inquiry group.

Our group was not immune from the dynamics that permeate similar groups. We uncovered ways in which people's hurts associated with skin color, relationships and power were affecting the group. There were three biracial women, who were untrusting of their darker complexioned sisters. Common experiences of the biracial group as children were taunts by their darker complexioned school mates; this mistrust was carried into the group. Similarly, five men expressed a mistrust of all black women regardless of complexion, which impacted how they related to women in the group. A heterosexual couple disclosed conflicts with their relationship, one of the issues we collectively felt was a concern in our community. We struggled to remain objective with their conflicts. Often among the group we dismissed each other's experiences because our own seemed more traumatic. And there were issues of power. Two of the women were friends and sometimes would join together to influence the group focus. By directly naming these dynamics, which usually cause discord in the African American community, we were able to use these issues as catalysts for our healing. We were a microcosm of the larger African American community.

We met one Sunday a month for the next year. Mariah recalls, 'We became committed to our own healing, but this was just the beginning of our commitment.' On these Sundays we would engage in breathing sessions and the process of integrating new information about ourselves. Each month we would return to our communities, attempting to live from this new information. Once a month we would return to our developing community to talk about our experiences in the world. We were able to see where we needed work and modify how Amber and Leo worked with us. These cycles served as an analysis that prompted a re-evaluation of our intent. In breath sessions, we gave voice to our anger, our rage and sense of power-lessness; however, our reflections unraveled the knowledge of how our internalization of racism was prominent in causing a continual reaction to the subtle racism that bombarded our daily worlds.

Our reflections revealed that our internal world was limiting our abilities to feel satis-faction in our lives. Susanne Lipsky from *Re-Evaluation Counseling* (1987) implies that the internal world holds distress patterns that

influence the way we react in the world. She states:

> We know that every hurt or mistreatment, if not discharged (healed), will create a distress pattern (some form of rigid, destructive, or ineffective feel-ing and behavior) in the victim of this mistreat-ment. This distress pattern, when restimulated, will tend to push the victim through a re-enactment of the original distress experience either with some-one else in the victim role or, when this is not pos-sible, with the original victim being the object of her/his distress pattern. (p. 1)

This distress pattern of reaction was observed by many members of the SASHA community. Mtundu, a carpenter and SASHA participant, recalls this pattern as a frequent experience as explained in the fol-lowing story.

> I was in a hardware store in a small town south of San Francisco. I saw this employee was not busy so I walked toward him for some assistance. He quickly turned and walked in the other direction. I really felt my body becoming tensed. You know when we go into stores we either get followed or we get ignored. Now I don't know if he just did not want to help me because I am Black, or if that is just my thought because it happens so often. All I know is that it really makes me feel bad and sorry for myself that I have to deal with those feelings again.

After two years of working with Amber and Leo, we ended our relationship with them and began to facilitate our own ses-sions. We paid ourselves, as we had paid Amber and Leo. We used this money to fund a yearly retreat. During one of our retreats Harold suggested that we read an article by Lipsky (1987) in which she wrote:

> Internalized racism has been the primary means by which we have been forced to perpetuate and 'agree' to our own oppression … Patterns of inter-nalized racism have caused us to accept many of the stereotypes of blacks created by the oppressive majority society … internalized racism … has given rise to patterns which cause us to mistrust our own thinking. (p. 1)

During our reflection we all agreed that there was a component of racism we had internalized.

We had all spoken of failed relationships, questioned why we were hyper-vigilant or overly cautious and, most importantly, wondered why we did not feel satisfied with our lives, at the same time accepting these feelings and attitudes as part of being Black in America.

> This has been a problem that no one has been able to solve and over which many have despaired. Some patterns of internalized racism had become so familiar that we, ourselves, accept them as part of our 'black culture.' We attribute them to 'the way we are.' (Lipsky, 1987: 2)

SHARING THE FRUITS OF OUR SECOND-PERSON INQUIRY

Our new clarity sustained us for many years as a self-supporting group. After our first year of working together we decided to call ourselves Self Affirming Soul Healing Africans (S.A.S.H.A.) in tribute to my daughter Sasha, who had died a year earlier. We were so inspired by our progress after our years of working together that we decided it was time to reach out to the larger African American community in order to help others learn how to use the SASHA process. Eventually a second group was formed. We then called ourselves SASHA One and the new group SASHA Two.

As action researchers, our SASHA One group was now engaged in third-person learning because we were now working with a larger community. Because this process had grown out of our own experience, we were using it intuitively to help others experience the same learning that had changed our lives. We had developed a process, but decided that if we wanted to be most effective in instructing others how to use the SASHA process, we needed a road map. Thus, we began the hard work of distilling our intuitive knowing into conceptual understanding. We gradually realized that we were using a process that was actually systematic. The result of our effort is the SASHA model.

Figure 32.1 describes the SASHA model which is a seven phase process: Building Community; Experiencing a Disorienting Experience; Feeling the Vulnerability; Experiencing Body, Mind and Spirit Split; A Culturally Corrective Experience; Body, Mind and Spirit Wholeness; and Entering a New Vulnerability. The first four stages are known as self-affirming, acknowledging that the subtle and obvious racial experiences are/were real. The subsequent three phases are known as the soul healing part of the equation, where there is an acceptance that 'Whatever one did to survive racism is okay.'

The SASHA process employs a series of exercises that support participants in accessing their frailty to historical racism. These exercises help the participant access feelings associated with habitual stereotyping, societal alienation, and customary marginalization because of skin color. SASHA is a body-based model that can be used for any type of recovery by any group, but the techniques we developed focus on the specific concerns of African Americans. From our experience we discovered a way to express our internal confusion. We found that when we sang together using 'call and response' (an African tradition which involves an interchange between the speaker/singer and the audience) we became aware of how our own isolation from community hurt us at the same time this technique assisted us with building community; when we used drums we unlocked our internalized thoughts of 'I should have rhythm, I am not black enough'; when we lined people up according to skin color tones, we saw how we isolated ourselves and devalued our natural beauty; when we told stories drawn out by our breath sessions or meditation we began to appreciate our culture. We found knowledge in our bodies that could help us heal from our oppression. This holistic approach invited the community members to retell their story with a blend of song, dance, cognitive process and meditation. Our emphasis on body was so important – we were reclaiming our whole.

One of the underlying beliefs of SASHA is that racism will always be present in the

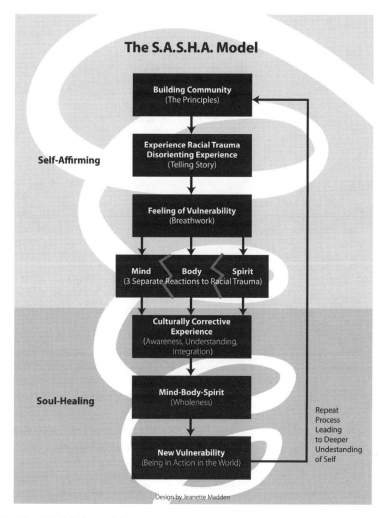

Figure 32.1 *The S.A.S.H.A model*

world and that we will always be vulnerable to racism. The SASHA model permits those who use it to be aware of a new type of vulnerability. With this new vulnerability, instead of being reactive in response to racial stimuli, one is open to receive and participate in life. The new vulnerability is an openness in one's self that brings heightened awareness and understanding of individual choice. You develop a closer relationship to the internal body process and remain connected to your feelings. There is a heightened sense of internal harmony and humanness, a positive feeling of being energetically vulnerable. With this openness comes an awareness of when this state of harmony has been interrupted by a racist action. While this awareness allows participants to realize their choices, more importantly, there is a high probability that they will not store the memory in their bodies or internalize the racial experience. Participants realize that they are open to choices, to alternatives and, hence, to new opportunities. Thomas Parham (1993) put it this way: 'You are now vulnerable to a different conceptual understanding of both your predicament, as well as your choices to be (as Spike Lee would say) "mo betta"' (p. 3).

OUR LEARNING PROCESS

There are several exercises that are documented in our archives, and as we continue to offer workshops we discover others that are developed spontaneously and intuitively. For this exemplar I focus on the spooning exercise. I selected this exercise because it demonstrates the power of an extended epistemology that guided all of our learning as well as our work in facilitating learning for the larger African American community.

When we first experimented with the spooning exercise, there were ten of us in attendance that day. Two members of our group facilitated this exercise. Participants were instructed to find a position on the floor, while the facilitators led us in a breathing meditation. Once relaxed we were told to form a line, lying stomach to back, stomach to back, until all of us were in a single row along the floor.

As we held on to one another we listened to 'Amazing Grace' being sung by Aretha Franklin. We thought this was just a connecting exercise that would bring us back into our bodies while allowing us the experience of connecting with other people. As the song progressed, the words 'Amazing grace how sweet the sound that saved a wretch like me' filled the room, we held each other feeling closeness. More words: ''Twas grace that taught my heart to fear, And grace my fears relieved'; we held on to one another with more force as if we were holding on for dear life. I remember feeling this was becoming my only connection to life. The words continued: ''Tis grace hath brought me safe thus far, And grace will lead me home.' I remember my eyes filling with tears because I was having a body memory of being in this position once before. I felt the body of the person I was holding, heaving with a release of tears. I felt the person holding me responding in a similar manner. In a few moments we all were in tears, the sounds of sighing were rippling throughout the room. The song persisted until the end: 'The Lord has promised good to me, His Word my hope secures.'

Although the positioning of our bodies was not similar to any of the available pictures depicting the positioning of slaves on the ship, the closeness of our bodies seemed to elicit a similar response. During our reflection time, the discussion focused on what seemed for all of us slave ship memories. We had all begun to imagine what it was like having to travel in close quarters for many months, what it felt like to live in vomit, and smell urine. What fear smelt like as the prisoners tried to understand what was happening and what would happen to them from day to day. These fears, although not as pronounced, sometimes parallel the fears we face today as African Americans.

Further dialoguing led to integrating the experience. Isis recalls that in our particular group individuals had difficulty with physical closeness. She states:

> Chinese Americans can stand on the bus and be inside anyone's personal space. At the market place you can see Middle Eastern people touching, holding hands while they are shopping. You very seldom see any of these behaviors with us, if you ever see it with us at all.

Watombu recalls the experience:

> It was a unique way to experience our history. Being great great grandchildren of slaves, we were able to access and release deep feeling about slavery. It was as if our souls were remembering our ancestors. What was remarkable for me was that there was a collective spirit, a oneness of our spirits and it came up in all of us as individuals and as a group.

The spooning experience revealed something to Watombu that he felt was very important to relate to the African American community. His individual experience told him that this very negative experience of slavery was being held in our bodies and we needed to see that as a community in order to heal from racism. He stated:

> We need to take professors, teachers, therapists and social workers through this exercise. They would understand our condition and know why young people act so ugly. They would have compassion for them and us.

Watombu felt hope – it sparked a dream, it fed his enthusiasm, he wanted to get the word to the people. Watombu's job allowed him to work with an understanding of his experience and model the truth he discovered for himself. In addition to relaying the new information through modeling in his work setting, he was able to model for his two sons the release experienced by the spooning event. He was able to establish communication with them that guided them through challenging times. Watombu remembers:

The experience and knowledge I obtained from spooning could not have come out in words during therapy. Our collective experience, our feelings, our feeling the slave dungeon really moved me and taught me a new way of feeling the world. Remarkable.

We began to explore the effects of the Diaspora on our abilities to be emotionally and physically close; to show affection and experience intimacy. With more discussion and integration, we began to reclaim our closeness with one another. This physical closeness led to trust, which deepened our commitments to each other. The structure of SASHA allowed us to go out into the larger community to share and live this new knowledge. It was safe to question others about their experiences and share our knowledge because, next month, we knew we could return to the safe community of SASHA.

We used the spooning exercise in several SASHA community workshops, always creating a response similar to our own. Spooning is effective in releasing a collective memory as well as an individual emotional release. The experience is an example of a collective culturally corrective experience, which is the fifth phase of the SASHA model. This phase addresses soul healing, where participants are given the opportunity to understand a meaning scheme that has formed some aspect of their worldview. Thus a culturally corrective experience is actually the integration of that new information. We arrive at this point by applying a planned stimulus that elicits an emotional and/or physical response from the participant. The

response that is elicited becomes an opportunity to address life events that have shaped our worldviews. The spooning exercise was a form of presentational knowing that served as the impetus for the surfacing unconscious emotional material. Some psychologists would call our collective response a collective consciousness event.

IDENTIFYING SASHA'S OPERATING PRINCIPLES

During our time of working together, we four women continued to meet, always exploring methods on how we could improve the workshops. Mariah had learned a technique called The Café. The Café is a method used to create 'collaborative dialogue around questions that matter' (Whole Systems Associates, 2002). At another yearly retreat we used this technique to elicit ideas from the SASHA participants on what they felt was necessary for them to feel safe doing this deep emotional work. The ideas coalesce into themes that helped us understand our effectiveness in the blossoming community. From an intensive reflection process, evaluating our experience, we identified four components that made the experiences a success: 1) our willingness to commit to our healing, 2) our ability to be compassionate with ourselves and others, 3) self-awareness of our perceptions, and 4) honesty and courage to speak the truth. These became the guiding principles of our work. Figure 32.2 explains the significant of each principle.

After three years of being in charge of our own learning and racial healing, which involved many cycles of culturally provocative actions and critical reflection that helped us integrate new information, our SASHA group experience led us to share our learning with the African American community. Through our action of offering our model to the larger community, we moved the fruits of our second-person inquiry once again into third-person learning. These third groups of participants were called the Weekenders.

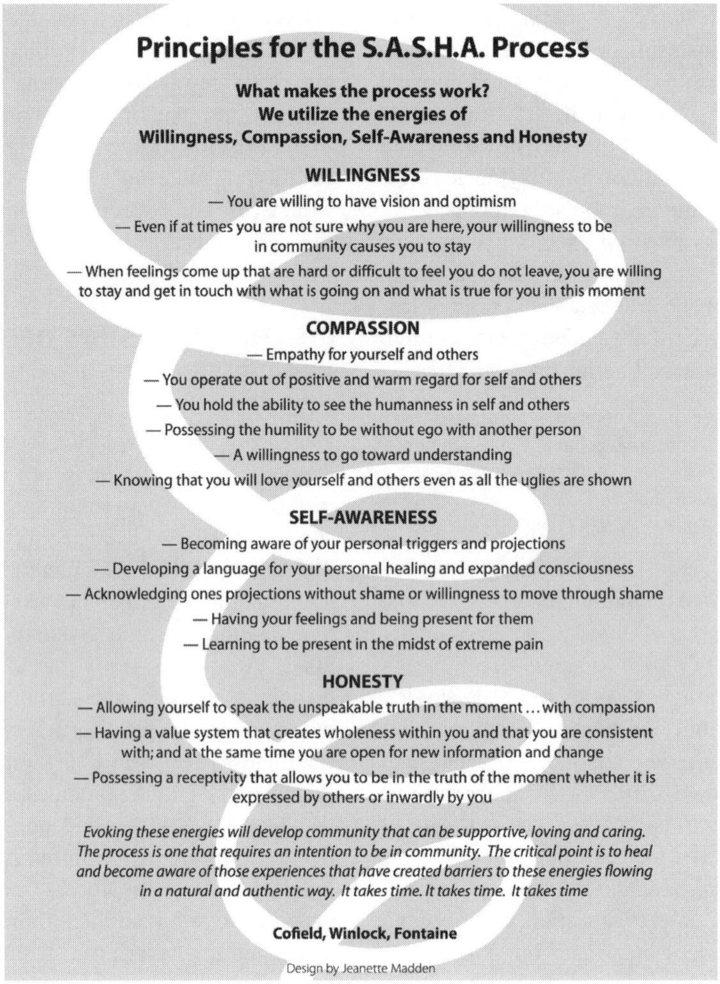

Principles for the S.A.S.H.A. Process

What makes the process work?
We utilize the energies of
Willingness, Compassion, Self-Awareness and Honesty

WILLINGNESS

— You are willing to have vision and optimism

— Even if at times you are not sure why you are here, your willingness to be
in community causes you to stay

— When feelings come up that are hard or difficult to feel you do not leave, you are willing
to stay and get in touch with what is going on and what is true for you in this moment

COMPASSION

— Empathy for yourself and others

— You operate out of positive and warm regard for self and others

— You hold the ability to see the humanness in self and others

— Possessing the humility to be without ego with another person

— A willingness to go toward understanding

— Knowing that you will love yourself and others even as all the uglies are shown

SELF-AWARENESS

— Becoming aware of your personal triggers and projections

— Developing a language for your personal healing and expanded consciousness

— Acknowledging ones projections without shame or willingness to move through shame

— Having your feelings and being present for them

— Learning to be present in the midst of extreme pain

HONESTY

— Allowing yourself to speak the unspeakable truth in the moment … with compassion

— Having a value system that creates wholeness within you and that you are consistent
with; and at the same time you are open for new information and change

— Possessing a receptivity that allows you to be in the truth of the moment whether it is
expressed by others or inwardly by you

Evoking these energies will develop community that can be supportive, loving and caring.
The process is one that requires an intention to be in community. The critical point is to heal
and become aware of those experiences that have created barriers to these energies flowing
in a natural and authentic way. It takes time. It takes time. It takes time

Cofield, Winlock, Fontaine

Design by Jeanette Madden

Figure 32.2   *Principles for the S.A.S.H.A process*

Our community expanded to include community workshops, lectures and writings about internalized oppression and the SASHA model. The SASHA Ones became the planners, learners and facilitators of the process. The SASHA Twos began, independently, to continue their first- and second-person learning. Finally, as a strong community we collectively worked with the Weekenders.

A SUMMARY VIEW OF OUR EXPERIENCE

In 1991 four women convened a meeting to address our personal unrest regarding racism and recovery. We wanted to liberate our minds of the internalized oppression that prevented us from living and participating fully in the world. My connection with these women expanded my first-person inquiry into our second-person inquiry. Our lack of knowledge of a body-based technique we decided to use for addressing oppression led us to an insider/outsider relationship with two white facilitators. After three years of being in charge of our own learning and racial healing, which involved many cycles of culturally provocative actions and critical reflection that helped us integrate new information, our SASHA group experience led us to share our learning with the African

American community. Through our action of offering our model to the larger community, we moved the fruits of our second-person inquiry once again into third-person learning. We called these third groups of participants the Weekenders.

As our community grew, our work on internalized racism continued to include a model that others could use who were involved in a similar healing process. SASHA Ones and Twos began to work together, continuing our first-person and second-person learning. We developed a community that could now offer third-person learning as we collectively gave birth to Weekenders.

For the next seven years, each member was going into the world to practice new skills. Our commitment to heal our community fueled our commitment to the process. Although we have since stopped meeting, our commitment is still strong in our community. The four women and two of the men continue our work. Mariah has organized several Black health fairs, Fatima is a body-based therapist, Isis participates in a national Black women's support group dealing with issues of racism, Mtundu does work with alcohol recovery groups, Watombu trains disabled people and I am a diversity trainer and community organizer. We all say that the SASHA work influences how we are in the world today. Isis explains:

With my personal life SASHA really helped me value my opinions and my sensitivities and passion for my own personal growth and the growth of people around me.

While Watombu offers:

I have a way of looking at things because of the [SASHA] process. And that's changing me, that's changing the way I deal with myself and others in the world, and even with working out there with different disabled people, I do things to try to enable them. I know we are all human beings – I believe that any human being, regardless of what they have, have the potential to achieve and improve, and I've seen it since I've been doing this work with SASHA. So I'm more about pushing the right buttons to keep myself and people moving forward.

Even though we knew nothing about the process of action research, we were in fact following a participative methodology that resulted in creating a conceptual model allowing our experiences to be carried into the larger community. We incorporated our cultural experiences to bring our model to life. Our approach to the question of internalized oppression was holistic. We wanted to address all aspects of the participants, instead of the traditional cognitive approach, with a focus on body-based interventions. We drew on the work of the action research community showing how issues such as racism can effectively be addressed from a holistic approach. Although the SASHA project placed more emphasis on a holistic approach to practical concerns, which is unusual in action research, this work offers another perspective that hopefully contributes to the action research community.

ACKNOWLEDGMENT

Thanks to Elizabeth Kasl, who helped me understand action research, Jeanette Madden, graphic designer, and to all the members of the SASHA community.

REFERENCES

Asante, M. (1995) *African American History: a Journey of Liberation*. Maywood, NJ: The People Publishing Group.

Bell, E.E. (2001/2006) 'Infusing race into the discourse of action research' in P. Reason and H. Bradbury (eds), *Handbook of Action Research: Participative Inquiry and Practice*, London: Sage. pp. 48–58. Also published in P. Reason and H. Bradbury (eds) (2006), *Handbook of Action Research: Concise Paperback Edition*, London: Sage. pp. 49–59.

Grier, W.H., and Cobbs, P.M. (1969) *Black Rage*. New York: Basic Books.

Harding, V. (1983) *There is a River*. New York: Random House.

Hendricks, G. and Hendricks, K. (1994) *At the Speed of Life: a New Approach to Personal Change through Body-centered Therapy*. New York: Bantam.

hooks, b. (1981) *Ain't I a Women?* Cambridge, MA: South End Press.

Lipsky, S. (1987) 'Internalized racism.' Seattle, WA: Rational Island Publishers. [http:/www.rc.org/publications/journals/black_reemergence/br2/br2_5_sl.html]

Parham, T.A. (1993) *Psychological Storms: the African American Struggle for Identity.* Chicago, IL: African American Images.

Russell, K., Wilson, M. and Hall, R. (1993) *The Color Complex.* New York: Anchor Books.

Whole Systems Associates (2002) 'The World Cafe presents … ' [ww.theworldcafe.com]

33

The Tapestry of Leadership: Lessons from Six Cooperative-Inquiry Groups of Social Justice Leaders

Lyle Yorks, Arnold Aprill, LaDon James, Anita M. Rees, Amparo Hofmann-Pinilla and Sonia Ospina

This chapter extracts lessons about social justice leadership and about the use of cooperative inquiry as a vehicle for conducting participatory social research from six cooperative inquiry (CI) groups comprised of awardees from the Leaders for a Changing World initiative that honors and convenes innovative, under-recognized social justice leaders, with the express intention of creating insight into the nature of effective progressive leadership. Three of the participants in the CI groups joined one of the facilitators in identifying themes and creating a tapestry of social justice leadership from the reports of six cooperative-inquiry groups. Three patterns are present in the tapestry: (1) developing democratic identity; (2) developing democratic agency; and (3) sustaining democracy, presented in eight values threads and six action threads. Lessons about the process of CI and insights into the motivation of participants are also discussed.

What can we learn about effective models of leadership from social justice organizations that work collaboratively with broad-based grassroots constituencies? And, what can we learn about cooperative-inquiry as a valuable practice for this kind of leadership? This chapter extracts lessons about social justice leadership and about the use of cooperative-inquiry as a vehicle for conducting

participatory social research from six cooperative-inquiry (CI) groups comprised of program participants from the Leaders for a Changing World initiative.

Leaders for a Changing World (hereafter called The Program) is supported by the Ford Foundation for honoring and convening innovative, under-recognized social justice leaders, with the express intention of creating insight into the nature of effective progressive leadership. The Program works in partnership with the Research Center for Leadership in Action (hereafter called The Center) at the Wagner School of Public Service, New York University. CI is one of three research components in The Program – the other two being ethnographies and narrative inquiries focusing on leadership in the organization receiving the award (see Chapter 28 by Sonia Ospina et al. in this Handbook).

Cooperative-inquiry groups were formed among the program participants to provide a systematic structure for learning from experience through a process of co-inquiry. Two inquiry groups were formed from each of three years of program participants, 2001, 2002, and 2003 respectively. Participation in these groups was voluntary. There is a political dimension to the principle of co-inquiry that maintains that people have a right to participate and express their own values in the design of an inquiry into their experience. Participants organize themselves in small groups to address a compelling question that brings the group together in order to construct new meaning related to their question through cycles of action and reflection and practicing validity procedures (Heron, 1996; Heron and Reason, 2001/2006; Kasl and Yorks, 2002).

WHY STUDY SOCIAL JUSTICE LEADERSHIP?

The Program is built on the premise that the images of leadership in the popular media and leadership structures promoted by social hierarchies are problematic for the creation of democratic culture. Popular images of leadership tend toward cults of personality. And while there is a vast academic leadership literature, much of it focuses on persons defined as leaders, describing their role, their actions and behaviors, and/or the sources of their influence and authority on others. The popular business literature has largely uncritically applauded successful CEOs, ascribing to them in a very idiosyncratic manner the

character of individuals as the source of the success of their organizations.

A more recent stream of literature focuses on leadership as a characteristic of a social system (Drath, 2001), while recognizing the roles played by leaders in sustaining systemic leadership (Ospina and Sorenson, 2006; Palus and Horth, 2002). It is this perspective that is a key premise of the research component of The Program (Cohen, 2005). The Center understands social change leadership as a collective achievement resulting from the meaning processes that a group of people committed to social justice successfully engage in to address a targeted social problem in the world (Minieri et al., 2005; RCLA, 2005).

WHY COOPERATIVE-INQUIRY?

Cooperative-inquiry is a method for conducting participatory research and facilitating adult learning through experience. The epistemic assumptions of CI have been developed by John Heron and Peter Reason (Heron, 1992; Heron and Reason, 1997; Chapter 24 by John Heron and Peter Reason in this Handbook). Broadly defined, CI 'is a process consisting of repeated episodes of reflection and action through which a group of peers strives to answer a question of importance to them' (Bray et al., 2000: 6). This approach to developing new understandings of practice grounded in a broad base of practitioner knowledge explicitly enacts the values of the leaders in The Program (Ospina and Schall, 2000).

There are remarkable parallels between the process of CI and the form of leadership described in the inquiries. These parallels are rooted in values of building human capacity through seeking connectedness while embracing the diversity in human experience, finding meaning through relationships, and affirming the right of people to be effective. We will return to these parallels at the conclusion of this chapter. First we provide an overview of the CI process as it was enacted in The Program. Then a summary of the analysis and insights that emerged from our meaning making from the learning from the six groups.

THE SIX CI GROUPS COMPRISING THE BASIS FOR THIS CHAPTER

Each of the six groups came to be known by an identifying name related to its inquiry question: *The Dance* (How can we create the space/opportunities for individuals to recognize themselves as leaders and develop leadership?); *The Council* (How do we as grassroots community organizers keep our organizational autonomy and build a wider movement to bring justice to our communities?); *Strategy* (How can we help people learn to be more strategic, conceptual, and creative in their thinking?); *Discovery* (What makes social change leadership successful and what values are held in common across such diverse leaders and organizations?); *The Arts* (How and when does art release, create, and sustain transforming power for social change?); *The Movement* (How do we engage and sustain a social justice movement that seizes power?).

The groups met five or six times for about two days over the course of approximately nine months, with each group determining the location and timing of meetings, as well as their overall process for inquiring into their inquiry questions. The meetings included visits to sites that illuminated the group's inquiry questions, discussion and analysis of the group's insights into their inquiry questions, and reports on new actions taken by group members based on insights from their collective discussion. Each CI group had a university-based facilitator whose role was to support the richness of the discussion rather than to serve as a discussant. Each co-operative-inquiry group produced a report on their findings. Yet, as our analysis demonstrates, commonalities about the role and characteristics of social justice leadership emerged across the groups. Their full co-operative-inquiry reports are posted

on The Center website (http://Leadershipfor change.org/insights/research/cooperative. php.). Additionally, a series of booklets summarizing the lessons learned from the inquiries is available from The Center at the Wagner School, NYU.

Forming the groups in the context of the larger Program was in and of itself a learning journey for The Center's staff. Program participants were exposed to the concept of cooperative-inquiry during the first program-wide meeting of their group, with the decision regarding whether or not to join one of the groups being made at a subsequent meeting. Many of the program participants harbored a suspicion of the research agenda, concerned that they were in fact subjects of research (Ospina et al., 2004). For many participants, the decision to join the CI process in The Program seems to have been a combination of interest in a compelling question put forward by one of their peers in The Program who would recruit other participants, interest in who was going to be at the table discussing it, and the idea that resources were being made available. The relative balance of these factors in motivating participation varied with different participants. The words of Vicky (member of the Strategy Group), who initially did not plan on participating in a research option of The Program, capture the interconnectedness of these factors as well as the initial skepticism about research:

> I remember my initial resistance to this whole [research] process and CI. There wasn't a compelling question, I didn't have a relationship with the people who were making the invitation and at that point ... Then Larry came up to me with this idea and I am thinking that is something I can get my teeth into. Because he had an interesting question it drew me in .... Plus the other people who would be around the table talking and taking action on the question, I could see that as being valuable.

As the program evolved over the three-year period, concerns over the issue of being 'research subjects' became lessened by the experience of the CI participants in the proceeding groups, who were willing to speak about the co-inquiry aspects of the process and their learning. Also The Center's facilitators evolved an open process for facilitating the emergence and integration of potential inquiry topics during a program-wide meeting. This process involved open brainstorming of potential topics that were subsequently integrated through dialogue and discussion into two topics that held broad interest as a basis for organizing a CI group.

The experience of each of the CI groups was unique and varied as a function of how they were initiated, the mix of participants, and the focus of the question. Most broadly the process unfolded along three phases. The first phase involved *refining the topic into an inquiry question* that resonated with all of the members of the group. This could take one or two meetings and involved open dialogue and discussion about possible phrasing of the question and what was engaging to each participant. The second phase involved *developing a deeper understanding of the question* through activities involving sharing materials and experience among participants, visits to exemplary field sites relevant to the inquiry question, and with participants starting to 'experiment' through taking actions between meetings. This would typically start with the second meeting and continue throughout the remaining meetings. The third phase involved *sensemaking*, through cataloging their learning, developing a report and other materials about their experience. These were not discrete, linear phases, but emergent and somewhat iterative processes. The motives, experiences, personalities, and domains of work among the participants within each group were diverse.

There is no 'orthodox' way of conducting a CI group, although the epistemic (Heron and Reason, Chapter 24) and political foundations are critical. Some of the groups strove to incorporate all four kinds of knowing into each meeting. Other groups had the various ways of knowing emerge across the meetings. Attention was paid to use of inquiry methods. Some groups adopted metaphoric learning practices such as reference to the learning window (what we know

we know, what we think we know, and what we know we don't know; Stewart, 1997; Yorks, 2005), and the ladder of inference (what we have observed – first rung of the ladder; what interpretations we have made – second rung of the ladder; attributions that are the basis for these interpretations; and generalizations we are making – fourth rung of the ladder; Argyris, 1993). The goal was to develop a group culture of transparency.

The diversity of the groups was important. Some of the richest insights come from groups with participants from different arenas of social justice practice. In the arts group, this was reflected in the mixture of artists, organizers, and those playing mediating roles between the two. In the Strategy CI there were organizers, and a participant with foundation experience. One of the participants was transitioning to teaching and was making creative connections between organizing and teaching. In another group there were people working on human rights, and others on sustainability. The diverse perspectives provided by different practices, but sharing a common vision and set of values, seems fundamental to the process of engaging in critical reflection. The distinct perspectives offered by these roles added richness to the conversations about the experiences of the groups.

The facilitators had to pay careful attention to providing light control (Cumming and Collier, 2005) or light touch (Yorks and Nicolaides, 2006), offering enough structure to sustain the dynamic and inviting the freedom that surfaces innovative responses to the experiences participants were having to the various activities and actions being experienced. Relationships are at the heart of light touch, with participants and facilitators establishing boundaries that are mutually beneficial for all concerned. Essentially the facilitators were holding the space for the inquiry process to unfold. The reports reflect the value of establishing and sustaining a 'learning space' or 'container'. In the words of one of the members of the Strategy CI:

'These meetings have become an important place for stepping out of my hectic life and connecting with ideas and thinking about what I have been doing.' The Discovery CI writes about how the CI allowed them to 'see our work both 'up close' and 'from a distance'. Abby (a member of the Arts Group) reflected on the experience: 'All of us are extremely strong-willed people ... and we were all grateful, I think, to have the time to reflect on the work that is at the center of our lives. We grooved on each other's ideas, and the conveners of the group did not interfere. They nicely restated things, reminded us of forgotten insights, but respected our power.'

MAKING MEANING ACROSS THE SIX INQUIRIES

CI is both an adult learning strategy and a research strategy (Yorks and Kasl, 2002). The Group for Collaborative Inquiry and thINQ (1994) have argued that failure to communicate findings from such inquiries to the outside world unintentionally impoverishes fields in which the experiences of practitioners should be part of the knowledge base that informs theory. This chapter represents a process of learning from a secondary analysis of the written descriptions and findings of the CI groups by one of the lead academic facilitators, and three program participants who had participatcd in thc CIs and expressed an interest in being part of this analysis process. The analysis was complemented with feedback and comments from two members of the team that lead the research component of The Program.

The process involved each participant in the analysis independently reading the reports, and marking themes around the questions of 'characteristics of social justice leadership embedded in the reports' and 'reactions of participants to the CI experience'. These themes were then comparatively discussed. Later, they were organized under a framework of broader themes that

gave more meaning to them in terms of actionable knowledge. This took place in the context of three separate meetings. Along the way, numerous stories and reflections on The Program experience were shared. This was a process of inductive analysis and comparative dialogue based on synthesized experience, providing a degree of 'analyst triangulation', but not a formal process of inter-rater reliability.

THE TAPESTRY OF LEADERSHIP

Two frameworks for analyzing the content of the reports emerged: the first framework produced by Lyle and Arnie involved eight themes naming goals, purposes, and values of social justice leadership, and the other framework produced by LaDon and Anita involved eight themes naming actions, strategies, and behaviors inherent in social justice leadership. The two frameworks are inextricably interwoven, from which an insight emerged that progressive leadership is a 'tapestry' of interdependent patterns, consisting of threads of values, and actions, like the bands of color in a family plaid (Table 33.1). Amparo and Sonia reviewed the emerging 'tapestry' in addition to contributing to the narrative.

The three identified patterns created by the interwoven threads were: (1) developing democratic identity, (2) developing democratic agency, and (3) sustaining democracy. The 'Values' threads were: (1) building and acting on democratic capacity, (2) role migration, (3) leadership as a relationship, not a personality, (4) thinking and speaking critically, (5) seeking connectedness, (6) embracing broad diversity as an essential asset, (7) affirming the right to be as effective as we actually are, and (8) hope.

The 'Actions' threads were: (1) shared learning, (2) shared experience, (3) building the broader community/connecting to something bigger, (4) action planning and message development, (5) movement, (6) space for developing and sustaining leadership, (7) continuous base building, and (8) celebration.

Table 33.1   *The tapestry of social justice leadership – an analytical framework*

Pattern **DEVELOPING DEMOCRATIC IDENTITY**

Values	*Actions*
Building and acting on democratic capacity	• Sharing learning • Sharing experience
Embracing broad diversity as an essential asset	• Sharing learning • Sharing experience • Continuous base building
Seeking connectedness	• Continuous base building • Building the broader community/connecting with something bigger

Pattern **DEVELOPING DEMOCRATIC AGENCY**

Values	*Actions*
Leadership as relationship, not personality	• Space for developing and sustaining leadership
Role migration	• Space for developing and sustaining leadership • Movement
Thinking and speaking critically	• Action planning and message development

Pattern **SUSTAINING DEMOCRACY**

Values	*Actions*
Affirming the right to be as effective as we actually are	• Affirming the right to be as effective as we actually are
Hope	• Celebration

Just as a tapestry cannot be reduced to its threads and maintain its essence, neither can the holistic nature of leadership be captured by these patterns and threads alone. The patterns and threads of values and actions that emerged from our analysis, while distinct, arc also interdependent.

Looking at the connections among the patterns and the threads reveals the nature of progressive leadership, which in turn can be discussed in terms of the stories reflected in the reports. For example, in discussing how leadership is embedded in relationship and not people, the discussion by the Council makes clear this goes beyond providing people with a 'feeling' of involvement. In two statements that illustrate the interconnection between threads [*shared learning, shared experience*, and *connecting to something bigger* as well as *creating space*], the group goes on to argue that 'where older models emphasize the leader as one who knows the most and empowers followers, the Council emphasizes that the leader must constantly learn'. Elsewhere they write that:

> In reference to the idea of 'building' a wider movement … the group is committed to being very clear on the idea that a movement is not theirs to build. The group feels that leadership is part of a movement – inside it, not outside it, and in that sense so-called leaders can only 'help to build' a movement in order to maintain a way of life. An alternative metaphor is 'growing with a natural movement'.

THE FIRST PATTERN: DEVELOPING DEMOCRATIC IDENTITY

Building and Acting on Democratic Capacity

Effective social justice leadership derives its power and capacity from the life experiences and consequent learning that people can offer to a group or community – especially the life experiences of those who are marginalized by the dominant culture in society. All people need opportunities to enact their power and capacity, and to assume responsibility for and to make choices about actions that matter. All people are equally valuable. Everybody's story counts. Close examination of the rationale underlying the inquiry questions defined by these groups reveals that the value structure embedded in this theme is central to social justice leadership. This value system is reflected in how the groups pursued their questions and in the meaning they made from their inquiry. Simply put, these groups pursued participation that was inclusive, not exclusive.

Valuing and building on *shared learning and shared experience* provide the substance for building democratic capacity and utilizing broad diversity. The Council noted an organizer 'must constantly learn and investigate' and learn 'from the people you work with' … 'plans and actions are shaped by the result of learning rather than the other way around'.

Embracing Broad Diversity as an Essential Asset: Innovation and Tradition

Effective social justice leadership draws on the creativity inherent in both innovation and the wisdom inherent in traditions. Inclusiveness of marginalized populations includes honoring and learning from the wisdom of diverse traditions as well as engaging in innovative actions. The embracing of broad diversity is more than issuing an invitation to join, but is a process of shared learning and experience – the river flows in all directions. In an interestingly coincidental way the action of cutting edge effective leadership mirrors the principles of co-inquiry and honoring learning derived from lived experience, and is open to diverse ways of thinking. These threads are expanded by continuous base building among diverse communities. Broad diversity suspends time, balancing innovation with the lessons of tradition.

Seeking Connectedness

Effective social justice leadership involves resisting fragmentation. There is a connectedness to the natural world, to other people and to each other's work. There is a growing recognition of the importance of systemic connectedness, connecting movements. Building this connectedness among movements is a leadership challenge for these leaders. Social justice movements work in varied arenas, and can find themselves competing for the attention of funders, the public, and politicians. They are continually wrestling with the challenge of *building the broader community – connecting with something bigger*. The Discovery Group developed a model a 'we-ness and bridge building' represented by a series of concentric circles of the individual, interpersonal relationships, and public coalitions.

THE SECOND PATTERN: DEVELOPING DEMOCRATIC AGENCY

Leadership as Relationship, Not Personality

Across the CI reports is the theme that 'Leader' is a role people assume to assist the enacting of leadership, but 'leadership' is actually enacted by communities. Through the inter-relationships of their members communities take the initiative and develop the political will to solve problems. When we say there is no leadership in a particular community, we may mean the lack of an organizing figure, but we are actually commenting on the obstacles to the community's marshalling its collective capacities. Leadership as a phenomenon exists in the space between and among people, not in the individuals themselves. The quality of its character is determined by the nature of the interaction among the roles that people enact. *Creating space for developing and sustaining leadership* and *movement* enact the power of leadership as a relationship and support role migration.

Role Migration

Effective social justice leadership, recognizing that capacity can only be developed by being enacted, facilitates fluid movement between roles for all people, from follower to leader, from teacher to learner, from expert to novice, and back again. The leader models growth by becoming a learner, learning with and from the community.

The CI group The Dance goes on to describe this shift in the leadership relationship as a process of 'stepping back and stepping up'. This is something other than traditional notions of delegating. Rather there is 'a genuine shift in the relationship, in which someone steps back (whether they do it consciously or not) and someone steps up (in our conversations we've termed the latter *crossing over*)'.

> Crossing over is different from being empowered. It is not something that is granted by others, but something that we claim for ourselves. Once people claim a space by crossing over there is a reframing of the way they see themselves in the world. They have taken up their authority to influence others.

The theme that runs throughout the Strategy CI is the need for fluidity between roles. 'You can't just tell them' is repeatedly emphasized. One of the members talks about the importance of 'getting people to work without a script'. In describing a meeting with the Mayor he states: 'We know what the outcome should be, what we were trying to

accomplish, who was going to do what, but no scripts. People had to think about what they were going to say.' Understanding the systemic nature of leadership and movement among roles provide what the Council describes as 'unity of view' and the Strategic Learners called 'a sense of shared fate'.

Thinking and Speaking Critically

Effective social justice leadership supports all people in developing an analysis of power relations, including its own. Special attention is given to the power of language, and to who controls expression. Effective social justice leadership sees and says what needs seeing and saying, and supports its communities in deconstructing propaganda, including its own. It speaks to power and speaks out against injustice. CI offers a model of leadership that is a cycle of investigation, planning, action, reflection, and investigation.

THE THIRD PATTERN: SUSTAINING DEMOCRACY

Affirming the Right to Be as Effective as We Actually Are

Effective social justice leadership involves not getting skewed from the core values of their movement by funders, institutions, politicians, and other structures of the dominant culture. There is a demand that the authority and expertise of diverse peoples be recognized.

Arnie, a member of the Arts CI, coined the term 'pralicy' as a companion term to 'praxis', capturing the group's belief that practice should influence the content of policy – a counter point to research influencing and shaping policy.

Hope

There is a belief in the capacity and power of people to think critically, to solve problems, and to be expressive and caring. Social justice leadership trusts in the power of the persistent human longing for a humane world and acts out of a hopeful vision for the human condition. *Celebrating* and believing in the dignity of people, and their capacity to bring about change, is perhaps the cornerstone sustaining social justice leadership. This translates into hope and, in the words of the Discovery Group, 'hope sustains us, hope compels us, and hope brings us together'.

COOPERATIVE-INQUIRY AS DEMOCRATIC LEADERSHIP THROUGH INQUIRY

As mentioned in the introduction to this chapter, there are remarkable parallels between CI and the framework of leadership that emerged from our analysis of the six CI reports. These parallels reveal the reach of culturally embedded epistemic values in society. The extended epistemology of co-inquiry (see Chapter 24 by Heron and Reason) is the foundation for the belief that 'good research is research conducted *with* people rather than *on* people' and 'that ordinary people are quite capable of developing their own ideas and can work together in a cooperative-inquiry group to see if these ideas make sense of their world and work in practice' (Heron and Reason, 2001/2006: 179). In CI 'everyone can take initiative and exert influence on the process' (Heron and Reason, Chapter 24). This is akin to the processes of 'stepping down', 'stepping up', and 'crossing over' described by The Dance.

An epistemology of inquiring with people is distinct from traditional research models in which researchers seek to remain outside the phenomena, often acting on them through experimental designs. This finds its parallel in the assumptions held by managers who see themselves as acting on the systems from which they are apart. The tapestry of leadership patterns that emerges is distinct from many traditional models in the literature that are linked to individual behaviors and contributions. In the words of the Council, 'leadership is part of a movement – inside it, not outside it'. Many traditional models place leadership in the context of supporting and sustaining hierarchical structures – corporations, military, foundations, and universities. Leadership is mixed, intertwined with a focus on control and management of resistance. Social justice leadership is more fluid and embedded in emerging relationships. In summarizing the overall analysis, Arnie comments that 'the main strength of social justice leadership is its distributed nature – drawing on broad bases of capacity. … It has more engines.'

One can speculate that there are underlying sociological forces working here derived from our epistemic assumptions in the primacy afforded to conventional models of leadership. It is beyond the scope of this chapter to explore this speculation. What has emerged is the value of creating space for inquiry and learning for both understanding and building social justice movements.

REFERENCES

Argyris, C. (1993) *Knowledge for Action.* San Francisco, CA: Jossey-Bass.

Bray, J., Lee, J., Smith, L. and Yorks, L. (2000) *Collaborative Inquiry in Practice: Action Reflection and Making Meaning.* Thousand Oaks, CA: Sage.

Cohen, D. (2005) *Internal working document, Leadership for a Changing World Program.* New York: Research Center for Leadership in Action, Robert F. Wagner Graduate School of Public Service, New York University.

Cumming, G.S. and Collier, J. (2005) 'Change and identity in complex systems', *Ecology and Society,* 10 (1): 29. [http://www.ecologyandsociety.org/vol10/issl/art29]

Drath, W. (2001) *The Deep Blue Sea: Rethinking the Sources of Leadership.* San Francisco, CA: Jossey-Bass.

Group for Collaborative Inquiry and thINQ (1994) 'Collaborative inquiry for the public arena', in A. Brooks and K. Watkins (eds), *The Emerging Power of Action Inquiry Technologies. (New Directions for Adult and Continuing Education No. 63).* San Francisco, CA: Jossey-Bass. pp. 57–67.

Heron, J. (1992) *Feeling and Personhood: Psychology in Another Key.* Thousand Oaks, CA: Sage.

Heron, J. (1996). *Co-operative Inquiry: Research into the Human Condition.* Thousand Oaks, CA: Sage.

Heron, J. and Reason, P. (1997) 'A participatory inquiry paradigm', *Qualitative Inquiry, 3:* 274–94.

Heron, J. and Reason, P. (2001/2006) 'The practice of co-operative inquiry: research "with" people, rather than "on" people', in P. Reason and H. Bradbury (eds), *Handbook of Action Research: Participative Inquiry and Practice.* London: Sage. pp. 179–88. Also published in P. Reason and H. Bradbury (eds) (2006), *Handbook of Action Research: Concise Paperback Edition.* London: Sage. pp. 144–54.

Kasl, E. and Yorks, L. (2002) 'An extended epistemology for transformative learning theory and its application through collaborative inquiry', *Teachers College Record on Line* [www.tcrecord.org, Content ID 10878].

Minieri, J., Dodge, J., Foldy, E., Hofmann-Pinilla, A., Krauskopf, M. and Ospina, S. (2005) *From Constituents to Stakeholders: Community-based Approaches to Building Organizational Ownership and Providing Opportunities to Lead.* New York: Research Center for Leadership in Action, Robert F. Wagner Graduate School of Public Service, New York University.

Ospina, S. and Schall, E. (2000) *Perspectives on Leadership: Our Approach to Research and Documentation for the LCW Program.* [http://leadership-forchange.org/insights/conversation/files/perspectives.php3]

Ospina, S. and Sorenson, G. (2006) 'A constructionist lens on leadership: charting new territory', in G. Goethals and G. Sorenson (eds), *The Quest for a General Theory of Leadership.* Cheltenham: Edward Elgar. pp. 188–204.

Ospina, S., Dodge J., Godsoe B., Mineri, J., Reza, S. and Schall, E. (2004) 'From consent to mutual inquiry: balancing democracy and authority in action research', *Journal of Action Research,* 2 (1): 47–69.

Palus, C.J. and Horth, D.M. (2002) *The Leaders's Edge: Six Creative Competencies for Navigating Complex Challenges.* San Francisco, CA: Jossey-Bass.

RCLA (2005) 'Internal draft working paper.' Research Center for Leadership in Action, Wagner School of Public Service, New York University.

Stewart, T.A. (1997) *Intellectual Capital: the New Wealth of Organizations.* Garden City, NY: Doubleday.

Yorks, L. (2005) 'Adult learning and the generation of new knowledge and meaning: creating liberating spaces for fostering adult learning through practitioner-based collaborative action inquiry', *Teachers College Record,* 107: 1217–44.

Yorks, L. and Kasl, E. (eds) (2002) *Collaborative Inquiry as a Strategy for Adult Learning. (New Directions for Adult and Continuing Education No. 94).* San Francisco, CA: Jossey-Bass.

Yorks, L. and Nicolaides, A. (2006) 'Complexity and emergent communicative learning: an opportunity for HRD Scholarship', *Human Resource Development Review,* 5: 143–7.

34

The Workplace Stress and Aggression Project: Ways of Knowing – Our Rosetta Stone for Practice

Rita Kowalski, Lyle Yorks and Mariann Jelinek

This chapter discusses how university- and organization-based researchers, working collaboratively, discovered how presentational knowing provided a key to transferring knowledge. Recognizing the importance of all forms of knowing helped generate knowledge about ourselves, the academic–practitioner collaboration, and the organization. To build capability and to apply learning, we had to accept individual voices and emotions along with academic theory. The chapter discusses how we as researchers accepted the changes co-inquiry and collaboration required and discovered that transferring our knowledge was not about maintaining an objective distance, but embracing all forms of knowing (experiential, presentational, propositional, practical). Using a descriptive voice, a personal voice and a collective voice, we recount how the discovery of the ways of knowing and, in particular, the power of presentational knowing unlocked a key to learning, knowledge creation and application in the world of practice.

Voices are central to our story, so it is important to know something about the authors and the voices used in this chapter. Rita Kowalski is an organizational researcher who participated in the first discussions about the project in 1998. Lyle Yorks is a university researcher who introduced the learning practices to the project and became a project team member in 2001. Mariann Jelinek is a university researcher who watched the project's evolution and who has helped the project team reflect and place in perspective its experience.

A descriptive voice begins our brief project overview, discussing the organization, the project team and the project's evolution.

A personal voice, that of a practitioner, then sets the stage, for the introduction of ways of knowing into the project. The last voice is a collective voice, representing the project team, whose experiences and voices often blended as our knowing became more holistic, more aware of the importance, in action research, of using all forms of 'knowing' (experiential, presentational, propositional, practical; Heron and Reason, 2001/2006, Chapter 24 in this volume). We conclude with lessons learned from our work.

A BRIEF PROJECT OVERVIEW

The US Department of Veterans Affairs (VA) is the project's setting. The VA is the second largest department in the US Federal Government, employing over 220,000 people, with an annual budget of over $50 billion. It has three major service lines that provide US military veterans with financial assistance through disability compensation and pensions, education and home loans; a broad range of medical, surgical and rehabilitative care; and burial services. Our project's ultimate objective was improving care and service to veterans by improving the working environment. It involved 11 pilot (experimental) sites with over 7000 employees, 15 comparison (control) facilities with over 6000 employees, and a highly diverse governing project team. This team included a physician executive responsible for a network of medical centers, three practitioners with extensive experience in human resources management, and four academics from different universities. The project team interacted with pilot site action teams composed of local site employees.

To become a project pilot site, both management and the union had to agree to participate and jointly selected action team members who represented a cross-section of the organization. Among the selection criteria were such things as an action orientation, a commitment to learn, credibility with

employees and leadership, plus good communications skills. The action teams briefed employees about the project, distributed and administered a survey, analyzed results, provided employees with feedback, designed and implemented interventions, and evaluated results (Kowalski et al., 2003).

The project used cycles characteristic of action research (Greenwood and Levin, 1998), involving the project team and actions teams in action and joint reflection about interventions and cycles involving individuals and teams, as they became more conscious and disciplined in engaging their voices. As the project matured, it evolved into a participatory action research project. This evolution occurred in direct response to deepening perceptions about the project's nature, various presenting problems (and thus their likely solutions), as well as deeper understanding of where important data might reside – both about our own tensions, as a team, and about the issues facing VA. Seeing ourselves as a proper focus of study if we were to affect VA was itself an important insight.

Project results for VA included significant reductions in workplace stress, and in all forms of aggression; a reduction in many of the behaviors related to occupational worker's compensation and equal opportunity claims; and a substantial increase in employee satisfaction at the pilot sites (Harmon, 2004; Keashly and Neuman, 2004; Neuman and Keashly, 2005, forthcoming). Project team outcomes included a much deeper understanding of organizational action from diverse viewpoints. The action teams adopted and adapted inquiry and learning practices, which added to the project's richness, providing participants with practices that changed their 'conversation' during the course of the effort. This new discourse created a special and highly effective 'space' for addressing difficult issues (Yorks, 2005) and enabled the project team to address sensitive issues involving gender and interpersonal behavior (Reid-Hector, 2006).

Variation in approaches and results evidenced across sites deepened the project's generated learning. The sites implementing the learning practices most deeply were the most successful. Implementation was not uniform. One site even dropped out of the project. (These issues of varying engagement involve what Reason and Bradbury (2001/2006) refer to as 'building infrastructure' are issues we are currently dealing with, and we will not address here.)

PROJECT EMERGENCE

University research did not initiate this project; it began quietly in the middle of the organization. In 1998, a long-time VA employee (an insider working in human resources who handled disciplinary and adverse actions against employees) became frustrated at having spent years providing advice on how to discipline employees whose behavior and actions were inappropriate and finding, despite his actions, inappropriate behavior reoccurred. Determined to find a remedy for the recurring pattern of aggressive behavior, he tapped into a network of diverse contacts to investigate what was known about behavioral change in organizations. Psychological research on workplace violence and emotional abuse caught his attention. He shared his findings with two other VA practitioners; one suggested contacting faculty from the Center for Human Resource Management Studies (CHRM) at Farleigh-Dickinson University, which encouraged collaboration between academics and practitioners. This led to a meeting in February 1999 of some 20 academic researchers and VA practitioners to discuss developing a proposal. While a number decided not to participate, this initial meeting's openness and willingness to listen to diverse views remained an enduring project characteristic. One project team member present at this meeting commented that

participants 'created a lot of trust ... everybody knew what was on the table that we had to balance'. However, the initial project design was not action research; it was quite traditional in its use of time one and time two quantitative survey data. The design fit the organization as VA was data-driven, expecting numbers to support a business case. Indeed, 'evidence-based medicine' was a deeply woven cultural theme inside VA.

THE CHANGE TO ACTION RESEARCH

Between August 1999 and January 2000, the project changed. One reason involves the project team's willingness to ask questions and involve outsiders to hear their questions and suggestions for improvements. The second was a very practical driver of change – the need to fund the academic researchers.

In August 1999, we attended a pre-conference action research workshop at the Academy of Management (AoM), where practitioners brought projects for discussion with university action researchers. A workshop discussion facilitator (Hilary Bradbury) asked, 'Where is the action in your research?' It was clear that our initial approach was cast as 'a study' that might not affect employees' behavior. Reflecting, the VA members attending realized that talk, study, or even data were insufficient; to make a difference inside their organization, they would have to model the behaviors of openness and participation that their project espoused to demonstrate as another way of being. Thus, the project's initial design had to fundamentally alter. A conventional research project would only provide the organization with yet another study that would sit on a shelf, useless except as a citation in subsequent studies on the same issue. For the organizational change impact sought, we needed to significantly involve people at each site – in analyzing data, developing and implementing interventions, and evaluating results. After all, their understanding and behavior was the intended target of change. Reflecting on the question ('Where is the action in your research?') made us aware of the value of diverse voices potentially present in participatory research. We had experienced this at our first meeting, where divergent disciplines spoke; now we wanted diverse, participative voices built into the project.

This change to a more openly participatory model, using collaborative action inquiry, while a significant design improvement, also created tension within the project team. Those attending the AoM meeting had largely made the decision to change without the input or understanding of those university-based researchers not present. So much for modeling participation! Moreover, the academics were quite focused on quantitative data analysis, while workshop attendees were more responsive to qualitative phenomena. This may seem surprising, but it is important to understanding how greatly we changed and how much we learned. An academic project team member who realized the organizational implications for the project team itself vigorously urged the addition of learning practices, such as the Ladder of Inference, Stop and Reflect, and the Learning Window (see, for example, Bray et al., 2000; Roth and Kleiner, 1999; see also Chapter 46). The practices enabled the team to discuss and eventually deal with the fallout from the fundamental shift in the research design (Reid-Hector, 2006) – and to affect the client organization as well, in ways alternative research designs would not permit.

We want to be transparent about team tensions, and admit that the issue festered for months, until a feedback session conducted by a doctoral candidate and another academic in October 2002. After interviewing project team members, they fed back data to the team, using the project's own processes to frame the discussion and help the project team candidly discuss their tensions. Working collaboratively across disciplines and involving academic researchers and organizational researchers as co-creators are difficult, so it is

not surprising that our multidisciplinary, multi-organizational team struggled for some time with a high-participation research model's meaning and implications. Taking the project to the AoM during its formative stage was a critical event that gave rise to another key operating behavior and value. We were willing to expose our thinking, learning, and uncertainties to critical questions and comments from the outside (Neuman, 2004; Yorks, 2005). The questions we heard helped us to inquire, both individually and as a team, into where we were and how we could improve what we were doing to meet emergent realities and circumstances we were facing. In retrospect, the benefits of such openness became apparent; thus we actively sought to replicate it in subsequent action.

Our need for project funding had an unintended consequence that proved to be invaluable; it resulted in our formally adding the learning practices to the project's design. We submitted a proposal to the National Science Foundation (NSF). The NSF approved the proposal in April 2000 to assess the effectiveness of organization change interventions designed to reduce workplace stress and aggression and improve performance, and examine whether (and how) using 'collaborative action inquiry' leads to organization learning and change (Harmon, 2000). Our team never anticipated how deeply inquiry and reflection would transform our view of collaboration, challenge our assumptions about the roles of researchers and practitioners, and serve as a significant transformational intervention (Reid-Hector, 2006). This decision to formally design assessment completed the transformation of the project's design to an action research project using inquiry and learning practices. Another academic interested in organizational learning helped write the NSF grant, became our learning coach, and joined the project team (Yorks, 2005).

The more traditional university-based researchers later commented that they felt, when they read the proposal, as if the 'project was hijacked' away from the focal issues of workplace stress and aggression that had initially attracted them. Ironically, the shift in focus extended the inquiry on stress and aggression into our own team. The new approaches provided a highly effective way to discuss project decisions, tensions and conflicts (Reid-Hector, 2006). As a result, we became aware, as the project unfolded, that the presenting topic of stress and aggression was also an issue we faced within the team; one that we would have to resolve if we were to be successful.

During the feedback session, what crystallized was how action research's emphasis on participation and co-creation had affected the relationship between the groups we had initially called 'the academics' and 'the practitioners'. We explicitly discussed our roles and how they had changed as we worked together. Recognition of this shift occurred when one university-based researcher wondered aloud about the project team's role, purposes and function: 'Is it to run the project? Is it to supervise the research?' We saw that we allowed natural leaders to emerge as issues and needs arose. Learning to share leadership and recognize how we each contributed took time. We were experts or novices depending upon the task, situation, or point in time.

From the beginning, we exhibited a willingness to listen, a desire to be participatory, reliance upon asking questions, a willingness to take our work to outsiders for their reactions, and a desire to learn: all elements that correspond to choice points for action researchers, as discussed by Bradbury and Reason (2001/2006). Unwittingly at first, we were enacting action research. We chose to be participatory, both in respecting the views of other academics and in deciding to involve all stakeholders as project participants. We also chose to go beyond our initial network with our ideas and questions, expanding the project's participants, both directly and peripherally. We were learning, and wanted to share *how* we learned and *what* we learned with others, inviting them to reflect on what they heard. We also began increasingly to use stories to explain our work, making our

learning and findings available to nonprofessionals as well, although it was not until later that we came to appreciate storytelling's implications. Because of our multidisciplinary team and array of methods for external validation, we were able to meet the often divergent interests of those interested in science, those interested in business results and those interested in learning. These characteristics' importance became more apparent in each action cycle, as we learned more about participation and ways of knowing. In short, in contrast to the stereotypical model of research as driven by a priori theory, arm's length data gathering, and hypothesis confirmation, our project was characterized by an iterative series of theory, action and reflection cycles that adapted the project to insights and contexts as these emerged. The project and researchers both changed, enhancing project outcomes as well as researcher capabilities. It seems self-evident that the outcomes achieved were unattainable in any other way.

WAYS OF KNOWING AND THE PROJECT

Heron and Reason (Heron, 1992, 1996; Heron and Reason, 2001/2006, Chapter 24) provide an epistemology applicable to our work, going beyond the traditional propositional academic knowledge to include other relevant and important 'ways of knowing'. Addressing the nature of knowledge is especially important for researchers concerned with human action, understanding, and inference and their interactions. The Heron/Reason model moves from 'experiential knowing' (occurring through direct face-to-face encounter with person, place or thing), to 'presentational knowing' that draws upon expressive forms of imagery (e.g. art, stories, music, drama, etc.), to 'propositional knowing' using 'ideas and theories, expressed in informative statements (e.g., books, speeches, etc.), moving finally to 'practical knowing' that involves applied knowledge – the tacit 'how to' knowledge seen in a skill or compe-tence (Heron and Reason, 2001/2006: 183).

As the project became more collaborative, we became increasingly comfortable with multiple forms of knowing: their value for the work was constantly reiterated. In the begin-ning, we seemed to be using a traditional propositional academic epistemology. Initially, we all encountered forms of experiential and what could be considered more propositional knowing in completing tasks and attending project events, but our emotional reactions were implicit; our learning from and about them unexpressed – indeed, inexpressible, because all but illegitimate under traditional propositional academic norms of 'objectivity'. To reduce workplace stress and aggression, however, emotional reactions were the heart of the matter. We had to improve and increase our ability both to express and explain emotions, thinking about how these affected our own learning and our knowing, as well as that of organizational members we hoped to affect. This realization grew slowly, but was eventu-ally central to our project.

AN INTERLUDE

As we have described the project so far, our voice sounds detached. This descriptive voice is important, but to understand how the project opened new ways of knowing to us, you need to hear a personal voice. Rita's story will provide a framework for our dis-cussion of ways of knowing and learning from the project.

Rita's Story

How does a practitioner become an organiza-tional researcher? Not intentionally in the begin-ning, but very deliberately as I began learning how to notice, inquire and act. When we began, I assumed that we would provide the sites with 'the answer'. After all, wasn't that what research does? I wanted the project to provide evidence about how aggressive, abusive behavior affected business results.

The project did build a business case for addressing workplace stress and aggression,

meeting my expectations. However, there were unexpected outcomes as well – additional benefits to me, personally. Reflection on the project, due to the nature of our presenting problem (stress and aggression), required acknowledging emo-tions and naming dysfunctional behaviors, so that we could improve our interactions and work. To hold my own and contribute to our work, I read more theory. These actions grounded my practice. As I incorporated inquiry in my practice and engaged my academic colleagues in my explo-rations, I made a discovery that improved my prac-tice, strengthening my contributions to the project. Several events prepared me for the dis-covery of my key to application and practice. Each was transformative, reframing my views of emo-tions and of the place of creative arts in action research.

The first took place in September 2001 at the Society for Organizational Learning's (SoL) Greenhouse where SoL invited groups to bring new and ongoing projects for discussion and learning. To encourage interaction across the pro-jects, teams were formed consisting of people from different projects. Each team was asked to develop a movie poster explaining a specific pro-ject. I left my home group to work on another pro-ject's poster. When I rejoined my project team members who had stayed behind and saw the poster, I was speechless. While the project team had talked about the impact of our own negative behaviors, seeing the poster was disconcertingly direct (see Figure 34.1). The poster touched upon accountability and each person's contribution to workplace behavior's dark side. I loved the poster's clarity, but did not yet see its potential for knowl-edge creation.

In January 2002, back at the VA, the project team began to use visual mapping to feed back a story we heard from action teams' members during site visit interviews. My first site feedback session using the map was the second transforma-tive event. While the map looked complicated, the team, and every other team we visited afterward, responded to maps based on their input with energy and appreciation for what they accom-plished. My analytical mind recognized a research artifact. I also saw how one word picture explained a site far more comprehensively and evocatively than a bulleted PowerPoint presentation, but I did not understand how it worked.

The next transformative event was our two-hour in-house VA broadcast in December 2003, pre-senting a panel discussion and action team activi-ties from the sites. We hoped that the broadcast would help us spread the word, giving us more credibility and support. I was skeptical, but I agreed to work on this effort. We sent crews to tape interviews and events with action team members at three different locations. They told

Figure 34.1   *Rita's poster*

their stories about stress, aggression, and changing those behaviors while the camera caught them interacting, laughing with and caring for veterans. As we worked with the producers for the live broadcast, they led us through several cycles of reflection and inquiry, refining the broadcast's message, reviewing the video clips and preparing the panel for the live broadcast. Sitting in the broadcast booth, I watched the producers and the crew work with the video and our panel. I saw the play within the play, liberating our work. I knew that the tape would help us spread our work, but I still did not get it.

Immediately after this broadcast, we began working with action team members to plan the knowledge transfer meeting. This meeting's purpose was to share and learn together, reflecting on what we had accomplished. I was not only working with the teams to plan the meeting, but was asked to develop a proposal for four new taped broadcasts about our learning. I had no idea about how to write the proposal, or how to incorporate the conference into the design. I had questions I could not answer, so I took the subway up to Columbia to meet with Lyle Yorks, the

project team member who had brought the learning practices to our project. We discussed my quandary. In passing, Lyle mentioned John Heron, whom he said was a major influence in his own work.

The next week I read Heron's *Co-Operative Inquiry* and then wrote the proposal in one sitting. This book introduced me to the four ways of knowing, giving me a way to integrate my experiences, my feelings, and my intellect into my practice. Bringing these insights back into the project helped me work more confidently with the conference's design team. We decided to tape the conference and to conduct interviews with action team members during the conference to discuss project learning. We used these tapes as part of the four, 30-minute broadcasts to visually display the conference's creativity, action and energy.

The ways of knowing became my Rosetta stone, enabling me to translate what I intuitively felt into action. I finally had a key to solving my frustrations with transferring knowledge and practices across an organization. For years I had been coached to rely solely on objective data, and being totally dispassionate. This approach was rewarded, but overlooked the fact that organizations consist of people with emotions and feelings. For any behavioral change project to be successful, emotions and feelings that drove behavior were central. We could not ignore their existence and impact, if we were trying to learn about ways to reduce workplace stress and aggression. Each of us had to learn from experience, from emotions and from conceptualization, if we wanted to develop 'know how' and impact practice.

THE PROJECT TEAM AND WAYS OF KNOWING

The project team, as it gained experience with the learning practices and action research, began to ask questions about participation, co-creation and knowledge. Action research cycles required the team to pause and notice what it was learning. Because of the presenting problem, issues involving aggression and stress within the team leaped into prominence and provided a practice field as the team learned how to walk the talk. Learning to deal with emotions constructively and to explain how they impacted our work were major challenges. They added dimensions to our research that our original design would not have noticed, or would have de-legitimated as we strove to enact an impossible 'objectivity'.

Making ourselves the subject of part of our exploration forced us to confront our own tensions, enabling us to understand and also to demonstrate in action the new behaviors we were asking organization members to accept. 'Knowing by doing' also made the team credible role models: we served as an existent proof of the efficacy of the new behaviors.[1] Learning to embrace four ways of knowing and, in particular, acknowledging presentational knowing opened up a new way to explore ourselves. As in Rita's story, the project team's experience and comfort with presentational knowing evolved over time. We first began to use

forms of presentational knowing unconsciously. Through the reflective practices, we were noticing more frequently not only what we were doing, but its affect on ourselves and others. Our reflection suggests that as we became more comfortable with the first and second voices of research (Torbert, 2001/2006; Reason and Torbert, 2001; Chandler and Torbert, 2003; see also Chapter 16), we also became more comfortable with the presentational ways of knowing that provided a key to the emotional side of our personal (first-person) and team (second-person) learning, which in turn made us more willing to bring our work to the outside world (third-person). With presentational knowing's key, we were better able to explain to others what we had done and experienced, and why it mattered.

Our insight's impact was not limited to emotions. We also became better at telling stories – accessing the qualitative data that illustrated the quantitative data we had collected – which emerged as a critical skill. A major crisis took place when we conducted our first action team training sessions. First impressions are important, and what the action teams saw was a project team in conflict. When responding to a question about the survey being planned, one of the university researchers responded for the team, without consulting another university researcher more directly involved with content and design. The pilot site action team members saw the anger that resulted. Our expert didactic design was also not working, as project team members not directly presenting material engaged in side bar conversations at the back of the room – an action distracting at best, but ironically aggressive and rude for an 'expert' team trying to reduce workplace stress and aggression. After the session, our discussion of what had happened deteriorated dramatically. We continued bickering over dinner at a restaurant. Finally, an organization-based researcher held up a pepper shaker and said, 'This is our talking stick. Whoever holds it is the only person who can talk.' The pepper shaker took on a life of its own, as people at first unconsciously, then deliberately, spoke into it like a microphone, while others listened. This experientially-cued 'stop and reflect' short-circuited the bickering and interruptions, helping us change what we were doing. Clarity and agreement around necessary workshop modifications emerged rapidly. We quickly agreed to share with the action teams what we felt was a 'breakthrough' experience, in an effort to be transparent and model the learning behavior we espoused (not an easy decision for those of us still concerned about maintaining some semblance of 'expert' status with an audience accustomed to such distinctions from their 'trainers').

The next morning when we met with the action teams, the same organization-based researcher who had suggested using the pepper shaker openly acknowledged to the action teams our difficulties the day before. He held up the pepper shaker and told the story of our using it at the restaurant. He acknowledged our dysfunctional behavior, and discussed how the pepper shaker helped us reflect on and reshape our work. Throughout that day, we noticed teams passing around crushed cans or bottles that they called 'pepper shakers' as they enacted our procedure to integrate 'stop and reflect' practices into their own behaviors (experiential knowing). Our story (presentational knowing) became a way for them to absorb the transferred lesson about reflection, and to immediately apply it (practical knowing). Acknowledging our own dysfunctional behavior and explicitly dealing with it, and then publicly sharing that acknowledgment and response, let them see us learning in action, warts and all. It vividly demonstrated that such issues occurred (even among experts), and that they could be productively addressed. This positive experience encouraged us towards further displaying our own process issues as they arose, to communicate and foster learning.

Having seen how interacting with researchers outside the project enhanced our project, we returned to the AoM in 2001. At a symposium about the project we spoke from a half circle and told our stories about first steps, conflicts, tensions, disagreements and solutions. Our modified 'fishbowl' design allowed a free flowing discussion that touched upon tensions dealing with project design, control, and evaluation, while the academic audience observed and then asked questions about our work, challenging us and making us more critical of our work.

In 2003, at another AoM symposium, we consciously turned the presentation into theater. We began with a grounded presentation of theoretical models, but also included our first person reflections in small set pieces, where we played out the tensions we felt as team members, interacting in the second person mode. Our scripted presentation contained notes specifying 'exaggerated' dialogues at key points. We wanted to depict the emotions and tensions surrounding co-creation with researchers drawn from different disciplines, experiences and organizations. At rehearsal, we talked about where and how to add 'drama'. During the presentation, somewhat to our surprise, we found ourselves reliving our moments of tension and discovery. One organization-based researcher reflected,

> I remember listening to [a university researcher] talk about the need to maintain the purity of our survey process. ... I got so caught up ... I became angry again. I sat down surprised. ... I let our listeners see and experience the emotions surrounding the debate. We could have read a paper, but we actually let them experience our anger and frustration about methods and control issues.

Without the emotion, these issues are abstract at best; in practice, because organizational participants have a genuine, very personal stake in the outcomes, these issues acquire power, salience and meanings almost wholly invisible in traditional research paradigms. By scripting the presentation, we were able to articulate and vividly share important facts of field research of critical importance to organizational research. In this sense, presentational knowing moved well beyond what is possible in more traditional research presentations.

Our insights have had further impact. Rita's story mentioned the 'movie poster' that visually explained personal accountability for dysfunctional behavior with an unsettlingly direct humor, tapping into emotional responses. Another organizational researcher began using this poster in presentations to leadership groups within VA. After seeing the poster, group participants first were silent, uncomfortable, and resistant – but then they began conversations about interactions they have faced with a fresh honesty. We were learning that the poster tapped into emotions and made legitimate discussions otherwise typically disqualified as inappropriate in organizational settings. We incorporated movie poster development into the project's 'close-out' conference in 2003, as a way for everyone to jointly and publicly evaluate their experience. Members from both the project team and action teams were randomly chosen to join in workgroups to develop the posters. Figure 34.2 is an example. When the designers presented their poster, an uncomfortable initial silence ensued; then it generated discussion that some found unsettling because it raised hitherto 'unidiscussible' topics, about perceptions and emotions within the organization.

The final project close-out session demonstrated how far the project team's concept of co-researchers had changed, as well as how far the action teams had come. The local pilot action team members were now involved in the meeting's design. They brought more aspects of propositional knowing to the design; because of our learning as a project team about collaboration and ways of knowing, we encouraged and relished their ideas and energy. We knew we had moved our work to a new level. As we later explained in a broadcast describing this meeting, 'We could have just used a sheet of paper and have someone read it, but we are dealing with people and relationships and emotions.' The teams' skits, which portrayed the things they felt and what they saw people doing, conveyed information far more powerfully that any report possibly could. One team, depicting a monthly meeting between randomly selected employees and a senior leader, acted out dysfunctional behavior. A university-based researcher reflected, 'people were having fun, but they knew serious learning was going on. … we are laughing … while … learning the message the team wanted to communicate to us.'

Not all of the skits were positive. One action team faced organizational barriers and leadership resistance. Their skit showed organization leaders holding hula hoops high in the air as the action team members tried jumping through them. Characterizing organizational hurdles as 'hula hoops' challenged the relevance and legitimacy of resistance by leaders to changes others viewed as constructive. The enacted metaphor conveyed powerful emotions, making them directly accessible to those who watched.

Collectively, the skits created 'a life story' about the project, creating a 'communicative action' that made sense of the project, its interventions, and all of our experiences (Shaw, 2002: 104–5). They added enormously to the discourse and to a broader understanding of organizational life and to the participants' ability to engage in meaningful interventions.

Rita's story discussed the broadcast series, a form of presentational knowing. These broadcasts captured the project's experiences through selected interviews, narrated glimpses of interventions and of the skits, posters and across-team learning sessions at the close-out conference. We developed the broadcast design using a series of reflection cycles culminating in a broadcast presentation that caught the emotions and learning that emerged 'as it happened'. This experience was a new way of going to the third person voice that captured experiences

Figure 34.2 *A movie poster*

through images and stories far more powerfully than written words.

OUR LEARNING

This chapter helped us realize that without presentational knowing, we would have seriously restricted our ability to affect practice and leave a legacy. We know now that the chosen presenting problem gave us an advantage, because human beings have a visceral reaction to aggression and stress. We realized as we worked together over time that dealing with our own aggression and stress – on the project team and with the action teams – helped us develop the 'know how' to explain and transfer what we learned to others.

In the past, we would have trained teams through lectures about learning practices, or about stress and aggression. Instead, we learned how to use learning practices more

naturally and 'taught' new teams by embodying the practices ourselves, without prior explanation, demonstrating the learning we wished to convey. The 'ways of knowing' provided a theoretical framework that made application to practice possible. Without the safety that reflection and testing assumptions provided, we would not have made this connection. The learning practices became our way of talking with new teams, not telling them but talking with them using our behaviors. We learned to do this from having discovered how the action teams had naturalized the learning practices. When we modeled the practices, we found that in a matter of hours, a new team would mirror them back to us. We learned how to accelerate this process experientially, in a way we would never have envisioned from within the traditional objective research paradigm.

In retrospect, we seem to have done this using the first voice of research to ask questions of ourselves individually, and using the second voice to discuss what we jointly had learned. We used the third voice not only to share what we had learned, but to engage the outside world in our work. Because we learned to bring the emotional side of our work in through stories, maps and posters, we enriched our third–person conversations, hearing new questions, which began our cycle of action research and discovery again. The 'ongoing research' paradigm of action research seems to have improved our research capabilities in real time, on the fly, even as our theoretical understandings deepened.

We never made this connection until we spent time reflecting on our work together and its implications. We are just beginning to appreciate how presentational knowing not only helps us apply what we learned in actual practice, but also to transfer our tacit knowledge to others. As we have talked with others about our work, they often remark about our candor. We acknowledge our research problems and frustrations, seeking to hide very little – because we have learned that openness facilitates learning and good results. Writing this chapter, we recognized that our journey as researchers was both hard work and unique. Would we start a project like this again, knowing what we know today? Maybe not; however, we are still together after five years, still talking and working together – and still making discoveries.

ACKNOWLEDGMENTS

Work on this project was partly supported by grant # 0080676 from the US National Science Foundation (NSF), Innovation and Change Division. Findings do not necessarily represent the views of the NSF. We also gratefully acknowledge the support of the VA Learning University, the Office of Resolution Management, the VA Office of Occupational Health and Safety and VHA's VISN 13.

The authors would like to acknowledge the other members of the Project Team whose efforts are part of our work: James Scaringi, the project's father, Joel Harmon, the Principal Investigator for the NSP grant whose insistence got the learning practices into the design, Loraleigh Keashly and Joel Neuman, the university researchers who brought their knowledge of workplace aggression to the project, and Daniel Kowalski, the organization researcher, who drew upon his knowledge of Native Americans to introduce the 'talking stick' (pepper shaker) to our campfire.

Figures 34.1 and 34.2 reprinted with permission.

NOTE

1 Embodying a new vision of being, 'walking the talk', has also been identified as an important component of charismatic and visionary leadership (House and Shamir, 1993; Boal and Bryson, 1987).

REFERENCES

Boal, K.B. and Bryson, J.M. (1987) 'Charismatic leadership: a phenomenological and structural approach,' in J.G. Hunt, B.R. Balinga, H.P. Dachler and C.A. Schriescheim (eds), *Emerging Leadership Vistas*. Lexington, MA: Lexington Books. pp. 11–28.

Bradbury, H. and Reason, P. (eds) (2001/2006) *Handbook of Action Research: Participative Inquiry and Practice*. London: Sage.

Bradbury, H. and Reason, P. (2003) 'Action research: an opportunity for revitalizing research purpose and practices', *Qualitative Social Work*, 2 (2): 155–75.

Bray, J., Lee, J., Smith, L. and Yorks, L. (2000) *Collaborative Inquiry in Practice: Action, Reflection, and Making Meaning*. Thousand Oaks, CA: Sage.

Chandler, D. and Torbert, B. (2003) 'Transforming inquiry and action: interweaving 27 flavors of action research', *Action Research*, 1 (2): 133–52.

Greenwood, D.J. and Levin, M. (1998) *Introduction to Action Research: Social Research of Social Change*. Thousand Oaks CA: Sage.

Harmon, J. (2000) *Reducing Workplace Aggression Using Action Science to Enhance Organizational Change* (*National Science Foundation*). [https://www.fastlane.nsf.gov/servlet/showaward?award=0080676]

Harmon, J. (2004) *Final Report on Award 0080676.* (*National Science Foundation*). [https://www.fastlane.nsf.gov/cgi-bin/NSF_PrjRpt]

Heron, J. (1992) *Feeling and Personhood: Psychology in Another Key*. London: Sage.

Heron, J. (1996) *Co-operative Inquiry: Research into the Human Condition*. London: Sage.

Heron, J. and Reason, P. (2001/2006) 'The practice of co-operative inquiry: research "with" rather than "on" people', in P. Reason and H. Bradbury (eds), *Handbook of Action Research: Participative Inquiry and Practice*. London: Sage. pp. 179–88. Also published in P. Reason and H. Bradbury (eds) (2006), *Handbook of Action Research: Concise Paperback Edition*. London: Sage. pp. 144–54.

House, R.J. and Shamir, B. (1993) 'Toward the integration of transformational, charismatic, and visionary theories of leadership', in M. Chemers and R. Ayman (eds), *Leadership: Perspectives and Research Directions*. New York: Academic Press. pp. 81–107.

Keashly, L. and Neuman, J.H. (2004) 'Bullying in the workplace: Its impact and management', *Employee Rights and Employment Policy Journal,* 8: 335–73.

Kowalski, R., Harmon, J., Yorks, L., and Kowalski, D. (2003) 'Reducing workplace stress and aggression: an action research project at the U.S. Department of Veterans Affairs', *Human Resource Planning,* 26 (2): 39–53.

Neuman, J.H. (2004) 'Injustice, stress, and aggression in organizations', in R.W. Griffin and A.M. O'Leary-Kelly (eds), *The Dark Side of Organizational Behavior*. San Francisco, CA: Jossey-Bass. pp. 62–102.

Neuman, J.H. and Keashly, L. (2005) 'Reducing stress and bullying: an intervention project in the U.S. Department of Veterans Affairs', in J. Raver (Chair), *Workplace Bullying: International Perspectives on Moving from Research to Practice* (symposium presented at the annual meeting of the Academy of Management, Honolulu, HI, August).

Neuman, J.H. and Keashly, L. (forthcoming) 'The means, motive and opportunity: framework and insidious workplace behavior', in J. Greenberg (ed.), *Insidious Workplace Behavior*. Hillsdale, NJ: Lawrence Erlbaum.

Reason, P. and Bradbury, H. (eds) (2001/2006) *Handbook of Action Research: Participative Inquiry and Practice*. London: Sage.

Reason, P. and Torbert, W.R. (2001) 'Toward a transformational science: a further look at the scientific merits of action research', *Concepts and Transformations,* 6 (1): 1–37.

Reid-Hector, J. (2006) 'Inquiry-based learning practices and team learning: a model for experienced-based adult learning'. Doctoral dissertation, Columbia University, New York.

Roth, G. and Kleiner, A. (1999) *Car Launch: the Human Side of Managing Change*. New York: Oxford University Press.

Shaw, P. (2002) *Changing the Conversations in Organizations: a Complexity Approach to Change*. London: Routledge.

Torbert, W.R. (2001/2006) 'The practice of action inquiry', in P. Reason and H. Bradbury (eds) *Handbook of Action Research: Participatory Inquiry and Practice*. London: Sage. pp. 207–18. Also published in P. Reason and H. Bradbury (eds) (2006), *Handbook of Action Research: Concise Paperback Edition*. London: Sage. pp. 207–17.

Yorks, L. (2005) 'Adult learning and the generation of new knowledge and meaning: creating liberating spaces for fostering adult learning through practitioner-based collaborative action inquiry', *Teachers College Record,* 107 (6): 1217–44.

35

Theatre in Participatory Action Research: Experiences from Bangladesh

Meghna Guhathakurta

This chapter describes and analyses the premises, processes, challenges and impact of interactive theatre used in conjunction with participatory action research (PAR) in Bangladesh. Research Initiative Bangladesh (RIB), a research support organization, has been employing PAR as a way of self-inquiry and self-development leading to holistic awareness and collective action to reach out to the marginalized in society. RIB found itself in a pioneering role of encouraging this kind of community-based research in what are often termed 'missing communities' – missing, that is, in terms of their absence in mainstream development agendas. As a consequence of this RIB also found itself having to engender a growing corps of new *researcher-animators*, who will take it upon themselves to 'animate' the underprivileged people to regard themselves as principal actors in their lives and not as subordinates to other social classes.

This chapter will describe and analyse the premises, processes, challenges and impact of interactive theatre used in conjunction with participatory action research (PAR) in the context of Bangladesh. It will also critically engage with the discourses of transformation that such work is producing or helping to produce. First I will trace how the concept of PAR had been used in the Bangladesh context and, second, I will look at how interactive theatre has been adapted in combination with PAR. Third, I will see how this practice has evolved within some of the marginalized communities with whom Research Initiative Bangladesh (RIB) has been working. Finally, I will try to reflect upon and generalize about some of the lessons learnt regarding discourses of transformation that the element of theatre introduces to the praxis of PAR.

CONCEPTUALIZING AND ACTIVATING PAR IN BANGLADESH

One of the foremost exponents of Participatory Action Research (PAR) from Bangladesh has been Md. Anisur Rahman (see also Chapter 3 in this volume), who writes that his own initiation in PAR has its roots in the 1971 Liberation War of Bangladesh which made him want to see the people of Bangladesh engage in carving out their own paths of development with collective creativity (Rahman, 2004: 5). While in the post-independence period in Bangladesh a space was found where various spontaneous attempts at collective participatory action could be recorded, subsequent developments in the larger political scenario were not conducive to its continuation. In the year 2000, when some eminent citizens including Md. Anisur Rahman established Research Initiatives, Bangladesh (RIB) to promote research on poverty groups, it adopted as its founding philosophy the idea of humanizing the poverty discourse. Through this perspective RIB sought to veer away from existing trends in poverty research, which reify the poor in terms of physical subsistence – in other words, treat them as 'livestock' to be kept alive to produce milk, eggs and flesh for the 'non-poor' (RIB, 2003: 6).

Participatory action research or its Bengali equivalent *Gonogobeshona*, as a way of collective self-inquiry and self-development leading to holistic awareness and collective action, therefore came to play an active part as one of the many ways in which the marginalized in society could be reached and awakened. RIB found itself in a pioneering role of encouraging this kind of community-based research of what are often termed 'missing communities' – missing, that is, in terms of their absence in mainstream development agendas. As a consequence of this RIB also found itself having to engender a growing corps of new *researcher-animators*, who will take it upon themselves to 'animate' the underprivileged people to regard themselves as principal actors in their lives and not as subordinates to other social classes. 'The central spirit behind this conception of animation is the view of women and men as *creative beings* and the desire to see the creative possibilities of the underprivileged people released' (Rahman, 2004: 19; see also Tilakratna, 1987). RIB has been working in this approach and building the capacities of local animators in marginalized communities such as the Bedays (river gypsies), Dalits, Sweepers, Rishis (leather workers), Kewras (pig-rearers), Mundas, Bunos and may other Adivasi communities. PAR has also been used very effectively to understand the problems of women and men in small cottage industries like mat weaving, silk sari weaving, wood-cutting or subordinate labour activities like women working in jute mills and tanneries or low cost restaurant workers. Apart from such communities, several projects have been devoted to refining the conceptual parameters and exploring new dimensions of animation techniques and pedagogic processes, like the capacity-building of animators' projects conducted by Alaudin Ali in Nilfamari district in northern Bangladesh and using interactive theatre in combination with PAR as a tool of animation conducted by Rajib Parves in the district of Kushtia in western Bangladesh. It is the latter project which I will focus on and elaborate here though lessons from the former project will be referred to as well.

THE ROLE OF INTERACTIVE THEATRE IN DEEPENING EXISTING TRENDS IN DEVELOPMENT THEATRE

The works of Augusto Boal and Paolo Freire have been an inspiration throughout the world to animators who have sought to work with the underprivileged and oppressed. Bangladesh has been no exception. Augusto Boal's (1985) theatre of the oppressed with its diverse forms such as forum theatre and invisible theatre and Paolo Freire's (1974) pedagogy of the oppressed with its emphasis on dialogue, praxis, conscientization and lived experience have found their place in the practice of different theatre groups in Bangladesh, more specifically in the realms of development. Popular theatre, puppet theatre, experimentation with indigenous forms like *pala gaan* (storytelling through songs) and *kobi gaan* (interchange between two rival bards and their respective teams) have been used quite effectively by existing development agencies, to raise awareness of issues like family planning, education, immunization and health issues.

However, whereas most developmental theatre offered solutions to existing problems and spectators remained passive observers, Rajib Parvez, a young theatre activist trained in Boal's forum theatre techniques, sought to use both theatre and pedagogy for the identification of problems by the people themselves and thereby to develop a consciousness with the potentiality to transform. In Augusto Boal's language, therefore, all human beings become Actors (they act!) and Spectators (they observe!) in brief ' Spect-Actors'.

Rajib Parvez, with the support from Research Initiatives Bangladesh (RIB), has been able to break new ground in this area. Rajib's work received new impetus from the parallel work on PAR (Gonogobeshona or people's research) being supported by RIB. As Executive Director of RIB it has been my pleasure as well as those of others in RIB to see his work develop from experimenting with this form within the confines of an existing project in the sweepers' community to a project designed for refining, broadening and deepening skills and techniques of animation and sharing it with a team of fellow actor-animators. It was a learning process for all of us and as such it gives me great pleasure to share moments of this with a broader community of people.

RAJIB'S PRELIMINARY WORK WITH THE SWEEPER COMMUNITY

Bangladesh is a country populated by a Muslim majority. In 1947, after the withdrawal of British colonial power, the Indian subcontinent was divided into two nation-states largely on the basis of religion, Hindus in India and Muslims in Pakistan. Bangladesh, as the erstwhile eastern wing of Pakistan at the time of Partition, had a Muslim preponderant population but also a sizeable number of Hindus. However, with the increase of state-instigated violence against the religious minorities, more and more Hindus – especially from the middle class – migrated to India. Currently, in the independent state of Bangladesh, there are about 10 per cent of Hindus still remaining, and a large proportion of them are from the lower rungs of the Hindu caste hierarchy. Although the caste system is originally derived from the Hindu religion it has become integrated with the social system practised over the years. As such, although the Hindu middle class has migrated to India, the Muslim powerful elites who took over in the rural areas continued the discriminatory practice against them. Thus in many areas of Bangladesh, sweeper communities and others like them are not treated equally in public places, for example not allowed to sit with others in restaurants and schools.

The sweepers' community is a marginalized, impoverished community in Kushtia, a district in western Bangladesh. They have been called Harijons (children of God) by M.K. Gandhi, but they often reject this nomenclature. I will therefore call them the sweeper community. They were stigmatized by society because they performed menial tasks such as sweeping and cleaning.

INTRODUCING AND ADAPTING INTERACTIVE THEATRE AMONG THE SWEEPER COMMUNITY IN KUSHTIA, BANGLADESH

A local NGO known as the Friends Association for Integrated Revolution (FAIR) decided to investigate the inhuman conditions of the lives and livelihood of this community. It was also their intention to follow the principles of action research in raising consciousness, awareness, self-reliance, self-motivation and confidence to fight for their basic needs and fundamental human rights as a community. In order to fore-ground them into the existing development discourse, their participation was considered essential. This was brought about by initially employing a variety of methods like focus group discussions, workshops and seminars bolstered by vocational training programmes, advocacy and cultural activities.

In preparing to work with the community Dewan Akhtaruzzaman, the principal researcher from FAIR, invited some of the Board members of RIB to visit the commu-nity. During this visit the Chairman, Shamsul Bari, and Anisur Rahman learnt of the trials and tribulations of the community from close quarters. They learnt that the community faced problems in sustaining their livelihood not only because they were considered finan-cially poor but also because of the social stigma attached to their profession that limited their acceptability and led to discrim-ination against them. They were thus pre-vented from participating fully in society and contributing to it as full citizens. As a result of this conversation, the Board Members were more than convinced that (a) the project should be designed on the model of partici-patory action research (PAR) whereby the primary objective should be to get the com-munity involved in determining their priori-ties, (b) the animator at FAIR should be assisted and guided by a resource person. In this respect the name of Alaudin Ali came up. He was involved in the project to help create animators in North Bangladesh.

The PAR exercise among the sweeper com-munity in Kushtia bore fruit. Through the help of Alaudin Ali, who came to Kushtia to hold a series of workshops on PAR, a batch of anima-tors were created among the sweepers them-selves who successfully guided the process of self-development among men, women and children of their community. This was not an easy task, as there were hierarchies embedded within the sweeper community, hierarchies which were gendered and intra-caste. The animators were well aware of this divide and effort was taken to constitute separate groups among women and men so that issues would be discussed openly within each group and then aired generally in larger all inclusive groups. It was interesting, though, that it was through facing the challenges of intra-caste hierarchies that the thought of a theatre workshop was borne.

In one of the PAR discussions held among the community it was suggested that some of the funds allocated for livelihood training as barbers be diverted to constituting a theatre group for the youth since no one was inter-ested in being a barber. When probed further it became apparent that it was due to the fact that barbers constituted one of the lowest rungs in the intra-caste hierarchy (even lower than sweepers) and hence no one was inter-ested in taking up this vocational training. When the idea was proposed to the RIB Secretariat, we found the idea of the theatre an interesting prospect but we made it a con-dition that the transfer of funds take place only if this issue of intra-caste hierarchy be addressed in PAR groups and also in the training of theatre activists. This was accepted by FAIR and Rajib Parvez, whose training in forum theatre techniques was brought into the picture.

However, since Rajib and his team were not informed of the practices of PAR it was sug-gested that Rajib could get acquainted with the principles and theory behind the process by visiting Alaudin Ali's field in Nilfamari. Rajib was therefore included as a member of a team of potential researchers who went to observe PAR as it was practised in the field in Alaudin Ali's project area in North Bangladesh. It was expected that as a dialogue with this process, the ideas of PAR would be enriched and strengthened in diverse areas as well as a net-work built among PAR researchers. After the workshop Rajib started to apply himself to adapting his theatre techniques alongside the practice of PAR and an amazing synergy emerged in the form of what he now called interactive theatre.

In applying his theatre techniques to this young group of adolescents whose problems ranged from drug addiction to truancy, Rajib met his first challenge of organizing these rather undisciplined and unpunctual youth. Rajib describes in his own words the steps he took to concretize this process: 'Some youth from the community came from another area and asked me whether they could do something. They were an unruly lot, who were renowned in their area for truancy and addiction. They had at one time even created hindrances for the community in their PAR activities.' Rajib decided to take them on as a challenge. He thought that it was because of a dearth of cultural outlets that the youth of this community was festering in negativity. The creation of a theatre group among these youth would be one way to address this problem and also to take the confidence-building measures among the community one step further. But the task would be an up hill one. The time for rehearsals were fixed from 7 to 9 pm, yet no one appeared. All kinds of excuses were given. Rajib then used an animator from his team who was younger and could become friends with them. He started to present the work so that it would be of interest to them. He got them to discuss themes which they thought were problems in their society. Once they came up with the themes he got them to portray them with action. Gradually their appearances increased and became more punctual. They started showing commitment towards the development of their own community, which went a long way in enabling them to come up with a significant production.

Rajib held a 15-day workshop with these youth. In his report to RIB he elaborated the steps that he followed in his workshop:

1st step: 'Our' (the community's) Poverty: Review the current situation of the Sweeper Community and discuss whether this could be changed.
2nd step: Do we want change? If so what kind of change and how would we bring that about?

3rd step: Transformation: To transform these problems into a story or representation, one that is realistic. To discuss what aspects of development we should give priority to and to construct a story on that basis.
4th step: Change the story or representation: At the time of presenting the story to the community, the story will be changed according to the suggestion of the audience. As a result of this collective inquiry, the potential for change will become clearer.
5th step: Return to reality and change: The theatre group will assemble once again to discuss the potentialities for change and to take steps to bring about change in the community through self-transformation.

The first three steps were taken during the 15-day workshop, while the second two were part of the performance and its aftermath. During the workshop Rajib also introduced elements of acting, drama, composition, movement, singing and choreography to the youth. For example, he would show the participants how to form a bridge by using their combined bodies, or a tubewell (hand pump).

After this stage he would ask them to form groups of four or five and discuss the problems they faced in their day-to-day lives. The youth have come up with problems like having to use a single tubewell for the whole community and hence stand in a long line just to brush their teeth, or they mentioned how their leader would cheat them of their daily wages because they did not know how to read or write. After presenting their problems in the form of 'scripts', each group would be asked to enact them as a performance. Dialogues would be free flowing. Rajib would guide only some of the actions to help make them more expressive.

THE THEMES OF THE PRODUCTION

In a series of discussions the youth groups decided to call their production 'Alor Shondhaney', literally meaning 'In Quest for Light', and implying their search for self-knowledge or raising their self-awareness; the following theme or themes for the production also emerged from these discussion:

Scene 1
Ram Lal was a sweeper in a large office. He wished to make his son Hari Lal into a high official. He sends his son to school after asking the blessings of his grandfather.

Scene 2
But at school other boys refuse to sit next to him. One boy makes him sit in the back-bench. A more progressive school-teacher intervenes and makes him sit in front. Another hot-tempered teacher, however, beats him and is lazy in his teaching methods. Generally there are no external markers to say that he is from a sweeper community but in a closely-knit community one generally knows the background of each person.

Scene 3
After returning from school, Hari starts to play marbles with his friends. At one point they start fighting.

Scene 4
In another scene the marriage ceremony of Chanda is enacted. Here Hari Lal is sitting with others at the wedding feast. But he is not allowed to sit and eat together with others even in his own community (this was the issue of intra-caste discrimination mentioned before, one that sparked the whole idea of demanding a theatre) as there is also an internal ranking system whereby some castes are considered more untouchable than others.

Scene 5
At the wedding ceremony, many in the sweeper community celebrated by drinking alchohol. One of them brought with him a friend called Proloy. But Proloy comes from the elite strata of society and refused to shake hands with the rest of the community.

Scene 6
The next scene is of a grandfather who gets depressed when telling stories to his grandsons because the sad ending of his stories are too real for him.

Scene 7
Several young boys were involved in gambling. They get into a wild fight and one boy gets killed.

As any theme in forum theatre should be, these scenes were simple, rough-shod and end in disastrous consequences. It is up to the audience and the animator to transform these scenes into better outcomes for the community. As it stands, they speak of the negative sides of the life of the sweeper community. The title speaks of the wish of the youth and community members to change this situation, to aspire for a world without discrimination and humiliation. As Rajib says, 'for the real development of villagers, "problem identifying" theatres are more important than "problem solving" theatres. This is because the audience, in this case, the community, takes initiative for collective inquiry into their problems and enters into dialogue with the actors to change the situation. This boosts their morale and self-confidence. Through this process, therefore, the theatrical method gradually becomes an "incessant social process" of problem identifying dialogues'.

EXAMPLE OF AN ACTUAL PERFORMANCE

To demonstrate how the interaction between the audience and the actors may generate a new discourse, I will draw some instances from an actual performance.

In scene one, when Ram Lal was sweeping the floor of the office of his boss, his boss scolded him in foul language for not doing his job during 'Holi', which was, as it turned out, one of their most important religious festivals. Someone in the audience pointed out that they did not get any official holiday during Holi, so technically the office was not closed. The boss then pointed out that if he had known it was 'Holi' he would have let him off for that day, but Ram Lal did not notify him. Ram Lal was therefore asked to notify on such occasions, so that his boss did not need to scold him again. In scene one, when Ram Lal sent his son Hari Lal to school, Hari went to get the blessings of his grandfather. But the grandfather was sceptical. He muttered that this should not be. From time immemorial they were sweepers, and a sweeper's son is destined to be a sweeper. Why waste time on education. A woman and girl in the audience protested and stopped the scene at this point. They reasoned with the grandfather to send his grandson off with his blessings, since times have changed, and education can change one's destiny. It was especially interesting and quite overwhelming to see two women come and argue on stage with the grandfather in a community, which was still very much steeped in patriarchal values. It should be mentioned that women generally do not have a voice in this society, but they were gradually becoming vocal about their rights during the discussions held in their PAR groups. They raised the question as to why it is only men who decide for the whole community as elders.

In scene 2, almost everyone in the audience stopped the scene when the Harijan boy was asked to sit at the back of the class. Here the animator, Rajib himself, came forward and took advantage of his special audience from RIB and asked Professor Anisur Rahman, who was in the audience, to give reasons as to why he thought that the boy should be allowed to sit with others. This created a warm feeling among the audience as they felt that their guests too were included in their collective inquiry. It gave a special meaning to their efforts.

THE CREATION OF ACTORS-ANIMATORS THROUGH INTERACTIVE THEATRE

Rajib's success in the sweeper community inspired him and RIB to undertake a follow up project where Rajib, with the help of his institution Centre for Development Theatre (CDT) based in Kushtia, would develop a body of animator-actor-musicians who would engage themselves in participatory action research as well as experiment in adopting the techniques of forum theatre to the rural Bangladesh scene by incorporating different indigenous folk elements like *Kobigaan* (a battle of wits through music between two bards) and *Palagaan* (songs through which a story is told) and by using invisible theatre in buses and trains on public

issues. In his experimentation, Rajib has deliberately chosen his animators from different sections of society – teachers, students, musicians, and folk theatre artists – so as to be able to reach different socio-economic groups. In the section below I will outline Rajib's efforts in his development of forum or interactive theatre.

PERSPECTIVES FROM THE FIELD

In the following section, I offer some observations from a field visit I made to Rajib's ongoing project. Rajib and his team of animators continued to work from Kushtia, but this time instead of a specific community, his field constituted a rural setting at the one-village union of Haripur, a kilometre or so across the sand-filled banks of the river Gorai. Haripur, as we heard later, was a huge village consisting of 28,000 voters and many neighbourhoods. As it was in commuting distance with Kushtia, there was a large number of professionals and small businesses in the area. Families like these were well educated, but in poorer neighbourhoods illiteracy went hand in hand with a high prevalence of dowry, child marriage, gambling, addiction and rape. It was reported that when gambling dens sit together, creditors lie in wait for people to lose so that they give them immediate credit to make good their losses. This has also been a theme for theatre activists to explore.

After introductions with his team of animators cum artists-musicians, Rajib showed us a video of the processes through which he gains validation from the people about the theme of his drama. The themes of his plays are usually drawn from real life situations, which surface in the discussions held by participatory action research groups. We were supposed to witness one such validation of a theme, the theme of a rape and consequent suicide of a 12-year-old girl. This was to be followed by a discussion with the animators. After lunch, we were then to see the actual performance of an interactive drama called

Putuler Biyey (literally Doll's wedding, a drama against child marriage). This too was to be followed by a discussion.

In order to gain credibility in the village Rajib had befriended the household of Omar Chacha (Uncle Omar), who has a tea shop outside Rajib's office in Kushtia and is a resident of the village. Whenever doing a show, Rajib and his team use his house as an anchor point. They also practise in a space which they rent out from a private coaching centre, whose teacher is one of their animators. All this gives them a platform in the village. Rajib has deliberately chosen his animators from different sections of society so as to be able to reach different socio-economic groups.

THE VALIDATION OF A THEME

Rajib and his team usually validate the theme of his drama from the area where the real life incident actually occurs. Rape is quite a common occurrence in that area. The issue of rape first surfaced in a PAR group discussion when a 12-year-old girl was gang raped by boys linked with the power structure. It seems that it was not an uncommon occurrence in that village due to the near total absence of law and order. Lacking a support system, which could give her some form of justice or reprieve, the girl committed suicide seven days after the rape. Daily, the mother was seen crying in the spot where she was raped. One day some persons brought her over to the group and asked her to tell the story. The theatre team then enacted the story in a play.

It was this play for which Rajib's team sought validation in the same neighbourhood where the incident occurred. Although the drum beats and the fanfare drew the crowds together rapidly, there was tension in the air. We were told that the mother of the raped girl, clad in a black *burqah* (Islamic dress), was in the audience. The crowd watched the play as if in a trance. Effort was made to keep a light tone at the beginning in order to give some relief and this contrasted with the tragic end of the play. By the time the play ended,

students returning from school and even teachers from the adjacent *madrasah* (Islamic school) joined the crowd. We heard later that the four rapists were also present during the play but had left just as the animators started seeking validation from the audience. The mother too had shifted to the back of the audience, peering out between two women to see the play. During the validation the animator asked the question whether such an incident was true in their lives and society and whether this should be turned into a play so as to prevent it from happening again. The audience all replied in the affirmative. One man and woman whose daughter had suffered such a fate three years ago and were still fighting a case in court in vain started to speak out, but their voices were restrained by the animator. Rajib later told us that they were poor and were under threat from the powerful elements in the village, and too much exposure on their part would endanger their position. They were sensitive to their situation.

After the validation, we met with the mother of the girl. She was in tears, but spoke of the incident. She kept lamenting that she could do nothing to prevent her suicide. Threatened by the rapists, both mother and daughter had been intimidated and had kept the incident to themselves and hence had felt isolated. It was only during the PAR discussions that these issues had been raised in public. If continued, it is expected that the PAR groups could act as counselling and solidarity groups to prevent future incidents like these, though one may also need counselling support or capacity-building workshops.

EXAMPLE OF AN INTERACTIVE THEATRE PERFORMANCE IN A VILLAGE

Rajib has been experimenting with different forms of drama. One of the standard forms he had been using was a modified and adapted version of the forum theatre. He had further adapted this form into the Bangladesh scenario by incorporating folk forms such as *pala gaan* (where a story is told through songs and dialogue). The essence of interactive theatre is the interaction with the audience, where the audience, after having seen the unfolding of the plot, then identifies the problem and helps to change it for the better.

The plot enacted that day was about child marriage. Two friends decided to get their teenage son and eight-year-old daughter married off without consulting their near and dear ones and even coerced the Imam Shahib (Islamic priest) and Union Parishad (local government) chairman into performing the marriage ceremony. Both bride and bridegroom were oblivious about what they were doing. As years went by the teenage boy grew up and developed relationships of his own, thus discarding the early marriage by sending divorce papers to his hapless 'child bride'. The animator then asked the audience whether they had seen this happen in their lives and whether they could change the turn of events.

As the scenes were re-enacted the audience stopped at the scene where the fathers had decided to marry their children without consultation with anyone else, especially the mother of the bride. Some people thought that mothers should be consulted. But the actors playing out their role contested and provoked the audience. Security of the girl-child, her sexuality and, women's decision-making power were all brought out as issues. This set off a heated discussion about women's sexuality, where men became openly aggressive and abusive in their views about women who do not observe *purdah* (i.e. segregation). But the day was saved by both Rajib as animator and a level-headed 13-year-old girl from the audience (later joined by another girl of her age) who argued logically with the bride's father and the groom and stopped the marriage from happening. Incited by the animator, she played out the role of a friend to the child-bride to be and went in search of the young groom to dissuade him from taking a step he did not fully comprehend. They urged him to continue his education and instead of getting angry

with his father urged him to level with him in his own terms. The theatre therefore demonstrated that some women in the audience as well as the future generation had a positive attitude towards the banning of child marriages. Men were more ambivalent about it.

DISCUSSION OF THE PERFORMANCE

After the validation and play, discussions were held with the animator-actors in a nearby coaching centre. The discussions after the play were especially interesting. While everyone agreed that the form that Rajib used was highly effective, they nevertheless had many questions relating to it. Some were more specific to the play, others had more generally to do with method.

It was pointed out specifically that though the drama had ended on a positive note as a result of interaction from the audience, the conclusion did not make it clear to the audience that the law of the land in fact forbade child marriage. Rajib replied that this was possibly due to the way the scenes were constructed and played out. Because the first scene depicted the social pressures of child marriage, the resolution veered towards a more social solution rather than a legalistic one. This could be looked at in a positive light as well and would have been ideal if it would have supported an already legally aware constituency rather than being placed at the cost of it.

This led to the discussion as to how much an animator or animator-actor should retain control in the interactive phase. Often it was found that the interaction led to a wide number of issues, which in turn led the discussion astray from the problem originally posed to the audience. A balance needed to be struck between discussing the core issues and other issues relevant to the core ones. It seemed that no one strategy would be adequate, but rather that the animator needed to retain a degree of flexibility as well as a conceptual grounding of the issues being raised. In order to do this effectively, it was felt that the animators needed some reading materials and discussions with resource persons in this matter.

The participatory element in Rajib's PAR practice was also discussed. Although empathy with the audience constitutes the epitome of such practice, it was found that emotionally high-strung individuals often got overexcited in their animation work. This had a tendency to impede participation. As many observed, the animators were often taking on too many issues all at once, often at the cost of going in depth into one particular issue. It was felt that follow-up discussions among animators would help resolve this dilemma.

CHARACTERIZING INTERACTIVE THEATRE AS A DISCOURSE OF TRANSFORMATION

Rajib's experiments with interactive theatre in the Bangladesh context seem to have contributed towards the construction of a discourse of transformation. First I will outline some of the characteristics of Rajib's interactive theatre, which have underpinned such a discourse. I will then go on to conceptualize as to those components or elements of theatre that have actually catalysed such discourses of transformation and, as such, have critically enhanced the traditional practice of PAR. First, the characteristics:

Interactive Theatre Situated Within the Context of PAR

The experiments of interactive theatre have been situated within the context of PAR. In both the case of the sweeper community as well as in the village of Haripur, the practice of PAR had to be introduced prior to or at least simultaneously with interactive theatre practices. Thus it is important to realize that interactive theatre in both cases was not practised in isolation but within a culture which engenders an 'incessant social process of problem identifying dialogues'.

Animation Techniques and Processes Unique to Interactive Theatre

Rajib has used the mirroring principle as a central concept in sharpening his animation technique. This has been at the core of the problem-identifying nature of interactive theatre. The audience observes the enactment of the scenes as in a mirror. The scenes reflect what happens in reality. They are therefore representations, which because of their closeness to reality elicit emotional responses from the audience but, because they are representations, may be intervened with, stopped at any stage and changed for the better. Such change may then be carried out by the audience members themselves through the continuing practice of PAR in the area.

Adaptation of Folk Forms

In order to help the audience relate more closely to the performance Rajib has adapted many indigenous folk forms into the performance because folk theatre in the rural scenario is often the only means of entertainment. People therefore only accept it on its entertainment value. Rajib has therefore tried to retain the entertainment even in sequences which are grim and serious, such as the consequences of rape or child marriage, in order to draw the attention of the crowd. Rajib also found a way to draw the attention of the crowd in the first place. When going to a location to perform, the group is usually accompanied by drummers. The sounds of the drums not only act as an announcement of their performance but, while drumming and dancing, they create a space for the performance to take place as crowds gather round them.

Self-Transformation of Animators and Catalysts

It was mentioned before that Rajib chose his animators from all walks of life, some professional musicians and actors, some teachers, in order to gain acceptability among all strata of society. But whatever their background, they were all required to be animators and performers. Each had to animate and perform in turn, so that no division of labour was imposed. Some refused to perform in the beginning, but had to give in to the requirements of the group. Later they developed into excellent performers, since what they were doing was so close to real life, and the characters they represented were really inside them and around them so that the expression of their traits became almost effortless. It must be mentioned that there was no learning of lines and the actors were only given a sketchy outline on which they were asked to improvise. One of the performers confided to us that he had no inkling of acting before he came and was hesitant in venturing into this field. But this very same person gave such a brilliant impersonation of a cunning and devious Union Parishad (local government) chairman that his appearance at once brought out vile words from the villagers. On probing deeply he revealed to us that he had in his mind a close uncle who had acted as his prototype!

Apart from the actors and performers, Rajib came across many people in the field who were touched both personally and professionally by his work. One such person was Forhad Hossain, the Social Welfare Officer of Meherpur Thana (Police Station), who accompanied Rajib in all his performances. He confided that he had dabbled in left politics during his student days, spurred on by idealism to do good for people. In his current position as social welfare officer his enthusiasm had been ebbing. Seeing Rajib's theatre technique gave him new impetus in his work. He was convinced that this was an ideal way to reach the ordinary people of Bangladesh. He admitted that he was so caught up with this endeavour that he often spent more time with the actor-animators than he did with his two-year-old daughter at home.

Follow-up Mechanisms

Perhaps one of the weakest points in Rajib's experimentation has been the dearth of follow-up mechanisms. Two kinds of follow-up may be mentioned. One is the follow-up immediate to the performance. Here some kind of follow-up mechanism could be found, when the audience continued to discuss the play in their daily conversations as part of the process of collective inquiry. Where PAR groups were already meeting, the discussions were more structured with the potential of resulting in collective or remedial action. The second kind of follow-up referred to the phase when Rajib and his team would withdraw from the area. In neither area where Rajib had operated were there any signs of the performances being continued after his departure, even when there were trained actor-animators around.

However, there has been an area where Rajib's effort has been successful, and that has been the practice of interactive theatre in another of RIB's PAR projects, among the very oppressed youth groups of the Rishi community (leather workers), who like the sweeper community have been structurally marginalized and discriminated against in mainstream society. Rajib has been asked to offer the teenagers of Paritran theatre a training workshop and in barely six months they have given over 20 performances in various districts in their area and have recently been invited to perform in Italy! Needless to say this was their first ever trip abroad. But more important for their development was their success in helping to project the problems of the Rishi community to villages near and far, thereby gaining support and solidarity for their cause.

CONCEPTUALIZING INTERACTIVE THEATRE AND PAR IN A DISCOURSE OF TRANSFORMATION

Both interactive theatre and PAR have common objectives. They aim to transform or change. Both employ the critical role of the animator and both engage collective and dialogic reasoning as opposed to individual rationality. But what are the components of interactive theatre which, through catalysing processes of change, have critically enhanced the praxis of PAR?

First, the element of role-playing, which engages both audience and actors in a dialogue is critical to the process of transformation. Generally in a PAR session, even familiar issues are often discussed with a general sense of distance or objectivity. One loses this sense when one plays the role of a victim of rape or discrimination. The person's being is therefore transformed. This is true both for actors and spectator. Moreover, the constant switching of roles, as in the case of the spect-actor, brings about a fluidity, which may be compared with the process of praxis in PAR. In PAR the cycles of reflection–action–reflection which constitute praxis are deliberated over a long period of time. In interactive theatre the timescale is reduced. In a matter of moments the spectator (observer) turns into an actor and back into a spectator. As such there is rapid movement from reality to representation and back to reality. This is a mental exercise which can greatly contribute to an ongoing practice of PAR.

Second, theatre implies an embodiment of emotion and drama, both of which are forms of expression. In PAR the animator's role is to assist the breaking of mental barriers and thereby reveal possibilities of change. Animation is effected through enabling a rational dialogue. Actor-animators, however, have the freedom to use emotions and a heightened sense of drama to engender and enable expression of views among the audience. Thus in a way they are more powerful than their PAR counterparts and therefore have to be more careful and skill about using such powers. But if skill orchestrated, the interaction may be very fulfilling in achieving the right result, as was the case in the example portrayed earlier.

Finally, as much as theatre enhances the expression of different emotions, and thereby provides a site for catharsis, it also gives a kind of protection to actors and audience alike to express those emotions in a safe manner. For theatre is after all a representation, not reality. In enactments of rape or violence in a rural setting it is possible for the audience to become visibly disturbed, but the presence of actor-animators are there to ensure that such expressions are conducted in a safe atmosphere. Since the theatre takes place in a public setting, where the general trust normally prevalent within PAR groups is absent, this is no doubt a more challenging and risky task for the actor-animator but one that is greatly rewarding.

REFERENCES

Boal, Augusto (1985) *Theatre of the Oppressed*. London: Pluto.

Freire, Paulo (1974) *Pedagogy of the Oppressed*. New York: Seabury.

Rahman, Md. Anisur (2004) *Participatory Action Research: Learning from the School of Life*. Dhaka: RIB.

RIB (2003) *Conception and Research Ideas of Research Initiatives*. Dhaka: RIB.

Tilakratna, S. (1987) *The Animator in Participatory Rural Development (Concept and Practice)*. Geneva: ILO.

36

Changing the Culture of Dependency to Allow for Successful Outcomes in Participatory Research: Fourteen Years of Experience in Yucatan, Mexico

María Teresa Castillo-Burguete, María Dolores Viga de Alva and Federico Dickinson

We report about a 14-year-long participatory research (PR) process in a coastal village in Yucatan, Mexico. In this process we identified several factors and dimensions that strengthen the PR process and should be taken into account when developing PR: communication and conscious interrelation between PR agents; visualization of the PR process from different points of view; recurrent and systematic motivation and empowerment. We also experienced some factors that limit attaining proposed PR objectives: patronage relationships; gossip; lack of seriousness; and technical errors made by us. After the analysis of this process we conclude that: (1) a long-range approach is useful in PR for understanding how the learning acquired in the process is applied to the facets of daily life; (2) young people use PR learnings to change their reality; (3) interdisciplinarity is highly useful since the problems addressed with PR are typically complex, involving social, political, economic, cultural and environmental aspects; (4) participation is part of a community's cultural capital; and (5) PR process agents must invest abundant time, effort and feedback to promote horizontal, multiple leaderships, manage resources, negotiate agreements, account for actions, understand group norms, patterns and behaviors, and facilitate learning in action.

In this chapter we report on and discuss a 14-year-long, participatory research (PR) project. This process was implemented in The Port, a small coastal village in Yucatan, Mexico, the 586 inhabitants of which share a strong Mayan cultural ancestry. Our main goal is to identify the strengths and weaknesses of the PR process, as well as some of the variables that supported or undermined what we suggest is a paradigmatic PR case involving an academic group and a community.

The process has included community organization and participation on health and environmental concerns. Issues addressed since 1992 include lack of healthcare services, design of a community health program, experimental implementation of a double-dry latrine, alcohol use patterns and building of several palafitte (i.e. houses built on stilts to avoid flooding) prototypes.

Our contributions include suggestions that: (1) a long-range approach is useful in PR for understanding how the learning acquired in the process is applied to the facets of daily life, both at the family and community levels; (2) young people use the look–judge–act routine to change their reality; (3) interdisciplinarity is highly useful since the problems addressed with PR are typically complex, involving social, political, economic, cultural and environmental aspects; (4) participation, understood as a component of the socialization and resocialization processes, is part of a community's cultural capital; and (5) PR process agents (i.e. *facilitadores* [facilitators] and *acompañantes* [companions]) must invest abundant time, effort and feedback to promote horizontal, multiple leaderships, manage resources, negotiate agreements, account for actions, understand group norms, patterns and behaviors, and facilitate learning in action. We can synthesize this last point in the words of Heron and Reason: 'good research is research conducted *with* people rather than *on* people', (2001/2006: 179).

In 1990 we began the Ecological, Social and Health Assessment Program in a rural municipality in the Mexican state of Yucatan (Ortega and Dickinson, 1991). The overall goal was to improve the studied community's health and well-being through their members' active participation in the formulation and evaluation of activities and programs aimed at satisfying needs they identified and/or sustainable resolution of priority problems identified by a research team. The project was planned as a long-term (10-year) applied human ecology program, and included participative research (PR) as a collaborative work methodology focused on creating bonds between scientific researchers and the community. In the spirit of collaboration between university and community proposed by Brulin (2001), over the years the Ecological, Social and Health Assessment Program has brought together natural and social scientists from the Center for Research and Advanced Studies-Merida (Cinvestav), a federal research center, the Autonomous University of Yucatan and other research and education institutions in Mexico.

Our choice of PR methodology for this project was influenced by the presence of a *patronage* or *paternalist* culture in Mexico that was actively fomented by the *Partido Revolucionario Institucional* (PRI) during its 71 years (1929 to 2000) as the sole political party in the country. In the words of Bobbio and Matteucci, paternalism is 'a social policy, tending to the citizenship and people's well being, that excludes their direct participation; it is an authoritative and benevolent policy, a popular relief activity, exercised vertically, applying administrative methods' (1982: 1193–4). Goods distribution in this kind of system is independent of the desires, needs and analysis of a country's citizens (Dieterlen, 1988). Indeed, it can be a negative force because it infringes upon the basic right of people to plan and implement their own life plans by making them dependent on government policies.

Patronage has deeply infiltrated Mexican culture and extends even to the family and community levels, where people have internalized the dynamic of receiving benefits in return for a minimum of effort, for example in exchange for their vote in elections. Aside from the negative consequences patronage has had in the political, ethical and social aspects of national life, it has also distorted the socialization of children. It has blocked development of the perception that participation is a cultural capital that must be fomented, as well as the recognition that individuals and groups can develop the skills needed to identify, analyze, and solve problems. The very nature of PR strengthens these civil and social values and is therefore a very effective tool in the fight to metamorphose this culture of patronage into a more socially-engaged system.

The initial phase (1990–1) of the Ecological, Social and Health Assessment Program was aimed at assessing the ecological, socioeconomic and health conditions of two human communities in Scorpion Tree Municipality: The Town and The Port. The results from this phase were to be used as baseline data for assessment of future changes, and to be presented in feedback workshops in both communities as potential inputs to the PR process we discuss here. From the very beginning of the program, we invited civil, educational and religious institutions, as well as people seen as prestigious within the communities, such as midwives, healers, and elderly people, to form an Advisory Committee for the program. This Committee helped the *acompañantes* (explained below) to better understand local background and the opinions and expectations of the people in both communities.

We chose the PR methodology for the Ecological, Social and Health Assessment Program because it is a theoretical-methodological tool for generating creative and intellectual processes that consciously involve a population, motivating its members to increase their understanding of, and ability to autonomously identify, prioritize and resolve their problems (Schutter, 1981, 1996; Hall, 1989; Castillo et al., 1997). This approach has been nourished over the years by the experience of hundreds of people in over 60 countries, actively involves communities in knowledge production, and combines social research, educational work and action (Schutter, 1981, 1996; Hall, 1989) while emphasizing that people involved in a PR process participate in knowledge production, research development and transformation of their reality (Barquera, 1986). Reason (1994) also suggests that this process moves towards empowerment and training (i.e. skills acquisition and development) as part of the construction and use of communities' own knowledge, as Reason and Bradbury (2001/2006) and Lykes and Mallona (Chapter 7 in this book) also argue.

Participatory research has benefited from the contributions of Paulo Freire and Orlando Fals Borda. Both have worked to make PR a tool people can use to solve their community's problems by adopting them as their own, and which they can appropriate for their own autonomous use to apply however they choose (Barquera, 1986).

PARTICIPATORY RESEARCH AND THE ECOLOGICAL, SOCIAL AND HEALTH ASSESSMENT PROGRAM PROCESS

The Setting for our Participatory Research

What we call 'The Port' is a small coastal village in Yucatan, in the southeast of Mexico, with a population of 586 inhabitants who share a strong Mayan cultural ancestry. The main productive activities are artisanal fishing, salt extraction and coconut production, though ecotourism is growing in importance. Most inhabitants profess to be Catholic (70%; other denominations include Pentecostal and, more recently, Jehovah's Witnesses), and half of those older than 12 years of age have not finished elementary school (Castillo, 2001).

Our application of PR requires two key groups: facilitators and *acompañantes*. *Acompañantes* is derived from the Spanish verb *acompañar* (to go with or accompany somebody). We use *acompañantes* (the noun) in the sense reported by Clinton (1991) of *acompañamiento* (the action) 'used by Latin American development workers to describe a relationship with communities, groups and individuals that fosters mutual support, trust, a common commitment and solidarity' (Whitmore and McKee, 2001/2006). Facilitators are community members skillful in the use of PR methodology who facilitate the process for the community as a whole. *Acompañantes*, in this case, are scientific research team members who train the facilitators in PR methodology, philosophy and use, accompany them during its application, provide feedback, systematize data and, upon request, contribute useful information to the community development process. In this chapter, we use the verb 'to train' to indicate development of skills or habits in the analysis and solving of community problems; in other words, the empowerment of people taking part in the PR process through guided experiential learning of skills and obtaining the information needed to negotiate with government agencies and NGOs. In training we work together with facilitators to assist them in learning how to more effectively access and negotiate with people and institutions outside the community that provide funding, information and other resources. This assistance is transitional and is, in fact, second-order learning, i.e. a type of learning to learn, development of skills for accessing sources of continuing information and the resources needed to defend their community and improve its well-being by way of recognizing and using new resources.

Our PR process typically includes a three-step routine with five stages. The steps are *look*, *think* and *act*; these allow the facilitators to diagnose and hierarchize their community's problems (Stringer, 1996; Viga et al., 1999). The stages are:

- *Convocation*, in which community facilitators are invited to form part of a group interested in addressing certain problems.
- *Training* of facilitators in PR methodology.
- *Analysis-Action* is implementation of the look–think–act problem-solving process for a selected problem.
- *Evaluation* of the results obtained and the difficulties faced during the process; of the didactic materials used; and of facilitator and community attendance, participation and interest during the different process stages.
- *Celebration* of the process.

Sometimes, as occurred in The Port, the PR group begins a new cycle at the analysis-action stage once the celebration stage has passed, making the on-going process a metaphorical spiral. The PR process ideally develops reiteratively, returning repeatedly to community problems but advancing with each curve in the spiral as knowledge acquired in the look–think–act cycle is applied to new challenges (Figure 36.1).

The PR process in The Port began when the *acompañantes* made a graphic presentation at a community workshop in 1991 of the main results produced by the Ecological, Social and Health Assessment Program scientific team; the workshop was attended by the program's Advisory Committee. At this presentation the *acompañantes* invited people interested in working towards solving community problems to form a PR group. This convocation was attended by men and women from the community, although mostly women came, some with their children. The first three or four meetings were devoted to explaining that we were not going to be giving away chicks, provisions, fruit trees or anything else that many other organizations often do, particularly the government. Our offer centered on generation of knowledge that would help them to improve their well-being, which initially brought laughter, since the attendees were a bit incredulous. Attendance diminished in progressive meetings until about 10 to 15 people remained who continued attending regularly. Later we were told that those who had stopped coming did so precisely because they realized that we were not going to give them what they had expected. We know from Castillo's (2001) work in The Port that the people who regularly enrolled in the PR process belong to the community's group of regular participants.

The training stage was done in about five sessions of 1.5 to 2 hours each, and was focused on showing the commonality of the situations to be analyzed, forming facilitators and *acompañantes* into a group, and demonstrating that the task ahead would not be easy; this is partially reported elsewhere (Dickinson et al., 1998; Pyrch and Castillo,

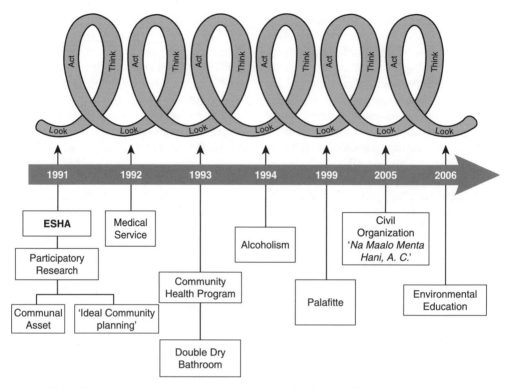

Figure 36.1 *Participatory research process in The Port, through time*

2001). It should be stressed that according to PR methodology *acompañantes* should form part of the PR group, on a par with the facilitators. Maintaining this role in practice has proved quite difficult because the facilitators have looked to the *acompañantes* for group leadership, asked them to solve problems, and expected them to make decisions, especially the hard ones. We have been extremely careful to follow the methodological rules controlling our role in the group. For the purposes of this chapter we treat the terms 'facilitators' and 'PR group' as synonymous, and make *acompañante* participation in the group explicit.

The first PR process activity involving the facilitators was an 'ideal community' exercise in which they formed five groups to analyze the community's shortcomings and express how they would like their community to be. Each group expressed its ideas in the form of

drawings and then presented them to the rest of the facilitators. Based on this activity they decided to work to remediate some of the problems and received training in PR methodology for this purpose. Once trained they carried out a diagnosis of the actual community that showed the community's main problems to be linked to water quality and supply, the limited electrical grid, narrow roads into town, alcoholism, lack of healthcare, lack of boats, pests in the coconut plantation, clearing of abandoned lots and summer homes, control and cleaning of the wetlands near the town center, and trash on the beach (Castillo et al., 1997). The facilitators then hierarchized the problems and identified the primary problem for resolution as lack of healthcare.

During the following meetings the PR group gathered information that would enable them to act. This information showed that The Port inhabitants could theoretically receive medical attention in the clinic in the municipal seat through *Solidaridad* (Solidarity), a federal health program servicing the unemployed or workers without social security. However, transport to the municipal seat was not easy and so they had to travel to the clinic the day before to get an appointment for the following day, or leave very early in the morning and risk there not being any appointments for that day. In emergencies they would go to other public or private health institutions.

As part of the *look* step of the PR methodology, the facilitators reported that, before beginning the PR process, community members had met with health authorities to arrange for a doctor from the *Solidaridad* clinic in the municipal seat to see patients in The Port. These authorities told them they would need to prepare a space in which to have the appointments, and they built a Mayan style, palm-roofed house, fulfilling their end of the agreement. The federal health authorities, however, did not fulfill their part of the agreement (Castillo et al., 1997), and The Port still had no health care services.

The facilitators continued gathering data to better understand their options, and realized they needed to comprehend the official criteria for healthcare resource allocation, including the number of physicians in the state, the towns where they were stationed, the number of towns in the state without healthcare service, the number of physicians coming to the state to fulfill their social service requirement, etc. One result of this research was that they found out that a physician was stationed in a state health services clinic in a nearby town, leading to comments such as:

The port right nearby is smaller than ours, here we're bigger ... but we don't have a doctor or a medical clinic, while they have a good clinic, doctor, nurse and they give them medicines ... if they [the people] need to visit the doctor they can because he's always there, he stays there almost all the time ... he [the physician] only leaves one day when he gets to rest; it's good there. (Several women, talking among themselves in a PR group meeting, 1993)

In the *think* phase the PR group analyzed the problem's origins and consequences, its relationship to other problems, and the possible strategies for obtaining the desired medical services, including directly requesting them from the state governor.

This analysis served to identify what to do in the *action* phase. By this time the facilitators already had a well-developed panorama of the available traditional treatments for some diseases, how long healthcare had been lacking and of the available state medical services. This knowledge and the facilitators' drive to have healthcare services led them to negotiate independently with authorities at different levels, such as the municipal president, the heads of different health services in the state and the personnel staffing these services. This was a crucial stage because the facilitators had to negotiate with both state and federal health authorities who tended to impose their power and tried to block the facilitators' initiatives (Castillo et al., 1997). Despite these counteractions, they maintained an autonomous approach, using documents and meetings with state and federal health authorities to negotiate healthcare services for the community.

With community backing, the facilitators arranged for the state government health services to provide medical attention in The Port once a week, and to train and maintain a medical assistant there. In our perception, the facilitators' success was the result of their greater organization capacity, which allowed them to more effectively negotiate with the health authorities. The community committed to pay the physician's transport costs and a fee for each patient. Representatives of the *Solidaridad* program committed to guaranteeing that the clinic in the municipal seat would remain open to provide medical attention to The Port community if they requested it. The state government health services met its commitments and *Solidaridad*, once again, did not, as shown by comments like this one:

In the meeting with the IMSS-Solidaridad doctors they said they would continue giving appointments in The Town, open for all those who wanted, but when we go, the nurses and doctors make fun of us, and say that despite everything we go to appointments there, but we made ourselves heard. We don't like this, it's bad that they do this, there's no reason for them to do this, they must meet their commitment without having to say anything to us or requiring anything from us. (Middle-aged woman, restaurant owner)

Among the facilitators who attended the meetings was the municipal commissary, who also attended council meetings in the municipal seat. On one occasion he commented to one of us (M.T. Castillo) that he had submitted a request for construction of a more formal clinic to the council to 'see if it came to anything'. Once he finished his term as commissary he stopped participating in the PR group, but a couple of years later the state government approved the first stage of a clinic for The Port. This highlights the utility of contacting the 'right' people as part of the process; it may not produce immediate results but can bring long-term benefits.

In 1992 the PR group began working towards obtaining healthcare services and by 2006 had succeeded in having a health center built of concrete with a waiting room, office, hospitalization space, and a living space for the physician with a kitchen and bath. The center is run by the state health services, which, since 1995, has staffed the clinic with physicians doing their social service. The physician remains in the community six days a week, and has a support staff of two nurses. The physician and nurses treat emergencies and implement a preventative healthcare program in tandem with a community committee. Both the medical attention and medications provided in the health center are free of charge. The community is now negotiating for a dental care unit.

As of 2006, people from the municipal seat come to appointments in The Port clinic. Community members say those from the municipal seat come because they are treated well, the physician is good and they are given their medicines. If there is no transport back to the town the physician takes them back in his car. They add:

it's a pleasure that at the clinic even people from The Town come to appointments here. This means they like it. (woman, homemaker, no children)

We're not envious, if the doctor sees them, great, it's always people who need the service and it's no inconvenience to us that they come here, on the contrary, we like it that people are well. (local fisher, father of two children)

STARTING AGAIN

Once the initial approval had been given for a physician to periodically see patients in The Port, the PR group (facilitators and *acompañantes*) evaluated the process, including accomplishments, to see what worked well, the mistakes made, and the materials and dynamics used. The facilitators expressed that:

at the beginning of the PR process we doubted the efficiency of its organization and negotiation to obtain medical care; this doubt was overcome by achieving the immediate objective, which coincided with the community workshops for the end of the second project stage in which the community was informed of the results of the scientific studies done in the first stage, including that there was a high incidence of parasitism in child and adult populations, which greatly surprised the community. (Castillo et al., 1997: 248)

After the evaluation, there was a party to celebrate the accomplishments, and the entire process, as a way of leaving a mark on the group's and the community's memories.

Upon re-entering the PR spiral (Figure 36.1) at the *look* stage an analysis was done showing that the medical service helped cover part of the health problem, though it did not completely solve it. In response, the facilitators developed a Community Health Program with four levels (individual, family, community and environment) intended to improve the living conditions of groups and individuals. This program guided two of the next three process stages: parasitism in humans (discovered in the first phase of the Ecological, Social and Health Assessment Program);

and local alcohol use patterns. In this chapter, we only want to stress relevant events within these stages.

To address the environmental and community levels of the Community Health Program, the PR group experimented with a 'double-dry toilet'. Two aspects stood out during this stage: (1) the PR group decided to experiment before taking large-scale measures; and (2) while the PR group was analyzing the human parasitism problem, the State Health Ministry offered to build the community bathrooms with conventional toilets. Using the PR methodology, the PR group decided that the Ministry's offer was inappropriate for The Port, given its environmental and economic costs, and the community as a whole agreed.

Outstanding aspects of the alcohol use patterns issue included that: (1) the PR group designed the research and, when discussing the timetable for application of a questionnaire to several groups in the community, the facilitators informed the *acompañantes* that they would do the work by themselves, in their free time during the day, and refused the *acompañantes*' offer of help; (2) some of the women in the PR group faced their husbands' opposition to participating in such a fractious issue; and (3) the PR group managed to convince municipal authorities to impose hours for the sale of alcohol in the community. Several years later, we learned that this last achievement is still considered a relevant success by several facilitators.

The latest issue addressed by the PR group has been the design and building of palafittes – houses built on stilts to avoid flooding. This stage of the PR process has produced a number of remarkable results: (1) the 'double-dry toilet' experience opened facilitators to experimenting with the building of a prototype palafitte; (2) they designed the house together with architects; (3) they took part in building the house; (4) they persisted in the project, even though the overall community was skeptical about the project's success and teased the people who would live in a raised house; and (5) the

facilitators decided to incorporate themselves into a formal civil organization called *Na Maalo Menta Hani* ('strong, tall house' in the Maya language). This civil association is focused on the building of palafittes and repair of existing family homes; it can also receive donations without them being channeled through CINVESTAV.

REFLECTION FOR FUTURE ACTIONS

Over the past 14 years we have identified a number of factors and dimensions that strengthen the PR process and should be taken into account by anyone interested in engaging in this kind of community work: communication and conscious interrelation between facilitators and *acompañantes*; visualization of the PR process from different points of view; recurrent and systematic motivation; empowerment; and linking facilitators with outside agents.

Communication among acompañantes, facilitators, the community and all kinds of authorities leads to an understanding of perceptions, feelings and expectations that generates confidence in participants, improves decision-making and problem-solving, and supports PR processes and their promotion. Conscious *interrelation among* all parties involved in the PR process, in all its stages, helps to strengthen mutual respect, the commitment and will to continue in the action, security and confidence in the problem's solution and credibility within the workgroup. This was manifest during the healthcare services negotiation process in which the state health authorities accepted the facilitators as legitimate interlocutors, made agreements with them and then fulfilled those commitments.

Comprehending the PR process from an anthropological point of view allows a deeper understanding of communal processes and adjustment to them, a strengthening of a community's own cultural decisions and elements, and blocking of any that might be imposed from outside. The PR process we have participated in as *acompañantes* has shown us that if a community has enough timely, accurate information it can make its own decisions, such as rejecting the plan to build bathrooms thought inadequate given the community's economic and environmental conditions. Understanding it from a psychological point of view prepares us for individual and group interaction in accordance with the interests of the majority of participants.

Motivation stimulates and maintains interest in participation, increases group confidence, results in more efficient decision-making, promotes multiple leaderships, and favors criticism, self-criticism, evaluation and the tenacity to confront problems. Lack of *motivation* within the PR group and community contributes to generating disinterest in problem-solving as well as producing boredom and apathy. This occurred when the facilitator group was analyzing the alcoholism problem and its members were discouraged when a new liquor store opened, the women had to confront criticism and faced arguments with their husbands, who reproached them for getting involved in this divisive issue.

Knowledge of PR allows facilitators to understand and independently apply the methodology, improve their learning, motivation and communication, as well as clarify participants' actions, and thus contribute to empowerment of community members and groups (e.g. women). Indeed, we have reports that the PR methodology has been spontaneously used by children who want to do things like sell lemonade to summer tourists.

Linking of facilitators with different types of authorities at different levels, institutions of higher education, research centers and non-governmental organizations has positive effects on meeting objectives, provides more information, a better knowledge of problems and greater understanding of communities. The civil association formed as part of the palafitte project has been able to successfully interact with official programs like the Mesoamerican Biological Corridor, an environmental preservation program financed by the World Bank to obtain resources for service projects (e.g. rental of umbrellas and lounge chairs for the beach) that help to raise community well-being.

We also experienced a number of factors that limit attaining proposed PR objectives, including: patronage relationships; gossip; lack of seriousness; and technical errors made by *acompañantes*.

According to our field notes, some facilitators reported that their understanding of PR had allowed them to act of their own volition to solve problems, without waiting for others to solve them, as is the custom in some paternalist government practices (Dickinson et al., 1998).

Gossip blocks and distorts communication between facilitators and other community members, and even with authorities, and favors interests external to the PR group. A recent example (Dickinson et al., 2006) was the dissemination of unfounded rumors about the financial contribution of the participants in construction of the first two palafittes; this caused a number of people to distance themselves from the PR group.

Lack of *seriousness* in commitments acquired by PR group members, be they *acompañantes* or facilitators, leads to lack of punctuality, absenteeism, loss of commitment and confidence, data repetition and limited accomplishments. This was problematic in The Port, where fishing and tourist services, the two main occupations, are seasonal, leading to absenteeism at community activities (Dickinson, et al., 2006).

Technical errors like repetition of data and activities by *acompañantes* notably lower interest in participating. To avoid these kinds of errors in our work at The Port we improved meeting planning and recording to prevent data repetition and were more attuned to non-verbal expressions showing boredom or disinterest.

WHAT WE LEARNED ABOUT PR THAT WE CAN TAKE WITH US

1. Uncertainty of the Medium-term and Hope of the Long-term

The experience we have gained in developing a PR process within a culture with strong anti-participation forces has forced us to visualize a broader time frame within which to propose the desirable future scenarios that were shaped and clarified in the rush of the short-term, the uncertainty of the medium-term and the hope of the long-term. This allowed us to observe some of the desired positive changes, like dominion of the PR steps by some of the participants and their generalization into private spaces and environments, such as the family, to help in decision-making.

It was especially rewarding to see the children and young people we knew yesterday become today's adults, and witness their different experiences using the *look–think–act* routine to change their reality. Thanks to this experience we remain hopeful, we now recognize that no dream can escape the passage of time, and that despite this reality, and no matter how audacious it may be, progress can be made in reaching that dream.

2. The Value of Interdisciplinarity

Another vital aspect derived from our PR work has been the value of *interdisciplinarity*. This collaborative work perspective has helped us understand the importance of approaching complex, interconnected problems with openness and flexibility, especially when faced with conflicting disciplinary perspectives. At times this also allows previously unknown and neglected individual abilities, like creativity, to fluoresce, and promotes the analysis and synthesis needed to support words and actions. All this is accompanied by constant movement among the incorporation, management and control of scientific and popular languages; it is no small challenge.

3. Training Facilitators or Acompañantes

Our experiences in training *human resources* during this long-term PR experience in The Port gave us a metaphorical perception of the learning process (skills, attitudes, knowledge and values needed to develop the PR process) as a kind of cone that widens over time, broadening with each new start. For us, this notion is implicit in PR and implies that facilitators need the capacity to invest lots of time, effort and feedback for the PR process's medium- and long-term development. When *acompañantes* participate for long periods of time, as is the case here, the resocialization process experienced by facilitators and *acompañantes* is based on mutual respect, self-criticism and openness to change. These aspects are fundamental to adopting horizontal, multiple leaderships; managing resources; negotiating agreements; accounting for actions; understanding group norms, patterns and behaviors; and facilitating learning in action. The capabilities (i.e. the skills, attitudes, knowledge and values) of both the facilitators and *acompañantes* taking part in a participatory research process should grow over time, expanding the number of tools available to confront and solve problems and then consequently improve lives.

4. Understanding Community as a Prerequisite to PR

Building on Castillo's (2001) proposals, we suggest that understanding *community* is fundamental to PR because a community's complexity transcends the physical place and the different groups of individuals and interests within it. It is a social system in which a number of interrelationships and interactions occur that constitute family, religious, legal, economic and cultural life. The field work experience in The Port (Castillo, 2001) made it clear to us that an efficient PR process requires previous knowledge of a community's annual calendar, the spaces and subjects around which participation occurs, which community members participate and in what activities (e.g. religious, civil, productive, recreational) and the existing relationship networks for participation and community life in general.

We believe that the experiences we share here can be replicated and improved because the methodological phases and steps needed to generate the PR process are conceptually simple – however, not everyone can easily behave in a way that is congruent with PR and especially not in a culture preconditioned by patronage. The greatest challenge is modifying the human factor, and particularly teaching individuals the value of respect for others and, given the current environmental crisis, for nature. Each community, region and country is home to valuable people just waiting to grow, and the PR process can allow them to do so. *Participation*, when grounded in and linked to the *socialization* of children and *resocialization* of adults, gives us a better understanding of how it becomes *cultural capital* (Bourdieu, 1987, 1988; Pérez et al., 2003). The incorporation of cultural capital can guarantee the maintenance and development of important social communication networks, facilitate data management and decision-making, and contribute to changing participants' adverse social reality to one of development and well-being. In our view this theoretical perspective strengthens the PR proposal.

Finally, we believe that in all these years of understanding, designing, implementing, evaluating and enriching, the PR process has given us an excellent opportunity to identify our own errors – trying to participate in a community without fully understanding it, not recognizing seasonal variations in participation due to the community's annual calendar (Castillo, 2001), not always using accessible, understandable language (Dickinson et al., 2006) – and then to correct them, share them and so learn to be better human beings.

DEDICATION

To loving memory of Armando Kantun-Reyes: his happiness and joy of life will be with us for ever.

ACKNOWLEDGMENTS

We acknowledge financial support of IDRC (3-P89-0270 and 91-0240), Fondo Mexicano para la Conservación de la Naturaleza (A2-99/002), CONACYT (28402-S) and Cinvestav. Especial thanks to Yoland Wadsworth and Peter Reason for their help and to Ernie Stringer, Robert Chambers and Hilary Bradbury for their criticism of early versions of this chapter, and the generous support of Betty Faust on reviewing proper meanings in English, her native language, for our Spanish constructs.

REFERENCES

Barquera, H. (1986) *Una revisión sintética de investigación participativa*. Pátzcuaro, México, Centro de Cooperación Regional para la Educación de Adultos en América Latina y el Caribe (CREFAL) 18: 36–49.

Bobbio, N. and Matteucci, N. (1982) *Diccionario de política*. Madrid: Siglo XXI.

Bourdieu, P. (1987) 'Los tres estados del capital cultural', *Sociológica*, 5: 11–17.

Bourdieu, P. (1988) *La distinción. Criterio y bases sociales del gusto* (trans. M.C. Ruiz). Madrid: Taurus.

Brulin, G. (2001) 'The third task of universities or how to get universities to serve their communities!', in P. Reason and H. Bradbury (eds), *Handbook of Action Research: Participative Inquiry and Practice*. London: Sage. pp. 440–6.

Castillo, M.T. (2001) *Relaciones de género en los ámbitos de participación comunitaria de un pueblo de la costa yucateca*, Tesis de Doctora en Antropología Social, Departamento de Ciencias Políticas y Sociales. México, D.F: Universidad Iberoamericana.

Castillo, T., Dickinson, F., et al. (1997) 'Investigación y participación comunitaria, experiencias de resocialización en Yucatán', in E. Krtoz (ed.), *Procesos de resocialización en Yucatán*. Mérida, México: Universidad Autónoma de Yucatán. pp. 227–57.

Clinton, R.L. (1991) 'Grassroots development where no grass grows: small-scale development efforts on the Peruvian coast', *Studies in Comparative International Development* 26 (2): 59–95, quoted in E. Whitmore and C. McKee (2001) 'Six street youth who could...', in P. Reason and H. Bradbury (eds) (2001), *Handbook of Action Research: Participative Inquiry and Practice.* London: Sage. pp. 396–402.

Dickinson, F., Viga, D., et al. (1998) 'Communal participation and sociocultural change in rural Yucatan: participatory research, health, and quality of life', *Human Ecology Review,* 5 (2): 58–65.

Dickinson, F., Viga, D., Lizarraga, I. and Castillo, T. (2006) 'Collaboration and difficulties in an applied human ecology project: implications for the local coastal environment', *Landscape and Urban Planning,* 74: 204–22.

Dieterlen, P. (1988) 'Paternalismo y estado de bienestar', *Doxa,* 5: 175–94.

Hall, B.L. (1989) 'Investigación participativa, conocimiento popular y poder: Una reflexión personal', in G. Vejarano M. (ed.), *La investigación participativa en América Latina.* Pátzcuaro, México, Centro de Cooperación Regional para la Educación de Adultos en América Latina y el Caribe (CREFAL), 10. pp. 15–34.

Heron, J. and Reason, P. (2001/2006) 'The practice of co-operative inquiry: Research "with" rather than "on" people' in P. Reason and H. Bradbury (eds), *Handbook of Action Research: Participative Inquiry and Practice.* London: Sage. pp. 179–88. Also published in P. Reason and H. Bradbury (eds) (2006), *Handbook of Action Research: Concise Paperback Edition.* London: Sage. pp. 144–54.

Ortega, J. and Dickinson, F. (1991) *Ecological, Social and Health Assessment (Mexico).* Final Technical Report of the Phase I. Mérida, México, Centro de Investigación y Estudios Avanzados del Instituto Politécnico Nacional-Unidad Mérida y Universidad Autónoma de Yucatán.

Pérez, A., Castillo, M.T. and Viga, D. (2003) 'Cultural capital, gender relationship and community participation', presented at the conference 'Social Science Beyond Bourdieu', University of East London, UK, (June).

Pyrch, T. and Castillo, M.T. (2001) 'The sights and sounds of indigenous knowledge', in P. Reason and H. Bradbury (eds), *Handbook of Action Research: Participative Inquiry and Practice.* London: Sage. pp. 379–85.

Reason, P. (1994) 'Three approaches to participative inquiry', in N.E. Denzin and S. Lincoln (eds), *Handbook of Qualitative Research.* London: Sage. pp. 445–62.

Reason, P. and Bradbury, H. (2001/2006) (eds) *Handbook of Action Research: Participative Inquiry and Practice.* London: Sage.

Schutter, A.D. (1981) 'Método y proceso de la investigación participativa en la capacidad rural', in F. Vío Grossi, V. Gianotten and T. d. Wit (eds), *Inestigación participativa y praxis rural. Nuevos conceptos en educación y desarrollo comunal.* Lima: Mosca Azul. pp. 155–94.

Schutter, A.D. (1996) *Investigación participativa: Una opción metodológica para la educación de adultos.* Pátzcuaro, México, Centro de Cooperación Regional para la Educación de Adultos en América Latina y el Caribe (CREFAL).

Stringer, E.T. (1996) *Action Research: a Handbook for Practitioners.* Thousand Oaks, CA: Sage.

Viga, M.D., Dickinson, F., et al. (1999) 'The impact of training in participatory research on the behavior of school children: an experiment in the Yucatan', *Human Ecology Review,* 6 (2): 62–71.

Whitmore, E. and McKee, C. (2001/2006) 'Six street youth who could...', in P. Reason and H. Bradbury (eds), *Handbook of Action Research: Participative Inquiry and Practice.* London: Sage. pp. 396–402. Also published in P. Reason and H. Bradbury (eds) (2006), *Handbook of Action Research: Concise Paperback Edition.* London: Sage. pp. 297–303.

37

Health Promotion and Participatory Action Research: The Significance of Participatory Praxis in Developing Participatory Health Intervention

Lai Fong Chiu

The public health movement has spurred an increasing number of community-based parti-cipatory interventions. Although participation is asserted as an important quality criterion, how such quality can be achieved in practice has been less well understood. This chapter explores participation as a set of practices that embodies first-, second- and third-person research perspectives through an inquiry into the 'what', 'who', and 'how' of participation. The concept of participation that emerges from the exploration is complex. It is evident that participatory practice is multi-faceted and is contingent upon situational and structural power relations. Researchers are urged to seek a clear conceptualization of participation through reflection upon its practical consequences. Only by facing contradictions, predica-ments and uncertainties that arise when working towards participation can the potential and limitations of participatory health intervention practice be better understood.

The core principle of the new public health movement is the recognition of the need for tackling the wider determinants of health – the social and environmental factors. Empower-ment, community participation and capacity building are increasingly seen as strategies for achieving systemic change. Lending support to this movement is a broad knowledge base developed under the rubric of health inequali-ties. This ranges from the influence of income, ethnicity, and class (Townsend et al., 1992; Davey Smith et al., 2000), through social inclusion (Shaw et al., 1999; Percy-Smith, 2000) to the importance of lay knowledge and citizen participation (Williams and Popay, 1997). Yet contrary to this development, health intervention research in the UK is dominated by research practice that remains by and large conventional. Health improvement programmes continue to focus narrowly on ill health and diseases, e.g. diabetes and obesities, and tend to seek solutions from cognitive and behavioural sciences in the hope of changing individuals' behaviour (Crowley and Hunter, 2005).

Nevertheless, and despite this contradiction, the popularity of community-based participatory intervention across countries such as Canada (e.g. Potvin et al., 2003), the USA (e.g. see review by Viswanathan et al., 2004), and in Wales in the UK (Whitelaw et al., 2003) is on the rise. Community participation is often asserted in theory as an important quality criterion of this type of intervention, but in practice it appears to be less well understood. Attempts have been made to generate principles for implementing participation (Potvin et al., 2003) and to devise 'objective measures' or indicators for evaluating the process (Naylor et al., 2002). However, the principles generated by and large merely restate the principles of participatory action research (PAR) and measurements devised are too crude to provide insights into the participatory process. Attempting to rationalize complex processes such as participation at the expense of research reflectivity and reflexivity has meant that the strategic and contingent nature of participation has been overlooked. The opportunity to understand the very process – participation – that has been advanced as a crucial strategy for the new public health movement thus appears to have been missed.

Perhaps, the influence of the rationalist account of participation in health intervention can be traced back to the unproblematic appropriation of the concept of 'ladder of participation' propounded by Arnstein (1969). In PAR discourse, participation[1] is frequently asserted to be a continuum with the extremes defined by co-option and collective action, and with the quality of participation determined by who has power to control the research process (Hart, 1992; Pretty, 1995). From this position, quality is assumed to be negatively correlated with the degree of control exerted by the researcher (Cornwall and Jewkes, 1995). Although the assertion that community participation brings unqualified benefits has since been revised (Irvin and Stansbury, 2004) as well as refined (Webler, 1999) in other disciplines, the bi-variate (power and control) theory of participation has remained unchallenged in PAR.

Like many other health promotion practitioners, I was enthused by the empowerment and participation principles enshrined in the Ottawa Charter of Health Promotion (World Health Organization, 1986)[2] and found these principles converged with PAR/practice. I have since conducted my health promotion research in the PAR tradition. Three key projects that furnish much of my PAR experience in health promotion are: (1) Communicating Breast Screening Messages to Minority Ethnic Women: constructing a community health education model (Chiu, 1993); (2) Woman-To-Woman (W2W): promoting cervical screening to minority ethnic women in primary care (Chiu, 1997, 2000): 3); Straight Talking: communicating breast-screening messages in primary care (Chiu, 2002).

The iterative critical learning that I have gained from each successive project has challenged my conception of participation and empowerment. My current experience from the project entitled: Communication for Health (C4H): The Efficacy of Participation Videos in Promoting Access to Breast Screening Information among South Asian and Chinese Communities (2004–December 2005) has provided insights into different aspects of participatory practice that challenge further some of the paradigmatic and hegemonic assumptions made in PAR about participation, empowerment and their relations to social transformation. I began to question my own understanding of and skills in facilitating participation and began to re-examine the notion of participation.

This chapter is an exploration of participation practice (praxis) grounded in my own experience of PAR. Critical reflection on relevant examples of my research experiences from the first-, second- and third-person perspectives reveals the obvious limitations offered by the bi-variate conception of participation. Indeed, the concept of participation that emerges through iterative cycles of action and reflection is complex. It becomes evident that participatory practice is multi-faceted and is contingent upon situational and structural power relations. Therefore, the challenges ahead in practising participatory health intervention in the context of public health and health promotion are considerable. In my view, these challenges can better be met by achieving a clear conceptualization of participation through reflection upon its practical consequences (Burch, 2006). The following is an illustration of this perspective.

PARTICIPATORY PRAXIS

The early characterization of PAR – specifically those projects that are perceived at the emancipatory wing of action research – as third-person inquiry (Reason, 1994; see also Introduction and Chapter 16 in this volume) might have influenced the ways we think about our research conduct (Chiu, 2006). In a complex social system, existing institutional and organizational practices play a major role in facilitating or impeding people's involvement. The key role of the researcher, his or her competence in first-person research practice, is central to participatory practice and is often ignored or omitted in the reporting of research results (e.g. Naylor et al., 2002; Potvin et al., 2003). As Fisher and Torbert (1995) have suggested, first- and second-person inquiries often presuppose the success of third-person inquiry. To ignore these components would be to distort participatory processes and to obscure power relations between the researchers and the

participants. To aid discussion, I will define the set of complex practices that facilitate participation as participatory praxis, which describes transformational research practice that embodies the first-, second- and third-person's perspectives. This term has its roots in the Marxist philosophy of praxis in which transformative social action is brought about by the dialectic of theory and practice (Korsch, 1970 [1923]), and in the more recent interpretation by Freire in which transformational social practice is based upon cycles of action-reflection, where deliberation, choice and rationality are emphasized (Gadotti, 1996). It acknowledges the different forms of participation and the multi-faceted ways in which these can be facilitated through the plurality of knowing and doing. Deliberation, choice, rationality, aesthetic and affective sensibilities are all important elements for facilitating participation. While much of the quality of the research relies on the quality of participation praxis, the development of a researcher's participatory praxis is always subject to the limits of his or her history and a necessary situated perspective. These assertions are explored below.

WHAT TO PARTICIPATE IN?

Influenced by the community development movement and the Ottawa Charter, heath promotion practitioners often perceive the way to bring about changes is to immediately tackle the social determinants of health, e.g. income distribution, unemployment, poor transport and housing. However, what they can actually do or research into is often constrained by their structural position as well as their own personal disposition. On reflection, my appropriation of PAR as a form of research/practice was driven by my practical experience in community work and my frustration with the inadequacy of orthodox research to address the immediate needs of minority ethnic and low-income groups. However, I soon found that under the political, organizational and practical constraints of the UK National Health Service, there were limits to which and how these needs could be addressed. While successive health policies have emphasized user involvement (Department of Health, 1999a, 1999b, 2002), no substantial resources have been allocated to develop this approach in health promotion. Contemporaneously, health agendas and targets have been set centrally. The first breast screening project was an attempt to mobilize resources that were directed at providing services to instead develop participatory health intervention, hoping that by its introduction into the medical environment it would redress the consistent failure of orthodox research to inform practice. However, this attracted criticisms from both sides. Many practitioners saw this as an opportunistic grafting of community development on to service improvement and a sell-out to the medical model, while medical practitioners were sceptical or even felt threatened by the involvement of lay people to deliver health education/promotion initiatives. Outwardly, they were concerned as to how complex medical information could be understood by untrained community members. But inwardly, they were possibly worried that their professional authority was being undermined (Allen et al., 2001).

Practising PAR in a period in which progressive health policies have collided with deep-rooted traditional professional practice has been challenging both intellectually and emotionally. Paradoxically, it has become a fertile training ground for the plurality of knowing and doing through self-reflection, mutuality and collective learning (Torbert, 2001/2006). Admittedly, participatory praxis developed out of the series of PAR projects mentioned above cannot be compared with the community development practice of large demonstration development projects such as those carried out by community development corporations in the United States (Gittell and Vidal, 1998), as our projects are small in scale and their influences are confined to a health service setting. Paradoxically, the pragmatic goals and clear boundaries of these projects

have enabled PAR to develop systematically and iteratively. Successful completions of these projects have demonstrated that the idea of participatory health intervention is capable of yielding interesting results. This experience is encapsulated in the Community Health Educator Model (Chiu, 2003), through which the philosophy, theories and practice of PAR are articulated. This model has now been adopted by many health districts across the UK, in different shapes or forms. So, I have in effect turned the constraints of my social (minority ethnic) and professional (researcher) position into opportunities and strengths, through which I can continue to develop PAR within the area of cancer screening.

THE 'WHO' OF PARTICIPATION

While conventional researchers formulate sampling strategies to study particular populations, PAR researchers face choice points as to which communities to involve in the projects. In the UK, epidemiologists have long highlighted the health differentials between ethnic groups (Balarajan and Soni Raleigh, 1993; Senior and Bhopol, 1994). In addressing inequalities, conventional intervention research influenced by epidemiology often targets certain particular disadvantaged groups such as minority ethnic[3] and low-income groups. This, coupled with studies that attribute ethnicity in the forms of language(s) and culture(s) as key barriers to low uptakes of service, means these groups are often portrayed as not only having information deficits but also as being socio-cultural deviants. This reification of social grouping in conventional intervention research through the adoption of social groups as independent variables is so common that individuals or groups are imperceptibly stripped of their agency, thus creating its own contradiction in bringing about change in health interventions.[4]

The distorting influence of the conventional research paradigm may be seen even in the choices of groups that a project could involve. When constructing our research proposals, terms such as 'African Caribbean' and 'Asian' suggested by funders were often found to be too broad to inform strategies for local involvement on the ground. The former might, for example, encompass people from Jamaica, Trinidad, Haiti, and the Dominican Republic, as well as people from the whole of the African continent, while the latter includes Indians, Pakistanis, and Bangladeshis but in practice might exclude Sri Lankans. Because these short-hand abstract terms tend to ignore the complex socio-political and migration histories of minority groups, the huge ethnic, linguistic and cultural variations among them are subsequently obliterated. For example, South Asian dialects such as Murpuri, Punjabi, and Urdu as well as English were simultaneously spoken in the Pakistani community. The Ugandan Asians speak English, Gujarati, Hindi and/or Punjabi; and Syhleti was the major dialect of the Bangladeshi community. Depending on their birthplace and education, the Vietnamese might speak French, English, Mandarin Chinese or Cantonese; younger members of the Chinese community might speak English, Cantonese or Mandarin; while most of the older members of the community in Britain speak Hakka as their mother tongue and Cantonese as their second language.

Understanding and acknowledging linguistic and cultural diversity is fundamental in engaging minority ethnic groups in participatory health intervention. The concept of 'language community' is not only a useful organizing tool for recruitment of participants but also a tool for dialogue and conscientization. How otherwise could we facilitate open communication that focused around critical inquiry and analysis of participants' own circumstances? If we could not provide conversational space where they could 'speak a true word' and overcome their 'silencing' (Freire, 1970, 1994) about their cultural conditions and identities, how could we know what they are thinking or feeling about their own sufferings, and how could we know what to do to support any changes that might improve their predicaments? Without attending to and respecting participants' diverse

everyday languages, understandings, and ways of life, it is hard to say that our practice adheres to the emancipatory tenets of PAR. In addition, language, be it spoken or written, is central to the subject of our research (communicating breast screening messages) and to the products of our study (producing a community health education model and multilingual materials to support it). We thus decided to give it primacy over ethnic category. As a result, this approach enabled us to recruit a total of eight language/ethnic groups and six language/ethnic groups in the breast screening project and the Woman-to-Woman project respectively (see Table 37.1).

Other problems that we had in involving local groups based on official abstract ethnic categories stemmed from the variations of settlement patterns of different ethnic groups. For example, while it is relatively easier to involve the Pakistanis in major cities as their communities are larger in number and are likely to have well-established local political and social infrastructure, the reverse is true for small market towns. It is also difficult to involve the Chinese and Vietnamese groups, as they are small in numbers and tend to have a scattered settlement pattern. When I was working in small health trusts located in northern small mining/market towns in the mid and late 1990s, I had to make strenuous efforts to liaise with other health organizations in the surrounding districts to formulate involvement strategies that could reach these groups. This was further complicated by the fact that these surrounding districts had their own small but needy communities such as the Somalis and the Yemenis, whose needs local stakeholders were hoping could be addressed in these projects. Extra funding was needed to support their involvement. After a process of negotiation, funding was only found for the Yemenis but not the Somalis because the latter were not defined either locally or nationally as an 'ethnic' group. By contrast, although the Yemenis were also not identified as an ethnic group by the national census, they were included in the project because the local authorities officially recognized them as

Table 37.1 Various ethnic groups involved in the three PAR projects between 1990 and 2002

Project	Researcher's job role (1st person)	Professional group (2nd person)	Ethnic/ language group (3rd person)							
Breast Screening	Health promotion practitioner/ researcher	University researcher, regional health promotion practitioner, radiographers	African Caribbean (English)	Bengali (Syhleti)	Chinese (Cantonese)	Indian (Hindi)	Indian (Gujarati)	Pakistani (Mirpuri)	Sikh (Punjabi)	Vietnamese (Vietnamese and Cantonese)
WTW	Health promotion practitioner/ researcher	Local health promotion practitioners, practice nurses	African Caribbean (English)	Bengali (Syhleti)	Chinese (Cantonese)	Yemeni (Arabic)		Pakistani (Mirpuri)		Vietnamese (Vietnamese and Cantonese)
Straight Talking	Researcher in a NHS Trust	Local public health specialist, practice nurses	White (English)	Bengali (Syhleti)	Chinese (Cantonese)	Pakistani (Mirpuri)				

a distinct and separate ethnic group. Their local socio-political infrastructure was well established to enable them to negotiate with agencies and authorities for resources.

Because official recognition of ethnicity status confers resources and benefits, minority ethnic groups are constantly struggling for self-identification that can maximize access to such advantages. For example, despite the label, members of the local Vietnamese group were mostly ethnic Chinese in origin. They nevertheless defined themselves as Vietnamese rather than Chinese. This self-identification might seem illogical to those who contend that the meaning of ethnicity derives from shared ancestry, language and culture. However, if we understand how resources were allocated to minority groups under different budgetary arrangements and policies, we can understand the reason for this self-identification. Defining themselves as Vietnamese rather than Chinese, they avoided competing with existing Chinese communities for resources.[5]

Social identification might generate trust; and trust is one of the major building blocks of participation. However, identification also operates on levels sometimes difficult to anticipate. For example, we sought to organize our involvement of individuals based on the languages they spoke, as we had seen that language was a fine-tuning tool for ethnic categories. Yet involvement can remain problematic due to the further unpredictability of individual or group ethnic identification. The strategy to engage the wider base of the minority ethnic communities, particularly those whose first language is not English, was through the recruitment of the bilingual community health educators (CHE). However, not long into the Woman-to-Woman project, the Vietnamese/Cantonese speaking CHE [Wendy] who was recruited through the local community centre reported difficulties in engaging with members of her community as she was identified as a Southerner while the majority of the community were from North Vietnam. I observed that in the focus groups, Wendy's attempts to facilitate

the discussion were ignored, and participants' responses were often directed to me (as I am also a Cantonese speaker), rather than to her (Chiu and Knight, 1999). This lack of identification between Wendy and her own community demoralized her and she wished to leave the project. Only after the (Vietnamese) community centre manager vouched his support was she willing to continue her involvement with the project. In a small community such as this, few women were educated or available to be involved. Moreover, because the project is time-limited, re-recruitment and re-training of another CHE was not an option. Wendy's disengagement would have dealt a heavy blow to the project.

The above observations highlight some of the complexity, indeterminacy and unpredictability of participation. Its practice requires complex negotiation between top-down interests and local conditions, and between individuals and groups. The researcher is required to understand that although everyday articulation of ethnic identities is around ancestry, culture and language, these are all subject to change, redefinition and contestation, both by individuals and the collective (Fenton, 1999). Different strategies need to develop to respond to the fluid and constructed/co-constructing nature of ethnic identities that one finds in real life.

In engaging with communities, the mismatches between the collective and the individual identification can often be found to arise at the boundary between the collective assertion of group identity and the individual's day-to-day experience of shared language and culture. The researcher has to find what unites different individuals and groups in their struggle, and seek to facilitate their co-operation with each other. It is to this aspect of participatory praxis that I now turn.

THE 'HOW' OF PARTICIPATION

The practice of PAR in health promotion has been closely associated with the 'Southern'

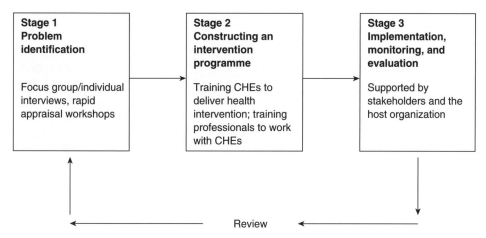

Figure 37.1 *The Community Health Educator Model in a three-stage action research framework*

tradition in which the power, dimension is explicitly addressed. However, the often too-blunt and too-simplistic description of a bi-variate theory of power, i.e. the powerful versus the powerless, system versus individuals etc., often provides little insight into how power itself can be transformed (Torbert, 2001/2006: 256). Involving minority ethnic and low-income women in our PAR projects has enabled me to deal with and reflect on the power dynamics and its transformation more attentively. The following examples illustrate how power in practice permeates all aspects and at all levels of participatory praxis and how it is enmeshed and embedded in first-, second- and third-person research practice.

Participatory Boundaries, Limits and Commitments

Perhaps the fundamental difference between participatory health intervention and conventional health intervention relates to the levels of commitment expressed by or expected of their participants. PAR's relationship to participants goes beyond a willingness to be interviewed. Or even the need for them to perceive the need for change and be willing to play an active role in both the research and change processes (Meyer, 2000). At best it can express participants' own purposes and determination. Power is deeply implicated in the notion of participation, and the transformation of power cannot simply be an issue of transfer of control as suggested in early participatory discourse. Specifically, introducing PAR in the public health/promotion arena in the Anglophone countries necessitates an awareness of political and organizational dynamics of the health systems with which researchers and participants have to negotiate. Therefore, conceiving an intervention that will take participants through the process of change requires the researcher to be able to organize both the research and action elements of the project systematically. I have found the adaptation of Lewin's research cycle useful (Lewin, 1946). The three-stage cycle – problem identification, solution generation, fieldwork and evaluation – illustrated in Figure 37.1 provides not only the basis for research plans in our PAR projects but also a platform for negotiation of involvement. This framework also gives participants and stakeholders a clear indication of the extent of their commitments and a good estimate of the resources required.

A well considered research plan communicates clarity and confidence to existing would-be participants. It also connotes the message that there are boundaries and limits within which transformation could occur and what kinds of changes might be realistically desired or anticipated.

A clear indication of the level of commitment expected of individuals is also important for second-person research/practice, as colleagues and other professionals who will most likely need to negotiate their involvement in the project with other commitments, resources and authorities. For example, in the W2W project, practice nurses of six general practices were enlisted. Many of them worked part-time on a sessional basis with their practices. Although their involvement with the project was remunerated pro-rata according to their stipend, they were not entirely free to participate on an 'as-and-when' basis, even though their involvement was linked to their professional role and the cervical screening service provided by their general practices. The transformation of their professional practice would have a knock-on effect to how these services are organized. The required changes of service provision might or might not be welcomed by practice managers or senior partners who had the ultimate power to sanction practice nurses' involvement or simply ignore their feedback from the projects. Therefore, while we might view these nurses as the more powerful partners as compared to the relative powerlessness of minority ethnic women, their power remained limited and circumscribed and subjected to the control of organizational practice. To ensure the participation of the practice nurses would be fruitful, formal letters were issued to the practices by the Directors of Public Health/Promotion to support their involvement and to recommend that nurses' feedback from the project be placed on the agenda of monthly Senior Partners' meetings of their respective practices.

I also learned that although participants were willing to be involved, the goals and plans of the projects were not necessarily fully understood by everyone, nor were they necessarily aligned with participants' interests.

Initial exploratory workshops were important to address these issues; and continual explanation, guidance and feedback were necessary to maintain or renew everyone's commitment to the project. In these workshops would-be participants were given public health information so as to sensitize them to the unequal health status suffered by some sections of their communities and the specific issues concerning access to services. They also had an opportunity to take part in visioning and self-image exercises that were designed to explore their own capacity to address these issues (e.g. Chiu, 2000). Other exercises such as values clarification, social networks and relationship awareness, conflict and negotiation skills, etc., which served to stimulate the energies of the participants, were integrated into a training programme based upon a self-analysis of participants' own training needs. Continuing commitments to the project by participants relied on programmatic feedback, setting of sub-goals, and planning actions and evaluation of these actions.

Co-researching with Participants

In all the above projects, CHEs were invited to become co-researchers. They received training and support to work with the research team to undertake various research activities, e.g. focus groups, surveys, individual interviews, data analysis as well as conducting health education sessions in their own language communities. Their roles were not necessarily well understood by conventional researchers in the team. Because of CHEs' bilingual capacity, they were often perceived as interpreters or interviewers. There can be little understanding of what co-researchers can bring to the research and how more appropriate methods can be designed through their involvement. Thus the process of co-researching with participants is educational to conventional researchers themselves.

In the Straight Talking project, CHEs were involved explicitly as co-researchers right from the outset. They conducted focus groups with participants in their own language/ethnic group, helping them to voice their experiences of services. At the evaluation stage, they were also involved in the methodological design which aimed to measure the effects of their own intervention with non-attenders of breast screening. The discussions with conventional researchers were skewed to methods such as randomized controlled trial which did not allow for the 'fuzziness' of the intervention of which CHEs were an intrinsic part. After much discussion, a compromise was reached – the design that emerged was a quasi-experiment in which pre- and post-questionnaire interviews were used to gauge changes in women's knowledge, attitude and intention to accept/refuse screening. A workshop focusing on interviewing skills and the explanation of the evaluation method was provided for CHEs. Helping them to 'pilot' the questionnaires was a key task in this workshop. To ensure the successful adoption of the interviewing method, further meetings were held with CHEs in which the process was carefully rehearsed so as to detect any translation difficulties that might arise, as well as give plenty of opportunities for CHEs to practise their interviewing skills.

Through the pilot, CHEs helped to redesign the questionnaire and they discovered that the measurement of health anxiety was also culturally inappropriate. This was specifically so for the Mirpuri and Sylheti language groups. For example, a question asking a woman whether she thinks about death frequently was perceived as meaningless, as the Islamic religion specifically requires its adherents to think of death several times a day. The Cantonese CHE also found this question culturally awkward to ask, as many Chinese people would find it 'unlucky' to answer such a question. They would also be uncomfortable with the CHE as they would think she should know better than to ask such a question. In addition, CHEs discovered that the length of the questionnaires made it difficult to maintain the woman's attention in the interview. Many questions

thought necessary from the professional researcher's point of view were perceived as repetitive and interviewees reported becoming frustrated and losing interest. Most importantly, because CHEs and interviewees usually belonged to the same community group and were familiar with each other, the 'interview' itself was perceived by women as a strange and awkward way of questioning their opinions. As a result, alterations were made to many of the questions.

CHEs' involvement in the 'piloting' and designing of the final questionnaires, to make them linguistically and culturally applicable to their respective community, was a reflection of the participatory nature of the project and, arguably, illustrative of the potential for a research design to encompass empowering elements. The responsibilities and activities of CHEs in this stage of the project represented a further development of their 'co-researcher' role established in the focus group stage. As conduits to their respective communities, the pro-active role of CHEs in the design and administration of questionnaires created a direct link between the voices of women in the community and the interpretation and dissemination of research findings.

The research processes and problems encountered during the fieldwork design were documented and reported. This allowed us to lay bare the challenges that we met. The researchers' assumptions about how best to collect information or 'data' were challenged by the realities of women's lives and how they related to each other. Together, with the CHEs as co-researchers, the team learned that interviewing with a questionnaire was a constructed social encounter, in which most women refused to take part. It is clear that had the original questionnaire been implemented, the results would have been largely meaningless, but this might not have been apparent in the absence of the insights provided by the CHEs. The dangers of a conventional, non-participatory approach to health interventions in health promotion are many and obvious. A vigorous researcher will recognize that data collection is effectively 'data construction' (Farran, 1990), and that the process of creating the measurements was crucial to the outcomes. In PAR, this process is revealed, so that the results would make sense to participants and research beneficiaries. Paradoxically, this processual knowledge is not only ignored but is seen by conventional health intervention researchers as data contamination, undermining the validity of research results.

Advancing Participation through Symbolic and Cultural Representation

The example of engaging a video production company to support the C4H (participatory videos) project highlights yet another complex dimension of participation which cannot be simply labelled as action, or co-operative, or participatory inquiries, but is in practice a mixture of all three. In this project, women from four language/ethnic communities (both bilingual and monolingual) and other stakeholders, e.g. two primary care trusts and two breast screening services, were involved in the planning, production and post-production and evaluation of the videos (see note 1). Because of the key role played by the production team in this project, the three-staged research cycle was modified into a production/research process – pre-production, production and post-production processes that everyone found easy to understand.

This project was informed by my earlier work with women on their photostories about breast and cervical cancer screening. It drew on a body of work on participatory communication for social change in which a variety of experiences from the South were represented (Gumucio Dagron, 2001; White, 2003). Rather than focusing on problems, its emphasis was on creativity and the use of symbolic representation as resources for development. On completion of the consultation process, in collaborations with the production team and other colleagues from the primary care trusts,

participants were invited to join a two-day workshop in which drama exercises and group discussions were facilitated to explore the storyline and ideas for the videos. They also had opportunities to learn camera work, as well as to construct characters and storyboards.

Through the drama exercises, participants were able to explore their feelings about breast screening in a safe environment. The drama exercises helped participants to experience the complicated feelings that a woman might go through when she first receives her screening invitation. There were also explorations of ethnic identities, culture, and language in relation to health and cancer screening. In putting the story together, while acknowledging the many barriers that women face in gaining access to screening services, participants firmly rejected the traditional portrayal of minority women as lone victims of the health system in favour of images that projected diversity and variation within their respective communities. The actions and interactions of the workshops were recorded on audio and video tapes, and formed the basis upon which the final screen scripts were written with the support of the professional writers.

The health professionals involved also checked the accuracy of technical information about breast cancer and cancer screening, while the community participants examined the cultural sensitivity of the proposed storyline. In the videos, women raised the subject of breast screening in the context of a range of family relationships and friendships – mother and daughter, sisters, cousins, and friends – and in different social settings. The diversity and differences were played out by four or five characters of different social backgrounds, presenting the audience with different emotional responses that women can have to the breast screening invitation. The story begins with one woman raising the subject in a conversation with her friends at a café. These friends play other characters in different parts of the story. These characters

Figure 37.2   *Drama workshop*

Figure 37.3   *On location*

are vehicles for exploring cancer myths and other concerns about breast screening. They end with all the friends meeting again in the café and with one of them telling the others that she went for breast screening.

As a participatory action researcher, I am mindful that the world is suffused with images, e.g. TV ads, movies, and press photographs, that perpetuate race and gender stereotypes, that in turn serve to maintain unequal social power relations. Allowing the improvization of dialogue had not only made it easier for those who were non-literate to participate in the filming but also enabled their voices to be heard in their own terms. When participants brought along their own props like roti-pans, scrolls, and wardrobe on sets, they participated more freely in the making of their own cultural images. By the very act of participating in filming on location, minority ethnic women laid a symbolic claim to these public spaces, creating a new

Figure 37.4 *Screen design*

form of social visibility, a new way of seeing our world. Thus the balance of symbolic and cultural power was transformed.

The C4H project highlighted the different dimensions that we needed to work towards in transforming power. While minority ethnic women might seem powerless in their clinical encounters with health professionals, given the opportunity, they can mobilize their symbolic and cultural resources to contest the usefulness of health education knowledge produced by routinized practice, challenging the medical orthodoxy that had hitherto paid little attention to people's languages and cultures.

CONCLUSION

In contemplating participation and power relations in the light of the above experience, it is hard to ignore the key contributions of the researcher to the process. The development of participatory praxis requires the constant engagement of oneself in a process of negotiation with a myriad of obstacles as events unfold. The reflections presented above illustrate that greater effectiveness of participation can be achieved by the awareness of one's structural relations with others vis-à-vis the system within which one works. This awareness helps one to unearth one's own assumptions and to develop 'alternative frames' (Torbert, 1991) that lead to strategic actions in response to local conditions at different choice points such as that demonstrated above, i.e. the practical and strategic use of language/ ethnic group as a tool for engaging diverse groups and communities. The emergent consequence of this strategic action was a more conscious recognition of the linguistic and symbolic power for transformation. Co-researching with participants in adopting conventional evaluation methods in the Straight Talking project has brought this power into sharp focus. The involvement of the CHEs and the problems that they encountered in conducting conventional interviews in their respective communities is a constant reminder of the gaps between the idealistic abstractions of conventional research and the social reality of inquiry. Without their contribution, results obtained – whether quantitative or qualitative – would be divorced from the life they are supposed to represent.

Working with CHEs and their respective language/ethnic communities has opened up possibilities for creative mobilization of symbolic and cultural power embedded in agency for transformation. The C4H participatory video project was a particular case in point. The opportunity for participants to construct their own cultural images and to produce their own health education resources has the greater potential to be both participatory and empowering. The videos [produced as a single DVD] epitomized the different forms of representation on different levels. The potential of these representations for cultural and psychological transformation cannot be underestimated though they are yet to be more thoroughly explored.

From this vantage point, the transformations of power that occur are often the product of first-, second- and third-person research/practice. This is a far cry from the bi-variate view of participation in which quality is determined by the power and control held or ceded by the researcher to the participants. Only by facing contradictions, predicaments and uncertainties that arise when working towards participation can the potential and limitations of participatory health intervention practice be better understood.

NOTES

1 It is unclear exactly how the concept – 'ladder of participation' developed in the field of planning (Arnstein, 1969) – has entered the knowledge/practice of PAR. According to Arnstein, participation is associated with power. The participatory ladder has eight rungs with manipulation at the bottom and citizen control at the top. Each rung represents a degree of power in influencing decisions. This bi-variate view (control and power as determinants of participation) of participation is simplistic but phenomenally influential.

2 The Ottawa Charter of Health Promotion (1986) has been phenomenally influential in developing the concept of health promotion and in shaping public health practice. The principles of empowerment and participation are enshrined in the Charter. These principals underpin the three basic strategies, i.e. advocate, enable and mediate, to enable people to increase control over, and improve their health. However, over the past 20 years there has been a recognition that the Ottawa Charter might have become a mantra, while practice is increasingly compromised to fit reality

(Kickbusch, 2005). It is, however, unclear what has been assumed under the terms 'practice' and 'reality'. This pronouncement somehow affords much about health promotion practice and implies the all too constraining properties of the socio-political environment. This chapter through participation reveals the complexity and interactive nature of practice and social conditions.

3 In both academic and lay discourse, the term 'minority ethnic groups' is used to denote population groups that have different ethnic and cultural origin or backgrounds from the majority white English-speaking populations. The term differs from the term 'people of colour' used in the US to avoid defining racial groups in terms of colours and to include other minority groups that have migrated from Ireland and other parts of Europe and, most recently, following the accession of the Czech Republic, Estonia, Latvia, Lithuania, Hungary, Malta, Poland, Slovenia, and Slovakia to the European Union.

4 The tension between structure and agency that underpins all social actions is at the heart of the debate in the new health promotion movement (Robertson and Minkler, 1994). Although epidemiologists have called attention to the materialist/structrualist's explanation of health inequalities, their approach has rendered invisible the very social relations of power structuring material and psychic conditions that contribute to the stratification of health and illness (Shim, 2002). More importantly, the notion of agency (the ability and activities of people to deploy a range of power to make and shape and reshape their world) that is crucial for transformation is imperceptibly lost.

5 Throughout the 1980s and the early 1990s under the UK Government's Urban Programme – Section 11, funding was made available to develop 'ethnic minorities' communities. The diversity that existed among minority communities had made the funding programme difficult to manage and was seen as divisive. The programme was terminated in 1995 and replaced by a single regeneration budget which is open to applications from all community groups regardless of their ethnic status.

REFERENCES

Allen, S.M., Petrisek, A.C. and Lalibert, L.L. (2001) 'Problems in doctor–patient communication: the case of young women in breast cancer', *Critical Public Health*, 11 (1): 39–58.

Arnstein, S. (1969) 'A ladder of citizen participation', *JAIP*, 35 (4): 216–24.

Balarajan, R. and Soni Raleigh, V. (1993) *The Health of the Nation: Ethnicity and Health, a Guide for the NHS*. London: Department of Health.

Burch, R. (2006) 'Charles Sanders Peirce', *The Stanford Encyclopaedia of Philosophy* (Fall), Edward N. Zalta (ed.)

[forthcoming URL: http://plato.stanford.edu/archives/fall2006/entries/peirce) (accessed 7 August 2006]

Chiu, L.F. (ed.) (1993) *Communicating Breast Screening Messages to Minority Women: a Conference Report.* Leeds: Leeds Health Promotion Service.

Chiu, L.F. (1997) *Woman-to-Woman: Promoting Cervical Screening among Minority Ethnic Women in Primary Care, a Participatory Action Research Project (1995–1997).* Department of Health Promotion, Rotherham Health Authority, Rotherham.

Chiu, L.F. (2000) 'A participatory action research study of an intercultural communication strategy for improving the experience of cervical screening among minority ethnic women in the primary care setting.' PhD thesis (unpublished), University of Leeds, Leeds.

Chiu, L.F. (2002) *Straight Talking: Communicating Breast Screening Information in Primary Care.* Leads: Nuffield Institute for Health, University of Leeds.

Chiu, L.F. (2003) *Application and Management of the Community Health Educator Model: A Handbook for Practitioners.* Leeds: Nuffield Institute for Health, University of Leeds.

Chiu, L.F. (2006) 'Critical reflection: more than nuts and bolts', *Action Research,* 4 (2):183–203.

Chiu, L.F. and Knight, D. (1999) 'How useful are focus groups for obtaining the views of minority groups?', in R. Barbour and J. Kitzinger (ed.), *Developing Focus Group Research: Theory, Practice and Politics.* London: Sage. pp. 99–112.

Cornwall, A. and Jewkes, R. (1995) 'What is participatory research?', *Social Science Medicine,* 41(12): 1667–76.

Crowley, P. and Hunter, D.J. (2005) 'Putting the public back into public health', *Journal of Epidemiology and Community Health,* 59: 265–7.

Davey Smith, G., Charsley, K., Lambert, H., et al. (2000) 'Ethnicity, health and the meaning of socio-economic position', in H. Graham (ed.), *Understanding Health Inequalities.* Milton Keynes: Open University Press. pp. 25–37.

Department of Health (1999a) *Building Healthy Communities and Tackling Inequalities.* London: HMSO.

Department of Health (1999b) *Involvement Works: the Second Report of the Standing Group on Consumers in NHS Research.* London: HMSO.

Department of Health (2002) *Shifting the Balance of Power within the NHS: Communications.* London: HMSO.

Farran, D. (1990) '"Seeking Susan": producing statistical information on young people's leisure', in L. Stanley (ed.), *Feminist Praxis.* London: Routledge. pp. 91–103.

Fenton, S. (1999). *Ethnicity: Racism, Class & Culture.* London: Macmillian.

Fisher, D. and Torbert, W.R. (1995) *Personal and Organisational Transformation: the True Challenge of Continual Quality Improvement.* London: McGraw-Hill.

Freire, P. (1970) *Pedagogy of the Oppressed.* New York: Herder and Herder.

Freire, P. (1994) *Pedagogy of Hope* (trans. M.B. Ramos). New York: Continuum.

Gadotti, M. (1996) *Pedagogy of Praxis.* New York: SUNY Press.

Gittell, R. and Vidal, A. (1998) *Community Organizing: Building Social Capital as a Development Strategy.* Thousand Oaks, CA: Sage.

Gumucia Dagron, A. (2001) *Making Waves: Stories of Participatory Communication for Social Change* (A report to the Rockefeller Foundation). New York: Rockefeller Foundation.

Hart, R. (1992) 'Children's participation: from tokenism to citizenship', *Innocenti Essay* No. 4, UNICEF.

Irvin, R.A. and Stansbury, J. (2004) 'Citizen participation in decision-making. Is it worth the effort?', *Public Administration Review,* 64 (1): 55–65.

Kickbush, I. (2005) *The Dynamics of Health Promotion: From Ottawa to Bangkok, Reviews of Health Promotion and Education Online.* [URL:http://www.rhpeo.org/reviews/2005/1/index.htm.] (access 5 June 2006)

Korsch, K. (1970 [1923]) *Marxism and Philosophy* (trans. F. Halliday]. London: New Left Books.

Lewin, K. (1946) 'Action research and minority problems', in K. Lewin (ed.), *Resolving Social Conflicts: Selected Papers on Group Dynamics.* New York: Harper and Brothers. pp. 201–16.

Meyer, J. (2000) 'Using qualitative methods in health-related action research', in C. Pope, and N. Mays (eds), *Qualitative Research in Health Care.* London: British Medical Journal Publications. 320: 178–81.

Naylor, P., Wharf-Higgins, J., Blair, L., Green, L., O'Connor, B. (2002) 'Evaluating the participatory process in a community-based heart health project', *Social Science & Medicine,* 55: 1173–87.

Percy-Smith, J. (2000) *Policy Responses to Social Exclusion: Towards Unclusion?* Milton Keynes: Open University Press.

Potvin, L., Cargo, M., McComber, A.M., Delormier, T. and Macaulay, A.C. (2003) 'Implementing participatory intervention and research in communities: lessons from the Kahnawake schools diabetes prevention project in Canada', *Social Science & Medicine,* 56: 1295–1305.

Pretty, J. (1995) 'Participatory learning for sustainable agriculture', *World Development,* 23 (8): 1247–63.

Reason, P. (1994) 'Three approaches to participatory inquiry', in N.K. Denzin and Y.S. Lincoln (eds),

Handbook of Qualitative Research. Thousand Oaks, CA: Sage. pp. 324–39.

Robertson, A. and Minkler, M. (1994) 'New health promotion movement: a critical examination', *Health Education Quarterly*, 21 (3): 295–312.

Senior, P. and Bhopal, R.S. (1994) 'Ethnicity as a variable in epidemiological research', *BMJ*, 309: 327–9.

Shaw, M., Dorling, D., Gordon, D. and Davey Smith, G. (1999) 'Poverty, social exclusion, and minorities', in M.G. Mormot and R.G. Wilkinson (eds), *Social Determinants of Health.* Oxford: Oxford University Press. pp. 211–39.

Shim, J.K. (2002) 'Understanding the routinised inclusion of race, socio-economic and sex in epidemiology: the utility of concepts from technoscience study', *Sociology of Health and Illness*, 24: 129–50.

Torbert, W.R. (1991) *The Power of Balance: Transforming Self, Society, and Scientific Inquiry.* Newbury Park, CA: Sage.

Torbert, W.R. (2001/2006) 'The practice of action inquiry', in P. Reason and H. Bradbury (eds), *Handbook of Action Research: Participative Inquiry and Practice.* London: Sage. pp. 250–60. Also published in P. Reason and H. Bradbury (eds) (2006), *Handbook of Action Research: Concise Paperback Edition.* London: Sage. pp. 207–17.

Townsend, P., Davidson, N. and Whitehead, M. (eds) (1992) *Inequalities in Health: The Black Report and the Health Divide.* New York: Penguin.

Viswanathan, M., Ammerman, A., Eng, E., Gartlehner, G., Lohr, K.N., Griffith, D., Rhodes, S., Webb, L., Sutton, S.F., Swinson, T., Jackman, A. and Whitener, L. (2004) *Community-Based Participatory Research.* Agency for Healthcare Research and Quality, US Department of Health and Human Services (Final Evidence Report).

Webler, T. (1999) 'The craft and theory of public participation: a dialectic process', *Journal of Risk Research*, 2 (1): 55–71.

White, S.A. (ed.) (2003) *Participatory Video: Images that Transform and Empower.* Thousand Oaks, CA: Sage.

Whitelaw, S., Beattie, A., Balough, R. and Watson, J. (2003) *A Review of the Nature of Action Research.* Sustainable Health Action Research Programme, Welsh Assembly Government.

Williams, G. and Popay, J. (1997) 'Social sciences and the future of population health', in L. Jones and M. Sidell (eds), *The Challenge of Promoting Health.* London: The Open University. pp. 260–73.

World Health Organization (1986) *The Ottawa Charter for Health Promotion* (First International Conference on Health Promotion, Ottawa, 21 November, WHO/HPR/HEP/95.1) [http://www.who.int/hpr/NPH/docs/ottawa_charter_hp.pdf] (accessed 9 August 2006).

38

'This Is So Democratic!' Action Research and Policy Development in East Timor

Ernie Stringer

Action research sometimes is envisaged as applicable only to localized processes within an institution or organization. As this chapter demonstrates, however, both the practices and values of action research may be incorporated into much broader procedures of national policy development and implementation. In the context of East Timor, a newly independent nation in the first stages of its emergence from a long history of colonialism, action research was used as a means of both formulating and implementing national policy. Participatory action research was used to initiate and sustain the continued development of a system of parent organizations in schools across the nation, a process of development that was consonant with the democratic values that were such an important feature of East Timorese independence. As the chapter demonstrates, action research provided the basis for development of policy related to parent teacher associations and the institution of a system of participatory development that built the capacity of East Timorese people to sustain the ongoing operation and further development of their schools.

FROM MICRO TO MACRO: POLICY DEVELOPMENT AND CAPACITY BUILDING

Much of the development literature currently focuses on the need for appropriate micro-level processes that complement structural developments at the macro-level. Stiglitz (2002) suggests that, in conjunction with pragmatic, utilitarian concerns of efficacy, development should take into account the desires and needs of those affected by government policies; to overcome the feelings of powerlessness experienced especially by the poor who feel they are voiceless and lack control over their own destiny. He notes the need for people to feel that their concerns are heard and suggests that policies, programs and services thus will gain the widespread support required of any developmental process.

This perspective is echoed throughout the literature. Krishna (2002) suggests that 'Concerted action made possible by civic associations enables citizens to engage state and market agencies more effectively … service delivery is improved, accountability and transparency are enhanced, and the pool of resources is enlarged when organized groups of citizens engage constructively with the state' (p. 1), and that 'A larger vision of human development is served when citizens' associations participate widely in diverse tasks of provisioning and self-governance' (p. 2).

As the literature recognizes, however, participatory processes are not inherently efficacious. There is a concurrent need to build the capacity of community groups to enact this vision; to acquire the social capital that will enable them to effectively work. As Krishna (2002) recognizes, a fundamental aspect of the operation of civil society organizations (CSOs) concerns the mediating role that they play between the individual and the state. The performance of government programs is improved when, instead of interacting with citizens as atomized individuals, state agencies deal with organized community groups. Citizens derive greater benefits from government programs and from market opportunities when their individual efforts are organized and made more cohesive by CSOs that apply participatory processes in the development and operation of services (Fukuyama, 2004; Putnam et al., 1993; Krishna and Prewitt, 2002).

THE CONTEXT

In the aftermath of the destructive withdrawal of Indonesia from East Timor, the nation set about rebuilding its infrastructure, creating institutions and services that would provide for the needs of the populace. Beset by the lack of both financial and human resources, the new national government, with the assistance and support of the UN and other international agencies and organizations, commenced the arduous task of building an independent 'civil society' in East Tiimor.

In conjunction with UNMISET (United Nations Mission in Support of East Timor), the new government formulated a series of national development plans that focused on the organization of government departments and institutions to provide services to the people of the nation (Planning Commission, 2002a, 2002b). As part of this process, the rebuilding of the education system was a priority, but was hampered by lack of human resources, since Indonesian professionals had comprised over 30 percent of the teachers and school administrators. Further, and most fundamentally, the Indonesian military had destroyed 70 percent of schools as they left the country, requiring East Timor to literally rebuild and re-equip the school system from the ground up.

Early in the process of redevelopment of the education system it became apparent that economic conditions would not allow the government to provide all the resources needed for the task. The fledgling Ministry for Education, Culture, Youth and Sports made the decision to engage the community in the process of rebuilding the schools through the formation of parent teacher associations. This would be a difficult task, since the equivalent bodies in Indonesian times (Baden Penyelurygara Pelaksanaan Pendidikan – BP3) were highly authoritarian and largely distrusted by local people due to their emphasis on extracting school fees from parents. Attaining parent participation in the redevelopment of the schools would be inhibited by their suspicion that authorities would once again make significant demands on the already meagre resources of East Timorese families.

THE PURPOSE: DEVELOPING POLICY FOR CIVIL SOCIETY IN A DEMOCRATIC NATION

As consultant to UNICEF I was engaged to work within the Ministry of Education, Culture, Youth and Sports (MECYS) to write a concept paper to explain how parent teacher associations (PTAs) could be developed in the nation's schools. The intent was not only to assist parents to participate in the reconstruction and operation of the schools, but in the process to demonstrate the ongoing commitment of the nation to democratic values. To accomplish this it would be necessary to engage the energy and enthusiasm of the people, to provide ideas of the way parent teacher organizations could operate, and show how parents might participate more fully in the organization, management and operation of local schools.

PROCESS: DEVELOPING PTAs IN EAST TIMOR

The establishment of PTAs in schools across the nation emerged in a number of phases (see Figure 38.1), each following, in iterative fashion, from the outcomes of the previous phase. The project covered a period of $2\frac{1}{2}$ years, and included:

1. Development of a concept paper
2. Initiating developmental processes: formulating an operation manual and demonstrating consultation processes
3. Trialing of PTA development in seven schools facilitated by the local team
4. National development: implementing a national process

At each stage, action research processes were central to the attainment of desired outcomes. Individual interviews with a sample of key stakeholders within the ministry (Minister, Director General, Deputy Director General, Directors), the schools, community leaders, and aid agencies (UNICEF, World Bank, Japanaid, IrelandAid, Oxfam, the Catholic Church, etc.) complemented consultation workshops with parents, principals, teachers, superintendents and community leaders in selected schools/areas. The results of these consultations were initially monitored by a committee comprised of Ministry stakeholders and representatives from major government, church and aid agencies (PTA Roundtable), then through a MECYS planning body – the PTA Technical Working Group – established for the purpose. The outcomes of each stage were fed into the action plans that emerged to further extend the developmental process – from a single trial school, to a sample of district schools, to core schools in all districts, and then to cluster schools in all districts. The support system that was constructed to support initial developments became a permanent feature of the organization of district education offices, and was used to sustain other needed developments – school-based management, teacher training and the introduction of a new curriculum. Thus the developmental support system that initially focused on the formation of PTAs became institutionalized, providing the means to accomplish the sustainable development of schools across the nation.

INITIATING PTAs: DEVELOPMENT AND CAPACITY BUILDING PROCESSES

On the face of it, developing a PTA in each school was a relatively simple task, requiring an elected body comprised mainly of parents to make plans for parent activities in the school. It was evident, however, that all stakeholders would need to acquire a new way of thinking about the nature of parent organizations, and new ways of doing the work so that they would not merely reinstitute the old system of parent organizations (BP3s). They would need, in other words, to acquire a new set of skills that would enable

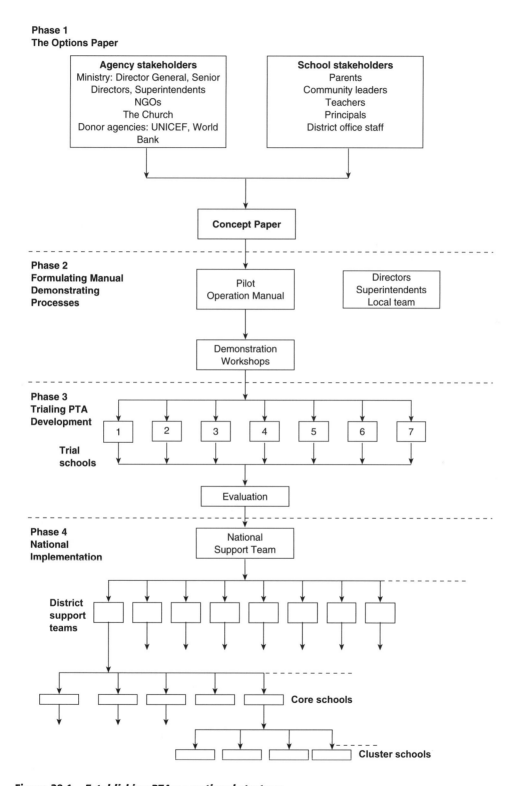

Figure 38.1 *Establishing PTAs: a national strategy*

them to create a radically different type of organization, and to carry out the diverse activities that were signaled in preliminary consultations. Developmental activities therefore needed to incorporate capacity building processes that would enable schools to achieve the outcomes that were the desired intent of the project. These became embedded into the processes, so that at each phase the different stakeholders engaged in action research routines that enabled them to acquire needed capacities 'on the job'.

Phase 1: The 'Options' Paper

Action research processes depicted in Stringer (1999, 2004, 2005; Stringer and Dwyer, 2004) were chosen as the basis for formulating a PTA policy for the Ministry for Education, Culture, Youth and Sports (MECYS). Procedures were implemented cyclically, the information and analysis from each phase being incorporated into a concept paper that was eventually presented to the Ministry and other stakeholders. Each cycle of research included:

- Framing and focusing of the issue
- Identification of stakeholders having an impact on the issue
- Gathering information from stakeholders and other relevant sources
- Distilling the information to identify key issues, ideas and elements
- Reporting on what has been discovered
- Formulating next steps (planning the next research cycle)

The purpose was to formulate joint and collective accounts that took into account the agendas and perspectives of each stakeholding group, incorporating that information into a report that clarified the issues and agendas. In the first phase of the research in November 2002 I, as project consultant, met with stakeholding agencies, including directors in the MECYS, and representatives of United Nations agencies and non-government donor organizations (NGOs) to clarify the various activities related to parent involvement in schools.

Over a period of four weeks consultative workshops were held in six schools from a variety of regions in East Timor, from middle-class urban to poor rural environments. Workshops were held in school classrooms and participating parents and teachers encouraged to express their views about the issues and problems experienced by the schools since independence, and whether or not a parent organization was needed. The meetings were well attended, with large groups of parents demonstrating by their participation their concern about the education of their children. The local language, Tetum, was used throughout, though a translator was used at times when the consultant found it necessary to speak to the meeting.

Many of the issues were somewhat contentious, and both parents and teachers sometimes became quite passionate in expressing their views about the rundown state of the schools, and the lack of available resources. In the end, though, many parents accepted the fact that in the immediate future they would need to take action if their children were to gain an adequate education. Such was the interest in these discussions that at a number of schools parents and teachers continued their meetings for some considerable time after the departure of the consultation team. Often they had creative ideas about the ways that parents could participate in the school, including teaching of traditional songs, dances and arts, assistance with maintenance of the school infrastructure, monitoring of the quality of teaching, and assistance with the behaviour and attendance of children.

On the basis of this limited number of consultation workshops, it was clear that the participative nature of the workshops was highly effective in mobilizing the potential of parents and the community. My field notes, written as I reflected on these activities, provide an indication of the extent to which the action research processes had enabled people to engage issues that were obviously of great interest to them – the education of their children:

The worn, crumbling, bare concrete floor of the classroom is framed by cracked, corroded and unpainted walls. The spaces for windows are likewise bare, not a pane of glass to be seen in the school, and window openings have no coverings except for remnants of rusted link fencing wire. A new corrugated iron roof has been inexpertly attached to the classroom walls, and lack of any ceiling means that heat from the tropical sun is radiated directly into the room. There are no doors, no furnishing, except for children's bare wooden desks and chairs, and a 'blackboard' consisting of a square of black paint on the concrete wall at the front of the room. There is no wiring for electricity and, I am told, no running water in the school. The room contained no shelving, books, charts, pictures, learning materials, and was devoid of anything resembling teaching materials.

The heart of the school is not in its physical resources, however, but is reflected in the faces of the people in the room – parents, teachers, community leaders and some educational administrators. Eager, concerned, interested, impassioned, their foreheads wrinkle in concentration as they listen to each speaker reporting back on the outcomes of their small group discussion. The apparent poverty of the bare surroundings and the heat from the tin roof are forgotten as they focus on the issues at hand – how could they ensure an adequate education for our children at a time when the new nation has so few resources.

The last speaker completes his oration and the written record of his presentation is read back to the assembled group, proof that their words have been heard and note taken of their thoughts and ideas. During a break for refreshments the team leader writes down key issues from each presentation on small charts and fastens them to the wall. As the meeting re-commences, parents gaze in awe at the sight of the representation of their own words. They talk animatedly about the issues displayed and the possibilities emerging from their intention to help teachers develop a better school for their children. An excited buzz emerges as the final comments from the principal and district superintendent thank people for their participation, pointing out that these processes represent the new ways of a democracy – the people's voice has been heard and will be acted upon.

As people disperse there is jubilation among the visiting facilitators and the administrators. Here is a process of working with the people, of building their capacity to participate in the reconstruction of the school system, of mobilizing their energies to fashion a new institution for a new nation. It gives lie to the often-heard sentiment 'The parents aren't interested in their children's education'. Given the appropriate context and the right processes they have come out in force and demonstrate both their

interest and willingness. A community of action is in the process of formation.

On the basis of information gained from these consultations a draft concept paper was formulated, outlining three possible options for the structure of a parent teacher association. This paper formed the basis for a two-day workshop with MECYS directors and superintendents, and was also distributed to other agencies and NGOs. Senior ministry directors and the Minister of MECYS were briefed on its contents prior to presentation of the final concept paper – *Parent Teacher Associations in East Timor* – to a roundtable meeting in late December 2002. The paper was accepted enthusiastically by participants at the roundtable meeting, and the Minister asked the Director General to form a Technical Working Group, comprised of senior directors, to facilitate the implementation of its recommendations.

An unanticipated outcome, at this stage, was the broad acceptance by all stakeholders of the participatory procedures used in formulating the paper. Workshops had been participatory in nature, and though they ran against the grain of traditional authoritarian styles of operation, the energy and enthusiasm that emerged was palpable. This not only set the scene for the productive engagement of parents and community leaders, but also was a clear demonstration of the efficacy of participatory, democratic procedures.

Phase 2: Initiating Developmental Processes: Formulating an Operational 'Manual' and Demonstrating Consultation Processes

The enthusiastic acceptance of the concept paper was followed by requests for the consultant to write a 'manual' that would provide guidance to those responsible for establishing PTAs in local schools. The resulting publication – *Parent Teacher Associations: Pilot Operation Manual* (Democratic Republic of East Timor,

Ministry of Education, Culture, Youth and Sports, 2003) – described processes for consulting with parents and the local community, and outlined procedures for identifying and initiating parent activities within the local school. The manual also suggested procedures for supporting parent activities, describing possible options for the structure and operation of organizations that not only could sustain identified parent activities, but also enable parents to participate more broadly in the operation and management of the school – school councils, parent councils, and so on.

The manual went through a number of drafts to accommodate inputs from key stakeholders. A workshop for key Directors of Education within the Ministry and all District Superintendents provided the means to familiarize them with details of the project, and enable them to comment on and critique the material contained in the manual.

The processes incorporated in the manual were then trialed by an East Timorese team who, in conjunction with the consultant, initiated the development of a PTA in one rural East Timorese school. Two preliminary workshops were held with teachers, the principal and community leaders to clarify the purposes and processes that would form the basis of parent workshops. This proved an important part of the process, since these key stakeholders were being asked to make a transition from well-established practices, and to understand the desired outcomes. A key epiphany emerged, particularly for village traditional leaders, when they realized that the focus was not on school fees, but on parent activities. It was a clear indication that one word can make a difference – that, in this case, the interpretation of the words 'parent contribution' related not to money, but to activities in which the parents could engage. An excited buzz resulted when, in response to a question, the audience was informed that we were talking about 'non-financial contributions'. The tenor and tone of the meeting changed immediately, and the rather hesitant response of community

leaders was replaced by enthusiastic comments and discussions about the possibilities that might emerge.

In the workshop that followed, parent groups articulated a wide range of activities in which they would be willing to participate, ranging from the construction of a fish pond,[1] to fencing for the school, and security for the classrooms. The fish pond was used as an example to demonstrate planning processes, the group of male parents responsible for the idea clearly articulating how they would acquire land, build dykes, obtain a net, obtain fish, raise them and market them. Photographs taken some months later show parents proudly displaying their fish farm, the result of their carefully planned labours.

The delight of my East Timorese colleagues was palpable. Familiar with traditional processes where passive audiences sat passively listening to extended speeches, some of which took on the air of an harangue, they were delighted by the purposeful and active participation of parents that resulted from the small group processes. As I recorded in my field notes:

> As we left the village late in the afternoon my colleagues were buzzing with excitement, their eyes shining and their conversation bubbling with the events of the day. 'Streen-gere,' they said. 'This is so exciting. This is so democratic. The people were so interested.'

Phase 3: Trialling of PTA Development

In the months following, a UNICEF/MECYS team initiated PTA consultation and development processes in six core schools in diverse locations across the nation. Workshops with parents, teachers, principals, and community leaders in each of these schools assisted participants to identify activities, create action plans, and develop the organizational basis for a PTA. Working under the direction of the Ministry Technical Working Group (TWG) comprised of Directors of Education, the field support team visited pilot schools, working in conjunction with a staff member from each district office.

Some months later a one-day evaluation and planning workshop was held in each of the pilot schools. This provided an opportunity for participating pilot schools to review the progress of their PTA developments and to plan their 'next steps', enabling Ministry and UNICEF stakeholders to judge the effectiveness of the initial developments in the process.

The enthusiasm and dedication for participants was most evident. Under the most trying of conditions parents waited patiently for workshops to commence – sometimes waiting an hour or two when travel difficulties delayed the facilitators – and continued in the tropical heat to concentrate on the issues at hand throughout the day. My field notes record the context in the following terms:

> The heat and humidity are oppressive. My face is wet with sweat and my drenched shirt clings to my body, and even the participants fan their faces and mop their brows. An occasional waft of breeze serves only to accentuate the heat of the day. But the people are active and interested. They focus on the issues at hand and continue to work, concentrating, thinking, discussing. [They talk of] what they are doing, how they have organized themselves. The process gives them voice and to actively participate in decision making seems very affirming to them. The term 'ownership' comes to mind as I watch them work.

The results of 'review and planning' workshops were most encouraging. In some schools the outcomes were dramatically successful, with parents initiating a wide range of activities, ranging from teaching local arts, crafts, songs and dances, to rebuilding classrooms and providing services (water, security, fencing, teaching aids, and so on). The evaluation report noted:

- Evaluation workshops at the seven pilot schools indicate that the processes for PTA development described in the *Pilot Operation Manual* are effective.
- Though schools differ in the degree and nature of development, pilot activity has generated high degrees of awareness of the need to increase parent participation in the schools.
- In most schools principals are eager to engage in developmental activities, though they express the need for support (training) to do so.
- In most schools the enthusiasm of participating parents is most evident. They express great satisfaction in their achievements, and are keen to extend their activities. With principals, they wish to develop ways to increase and extend parent participation. Some also express the desire for support (training).
- Highly effective local PTA models have been developed in some schools. Both the structure and operation enacted by these schools creates considerable interest when presented to principals, teachers and parents in other schools.
- Some pilot schools are still locked into rigid formats and directive operations of the old BP3 models. These schools will need extended support to assist them to modify processes for engaging parent participation.

The potential of these processes was clearly evident in most schools, but some were particularly successful. In one village the parents applied their newly developed organizational skills to the broader needs of the community, so that a project to provide water to the school was extended to include the development of a water supply for the village. Having achieved these ends, parents then focused on the construction of a new health clinic. The action research activities instituted in the schools therefore became the genesis of a more general community development process. Though not all PTAs emerged in such dramatic fashion, successful local models began to appear in a number of places, and the awareness of possibilities for engaging parents spread throughout each district. Principals and parent groups in other schools began to ask for workshops, and even where nascent PTAs evolved in relatively passive fashion, a keen awareness of the need to 'do it better' was evident.

What also became evident was that the PTA project was just one of a number that focused on development of the school, and that it would be necessary to integrate many of these other activities. The impact would obviously be so much greater where projects became complementary parts of the same process, rather than competing for the time and energies of parents, teachers and principals. Developmental processes therefore became envisaged in more strategic terms, as an integrated set of activities, rather than a random application of different developmental agendas. This is particularly relevant to many development contexts, where a range of agencies and institutions often compete for space in the context, each with their own agendas, and their own developmental processes. The strength of this project, as becomes evident in the following sections, is that it came as part of a 'package' that was introduced under the auspice of a team designated by the district offices.

Phase 4: A Schools Development Program: Implementing a National Process

The evident success of the pilot project set the scene for further extension of the process. Meetings between key stakeholders within the Ministry and UNICEF, the principal funding agency for this project, resulted in a plan to extend the development of PTAs throughout the schools of the nation. The Ministry's Technical Working Group, using information derived from the evaluation of PTA pilot projects, planned the structural supports for the developmental processes required in schools in each of the national districts. A National Support Team funded jointly by the Ministry and UNICEF was created that would coordinate and support the work of District Support Teams (see Figure 38.1).

The support system mooted for this project was so obviously effective that, even before its inception, it was extended to incorporate other necessary developments in the school system – teacher training, school-based management training, and later, the introduction of a new curriculum. To facilitate and support these developments in local schools,

funds were allocated to enable each district to employ three people as either district coordinators or training officers. A national team of six people comprised of three national coordinators and three international consultants provided training, mentoring and operational support for district teams.

A series of three training workshops, held over a period of 12 months enabled the national team, in conjunction with the UNICEF consultant, to provide initial training to district teams, review their progress and plan the next phases of development. The workshops reflected the manner and style of the approaches to be used by district facilitators with parent and teacher groups, providing opportunities for participants to clarify the nature of the work they would do through small group discussions, and enabling them to reflectively plan a schedule of activities. People who had experienced these procedures in the pilot schools were particularly useful in this process as they had first-hand experience of the efficacy of participatory processes.

Workshops provided clear evidence that most district teams, despite numerous problems, had successfully implemented the processes of development in a sample of core schools in their district. The changes in their demeanour were evident as they reviewed their activities, describing both their successes and the challenges they faced in facilitating developmental activities. In the four-day workshop that marked the final stage of the training process national and district teams were able to demonstrate the high degrees of understanding and competence they had attained. Not only did they demonstrate a clear understanding of the processes involved, but their detailed action plans enabled them to 'hold' the multiple dimensions of the key tasks for which they were responsible. Their skill and professionalism are evident in photographs taken during the final workshop. The intensity of their faces as they engage in planning processes, the life and vitality that permeated almost all of their work, and the long hours worked in difficult conditions were testament to the work they had accomplished. In doing so they embodied the spirit of a resource that would continue to enrich development of the schools in East Timor.

> The continued gentle rattle of small, inadequate fans serves to accentuate the heat, and an occasional waft of breeze out of the mountains that hang as spectacular backdrop to the city gives promise of cool showers in the early evening. …
>
> So it is, at 3.00 p.m. on this steamy day that I sit quietly, sweating profusely into my clothes, and watch the national team facilitate the review and planning processes we had planned so carefully the previous week. I look on with a sense of satisfaction as the team works competently with district facilitators from across the nation, engaging their attention and enthusiasm, and this late in the afternoon, continuing to evoke energy and clarity as people focused on the issues they had identified that morning.
>
> A wonderful feeling that I had become blessedly redundant pervaded me, the facilitators clearly having the capacity to carry on the business at hand, in a competent and well organized manner. The work of the district teams is exemplary, their creative, detailed and carefully articulated plans providing the basis for rational developments within the schools.
>
> As a group they are indicative of a powerful resource that is now available within the education system. They provide the means to resource the continuing development of the nation's education system, so that the capacity for development has been built into the system in the process of development. …
>
> 4.45 p.m. on the final day. Participant energies are flagging, but they are still wonderfully engaged. Though a few are distracted, the majority are still focused as they grapple with the issues and ask challenging questions of each other.

CONCLUSION

The excitement and commitment that was characteristic of much of the work in this project was demonstrated clearly in the final workshop. Participants laboured intensively for long hours in climatically difficult conditions, working in collaborative groups, demanding a high quality of performance from each other, but also providing mutual

support and encouragement throughout the arduous journey through the complex tasks they were assigned. In many ways they epitomized the success of the project, for not only was their skill and dedication clearly apparent, but they were able to demonstrate in their operations the understanding of the value and effectiveness of participatory processes. Clearly, not only had a powerful resource been built into the education system, providing the means for continuing and sustainable development, but in their operation project participants were able to demonstrate the democratic processes that this new nation held in such high regard.

The world of government policy-making and implementation has for centuries rested on the work of an expert and/or political elite. Government functionaries, sometimes with the assistance of experts, formulate policy that is then translated into directives stipulating the nature of programs and services, how they will be implemented, and the way they will operate. Little wonder that in many instances government services are ineffective or inefficient, deficiencies that are particularly harmful to the well-being of poorer, marginalized groups. These processes are particularly significant in developing nations, where a social elite often directs resources to their own benefit, or funnels off funds for their own purposes, the closed nature of operations providing a breeding ground for corruption and inefficient or ineffective services.

The participatory nature of the processes described in this chapter provides evidence that government programs and services can be formulated and implemented in ways that not only increase the possibility of effective services, but also provide high degrees of transparency that mitigate against institutionalized corruption and inefficiency. The East Timor experience also demonstrates that policy does not have to be universally applied nationwide; that staged or phased implementation provides the means to ensure that systems and services take into account the exigencies and circumstances of the particular locality. It also demonstrates that all wisdom does not reside with experts or those in positions of power and authority; that utilizing the knowledge, experience and wisdom of local people can both enrich and enhance government services.

The effectiveness works at a number of levels, since the active participation of the people not only provides a fund of local expertise, but it enhances the life of the community in a direct way. The empowerment of the people in the process, the energy and excitement that results when they are able to successfully contribute to events that move their lives provides the basis for a healthy and harmonious society. People working in concert to achieve common purposes are able to make significant contributions to the wellbeing of their community, providing possibilities for further development derived from the capacities – social capital – that has been built into their lives.

The path to development does not always happen in peaceful environments. During the project riots occurred in Dili, and further disturbances at the time of writing are indicative of the undercurrent of violence that has resulted from years of oppression. The transparent and participatory processes involved in action research can only assist, over a period of time, in ameliorating the underlying tensions in the fabric of the community. Certainly the work of this project was able to continue throughout the period of unrest that surrounded its first stages.

The big lesson of this project is that delivery of services is only part of the developmental equation – the *way* they are developed and delivered is as important as the actual services themselves. Participatory processes provide the means to ensure that developments fit the social and cultural realities of each locality and build the capacity of the people to enrich and enhance the services that serve them.

The picture presented is somewhat simplified, and it has not been possible to provide, in this short chapter, a full account of the struggles and difficulties that were a constant part of the process. After hundreds of years of colonial rule it would be naïve to assume that fully participatory and democratic processes suddenly and unproblematically became institutionalized across the nation. What is clear, however, is that there is now a widespread and well-received set of processes that provide the basis for future developments. Successful local models that exhibit the effective and democratic processes so desirable in modern democracies/civil society have now been implemented in many towns and villages across the nation. Over time they will continue to influence events as people confront the new social model that is emerging in their nation, opening the possibility that they will gradually infuse those styles of operation into their daily lives. Systematic and participatory processes of development that are an integral part of action research in this instance has provided an effective means for instituting national policy in a developing nation.

NOTE

1 I sat puzzled as this idea emerged. 'This school needs many things,' I pondered, 'But an ornamental fish pond?!!!' When I questioned my interpreter he explained, with a laugh, that the pond was to farm fish, and would be part of a rice paddy.

REFERENCES

Democratic Republic of East Timor, Ministry of Education, Culture, Youth and Sports (2003) *Parent Teacher Associations: Pilot Operation Manual*. Dili, East Timor: UNICEF.

Fukuyama, F. (2004) *State-Building: Governance and the World Order in the 21st Century*. New York: Cornell University Press.

Krishna, A. (2002) *Active Social Capital: Tracing the Roots of Development and Democracy*. New York: Columbia University Press.

Krishna, A. and Prewitt, G. (2002) 'How are civil society organizations important for development?', in A. Krishna, C. Wiesen, G. Prewitt and B. Sobhan, *Changing Policy and Practice from Below:*

Community Experiences in Poverty Reduction. Durham, NC: Duke University Press. pp. 4–14.

Planning Commission (2002a) *East Timor National Development Plan.* Dili, East Timor.

Planning Commission (2002b) *East Timor: State of the Nation Report.* Dili, East Timor.

Putnam, R., Leonardi, R. and Nanetti, R. (1993) *Making Democracy Work.* Princeton, NJ: Princeton University Press.

Stiglitz, J. (2002) *Globalization and Its Discontents.* London: Penguin.

Stringer, E. (1999) *Action Research.* Thousand Oaks, CA: Sage.

Stringer, E. (2004) *Action Research in Education.* Upper Saddle River, NJ: Pearson Prentice Hall.

Stringer, E. (2005) *Action Research in Human Services.* Upper Saddle River, NJ: Pearson Prentice Hall.

Stringer, E. and Dwyer, R. (2004) *Action Research in Human Services.* Upper Saddle River, NJ: Pearson Prentice Hall.

39

'No – You *Don't* Know How We Feel!': Collaborative Inquiry Using Video with Children Facing the Life-threatening Illness of a Parent

Gillian Chowns

This chapter describes a collaborative inquiry conducted with nine children who were facing the serious illness and possible death of a parent. It describes the impetus for the research, some of the obstacles and ethical issues, and the practicalities of working in this way with a group that is conventionally seen as very vulnerable and a topic that is also considered highly sensitive. The concepts of competence, power and capacity are then discussed in the light of both the findings and the experience of the inquiry.

'Sometimes people don't always listen to us' is a comment from children that I have heard throughout my professional life as a social worker and an educator, as well as in my personal life as a parent. This chapter tells just part of the story of a collaborative inquiry that sought to enable children to be listened to, and respected for their expertise and experience, and focuses on two central issues – power and competence. Both of these challenge the production of knowledge, the practice

of palliative care and contemporary understandings of childhood.

If action research is 'best understood as a way of being and doing in the world' (Heron and Reason, 2001), it must be transparent about its choices – and the consequences that follow, foreseen and unintended. As author of this chapter, I acknowledge that the interpretation of those choices and consequences is mine; although other voices (the children's and the adult co-facilitators') may briefly feature, this story of a collaborative inquiry is, paradoxically, an individual, personal representation. In the spirit of transparency, I begin with a brief summary of the selves that inform this telling, and the purpose of both the research itself and this chapter's account of it.

My primary professional identity is as a social worker with children and families. For the last decade I have been a specialist palliative care social worker, working directly with children who are themselves healthy but whose parent is seriously ill with cancer. In the past, I have taught in both the UK and in Africa at playgroup/kindergarten, primary, and secondary levels. Currently I am a senior lecturer in palliative care in an English university. From my personal life I bring the experience of a happy childhood, an enduring marriage, continuing parenthood and, now, the role of grandparenting.

Although it is possible to separate these roles on paper, in practice they coalesced and collided, each contributing to the values and beliefs that informed my work. Researching the experience of these children *as they saw it* was both an expression of those values and an intention to contribute, however modestly, to changing the understanding and practice of both professionals and families. I chose collaborative inquiry as an approach that offered a more ethical, respectful and democratic way of working with these children, a marginalized group (Lykes and Mallona, this volume) in the world of palliative care. Collaboratively producing a video on the topic made the findings more readily accessible to both the above groups as well as being a contemporary, attractive medium for the young co-researchers.

This brief account of our work is not presented as a blueprint for other inquirers, but to highlight some of the issues raised in working with this age range, to contribute to ongoing debates on research methods, ethics, interpretation and much more, and to encourage more adult–child collaboration.

BACKGROUND

Palliative care is 'an approach that improves the quality of life of patients and their families facing … life-threatening illness' (World Health Organization, 2002). In the West, it has been offered most readily to people with cancer; in the developing world it is HIV/AIDS that is the dominant disease. The definition recognizes that the family are part of the 'unit of care', but in practice 'family' has been largely interpreted as adult members (Ferrel et al., 2002; Lewis, 2004; Northouse et al., 2002); the children of seriously ill parents receive comparatively little attention. While research into bereaved children has grown considerably (Klass et al., 1996; Worden, 2002), research about children who are likely to become, but are not yet, bereaved, is scarce. Most research on the impact of cancer on families has been adult-focused, adult-conducted and adult-interpreted (Barnes et al., 2000; Davis Kirsch et al., 2003; Beale et al., 2004). Children's views have often been obtained by proxy and, even when accessed directly, the researchers have then sought 'confirmation' from the parents (Nelson and While, 2002). The authentic voice of the child (defined here as under 18) has been absent.

METHOD

My work with children in a variety of settings left me increasingly frustrated at the failure of parents and professionals to attend to their experiences, but also convinced of children's ability to cope with difficult situations. In my doctoral research, I wanted to challenge the first and honour the second.

Key ethical issues were consent, confidentiality, and ownership. In keeping with my position on children's rights and abilities, I sought consent from the children first, and only afterwards from their parents. Inevitably, anonymity was impossible with the use of video, but what we could guarantee was control of all the material;

each of the children would have the option to give or withhold consent to the public use of any of the footage taken during the project. Whatever they said or did during the sessions would remain confidential unless or until they themselves decided it could be included in the final video. The principles of participatory video were both explained and demonstrated at our first meeting – that all the participants were involved in all the stages, from deciding the themes, to filming, interviewing, editing and dissemination. Although the doctoral thesis would be exclusively written by me, the young co-researchers would have the option to be co-presenters at the launch of the video and at subsequent conferences, thus carrying the principle of collaboration right through to dissemination.

This approach to research had been an unfamiliar one for the National Health Service local Ethics committee, who were unused to having notions of 'bias', 'objectivity' and 'consent' contested; nevertheless, approval was given at first submission.

I then talked to the children whom we were currently supporting through their parents' illness and invited them and their parents to a meeting to discuss the idea of acting as co-researchers of their own experiences to make a video to help other families. Nine children aged from seven to 15 years participated, together with four adults – three social workers and a 'participatory video' (PV) expert. The group included three sibling sets; there was a mix of lone-parent and two-parent families; the cancer diagnoses included breast, bone and cervix; prognoses were very variable.

Despite the well-rehearsed difficulties of recruitment in palliative care research, we not only had a sufficient number of children interested in the project but we also had parents who were supportive. Since the research was focused on the pre-bereavement period, the fieldwork was conducted over an intense but short seven weeks, to minimize the risk of a bereavement during the making of the video. Nevertheless, the crucial planning, preparation and dissemination phases extended the whole project by many months either side of the group sessions.

PREPARATION

Two social work colleagues with expertise in palliative care and group work, Sue and Alison, were keen to be involved, but this did not mean that we all had a shared understanding of how the video project would be realized. Sue writes below of her concerns during this early stage:

> Planning a children's group, particularly one that involves painful and sensitive issues, and where the situation for individual members can change dramatically at any time, feels seriously problematic. Add into the equation a plan to make a video with the group which will be for public consumption, and the hurdles are likely to feel insurmountable. ... Although wanting to be supportive, I was sceptical that it would ever be possible because of a whole variety of problems: engaging a viable group; finding sufficient time; overcoming the issues of consent and confidentiality; getting funding; finding a suitable venue; coping with the group if one of the parents dies; and, finally, producing a suitably professional product when I, for one, knew absolutely nothing about video. Talking to children about difficult issues was the least of my worries, given that it was my daily work within a palliative care team, but the practicalities of this project seemed impossibly complex.

An additional challenge was the integration of the cameraman Nick. I had been seeking a video expert, and he was recommended by a colleague. However, he then argued persuasively for a more participatory approach (Robertson and Shaw, 1997; Brinton Lykes, 2001; Lunch and Lunch, 2006), in which the children would be in control of the camera, and although this was entirely congruent with the espoused values of collaborative inquiry, it shifted his original role from unobtrusive recorder to active co-facilitator. It became imperative to invest time in bringing the facilitators together, build trust and agree a common understanding about collaboration. Two meetings at which some group-work exercises (Doel and Sawdon, 1999) proved effective, began the essential process of developing mutual respect and trust. These exercises, in which we each identified our hopes for the project, the fears that we had, and the skills that we brought to it, highlighted and reduced some of the existing tensions between us, and helped to integrate Nick within the team. My colleagues all identified 'fun' as an important part of the project – a salutary reminder for me, the project leader, as I had entirely forgotten that aspect. The honesty of our responses helped us to understand and support each other through the fieldwork phase.

In the preliminary Open meeting for families, held to explain our thinking, we modelled our commitment to collaboration by having the video equipment available and literally handing it over to the children. Then, in the first session of the fieldwork phase, we brainstormed the themes that were the young people's own concerns. The adults provided flip-chart paper, pens and the reiterated principle – that the children were the 'experts' in this situation and it was their themes that were the starting point. The original vision of collaborative inquiry through making a video had been mine alone – a slow germination of a seed of an idea that had been nourished by a multitude of conversations, readings, incidents and ideas – but the research questions were defined by the young co-researchers rather than by 'expert' adults. Throughout the project, these issues were explored through interviews, games, explicit discussion and casual conversations over refreshments. In addition, the 'Good/bad' feedback slots at the beginning and end of each session provided opportunities to reflect in a more considered way on all that was happening.

DATA COLLECTION, EDITING AND DISSEMINATION

Over the seven weekly sessions, many hours of tape were amassed. One camera had been used specifically to record the *process* of the collaborative inquiry – a running record of the whole of each session – while the other had been designated for 'proper' footage – material deliberately recorded for potential inclusion in the final video. However, these two sets of tapes were not mutually exclusive. The young people reviewed all the 'proper' footage and, as indicated earlier, gave or withheld consent for its inclusion in the public film. They agreed that I should review all the process tapes (on which I drew for the part of my thesis researching the practice of collaborative inquiry with children) and any extracts that I felt would be useful for the video would then also be reviewed, vetoed or accepted by them. Thus, all material remained 'private' to the group until unanimous consent for its public use was forthcoming.

Nick, the technical expert, produced the first rough video draft. Several weeks had passed, which offered an opportunity for a perhaps more dispassionate appraisal of their contributions. The draft was reviewed – with brutal honesty: 'Too boring'; 'Not enough fun'; 'I don't like the bit where it keeps zooming in and out.' So it went back for further revisions before being finally launched as the 25-minute film 'No – You *Don't* Know How We Feel' (Chowns et al., 2004).

Collaborative dissemination was equally challenging. In the first year after the film was made, four of the young people made conference presentations. Notwithstanding organizers' assumptions that all presenters are adult, academic and professional, the project has enabled a marginalized group of service users – children – to communicate their research directly to the wider public. Those children who have presented an aspect of the research (of their own choosing) have clearly made an impact on their audience, and equally the experience of presenting has impacted on them, enabling them both to properly value themselves as worthwhile contributors to society rather than as passive victims needing help, and also to continue the iterative process as they negotiate new understandings of their experience of living with life-threatening parental illness.

Ellis, sparing with words, and at 15 our oldest co-researcher, publicly reflected on this:

At first I was very wary about doing the video. As a private person I wasn't sure how much or how little I was prepared to say. However, after meeting the group and talking with my Mum I decided to go ahead. ... It [the video] gave me a chance to tell people, especially my Mum, of how I really felt about her cancer. I know my Mum found this really helped her to deal with it. When she was very low and tired we always tried to be there for each other.

At another national conference he expanded further:

This experience has affected my life as it made me realize that there are others in my unique situation and I hope other children and young adults will benefit from our own experiences as told through the video. ... There were a lot of personal issues raised in this video and at first I was unsure, but after watching the final video I realized how much it could help others and my concerns about [it] being released into the general public went [disappeared].

This demonstrates the three levels on which the video project operated – first, second and third person. It was a positive experience for Ellis himself; it impacted on his mother, and their relationship with each other; and he began to understand its potential impact on the wider world. It also articulates some of the dynamics and dilemmas of 'consent' – which in practice is provisional, fluid, incremental and open to influence (here, by his parent and the group).

COMPETENCE AND CAPACITY-BUILDING

On hearing of the original research proposal, many individuals and agencies presupposed children, as a class, to be unreliable or vulnerable (at risk of wounds) rather than able. They feared that collaborative inquiry would either make too many demands on the children or that they would 'play up' to the camera.

My own position was liberationist rather than protectionist. That is to say, I recognized that young people were no more and no less vulnerable than any other researcher/participant

(Brydon-Miller, Chapter 13 in this volume), and that I needed to be rigorous in my ethical approach (Farrell, 2005) to consent and much else, as discussed earlier, but as a practising social worker I usually began with an assumption of ability rather than vulnerability. I always acknowledged, on first meeting, that the child had the ability either to make this the only meeting, or the beginning of some joint work. And both my practice (supporting children before and *after* bereavement) and my reading of the bereavement literature (Christ, 2001; Klass et al., 1996; Monroe and Kraus, 2005) provided evidence that children could survive parental bereavement. Moreover, Barnard et al. (1999), Holland (2005) and Alderson (2000) argue that adult assumptions of ability or incompetence will enhance or diminish a child's actual performance, and one must distinguish between children's relatively poor performance in research on hypothetical situations and their maturity when responding to research on real-life experience (Alderson, 2000). I brought this awareness to the research study and thus began with a standpoint (contested, as all standpoints may be) that favoured capacity and competence.

Each session began by identifying the good and difficult things about the previous week and ended with a review of the day's footage. Thus reflection was a key component of the work, whether or not it was so labelled by our co-researchers. Over the weeks, the children's critical faculties were honed as they critiqued their contributions and made constructive suggestions for generating better footage. Megan, aged 13, was critical of some stilted interviews that three of them had conducted in Session Two and commented: 'We could use some stuff from the process tapes – when we were discussing it before [filming] it was much better, we said some really important things.'

The study also provided evidence that living with life-threatening parental illness gave the young people a more mature approach to life than their peers'. One girl commented negatively on how childish and irritating her friends could be, while several youngsters highlighted the need to support and protect parents or siblings, and therefore put their own preferences aside. Eleven-year-old Laura, an only child of a separated mother, explained. 'I wanted to tell my Mum that I didn't like what was happening, but I didn't want to upset her.' And the 14-year-old twins, Gemma and Natalie, commented; 'When we're round our Dad … he does things a lot slower. You have to put up with it.'

Thus, one positive consequence of recognizing a parent's vulnerability was that the child's capacity for *other-centred* behaviour – standing in the other person's shoes, and meeting those needs rather than their own (self-centred) needs – was increased, and in *practising* this other-centred behaviour they became even more competent at it and therefore more competent participants in society. This was not a primary aim of the video project, more a by-product of living with life-threatening parental illness. Although they all wanted their parents to be more understanding of the stresses that they, as children, experienced, they saw this as a question of reciprocity – just as they were actively trying to support their parents, so they hoped their parents would actively support them. However, the children gave their support freely; it was not conditional upon it being returned.

This capacity for a more mature outlook and behaviour pre-dated the video project but the youngsters' participation as collaborative inquirers further enhanced their capacity and competence. For example, after seven sessions in which we had consistently told them that it was their experience which mattered, their choices that would count, and their feedback on the previous sessions that needed to be heard, their capacity to critically appraise the first edit of the video was clearly evident, as illustrated earlier. Similarly, in Session Five there was a long, complex and lively debate about truth-telling wherein they demonstrated an impressive capacity to marshal their thoughts, construct an argument and respond respectfully but robustly to challenges, all on a difficult and semi-abstract topic. The collaborative ethos of the project contributed to capacity-building. The expectation of competence inherent in the underpinning values of collaborative inquiry brought forth competence, and the constant sharing of power provided frequent opportunities to display and hone that competence. For example, in Session Two, the adults divided them into small groups to discuss and plan an interview, and then withdrew. My field notes of the video tape record: 'Silence … all looking down at their feet – then Laura gets clock, takes on role of time-keeper, Megan picks up paper and pen to write captions for interview (her idea).' The ensuing discussion, too long to reproduce here, was animated, rich, wide-ranging and entirely independent of any adult input.

However, this ability to exercise power competently and take responsibility was not a static state; it shifted, slipped, disappeared and re-formed, in response to many factors beyond the study's remit. Two siblings illustrate its dynamic nature in their attendance and involvement in the project. Superficially less focused than his co-researchers, Jack, a young-acting seven, was nevertheless committed to the group and, despite his mother's rapidly deteriorating health, the deepening uncertainty of his daily life, and his general dependence on adults, he attended every session and was never a presence that could be ignored. His limited concentration span meant that he frequently tired of activities before the rest of the group, but when it came to the painting exercise, a valuable example of presentational knowledge, he was completely focused and his simple explanation was heard with rapt attention by the whole room: 'This is a sad picture' (an enormous face that filled the paper, with a red, screaming mouth). When one of the girls suggested that it looked as if the face was screaming because it was scared, Jack nodded silently. 'What makes you scared, Jack?', she asked. 'When my Mummy's not well', he whispered. The silence that followed was profound.

By contrast, his sister Becky was equally competent at having her very different wishes honoured; her energies were focused on her dying mother, her attendance sporadic, and her contribution limited. What is less certain is whether the siblings were as capable of getting their wishes met once the main phase of the study was completed. Neither attended the first edit review, nor the pre-launch showing to the parents, nor the public launch some months later. It may be that this was entirely consonant with their own preferences, but one cannot be confident that the collaborative inquiry had *sufficiently* strengthened their capacity and competence to achieve their own wishes. They each participated as much or as little as they wished in the group sessions, but it may well be that their subsequent non-participation reflected their father's views rather than their own preferences.

This non-particpation, for whatever reason, highlights the limitations of 'real-world research' (Robson, 2002). While this study sought, inter alia, to help children become effective inquirers, it could not impact so directly on the many other parts of the system that is society. The *output* of the study, the video (Chowns et al., 2004), sought to enable others – teachers, families, professionals, peers and siblings – to become more enquiring, but this was a future impact; the research itself had limited power to change the broader *context* in which it took place. Competence was recognized and celebrated within the study, but in the outside world it was often dismissed and devalued. The children's own understandings of themselves as competent and capable were challenged by the reluctance of their social networks – parents, school and the wider community, all of whom appeared to be working to older models – to acknowledge competence in children. Knowledge may be power, but if that knowledge is not respected or sanctioned as knowledge by those currently in power (adults), then it may yet not bring power to the knowers (children).

POWER

The ascription of power to children remains contested. And the broader debate usually assumes that increased power for one group means a loss of power for the other (Gaventa and Cornwall, Chapter 11 in this volume). I had been guilty of this assumption when I agreed to the participatory video approach. I recognized its strengths, but felt that I would be handing over some of my power to Nick and the children; I would no longer control the direction of the project. However, the reality was more subtle and rewarding; shared power begat reciprocity and increased collective power. Our experience was that we all, facilitators and co-researchers, were more effective than if we had not shared that power.

However, the limitations of empowerment bear further reflection. Collaborative inquiry seeks to empower those whose expertise is often not recognized and validated as 'proper' knowledge. Our co-researchers, as children and as users of palliative care services, were located on the fringes of both society and research; and the espoused values of social work and collaborative inquiry had to compete with the normal, everyday experience of their lives as less-than-powerful people. Collaborative inquiry constructed them as knowers, actors and equals, and we adults endeavoured to assert this in word and action. Phrases such as 'it's up to you, it's your choice' and 'You decide, you're the experts in living with this' were reiterated frequently, and, importantly, the ensuing choices were then respected.

However, this was an unfamiliar construction for the children, who did not see themselves as having choice and power, initially – because society did not construct them as holding this much power. Theirs was a world where they occupied positions of relative powerlessness, as dependants and pupils – an adult-dominated world, in which adults controlled the agenda and, sadly, could not always be trusted to keep their promises. So our group did not accept our protestations of power-sharing with open arms. Indeed, one

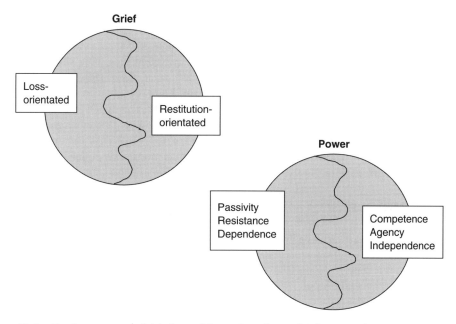

Figure 39.1 *Dual process model (adapted from Stroebe and Schut, 1999)*

could argue that this was just one small way in which children learn to exercise some power and control – discounting adult promises enables the child to survive better when those promises are experienced as broken. So, a review of Session One tapes showed a group who were largely passive, wary, and apparently conforming. In later sessions, the children more readily made statement of intent – 'Let's do that' or 'We can act a story' or 'I'm not going to say anything', but in the earlier ones, they were in permission-seeking mode: 'Could we ask the others some questions?' 'If we don't want to be filmed, can we sit it out?'

Some children were also inhibited when it came to everyone doing a section of a story board; they got up to draw their picture, then promptly returned to their chair, while others stayed down on the floor, crowding round the drawings, and commenting on the contributions. As one facilitator reflected: 'They're playing the game, aren't they, doing what they think we want … and making up their minds about us?'

Collaborative inquiry attempts to shift the power dynamics of 'user' and 'academic', but methodology and method are insufficient in themselves. It was in the day-to-day details of the project that the adults modelled the principles of collaboration, and thereby enabled the whole group to *live* them.

We adults held considerable power, simply by virtue of being adults, as well as by being either camera or palliative care experts, but the children had their own, not inconsiderable, power as well. Their trust and collaboration was theirs to give or withhold, and they did not do either unthinkingly.

This negotiation of power was a continuous, dynamic process – an oscillation. It has parallels with Stroebe and Schut's dual process model of grief (1999), which recognizes that a bereaved person does not make steady progress but may swing wildly from loss-oriented to restitution-oriented activity and thinking (see Figure 39.1).

Similarly, the young people in the study oscillated, not only between but also within each session, between power and powerless orientations. Thus, in Session One, when they were invited to brainstorm ideas for what should go into the video, the contributions came thick and fast, individuals endorsed or qualified others' ideas uninhibitedly and there was a palpable sense of energy and power within the group that in some cases was physically translated into jumping up from the chair. Yet at other times they had been very much in teacher–pupil mode despite our best efforts – in the way we had arranged the chairs (in a circle), ourselves (scattered among the children), and the programme (contributions from them as well as us, acting and filming as well as talking and listening) – to challenge these daily norms.

In one of the later sessions, the oldest group, Ellis, Gemma and Megan, appeared to revert to powerlessness as they struggled to generate a discussion on cancer information; they wanted someone to ask direct questions, declined to choose one of their own number, and wanted an adult to move in and organize them – 'We can't do it, it's easier if you do it.' In the asking, of course, they nevertheless demonstrated the use of both positive and negative power, as well as a recognition of differing areas of expertise in adults and children.

The power balance shifted considerably over the life of the project, but it was an uneven process. In Session Three one teenager facilitated the discussion on painting, and in Session Six another independently raised the topic of advice for other children and started a discussion with his co-researchers. However, as illustrated above, there were also clear instances of children reverting to the less-powerful orientation, asking the adults to direct interviews and generally take charge.

One partial explanation for this oscillation may be the capacity for sustainability – in the sense of the ability to maintain this approach consistently. Although the offer of shared power was consistently made, its acceptance and use required considerable mental and emotional energy and, at times, none of us was able to sustain this level of energy so we each reverted to more conventional modes-of-being.

For example, while filming the section on 'Cancer Information', one group managed independently, and the other, as highlighted above, reverted to a more dependent role. It seemed as if they had simply run out of energy. Later on, it was an adult who 'reverted to type'; she moved back into professional mode, trying to organize the group and elicit views, with little success, despite earlier maintaining an effortlessly collaborative style.

Occasionally, the adults failed to use their legitimate power to empower the children. During a discussion of how to cope with enquiries about a parent's health, several children suggested the response 'She's fine' in the hope of shutting down the conversation. We adults simply acknowledged this, whereas encouraging the group to explore ways of explaining why this was an unwelcome question might have then enabled them to change a difficult situation. Instead, our failure to exercise appropriate power disempowered the children and left them masking rather than controlling a problem.

Elsewhere, we used our authority appropriately. Midway through the inquiry, when collaboration was well-established, we consciously took more control of the session *structure* which freed the children to focus on the *content,* where they were the experts. So the adults selected video diaries and an activity which involved ranking statements as key items, but the opinions, debate and counter-challenges were all the children's own. One statement (drawn from a palliative care textbook) that 'children need to know the truth' provoked an excellent debate about timeliness and honesty, as well as some sharing of personal experiences of unwelcome parental protectiveness. This working to particular members' strengths (Heron and Reason, 2001/2006) values difference without compromising collaboration.

Planning the painting session, however, was an example of deliberately refraining from the use of power. All my co-researchers were keen to paint their emotions at the next, short, Friday session. I pointed out just how much time painting requires, but accepted, with public grace and private reluctance, the group preference not to wait for a longer Saturday session.

In the event, the painting was very rushed, but we nevertheless captured some excellent footage. Equally importantly, it enabled the young people to articulate in greater depth the emotions that dominated their life as off-spring of seriously ill parents and to learn from each other. One of the twins drew a solitary teardrop and spoke of how alone she felt, which led to a discussion about telling friends at school, the attendant risks and likely reactions. The ensuing debate enabled the children to learn about others' coping strategies and consider alternative behaviours.

The exercise of power, whether by children or adults, is a complex and contested activity. Reflection before, during and after each session (reflection-on-action and in-action) was an important tool to help us all explore the subtleties of its use in collaborative inquiry, and led us to conclude that multiple perceptions may co-exist – there may be no 'right' answer.

CONCLUSION

Both power and competence were central issues in the video project, which demonstrated that young people are more capable and articulate than most adults recognize. It is not protection that our co-researchers sought, but understanding. They wanted their coping strategies to be acknowledged and respected. They wanted to be included and involved, as supportive family members, change agents and givers of knowledge to other families, and as persons in their own right, not ignored or marginalized. They saw themselves not as passive victims but as active contributors to the good of others facing serious illness in the family. Above all, they wanted to be heard. Together, the methodology – collaborative inquiry – and the method – participatory video – have enabled co-researchers to present their work in a way that is accessible to the wider community and also faithful to their own perspective.

Collaborative inquiry has been almost entirely theorized and practised in terms of adults (Reason and Bradbury, 2001/2006), and there are to date few accounts of its application to children. The combination of a sensitive issue (death and dying) and a research population (children) seen as particularly vulnerable was considered daunting by many colleagues, but the use of participatory video with collaborative inquiry's attention to power dynamics, participatory principles and respect for differing typologies of knowledge (Heron and Reason, 2001/2006) enabled the young people to articulate their experience and expertise and also challenged contemporary assumptions about children's capacity and competence. The account of this research invites other practitioners considering collaborative inquiry to freely adapt, amend, and debate its ideas and activities, but also to recognize and respect children's competence and capacity (largely unacknowledged) alongside their vulnerability (an attribute of all humanity).

While collaborative inquiry continues to be constrained by the wider society in which it operates, it has the potential to shift the broader social context from one where the silencing of children is unremarked, to one where their voice and competence may eventually be credited – and celebrated.

REFERENCES

Alderson, P. (2000) *Young Children's Rights: Exploring Beliefs, Principles and Practice*. London: Jessica Kingsley.

Aries, P. (1973) *Centuries of Childhood*. London: Jonathan Cape.

Barnard, P., Morland, I. and Nagy, J. (1999) *Children, Bereavement and Trauma*. London: Jessica Kingsley.

Barnes, J. et al. (2000) 'Qualitative interview study of communication between parents and children about maternal breast cancer', *British Medical Journal*, 321: 479–82.

Beale, E., Sivisend, D. and Bruera, E. (2004) 'Parents dying of cancer and their children', *Palliative and Supportive Care*, 2: 387–93.

Beresford, P. (2002) 'Maturity needed', *Community Care*, 11 (17 July).

Brinton Lykes, M. (2001) 'Creative arts and photography in participatory action research in Guatemala', *in* P. Reason, and H. Bradbury, (eds), *Handbook of Action Research: Participative Inquiry and Practice*. London: Sage. pp. 363–71.

Chowns, G. et al. (2004) 'No – You *Don't* Know How we Feel', video, available from gpatgc@aol.com or sue.bussey@berkshire.nhs.uk

Christ, G. (2000) *Healing Children's Grief*. Oxford: Oxford University Press.

Cunningham, H. (2005) *Children and Childhood in Western Society since 1500*. Harlow: Pearson.

Davis Kirsch, S., Brandt, P. and Lewis, F. (2003) 'Making the most of the moment', *Cancer Nursing*, 26 (1): 47–54.

Doel, M. and Sawdon, C. (1999) *The Essential Group-worker*. London: Jessica Kinsley.

Farrell, A. (ed.) (2005) *Ethical Research with Children*. Maidenhead: Open University Press.

Ferrel, B. et al. (2002) 'Family perspectives of ovarian cancer', *Cancer Practice*, 10 (6): 269–76.

Geldard, K. and Geldard, D. (1997) *Counselling Children*. London: Sage.

Heron, J. and Reason, P. (2001) 'The practice of cooperative inquiry', in P. Reason and H. Bradbury (eds), *Handbook of Action Research: Participative Inquiry and Practice*. London: Sage. pp. 179–88.

Holland, J. (2005) *Lost for Words*. London: Jessica Kingsley.

Jarrett, L. (2006) *A Creative Guide for User Involvement in Palliative Care*. Oxford: Radcliffe.

Klass, D., Silverman, P. and Nickman, S. (1996) *Continuing Bonds*. Washington, DC: Taylor and Francis.

Lewis, F.M. (2004) 'Family focused oncology nursing research', *Oncology Nursing Forum*, 31(2): 288–91.

Lindsay, G. (2000) 'Researching children's perspectives: ethical issues', in *Researching Children's Perspectives*.

A. Lewis and G. Lindsay (eds) Buckingham: Open University Press. pp. 3–20.

Lister, R. (2005) 'Growing pains' *The Guardian*, 6 October: 29.

Lowden, J. (2002) 'Children's rights: a decade of dispute', *Journal of Advanced Nursing*, 37(1) 100–7.

Lunch, N. and Lunch, C. (2006) *Insights in Participatory Video*. Oxford: Insightshare.

Monroe, B. and Kraus, F. (eds) (2005) *Brief Interventions with Bereaved Children*. Oxford: Oxford University Press.

Nelson, E. and While, D. (2002) 'Children's adjustment during the first year of a parent's cancer diagnosis', *Journal of Psychosocial Oncology*, 20 (1): 15–36.

Northouse, L. et al. (2002) 'A family-based program of care for women with recurrent breast cancer and their family members', *Oncology Nursing Forum*, 29 (10): 1411–19.

Reason, P. and Bradbury, H. (eds) (2001) *Handbook of Action Research: Participative Inquiry and Practice*. London: Sage.

Robertson, C. and Shaw, J. (1997) *Participatory Video*. London: Routledge and Keegan & Paul.

Robson, C. (2002) *Real World Research*. Oxford: Blackwell.

Stroebe, M. and Schut, H. (1999) 'The dual process model of coping with bereavement', *Death Studies*, 23: 197–224.

Toffler, A. (1981) *The Third Wave*. London: Pan Books.

Twigg, J. and Atkin, K. (1994) *Carers Perceived*. Buckingham: Open University Press.

United Nations (1989) *Convention on the rights of the child*. Geneva: United Nations.

Worden, J.W.W. (1996) *Children and Grief: When a Parent Dies*. New York: Guilford Press.

World Health Organization (2002) *Definition of Palliative Care*. Geneva: World Health Organization.

40

IT and Action Sensemaking: Making Sense of New Technology

Chris Dymek

Often, organizations feel compelled to explore the use of new technologies for either competitive advantage or to ward off the threat of obsolescence. Depending on the technology in question, use of it might have very disruptive effects within the organization. Having been both an initiator and on the receiving end of new technology implementations, I have searched for more satisfying, less disruptive ways to introduce them into organizations – ways that are both socially and organizationally valid. This search led me to think about using action research to make sense of the use of a new technology. Ultimately, my dissertation work resulted in developing a model for such a process, which I call 'action sensemaking'. This chapter describes one organization's effort to use this model while developing a conceptual design for use of a new information technology (IT). The co-researchers involved in this participatory action research project engaged in both second- and third-person research/practice, thereby ensuring social and organizational validity of the resulting conceptual design.

This chapter describes one organization's effort to develop a new IT approach using an AR model I have come to call 'action sensemaking'. Briefly, action sensemaking is a collaborative inquiry focusing on at least two action/reflection cycles that involve: (1) the combining of both internal and external organizational knowledge to generate relevant cues to sensemaking, and (2) linking the generated cues with existing organizational frames to generate ideas for utilizing a new technology and, potentially, new organizational meanings and frames. In this context, sensemaking is a deliberate process undertaken to seek out relevant cues, which would, when consciously combined with existing organizational schema or 'frames', result in the creation of new meanings within the organization. An organizational schema or frame is present when a particular, set, way of perceiving cognitively and responding to stimuli occurs. Accountants, for example, are likely to have a different organizational frame from the IT staff in an organization.

The organizational members involved in the AR project on which my work is based engaged in both team work and reflection with the purpose of extending the work beyond themselves. In so doing they also added to the social and organizational aspects of the resulting AR design by creating a sense of partnership, which left the system stronger – stronger in that there was a solidarity about the direction we were headed and in that we learned some productive ways of engaging during our work. Also, the work produced was practical in that it was grounded in new workflows incorporating the new technology. The workflows and documented resulting efficiencies were produced by those who were actually engaged in the work.

PROJECT BACKGROUND

In the spring of 2002 the company, which will be referred to as ORG in the remainder of this chapter, embarked upon a total replacement of its core information system. This project was called Release One and was implemented with mixed results in the company. Technically, the result was flawless. Practically, however, some users of the new system felt this system was designed to facilitate work processes for only one area of the company. Since all areas of the company were represented on the project team for Release One, this was a puzzle. Further probing revealed that the core issue stemmed from a perception that dissent was stifled in

the design sessions of the project. Members of the project team were afraid to publicly disagree with the ideas of a powerful participant during design sessions.

Given this background, the Steering Committee for Release Two (as the project that underlies the work here was called) desired a project design that would allow for all needed voices to be heard in a setting that would mitigate power issues. The steering committee was comprised of a group of senior leaders in the company. I submitted a preliminary project charter document to the steering committee outlining the overall project design, which was based on the action sensemaking model in Figure 40.1, and clarified the project goals, scope and timeline. I did so in the context of an AR dissertation that I undertook as part of my doctoral studies at Pepperdine University. The project co-researchers were not involved in these early project charter discussions because the culture of ORG was such that prior to allocating any human resources to a project, senior management required at least a high-level project plan. However, they were involved in many facets of the design stage of the project including planning what data were needed and how to acquire the data.

The goal for our project team was to determine a design for use of a software product called eService. eService was intended to provide a feature-rich web portal for ORG customers and partners. eService contained some standard features but could be customized to do most anything required of a customer interface. Any customer data could be retrieved or updated using eService. The CEO of ORG intended that this technology provide new services and increased productivity for ORG its customers and partners. ORG devoted roughly one-tenth of its yearly budget to this project combined with the earlier Release One. Both releases were viewed by senior management as having strategic significance.

The steering committee, on which I was also a member while acting in the capacity of project manager for the team, allocated one team member from each of ORG's four customer service areas, two members from operations, two from research and education, and two from technology services to the project team. In addition, the facilitator for the team of co-researchers was allocated from human resources. The facilitator was an experienced human resources professional with a background in organization development. Human resources was not affected by this software implementation and, so, its personnel were thought to be relatively unbiased as to any chosen outcome.

Prior to the team's work commencing, I met individually with potential members recommended by the steering committee to inform them about the project, review the commitment we were asking them to make to take part in an AR project, and to converse about any concerns they might have regarding the project. They were also informed that all meetings were going to be taped and that the tapes would be transcribed for analysis purposes. Potential members had the option not to partake in the project, but all seemed willing to try a new approach in an effort to improve upon the earlier Release One project. Next I describe the approach.

PROJECT METHODS

The overall approach we followed was based on the earlier-mentioned action sensemaking model depicted in Figure 40.1. Several years ago, I came across Karl Weick's work on sensemaking and it occurred to me that project teams trying to implement new technologies in organizations were really engaged in deliberate sensemaking initiatives (Weick, 1995). Since my work at the time required me to implement new technologies, I wondered what benefit might accrue to teams if they applied insights from Weick's sensemaking theory – particularly

the idea that, during sensemaking, new meanings are created by combining existing frames with new cues (i.e. where frame equates to schemata and cue equates to input that gets noticed).

The Action Sensemaking Model Explained

While working on my dissertation and the research presented here, I constructed a model for teams trying to determine how best to use new technologies. The result of my model attempt is depicted in Figure 40.1.

This model presents a picture of the action/reflection cycles mentioned at the beginning of this chapter. The first cycle in the model shows that linking both internal and external organizational knowledge can generate relevant cues to sensemaking. These cues are then linked consciously with existing organizational frames in the second action/reflection cycle to generate ideas for utilizing a new technology and, potentially, new organizational meanings and frames. Frame change is depicted as leading to organization change. The 'A's in Figure 40.1 represent the linking actions taken in each of the action/reflection cycles.

In addition to Weick's sensemaking theory, the model draws heavily on the organization change research of Bartunek and Mohrman. For both Mohrman (2001) and Bartunek (1984), planned change requires the modification of schemata or frames that are embedded in a system. For Mohrman (2001), schemata change can occur through social networks and the establishment of network connections that link knowledge from different sources and perspectives. Bartunek (1984), like many from the Hegelian tradition, suggests that dialectical processes need to occur for fundamental change to take place. Her work draws upon other social science work on change in interpretive schemes (Argyris and Schön, 1978; Sheldon, 1980; Hedburg, 1981; Tushman and Romanelli, 1985).

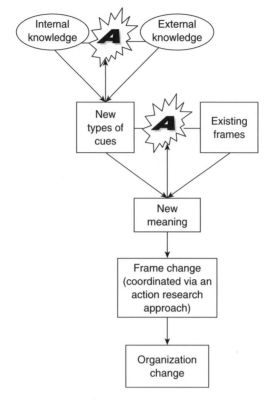

Figure 40.1 *Model depicting how organization change occurs given a sensemaking framework*

Combining the work of Mohrman and Bartunek suggests that fundamental change in organizations requires schemata change and that schemata change requires dialectical processes, which are applied within network connections that link knowledge from different areas – within and external to the organization. Translating the above into sensemaking language, it could be said that fundamental change in organizations requires a change in the frames within an organization. A frame change requires a dialectical process, which allows for new connections to be made by bracketing new types of cues (i.e. represented by the second 'A' in Figure 40.1). Linking knowledge within and external to the organization can generate these new cues (i.e. represented by the first 'A' in Figure 40.1).

In large IT projects, where many departments are affected, there are typically wide variations in views about how best to implement the new systems. These views result, in part, from different schemata or frames held by members of the different departments of an organization. Moreover, power issues come into play in IT projects – the powerful voices typically hold sway around what gets implemented. Reconciling diverse frames and power bases in IT projects had been successfully accomplished in another action research project (McDonagh and Coghlan, 2001/2006). Hence, its use in the action sensemaking model depicted in Figure 40.1 seemed appropriate. Moreover, conscious group learning as a result of action/reflection cycles in AR projects would be useful during the action-required points (indicated by 'A') in the model.

Data Gathering: The First Action/Reflection Cycle

For the first action/reflection cycle, the team decided to use a variety of methods to gather external and internal knowledge. The group decided to divide into two – one group would gather customer data (the research sub-group) via survey instruments and one group would gather internal organizational data by interviewing process experts and create flow-charts of key processes that touched the customer (the process sub-group). The process sub-group would also attempt to define how much time was involved in key process steps and what if any additional costs (i.e. other than time) might be involved.

In addition, the group felt it needed input about what ORG's competitors were doing regarding electronic, internet-based services. So, some members agreed to research competitor web portals and do a show and tell for the team. The technology portion of the team agreed to also conduct a show and tell of the new eService technology product and how it is used in one particular organization. It is important to note that while the co-researchers formed sub-groups to facilitate gathering the data they felt were needed, the group of co-researchers as a 'whole' discussed and reflected upon the data.

Understanding Existing Frames: The Key Concept Questionnaire

Prior to gathering, discussing and reflecting upon the data, co-researchers were asked to answer, with input from their respective work groups, what I termed a 'key concept questionnaire'. Questionnaire responses were to be discussed at a team meeting. The thinking behind the key concept questionnaire was that each of the co-researchers was coming to this project with a theory or frame about key concepts important to this project. I believed that it would be an empowering learning experience to see how (if at all) those concepts might change or be transformed as a result of our work together.

Since the goal of our work was to create a conceptual design for use of eService that would enhance customer service and productivity, the key, going-in concepts to this project were: customer, customer service and productivity. Below are a few of the questions from the key concept questionnaire that are germane to this chapter:

- Who are ORG's customers? What makes them a customer of ORG?
- What is good customer service?
- When you hear the word productivity, what comes to mind?

Brainstorming: The Second Action/Reflection Cycle

For the second action/reflection cycle, the group chose to conduct brainstorming sessions in order to combine all the relevant cues received from data gathering with existing organization frames. The group then prioritized ideas using a technique called the Full Analytical Criteria Method (Brassard and Ritter, 1994). In keeping with the overall project goals, the criteria we decided to prioritize against were cost, efficiency and maximizing customer desires. The top three process ideas resulting from our prioritization work would be those that we would recommend implementing. Emergent within our group process was the involvement of most of the organization in further brainstorming around the top three process ideas.

While the action sensemaking model served as a going-in frame of reference to guide this project, we were open to its modification and embellishment as our group of co-researchers engaged in the work.

PROJECT CHALLENGES AND LEARNINGS

While ultimately a successful effort in that our team met its stated goals, this work was not without challenges. I highlight those challenges here and our learnings from them.

Methodological Challenges/Learnings

The two significant methodological challenges that arose involved (1) the team creating a common frame around key project concepts and (2) the need to involve other organizational members in the sensemaking of this new technology.

Concept Issue 1: Who Are Our Customers?

Concept frame issues occurred early in the project. During the second team meeting, the dialogue that ensued in response to the key concept questionnaire was quite lively. The most dissent occurred around who ORG's customers were. ORG is an internationally recognized accrediting body. Since ORG directly serves a variety of human service providers and its mission is to enhance the lives of people served by those human service providers, at one point in the discussion it seemed that almost anyone on the planet could potentially be someone, albeit indirectly, served by ORG..

Some in the group felt that we needed to narrow our focus to customers that paid for direct ORG services, including trainings and conferences. If we did not narrow our focus, it was thought that we would be spinning our wheels trying to accommodate everyone's interests and not accomplish anything timely. The other point was that if ORG neglected its paying customers, ORG might lose them as customers to ORG's competitors.

Others in the group felt strongly, however, that because of ORG's mission, we needed to pay attention to those persons served by our direct customers as well in this process. Since one of our group's ground rules was to strive for consensus-based decision-making, the facilitator and team worked hard to come up with a resolution. An agreement was reached to focus on customers that paid for ORG services but to note in the team's status report to the steering committee that this was an issue and to further note that mitigating actions to design specific electronic interfaces for persons served would take place outside of this project in the near future.

While originally meant to serve as a 'before snapshot' of frames around key concepts within the group, the dialogue at this point served other significant purposes. Firstly, it created a common frame for the co-researchers, which enabled us to be clear about where we were headed – for example, how could we gather customer data if we weren't clear about who our customer was? Secondly, the dialogue itself set an important tone for the group going forward. It demonstrated that within our project context all voices were important in achieving a common frame and that consensus could be reached.

Concept Issue 2: To Flowchart or Not?

The other concept issue that surfaced was with regard to a methodological concept, which we neglected to discuss upfront. At a meeting where the process sub-group described in detail the flow of one particularly complex ORG process, an intense debate was sparked about the value of looking at flowcharts at that level of detail for our conceptual design deliverable. The more technically oriented members of the group felt that we needed to create flowcharts of existing processes at that level of detail – if we didn't, then we would not be able to clearly see how we could improve organizational effectiveness with eService. Other members of the group felt that creating and assessing this level of detail were not what they signed up for when they agreed to become members of this project team; they felt that 'conceptual' in conceptual design implied a higher level, not quite so detailed type of design. The team agreed to meet at another time to discuss this issue further.

In discussing an approach to the next meeting with the project facilitator, the facilitator and I agreed that simply allowing time for all concerns to be heard and talked about would be the best approach; we also wanted to hear if the team felt that there were alternative methods of achieving the project goals. When the group reconvened, three issues emerged. One was a competence issue – a manager from the customer service area said that she did not feel qualified to assess the flowcharts because she did not know at that level of detail what her staff did. The second issue was the already mentioned issue around the level of detail that was appropriate for a conceptual design. The third issue, which was related to the second, was the time constraint that certain co-researchers felt was imposed upon them – they believed that we simply could not complete creating and assessing the flowcharts with the current project timelines.

The eventual consensus that was reached was that we could continue creating and assessing the flowcharts if we (a) were able to get more time to do so from the steering committee and (b) had validations of the flows from the actual workers connected with those process flows. Both conditions (a) and (b) were ultimately satisfied.

Further reflection on this major division in the group, however, suggested that different frames existed in the group around 'conceptual design'. Moreover, no frame existed concerning flowcharting for this type of work for those members of the group who did not take part in projects which had previously used this technique. So, when the flowcharting cues were presented initially to the group, those members without this frame naturally had difficulty making sense of how this helped the group effort.

One learning from this conflict was that work needed to be done around methodological concepts during our creation of a common frame around key project goal concepts. What is a conceptual design? Which methods are best used to arrive at a conceptual design? These questions would have been best addressed earlier in the project.

Involving Other Organization Members in the Sensemaking

Regarding satisfying condition (b) mentioned above and involving more process workers in the work, we organized group meetings of nearly all the workers involved in the designated, high priority processes – some of these workers were members from the core team. There were at least two, two-hour meetings for each of the processes. The initial meeting included a show-and-tell similar to what the core team saw on the capabilities of the new software. Next, members from the core team explained some of the team's initial, brainstormed ideas. Most work groups were familiar with these ideas prior to the meeting because their core team representatives were constantly sharing project information/output with them. A public folder was also created on a company file server to let anyone in the company view project documents.

The work groups were encouraged to generate more ideas and to continue to do so as they went through the effort of revising their process flows to accommodate the new ideas. A business analyst skilled in using a flowcharting product called VISIO took the as-is process flows developed by the core team and recreated them on the spot as the work groups revised them during the meetings. They were projected on the wall so everyone in the room could see them as the group worked and thought together.

These work groups generated several additional ideas to the core team's, which were then incorporated into the new workflows. During the meetings where these new ideas were generated, there was more group pushback than in the core team meetings. Fellow process workers would probe and question each other more. Good questions like 'How could we handle condition Y if we did X?' would occur or 'If we used feature F, we will need to account for possibility P'. As I sat in these meetings and heard this pushback and the resulting conversation, I realized that this was what we needed to ensure a design that was practical and workable – these people were in the trenches, so to speak, and knew all the potential process variations that could occur. Taking the time to engage in this extension of the core group's work was key to ensuring the quality of our deliverable.

Organizational Challenges/Learnings

Broadly speaking, the organizational challenges we faced in this work involved the amount of time it took to work through issues via a dialogic approach and an overarching contributor to the length of time, which was the existence of competing, entrenched frames or the lack of needed frames within the group.

Competing Frame 1: 'Formal'

An example of competing, entrenched frames occurred as we were trying to accommodate customer stated needs to provide documents electronically. Due to ORG's official capacity as an accrediting body, it was thought by some in the group that official ORG correspondence (e.g. invoices, request for annual conformance report, etc.) should still be sent via a more formal hardcopy letter as opposed to electronic methods. Others in the group who had experience with electronic formal correspondence did not equate formal with hardcopy. In this case, we agreed to seek more data to resolve the issue including obtaining legal advice and researching competitor practices, thereby generating another research/reflection cycle.

Competing Frame 2: Different Approaches to Decision-making

What emerged as a significant frame divergence during the process prioritization portion of our work was a difference in overall *approach* toward reaching a decision about a relative ranking. Some co-researchers needed to validate their ranking more precisely against the data, while others

believed they had a good sense of the data in general and that that was enough for them to determine a ranking. So, where we could reach consensus quickly with a ranking given the latter approach, we did. Where we could not, we devoted the time to resolving differences via dialogue and, at times, painstaking review of the data. This led some co-researchers to question the significance of our work at this point – they felt we were focusing on too much minutiae. After much dialogue, the group conceded that this was important (even though we didn't all like it) because, as one co-researcher articulated, 'it validates it' – where 'it' referred to our final result.

The Challenge of Non-existent or Vague Frames

While our dialogic approach and more data assisted with resolving entrenched frames, helpful analogies were found to be useful in cases where no frame existed for some co-researchers. An example of this occurred when an idea was presented to put ORG's accreditation application online for customers. It was suggested that since this is a difficult document for customers to fill out, we could incorporate help features in the form of drop-downs just like TurboTax. For those team members who had no frame to help make sense of this idea, the TurboTax analogy was helpful in creating such a frame by allowing those members to relate the idea to an existing frame. TurboTax is a tax return preparation software package familiar to many of the co-researchers.

During our first action/reflection cycle most team members were not familiar with many of the competitor website functions and the new types of features available to the company with eService. What helped make these cues salient for those team members was conversation by team members comparing what our competitors did to what we could do and even how we could do it better. For example, the presenter in one instance showed the group how a competitor had many forms available electronically, but they were not interactive and did not feed directly into a database. A team member noted that we could design that better and this was confirmed by a verbal affirmation from another team member. This type of conversation – where a cue was presented, noted and expanded upon by another team member and positively confirmed by one or more additional team members – turned out to be an important facet of the group sensemaking and occurred in later sessions as well. It helped solidify frames where either none existed or only existed vaguely.

POST PROJECT REFLECTION ON ORGANIZATION AND MEANING CHANGE

During a celebratory breakfast after our deliverable was accepted by the steering committee, we reflected upon potential meaning changes occurring in our organization as a result of our work. We realized that our concept of good customer service was expanding to include anytime service – anytime a customer needed a service, it should be available via a web service if possible. Frame transformation was beginning in certain areas as well. Productivity in a web services environment can't mean efficient use of labor and materials to provide that service – once the web service is constructed, no additional labor or material is required for a customer to access that service. Also, 'official' in such an environment can no longer connote 'hardcopy' – secure, password protected, or encrypted are descriptors that might be more appropriately connected with 'official'.

But not all organization change in this work resulted from meaning change. Some of the new ideas generated were simply process changes that incorporated new technology features without changing previously held organizational meanings. Hence, the original model depicted in Figure 40.1 was

modified in Figure 40.2 to reflect the fact that there were two paths to organization change in this project. It might be said, however, that where meaning or frame change was detected, the change was more transformational in nature. Figure 40.2 also captures our initial dialogue about key concepts and what had been noted earlier in this chapter as enablers and distractors of the key action/reflection cycles. Although noted as a distractor, the co-researchers' lack of comfort in making decisions without the larger group actually contributed to the work as a whole.

CONCLUSION: ADDITIONAL THOUGHTS ON DEMOCRATIC PARTICIPATION

Through this work and other IT projects, I have learned that if the work is to be truly 'democratic', the work needs more than just the consent or 'vote' of those affected. After all, the consent may not be informed or it may be coerced. How does one ensure informed, non-coerced consent? I believe three factors, which were incorporated in this work, are important here: the organization must want it; power plays must be actively eliminated; and during the project, active questioning of methodological concepts must occur in addition to other conceptual questioning.

Some organizations simply believe they can't afford the time or cost involved in real, democratic participation – perhaps they may lose market share if they don't move quickly enough to embrace a new technology. These organizations may be prepared to accept the social 'fallout' of such implementations like disgruntled workers and, potentially, the need to terminate employees who don't buy-in. The commitment to a democratic process must be there before utilizing action sensemaking. Typically, it is difficult to obtain such a commitment for IT projects.

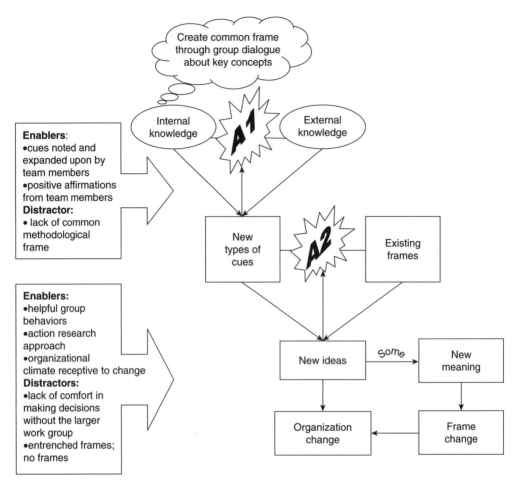

Figure 40.2 *Model depicting how organization change occurred during the action sensemaking project.*

The organization also should employ a facilitator who is not affected by the technology to help with any power issues that might arise. Good facilitation can ensure that all voices are heard during key discussions and that consensus was not coerced.

The new learning for me in this project was that methodological concepts like 'flowcharting' need to be explained and agreed to prior to their use. The issue that arose for our team around flowcharting suggests why many IT projects run into trouble when the IT 'experts' impose methodologies on user teams during system design and implementation. Unless the users understand and buy into the methodologies utilized, they may merely be going through the motions and may resent and, therefore, not fully contribute to the system design and implementation. IT professionals are trained to use various system development methodologies, but are typically not trained to gain informed consent around use of those methodologies.

This work differed from typical IT projects in that we actively sought quality of participation via the above-mentioned democratic processes.

REFERENCES

Argyris, C. and Schön, D.A. (1978) *Organizational Learning: a Theory of Action Perspective.* Reading, MA: Addison-Wesley.

Bartunek, J.M. (1984) 'Changing interpretive schemes and organizational restructuring: the example of a religious order', *Administrative Science Quarterly,* 29: 355–72.

Brassard, M. and Ritter, D. (1994) *The Memory Jogger II.* Methuen, MA: GOAL/QPC.

Hedburg, B. (1981) 'How organizations learn and unlearn', in P. Nystrom and W. Starbuck (eds), *Handbook of Organizational Design.* Oxford: Oxford University Press. pp. 3–27.

McDonagh, J. and Coghlan, D. (2001/2006) 'The art of clinical inquiry in information technology-related change', in P. Reason and H. Bradbury (eds), *Handbook of Action Research: Participative Inquiry and Practice.* London: Sage. pp. 372–8.

Mohrman, S.A. (2001) 'Fundamental organization change and the importance of networks.' Paper presented at the Academy of Management meetings, Washington, DC, August.

Sheldon, A. (1980) 'Organizational paradigms: a theory of organizational change', *Organizational Dynamics,* 8 (3): 61–79.

Tushman, M.L. and Romanelli, E. (1985) 'Organizational evolution: a metamorphosis model of convergence and reorientation', in L. Cummings and B. Staw (eds), *Research in Organizational Behavior (6).* Greenwich, CT: JAI Press.

Weick, K.E. (1995) *Sensemaking in Organizations.* Thousand Oaks, CA: Sage.

PART FOUR

Skills

INTRODUCTION TO SKILLS

As we emphasize throughout this volume, while action research is informed by a variety of epistemological and political perspectives, it is always importantly grounded in practice. So the question 'How do we engage in practice?' is significant and probably under-explored. The people who initiate action research are variously called 'action researchers', 'animators', 'facilitators', 'initiating co-researchers' and so on. What attitudes, skills and qualities of being do they require in order to do their work?

As Morten Levin notes in his contribution, it is quite extraordinary that so little has been written in the action research literature about the education of action researchers and the development of their skills. Looking back at early chapters in the Handbook, we can see that they are alluded to in many places. Marja Liisa Swantz (Chapter 2) writes of the importance of researchers truly living alongside the people they are working with; Anisur Rahman (Chapter 4) writes about the requirement for animators to experience a sense of critical liberated consciousness before they can help others develop similarly. Robert Chambers

(Chapter 20) writes about the behaviour, attitudes and mindsets that underlie the techniques of PRA. Bill Torbert and Steve Taylor (Chapter 16) write of the qualities of moment to moment attention that are required for truly reflective practice. Many of the chapters in the Exemplars section draw attention to these kinds of skills in practice.

By their nature, skills are not easy to write about. They are necessarily embodied. A while ago John Heron uses the term 'knack' to describe that inner core of action which transcends verbal description and is known only to the doer at the moment of doing. At the heart of the practice of a skill is 'a knowing of the excellence of its doing' (Heron, 1996: 44). At the same time Heron points out that 'Skills are a blessed relief. They bring us to the business of living' (Heron, 1992: 173).

While we agree with Levin that little has been written directly about action research skills, there were important contributions in the first edition of this Handbook, notably the chapters by Jenny Rudolph, Steve Taylor and Erica Foldy (2001/2006), Yoland Wadsworth (2001/2006), Reason and Marshall (2001/2006) and Judi Marshall (2001/2006). There are also important things we can draw on from the wider literature on facilitation and group dynamics (e.g. Baldwin, 1996; Egan, 1994; Heron, 1999; Randall and Southgate, 1980; Srivastva et al., 1977; Tuckman, 1965), psychotherapy (e.g. Hillman, 1975; Perls et al., 1951; Rogers, 1961), education as liberation (Freire, 1970; Mezirow, 1981) and spiritual practice (Coghlan, 2005; Winter, 2003; Heron and Lahood, Chapter 29).

As I (Peter) write this, I am drawn to reflect on the development of my own abilities as an action researcher. Certainly, a long history of working in a variety of T-groups and encounter groups, in co-counselling and psychotherapy helped unhook me from some of my most engrained patterns. My encounter with feminism in the 1960s and 1970s was quite shocking, bouncing out of at least some of my patriarchal assumptions. In more recent years I have learned most through attempting to live the values I espouse as an action researcher in my life as an educator. Judi Marshall and I described one aspect of this as 'dancing in beauty rather than fighting ugliness' which, in the context of modern university life, is not always easy:

> Taking an attitude of inquiry involves noticing our current state, gently taking its messages ('ah, I have let that unsettle me') and seeking to adjust it if appropriate. Our practices for stepping aside into dancing with beauty are simple, when we can access them. They include: noticing the breath; sitting in committee meetings in a position of meditation, allowing and noticing what comes, internally and externally, but not attaching to it; taking time; maintaining a life beyond 'work' … being embodied; being in nature; noticing and contradicting the messages of duty to workaholic behaviour and frames of mind; and meeting with people fully, not instrumentally, looking them in the eye. When we practice these approaches, and others, the world is a different place. And they need repeatedly re-inscribing, the context does not seem to foster them, sometimes they seem beyond our reach. (Marshall and Reason, 2006)

So bearing in mind that the skills of action research are both a 'blessed relief', profoundly simply, maddeningly elusive and most difficult to describe, we offer eight different perspectives. Jill Grant, Geoff Nelson, and Terry Mitchell provide an overview of five challenges in PAR practice: building relationships, acknowledging and sharing power, encouraging participation, making change, and establishing credible accounts. Kate McArdle then pays particular attention to the establishment, facilitation and conclusion of a co-operative inquiry group. Jenny Mackewn explores facilitation both for action research, but also as action research. Moving up the scale to the management of larger action research practices, Geoff Mead reflects on his experience of managing a large-scale leadership programme based in action inquiry groups and draws lessons for the management of such large complex projects; following which David Coghlan and Rami Shani reflect on the skills of the organizational insider as action researcher.

We then turn to the issue of the education of action researchers with two complementary chapters: Steve Taylor, Jenny Rudolph and Erica Foldy provide a detailed account of their practice of teaching reflective practice; and Morten Levin draws on his experience to reflect more broadly on the nature of university education and the place of action research in both undergraduate and doctoral programmes. Finally, Judi Marshall reflects on the issues that arise when searching for appropriate form in writing for action research

REFERENCES

Baldwin, C. (1996) *Calling the Circle: the First and Future Culture*. Bath: Gateway Books.

Coghlan, D. (2005) 'Ignatian spirituality as transformational social science', *Action Research*, 3 (1): 89–107.

Egan, G. (1994) *The Skilled Helper*, 5th edn. Monterey, CA: Brooks/Cole Publishing.

Freire, P. (1970) *Pedagogy of the Oppressed*. New York: Herder & Herder.

Heron, J. (1992) *Feeling and Personhood: Psychology in Another Key*. London: Sage.

Heron, J. (1996) 'Quality as primacy of the practical', *Qualitative Inquiry*, 2 (1): 41–56.

Heron, J. (1999) *The Complete Facilitator's Handbook*. London: Kogan Page.

Hillman, J. (1975) *Revisioning Psychology*. New York: Harper Collophon.

Marshall, J. (2001/2006) 'Self-reflective inquiry practices', in P. Reason and H. Bradbury (eds), *Handbook of Action Research: Participative Inquiry and Practice.* London: Sage. pp. 439–9. Also published in P. Reason and H. Bradbury (eds) (2006), *Handbook of Action Research: Concise Paperback Edition.* London: Sage. pp. 335–42.

Marshall, J. and Reason, P. (2006) 'Keynote address: Taking an attitude of inquiry.' Paper presented at the ALARPM 7th and PAR 11th World Congress, Groningen, The Netherlands, 22 August.

Mezirow, J. (1981) 'A critical theory of adult learning and education', *Adult Education,* 32 (1): 3–24.

Perls, F., Hefferline, R. and Goodman, P. (1951) *Gestalt Therapy.* New York: Dell.

Randall, R. and Southgate, J. (1980) *Co-operative and Community Group Dynamics … Or Your Meetings Needn't Be So Appalling.* London: Barefoot Books.

Reason, P. and Marshall, J. (2001/2006) 'On supervising graduate research students', in P. Reason and H. Bradbury (eds), *Handbook of Action Research: Participative Inquiry and Practice.* London: Sage. pp. 413–19. Also published in P. Reason and H. Bradbury (eds) (2006), *Handbook of Action Research: Concise Paperback Edition.* London: Sage. pp. 315–21.

Rogers, C.R. (1961) *On Becoming a Person.* London: Constable.

Rudolph, J.W., Taylor, S.S. and Foldy, E.G. (2001/2006) 'Collaborative off-line reflection: a way to develop skill in action science and action inquiry', in P. Reason and H. Bradbury (eds), *Handbook of Action Research: Participative Inquiry and Practice.* London: Sage. pp. 405–12. Also published in P. Reason and H. Bradbury (eds) (2006), *Handbook of Action Research: Concise Paperback Edition.* London: Sage. pp. 307–14.

Srivastva, S., Obert, S.L. and Neilson, E. (1977) 'Organizational analysis through group processes: a theoretical perspective', in C.L. Cooper (ed.), *Organizational Development in the UK and USA.* London: Macmillan. pp. 83–111.

Tuckman, B. (1965) 'Development sequences in small groups', *Psychological Bulletin,* 63: 419–27.

Wadsworth, Y. (2001/2006) 'The mirror, the magnifying glass, the compass and the map: facilitating participatory action research', in P. Reason and H. Bradbury (eds), *Handbook of Action Research: Participative Inquiry and Practice.* London: Sage. pp. 420–32. Also published in P. Reason and H. Bradbury (eds) (2006), *Handbook of Action Research: Concise Paperback Edition.* London: Sage. pp. 322–34.

Winter, R. (2003) 'Buddhism and action research: towards an appropriate model of inquiry for the caring professions', *Educational Action Research,* 11 (1): 141–60.

41

Negotiating the Challenges of Participatory Action Research: Relationships, Power, Participation, Change and Credibility

Jill Grant, Geoffrey Nelson and Terry Mitchell

In this chapter we explore some of the issues that researchers and participants face when engaging in participatory action research (PAR). We suggest negotiation processes and skills that may be helpful in co-creating meaningful research accounts that arise from the lived experiences of communities as well as the subjectivity of ourselves as researchers. We reflect on power issues, self-reflexivity and the potential to develop credible accounts that can be transformative and transgressive. We consider PAR challenges, negotiation processes, and identified skills for building relationships, acknowledging and sharing power, encouraging participation, making change, and establishing credible accounts. As we discuss each area of challenge, we present vignettes from our own research that serve as examples of the challenges and possible strategies for achieving the goals of participatory research.

Participatory action research (PAR) is a research methodology that attempts to address power imbalances and oppressive social structures. It values the 'researched' community as a vital part of the research project and its members as experts of their own experiences. PAR is particularly concerned with oppressed communities and attempts to create action as a catalyst for social change (see in particular Chapters 2, 3, 27 and 35). While definitions of what 'counts' as PAR may vary, it is generally recognized that PAR includes some important dimensions. PAR identifies as goals emancipation, empowerment, participatory democracy, and the illumination of social problems and is a cyclical process of research, learning, and action. These cycles are understood to be iterative, with each building upon the other (Altpeter et al., 1999; Boog, 2003; Brydon-Miller, 2001; Coenen and Khonraad, 2003; Green et al., 1995; Kemmis and McTaggart, 2005; Minkler and Wallerstein, 2003; Reason and Bradbury, 2001/2006; Stringer, 1996). It emphasizes these values as it asserts that new knowledge is gained through mutual understanding and collaboration, considering the research project and its evaluation as a shared process between researchers and communities (Reid, 2000; Roberts and Dick, 2003). Further, PAR has as a goal the outcome of capacity-building within the community involved in the research (Alvarez and Gutierrez, 2001).

In this chapter we explore some of the issues that researchers and participants in PAR may face and suggest negotiation processes that may be helpful in developing credible accounts that are both based in the subjectivity of researchers and communities and that have the potential to be transformative and transgressive. In doing so, we emphasize the large responsibility that we as researchers have in exploring our own subjectivity and in being clear and reflexive about our values and power. Ultimately the goal of this chapter is not to provide straightforward answers to challenges faced in pursuing PAR, but to highlight tensions with the goal of making the research process and its challenges more transparent.

We are three researchers from Canada: two working in the field of Community Psychology (GN and TM) and one in Social Work (JG). Jill is a recent PhD graduate who is interested in partnerships with those who have experienced the mental health system (who often refer to themselves, in Canada, as 'consumer-survivors') and who has conducted PAR projects with mental health organizations. Geoff has also done research and action with consumer-survivors around issues of housing and self-help and with neighbourhood organizations serving low-income families with young children. Terry conducts and teaches participatory action research. Her research focus is on Aboriginal health issues and women's experiences of cancer and cancer care.

Although we have varying interests and experiences, we all share a commitment to research that is values-based and focused on partnership and action. We believe that central to the success of PAR is a commitment to clarifying and enacting values that contribute to the relationships and end results desired by partners in PAR projects. We understand values to be guidelines that help us to make choices and to navigate the various challenges within a PAR research project. The values we identify as central to our work mirror those that Nelson et al. (2001) present as central to Community Psychology: caring, compassion, community, health, self-determination, participation, power-sharing, human diversity, and social justice. Because of our values stance, we do comment on both the 'is' and the 'ought': that is, how we conduct research (is) and how we believe, from our particular value stance, challenges in PAR should be negotiated (ought).

Current literature addressing the challenges of PAR, discussed below, while helpful in its recognition of some of the issues facing PAR researchers, reveals definite gaps in its recognition of the skills required to negotiate PAR and in its illustration of the required negotiation processes. After summarizing the challenges, strategies for addressing them, and the skills required, we provide examples of our research in vignettes as illustrations of possible ways to negotiate the challenges.

PRESENTING AND ADDRESSING CHALLENGES

Since it is essentially a dialogical process, participating in PAR gives rise to challenges, many of which may be based in differences between researchers (as outsiders) and participants (as insiders). The ways in which researchers meet these challenges has impacts on both the participatory nature of the research project and on how emancipatory the knowledge created may be (Roberts and Dick, 2003). We have categorized challenges raised in the PAR literature in this way: *building relationships, acknowledging and sharing power, encouraging participation, making change,* and *establishing credible accounts.* We present challenges and suggestions for facing these challenges, as well as the skills required. Much of the literature tends to provide ways to address challenges that, in the attempt to make PAR accessible, may actually minimize the complexity of it. We present suggested resolutions, as well as our own thoughts about these resolutions. However, it is important to recognize that in doing so we do not wish to provide a recipe book answer to negotiating PAR: we *do* see it as an exceedingly complex process. Rather, this summary is provided as a starting point for reflection on the intricacies of PAR and for an awareness of the impact of the researcher's own position in the research process. As important as it is to resolve conflicts, it is arguably more imperative to develop the ability to recognize the occasions when conflicts will not be resolved and to reflect on one's ability to accept the extant conflict. As Isenberg et al. (2004) remind us, 'Collaboration necessarily includes conflicts, not all of which can be easily resolved' (p. 126).

Building Relationships

Gray et al. (2000) note that PAR is based on relationships. We agree: we consider relationships to be the foundation on which the success of PAR depends. Within relationships between researchers and community members, trust is the central challenge, giving rise to the need to question whether researchers are adequately trained to develop relationships with the communities into which they venture. The researcher is often the outsider and has the responsibility to gain the trust of community members. This may be difficult for a variety of reasons, including

the fact that the community may see the researcher as more similar to service providers than to community members (Reid, 2000), and/or as members of an historically oppressive group. Addressing challenges vis-à-vis relationships requires a unique blend of skills and values: skills and values that are not often addressed in the training one receives in preparation to become a researcher. Relationships represent, instead, a way of being with people and often require us to unlearn approaches advocating distance and 'objectivity'.

It is important for researchers to approach relationships with communities with transparency and clarity about one's positions and about the expectations one has of community members. By being transparent and clear about expectations, a researcher and community may be better able to contract about mutual expectations, an important step in negotiating the research process (Coenen and Khonradd, 2003; Hagey, n.d.; Heron and Reason, 2001/2006; Roberts and Dick, 2003). In order to build relationships with community members, it is vital that researchers take time to learn about the community and build informal relationships with community members. Such relationships may be facilitated through open and honest communication, begun, as stated previously, with open discussion of mutual expectations. Regular team meetings to check in on process and progress also assist in building relationships and in keeping dialogue open (Alvarez and Gutierrez, 2001; Isenberg et al., 2004; Ochocka et al., 2002).

In order to successfully navigate relationships with communities, we as researchers need to communicate our expectations honestly and authentically, while maintaining the commitment to participation, empowerment and democracy as well as a sincere interest in participants as individuals. Researchers often require certain outputs (e.g. published articles, evaluation reports) as a function of their employment, and we encourage researchers to reflect on this and to share their needs openly with participants. Reflection will also

Table 41. 1 *Building relationships: challenges, strategies and skills*

Challenges	Strategies	Required skills
• Community mistrust of outside researchers • Inadequate preparation and training of researchers	• Communicate openly and honestly • Contract • Learn about community • Build informal relationship • Hold regular team meetings	• Communication skills • Ability to express needs • Ability to help others express needs

---

Vignette 1 *Building relationships with service user researchers*

After being approached by a mental health housing provider to conduct an evaluation of its new services, Jill and a co-investigator are currently working in partnership with service users of this organization to evaluate the process of developing this supported housing facility and the outcomes for tenants of the facility. Service user researchers are working in collaboration with the outside researchers to collect and analyze the data for this three year project. During the training for the service user researchers, it has been important to focus on building relationships. This has meant more frequent meetings than absolutely required and informal time to get to know each other at the beginning of each meeting. In addition, Jill and her co-investigator have shared openly with the service user researchers the benefits to us of conducting the research project, i.e. opportunities for research funding, publications, and networking with mental health service users and service providers. The service user researchers have also taken time to discuss the ways in which they hope to benefit from the project and the relationships. The time invested in this relationship-building is helping to build trust among the team of researchers.

---

assist a researcher in identifying any existing attitudes toward the community and to understand the ways in which these attitudes may influence the ability to build relationships. Table 41.1 summarizes the challenges, strategies and skills for building relationships in a participatory project.

In Vignette 1, Jill discusses some of the ongoing strategies to build relationships and trust with members of a community who are both service users and, for the research project, researchers.

While incorporating informal time within the context of meetings may reduce the efficiency of the project, the focus on building relationships and getting to know community partners both builds trust and provides transparency regarding the research process. Jill and her co-investigator hope that the time spent building relationships will prove beneficial throughout the research project. The ability to build relationships is also affected by the treatment of power, the next challenge raised.

Acknowledging and Sharing Power

PAR has as one of its central tenets the importance of addressing power inequities in society; it endeavours to begin this process within the research relationship. Power, as we define it, is a potential (Giddens, 1979) which is created within the interaction of relationships (Foucault, 1994) and which can be used *over* others as domination (Giddens, 1993), or *with* others to make positive change (see also Chapter 11). Most researchers enjoy a place of relative and actual power in comparison to most participants in PAR. It may be difficult, therefore, to prepare oneself as a researcher for relinquishing the control that normally comes as a perquisite of power (Gray et al., 2000). It is vital to note that research participants are not powerless in the research relationship – indeed, without their consent, the research relationship would not exist. It is also important to remember that power is not limited, but rather can be shared and this sharing can generate more power. In order to share power resources with communities to foster the existing potential for social action it is necessary for researchers to specifically acknowledge our sources of power. Moreover, researchers need to acknowledge that power inequities within the research relationship are not erased, only reduced through processes of PAR. Indeed, the institutional, structural and dominant forces within the context of the researcher, as well as the researched, must be considered (Kemmis, 2001/2006). Without identifying and discussing power issues within the research relationship, as Bond (1990), Healy (2001), and Reid (2000) point out, and power dynamics within the researcher's setting, non-reflexive claims to equality of power may result. This can lead to oppressive relationships, where power is used over communities and where the rights and privileges of researchers dominate, as researchers inadvertently reproduce oppressive dynamics. It is also suggested that most research benefits the researcher more than the community (the researched) and that this inequity further reinforces the power differential (Reid, 2000). Further, since research unfolds within a context or setting that contains its own power dynamics, it is necessary for the researcher to gain awareness of this context (Altpeter et al., 1999; Boog, 2003; Coenen and Khonraad, 2003; Reid, 2000) as well as the professional challenges and restraints within their academic setting.

As with building relationships, we assert the importance of researcher reflexivity, taking time to consider our positions of power and the ways in which we can share our power. One strategy for sharing power is an open discussion with communities, examining sources of power, especially those that are less apparent, acknowledging power differentials and encouraging discussion about how to address them. Community members are likely to envision ways in which to address power differentials, but a researcher has a responsibility to consider strategies ahead of time. One important step is for the researcher to acknowledge that the research project is a learning opportunity for all; with this understanding comes a commitment to recognize and value varying sources of knowledge (Boog, 2003; Coenen and Khonraad, 2003; Fadem et al., 2003; Hagey, n.d.; Healy, 2001; Ochocka et al., 2002; Reid, 2000; Roberts and Dick, 2003). Recognizing and valuing various sources of knowledge is the first step toward sharing knowledge. The PAR researcher can facilitate this by demystifying the research process and learning to engage research participants in the research by sharing her/his technical knowledge and building research capacity within the community. PAR moves us from the traditional power dynamic of the researcher researching 'the researched' to the bi-directional sharing of various skills, resources and expertise in the co-construction of knowledge. Isenberg et al. (2004) and Ochocka et al. (2002) suggest training communities, teaching them research vocabulary, and avoiding jargon as strategies for demystifying the process. Gray et al. (2000) and Isenberg et al. (2004) also add the importance, as we asserted above, of being clear about needed or expected outcomes of the research project.

It is also vital to include the community in all phases of the research project, and Roberts and Dick (2003) suggest that, as community members become increasingly competent, the amount of control they hold be increased. In an emphasis on co-constructed knowledge this would include an increased emphasis on participation in the textual aspects of meaning making: analysis, interpretation, reporting, and dissemination. Members of a community involved in a research project also suggested that there be a mechanism built into the research process to address abuses of power (Reeve et al., 2002).

It may be helpful, at the outset of a project, for researcher and communities to agree on how decisions will be made. Another strategy is to ensure that 50 per cent of the research budget directly benefits the research population and members of the identified population though employment, training, and other resources that may go directly to the community for access to and use of community resources, space, and services.

Table 41.2 *Sharing power: challenges, strategies and skills*

Challenges	Strategies	Required skills
• Researcher is generally in a position of power relative to community members • Researcher may be reluctant to acknowledge privilege and share power	• Reflect on and discuss positions of power and sources of inequity • View research project as learning opportunity for all • Demystify research process • Encourage community involvement in all stages of project, with increasing control • Create mechanisms to address abuses of power	• Reflexivity • Humility • Facilitation and group process skills • Awareness of the mechanisms of power and oppression • Willingness to cede power • Capacity building

---

Vignette 2   *Sharing power in PAR with Aboriginal communities*

Terry is a non-Aboriginal woman who has been conducting research with Aboriginal people since 1991. She has learned to recognize that neither individuals nor groups of people are inherently powerless; rather their ability to exercise their personal and collective power may be constrained by structural inequalities, be they researchers or the researched. While PAR researchers may strive to document these structural inequalities, they must actively resist reinforcing or replicating them within the research relationship. Terry has found that Aboriginal communities, due to a history of colonization and a record of harmful research practices, do not view a participatory action research methodology as sufficient to counterbalance the many harms that have been created by outside researchers. While the Aboriginal Women's Cancer Care Study was participatory and was guided by an Aboriginal Advisory Group, coordinated by an Aboriginal woman, and employed Aboriginal interviewers in each of the communities, this was not enough to ensure the adequate protection of culture and communities. They had to further demonstrate their willingness and ability to share power by engaging in and meeting new standards for Aboriginal research. OCAP, which stands for Ownership, Control, Access, and Possession (of research data), is part of an active process of restoring the power and control of research and indigenous knowledge back to Aboriginal communities and individuals. They conducted a separate ethics review, meeting the criteria of OCAP, for each of the four communities that they approached for participation. This process took over a year and a half of relationship building and community decision-making in clarifying the definition and dynamics of power sharing in these multiple research relationships (Mitchell and Baker, 2005).

Once again, a researcher must be reflexive about power sources and needs. This requires insight into the mechanisms of power and oppression and honest commitment to challenging them (Hagey, n.d.). While this reflexivity is not enough to actually address power imbalances, it is the first step, directing our attention to the sources of inequity and to our degree of commitment to challenging inequity (Martin-Baro, 1994). As one way to become more reflexive about power imbalances, Kondrat (1999) suggests a series of questions that we can ask ourselves and that direct our attention to structural inequities and sources of oppression we may wish to challenge through our relationships. The next step, the actual sharing of power, requires a commitment to empowerment and democracy as well as respect for the knowledge and abilities of community members. Along with this respect, we find it important to search for a healthy dose of humility, which may lead to a greater willingness to cede power. In order to implement sharing of power, a researcher requires group facilitation skills (Nelson et al., 2004b) and skills in drawing out the strengths of others. Table 41.2 summarizes the challenges, strategies and skills of sharing power in a participatory project.

In Vignette 2, Terry provides an example of some of the negotiation processes in a project with a community living with a legacy of institutionalized oppression. In doing so, she demonstrates some of the possible ways to begin to share power.

By noting the unique characteristics of the community with whom they were working, by respecting community-identified needs, by committing to a devolution of power, and by honouring community members' expertise, Terry and her colleagues were able to actively challenge structural inequities through interactions, responding to the need for community ownership of their own forms of knowledge and action. The ability to share power has as one of its possible outcomes increased participation from the community, the next challenge to be presented.

Encouraging Participation

While different projects have varying goals with regard to level of participation (Isenberg et al., 2004), the question of possible and desired participation arises in PAR projects. It is important for researchers, in our enthusiasm for participatory research, to avoid making assumptions about the level of participation desired by a community (Bond, 1990). As Chambers and Gaventa and Cornwall (Chapters 20 and 11) also note, Cooke and Kothari (2001) have described participation as a 'new tyranny', arguing that, in efforts to encourage community participation, researchers and community developers may intentionally or unintentionally reinforce existing power inequalities. It is, thus, important to attempt to gain an understanding of community members' interests in participation, while striving toward making participation accessible to as many as possible. This requires open discussion with communities about their wishes, rather than researchers making assumptions that meet our agendas.

There are a number of barriers to participation of community members in a research project: time constraints (Altpeter et al., 1999; Gray et al., 2000), financial barriers (Green et al., 1995), language barriers, community members being overwhelmed or intimidated, and some community members burning out, since often the same individuals are repeatedly invited to participate in projects. Prior to commencing a PAR project, it is important for the community and the researcher to assess its feasibility. If feasible, the community and researcher may wish to imagine potential barriers to participation and discover ways to address them, keeping an eye on being flexible and searching for possible accommodations and offering various options for participation (Bond, 1990; Ochocka et al., 2002). For example, advocating with a funder for funds to support participation may help to address financial barriers (Fadem et al., 2003). This conversation requires communication skills, especially listening and negotiation.

If barriers are addressed, it is expected that community members' levels of commitment will vary across individuals and throughout the life of the project. As researchers, we must be respectful of participants' needs and constraints. This raises the importance of contracting about roles and renegotiating roles throughout the project, as individuals' abilities to participate may change over time. As participation increases, the organizational challenges become more complex. It may be fruitful for a coordinating committee to be formed with the responsibility of communicating with all committees, and it is important to regularly check in with all participants (Altpeter et al., 1999; Fadem et al., 2003; Gray et al., 2000; Reeve et al., 2002; Roberts and Dick, 2003).

Varying levels of participation may mean that those community members who are less able to participate may feel excluded. For this reason, communication with all stakeholders is encouraged (Boog, 2003; Fadem et al., 2003; Isenberg et al., 2004). This feeling of exclusion, however, may signal a desire to become involved, and skills in motivation and capacity-building may help reluctant community members to recognize the strengths they may bring. Table 41.3 summarizes considerations in encouraging participation.

In Vignette 3, Terry discusses some processes of encouraging participation in a

Table 41.3   *Encouraging participation: challenges, strategies and skills*

Challenges to participation	Strategies	Skills required
• Barriers to participation • Varying levels of commitment • Organizational challenges • Feelings of exclusion or intimidation	• Assess feasibility of PAR • Find accommodations to address barriers • Offer options for participation • Contract and renegotiate • Establish a coordinating committee • Communicate regularly with all stakeholders	• Communication skills • Organizational skills • Flexibility • Motivational skills • Capacity-building skills

---

Vignette 3   *Community participation in PAR focusing on the Swiss Air disaster*

In October 1998 Swiss Air Flight 111 crashed into the Atlantic Ocean outside of Halifax, Nova Scotia. Through an extensive community consultation and snowballing process, Terry was able to identify individuals who would form a Community Advisory Group (CAG) to inform and guide community entry, access, data collection, interpretation and dissemination. The CAG (volunteer fire chief, Emergency Measures Coordinator, Ground Search and Rescue Captain, three social workers, three clergy, a retired fisherman, and three civic leaders) met approximately once every two months for the next two years. Individuals also attended additional special committee meetings to develop community information releases about the study, to review and provide feedback on all research instruments, and to develop community mental health protocols for responding to research participants' potential needs for service, and the development of a support service brochure. The ongoing and extensive participation of the CAG group was facilitated by the investigators and research coordinator traveling 45 minutes to 2 hours to the rural coastal communities. Terry and the research coordinator expressed their commitment to the communities by traveling to meet in their homes, churches, and fire halls rather than the university and arranging for local businesses to cater meetings. A donation was also made to the local fire hall for the use of their facilities. Significantly, a contract was drafted and signed by all research collaborators that outlined the roles and responsibilities of both the large interdisciplinary team and the CAG. The ongoing commitment and participation of CAG members was sustained through clear and constant communication, researcher presence in the coastal communities and legitimate opportunities for participation including national and international conference presentations and co-authorship on a published article (Mitchell et al., 2003).

---

community. At the same time, her vignette illustrates the vital role that a coordinating committee may play as well as the positive impact of careful communication with community members.

The level of participation and its quality impacts on the next two areas of challenge: making change and establishing credible accounts.

Making Change

Since PAR arises out of a desire to effect change, this is an important outcome to explore. As Healy (2001) notes, there is often confusion about what constitutes change for PAR projects. Is comprehensive social change the only true form of change in PAR? The desired change varies with each research project, but we find it important to negotiate with community members about the desired change. The pace of this change is intertwined with this challenge: it is possible that a community may want and need quick results in the form of local change while a researcher may be focused on comprehensive social change (Healy, 2001). The reality is that change, and thus, PAR, is often a slow process, and it is important to be upfront with a community about this. Weick (1984) asserted that, in social change work, it is important to achieve 'small wins' rather than expecting large-scale change

Table 41.4 *Making change: challenges, strategies and skills*

Challenges	Strategies	Required skills
• Differing definitions of needed change • Change and PAR are often a slow process	• Discuss and negotiate purposes of project and the definition and pace of change • Work together to create and implement a plan for change • Recognize times for the researcher to step away • Understand action and research as complementary and iterative	• Knowledge of intervention strategies • Negotiation skills • Facilitation skills • Capacity-building

---

Vignette 4 *PAR and advocacy for housing for people with mental health challenges*

In the early 1980s, Geoff, along with Mary Earls, who was a graduate student in Community Psychology at Wilfrid Laurier University, conducted an action-oriented needs assessment of housing and support for mental health consumer/survivors in Waterloo Region (Nelson and Earls, 1986). The results of this multi-method assessment clearly documented the need for supportive housing and were shared at a community forum hosted by the local social planning council that was attended by roughly 70 people. Politicians running for office in the upcoming provincial election were invited to attend and to comment on the findings and their parties' platforms regarding the issue at hand. Participants at the meeting were invited to join a mental health housing coalition to address the issue. This coalition operated for more than six years and included mental health consumer/survivors, family members, service-providers, planners, housing providers, and interested community members. Geoff and Mary acted as Chairs for part of that time, while other stakeholders stepped forward and assumed leadership roles at other times. The coalition was very successful in advocating with government, using a variety of strategies (letter-writing, newspaper articles, meeting with government officials) for more housing and support for mental health consumers during this time period (Nelson, 1994).

---

to occur dramatically. Deciding upon a focus for change requires negotiation about the purposes of the research project between community and researcher, balancing the needs of each (Alvarez and Guttierez, 2001). In this way, the community and researcher work together to create and implement the action plan for the research project (Isenberg et al., 2004), with the researcher taking responsibility for recognizing times when it makes sense for her/him to step aside and allow the community to take responsibility for the project (Fadem et al., 2003). One attitude that may help researchers and community members to be comfortable with the process is an awareness that research and action are complementary and iterative (Roberts and Dick, 2003).

It is vital for a researcher to be aware of intervention strategies, to be skilled at both

facilitation and negotiation, and to have an ability to identify and develop strengths in the community. Table 41.4 summarizes the challenges, strategies, and skills related to making change.

While we agree with Alvarez and Gutierrez (2001) when they remind us that change and PAR are often slow processes, we also have found that the timing of a project is important, and that, by expecting PAR to be a slow process, researchers may miss an opportunity for change. The reality is that PAR depends on our ability to build positive relationships with communities: relationships take time to build. But we advise researchers to be open to the possibility that timing may allow the research project to unfold in a timely manner.

In Vignette 4, Geoff shares an example from his early work, where including representatives from various groups helped to define and enable change. It highlights the researchers' abilities to effectively facilitate partnerships while also identifying and building capacity among a large group of stakeholders. The effectiveness of timing the transfer of responsibility to other members of the team was borne out in the positive change-making results.

Establishing Credible Accounts

Some question whether PAR confuses community development with research (Krimerman, 2001). We maintain that PAR is, in fact, research that *also* leads to community development. As a legitimate research approach, PAR must endeavour to establish credible accounts at the same time that it attempts to create change. We define credible accounts as those that adequately capture the experiences of participants. As in any research methodology, there exist in PAR certain threats to creating credible accounts. In order to evaluate research, a researcher and community must collaboratively decide on the criteria for credibility. Following a constructivist understanding of reality as created by local experiences (Alvesson and Skoldberg, 2000), we believe that credibility in PAR means that the truth and knowledge of the community is both privileged and communicated. For us, this is the important question in research which is attempting to illuminate human experience, whether PAR or another methodology: Does it adequately reflect the community and the experience and interests of its members?

Due to the power differentials often present between researchers and communities, there exists the constant risk that community members' local knowledges will be subjugated by researchers' 'generalizable' knowledge, and that researchers' interpretations will be privileged over communities' (Coenen and Khonraad, 2003; Fadem et al., 2003; Reid, 2000; Roberts and Dick, 2003). It is important, then, to commit to community control of the research project, which

suggests involvement of the community in all stages of the project and creating space for community knowledge. This means that, in the co-construction of knowledge, researchers may well frequently seek the input of community members prior to offering their own interpretations or understandings. It also means that, if there are tensions between the understandings of communities and of researchers, the texts produced would emphasize these tensions, as they may serve to highlight the complexity of knowledge construction. Coenen and Khonraad (2003) assert that the researcher also has a responsibility to be clear about decisions made during the research process and their rationale. This means tracking carefully the rationale for decisions and reporting these in the texts we produce. Relinquishing control and still maintaining integrity requires knowledge and skills in a variety of research paradigms (Brydon-Miller, 2001; Green et al., 1995) and a respect for the community's knowledge that requires researcher humility.

Another potential barrier to creating credible accounts is the lack of continuity of participants that often exists in PAR. As stated previously, community members' abilities to participate may change throughout the process of a PAR project. To address this, Wadsworth (2001/2006) suggests that PAR researchers work with community members who are the most dedicated to the project since they are the most likely to endure. Retaining participants requires skills in motivation, facilitation, and capacity-building. Table 41.5 summarizes the above material.

In Vignette 5, Geoff highlights the positive effects of privileging the knowledge of the consumer-survivor community. It illustrates both the importance and the possibility of adapting research methodologies according to the purpose of the project and the needs of the communities. By drawing on their vast knowledge of different research approaches and starting from the perspective of the community, Geoff and colleagues were able to create credible accounts that reflect the

Table 41.5 *Creating credible accounts: challenges, strategies and skills*

Challenges	Strategies	Required skills
• Researcher's interpretations may be privileged • Researcher's 'generalizable' knowledge may subjugate community's local knowledge • Lack of continuity of participation	• Encourage community control and participation at all stages • Privilege community knowledge • Be clear about decisions • Work with most interested community members	• Knowledge/skill related to a variety of research paradigms • Humility • Motivation skills • Facilitation skills • Capacity-building skills

---

Vignette 5 *Establishing credible accounts in PAR with consumer/survivor-run organizations*

Geoff and colleagues have just completed a participatory action research project that is a longitudinal evaluation of mental health consumer/survivor organizations in southwestern Ontario (Nelson et al., 2004a). These organizations are operated exclusively by and for people who have experienced mental health challenges. Participatory action research is an excellent fit with the ethos of these settings (Nelson et al., 1998). This study utilizes both quantitative and qualitative methods to examine the activities and impacts of these organizations on both individuals (new members) and systems (community, service systems, and policy). It has been important to establish the credibility of the methods and findings to the consumer/survivor community, service-providers, policy-makers, and researchers. Rigorous quantitative and qualitative methods within the framework of a PAR study that passed the scrutiny of peer reviewers (researchers) for funding and which was developed with and supported by the consumer/survivor community have been key in establishing credible accounts of the nature and effects of these organizations (Nelson et al., 2004a).

---

knowledge of the community and meet rigourous academic standards.

CONCLUSIONS

We have attempted to emphasize the importance of researchers being reflexive and responsive to community needs through the willingness to share and cede power. We provided specific examples that illustrate and serve to address various challenges in PAR. With this reflexivity and commitment to devolution of power, a researcher is better prepared to approach the inevitable unmentioned and unexpected challenges that arise. By spending time reflecting on one's position vis-à-vis community members, actively searching for ways to decrease barriers to their participation, and striving for open communication, researchers will be more prepared to honestly approach PAR projects

and to share the research process and product with communities. Recognition of the responsibility that comes with a decision to enter into partnership with communities is vital as a first step to sharing power and negotiating processes.

PAR is an approach to research that represents radical changes to the ways in which research is conducted, to what is valued as knowledge (Altpeter et al., 1999; Alvarez and Gutierrez, 2001), and to the way research must be taught (Nelson et al., 2004b). In order for PAR to be a positive experience, where benefits to the community are maximized and risks minimized, PAR requires adjustments to the ways in which researchers approach a project. It also requires some skills that may not be commonly needed in traditional forms of research. In this chapter we have presented some of the challenges of PAR, suggestions for facing these challenges and the required skills for confronting the challenges. The above strategies and skills allow us to begin to negotiate values and power, allowing for a pooling of resources and a richer creation of knowledge – the very process that makes PAR a unique approach to research.

REFERENCES

Altpeter, M., Schopler, J.H., Galinsky, M.J. and Pennell, J. (1999) 'Participatory research as social work practice: when is it viable?', *Journal of Progressive Human Services*, 10 (2): 31–53.

Alvarez, A.R. and Gutierrez, L.M. (2001) 'Choosing to do participatory research: an example and issues of fit to consider', *Journal of Community Practice*, 9 (1): 1–20.

Alvesson, M. and Skoldberg, K. (2000) *Reflexive Methodology*. Thousand Oaks, CA: Sage.

Bond, M.A. (1990) 'Defining the research relationship: maximizing participation in an unequal world', in P. Tolan, C. Keys, F. Chertok, and L. Jason (eds), *Researching Community Psychology: Issues of Theory and Methods.* Washington, DC: American Psychological Association. pp. 183–7.

Boog, B. (2003) 'The emancipatory character of action research, its history and the present state of the art', *Journal of Community and Applied Social Psychology*, 13: 426–38.

Brydon-Miller, M. (2001) 'Education, research, and action: theory and methods of participatory action research', in D. Tolman and M. Brydon-Miller (eds), *From Subjects to Subjectivities: a Handbook of Interpretive and Participatory Methods.* New York: New York University Press. pp. 76–89.

Coenen, H. and Khonraad, S. (2003) 'Inspirations and aspirations of exemplarian action research', *Journal of Community and Applied Social Psychology*, 13: 439–50.

Cooke, B. and Kothari, U. (eds) (2001) *Participation: the New Tyranny.* London: Zed Books.

Fadem, P., Minkler, M., Perry, M., Blum, K., Moore, L. and Rogers, J. (2003) 'Ethical challenges in community based participatory research: a case study from the San Francisco Bay area disability community', in M. Minkler and N. Wallerstein (eds), *Community-based Participatory Research for Health.* San Francisco, CA: Jossey-Bass. pp. 242–62.

Foucault, M. (1994) 'The subject and power', in J.D. Faubion (ed.), *Michel Foucault: Power.* New York: The New Press. pp. 326–48.

Giddens, A. (1979) *Central Problems in Social Theory: Action, Structure and Contradiction in Social Analysis.* Berkeley: University of California Press.

Giddens, A. (1993) 'Problems of action and structure', in P. Cassell (ed.), *The Giddens Reader.* Stanford: Stanford University Press. pp. 88–175.

Gray, R.E., Fitch, M., Davis, C. and Phillips, C. (2000) 'Challenges of participatory research: reflections on a study with breast cancer self-help groups', *Health Expectations*, 3: 243–52.

Green, L.W., George, M.A., Daniel, M., Frankish, C.J., Herbert, C.J., Bowie, W.R., et al. (1995) *Institute of Health Promotion Research Study of Participatory Research in Health Promotion.* University of British Columbia: The Royal Society of Canada.

Hagey, R.S. (n.d.) *The Use and Abuse of Participatory Action Research.* [www.hc-sc.gc.ca/hpb/icdc/publicat/cdic/cdic181/cd181a_e.html] (accessed 18 June 2004).

Healy, K. (2001) 'Participatory action research and social work: a critical appraisal', *International Social Work*, 44 (1): 93–105.

Heron, J. and Reason, P. (2001/2006) 'The practice of cooperative inquiry', in P. Reason and H. Bradbury (eds), *Handbook of Action Research: Participative Inquiry and Practice.* London: Sage. pp. 179–88. Also published in P. Reason and H. Bradbury (eds) (2006), *Handbook of Action Research: Concise Paperback Edition.* London: Sage. pp. 144–54.

Isenberg, D.H., Loomis, C., Humphreys, K. and Maton, K.I. (2004) 'Self-help research: issues of power sharing', in L.A. Jason, C.B. Keys, Y. Suarez-Balcazar, R.R. Taylor, M.I. Davis, J.A. Durlak and D.H. Isenberg (eds), *Participatory Community Research.* Washington, DC: American Psychological Association. pp. 123–37.

Kemmis, S. (2001/2006) 'Exploring the relevance of critical theory for action research: emancipatory action research in the footsteps of Jürgen Habermas', in P. Reason and H. Bradbury (eds), *Handbook of Action Research: Participative Inquiry and Practice.* London: Sage. pp. 91–100. Also published in P. Reason and H. Bradbury (eds) (2006), *Handbook of Action Research: Concise Paperback Edition.* London: Sage. pp. 94–105.

Kemmis, S. and McTaggart, R. (2005) 'Participatory action research: communicative action and the public sphere', in N.K. Denzin and Y. Lincoln (eds), *The Sage Handbook of Qualitative Research.* Thousand Oaks, CA: Sage. pp. 559–603.

Kondrat, M.E. (1999) 'Who is the "Self" in self-aware: professional self-awareness from a critical theory perspective', *Social Service Review,* Dec: 451–76.

Krimerman, L. (2001) 'Participatory action research: should social inquiry be conducted democratically?', *Philosophy of the Social Sciences*, 31 (1): 60–82.

Martin-Baro, I. (1994) *Writings for a Liberation Psychology.* Cambridge, MA: Harvard University Press.

Minkler, M. (2004) 'Ethical challenges for the "outside", researcher in community-based participatory research', *Health Education and Behavior,* 31: 684–97.

Minkler, M. and Wallerstein, N. (eds) (2003) *Community-based Participatory Research for Health.* San Francisco, CA: Jossey-Bass.

Mitchell, T. and Baker, E. (2005) 'Community building vs career building research: The challenges, risks, and responsibilities of conducting participatory cancer research with Aboriginal communities', *Journal of Cancer Education* (Special supplement, Spring), 20: 41–6.

Mitchell T., Townsend, R. and Schnare, J. (2003) 'Community resilience or unidentified health risk?: Health professional perceptions on the impact of the Swissair Flight 111 disaster on surrounding communities', *Canadian Journal of Community Mental Health,* 22 (1): 69–84.

Nelson, G. (1994) 'The development of a mental health coalition: a case study', *American Journal of Community Psychology,* 22: 229–55.

Nelson, G. and Earls, M. (1986) 'An action-oriented assessment of the housing and social support needs of long-term psychiatric clients', *Canadian Journal of Community Mental Health,* 5 (1): 19–30.

Nelson, G., Ochocka, J., Griffin, K. and Lord, J. (1998) 'Nothing about me, without me: participatory action research with self-help/mutual aid organizations for psychiatric consumer/survivors', *American Journal of Community Psychology,* 26: 881–912.

Nelson, G., Ochocka, J., Janzen, R., Trainor, J. and Lauzon, S. (2004a) 'A comprehensive evaluation approach for mental health consumer-run organizations: values, conceptualization, design, and action', *Canadian Journal of Program Evaluation,* 19 (3): 29–53.

Nelson, G., Poland, B., Murray, M. and Maticka-Tyndale, E. (2004b) 'Community health action research: towards a praxis framework for graduate education', *Action Research,* 2: 389–408.

Nelson, G., Prilleltensky, I. and MacGillivary, H. (2001) 'Building value-based partnerships: toward solidarity with oppressed groups', *American Journal of Community Psychology,* 29 (5): 649–77.

Ochocka, J., Janzen, R. and Nelson, G. (2002) 'Sharing power and knowledge: professional and mental health consumer-survivor researchers working together in a participatory action research project', *Psychiatric Rehabilitation Journal,* 25 (4): 379–87.

Prilletensky, I. (2001) 'Value-based praxis in community psychology: moving toward social justice and social action', *American Journal of Community Psychology,* 29 (5): 747–78.

Reason, P. and Bradbury, H. (eds) (2001/2006) *Handbook of Action Research: Participative Inquiry and Practice,* London: Sage.

Reeve, P., Cornell, S., D'Costa, B., Janzen, R. and Ochocka, J. (2002) 'From our perspective: consumer researchers speak about their experience in a community mental health research project', *Psychiatric Rehabilitation Journal,* 25 (4): 403–8.

Reid, C. (2000) 'Seduction and enlightenment in feminist action research', *Resources for Feminist Research,* 29 (1/2): 169–88.

Roberts, G. and Dick, B. (2003) 'Emancipatory design choices for action research practitioners', *Journal of Community and Applied Social Psychology,* 13: 486–95.

Stringer, E.T. (1996) *Action Research: a Handbook for Practitioners.* Thousand Oaks, CA: Sage.

Wadsworth, Y. (2001/2006) 'The mirror, the magnifying glass, the compass and the map: facilitating participatory action research', in P. Reason and H. Bradbury (eds), *Handbook of Action Research: Participative Inquiry and Practice.* London: Sage. pp. 420–32. Also published in P. Reason and H. Bradbury (eds) (2006), *Handbook of Action Research: Concise Paperback Edition.* London: Sage. pp. 322–34.

Weick, K.L. (1984) 'Small wins: Redefining the scale of social problems', *American Psychologist,* 39: 40–9.

42

Getting in, Getting on, Getting out: On Working with Second-person Inquiry Groups

Kate Louise McArdle

Observations from the author's practice of establishing and facilitating second-person inquiry processes inform this chapter's discussion of the types of issues requiring facilitative attention during the beginning (getting in), the middle (getting on) and the ending (getting out) of such inquiry. The aim in writing has been particularly to open conversations about the beginnings and endings of inquiry practice, which seem scarcely discussed.

In this chapter, I seek to explore some of the skills that seem important when engaging others in inquiry work focused in small, face-to-face groups. In Torbert's (2001/2006) terms, the type of process I discuss would be termed 'second-person inquiry'. The backgrounding experience from which I offer this discussion includes PhD and ongoing action research work as an academic based at CARPP (Centre for Action Research in Professional Practice) at the University of Bath (McArdle, 2002, 2004) and as a consultant. In this writing I have outlined some issues that seem interesting to attend to when working with second-person inquiry processes, and in writing have assumed

the reader is familiar with approaches to second-person inquiry practice. Examples of such practice can be found in this volume (see Chapters 28, 30, 33, 39).

I have constructed my writing here around three key stages in the life of an inquiry group – the starting-up phase ('Getting in'), the time spent learning about and engaging in inquiry over time ('Getting on') and finally the process of ending the group ('Getting out'). This is not, however, to suggest that these stages are discreet, but it makes sense here to highlight that at different times some issues seem more pressing than at others. Prior to discussing these various elements, however, I begin by positioning myself in this work.

WHERE I'M COMING FROM

Being (among many other things) a 30-year-old woman who makes her living from being an action research professional may make it likely that I am going to see different things, and be seen differently, from you as I engage in inquiry practice. Where each of us is in our life no doubt colours what appears to matter to us as we inquire – the following is an incomplete snapshot account of what matters to me right now. I'd like you to notice as you read how our different positionings can inform what we understand about working with second-person inquiry groups. Alongside this personal positioning, the context in which inquiry work is established obviously has a huge role to play in shaping the inquiry process. Working the politics of inquiry will feel different and happen differently depending on what the inquiry is established to explore, your role in that process, and whom the process includes. The bulk of my practice takes place in organizational settings, and it is this practice that informs my writing here. In such settings, as a researcher or consultant, I create and facilitate second-person inquiry processes to explore issues of organizational interest – recent examples include working with organizations to help them explore issues of organizational diversity and the development of group facilitation skills. Within such organizational remits people come together (equating to a 'convergence' of interest, in Heron's terms), and ultimately pursue their own related questions of direct relevance to their own practice ('divergence').

GETTING IN

Establishing an inquiry group can be a particularly demanding time – one where the action researcher might experience a vast range of pressures from different stakeholders (funding bodies, corporate sponsors, potential inquiry group members) scattered across different contexts (in the organization where you work, family members, friends or members of your community) coupled with the pressures they apply to themselves (How do I get this right? How can I ensure people want to be involved? How will my lack of/vast experiences of second-person inquiry affect how participants see me?).

During my PhD years, I discovered and later wrote about the absence of detailed accounts of the practice of establishing inquiry groups (McArdle, 2002, 2004). Below I round up some of the key issues that seem to arise when seeking to 'get in' and the types of skills they draw on from the action researcher. In summary, it seems that when seeking to 'get in', the nub of inquiry practice is related, as Reason and Goodwin (1999) phrased it, to 'establishing the conditions' from which inquiry – as a pattern of behaviour between people rather than a 'thing' – can emerge.

This notion of 'establishing conditions' will draw on a broad territory of skills from the action researcher. Among other things, at a macro level, stakeholders and their expectations need to be managed (see Charles and Glennie, 2002), as do budgets and the (often very advance) diarizing of the inquiry process. At the micro level, as we seek to energize people to engage in inquiry, it is necessary to attend to modelling the types of inquiring behaviours we'd encourage others to enact should they join in the inquiry process – giving them a 'taster' of what might be involved in our work ahead. Alongside this, attention is appropriately directed towards the creation and holding of appropriate boundaries between the micro and the macro – the group and the organization. Sounds exhausting, doesn't it? Wadsworth's discussion of facilitator[1] as energy worker in the first edition of this Handbook (Wadsworth, 2001/2006: 420–32) is helpful when thinking about how to begin. 'Working' energies is not about giving energy or taking it; Wadsworth describes it as a process of understanding the energies that are in your particular context and responding to them. I find it useful to consciously *attend* to energies – to awarely tune into my own and others' energy in order that I might 'work' them.

As with any project we might undertake, the beginning is when we become visible (to others and to ourselves) in our affiliation with an agenda, as we express our desire to pursue this agenda and seek resource to do so. In this sense beginnings are political (as are all stages, but for me, 'getting in' is when I feel the politics more!). Below I outline some of choice points I've attended to when proposing such work, and then relate this to examples from my practice.

A PROPOSAL

In order that inquiry may begin, someone needs to propose it does so. Whether this proposal takes the form of talking the idea through with a friend, who may join in, or writing the proposal formally and sending it to a funding body or corporate sponsor, we all need to begin somewhere. Working energies is evident in the choices we make regarding the proposal itself – who will 'speak' in the proposal and what does this mean? During my PhD years it mattered to me that 'I' got access to organizations, rather than the director of our research centre doing this on my behalf (McArdle, 2004). This choice was about 'establishing the conditions' in which I could inquire – 'getting in' myself would indicate that I was trusted to do the work. Such choices are differently effective depending upon the audience for the proposal – if funding is sought from a research body (see Chapters 30 and 33, this volume), host organization (Mead, 2001) or potential participants. Once careful attention has been given to who will speak and be spoken to in the proposal, there is the obvious issue of what to say. There are some elements of any inquiry process that will be included almost

irrespectively – the time frames or necessary resources are perhaps obvious candidates here. However, more discerning choices need to be made around content for sponsors as opposed to participants, or differently positioned participants (children and adults) for example. Making such choices is tricky given the nature of the approach to be employed – second-person action research cannot be 'sold in' on guarantees of outcome. Attention to holding uncertainty of 'outcome' with sufficient certainty – sufficient offering to get people energized and excited to be involved – seems important here, as Traylen (1994) suggests:

> I was aware that [co-operative inquiry] could evoke anxiety with its lack of structure, excitement with its open-endedness, and uncertainty with its unpredictability regarding specifically desired outcomes. (Traylen, 1994).

The challenge of balancing (and selling in) certainty and uncertainty is embedded in the nature of the relationship that exists between the parties involved. For example, being an 'outsider' – making a proposal to an organization you don't know – can feel very challenging, as it's difficult to know what type of communication is going to get you heard well. How can you do it in a way that is both authentic and appropriate to the context? Developing a sense of this is undoubtedly a skill that helps in pitching successfully for such work,[2] particularly when you don't already have a reputation before you.

The opposite positioning – being an 'insider' to the inquiry context – can make proposing such work feel exposing and vulnerable-making, which in turn can make you feel a bit like an 'outsider'. A very visible expression of interest in (often) issues that your organization, family or community might have difficulty confronting, and might therefore be unwilling to sponsor (financially or in terms of participation in the inquiry), can, in real or imagined ways, leave the proposer compromised as a potential 'trouble maker' (see Meyerson and Scully (1995) on the notion of the Tempered Radical; also

Coghlan and Shani, Chapter 45 in this volume). For example, I am currently trying to convince myself to call other women in my organization together to explore the gendered nature of our organization's culture and the impact this has on aspiration and practice. Just airing the thought here feels like I'm making steps towards marginalizing myself already! Getting in is political.

Making 'getting in' more possible therefore requires some matching of the language or behaviour of the stakeholders you endeavour to 'get in' with. It is both about 'sameness' – making the intervention less visible, less different, from 'what normally goes on around here'– and about 'difference' – making the intervention more visible, different, in ways that you feel will engage people's interest in the potential inquiry. If the visibility of either is extreme, getting in can be less possible (potential participants or sponsors can feel either 'scared-off' or insufficiently engaged). There is some working of energy to be done at this early stage – reading how individuals respond to your ideas and using this as 'data' to inform what needs to be done next (Do they need me to push a boundary here, or do they need me to emphasize things they are more familiar with?).

Proposing Inquiry to P&G

During my doctoral research I facilitated a 15-month long co-operative inquiry process (Heron, 1996) for a group of 'Young Women Managers' (eventually known as the 'YoWiM' group) within Procter & Gamble. At the time I was a full-time student, so was 'outside' the organization. In my own 'getting in' phase with P&G I first submitted a proposal to senior managers. Then, following a successful pitch, I distributed flyers to young women in the organization, indicating the kind of work I hoped to do, and ran two two-hour long taster sessions at P&G's offices. Through seeking feedback during the subsequent YoWiM inquiry process I was able to begin to discover why these various 'pitches' worked. I consider they did so

because of an appropriate balance of 'sameness' and 'difference', as discussed above:

My sponsors essentially liked the proposal because:

1. It 'told them what they needed to know'. (*Sameness* – the proposal looked and read like the type of proposal document they are familiar with.)
2. They liked the idea of hearing stories from 'inside the organization' about 'how it really is as opposed to how we imagine it is'. (*Difference* – the proposal named and explained a different approach to knowledge generation, and they felt this would be valuable to them.)

The young women who participated initially wanted to be involved because:

1. 'It sounded like it'd be different from the kind of things we normally do here.' (*Difference* – diversity of learning experience being read as intrinsically valuable, meaning that *Difference* in itself is about *Sameness* – the desirable act of exploring alternatives in order 'to become more efficient'.)
2. 'It sounded like fun'. (*Difference* – having fun at work was 'unusual', particularly in an organizationally sponsored 'work' activity. Such sponsorship, however, indicated that the activity was understood to be of benefit to the organization – *Sameness*. Having 'fun' during working hours was therefore understood to be safe.)
3. 'I thought it would be a good opportunity to meet other young women.' (*Difference* – young women, and women generally, in P&G were a minority – all of the participants in YoWiM felt that they did not have ways of spending time with other women. *Sameness* – networking is an organizationally 'robust'/'approved' activity.)
4. 'Coming to the first session was not a big deal as it was going to be on-site, so if it was rubbish I could leave and would only have wasted ten minutes, rather than having to be somewhere else for a whole day.' (*Sameness* – being 'on-site' meant the *Difference* of the proposed work was not in obvious, sharp contrast to the process of a normal working day.)

In managing our own energies at the very early stages, it seems important to remember that the initial proposal – be it over coffee or in a formal report – only needs to do the job of creating interest in the possibility of inquiry. It just has to 'get you in *a bit*'. I like the idea of 'getting in' being a nested inquiry process, with lots of different layers (lots of different chances to get a bit further in) which inform those involved about each other and the nature of the work they might do together. Moreover, learning together and moving with each other progressively further 'in' means that participants' energy becomes engaged in shaping the inquiry and the choices that need to be made about how to proceed. Collaborating in such a way so early on can develop a strong sense of ownership of the inquiry process.

Once we have a group of people 'signed up' and ready to meet together for their first session, the pressure of success or failure can feel as if it rests firmly on our shoulders and that it will be determined by our facilitation of the first meeting! This makes the point that there is no such thing as 'being in' indefinitely – it is an ongoing negotiation, as the example below illustrates.

ELCAM

I recently worked in a supervisory role on a co-operative inquiry project with a private client (referred to here as ELCAM). Ella, a researcher from ELCAM, was tasked by the organization to design and facilitate a six-month co-operative inquiry process for 12 senior ELCAM managers who had already 'signed up'. Ella had not used action research methods nor facilitated a group such as this before. My role was to mentor Ella and for this purpose she and I would meet for a two-hour session in between each group meeting. Prior to the first group meeting Ella's attention was focused on the following themes:

Questions of confidence: Will I be okay? Will I be good enough, clever enough, skilled enough, credible enough? What will I do if they don't understand the method? What will I do if I don't understand the method? What happens if I can't explain it well?
Concerns about structure: What kind of things should I be asking them to do in the session? What

if they finish everything we've planned and I've got loads of time left? What if they forget to do anything in the month between sessions? What if they won't talk? What if they don't like being there? What if people won't tell the truth because of the senior women being there?
Anxiety over authority: I'm worried [my boss] will want to take over that task/not want me to ask those kinds of questions. What if they don't listen to me? What if they don't do what I ask them to do in the breakout sessions?

The above themes illustrate to me the notion of 'being in' as an ongoing, temporal, state – a framing that maybe even helps 'staying in' to become more likely as we actively continue to work the energies rather than just relying on people wanting to be part of our inquiry process. Rather than thinking of ourselves as 'out' or 'in' we might instead envisage ourselves, and all others associated in the work, on a continuum of 'getting in' – perhaps across the entirety of the life of the work. 'Being in' seems at best only what we give each other permission to be. Feeling 'in' is about being clear on what we and others contribute to the process it seems, and our understanding of the value of this contribution can yo-yo throughout the life of the group as time passes and roles change. The intimate nature of second-person inquiry group processes – most usually involving getting to know only a few others in quite some depth over time – has the potential to make all involved sensitive to feelings of being 'in' or 'out' – valuable and appreciated, or redundant and defunct.

GETTING ON

I mentioned earlier that my demarcation of three 'phases' of practice is, though somewhat artificial, a useful way of thinking about core skills and how they are differently suited at different times in inquiry practice. Indeed, I evidence above how 'getting in' is in many ways nothing more than a state of mind that is at best only ever temporary and experienced in varying degrees, quite possibly throughout the life of the group.

'Getting on', however, feels different. As the inquiry group takes on a life of its own, patterns of relationship and practice develop and change. Roles and relationships shift. Shared history creates 'baggage'. Energies peak and trough. People may leave or join. When people are getting on with 'getting on', the practice of inquiry facilitation can become scattered across the divergent practices of perhaps ten participants and all of those they are engaging in inquiry beyond the group. Perhaps the question that absorbs the attention of everyone involved at this stage is 'what is my role here?' If, as we suggest in second-person inquiry, we intend to move towards a practice of co-inquiry over time, it seems necessary and 'right' that we attend to this question.

For me, attention to this question is evident most particularly when we start to wonder what elements of our original role we might appropriately be holding onto, and which we should be letting go of. This applies to facilitators and other participants alike as we feel our way though our experience of the inquiry process and evidence bubbles up of people testing out new ways of being in the group. Facilitators may initially seek to trade the administrative elements they have been managing as a way of helping others to assume responsibility for the group – emailing to arrange where to meet next time or typing up and circulating notes from the meeting are good examples of these early (low risk) steps. Other 'higher risk' trades tend to come later – sharing the facilitation of the group or designing the programme of work – hopefully when there is mutual understanding of the skills and intentions that are preferable in such roles and some explicit intention on everyone's part to support these shifts and be forgiving of skill gaps. Despite our best intentions and careful planning, as facilitators of second-person inquiry we all at some point experience group members moving into facilitative roles and (if we can bear to be honest enough to admit it) 'getting it wrong' (in comparison to what we would have done), hurting each other, being unforgiving about each other's lack of skill, looking back to us to sort out the tangles they get into. We also see group members move elegantly into such roles and in Heron's terms, enact practical knowing (Heron, 1996) of the skills required. Whatever happens, and whenever it happens, it seems fair to suggest that inquiry groups can't 'get on' with the business of becoming a community of inquiry unless the initiator/lead facilitator is prepared to carefully 'let go' of their initial role.

Letting go does not mean a literal abandonment of the group to their own devices. Quite the opposite. It is about becoming more and differently engaged, rather than less so. For me this time is about shifting from modelling the 'doing' of facilitative skill to modelling noticing others 'doing' facilitative skill – helping participants to notice what they are doing and how it contributes inquiring rigour to the process of the group. This, quite apparently, is in itself a facilitative behaviour, but as opposed to one that moves the group forwards in a particular direction (be this towards following a theme of discussion, getting people back on track, 'getting started again' after a coffee break). This is about supporting the group and holding the space for them to notice where they are and what they are doing. As one of the young women in YoWiM described it: 'When we got stuck you didn't leap in and sort us out, even though I wanted you to sometimes! You just kind of helped us not panic about being stuck' (YoWiM, October 2001).

So, what happens when second-person inquiry groups 'get on'? I will refer again to my work with ELCAM and YoWiM at P&G to pick up examples of the above challenges I have faced. Given that we perhaps consider the bulk of the life of an inquiry group as being about 'getting on', it might also be – rightly or otherwise – our main reference point for the answer to the question about quality in action research practice that Reason and Bradbury posed in the first edition of this Handbook – 'How do I know this is good work?'

ELCAM

Over time as Ella's confidence in her own ability has shifted, her questions and attention have also moved. Without doubt, this shift is due to things having gone 'well' in the group – both in the sense that people are energized and turning up to the sessions, but also in that they are tackling difficult issues, falling out with each other, feeling safe enough to ask big questions.

However, just as Ella was beginning to enjoy being less anxious about her practice, the one thing she describes herself as 'hating'/'being afraid to confront' – conflict – happened in the group. In this particular instance confidentiality was broken and knowledge of this found its way into the group. The impact was people feeling scared and upset. Ella arrived for her session with me full of anxiety about 'what she should do about it'. Her attention shifted back to her initial position of anxiety-driven desire to 'fix' things. My role here was to help her notice her behaviour and to encourage her to reframe what had happened from 'conflict' to 'people being upset and confused and needing to be helped to move through it'. Armed with renewed confidence by reframing the situation, Ella went to her next session prepared to join others in working through their upset in an unrushed way. She, through taking time to think about her own practice, remembered that her role had shifted to one of holding inquiring space for others, rather than fixing their 'problems'.

Sometimes a marker of doing good work well is about putting such structures in place that explicitly enable time to be spent focusing on our own practice and not getting carried away with the anxiety-driven responses of ourselves or other group members. As here, the knock-on effect of creating such structures can be that space is created in the group for others to more fully participate in generating knowledge about their own inquiry – rather than having it squashed by your desire to 'save them'. Framing mentoring relationships in this way moves the 'novice' inquirer (Ella) out of a frame of 'I need help from an expert' (Me) to 'I am developing competence in building a robust first-person inquiry structure into my practice' (or something along those lines!).

Engaging in the practices and processes of second-person inquiry over time means that we will be faced with situations we don't like, perhaps with people we find difficult. Getting good quality support and/or attending carefully to our own first-person inquiry (Torbert, 2001/2006) – our practice and the questions that emerge from it – will mean that we begin to frame things differently and make different choices in our practice, as here. I almost want to say that there is something going well in your group if being in it hurts from time to time – it's a sign of 'getting on', that relationships and roles are shifting, that people are working on things that matter, that boundaries of process and content are being tested.

YoWiM

In working with Ella at ELCAM, I relived in some ways my own first experience of conflict in the YoWiM group at P&G. This happened quite early in the life of the group and took me by surprise. One of the women in the group, Ann, confronted what she saw as lack of engagement on the part of two other participants. She told the other two women that she felt they were doing nothing in the action element of the cycle when she was 'doing lots and filling a journal with things to talk about with you all', that she felt this 'lack of commitment' was 'bad for our group' and that it 'drained her energy'. You could almost hear the collective intake of breath in the group as people prepared for their safe space to come crashing down around their ears. What actually happened was the women who the feedback had been directed at became upset and tried to 'explain' that they were engaged. I 'let' this happen without interruption – considering that some clear exploration of difference was likely to be helpful to the group's progression and that I wanted to model being supportive of people raising concerns.

When the conversation began to shift away I drew us back, pointing out the directness of the feedback and by checking if those directly involved were okay. Our space was no longer safe by that point and everyone said they were 'fine' (some with tears in their eyes). Looking back, it was pretty brutal – Ann was very direct, very judgemental, very blaming and sounded disappointed. I helped people feel less safe by not slowing things down, naming (more broadly) what I saw happening, nor inviting others to think about how we might reframe this incident as 'data' that we could inquire into. The net result of this was that the two women who had been 'judged' left the group, citing work pressure, Ann missed the next two sessions and I felt less credible.

The above illustrates how, as inquiry groups work together over time, there can emerge a mismatch between different participants' views of the *'significance' of the work undertaken*. Linking back to the earlier discussion of sameness and difference, Ann was, due to her own considerable engagement, experiencing her process as becoming very 'different' from that of other group members, which in turn made her feel 'different' from them.

Being 'different' can result in feeling like you've somehow managed to get yourself 'back out' of an inquiry group, when you'd been investing so much in 'getting in' and 'getting on'. Unless the group shifts its understanding of what is going on, being back 'outside' can get to feel like the best (safest, easiest?) place to be. In this work I could, if faster on my feet, have encouraged the group to move into a more appreciative frame of the different types of engagement underway – we might have agreed to walk in each other's shoes for a cycle, either matching Ann's depth of inquiry or working tentatively at breadth, as the rest of the group. With hindsight, this may have made us feel more sameness in our intention to inquire, irrespective of how we did it – this might have been a good reframing. Such instances

are not unrecoverable, and they are certainly not wasted if we attempt to learn from them (in the group and also by sharing stories, as here, in a broader community).

In 'getting on', when people begin to feel safe and confident in their emerging inquiry practice, they can stumble across terrain where their lack of skill (in this instance, in giving feedback, in holding a safe space to debrief it, in naming that actually they are not okay) becomes painfully evident, and people limp away from inquiring in the moment, or their membership of an inquiry group, rather than growing through it. 'Getting it wrong' seems to be part of the process of 'getting on' and in happening can – if we manage to handle it – create the conditions from which inquiry can emerge.

GETTING OUT

In theoretical terms, the ending of a group is a time for clearing the air, creating shared meaning about what we have achieved, processing left-over emotional upset, making space to hear about regrets and appreciations, celebrating the work we have done, and exploring how our learning informs our future work alone or together (Srivastva, et al, 1977; Randall and Southgate, 1980). Given the reflective nature of such attention – that we are looking backwards and appraising what has happened – we might consider that endings are about slowing down in order that we might really 'get clear' on what we've achieved. Of course 'speed' is hardly synonymous with the notion of rigorous inquiry at any point, but the fact that the group is engaging in its last meeting or cycle together by definition focuses attention on completion, on ensuring we do what needs to be done.

The reasons for ending obviously differ – it may be due to the agreed period of the work passing or the purpose of the group having either been realized or having shifted to a point of such divergence that it no longer makes sense for the group members to work together. Furthermore, it is arguable that the group ends in its current form when its membership changes markedly (particularly if the membership has been constant for an extended period). Less obviously, and for many different reasons, participants might end or begin to withdraw their individual involvement in a group before the agreed period of work is over. Ending, therefore, is not a discrete process either – 'getting out' seems both curiously slippery as a concept ('ending behaviour' is seemingly enacted at different times by different group members, and is not easy to spot in the moment) and entirely obvious (following an 'ending' meeting, the group no longer works together).

Getting into 'Getting Out': Ending Inquiringly

Endings, similarly to beginnings, seem to be a time that inquiry participants remember – the early sessions can seem to set the pattern for what comes, and final sessions can be seen as the time when 'what has meant to be here' is decided upon. Therefore, all involved can feel that endings are significant in many different ways. This significance can lead people to really engage in creating an ending process that explicitly seeks to enable all involved to take time to end in a satisfying way together. Several of the endings I have been involved with have, in a way, showcased the inquiry group. Working together over time means that inquiry skills are created and honed, so by the time the ending has come these skills are flourishing and are evident in the practice of the group as they join together to construct an ending process that meets their needs – something to be delighted by and to ~~celebrate~~.

Getting into 'ge~~tting out~~' is in my experience been most pos~~itive with~~ group members who have engaged in their first-person inquiry with rigour for much of the time they have worked with the group. They seem to feel less blocked and more likely to engage in ending well as they have largely come to terms with and processed disappointments and delights along the way, and have developed

inquiry skills that will sustain them and continue beyond the life of the group. They have managed, overall, to be aware of their role in the group and are clear on what they contribute. This has left me feeling that engaged inquirers have nothing to fear from ending and they can therefore hold an inquiring attitude towards 'it' as an event, and towards their own creation of an ending experience. This is essentially what I mean by 'getting into getting out' – framing the notion of ending as an inquiry in its own right.

This, of course, will not be the case for all group members, and I will move on to discuss this shortly. However, firstly, I consider how this intention to end inquiringly looks when enacted.

Getting On with 'Getting Out'

If group members are into ending inquiringly, there can be a desire to trial yet more new behaviours in the familiar space of the group before it ends. Risk in this sense exists differently than at any other point in the inquiry process, as the relationship with the group is not going to continue in its current form. Often in ending processes group members will chose to foreground presentational knowing (Heron, 1996; Heron and Reason, Chapter 24) in the form of story, dance, bodywork, poetry, and metaphor. Perhaps this is due to a desire for meaning making about the experience of inquiry to be done in a way that holds open the potential both for collaborative as well as individual sense making. Stories, bodysculpts and other presentational forms seem to retain a sense of ownership at an individual level about what they mean or represent, irrespective of how we might rework them to represent a group experience (see McArdle, 2004: Ch. 5).

Ending Presentationally with YoWiM

Examples of such new types of choices were evident in ending with YoWiM. Though presentational work had been used throughout our process, it had particular significance during the ending phase. We chose to change the location of our session (from a half-day session at the P&G offices, where the participants worked, to a two-day session in Bath) to physically move us into a different type of space where we could focus on ending and make us very aware that things were changing. We carefully considered the relationship between the location of the inquiry and what we sought to know. Being somewhere new in this sense was a form of presentational knowing about the impact of context on inquiry.

During our two days together, we constructed a timeline of our work together across the entire length of the wall of our meeting room – without talking, we all stuck post-it notes of key incidents, energy levels and emotions to the relevant point on the line, then spent half a day telling our own stories from our most important notes. We employed sculpting with clay to explore what had been learnt and experienced over the preceding year together. We wrote letters to each other about what we felt each other had done brilliantly and what we needed to work on. At the very end of the session we stood in turn from our seat in the circle, said our goodbyes, said 'this is over now for me', then stepped outside of our circle, and just stood quietly noticing that all that was left was empty chairs.

Each of these activities represented a new choice for the group – the new location, the length of our time together, the nature of the activities engaged in. Perhaps the most striking element of this work was that we stayed in experiential (doing/experiencing things together) and presentational modes for much of our time together, shifting into propositional mode (Heron, 1996) on an individual level, rather than 'deciding on what was true for everyone'. The power of the presentational form in enabling individual and joint sensemaking seems appropriate and poignant when groups get into ending inquiringly.

Getting Out of Getting Out: Avoiding Ending?

As mentioned earlier, endings are not always experienced at the same time or in the same way by all group participants. This may be a reason for endings not being reported out (or perhaps even planned in) with great regularity – because people begin to leave groups before they are 'over' (so that groups fizzle out or just stop). Signs of this happening include:

1. *Participation dwindling for the kind of reason that makes you wonder if people are telling you the truth:* Vagueness about continual diary clashes is an obvious example.
2. *People being difficult to contact:* Emails about the inquiry not being responded to and voicemail seemingly always being on are symptoms displayed by people wanting to leave or finding involvement difficult. When you begin to wonder if you are helpfully doing your best to contact a fellow group member, or unhelpfully pursuing someone who would rather you didn't bother, this is an indication that things are not as they might be.
3. *Group members attending sessions as passengers rather than participants:* Simply turning up to meetings doesn't make any of us a member of an inquiry group. Ongoing lack of engagement in group discussions or activities is a sign that people have either left or are in the process of doing so. This seems most obvious when other group members are strongly emotionally attached to issues under discussion whilst the 'passengers' seem incapable of engaging to the same kind of extent.
4. *Group members suggesting alternative ways of staying linked in with the work:* Blaming location/timings of the inquiry group for their inability to attend group meetings. Some group members request alternative arrangements that would suit them better (a different type of supervision or mentoring, for example), and then find reasons for these new arrangements not to work either. This can become a process of gradual extraction throughout which 'others' are blamed for the participants eventually not being able to be involved.

This list is not exhaustive, and the types of behaviours listed are not always about 'leaving'. Indeed sometimes they are symptomatic of the difficulties of being involved – more of a 'cry for help' than a 'goodbye' – which all involved would benefit from surfacing and dealing with. This was indeed the case in a project I am currently running for an organization referred to here as GESS.

GESS

In this work, I facilitate a co-operative inquiry process for a staff team, who are in turn taking the learning from our process into their facilitation of other inquiry groups. GESS requested I take over the project from another facilitator. Participation in meetings had been dwindling, meeting dates had been difficult to pin down and everyone involved was unhappy. There was something very permission-giving in 'getting a new facilitator in' – all participants attended the first session I facilitated and openly discussed why it wasn't working out. It seemed that they felt there was no risk in naming all the dynamics and confronting all the issues with me, as it was not my practice as a facilitator, or our group history, they were critiquing. Similarly I felt no risk in asking them about what hadn't worked. The project and the group were already in crisis – no one had anything to lose. This group could have 'stopped' as a direct result of behaviour symptomatic of involvement being 'difficult', being misread as 'leaving' or 'ending' behaviour, or just continued limping along. We salvaged the process, and have gone on to complete a further year of useful work together.

Recently, as we approach our ending, I have been attending to how actual endings outside of the staff inquiry group at GESS have impacted upon ending behaviours within the group. One parallel inquiry group (G1), run by two of the GESS team, began to experience dwindling attendance (from 10 participants to sometimes just one or two, plus the two GESS staff), following a high profile and successful conference presentation by the group members six months prior to the planned period of work ending. The GESS staff responded to this by being very

positive (sending emails and text messages indicating that they were looking forward to seeing participants at the session the following week) though not mentioning that participation was an issue. In effect they did the opposite of 'matching' as discussed in 'getting in' – as participant energy dropped and people disengaged, they raised their energy and became more and more engaged in jollying people along (in the hope that doing so would make people want to join in again) but in doing so modelled non-inquiring behaviour – not naming what was happening, how they felt, reverting to the old blocked pattern they had enacted in the GESS staff group prior to my joining (which they have since referred to as 'sticking our heads in the sand and hoping it would all just stop').

In working through these issues with the two GESS staff, we have considered that G1 'ended' for some of the participants following their presentation earlier in the year – they had achieved what they wanted to achieve from their involvement and quite understandably started to 'leave'. Without the GESS staff attending inquiringly to these diminishing energies, G1 participants were left without the skills or the support they needed to explore what was going on. Their involvement in the group became an exercise in avoidance and denial. The dip in G1 participant energy was matched by the two GESS staff members in the staff inquiry group. Their participation became sketchy, their engagement seemed blocked – they seemed to tell stories that were interesting or entertaining for others, rather than of any particular use for their inquiries. They were, in my opinion, beginning to 'leave' our group. I raised this with them. Out tumbled stories of them feeling incompetent as facilitators, embarrassed about their apparent denial of what had been going on for them and for members of their group, upset and frustrated that they had not been forewarned about what might happen, disappointed that they hadn't 'done better' for each other as colleagues. In beginning my work with this group (as above), and in this instance, I learnt just how close an inquiry group and its individual participants can be to 'getting out' of inquiring (deliberately or accidentally) at any time.

The point I raised earlier about the intimate nature of the second-person inquiry group seems important to refer to here. The second-person inquiry group by its nature (few people, with similar interests, meeting regularly over an extended period) has the potential to go very deep very quickly and, where matched with inquiry skill-building, this can become a 'transformative' (Kemmis, 2001/2006) process. However, where there is an absence of such skill development the intimacy of relationship can block progress – saying 'this isn't working for me anymore' can feel like a judgement on others that may hurt them, or might make the individual feel incompetent for not being able to make it work. Sometimes it's easier to fail to attend meetings and not return calls.

The experience of the GESS inquiry illustrates that throughout the life of the inquiry, things happen within and beyond any group that can make us feel as though we aren't 'in' the group at all – even when we are approaching the 'getting out' phase (or indeed as we are engaging in it), issues we confront and things we experience might make us begin to wonder if we were ever really 'in' at all. Perhaps we are more vulnerable to such feelings (I didn't do as well as others/my group would have got more by working with someone else) as inquiry ends and self-doubt and feelings of aloneness creep in. The potential for such vulnerability makes 'getting out' in: an inquiring manner vital – there needs to be time for mutuality of sensemaking to help us really know, at a shared level, what we have achieved and who we are as we 'get out'.

irrespective of the stage we may think we are in (be this in, on, or out) chances are we are more likely to be in some sort of muddy overlap between them, or somewhere else entirely different. As mentioned above, some groups finally really 'get on' with inquiry as they 'get out'. Furthermore, if we end or 'get out' knowing that 'this was good work' we can finally feel wholly 'in' (wholly accepted by, understood by, valued by and valuing of) the group for the first time. In addition, the P&G and GESS examples show how very differently positioned group members can be – with some really 'getting on' whilst others feel barely 'in' or are actively trying to 'get out'. This complexity is part of what I love about working with second-person inquiry processes. I feel there is value in carving the process up into the three stages offered here so that we might begin to notice a little more clearly the different skills needed, or issues we need to watch out for, at each stage. As mentioned earlier, the real skill lies perhaps in 'matching' – complexity and muddiness require a complex facilitative response. Which sometimes means we get muddy too…

NOTES

1 I use the term 'facilitator' throughout this chapter as this is the label most usually applied to my role by the organizations I work with. It is a term with baggage, suggesting all kinds of assumptions about power and authority in the group, which I spend much time actively dismantling. It makes sense to use the term here to denote an 'initiating' or 'methodology expert' role.

2 Yorks and Kasl (2002) give a good description of what might be considered 'necessary' to include in a proposal or negotiations for such work.

BEING IN, ON AND OUT ALL AT ONCE: A KEY CHALLENGE IN FACILITATING SECOND-PERSON INQUIRY

It seems to me, through my ongoing second-person inquiry work as illustrated here, that

REFERENCES

Charles, M. and Glennie, S. (2002) 'Co-operative inquiry: changing interprofessional practice', *Systemic Practice and Action Research*, 15 (3): 207–21.

Heron, J. (1996) *Co-operative Inquiry: Research into the Human Condition*. London: Sage.

Heron, J. and Reason, P. (2001/2006) 'The practice of co-operative inquiry: research "with" rather than "on" people', in P. Reason and H. Bradbury (eds), *Handbook of Action Research: Participative Inquiry and Practice*. London: Sage. pp. 179–88. Also published in P. Reason and H. Bradbury (eds) (2006), *Handbook of Action Research: Concise Paperback Edition*. London: Sage. pp. 144–54.

Kasl, E. and Yorks, L. (2002) 'Collaborative inquiry for adult learning', in L. Yorks and E. Kasl, *Collaborative Inquiry as a Strategy for Adult Learning*. San Francisco, CA: Jossey-Bass. pp. 3–12.

Kemmis, S. (2001/2006) 'Exploring the relevance of critical theory for action research: Emancipatory action research in the footsteps of Jürgen Habermas', in P. Reason and H. Bradbury (eds), *Handbook of Action Research: Participative Inquiry and Practice*. London: Sage. pp. 91–102. Also published in P. Reason and H. Bradbury (eds) (2006), *Handbook of Action Research: Concise Paperback Edition*. London: Sage. pp. 94–105.

Ludema, J.D., Cooperrider, D.L. and Barrett, F.J. (2001/2006) 'Appreciative inquiry: the power of the unconditional positive question', in P. Reason and H. Bradbury (eds), *Handbook of Action Research: Participative Inquiry and Practice*. London: Sage. pp. 189–99. Also published in P. Reason and H. Bradbury (eds) (2006), *Handbook of Action Research: Concise Paperback Edition*. London: Sage. pp. 155–165.

McArdle, K.L. (2002) 'Establishing a co-operative inquiry group: the perspective of a "first-time" inquirer', *Systemic Practice and Action Research* 15 (3): 177–89. [www.bath.ac.uk/carpp]

McArdle, K.L. (2004) 'In-powering spaces: a co-operative inquiry with young women in management.' Unpublished PhD thesis, School of Management, University of Bath. [www.bath.ac.uk/carpp]

Mead, G. (2001) *Unlatching the Gate: Realising my Scholarship of Living Inquiry*. Centre for Action Research in Professional Practice, School of Management, University of Bath.

Meyerson, D.E. and Scully, M.A. (1995) 'Tempered radicalism and the politics of ambivalence and change', *Organization Science,* 6 (5): 585–600.

Randall, R. and Southgate, J. (1980) *Co-operative and Community Group Dynamics. ... Or Your Meetings Needn't Be So Appalling*. London: Barefoot Books.

Reason, P. and Bradbury, H. (eds) (2001/2006) *Handbook of Action Research: Participative Inquiry and Practice*. London: Sage.

Reason, P. and Goodwin, B.C. (1999) 'Toward a science of qualities in organizations: lessons from complexity theory and postmodern biology', *Concepts and Transformations*, 4 (3): 281–317.

Srivastva, S. and Obert, S.L., et al. (1977) 'Organizational analysis through group processes: a theoretical perspective', in C.L. Cooper (ed.), *Organizational Development in the UK and USA*. London: Macmillan. pp. 83–111.

Torbert, W.R. (2001/2006) 'The practice of action inquiry', in P. Reason and H. Bradbury (eds), *Handbook of Action Research: Participative Inquiry and Practice*. London: Sage. pp. 250–60. Also published in P. Reason and H. Bradbury (eds) (2006), *Handbook of Action Research: Concise Paperback Edition*. London: Sage. pp. 207–17.

Traylen, H. (1994) 'Confronting hidden agendas: co-operative inquiry with health visitors', in P. Reason (ed.), *Participation in Human Inquiry*. London: Sage. pp. 59–81.

Wadsworth, Y. (2001/2006) 'The mirror, the magnifying glass, the compass and the map: facilitating participatory action research', in P. Reason and H. Bradbury (eds), *Handbook of Action Research: Participative Inquiry and Practice*. London: Sage. pp. 420–32. Also in P. Reason and H. Bradbury *Handbook of Action Research: Concise Paperback Edition*. London: Sage. pp. 322–34.

Yorks, L. and Kasl, E. (2002) 'Learning from inquiries: lessons for using collaborative inquiry as an adult learning strategy', in L. Yorks and E. Kasl, *Collaborative Inquiry as a Strategy for Adult Learning,* No. 94. San Francisco, CA: Jossey-Bass.

43

Facilitation as Action Research in the Moment

Jenny Mackewn

This chapter presents a model of action research which resolves the contradictions and choices of facilitative practice by regarding it as a continual process of inquiry. Four dimensions of this inquiry are outlined and exemplified: the purpose of the group, organization or community; the conceptualization of how facilitators make meaning of their art and of the community or group phenomena which they are facilitating; the wider field; and the choreography of energy.

In this chapter I describe a model of facilitation that I find to be useful both in my own practice and in support of the practice of other facilitators. I regularly offer this model in workshops and shadow (a type of supervisory or meta-) consultation to facilitators and consultants. I briefly discuss the nature of facilitation and the dilemmas which face me and others who try to explore what facilitation is. I see facilitation as encompassing a wide range of practices embedded within an even wider range of unarticulated philosophies. I focus on the spectrum of skills and qualities required to practice well as a facilitator, which I describe as existing as dualities. I develop to an approach I call 'Facilitation as Action Research in the Moment', in which the crucial dimensions

that need consideration when deciding what to do when as a facilitator are subject to continual inquiry. These crucial dimensions are: the purpose of the group, organization or community; the theoretical conceptualization which the facilitators bring to their meaning making of the events; the wider field or context in which they are operating; the energy or atmosphere in the group at any particular time and the choreography of that energy.

MY BACKGROUND

I have been a practising facilitator for 20 years, earning a part of my living through that work. I practise in a wide range of guises. I act as a design facilitator and consultant in organizational and community settings – in successful commercial enterprises, in public and voluntary sector services and with communities. I lecture in different university settings. Additionally, I have initiated, designed and led workshops in facilitation as action research for seven years. During that period I have been able to develop the approach to facilitation that is described in this chapter with the active contribution of the people who have attended those workshops.

I am a 60-year-old woman, newly a grandmother, of Scots and partially unknown cultural background; fit and athletic; persistently interested in learning new approaches to work and living; committed to cycles of action, reflection, learning, co-creating. I have lived and worked for substantial periods of time on two continents. This descriptive list is inevitably partial and incomplete but it may give you some idea of what matters from my perspective at this time.

At the same time I wonder how this brief description of me will have coloured your own judgement and degree of interest in reading the rest of this chapter. Has it sharpened or dampened your interest? Either way, are you aware of what – in my self-description – sharpened or dampened that interest? Because of course you, like me, will be influenced by your own conditioning, experiences, cultural norms, training and conceptual models. And may have been unwittingly switched on or off by any aspect of my description – in ways I did not intend or anticipate in offering it

SO WHAT DO WE MEAN BY FACILITATION?

Facilitation is understood in different ways by different people (see, for example, Heron, 2000; Shaw, 2002; Spinks and Clements, 1993; Stacey, 1995; Wadsworth, 2001/2006). Yet many practitioners and authors (as well as group participants) who talk or write about facilitation do not articulate their underlying assumptions. Nor do they identify which particular definition or type of facilitation they espouse. This means often people will discuss and disagree about the practice of the facilitator without being aware of either their

own or the other person's embedded belief systems about the nature of facilitation and without ensuring that they are comparing like for like. Overall we might say that the differences that emerge in facilitation relate to the degree to which the facilitator combines the roles of a participant, mover and/or observer.

WHAT ARE THE SKILLS OF FACILITATION?

There is almost as much variety and range in the skills that people believe are needed to be a good facilitator as there is in people's definitions of facilitation. During the facilitation as action research workshops that I design and run, we invite people to inquire into the meaning of facilitation and the skills that they think are involved. Table 43.1 offers a useful crystallization of our reflection on the question of important skills for facilitation.

Faced with such a demanding range skills, many will feel overwhelmed by the sheer breadth of skills. Won't it take a lifetime to acquire all those skills? Where do we start? Which are the most important skills? How would we prioritize them? The outcome of one group' s conversation about how they would prioritize the long list of facilitation skills is given in Table 43.2. Naturally the way the skills are prioritized will depend upon the subjective mindset of the people discussing the prioritization and the subjective mindset of the facilitator as he or she is practising their art.

PARADOX IN FACILITATION: CONTRADICTORY SKILLS

It is important to note that many of these skills are contradictory and paradoxical, which has led me to develop a table of Polarity and Paradox in Facilitation (see Table 43.3). Sometimes facilitators need to follow the group's agenda, while at other times facilitators need to lead the group's agenda. Sometimes the facilitators need to question, inquire and consult, while at other times they need to direct. Sometimes facilitators need to listen; other times they need to tell people

Table 43.1 *Facilitation skills and qualities*

Created by participants on Facilitation as Action Research Workshop, Centre for Action Research in Professional Practice, University of Bath, 2004

- Tolerating silence … Creating silence
- Modelling
- Gender awareness
- Self-awareness
- Preparation
- Respecting self and others
- Formulating questions and questioning
- Offering choices, taking decisions
- Making decisions at group and individual level at all times
- Inspiring
- Listening to self and others
- Attending to inclusionality, attending to others
- Energy in self and others and group – linking level of energy with type of activity and intervention
- Structuring, creating structure for self, for group … . Flexing structure
- Pace and variety
- Guiding, managing, creating
- Holding authority and credibility
- Creating fun experience; having and appreciating humour
- Inventing research on the spot
- Listening, seeing and observing – eyes in bottom, back of head
- Affirming and confronting
- Knowing how to use own power and presence
- Knowing how to relate to power structures in organizations
- Knowing how to relate to power and presence of others
- Confronting + supporting, challenging and nurturing
- Holding interest and enjoyment
- Holding intentions of self and of group through turbulence and diversions
- Noticing connections; noticing patterns
- Linking events and patterns in the team or group to organizational patterns and to business behaviour and outcomes
- Creating space … . Holding space
- Providing or helping others to provide clarity and purpose
- Making group level interventions.
- Attending to meaning, giving meaning, inviting group meaning-making
- Imparting of learning, drawing out learning from experiential exercises
- Drawing out learning (at group and individual level) from unexpected events or experiences in team
- Generosity
- Containing and opening up
- Follow group's agenda … . Lead group's agenda

what to do. Sometimes they need to nurture and support the people in the group or community; other times they need to challenge. Sometimes facilitators need to provide structure and time boundaries; at other times they need to flex structure and time boundaries.

Both ends of the polarities given in the table are part of the whole skill of facilitation. One end of the spectrum gives meaning and definition to the other, just as night defines day and day defines night. So facilitators should not be asking themselves 'Do I want to be a supportive *or* a challenging type

of facilitator? Do I think I am a consulting *or* a directing type of facilitator?' Instead, an artful facilitator needs to be able to embrace the paradox of valuing both ends of the spectrum and acting in a timely, elegant and skilful way at both ends of the spectrum of polarities and indeed at finally graded points anywhere along the spectrum.

If facilitators need to embrace these paradoxes, then the all-important questions become: When shall I act at which end of the spectrum of polarities? When shall I follow the group's agenda? When shall I lead it? When

Table 43.2 *Prioritizing facilitation skills*

Created by participants on Facilitation as Action Research Workshop, Centre for Action Research in Professional Practice, University of Bath, 2004

Preparing self

- Physical, breathing
- Posture, visualization
- Protection, grounding
- Centring, developing own presence or aligned energy

Observing

- Energy levels at individual and collective level
- Interest levels at individual and collective level
- Body language at individual and collective level
- Own reactions and feelings (in body, in mind, in heart); hunches in self
- Groupings and subgroupings in group
- Behaviour (of individuals, subgroups, groups) in sessions
- Behaviour (of individuals, subgroups, groups) in breaks

Listening and attending

- To words (i.e. content) at individual and collective level
- To process, e.g. to non-verbal sounds; to breathing; to sighs; to what is not said; to congruence (or incongruence) between words and body/energy; to energy and interest levels
- Listening between the lines

Ensuring all voices are heard, while dealing with dominant voices; making space for quiet ones. Acting as a traffic controller.

Noticing what is going on in self (as possible measure of issues of group, as well as personal data). Sharing some of own process.

Regularly attending to self

- Grounding, protecting, caring for own energy
- How use self – variety of styles and ways of using self

Following or leading group's agenda and process
Presenting/imparting information
Making meaning and inviting others to make meaning
Structuring, e.g. breaking group into pairs or small groups; planning and implementing exercises or activities

---

shall I listen? When shall I tell people what to do? When do I make which intervention?

FACILITATION AS ACTION RESEARCH IN THE MOMENT

I am proposing that the answer to these questions lies in a lively and personally demanding model of *facilitation as a form of ongoing action research* in which facilitators are continually asking themselves, and sometimes the group, what is needed here?

I suggest that the most crucial four dimensions to consider in this inquiry are:

- the *purpose* of the group, organization or community;
- the *conceptualization* of how facilitators make meaning of their art and of the community or group phenomena which they are facilitating;
- the *wider field* in which we are operating,
- the *choreography of energy*

These four dimensions (see Figure 43.1) are not dissimilar to Torbert and Taylor's four territories of experience (see Chapter 16). Nor are they too different from the emphasis placed on 'meaning choice and relationship' that is emphasized in the recently published edited volume on facilitating cultures of collaboration by Schuman (2006). Of course, the four

Table 43.3 *Polarities and paradox in facilitation*

Following team's or group's agenda	Leading team's or group's agenda
◄──►	
Consulting, questioning	Directing
◄──►	
Listening	Telling people what to do
◄──►	
Nurturing, supporting	Challenging
◄──►	
Providing structure and time boundaries	Dropping structure and time boundaries
◄──►	
Suggesting/providing meaning	Inviting group to make meaning
◄──►	
Allowing multiple meanings and possibilities	Settling on one meaning and possibility
◄──►	
Attending to individuals	Making team or system level interventions
◄──►	
Using own presence, power to influence	Attending to and enhancing power and presence of other participants
◄──►	
Noticing patterns	Ignoring patterns
◄──►	
Listening to words spoken	Attending to body language and energy levels
◄──►	
Ensuring all voices are heard	Dealing with over-dominant voices

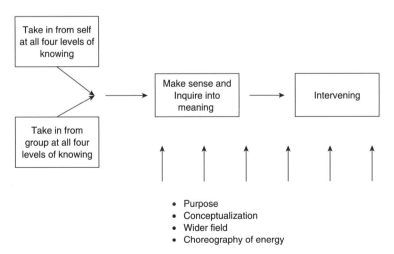

Figure 43.1 *The four interrelated dimensions of facilitation as action research in the moment*

dimensions are not separate; they merge, overlap and exist simultaneously. But facilitators will be able to distinguish between them in practice.

FACILITATION AS ACTION RESEARCH IN THE MOMENT

Dimension 1: Purpose

The objectives and overall purpose of the group/team/organization profoundly influence how we work as facilitators. If a purpose energizes and motivates, it can catalyse the group's energy to achieve breakthrough into transformative action. Therefore it needs to be the lodestar which guides the facilitator's planning, design and ongoing action research in the moment throughout the event(s) which they are facilitating.

We can consider purpose in the conception of events; in the design of events; in the objectives and purpose of each particular event; and in the interventions that facilitators make during the events to support these purposes.

Facilitators cannot, of course, identify an organization's or community's purpose alone. They must co-create purpose with the people within the organization who are concerned and affected by the need, as well as with people who have power enough in the community or organization to carry influence. The facilitators must ask themselves who are the right people to engage in conversation regarding purpose. To be effective, facilitators will usually need to develop strategic partnerships with sponsors or leaders within the organization or community, while at the same time creating connection with those who may have no voice or feel disempowered within the larger system. Sometimes facilitators may choose to get together a small design group that consists of facilitators, the relevant organizational leaders, one or two stakeholders and one or two participants of the event. I have learnt that co-planning and co-designing are iterative and emergent processes which continue throughout the design and planning period and right into the event-time itself, as each successive design is refined and replaced by a better one that more closely meets

the emerging needs, interests and energies of the participants, facilitators and leaders and sometimes responds to the impact of the wider field.

> At a recent planning meeting for a two-day skills review event for a group of experienced facilitators, the design group decided upon the following purpose: *To use the action inquiry engine to power independent facilitation in the service of the updated strategic agenda.*
> This purpose inspired and energized the design team. They felt that it distilled their reason for spending the day together and would inspire and motivate them to make the most it.
> As facilitators we continuously referred back to the purpose and objectives as a guide to our design and to our facilitative interventions.

In intentional striking contrast to the above example, I facilitate an ongoing support and supervision group for massage and shiatsu therapists operating within the context of a cancer support hospice. The purpose of this group (as worked out with both the organization and the group) is to provide spiritual, emotional and intellectual support to the practitioners who work with seriously ill and dying patients.

> The two hours we spend together once every four or five weeks are disciplined and yet relaxed. We manage to attend to case discussions, team and organizational issues, do some relaxation, cleansing or meditation, co-create simple ceremonial work to honour the dying of a patient or the life transition of a practitioner, without feeling hurried. We are on purpose together.

There is a creative tension between following the agreed purpose and deciding to deviate from that agreed purpose. Facilitators practising facilitation as action research in the moment need to be aware of the complexity interaction and be alert to the possibility that at some point in the planned programme it may no longer be 'right' to follow the agreed purpose – because a new or greater purpose/need becomes evident (or because some aspect of the greater field is now demanding attention in a way that was not anticipated when designing). The new purpose or need is often one which could not emerge in the earlier design meetings because it had not yet ripened but which now emerges as a result of the actual exchange or dialogue between the people.

One of the small miracles of changing direction to attend to a deeper purpose that emerges is that time can take on a new elasticity and texture when a group is working and playing with the matters that truly engage it. Often the group and the facilitator(s) can find a way to attend to both their deepest concerns and their immediate responsibilities.

Dimension 2: Conceptualization

Facilitators all have a variety of theories and theoretical models through which they make meaning of their art and of the community or group phenomena which they are studying and attempting to facilitate. Some of these theories are consciously known by the facilitators and can be relatively easily articulated. Other theories are embedded as unconscious beliefs and will be harder to access, let alone articulate. Consciously or unconsciously, our theoretical conceptualization influences how we think about our work, and how we make meaning of the phenomena we encounter in our work. It informs our definition of facilitation, as I have pointed out above, and the decisions that we make from moment to moment when we consider which of the paradoxical skills of facilitation to use in what circumstances. Different theoretical conceptualizations of what a community, organization or group is and how it may develop can radically alter what we decide to do as facilitator.

Some theories suggest that groups and teams go through several stages of development and that participants are likely to experience certain fairly predictable concerns and feelings associated with each stage (Neilsen, 1986; Srivastva et al., 1977; Tuckman, 1965). This relatively linear model of group development and dynamics is widely taught on group facilitation training courses and such models are often presented as though they were the only way to conceptualize a group and its development. Other theorists have suggested that a group, organization or community is a system which consists of tops, middles or bottoms (Oshry, 1995) or which is made up of multiple feedback loops (Senge, 1999). Then again, writers drawing

on complexity theory (Stacey, 1995; Shaw, 2002) have described groups, organizations and communities as complex adaptive self-organizing systems. In my workshops for facilitators we take each of these ways of conceptualizing groups, organizations and communities in turn and devote a couple of days to exploring each model and inquiring into how that particular way of conceptualizing a group, organization or community influences what we actually do as facilitators. This too brief discussion reminds us that there are many different ways to conceptualize the group, organization or community with which we are working; and that the way we conceptualize it is likely to radically alter our style of facilitation and choice of intervention.

To give a flavour of how the way we conceptualize a group or organization influences our facilitation as action researcher, I will take the idea that groups and communities go through relatively predictable stages of development and give an example of the sorts of first-person inquiry that go through my head while facilitating a group which is at the first-or forming – stage of group development. Table 43.4 offers an integrative model of the stages of group development, together with an outline of the likely concerns and feelings of the participants and guidelines about possible facilitator behaviours for each stage.

I am facilitating a group which is forming. I remember that a new group needs to be welcomed, made to feel safe and valued, needs to understand the purpose, limits and structure of the group. *So I ask myself – what can I as facilitator do that will help the members of the group feel safe and welcomed? In response to my own inquiry, I may ensure that I am there early. I ensure the room is organized in advance. I greet each person individually, creating connection, making eye contact, shaking hands, being personally present.*

I ask myself *how can I provide enough structure to help people feel safe and contained and give them an understanding of the purpose of the group?*

In response to my own inquiry, *I may provide a light but firm structure, in which I temporarily lead a team's or group's agenda by setting up and directing introductory activities, presenting a proposed programme, temporarily telling people what to do. Generally I tell myself to be supportive and welcoming rather than challenging at this point.*

Table 43.4 *Facilitator behaviours and stages of group or team development*

Stage 1   Forming or inclusion, identity and dependence
Key facilitator behaviours

- Create safety and comfort
- Make objectives and task clear and explicit
- Help people feel welcome and involved
- Create opportunities and time for people to get to know one another
- Be directive without being authoritarian, create clear structures for meetings, the way the group or team is to work, that can evolve and change over time and in which participation can occur

Concerns and feelings of participants associated with this stage

- What do I have to do to belong here?
- Am I going to be liked/respected/accepted?
- Who is like me? Who am I like?
- Is this event/group/team going to be on purpose and is its purpose going to align with my purpose?
- How safe, comfortable, anxious or apparently cool and collected do I feel?

Stage 2   Storming or influencing, conflict and identity
Key facilitator behaviours

- Allow conflict to surface in the group; don't avoid or reject conflict
- Legitimate and support the expression of different opinions and feelings
- Accept responsibility for and confirm own facilitation
- Avoid scape-goating and polarization
- Be clear about limits; what is and what is not negotiable
- Try and take feedback seriously without collapsing under criticism

Concerns and feelings of participants associated with this stage

- Who am I dissimilar from? Who is dissimilar to me?
- Who has influence, authority and control? Who has most influence?
- If differences get expressed, is all this going to fall apart?
- Likely feelings of anger, frustration, resentment, apathy amongst team members and possibly responding feelings in facilitator-leader

Stage 3   Norming or consolidation of roles
Key facilitator behaviours

- Allow norms to be created by the team and by the facilitator
- Validate both formal and informal roles that evolve (e.g. chair, secretary and carer, placator and organizer of social events). Develop such roles
- Create climate where feedback can be more openly given and received

Concerns and feelings associated with this stage

- Likely feelings of relief and sense of progress as roles and norms are established, followed by possible boredom now that life is more settled.

NB Many functional teams do not need/want to go beyond Stage 3

Stage 4   Role and norm destructuring
Key facilitator behaviours

- Draw attention to roles (both formal and informal) and raise awareness re how much the group allows members to behave flexibly (e.g. in several roles)
- Draw attention to ways in which group may reinforce each other's role rigidity
- Raise awareness of existing norms; introduce inquiry re continued value of current norms
- Normalize and accept increased vulnerability, conflict, differentiation and awkwardness as roles and norms crumble and become more open

Table 43.4   *(Continued)*

Concerns and feelings associated with this stage

- Feelings of increased vulnerability and awkwardness for some as norms and roles dissolve, accompanied by possible excitement and anxiety about how the group or team will function in the future

Stage 5   Performing or high cohesiveness and high differentiation, intimacy and interdependence
Key facilitator behaviours

- Challenge existing norms and assumptions
- Develop creativity, allow room for mistakes and experimentation
- Encourage others to lead and/or facilitate, let go of control
- Create more sense of equality in team, partnership and interdependence
- Don't allow team to get too cosy and internally focused
- Become more of a consultant to the group

Concerns and feelings associated with this stage

- Feeling good, involved, committed, that the whole of both individuals and group is being seen, validated and used
- More able to relax with and enjoy the group or team
- Excitement of achievement
- Flow

Stage 6   Completing, celebrating, mourning
Key facilitator behaviours

- Anticipate varied reactions to ending
- Let people know of ending well in advance, if at all possible
- Help create appropriate ending rituals e.g. meals, parties
- Help individuals and team learn from their work together, e.g. encourage reminiscing, and storytelling
- Allow and facilitate expression of appreciation and acknowledgement
- Help individuals plan and prepare for the future, e.g. next job/project
- Celebrate successful outcome(s)
- Create space for expression of feelings re ending (from sadness to relief)

Concerns and feelings associated with this stage

- Feelings of sadness or relief at ending
- Satisfaction with successful outcome(s)
- Wish to move on without paying too much attention to this stage is common in many western and business cultures due to a tendency to always be moving on to the next new action or engagement, avoidance of endings and possible embarrassment about feelings associated

So from the first six of the polarities and paradoxes in facilitation, I follow the right-hand polarities at this stage in the group/team's development.

Dimension 3: The Wider Field

The wider field is the total situation consisting of all the complex interactive phenomena of the individuals and their environment, the whole system that impinges on the focal group we are facilitating. As facilitators, we are always operating in a wider and more complex context than the one on which the organization is choosing to focus. Whatever is in focus, something else will be out of focus or in the background. We facilitators have important responsibility regarding whether to accept the choice of focus of the organization or to shift the attention to what we notice is missing from the scope of the events which we are facilitating.

A simple and localized example of the crucial choice of focus in the context of the wider field occurred at a recent discussion about future roles amongst the team of therapists in the hospice for cancer sufferers.

I noticed that the conversation had taken a completely different flavour than previous discussions – one or two people are speaking animatedly while most are silent. The overall energy feels inhibited. *I reflect upon this change and feel I have a choice – I can go on listening to and supporting those who have the energy to speak. Or I can draw attention to the wider context (the hospice is about to move premises and a number of the current team are not able to make the journey).* I choose to refer to the wider context and gradually new perspectives emerge – some people express sadness, fear or anger about the changes while others own that they are delighted. They have felt embarrassed to share their delight because the change affects others badly. My referring to the wider context has opened a space for people to speak about the move and how it is impacting upon their lives.

The wider field can be interpreted in a far broader way than in the above example, and this far broader field may also impact upon our choices as facilitators doing action research in the moment. For example, an exploration of future commercial markets in the oil industry will be very different if it is focused upon an expansion of the markets as they are currently envisaged, as opposed to a consideration of markets as they may develop after post peak oil production. If the facilitator or other participants choose to mention an aspect of the larger field conditions such as the idea, in some places still controversial, that oil production is peaking and an energy crisis looming, then the conversation about future markets or developments in the organization may change dramatically. Doing so may be experienced as risky; facilitation is also political.

There is evidently an interesting and creative tension between prioritizing the purpose of the event (as identified by the organizational sponsors, the stakeholders and participants) and referring to the wider field or context.

Dimension 4: Choreography of Energy:

For our moment to moment practice as facilitators, the most crucial of the four dimensions of facilitation as action research is energy. The capacity to work with the energy flows in a group is a 'meta-skill', core and difficult to practice.

First, facilitation requires us to be aware of our own intrinsic energy as facilitators. We facilitators can easily be so busy with building the strategic relationships with the organizational or community sponsors, working out the design, and asking ourselves what interventions we should be using, etc., that we readily get out of touch with ourselves and our experiential and imaginative knowing – thus cutting ourselves off from how we impact the space we then in turn facilitate. As a matter of discipline, I am training myself to develop a centred state and to ask myself: *what is going on within my own body and my own imagination? How do I feel energetically?* This disciplined attention to and inquiry into my own energetic state helps me to stay energetically centred and alert.

Such an attention to our own energetic state is an essential prerequisite to doing facilitation as action research from moment to moment. If we are not centred, we cannot have real awareness of the complexity of dimensions discussed here; we cannot notice the unfolding options and cannot make discerning choices. Instead, we are likely to either be swayed by the whims of the group or be too defensively attached to our own ideas of what is needed.

Second, facilitation requires us to be aware of the group's energy, paying attention to the atmosphere in the room, noticing the body language of the people. From moment to moment, I ask myself: *are they leaning forward, engaged? Are they wary, cautious? Are they relaxed, happy? Are they turned off or turned inward? Or are some energetically engaged while others are not contributing? If so why is this? How can I explore the different levels of response? Or if the energy has merely got stale, how shall I attend to or shift the energy?*

Third, facilitation requires us to learn how to connect our energy to the group's energy and vice versa. When we have got the energetic connection we will know it in our bones. Sometimes we will feel like we are riding a huge wave, planing in front of it. Other times we will feel as though we are bobbing along nicely with an energetic swell. At still other times, we will feel as though – despite our best efforts – we have not quite engaged with the energy of the group.

Nothing we suggest inspires or excites. The energy of the group is more than the sum of the individual energies in the room, and is therefore very powerful – far greater than our individual power as facilitator.

Yet we can learn to influence (as well as be influenced by) the energy of the group. For as facilitators we can learn to ride with, stir up, calm, respond and dance with the energy in the group. Facilitators who inquire into and learn to build these energetic connections can act as catalysts to the group's energies – as in chemistry, they act as catalysts, to stimulate a breakthrough or transformation which would have been unlikely to happen without the presence and particular energies of those catalytic facilitators or animators.

Important ways of working with our own and with the group's energy include: (a) sensitizing ourselves to work with our own and the group's energy; (b) developing ourselves as energy-sensitive instruments; and (c) integrating creative approaches and presentational knowing. Given their importance, I will take up each of these in turn.

a) Sensitizing Ourselves to Work with Our Own and the Group's Energy

How do we know when to choose to do what with our energy and with the group's energy?

There can be no definitive answer. I have learned that we need to re-sensitize our bodies so we can tell what is going on. If we have become desensitized this may take time, concentration and new disciplines. We need to ground ourselves so our energy is in our bodies rather than in our heads. I find running, yoga, massage and the gym are wonderfully grounding. Others tell me *chi gung* may be better still. Whatever, we need to practise so that we can *trust* that we can pick up the energetic state of ourselves and of others in the group with which we are working. Our minds are full of chatter and ideas and this tends to get in the way of learning what our bodies and our imaginations are telling us. Some tips for learning to dance the facilitator's energetic exchange are shown in Table 43.5.

b) Developing Ourselves as Energy-sensitive Instruments

An important way of learning how to feel and choreograph energy is to develop ourselves as energy-sensitive instruments and to have some ideas about the possible meanings of the energy we experience. So we need to develop a discipline of inquiring systematically:

What is the quality of the energy within the group from moment to moment? What are the likely meanings of that group energy?

What is happening within myself and what does that mean about me and what might it mean about the group?

In learning how to develop ourselves as energy-sensitive instruments we will need to use a truly integrative knowing, drawing on many ways of knowing, similar to the 'extended epistemology' discussed in Chapter 24, which is grounded in our experience; expressed through stories and images; articulated through theories that make sense to us and put into practice in the complex discipline of facilitation as action research in the moment. For energy is usually experienced in our bodies through experiential knowing and in our images or stories through imaginal or presentational knowing, channelled through our minds and expressed through our practice.

As consultants developing ourselves as instruments, we can learn to be aware of ourselves as part of an energetic relational system, for we are most interestingly in relationship with the individuals, group or organization with which we are working. And the more we can tell about the quality of the relationship between us and the group, the more we can guess about the group, organization or community and its likely internal patterns of relating and its unexpressed culture.

Our own reactions (at all four levels of knowing) will obviously tell us about ourselves. But our reactions will also tell us about the group or organization relational system in which we are working. In order to understand a group, organization or community, we need to get close to them, establish rapport and relate in an empathetic way. At the same time, our very empathy with the team can lead us to (unconsciously) begin to

Table 43.5 *Dancing the facilitator's energetic exchange*

- Develop our capacity to be energetically centred and sensitive by following appropriate disciplines such as sport, yoga, t'ai chi, meditation
- Sensitize
- Ground
- Believe we can
- Still our minds
- Pay attention to what we notice externally in the group and internally in our bodies
- Share some of what we notice and what sense we make of it
- See what happens
- Keep inquiring and experimenting (both within ourselves and with the group/community with whom we are working)
- Trust we'll get better and better at dancing the dance of energetic exchange
- Integrate creative exploration and approaches into our facilitation so as to harness the whole energy of the group, not just their brains and verbal language

act or feel like the system we are facilitating and become so immersed in the world of the people we are facilitating that we become confluent with it.

Hawkins (2003) has referred to these phenomena as parallel process: our own reactions may resonate with and represent the unarticulated experiences and feelings of the people in the organization or community in which we are working. Or they may represent the energetic complement to the person/team we are dealing with: we may react to a person or team in a way in which other people in the organization typically react to that person or team.

When we begin to enact this parallel process, it is important to first notice those feelings when they are not the typical ones we would normally feel in a set of circumstances; and, second, to inquire what are the possible meanings of these atypical behaviours and feelings.

We wanted to have a conversation with one of the directors of the organization we were working with. We found we were highly nervous and uncertain about how to approach him. We were unusually giggly and behaving like two young girls. *We wondered if other people experienced the director as frightening and also responded in child-like or compliant ways to his authority figure?* If this was the case it would be especially significant as the organization wanted to increase its capacity for creative innovation. Authority, fear and compliance are not the most fertile grounds in which to develop collaborative creativity and innovation!

We introduced our hypotheses to the team. Both director and team members recognized the truth of the suggestions. With coaching and support from both a team consultant and an individual mentor to the director, the director became more aware of how he unintentionally evoked fear and cut off exploratory conversations, while the team members became more aware of how they failed to challenge the director when he behaved in ways that evoked fear or cut off the very sort of exploratory and creative dialogue that could lead to greater innovation.

c) Integrating Creative Approaches and Presentational Knowing into Our Facilitation

Learning and development which draws on all four ways of knowing is likely to be fuller and much more memorable than knowing which draws on only one or two ways. Programmes and events are often designed as primarily verbal and rational and thus stay within a comfort zone for both facilitators and participants.

As discussed elsewhere in this Handbook (Chapters 20, 27, 30, 34, 35), creative and non-verbal approaches harness the greater energy and commitment which lie locked up in the often unused experiential and presentational (or imaginal) knowing of the leaders, facilitators and the group. Creative and non-verbal approaches allow the participants to integrate their rational and intuitive minds, the left and right hand side of the brain (Ornstein, 1972; Mackewn, 1997). They also allow participants and facilitators alike to access their dreams, their body memories, their collective wisdom, their intuitive hunches and voice them in the service of the group to which they belong – often leading to remarkable insight or benefits for that group, organization or community.

An example took place in a commercial organizational setting with the finance department (traditionally averse to creative or 'touchy feely' approaches). We had been working with internal sponsors to initiate, develop and nurture an internal mentoring scheme. The mentees, young managers, have been invited to attend a meeting in which they debrief their early experiences of the mentoring programme and tell how things are going from their perspective.

> The young managers come in polite, well pre-sented, slightly formal, seem keen to impress, pos-sibly slightly suspicious. We invite them to do a brief check-in and then to tell their stories of being a mentee. They do this with growing enthusiasm – sharing 'successful' experiences and challenging moments, amusing each other and us in the process – as well as alerting us to problem areas which may need attention later. In this storytelling they are already integrating rational sequencing and the organization's need for evaluation with creative right brain storytelling and imaginative description. As they do so they integrate their whole selves. Naturally their energy increases, and ours as well.
>
> Then I draw a stick figure cartoon of the mentee's worst nightmares and show it to them. I ask them to draw a cartoon of their own worst nightmares and their best moments. At this point I choose to speak with authority and energy and don't hesitate or consult them. I want to introduce another creative medium and right brain activity and so I model doing so. I set them up in pairs with flip chart paper and give them 3 minutes to com-plete the cartoon task. My intention is to introduce a fresh, vital and unexpected energy to further help their functioning to flow between rational thought and intuition/creativity.
>
> The effect is electric. The meeting had already been going well. But now it takes off. The young managers speak fluently of the things that are really troubling them. The group is inspired. They offer each other support and innovative possibili-ties for resolution.

Yet many facilitators (and some group partic-ipants) are hesitant to try creative approaches. They fear that people will feel infantilized by the introduction of coloured pens and papers or awkward at the request that they move or mime a group situation or business challenge. Or they just do not see these creative, non-verbal approaches as relevant or an effective use of time. The energetic and holistic bene-fits as explained here are so enormous that it is important for facilitators to learn to inte-grate creative approaches into our work in skilful ways that minimize the discomfort of the group. We need first to familiarize *our-selves* with the experiences and depth of working with creative media and presenta-tional knowing, then think about how to adjust creative media so that we can introduce them smoothly into the groups in which we are working. The art of facilitation is to intro-duce creative experiences that take people just outside their comfort zone but not into their panic zone; to give a really good rele-vant and rational reason for why you are sug-gesting they try this (so that their rational mind is settled); to demonstrate confidence; and to set an example ourselves.

The resulting payback is enormous. The group is energized by the novel approach, the individuals are inspired because their ratio-nal and intuitive minds are working together, both individual and group have access to intuitive hunches and personal and collective wisdom which were previously missing or unvoiced.

CONCLUSION

The facilitator's job is complex. It is already quite challenging to remain mindful of one of these four dimensions I have outlined. But of course facilitators need to multi-task, remain mindful of and interweave all four dimen-sions almost simultaneously: purpose *and* theoretical conceptualization; theoretical conceptualization *and* the wider field in which we are operating; the wider field *and* the observation and choreography of energy. In this view, facilitators must continuously inquire in the moment from multiple per-spectives – that is, how does the purpose of the group (purpose) *and* the stage of devel-opment of the group (theoretical conception) *and* the impact of the wider field *and* the observation of energy simultaneously inform the inquiry into what we do as facilitators from moment to moment?

Thus facilitation as action research in the moment is itself a paradoxical form, both a science and an art. It is a science in that it draws on theory and evidence; it is an art in that it requires precision, attention and timely action. As an art form it does not and cannot follow any one methodology or pre-determined plan. It is an art in which we facilitators can with practice and reflection develop our skill, commitment, creativity and sensitivity to the specific dynamics of any given situation so that we can rise to the challenge of our task and make our own discernments from moment to moment about what is needed in that particular situation.

All our relevant skills and our consciousness of the four domains outlined here are needed to cope with the challenges of each situation. When facilitating in the ways described we will often feel as if we have eyes in the back of our heads, sensory perception points throughout our bodies. We are taking in information from the group/system though all our perceptions, we are making sense of that information, we are designing our immediate responses, while considering possible redesigns of the whole event and wondering how we can serve the purpose and yet address the new issues emerging from the current dialogue or the wider field. We are completely absorbed by our complex art. There is no excess psychic energy left over to process any information beyond what the demanding activity of facilitation offers. All the attention is concentrated. Thus facilitation as action research in the moment can offer a flow experience similar to those described by rock climbers and dancers: 'Your concentration is very complete. Your mind is not wandering. You are not thinking of anything else. You are totally involved in what you are doing; your energy is flowing very smoothly. You feel alert, relaxed, comfortable, energetic' (Csikszentmihalyi, 2002: 53).

REFERENCES

Csikszentmihalyi, M. (2002) *Flow*. London: Rider.

Hawkins, P. (2003) *Systemic Shadow Consultancy*. A Bath Consultancy Group working paper.

Heron, J. (2000) *The Complete Facilitator's Handbook*, London: Kogan Page.

Mackewn, J. (1997) *Developing Gestalt Counselling*. London: Sage.

Neilsen, E.H. (1986) 'Empowerment strategies: balancing authority and responsibility', in S. Srivastva (ed.), *Executive Power*. San Francisco, CA: Jossey-Bass. pp. 78–110.

Ornstein, R.E. (1972) *The Psychology of Consciousness*. San Francisco: W.H. Freeman.

Oshry, B. (1995) *Seeing Systems*. San Francisco, CA: Berrett-Koehler.

Schuman, S.P. (ed.) (2006) *The IAF Handbook of Group Facilitation: Best Practices from the Leading Organization in Facilitation*. San Francisco, CA: Jossey-Bass.

Senge, P. (1999) *The Fifth Discipline: the Art and Practice of The Learning Organisation*. London: Random House.

Shaw, P. (2002) *Changing Conversations in Organizations*. London: Routledge.

Spinks, T. and Clements, P. (1993) *A Practical Guide of Facilitation Skills*. London: Kogan Page.

Srivastva, S., Obert, S.L. and Neilson, E. (1977) 'Organizational analysis through group processes: a theoretical perspective', in C.L. Cooper (ed.), *Organizational Development in the UK and USA*. London: Macmillan. pp. 83–111.

Stacey, R.(1995) 'Creativity in organizations: *the importance of mess'*, Complexity Management Centre Working Paper, University of Hertfordshire.

Torbert, W.R. and Taylor, S.S. (2006) 'Action inquiry: interweaving multiple qualities of attention for timely action', in P. Reason and H. Bradbury (eds), *Handbook of Action Research: Participative Inquiry and Practice*. London: Sage.

Tuckman, B. (1965) 'Development sequences in small groups', *Psychological Bulletin*, 63: 419–27.

Wadsworth, Y. (2001/2006) 'The mirror, the magnifying glass, the compass and the map: facilitating participatory action research', in P. Reason and H. Bradbury (eds) *Handbook of Action Research: Participative Inquiry and Practice*. London: Sage. Also published in P. Reason and H. Bradury (eds) (2006), *Handbook of Action Research: Concise Paperback Edition*. London: Sage. pp. 322–34.

44

Muddling Through: Facing the Challenges of Managing a Large-scale Action Research Project

Geoff Mead

This chapter takes a practical view of the complex demands of managing a real-life large-scale project involving multiple action research groups over an extended period of time. The different perspectives of the various stakeholders in the project, the tensions between them and the consequent unanticipated issues that arose are explored. The narrative charts a gradual shift from hierarchical line management of the project towards a more relational approach, consciously developing a network of relationships among the stakeholders. It closes by identifying some of the capacities and qualities demanded of someone charged with managing such a project and concludes that whilst good planning is essential it is no substitute for an active and curious engagement with the phenomenology of the process as it unfolds.

A considerable amount has been written about the skills of facilitating action research in groups, including those particularly relevant for co-operative inquiry (Heron, 1996; Heron and Reason, 2001/2006; McArdle, Chapter 42; McKardle, 2002; McKewn, Chapter 43; Wadsworth 2001/2006). In this chapter, I want to take a slightly different perspective and consider some of the challenges of managing a large-scale project involving multiple action research groups over an extended period of time. I also want to identify and illustrate some of the qualities and capacities that might be called upon in attempting to manage this kind of large-scale action research project.

In the ongoing debate about the scope and influence of action research, this kind of approach potentially offers a middle ground – perhaps even a creative synthesis – between depth of intervention (e.g. single case action research groups) and breadth of intervention (e.g. dialogue conferences; Gustavsen, 2003; Chapter 4). I am interested to see if we can move beyond the polarization of intense, small-scale, local interventions on the one hand and diffuse widespread, systemic interventions on the other

I will offer a partial and tentative view grounded in the 'messy lowlands' of my own practice, drawing on the experience of working with the UK Cabinet Office sponsored Public Service Leaders Scheme (PSLS) over a five year period, from its inception in 2001 to its conclusion in 2006, variously as the designer, co-ordinator, supervisor, manager, and director of the action inquiry element of the programme. I hope this will be useful for other practitioners faced with similar challenges but, as suggested by the adoption of Charles Lindblom's term 'muddling through' (Lindblom, 1959) in the title of this chapter, there are limits to how accurately such challenges can be anticipated and prepared for.

In the following sections I will give some background and context for the PSLS and describe the part played by the action inquiry groups in the scheme – enough, I hope, to enable you to locate what follows in subsequent sections. I will then focus on the particular demands and challenges that arose during the first three years of the scheme, how other stakeholders and I made sense of them and how we responded. In describing and reflecting on these experiences I shall attempt to stay close to the spirit of 'muddling through' to give you a feel for unfolding events without undue post-hoc rationalization. In a separate section I will go on to show how using the *four territories of experience – visioning, strategizing, performing and assessing*[1] – theorized by Torbert and others (Fisher et al., 2000; Torbert, 2004) helped me to understand some of the tensions that arose between the different stakeholders in the scheme. I will also summarize how this new understanding enabled my practice to develop. Finally, I will seek to identify some of the capacities and qualities that managing the project demanded and draw some tentative

conclusions about how best to approach such a role.

ACTION INQUIRY GROUPS AND THE PSLS

The PSLS was commissioned by the Cabinet Office, in response to governmental concerns about the quality of public service leadership. The contract to design and deliver the programme was awarded on the basis of a competitive tender to a consortium of organizations including the National School of Government, the Institute of Local Government at the University of Birmingham, and Clutterbuck Associates – a niche consultancy specializing in coaching and mentoring. I was closely involved with the scheme from its inception (as an associate of the National School of Government), having been invited to propose a design for the learning groups on the strength of an earlier small-scale collaborative inquiry into 'Developing ourselves as leaders' in the police service that I had undertaken whilst serving as a Chief Superintendent in the Hertfordshire Constabulary (Mead, 2002).

The scheme was intended – according to the PSLS website (www.publicserviceleadersscheme.gov.uk) – to develop a new generation of public service leaders with the appropriate skills, abilities, knowledge and experience to work effectively in positions of leadership within – and across – the public sector. Participants were drawn mainly from central government (civil service), local government and the National Health Service with a small minority of police and voluntary sector representatives. They ranged in age from late twenties to late forties, with most in their thirties. Many had already been through some kind of fast-track scheme and were selected on the basis of perceived potential to progress to senior public service leadership roles. Each cohort had a fairly even balance of men and women overall, though with disproportionately (and disappointingly) few members from visible ethnic minorities.

The programme, which I have described more fully elsewhere (Mead, 2006), comprised several related elements. Participants attended a two-day *foundation event* to introduce them to the programme and make an initial identification of learning and development needs through small group exercises and the results of a 360° feedback tool (Transformational Leadership Questionnaire™). On the basis of this information and in dialogue with their organizational sponsor, they prepared a written *personal learning contract* against which to gauge and evidence their development over their time on the scheme. Participants were expected to attend at least 80 per cent of the nine two- or three-day residential *network learning events* with inputs on leadership and public service delivery and large group inquiry processes such as world café (Brown, 2002) and open space technology (Owen, 1992). All participants had the opportunity to select a *mentor* from a pool of trained volunteers, mostly senior public service leaders and all had access to the *virtual learning centre*, an on-line repository of information, articles and notices of events. As part of the programme, participants were expected to arrange a period of *interchange* in another organization, probably in a sector different from their own. Finally, all participants were expected to work as members of facilitated *action inquiry groups*.[2]

Each action inquiry group (AIG) had 11 or 12 members and a professional external facilitator drawn from the staff and associates of the supplier consortium. Over time, as some participants left the scheme, most groups developed a stable core of 8 to 10 attendees. The composition of the groups was determined on the basis of a few simple criteria. First, we clustered participants regionally to minimize travel and for ease of contact between meetings. Second, we looked for the optimum mix of sector and professional background. Third, without applying quotas, we attempted to achieve a reasonable gender[3] balance. As a safeguard, participants were invited to swap groups at the beginning of the

process if they felt that, for any reason, the proposed membership was unsuitable. Each AIG met six times per year for a full day. Group members hosted meetings at their place of work, on dates mutually agreed between the members and facilitator.

As the member of the consortium responsible for designing this element of the programme, I wanted to create a process that would integrate with the other elements of the PSLS and, whilst giving some structure, have enough flexibility to address a wide range of needs among a large population of participants, and I coined the term *action inquiry group*. In the course of the two-day preparation seminar for AIG facilitators and later at the opening session of the PSLS when introducing participants to the idea of action inquiry groups, I described their distinctive features as cycles of action and reflection, ongoing inquiry questions, a focus on improving practice, the possibility of collaborative inquiries emerging, an egalitarian and participative ethos, a form that values many different ways of knowing. I also explained that AIGs were intended to provide continuity and a sense of community, a safe and challenging space, both personal and professional development, individual and collective learning, and a source of long-term cross-sector relationships as well as integration with other elements of PSLS.

During the five-year lifetime of the PSLS, over 250 rising public service leaders participated in a total of 21 action inquiry groups, each lasting up to three years. Anticipating the need to support the group facilitators, the design incorporated a process for monitoring, supervising and co-ordinating their work. Prior to taking up their roles, all facilitators attended a two-day workshop to be briefed on the scheme and prepare for the opening sessions of their groups. Facilitators submitted a confidential monitoring form after each group meeting, describing what the group (not individuals) had done and were planning to do plus any issues, themes or problems that had arisen. My role was to supervise their practice and oversee this element of the scheme on behalf of the consortium through telephone and email contact and occasional face-to-face meetings of all facilitators, a process we called the *meta-set*. My intention in creating the meta-set was to bring the AIG facilitators together as a community of inquiry as well as a community of practice (Lave and Wenger, 1991; Wenger, 1998). It seemed to me that we could only learn how to manage and facilitate the AIGs well by attending to our own learning and development as a parallel process to working with the participants.

ISSUES, CHALLENGES AND RESPONSES

Despite our good intentions, the route we actually followed in managing the action inquiry group element of the PSLS was much rockier and more complex than we had imagined. It was in seeking to respond to these twists and turns that some of the qualities and capacities required to manage such a large-scale project gradually became apparent.

As you will see below, the various stakeholders in PSLS held quite different perspectives on what they thought the action inquiry groups should focus on and what they wanted from them. These different perspectives took some time to tease apart and articulate clearly although, from very early on, tensions between them were apparent and they caused a lot of 'noise' in the system (e.g. confusion about action inquiry, facilitators resigning from their roles, demands for progress reports, and an external evaluation of the scheme). Whilst I did my best to engage with these tensions I tended, in the early stages at least, to think of them as unfortunate obstacles to be overcome, as a distraction from the main business of supervising the professional practice of a group of AIG facilitators.

Gradually I realized that addressing these tensions, far from being a distraction, was a crucial dimension of managing the process effectively. Furthermore, I came to understand that these tensions were not a problem to be designed out or solved through the exercise of hierarchical authority and accountability. Rather, they were a systemic property, an ongoing phenomenon to be actively managed by building a network of relationships between the various stakeholders.

Early Days: Unexpected Confusion

Participants, facilitators, colleagues from the consortium, and members of the Cabinet Office PSLS secretariat gathered together for the opening day of the scheme in July 2001. As part of the opening proceedings I gave a half-hour presentation on the structure and purpose of the action inquiry groups. Participants had already been given a copy of 'A layperson's guide to co-operative inquiry' (Reason and Heron, 1999) and they seemed interested and attentive as I spoke. I offered an overarching inquiry question for them to consider – 'How can I/we improve my/our practice as public service leader(s)?' – and sent them off for their first meeting with their facilitators. I waited excitedly as the groups commenced their work, available for support if needed but expecting a smooth passage.

Within 40 minutes one of the facilitators came into the room looking flushed. 'They don't get it,' he said. 'They don't understand what this action inquiry stuff is all about and I cannot tell them. Can you help please?' I returned with him to the group, my heart sinking. 'What is there not to understand? I've explained it quite clearly and they have had the reading,' I thought. As I entered the room, the participants' frustration was evident: 'This all seems very woolly. What exactly are you asking us to do?' queried a spokesman. There followed an hour of fairly unsatisfactory and heated discussion ending with my encouragement to them to 'find their own way'.

Although this was the only group I was called in to speak with that day, it became clear when the meta-set debriefed immediately after the groups had finished that there was a lot of confusion amongst participants (and some facilitators) about what was expected. I wondered how I might have better prepared both participants and facilitators to move into what, it had transpired, was new and unfamiliar territory. Could the framing have been stronger? Could the contracting with participants have been clearer? Perhaps, but given that participants were required to take part in the AIGs, I had taken the view that being overly prescriptive about process and content would have been oppressive. I decided to hold firm to this line – for the time being at least – and found that reassuring comments like: 'it will be all right', 'it is important that they find their own way', 'there is often some confusion early on', 'it's all part of the process', tripped off my tongue with more apparent confidence than I actually felt at the time.

Six Months: the Wheels are Wobbling

The initial sense of turbulence amongst the group of facilitators seemed to amplify rather than diminish in the early months of the scheme. For the first cohort, ten facilitators (eight plus two reserves) had been selected from staff and associates of the organizations forming the supplier consortium. All were experienced and well-regarded facilitators in their own fields though few had any first-hand experience of action research or action inquiry and the relative looseness of the design proved to be very demanding for those used solely to facilitating learning through structured exercises in a training environment. Within a few weeks, three notified me that they were unable to continue for various reasons, and later a fourth left at my request after their group had expressed concerns about an over-directive style of facilitation.

These problems with facilitators brought me face to face with the politics of managing a large-scale action research project in a commercial environment as there was a strong financial incentive to use only staff and associates of the supplier consortium as facilitators (since this attracted revenue). However, this seriously limited the size of the pool from which they were chosen. In

order to develop sufficient competence in action research/inquiry amongst the remaining facilitators, I had to persuade my colleagues from the consortium that we should bring in some facilitators with specific expertise in facilitating action research/inquiry even if that meant reducing our revenues by going outside our own organizations to find them. They agreed that the downside risk of not doing so was too great and, over the next few months, we recruited an able group of facilitators drawn from within and outside the consortium, including some colleagues from the Centre for Action Research in Professional Practice, University of Bath.

All these issues were discussed in the meta-set, which quickly took on added significance as a forum for the management of the action inquiry groups as well as the supervision of facilitation practice. Although I had originally envisaged acting solely as an 'expert' adviser and supervisor, I found that I needed to become much more involved in the management of the PSLS as a whole in order to position the work of the AIGs and to support the work of the facilitators. After some months, my colleagues in the consortium invited me to act as 'director of action inquiry', taking formal responsibility not just for the development of AIG facilitation but also for the overall effectiveness of this element of the scheme and its integration with the rest of the programme. In hindsight, the need to take on a wider management role from the outset seems obvious. However, it came as an unforeseen and (given other professional demands on my time) a not entirely welcome development.

With eight AIGs running at the same time (growing to a maximum of 21 groups over the next three years with additional annual intakes into the PSLS), a crucial issue for me was to affirm the inevitable diversity of practice within the AIGs whilst seeking to provide overall coherence by holding firmly to an ethos or stance of action inquiry. As the meta-set matured, facilitators spent increasing amounts of time sharing, critiquing and comparing their practice. At the same time, the facilitators were also de facto the main point of contact with the scheme for participants and needed information and guidance about many other aspects of the programme (e.g. *mentoring, interchange, personal learning contracts, graduation criteria*) to allay the anxieties and concerns of their groups. Colleagues in the consortium and members of the Cabinet Office secretariat were invited in for parts of the meta-set meetings to cover some of these aspects. By opening up in this way, we began to develop useful personal relationships with stakeholders across the wider PSLS system.

Twelve Months: Crisis of Confidence

Managing the project in the first year involved holding a lot of uncertainty and anxiety among participants, facilitators, colleagues in the consortium and the client group, all of whom were unsettled by the initial lack of clarity experienced in the groups and their apparent reluctance to engage in formally constituted co-operative inquiries. After about 12 months, the Cabinet Office secretariat (our clients for this contract) began to express their concerns directly and asked the consortium for a formal report on the progress of the AIGs which were, by virtue of the confidentiality of their proceedings, a 'black box', as one member of the secretariat put it.

Faced with this demand, I turned to the group of facilitators in the meta-set and asked them what evidence we could provide of common inquiry themes emerging in their groups. Their responses revealed that, on the whole, participants were much more interested in exploring the difficulties they were experiencing in reconciling the conflicting demands of home and work life than inquiring into wider organizational and systemic issues. Participants on the whole, they said, had come to value membership of AIGs but for reasons different from those we had originally envisaged. I was persuaded by the facilitators that the groups were settling in to worthwhile ways of working, opening up

'communicative spaces' (Kemmis, 2001/2006) that they found useful and supportive. We decided that we should apply ourselves to bringing some rigour, depth and challenge to the work that they wanted to do rather than 'beating them up' for not doing formal co-operative inquiries.

This was a pivotal point in the development of the action inquiry groups and of our relationships within the meta-set. The facilitators and I agreed that we needed to find a way to hold open the space for the work the groups were actually doing until it matured to the point where convincing evidence for its value would emerge. We needed to gather stories or at least snippets of stories that could be shared to satisfy the Cabinet Office secretariat that the groups were making satisfactory progress. We combed our collective experience of the past 12 months and found examples of focused discussions in the groups around such topics as 'ways of improving motivation', 'the policy/service interface', 'being transformational in a transactional world', and 'the implications of immigration for service delivery' that we labelled as inquiries.

Rather than offer a written report that could be dissected and picked over out of context, I arranged an hour-long meeting with the secretariat and, accompanied by consortium colleagues, gave a half-hour oral presentation supported by visual aids. We acknowledged the early confusion, commented frankly on perceived difficulties in particular groups, invited their suggestions for future improvements and sought to demonstrate that we had actively and constructively managed this element of the scheme. It became clear that the secretariat felt under some pressure from the high-level sectoral sponsors of the scheme to demonstrate that, after 12 months, it had begun to deliver substantive benefits. In short, they needed the stories even more than we did and found the examples we provided very helpful in building the credibility of the scheme with sponsors. For our part, we were learning that rather than adopting a defensive posture, keeping the secretariat at arm's length from the AIGs, it served us better to help them meet the perceived needs of their clients – the high-level sectoral sponsors of the scheme. We (and the shift from I to we is significant here) were beginning to take a much wider and more systemic view of what was involved in managing the whole scheme.

Two Years: Loss of Energy

Towards the end of the second year, most groups had settled into a regular pattern of meetings with favoured ways of working and a stable core of attendees. Facilitators were able to pass on many examples of valuable personal work and wider learning about leadership practice. However, they also reported a general slump in energy and enthusiasm in the groups. In the meta-set we surmised that this might in part be due to the fact that some of each group had decided to leave the scheme after two years (either because they were eligible for early graduation or because their organizations were not in a position to pay the unsubsidized third year fee). Facilitators exchanged ideas, drawn from their own successful practice, for activities and processes that they might use to enliven the groups. Thinking more systemically, we felt that more communication between the groups might create more energy and we decided to expose the groups to the wide variety of approaches and experiences that had occurred across the whole cohort.

First, we arranged a special event at a meeting of the whole cohort. Each group was given time with its facilitator to consider what they wanted to share about their experience (process, content, and learning) with other groups and what they would like to find out about the experience of other groups. They prepared questions to ask other groups and some visual display material, ranging from flip charts, to collages, photographs and artefacts to exemplify and represent their own experience. Groups then assembled with their display materials in one large room and enjoyed several rounds of exchanges with

other groups. Following this they met again with their own facilitators to consider what they had learned and what possibilities they could see for extending and enriching their future meetings. The group exchanges were characterized by high levels of interest and intense conversations interspersed with laughter and expressions of recognition – 'yes, we did that too' – and of discovery – 'we never thought of that, how did it work?' Subsequently, facilitators reported renewed levels of energy and engagement in their groups.

Second, we asked participants to reflect appreciatively on their experience in their inquiry groups. They were introduced to the concept of appreciative inquiry (Hammond, 1998; Cooperrider Jr et al., 2000; Ludema and Fry, Chapter 19 in this volume) and then asked to interview each other in pairs to elicit specific examples of learning in their AIG that were significant to them in some way and of times when they felt members of their AIG worked really well together. Following this, they were invited to write any observations about their experience of action inquiry groups that came to mind. The text generated by this process painted a very rich (though not definitive or objective) picture of how the groups worked and what participants saw as the benefits they had obtained from the experience. I would like to offer just one quotation from the exercise that encapsulates something of the spirit of what was said by many participants about their experience:

> My action inquiry group is important to me in many ways ... The key thing is that it is a safe environment where you don't have to play a role: i.e. wife, boss, senior manager, friend, or colleague. You are literally 'laid bare'. There is no need for being brave, or trying to look clever. You can exhibit all your frailties. An important part of the learning has been that we are all frail, but even more interesting is that actually our problems and issues seem to be common: the difficult boss, being consumed with work, [or] really properly scared of being 'found out'. It's silly because we still all hold on to some belief that we are the only ones to have these problems [and that] everyone else is more capable than [we are].

Table 44.1 *Perceived usefulness of AIGs*

	Cohort one	Cohort two	Cohort three	All cohorts
Action inquiry groups	4.6	4.9	3.6	4.4
Whole PSLS programme	3.4	4.4	3.6	3.9

The fruits of this appreciative reflection were fed back into the whole PSLS system: participants, facilitators, consortium and secretariat (and onwards to some sectoral sponsors). We found that sharing these verbatim, anonymized accounts of participants' experiences in their AIGs helped all the different stakeholders to understand and talk about the benefits of the scheme. For the first time we developed a common language, grounded in shared narratives, to describe the process of the AIGs. This was to prove invaluable a year later when the secretariat commissioned an external evaluation of the PSLS.

Three Years: Pulling the Strands Together

Two particular actions in the third year of the scheme illustrate the continuing move towards more relational management. The first of these was the way that we worked with the external evaluators to help them dig down deeply into participants' actual experience of the scheme to find the kinds of benefit they were reporting to us but which might escape a more conventional evaluation.

As an opening move, we gave the evaluators a copy of the text generated by the appreciative reflection conducted at the end of the second year. We also arranged, with participants' consent, for them to attend an AIG meeting and to interview participants about their AIG experience. Having discussed the wider issues involved in promoting and sustaining the scheme in the meta-set, facilitators also co-operated readily with the external evaluation, arranging interviews and inviting them into meetings of their AIGs.

The evaluation report (Foster and Turner, 2003), based on a combination of interviews,

and focus group sessions with participants, their line managers and organizational sponsors plus a questionnaire for qualitative and quantitative responses concluded:

> The scheme is having a positive impact on participants' development, in particular:
>
> - increasing self-awareness
> - increasing confidence
> - broadening perspectives in decision-making
> - encouraging a consultative approach; and
> - developing partnership working

The numerical data in the report show a high level of participant satisfaction with the AIGs. On a scale of 1 (not at all useful) to 6 (very useful), cohort one rated action inquiry groups at 4.6, cohort two at 4.9 and cohort three at 3.6. At this time (July– October 2003) cohort one was in its third year, cohort two in its second year, and cohort three barely three months into the scheme. The full results are shown in Table 44.1.

I include these paragraphs about the evaluation less to show how well the scheme was regarded (though I think that is relevant and of interest) than to highlight the kind of evaluative processes that are likely to be used by clients of large-scale commercially-based schemes such as PSLS. There is a need to bridge the divide between an action research/inquiry based approach and conventional evaluation methods which may undervalue or not even recognize the embodied and tacit forms of learning claimed by participants. In our case, pre-empting the formal evaluation with the verbatim accounts of the benefits participants had previously identified in their appreciative reflection on the AIGs provided a substantial body of evidence that would have been difficult to ignore. I suggest that it also set the tone for the external evaluators' contact with participants and predisposed them to evaluate the scheme from a broader and more inclusive standpoint than they might otherwise have done.

The second action illustrating the move towards more relational management of the scheme was the way in which we brought stakeholders together at a plenary event to hear participants' unmediated feedback. Working in small groups based on their AIGs, participants reported their experience of the PSLS directly to senior members of the Cabinet Office and other high-level sectoral sponsors. They presented, often in quite moving tones, stories and examples of how they believed they and their organizations had benefited from the PSLS. Frequently, they cited the AIG as the highlight of the scheme and some declared their intention (subsequently fulfilled) for their groups to continue to meet after the formal end of the programme. One participant, when gently challenged by a visiting sponsor to describe what outcomes the course had produced, declared passionately: '*We* are the products of the Public Service Leaders Scheme'.

Moments such as that one, and another occasion when a visiting sponsor was so impressed by his contact with the members of one AIG that he acted as their spokesperson and proudly presented their feedback to the whole group, including the other sponsors, illustrate the potential benefits of facilitating connections between the different stakeholders in the system.

In the next section I will show how my understanding of the dynamics involved in the PSLS benefited from applying a particular theoretical perspective and then summarize how this understanding was gradually reflected in my approach towards managing the AIG process.

TOWARDS A SYSTEMIC UNDERSTANDING

The crisis of confidence in the AIG process that resulted in the demand for a formal progress report to the Cabinet Office secretariat after about 12 months starkly revealed the existence of tensions between the different stakeholders: the secretariat wanted evidence of 'tangible results' from the groups, participants were more interested in focusing on their own life situations, facilitators wanted the freedom to follow their own preferred ways of working with groups, and I found myself somewhere in the middle of all this putting pressure on the facilitators to bring some coherence to the work of the groups whilst simultaneously trying to convince the secretariat that everything was all right. I could see the issues quite clearly but felt stymied by not understanding how we had come to occupy such different positions. I wanted to find a theoretical model or framework that would help me understand and thus offer up possibilities for acting differently and more effectively. Kurt Lewin, sometimes referred to as the grandparent of action research, is reputed to have said 'there is nothing so practical as a good theory', and I was short of a good theory.

In conversation with colleagues at CARPP, it occurred to me to look at the different perspectives of the stakeholders through the 'four territories of experience' proposed by Torbert and others (Fisher et al., 2000; Torbert, 2004) as critical for effective action in the world: *visioning, strategizing, performing and assessing*. By their definition, *visioning* is concerned with long-term intentions, purposes, and aims: *strategizing* with planning and implementing overall delivery: *performing* with acting in pursuit of role-defined responsibilities: *assessing* with observed behavioural consequences and the effects of action. Applying these perspectives to the action inquiry group element of the PSLS, it seemed obvious that they were 'owned' by different stakeholders and that this might explain the roots of some of the tensions and difficulties we were experiencing.

In Table 44.2, I have sought to follow the logic of this through, assigning each of the four territories of experience to one of the stakeholder groups. These are defined as:

Table 44.2 Different perspectives on action inquiry groups (adapted from Mead, 2006)

Stakeholders	PSLS Secretariat Cabinet Office	Director of Action Inquiry Groups	Action Inquiry Group Facilitators	Individual PSLS Participants
	Visioning	*Strategizing*	*Performing*	*Assessing*
Perspective	Long-term impact of PSLS as a whole on public service leadership	Medium- to long-term impact and sustainability of action inquiry group process	Medium- to short-term exercise of facilitator role to sustain life of the group	Short- to medium-term impact of learning in the group on my work and life
Question	How do we know action inquiry groups are 'working well' and represent good value for money for sectoral sponsors?	How can we satisfy the client that we are doing good work whilst keeping the space open for very different needs of each group?	How can we meet the specific needs of our groups which may not look much like the original plan whilst 'playing the game'?	How can this group meet my needs well enough to justify the time I have to take out of my busy life to be here?
	Control	*Co-ordinate*	*Facilitate*	*Relate*
Pull towards	Tangible products that can be shown to others to prove value of PSLS	Coherent stories of what groups are doing in relation to aims of PSLS	Activities that promote reflection and improve practice of participants	Friendships that help me cope with demands and pressures of life and work
Tensions	Holding the space between the sectoral sponsors and the deliverers	Holding the space between the secretariat and action inquiry group facilitators	Holding the space between director of action inquiry and participants	Holding the space between 'system world' and 'life world'

PSLS participants (participants), AIG facilitators (facilitators), director of AIGs (director), and Cabinet Office PSLS secretariat (secretariat). This nomenclature does not include the wider sectoral sponsors of the scheme but for the sake of simplicity I have assumed their influence was primarily exercised on and through the secretariat.

We might say that the secretariat was the primary custodian or owner of *visioning* with a long-term perspective on the impact of the PSLS as a whole on the quality of public service leadership (and, not shown in Table 44.2, probably a short-term concern for their own credibility in the eyes of sectoral sponsors and other senior governmental figures). The iconic question they held towards the AIGs might be expressed as: 'How do we know action inquiry groups are "working well" – and represent good value for money for sectoral sponsors?' They were pulled by these concerns towards controlling the

process in order to produce tangible outcomes that could be shown to others to prove the value of the PSLS (and, perhaps, their own effectiveness in overseeing the scheme). We can surmise that the primary tension they experienced was that of holding the space between the demands of sectoral sponsors and the ability of the consortium to deliver results in accordance with the contract.

As director I certainly felt that, together with colleagues in the consortium, I owned *strategizing*. Although I was concerned about the success of PSLS as a whole, my primary perspective (and what I was accountable to the client and colleagues for) was the medium- to long-term impact and sustainability of the AIG process. The question I often asked myself was: 'How can we satisfy the client that we are doing good work whilst keeping the space open for the very different needs of each group?' I was pulled to co-ordinate the work of the facilitators and wanted coherent stories of what the groups were doing in relation to the avowed aims of the PSLS. This particularly manifested itself in the conflicting expectations of the client and participants about undertaking inquiries with an organizational focus versus creating safe *communicative spaces* (Kemmis 2001/ 2006) for dialogues of a more personal nature to happen. In the early stages, at least, my role was characterized by holding the space between the secretariat and the action inquiry group facilitators.

The facilitators were the primary custodians of the *performing* perspective for the AIGs, with a medium- to short-term focus on the exercise of their role in promoting and sustaining the life of the group and the quality of inquiry undertaken. In our meta-set meetings it seemed that their iconic question might be phrased as: 'How can we meet the specific needs of our groups (which may not look much like what was originally envisaged) whilst 'playing the game' sufficiently for an appearance of cohesion?' They were clearly pulled towards facilitating activities in their groups that promoted reflection and helped to improve participants' leadership practice. It is also clear from our discussions that they experienced the tension of holding the space between the demands of the director of action inquiry (me) and of the perceived needs of participants. I think the extent of this tension is evident in a remark made recently to me – with the benefit of hindsight – by one of the facilitators:

> In all those meta-set meetings I never felt you were fully present. I really only trusted you because I knew you well in other contexts. You often seemed to be holding issues for other people and I don't think you always told us what was going on. ... I also want to acknowledge the difficulties of your position and to thank you for doing a 'good enough' job.

The participants were the primary owners of the *assessing* perspective, concerned for the most part with the short- to medium-term impact of learning in the group on their work and lives. We could imagine their

characteristic question to be something like: 'How can this group meet my needs well enough to justify the time I have to take out of my busy life to be here?' Despite our encouragement for them to engage in collaborative inquiries into issues and questions with obvious organizational relevance, they were pulled strongly towards forming relationships, friendships that might help them personally cope with the often conflicting demands and pressures of life and work.

The distinction made by Jürgen Habermas (Habermas, 1987; Kemmis, 2001/2006) between the dynamics of the *system world* and the *life world* and the colonization of the latter by the former in modern industrialized and post-industrialized societies provides a powerful explanation for the 'pull to the personal' in the action inquiry groups as participants sought to reconcile the demands and constraints of their roles as public service leaders with their more holistic sense of self outside the work environment. This might be expressed as a tension in holding the space between the system world and the life world.

Torbert and others (Fisher et al., 2000; Torbert, 2004) argue that we achieve the greatest possibility for appropriate, timely and effective action when the four territories of experience (four perspectives or categories of action) are aligned either internally within one person or through close interrelationships and mutual feedback within a system. Applying this new understanding to my role as director of AIGs encouraged me to shift my practice to a more relational and systemic perspective. Originally I had tried to manage the process by a carefully controlled flow of information up and down a chain, from participants to facilitators, to me (in the form of monitoring reports) to the Cabinet Office secretariat (via formal progress reports) and back down again. Now, with greater understanding of the system dynamics and with more confidence in the value of the work done in the AIGs, I consciously sought to build multiple connections between all the stakeholders in the system. This shift is represented in Figure 44.1.

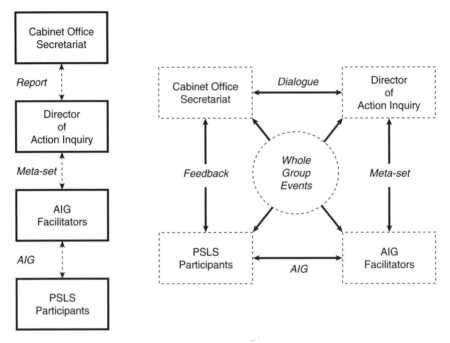

Figure 44.1 *From a flow of information to a network of relationships*

The model on the left-hand side shows the limited and linear connections with which we began between the four stakeholder groups. The perimeters of the boxes are shown in bold and the arrows indicating the connective processes as dotted lines to indicate both an attitude of mind and the relative emphasis placed on each. The model on the right-hand side shows the development of a more complex network of relationships in which all the stakeholders have direct contact with each other. The perimeters of the boxes are shown as dotted lines and the arrows indicating the connective processes in bold; again, to indicate both an attitude of mind and the relative emphasis placed on each. The right-hand model also shows new opportunities for direct communication between participants, facilitators and the secretariat through feedback and by bringing all parts of the system (including, but not shown on the diagram, sectoral sponsors) together at whole group events such as network learning events to interact informally at social occasions and more formally through presentations and discussions.

It took a couple of years to make this shift for the first cohort but, once made, it continued for subsequent cohorts. We can speculate why it took so long: perhaps we (consortium colleagues and I) needed time for the benefits claimed by participants to come through before feeling sufficiently confident in the action inquiry group process to 'let the stakeholders loose on each other'. Certainly we can agree with Gustavsen et al. (Chapter 4) in recognizing that 'relationships with dynamic problem-solving capability do not emerge by themselves' and that considerable effort is required by all those involved.

This reinforces the point that the move towards more relational management of the project did not come about through my agency alone. Alongside the role-based tensions of the different stakeholders there was also their natural impetus to communicate, to connect and to form mutually satisfying relationships, which also took time. Perhaps the most important thing I did was to recognize this countervailing human tendency and help it find expression in the scheme.

The good news is that it got easier as the network of relationships built up and as each successive cohort of participants was 'held' by its predecessors. My role felt less burdensome as time went on and I felt able to exercise it with a lighter touch.

CAPACITIES AND QUALITIES

So, what can be said of the capacities and qualities demanded of someone managing a large-scale action research project such as the action inquiry group element of the PSLS. I would like to close by highlighting ten that seem to flow from the experiences I have shared with you in this chapter – though I do not claim always to have demonstrated them myself.

1. Ability to articulate the benefits, ethos and principles of an action research/inquiry approach in straightforward language that makes sense to participants and other stakeholders.
2. Non-attachment to particular methods and ways of working. It is more important to respond to the real and emergent needs of participants than it is to implement a pre-determined design, no matter how good.
3. Capacity to bear anxiety and hold uncertainty on behalf of the system, expressing confidence (not complacency) before the benefits of the project become apparent.
4. Political *nous* to read the concerns, wants and needs of multiple stakeholders, recognizing the legitimacy of different perspectives and being willing to address them without being precious.
5. Willingness to step into a leadership role, especially if there is a vacuum, and stand up for the project in the face of doubts and criticism. Acting decisively when needed (e.g. responding to concerns about the quality or appropriateness of facilitation).
6. Determination to insist on what is needed to make the project work, including the recruitment, development and supervision of those actually delivering the action research/inquiry project.
7. Systemic perspective that brings different stakeholders together and builds networks of relationships to support and sustain the project.

This also requires a willingness to stand back out of the limelight.
8. High level of personal energy to take a proactive stance, to manage the project actively for success rather than managing by exception when problems arise or, even worse, laissez-faire.
9. Patience and persistence are needed to stay with a long-term project – commitment to the project in hand is an essential requirement, especially when new and exciting alternatives offer themselves.
10. Optimism in the face of delays and disappointments needs to be balanced with a willingness to face the facts and make a realistic assessment of how the project is going at all times.

Finally, let me return to where I started out. I borrowed Charles Lindblom's phrase 'muddling through' for the title of this chapter as, to my mind, it accurately reflects the experience of decision-making in a complex environment in the midst of action: surrounded (sometimes overwhelmed) by inchoate and partial data, assailed by strong emotions, faced with unclear personal motivations, political machinations and plurality of choice. It is therefore crucial that practitioners charged with managing large-scale action research projects hold open and inquiring attitudes to their roles and to the schemes they manage. Good planning is essential but no substitute for an active and curious engagement with the phenomenology of the process as it unfolds.

NOTES

1 Torbert uses various alternative forms of language to describe these territories (e.g. purpose, thinking/feeling, behaviour, outside world) but I find the formulation quoted in the text the most helpful in this case.

2 The term 'action inquiry' was first used by Torbert (1991) as a development of 'action science' as practised by Chris Argyris and colleagues (Argyris et al., 1985).

3 As previously mentioned, the scheme attracted disappointingly few members of visible ethnic minorities and, though this was a significant issue for sponsors of the scheme, it was not a factor that we took into account when composing the AIGs.

REFERENCES

Argyris, C., Putnam, R., et al. (1985) *Action Science: Concepts, Methods and Skills for Research and Intervention.* New York: Academic Press.

Brown, J. (2002) *The World Café: a Resource Guide for Hosting Conversations that Matter.* Mill Valley, CA: Whole System Associates.

Cooperrider, D., Sorensen Jr, P., et al. (eds) (2000) *Appreciative Inquiry: Rethinking Human Organization Toward a Positive Theory Of Change.* Champaign, IL: Stipes Publishing.

Fisher, D., Rooke, D., et al. (2000) *Personal and Organisational Transformations through Action Inquiry.* Boston: Edge/Work Press.

Foster, E. and Turner, J. (2003) 'Evaluation of the Public Service Leaders Scheme', *Cabinet Office,* 35.

Gustavsen, B. (2003) 'Action research and the problem of the single case', *Concepts and Transformations,* 8 (1): 93–9.

Habermas, J. (1987) 'Lifeworld and system: a critique of functionlist reason', *The Theory of Communicative Action,* 2: 381–3.

Hammond, S.A. (1998) *The Thin Book of Appreciative Inquiry.* Plano, TX: Thin Book Publishing Co.

Heron, J. (1996) *Co-operative Inquiry.* London: Sage.

Heron, J. and Reason, P. (2001/2006) 'The practice of co-operative inquiry: research "with" rather than "on" people', in P. Reason and H. Bradbury (eds), *Handbook of Action Research: Participative Inquiry and Practice.* London: Sage. Also published in P. Reason and H. Bradbury (eds) (2006), *Handbook of Action Research: Concise Paperback Edition.* London: Sage. pp. 144–54.

Kemmis, S. (2001/2006) 'Exploring the relevance of critical theory for action research: emancipatory action research in the footsteps of Jürgen Habermas', in P. Reason and H. Bradbury (eds), *Handbook of Action Research: Participative Inquiry and Practice.* London: Sage. Also published in P. Reason and H. Bradbury (eds) (2006), *Handbook of Action*
Research: Concise Paperback Edition. London: Sage. pp. 94–105.

Lave, J. and Wenger, E. (1991) *Situated Learning: Legitimate Peripheral Participation.* Cambridge: Cambridge University Press.

Lindblom, C.E. (1959) 'The science of "muddling through"', *Public Administration,* 19: 79–88.

McKardle, K.L. (2002) 'Establishing a co-operative inquiry group: the perspective of a "first-time" inquirer.' *Systemic Practice and Action Research,* 15 (3): 177–89.

Mead, G. (2002) 'Developing ourselves as police leaders: how can we inquire collaboratively in a hierarchical organisation?', *Systemic Practice and Action Research,* 15 (3): 191–206.

Mead, G. (2006) 'Developing public service leaders through action inquiry', in C. Rigg and S. Richards (eds), *Action Learning, Leadership and Organizational Development in Public Services.* London: Routledge.

Owen, H. (1992) *Open Space Technology.* Potomac, MD: Abbott Publishing.

Reason, P. and Heron, J. (1999) 'A layperson's guide to co-operative inquiry.' [http://www.bath.ac.uk/carpp/layguide.htm]

Torbert, W.R. (1991) *The Power of Balance.* Newbury Park, CA: Sage.

Torbert, B. (2004) *Action Inquiry: the Secret of Timely and Transforming Leadership.* San Francisco, CA: Berrett Koehler.

Wadsworth, Y. (2001/2006) 'The mirror, the magnifying glass, the compass and the map: facilitating participatory action research', in P. Reason and H. Bradbury (eds), *Handbook of Action Research: Participative Inquiry and Practice.* London: Sage. Also published in P. Reason and H. Bradbury (eds) (2006), *Handbook of Action Research: Concise Paperback Edition.* London: Sage. pp. 322–34.

Wenger, E. (1998) *Communities of Practice: Learning, Meaning and Identity.* Cambridge: Cambridge University Press.

45

Insider Action Research: The Dynamics of Developing New Capabilities

David Coghlan and A.B. (Rami) Shani

Capabilities are the know-how that enables an organization to achieve its intended out-comes. This chapter outlines insider action researchers' tasks and issues in developing learning capabilities for first-, second- and third-person practice in relation to preunderstanding, role duality and organizational politics. It shows how the outcome with regard to the tasks and skills relating to preunderstanding is the capability to inquire into what is close and familiar; with regard to role duality it is the effective utilization and understanding of the insider action research role as a learning mechanism, and with respect to organizational politics it is building learning mechanisms that are effective politically.

Capabilities are the know-how that enables an organization to achieve its intended outcomes (Dosi et al., 2000). In an ever changing world, developing new capabilities is widely viewed as a strategic necessity for organizations across all sectors (Mohrman et al., 2006). Despite their importance, relatively little is known about how organizations actually develop new capabilities. Insider action research is viewed as one way to develop new capabilities.

When full members of an organization seek to inquire into the working of their organizational system in order to change something in it, they can be understood as undertaking insider action research (Coghlan, forthcoming; Coghlan and Brannick, 2005). Complete membership is contrasted with those who enter a system temporarily for the sake of conducting research and may be viewed in terms of wanting to remain a member within a desired career path when the research is completed. Insider action research offers a unique perspective on systems, precisely because it is from the inside. The insights generated by insider action researchers in action research projects allow the organization to continuously examine existing capabilities and develop new capabilities (Shani, et al., 2004). We are all insiders of many systems – our own families, communities, organizations and associations. As members we play active roles in the development of these systems, e.g. in child-rearing, in enabling our organization to function and fulfil its goals. We typically bring our knowledge, developed in-action from these situations, and extrapolate it to others, while at the same time adapting to the characteristics of each local situation. The process of generating new knowledge is a capability that triggers the ongoing development of new capabilities.

The organization development literature points out that the development of new capabilities entails a slow, difficult, and costly process with uncertain outcomes (Cummings, 2008). Furthermore, the development of new capabilities and the evolution of existing capabilities surface ongoing challenges. Existing capabilities are deeply embedded in organizations' routines, culture and frameworks. They reflect a dominant logic or design and evolve through a series of incremental changes that build on and reinforce that logic (Coghlan and Rashford, 2006; Mohrman et al., 2006). Thus, an effort to develop new capabilities requires a deep level insight, inquiry and understanding of the organization, its dynamics, culture and evolution. The insider action research can serve as a catalyst for the development of new capabilities, yet the challenges for triggering and facilitating such an effort are many.

In this chapter we examine the skills and challenges of insider action research in terms of the three voices and practices of inquiry (see Torbert and Taylor, Chapter 16 in this volume) and the particular challenges of insider action research (Coghlan and Brannick, 2005; Roth et al., 2007). The tasks and skills we discuss are summarized in Table 45.1, which draws together insider action

researchers' tasks and issues in developing learning capabilities for first-, second- and third-person voice and practice in relation to preunderstanding, role duality and organizational politics. The desired outcome in working with preunderstanding is the capability to inquire into what is close and familiar. The outcome for working with role duality is the effective utilization and understanding of the insider action research role as a learning mechanism, and the outcome for working with organizational politics is building learning mechanisms that are effective politically.

FIRST-, SECOND- AND THIRD-PERSON INQUIRY

There are several modes by which we can participate and inquire into our experience (see Introduction and Torbert and Taylor, Chapter 16). Through *first-person voice/ practice* we can reflect on our own values and assumptions and how we behave and so develop self-reflective skills. As Buchanan and Boddy (1992) remind us, the desire to be involved in or to lead radical change involves high hassle and high vulnerability. This requires a combination of self-reflection with vulnerability, realistic expectations, tolerance, humility, self-giving, self-containment and an ability to learn (Bell, 1998). Through *second-person voice/practice* we engage in inquiry with others and work to create a community of inquiry. This involves not only the actual processes of collaboration, but also the design and management of shared responsibility for the design and execution of the project that enhances co-inquiry. The collaborative nature of the inquiry is central to the quality of action research process and its outcomes (Shani and Pasmore, 1985). Through *third-person voice* we move beyond immediate first- and second-person audiences to the impersonal wider community and make a contribution to the body of knowledge of what it is really like in these systems and how we can learn to manage change while in the middle of it. Contributions might include

Table 45.1 *Preunderstanding, role duality and organizational politics in first-, second- and third-person practice as learning capabilities*

	Preunderstanding	Role duality	Organizational politics
First-person	*Task*: Developing spirit of inquiry in familiar situations where things are taken for granted *Skills*: Attending; questioning own assumptions; self-awareness/reflection skills	*Task*: Holding and valuing both sets of roles simultaneously *Skills*: Catching internal responses to conflicting demands and dealing with them	*Task*: Learning to act politically in mode within values of action research *Skills*: Acting politically and authentically
Second-person	*Task*: Developing collaborative inquiry/action in familiar situations where the spirit of inquiry may be diminished *Skills*: Collaborative action and inquiry: • combining advocacy with inquiry • intervention typology • testing assumptions and inferences • learning window	*Task*: Holding and managing the demands of both roles, particularly in situations of conflicting role demands. *Skills*: Role negotiation with significant others, especially superiors	*Task*: Surviving and thriving political dynamics *Skills*: Performance and back-staging
Third-person	*Task*: Developing practical knowledge of how to inquire as a 'native' *Skills*: Linking practice with theory	*Task*: Develop practical knowledge of how the dual roles impact on action research and contribute to insider action research role identity theory *Skills*: Linking experience of role duality with theory	*Task*: Articulating knowledge out of action that is actionable politically; contributing knowledge of what organizations are really like *Skills*: Linking political experience with theory
Outcomes in developing new capabilities	Learning capabilities to inquire into what is close and familiar	Effective utilization and understanding of insider action research role as a learning mechanism and development of new organizational capabilities	Building learning mechanisms that are sustainable politically

shared knowledge and continuous learning via the facilitation of shared sensemaking, interpretation and continuous experimentation and how the ability to suspend preconceived and well indoctrinated categories and analytic rules enables new knowledge to be created and acted upon. Through *third-person practice*, we work to extend the scale of the first- and second-person practice to a

wider system, such as other organizations, or to influence policy-making and implementation. In this chapter we advance the notion that the engagement of the three voices/practices is crucial in the development of new organizational capabilities.

Doing action research within one's own system can be seen to involve managing three interlocking challenges (Coghlan and

Brannick, 2005). Insider action researchers need to build on the closeness they have with the setting while, at the same time, create distance from it in order to see things critically and enable change to happen. This we refer to as *preunderstanding*. They have to hold *dual roles*, their organizational member role(s) and the action researcher role, and the consequent ambiguities and conflicts between these that can arise. They also have to manage *organizational politics* and balance the requirements of their future career plans with requirements for the success and quality of their action research. Each of these three challenges makes demands on first-, second- and third-person voice/practice and, through confronting them, insider action researchers can contribute to the development of capabilities.

We also note that these three challenges are not static. Action research is a dynamic process where the situation changes and changes as a consequence of deliberate action. Action researchers have to deal with emergent processes, not as distractions but as central to the research process. Design considerations such as socio-technical processes, co-inquiry and experimentation are emergent and cannot all be designed in advance (Shani and Bushe, 1987). Preunderstanding, role duality and organizational politics are likely to shift as the consequence of deliberate action or as unintended consequences of actions. Lewin's often cited maxim that one only understands a system when one tries to change it is illustrative of the development of preunderstanding that occurs in the course of an action research project. Similarly, in the emergent nature of the shifting situation in a system's change process, how the insider action researchers hold their dual roles and survive and thrive politically are challenges that need constant attention and renegotiation. They not only need to cope with and manage these three challenges within their projects, but they also need to inquire into them and offer their learning to the wider community as to what it is like to engage in insider action research.

Based on the philosophy of Bernard Lonergan, the Canadian philosopher-theologian, the structure of knowing which underpins inquiry at first-, second- and third-person is a three step process: experience, understanding and judgement (Lonergan, 1992; Flanagan, 1997). We attend to our experience both within and outside of ourselves, what Marshall (1999) refers to as inner and outer arcs of attention. Then we subject our experience to questioning. What is happening? Why is it happening? The insight comes and we follow it up by reflecting and weighing up the evidence as to whether the insight is correct or not (judgement). A similar process for a course of action takes us through the same set of (a) experiencing the situation, (b) using sensitivity, imagination and intelligence to answer the question for understanding as to what possible courses of action might be, (c) reflecting on the possible value judgements as to what is the best option and (d) deciding to follow through the best value judgement and being responsible for consistency in knowing and doing. Of course, there is no guarantee that we will attend to experience and the search for insight. We can easily fly from insight, resist the reasonable judgement and try to escape responsibility. Lonergan's methodology forms the basis for attending to (a) our own cognitive and acting operations (first-person), (b) working with other persons' cognitive and acting operations (second-person) and (c) seeking to contribute to the wider community of knowledge and action (third-person). A praxis-reflection methodology of attention to experience, understanding and judgement which lead to action, such as presented by Lonergan and Marshall, are the basis for engaging in insider action research and for addressing the challenges of preunderstanding, role duality and organizational politics.

PREUNDERSTANDING

Preunderstanding refers to such things as people's knowledge, insights and experience before they engage in a research programme. The knowledge, insights and experience of insider-researchers apply not only to theoretical understanding of organizational dynamics, but also to the lived experience of their own organization. It is a blend of experiential, presentational and propositional knowing. Personal experience and knowledge of their own system and job are a distinctive preunderstanding for insider researchers. For insider action researchers, knowledge of their own system has great advantages; they know who's who and what's what. They know where disparities exist between the formal and informal organizations. They know how the informal system works, particularly where informal power lies and how informal information networks function. Such knowledge enables a direct access to sources of power, influence and information. This knowledge is not always explicit. Insider researchers are part of their organizational culture and, therefore, there is much that they don't see, and they may find it difficult to stand back from it in order to assess and critique it, particularly as they may be colluding with the premises that underpin organizational actions. Their perspective may be partial as their experience may be based in one functional area of the system and thus lack understanding of other areas. Their professional background may give them membership of one occupational community, thus excluding understanding of other occupational communities. They need to be in tune with their own feelings as an organizational member – where their feelings of good will are directed, where their frustrations are and so on. In short, preunderstanding for insider action researchers involves building on closeness and achieving distance.

At the same time, familiarity also inhibits inquiry. When we are in new situations we are conscious of what we don't know and we work hard at figuring out what's going on and how to respond. In insider situations, we are meeting the same people that we meet every day. We engage in the same organizational rituals where we attend meetings with the same people and discuss the same topics that we discussed last week. Thus, one of the challenges of preunderstanding is, where the ritual appears to be the same, developing the mechanism that will enhance the ability to inquire into such situations.

Within the challenge of preunderstanding, *first-person skills* focus on holding and managing this tension between closeness and distance through developing skills of inquiry in familiar situations where things are taken for granted. The praxis-reflection methodology is central to holding this tension and to making sense of it in a dynamic setting where familiarity inhibits inquiry and where subtle shifts may be missed. Asking what evidence I am being presented with as I work in a familiar setting and what it is that I take for granted are examples of inquiry into preunderstanding.

Praxis-reflection skills may be developed in several ways.

- One way is to attend to your own experience and how you move from experience to knowing and action. For example, if you do crosswords, notice your questions about a clue, the flashes of insight that you get (eventually!), how you check those insights with how they fit with the blank spaces for the letters and the other words that cross it. Then you verify; this must be the answer. Attending to the process of knowing enables insider action researchers to learn the different processes in knowing (the role of experience, insight, judgement) and to catch how they weigh up evidence, make judgements and decide on action. Of course, in human and organizational settings, issues, such as the crossword example, are not as clear cut. In organizational settings our knowing is always incomplete and can only be completed by attending to particular tasks and situations in which we are at a given time. A remembered set of insights are only approximately appropriate to the new situation. They are insights into situations which are similar but not identical. No two situations are identical. Time has passed, place has changed, we remember differently. Accordingly, our judgements are provisional and open to revision as events unfold. We learn to treat facts as hypotheses (see Friedman and Rogers, Chapter 17 in this volume).

- Journaling is another important mechanism for learning to reflect on and gain insights into preunderstanding. Insider action researchers can record their experiences, thoughts and feelings over time as they move through their project and, through the reflective process, can begin to identify gaps between what they know and what they think they know and what they find that they don't know. They can begin to learn to stand back and critique what they have taken for granted hitherto. As Raelin (2000) argues, reflection must be brought into the open so that it goes beyond privately held taken for granted assumptions and helps action researchers to see how their knowledge is constructed. Otherwise, it may simply reinforce unexamined prejudices. In this manner, first-person reflection moves to incorporate second-person practice as assumptions and intepretations are shared and tested. Another element of first-person practice in this regard is how action researchers model the process of inquiry-in-action. We develop this in the following section on second-person skills.
- A third way of developing praxis skills is through second-person practice with a mentor, consultant or academic supervisor. We discuss this way under second-person practice below.

Second-person skills within preunderstanding require collaborative inquiry/action with people with whom insider action researchers are likely to have long-standing relationships, people whom they know well and with whom they have become so familiar so as to diminish the spirit of inquiry. Some of these relationships are close; others may be overtly political. Schein's (1999) typology of helper/consultant inquiry provides a useful framework for insider action researcher second-person skills. His first category is what he calls *pure inquiry*. This is where researchers prompt the elicitation of the story of what is taking place and listen carefully and neutrally. They ask, 'What is going on?' 'Tell me what happened'. The second type of inquiry is what Schein calls *exploratory diagnostic inquiry,* in which action researchers begin to manage the process of how the content is analysed by the other by exploring (a) emotional processes, (b) reasoning, and (c) actions. So they may ask, 'How do you feel about this?' 'Why do you think this happened?' 'What did you do?'

'What are you going to do?' and so on. The third type of inquiry is what Schein calls *confrontive inquiry*. This is where action researchers, by sharing their own ideas, challenge the other to think from a new perspective. These ideas may refer to (a) process and (b) content. Examples of confrontive questions would be, 'Have you thought about doing this?' 'Have you considered that ... might be a solution?'

Because insider action researchers are part of the situation, they may not always act as an external consultant might, that is, be solely the enabler of emergent information and action. Of necessity they have a view of things as they are and what needs to change, and are expected to share and argue that view. Accordingly, a critical skill for insider action researchers is to be able to combine advocacy with inquiry, that is to present their own inferences, attributions, opinions and viewpoints as open to testing and critique. This involves illustrating inferences with relatively directly observable data and making reasoning explicit and publicly testable in the service of learning.

Action science and developmental action inquiry provide useful skills on which insider action researchers may draw in order to work with preunderstanding in a second-person context. These are intervention skills which aim to minimize inference, attribution and privately held assumptions which impede second-person inquiry. Within action science, the use of the ladder of inference and the right- and left-hand column provide useful techniques for uncovering privately held inference and attribution (see Friedman and Rogers, Chapter 17). In a not dissimilar vein, Torbert and Taylor (Chapter 16) suggest four 'parts of speech' as useful to the action inquiry role, and which minimize inference and attributions:

- *framing* – explicitly stating the purpose of speaking for the present occasion: what dilemma you are trying to resolve, sharing assumptions about the situation, etc.
- *advocating* – explicitly stating the goal to be achieved, asserting and option, perception, feeling or proposal for action.

- *illustrating* – telling a bit of the concrete story that makes the advocacy concrete and orients the others more clearly
- *inquiring* – questioning others to understand their perspectives and views.

These interventions may occur in one-to-one or group situations.

The learning window presents a useful synthesis for second-person preunderstanding issues (Yorks, 2005). The learning window is a 2×2 matrix that provides an analytic tool for testing the level of confidence in data/findings, exposing gaps in knowledge and pinpointing areas where the differences between inference and knowledge need to be learned. Quadrant 1, reflecting what the group knows, has to contain solid data that have been tested and meet with consensual agreement among group members. Quadrant 2, what the group thinks it knows, catches the inferences and attributions that group members are making and challenges the group to make those inferences explicit, to locate them in directly observable behaviour through the ladder of inference and to see them as hypotheses to be tested, rather than accepting them as facts. Quadrant 3 identifies the gaps in knowledge that the group knows it needs to address and opens up an agenda for further data collection and hypothesis testing in action. Quadrant 4 opens up the new knowledge that is yet to come and which may be unexpected.

Engagement with a mentor, role analysis specialist or academic supervisor is a valuable mechanism for attending to and reflecting on the challenges of preunderstanding. Through second-person interaction with such a person who listens attentively, supports and challenges, insider action researchers can explore their preunderstanding and expose its limitations.

The *third-person* voice shares the learning that comes from holding closeness and distance with the wider community of theory and practice. As we've said, familiarity inhibits inquiry, so contributing lessons learned and tools developed for inquiry-in-action into 'at home' situations is an important contribution to both the world of practice and of theory. For the world of practice, such insider learning contributes to the knowledge of insider interventionists, such as managers, internal consultants and others who work at changing their own systems from within. For the world of theory that traditionally has a deep-rooted suspicion of closeness and of being 'native', such insider experience contributes to the growing reflection on reflexivity (Brannick and Coghlan, 2007).

Preunderstanding and the existing interpersonal dynamics between insider action researchers and their peers in the workplace present both major strengths and a major set of challenges to the quality of the insider action research. The questioning of assumptions at the individual level and facilitating dialogue with relevant others in the workplace is likely to validate the importance of the research focus.

The challenge of preunderstanding through first-, second- and third-person voice/practice is to build on the closeness insider action researchers have with their systems and to develop distance in order to inquire critically and to intervene. As familiarity inhibits inquiry, confronting these challenges of preunderstanding is a critical step to developing learning capabilities from within.

ROLE DUALITY: ORGANIZATIONAL AND RESEARCHER ROLES

Augmenting one's normal organizational membership roles with the research enterprise can be difficult and awkward, and can become confusing for insider action researchers. Within their organizational roles they are managing within the boundaries of formal hierarchical and functional roles and informal roles of colleagueship and possible friendship and having desires to influence and change the organization. Insiders' organizational relationships are typically lodged and enmeshed in a network of membership affiliations, as they have been and continue to be a participant in the organization. These friendships and research ties can vary in character from openness to restrictiveness. Insider researchers are likely to find that their associations with various individuals or groups in the setting influence their relations with others whom they encounter, affecting the character of the data they can gather with them. Within their action researcher roles, they are working at enabling participation and as deep reflection-in-action as possible. As a result, insider action researchers are likely to encounter role conflict in trying to sustain a full organizational membership role and the research perspective simultaneously. Their organizational role may demand total involvement and active commitment, while the research role may demand a more detached, reflective, more theoretic position. This conflict may lead to an experience of role detachment, where insider action researchers begin to feel as an outsider in both roles.

As Coghlan and Shani (2005) explore, action researchers, and in this case insider action researchers, have to deal with the role expectations and sent-role of the members of the system in which they are working. The system may not have unified expectations of the action research project and so there are intra-sender ambiguities and conflicts as different members or factions hold different expectations of what role the action researchers are to play. At the same time, action researchers may have expectations of what their role is or what they want it to be, which may or may not accord with the sent-role or varieties of sent-role from the system and its constituent factions.

Ashforth et al. (2000) provide some role constructs that are useful for insider action researchers. Role boundaries can be flexible (that is, their boundaries can be pliable spatially and temporally) and they can be permeable (one can be physically in one role and psychologically and/or behaviourally in another), for these constructs of role flexibility and permeability enable transition from one role to another. In terms of insider action

research, the insider researchers may be in their office or at a meeting in their organization exercising their organizational role (physical and spatial) and, at the same time, probing for answers to questions in their research role.

First-person skills involve holding and valuing both sets of roles simultaneously and catching internal responses to conflicting demands and dealing with them. Once again we emphasize the praxis-reflection methodology and the value of journaling in exploring role duality. A continuous examination of the role conflict and dynamics seems to characterize the nature of the issues that the insider action researcher struggles with as the role duality evolves.

Second-person skills involve role negotiation with significant others, especially superiors. Holding and managing the demands of both roles, particularly in situations of high work intensity and conflicting role demands, are challenging. Roth (2002) claims that learning to manage the dual role dynamics is an emergent skill. He views the role duality as a continuum, ranging from role segmentation to role integration. At the beginning of the action research project, the researcher role was segmented from the practitioner role but, as the project evolved, staying within the two roles became more manageable, as captured in his words: 'I did not act as a practitioner or as a researcher, rather as practitioner and researcher'. Dialogue and continuous renegotiation of roles is crucial. At the same time, the struggle to contribute to both and the ongoing conflicting agenda and the need to continuously renegotiate with superiors at times might lead to a sense of being an outsider in both worlds.

The *third-person* voice can contribute to knowledge of roles in systems – how, for example, role flexibility and permeability pertain to insider action research and affect role identity as well as to some of the mechanisms that can be created in order to help gain new insights. The challenge is to create the time and space for this crucial activity to occur. Learning mechanisms are viewed as conscious, planned proactive features that enable and encourage reflection and learning (Popper and Lipshitz, 1998; Shani and Docherty, 2008). We propose that the capability to learn can be designed rather than left to evolve or be encouraged through the current activities of the organization (Ellström, 2001; Fenwick, 2003; Shani and Docherty, 2003). The learning processes needed to create a new organizational capability can be planned at the individual and collective levels, and specific features can be designed to initiate, facilitate, monitor, and reward this learning. By their very nature, learning mechanisms are multi-faceted, including cognitive or cultural, structural and procedural elements (Lipshitz et al., 2002; Shani and Docherty, 2003).

Learning mechanisms provide the time and space for the challenges of role duality to be supported and worked through. It is within this arena that the insider action researcher can play both roles as needed.

ORGANIZATIONAL POLITICS

Organizations are social systems. As such, an integral part of organizational life is political dynamics. Any form of action and clearly any form of research in an organization has its political dynamics. Political forces can undermine research endeavours and block planned change. Gaining access, using data, disseminating and publishing reports are intensely political acts. Insider action research is political. Indeed, it might be considered subversive. Action research has a subversive quality about it. It examines everything. It stresses listening. It emphasizes questioning. It fosters courage. It incites action. It abets reflection and it endorses democratic participation. Any or all of these characteristics may be threatening to existing organizational norms, particularly in those organizations that lean towards a hierarchical control culture. Meyerson (2001) calls those who quietly enact change in their own organizations 'tempered radicals'.

Cooklin (1999) refers to the insider change agent as the 'irreverent inmate', one who is a supporter of the people in the organization, is a saboteur of the organization's rituals and is a questioner of some of its beliefs. While as insider action researchers may see themselves as attempting to generate valid and useful information in order to facilitate free and informed choice so that there will be commitment to those choices in accordance with the theory and practice of action research (see Friedman and Rogers, Chapter 17), they find that, as Kakabadse (1991) argues, what constitutes valid information is intensely political.

First-person skills entail learning to act politically within values of action research. Recognizing that politics are not only a fact of organizational life but *the* fact, insiders need to reflect on their own values and how they hold their roles, politics and ethics together (Coghlan and Shani, 2005). Buchanan and Badham (1999) lay out the challenges of being effective in organizations as political systems and pose the question, 'how far are you prepared to go?' The praxis-reflection methodology involves attention to and reflection on the personal questions and dilemmas which arise in the political dynamics of the action research projects.

The *second-person* political skills for the insider action researcher involve being able to work the political system, which involves balancing the organization's formal justification of what it wants in the project with their own tacit personal justification for political activity. Throughout the project they have to maintain their credibility as an effective driver of change and as an astute political player. The key to this is assessing the power and interests of relevant stakeholders in relation to aspects of the project. One particular manager may have a great deal of influence with regard to budget allocation, but little influence with regard to strategic decision-making.

Buchanan and Badham (1999) coined the term 'political entrepreneur', a role which implies a behaviour repertoire of political strategies and tactics and a reflective self-critical perspective on how those political behaviours may be deployed. Buchanan and Boddy (1992) describe the management of the political role in terms of two activities, performing and back-staging, and these activities form the basis of political *second-person* skills. *Performing* involves the public performance role of being active in the change process, building participation for change, pursuing the change agenda rationally and logically and managing conflict, while backstage activity involves the recruitment and maintenance of support and the reduction of resistance. *Back-staging* comprises skills at intervening in the political and cultural systems, through justifying, influencing and negotiating, defeating opposition and so on. Insiders have a preunderstanding of the organization's power structures and politics, and are able to work in ways that are in keeping with the political conditions without compromising the project or their own career. Smyth and Holian (1999) point out that there's a perceived risk in becoming a 'sacrificial lamb' or a 'Joan of Arc' if insider action researchers don't handle politics successfully.

Bjorkman and Sundgren (2005) suggest that insider action researchers view themselves as political entrepreneurs. The political entrepreneurship role requires the ability to be congruent with one's value set, the value set of action research and finding a way to exploit learning opportunities within the organization. Working through the issues of value congruence is a challenging but required task. The process allows the individual to develop new personal capabilities that are critical for one's own role and performance as an organization member and as an insider action researcher.

Pettigrew (2003) reflects on his own role as a political entrepreneur. He notes that it can be exhilarating when it appears that one's advocacy, enthusiasm and energy have created desired effects towards some defined outcomes and equal and opposite despair when things go wrong. He reflects that there's a fine line between acting in a

politically astute manner and acting unethically. In his view, action researchers have to build relationships and trust with people who operate from different mental models and at different levels. Yet working as a change agent cannot always be done with openness, honesty and transparency. He judges that the real skill is the political entrepreneur knowing that the game is everything and that it is 'theories-in-action' rather than espoused theories that count.

Friedman (2001) provides more specific second-person guidelines:

a) Describe your own reality image and situation as concretely as possible.
b) Ask senior and middle management if this explanation accurately fits as they see it.
c) If there are significant differences, inquire into the sources of these differences.
d) Continuously inquire into the reasoning behind actions.
e) Design strategies dealing with the current situation and similar future ones.

Politics are integrally linked to what capabilities are developed and what are not. If organizational politics are not managed successfully, the learning mechanisms that are sustainable politically are not built.

Holian (1999) provides a case which integrates all three challenges. She reports how her additional researcher role added complex dimension to her senior executive role. The role conflict between her senior executive position and her action researcher role that she experienced when organizational members provided her with information which she did not know if she could use in her researcher role and which she thought she should use in her executive role created an ethical dilemma for her. As her research subject was ethical decision-making she faced a double dilemma, a content one for her organization and a process one for the research. She established and participated in a cooperative inquiry group comprising people in decision-making roles from a diverse range of organizations. The members of this group discussed ethical issues they were experiencing, and encouraged one another to reflect on their own experience and find new ways of working with ethical issues in their own organizations. She reported how she felt unprepared for the backlash which resulted from surfacing 'undiscussables' within the organization related to cover-ups, perceived abuse of power, nepotism, harassment, allocation of rewards and unfair discrimination. While these issues were deeper, more shocking and troubling than anticipated, she reflected that she was not adequately prepared to look after herself or others when the backlash came. Consequently, she was not able to balance the multiple roles of researcher, senior executive and programme facilitator, and she resigned.

Holian's preunderstanding, role duality and organizational politics were radically challenged in her insider action research. As she reports, she was unprepared for the reactions she received. We might infer from her story that the skills she needed to manage this project could not be foreseen but emerged through the process of her inquiry. As we noted earlier, preunderstanding, role duality and organizational politics are not static, and for Holian they shifted as she got deeper into her action research. So the skills she needed developed through the process of inquiry itself.

CONCLUSIONS

Our point of departure was that insider action research is viewed as one way to develop new capabilities. In this chapter we have shown that first, second and third voice/practice of insider action research provide unique opportunities to address the issues of preunderstanding, role duality and organizational politics and explore their role in the development of new capabilities. At the most basic level, new capabilities are viewed as composite bundles of competences, skills and technologies that are bound together to enable particular salient performances (Hamel, 1994). Bogner and Thomas (1994) argue that a capability exists on two levels.

On one level is the active component of the capability, the 'doing' of activities that exploit knowledge and skills better than the competition. On a second level there is a cognitive component of the capability. They propose that all relevant actions and skills are driven by a distinctive set of cognitive traits (e.g. shared values, recipes, integrated understandings of different aspects of competitive dynamics) that lie behind core skills and transform the mere doing of an act into a capability (Mohrman et al., 2006).

The tasks and skills we have discussed are summarized in Table 45.1, which draws together insider action researchers' tasks and issues in developing learning capabilities for first-, second- and third-person practice in relation to preunderstanding, role duality and organizational politics. We have shown how the outcome with regard to the tasks and skills relating to preunderstanding is the capability to inquire into what is close and familiar, with regard to role duality it is the effective utilization and understanding of the insider action research role as a learning mechanism and with respect to organizational politics it is building learning mechanisms that are effective politically.

What then can we say in conclusion? Insider action research is an exciting, demanding and invigorating prospect that contributes considerably to researchers' own learning and contributes to the development of organizational learning capabilities. It is also daunting, with a high potential for self-destruction, particularly if politics are not managed well. We conclude with advice from Friedman (2001) who suggests four attributes for insider action researchers: be proactive and reflective, be critical and committed, be independent and work well with others, and have aspirations and be realistic about limits.

REFERENCES

Ashforth, B., Kreiner, G. and Fugate, M. (2000) 'All in a day's work: boundaries and micro role transitions', *Academy of Management Review*, 25: 472–91.

Bell, C. (1998) 'Self-reflection and vulnerability in action research: bringing forth new worlds in our learning', *Systemic Practice and Action Research*, 11 (2): 179–91.

Bjorkman, H. and Sundgren, M. (2005) 'Political entrepreneurship in action research: learning from two cases', *Journal of Organizational Change Management,* 18 (5): 399–415.

Bogner, W.C. and Thomas, H. (1994) 'Core competence and competitive advantage: a model and illustrative evidence from the pharmaceutical industry', in G. Hamel and A. Heene (eds), *Competence-based Competition.* Chichester: Wiley. pp. 111–44.

Brannick, T. and Coghlan, D. (2007) 'In defense of being "native": the case for insider academic research', *Organizational Research Methods*, 10: 59–74.

Buchanan, D. and Badham, R. (1999) *Power, Politics and Organizational Change: Winning the Turf Game.* London: Sage.

Buchanan, D. and Boddy, D. (1992) *The Expertise of the Change Agent.* London: Prentice-Hall.

Coghlan, D. (forthcoming) 'Insider action research doctorates: generating actionable knowledge', *Higher Education.*

Coghlan, D. and Brannick, T. (2005) *Doing Action Research in Your Own Organization*, 2nd edn. London: Sage.

Coghlan, D. and Rashford, N. (2006) *Organizational Change and Strategy: An Interlevel Dynamics Approach.* Abingdon: Routledge.

Coghlan, D. and Shani, A.B. (Rami) (2005) 'Roles, politics and ethics in action research design', *Systemic Practice and Action Research*, 18 (6): 533–46.

Cooklin, A. (ed.) (1999) *Changing Organizations: Clinicians as Agents of Change.* London: Karnac.

Cummings, T.G. (2008) *Handbook of Organizational Change and Development.* Thousand Oaks, CA: Sage.

Dosi, G., Hobday, M. and Marengo, L. (2000) *Problem-solving Behaviours, Organizational Forms and the Complexity of Tasks.* LEM Papers Series 2000/6. Pisa: Sant' Anna School of Advanced Studies, Laboratory of Economics and Management.

Ellström, Y. (2001) 'Expansive learning at work: toward an activity theory reconceptualization', *Journal of Education and Work*, 14: 133–56.

Fenwick, T. (2003) 'Professional growth plans: possibilities and limitations of an organization-side employee development strategy', *Human Resource Development Quarterly*, 14: 59–77.

Flanagan, J. (1997) *The Quest for Self-Knowledge: An Essay in Lonergan's Philosophy.* Toronto: Toronto University Press.

Friedman, V. (2001) 'The individual as agent of organizational learning', in M. Dierkes, J. Child, I. Nonaka and A. Berthoin Antal (eds), *Handbook of Organizational Learning.* Oxford: Oxford University Press. pp. 398–414.

Hamel, G. (1994) 'The concept of core competence', in G. Hamel and A. Heene (eds), *Competence-based Competition.* Chichester: Wiley. pp. 11–33.

Holian, R. (1999) 'Doing action research in my own organization: ethical dilemmas, hopes and triumphs', *Action Research International*, Paper 3. [http://www.scu.edu.au/schools/sawd/ari/ari/holian.html]

Kakabadse, A. (1991) 'Politics and ethics in action research', in N. Craig Smith and P. Dainty (eds), *The Management Research Handbook.* London: Routledge. pp. 289–99.

Lipshitz, R., Popper, M. and Friedman, V.J. (2002) 'A multifacet model of organizational learning', *Journal of Applied Behavioral Science*, 38 (1): 78–98.

Lonergan, B.J. (1992) *Insight: An Essay in Human Understanding. The Complete Works of Bernard Lonergan*, Vol. 3 (ed. F. Crowe and R. Doran). Toronto: University of Toronto Press. (original publication, London: Longmans, 1957)

Marshall, J. (1999) 'Living life as inquiry', *Systemic Practice and Action Research*, 12 (2): 155–71.

Meyerson, D. (2001) *Tempered Radicals: How People Use Difference to Inspire Change at Work.* Boston: Harvard Business School Press.

Mohrman, S., Docherty, P., Shani, A.B. (Rami), Schenkel, A.J. and Teigland, R. (2006) 'The development of new organizational capabilities: a design-based model for managerial action.' 'Paper presented at the Academy of Management Annual Conference, August, Atlanta. USA.

Pettigrew, P. (2003) 'Power, conflicts and resolutions: a change agent's perspective on conducting action research within a multi organizational partnership', *Systemic Practice and Action Research*, 16 (6): 375–91.

Popper, M. and Lipshitz, R. (1998) 'Organizational learning mechanisms: a structural and cultural approach to organizational learning', *Journal of Applied Behavioral Science*, 34: 161–79.

Raelin, J.A. (2000) *Work-Based Learning: The New Frontier of Management Development.* Upper Saddle River, NJ: Prentice-Hall.

Roth, J. (2002) 'Knowledge unplugged: an action research approach to enhancing knowing in R&D Organizations.' Doctoral Thesis, Fenix Research Program, Gothenburg, Sweden: Chalmers University of Technology.

Roth, J., Shani, A.B. (Rami) and Leary, M. (2007) 'Insider action research: facing the challenges of new capability development within a biopharm company.' *Action Research*, 5 (1): 41–60.

Schein, E.H. (1999) *Process Consultation Revisited: Building the Helping Relationship.* Reading, MA: Addison-Wesley.

Shani, A.B. (Rami) and Bushe, G.R. (1987) 'Visionary action research: a consultation process perspective', *Consultation,* 6 (1): 3–19.

Shani, A.B. (Rami), David, A. and Willson, C. (2004) 'Collaborative research: alternative roadmaps', in N. Adler, A.B. (Rami) Shani and A. Styhre (eds), *Collaborative Research in Organizations: Foundations for Learning, Change, and Theoretical Development.* Thousand Oaks, CA: Sage. pp. 83–100.

Shani, A.B. (Rami) and Docherty, P. (2003) *Learning by Design: Building Sustainable Organizations.* Oxford: Blackwell.

Shani, A.B. (Rami) and Docherty, P. (2008) 'Learning by design: Key mechanisms in organization development', in T. Cummings (ed.), *Handbook of Organizational Change and Development.* Thousand Oaks, CA: Sage.

Shani, A.B. (Rami) and Pasmore, W.A. (1985) 'Organization inquiry: towards a new model of the action research process', in D.D. Warrick (ed.), *Contemporary Organization Development: Current Thinking and Applications.* Glenview, IL: Scott, Foresman. pp. 438–48.

Smyth, A. and Holian, R. (1999) 'The credibility of the researcher who does research in their own organization.' [http://www.latrobe.edu.au/aqr/offer/papers/RHolian.htm]

Yorks, L. (2005) *Strategic Human Resource Development.* Mason, OH: South-Western.

46

Teaching Reflective Practice in the Action Science/Action Inquiry Tradition: Key Stages, Concepts and Practices

Steven S. Taylor, Jenny W. Rudolph and
Erica Gabrielle Foldy

This chapter describes an approach for teaching reflective practice in the action science/action inquiry tradition. We offer a theoretical background for our approach and then break it down into three key stages: (1) understanding the social construction of reality; (2) recognizing one's own contribution to that construction; and (3) taking action to reshape that construction. We articulate key concepts (e.g. the ladder of inference and competing commitments) and tools (e.g. the change immunity map and the learning pathways grid) for each stage. We end with suggestions for assignments that integrate learning across stages and concepts. In short, we offer a conceptually grounded set of concrete practices for teaching reflective practice.

Reflective practice, the process of examining one's own actions and learning about oneself, has long been part of many great transformational traditions, from Buddhism (Goldstein, 1983) to the Jesuit (Coghlan, 2004) spiritual exercises to Socrates and the transcendentalists' call to 'know thyself' (Emerson, 1903). In modern social science, reflective practice is also known as 'first- person research' (e.g. Marshall and Mead, 2005). Our particular approach draws heavily on the definitions and disciplines of reflective practice as articulated by Agyris and Schön's Action Science and Reflective Practitioner work (Argyris and Schön, 1974; Argyris et al., 1985; Schön, 1983, 1987; Schön and Rein, 1994), and Torbert's action inquiry (Torbert, 1972, 1991; Torbert et al., 2004).

We draw upon this work to teach graduate students the theory and skills of reflective practice. Steve Taylor teaches management students at Worcester Polytechnic Institute, a largely technically oriented population. Jenny Rudolph teaches healthcare management and policy students at Boston University and clinicians at the Center for Medical Simulation, Boston. Erica Foldy teaches public administration and policy students at the Wagner School of Public Service at New York University. Together we have been learning the theory and skills of reflective practice for over a decade and teaching those skills in various contexts for the majority of that time (e.g. Rudolph et al., 2001). Over time we have synthesized an approach that pulls together concepts and practices from a wide variety of scholars working in this tradition (e.g. Friedman, 2001/2006; Friedman and Lipshitz, 1992; Kegan and Lahey, 2001; Mazen, 2000; Reason, 1996; Senge et al., 1994; Stone et al., 2000). Our pedagogic goal is to enable students to enhance their personal and professional effectiveness by having greater self-knowledge along with a broader repertoire of cognitive frames, emotional reactions, and behaviors on which to draw. We focus on students' ability to reflect *on* action as a step towards being able to reflect *in* action.

Although each of us tailors this approach to our own teaching context, we have identified important commonalities: key stages in the learning of reflective practice, as well as supporting concepts and practice exercises. In this chapter, we draw on these commonalities to present one integrated approach to teaching reflective practice.

The chapter is organized as follows. We start by laying out the theoretical foundations for our pedagogical approach to teaching reflective practice. We then describe the concepts we use in building reflective practice skills in our students: helping them understand in a visceral way what it means for social reality to be constructed and how their own construction of reality contributes to many of the challenges they face; helping them discover how they are personally implicated in problems they have previously understood as exogenous to themselves; and offering prescriptive actions for intervening in these problems. We then describe take-home assignments that build their skills in all these areas and help them take effective action based in reflective practice.

THEORETICAL FOUNDATIONS

Our approach to teaching reflective practice is built on theoretical work broadly related to self-awareness directed at effective action. At the heart of the work is Argyris's (Argyris et al., 1985) Action Science which begins with the core idea that our frames (in a broad sense which includes mental models, schemas, etc.) lead us to act in certain ways and those actions produce outcomes. We also draw on Torbert's discipline of Action Inquiry which offers us the fundamental notion that by consciously paying attention to the alignment (or misalignment) among our intentions, strategies used to carry out these intentions, and our own actions, we can continue to develop psychologically as adults (Torbert, 1991; Torbert et al., 2004).

We also draw upon Quinn's (Quinn, 2000; Quinn et al., 2000) Advanced Change Theory to explain why reflective practice is critical for enhancing personal and professional effectiveness. This theory argues that change processes that resort to telling, forcing, and even participation of others without self-change have limited effectiveness. Quinn argues that without changing one's own behavior, significant, sustainable, and systemic change is unlikely. Advanced Change Theory follows the process of identifying the problem, identifying one's own role in that problem, changing one's own behavior, and then letting the system respond to the change. While there are structural limits to the effects of such actions, we believe it is a starting point and one that most students may overlook. Identifying one's own role in the problem is not easy and requires reflective practice skills.

Our approach is informed by the following concepts. First, we attempt to move students from 'Mystery-Mastery' or 'Model I' frames or governing values to 'Collaborative Inquiry' or 'Model II' governing values (Argyris and Schön, 1974; Torbert, 1972). In other words, we are attempting to help them move from an approach that emphasizes keeping their own concerns and goals a mystery while unilaterally attempting to master the outside world to an approach that values transparent thinking and collaborative dialogue (Torbert, 1972). Second, we are attempting to create a context for learning that allows students to become increasingly 'self-authoring' in a process that allows them to 'have their beliefs' rather than 'their beliefs having them' (Kegan, 1982, 1994; Kegan and Lahey, 2001). This means that instead of being ruled by assumptions, or theories-in-use (Argyris et al., 1985) of which they are unaware, they become aware of these governing frames and decide whether they are in alignment with their goals.

The concepts and practices we propose are grounded in a pedagogical approach that Torbert (1991) calls 'Liberating Disciplines'. In this paradoxical approach to transformation, we exercise our available forms of power to unilaterally try and force the students to develop their own power which, over time, can free them of the unilateral power of others. We are transparent about this approach which makes our actions discussable, thereby making us vulnerable, even as we wield power. Some students are disconcerted by that vulnerability; upending conventional power relations leaves them feeling insecure. Others try to take advantage of the instructor's vulnerability as they attempt to assert their own power. A liberating disciplines approach means treating students' discomfort with the unusual deployment of power as real-time opportunities for teacher and student to learn. This is a very difficult challenge that requires the instructor to tolerate uncertainty as new class structures emerge. We use power openly to create a situation in which students can begin (indeed are required) to experiment with their own creative power to transform themselves, their teams and the class.

In this approach we help students develop the skills and awareness to see themselves as authors (rather than characters) of their work or personal lives. The paradox in this approach is that we force students to become self-authoring by obliging them to conform to the requirements of the class using grades and other tools

that come from our power as the instructor. We complement these forcing strategies with three supportive elements: building mutuality by allowing students to influence the course of the class (see course feedback memo below as an example); establishing oneself as ally in students developing their professional skills; and revealing one's own weaknesses (and strengths) as reflective practitioner (by 'telling stories on oneself', using examples that show one's own mistakes and breakthroughs in the process). Many teachers may already use 'liberating structures' intuitively, but we believe that being explicit (explaining the process to students mid-way through a semester, for example) and purposive about using them can enhance success.

THREE KEY STAGES IN LEARNING REFLECTIVE PRACTICE

Based on these broad conceptual groundings we have broken down learning reflective practice into three core stages. The stages are (1) understanding the social construction of reality, (2) recognizing one's own contribution to that construction, and (3) taking action to reshape that construction. This breaks down the complex process of reflecting in action into simpler steps. Of course, reflective practice requires a constant intermingling of the three stages and even in teaching the separation is seldom neat and tidy; nonetheless, we find this a useful way to structure the material. Table 46.1 outlines the three stages with their key supporting concepts and practice exercises. The rest of this chapter fleshes out this table in greater detail.

KEY CONCEPTS AND PRACTICES

Social Construction of Reality

Concept: Internal perceptions shape external reality. A foundational concept for teaching reflective practice is the idea that people's perception of external reality is influenced by internal images and that these internal

Table 46.1 *Key stages, concepts and practices in learning reflective practice*

Stage	Supporting concepts	Practice
Understanding the social construction of reality	Internal perceptions shape external reality	Social construction of the physical room
	Ladder of inference	Uncritical inference test
	Unconscious filters/frames	The implicit association test
Recognizing one's own contribution to that construction	Competing commitments that cause stasis	Change immunity map
	Impact of frames on actions and outcomes	Two-column Case and Learning pathways grid
Taking action to reshape that construction	Types of speech	Two-column Case and Learning Pathways Grid Clean and dirty questions

images shape how they act. We want our managers-in-training to understand, both intellectually and viscerally, that, like all of us, they co-create the organizational reality in which they move. Our goal is to help students see how their internal frames, emotional reactions, and actions influence and co-create organizational structures and practices that they previously viewed as immutable, external facts (see Figure 46.1). Establishing a gut-level sense that their internal reality images shape their own action and the reality around them is the foundation that motivates and makes possible further reflective practice (Friedman, 2001; Friedman and Lipshitz., 1992).

Practice: Social construction of the physical classroom (Gergen and Gergen, 2004). We begin this process experientially – by allowing students to experience how the frames provided by different professions cause people to view the same apparently objective reality differently. We break a class into groups, and give each subgroup a slip of paper (privately) that names a profession to which they belong during the exercise. The subgroup's task is to describe the room in which we are working from the standpoint of their profession. Professions might include teachers, fire inspectors, interior decorators, janitors and burglars. When the subgroups have completed their internal discussions they then share with the group as a whole (it works best to have the burglars report out last). Each group comes up with entirely different accounts of 'what is here'. Students generally

grasp, at a gut level, the idea that seemingly concrete realities are socially constructed.

Concept: Ladder of inference. A practical tool for working with the social construction of reality is the ladder of inference, which is a 'schematic representation of the steps by which human beings select from and read into interactions as they make sense of everyday life' (Argyris et al., 1985: 57) and is described extensively elsewhere (e.g. Senge et al., 1994).

We want students to understand that all of us instantaneously, unconsciously, and automatically select, name, and draw conclusions as we move up the ladder, reaching internally-derived conclusions we often then mistake for external reality. We also attempt to convey that: (1) categorizing and drawing inferences is absolutely necessary to allow us to act in the world – otherwise we face a world of undifferentiated 'buzzing, blooming confusion' (James, 1890: 462); (2) inference drawing is so powerful and potentially dangerous because it is easy to lose sight of the fact that we have drawn an inference; and (3) if people forget to treat their inferences as inferences, it undermines effective action (Kegan and Lahey, 2001).

Practice related to ladder of inference: Haney's 'uncritical inference test'. To help students do a 'slow motion' analysis of how they climb the ladder of inference, selecting and naming data and then linking it with previous belief systems to arrive at inferences about a given situation, we use an exercise based on William Haney's (1955) uncritical

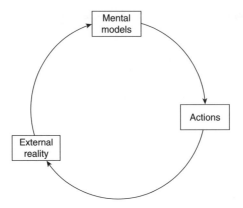

Figure: 46.1 *Simple model of social construction of reality for class use*

inference test in which students answer true/false questions about a four-sentence story. In debriefing the 'test' they quickly discover that their process of interpreting the story was informed by (or fraught with) numerous inferences about which they were totally unaware (such as the businessman and the owner are the same person).

Concept: Unconscious filters/frames. The ladder of inference and similar practices assume that, if we are self-reflective, we can identify the frames or ways of thinking that are affecting our behaviors. Some work suggests that it may help to work with a group, since others may be able to point out our ways of thinking that are so automatic we can't identify them without help. But the assumption in both cases is that our mental models are lurking just below the surface. Once surfaced, we can decide if they are, in fact, one of our frames and then assess them

and decide whether they are helping us or hurting us.

However, we believe that some of our most powerful ways of thinking may simply not be available to us. Of course, a long history of work in psychology suggests that we have unconscious motives that drive behavior. More recently, researchers have sought ways of uncovering unconscious preferences or attitudes related to race, gender and other social identities. We draw on this research to illustrate to students that not all of their ways of thinking are necessarily subject to their own control.

Practice: The implicit association test. The implicit association test (IAT) is a web-based instrument that purports to measure automatic and, often, unconscious preferences and attitudes. Researchers have developed tests related to race, age, gender, disability and others. The test asks the test-taker to associate

---

The Haney Uncritical Inference Test Story: A businessman had just turned off the lights in the store when a man appeared and demanded money. The owner opened a cash register. The contents of the cash register were scooped up, and the man sped away. A member of the police force was notified promptly. *Sample of the 15 Statements Students Assess as (T/F)* A man appeared after the owner had turned off his store lights; the robber was a man; the man who appeared did not demand money; the man who opened the cash register was the owner; the store owner scooped up the contents of the cash register and ran away.

two sets of terms or images. One set of terms or images represents two groups of individuals: white and black Americans, women and men, old people and young people, etc. The other set of terms or images represents positive statements or images vs. negative statements or images. The rationale of the test is that we will take longer to associate positive statements with some groups than other groups, and take longer to associate negative statements with some groups than with other groups. For example, in one version of the test designed for people in the United States, pictures of people that are easily characterized as either white or African American are flashed on the screen at the same time as positive and negative words and images. The majority of people who take the test take a longer time to associate positive words with African Americans (and a shorter time to associate positive words with whites) and longer to associate negative words with whites (and shorter to associate negative words with blacks). The researchers behind this work argue that the length of time that it takes to make the association manifests preferences for some kind of people over others. They argue further that these preferences are often unconscious and inaccessible to the test-taker and that only an instrument like the IAT can document them. While this research is controversial, it has a long track record and has been vetted by a number of psychology journals (Banaji et al., 1993; Greenwald and Banaji, 1995).

We also use the IAT to add a social and political dimension to the often apolitical approaches that make up the core of the literature on reflective practice. Reflective practice approaches often make it seem like, with work, we can have full control over how we think. The IAT reminds us that we are shaped by racism, ethnocentrism, sexism and other embedded ways of thinking about each other and that we have less control than we think. When someone takes the IAT and, according to the test, has a strong preference for Europeans over Asians, or the opposite, that won't necessarily resonate for the test-taker. In fact, it may come as a rude shock. The IAT doesn't solve these issues, but it does spur individuals and groups to think more about how much awareness and how much control we have over our own frames or mental models.

The Self's Contribution to the Social Construction of Reality

The next stage is for students to realize that they are implicated. That is, they need to see how our frames lead us to act in ways that contribute to a situation being problematic. This is often difficult: we tend to blame our problems on others rather than considering how we ourselves have contributed (Ross, 1977). Recognizing one's own contribution is a logical extension of the idea that our social reality is constructed: if we have participated in that construction then we have some responsibility for how it is constructed – and for changing it. From a systems point of view, we are part of the system and thus our own behavior is part of the explanation for how the system behaved (Senge, 1990).

Concept: Competing commitments. At this point in the process, we begin to encourage students to consider changing thoughts and behaviors. It is helpful, therefore, for students to understand why it is difficult to change. Kegan and Lahey (2001) developed the concept of 'competing commitments' as a replacement for the notion of resistance to change. They argue that change is difficult not because we are resistant for its own sake, but because we have very good reasons to avoid change – just as we do to pursue it. In fact, when change is difficult, it is the result of competing commitments which pull us in opposite directions. Only by surfacing these competing commitments do we surface our internal conflict. For example, powerful desires to stay safe can be in dynamic tension with desires to try new things. Once made explicit, we can develop experiments that resolve the conflict in a way that feels truly integral rather than imposed. Exploring our competing commitments is one way to explore how we contribute to outcomes we may or may not want.

Complaint	Commitment	Doing/Not doing	Competing commitment	Big assumption
'Walking on eggshells' around my sister.	A real, open and honest relationship between two caring people.	Suppress true feelings.	I am committed to not fighting with my sister.	If I share my true feelings with my sister, we will get in a big fight and I will lose the relationship.

Figure 46.2 *'Walking on Eggshells': Change immunity map*

Practice: The Change Immunity Map. To help students uncover their own competing commitments, we use Kegan and Lahey's (2001) change immunity map. This map starts with students' complaints and thus provides an easy way in. It moves from complaints to the commitments underneath the complaint, then onto what the student is doing or not doing that prevents the commitment from being fully realized. It is here that the students really start to see how they are implicated. In the example in Figure 46.2, one student analyzes his relationship with his sister, beginning with his complaint that he felt he was constantly walking on eggshells around her. The process took him through unfolding realizations which ultimately revealed his 'big assumption' – that he was scared of losing this relationship. The change immunity map offers a view of how the students' own competing commitments and internal protective routines lead to the very outcomes that they complain about, thus implicating themselves. The big assumption suggests a potential point of leverage, a problematic frame for the student to address.

Concept: Impact of frames on action and outcomes. We use the generic term 'frames' (Bolman and Deal, 2003) to denote the knowledge structures or 'mental template[s] that individuals impose on an information environment to give it form or meaning' (Walsh, 1995; 281). There are myriad other terms for these internal filters such as schemas, mental models, or scripts. These frames determine how we understand the world and how we translate that understanding into action. For example, if I believe a person I am dealing with is stupid I will act differently towards them than if I believe they are a genius. Taking action, based on these frames, will lead to particular outcomes. Identifying the causal chain of frames leading to actions which lead to outcomes offers a useful analytic map for understanding behavior (Argyris et al., 1985).

Practice: Two-column case and the learning pathways grid. We begin the practice of this concept by having each student write a short two-column case about an interpersonal interaction that turned out badly. The case includes a brief description of the context of the interaction, actual or remembered dialogue from the encounter in the right-hand column, and a left-hand column that captures what the casewriter thought and felt, but did not say (Argyris et al., 1985; Senge et al., 1994). Simply writing the case often triggers learning – the casewriter can become uncomfortably aware of the kinds of language she used or how her thoughts seem oddly disconnected with what she is saying.

However, systematic analysis of the case generally provides the richest insights into how we contribute to problematic outcomes. We use the Learning Pathways Grid (developed by Action Design [www.actiondesign.com], see Rudolph et al., 2001/2006; Taylor, 2004, for examples). The LPG analysis makes very explicit the connections between the casewriter's frames and actions and the outcomes of the interaction. The analysis identifies the actual outcomes in the situation, the actual actions that were taken that led to the outcomes, and the salient actual frames that led to those actions (see Figure 46.3).

Actual frames	Actual actions	Actual outcomes
Desired frames	Desired actions	Desired outcomes

Figure 46.3 *The learning pathways grid*

In addition to analyzing what actually happened, the LPG includes a space for suggesting different ways of framing and acting that might lead to better outcomes for the casewriter. Therefore, it acts as a bridge from the stage of Recognizing One's Own Contribution to the stage of Taking Action. Although the LPG analysis provides compelling evidence of how the casewriter is implicated in co-creating the problematic situation, students are often still too deep within their own frames to be able to see and enact different frames. Prescriptive frameworks provide off-the-shelf blueprints that create a starting place for how to act differently.

Taking Action to Reshape our Reality

Once students have internalized the social construction of reality and how they are implicated in that construction, the next step is to act on that knowledge. Even when we have recognized how our own frames lead to actions that produce undesirable results, we are often unable to act differently because those frames have been our reality for so long that we can't imagine alternatives. At this point it is useful to provide generic approaches to action that suggest new and different ways of acting that may produce more desirable results.

Concept: Types of speech. Once managers have a well-developed map of how their own frames and emotional reactions contribute to problems they face, our next move is to help them characterize and improve the actions they take, particularly the types of speech they use. We start by conveying that talk, aphorisms to the contrary (e.g. sticks and stones …) not withstanding, is action (Austin, 1962; Searle, 1969). Operating on the premise that social and organizational realities are socially

constructed, we argue that it is through talk that these realities are iteratively and continually re-enacted (Weick, 1995). To help students explore how different types of speech enact different social and organizational realities, we introduce Torbert's typology of four types of speech (Torbert et al., 2004). 'Advocating' asserts a point of view or judgment; 'illustration' offers data or anecdote to back up the advocacy; 'inquiry' is a question that helps people find out about information or other people's points of view. Finally, and most rarely, people use 'framing' to set out a charter and seek a public agreement for the direction of the current conversation or formal meeting.

Practice: The two column case and the learning pathways grid. We continue our work with the two-column case that we introduced in the last section. The Four Types of Speech provide a simple and useful framework for analyzing these cases. By reading through the dialogue in the right-hand column of the case and labeling the types of speech, students usually find that they use advocacy exclusively or heavily, with no inquiry, contributing to a pattern of dueling arguments with little inquiry and low levels of interpersonal influence and learning on both sides. Students then experiment with new ways of talking to improve their problem-solving ability by, for example, adding the simple (but not easy to execute) move of pairing advocacy and inquiry in their interactions. They can do this first by writing out sample advocacy-inquiry statements and then by redoing the problematic conversation in a role play.

Practice: Clean and dirty questions. To strengthen students' ability to pair advocacy and inquiry, we ask students to practice moving from a 'dirty' question to a 'clean' advocacy paired with an inquiry. A 'dirty' question is a term developed by Schön to denote questions that have judgments or solutions embedded in them. An example is 'Wouldn't it be better to finish that marketing report early?' The exercise is detailed in the following box.

Exercise : To practice this skill, we form students into groups of four to six. Two people will interact as role play partners; others will observe and consult to the roleplayer in the pair. Each person picks a problem or mistake made by someone else (outside the group) that annoyed or upset them. The first role player in the group very briefly (1 minute) describes the situation. Then interacting with his roleplay partner, he states the feelings and judgment about the situation as a 'filthy' question or statement. This statement usually berates or exhorts. For example, 'I can't believe you're still tinkering with that marketing report. Everyone else is going to get their ideas in ahead of us! What are you thinking?!' Using clues from this 'filthy' question, the roleplayer then reflects with his partner and group about what thoughts, feelings, or identity issues underlie this filthy intervention. Using this input, the roleplayer attempts to put some of these feelings and judgment into the advocacy and then pairs it with an inquiry to find out what is going on with the other person. For example, 'I'm frustrated that you're still working on that report. Can you help me understand why you think the report needs more work?' The roleplayer then checks with his roleplay partner about how the statement made the partner feel. Using this input and ideas from others in the group, the roleplayer makes further improvements if needed. Students then switch their roles in the pair.

Bringing it All Together: Assignments for Building Reflective Practice Skills

At this point, we have developed a number of different theoretical concepts. We have also described how we use in-class exercises and discussion to allow students to engage those concepts, making them more concrete and connecting them to their own life experiences. We also use two take-home assignments that require students to integrate a number of these concepts into one project. We describe each here.

Course feedback memo. The course feedback assignment requires students to practice giving feedback, a key life skill. The assignment asks students to write a three-page memo to their professor, highlighting what is useful and what could be changed about the course. Not only does it help us get information on how students are experiencing the course, it also provides a real-life exercise in giving feedback, rather than using made-up scenarios as is often done in these circumstances. Giving feedback is difficult precisely because there is generally a relationship between feedback-giver and

feedback-receiver and both parties can be concerned about harming that relationship. When that relationship is completely hypothetical, as with made-up scenarios, some of the challenge is lost.

In preparation for writing the memo, students read several chapters of *How the Way We Talk Can Change the Way We Work* (Kegan and Lahey, 2001) and all of *Difficult Conversations* (Stone et al., 2000). The assignment instructs students to give feedback, drawing on those two sources for guidelines. The assignment is peer graded, given the potential for conflict of interest. Students bring two hard copies to class. They exchange one copy with another student; each grades the other's paper. We take the second copy and make comments and hand them back, but do not grade them.

On the day the assignment is due, we also practice verbal feedback, based on what they've written in their papers. They gather in groups of four or five to decide on several points they wish to raise with their professor. (We leave the room for this discussion so they won't feel inhibited by our presence.) On our return, we meet with one group at a time, while the whole class watches. We also ask for a second group to act as observers so that they can provide suggestions on giving feedback to the first group that is speaking directly to the professor. We try to meet with each group and give each group a chance to be the observer group as well.

This exercise is meant not only to give practice in giving feedback, but also to model openness to feedback and a willingness to be vulnerable, in order to learn. One of the predominant messages of our teaching is that we only learn by such openness and vulnerability; if, as the professor, we do not model those qualities, then the force of the message will be undermined if not totally erased.

Personal inquiry projects. At the heart of action research is cycles of analysis, action based on that analysis, and further analysis (Reason and Bradbury, 2001/2006). This cycle can be embodied in a personal inquiry project assignment. The assignment includes (1) a description of a situation where they believe their own frames/assumptions about the world may be problematic; (2) an analysis of the situation that shows how their own frames/assumptions lead them to act in specific ways that contribute to causing the problem (this analysis should produce a testable hypothesis about the situation); (3) a plan of action to test their hypothesis including what results they might expect and how they will know if their test has been successful or not; (4) the results of their test in the form of concrete data, such as dialogue presented in a two-column format; and (5) analysis of the results of their experiment.

Although the personal inquiry projects vary tremendously, here is one example. A student has repeated difficult interactions with his sister in which he offers her advice on her job search and they end up having an argument. He writes a two-column case of one of the interactions. He then analyzes the two-column case using the ladder of inference and the Learning Pathways Grid with the help of his inquiry group. The analysis provides the insight that when he is in a position to offer someone advice in order to try and get them to change their behavior, he assumes that rational data is

all that is needed to convince people, that people are predisposed to not take his advice, and that people don't mind him giving them advice. This leads him to use accusatory language to try and indict the person with data and, when that doesn't work, he becomes frustrated and attacks them with sarcasm, which leads to the arguments and tension that are problematic.

He then tests this insight in a series of experiments (see Schön, 1983, for an excellent discussion of ways of experimenting). First he asks an assortment of people (that he often has this dynamic with) what they are looking for in someone who is giving them advice. He finds that his focus on rational data that is intended to get people to listen to him makes him appear arrogant or condescending and thus leads people to not listen to him. He also discovers that people are not predisposed to not listen to him but that they are not always interested in hearing his advice – thus all three of his primary frames are wrong. He then goes on to experiment with enacting different frames, such as first asking his sister whether she wants his advice or not, and generally avoids the tension and arguments. Thus he has managed to look at his own behavior, see how he is implicated in the problematic situation, test his own frames, and finally act differently in the situation, which in this case (and in most cases, but not all) produced vastly better results.

CONCLUSION

This chapter presents one approach to teaching reflective practice, building on well-established theoretical foundations. The approach is based on three stages in the learning process: understanding the social construction of reality, recognizing the self's contribution to that construction, and taking action to shape that construction. We then suggest specific concepts and practices associated with each stage.

While we do see the three stages as sequential, with each stage building on the previous one, we do not argue that the teaching design should strictly follow what we outline here. Each of the different stages and concepts can be taught on its own; indeed many of the practices can also stand on their own, depending on the course context and what the instructor hopes to teach. Some courses, like those in leadership, consulting or developing management skills, could incorporate the full succession. However, the topics can also be interspersed in courses on negotiation, human resources, organizational behavior, business and society, and the like.

Regardless of how the concepts are introduced, we do believe that the concepts are best reinforced through a consistent and transparent pedagogy. By consistency, we mean that we try to model the sort of reflective practice that we are trying to teach in the class. This can manifest in many different ways: acknowledging our own frames – and their implications – related to the lesson material; explicitly pairing advocacy and inquiry in class discussion; a willingness to change aspects of the course that aren't working for students. By transparency we mean being explicit about our own practice as much as possible, especially when it can connect to the subject matter. For example, teachers make many choices that are similar to the kinds of choices or decisions that managers have to make. Grading is a form of performance appraisal. We make our grading style transparent, explain why we grade the way we do, connect that with how managers assess performance, and suggest that they, as managers, will face similar issues. We allow them time to think about how they might handle those situations, given their experience in this class and in other classes. We are also explicit about our use of positional power, late in the class explaining how we have used our position as instructors to 'force' them to develop as reflective practitioners. We then draw parallels to choices they can make as peers, managers, and subordinates.

We see this chapter as an orientation to teaching the fundamentals of reflective practice. It does not cover a number of other more complex topics in reflective practice that

we also teach, if we have the time. There are also other theoretical approaches to reflective practice. For example, psychoanalytic approaches have also been very influential in the fields of management and organizational behavior (e.g. Berg and Smith, 1985).

Finally, we want to acknowledge the challenges of this kind of teaching. Because it does not conform to the 'sage on the stage' archetype of teaching, some students are wary of it, mistaking the professor's acknowledgment of multiple perspectives for insecurity or lack of knowledge on the professor's part. With undergraduate and master's students, we sometimes find it useful to lead off with a style of teaching slightly more in sync with the 'sage on the stage' approach and gradually move to a more mutuality-enhancing 'guide on the side' approach once we have developed credibility as content experts. We then, eventually, make the topic of how they assess and evaluate knowledge and competence in authority figures and others part of the class dialogue.

We have found that this kind of teaching not only enhances our students' learning, but our own. Certainly, teaching reflective practice keeps us out of teaching ruts: it is never routine because it is never the same. It means being exquisitely attentive in the moment to students and the class dynamics – and the effect those dynamics are having on us. We are aware of our own fallibility and our capacity to fall into many of the traps that we explicate for our students. We do think we are relatively good at catching ourselves – and when we do, we try and offer that as a lesson to our students – and to ourselves.

REFERENCES

Argyris, C. and Schön, D. (1974) *Theory in Practice: Increasing Professional Effectiveness*. San Francisco, CA: Jossey-Bass.

Argyris, C., Putnam, R. and Smith, D. (1985) *Action Science: Concepts, Methods, and Skills for Research and Intervention*. San Francisco, CA: Jossey-Bass.

Austin, J. L. (1962) *How to Do Things with Words*. Oxford: Clarendon Press.

Banaji, M.R., Hardin, C. and Rothman, A.J. (1993) 'Implicit stereotyping in person judgment', *Journal of Personality and Social Psychology*, 65: 272–81.

Berg, D.N. and Smith, K.K. (1985) *Exploring Clinical Methods for Social Research*. London: Sage.

Bolman, L.G. and Deal, T.E. (2003) *Reframing Organizations: Artistry, Choice, and Leadership*. San Francisco, CA: Jossey-Bass.

Coghlan, D. (2004) 'Seeking God in all things: Ignatian spirituality as action research', *The Way*, 43 (1): 1–14.

Emerson, R.W. (1903) *Essays by Ralph Waldo Emerson*. London: Isbister.

Friedman, V.J. (2001/2006) 'Action science: creating communities of inquiry in communities of practice', in P. Reason, and H. Bradbury (eds), *Handbook of Action Research: Participative Inquiry and Practice*: London: Sage. pp. 1–14. Also published in P. Reason and H. Bradbury (eds) (2006), *Handbook of Action Research: Concise Paperback Edition*. London: Sage. pp. 131–43.

Friedman, V. J. and Lipshitz, R. (1992) 'Teaching people to shift cognitive gears: overcoming resistance on the road to model II', *Journal of Applied Behavioral Science*, 28 (1): 118–137.

Gergen, K.J. and Gergen, M. (2004) *Social Construction: Entering the Dialogue*. Chagrin Falls, OH: Taos Institute Publications.

Goldstein, J. (1983) *The Experience of Insight: A Simple and Direct Guide to Buddhist Meditation*. Boulder, CO: Shambhala.

Greenwald, A.G. and Banaji, M.R. (1995) 'Implicit social cognition: attitudes, self-esteem and stereotypes', *Psychological Review*, 102 (1): 4–27.

Haney, W.V. (1955) *The Uncritical Inference Test*. San Francisco, CA: International Society for General Semantics.

James, W. (1890) *The Principles of Psychology*. New York: Henry Holt & Co.

Kegan, R. (1974) *In Over our Heads: The Mental Demands of Human Life*. Cambridge, MA: Harvard University Press.

Kegan, R. (1982) Th*e Evolving Self: Problems and Process in Human Development*. Cambridge, MA: Harvard University Press.

Kegan, R. (1994) *In Over Our Heads: The Mental Demands of Modern Life*. Cambridge, MA: Harvard University Press.

Kegan, R., and Lahey, L.L. (2001) *How the Way We Talk Can Change the Way We Work*. San Francisco, CA: Jossey-Bass.

Marshall, J. and Mead, G. (2005) 'Special Issue: Self-reflective practice and first-person action research', *Action Research*, 3 (4): 233–332.

Mazen, A.M. (2000) 'Like water for chocolate: action theory for the OB class', *Journal of Management Education*, 24 (3): 304–21.

Quinn, R.E. (2000) *Change the World: How Extraordinary People Can Accomplish Extraordinary Results*. San Francisco, CA: Jossey-Bass.

Quinn, R.E., Spreitzer, G.M. and Brown, M.V. (2000) 'Changing others through changing ourselves: the transformation of human systems', *The Journal of Management Inquiry*, 9 (2): 147–164.

Reason, P. 1996. *A Participative Inquiry Paradigm*. University of Bath.

Reason, P., and Bradbury, H. (2001/2006) 'Introduction: Inquiry and participation in search of a world view worthy of human aspiration', in P. Reason, and H. Bradbury (eds), *Handbook of Action Research: Participative Inquiry and Practice*: London: Sage. pp. 1–14.

Ross, L. (1977) 'The intuitive psychologist and his short-comings: distortions in the attribution process', in L. Berkowitz (ed.), *Advances in Experimental Social Psychology*, *Vol. 10*: London: Academic Press. pp. 173–240.

Rudolph, J.W., Taylor, S.S. and Foldy, E.G. (2001/2006) Collaborative off-line reflection: a way to develop skill in action science and action inquiry', in P. Reason, and H. Bradbury (eds), *Handbook of Action Research: Participative Inquiry and Practice*. London: Sage. pp. 405–12. Also published in P. Reason and H. Bradbury (2006) (eds), *Handbook of Action Research: Concise Paperback Edition*. London: Sage. pp. 307–14.

Schön, D.A. (1983) *The Reflective Practitioner: How Professionals Think in Action*. New York: Basic Books.

Schön, D.A. (1987) *Educating the Reflective Practitioner*. San Francisco, CA: Jossey-Bass.

Schön, D. and Rein, M. (1994) *Frame Reflection*. New York: Basic Books.

Searle, J.R. (1969) *Speech Acts*. Cambridge: Cambridge University Press.

Senge, P.M. (1990) *The Fifth Discipline: The Art and Practice of the Learning Organization*. New York: Currency Doubleday.

Senge, P.M., Roberts, C., Ross, R.B., Smith, B.J. and Kleiner, A. (1994) *The Fifth Discipline Fieldbook: Strategies and Tools for Building a Learning Organization*. New York: Doubleday.

Stone, D., Patton, B. and Heen, S. (2000) *Difficult Conversations: How to Discuss What Matters Most*. Penguin Books.

Taylor, S.S. (2004) 'Presentational form in first person research: off-line collaborative reflection using art', *Action Research*, 2 (1): 71–88.

Torbert, B. et al. (2004) *Action Inquiry: The Secret of Timely and Transforming Leadership.* San Francisco, CA: Berrett-Koehler.

Torbert, W.R. (1972) *Learning from Experience: Toward Consciousness.* New York: Columbia University Press.

Torbert, W.R. (1991) *The Power of Balance: Transforming Self, Society, and Scientific Inquiry.* Newbury Park, CA: Sage.

Walsh, J.P. (1995) 'Managerial and organizational cognition: notes from a trip down memory lane', *Organization Science*, 6 (3): 280–321.

Weick, K.E. (1995) *Sensemaking in Organizations.* Thousand Oaks, CA: Sage.

47

The Praxis of Educating Action Researchers

Morten Levin

The thesis of this chapter is that action research involves both action and research and that any practitioner must have the ability to initiate and support involvement in actions as well as capability to critically reflect on process and outcomes of the action engagement. First, proficiency is needed in order to concretely and practically work with social change in order to solve participants' pertinent problems. Second, skills are needed to enable creation of sustainable cogenerative learning processes involving both problem owners and researchers in the same learning cycle. Third, the researchers must have the capability, either alone or together with the participants, to create knowledge that can be published (communicated in the broader sense) in order to contribute in the ongoing scientific and the broader societal discourses. No other role in social science demands a broader spectrum of capacities, bridging practical problem-solving, reflective and analytical thinking than an action researcher.

Action research can be mapped as a wide variety of strategies for research. Different positions emphasize a variety of capacities for the involved action researcher. The presentations of 'groundings' in this volume and in the first edition of the Handbook clearly point to this diversity through the conceptualization of action research as a knowledge-generating strategy and as professional praxis. This chapter does not intend to comprehensively cover the varied field. Rather, what I understand as skills in action

research is constructed on the basis of the epistemological position and the researcher role that is presented in Greenwood and Levin (1998/2006, 2000, 2005) and Levin and Greenwood (2001, 2007).

The thesis of this chapter is that action research involves both action and research and that any practitioner must have the ability to initiate and support involvement in action as well as capability to critically reflect on process and outcomes of the action engagement. First, proficiency is needed in order to concretely and practically work with social change in order to solve participants' pertinent problems. Second, skills are needed to enable creation of sustainable cogenerative learning processes involving both problem owners and researchers in the same learning cycle. Third, the researchers must have the capability, either alone or together with the participants, to create knowledge that can be published (communicated in the broader sense) in order to contribute in the ongoing scientific and the broader societal discourses.

No other role in social science demands a broader spectrum of capacities, bridging practical problem solving, reflective and analytical thinking than an action researcher. Various dimensions of the role are treated in books on action research (see, for example, Coghlan and Brannick, 2005; Greenwood and Levin, 1998/2006; Reason and Bradbury, 2001/2006; Stringer, 1999; also other chapters in this section), but given the complexity and the diversity of skills needed, it is astounding how little is written in the texts of action research on the researcher's role and skills.

The action research role is bi-polar because it demands both practical skills in order to advance the solution of practical problems and that the researcher has an analytical and reflective mind which provides the intellectual capability to produce texts for the scientific community. The action research professional must be both capable to intervene in concrete practical activity and to generate scientific insights. We are not used to seeing an integration of *on the spot extrovert actions* and *deep and sustained systematic introverted reflective processes* in the same person. In training action researchers, the task is both to nurture action capability and to facilitate reflective capacity.

Conventional teaching at universities unilaterally focuses on reflective and theoretical training. Even in professional training such as engineering and medicine practical skills are only moderately attended to; within the core social sciences practice is almost completely ignored.

The ethos of the Humboldtian University, which emerged in Germany in the 19th century, created a tight link between teaching and research. A professor's primary task was to build proficiency in teaching or research; a secondary effect of this was to create a disjunction between theory and praxis. The product of university work was narrowed down to researching and teaching theoretical knowledge, while practical applications were seen as a responsibility for other actors. In addition, this ethos dictated that the identification of relevant research questions should emerge from the inner circles of academia. In action research, the knowledge generation process is understood as an inquiry into a holistic real life situation where knowledge is generated through active experimentation in which problem owners and researchers co-generate knowledge (Greenwood and Levin, 1998/2006). The modern university pays little attention to the link between research, teaching, and practical problem solving. These three-dimensional tasks have to be accommodated within the ideology of a two-dimensional institution. This is the fundamental challenge of training action researchers in universities.

Academic environments have always shown hostility to activities that would break the code of the orthodox Humboldtian ideal. Would it be a contradiction in terms to aspire for a different and involved knowledge production in institutions that honor distance and disconnectedness? Could a pedagogical approach that is built on reflection and learning together with the involved problem owners, based on concrete experimentation in order to solve real life problems, grow on this potential hostile ground? Is it possible to overcome this obvious contradiction between top-down professorial lecturing to a bottom-up inquiry process lending learning opportunities for everyone involved?

The data and analysis that this chapter is built on is my own teaching experiences. The first major part of the chapter conveys in narrative form the data and experiences from where the analysis of skills is drawn. This creates, then, the backdrop for the discussion of skills in action research. The conclusion will present a perspective on the historical possibility for action research in academic institutions.

BREAKING THE PATTERN – MY JOURNEY TEACHING ACTION RESEARCH

Changing the curriculum in universities is a bureaucratic process controlled by local power-holders and strongly influenced by different professions (Clark, 1995; Silva and Slaughter, 1984). Universities are conservative mastodons that change very slowly. Individual experimentation is possible but institutionalizing change takes a long time. What follows is a narrative of how I navigated this institutional context in order to teach action research through an experimental activity which can itself be conceptualized as an action research process based on cycles of experimentation, reflection, learning, and new experimentation. Throughout this process I have balanced the innovation activity with not stirring the powerholders. 'Get it done' has been my motto.

In 1982, I was appointed associate professor at the Norwegian University of Science and Technology (NTNU). Since graduating in engineering and subsequently in sociology, prior to taking the NTNU position my main experience was with trade union education. The differences between those two worlds – the deep involvement in trade union education and the clear analytical distance as expected in university lecturing – could hardly be larger and were not easy to integrate. Over the first years, I taught in the traditional academic way. This conventional teaching soon became unsatisfactory and the accompanying frustration motivated me to seek alternatives.

I became passionately involved with experimenting with pedagogical structures, developing a surge of energy to create alternative practical teaching that gradually enhanced my understanding of what could be alternatives and what was possible in praxis. I was repeatedly surprised by the flexibility

that actually existed in the teaching system: none of my colleagues or any other official at the university ever bothered about what I was doing in my classes. In fact, I had 'carte blanche' for experimentation. It was up to my creativity and my own naiveté to create a different take on knowledge generation in an academic setting. I plunged ahead.

One structural obstacle was large classes. If the number of students in a class was higher then 50, a dramatic reduction in communication between teacher and students was evident. A second obstacle was the physical construction of the classrooms or auditoriums. The simple design of an auditorium with students roosted in a semi-circle is a dramatic hindrance to dialogues between students and instructors, whereas a classroom with a flat floor creates a very different flexibility. Time slotted in segments of 45 minutes was another constraint that administratively had its rationale but hardly could be supported by pedagogical arguments.

In developing my university teaching and subsequently teaching of action research I was 'making the road by walking', to borrow from the title of Myles Horton's and Paulo Freire's (1970/1995) book on adult education. Numerous small steps along that road, some successful and many failures, slowly created an action research praxis in teaching. This history is undoubtedly mundane; it lasted for a long period and was sprinkled with quite a lot of tripwires. Teaching for 23 years has had its 'ups and downs', but amazingly enough it created energy to continue on the road. The concrete experience from learning that students 'took off' on their own knowledge journey kept the excitement alive. Without that sense, I would never have had energy to continue.

THE FIRST MOVE – DIALOGICAL PEDAGOGY

My point of departure was not only a devotion to action research, but devastating experiences of teaching large classes (200–400 students). These large classes demanded skills in staging and acting a high-energy teacher performance, while the students learned fast to 'survive' class in total passivity. The accumulation of such experiences over some few semesters inspired me to see if I could figure out a different approach to teaching. I soon abandoned larger classes as an arena for experimentation. The smaller classes were more promising. Dialogues and conversations could easily 'criss-cross' a small class while non-teacher centric communication was practically impossible in large classes.

My first experimental arena was a class in public planning and administration. Teaching such a topic in a science and engineering university attracted few students. The class had between 8 and 15 students and diverse dialogues were possible. The communication platform existed, but the vital issue was how to bring real life problems into the classroom. The initial solution was to divide the class into teams of three to five students and make the teams figure out a regional public planning issue. It was easy for the students to find interesting and motivating real life problems. The teams had to develop their own knowledge generation question and to engage in fieldwork. My role was transformed to a critical listener, a developer of questions, and often but not always a creator of an entry point to the actual field. The students had to manage the fieldwork quite by themselves. In fact, I experienced few problems with students not being responsible and mature fieldworkers. Most of their methodological skills were learned in the field working with the concrete problem issue. This class represented one of five courses that the students had to take each semester. The learning process in class was designed to develop the students' 'projects', balanced by study of what were considered necessary substantive texts. One 'spectacular' year all four projects in the class made it to the front page of the regional newspaper, so at least the relevance was not in question.

It was amazing to observe the strong motivation created by working on real life problems. Students devoted so much time and energy to these assignments that they complained of not having enough time for their other courses. However, a clear signal of the effectiveness of this approach was that they in no way wanted to reduce their engagement in the projects. Talking to and learning from people for whom the problem situation was real created this extreme energy for hard and concentrated work. I could see how it was possible to bring in real life problems, but it was still a mystery how potential change activity could be integrated into the teaching activity. For many years I refined this model of teaching and actually wrote a technical report identifying it as 'dialogical pedagogy' (Levin, 1989).

This way of teaching in small classes was not only stimulating for students, but equally rewarding for myself as teacher and co-learner. One of the unexpected and nice experiences was the day I dropped by the students' workspace and found a flip-chart from one class taped up on the backside of the entrance door. It was of course incomprehensible for anyone that had not been present in the class, and hardly possible in the aftermath of the engaged classroom discussion to interpret. When I asked the students why they had kept this flip-chart, they told me that it signified the learning dynamic in the class and their commitment to the joint learning process. This pedagogical approach was obviously a route to follow, but it took many years before I managed to create a design that would be closer to that of the action research process.

SECOND WAVE – TOWARDS TEACHING ACTION RESEARCH

The public planning and administration course was replaced by a new course in organizational development (OD) which was primarily a course for students in technology management. This course made possible a new take on teaching in the style of action research. First, the modeling of OD was built on the co-generative model of action research (Elden and Levin, 1991; Greeenwood and Levin, 1998/2006). Second, it was natural in a course modeled on action research to plan for and reflect on change processes in time-line perspective. Change does not happen in the blink of an eye, but is a process that evolves over time. Initially I worked out a concept based on using a written up case. These cases were built on my own field experience, and as such were clearly influenced by my own analytical perspective. The cases indicated a transparent problem statement and the OD literature created the backdrop for a structured project design and development. The general framing of the assignment was to make sense of what issues were at stake in the actual organization and to develop a plan for an OD process.

I worked along these lines for some time and the teaching was quite well received by the students and obviously socially and intellectually stimulating for myself. Student enrollment was high (30 to 50). The classes worked well, almost to the extent that I every now and then envisioned it as the best teaching I had ever done. Students' evaluation was quite favorable and the status of the course was respectable. Feedback from students included: 'You take this course in order to learn; you have to work as much in this course as in all the other courses together this semester; you will need what you learn in this course when you start your professional life.' Altogether, this was quite stimulating and led me to search for even better solutions to making the knowledge generation process in the class look more like real life.

The first development was easy as it involved the simple trick of asking the students to write an OD plan that was built on stating the goal for the activity, arguing for practical developmental activity and how to evaluate and restructure the learning and change activity as it unfolded. The assignment had three stages. First, the students had to develop an assessment of the organization's strengths and weaknesses. This analysis was the foundation for the first OD plan.

Subsequently, the students received a simulated feedback on this plan, based on experiences I had gained from working with OD in a number of organizations, that forced them to change or redevelop initial plans. The simulated development was handed to students in the form of half a page of text. These simulations were built on years of experience with running action research processes in organizations. This very modest change in structure created a dramatic change in the whole assignment. In fact, it simulated a dynamic change situation and clarified that planning an OD process is only a forecast and not a final blueprint for how things would evolve. Students took the simulation seriously and we had many fierce battles over the potential incomprehensibility and inconsistency of the simulated feedback. This was of course perfect since the students first had to make sense of the feedback. This small 'trick' was a way to formulate an open question and make the whole teaching situation somewhat like real life. This was a very simple idea, but it crossed most of what I considered to be untouchable boundaries for teaching at NTNU.

The further development of this open question approach was that data could be used in a much more sophisticated way in classes. What about presenting a case without a clear or intended focus of attention? The technological option created by computerized streaming of video opened new possibilities. What about taping on video a number of moderately structured conversations with some people in an organization and then streaming them to make them accessible for looking at and listening to on a computer? This video streaming approach turned out to be fairly time consuming. First, I had to use my contacts in industry or public administration to get access to the organization. Confidentiality issues had to be solved, relevant persons to be identified and subsequently interviewed, and finally I had to create a CD for viewing on PCs. The recording sessions usually lasted for a full day. Initially I played with the idea that the video could be uploaded to a server, but this was abandoned due to issues of confidentiality. The contract with the actual organization was based on the expectation that the material and the reports were confidential and only used for teaching purposes. Confidentiality was secured as the students signed a declaration of confidentiality and we guaranteed to keep close track of the CDs. In an early phase of the teaching members from the 'case' organization were invited to give a guest lecture which created an opportunity to present their experiences and perspectives of their own organization. This was usually done in a two or three hour session in the class. Some weeks into the semester, either at a video conference or in class, people from the 'case' organization attended a 'questioning' session where students could seek additional information.

The assignment was simple: 'Develop an OD plan that improves this organization's operation.' This straightforward and un-precise problem statement (actually lack of it) frustrated many students. The formidable experiential situation highlighted how real life situations are messy and unclear. An important segment of professional capability is actually to make sense of a holistic and complex real life situation and to be able to formulate a grounded understanding.

Finally, at the end of the course, members of the actual organization were invited to participate in the students' final presentation where direct and grounded feedback was given from the problem owners. The students' analysis and OD planning were always well received by the organizational members, even though the report often had a critical stance.

A demanding and time-consuming part of this assignment was to analyze the interviews. This was problematic and challenging as the students had only rudimentary knowledge of data gathering and analysis. It was necessary to give a crash course in data analysis and the students were advised to watch the CDs in pairs to enable a necessary minimal control over the understanding and sensemaking process.

This approach to teaching was engaging but also very demanding for the students because it differed so much from what they experienced in other courses. The reception by students and by my colleagues was quite positive, the teaching was quite successful, and I was awarded the university's prize for innovative pedagogy. But is it fundamentally a way to train students in action research? The most evident disconnection from an action research process is the lack of direct exposure to the field. It is simply impossible to send out 30 to 50 students to almost any kind of location. In addition, it is certainly impossible for the students to take on responsibility for running an action research based change process. This would be neither socially nor logistically possible. Involving students in the field is not an option unless there are less than perhaps 10 students in the class. However, this video-based presentation and later simulation of a change process was sufficiently realistic to train undergraduates in some elements of action research. The focus for intervention had to a certain degree to be negotiated with locals, and students had to seriously think through and argue for what kind of learning arenas they suggested in order to support change.

THIRD THEATER – ACTION RESEARCH PHD PROGRAMS

The quintessence of an action research intervention is to create opportunities for collective learning through integrating local members and action researchers in the same reflection and learning process. For me, the most promising educational action research activity has been the PhD training, for the students are more mature when they enroll and the program involves at least four years of deep intellectual engagement. One obvious way to organize a PhD program is to center it on individual action research projects, where the advisor(s) directly support and guide the student both in the field and in academic reflection and writing. This individualistic type of advising recreates the one-to-one relationship seen in conventional PhD programs. Throughout my career, I have designed three larger PhD programs (a more detailed presentation of these programs is contained in Levin, 2003). The first generation program was built around a larger Norwegian evaluation effort. The program had seven students in the cohort and two responsible professors, one of whom left after the first year of operation. In order to manage the work load I involved a number of national and international scholars both to teach and to advise. The student group developed a strong collective spirit, and gradually took initiatives to organize seminars and invite professionals to speak. This created a different and more symmetrical balance between students and mentors. The structured progression of the advising sessions also supported the individual progression. All participating students graduated from the program.

The next program had a focus on creating transdisciplinary knowledge in the field of operation of a chemical process plant. The program had nine students, four with engineering background and five with a background from organization and leadership. The staff comprised four professors, two engineers and two from social science. The program was organized around bi-weekly seminars, enabling in-depth discussion that included all students and professors. These discussions were probably the most successful part of the program, and greatly enjoyed by all participants. The students worked in peer groups and in the earlier phases the cooperation and integrated development created elements of transdisciplinary knowledge, but when students started to dig deep into the thesis research they reverted more to disciplinary perspectives. The student group was more fragmented and did not develop the same strong peer culture as in the previous program. In many respects, the most interesting outcome was for the participating professors, who managed to create a playful transdisciplinary discourse broadening the perspectives created by the conventional disciplines. The group did not produce much in terms of conventional academic output, but the one paper we managed to create collectively won the best prize award at an international conference.

The third PhD effort intended to create an international program in work life action research. The program had initially 24 students and a staff of nine – five Norwegian members and four international – and was planned to operate for four years. The program was funded by the Norwegian Research Council and was closely connected to a regional developmental program (Value Creation 2010; see also Chapter 4 in this Handbook). The program was organized in four yearly one week sessions (16 weeks altogether) and with a strong emphasis that students should follow the pre-programmed plan to enable them to finish by the end of the fourth year. The program has so far been successful in creating a network among participating students, but the broad spectrum of competence held by the nine staff members turned easily dysfunctional because it was difficult to coordinate positions in such a way that they made sense for the students. The program will end by December 2006 and a preliminary analysis indicates that the program had too many students and too large a staff. The next generation program, which will start in January 2007, will only have 16 students and a permanent staff of five.

THE CHALLENGES IN ACTION RESEARCH EDUCATION AND THE ASSOCIATED SKILLS

Action research obviously includes both action and research. It presupposes an ability to *act* in order to solve pertinent problems and it demands that these actions aiming to resolve pertinent questions also lead to a *research based* reflection process. Skills to promote action and intellectual capacity to enable social science research must be contained in the same person.

I now devote attention to identifying and discussing skills involved in educating action researchers. Two perspectives on skills will be relevant for this discussion. First, educating action researchers will demand professorial skills understood as competencies of a substantial and pedagogical nature that *teachers would have to master in order to be competent facilitators* for action research education. Second, educating action researchers will have to be grounded on an understanding of what kind of *skills are mandatory for professional work* as an action researcher. These two sets of skills are separate but interconnected. A professor cannot teach action research unless the pedagogical perspective is aligned to the core values and processes of action research. In addition, the teaching has to include training in skills that are necessary for engaging in action research.

The discussion will be structured around an identification of the current challenges in action research education. This is the point of departure for discussing skills for the action researchers and skills for teachers. Its focus is to raise the principal issue of what level should action research be taught at and should it be organized in separate courses.

Should Action Research be a Separate Course or Integrated in Ordinary Undergraduate Courses?

A general learning from teaching methods in social science is that it is very difficult if not impossible to teach method separate from substantial issues. Method is intrinsically linked to the theories, concepts and the praxis of research within each profession. Disconnecting methods from the professional content leads to loss of epistemological underpinning, so integrating teaching of method with content in everyday teaching is essential. Introducing action research as a method in teaching different disciplines is very important in order to show that it is a useful alternative that can be integrated into the methodological repertoire giving access to new types of data, different experiences from the field, a different take on sensemaking, and alternative ways of dealing with reliability and validity.

Introducing action research in social science teaching creates a praxis where students take more responsibility for their own learning process simply because the teaching will be driven by the actual problem focus. In this perspective, the teacher will have to connect the students to people's working and living conditions outside of the university or to create opportunities that have similarities with a real life situation through elaborate use of multi-media technologies.

I am clearly in favor of integrating action research in everyday teaching but I realize also that there are courses that cannot be designed to accommodate action research principles. Two issues are important. First, action research calls for the teaching to be constructed from real life problems. With this premise, the pedagogical process must integrate theoretical reflection and reasoning with the concrete problem solving process. Students will acquire understanding of the research process, but in undergraduate education they will not have the capabilities to enable quality research. Second, dealing with real life problems creates a sound platform for substantial professional knowledge because everyday social practice will create the opportunity to reflect on social science theories. In addition, the action research teaching directs attention to how social change processes can contribute to a resolution of a concrete practical problem. From my own experience, this action-oriented approach to social science is a premise for engaging in change activity. Students who have finished undergraduate education without this perspective in their hands and mind have real difficulties later in engaging in change related practice. The distant analytical perspectives of traditional teaching and research hamper the ability and willingness to risk involvment in change activity because the grounded role model for a professional is the distant observer.

The core argument is that action research should be integrated in teaching social science, but such integration will demand new pedagogical approaches and a focus on the dynamics of social systems instead of promoting a static conceptualization.

Mentor/Apprentice and Collective Reflection

The skills required in action research cannot be precisely formulated as written role requirements simply because they are deeply integrated with the action researcher's actions (Ryle, 1949). The heart of the mentor/ apprentice relationship is the creation of learning possibilities directly linked to concrete praxis, either through mutual engagement in the shared work or in reflecting on shared work experiences. This training can only take place in real life situations. Students and advisors have to share responsibility for the design of learning processes that enable both reflection in action and reflection on action (Schön, 1983). The advisor must concretely be engaged in the field and be able to manage the art of *reflection in action* and through that make it possible to see and understand why and how actions are taken (see also Chapter 46 in this Handbook). *Reflection on action* is much easier as this has the character of experiential learning and there is some distance to the actual events.

This alliance of an experienced mentor and an apprentice eager to learn can, if all goes well, lead to valuable in-depth cooperation. In contrast, if it doesn't work, it can easily become a disaster. Insights necessary for running action research projects are acquired through working in the field and in conversations with experienced actors. The essence of the learning process is conversations between mentors and apprentice through concrete problem-solving and common reflections on actions taken. The mentor/apprentice relationship is asymmetrical and unbalanced. The mentor has the power grounded in the skills of a proficient action researcher and in control over the project's social and economic resources. A key issue in the mentor/apprentice relationship is the gradual transfer of control to the apprentice. This challenging situation has to be dealt with very consciously and carefully by the mentor. In the three major PhD programs described above, the asymmetrical one-to-one relationship has been compensated through creating advising teams consisting of more than one professor.

A strength of the mutual presence in the field is that the experiences are shared, whereas it is possible to engage in 'reflection on' processes without necessarily sharing the same experiences. The mentor/apprentice relationships are obviously most powerful when the mentors also are present in the field but, to a certain degree, the same relations can be developed when mentor and apprentice reflect on experiences. However, the very important reflection in action process can never be substituted by working together in the field as this reflection process is inevitably linked to the concrete project activity.

Furthermore, the relationship between students and professor in everyday teaching models a mentor/apprentice relationship. The kind of dialogues that shape the learning situation will model how professional knowledge can be communicated and made relevant for the students, a conversation that actually is the same as the one that underpins concrete action research activity.

Collective Reflection for Advisors and Students

In conventional PhD programs individual students meets individual professors, creating what we have identified as an asymmetrical relationship. The asymmetry is equally problematic for the powerholder and for the students subject to authority, as I have pointed out in the previous section. One solution to this problem has been to build peer groups of students and faculty cooperation in teaching and advising. It seems important to create PhD programs that have a minimum intellectual 'mass' to enable broad and diverse discourse on the epistemology and the praxis of action research. This enables a reflective space that is important both for the student community and for the communication between students and professors. A secondary effect of creating a PhD program in action research is that it also makes it possible to create a team of teachers cooperating in advising students.

In addition, cooperation between teachers in mentoring and teaching has the important side effect of creating a reflection space for advisors, both regarding professional knowledge and in advising. This kind of cooperation does not come easily to professors. Large egos and fierce competition might easily destroy the potential of peer learning. Good cooperation is extremely valuable but hard to achieve.

For students it is even more important to gain access to colloquial groups. Probably the most recorded single dissatisfactory factor in a traditional PhD program is the disconnectedness from other students. In undergraduate education, this is equally important, but probably easier to shape the conditions for. One way forward is to create a group of students that are involved in action research and use this peer group as a joint learning arena (Levin, 2003). It has turned out that much of what is needed to become a professional takes place in peer-based discourses, both with regard to fieldwork and to make sense of the relevant literature. This is the road I am now following in PhD programs where a cohort of students (9 to 20) follow in parallel the teaching and advising. Each student has more then one advisor, and the whole faculty cooperates in teaching and advising. The underlying idea is to have both a student collective and a collective spirit among the faculty. With a smaller faculty, it has been possible to create good cooperation.

Training Must Include Tacit Components (Knowing How)

Running action research projects is practical work. Learning arenas have to be envisioned and practically made operational. Communicating, cooperating, and engaging in practical problem solving are all practical and concrete tasks. The necessary 'knowing how' (Ryle, 1949) to do such work is undoubtedly one of the most important skills in the action research repertoire. These knowing how skills embedded in action are vital to action research: no one can become a proficient practitioner unless they have appropriated the necessary tacit knowing. The best way to enhance the students' inventory in knowing how is to have them engaged in the concrete practical activity of projects. In addition, two teaching strategies have been shown to be feasible. First, as has been discussed above, creating video-based simulation exercises forces the student to actively engage in making decisions on how a change process should be conducted. Second, exercises can be created that engage the students both as executors and as participants, as in the well developed tradition of group dynamic exercises (Kolb et al., 1971). Alternatively, the students can be asked to design and conduct a search conference (Emery, 1999) on issues of importance for the class, which give students experience both as facilitators and participants in change and learning processes. Through planning for participation in learning processes and as a consequence of being a participant, students can have access to the know how necessary for running change processes and the tacit knowing of being a participant in the same processes.

Framing Research Questions From Everyday Life Experiences

In conventional social science the modus operandi is to develop research questions from a reading of the literature which makes the research frontier solely dependent on the issues of concern to the research community. In action research, the research should support the effort to solve pertinent local problems that are shaped by everyday experience.

However, this is only half the truth for, as Greenwood and Levin (1998/2006) demonstrate through their cogenerative model of action research, good research questions are developed at the borderline between local understanding and academic-based insights. The action research practitioner needs skills to enable such a fusion of perspectives and this proficiency must be developed through the teaching process. The primary ability is to listen and understand the problem owners' points of view, to relate that to substantive knowledge in the area, to seek out potential alternative ways of making sense of the situation and to communicate this position back in such a way that it creates new insights for all involved.

In practical teaching, the core problem is get access to how local people construct a problem horizon. If the students are working in a real life situation this is straightforward, they automatically have access to local problem statements. If this is not possible the option of the multi-media approach described above is available. The task is to create a bridge between local problems and scientific questions. This forces the students (and the professors) to have an understanding of the relationship between theory and practice. I have often experienced this as a very difficult issue simply because students seldom are asked to reflect more than on the theoretical level. Connecting theory and practice raises issues that span beyond the description and understanding of a social situation by making visible questions of how this knowledge can be used for improving the participants' life situation. It is easy to see how university education creates barriers for shaping research questions from everyday experiences. But this issue is not really so difficult to tackle in everyday teaching, for the teacher can confront students with the practical implications of theoretical positions by always asking students to consider what their practical recommendation would be in a given practical problem situation, drawing on theoretical insights. The second and more difficult element is to create communication

skills for students that will enable them to understand what problem owners are talking about and enable students to talk back on the premises of professional knowledge. These communication skills penetrate all practical action research work, and they are impossible to teach in the classroom without practical experience.

Writing the Action Research PhD Thesis

The hallmark for PhD education is the ability to transform the research into a PhD thesis. A PhD is conventionally understood as a sign of craft competence in research and it is now more than ever a mandatory prerequisite for an academic career and the ability to compete for research funds. There is no future road for action research unless it finds a sound location in academia (Greenwood and Levin 2005; Levin and Greenwood, 2001, Chapter 14 in this Handbook), and the prerequisite for that is to ensure that enough action researchers have the necessary qualifications to compete for and win academic positions. The major challenge is to integrate both the deep involvement and reflective distance, to write a thesis that captures the richness of active engagement in the social change process and at the same time lends enough weight to the researcher's critical distance to the process that he or she has been engaged in. One mode of writing is to organize the thesis to communicate the gradual learning that takes place in an action research process, singling out major incidents, identifying what has been learnt through the practical achievements and what new actions were taken. In this way the thesis shifts from the traditional linear structure to a cyclical spiral of reflection and action that gradually creates new practical results and new conceptual insights.

A PhD will demand command over all the skills elements I have been arguing for in the previous sections. It is also evident that it would be beneficial for the students to have met action research based teaching before entering a PhD program. If not, they will have to be in the fast lane in order to both handle action elements as well as the critical reflections that are engraved in the research practice.

CONCLUSION

The thrust of my argument is that PhD training is key and this is where we should concentrate our efforts. It is at the PhD level that students learn the craft of research. But this does not mean that all training in action research should be postponed until PhD training. This is a too simple a conclusion. Even though the argument is that in action research action and reflection are intertwined, this does not necessarily imply that all training in action and reflection have to be simultaneous and parallel. One option is to have a major focus on processes of change in courses at undergraduate level. Such training would shape professionals that can master participative change processes with an emphasis on collective and mutual learning. These skills are necessary for an action researcher, and they should be present in a repertoire of proficiencies that are one important building block for the training in action research.

In conventional social science training, the students learn the basics of the discipline's vocabulary, theories, and knowledge generating procedures. This enables them to work later as professionals. These grounding concepts of social life create the backdrop for interpreting social reality and subsequently advising concrete actions to solve pertinent problems. These courses seldom make it to the point that the students learn how to support concrete actions. An in-depth understanding of social process and social structures are the knowledge base upon which social change activity is founded. Practicing change is not disconnected from theoretical reflections and it is my experience that if basic skills in organizing social change are not engraved in the student's mind

through the undergraduate program, it is very hard later to acquire the competency. The socialization to an analytical and detached social scientist is all too strong.

These capabilities in change are important to enable an integration of research and action. This combination will necessarily have to take place in PhD programs. It is at this level students gain the necessary proficiencies theoretically, methodologically, and analytically to operate as a skilled researcher. If action research intends to be part of the current international debate in the research community, there is no option to bypass proficiency in research. Accordingly, PhD education for action researchers is necessary. The challenge is to create PhD programs that really combine action and research.

Institutions of higher education can accommodate the education of action researchers. Constraints created by conventional academic practice shape a background from which action research education will have to be crafted. My experiences have shown that action research teaching can be accommodated in higher education. In an earlier paper I have described the introduction of PhD education action research as a process in disguise until it is shown to be practically feasible through making it happen (Levin, 2003).

In the changing university of today (see Levin and Greenwood, 2001, Chapter 14; Greenwood and Levin, 2005) there is a swing away from disconnected and abstract towards contextualized and concrete social science. Training action researchers in universities has also potentially a much broader perspective. In this chapter I have suggested that teaching action research creates a different type of professional able to combine contextualized problem-solving, knowledge generation that includes local actors and insights communicated to the scientific world. This is precisely what Gibbons et al. (1994) and Nowotny et al. (2001) envisage as the essence of the new situated knowledge generation where the new knowledge is negotiated between scientists and problem owners. This is what cogeneration of knowledge is all about. If the Gibbons/Nowotny perspectives sketch the direction which university knowledge production will take, action research is currently the mode of doing research that is closest to this ideal. This should be a strong argument for pursuing on a broad basis the education of action researchers in institutions of higher education. This is the road to follow in order to not only expand action research but also to change higher education and revitalize it to become a knowledge producer that impacts social development.

ACKNOWLEDGMENT

Davydd J. Greenwood, Ann W. Martin, David Coghlan, and Peter Reason have contributed with critical and constructive comments to earlier drafts of this chapter. The comments have been most helpful for the development of the chapter.

REFERENCES

Clark, R.B. (1995) *Places of Inquiry: Research and Education in Modern Universities.* Los Angeles, CA: University of California Press.

Coghlan, D. and Brannick, T. (2005) *Doing Research in Your Own Organization, 2nd edn.* London: Sage.

Denzin, N.K. and Lincoln, Y.S (2000) *The Sage Handbook of Qualitative Research, 2nd edn.* Thousand Oaks, CA: Sage.

Denzin, N.K. and Lincoln, Y.S. (2005) *The Sage Handbook of Qualitative Research, 3rd edn.* Thousand Oaks, CA: Sage.

Elden, M. and Levin, M. (1991) 'Cogenerative learning: bringing participation into action research', in White (ed.), *Participatory Action Research.* Newbury Park, CA: Sage.

Emery, F.E. (ed.) (1999) *Systems Thinking.* London: Penguin.

Freire, P (1970) *The Pedagogy of the Oppressed.* New York: Herder & Herder.

Gibbons, M., Limoges, C., Nowotny, H., Schwartzman, S., Scott, P. and Trow, M. (1994) *The New Production of Knowledge: the Dynamics of Science and Research in Contemporary Societies.* London: Sage.

Greenwood, D.J. and Levin, M. (1998/2006) *Introduction to Action Research: Social Research for Social Change.* Newbury Park, CA: Sage.

Greenwood, D.J. and Levin, M. (2000) 'Reconstructing the relationship between universities and society through action research', in N.K. Denzin and Y.S. Lincoln (eds), *The Sage Handbook of Qualitative Research, 2nd edn.* Newbury Park, CA: Sage. pp. 85–106.

Greenwood, D.J. and Levin, M. (2005) 'Reform of the social sciences and of universities through action research', in N.K. Denzin and Y.S. Lincoln (eds), *The Sage Handbook of Qualitative Research, 3rd edn.* Thousand Oaks, CA: Sage. pp. 43–64.

Horton, M. and Freire, P. (1970/1995) *We Make the Road by Walking* (ed. B. Bell, J. Gaventa and J. Peters). Philadelphia: Temple University Press.

Kolb, D.A., Rubin, M. and McIntyre, J.M. (1971) *Organizational Psychology: An Experiential Approach.* Englewood Cliffs, NJ: Prentice Hall.

Levin, M (1989) *Dialogisk pedagogikk* (Dialogical Pedagogy). Trondheim: ORAL-NTH.

Levin, M. (2003) 'Ph.D. programs in action research: can they be housed in universities?', *Concepts and Transformation,* 8 (3): 219–38.

Levin, M. and Greenwood, D.J. (2001) 'Pragmatic action research and the struggle to transform universities into learning communities', in P. Reason and H. Bradbury (eds), *Handbook of Action Research: Participative Inquiry and Practice.* London: Sage. pp. 103–13.

Levin, M. and Greenwood, D. (2007) 'The future of universities: Action research and the transformation of higher education' in P. Reason and H. Bradbury *The SAGE Handbook of Action Research: Participative Inquiry and Practice, 2nd edn.* London: Sage. pp. 211–26.

Nowotny, H., Scott, P. and Gibbons, M. (2001) *Re-Thinking Science Knowledge and the Public in an Age of Uncertainty.* London: Sage.

Reason, P. and Bradbury, H. (2001/2006) *Handbook of Action Research: Participative Inquiry and Practice.* London: Sage.

Ryle, G (1949) *The Concept of Mind.* London: Hutchinson.

Schön, D.A. (1983) *The Reflective Practitioner: How Professionals Think in Action.* New York: Basic Books

Silva, E.T. and Slaughter, S.A. (1984) *Serving Power: The Making of the Academic Social Science Expert.* Westport: Greenwood Press.

Stringer, E.T. (1999) *Action Research, 2nd edn.* Thousand Oaks, CA: Sage.

Whyte, W. F. (ed.) (1991) *Participatory Action Research.* Newbury Park, CA: Sage Publications.

48

Finding Form in Writing for Action Research

Judi Marshall

This chapter explores how form emerges and can be worked with in writing action research. It considers notions of form, and advocates writing in which form, content and thematic contribution are analogically congruent. Virginia Woolf's *The Waves* (which explores patterns of thought and the nature of identity) is taken as an exemplar of such resonance. A strand in the chapter considers what can be learnt from Woolf's approach to writing. Conventions and the politics of form in writing are discussed. The chapter offers practices for enabling writers to find appropriate form. It gives a range of illustrations of the processes involved. Attention is paid to the need to craft writing to achieve desired effects, so that it can communicate artfully to the reader. Issues of voice and potential silencing are also considered.

ASPIRATIONS

The sun had not yet risen. The sea was indistinguishable from the sky, except that the sea was slightly creased as if a cloth had wrinkles in it. Gradually as the sky whitened a dark line lay on the horizon dividing the sea from the sky and the grey cloth became barred with thick strokes moving, one after another, beneath the surface, following each other, pursuing each other, perpetually.

As they neared the shore each bar rose, heaped itself, broke and swept a thin veil of white water across the sand. The wave paused, and then drew out again, sighing like a sleeper whose breath comes and goes unconsciously.

(opening lines of *The Waves*; Woolf, 1931/1992: 3)

[*The Waves*] is an exploration of the workings of the minds of the six named characters within the text. … The life-span of the six. … is conveyed through a series of 'dramatic soliloquies', interspersed with passages of depersonalized prose which describe constantly shifting patterns of light and water passing from dawn to dusk, spring to winter, across the globe. (Flint, 1992: ix)

No author's comment or interpretation is offered. The novel can be read as Woolf's investigation of patterns of thought and the nature of identity (Briggs, 2005; Flint, 1992). Identity is not portrayed as information about the characters, but as primarily constructed from within, through an individual's deployment of language. ... All the speakers in *The Waves* have certain set phrases or habits of thinking to which they return, carrying them through life like talismans. .... It is through such verbal accretion, Woolf suggests, that identity establishes itself .... the image of waves, with their incessant, recurrent dips and crests, provides a far more helpful [than 'stream of consciousness'] means of understanding Woolf's representation of consciousness as something which is certainly fluid, but cyclical and repetitive, rather than linear. (Flint, 1992: x–xi)

When I first read *The Waves* I was so excited. Academic writing seldom does this for me. The form and informing motif of the novel were so congruent with its themes that I lived the latter richly, without that strong a conceptual sense of all I was exploring. Only later did I articulate what I felt in the novel's construction and ideas, and seek out commentaries.

In this chapter I explore how form emerges and can be worked with in writing. I draw on my experiences of writing and of supporting other writers, especially graduate students doing action research. In these activities I have pursued long-term interests in issues of voice, overcoming silencing, multiple forms of knowing and finding form. I use examples from my own experience and from other people I know as I can tell the processes involved more fully.

Some features of who I am may be relevant to this chapter. For example, I tend towards introversion and working through intuition. Whilst these are not fixed preferences, they may explain my wish when writing alone to scurry away into a protected corner with a view of interesting surroundings (especially of hills and trees). Your preferences may be different. But, in my experience, for many people writing involves a movement inwards to enable their movement outwards into expression.

This chapter incorporates different forms. As I write and publicly present this material, the tone of advocacy, of making a case, keeps coming through, and so shapes the first half of the chapter. Some of my thinking about finding form finds expression as direct invitations or injunctions to the potential

writer. This voice is appropriate in the writing workshops I run. I adopt it in the second half of the chapter, offering practices to enable writing, with illustrative stories. The analysis and processes presented imply a solo writer (perhaps in a phase of writing alone in order to present drafts to co-inquirers), but can be adapted to writing with others. Thirdly, I thread into the chapter notes *in italics* on what I learn from Virginia Woolf's writing of *The Waves*, my aspirational exemplar of the kind of congruence between form, content and thematic contribution which I am advocating here.

I have held my process open, but a more 'creative' form has not emerged for this chapter. So I feel a sense of paradox; I advocate experimentation and yet this writing is relatively conventional. This, then, is an aspirational text.

This chapter is a small addition to the burgeoning literature about writing and representation. There is a great deal happening, for example in qualitative research, as scholars work creatively beyond the crises of legitimation and representation outlined by Denzin and Lincoln (2005). Conventions of realism in writing have been fundamentally, irrevocably, challenged. I can assume, rather than argue, therefore, that there is no one objective reality to be discovered and portrayed, that there are multiple (potentially shifting) 'truths' seen from different perspectives, and that writing only, but potentially valuably, represents the constructed perspective of the author(s). I welcome experiments with diverse forms of writing which reflect the contentious, provisional, perspectival and multi-faceted nature of knowing (Denzin and Lincoln, 2005; Eisner, 1993; Ellis and Bochner, 2000; Lather et al., 1997; Richardson, 2000; Sparkes, 2003; Weil, 1996).

I do not seek to encompass all these developments here lest I lose my own intent, which is to offer a focused contribution on working with those tentative, precious moments in which form is coming into being. I shall suggest that often we need to 'listen' to what form our writing is seeking to take because this has analogic congruence, in some way, with the substantive themes we are exploring or to our relationship with them as inquirers. We can then craft the emerging form, to communicate out to the reader.

In the next section I say what I mean by form and why I think it so important as a focus of attention.

NOTIONS OF FORM

By form, I mean the shape of the writing – its pattern, style, flow and eventual structure. While form can be distinguished notionally from content – what the text purports to be about – in practice these are inseparable. No content can appear without form of some kind. Czarniawska (1997) thinks this language potentially misleading. Talking about analyzing identity as narrative, she says 'the traditional "form and content" dichotomy unavoidably brings to mind an image of form as something external, holding the content within it ("a container"). This makes it seem perfectly possible to analyze form regardless of content and content regardless of form' (p. 47). She prefers to borrow the terminology of *material* and *device* from the Russian formalist Bakhtin (1928/1985), because the notion of an 'outer/inner dichotomy vanishes and it is thus easier to see why one cannot be considered without the other' (p. 47). There can, then, be no material without device, no device without material. Even if we seek to analyze a device, 'it simply becomes a material to be elaborated with the use of a meta-device, as it were' (p. 47). In this chapter I work with Czarniawska's appropriate cautions, but continue to use the terminology of 'form', because it is widespread and because I enjoy its associations – in-forming, formative and so on.

All writing has form. All form communicates, something. In conventional academic scholarship, which seems alarmingly impervious to any crises of representation and legitimacy (Denzin and Lincoln, 2005), much form communicates a deadening and suppression of voice, depersonalization, acquiescence to norms. Well established conventions favour linear arguments, rationalized discourse, quantitative analysis (or similar principles applied to qualitative data), value neutrality and so on. Understanding is expected to confer potential control. These are political, gender-associated, issues about how knowledge is framed. And much of the resulting writing is dull, boring and poorly contextualized as a result.

To reach beyond these conventions and pay more attention to form, I draw on a distinction between digital and analogic aspects of communication (Watzlawick et al., 1967). In digital communication 'the relation between the name and the thing named is an arbitrarily established one' (p. 61). Meaning can be conveyed with some precision within the conventions of such a language system, and it is possible to communicate negation, that something is not. 'In analogic communication, on the other hand, there is something particularly "thing-like" in what is used to express the thing' (p. 62). It is based on likeness, similarity. It includes 'virtually all non-verbal communication', including body movement, 'posture, gesture, facial expression, voice inflection, the sequence, rhythm, and cadence of the words themselves. … as well as the communicational clues unfailingly present in any *context* in which an interaction takes place' (p. 62). Watzlawick et al. suggest that analogic communication has its roots in more archaic periods of evolution, and is therefore of more 'general validity' (p. 62).

Analogic communication is especially used to convey the nature of relationship (Bateson, 1973) and therefore signals the status of digital messages. 'It is easy to profess something verbally, but difficult to carry a lie into the realm of the analogic' (Watzlawick et al., 1967: 63).

However much we name and frame what we think we are doing (Fisher et al., 2003), form is a meta communication, analogically 'framing' that digital attempt at clarification, which may thus be contradicted or rendered meaningless (Watzlawick et al., 1967).

Analogic communication typically has a 'curiously ambiguous quality' as it 'has no qualifiers to indicate which of ... discrepant meanings is implied' (p. 65). Digital and analogic communication complement each other, and the former is always accompanied by the latter. We can seek to translate from one to the other, but there are always irreducible differences; 'information' of some kind is always beyond translation.

I am interested in analogic aspects of writing, because form is often taken for granted or conventionalized. As writers we need to be thoughtful about analogic communication, and the ways of knowing we depict and invoke. And we cannot choose how form will be received and interpreted.

ADVOCATING CONGRUENCE OF FORM AND CONTENT

I advocate a notion of 'analogic appropriateness', in which form and content are congruent in some way – when the analogic reflects the issues explored, and therefore the digital symbolic messages, in a kind of mirroring, when something is an example of itself (a concatenation of resonances as achieved in *The Waves*). Apprehending this is as much a felt experience as a cognitive understanding. For example, a piece of writing about fragmented knowing can itself be fragmented, providing a mirroring or resonance that also communicates. Then the text is 'informative' in itself, although what we experience may be partly tacit.

Finding form is partly an aesthetic matter. But it is not only about potential beauty, harmony, elegance. It is about the aesthetics of whatever needs to be, including that of ugliness, fragmentation or discord, if appropriate. Artists know this. For example Edward and Nancy Reddin Kienholz confront us with political and systemic conundrums and abuses of power through their pieced together, sometimes rough hewn, figures and scenes that are *crafted* to achieve that effect. This is my aspiration. But sadly, most action

researchers are not artists. 'The greater freedom to experiment with textual form. ... does not guarantee a better product' (Richardson, 2000: 936).

Nonetheless, we need to develop the crafts of working multi-dimensionally through representation, so that all scholars question their processes of knowing and forms of representation as an artist or novelist might do.

Finding form is also an epistemological and political matter (see Chapter 27). Generating appropriate forms to express our work draws from and therefore has the potential to communicate or evoke multiple ways of knowing – intuitive, emotional, tacit, embodied knowing alongside the propositional. Sometimes content cannot be expressed until a compatible version of form is achieved.

With others (Clough, 1992; Denzin and Lincoln, 2005; Richardson, 2000), I advocate writing as a method of inquiry, as a formative, integrated research process rather than a later stage when what is already known is 'written up'. 'There is, in the final analysis, no difference between writing and fieldwork' (Clough, 1992: 10).

And I see the presentation of the resulting writing as also often a continuation of inquiry, an offering to engage the reader and stimulate debate. In this we can be more or less deliberately provocative. I enjoy work in which the core issues of contention in sensemaking are made available to the reader – through form as well as content, for example in devices which render interpretation problematic – to stimulate their exploration. This is a genre of third person action research (Reason and Torbert, 2001).

Learning from Woolf: Working with intent

Woolf wanted to develop 'a new kind of play ... prose yet poetry; a novel and a play' (Woolf in Briggs, 2005: 240). This would allow and require the writing to have an abstract and compressed quality and a sense of rhythm (Flint, 1992). 'Could one not get the waves to be heard all through?' Woolf asked (Flint, 1992: xxi). I think the realization of these intentions contributes significantly to how dense The Waves is with explicit and tacit association and potential meaning, and its sense of having emergent properties. 'Nothing in The Waves is simply one thing' (Dick, 2000: 67).

Woolf also wanted to avoid linear form (Whitworth, 2000, associates this with her critique of patriarchy) and realism (the 'appalling narrative business of the realist: getting on from lunch to dinner'; (Woolf in Whitworth, 2000: 155). I resonate with these very contemporary intentions. And I admire and agree with Woolf for choosing to address them through radically experimenting with form.

These aspirations gave her criteria to judge her work. As she wrote, she could assess whether it was achieving the desired effects. On completing the first draft she said: 'I begin to see what I had in my mind' (Woolf in Briggs, 2005: 256).

And she was aware that her style might challenge the reader. 'I am writing to a rhythm and not to a plot ... it is completely opposed to the tradition of fiction and I am casting about all the time for some rope to throw the reader'; Woolf in Briggs, 2005: 257).

THE POLITICS OF FORM

Going beyond rational, analytic conventions of writing can be risky, and therefore political.

Of course, what I say here will be of little use to you (could actively mislead) if you want to or must publish in 'mainstream' academic journals with their conventions of academic style. Then you can look to advice like that of Golden-Biddle and Locke (1997) who analyze different forms of academic storyline. They offer an interesting aid to successful journal publication for qualitative researchers, although they assert that they 'want to avoid espousing a normative "how to" guide' (p. xx). They depict writing as seeking to join in a conversation with a particular theoretical disciplinary audience. Texts need, then, to be persuasive within the

conventions, including the demands for demonstrating expertise, of particular knowledge communities. Golden-Biddle and Locke's own metaphor is that of crafting storylines – the 'macrostory' of theory within which the fieldwork story is nested.

They have systematically analyzed the different storylines people use at each stage of an article. These stages are assumed to be reasonably straightforward and usually take a linear path through gaining attention, positioning oneself in relation to existing theory (with choices of being more appreciative or more disparaging towards other people's work), and constructing a fieldwork based analysis which contextualizes the article's theoretical points. There are parallel processes in which writers characterize themselves as storytellers, either invoking images of institutional scientist and objectivity or distinguishing themselves in atypical ways.

Work of this kind has value in making some of the implicit codes of writing explicit. Such stories may well be your preference. And it is a highly socialized, adaptive view of writing. I should aspire to this writing competence, but do not. Over many years I have been seeking not to have the richness and political aspects of my research subverted by subordinating it to dominant forms of writing, seeking not to have to 'tell it slant' (Olsen, 1977). These issues clarified for me in researching women in management, when I was developing a feminist perspective and therefore especially aware of the politics of knowing and of potential silencing (Marshall, 1984). They have tracked my steps ever since, as I have explored other topics, always wanting to pay due respect to multiple ways of knowing.

WORKING OPENLY WITH FORM

Here I am especially interested in those precious moments as experiences, ideas and inquiry move towards expression in writing. As this happens, form is taking shape in a mutual process through the articulation of the content. When we work with an open sense of possibility about form we are engaging in the processes of knowledge-making and can glimpse their contentiousness in action in our own self-reflective practice. Form often becomes established early in the writing process, and what shape it takes can be fateful. It can also be worked with and changed later, throughout drafting and redrafting, if we allow. We need a double move to go beyond conventional academic storylines, one in which content and form are both radicalized.

Learning from Woolf: Opening all to Question

Often Woolf explores issues and then questions the ground she has just set out. In her autobiographic writing (Woolf, 2002), for example, she identifies her first memories and names one (in which waves are figural) as the base for her life. But she then ponders whether it is possible to know and write about a life with any assurance, one's own or anyone else's as a biographer or novelist. Can she/we say who the person is to whom things happen, or which memories are more important, or how to account for the extensive times of non-being which surround our 'moments of being' (p. 90)? She also suggests that unless we analyze the forces of society which influence us – she later notes 'the patriarchal society of the Victorian age [which] was in full swing in [their family] drawing room' (p. 154), then life writing becomes 'futile' (p. 92). We see Woolf's constant sense of inquiry; she cannot write autobiographically without questioning the foundations of the genre. The issues she identifies as contentious are played out in The Waves, *explored and left open. Some of Woolf's questioning – about identity, writing, biography – is given to the book's characters to speak (Marcus, 2004). I admire the fluidity of meaning-making achieved.*

I have come to enjoy, but also sometimes to dread too, holding on expectantly, allowing the uncertainty, as form is arising. And I enjoy being there for other writers as this happens for them. I see this as the realm of what Heron (1992) and Heron and Reason (Chapter 24 in this volume) call *presentational knowing*, in their modelling of a radical epistemology. I am interested in the movement to *presentational knowing* which 'emerges from the encounters of experiential knowing, by intuiting significant form and process in that which is met' (Heron and Reason, Chapter 24). Presentational knowing can be expressed in 'the arts' such as storytelling, music, dance and painting. And I take it also to be a mundane, continuous, moment-by-moment process, as experience takes shape or pattern and some sense of form emerges. When writing is inquiry, this boundary is always open.

I am seeking to notice presentational knowing arising, to catch it in process, before it is overtaken, discounted, devalued by conventionalized forming. And I appreciate that this process may not be fully accessible to the conscious mind (Heron, 1992). In this venture I aspire to the multiple attentions of the first person action researcher (Marshall, 2001/2006; Fisher et al., 2003).

Learning from Woolf: Engaging in Continuing Self-reflection

Working on The Waves *Woolf said, 'I want to trace my own process' (Woolf in Briggs, 2005: 246). This is shown as a continuing preoccupation in her diaries, which I know through commentators (Briggs, 2005; Flint, 1992; Marcus, 2004) who record and analyze the complex pathway of the book's long gestation, showing Woolf's tenacity, her sense of questing exploration. 'Writing it required a long and dedicated expedition into the interior' (Briggs, 2005: 238). Woolf thought about the novel for 3 years before starting to write. She then did four revisions between July 1929 and its completion in July 1931.*

Appropriate form needs to emerge from working with the phenomena we study; it should not be imposed or turned into technique, otherwise it will lose its resonant and evocative quality and will not work analogically. There are conformist tendencies even in experimenting genres, such as a current tendency for everything to become 'narrative'. Any new development can become orthodoxy by reaching for new conventions (Clough, 1992; Denzin and Lincoln, 2005).

I have a notion of emergent form, being 'grounded' in some appropriate practices of engagement with the stuff of inquiry – experience, data, issues – within a sense of the larger context or field (Senge et al., 2005), making it analogically appropriate to the material it expresses. It then becomes a process equivalent to that of 'grounded theory' (Glaser and Strauss, 1967). My notion of *grounded form* aligns with constructivist re-visions of grounded theory, which do 'not subscribe to the objectivist, positivist assumptions in its earlier formulations' (Charmaz, 2005: 509), and see the entire research process as interactive. Thus questions of the nature of knowing are brought into contention. There is no one way to write the material, someone 'chooses' how to write it. What, then, might be the quality, validity, equivalents to the constant comparative method, the care of iterative coding and categorizing, theoretical sampling and theoretical saturation (Glaser and Strauss, 1967)? I suggest that an engaged, emergent, iterative process is required to facilitate the generation of analogically appropriate form. Is it possible to account for the processes involved? Not fully, as they cannot be fully translated into digital expression. But whilst there might be limits to any account we can give, we can still strive for some account. This is a highly process based notion of quality, drawing on disciplines of writing as inquiry (Richardson, 2000). We can, for example, ask: How did this writing come to be like this? What quality processes did the author engage in? How did they expose them to critique?

In the second half of this chapter I offer practices for working towards grounded form, each implying quality processes we can track as we develop our writing.

PRACTICES FOR WORKING WITH ARISING FORM

The practices for working with finding form set out below are drawn from my own writing experience and from enabling other writers. The examples show two phases of activity. There is the initial, sometimes challenging, process of catching presentational knowing arising and finding form of some kind. But this alone is seldom enough to present our work artfully to the reader. In a second phase, the writer needs to craft the emergent form with some care and skill to realize its potential in practice. Finding appropriate form provides clues about what sort of writing craft to develop. We can also explore established writing genres which have similarities, and engage in active dialogue with (rather than con-form to) their disciplines and quality processes.

Below, I address you as a writer directly. This seems somewhat presumptive – you may well not need my encouragement. But in running writing workshops I find this voice appropriate – speaking to the writer in each participant, the person who knows how to write what it is theirs to write – and so have replicated it here. As enablers of writers, one of our strongest interventions is to invite people to keep faith with their own process.

Writing processes are highly individual, as the accounts of novelists show. But on this edge of writing creatively for academic study I find that some practices for enabling writing are sometimes transferable. And each person needs to develop their own approach.

Accept and Seek to Express What Is Rather than What Should Be

At the core of my notion of grounded form is the suggestion that form should be congruent with content. We are therefore seeking to express 'what is', for us in relation to the world we are seeking to know and articulate, not as an objective reality. Finding appropriate form can give the confidence of fit with, allowance into expression of, voices that matter, one's own and those of co-inquirers.

I often find that the 'problem' that obstructs writing is a key to form. 'I cannot write that because ...' a graduate student will say. And then they proceed to articulate their perspective, with its conceptual quality, which becomes what they must write. This example illustrates too that speaking what we know can surprise us. 'How can I know what I think till I see what I say?' (a little girl quoted in Wallas, 1926: 106). Also, being heard and affirmed can provide valuable encouragement.

> I sit at the side of a seminar room only half attending to the speaker on some aspect of qualitative research methods. I have been worrying for days about how to write the logical bridge between chapters 2 and 3 of a book on women in management. Chapter 2 reviews women in management literature, which accepts male as the norm and argues women are only suitable as managers if they demonstrate their similarity to this, doubts women's career motivations and so on. (It is the early 1980s.) Chapter 3 reports where my dissatisfaction with this literature took me, my unsettling journey into feminist analysis – questioning stereotyping, meaning-making, language and more. I realize suddenly, after all my logical, conceptual trying, that there is no clear progression from Chapter 2 to Chapter 3 and that **that** is the point. I am relieved and excited. I can approach the writing differently. And the form I now have is conceptually based (it mirrors the sense-making), not a trivial, discretionary artifact. I write a few sentences reporting this insight – naming and owning 'my changing orientation: from reform to radical feminism' (Marshall, 1984: 43) – with a sense of clear, direct knowing and voice. These become the opening to Chapter 3.
>
> Now that I have the potential device I can work with it and craft it. I decide to tell my sense-making journey more explicitly as the book's conceptual storyline, as an appropriate form to lead me through theoretical and fieldwork explorations.
>
> (Account written July 2006 in Freefall writing mode – see below – from placing myself back in that moment.)

Telling 'what is' may not be a straightforward matter, depending on the issues of representation involved.

> Riley and Phillipson (1993) wanted to depict the experiences of women managers in social services

organizations in the UK. Their data, gathered through their work as trainers, was contentious. If reported directly, it could expose women, increase the vulnerability and marginality they sometimes experienced. Riley and Phillipson therefore transposed their understandings and data into an 'imagined scenario in which a group of women meet together to decide how to "help" their male Director understand what it is like to manage as a woman, a request he has made of them' (p. 43). In this way they could explicitly address the politics of articulating women's experience through research, using a form analogically resonant with issues about voicing and silencing. The fictionalized women debate what motives the manager might have in asking, how much to reveal, whether they can speak for other women, what language to use and so on. They experience 'a relief in sharing ... examples of the daily bruising' (p. 53) which they had learnt to pretend was not happening. They devise a presentation to the management meeting to communicate their multi-layered understanding.

Repeatedly, I find that people's writing flourishes, and achieves more conceptual quality, when they engage the dilemmas they perceive by finding form that addresses rather than avoids them.

Finding form is an ongoing process, to be worked with throughout writing. Sometimes a form we have adopted early on needs to be changed radically, because we realize it is not working and another breaks through, or needs to be allowed to do so.

Learning from Woolf: Finding Appropriate Form both Frees and Sharpens Writing

How the characters in The Waves *could be portrayed and the nature of the impersonal interludes took shape as the writing progressed. Commentators report the exciting moments in which Woolf discovered answers to her dilemmas of form. Once each of these occurred, specifics of content could be crafted with more confidence. And she iteratively reconceived form as detailed working brought her new insights. For example, when she finally hit upon the device of the characters speaking through soliloquies, she experienced a sense of release and could rush on to finish that draft (Briggs, 2005: 253). In a later phase of revision she wanted to clear out irrelevances, sharpen and make 'the good phrases shine. One wave after another' (Woolf in Briggs, 2005: 256). As Briggs notes 'even the process of writing had begun to echo the primal rhythm of waves' (pp. 256–7). We see, then, a mirroring of content, form and writing process.*

Perhaps finding form is as simple as that and there is no more to say. Yes, and no. It can be difficult to sit with the tentative uncertainty and hope that a unique articulation in its uniquely appropriate form will emerge. In the rest of this section I offer some practices for being there. They are by no means guaranteed, and this is not a comprehensive array.

Employ disciplines and respect emergence

Writing takes time. We need to learn to tolerate slow starts and uneven processes, and stick with them. If it is difficult, it is worth persisting. But if it is *very* difficult perhaps something is not right; I need to pause and pay attention to the process, for its potential to be in-forming. I often write side-notes on the writing process and arising issues as a holding device. Some notes initially seem to reflect on me as a sensemaker, some might seem quite personal. But they might become apparent as themes in the topics I am exploring or political aspects of sensemaking. They might then take on a significance of their own, becoming figural in the text and giving it form.

Example of a discipline: Freefall Writing

Just writing and seeing what came has long been an approach I followed. Learning about 'Freefall' writing – Goldberg (1986) and Turner-Vesselago (1995) who calls it 'writing without a parachute' – has added texture to this approach.

In our research community we find Freefall writing especially helpful as a simple disciplined process inviting the writer to speak in their own voice and articulate their knowing. We take practices from these two sources and apply them to writing research. The basics of Freefall are: keep the hand moving; don't cross out; don't worry about spelling, punctuation, grammar; don't think – write; show, don't tell – give the sensuous detail; and go where the energy is, which may be fearward. Both authors suggest that writing practice can be built up through doing timed exercises.

Learning from Woolf: Working Between Uncertainty and Confidence

In the early stages of writing, Woolf's 'diary entries alternate between the repeated admission "I don't know", and the firm conviction that "there is something there"' (Briggs, 2005: 249). Throughout the writing process, she questioned the appropriateness of emerging structures. I admire her persistence, the combination of restless creativity, purposefulness, hard work and inquiry that I see in the accounts of her process – her willingness to take this as her task.

Invoke the Writer in You and Your Own Direct Voice, Whatever Shapes it Takes

Finding form requires bypassing the censors, accrediting your right to write, identifying and dismissing internalized notions of 'standards' which are inviting your conformity or subduing your voice. Freed from such expectations you may then know how to write what is yours to write. In writing workshops I use a range of approaches, including Freefall writing, to invite people into their competence as knowers and writers.

Learning from Woolf: Respecting What We Bring to Writing

The Waves echoes Woolf's first, most important, memory. 'It is of lying half asleep, half awake, in bed in the nursery at St Ives. It is of hearing the waves breaking, one, two, one, two, and sending a splash of water over the beach' (Woolf, 2002: 78). Woolf brought herself and her life fully to her writing. Her reflective process appears thorough, self-engrossed but working with issues in a personal/universal sense, seemingly unashamed.

Create Resonant Spaces and Cditions for Writing

How do you ready yourself to have the internal attentions and the external conditions to write? Woolf (1929/1977) argued that 'a woman must have money and a room of her own if she is to write fiction' (p. 6). This can be taken literally and metaphorically.

You can pay attention to:

- How you come to writing. There is a sense of inquiry here. When are you prevaricating and need to push yourself? When are you gently moving towards writing emerging? When do apparent difficulties offer understanding about the writing?
- Whether certain times of day enable, or constrain, your writing. I can often write well first thing in the morning, especially when I speak to no one before I start. Form is often clear to me then, confident.
- What kinds of writing spaces work for you.
- How you work with the physicality, the embodiedness, of writing/thinking. Sometimes we need to turn away, go for a walk, do something else. And the notion of form we have been seeking comes to us.

Michelsohn (2006) had to write his final thesis for the Masters in Responsibility and Business Practice. He is a banker, musician, very concerned about issues of ecological sustainability, a Brazilian living in Europe. His first draft portrayed some of the identity and issue-based tensions he experiences. But the tutors said it did not do his thinking and engagement justice. They both suggested independently that he create special circumstances to allow him to write up the project. He went to Rio de Janiero, to the library in his grandparents' house, a positioning full of analogic resonance with the issues he was addressing. He wrote the final thesis, in only eight days, as a conversation with his departed grandfather, a kindred radical spirit, and drawing on imagery from a cartoon book from his childhood, Mafalda. He created a text which is rich, multi-layered, questioning, portraying his tensions from a more encompassing consciousness.

Defend Emergent Form, Claim Authority

Sometimes our emerging form does not meet with approval or later seems inappropriate, and we have to decide how vital it is to our writing, or whether it was a temporarily significant device that we can now relinquish.

I was invited to write a chapter from a feminist perspective for A *Handbook of Career Theory* (Marshall, 1989). I explored themes of being, inaction, interdependence, cyclic patterns and whole lives, drawing on notions of communion to accompany the more control and anticipation based foundations of career theory informed by agency. The editorial review process was challenging. The editors liked the content, but were concerned that the chapter sometimes had a 'non-linear style', especially given their North American base. They asked me to revise accordingly. I tried, but could not achieve a more linear storyline. I came to realize that as the form mirrored my argument for less linear notions of career, abandoning it could threaten the foundations and integrity of the chapter. So I sought both to explain and protect it by being explicit about how the style reflected the content, and about the reviewers' reservations, in the introduction.

The editor in charge of my chapter still tells this story as an abiding memory of my work; some indication that it was an unusual experience for them.

In this case I claimed author-ity for my style of writing and this was accepted. Had this been a journal article, I doubt if I would have been so 'lucky'.

Gloria Bravette (1997), a British woman of African descent, was using writing as inquiry. She felt a strong imperative to write the final section of her PhD thesis in a direct voice to a composite white 'other' which contained people and experiences to which she had failed to respond during her life because of fear and shame. 'I realise that I have broken my silences [about race] in defiance of you – it was the only way that I knew how to break away from the hold that you were having over me' (p. 225). She explored the challenge of claiming her right to know as 'black, and therefore inferior' (p. 223), and the difficulties of distinguishing 'white' people who love humanity from racists.

Gloria wondered whether or not to explain this device to the reader, and decided to do so. Her articulate framing, accompanied by her conceptual model of 'unleashing creative potential through the unblocking process' (p. 224), explained how necessary it was to adopt this direct, confronting voice to break the bonds that bound her, to place limits on her fear. Only then could she write the earlier sections of the thesis fully.

One choice to be worked with is when and how to read the work of others and when and how to allow one's own voice, inquiry and accumulated sense of others' work to come to some articulation. Especially in finding form, it is important not to swamp or stifle your own voice, authorship, authority. And, usually, eventually, a blending and integration is appropriate.

Value the Imaginal and Metaphorical as Guides to Form

Catching moments of form taking shape often involves a sense of knowing beyond language. Sometimes this can be encapsulated in an image or metaphor that can then be articulated, explored and worked with.

Some years ago I studied women who had reached middle or senior level management positions and then left, contemplated leaving or been forced out of employment. I wanted to tell the stories of such women, because their behaviour seemed a mystery or was taken by some commentators as evidence that women are not tough enough for senior management jobs.

Two images that arose from the processes of sensemaking provided forms that shaped the resulting book (Marshall, 1995). Both emerged, as if spontaneously, following sustained immersion in the study's material and puzzling about how to write it.

They relate to self-reflexive sensemaking in political and contested terrain. They provide articulations of the warrant I had to speak from the research study, and address issues of validity in interpretive social science. Neither is unique to me. But in this project they were fitting epistemologically and therefore carried a felt sense of 'insight'.

The first image was that of 'turning things in the light' (p. 7). I had worked with 16 women in depth, hearing their experiences and writing versions of their stories which could be told publicly. The image referred to my wish to offer the potential for different interpretations of the women's experiences to be considered. Each story was like a crystal or prism, reflecting and refracting light, always offering new impressions. This affected how I wrote the stories and accompanying text.

The second image arose when I was reflecting on what warrant I had for drawing out shared and contrasting themes from the women's stories. During a Freefall writing exercise, I found myself likening the kind of sensemaking I was seeking to trying to free the ends in a multi-coloured, multi-stranded tangle of wool. I realized, *inter alia*, that 'If I pull too tightly, if I interpret beyond my warrant, the wool/theme will tense and lose its texture' (p. 37). This image provided the rationale for the book's structure. Short analytic commentary pieces (for example 'Is gender at issue?', pp. 98–101) were interspersed amongst the women's stories to offer conceptual threads and questions relevant to interpreting them, and to treating their interpretation as provisional, open, worthy of reflection. Happily the publisher was willing to accept a manuscript with 42 'chapters', as long as we did not call them that.

In both cases, once the image had emerged as an articulation of the form the writing was beginning to show, I could use it more deliberately, amplify it, develop and craft that incipient way of working.

These devices allowed several dilemmas in the sensemaking process, which I realized were important features of the field being explored, to be engaged with rather than controlled. They were an attempt to offer a sense of 'truth' relevant to the topic area at a process rather than content level. The book sought, then, to be a continuation of inquiry, wanting to throw the questions it raised back into lives and organizational worlds akin to those I studied.

Learning from Woolf: Working With, Developing, Imagery

As Woolf developed The Waves *there were significant shifts in her guiding images which she sought, embraced. Moths and the maternal instinct were early potential devices. Waves appeared too, and then replaced moths as a central motif (Briggs, 2005; Flint, 1992; Marcus, 2004).*

CLOSING THEMES AND QUESTIONS

In this closing section, I return to some themes considered earlier and explore their implications for action research.

If we work with a sensitivity to form, whether, how much and how to explain form are open choices. Should we show rather than tell, letting the reader make sense and experience for themselves? We are open to analogic ambiguity. Interpretation of our writing is even more than usually beyond our control. I generally favour some attempts at framing, some signposting to help the reader, and writer, through. And yet, if form is fundamental to our meaning-making, explaining it can seem like appeasement, aesthetically inappropriate, a conventionalizing, taming, move. *The Waves* was well received by friends, critics and public, who coped with what it offered.

'Un-conventional' writing forms can be demanding of the reader, who cannot scan or read to formula. Often texts have emergent, holistic, properties which will not be understood unless engaged with fully. I cannot show you a short section of *The Waves* to illustrate all I have claimed for its qualities. As readers we may, then, need to develop an extended aesthetic, with an associated language of appreciation and critique, which goes beyond our analytic frames of understanding.

What is our writing for? If form and content are congruent, our writing can pass on more of the alive complexity of the issues explored, and more of the dilemmas and provisionality of meaning-making, to the reader. This can become an invitation or provocation, an extension into third person inquiry.

What I am advocating here is obviously politically risky for academic scholars given the, increasing, conformity and surveillance of many mainstream disciplines. And yet, experimentation is rife. Perhaps we can re-vise tolerances applied to writing. If, however, academic writing wants to stay dull, boring and poorly contextualized, what choices can we generate?

How can we judge quality in the realms of analogic congruence and grounded form? Criteria can include writing that:

- evokes the experiences, themes and issues of the inquiry for the reader;
- communicates conceptually through the congruence of content and form;
- accounts for the writer's process, and its resonances with form and content;
- renders the sensemaking appropriately contentious, in ways which illuminate the issues explored; and
- provokes readers' engagement and debate.

Finding form is a profoundly conceptual matter, and we need to work actively with it. Exploring the qualities our writing aspires to, perhaps through imagery, can guide how we craft our work. This will include finding devices for showing the provisionality of knowing, as Woolf did, as aspects of what we offer.

REFERENCES

Bakhtin, M./Medvedev, P.N. (1928/1985) *The Formal Method in Literary Scholarship: a Critical Introduction to Sociological Poetics.* Cambridge, MA: Harvard University Press.

Bateson, G. (1973) 'A theory of play and fantasy', in *Steps to an Ecology of Mind.* London: Paladin. pp. 150–66.

Bravette, G. (1997) 'Towards bicultural competence: researching for personal and professional transformation.' PhD thesis, University of Bath, UK.

Briggs, J. (2000) 'The novels of the 1930s and the impact of history', in S. Roe and S. Sellers (eds), *The Cambridge Companion to Virginia Woolf.* Cambridge: Cambridge University Press. pp. 72–90.

Briggs, J. (2005) *Virginia Woolf: an Inner Life.* London: Allen Lane.

Charmaz, K. (2005) 'Grounded theory in the 21st century: applications for advancing social justice studies', in N.K. Denzin and Y.S Lincoln (eds), *The Sage Handbook of Qualitative Research, 3rd edn.* Thousand Oaks, CA: Sage. pp. 507–36.

Clough, P.T. (1992) *The End(s) of Ethnography: From Realism to Social Criticism.* Newbury Park, CA: Sage.

Czarniawska, B. (1997) *Narrating the Organization.* Chicago: University of Chicago Press.

Denzin, N.K. and Lincoln, Y.S. (2005) 'Introduction: the discipline and practice of qualitative research', in N.K. Denzin and Y.S Lincoln (eds), *The Sage Handbook of Qualitative Research, 3rd edn.* Thousand Oaks, CA: Sage. pp. 1–32.

Dick, S. (2000) 'Literary realism in *Mrs Dalloway, To the Lighthouse, Orlando* and *The Waves*', in S. Roe and S. Sellers (eds), *The Cambridge Companion to Virginia Woolf.* Cambridge: Cambridge University Press. pp. 50–71.

Eisner, E.W. (1993) 'Forms of understanding and the future of educational research', *Educational Researcher,* 22 (7): 5–11.

Ellis, C. and Bochner, A.P. (2000) 'Autoethnography, personal narrative and reflexivity', in N.K. Denzin and Y.S. Lincoln (eds), *Handbook of Qualitative Research, 2nd edn.* Thousand Oaks, CA: Sage. pp. 733–69.

Fisher, D., Rooke, D. and Torbert, B. (2003) *Personal and Organizational Transformations through Action Inquiry.* Boston: Edge\Work Press.

Flint, K. (1992) 'Introduction', in V. Woolf, *The Waves*. London: Penguin Books. pp. ix–xl.

Glaser, B.G. and Strauss, A.L. (1967) *The Discovery of Grounded Theory: Strategies for Qualitative Research*. New York: Aldine Publishing Co.

Goldberg, N. (1986) *Writing down the Bones: Freeing the Writer Within*. Boston: Shambhala.

Golden-Biddle, K. and Locke, K.D. (1997) *Composing Qualitative Research*. Thousand Oaks, CA: Sage.

Heron, J. (1992) *Feeling and Personhood: Psychology in Another Key*. London: Sage.

Kienholz, E. and Kienholz, N.R. (n.d.) [http://theochem.chem.rug.nl/~heijnen/Kienholz/MGW/wheel/entranc e.html] (accessed October 2006).

Lather, P., Lather, P.A. and Smithies, C. (1997) *Troubling the Angels: Women Living with HIV/Aids*. Boulder, CO: Westview Press/Harper Collins.

Marcus, L. (2004) *Virginia Woolf, 2nd edn*. Tavistock: Northcote House Publishers.

Marshall, J. (1984) *Women Managers: Travellers in a Male World*. Chichester: Wiley.

Marshall, J. (1989) 'Re-visioning career concepts: a feminist invitation', in M.B. Arthur, D.T. Hall and B.S. Lawrence (eds), *A Handbook of Career Theory*. Cambridge: Cambridge University Press. pp. 275–91.

Marshall, J. (1995) *Women Managers Moving On: Exploring Career and Life Choices*. London: International Thomson Publishing Europe.

Marshall, J. (2001/2006) 'Self-reflective inquiry practices', in P. Reason and H. Bradbury (eds), *Handbook of Action Research: Participative Inquiry and Practice*. London: Sage. pp. 433–9. Also published in P. Reason and H. Bradbury (eds) (2006), *Handbook of Action Research: Concise Paperback Edition*. London: Sage. pp. 335–42.

Michelsohn, M. (2006) 'Becoming a juggler: holding the tensions of a complex life through a search for purpose and creativity.' MSc in Responsibility and Business Practice, Final Project, unpublished. University of Bath, UK.

Olsen, T. (1977) 'One out of twelve: women who are writers in our century', in S. Ruddick and P. Daniels (eds), *Working it Out*. New York: Pantheon. pp. 323–40.

Reason, P. and Torbert, W.R. (2001) 'The action turn: toward a transformational social science', *Concepts and Transformations*, 6 (1): 1–37.

Richardson, L. (2000) 'Writing: a method of inquiry', in N.K. Denzin and Y. Lincoln (eds), *Handbook of Qualitative Research, 2nd edn*. Thousand Oaks, CA: Sage. pp. 923–48.

Riley, M. and Phillipson, J. (1993) 'Women in social services management', in B. Broad and C. Fletcher (eds), *Practitioner Social Work Research in Action*. London: Whiting and Birch. pp. 42–54.

Senge, P., Scharmer, C.O., Jaworski, J. and Flowers, B.S. (2005) *Presence*. London: Nicholas Brealey.

Sparkes, A.C. (2003) 'From performance to impairment: a patchwork of embodied memories', in J. Evans, B. Davies and J. Wright (eds), *Body Knowledge and Control*. London: Routledge. pp. 157–72.

Turner-Vesselago, B. (1995) *Freefall: Writing without a Parachute*. Toronto: The Writing Space.

Wallas, G. (1926) *The Art of Thought*. New York: Harcourt Brace.

Watzlawick, P., Bavelas, J.B. and Jackson, D.D. (1967) *Pragmatics of Human Communication*. New York: W.W. Norton & Co.

Weil, S. (1996) 'From the other side of silence: new possibilities for dialogue in academic writing', *Changes*, 14 (3): 223–31.

Whitworth, M. (2000) 'Virginia Woolf and modernism', in S. Roe and S. Sellers (eds), *The Cambridge Companion to Virginia Woolf*. Cambridge: Cambridge University Press. pp. 146–63.

Woolf, V. (1931/1992) *The Waves*. London: Penguin Books.

Woolf, V. (1929/1977) *A Room of One's Own*. St Albans: Granada.

Woolf, V. (2002) 'Sketch of the past', in *Moments of Being: Autobiographical Writings*. London: Pimlico.

49

Concluding Reflections: Whither Action Research?

Peter Reason and Hilary Bradbury

To conclude this volume, the editors asked all contributors to reflect on the future of action research. This chapter outlines the action research community's aspirations to work on the 'big issues' of our time. It explores the different definitions of action research, the institutions that do and do not support action research practice, the development of practitioners, and the tension between supporting those who are marginalized and attempting to influence the powerful and privileged.

For this closing chapter we asked all contributors to respond to the question 'Wither Action Research?', inviting them to help identify the key issues that our broad community should be addressing. It is a bookend of sorts to Chapter 1, where we asked our Editorial Board to tell us about the personal and theoretical grounds of their practice. Our specific questions included: What is the future of action research? Who are its future leaders? What are the issues to which action researchers need to respond?

THE BIG ISSUES

The first response was from Rajesh Tandon,[1] and reflected the ambitions of many action researchers to contribute to the big issues of our time, and the imaginative capacity of so many of our community. Picture, if you will, the front page of the *International Herald Tribune* circa 2020

Action research in global peace-building! Action research practitioners are engaged in a major exercise of global peace-building; their professional network is offering hands-on methodology for understanding and addressing the pressing concerns of divided communities and humanity. This network of action researchers had grown out of the 'new' paradigm of community-based participatory research, where the worlds of academe and practice organically collaborate in educating and training a new generation of professionals.

This global ambition was echoed by Ernie Stringer[2] and Dave Brown.[3] Ernie wondered.

How do we in wealthy nations, where many of the discourses and practices of action research take place, make the resources we embody available to those in poorer nations? This is especially important in a climate dominated by economic rationalism and user-pays knowledge production processes. I believe we have much to gain … from interacting with this issue.

And Dave wrote:

I think action researchers should and will get more involved with the 'big issues' of our shrinking world – poverty, ecological catastrophes, water distribution, HIV/AIDS – to help with the construction or reconstruction of global institutions and problem-solving arrangements. … Since many of the most difficult problems involve social construction processes and interventions, some AR approaches could be very helpful.

This issue is explored at the end of Chapter 5 (this volume, Bradbury et al.) with reference to some consensus among social scientists on how successful large-scale change might occur.

Kenneth Gergen[4] makes the important point that action research has quite different ambitions from traditional research models which look to the past in order to predict and control the future.

If we live primarily in worlds of constructed meaning, and these meanings are of pivotal significance to our actions, then the traditional goals of prediction and control should be abandoned. Rather, the point of the sciences ceases to be that of looking backwards in hopes that we can make future predictions. Rather, we are challenged to engage in the kind of research that creates futures about which we care. In this sense action research is a vanguard orientation. It represents the most forward looking orientation to practice existing within the social sciences. Its potentials must be nurtured with utmost care.

John Heron and Gregg Lahood[5] point to the central role of AR in realizing justice for the human community:

such justice seen primarily as empowering participative and transformative decision-making in every kind of human association and in every field of human endeavour.

As editors of this volume, our concern and interest in action research has never been limited to the challenges of theory and practice. Our purpose always, to quote Orlando Fals Borda,[6] has been to 'transform and re-enchant our plural worlds'. Peter has, at the time of writing, drafted a statement of purpose for the next action research doctoral programme at Bath:

The staff associated with this programme share a profound concern for the state of the planetary ecology. We are alarmed at the failure of western society and its institutions to recognize the severity of the challenge of global warming and the degradation of ecosystems and to address these with the urgency they call for. We believe that significant changes will be needed in all aspects of economic and cultural life.

Our intention is that by initiating and facilitating this programme we will be playing our part in the 'Great Turning' which Joanna Macy writes about, the shift toward a life-sustaining civilization.

We believe that the practices of action research which we have developed over the past 25 years might play a significant part in developing our shared capacity to approach these challenges in a spirit of mutual inquiry.

DEFINITIONS

Do we need to define action research and clarify its boundaries more clearly? Do we need, as Ian Hughes asked, to clearly distinguish between action research, participatory research and participatory action research? Do definitions matter? As Lai Fong Chiu[7] wrote:

Action research is an umbrella term for a variety of practical and intellectual efforts for change. Its seemingly broad outlook, fluid boundaries and inter-disciplinarity provide both opportunities and danger for future development.

Ed Schein[8] raised a similar question:

The future of action research will depend upon what we mean by that concept and how we show both academics and practitioners the value of collaboration for learning and helping. I think we are still very confused about the 'essence' of what we are talking about. Note that we still have in our lexicon 'action research,' 'action learning,' 'action science,' 'collaborative interactive action research,' 'participatory inquiry,' and several other labels that seem to deal with various aspects of this so called field of practice. We are still uncertain whether we should 1) be scientific and rigorous, allying ourselves with our academic colleagues who are concerned with knowledge production or 2) be helpful, allying ourselves with our clients and with other practitioners for whom data production itself is secondary to learning and change.

Robert Chambers[9] asked also about labels and limits:

Are there boundaries to what it is useful to call action research? Does it, for example, include 'Reflect' and other movements where local people are facilitated (or on their own) conduct their own research and analysis (see Chapter 20)? Does it include Integrated Pest Management, where farmers are facilitated to do their own research on the ecology of pests? Is the implicit definition in the volume a bit more restricted, a bit more intellectual, academic … ? If the answer is yes, they should be included, do they join popular education and other mass movements as sources of insight? And if so, what are the implications for future priorities?

One way to approach these questions is to attempt to tie down definitions. Another approach is to be expansive and inclusive, to hold open the ambiguity and unpredictability of our work, as indeed does Ed Schein in answering the challenge he has posed:

I believe the essence of this process, whatever we end up calling it, is the initial definition of the situation as being a collaboration between someone with a question, problem or issue and someone with some helping skills. How we then proceed is always a joint effort between the 'client' and the 'consultant/helper' and, as my own process consulting experience has taught me, is quite unpredictable. And it should be. We should not at this stage of the game have a model of these human processes that we impose, but, rather, continue the inquiry of what collaboration between clients and helpers reveals as we get into ever more interesting problem arenas.

Lyle Yorks[10] writes in a similar vein:

The future of AR lies in the combination of robust epistemological awareness with flexible and adaptable methodology. This combination holds the potential for enabling people to develop the capacity for responding to the complex demands of our time which are characterized by

interconnections that are complex and unpredictable. It is simplistic to think one can create boundaries around them that allow for traditional problem solving approaches. Working with such demands requires having a capacity for remaining in relationship with emerging experience through time, working with co-inquirers who are socially and professionally diverse.

Bill Torbert[11] reaches for a challenging definition:

Action research can reach its potential only when it is recognized and practiced as a far more challenging and inclusive art and science than modernist empirical research and postmodernist critical/constructive research. Modernist social science research predominantly involves separating the researcher from the object of study, analyzing the data only after the events researched, and reporting primarily single-loop incremental results only in a third-person voice to the community of academic scientists. Postmodern constructivist research attempts a double-loop critique of naïve empiricism and occasionally introduces a first-person voice but fails to engage in real time practice. Full-blown action research represents a double-loop paradigmatic transformation which interweaves action and inquiry in real time and including participants as co-researchers [see Chapter 16 for a fuller discussion of Torbert's vision].

Others are clear that action research must make links with other post-objectivist disciplines. As Sonia Ospina[12] and her colleagues write in Chapter 28, there are fruitful links to be made with the emerging qualitative research disciplines. Bjørn Gustavsen points to the importance of:

developing platforms of co-operation with forms of research that do not use the concept of 'action research' but which are nonetheless involved in the generation of practical change. Many such researchers shy away from entering the action research discourse (which is sometimes seen as quite difficult) and it is better to create platforms of co-operation based on complementarity than to demand that other researchers should understand and accept action research 'from inside'.

Victor Friedman[13] asserts that the war with positivism is more or less over, while positivist, mainstream social science is still dominant and powerful, it is now widely accepted that its account is deeply flawed. In consequence:

Doors are opening for new and innovative research approaches – many fall within the realm of action research. The implication of this is that positivism/positivists are no longer the 'enemy'. To the contrary, the time may have come to look for new allies among our old enemies and to create new coalitions in order to face the big challenges.

Our own inclination has always been to be eclectic, inclusive and expansive, to see action research as a family of approaches where different needs and interests will pull practitioners and participants in different ways. If action research is about engaging with people to address issues in their lives, then the whole range of practices that Chambers points to must be included; if action research is to address the pathologies of epistemology and politics that beset our universities (of which see more below), then we must also be addressing philosophical questions about the nature of knowledge in action, about quality and 'validity', and the organizational issues that divide academics into scholarly silos. Action research is about creating forms of inquiry that people can use in the everyday conduct of their lives; *and* action research is part of revisioning our worldview, a paradigm shift, changing what we take as knowledge.

As we have argued elsewhere, while we can point to broad characteristics of action research – we have written of an emergent process which seeks human and ecological flourishing through practical focus, participation, and many ways of knowing – action research is a complex living process which cannot be tied to definitions. Action research is far more a work of art than a set of procedures; there are always more possibilities than can be encompassed, and *quality in inquiry comes from awareness of and transparency about the choices open to you and that you make at each stage of the inquiry* (Bradbury, 2007; Reason, 2006).

POLICY, SCOPE AND SCALE

Bjørn Gustavsen[14] reminds us of what he has also written elsewhere (Gustavsen, 2003)

namely that action research has won all debates on ethics and epistemology but has been less influential in creating large scale-change and influencing national policy. He argues that 'the action research entrepreneur' of the future will have to find a new context and purpose for action research that turns it into a major actor that has impact at the societal level. He writes that while action research is gaining ground, and research in all disciplines is to a growing extent dependent upon practical contexts and developments, action research has still not truly established itself at the level of institutionalizing change. He is impatient with the 'continued production and reproduction of the epistemological and ethical arguments for action research' and sees as inadequate the 'flow of individual action research cases, limited in time and space'. Thus action research must demonstrate ability to reach out in scope and create effects that are visible in society. This has implications: projects must be linked into networks so they can speak together, the emphasis must be on practices that link projects, action researchers must stop being exclusive and collaborate with other forms of research.

Bjørn is likely correct most of the time, but it's also important to note the degree to which the work of action researchers does have significant impact, as the work of Rajesh Tandon, Dave Brown, Ernie Stringer, Meghna Guhathakurta, Ann Martin as well as others in this book, evidences.

Meghna Guhathakurta[15] and her colleagues have ambitions to contribute to the transformation of Bangladesh, a country of many millions:

Several of RIB's projects are on the verge of moving beyond individual projects to that of a movement. They are a telecentre movement providing rural livelihood information through ICT disseminated through locally owned information centers (Pallitathya Kendros) across villages in Bangladesh; the Kajoli early childhood learning centers for children of extreme poor families; interactive theatre activism and PAR by volunteers; the Sannyasi, a village of pre-literate mendicants who as a result of PAR decided that they must learn to read and write!

Some of the common themes evident in these endeavours of RIB are:

(a) how far the community is involved
(b) whether the area of involvement has to do with their existential needs
(c) the sincerity and capacity of the animator
(d) whether there are adequate and qualified internal animators (i.e. animators internal to the community) to take the movement forward
(e) how far they are adaptable and flexible to changing circumstances
(f) existence of supportive action groups and organizations to help them on their way.

STAYING RADICAL OR SELLING OUT

Geoff Mead[16] raises some of the questions that action researchers may experience as they work to influence mainstream organizations:

An issue which continues to interest and concern me is how to take action research into mainstream environments and still maintain rigour and quality. By the mainstream I mean the institutions of the democratic/capitalist society in which we function. If we hold back we run the risk of being an elitist academic pursuit with no real claim to be trying to make significant change. If we allow the 'system' to colonise our practice as action researchers then we run the risk of dilution and becoming just another instrumental technique. The challenges are heightened by the overt commercial pressures on the process when we take it out of the academy. I think this dimension of action research brings its own pressures. The empowerment offered by action inquiry/research to the managers etc. we sometimes work with is subversive of the status quo and of existing power structures. Doing action research in organisations often feels to me like a subtle form of guerrilla warfare – perhaps this is inevitable?

Marianne Kristiansen[17] was disturbed at the 2006 ALARMP-PAR World Congress in Groningen as she experienced a broad tendency towards reducing action research to change management and an instrumental tool without questioning change itself. She emphasizes the importance of 'action research as emergent ways of being' and that the tools and methods are not aims in themselves. She argues for the importance of first-person practices to provide a critical

reflective base to our work. Mary Brydon Miller[18] writes similarly:

The trick is staying rooted while moving ahead. I worry that unless we can find ways of remaining firmly grounded in the values that brought so many of us to the practice of action research – the commitment to social justice, democratic practice, and respect for people's knowledge – that we will lose our way. Action research seems to have gained a certain popularity of late, and it's this very popularity and the potential watering down of our vision for social change that will accompany it that are of greatest concern to me. And yet I think it is vitally important that we do find ways of moving forward rather than staying locked in the past worshipping our departed heroes. My hope is that we can remain mindful of our shared history and values while embracing new practices and new technologies that will enhance our ability to bring about positive change.

Brinton Lykes[19] writes about her recent experiences in the USA, with feminist-informed PAR in local communities in Boston, anti-racist activism on her campus and in her community, and activism and protest within/among the profession of psychologists (specifically vis-à-vis the growing evidence of psychologists' participation in cruel and unusual treatment of prisoners at Guantánamo and the profession's refusal to condemn this work):

In all instances I have collaborated more closely with US-based peoples of color across the educational and professional spectrum and interacted more directly with white privileged academics, my peers in the profession. And in each situation I have become ever more aware of how even those of us engaged in PAR, AR, PR and feminist research, that is, on the 'intellectual margins' of the university, are central players in a 'professional-managerial class' (Ehrenreich and Ehrenreich, 1977), serving as buffers between the elite and peoples of color, youth, workers, environmentalists, etc. From the comfort of our university's professorships – where we worry about tenure and promotion, the legitimacy of our research, the source of funds to support the next study, etc. – we generate discourses of liberation and transformation as our governments and elected or appointed leaders transform democratic systems into police states where a darker tint to your skin, a head scarf or other covering of the body, or an accent are grounds for imprisonment, interrogation without the right of *habeas corpus*, and torture, particularly if you are not a US citizen and are living in post-9/11 Amerika. Although there is plenty of reason for those targeted by US policies and laws to crouch in fear it is rather those of us within the professional-managerial class who seemed paralyzed into apathy or the agitated activities of our profession in lieu of activism, building solidarity, and mass-based organizing. One is reminded daily of Germany during the ascendancy of Hitler and of the words of Rev. Martin Niemoller, who in 1945 upon his emergence from prison said: 'Then they came for me, and by that time there was no one left to speak up for me'.

As we labor for quality and validity – which are, are they not, legitimacy and recognition – and celebrate the recognition of AR within the panoply of legitimate research methodologies in universities, NGOs, the World Bank and the UN, can we simultaneously press for the revolutionary change needed to ensure life on earth and justice for the human community? Can action, participatory and feminist research contribute to elite intellectuals in a professional-managerial class of the condescension, white privilege, and objectifying rhetoric which make it difficult if not impossible to forge a mass-based movement for social justice? Must we clearly re-articulate our work and ourselves as *activist*, not action, research(ers) and choose lives that more fully reflect the discourse that we generate **and** the material realities of those with whom we generate knowledge, that is, the majority populations of the world? What is the meaning of earning wages including research dollars that situate us within the top quartile of the world's income distribution when those with whom we collaborate frequently live on less than $2 a day or lack healthcare or housing? These are the challenges that face us today; if we fail to engage them, then we and our research take a place alongside those in the academy that have come before us, domesticated by our quest for legitimacy, absorbed into a system of power and resources that assuage our fear and guilt, and protect us, at least temporarily, from those who will 'come for us' when there will be 'no one left to speak up'.

And as Wendy Frisby and Colleen Reid [20] point out, while more and more marginalized groups are getting engaged in different forms of action research, there remain numerous silences and omissions. We must be careful not to silence each other.

PEDAGOGY OF THE OPPRESSED *AND* PEDAGOGY OF THE PRIVILEGED

These arguments could easily become polarized, with some action researchers emphasizing the importance of standing alongside the oppressed and disadvantaged and others emphasizing the need to influence mainstream decisions and get involved in policy matters. We would argue that both matter enormously, and while we must open our minds to challenges such as those offered by Brinton Lykes and follow Anisur Rahman in supporting the self-reliance of ordinary people, we must also recognize that some things won't change unless we are also able to enter and work effectively in the corridors of power, influence and have an impact on questions of policy and gradually change the quality of discourse in mainstream organizations. We must seek to link the grassroots with the governmental and global, as Marja Liisa Swantz, Dave Brown and Rajesh Tandon argue in their chapters.

The pedagogy of the oppressed must be matched by a pedagogy of the privileged if we are to move our world toward justice and sustainability.

REFORM OF UNIVERSITIES

One set of institutions that action researchers would dearly love to change is the academic institutions in which many of us live. We will not rehearse the problems that action researchers experience in universities at length, because they are already well covered by Morten Levin and Davydd Greenwood in Chapter 14.

Davydd Greenwood [21] argues that we must 'move institutions of higher education in the direction of Mode 2 knowledge production, i.e., the co-generative creation of "socially robust" knowledge'. John Burgoyne [22] dreams of a business school 'in which teaching and research, action learning and action research, fuse into a combined process of mutual inquiry and learning, a meeting of critically reflective practitioner researchers and facilitators which develop themselves and their practice, contribute to, share and draw on a collective body of knowledge and understanding'. Morten Levin[23] argues that it is vital to 'locate AR in institutions of higher education because this creates legitimacy for AR. … Institutions of higher education are probably the most fruitful arena that can connect legitimacy and diffusion'. David Coghlan[24] points to the paradox that while there are continual complaints about relevance and the gap between academic research and practitioners, academic institutions continue to support a mode of research that apes the natural sciences and separates theory from practice. He argues that we must 'continue to batter at that door … however firmly it is locked and barred so that action research does not disappear' and 'publish strong action research that contains clear evidence that can be accepted in major journals'. Jennifer Mullett[25] is concerned about the tidal wave of 'evidence based research' which is usually based on positivist foundations but is of dubious value; and on the other hand the espousal of 'participation' as developing purely instrumental rather than authentic relations. John Heron and Gregg Lahood call for greater explicit attention to the transformation of academic departments into ongoing AR projects.

On the one hand these challenges of reforming institutions of research and learning are important: they clearly have monopolized the criteria by which 'knowledge' is judged and have a huge influence on what is seen as legitimate. On the other hand, in the light of our discussion above about mainstreaming and challenges such as those from Brinton Lykes, these issues can look like academic concerns of the worried privileged.

There is a delicate balance to be struck here. Our task is not to worry about gaining legitimacy on the terms of institutional criteria, but to use our positions to create spaces for genuine learning and inquiry-oriented universities, and to create new forms of

legitimacy so in the longer run we can contribute to a transformation of higher education. Ernie Stringer catches some of this mood:

> My reading of these issues is that action research is now in a similar position to that attained by qualitative research in the 1970s. Issues of legitimacy, its place in academic research and the need for institutional support have now largely been won in relation to qualitative research. I think we action researchers now need to find ways to support and inform our institutional stakeholders as they struggle with a methodology that doesn't seem to fit into the frameworks that have been formulated to accommodate other types of research. This process can be very productive, since it challenges the very assumptions that are built into those structures and therefore holds the possibility of focusing on their intent. By going 'back to the basics' of institutional practice we may assist in enhancing or improving the processes of research in academic and other institutional settings. If we see this as a developmental process that we work through with institutional stakeholders we can enhance the life of the institutions within which we work as well as the people we and they serve.

While Victor Friedman strikes a more cautious note:

> There is a need for a new political economy of knowledge. One of the fundamental assumptions of PAR has been that 'knowledge is power'. However, power in the world today does not seem to have much connection to knowledge. As one World Congress participant put it, the US decision to invade Iraq was not the result of positivist thinking. Indeed, the contrary may be true – knowledge does not carry much weight.

There is another dimension to this, which rings with Bjørn Gustavsen's call that we stop underplaying the practical impacts that actually emerge out of action research projects, and other calls for us to work with rather than against other academic practices. Jenny Rudolph[26] points to her work with what is called 'translational research' to support 'evidence-based' practices in healthcare, where the challenge is 'how findings published in scholarly and professional journals should be implemented in practice':

> How should these findings be translated into practice? This challenge presents a classic action

research challenge: how should propositional knowledge found in leading healthcare journals be made actionable by clinicians on the ground? In the US, the Agency for Healthcare Quality and Research (AHRQ), for example, has been a leader in putting an emphasis on clarifying the processes by which such translational research, research focused on the barriers and catalysts for implementation, should be done. The tenets of participatory action research (PAR), and of action science/action inquiry, both have much to offer in clarifying this process. PAR-based approaches could help illuminate how practitioners themselves choose and utilize evidence-based practice. Action science/action inquiry based approaches could help clarify how to surface the underlying values and assumptions that guide current practice and the adoption of new practices. Together these two approaches could make the adoption of evidence-based practice and learning from this practice more robust.

DEVELOPING ALTERNATIVE INSTITUTIONS

Another response to the challenges posed by the politics and epistemology of higher education is to create new alternative institutions. As Dave Brown writes:

This kind of work ('tackling big issues') may require creating institutions that are independent of, or at least not wholly dependent on, academic institutions that are almost entirely controlled by academic disciplines. Creating thinktanks or institutes that are good at knowledge production but also responsive and accountable to external constituents will be a key piece of this development.

Lai Fong Chiu, pointing to issues of legitimacy, suggests:

Alternative institutional support such as action research regional groups which could come together at least twice a year to exchange ideas or to work on practical educational projects such as training new researchers in various kinds of AR practices would be helpful. Maybe leaders in the field should seek financial support from the ESRC (Research Council) for such activities.

John Heron and Gregg Lahood call for more attention to fostering the development of AR in alternative education and research

centres, e.g. in those to do with complementary therapies of all kinds, with green, environmental and eco-sensitive issues.

We have pointed to the importance of such independent and quasi-independent institutions in our introduction. Such places and networks are often communities of inquiry in their own right, with more or less explicit ongoing inquiries into how to establish and maintain quality action research work within a broader institutional setting and wider context. It is entirely possible to gain credits within a university system and gain an external reputation while operating within an action research paradigm, although we should not underestimate the challenges of managing this kind of situation which demands the kind of 'late stage' leadership development Torbert and Taylor briefly describe in Chapter 16 which is 'self-conscious [about] mission/philosophy … invites conversation among multiple voices and reframing of boundaries … cultivating interplay, reattunement and continual triple-loop feedback among purpose, strategy, practice, and outcomes' (p. 527).

A comment Victor Friedman heard at the World Congress from a participant from Manila challenged this view:

Action research should focus on expansion and development through emerging organizations and institutions in the rapidly developing world (e.g. Asia). He argued that attempts to infiltrate, influence and transform established institutions (like CARPP or our action research center [Max Stern Academic College of Emek Yezreel in Israel] or many similar efforts around the world) are a waste. The thinking was that past attempts to influence deeply entrenched institutions have had only limited success and only for short periods of time (and we haven't really learned from those experiences). Rather than investing energy and resources swimming against the current of the establishment, we might ride the enormous wave of change that is sweeping across other parts of the globe.

Again, we doubt whether this is an either/or choice, and point rather to the potential for complementarity between institutions in different contexts and with different missions and approaches. This is all the more reason for holding open the boundaries of action research rather than closing on one definition and seeing the community of action research as inclusive rather than exclusive. To misquote Tennyson, we must beware 'lest one good purpose should corrupt the world'.

BUILDING COMMUNITY

If we are to embrace a pluralist view of action research and a pluralist community then that community itself needs nurturing and developing. Mary Gergen[27] writes:

> One of my oldest concerns/interests in AR has been with the embedded, interactive, but solitary stories of individual researcher teams working in a particular setting without much cross-fertilization from others, both within AR and without. I think this has been picked up on by yourself and your colleagues across the world, and much has happened to publicize AR activities and to raise questions and generate conversations both within the community and without. I think you and those you work closely with have done a remarkable job in holding conferences (to support and inform the AR community and close-in others), the journal, which I am sure will wobble and then walk, if not fly, and in the handbook, and in conversations such as this.

Robert Chambers writes about the importance of this wide community learning from the spread of good (and bad) practice:

> There are the huge challenges in spreading participatory action research in and through big bureaucracies with their hierarchies, tendencies to standardise, set targets, regulate. ... Is a big future frontier of knowledge, and of action research itself, to understand better what can work and what not, and how to do better?

It is not just exchange of information that keeps community going: it is appreciating both our common purposes and our differences and cherishing ourselves and other people round the world. Orlando Fals Borda has done wonderful service here in both stimulating and offering legitimacy to the dialogue between South and North (Fals Borda, 1996, 2001/2006), for we have so much to learn from each other intellectually and emotionally: often, when we hear of the brave and creative work of others round the world we are touched at times almost to tears.

One means of supporting the development of community, through valuable websites suggests the kinds of concrete steps – first order results – that are needed for communities of practice to flourish (see, for example, http://www.alarpm.org.au/public/home; and the comprehensive list of websites to be found on Jack Whitehead's Living Inquiry pages at http://people.bath.ac.uk/edsajw/).

THE NATURE OF KNOWING

There was curiously little written in the responses about epistemological issues, almost as if everyone was in agreement with Bjørn Gustavsen that 'action research has won all debates on ethics and epistemology' and Victor Friedman's remark that 'The war with positivism is more or less over'. More generally Lyle Yorks calls for 'robust epistemological awareness with flexible and adaptable methodology'. Apart from this, two important themes are raised.

Participative knowing

John Heron raises an important point concerning what he calls 'declarative validity' which he sees as resting at the heart of a participative worldview. How do we recognize the 'authentic signature' of participative relationship, the quality of experience that provides warrant for claims that we are engaged in empathic participative knowing? If we are to lay claim to experiential knowing in participative relationship as the grounding of our work, are there qualities which 'declare themselves' which we can point to as touchstones of the authenticity of these experiences?

Presentational knowing

Rita Kowlaski[28] and Steve Taylor[29] both point to the importance of presentational knowing in action research, knowing that is conveyed through aesthetic forms of graphic arts, poetry, movement and dance. Rita writes:

> I have found presentational knowing freeing and essential for application. I have learned more about relationships, behavior and creative tension conflict consciously using forms of presentational knowing in my work. There is something about conflict and creative tension we could learn more about if we watched it ourselves.

After giving a short account of a project in which team members are using presentational forms to communicate with each other and noticing the powerful effect this can have, and contrasting this with the way organizations 'take pride in objectifying people', she goes on to write:

> Until I understood how art and stories and music bring life to experience and concepts, I could not help others use or apply what I had learned. I lost opportunities since I had cut myself off from an important source of knowledge.

Steve Taylor articulated the same issues:

> I think one of the real issues with working across different ways of knowing and different forms of representation is with the movement between the different ways of knowing. If we start with richness of experience, we then need to be an artist to represent that richness with presentational knowing. The real difficulty is then in moving from the richness of experience and the artfulness of presentational form to propositional form. So often the move to propositional knowing is done with an incredible violence to the richness of experience and the artfulness of presentation. As we try to be precise, we often strip away feeling and are left with dry, banal concepts that trivialize the experience they are supposed to describe. We need to find ways to artfully capture and honor the richness of the experience as we try to also use the precision of propositional forms. As we try to be rigorous scholars we must also be passionate artists, not only in our presentational and propositional knowing, but also in our pragmatic knowing – in our action in the world.

These contributions suggest that while action research may in broad terms have 'won' the epistemological arguments, there is much more we can do to fully articulate and deepen and widen our understanding of the many ways of knowing we engage in. There is much to do to fully understand the quality claims of knowing that is rooted in experience and expressed in presentation, practical and propositional forms.

THE ART OF PRACTICE

As Bill Torbert wrote:

> I hope you will emphasize that … action research can reach its potential only when it is recognized and practiced as a far more challenging and inclusive art and science …

Rita Kowalski writes more personally of the challenges of practice:

> Action research is challenging not simply because it involves choices points, but because as you do action research the reflection needed to complete a cycle reminds you about choices. It isn't neat, but very human, open to different possibilities and uses time differently. It doesn't end; the impact of action research continues when we are mindful of leaving a legacy, an infrastructure behind.

These comments point to a theme that we see as important but find underplayed in the responses we have. If, as Stephen Kemmis so clearly writes, the first and central step in action research is 'the formation of communicative space' (Kemmis, 2001/2006: 100), what are the qualities and abilities that action research needs to develop in order to do this?

There is an art to engaging with people that is intensely human whether we are running a dialogue conference in Scandinavia, a feminist project in Canada or a village meeting in Bangladesh. There are embodied, tactile, emotional, rhetorical, even seductive skills that bring bodies and energies together in a way that opens the possibility of collaboration. If we dare, in a school of management, to sit our students in a circle with a table of flowers in the middle, we create a different form from when we sit in a tiered lecture hall, with both obvious and subtle differences in communicative possibilities. If as

PRA practitioners we get literally close to the ground, as Chambers describes (Chapter 20), we open new possibilities for empowerment. Maybe we can say we evoke different archetypal patterns (Hillman, 1975) and spiritual qualities in the different ways we engage with each other. What qualities of individual and collective leadership are appropriate? There is a huge amount of work needed to fully understand and articulate the many forms of the art and practice of action research.

TRAINING AND DEVELOPMENT OF PRACTITIONERS

These considerations all point to the importance of the development of the next generation, with several people pointing to the need for training and development of action research practitioners, facilitators and animators. Anisur Rahman in Chapter 3 describes animation in PAR as an 'art in which one can, with practice and reflection, develop one's skill, given the necessary commitment, creativity and sensitivity to the specifics and dynamics of a given situation'. He argues that animators must learn to unlock their own spirit of inquiry if they are to be able to help others do the same. Meghna Guhathakurta points out that the expansion of PAR work in Bangladesh depends not only on such 'professional' animators but also on whether there are adequate and qualified animators internal to the community to take the work forward. Robert Chambers suggests that the training and development of action research facilitators is a project for action research in itself.

Morten Levin from a very different context argues that:

The most fundamental task for action research in academia is to train professionals as action researchers. Without new trained cadres of researchers there will be no future for action research. Institutional arrangements and different political economies indicate that there must be different strategies that are applicable. In the Scandinavian context (maybe only Norwegian) it is possible to create large national programs building

on action research which have played an important role locating action research in higher education and supporting high level scientific training in AR. In economies dominated by a rougher type of capitalism other strategies have to be implemented. This is a process that must have a perspective of many, many years. Sustained effort is important.

Hilary responded to Dave Brown's suggestion that alternative institutions were needed with concern that if many action researchers leave the tenure track (in the USA) and create or join 'think tanks' it may be more difficult to ensure we train future action researchers.

As research professor at USC rather than associate professor at Case, I am not in direct line any more for mentoring PhD students – they have to come find me. But I see also that this means that fewer students are trained/encouraged as a result. ... I wonder if there is a way we can combine admittedly slim resources here in the US (and abroad?) and offer a place (maybe virtual) for inter-institute support and development of training for action researchers?

This is clearly an area for future conversations in the action research community, hopefully linking and learning from a wide variety of sources: the concerns of animators in PAR endeavours; the work on national projects in Scandinavia; the development of doctoral candidates in higher institutions; the practice of those supposedly established in the field; and many more.

CONCLUDING REFLECTIONS

As we opened this volume with accounts from the Editorial Board of the grounding influences on their action research practice, so we close with reflections on the future from those who actually contributed to this volume. This last chapter clearly has limitations: we could, maybe should, have extended the conversation by establishing an internet discussion forum and engaged in more cycles of inquiry; we could have found ways in which the interpretive work that we as editors have undertaken was more collaborative. But these limitations in the final product are less important than the ongoing debates and conversations which are opening up both within and between different action research groupings. As a broad community of action researchers we have opened many possibilities for creative conversations across disciplines, across countries, and across generations where we can and will continue to reflect on how to continue to make our presence felt.

In closing on our shared reflections on the question of whither action research, Judi Marshall[30] reminds us that we need to be attuned to the future:

> I have a strong sense of responsibility to younger people wanting to work through action research. Many seem to be mashed up in the politics of academia (as shown by people's stories at the World Congress). What field of legitimacy, imagination and proliferating practices are we creating for them? This does not have to be a conformist space, but we need to recognise the ethics of responsibility in this direction too.

We therefore give the last word to Victor's words of wisdom. Victor Friedman, returning from the World Congress in Gronigen, writes of his impressions of a coming change in the field and a new generation of action researchers beginning to emerge:

> My impression was that their perspective on action research, the role it should play, and how it should move ahead are very different from the dominant views of the past 20 years or so. … I found it difficult to clearly articulate all I heard, so if I were to go to this conference all over again, I would try to spend most of my time listening to this new generation of action researchers (people just emerging from graduate school or initial involvement in the field). I would want to hear about what attracts them to AR, what they would like from it, what they see as problematic, and where they see the future of the field. Perhaps it's an idea for a special issue of *Action Research*.

NOTES

1 Rajesh Tandon (India) writes as Founder and Director of PRIA (Participatory Research in Asia) which has pioneered PAR with communities in India for 20 years.

2 Ernie Stringer (Australia) is a white Australian who has worked for many years with Aboriginal people.

3 Dave Brown (USA) is Associate Director for International Programs at the Hauser Center for Nonprofit Organizations and Lecturer in Public Policy at the Kennedy School of Government.

4 Ken Gergen (USA) is a leading social constructionist who has been closely related with the development of appreciative inquiry.

5 John Heron and Gregg Lahood (New Zealand) have been engaged in co-operative inquiry into spirituality. John is a humanistic and transpersonal psychologist who developed the practice of co-operative inquiry.

6 Orlando Fals Borda (Colombia) is one of the elders of the participatory action research movement.

7 Lai Fong Chiu uses participatory research in medical work, in particular with immigrant communities in the UK.

8 Ed Schein (USA) is one of the elders and founding figures of organization development and process consultation.

9 Robert Chambers (UK) has been a key figure in the development of participatory approaches to development.

10 Lyle Yorks (USA) works at Teachers College, Columbia University, where he teaches and uses action research for transformative education.

11 Bill Torbert (USA) developed the theory and practices of action inquiry.

12 Sonia Ospina (USA) heads the Research Center for Leadership in Action at Wagner School, New York University.

13 Victor Friedman (Israel) works with action science to help individuals, groups, organizations, and communities learn.

14 Bjørn Gustavsen (Norway) is senior researcher at the Work Research Institute, Oslo.

15 Meghna Guhathakurta (Bangladesh) is Executive Director of Research Initiatives Bangladesh.

16 Geoff Mead (UK) is a former police officer whose work is increasingly focused on the role of story and narrative in leadership and organizational development.

17 Marianne Kristiansen (Denmark) is founder of the Centre of Interpersonal Organizational Communication at Aalborg University.

18 Mary Brydon-Miller (USA) is a participatory action researcher who engages in both community-based and educational action research.

19 Brinton Lykes (USA) works with community-based participatory action research to respond to and understand the effects of structural violence including war, poverty and gender oppression.

20 Wendy Frisby and Colleen Reid (Canada) work with women using feminist participatory action research in Western Canada.

21 Davydd Greenwood (USA) supports participatory action research work from Cornell University.

22 John Burgoyne (UK) is Professor of Management Education at Lancaster University who draws on action learning approaches.

23 Morten Levin (Norway) uses and teaches action research from Trondheim University.

24 David Coghlan (Ireland) uses and teaches action research at Trinity College Dublin.

25 Jennifer Mullett (Canada) is a community psychologist in private practice involved in community action research projects in Western Canada.

26 Jenny Rudolph (USA) works with medical practitioners at Boston University.

27 Mary Gergen (USA) is a scholar at the intersection of feminist theory and social constructionism.

28 Rita Kowalski (USA) works in organization development with the US Veterans' Adminstration.

29 Steve Taylor (USA) teaches management at Worcester Polytechnic Institute and works with organizational aesthetics and reflective practice.

30 Judi Marshall (UK) teaches and researches 'living life as inquiry' at the University of Bath.

REFERENCES

Bradbury, H. (2007) 'Quality, consequence and "actionability": what action researchers offer from the tradition of Pragmatism', in R. Shani et al. (eds) *The Sage Handbook of Collaborative Research*. Los Angeles, CA: Sage Publications.

Ehrenreich, B., and Ehrenreich, J. (1977),' The professional-managerial class'. *Radical America*, 11: 7–31.

Fals Borda, O. (1996) 'A North-South convergence on the quest for meaning', *Special Issue of Qualitative Inquiry 'Quality in Human Inquiry'*, 2 (1): 73–5.

Fals Borda, O. (2001/2006) 'Participatory (action) research in social theory: origins and challenges', in P. Reason and H. Bradbury (eds), *Handbook of Action Research: Participatory Inquiry and Practice*. London: Sage. pp. 27–37.

Gustavsen, B. (2003) 'Action research and the problem of the single case', *Concepts and Transformation*, 8 (1): 93–9.

Hillman, J. (1975) *Revisioning Psychology*. New York: Harper Collophon.

Kemmis, S. (2001/2006) 'Exploring the relevance of critical theory for action research: emancipatory action research in the footsteps of Jürgen Habermas', in P. Reason and H. Bradbury (eds), *Handbook of Action Research: Participative inquiry and Practice*. London: Sage. pp. 91–102. Also published in P. Reason and H. Bradbury (eds) (2006), *Handbook of Action Research: Concise Paperback Edition*. London: Sage. pp. 94–105.

Reason, P. (2006) 'Choice and quality in action research practice', *Journal of Management Inquiry*, 15 (2): 187–203.

Index